P9-CSU-239

"An utterly gripping Anna Karenina of ... ...Government... ...privile... ...fall in love and ...re arrested ...f Bolshevism ...s compelling brilliance is its living organic nature—a mixture of historical narrative, novel, and family saga with echoes of Grossman, Pasternak, Solzhenitsyn, and even Tolstoy."

SIMON SEBAG MONTEFIORE, author of *Stalin: The Court of the Red Tsar*

"Few books are truly visionary, but *The House of Government* earns this description. The cumulative effect of this massive chronicle of the Soviet era is devastating and, more important, utterly satisfying. It's a work of art in itself, a beautifully written exploration of a central phase of modern history, and one that has never seemed as terrifyingly relevant. Tolstoy himself would have recognized Yuri Slezkine as an artist, as the author of a narrative with transmogrifying power, an epic that functions on countless levels at the same time."

JAY PARINI, author of *The Last Station: A Novel of Tolstoy's Final Year*

"*The House of Government* traces the public and personal lives of residents of a unique, elite Moscow housing complex as they evolve from fanatic Bolshevik revolutionaries—dreaming of a Marxist utopia and determined to shed blood to create it—to victims of Stalin's terror. Based on diaries, letters, memoirs, and interviews, featuring hundreds of rare photos, and combining history, biography, and social theory, this cornucopia of a book is a tour de force."

WILLIAM TAUBMAN, Pulitzer Prize–winning author of *Khrushchev: The Man and His Era* and *Gorbachev: His Life and Times*

THE HOUSE OF GOVERNMENT

THE HOUSE OF GOVERNMENT

A SAGA OF THE RUSSIAN REVOLUTION

YURI SLEZKINE

PRINCETON UNIVERSITY PRESS
PRINCETON AND OXFORD

Published by Princeton University Press
41 William Street, Princeton, New Jersey 08540

In the United Kingdom: Princeton University Press
6 Oxford Street, Woodstock, Oxfordshire OX20 1TR

press.princeton.edu

Jacket illustration by Francesco Bongiorni / Marlena Agency
Jacket design by Chris Ferrante

Frontispiece: The House of Government.
(Courtesy of the House on the Embankment Museum, Moscow.)

Unless otherwise noted in the caption, all images are
courtesy of the House on the Embankment Museum.

Library of Congress Cataloging-in-Publication Data

Names: Slezkine, Yuri, 1956- author.
Title: The House of Government : a saga of the Russian Revolution / Yuri Slezkine.
Description: Princeton : Princeton University Press, 2017.
Identifiers: LCCN 2016049071 | ISBN 9780691176949 (hardcover : acid-free paper)
Subjects: LCSH: Moscow (Russia)—Politics and government—20th century. | Communists—
Russia (Federation)—Moscow—Biography. | Apartment dwellers—Russia (Federation)—
Moscow—Biography. | Victims of state-sponsored terrorism—Russia (Federation)—
Moscow—Biography. | Moscow (Russia)—Biography. | Apartment houses—Russia
(Federation)—Moscow—History—20th century. | Moscow (Russia)—Buildings, structures, etc.
| Political purges—Soviet Union—History. | State-sponsored terrorism—Soviet Union—
History. | Soviet Union—Politics and government—1936–1953. | BISAC: HISTORY / Europe /
Russia & the Former Soviet Union. | HISTORY / Revolutionary. | HISTORY / Social History. |
POLITICAL SCIENCE / Political Ideologies / Communism & Socialism.
Classification: LCC DK601 .S57 2017 | DDC 947.084/10922—dc23 LC record available at https://
lccn.loc.gov/2016049071

British Library Cataloging-in-Publication Data is available

This book has been composed in Kazimir Text and Kremlin II Pro

Printed on acid-free paper. ∞

Printed in the United States of America

10 9 8 7 6 5 4 3 2 1

This is a work of history. Any resemblance to fictional characters, dead or alive, is entirely coincidental.

Sometimes it seemed to Valène that time had come to a stop, suspended and frozen around an expectation he could not define. The very idea of his projected tableau, whose exposed, fragmented images had begun to haunt every second of his life, furnishing his dreams and ordering his memories; the very idea of this eviscerated building laying bare the cracks of its past and the crumbling of its present; this haphazard piling up of stories grandiose and trivial, frivolous and pathetic, made him think of a grotesque mausoleum erected in memory of companions petrified in terminal poses equally insignificant in their solemnity and banality, as if he had wanted to both prevent and delay these slow or quick deaths that seemed to engulf the entire building, story by story: Monsieur Marcia, Madame Moreau, Madame de Beaumont, Bartlebooth, Rorschash, Mademoiselle Crespi, Madame Albin, Smautf. And him, of course, Valène himself, the house's oldest inhabitant.

GEORGES PEREC, *LIFE: A USER'S MANUAL*

Mephisto:
There lies the body; if the soul would fly away,
I shall confront it with the blood-signed scroll.
Alas, they have so many means today
To rob the Devil of a soul.

JOHANN WOLFGANG VON GOETHE, *FAUST*,
TRANS. WALTER KAUFMANN

CONTENTS

BOOK THREE | ON TRIAL

PREFACE

During the First Five-Year Plan (1928–32), the Soviet government built a new socialist state and a fully nationalized economy. At the same time, it built a house for itself. The House of Government was located in a low-lying area called "the Swamp," across the Moskva River from the Kremlin. The largest residential building in Europe, it consisted of eleven units of varying heights organized around three interconnected courtyards, each one with its own fountain.

It was conceived as a historic compromise and a structure "of the transitional type." Halfway between revolutionary avant-garde and socialist realism, it combined clean, straight lines and a transparent design with massive bulk and a solemn neoclassical facade. Halfway between bourgeois individualism and communist collectivism, it combined 505 fully furnished family apartments with public spaces, including a cafeteria, grocery store, walk-in clinic, child-care center, hairdresser's salon, post office, telegraph, bank, gym, laundry, library, tennis court, and several dozen rooms for various activities (from billiards and target shooting to painting and orchestra rehearsals). Anchoring the ensemble were the State New Theater for 1,300 spectators on the riverfront and the Shock Worker movie theater for 1,500 spectators near the Drainage Canal.

Sharing these facilities, raising their families, employing maids and governesses, and moving from apartment to apartment to keep up with promotions were people's commissars, deputy commissars, Red Army commanders, Marxist scholars, Gulag officials, industrial managers, foreign communists, socialist-realist writers, record-breaking Stakhanovites (including Aleksei Stakhanov himself) and assorted worthies, including Lenin's secretary and Stalin's relatives. (Stalin himself remained across the river in the Kremlin.)

In 1935, the House of Government had 2,655 registered tenants. About 700 of them were state and Party officials assigned to particular apartments; most of the rest were their dependents, including 588 children. Serving the residents and maintaining the building were between six hundred and eight hundred waiters, painters, gardeners, plumbers, janitors, laundresses, floor polishers, and other House of Government employees (including fifty-seven administrators). It was the vanguard's backyard; a fortress protected by metal gates and armed guards; a dormitory where state officials lived as husbands, wives, parents, and neighbors; a place where revolutionaries came home and the revolution came to die.

In the 1930s and 1940s, about eight hundred House residents and an unspecified number of employees were evicted from their apartments and accused of duplicity, degeneracy, counterrevolutionary activity, or general unreliability. They were all found guilty, one way or another. Three hundred forty-four residents are known to have been shot; the rest were sentenced to various forms of imprisonment. In October 1941, as the Nazis approached Moscow, the remaining residents were evacuated. When they returned, they found many new neighbors, but not many top officials. The House was still there, but it was no longer of Government.

It is still there today, repainted and repopulated. The theater, cinema, and grocery store are in their original locations. One of the apartments is now a museum; the rest are private residencies. Most private residencies contain family archives. The square in front of the building is once again called "Swamp Square."

■ ■ ■

This book consists of three strains. The first is a family saga involving numerous named and unnamed residents of the House of Government. Readers are urged to think of them as characters in an epic or people in their own lives: some we see and soon forget, some we may or may not recognize (or care to look up), some we are able to identify but do not know much about, and some we know fairly well and are pleased or annoyed to see again. Unlike characters in most epics or people in our own lives, however, no family or individual is indispensable to the story. Only the House of Government is.

The second strain is analytical. Early in the book, the Bolsheviks are identified as millenarian sectarians preparing for the apocalypse. In subsequent chapters, consecutive episodes in the Bolshevik family saga are related to stages in the history of a failed prophecy, from an apparent fulfillment to the great disappointment to a series of postponements to the desperate offer of a last sacrifice. Compared to other sects with similar commitments, the Bolsheviks were remarkable for both their success and their failure. They managed to take over Rome long before their faith could become an inherited habit, but they never figured out how to transform their certainty into a habit that their children or subordinates could inherit.

The third strain is literary. For the Old Bolsheviks, reading the "treasures of world literature" was a crucial part of conversion experiences, courtship rituals, prison "universities," and House of Government domesticity. For their children, it was the single most important leisure activity and educational requirement. In the chapters that follow, each episode in the Bolshevik family saga and each stage in the history of the Bolshevik prophecy is accompanied by a discussion of the literary works that sought to interpret and mythologize them. Some themes from those works—the flood of revolution, the exodus from slavery, the terror of home life, the rebuilding of the Tower of Babel—are reincorporated into the story of the

House of Government. Some literary characters helped to build it, some had apartments there, and one—Goethe's Faust—was repeatedly invoked as an ideal tenant.

The story of the House of Government consists of three parts. Book 1, "En Route," introduces the Old Bolsheviks as young men and women and follows them from one temporary shelter to another as they convert to radical socialism, survive in prison and exile, preach the coming revolution, prevail in the Civil War, build the dictatorship of the proletariat, debate the postponement of socialism, and wonder what to do in the meantime (and whether the dictatorship is, indeed, of the proletariat).

Book 2, "At Home," describes the return of the revolution as a five-year plan; the building of the House of Government and the rest of the Soviet Union; the division of labor, space, and affection within family apartments; the pleasures and dangers of unsupervised domesticity; the problem of personal mortality before the coming of communism; and the magical world of "happy childhood."

Book 3, "On Trial," recounts the purge of the House of Government, the last sacrifice of the Old Bolsheviks, the "mass operations" against hidden heretics, the main differences between loyalty and betrayal, the home life of professional executioners, the long old age of the enemies' widows, the redemption and apostasy of the Revolution's children, and the end of Bolshevism as a millenarian faith.

The epilogue unites the book's three strains by discussing the work of the writer Yuri Trifonov, who grew up in the House of Government and whose fiction transformed it into a setting for Bolshevik family history, a monument to a lost faith, and a treasure of world literature.

■ ■ ■

In the House of Government, some residents were more important than others because of their position within the Party and state bureaucracy, length of service as Old Bolsheviks, or particular accomplishments on the battlefield and the "labor front." In this book, some characters are more important than others because they made provisions for their own memorialization or because someone else did it in their behalf.

One of the leaders of the Bolshevik takeover in Moscow and chairman of the All-Union Society for Cultural Ties with Foreign Countries, Aleksandr Arosev (Apts. 103 and 104), kept a diary that his sister preserved and one of his daughters published. One of the ideologues of Left Communism and the first head of the Supreme Council of the National Economy, Valerian Osinsky (Apts. 18, 389), maintained a twenty-year correspondence with Anna Shaternikova, who kept his letters and handed them to his daughter, who deposited them in a state archive before writing a book of memoirs, which she posted on the Internet and her daughter later published. The most influential Bolshevik literary critic and Party supervisor of Soviet literature in the 1920s, Aleksandr Voronsky (Apt. 357), wrote several books of memoirs and had a great many essays written about him (including several by his daughter). The director of the Lenin Mausoleum Laboratory, Boris Zbarsky (Apt. 28), immortalized himself by embalming Lenin's body. His son and colleague, Ilya Zbarsky, took professional care of Lenin's body and wrote an autobiography memorializing himself and his father. "The Party's Conscience" and deputy prosecutor general, Aron Solts (Apt. 393), wrote numerous articles about Communist ethics and sheltered his recently divorced niece, who wrote a book about him (and sent the manuscript to an archive). The prosecutor at the Filipp Mironov treason trial in 1919, Ivar Smilga (Apt. 230), was the subject of several interviews given by his daughter Tatiana, who had inherited his gift of eloquence and put a great deal of effort into preserving his memory. The chairman of the Flour Milling Industry Directorate, Boris Ivanov, "the Baker" (Apt. 372), was remembered by many of his House of Government neighbors for his extraordinary generosity.

Lyova Fedotov, the son of the late Central Committee instructor, Fedor Fedotov (Apt. 262), kept a diary and believed that "everything is important for history." Inna Gaister, the daughter of the deputy people's commissar of agriculture, Aron Gaister (Apt. 162), published a detailed "family chronicle." Anatoly Granovsky, the son of the director of the Berezniki Chemical Plant, Mikhail Granovsky (Apt. 418), defected to the United States and wrote a memoir about his work as a secret agent under the command of Andrei Sverdlov, the son of the first head of the Soviet state and organizer of the Red Terror, Yakov Sverdlov. As a young revolutionary, Yakov Sverdlov wrote several revealing letters to Andrei's mother, Klavdia Novgorodtseva (Apt. 319), and to his young friend and disciple, Kira Egon-Besser. Both women preserved his letters and wrote memoirs about him. Boris Ivanov, the "Baker," wrote memoirs about Yakov's and Klavdia's life in Siberian exile. Andrei Sverdlov (Apt. 319) helped edit his mother's memoirs, coauthored three detective stories based on his experience as a secret police official, and was featured in the memoirs of Anna Larina-Bukharina (Apt. 470) as one of her interrogators. After the arrest of the former head of the secret police investigations department, Grigory Moroz (Apt. 39), his wife, Fanni Kreindel, and eldest son, Samuil, were sent to labor camps, and his two younger sons, Vladimir and Aleksandr, to an orphanage. Vladimir kept a diary and wrote several defiant letters that were used as evidence against him (and published by later historians); Samuil wrote his memoirs and sent them to a museum. Eva Levina-Rozengolts, a professional artist and sister of the people's commissar of foreign trade, Arkady Rozengolts (Apt. 237), spent seven years in exile and produced several graphic cycles dedicated to those who came back and those who did not. The oldest of the Old Bolsheviks, Elena Stasova (Apts. 245, 291), devoted the last ten years of her life to the "rehabilitation" of those who came back and those who did not.

Yulia Piatnitskaia, the wife of the secretary of the Comintern Executive Committee, Osip Piatnitsky (Apt. 400), started a diary shortly before his arrest and kept it until she, too, was arrested. Her diary was published by her son, Vladimir, who also wrote a book about his father. Tatiana ("Tania") Miagkova, the wife of the chairman of the State Planning Committee of Ukraine, Mikhail Poloz (Apt. 199), regularly wrote to her family from prison, exile, and labor camps. Her letters were preserved and typed up by her daughter, Rada Poloz. Natalia Sats, the wife of the people's commissar of internal trade, Izrail Veitser (Apt. 159), founded the world's first children's theater and wrote two autobiographies, one of which dealt with her time in prison, exile, and labor camps. Agnessa Argiropulo, the wife of the secret police official who proposed the use of extrajudicial troikas during the Great Terror, Sergei Mironov, told the story of their life together to a Memorial Society researcher, who published it as a book. Maria Denisova, the wife of the Red Cavalry commissar, Efim Shchadenko (Apts. 10, 505), served as the prototype for Maria in Vladimir Mayakovsky's poem *A Cloud in Pants*. The director of the Moscow-Kazan Railway, Ivan Kuchmin (Apt. 226), served as the prototype for Aleksei Kurilov in Leonid Leonov's novel, *The Road to Ocean*. The *Pravda* correspondent, Mikhail Koltsov (Apt. 143), served as the prototype for Karkov in Ernest Hemingway's novel, *For Whom the Bell Tolls*. "Doubting Makar," from Andrei Platonov's short story by the same name, participated in the building of the House of Government. All Saints Street, on which the House of Government was built, was renamed in honor of Aleksandr Serafimovich, the author of *The Iron Flood* (Apt. 82). Yuri Trifonov, the son of the Red Army commissar and chairman of the Main Committee on Foreign Concessions, Valentin Trifonov (Apt. 137), wrote a novella, *The House on the Embankment*, that immortalized the House of Government. His widow, Olga Trifonova, would become the director of the House on the Embankment Museum, which continues to collect books, letters, diaries, stories, paintings, photographs, gramophones, and other remnants of the House of Government.

ACKNOWLEDGMENTS

This book took many years to write. I am grateful to the Hoover Institution for one of the quietest years of my life and the Wissenschaftskolleg zu Berlin, for one of the happiest; to the American Council of Learned Societies, National Endowment for the Humanities, the National Council for Eurasian and East European Research, and the University of California, Berkeley, for financial support; to Christiane Büchner, for letting me watch the making of her film and teaching me how to record interviews; to Olga Bandrimer, for transcribing those interviews and contributing her own stories; to Artem Zadikian, for being the world's most observant and generous photographer; and to Michael Coates, Nicole Eaton, Eleonor Gilburd, Clarissa Ibarra, Jason R. Morton, Brandon Schechter, Charles Shaw, I. T. Sidorova, Victoria Smolkin, A. G. Tepliakov, and Katherine Zubovich, for help with research. I am particularly grateful to the friends and colleagues who have read the entire manuscript and offered suggestions ranging from the inspiring to the debilitating: Victoria E. Bonnell, George Breslauer, John Connelly, Brian DeLay, Victoria Frede-Montemayor, Gregory Freidin, David Hollinger, Sergei Ivanov, Joseph Kellner, Joachim Klein, Thomas Laqueur, Olga Matich, Elizabeth McGuire, Eric Naiman, Benjamin Nathans, Anne Nesbet, Joy Neumeyer, Daniel Orlovsky, Irina Paperno, Ethan Pollock, Hank Reichman, Irwin Scheiner, James Vernon, Mirjam Voerkelius, Edward W. Walker, Amir Weiner, Katherine Zubovich, and all the members of the Berkeley Russian History Reading Group (*kruzhok*).

Jon Gjerde kept asking me how I would go about writing this book until I decided to go ahead and write it; Reggie Zelnik would have noticed the presence of a character who never lived in the House of Government; Brigitta van Rheinberg never wavered in her enthusiasm and helped reshape and rethink the manuscript; Chris Ferrante, Beth Gianfagna, Dimitri Karetnikov, and Terri O'Prey turned the manuscript into *The House of Government*; and Zoë Pagnamenta showed me what a good agent can do.

My greatest debt is to the women who created the House on the Embankment Museum and invited me in: the late Elena Ivanovna Perepechko, Tamara Andreevna Ter-Egiazarian, and Viktoria Borisovna Volina, and my very special teachers and friends Inna Nikolaevna Lobanova, Tatiana Ivanovna Shmidt, and Olga Romanovna Trifonova. This book is for them.

Finally, reciprocity is inversely related to intimacy. A stranger's favor must be returned promptly; a close friend can wait twenty years for a book to get written; all happy families are happy in the same way because they lie outside the cycle of fair exchange. Which is the reason I do not have to thank Peter Slezkine and Lisa Little for their contribution to the writing of this book.

BOOK ONE
EN ROUTE

PART I
ANTICIPATION

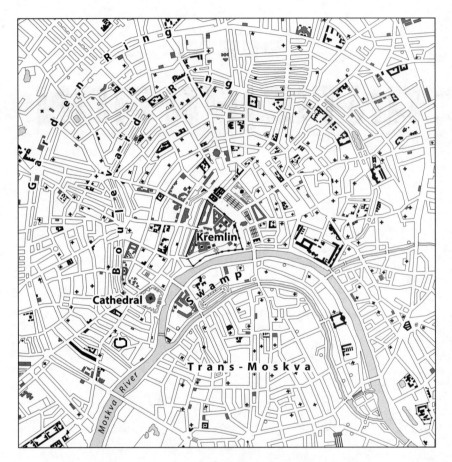

Moscow

1
THE SWAMP

Moscow was founded on the high left bank of the river it was named after. The wide-open and frequently invaded "Trans-Moskva" fields on the right side gradually filled up with quarters of coopers, weavers, shearers, carters, soldiers, blacksmiths, interpreters, and tribute-collectors, but the floodplain just opposite the Kremlin remained a chain of swamps and marshy meadows. In 1495, Ivan III decreed that all buildings along the right bank of the river be torn down and replaced by Royal Gardens. The gardens were planted and, under Tsar Aleksei Mikhailovich, neatly landscaped, but the mud kept creeping in. The Middle Garden was bounded on the west by the Boloto ("swamp" in Russian); on the east by the Balchug ("swamp" in Turkic); and on the south by nameless puddles and lakes. The construction of the All Saints Stone Bridge in 1693 transformed the old southern crossing into a causeway lined with shops, taverns, and warehouses (including the Royal Wool Yard and Royal Wine and Salt Yard). After the fire of 1701, the gardens were abandoned, and one part of the swamp began to be used as a market square and a place for recreational fistfighting, fireworks displays, and public executions.[1]

After the spring flood of 1783, the Vodootvodnyi (or "Drainage") Canal was built along the southern edge of the Moskva floodplain. The embankments were reinforced; the perpendicular ditches became alleys; and the former Royal Gardens were transformed into a crescent-shaped, densely populated island. The fire of 1812, which smoked Napoleon out of Moscow, destroyed most of the buildings and drove away most of the residents. The new structures—including inns, schools, factories, and merchant mansions—were largely built of stone. The Babyegorodskaia Dam at the western tip of the island made the canal navigable and floods less frequent. Next to the dam, on the Kremlin side, arose the Cathedral of Christ the Savior, consecrated in 1883 and dedicated "to the eternal memory of the unrivaled diligence, loyalty, and love of Faith and Fatherland, with which, in those difficult times, the Russian people acquitted themselves, and in commemoration of Our gratitude to the Divine Providence that saved Russia from the calamity that threatened to befall it."[2]

On the eve of World War I, the western section of the island ("the Swamp") was dominated and partially owned by the F. T. Einem Chocolate, Candy, and Cookie Factory, famous for its Dutch cocoa, bridal baskets, colorful marzipan figures, and "Fall in Love with Me" chocolate cakes.

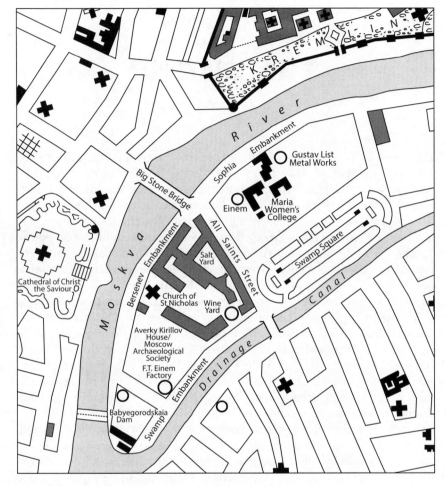

The Swamp

Founded in 1867 by two German entrepreneurs who made their fortune selling syrups and jams to the Russian army, the factory had several steam engines, brand new hydraulic presses, and the title of official supplier of the Imperial Court. Its director, Oskar Heuss (the son of one of the co-founders), lived nearby in a large, two-story house with bathrooms on both floors, a greenhouse, and a big stable. On the opposite side of the courtyard were apartments for the factory's engineers (mostly Germans), doctors' assistants, married and unmarried employees, housekeepers, and coachmen, as well as a library, laundry, and several dormitories and cafeterias for the workers. The factory was known for its high wages, good working conditions, amateur theater, and active police-sponsored mutual aid fund. Sunday lunches included a shot of vodka or half bottle of beer; boarders under sixteen received free clothing, sang in a choir, worked in

View of the Swamp from the Kremlin.
The Cathedral of Christ the Savior is on the far right.

View of the Einem Factory from the Cathedral of Christ the Savior

the store (for about eleven hours a day), and had an 8:00 p.m. curfew. About half the workers had been there for more than fifteen years; the hardest work was done by day laborers, mostly women.[3]

To the west of the chocolate factory were army barracks, a collection of shops, and, on the island's "Arrowhead," the Moscow Sailing Club. To the east was the seventeenth-century residence of the Duma clerk Averky Kirillov, which contained the Moscow Archaeological Society, and the Church of St. Nicholas the Miracle Worker, which contained the remains of Averky Kirillov. The deacons, sextons, psalm-readers, holy bread bakers, and priests (Father Orlov and Father Dmitriev) all lived in the churchyard, alongside dozens of lodgers and the wards of St. Nicholas Almshouse.[4]

According to Nikolai Bukharin, who grew up a short walk away on Bolshaia Ordynka Street, the Trans-Moskva churches were usually full.

Sailing Club

Averky Kirillov Residence

In the front stood the merchants' wives, rustling their silk skirts and blouses and crossing themselves with plump, rosy fingers, while, beside them, their husbands prayed gravely and fervently. Farther back one could see household dependents and poor relations: old women in black, God-fearing gossips, matchmakers, keepers of the family hearth, aunts with nieces still hoping for bridegrooms and swooning from fat and longing, confidantes, and housemaids. The government officials and their wives stood nearby looking fashionable. And at the back, pressing together as they stood or knelt, were exhausted laborers, waiting for consolation and salvation from the all-merciful God, our Savior. But the Savior remained silent as he looked sadly down at the hunched bodies and bent backs. . . . Joking and laughing a little nervously, young boys and girls spat on their fingertips and tried to put each other's candles out. As the candles sputtered, they would snicker, then stifle their laughter under the stern gaze of the grown-ups. Here and there, lovers could be seen exchanging glances. The porch was full of wall-eyed beggars in pitiful rags, with turned-up eyelids and stumps instead of hands and feet; the blind, lame, and holy fools for Christ's sake.[5]

Most of them lived close by. Next to the church, along the Drainage Canal (also known as the Ditch), and all around the chocolate factory were courtyards filled with wooden or stone buildings with assorted annexes, mezzanines, wings, porches, basements, and lofts. Inside were apartments, rooms, "small chambers," and "corners with cots" inhabited by a motley mix of people who might or might not attend the Mass celebrated by Father Orlov and Father Dmitriev. A sixteen-year-old factory apprentice, Semen Kanatchikov, who lived in the neighborhood in the second half of the 1890s and went to Mass regularly before converting to socialism, described his building as a "huge stone house with a courtyard that looked like a large stone well. Wet linens dangled from taut clotheslines all along

Church of St. Nicholas the Miracle Worker

View of Bersenev Embankment from the dam

View of Trans-Moskva from the Ditch

the upper stories. The courtyard had an acrid stench of carbolic acid. Throughout the courtyard were dirty puddles of water and discarded vegetables. In the apartments and all around the courtyard people were crowding, making noise, cursing." Kanatchikov lived in one of those apartments with about fifteen other men from his native region, who shared the rent. "Some were bachelors, others had wives who lived in the villages and ran their households."[6]

Next to the church of St. Nicholas was the Ivan Smirnov and Sons' Vodka Factory, owned by Ivan's grandson, Sergei Sergeevich Smirnov, and famous for its brightly labeled bottles of cheap alcohol—made, as one government commission charged, from low-quality moonshine distilled by Tula Province peasants. At the end of the block, between the Smirnov Factory and All Saints Street, was the former Wine and Salt Yard, which

Entrance to the Wine and Salt Yard

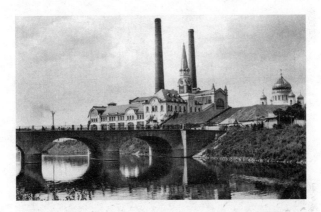

The power station

House next to the power station

housed the Moscow Assembly of Justices of the Peace, the office and residence of the city's sewage administrator, a water-supply office, several stone warehouses (including three for apples and one for eggs), and the Main Electric Tram Power Station, crowned by two chimneys and a little tower with a spire.[7]

The All Saints Bridge, commonly known as the Big Stone Bridge (even though it had been mostly metal since 1858), was a gathering place for pilgrims, vagrants, and beggars—except for the first week of Lent, when the surrounding area became the city's largest mushroom market. According to newspaper reports, mushrooms—dried and pickled—predominated, but there were also "mountains of bagels and white radishes," "lots of honey, preserves, cheap sweets, and sacks of dried fruit," and "long rows of stalls with crockery, cheap furniture, and all sorts of plain household utensils." One could hear "the shouting, laughter, whistling, and not-so-Lenten joking of thousands of people, many of them still hungover from the Shrovetide feast." "People wade through muddy slush, but no

Big Stone Bridge

Mushroom market by the Big Stone Bridge

one seems to notice. Pranksters stomp on puddles, in order to splash the women with dirt. There are quite a few pickpockets, who try to start stampedes."[8]

Across the road from the Wine and Salt Yard and next to the Birliukovskaia Hermitage, stood the Chapel of St. Nicholas the Miracle Worker, with two small wings that housed the monks' rooms, a drapery, and a vegetable stall. Next to the chapel were several pubs, a cheap bathhouse doubling as a brothel, and several former Wool Yard buildings filled with crowded apartments and shops occupied by various tradesmen, including a dyer, hairdresser, tinsmith, cobbler, seamstress, embroiderer, dressmaker, and "phonographer."[9]

Farther along the embankment, facing the Kremlin but partially hidden from view by tall trees in the front yard, was the three-story Maria Women's College, dedicated to "using the students' talents not only for the education of the mind, but also for the education of the heart and character." Most of the heart's education took place in the music rooms on the first floor between the administration office and the dining hall. From 1894 to 1906, one of the instructors at the college was Sergei Rachmaninoff, who did not like teaching but needed the exemption from military service that came with it. According to one of his students, upon entering the classroom, Rachmaninoff, who was twenty-three at the time, "would sit down at his desk, pull out his handkerchief, wipe his face with it for a long time, rest his head on his fingers, and, usually without looking up, call on a pupil and ask her to recite her lesson." One morning he walked out of the class because his students had not done their homework. He wrote to the principal to apologize: "I am generally a bad teacher, but today I was also unpardonably ill-tempered. If I had known that my pupils would have to pay for my behavior, I would not have allowed myself to act in such a way." Perhaps as penance, Rachmaninoff composed his Six Choruses for Women's or Children's Voices, op. 15, and also played at several school performances.[10]

Maria Women's College   Sergei Rachmaninoff in 1904

Behind the school was the sprawling Gustav List Metal Works, which employed more than a thousand workers and produced steam engines, fire hydrants, and water pipes, among other things. Gustav List himself lived above the factory office in a large apartment with a winter garden. He had arrived from Germany in 1856, worked as a mechanic at the Voronezh Sugar Mill, started his Moscow factory in 1863, and turned it into a joint-stock company in 1897.[11]

The factory's shops, warehouses, and dormitories took up the rest of the block. Semen Kanatchikov worked in the "aristocratic" pattern workshop. "Most of the pattern-makers were urban types—they dressed neatly, wore their trousers over their boots, wore their shirts 'fantasia' style, tucked into their trousers, fastened their collars with a colored lace instead of a necktie, and on holidays some of them even wore bowler hats. . . . They used foul language only when they lost their tempers and in extreme situations, or on paydays, when they got drunk, and not even all of them at that."[12]

In the foundry, where the finished patterns ended up, "dirty, dark-colored people, whose blackened, soot-covered faces revealed only the whites of their eyes, rummaged like moles in the earth and dust of the earthen floor." To the roar of the "enormous lifting cranes and turning gears," the "heavy fire-red stream of molten pig iron spewed forth large blazing sparks and illuminated the dark faces of the smelters standing by. . . . The heat near the pots and the furnaces was unbearable and the clothes of the smelters would repeatedly catch fire and have to be doused with water."[13]

When Kanatchikov first arrived at the plant, the workday was eleven and a half hours, not counting overtime night shifts during the busy fall and winter seasons, but after the St. Petersburg weavers' strike of 1896, List introduced the ten-hour day. Most workers, both the "urban types" and the "peasants" (who "wore high boots, traditional cotton-print blouses girdled with a sash, had their hair cut 'under a pot,' and wore beards that

Gustav List Metal Works

were rarely touched by a barber's hand"), lived in and around the Swamp. When they were not working, they drank Smirnov vodka; brawled at weddings; told funny stories about priests; fished in the Moskva and the Ditch; consorted with local prostitutes; courted stocking-knitters, milliners, and cooks in the Alexander Garden next to the Kremlin; read crime chronicles, serialized novels, and Christian and socialist tracts; attended church services and various conspiratorial meetings; staged bloody fistfights on the frozen river by the dam (usually with the Butikov textile workers from across the river); and visited the nearby Tretyakov Gallery of Russian Art, Imperial Museum of Russian History, and Rumiantsev Museum (of just about everything). On Sundays, museum admission was free, but the most popular "free spectacles," according to Kanatchikov, were Moscow fires, which, "no matter how tired," the workers "would run at breakneck speed to see."[14]

Twice a month, on Saturday paydays, most of Kanatchikov's housemates "indulged in wild carousing. Some, as soon as they had collected their pay, would go directly from the factory to beer halls, taverns, or to some grassy spot, whereas others—the somewhat more dandified types—first went back to the apartment to change their clothes." On the following Mondays, the "sufferers . . . with swollen red faces and glazed eyes" would treat their hangovers with shots of alcohol-based varnish kept in a special tin can. "After lunch half the shop would be drunk. Some would loaf on other people's workbenches; others would sit it out in the lavatory. Those whose morning-after drinking had gone too far went to sleep in the drying room or in the shop shed."[15]

East of the Gustav List Metal Works was the "Renaissance" mansion of the sugar millionaire, Kharitonenko, with Gothic interiors by Fedor Schechtel and a large gallery of Russian art. Between Gustav List and the Ditch was the Swamp proper: a large square filled with long sheds, filled with small shops, filled with all kinds of things, mostly edible. In late summer and early fall, the space between the sheds became Moscow's largest farmers' market. Every night, the dealers would gather in Afanasyev's tea room to agree on prices. At about two in the morning, they would come out to greet the arriving peasants, and, according to one newspaper report, each would "walk unhurriedly along the line of carts, glancing indifferently at the mountains of berries. Having made a choice, he would name a price and, if the peasant began to object, would shrug and walk away, lighting up a cigarette." In the ensuing haggling, "various numbers, promises, oaths, and jokes would be jumbled together, passed on, and spread around the square." At sunrise, the peasants would leave, the selling of berries to the public would begin, and, "as if by magic, everything would come alive and turn bright and cheerful. . . . There was so much of everything that one could not help wondering about the size and appetite of Moscow's belly, which, day after day, devoured these gifts of the Swamp quite casually—a mere tasty morsel or idle amusement."[16]

Swamp Square, view from the Kremlin

Swamp market

Later in the day, the berries would be replaced by mushrooms, vegetables, and, on holidays, promenaders and tavern regulars. The inhabitants of "the hovels where naked children crawled amidst soiled rags and which smelled of untreated leather, sauerkraut, the outhouse, and dank mold" would, in Nikolai Bukharin's words, "spill out onto the streets or suffocate in the fumes of taverns and bars with red and blue signs that read 'Beer-hall with Garden' or, in fancy script, 'The "Meeting of Friends" Inn.' Waiters, in jackets that were white in name only, would scurry around through the smoke while in the background, a 'music machine' played, glasses clinked, an accordion wailed, and a voice sang mournful, heart-rending songs. And this motley, mixed-up world was full of moaning, brawling, drinking, screaming, hugging, fighting, kissing, and crying."[17]

■ ■ ■

The state, through a variety of offices and officials, did its best to regulate and sanitize the life of the Swamp and the rest of the city. It inspected the goods sold at the markets and the products manufactured at the Einem, Smirnov, and List factories; repaired the streets, sidewalks, and embankments (the Bersenev and Sophia ones were among the best maintained in the city); fished the bodies of drunks and suicides out of the Ditch; counted every door, window, and tenant for taxation and surveillance purposes; supplied running water, gas, and electricity, along with detailed sign-up and use regulations; installed Gustav List fire hydrants every one hundred meters and put out fires (increasingly using telephones rather than fire towers for signaling the alarm); created a sewage system and, in 1914, made its use compulsory for property owners (who were to collect reports of any "foul odor emanating from water closets and pissoirs"); drained water out of flooded areas and transported solid trash to special dumps; carved, stored, and sorted meat at municipal slaughterhouses; issued numbered badges for cab drivers and enforced parking and traffic regulations; administered the growing streetcar network, powered by electricity that was generated on the site of the former Wine and Salt Yard (using Baku oil brought by rail and water to a special tank by the Simonov Monastery and pumped to the Swamp through an underground pipeline); delivered letters, parcels, and telegrams; replaced kerosene street lamps with gas burners and, in front of Christ the Savior Cathedral and along tram lines, with electric lighting; obligated landlords to cart off their dirty snow beyond the city limits and hire janitors and night guards (who doubled as police agents); planted trees and kept up city parks complete with gazebos, pavilions, and concert stages; built, funded, and staffed most of the schools; paid for about one half of the city's hospital beds; supervised and censored performances and publications; ran foundling homes, almshouses, workhouses, and poor relief offices; and required that all duly classified imperial subjects be registered at their place of residence and that all births, deaths, and marriages be recorded by the appropriate religious authorities. (In order to be allowed to marry his cousin, Rachmaninoff had to procure a written certificate confirming that he had been to confession, find a priest who was willing to risk the displeasure of the Holy Synod, and receive special permission from the tsar.)[18]

The modern state, more or less by definition, does too much or not enough; its many services are both intrusions and entitlements. Early-twentieth-century Russia was not a modern state because its services could not keep up with its industrializing efforts (Moscow was one of the fastest-growing cities in the world, with new immigrants, mostly peasant men like Kanatchikov, making up about 70 percent of the population) and because most bureaucratic rules were seen as optional or negotiable by both citizens and bureaucrats (Sergei Rachmaninoff took care of his incest problem by obtaining his confession certificate without ever going to confession, celebrating his wedding in the barracks chapel of the Sixth Grenadier Regiment, and receiving a note from the tsar that said: "whatever God has bound together, may no man tear asunder"). But mostly, late imperial Russia was not a modern state because it never quite recognized that its services were fulfillments of inalienable rights or that its subjects were responsible citizens (that is, individuals actively complicit in their own nationalization). It never tried to claim, with any degree of conviction, that Russians had a part in building up their state, a stake in its continued growth, and a self-generated desire, however ambivalent, to keep asking for more institutional intrusions.[19]

Instead, the imperial state continued to create more unacknowledged rights while disciplining as many potential usurpers as possible. On the eve of World War I, Moscow was the most policed city in Europe (with about 278 residents per policeman compared with 325 in Berlin, 336 in Paris, and 442 in Vienna). The Yakimanka Police Station, which included the Swamp, kept records of all resident foreigners, Jews, students, cabmen, workers, and unemployed, among others, as well as "commercial, inn-keeping, factory, and artisanal establishments." In addition to routine reporting and recording, police agents were to describe the "mood" of particular groups of people (especially those likely to "have a bad effect on their coworkers"); encourage residents to put out flags on public holidays; and "keep a close watch" on all "persons placed under open or secret police surveillance." Under "characteristic traits" in the police registration books, some of these persons were described as "quick-tempered"; others, as "talkative"; and still others—the majority—as "contemplative." The harder the police worked, the more quick-tempered, talkative, and contemplative their wards became.[20]

In September 1905, the Gustav List workers were among the first in Moscow to go on strike and to demand civil liberties and "personal inviolability" along with improved working conditions. After a rally on the Sophia Embankment, approximately three hundred of them walked over to the Einem Chocolate Factory and forced it to shut down. In November 1905, the Einem mechanical shop was turned into a weapons stockpile as workers made knives and daggers in the expectation of a "St. Bartholomew's Night" (which, according to an early Soviet oral historian, they understood as "a general slaughter"). There was sporadic shooting and barricade building in December 1905; more strikes in 1906 and 1913; a disastrous flood in April 1908 that made most of the basements uninhabitable; and massive anti-German riots in 1915 that involved a pogrom at the Einem factory and the destruction of six of its candy stores in the city. The Swamp and the rest of Russia were becoming quick-tempered, talkative, and contemplative to the exclusion of all other dispositions. The state's expectations and classifications (the "peasant" Kanatchikov, the "nobleman" Rachmaninoff) had little to do with what most people actually did or imagined; church truths (from the divinity of autocracy to the efficacy of confession) were routinely questioned and ridiculed; the new institutions that organized economic life (including the large foreign-owned factories such as List and Einem) had trouble attaching themselves to any existing representation of virtuous living; the new system of railway lines with its center in northern Moscow (along with the new industrial and commercial districts gravitating toward it) clashed with the old street diagram radiating from the Kremlin; and high literature (increasingly remote from the mass-produced kind) had mostly forsaken its job of providing meaningful connections between "once upon a time" and "happily ever after." Russia was not the only casualty of industrialization's encounter with the fin-de-siècle, but the ancien regime's rigidity made its plight seem universal and revelatory. The empire was crawling with prophets, soothsayers, and itinerant preachers. Everyone seemed to believe that the world was sick and would not last much longer.[21]

In addition to the orthodox Orthodox, who tended to read more devotional literature, go on more pilgrimages, and report more miraculous healings and apparitions than they had half a century earlier, there were the newly literate proletarian writers, who wrote about the "chains of suffering" and the coming deliverance; the Ioannites, who venerated Father John of Kronstadt as the herald of the coming apocalypse; the Brethren, who preached personal redemption through temperance, sobriety, and charismatic spiritualism; the Tolstoyans, who foresaw a universal moral transformation through vegetarianism and nonviolence; the Dukhobors, who resisted the growing demands for conscription and civil registration by emigrating to Canada with the help of the Tolstoyans (and their brethren, the Quakers); the Baptists, who proselytized vigorously and successfully in behalf of the priesthood of all believers; the Socialist Revolutionaries, who believed in the Russian peasant as both the instrument and principal beneficiary of universal emancipation; the Social Democrats (divided into the Bolsheviks, Mensheviks, and a variety of short-lived subsects, including the God-builders), who believed in the redemptive mission of the urban working class; the Anarchists, who expected free individuals to create a world without coercion; the Decadents, who had "the sense, both oppressive and exalting, of being the last of a series"; and the Symbolists, who approached "every object and phenomenon," including their own lives, "from the point of view of its ultimate state, or in the light of the future world" (as Vladimir Solovyov put it).[22]

In and around the Swamp, everyone was a Symbolist. Nikolai Bukharin's favorite book, as a ten-year-old, was the Book of Revelation—"its solemn and obscure mood, cosmic cataclysms, the archangels' trumpets, the resurrection of the dead, the Beast, the last days, the Whore of Babylon, the magic vials." After reading Solovyov's "The Tale of the Antichrist," he felt "shivers run down his spine" and rushed off to find his mother to ask if she was a harlot. Aleksandr Voronsky, a Tambov priest's son who lived in an attic above a Trans-Moskva holy bread bakery and taught Marxism to leather workers in a basement next to the church gate, "kept repeating" the verses he had memorized as an adolescent—about the divine gift of an "undivided heart" and the kind of "inspiring hatred" that engenders "the powerful, ferocious, and monstrous hymns of vengeance and retribution": "They will plunder your wealth and loot your merchandise; they will break down your walls and demolish your fine houses and throw your stones, timber and rubble into the sea. I will put an end to your noisy songs, and the music of your harps will be heard no more."[23]

Nikolai Fedorov, who worked as a librarian in the Rumiantsev Museum, proposed a practical plan to resurrect the dead and institute the reign of "complete and perfect kinship"; Semen Kanatchikov, who went to the Rumiantsev Museum "to look at pictures," discovered that soon "everything would become the common property of the toilers"; Alexander Scriabin (Rachmaninoff's classmate at the Moscow Conservatory) set out to write a work of art to end all life as well as all art; and Rachmaninoff himself based his First Symphony (composed and performed when he was a teacher at the Maria Women's College) on "Dies irae," a thirteenth-century Latin hymn about the Last Judgment. César Cui probably did not know how right he was when he began his review of the first performance with the words: "If there were a conservatory in Hell, and if one of its gifted students received the assignment to write a programmatic symphony on 'the seven plagues of Egypt' . . ."[24]

The conservatory (a short walk from the Sophia Embankment across the Big Stone Bridge and past the Rumiantsev Museum) was not the only doomed institution in Moscow, and the symphony about the coming plagues was not Rachmaninoff's only endeavor. While he was working on the First Symphony about the last days (op. 13) and the Six Choruses for his Maria College students (op. 15), he also wrote a song (op. 14, no. 11) that soon became "a symbol of social awakening" and a popular anthem of hope and redemption. The lyrics, originally written around 1829, were by Fedor Tyutchev, one of the Symbolists' favorite poets.[25]

The fields are still white with snow,
But the streams are astir with the clamor of spring.
They flow and awaken the somnolent shores
They flow and sparkle and proclaim . . .

They proclaim to the four corners of the world:
"Spring is on its way, spring is on its way!
We are the young spring's messengers,
She has sent us on ahead!

Spring is on its way, spring is on its way,
And, crowding merrily behind her,
Is the red-cheeked, bright dancing circle
Of the quiet, warm days of May."

On May 12, 1904, the police intercepted a letter from a certain "Y" in Nizhnii Novgorod to S. P. Mironycheva, a resident of the "Dormitory for Female Students" on the Sophia Embankment. Referring as much to Rach-

Spring flooding in the Swamp (1908)

maninoff's song as to Nikolai Dobroliubov's 1860 essay, "When Will the Real Day Finally Come?," the author urges his correspondent not to give in to despair: "Let this be a momentary concession to a time of uncertainty, oppression, and doubt. Surely, even now, the coming renewal is capable of lifting up the best people of our time toward energy and faith. The real day is coming, after all. It is coming—noisy and tempestuous, sweeping away everything weak, feeble, and old. . . . The dawn, which sheds its fantastic, enchanting, and transparent light over everything and everyone, is near."[26]

It is not clear whether the police agent who read the letter knew that "Y" was Yakov Sverdlov, a nineteen-year-old gymnasium dropout, pharmacist's apprentice, and "professional revolutionary."

Spring flooding in the Swamp

2

THE PREACHERS

Most prophets of the Real Day were either Christians or socialists. The majority of Christians continued to think of "the Second Coming" as a metaphor for endless postponement, but a growing minority, including a few decadent intellectuals and the rapidly multiplying Evangelical Protestants, expected the Last Judgment in their lifetimes. This belief was shared by those who associated Babylon with capitalism and looked forward to a violent revolution followed by a reign of social justice.

The two groups had a great deal in common. Some people believed that revolutionary socialism was a form of Christianity; others believed that Christianity was a form of revolutionary socialism. Sergei Bulgakov and Nikolai Berdyaev proposed to incorporate political apocalypticism into Christianity; Anatoly Lunacharsky and Maxim Gorky considered Marxism a religion of earthly salvation; Vladimir Bonch-Bruevich referred to Baptists and Flagellants as natural "transmission points" of Bolshevik propaganda; and the Bolshevik propagandist (and priest's son) Aleksandr Voronsky claimed to have met a revolutionary terrorist who was using the Gospels as a guide to "the violent overthrow of the tsarist regime."[1]

But normally they saw each other as opposites. Christians tended to think of socialists as atheists or Antichrists, and socialists tended to agree (while considering Christians backward or hypocritical). In standard socialist autobiographies, the loss of "religious" faith was a prerequisite for spiritual awakening. One crucial difference was that most preachers of a Christian apocalypse were workers and peasants, while most theorists of workers' and peasants' revolutions were students and "eternal students." The students were usually the children of clerks, clergymen, teachers, doctors, Jews, and other "proletarians of mental labor": professional intellectuals as metaphorical Jews (chosen, learned, and alienated) and Jews as honorary intellectuals irrespective of what they did for a living. They all grew up as perennial prodigies, as heirs to a lost sacred mission, as strangers among people they called "the people." They were, for the most part, hereditary members of the intelligentsia.

The Vilno Bolshevik Aron Solts believed that the source of his "opposition to the powers that be" was his Jewishness, which he associated with legal inequality, "relative intellectualism," and sympathy for revolutionary terrorists. Nikolai Bukharin claimed that his father, a teacher and sometime tax inspector, did not believe in God, "enjoyed saying something radical every once in a while," and often asked Nikolai, who had learned to read

Aron Solts   Nikolai Bukharin   Valerian Obolensky (Osinsky)
(Courtesy of Elena Simakova)

at the age of four, to recite poetry for family friends. Bukharin's friend and
Swamp "agitator" Valerian Obolensky (whose job in the winter of 1907–8
was to write leaflets for the Gustav List workers) grew up in the family of
a veterinarian of "radical convictions and high culture" who taught his
children French and German and encouraged them to read Belinsky and
Dobroliubov ("not to mention the great fiction writers"). Another early
convert to Bolshevism, Aleksei Stankevich, attributed his awakening to
the feeling "that Mother and Father were much better educated, more intelligent, and more honest than their milieu." (His father, a teacher in
Kostroma and Kologriv, was "driven to drink" by the idiocy of provincial
life.) "All this led our youthful minds deeper and deeper into doubt and
confusion."[2]

To be a true *intelligent* meant being religious about being secular; asking "the accursed questions" over lunch and dinner; falling deeper and
deeper into doubt and confusion as a matter of principle; and feeling both
chosen and damned for being better educated, more intelligent, and more
honest than one's milieu. Whether a member of the intelligentsia could
find the answers to the accursed questions and still be a member of the
intelligentsia was open to question. Lenin thought not (and did not consider himself one). The authors of the antiradical manifesto *Signposts* believed there were no nondoctrinaire intelligentsia members left (and considered themselves an exception). Most people used the term to refer to
both the confused and the confident—as long as they remained self-
conscious about being better educated, more intelligent, and more honest
than their milieu. The proportion of those who had overcome doubt kept
growing. Most believed in the coming revolution; more and more knew
that it would be followed by socialism.

There were two kinds of socialists: Marxists and nationalists. Or rather,
there was a wide range of possible definitions of collective martyrdom—
from the Mensheviks' reliance on the timely self-realization of the sociologically correct proletarians; to the Bolsheviks' expectation that Russian

workers and peasants might start a revolution out of turn, by way of exception; to the Populists' faith in the Russian peasant as a universal redeemer by virtue of his uniquely Russian communalism; to the Bundists' insistence on the need for a Jewish specificity within Marxist cosmopolitanism; to the uncompromising tribal millenarianism of the Armenian Dashnaks, socialist Zionists, and Polish nationalists. Even at the extremes, the distinction was not always clear: the Marxists talked of "hereditary proletarians" as a caste with its own culture and genealogy; the most radical Russian nationalists

Feliks Kon

were known as Socialist Revolutionaries (SRs), not Russian nationalists; and the most radical non-Russian nationalists represented their nations as the world's original proletarians. Everyone spoke the biblical language of tribal chosenness and suffering for humanity.

One of the oldest Bolsheviks, Feliks Kon, grew up in Warsaw, in a Jewish family of Polish nationalists. "Patriotism was a substitute for religion," he wrote in his memoirs. "Of the latter, only the formal, ritualistic side remained." Once, on Passover, as his grandfather "was presiding over the table and leading the prayers," an uncle returned from foreign exile, where he had been hiding from "the Muscovites": "The prayers were forgotten. Everyone, from the little ones to my old grandfather, sat listening to his stories with rapt attention. 'Rather than talking about the flight of the Jews from Egypt,' said Uncle to Grandfather, 'let's talk about the martyrdom of Poland.' Grandfather readily agreed."

At seventeen, Kon learned of the heroism of the Muscovite revolutionary terrorists and stopped talking about the martyrdom of Poland. The exodus came to represent universal liberation.

It was a change of faith, of cult. . . . A dead, ossified faith had been replaced by a living, vibrant one. . . . I was ready to do battle with the whole world of lies, hypocrisy, humiliation, and falsehood, the world of grief and servitude. . . . It was clear as day to me that I must go to other seventeen- and eighteen-year-old ardent young men and share with them my faith and my truth, for us to unite, come together, "do more studying"—I vaguely understood the necessity of that—and then, all of us together, leave behind "the gloaters, idle blabberers, and blood-stained executioners" for "the camp of the dying," to reveal to them the reasons for their grinding slavery, open their eyes to the force living within them, awaken that force, and then . . . then . . . then . . . the great deed would be done: the world of slavery and untruth would sink into the abyss, and the bright sun of liberty would shine over the earth.[3]

Karl Radek

Serial conversions involving a variety of national and cosmopolitan options were common on the Russian Empire's western periphery. Another ardent young man, Karl Sobelson, moved from the cult of Heinrich Heine and *Nathan the Wise* (which he described as typical of Galician Jews), to Polish patriotism "complete with its Catholic shell" (at which point he became "Radek"), to socialism "understood as a quest for Polish independence," to radical Marxism in a variety of national guises. Closer to the imperial center, spiritual awakening tended to be represented as a generic revelation of the misery of the surrounding world, with the finer distinctions regarding the nature of the last days becoming apparent later, as a result of sober reflection.[4]

Some well-off socialists remembered having been impressionable or rebellious children sensitive to injustice and subject to "feelings of discomfort and shame" on account of their unearned privilege. Elena Stasova—the granddaughter of a prominent architect, daughter of an even more prominent lawyer, and niece of a famous art critic—suffered from a growing "feeling of indebtedness" to the people "who made it possible for us, the intelligentsia, to live the way we did."[5]

But most, like Feliks Kon, were changed forever by reading, and even Stasova's feelings of guilt "were partly derived from books." The officer's son and cadet corps student, Sergei Mitskevich, lived in the dark until the age of fourteen: "I read Turgenev's *The Virgin Soil*, and my eyes were opened: I understood that revolutionaries were not the evil men our officials said they were, but people struggling for freedom, for the people. This realization led to a complete revolution in my thinking. I began to read a lot." New reading led to new insights and the eventual "discovery of the key to the understanding of reality," but it was the first youthful epiphany that separated life without "sense or meaning" from a purposeful quest for true knowledge.[6]

Kon (born 1864), Stasova (1873), and Mitskevich (1869) were among the oldest Bolsheviks. The vast majority—those born in the 1880s and 1890s—had their eyes opened in school, alongside their classmates. In Nikolai Bukharin's Moscow Gymnasium No. 1 (on Volkhonka across from the Cathedral of Christ the Savior), some boys "went on living aimlessly—reading whatever was assigned and horsing around in the hallways," but "the class elite" consisted of two groups of self-conscious apocalyptics: the decadents and the revolutionaries. According to Bukharin's partisan account,

the aristocratic group—the loners, the sons of the nobility and the upper bourgeoisie (rich merchants, bankers, stock exchange speculators, and Jewish moneybags, who were trying desperately to make their way into the most refined spheres)—aped their older brothers, playing earnestly at beings snobs and dandies. They wore jodhpurs, pointy English dress shoes, expensive narrow-waisted, light-colored jackets made by well-known Moscow tailors, and wide, fancy leather sashes. Their collars were starched and their hair neatly combed, with impeccably straight parts and not a hair out of place. They acted as if they were doing the gymnasium a great favor by attending classes. They kept to themselves and often brought French books, from Baudelaire to Maeterlinck and Rodenbach, which they read with melancholy miens, to make clear that they lived in a world of altogether different dimensions. They were loose-limbed, pointedly polite, fond of exchanging remarks in French or English and conversing about art, and seemed to regard normal life as something to be held squeamishly between two fingers, pinkie extended. They dropped the names of Nietzsche and Solovyov but did not read them; carried around reproductions of the exquisitely depraved, elegant graphic masterpieces by Aubrey Beardsley and Félicien Rops; and talked in church whispers of Oscar Wilde. Of the new Russian poets, they only recognized the Symbolists, showing off by sharing the latest news of their literary and personal lives, which bordered on refined gossip.

The rival group consisted mainly of children from intelligentsia families. They wore Tolstoy shirts under their jackets and kept their hair deliberately shaggy and often uncombed; some older boys were beginning to grow beards. In class they secretly read Pisarev, Dobroliubov, and Shchedrin. . . . They worshiped Gorky, despised everything official, scorned all kinds of "pomp and circumstance," and ridiculed "the white satin lining crowd," their ideals, and the way they walked, giving them cutting and rather accurate nicknames, such as "the heavenly wagtail," and occasionally entering into lively arguments with them, often on literary subjects. They sensed vaguely that the unstoppable stream of life would soon answer the question "When will the real day finally come?" They were impressed by every manifestation of open protest, every word of condemnation, every act of heroic resistance to established order. Even routine pranks had a certain value in their eyes: they were instinctively attracted to "undermining the foundations," even in little things. They were impertinent, sharp-tongued, and prone to mocking their sheeplike neighbors.[7]

According to his classmate Ilya Ehrenburg, Bukharin was less morbidly earnest than most of his fellow underminers (especially his best friend, the unsmiling Grigory Brilliant), but he was just as cutting. He laughed a lot and "constantly interrupted the conversation with jokes and made-up or absurd words," but "it was dangerous to argue with him: he tenderly ridiculed his opponents."[8]

Yakov Sverdlov

Yakov Sverdlov's (Y's) biographers describe him as boisterously argumentative. One of six children in the family of a Jewish engraver in Nizhnii Novgorod, he excelled in elementary school and was sent to a gymnasium, where he fought with the children of noblemen and "baffled" his teachers with unexpected questions. "Bored in his classes, he figured out a way to read regular books instead of textbooks while sitting at his desk. Once, when he had been caught in the act and heard the teacher's threatening 'What are you doing?', he answered calmly: 'Reading an interesting book.' 'What kind of book?' roared the teacher even more threateningly. 'An ordinary, paper one,' answered the student even more calmly." True or not, this story is an accurate representation of a young rebel's ideal ("quick-tempered," "talkative," and "contemplative") disposition. After four years, Sverdlov left the gymnasium to become a pharmacist's apprentice and a "professional revolutionary." Sverdlov's father cheered him on: all of Yakov's five siblings were, in one way or another, waiting for the coming of the real day.[9]

The road to belief began with friendship. Sverdlov had Vladimir Lubotsky (later "Zagorsky," the man after whom the town of Sergiev-Posad would be renamed); Kon had Ludowik Sawicki (who committed suicide in Paris in 1893); and Bukharin had Grigory Brilliant (the future people's commissar of finance, Grigory Sokolnikov). The son of a Kazan merchant, Aleksandr Arosev, remembered finding a friend early on in his *Realschule* career: "At one point I was told there was a strong boy named Skriabin in Grade 3, Section B. I sought him out. One day he was in the hall washing the blackboard sponge under a faucet. He looked rather gloomy (the way he always did, as I found out later). I came up to him and proposed fighting. Skriabin agreed. Having exchanged several preliminary punches, we got into a stranglehold, to the delight of the whole hall. I don't remember who won, but we became acquainted."[10]

Acquaintance led to conversations, conversations to confessions, and confessions to intimacy. As Arosev wrote in one of his many memoirs, "Friendship begins when one reveals to the other a mystery that has never been revealed before. And when you are young, anything can become a mystery: the way you notice a passing cloud, delight in a thunderstorm, admire a girl, or dream of a faraway land." For Skriabin, the mystery was music (he was a violinist and played quartets with his three brothers); for Arosev, it was novels. For both of them, it was the search for the true path to revolution. Arosev continues:

One night, . . . we were walking through the deserted streets, sprinkled with snow. The silence of the streets gave us a sense of intimacy, and the cold forced us to move closer to one another. We were walking arm in arm. It was well past midnight. From street corners, roadside posts, and porch awnings, shapeless shadows slid over the darkly glistening snow that looked like so many fish scales. Sometimes it seemed to us that those were the shadows of spies following us wherever we went, but there were no spies anywhere. Those shadows—the uncertain silvery flickerings in the night—were listening to our halting speeches, our words that sparkled with one thing only: a desperate eagerness to find a truth that we could give all of ourselves to in the name of struggle.[11]

The truth, they knew, was to be found in larger groups of like-minded believers. After more conversations and confessions, several clusters of friends would come together as a secret reading circle:

Seven or eight fifth-grade *Realschule* students were sitting on the chairs, bed, and couch of the low attic room lit up by a kerosene lamp with a white glass lampshade. The portraits of Kautsky, Engels, Marx, Mikhailovsky, Uspensky, Korolenko, and Tolstoy looked down sternly and protectively. On the bookshelf in the corner, one could see the names of the same heroes of the age. . . .

The air was filled with an energy that could only be sensed by the nerves, which, like little cobwebs, connected everyone and made them feel related and bound together forever, for many centuries to come. The young men barely knew each other, but each looked at the others with an almost ecstatic affection, proud to be there, next to all those others, who were so mysterious and, just like him, full of fire. Every face seemed to be saying: "Starting today, this very minute, I, so-and-so, have joined the ranks of fighters."[12]

They would then elect a chairman (on this occasion, Skriabin) and decide on book lists, passwords, and nicknames. Skriabin became "Uncle," and later "Molotov"; Arosev became "Z"; and, in other rooms in other towns, Sverdlov became "Comrade Andrei"; Brilliant became "Sokolnikov"; Obolensky became "Osinsky"; and Voronsky—"a pale, thin, curly-haired, blue-eyed young man with full, bright red lips" —became "Valentin."

Voronsky's circle of Tambov seminarians was born "within the damp, musty walls steeped in the balm and incense of Orthodox Christianity," but its members—"adolescent runts with prominent collarbones and awkwardly flailing arms"—read the same books as their Kazan and Moscow contemporaries—and held similar meetings:

Imagine a tiny room somewhere on First Dolevaia Street, in the house of a clerk's widow: faded wallpaper, calico curtains on the windows, three or four chairs with holes in the seats, a table, an iron bed, a bookshelf, a tin lamp with a paper lampshade (with a burnt trace left by the light bulb), fresh faces with downy upper lips, and open double-breasted gray jackets with faded white buttons. Two gymnasium girls in brown dresses are hiding in a dark corner; their hair is pulled back tightly in braids; one of them is so shy she almost never lifts her eyes. We are arguing about the commune, the land strips, and the relationship between the hero and the crowd. We are overconfident and full of peremptory fervor. Someone is plucking the strings of an old guitar or mandolin.[13]

What bound them together were the books they read and the omnipresent lampshades—white, brown, or green—which stood for both common reading and shared spaces. Sometimes Arosev's friends would just sit quietly reading by lamplight, with "cups of hot tea steaming on a little round table."

The open pages of [Plekhanov, Pisarev, and Belinsky] filled us up so completely and blinded our eyes to such an extent that sometimes, lifting our tired heads, we would be surprised to find ourselves in a room cast into shadows by a green lampshade. The lampshade would veil the sinful, messy world outside, while shedding its bright light on white sheets and black lines—those streams of intricate thought. I don't know about the others, but I was in awe of the tenacity, durability, and terrible fearlessness of human thought, especially that thought within which—or rather, beneath which—there loomed something larger than thought, something primeval and incomprehensible, something that made it impossible for men not to act in a certain way, not to experience the urge for action so powerful that even death, were it to stand in the way of this urge, would appear powerless.[14]

Aleksandr Arosev   Viacheslav Skriabin (Molotov)
(Courtesy of V. A. Nikonov)

Joining "the camp of the dying" was a vital ingredient of the urge for action nurtured by collective reading. As Kon put it, from a position of nostalgic immortality, "we were all going to die, of course, this much was clear. In fact, as I saw it at the time, it was even necessary," especially since death was "a wonderful, beautiful detail," remote and perhaps fleeting. "My state of mind at the time resembled the mood of a young knight who is determined to wake up a sleeping princess even if he has to undergo severe personal trials. . . . Awakened by the miraculous touch of socialism, the working people would wake up, rise, shed the terrible shackles of slavery, and liberate themselves and everyone else. The capacity for friendship and willingness to die is what separated "the sensitive and young at heart" from those Feliks Kon and his friends called the "Zulus"—or, "in the terminology of the time, the savages who only cared about their future careers and present comforts and had no interest whatsoever in the rest of humanity." The Zulus were divided into the "naked ones" and the "hypocrites." The sensitive and young at heart were divided into reading circles.[15]

As students moved into higher grades, the circles became ranked and specialized. The "lower circles" studied basic socialist literature; the "middle" ones organized presentations on particular topics or authors; and the "higher" ones sponsored papers on freely chosen subjects and formal debates with invited participants. Different circles, including those from different schools, formed interlocking networks of common reading, conversation, and belief. In Arosev's *Realschule*, all the reading groups were united into a single "Non-Party Revolutionary Organization" with its own statutes ("a kind of teaching plan for a short-term course designed to produce revolutionaries of both kinds: SRs and Marxists.")[16]

For most people, the choice between the SRs and Marxists happened some time after their separation from the Zulus. Unlike the original election, it is usually remembered as a rational act subject to testing, reconsideration, and public scrutiny. At the age of sixteen, the veterans of Osinsky's (Obolensky's) circle in Moscow Gymnasium No. 7 decided it was time to make up their minds and "self-identify politically." To that end, they invited a Moscow University student, Platon Lebedev (the future "Kerzhentsev"), and launched a series of presentations on the history of the Russian revolutionary movement. Osinsky spent three months in the Rumiantsev Library reading about the Decembrists.

I have always done my best to resist everything "fashionable," everything accepted by the intelligentsia in the manner of a psychological contagion. At that time [1904], I considered Marxism, which was spreading rapidly among the intelligentsia, just another fashionable trend (for the intelligentsia, including some of my friends, it did turn out to be only a fashion). So, I tried very hard to give the Decembrist movement a non-Marxist explanation. This explanation

contradicted my own evidence and the paper kept sliding into a
meaningless liberal rut. It was not difficult for Lebedev-Kerzhentsev,
with the obvious support of my own comrades, to rout me utterly.
Having given my "defeat" a great deal of serious thought, I arrived at
the conclusion that I had chosen the wrong path and that old Marx
was right, after all. The revolution of 1905 provided plenty of further—much more tangible—proof.[17]

In Kazan, Arosev (Z) and Skriabin (Molotov) chose their political affili-
ations without a great deal of serious thought. In the spring of 1907, at the
age of seventeen, they decided to test their convictions by reading the
relevant texts and holding a public debate at the Non-Party Revolutionary
Organization's fall meeting. Arosev's topic was "The Philosophical Foundations of the Socialist Revolutionary Party"; Skriabin's, "The Philosophical Foundations of the Social-Democratic Party." According to Arosev,
"Skriabin and I stocked up on the literature, left behind the noise of the
city—he, for Viatka Province, I, for the village of Malye Derbyshki—and immersed ourselves in Marx, Mikhailovsky, Engels, Lavrov, Plekhanov, De-
levsky [sic]. . . . We had agreed to read the same books, so that, during the
debate, he would be familiar with my sources and I, with his."

For three months, they read, took notes, and wrote long letters to each
other. "Those were not letters, but theoretical position papers and
counter-papers, a sort of written exam on material covered." At the end of
the summer, they reassembled in Skriabin's room. "The soft August twi-
light came in through the large windows. Out in the courtyard we could
see chickens walking around and a cat stretching itself by the water pipe.
The room slowly grew dark. A copy of Aivazovsky's 'The Waves of the Surf,'
painted by Nikolai Skriabin [Viacheslav's brother], looked down at us from
the wall. On the table, the samovar was wheezing softly. Next to it were
cups of unfinished tea and a large tome, open and unread." Suddenly
Arosev announced that his summer reading had convinced him of the superiority of Marxism over populism, and that he could not, in good conscience, defend the SR position (which favored Russian peasants over
rootless workers as agents of revolutionary change). After a brief pause,
Skriabin said that, in that case, he was not going to speak, either. At the
general meeting, the two friends' declarations "were met with loud applause from one side and a buzz of disapproval, from the other. . . . But no
one called Z a traitor. They knew that Z had taken a sharp ideological turn,
that he had stepped over the threshold separating a spontaneous study
of the world from its conscious understanding."[18]

Not all debates between the SRs and Marxists were this one-sided, even
in later retellings by eventual victors. The "decisive battle" Bukharin describes in his memoir involved two teams of earnest boys and girls (reinforced, in the case of the SRs, by one university student) and covered all
the usual points of disagreement: the "working class" versus "the people";

"sober calculation" versus "great deeds and self-sacrifice"; "objectivism" versus "subjectivism"; and "universal laws of development" versus "Russia's uniqueness." The Marxist charge that the SRs put heroes above the crowd met with the countercharge that Lenin's *What Is to Be Done?* amounted to the same thing; to which the Bolsheviks said that their leaders objectively represented the interests of the workers; to which the SRs responded that the Bolsheviks had "turned their party into a barracks, enforced total unanimity, killed all freedom of criticism in their own midst, and were now trying to spread the same thing everywhere"; to which the Bolsheviks responded by quoting from Lenin's *What Is to Be Done?*:

> We are a tight group walking along a precipitous and difficult path, holding each other firmly by the hand. We are surrounded on all sides by enemies, and we have to advance almost constantly under their fire. We have come together, as a result of a decision freely taken, precisely for the purpose of fighting the enemy, and not of stumbling into the nearby swamp, the inhabitants of which, from the very outset, have reproached us with having separated ourselves into an exclusive group and having chosen the path of struggle instead of the path of conciliation. And now some among us are beginning to shout: Let's go into the swamp! And when we begin to shame them, they retort: What backward people you are! Are you not ashamed to deny us the freedom to urge you to take a better road! Oh, yes, gentlemen! You are free not only to urge us, but to go yourselves wherever you please, even into the swamp. In fact, we believe that the swamp is just where you belong, and we are prepared to do whatever we can to help *you* take up residence there. But then let go of our hands, don't clutch at us, and don't soil the noble word "freedom," for we too are "free" to go where we please, free to fight not only against the swamp, but also against those who are turning toward the swamp![19]

At this point the Bolsheviks proclaimed themselves the winners and ended the debate. Everyone got up and, one at a time ("young ladies excepted!"), walked out of the smoke-filled room with "heavy dark-red curtains" into a back alley off the Arbat, a few blocks north of Bukharin's gymnasium and the Big Stone Bridge. "It was quiet in the street. . . . The sound of footsteps echoed through the alley. . . . Large flakes of snow were falling silently, floating out of the darkness, whirling around streetlamps, and covering, like a soft, fluffy eiderdown, the sidewalks, hitching posts, sleds, and the back of a coachman on the corner, half asleep and not fully sober."[20]

As student circles and various "non-party revolutionary organizations" established links with each other and joined formal revolutionary parties, they progressed from just reading to reading and writing essays

Valerian Kuibyshev

(Osinsky's first was about the utilitarian theory of ethics); to reading and writing leaflets (Voronsky's first ran: "All we can hear are the rattling of chains and the screeching of cell locks, but the new day is dawning, and the sun of social independence and equality, the sun of labor and liberty will rise"); to reading and transporting illegal literature, printing proclamations, holding rallies, making bombs, and, in the case of the SR Maximalists, killing state officials. All over the empire, schoolchildren, seminarians, college students, and eternal students were in the grips of a "living, vibrant faith," eager to fight "not only against the swamp, but also against those who are turning toward the swamp."[21]

In 1909, the twenty-one-year-old Valerian Kuibyshev—graduate of the Siberian Cadet Corps, student of Tomsk University, and member of the Bolshevik Party since the age of sixteen—was arrested for receiving a parcel with illegal books. His father, the military commander of Kainsk, in the Siberian steppe, was promptly summoned to appear before his commanding officer, General Maslennikov. Valerian describes his father as a simple man, honest soldier, and loving parent, in the manner of Pushkin's fort commander from *The Captain's Daughter*. He was a "servitor who never had any property, so we were raised very modestly; patched and threadbare suits were handed down from older brothers and sisters to the younger ones." He was also, like Sverdlov's father, understanding and perhaps proud of his son's rebellion. There were eight children in the Kuibyshev family, and every one of them was listed by the police as politically unreliable. According to a story Valerian told several friends in August 1931,

Father arrived in Omsk in low spirits and presented himself to General Maslennikov.

As soon as he entered, the general started yelling at him:

"You can't even raise your own children properly, so how are you going to train your soldiers? Your home address is being used for receiving subversive literature. You should be shot."

General Maslennikov did not stop yelling for half an hour. Father stood at attention, his arms at his sides, not allowed to respond while his commander was speaking.

Having exhausted himself, General Maslennikov fell silent for a while and then said: "I am having you transferred to Tiumen."

Tiumen was, of course, a much bigger town than Kainsk. This was a promotion. . . .

Father was taken aback: "Excuse me, Your Excellency?"

"You are being transferred to Tiumen." Then, after a short pause: "I have two sons in prison in Kiev myself."[22]

■ ■ ■

The young revolutionaries' main job was "propaganda and agitation." "Propaganda" consisted in extending school reading circles to "the masses." Aleksandr Voronsky's circle used to meet underground.

> The basement was dimly lit with a lamp. It smelled of kerosene and cheap tobacco. The curtains were closely drawn. Casting somber, monstrous shadows, the workers would silently sit down at the table covered with dark oilcloth that was torn and stained with ink. It was always cold in the room. Someone would move the iron stove closer, and the smoke would make your throat itch and eyes burn. They felt like meetings of mysterious conspirators, but the faces of those present were always perfectly ordinary. Sternly and possessively, Nikita would examine the members of the circle, as if testing them, tap on the table with his knuckle or a pencil, and say solemnly: "Listen to the Comrade Speaker."[23]

Nikita was an older worker who "loved 'learning,' put on ancient glasses to read books and newspapers, did not tolerate teasing, and never joked himself, or indeed knew how." The Comrade Speaker's learning was partly offset by his awkwardness in front of those whose social and intellectual inferiority was offset by their maturity and redemptive mission.[24]

"Agitation" (as opposed to "propaganda") referred to making speeches at factories or outdoor rallies. The speeches were to be short and more or less to the point. The point, according to the the agitators' instructions, was to make sure that "the flame of hatred . . . burned in the listeners' hearts." Voronsky delivered his "in one violent burst, without catching his breath, gesticulating volubly."[25]

> Once, I was rhapsodizing at an improvised open-air meeting from the caboose of a freight train. Below me was a crowd of railway workers. I ardently prophesied "the hour of vengeance and retribution" and was passionately urging them "not to give way to provocation" and "to fight to the end," while piling on the appeals and not sparing the slogans. Transported by my revolutionary fervor, I did not notice the clanking and the jerking of the train as, before the eyes of the amazed workers, I began to float away, first slowly, then faster and faster, farther and farther away, still waving my arms and shouting out fiery words.[26]

Words—written or spoken—are at the center of all missionary work. Voronsky and his fellow agitators spent most of their time talking, whether the train was moving or not. Reading (often out loud) was incorporated into discussion; writing (Lenin's, in particular) was like shouting out fiery words; and some of the most important silences in socialist autobiographies are memories of being spellbound by someone else's eloquence: Lenin's, Trotsky's, Chernov's. Everyone seemed quick-tempered, talkative, and contemplative at the same time.

Socialist proselytizing was different from the Christian kind in two fundamental ways. First, it was not universalist. The Christian message was, in theory, for everyone; the socialist one was aimed exclusively at the elect (Russian peasants for the SRs, industrial workers for the Marxists). Even the Calvinists, who preached members-only salvation for the chosen, did not claim to know who the chosen were. Socialists, by contrast, assumed that a particular, objectively defined part of humanity was the exclusive means of universal redemption and the indigenous population of the kingdom of freedom. The original preachers could come from anywhere—indeed, they were all intellectuals (unapologetically so, in the case of the Bolsheviks)—but the real meaning of their "agitation and propaganda" and the only chance for the coming of the real day was to convert the convertible. The prince was to wake up the sleeping beauty, not the ugly step-sisters.

The Bolsheviks were particularly forceful on this score. By being the most skeptical of "spontaneity" ("class political consciousness can be brought to the workers *only from without*," according to Lenin), they were the most intent on proselytizing. And proselytizing demanded organizational rigor. As the agitator's instructions put it, "explicating the role of our party as the most advanced detachment of the working class, you must not forget that our party is a fighting army, and not a debating society." And as a member of Bukharin's debating society put it, having followed his instructions, "my opponent tried to frighten us with talk about the barracks. I am not afraid of words. There are barracks and barracks, just as there are soldiers and soldiers. We are building our party not as a, I am sorry, motley collection of swans, crawfish, and pikes, but as a party of the truly like-minded, and a military party at that. Yes, military." And the reason they could do that was that they were the only party led by an uncontested charismatic leader. Lenin was both the creature and the guarantee of the unity of the like-minded.[27]

The second way in which socialist evangelism differed from its Christian counterpart was its intellectualism—the degree to which it was, indeed, a debating society. Most Russian Orthodox converts to Protestant Christianity seemed to be after personal salvation and independent work on the self, much of it through reading and conversation. Socialists were after the same thing, but they went much further. A conversion to socialism was a conversion to the intelligentsia, to a fusion of millenarian faith and lifelong learning. It was an immediate step up socially and intellectually, as well as spiritually. The student preachers of Bolshevism were asking the workers to become students while remaining workers. The would-be converts had a special role because of who they were, but they could not perform that role without an altered "consciousness."

This combination of proletarian chosenness with committed intellectualism—self-affirmation through change and upward mobility without betrayal—seemed to appeal to some workers. As one of Voronsky's pupils put it, "'It's really strange, all these people wearing glasses coming to serve us, for God's sake! And why are they serving us? They are serving us because they're beginning to understand our untold strength, because,' he would start beating himself on the chest, 'because proletarians of all countries unite! Simple as that.'" In Kon's version of a popular fairy-tale metaphor (also used in the title of Voronsky's memoirs), "the work was going well. Having been sprinkled with the magic water of life, the sleeping kingdom was waking up and coming to life."[28]

Karl Lander (Kārlis Landers), the son of Latvian day laborers, was fifteen years old when he saw a May Day demonstration and suddenly felt "drawn by a new powerful force." As he writes in his autobiography, "I knew the everyday life of workers well because of my relatives and close friends, but, suddenly, it appeared in a completely new light, as a carrier and keeper of some great mystery." His first mentor was a "Christian socialist in the best sense of the word," a man "who would have been at home during the peasant wars of the Reformation." Impressed by the message, Lander "dropped everything" and set out in search of sectarians "who did not recognize secular or religious authority and owned all things in common." What he found he did not like—because the "Dukhobor" sectarians who welcomed him did not allow secular books, whereas he was convinced that "in order to understand all these things, it was necessary to study, and study long and hard." The police did him the favor of sending him to prison, where he "spent whole nights in animated conversations." Having "cleared up many unresolved questions," he joined a Social-Democrat reading circle "united by common intellectual interests and bonds of close friendship."[29]

Pavel Postyshev, a "calico printer" from Ivanovo-Voznesensk, was sent to the Vladimir Central Prison in 1908, when he was twenty-one. His savior was a local doctor's wife, Lubov Matveevna Belokonskaia, who procured food, books, money, clothing, and fictitious brides for the prisoners. Four years later, he wrote to Belokonskaia from his place of "eternal exile" on Lake

Pavel Postyshev

Baikal: "Dear L.M., I am a working man and am proud to belong to that class because it is destined to perform a great deed. Treasuring my title or rank of proletarian, and determined to keep that title pure and unsullied, especially as a conscious proletarian, I must not lie to you. You have dedicated your life to the great cause of the workers, and how can we not love you as children love a kind mother."[30]

The Donbass miner, Roman Terekhov, claims to have started wondering, at the age of fifteen,

> why some people did nothing and lived in luxury, while others worked day and night and lived in misery. This provoked in me a feeling of great hatred for those who did not work but lived well, especially the bosses. My goal was to do everything I could to find a person who would untie the tightly fastened knot of life for me. I found such a person in Danil Oguliaev, a tool maker in our mechanical shop. He explained to me the reasons for our life. After this I began to love him and always did all of his errands and assignments, such as distributing proclamations, posting them where they could be seen clearly, etc., and also stood guard at secret meetings.

Once, he was allowed to participate in one of those meetings. "The night was dark and the steppe prickly as we walked toward the woods, where a comrade, who had been waiting for us, showed us the spot. There were about fifty people at the meeting. One young man made a presentation, and then another young man spoke against him. I didn't like their argument and felt very bad they hadn't been able to make up. I got back home with a bad taste in my mouth. The only valuable thing I took from that meeting were the words of one of the comrades about needing to arm ourselves." Terekhov began his armed struggle by trying to kill a mechanic in his shop, but the attempt failed because he could not find an appropriate weapon. Some time later, a student propagandist showed him an issue of *Pravda*, and he organized a newspaper-reading circle.[31]

Orphaned at four, Vasily Orekhov worked as a shepherd in his native village before running away to Moscow. At ten, he got a job at the Renommée candy factory (one of Einem's more serious competitors) but was soon fired "for the non-allowance of an administration of a beating upon his person." At seventeen, while working as a cook at a homeopathic hospital, he had some of his questions answered by a nurse named Aleksandrova. As he wrote in the mid-1920s in his typed, but unedited autobiography, "[She] prepared me for political literacy and the trade union movement having prepared my consciousness and her knowledge of my understanding and took into account my social status and everything I had lived through my spirit and my inclinations and my thirst for knowledge and work. Simply put, between July 1901 and March 1902 I was her probationer. In March I was accepted into a circle of democrats."

After several more jobs and a few beatings, and having joined a new Bolshevik circle and made a speech at a rally on the significance of May 1, Orekhov was hired at Kudelkin's box-making shop. He did not stay long. "In 1908 I was exiled from Moscow for overturning a bowl of cabbage soup onto Kudelkin's head and boiling his whole head, 'cause in those days the bosses used to provide their own boss food for us workers, and during Lent Kudelkin used to make this disgusting watery soup from cabbage with worms in it, and once he made this soup and I suggested that he keep his maggoty cabbage

Semen Kanatchikov

soup and give me something better, but Kudelkin said, 'you'll eat what you're given,' and so I turned the bowl of soup over his head, for which reason I spent two weeks in jail and was then exiled from Moscow." Having left for Podolsk, Orekhov joined a local Bolshevik circle and became a propagandist.[32]

Semen Kanatchikov's "beliefs, views of the surrounding world, [and] the moral foundations with which [he] had lived and grown up" began to crumble after he became an apprentice at the Gustav List plant in the Swamp. A fellow worker told him that there was no hell other than the one they were living in; that the relics of saints were no different from the Egyptian mummies in the nearby Historical Museum; that the Dukhobors were "wonderful human beings" because they considered all people brothers; and that the nonexistence of God could be proven by watching worms and maggots appear out of nothing ("and then other creatures will begin to develop from the insects, and so on. . . . And, in the course of four, five, or maybe even ten thousand years, man himself will emerge"). But it was a book (*What Should Every Worker Know and Remember?*) that brought about the epiphany. "For an entire week I was in a state of virtual ecstasy, as if I were standing up high on some tall stilts, from where all other people appeared to me like some kind of bugs, like beetles rummaging in dung, while I alone had grasped the mechanics and the meaning of existence. . . . I now withdrew from my [cooperative] and settled in a separate room with one of my comrades. I stopped going to the priest for "confession," no longer attended church, and began to eat "forbidden" food during Lenten fast days."[33]

The workers' conversions were similar to those of the students in that they seemed to result from a combinaton of an innate moral sense with eye-opening readings and conversations. But whereas the students "stepped over the threshold" in the company of other students, the workers, according to their own recollections, needed a guide "from without." As one of them put it, using a reading-circle commonplace, "it's sad to say, but it's obvious that the working people will not awaken from their slumber very soon"—unless a "comrade student" has sprinkled them with the magic water of life.[34]

One such student, according to his comrades, was Yakov Sverdlov. "With his medium height, unruly brown hair, glasses continuously perched on his nose, and Tolstoy shirt worn under his student jacket, Sverdlov looked like a student, and for us, the young people as well as the workers, a 'student' meant a 'revolutionary.'" In theory, anyone could become a revolutionary by acquiring consciousness and engaging in propaganda and agitation, and anybody could look like a student by wearing glasses and a jacket over a Tolstoy shirt. Sverdlov, for one, left the gymnasium after four years, never went to college, and only adopted the "student" uniform (which also included high boots and a cap and amounted to a combination of gymnasium and proletarian styles) when he was no longer a student.[35]

In fact, however, Orekhov, Terekhov, Postyshev, Kanatchikov, and most other workers would become revolutionaries without ever becoming students, no matter how hard they studied, what positions they attained, or whether they wore glasses and jackets over Tolstoy shirts (Kanatchikov did). One reason for the difference was their speech, style, taste, gestures, and other birthmarks that might or might not be compatible with an altered consciousness. Another was the worker's need for "the never-ending pursuit of a miserable piece of bread." As Postyshev wrote to his adopted mother, Liubov Belokonskaia, "while my soul is yearning for light, screaming and struggling to break out of the embrace of unrelieved darkness, my body is drowning out my soul's cry with its groaning for bread. Oh, how hard it all is!"[36]

The third reason had to do with the consciousness of those left behind. The "students" were almost always abetted at home while still in school and almost never damned when they became revolutionaries. As Kanatchikov put it, "Rare indeed were the occasions when a member of the intelligentsia completely broke his ties with his bourgeois or petty-bourgeois family.... What usually happened was that even after expelling the recalcitrant child from the family hearth, the kind-hearted relatives would soften, be filled with pity for the imprisoned martyr, and manifest more and more concern for him. They would visit him in prison, provide him with necessities, petition the authorities, request that his situation be mollified, and so on."[37]

According to Sverdlov's sisters Sarra and Sofia and his brother Veniamin, their father, the owner of an engraving shop, was a short-tempered but docile man who, after an initial struggle, grew to accept and eventually support the transformation of his house into "a meeting place for Nizhny Novgorod's Social Democrats," and his shop, into a place for manufacturing revolutionary proclamations and stamps for false passports. Voronsky's father, the priest, died when Voronsky was very young, but one of his fictional doubles visits his son's commune and, along with everyone else, drinks to Marxism, terror, Russian literature, new engines, and, at his son's request, "to the unequal struggle, brave souls, and those who sacrifice themselves without asking anything in return." (The toast "To the Clergy!" is roundly rejected by the seminarians, so Father Khristofor has to drink it alone.) In 1906, Kuibyshev's father, a lieutenant colonel and, at the time, military commander of Kuznetsk, received a telegram from his daughter that Valerian was about to be court-martialed ("everyone knows what a court-martial is: today they arrest you and within forty-eight hours you get your sentence: acquittal or death"). According to Valerian's account recorded in the early 1930s, "Father almost lost his mind: without wasting a single moment, he jumped into a carriage and rushed to the train station (in those days, there was no line connecting Kuznetsk to the Trans-Siberian). He told me later that he had spent an enormous sum on that trip because he demanded such speed that several horses died along the way."

Having arrived at the prison, Kuibyshev senior discovered that his son would be tried by a military district court, not a field court-martial. Valerian knew nothing about the telegram.

> When they told me that my father had come to see me, I felt very bad. I was expecting all kinds of reproaches, tears, and remonstrations (it was my first arrest). I would have no choice but to break with my father, and break for good....
>
> Having prepared myself to rebuff any attempt to talk me into straying from my chosen path in life, I entered the visitors' cell. But instead of finding my father angry, I found him crying like a child, with tears in his eyes, rushing toward me to embrace me. He kept kissing and hugging me, laughing happily, patting me all over, assuring himself I was alive. I was taken aback.
>
> "Father, what's the matter, why are you so happy?"
>
> He told me about the telegram.
>
> This is how my father found out about my first arrest. My sister's mistake helped reconcile my father to my chosen path.[38]

"The worker's story is very different," writes Kanatchikov. "He has no bonds, he has no 'hearth,' and he has no connections in the camp of his oppressors." Not only was his family less likely to be reconciled with his chosen path—he was less likely to be reconciled with his family (which he sometimes called "the swamp").[39]

> It usually happened that no sooner did a worker become conscious than he ceased being satisfied with his social environment; he would begin to feel burdened by it and would then try to socialize only with persons like himself and to spend his free time in more rational and cultured ways. At that moment his personal tragedy would begin. If the worker was an older family man, conflicts would immediately arise within his family, primarily with his wife, who was usually backward and uncultured. She could not understand his

spiritual needs, did not share his ideals, feared and hated his friends, and grumbled and railed at him for spending money uselessly on books and for other cultural and revolutionary goals; most of all, she feared losing her bread-winner. If the worker was a young man, he inevitably came into conflict with his parents or other relatives, who had various powers over him. It was on this basis that conscious workers developed a negative attitude toward the family, toward marriage, and even toward women.[40]

In student circles, women were less numerous and less prominent than men, but their roles as writers' muses, debate audiences, prison liaisons, model martyrs, and "technical workers" were crucially important in the life of revolutionary communities. (Only among Jewish revolutionaries was the number of women comparable to that of men, making Jewish women even more "overrepresented" among revolutionaries than Jewish men.) Among worker revolutionaries, there were almost no women. Workers joining socialist circles and waiting to be fully "awakened" were the only proletarians with nothing but their chains to lose. They had the advantage of belonging to the chosen class, but they had no proper consciousness, no "culture," no families, and no female companionship other than the awkward and often humiliating contact with Jewish and intelligentsia women. They had to remake themselves through study in order to become eligible for romance even as they were remaking themselves through study in order to redeem humanity. In the meantime, they had only their faith, each other, and the kind of existential freedom that seemed a mirror image of what they were promised in the kingdom of freedom. When Kanatchikov received a letter from his brother "enforming" him that the soul of their father, Ivan Egorych, had been delivered to God, he threw himself on his cot, buried his face in his pillow, and gave vent to a flood of tears. "But in the depth of my soul," he writes in his autobiography, "another feeling was simmering and growing—a feeling of freedom and proud independence."[41]

■　■　■

One place where students and workers came together—to coalesce into a "party" and be free from "the swamp"—was prison. Students tempered their steel, workers acquired consciousness, and both learned to live side by side in close intimacy and relative equality. Arosev was arrested for the first time in 1909, when he was still in school in Kazan. "I liked the prison right away: everything was efficient and serious, as if we were in the capital. As I was being taken to my cell and saw my slightly stooped shadow on the wall of the prison corridor, I was filled with great respect for myself. . . . We were put in a cell with eight other students. Two of them were SRs we knew. It all looked more like a jolly student party than a prison. There were books, more books, notebooks filled with notes, slices of sausage on the long wooden table, tin teapots, mugs, loud laughter, joking, discussions, and chess games."[42]

The prisoners walked along prison corridors "as if in university halls," played leapfrog in the courtyard, and observed strict silence before bedtime "in order to allow those who wished to read and write to do so." Life in the Ekaterinburg prison in 1907 was similar. According to one of Yakov Sverdlov's cellmates,

> All day long the cells on our block were open, and the inmates could walk freely from one cell to another, play games ["Sverdlov was one of the ringleaders when it came to leapfrog"], sing songs, listen to presentations, and conduct debates. All this was regulated by a "constitution," which established a strict order enforced by cell elders who had been elected by the political prisoners. There were certain hours reserved for silence and collective walks. . . . Our cell was always crowded. In those days most of the prisoners were Social-Democrats, but there were also some SRs and anarchists. People from other cells often came over to listen to Y. M. Sverdlov.[43]

Sverdlov knew, and Arosev soon found out, that "such freedom in prison was a direct reflection of the relative positions of the combatants outside." A great deal depended on the time, place, sentence, chief warden, and prisoner's social class. Orekhov, the worker who poured boiling cabbage soup over his employer's head, describes "having his arms twisted, being tied up in a sack, and being force-fed finely ground glass," as well as "lying unconscious for eight hours as a result of a single blow delivered to the head." The Don Cossack Valentin Trifonov remembers wearing a winter coat in prison in order to soften the blows of the guards. According to his son, Yuri, "the inmates were constantly protesting against something: from the authorities' use of the informal form of address, to the wardens' demands that they greet them by shouting 'Good day, Sir!' and taking off their hats, to corporal punishment, forced haircuts, and petitioners who asked for pardons and shorter sentences."[44]

There were riots, escapes, suicides, and executions. Even Arosev, in his comfortable prison, might be playing leapfrog in the courtyard when, "suddenly, they would bring in a comrade who had been sentenced to death, and we knew that tomorrow or the day after he would be led out into this courtyard, not far from where we were playing, and hanged, and this comrade would be no more."[45]

But most Bolshevik prison memoirs are about the education of a true Bolshevik, and most of them refer to prison as a "university." "Strange as it may sound," writes Kon, "the years I spent

Valentin Trifonov
(Courtesy of Olga Trifonova)

in prison were the best years of my life. I did a lot of studying, tested my strength in a long and bitter struggle, and, in constant interaction with other prisoners, learned the difference between words and deeds, firm convictions and fleeting fancies. It was in prison that I learned how to judge my own life and the lives of others from the point of view of the good of the cause." Osinsky and Bukharin cemented their friendship when they lived "in perfect harmony" in the same prison cell, and Platon Kerzhentsev, who had defeated Osinsky in the high school debate on the Decembrists, "studied thoroughly . . . the literature of both Marxism and populism and left prison—the best university of [his] life—as a Bolshevik." Iosif Tarshis's (Osip Piatnitsky's) time in prison was "a university" because he "studied systematically under the guidance of a comrade who knew Marxist revolutionary literature," and Grigory Petrovsky's time in prison was a university because he "not only read the best Marxist literature, but also studied arithmetic, geometry, and German."[46]

The education of a true Bolshevik consisted in learning how to judge his own life and the lives of others from the point of view of the good of the cause, but it also consisted in learning as much as possible about everything else. Once the faith in the coming of the real day was in place and "the key to the understanding of reality," in hand, the study of arithmetic, geometry, and German helped enlist all things for the good of the cause. The more one knew, the easier it was to perceive the "moving forces" behind people and things and "the fantastic, enchanting, and transparent light over everything and everyone."

During his first stay in prison, and with nothing but the prison library at his disposal, Kanatchikov read "Turgenev, Uspensky, Dostoevsky, Spielhagen (*Between the Hammer and the Anvil*), Shchedrin, and others." Shchedrin was his particular favorite. "I laughed so hard that the guard repeatedly opened the transom and stared at my face, evidently wondering if I'd lost my mind." By the time he was arrested again, he had more experience, a higher consciousness, and much better comrades. Faina Rykova (the sister of the student revolutionary, Aleksei Rykov), brought him a year's worth of books. "The selection had not been made very systematically, but that really didn't matter; I wanted to know everything there was that could aid the cause of the revolution, whether directly or indirectly. . . . I recall that my collection included Lippert's *History of Primitive Culture*, Kliuchevsky's lectures on Russian history, Timiriazev's *Popular Exposition of Darwin's Theory*, Zheleznov's *Political Economy*, and V. Ilyin's *The Development of Capitalism in Russia*. At that time, I still didn't know that Ilyin was the pseudonym of Lenin."[47]

Voronsky began by reading Marx, Kropotkin, Balzac, Flaubert, and Dostoevsky, but when he was put in a "semi-dungeon" with "damp corners crawling with woodlice," he relaxed his schedule. "Morning and evening—calisthenics and a brisk towel rubdown; three hours of German; and the remaining hours I reserved for Homer, Dickens, Ibsen, Tolstoy,

Leskov, indolent and sluggish daydreaming, and unhurried reflections and recollections."[48]

Yakov Sverdlov seems to have been incapable of anything indolent or unhurried. He walked fast, talked loudly, followed the "Mueller system" of calisthenics, slept no more than five hours a night, and kept his personal "consumption statistics" (ten cigarettes, one prison lunch, one bottle of milk, one pound of white bread, and three cups of tea a day, four to six pounds of sugar a month . . .). In the Ekaterinburg prison, when he was not doing some combination of the above or playing leapfrog, he was reading Lenin, Marx, Kautsky, Plekhanov, and Mehring, as well as Werner Sombart on capitalism, Paul Louis on socialism, Sidney and Beatrice Webb on trade unionism, Charles Gide on cooperation, and Victor S. Clark on the Australian labor movement. He read German books in the original, worked hard on his French and mathematics, and picked up a teach-yourself-English textbook. His constant rereading of *Das Kapital*, *What Is to Be Done?*, and the Marx–Engels correspondence allowed him to profit from reading journal articles about women's history (the author "is correct to relate the rise of individualism to the capitalist mode of production, which has led to the economic independence of women"), sports ("in different historical periods, sports have always served the interests of the ruling classes"), and a great variety of poetry, from proletarian autodidacts to Shelley, Verhaeren, Verlaine, Baudelaire, Poe, Kipling, and his particular favorite, Heinrich Heine. "Literature and the arts interest me very much," he wrote in a letter. "They help me understand the development of mankind, which has already been explained theoretically." According to Sverdlov's common-law wife and Bolshevik party comrade, Klavdia Novgorodtseva, his motto was: "I put books to the test of life, and life to the test of books."[49]

In March 1911, when Sverdlov was in the St. Petersburg House of Pretrial Detention and Novgorodtseva was about to have their first child, his reading turned to "various approaches to the sexual question and, in particular, the question of reproduction." She was thirty-four; he was twenty-five and had a seven-year-old daughter by another comrade (although he does not seem to have stayed in close touch with them). Among the "questions" he was considering were:

> The special selection of partners for the production of offspring in Plato's ideal state; More's Utopia, where, before marriage, the two sides appeared before each other with nothing on; the most recent theories, principally by the so-called men of science, at the head of which one would have to put Auguste Forel [the author of the recently published *The Sexual Question*], who recommends a preliminary medical examination of the whole organism in order to determine whether reproduction is desirable. I am also reminded of various descriptions of the act of birth in different cultural epochs, contained in both histories of culture and works of literature.

Yakov Sverdlov   Klavdia Novgorodtseva

Everything leads me to believe that the "pangs of birth" are directly related to the condition of the mother's organism: the more normal the organism, the less acute the pain, less frequent the accidents, etc. I am also thinking of various political programs that rely on scientific data to demand the termination of work for a certain period of time before birth, etc. Thinking of all these things and weighing them relative to each other, I am inclined to reach a favorable conclusion, although of course I am not a specialist and there is so much I still don't know.

He kept putting his reproductive life to the test of books until, on April 4, their son was born. Novgorodtseva named him Andrei, after Sverdlov's party nickname. When she wrote to Yakov that her body was much changed, he reassured her that it would not last and said that when he had written to her about literary depictions of childbirth, he had—"of course"— been thinking of Natasha Rostova from *War and Peace*.[50]

∎ ∎ ∎

If prison was a university, then exile was the ultimate test—a test of one's character and convictions by life when reduced to its essentials. There were two kinds of exile. One was voluntary flight to the west, known as "emigration" and mostly remembered as a time of homelessness, secret conferences, frequent moves, fractious votes, work in libraries, meetings with leaders, and loneliness in a variety of strange and mostly uninteresting cities and countries—or not remembered at all as a time spent away from both the beauty and the beast. The other kind was exile proper—an "administrative" banishment to Siberia or Russia's European north that combined martyrdom and fulfillment, confinement and freedom to a much more concentrated degree than prison—because it was both banishment to an inferno and a full-fledged, self-administered community of true believers complete with courtship, marriage, and childbirth. In most retrospective accounts and some contemporary ones, exile was an epic, mythic experience—the most important one in the lives of revolutionaries short of the revolution itself.[51]

After months of travel in a convoy, accompanied by more or less drunk and more or less indulgent soldiers, the exile would be delivered to the end of the world (usually a village in the tundra) and met by a local "political," who would ask him whether he was a "Bek" (a Bolshevik), a "Mek" (Menshevik), or something else entirely. Depending on the answer, the new arrival would be taken to a particular cabin, given tea, asked

Osip Piatnitsky

about life outside, and inducted into the local community, which, depending on its size, might or might not be divided along sectarian lines. The most important line was the one separating the "politicals" from everyone else. As Kanatchikov put it, "We jealously guarded the high calling of the revolutionary and strictly punished anyone who sullied and abased it. . . . We had to expend a great deal of energy in order to draw a sharp and distinct line between ourselves—political people who were struggling for an idea and suffering for our convictions—and the ordinary criminal offenders."[52]

Most of the larger communities were run as communes—with mutual aid accounts, communal dining rooms, conflict resolution committees, libraries, choirs, and regularly scheduled meetings and debates. Government stipends (higher for "students" than for workers) were supplemented with money sent by comrades and relatives, as well as with earnings from teaching, publishing, and occasional work in the area. (Sverdlov wrote about local life for a Tomsk newspaper; Novgorodtseva worked as a meteorologist; Voronsky bound books; and Piatnitsky felled trees.) Many of the exiles taught, treated, or studied the locals, but they could find no place for them in the coming revolution. Piatnitsky, a ladies' tailor from a Lithuanian shtetl (described in one police report as "below average height, thin, with a narrow chest)," marveled at how "dreadfully inept" the Siberian peasants were at being peasants. He wondered why, after they had listened to Marxist explanations with apparent interest, they would go straight to the local policeman "to ask if what the political exiles were saying was true." There were exceptions, however. Sergei Mitskevich married a local sixteen-year-old girl named Olympiada, who decided to "be useful to the people" by becoming a nurse; Boris Ivanov, a baker from St. Petersburg, came close to developing a "genuinely deep attachment" to his landlord's daughter Matrena; and Aleksandr Voronsky's literary double, "Valentin," preached so eloquently to his landlady, an Old Believer widow of about thirty-two, "broad-shouldered and stout," that once, after sitting and listening to one of his monologues she "got up, walked over to the double bed with a mountain of down pillows and a gloriously puffy eiderdown, slowly turned back the quilt, then turned to Valentin and said, calmly and meekly: 'I understand now. Come here and let me comfort you.' Having said this, she began, just as slowly and meekly, and with deep sighs, to unbutton her bodice."[53]

But mostly, they courted each other, married each other (unofficially), and lectured each other. Some exiles also exchanged lessons, but usually the students were the teachers and the workers their students. Valentin Trifonov, the orphaned Don Cossack who had worked in a railroad depot before becoming a Bolshevik, claimed to have learned everything, including "simply culture," from his fellow exile, Aron Solts. Boris Ivanov, the "barely literate and politically underdeveloped" baker (as he described himself), had Sverdlov tutor him in Russian, algebra, geometry, and political economy, as well as "basic literacy and political development." The exiles hiked, talked, celebrated revolutionary holidays, waited for new arrivals, and read (many publishers provided exiles with free copies). "Despite the administrative constraints, we lived fairly freely," wrote Voronsky about his time on the White Sea coast. "We were surrounded on all sides by snow, ice, the sea, the river, cliffs, and the rather primitive, but solid and healthy life of the native Pomors. We received free newspapers, journals, and books. Our days were uneventful but not dreary, at least during the first year of exile. We often got together, argued, and regularly received illegal literature. The police bothered us, but not very persistently. . . . The superintendent and the guards were a little scared of us."[54]

The exiles' worst enemy was melancholy and depression. "How could you not be melancholy and depressed," wrote Piatnitsky, "if all around you there was snow for eight months of the year, and it hurt your eyes to look at it, and you could only walk on a road because otherwise you were in danger of falling through the snow, which was almost five feet deep?" And how could you not be melancholy and depressed, wrote Boris Ivanov, "when, for several months in a row, the sun hides behind the horizon, and the pale, sullen, overcast day appears for half an hour to an hour, and then it's night again, for months on end"?[55]

Some would refuse to get out of bed; others would start drinking; yet others would suffer from doubt or stop reading and writing altogether. Local peasants would come uninvited, and, according to Sverdlov, "sit silently for half an hour before getting up to say, 'Well, I've got to get going, good bye.'" Visiting nomads would stop by "to marvel at how quickly the pen moved across the page and how much got written, and stand there looking over your shoulder until you couldn't write anymore." Postyshev could not always keep his promise to write to Belokonskaia. "How many times I have sat down at a moment of overwhelming sadness in order to share my loneliness with you, but was never able to finish a single letter. My dear, much respected Lubov Matveevna, if only you knew how much I suffered, you would forgive my silence."[56]

Even the company of fellow exiles could become unbearable. In the spring of 1914, Sverdlov was transferred to a tiny village beyond the Arctic Circle, along with one other political, "a Georgian named Dzhugashvili." "He's a good fellow," wrote Sverdlov to a friend, "but too much of an individualist in everyday life. I, on the other hand, require some minimal degree of order, so it bothers me sometimes." "The saddest thing of all," he wrote a month later, "is that, in the conditions of exile or prison, a person is fully exposed and reveals himself in the smallest details. The worst part is that all you see are the 'small details of life.' There is no room for bigger traits to manifest themselves. My comrade and I are in different houses now, and we don't see much of each other." Having been allowed to move to a different village, he wrote to Novgorodtseva: "You know, my dear, how horrible the conditions in Kureika were. The comrade I was with turned out to be such a person, socially, that we didn't talk or see each other. It was terrible. And it was all the more terrible because, for a variety of reasons, I didn't—couldn't, really—study. I reached the point of total intellectual torpor, a kind of anabiosis of the brain." (Three days later, Dzhugashvili wrote to Tatiana Slovatinskaia, in whose apartment in Petrograd he had lived before his arrest: "Dearest, my misery grows by the hour. I am in desperate straits. On top of everything, I have come down with something and have a suspicious cough. I need milk, but . . . I don't have any money. My dear, if you can scrape some money together, send it immediately, by telegraph. I can't bear it any longer.")[57]

Moving in with a close friend helped Sverdlov, but did not bring full relief. The friend, Filipp Goloshchekin, born "Shaia Itskov" but known as "Georges," "contributed quite a bit" to Sverdlov's reawakening. "He is a lively person. He raises countless questions, which he tries to resolve through dialog. . . . But don't start thinking that it's so great for the two of us, that we have a vibrant comradely atmosphere here. After all, we are only two." And still worse: "Georges has become a certified neurotic and is on his way to becoming a misanthrope. He has a good opinion of people in general, of abstract people, but he is terribly quarrelsome with particular human beings he comes into contact with. The result is that he is on the outs with everyone—except for me, of course, because I know what a good fellow he is, what a kind soul he has." Finally, they parted—"not because of a quarrel, nothing of the kind," but because "a separate apartment is better, after all." They had been going to bed at different times and studying at different times, "and, moreover, I can't write intimate letters when there's someone else around who is awake."[58]

Sverdlov wrote many intimate letters, especially when there was no one else around. "You know, my little one," he wrote to Novgorodtseva from Kureika, after he and Dzhugashvili had stopped talking to each other, "I really do love you so—so very, very much. Are you asleep and cannot hear? Sleep then, sleep, my darling, I won't disturb you. Oh my, oh my!" A year after the birth of Andrei, he still had not seen his son and wife (he called her his "wife" in his letters, although some Bolsheviks were wary of the term).

> I feel so strongly that my existence is inseparable from yours, and talk to you in my soul so often that it seems strange somehow that we haven't seen each other for so long. Oh how I want to be near you, to see you and our little one. But I'll confess that my greatest desire is to be with you; you are in my thoughts much more, you and you and you again, and then our little one. Don't misunderstand me. Yes, I do want your caress, sometimes I want it so much it hurts, and I don't think there's anything wrong with that. I want to lay my head in your lap and gaze endlessly at your dear, beloved, beautiful face, peer into your eyes, turn into a tiny babe and feel the touch of your hand on my hair. Yes, there is inexpressible joy in this, but even stronger, much much greater is my desire to share with you all my feelings, my thoughts, and in sharing them to gain new strength, to ensure that you are carried along by my mood, that we become one person within that mood.... I want to caress you, take care of you, fill your life with new energy and joy.... I want to give you so, so much. But what can I do?[59]

Meanwhile, Sverdlov's pupil, Boris Ivanov, was writing to a "dear, distant friend" Bliuma Faktorovich. "I am writing to you in the dusk. You are standing before me in my cabin the way you did back then at the New Year's Eve party in our workers' club. Your thick brown hair is like a crown, and your dark, fiery eyes are sparkling in the glow of the lights." The letter ends with a poem that transforms his loneliness and longing into their common—and tragic—devotion to the cause.

> We'll welcome the New Year with a kiss
> This night of joy is not for you and me.
> We'll kiss like brothers, as we struggle for the people
> Who suffer from oppression and from want.
> Please don't be jealous of the feasting all around,
> Let's drink our cup of tears to the bottom.[60]

Thousands of miles away, Voronsky was drinking from the same cup.

> During those long, dull nights, I used to read until my head spun, then stoke the stove, and turn down the lamp. The birch logs would hiss, crackle drily, and pop, like roasting nuts, while ugly, furry shadows wandered around the room. The coals covered in gray ashes reminded me of things lost and extinguished. Life in the capitals and big cities seemed far away and gone forever.... Enchanting female images would come alive and disappear, those past passions

turned into ghostly, elusive shadows. In a
rush I would finish stoking up the stove, close
the stove doors and shutters with a bang,
get dressed, cast a last worried, melancholy
look around the dark room, and set off to see
Vadim, Jan, or Valentin. The dark heavenly
depths used to crush me with their frightening immensity.[61]

Boris Ivanov

Even Sverdlov, whose "cheerfulness and optimism" were, according to Ivanov, the colony's
main "support for the weak," would occasionally
give way to despair. Once, when he had not re-
ceived any letters for several weeks, his lip was swollen, and he was "shivering from the cold (or a cold, he wasn't sure)," he wrote to Novgorodtseva,
"Yesterday it got so bad that I felt like crying and moaning, and could not
sleep. I had to use all my strength not to let myself go. I managed to pull
myself together somewhat, but then got to the point of regretting that I
didn't have any potassium bromide pills with me—and I'm not sure I
would've been able to keep from taking them, either."[62]

Those were rare moments, however, and they were always followed by
expressions of hope based on some combination of comradeship, love, and
faith in the truth of the prophecy. "The days of light will come; believe in
it firmly, be full of this faith," was the main theme of Sverdlov's letters to
his, sisters, and friends. Most of them, including Sverdlov himself,
followed this injunction. Voronsky's visions and doubts are dispelled by
"conversations with comrades"; Piatnitsky's passage about melancholy
and depression is followed by an account of mutual support among the
exiles; and Ivanov's description of the long Arctic nights ends with an
image of the "heavenly depths" that is sublime, not crushing. "The sky is
covered with countless stars, which shine much more brightly here than
they do at home or in the south. The fantastic bands of the northern lights
dance around like searchlights, and, every once in a while, a white fiery
pillar rises from the earth all the way to the sky or a spray of blue, red, and
violet lights might shoot up."[63]

Postyshev, too, found solace in nature (and in belles lettres):

It is not easy for me to describe these mountains in all their glory—
when they are painted golden by the rising sun and, high above
them, the turquoise sky is glistening, and the fiery dawn clings so
closely to the earth that it seems that the earth might catch fire. At
sunset, I prefer to walk between the mountains, in the "gashes," as
they are called here. Then the mountains are shrouded in a blue
haze; their tops seem to touch the clouds; and the rays of the setting sun radiate through the pine trees. At such moments, your

eyes can perceive magic; your soul becomes transcendent; and you wish to live and to hug everyone in sight and to forgive and be forgiven.[64]

A true Bolshevik could not indulge in such sentiments for too long, and neither could the wilderness. In 1913, Postyshev and two of his friends were celebrating "the great proletarian holiday, May First" in the taiga. "The noise of the giant trees was like the triumphant hymn of a million-strong army of the proletariat. That wild but majestic music penetrated to the very bottom of our hearts. We stood and listened to that powerful victory song. The chords kept changing: first a piercing scream full of hatred and thirst for vengeance, then the heavy moan of a huge, huge army."[65]

For Sverdlov, the "victory" referred to two things: his reunion with Novgorodtseva and the coming of the real day. The former came first. They met briefly in 1912 on the Ob River in West Siberia, and then, in May 1915, two years after the birth of their daughter Vera, Novgorodtseva came to join Sverdlov permanently in the village of Monastyrskoe, on the Enisei River. Boris Ivanov remembers first seeing their house:

> The forest came right up to the house, in the form of numerous low fir trees and bushes. The house had three rooms and four windows. The furniture was of the simplest kind: wooden benches, a table with a white tablecloth, a pile of books on a little stool. Among them, I could see the first volume of *Das Kapital*, a book in German, and an open issue of *The Russian Wealth*. On the windowsill, there was a huge heap of newspapers.
>
> A black-eyed boy of about six, dressed in a white linen suit, was looking at me with curiosity.
>
> "Adia, come on, stop staring! This comrade has just arrived from Petersburg. Say hello to him!," said Sverdlov, lightly pushing the boy toward me.
>
> "This is my little critter," he said with a smile.[66]

Andrei (Adia) Sverdlov was four, not six, but he had already traveled a great deal: visiting his father in the Tomsk prison, spending time in his mother's cell in St. Petersburg, and living in two different places of exile. Thanks to their extra earnings, the Sverdlovs had been able to buy a cow for fresh milk for the children.

Sverdlov usually got up around 6:00 a.m. and skied to the river bank to record meteorological data (Novgorodtseva's official job).

> Having come back from the Enisei [writes Novgorodtseva], Yakov Mikhailovich would chop wood, feed the cow, clean out the manure, start a fire in the stove, boil water, and make breakfast. Around eight the children would wake up. Yakov Mikhailovich always washed and

dressed them. The children were his responsibility: despite my protests, he never let me interfere.

   We usually had breakfast at about half past eight, and after that
I would set off on my round of lessons. Yakov Mikhailovich received
his pupils . . . at home. Around noon he would finish tutoring and
start making lunch.

The main staples in Monastyrskoe were fish and Siberian dumplings with
reindeer meat. Both Novgorodtseva and Ivanov claim that Sverdlov was
unsurpassed as a filling maker; Ivanov, a baker by trade, was the dough-
molding "artist." "We usually had lunch around 2:00 p.m. After that I
would do the dishes (having won this right after many a battle), and then
we would both do some sewing, mending, and, if need be, washing. By five
or six, Yakov Mikhailovich would be free from household chores, and by
seven, people would start coming over." About ten of Monastyrskoe's
twenty or so exiles came regularly. Sverdlov would "officiate" at the stove,
while the others tried to follow Ivanov's lead in molding the dumplings.
"There was no end to the jokes and laughter, but there was never any
alcohol. Yakov Mikhailovich never drank either vodka or wine." This
was true of most Bolshevik circle members, both the "students" and the
workers.[67]

   Sometimes they held formal lectures, debates, or party meetings. Such
gatherings were illegal, but in the winter, according to Ivanov,

   The windows [of Sverdlov's house] would be covered with a thick
   layer of ice, so you could not see anything from the outside. . . . Only
   the light of the kerosene lamp would show through the frozen glass
   and cast a pale reflection on the snow drifts near the house. . . . The
   Bolshevik exiles usually gathered in a small room that did not look
   like a setting for a lecture or a presentation. A pot of hot tea would
   be standing on the table. Valentina Sergushova would pour it out
   into mugs. Guests would be sitting in comfortable positions around
   the table, although some might be lying on reindeer skins spread out
   on the floor next to the iron stove with its burning cedar log. Their
   faces would be just barely visible in the semidarkness of the room.[68]

After the lectures they would often go for walks. Their favorite activity
was singing, and their favorite songs were "the roaring battle hymns of
the revolutionary proletariat of that time." Sometimes, during those
hikes, they would start playfully pushing each other around. "Occasionally such rough-housing would turn into real battles, with people throwing snowballs at each other and shoving each other into snow drifts. Sad
was the fate of those who could not react fast enough to an opponent's
sudden move!" Sverdlov, who was "the initiator and ringleader" of most
such battles, made up in aggression what he lacked in size. According to

Novgorodtseva, he particularly enjoyed "sitting astride his vanquished playmates and stuffing handfuls of snow down their collars."

> Finally, Yakov Mikhailovich would announce loudly, "Let's go have some tea!" and we would troop back to our place, exhausted, red-cheeked, loud, and happy. Once inside, everyone would get right to work: someone would start the samovar, others would get the dishes, set the table, etc. Then the tea drinking would begin, and the merry, free-flowing conversation would start up again. Andrei and Verushka, long used to all kinds of noise, would be fast asleep in the next room.
>
> Around nine or ten, everyone would head for home, and Yakov Mikhailovich would sit down to work. Night was the time for serious concentration. For at least four or five hours, he would sit over his books and manuscripts, reading, taking notes, copying out passages, and writing. He would not go to bed until one or two in the morning, and then at six or seven he would be up again.[69]

Exile stood for suffering, intimacy, and the sublime immensity of the heavenly depths. It offered a perfect metaphor for both what was wrong with the "world of lies" and what was central to the promise of socialism. "The gap between reason and what is beyond reason is created by deformations in social life," thought Voronsky as he "roamed through glades and climbed up slopes." "Only under socialism will the fundamental contradiction between the conscious and the unconscious be eliminated. The leap from the kingdom of necessity to the kingdom of freedom will be accomplished: there will be no tragic chasm between the conscious

Exiles in Monastyrskoe. Sverdlov is seated, in the white shirt.
Klavdia Novgorodtseva and Andrei Sverdlov are seated in front.
Between them, wearing a hat, is Grigory Petrovsky.
Stalin (Dzhugashvili) is in the back, in a black hat; on his left is
Lev Kamenev. Far right in a leather jacket is Filipp Goloshchekin.

and the unconscious; reason will tame the elements while remaining connected to their immense power." In the meantime, the memory of banishment would serve as a promise of liberation and a sacred bond among "comrades-in-arms, fellows in freedom, and friends." "They are my family, my country, my cherished past and glorious future. They blossom in my soul like rare flowers on a mountain slope, right next to the edge of the snow. Here's to our free, loyal fellowship, firm handshakes, sincere conversations on stormy nights, our laughter, jokes, bravery, daring, restless wanderings, our willingness to help each other at the cost of our lives, our certainty and faith in the bitterest of years, our marvelous, unique, valiant band!"[70]

■ ■ ■

The free fellowships preparing for the leap to the kingdom of freedom (by means of agitation and propaganda and through the trials of prison and exile) were organized into "parties," each one with its own program and statutes, but all of them sharing a fundamental rejection of the existing order of things and a withdrawal into a secret community of the self-chosen. The most important part of being a revolutionary was, in Voronsky's words, the "habit of dividing people into two camps: us and them."

> "Us" was the underground: a secret, exclusive circle of people fastened together by a voluntary, iron bond of mutual responsibility, with our own understanding of honor, right, and justice. This circle was invisible but always present, militant and unbending. It was like a volcanic island rising up in the middle of the ocean. Everything else—huge, ever multiplying, earthbound—was the world of the enemy. Everything else needed to be remade and reshaped; it was loathsome and deserved to die; it kept resisting, persecuting, expelling, pursuing, and living its own life. And so I learned how to despise everything that was outside our secret free fellowship.[71]

The first part of Voronsky's autobiography came out in *Novyi mir* in 1927; the full version appeared as a book in 1929. Some critics did not like its excessive "reflexivity," but, as Voronsky's wife wrote at the time, its "content could not possibly raise any objections." Gorky called it "the voice of a true revolutionary, who knows how to talk about himself as a real, live human being." The book's publication was approved by the censorship office and formally endorsed by Viacheslav Molotov (formerly Skriabin), on the recommendation of Platon Kerzhentsev (formerly Lebedev), under the "editorial responsibility" of Semen

Aleksandr Voronsky

Kanatchikov (formerly a Gustav List worker). Voronsky's underground self seemed no different from that of any other revolutionary.[72]

> I used to walk down Nevsky. The sight of the glittering shop windows, the carriages and trotting horses, the top hats and bowlers filled me with a sense of superiority. I would think to myself: here is a gentlemen with a bushy moustache wearing a shiny English suit, and here is a stout lady with a pink face rustling her silks. . . . They can walk into a store, casually pick out something expensive, have it delivered to their home by a delivery boy, walk into this or that restaurant, go to the opera in the evening and then sit down to dinner, unfolding a crisp, well-starched napkin. And here am I, with a fifty-kopeck coin in my pocket, wearing a ragged fall coat and rust-colored, worn-out shoes, but I don't mind: I am carrying out the will of the anonymous people who are marching unwaveringly toward their goal of destruction. I, too, am a member of their secret fraternity. In the shop window, precious stones sparkle with all the colors of the rainbow: they are for you, the full-bellied, the well-groomed, the satisfied. Inside my coat, piles of leaflets are stuffed under my tight belt. They are for you, too. They are just as good as dynamite or a Browning pistol. You walk by, shoving me aside, but you don't know what I know; you don't suspect anything; you don't realize the danger you're in. I am stronger and more powerful than you, and I enjoy walking among you, unnoticed.[73]

The underground men had a variety of names for the loathsome "everything else" that "kept living its own life" outside their secret free fellowship. The most common was "philistines" (*obyvateli*), or people without higher principles or interests, people absorbed in the pleasures and failures of everyday existence, people whose "opinions, thoughts, gossip, and desires were petty and pitiful," people who were not fully human because they had no spark of "consciousness." In Russia, according to Voronsky, they were doubly damned, and possibly not human at all, because they combined protocapitalist acquisitiveness with the "primeval and utter swinishness" of provincial backwardness: "the driveling, hiccuping, and lip-smacking gluttony, the unctuousness mixed with beastliness."[74]

> Have you ever been to the meat row at the market? Pig and cow carcasses hang from the ceiling, and counters and carts are all covered with chunks of fat, yellow grease, and coagulated blood. Pieces of bone and brain fly everywhere, attracting packs of dogs. Aprons are stiff with blood, and the sickly-sweet, nauseating stench of rotting flesh is stifling. I always imagine these to be the embodied feelings, hopes, and thoughts of the average inhabitant of our Okurovs, Rasteriaevs, and Mirgorods. They are his life, his world. Observe his excitement as he turns over and digs through the lumps of fat and

lard! His eyes are oily; his lower lip droops; his filthy, foul-smelling mouth fills with saliva; afraid that someone might snap up the coveted piece before him, he snarls hungrily and sticks out his elbows. Shove against him at this moment, touch him by accident, and he is ready to kill you on the spot. I've seen people standing by the meat counters with their eyes glassed over and their fingers trembling, looking at the hunks of meat the way some men stare at naked women. You think I'm exaggerating? Go see for yourself, but make sure you look closely.[75]

The "philistine" had long been the stock antipode of the "intelligent," and provincial Russia was his natural habitat. "The town of Okurov" was Gorky's version; "Rasteriaeva Street" was Gleb Uspensky's; and Mirgorod was Gogol's pastoral prototype. What the socialists did was to turn the philistine into a "bourgeois" and sentence him to death as a matter of Marxist inevitability and personal gratification. What the socialists feared was his ability to grow new heads and tempt new victims. The most common metaphor for "philistinism" was a "swamp" that posed as solid ground while seeping into homes, souls, and Bolshevik reading circles. Voronsky's native town of Tambov reminded him of the swamp he used to go to when he was a little boy. "Under its murky, dead film, the swamp bubbled, rumbled, rotted, and gurgled, exhaling foul odors and swarming with myriads of midges, soft, plump tadpoles, water spiders, red beetles, and frogs; it slurped and rustled with reeds and bulrushes. Farther in, if you made it across the shaky hillocks of grass to its depths, the quagmire yawned. Any calf, cow, or horse that lost its way would perish there."[76]

Whereas the SRs believed that the revolution would prevent the swamp from submerging the whole of the Russian countryside, the Marxists assumed that the flood was a fait accompli, welcomed it as a necessary interlude, and endorsed Engels's warning to the driveling gluttons: "You shall be allowed to rule for a short time. You shall be allowed to dictate your laws, to bask in the rays of the majesty you have created, to spread your banquets in the halls of kings, and to take the beautiful princess to wife—but do not forget that 'The hangman stands at the door!'" The Bolshevik-Menshevik disagreement concerned the question of who the hangman should be: the Mensheviks favored the proletariat; the Bolsheviks (some of whom recognized the original Heine in the prophet's words) demanded the leading role for themselves.[77]

Voronsky's alter ego Valentin was a true Bolshevik.

Some day soon the third angel will sound his trumpet. And then we will show all those who wish to enjoy life with some fat, a little manure, a bit of dirt, and a few legalized rapes what the end of the world is about. We will show them the price of categorical imperatives and civic cloaks. We will remind them of their little albums of those who have been hanged and the little amateur libraries they have collected about them. We won't forget anything: the innocent tears of the children, the wasted youth in the back alleys and basements, the destroyed talents, the mothers' grief, Sonechka Marmeladova and little Ilya, and all those hanged on the gallows as the sun was sending out its first, sinless rays.[78]

Valentin was deliberately, defiantly Dostoevskian. Few Russian socialists would have understood every one of his allusions or endorsed his combination of prophetic fire with self-doubting introspection, but most of them shared his vision. The revolutionaries were going to prevail because of the sheer power of their hatred. It cleansed the soul and swelled like the flood of the real day. "It rushes along to the gates of a new kingdom, drenching its path in human blood and leaving behind death, moaning, and cursing. It rushes past the cowardly and the petty, sweeping along the brave, the daring, and the strong." It was the main weapon of the weak and the guarantee of future salvation. "Man must return to his lost paradise, and he will return there—no longer as nature's slave or contemplator, but as its free master, ruler, and creator."[79]

Most of those who shared Valentin's vision were organized into groups located along the free will–predestination continuum. None was fully "objectivist" (the Mensheviks prepared for the inevitable by organizing trade unions), and none was free from "historical inevitability." They knew themselves to be closely related (as former members of the same reading circles and fellow "politicals" in prison and exile) and routinely accused each other of deliberate misrepresentation. They referred to themselves as "parties" but rejected meaningful comparisons to other political organizations. Lenin called the Bolsheviks "a party of a new type." Valentin abandoned the term altogether. "What sort of party are we?" he asked. "Parties are what they have in the West and in America. None of them, including the socialists, go beyond the legal struggle for reforms. We, on the other hand, are an army, men of fire and sword, warriors and destroyers."[80]

Parties are usually described as associations that seek power within a given society (or, in Max Weber's definition, "secure power within an organization for its leaders in order to attain ideal or material advantages for its active members"). None of the three main socialist groups in early-twentieth-century Russia were interested in securing power within the Russian state or society, however construed. Their purpose was to await and, to a greater or lesser degree, bring about, that society's replacement by a "kingdom of freedom" understood as life without politics. They were faith-based groups radically opposed to a corrupt world, dedicated to "the abandoned and the persecuted," and composed of voluntary members who had undergone a personal conversion and shared a strong sense of chosenness, exclusiveness, ethical austerity, and social egalitarianism. They were, by most definitions, sects.[81]

"Sects" are usually defined in opposition to "churches" (described as bureaucratic, specialized, world-accepting, all-inclusive, elite-friendly organizations into which most members are born) or to societies that they attempt to flee or undermine. Lists of attributes (voluntary, exclusive, egalitarian) are sometimes replaced by a continuum representing degrees of tension with the surrounding world, from a few hunted fugitives at one end to well-integrated institutions at the other. All scholarly definitions characterize sects as "religious" groups, but since the determination of whether a group is religious concerns the nature of the faith, not the degree of tension with the world, it is irrelevant to the sect/party distinction. The main three socialist groups in early-twentieth-century Russia can safely be called sects because no usable definition relies on doctrinal criteria (unless one counts group members who classify heretics in relation to a particular orthodoxy) and because all three decisively rejected the world and possessed the main structural features associated with world-rejection (and conventionally assumed to be sectarian).[82]

Membership in such a group gave one a great sense of purpose, power, and belonging (especially for the Bolsheviks, who stood out among the socialists as the only sect rigidly organized around a charismatic leader). But the radical abandonment of most conventional attachments, the continual sacrifice of the present for the sake of the future, and the violent casting out of money changers came—as all heroic commitments do—at the cost of recurring doubt. What if the discarded attachments were the true ones? What if the future came too late for there ever to have been a present? What if the "philistines" were only human? What if all the years in prison and exile were in vain? "What is my strength, that I should wait, and what is my end, that I should endure?" Job's plight is inherent in all forms of submission to a force presumed to be both all-powerful and benevolent. ("If it is a matter of strength, he is mighty! And if it is a matter of justice, who will summon him? Even if I were innocent, my mouth would condemn me; if I were blameless, it would pronounce me guilty.") It is particularly acute, however, among those who emphasize self-study and self-improvement as much as selflessness. A self that has been painstakingly worked on is not easy to sacrifice—especially if the work relies on as eclectic a reading list as Bukharin's or Voronsky's.[83]

Bukharin's autobiographical alter ego, Kolia, has his first "profound spiritual crisis" when his little brother dies. "Is there anything that is worth one of Andriusha's little tears? What is the point of all the actions, virtues, exploits, and expiations, if the past cannot be brought back?" The answer comes from the same source as the question:

> One day, Kolia was sitting quietly by himself reading Dostoevsky when, suddenly, he hit upon a passage that shook him to the depths of his being. It was the passage in *The Adolescent* that described how the people of the future ... would live without the consolation of their thousand-year faith. The great idea of immortality would disappear, and would have to be replaced with something else, and all of the great excess of love for Him who had embodied immortality

would be transferred to nature, the world, the people in it, to every little blade of grass. They would love life and the earth irrepressibly, insofar as they would gradually become aware of their own temporality and finitude, and it would be a special, different kind of love.[84]

Voronsky's autobiographical narrator has his first spiritual crisis when his sister dies:

How could this happen, I kept thinking, how could this happen? I yearn for universal happiness, I worry about the welfare and prosperity of others, and here I was, not noticing, not knowing anything about the life and hopes of my own sister. . . . In this way, won't I end up establishing universal fraternity by squashing and trampling over everything ruthlessly and coldly, not noticing not only clear enemies, but human life in general: children, brothers, sisters? Or is this a necessary stage, because you can't win unless your teeth are clenched, your heart steeled, and your head, clear and cold? Could it be so?[85]

This monologue leads up to the book's central episode. The narrator goes to see his uncle, Father Nikolai.

In the dusty courtyard, cluttered with a cart, traveling carriage, and droshky, the guard dog Milka and a dirty pink piglet lay head-to-head in front of the kennel. Both were sleeping. The piglet was dreamily wagging the taut end of its little tail.
   "Trough happiness," I said.
   Father Nikolai, a stout, calm, deliberate priest and a good farmer, glanced at the piglet and Milka, smiled, adjusted the silver cross on his chest, and continued on his way.

The narrator catches up with him, and they walk up a hill behind the village.

The lukewarm, watery sun slid toward the amber edge of the sky. To the right of the hill was a lush green meadow. Herds of cows and sheep plodded slowly and distractedly toward the village, casting long shadows behind them. We could hear the foolish bleating of the sheep and the dry cracking of the shepherds' whips. Two colts galloped by, bucking and shaking their flowing manes. The light-colored river lay tranquil, its gentle curves gleaming with copper flashes. Beyond the river, the fields stretched into the distance. Little hamlets dotted the hills. Behind them lay the silent, solemn pine forest. The cadenced tones of distant church bells floated lazily through the air.

"What a blessing," said Father Nikolai, stopping and leaning on his long staff. "Back in the courtyard, you said something about trough happiness. It may be the trough kind, but it's real. . . . Vegetation is at the root of all creation: the grass, the trees, the beasts of all kinds, the huts, the peasants, the birds, you and I. . . . Everything you see around you," he gestured broadly and unhurriedly with his hand, "has been created by vegetation, by trough happiness, as you call it."

"But vegetation is mindless and elemental," I objected.

Father Nikolai took off his wide-brimmed hat, ran his hand across his hair, and said:

"Indeed it is. . . . 'In the sweat of thy face shalt thou eat bread. Be fruitful, and multiply, and replenish the earth.'"[86]

They go on to argue about whether life is a miracle or a play of "blind and malicious forces," and whether "the real miracle" is life as we know it or the human desire and ability to subdue and transform it.

Father Nikolai gave it some thought, rolled up the sleeve of his cassock, and said:

. . . "Man needs to plow, sow, breed cattle, tend gardens, and raise children. That's the most important thing. Everything else is secondary. You, who are 'looking for the city that is to come,' do not know and cannot understand the joy of a farmer when he sees a brood of chickens, or the care with which he prunes and grafts an apple tree. You believe he only thinks of profit, but he doesn't always think of profit, and sometimes he doesn't think of profit at all: instead, he feels the joy of 'vegetation,' sees the fruit of his labor and takes pleasure in life. . . . Life is huge. It's like a mountain that can't be moved."

"We'll dig tunnels through it, Uncle."

"You think life is different on the other side? It's the same, the same."[87]

This dialogue—internal, external, or both—runs through Voronsky's book and, in one way or another, through most Bolshevik memoirs, from Kon's story of his grandfather presiding over a transformed Passover prayer to Kuibyshev's story of his father crying like a child in his son's prison cell. Could it be that it was inherent in human life?

"Have you ever read Ibsen's *Peer Gynt* and *Brand*?" I asked Valentin.

"I have. Why?"

"They represent two types, two psychological models. Peer Gynt lacks integrity; he is scattered and disorganized. All he can be is raw material for something else, but nothing human is alien to him. He

lulls, comforts, and deceives his dying mother. . . . He has no principles, but his heart is open. Brand, on the other hand, is a fighter,
he is all of a piece. He desires with his whole being. His motto is "all
or nothing," but his heart is closed to human joys and woes; he is
ruthless. He takes from his wife Agnes the little cap, her last memory of her dead child, and refuses to go to his mother's deathbed to
offer a few words of consolation."[88]

Every true Bolshevik has a purer, more consistently sectarian doppel-
gänger—an all-or-nothing Brand to his self-doubting underground man.
Ulianov has Lenin, Dzhugashvili has Stalin, Skriabin has Molotov, Arosev
has Z, and Voronsky has his Valentin.[89]

"There are millions of Peer Gynts. They are needed as manure, as
fertilizer. But don't you think, Valentin, that the Brand principle is
becoming too dominant among us? We are becoming harder,
tougher; we are turning into the revolution's promoters and apprentices; we are separating ourselves from everything 'human all too
human.'"

Fidgeting under his blanket, Valentin lit a match, drew on his
cigarette, and declared:

"That's the way it should be in our era. We must become more efficient and more resolute, we must give all of ourselves to our ideal.
We cannot show weakness and float in the wake of divergent and
contradictory emotions. We are warriors."[90]

In Voronsky's world, the real-life one as well as the fictional, there
is never an escape from dualism—even in his favorite refuge, a cottage in
a pine forest outside Tambov that belongs to Feoktista Yakovlevna
Miagkova, his older friend and socialist mentor. (She—also the child of a
priest—is the "mysterious revolutionary" who gave him his very first stack
of illegal leaflets when he was a seminarian.) Miagkova has three little
daughters. "This girls' world attracted me. Their pure, innocent eyes, the
braids tied with bright ribbons, the ink-stained notebooks, the stickers,
dolls, flowers, short colorful dresses, the carefree, inimitable, contagious
laughter, loud chatter, games, and all the running around helped me forget
my troubles and misfortunes." Two of the sisters love to listen to the silly
stories he makes up, but the third one, "the olive-skinned Tania," has a
"critical frame of mind" and refuses to play along. "You didn't really buy a
parrot, and you didn't really see a scary man, and he didn't really run after
you—you just made it all up." Voronsky may, in fact, have been chased by
a plainclothes policeman, but Tania isn't having any of it—she needs proof.
"Valentin" is Voronsky's fictional Brand-like alter ego. Tania was a real
all-or-nothing twelve-year-old. She would go on to join the Bolsheviks at
the age of twenty.[91]

. . .

Voronsky and Arosev may have been more self-consciously literary and programmatically self-reflexive than most Bolsheviks, and their memoirs may have absorbed some of the doubts and discoveries of the 1920s and early 1930s, but it seems clear—and was, for a while, universally accepted—that they were faithful chroniclers, not odd exceptions. Yakov Sverdlov, who never published anything other than articles on party politics and reports on Siberian social conditions, faced the same dilemmas and discussed them endlessly in his letters. What is the relationship between the coming general happiness and the present-day lives of individual believers? Which part of Father Nikolai's "vegetation" should be renounced as irredeemably philistine? What is to be done about the fact that—as Sverdlov writes apropos of the great mystery of his son's future life—"we mortals are not granted the ability to lift the veil of individual fate; all we can do is foresee the future of mankind as a whole"?[92]

The more terrible the trials, the greater the uncertainty and the temptations. "You cannot imagine [wrote Sverdlov to Novgorodtseva in January 1914], how badly I want to see the children. Such a sharp, piercing pain. Adka's photograph is on the table in front of me. So is yours. I stare and stare, for hours on end, and then I close my eyes and try to imagine little Vera, but I can't, really. I think until my head hurts. My eyes grow wet, and I am ready to burst out sobbing. My dear, dear, sweet little children. . . . Oh Kadia, Kadia! My darling, my love. . . . What will our future bring?"[93]

Sometimes it seems that their future life will bring nothing but trials: "There's much, much suffering ahead," he wrote in August 1914. Voronsky, the former seminarian, quotes the original passage from the confession of the Old Belief martyr, Archpriest Avvakum, who jouneyed to Calvary accompanied by his wife: "I came up, and the poor dear started in on me, saying, 'Will these sufferings go on for a long time, Archpriest?' And I said: 'Markovna, right up to our very death.' And so she sighed and answered, 'Good enough, Petrovich, then let's be getting on.'" (According to Voronsky's daughter, "let's be getting on" was his favorite saying.) But of course neither Sverdlov nor Voronsky is an Archpriest Avvakum. Or rather, they are, in the sense of being prepared to endure suffering for the sake of their faith, but they do not relish martyrdom or asceticism as virtues in their own right. As Sverdlov puts it in a letter to a young friend, "I also like Ibsen, but Brand's 'all or nothing' motto is not to my taste, for I consider it rootless and anarchist."[94]

Sverdlov's and Voronsky's faith, unlike Avvakum's, is to be strengthened by reading as broadly as possible. In Sverdlov's view, once a Marxist "consciousness" has been acquired, everything, without exception, becomes proof of its truth. "The greater the knowledge and the more wide-ranging it is, the vaster the space, the broader the horizons for creativity and, most important, the more conscious that creativity is." In 1916, with "the light of the kerosene lamp shining through the frozen glass and casting a pale reflection on the snow drifts" outside his house in Monastyrskoe, Sverdlov wrote to a young friend:

> For a better understanding of Ibsen, I would recommend reading everything by him, in a particular order. The best edition is the Skirmunt, reprinted by Znanie in eight volumes, in Hansen's translation. That is the best edition. It should be read in the order in which it was published, although you don't have to read the last volume: it's his correspondence, which, as I recall, is of little interest. But before you get started, it would be a good idea to read something appropriate about the history of Sweden and Norway over the last thirty or forty years, in order to become familiarized with the development of social relations there during this period. Such familiarity will help you understand Ibsen. For the same purpose, it would be good to read Lunacharsky's article ["Ibsen and Philistinism"] in the 1907 issue of *Obrazovanie*, the brochure about him by Roland-Holst, and Plekhanov's article in, I think, *Sovremennyi mir*, also from 1907.[95]

"Putting books to the test of life and putting life to the test of books" is hard work and requires constant vigilance and self-examination. In this sense, Sverdlov's faith is similar to Archpriest Avvakum's. "I watch myself very closely sometimes. You know my habit of self-analysis. I see clearly every fleeting movement of my soul. And right now I cannot detect any dangerous symptoms. There is none of the intellectual laziness and mental torpor that haunted me for a while. There is only a desire to study, to learn."[96]

But what if self-analysis revealed some dangerous signs of moral torpor? What happens when endless suffering breeds doubt, and doubt is deepened by reading and self-analysis? Are the Bolsheviks in danger of falling, one by one, into the chasm separating their ability to "foresee the future of mankind as a whole" and their all-too-human inability to "lift the veil of individual fate"? Sverdlov's answer is a thoughtful but resolute no. In 1913, he started writing to Kira Egon-Besser, the fourteen-year-old daughter of his close friends from Ekaterinburg, Aleksandr and Lydia Besser. Like many intelligentsia adolescents at the time, Kira suffered from chronic "pessimism" and occasional thoughts of suicide. Sverdlov's advice to her is remarkably consistent. "We were born at a good time," he wrote in January 1914, "in the period of human history when the final act of the human tragedy is at hand. . . . Today only the blind and those who do not want to see fail to notice the growing force that is fated to play the main part in this final act. And there is so much beauty in the rise of this force, and it fills one with so much energy, that, truly, it is good to be alive." Universal redemption is the key to personal fulfillment. "Allow me to kiss you on both cheeks when we meet," he wrote in May 1914, "for I have no doubt that I will see you and L. I. again. I'll kiss you in any case, whether you like it or not."[97]

They continued to correspond, and Sverdlov continued to urge hope and faith (hope as a function of faith). The first of his surviving letters was the one sent to the Dormitory for Female Students on Sophia Embankment in May 1904, when he was nineteen ("The real day is coming, after all. . . . The dawn, which sheds its fantastic, enchanting, and transparent light over everything and everyone, is near"). The last one, to Kira Egon-Besser in Petrograd, was written in Monastyrskoe on January 20, 1917, when he was thirty-two and she was eighteen:

My worldview ensures that my certainty in the triumph of a life of harmony, free from all manner of filth, cannot disappear. Just as unshakeable is my certainty that future life will produce pure human beings, beautiful in every respect. Yes, there is much evil in the world today. But to understand and discover its causes is to understand its transient nature. That is why isolated, but sometimes difficult, feelings of dejection are drowned out by the overall optimism of my approach to life. That's the whole secret. It has nothing to do with a rejection of private life. On the contrary, it is precisely this approach to life that makes a full private life possible, a life in which people are fused into a single whole not only physically, but also spiritually.[98]

Around the time this letter would have arrived in Petrograd, the workers of the Putilov Plant began the strike that would become the first phase of the February Revolution—and possibly the last act of the human tragedy. Sverdlov heard the news in early March, and, accompanied by Filipp ("Georges") Goloshchekin, jumped into a sled and set out up the Enisei in a mad rush to reach Krasnoiarsk before the ice began to break up. After more than two weeks of ceaseless travel, they arrived, and by March 29 had made it all the way to Petrograd.

According to Novgorodtseva, they went straight to the apartment of Sverdlov's sister Sarra.

Later she talked about how Yakov Mikhailovich had appeared out of nowhere and started peppering her with questions about what was happening in Petrograd, with their comrades, and in the Central Committee (at the time, Sarra was helping Elena Stasova in the Central Committee secretariat).

Having answered barely a tenth of the questions, Sarra suddenly remembered that her brother must be hungry after his long journey and started to fan the samovar when Yakov Mikhailovich suddenly grabbed his head and moaned:

"Oh no! Georges!"

"Georges? Georges who?"

"Goloshchekin! I left him downstairs by the entrance, told him I'd go see if you were in and be right back. It's been half an hour. Would you mind going to get him? He'll kill me for sure if I go. He's easy to spot: tall, skinny, with a goatee, and wearing a black hat. In other words, a regular Don Quixote."

Sarra ran out and immediately spotted Goloshchekin, who was shifting from one foot to the other, looking despondent. She brought him in, served them both tea, and then took them to the Tauride Palace, where, in a corridor, at the entrance to one of the rooms, Elena Dmitrievna Stasova had placed a desk under a large, hand-written sign that said: "RSDRP(b), Central Committee Secretariat."[99]

Kira Egon-Besser had to wait a day or two longer. "One evening in late March [she writes in her memoir], the doorbell rang. When I heard the sound of his familiar booming bass coming from the entryway, I came running and saw Yakov Mikhailovich. He kissed me on both cheeks."[100]

■   ■   ■

Revolution was inseparable from love. It demanded sacrifices for the sake of a future harmony, and it required harmony—in love, comradeship, and book learning—as a condition for fulfillment. Most revolutionary leaders were young men who identified the Revolution with womanhood; many of them were men in love who identified particular women with the Revolution. Becoming a Bolshevik meant joining a band of brothers (and, possibly, sisters); living as a Bolshevik meant favoring some brothers over others and loving some sisters as much as the Revolution. "Who do I confess my weakness to, if not to you, my dear, my sweetheart?" wrote Sverdlov to Novgorodtseva. "The more thorough the analysis to which

Valerian Osinsky
(Courtesy of Elena Simakova)

we subject our relationship, the more profound, I would even say, thrillingly profound, it becomes." Revolutionary introspection relied on "a union of two kindred spirits filled with the same emotion and faith." After 1914, Sverdlov's hope for the real day seemed fused with his wish to kiss Kira Egon-Besser.[101]

Sverdlov's last letter about the real day took about a month to come true. Valerian Osinsky wrote his in late February 1917, at the time of its fulfillment. Born "Valerian Obolensky" in the family of a veterinarian of noble birth, he had debated Kerzhentsev in his Moscow gymnasium, shared a prison cell with Bukharin, and served as an "agitator" in the Swamp after the 1905 Revolution. He was famously tall, studious, radical, and aloof. In February 1917, he was thirty years old and married to a fellow revolutionary, Ekaterina Mikhailovna Smirnova. They had a five-year-old son, Vadim, whom they called "Dima." His correspondent, Anna Mikhailovna Shaternikova, was in her mid-twenties, a devoted Marxist, and a volunteer nurse. They had met a few months earlier in a hospital in Yalta, where he was being treated for tuberculosis. They were in love, but could not, for the time being, be together. They knew that their individual fates depended on the future of mankind as a whole. They were certain that that future was near, but did not know that it had already reached Petrograd.[102] Osinsky's letter contains his prose translation of the last three stanzas of Émile Verhaeren's "Blacksmith" ("Le Forgeron"), with detailed line-by-line commentary:

> The mob, whose sacred fury always rises above itself, is an immensely inspired force, projected by the will of those to come, that will erect, with its merciless hands, a new world of insatiable utopia. . . .
> The blacksmith, whose hope does not ever stray toward doubt or fear, sees before him, as if they were already here, the days when the simplest ethical commandments will become the foundation of human existence, serene and harmonious. . . .
> Lit up by that luminous faith, the flames of which he has been stoking for many a year in his forge, by the side of the road, next to the tilled fields,
> The blacksmith, huge and massive, is hammering with mighty, full blows—as if he were tempering the steel of human souls—the immense blades of patience and silence.

This poem, according to Osinsky, is a prophetic depiction of "the psychology of revolution." The passage on the power of the mob confirms that "one of life's greatest pleasures" is to join collective humanity in its sacred fury. The "insatiability" of utopia refers both to the boundlessness of human aspiration and the "pitiless arms of the crowd." And what is liberation if not the embrace of "the simplest ethical commandments"? "For thousands of years, different moral teachers (Socrates, Christ, Buddha, etc.) have been preaching so-called good," but their prescriptions have been mutually contradictory and incomplete because they have been based on life in "antagonistic" societies. It has been "savage morality, slave morality, or beggars' morality—not the morality of a rational, free, and developed society, and thus not fully simple, not primary." True virtue is contingent on revolution. "Only in the world of insatiable utopia will the simplest ethical rules become real and free from exceptions and contradictions."

The same is true of love, the "moving force" of ethics in a society liberated from social contradictions. At present, it is circumscribed by personal interests, limited in forms of expression, and "mixed with hatred (albeit the 'sacred' kind)." "Over there," it will "reveal without shame all of its profound tenderness and its charity without embellishment, without the tinkling bells of magnanimity and philanthropy." This idea seems utopian because it sounds "ethereal, 'illuminated,' and a bit banal," but of course it is not a utopia because all it means is that people will be able to "live and work joyfully and intensely." It will be "the kind of 'good time when any grief is easy to bear,' . . . a time of real social health, as opposed to having one's head up in the clouds." (The "easy to bear" quotation comes from Knut Hamsun's *Victoria*, a universal "student" favorite about the life-sustaining power of ethereal love.)

This "luminous faith" (*lucide croyance*) is not only faith "but also certitude and clairvoyance." "It is with this luminous, radiant, burning certitude in his eyes that the huge, massive (*gourd*), heavy, and lumbering blacksmith . . . swings his hammer." At the end of his letter, Osinsky claims that his "sometimes spare, inaccurate, and not always rhythmical" translation is much truer to the original than Valery Briusov's smooth, rhymed version. "You cannot parrot the blacksmith, you have to be him—him . . . *dont l'éspoir ne dévie vers les doutes ni les affres—jamais* [him, whose hope does not ever stray toward doubt or fear]." To stress the point, Osinsky suddenly changes his tone and adds: "Tell me, A.M., does this blacksmith— *énorme et gourd*—remind you of anyone by any chance?"[103]

■   ■   ■

But the tallest, biggest, bluntest, and loudest of Russia's blacksmiths was the poet Vladimir Mayakovsky. In January 1914, "handsome and twenty-two," he arrived in Odessa as part of a Futurist traveling show also featuring David Burliuk and Vasily Kamensky. "All three," according to a newspaper report, "were wearing top hats, yellow blouses, and overcoats with radishes in their lapels." As they were walking along the embankment on the first evening of their visit, Kamensky noticed "an absolutely extraordinary girl: tall, shapely, with magnificent, shining eyes—in short, a real beauty." He pointed her out to Mayakovsky, who "turned around, looked her slowly up and down, and then suddenly seemed to become extremely agitated. 'Listen, you two stay here, or do whatever you want,' he said. 'I'll see you back at the hotel in . . . well, in a while.'"[104]

The girl's name was Maria Denisova, but Mayakovsky called her "La Gioconda." She was twenty years old. Originally from Kharkov, she had moved to Odessa to attend a gymnasium but had later dropped out and enrolled in sculpture classes at an art studio.[105] The next day, the three Futurists were invited to dinner at her older sister's house. According to Kamensky,

Vladimir Mayakovsky   Maria Denisova

The dinner at La Gioconda's turned into a triumph of poetry. We spent most of the time reciting poems and saying very special, festive things. Volodia was inspired. . . . He talked a great deal and was very smart and witty. . . . I will never forget the way he read his poetry that evening.

When we got back to our hotel, it took us a long time to get over the tremendous impression Maria had made on us.

Burliuk was silent, but looked meaningfully at Volodia, who kept pacing nervously back and forth, unsure about what to do or how to deal with this sudden eruption of love. . . . He kept asking quietly over and over again:

"What should I do? What can I do? Should I write a letter? But wouldn't that look stupid? I love you. What more can I say?"[106]

He did write a letter—not at all like the one from Tatiana to Onegin ("I am writing to you, what more can I say"), but a love letter nonetheless. He called it "The Thirteenth Apostle," but then, when the censors objected, renamed it *A Cloud in Pants*. Its addressee was God, among many others, and its subject was the end of love—and everything else.

On the Futurists' last day in Odessa, Maria told Mayakovsky to wait for her in his hotel room at 4:00 p.m. Two days later, on the train between Nikolaev and Kishinev, Mayakovsky began to recite:[107]

You think it's delirium? Malaria?
It happened.
Happened in Odessa,
"I'll see you at four," said Maria.
Eight,
Nine,
Ten.

Past midnight, and many anguished stanzas later, she finally came.

You entered,
brusque, matter-of-fact,
torturing the suede of your gloves,
and said:
"Guess what,
I'm getting married."
Fine.
Go ahead.
I'll be all right.
Can't you see I'm perfectly calm?
Like the pulse of a corpse.
Remember?
You used to say:
"Jack London,
money,
love,
passion,"
but all I could see
was you—La Gioconda
whom someone was bound to steal.
And did.

His revenge would be terrible. "Remember! Pompeii perished when they
mocked Vesuvius." But of course Pompeii was doomed in any case. Like
Sverdlov and Osinsky, Mayakovsky had known all along that there would
be earthquakes and famines, and that brother would betray brother to
death, and children would rebel against their parents and have them put
to death, and the sun would be darkened, and the moon would not give its
light, and the stars would fall from the sky, and the heavenly bodies would
be shaken. Like Sverdlov and Osinsky, Mayakovsky connected a doomed
love to a doomed world. Impossible loves were but reminders of impossible lives. The days of distress were but signs of the prophet's election and
the world's violent end.

I,
mocked and cast aside,
like an endless
dirty joke,
can see through the mountains of time
him
whom no one else can see.
There,
beyond the scope of feeble vision,
at the head of the hungry hordes,
in its thorny crown of revolutions,

strides the year
1916.
I am his John the Baptist;
I am where the pain is—
everywhere;
in each drop of the tear stream
I nailed myself to the cross.
It's too late for forgiveness,
I've burned the souls that nurtured compassion.
And that is much harder than taking
a hundred million Bastilles!
And when,
with rebellion
his advent heralding,
you step forth to greet your savior,
I'll rip out
my soul,
stomp on it,
make it big,
and hand it to you—
all bloodied, for a banner.

But no, it is he, the "spat-upon Calvarian," who is the Savior. His Maria is Mary, the Mother of God, and he is, "maybe, the most beautiful of her sons."

In Heaven, he asks God his Father to build a merry-go-round on the tree of knowledge of good and evil and offers to bring in the best-looking Eves from the city's back alleys.[108]

Not interested?
Shaking your shaggy head?
Giving me the big frown?
You don't really think
that creep with the wings
standing behind you
knows the meaning of love?

. . . .
You, the almighty,
came up with a pair of hands,
made sure everyone got a head,
so why couldn't you come up with a way
for us to kiss and kiss and kiss
without this torture?
I thought you were really powerful, a god almighty
but you're just a drop-out, a puny little godlet.
Look, I'm bending down

to pull out a cobbler's knife
from inside my boot.
Winged scoundrels!
Cringe in your paradise
Ruffle your feathers as you tremble in fright!
And you, the one with the incense breath,
I'll split you open from here to Alaska!

Heaven would be exposed for the joke it is, but—as in the original Revelation—the last and decisive slaughter would take place on earth. The hungry would crawl out of the swamp, and the well-fed—Voronsky's "driveling, hiccuping, lip-smacking" meat-market butchers—would hang in place of the bloody carcasses. The theft of La Gioconda would be avenged.

Come on, you
meek, sweaty little starvelings
festering in your flea-ridden muck!
Let's turn Mondays and Tuesdays
into holidays
by dipping them in blood!
Let the Earth, at knifepoint, think again
about whom it has chosen to pick on!
The Earth,
grown fat,
like Rothschild's lover,
used up and left to rot.
Let the flags flap in the heat of the gunfire
The way they do on any decent holiday—
And you, lampposts, hoist up
the shopkeepers'
bloody carcasses.
I outswore,
outbegged,
outstabbed myself,
sank my teeth into someone's flesh.
The sunset, red as the Marseillaise,
Shuddered as it breathed its last.[109]

3

THE FAITH

The most obvious question about Sverdlov's, Osinsky's and Mayakovsky's luminous faith is whether it is a religion. The most sensible answer is that it does not matter.

There are two principal approaches to defining religion: the substantive (what religion is) and the functional (what religion does). According to Steve Bruce's deliberately conventional version of the former, religion "consists of beliefs, actions, and institutions which assume the existence of supernatural entities with powers of action, or impersonal powers or processes possessed of moral purpose. Such a formulation seems to encompass what ordinary people mean when they talk about religion." The question, then, is whether the Marxist drama of universal degradation and salvation (preordained, independent of human will, and incapable of falsifiable verification) is an impersonal process possessed of moral purpose and whether communism as the end of recognizable human existence (all conflicts resolved, all needs satisfied, all of history's work done) is in some sense "supernatural." The usual answer is no: because the Marxist prediction is meant to be rational and this-worldly; because the "supernatural" is usually defined in opposition to reason; because "ordinary people" don't think of Marxism as a religion; and because the whole point of using the conventional definition is to exclude Marxism and other beliefs that assume the nonexistence of supernatural (science-defying) entities.[1]

The problem with this formulation is that it also excludes a lot of beliefs that ordinary people and professional scholars routinely describe as "religions." As Durkheim argues in *The Elementary Forms of Religious Life*, most human beings for most of human history had no basis for distinguishing between the "natural" and the "supernatural"; no way of questioning the legitimacy of their ancestors' ways; and no objection to sharing the same world with a variety of gods, spirits, and more or less dead forebears, not all of them human. Such beliefs may seem absurd in a world with a different sense of the "ordinary," but they are not about the supernatural as opposed to something else. In Christian and post-Christian societies, they have been seen to comprise "pagan religions," "primitive religions," "traditional religions," "primary religions," or simply a lot of foolishness. According to the definitions centered on the supernatural, such beliefs are either uniformly religious or not religious at all.[2]

One solution is to follow Auguste Comte and Karl Marx in associating religion with beliefs and practices that are absurd from the point of view of modern science. What matters is not what "they" believe, but what we believe they believe. If they believe in things we (as rational observers) know to be absurd, then they believe in the supernatural, whether they know it or not. The problem with this solution is that it offends against civility and possibly against the law without answering the question of whether communism belongs in the same category. If "animism" is a religion whether it realizes it or not, then Marx's claim that the coming of communism is a matter of scientific prediction (and not a supernatural prophecy) is irrelevant to whether rational observers judge it to be so. The problem with rational observers is that they seem unable to make up their minds and, according to their many detractors, may not be fully rational (or they would not be using non sequiturs such as "secular religion" and would not keep forgetting that "religion" as they define it is the bastard child of Christian Reformation and European Enlightenment). Some newly discovered "world religions" are named after their prophetic founders (Buddhism, Mohammedanism, Christianity); others, after the people whose beliefs they described (Hinduism, the Chukchi religion); and yet others, by using vernacular terms such as Islam ("submission"), Sikh ("disciple"), Jain ("conqueror"), or Tao ("path"). Most of the rest are usually grouped by region. Some regions (including China for much of its history and large sections of Europe in the "secular age") may or may not have religion, depending on what the compilers mean by the "supernatural."[3]

An attempt to stretch the definition (and accommodate Theravada Buddhism, for example) by replacing "supernatural" with "transcendental," "supra-empirical," or "other-worldly" provokes the same questions and makes the inclusion of Marxism—something the advocates of substantive definitions would like to avoid—more likely. Just how empirical or non-transcendental are humanism, Hindutva, manifest destiny, and the kingdom of freedom?

Durkheim suggests another approach. "Religion," according to his definition, is "a unified system of beliefs and practices relative to sacred things." Sacred things are things that "the profane must not and cannot touch with impunity." The function of the sacred is to unite humans into moral communities. Religion is a mirror in which human societies admire themselves. Subsequent elaborations of functionalism describe religion as a process by which humans create a sense of the self and an "'objective' and moral universe of meaning"; a "set of symbolic forms and acts that relate man to the ultimate conditions of his existence"; and, in Clifford Geertz's much cited version, "a system of symbols which acts to establish powerful, pervasive, and long-lasting moods and motivations in men by formulating conceptions of a general order of existence and clothing these conceptions with such an aura of factuality that the moods and motivations seem uniquely realistic." Whatever one's understanding of the "sacred," "ultimate," or "general" (Mircea Eliade describes the sacred as a "fixed center" or "absolute reality" amidst "the never-ceasing relativity of purely subjective experiences"), it seems impossible to avoid the conclusion that every society is by definition religious, that any comprehensive ideology (including secularism) creates and reflects a moral community, and that Osinsky's luminous faith provides a fixed center in the swamp of subjective experiences and relates humans to the ultimate conditions of their existence.[4]

In sum, most people who talk about religion do not know what it is, while those who do are divided into those who include Marxism because they feel they have no choice and those who exclude it according to criteria they have trouble defining. Compromise terms such as "quasi-religion" make no sense within the functionalist paradigm (a moral community is a moral community whether its sacred center is the Quran or the US Constitution) and raise awkward questions (Taoism, but not Maoism?) for the champions of the "supernatural." By extension, states that are "separate from the church" have no idea what they are separate from. The First Amendment to the US Constitution fails to define its subject and violates itself by creating a special constitutional status for "religion" while prohibiting any such legislation. In 1984, a University of California–Berkeley law professor, Phillip E. Johnson, surveyed the field and concluded that "no definition of religion for constitutional purposes exists, and no satisfactory definition is likely to be conceived." Three years later, he read Richard Dawkins's *The Blind Watchmaker*, had an epiphany, and founded the "intelligent design" movement.[5]

■ ■ ■

One reason for the trouble with definitions is the desire to apply the same name to two very different belief systems: one that did not know it was a belief system and one that did—and felt very strongly about it. In the first millennium BCE, much of urban Eurasia was afflicted with an epidemic of reflexivity and self-doubt. The arrival of Zoroaster in Iran; the Buddha, Jain dharma, and the Upanishads in India; Confucius, the Tao, and the "hundred schools" in China; classical tragedy and philosophy in Greece; and the prophetic era in ancient Israel had inaugurated what Karl Jaspers has called the "Axial Age"—an age "of standing back and looking beyond." They were not all about the "supernatural" in the strict sense, but they all posited an "absolute reality" radically distinct from a world inhabited by humans and their gods and ancestors. They shipped off as much of the sacred as they could to another plane or another time, allowing themselves occasional glimpses; posited an abyss separating humans from their true nature (as expressed in concepts or commandments); and made "alienation" the universal law of existence (leading a lot of people to believe that it had always been so). They proclaimed or implied, in other words, that humans were living incorrectly; that human life was, in some fundamental sense, a mistake, and possibly a crime.[6]

Ever since, these "Axial civilizations" and their numerous descendants—including Christianity (an offshoot of prophetic Judaism) and Islam (their close relative)—have been preoccupied, above all else, with the tasks of restoration, reformation, and "redemption" (as an escape from a human existence newly revealed to be misguided or meaningless). This has led to the emergence of "reason" independent of social ascription; the perception of the contingency—and, therefore, reformability—of the political order; the appearance of moral communities bound neither ethnically nor politically; the unification and codification of the sacred through written compilations of original solutions; the rise of elites specializing in interpreting the scripture and monopolizing access to salvation; and the possibility of the rise of counter-elites proposing alternative interpretations or entirely new solutions. Different traditions have different conceptual repertoires and escape routes, but all have offered more or less consistent and self-sufficient ways of "standing back and looking beyond."[7]

The fact of having lost one's way suggests the possibility of being able to find it again. All societies and the worlds they inhabit have had their beginnings, but it is only when human life turned out to be a problem that endings became solutions, and thus matters of serious concern. In ancient Greece, they tended to be political, metaphysical, provisional, and unintegrated. In southern Asia, the focus on individual reincarnation and escape allowed the collective resolution to remain remote (or perhaps it was the remoteness of the collective resolution that helped focus individual minds). In eastern and southeastern Asia, Confucian world-improvement and Buddhist and Taoist world-rejection came together to produce a tradition of expecting both at once (occasionally in the shape of an immediate world improvement by means of a violent world rejection). But even as they imagined an eventual return to wholeness and wondered about the effect of human choices on the unfolding of the cosmic drama, most heirs to the Axial predicament continued to expect a perennial cycle of corruption and rebirth. All final solutions were temporary. For the sun to rise, spring to return, hunted prey to submit, and the earth to give up its fruits, the hero had to keep killing the serpent and humans had to keep making mistakes and sacrifices. Holding chaos and its many agents at bay was a daily effort and the closest life could get to having a meaning. Everything was forever.[8]

Until it was no more. Sometime around the turn of the first millennium BCE, Zoroaster made history—literally, as well as figuratively—by prophesying the absolute end of the world. There was going to be one final battle between the forces of light and darkness and one last judgment of all human beings who had ever lived—and then there would be nothing but an all-encompassing, everlasting perfection: no hunger, no thirst, no disagreement, no childbirth, and no death. The hero would defeat the serpent one last time; chaos would be vanquished for good; only the good would remain—forever. This meant, among many other things, that time had become linear and irreversible (and thus, in a sense, properly historical). It also meant that the cost of individual moral choices had become almost impossibly high: not everyone was going to make it into timelessness, and no one was going to get a second chance.[9]

■ ■ ■

Perhaps influenced by Zoroaster, the ancient Israelites also came to think of time as a straight plot line. In some sense, Exodus is a conventional migration narrative explaining the legitimacy of a group's territorial claim. Such stories (themselves versions of a questing hero's return from the netherworld) tend to describe a hazardous march from a wrong temporary home to the right permanent one, indicated by the gods and discovered by the anointed leader-founder. But Exodus does much more than that. The story it tells is one of a final liberation from politics and a permanent solution to the "standing back and looking beyond" problem. Having escaped the Pharaoh, the Israelites did not establish a new state: they created a virtual one. Instead of a this-worldly king, they got themselves an other-worldly one, as powerful as their imagination would allow. The Israelites bridged the "Axial" chasm between the real and the ideal by submitting to a single ruler of unlimited power. They did not simply inherit him from their ancestors: they handed themselves over to him as part of a voluntary contract. They did not worship him through a polity that embodied his will: they worshipped him directly, as individuals (the Ten Commandments are in the second person singular) and as a community of the elect. After Moses, political and spiritual representation—indeed, any mediation between the Hebrews and their true ruler—became problematic or dispensable. They became "a kingdom of priests and a holy nation." Observance of the law became a matter of personal devotion and inner discipline. The Heavenly Father was to be loved, not simply served, and he was always watching and always listening: "Now what I am commanding you today is not too difficult for you or beyond your reach. It is not up in heaven, so that you have to ask, 'Who will ascend into heaven to get it and proclaim it to us so we may obey it?' Nor is it beyond the sea, so that you have to ask, 'Who will cross the sea to get it and proclaim it to us so we may obey it?' No, the word is very near you; it is in your mouth and in your heart so you may obey it."[10]

The key to the one-on-one relationship with the absolute was that it be the only one (that is, truly absolute). "Do not worship any other god, for the LORD, whose name is Jealous, is a jealous God." The Israelites escaped a rule that was transitory, contingent, and mostly tolerant of golden calves and local cults by subjecting themselves to a rule that was eternal, self-sufficient, and utterly inescapable. They fled a tyranny that was gratuitously arbitrary for a tyranny that was arbitrary out of principle—and thus, one hoped, just. When Job insisted on his innocence, he was questioning God's goodness. When Job's three friends defended God's goodness, they were questioning Job's innocence (because punishment, they reasoned, must be proof of sinfulness). But they were all wrong, as God himself explained. The Almighty was simply too mighty, too powerful, and too busy with matters of life and death to justify himself to anyone. He did as he pleased for reasons only he understood. Job had to "repent in dust and ashes" and do as he was told. He had no moral agency at all. The price of political freedom was absolute moral slavery.[11]

Absolute moral slavery to the source of all morality may equal freedom (although Job's possession of an independent moral sense seems to suggest otherwise), but even if it does not, the Hebrew god was remote and inconsistent enough to allow for some uncertainty. Unlike earthly kings and specialized gods, an all-powerful transcendental despot cannot be cheated ("there is no dark place, no deep shadow, where evildoers can hide"), but he just might be in a forgiving mood or otherwise engaged (he has so much more to do, after all). And of course the God of Israel gave Job and his friends plenty of reason to believe that the Covenant was well within human understanding and that all that was required of them was that they follow a few simple rules. "For I, the LORD your God, am a jealous God, punishing the children for the sin of the fathers to the third and fourth generation of those who hate me, but showing love to a thousand generations of those who love me and keep my commandments."[12]

Whatever the predicament of the individual subject, the fate of the chosen people as a whole was clear. The logic of the Book of Job did not apply to the Israelites as a group—or rather, the logic of the Book of Job seemed to suggest that individual moral slavery was a fair price for the guarantee of collective redemption. Some members of the tribe would be put to the sword, devoured by wild animals, or die of a plague (for breaking the law or for no reason at all), but the tribe as such would triumph no matter what. Its "great rebellions" and "many backslidings" might postpone the final deliverance, but they could do nothing to prevent it. The original election and final outcome were beyond morality or understanding: "The LORD your God has chosen you out of all the peoples on the face of the earth to be his people," and that was the end of it. Or rather, that was the beginning. The end was the restoration of the chosen people to the promised land, where "they will neither hunger nor thirst, nor will the desert heat or the sun beat upon them." Everything in between was history.[13]

The most obviously remarkable thing about the Hebrew God is that he was the first transcendental ruler to successfully eliminate all customary allegiances and proclaim himself an absolute monarch. But he did not stop there. After banning all rival cults and exterminating their adherents within the house of Israel, he denied the existence of all foreign gods, too. From being the only god of the Israelites, he became the only God, period.

A few vestiges of traditional tribal relativism persisted for a while (you take "what your god Chemosh gives you," and we'll take "whatever the LORD our God has given us"), but the tendency was clear enough. "I am the LORD, and there is no other; apart from me there is no God. I will strengthen you, though you have not acknowledged me, so that from the rising of the sun to the place of its setting men may know there is none besides me. I am the LORD, and there is no other."[14]

Some tribal gods are universal creators; the Hebrew God was the first universal autocrat. A small tribe repeatedly conquered by its much larger neighbors retaliated by conquering the world conceptually. Rather than recognizing the demonstrable superiority of their masters' spiritual sponsors, switching loyalties, and dissolving in the multitudes of fellow opportunists, the Israelites extended ad infinitum the powers and jurisdiction of their own patron. Everything that ever happened anywhere was part of a universal design centered on the drama of their wanderings and eventual deliverance. All human beings, including the rulers of the great empires, were pawns in the hands of Israel's heavenly pharaoh. History as the meaningful unfolding of time was the result of the Israelites' collective moral choices. Human life past and present was one continuous reason for the postponement of the Day of the Lord.[15]

There was not much mystery or inscrutability on this score. The End was predetermined; the Israelites kept making wrong choices; and the Lord kept blaming them for his continued unwillingness or inability to fulfill his promise. The world's first heavenly autocrat was also, by virtue of his chronic theodicy problem, the world's first Underground Man (or Adolescent). Constantly snubbed by his spiritual inferiors, he bragged about his great accomplishments, promised even greater accomplishments, nursed his many grudges, feigned humility, relished his ability to cause pain and thwart expectations, and fantasized obsessively about a spectacular public humiliation of the strong, the arrogant, and the well-connected. According to Isaiah, among others, he was not going to simply take his people to the assigned place and help them defeat the Hittites, Girgashites, Amorites, Canaanites, Perizzites, Hivites, and Jebusites who lived there. "The LORD is angry with all nations; his wrath is upon all their armies. He will totally destroy them, he will give them over to slaughter. Their slain will be thrown out, their dead bodies will send up a stench; the mountains will be soaked with their blood."[16]

As for those who will survive the slaughter (said the Sovereign Lord to his people), "They will bow down before you with their faces to the ground; they will lick the dust at your feet. Then you will know that I am the LORD; those who hope in me will not be disappointed. . . . I will make your oppressors eat their own flesh; they will be drunk on their own blood, as with wine. Then all mankind will know that I, the LORD, am your Savior, your Redeemer, the Mighty One of Jacob." All those who had ever offended against the Israelites and their mighty redeemer would get their comeuppance and eat their words. "And those tall Sabeans—they will come over to you and will be yours; they will trudge behind you, coming over to you in chains. They will bow down before you and plead with you, saying, 'Surely God is with you, and there is no other; there is no other god.'" And in case they were still unconvinced, Gog, of the Land of Magog, would be tricked into attacking the chosen people one last time: "I will summon a sword against Gog on all my mountains, declares the Sovereign LORD. Every man's sword will be against his brother. I will execute judgment upon him with plague and bloodshed; I will pour down torrents of rain, hailstones and burning sulfur on him and on his troops and on the many nations with him. And so I will show my greatness and my holiness, and I will make myself known in the sight of many nations. Then they will know that I am the LORD."[17]

The happy ending was subject to the same inflation as the violent resolution. The promise of a safe homecoming and peaceful life in the land of milk and honey evolved into a prophecy of entirely "new heavens and a new earth":

Then will the eyes of the blind be opened and the ears of the deaf unstopped.

Then will the lame leap like a deer, and the mute tongue shout for joy. Water will gush forth in the wilderness and streams in the desert.

The burning sand will become a pool, the thirsty ground bubbling springs. In the haunts where jackals once lay, grass and reeds and papyrus will grow.

And a highway will be there; it will be called the Way of Holiness. The unclean will not journey on it; it will be for those who walk in that Way; wicked fools will not go about on it.

No lion will be there, nor will any ferocious beast get up on it; they will not be found there. But only the redeemed will walk there, and the ransomed of the LORD will return. They will enter Zion with singing; everlasting joy will crown their heads. Gladness and joy will overtake them, and sorrow and sighing will flee away.

Sorrow and sighing would not simply flee away—they would disappear forever. The ferocious beasts would not simply walk off—they, too, would be overtaken by gladness and start feeding on milk and honey. "The wolf will live with the lamb, the leopard will lie down with the goat, the calf and the lion and the yearling together; and a little child will lead them."[18]

Meanwhile, the Israelites' earthly lot had not improved very much. The end of the Babylonian exile and the return of the ransomed was followed by a succession of more or less egregious Gogs. The worse the offenses against Zion and less likely the prospect that it would "no longer be plundered by the nations," the more cosmic and urgent the visions of the final retribution. The three centuries that were centered on the birth of a "new era" and bounded by the Maccabean Wars of the 160s BCE and the Bar Kochba revolt of the 130s CE were a time of a dramatic flourishing of Jewish apocalyptic eschatology ("revelations" of the End). All such revelations, beginning with the Book of Daniel, told the same story: the position of the righteous is worse than ever before; the history of their oppression is entering its highest and final stage; the corrupt ruling empire is about to fall; the ensuing time of troubles will involve general lawlessness, fratricidal wars, and natural disasters; God will finally intervene, directly or through a special representative; his army will defeat the united forces of evil; and the righteous will live happily ever after. "The sovereignty, power and greatness of the kingdoms under the whole heaven will be handed over to the saints, the people of the Most High. His kingdom will be an everlasting kingdom, and all rulers will worship and obey him."[19]

There were different ways of welcoming the inevitable. The members of the Qumran sect withdrew to the shores of the Dead Sea, renounced property and marriage, condemned Jewish appeasers along with Roman invaders, and strove after absolute ritual purity in preparation for the approaching slaughter. Others, often collectively known as "zealots," took up arms on the assumption that, as Josephus put it, "the Deity does not cooperate in restoring liberty otherwise than by influencing man's decision, and God will be much more ready to assist us if we do not shirk the toil entailed by the great cause which we have at heart."[20]

First-century Jewish Palestine was teeming with teachers, preachers, prophets, healers, exorcists, messiahs, and miracle workers inspired by the expectation of the imminent End. "A certain impostor named Theudas," writes Josephus, "persuaded the mass of the rabble to take their belongings with them and follow him to the river Jordan; for he said that he was a prophet and would by a word of command divide the river and afford them an easy passage; and by these words he deceived many." A "charlatan" from Egypt "gained for himself the reputation of a prophet, . . . collected about thirty thousand of his dupes, entered the country and led his force round from the desert to the mount called Olivet." A "body of villains . . . under the pretense of divine inspiration fostering revolutionary changes . . . persuaded the multitude to act like madmen and led them out into the desert under the belief that God would there give them tokens of deliverance."[21]

According to Mark, a preacher named John "wore clothing made of camel's hair, with a leather belt around his waist," ate "locusts and wild honey," and preached "a baptism of repentance for the forgiveness of sins." And according to Celsus, a second-century Greek writer,

> there are many, who, although of no name, with the greatest facility and on the slightest occasion, whether within or without temples, assume the motions and gestures of inspired persons; while others

do it in cities or among armies, for the purpose of attracting attention and exciting surprise. These are accustomed to say, each for
himself, "I am God; I am the Son of God; or, I am the Divine Spirit; I
have come because the world is perishing, and you, O men, are perishing for your iniquities. But I wish to save you, and you shall see
me returning again with heavenly power. Blessed is he who now
does me homage. On all the rest I will send down eternal fire, both
on cities and on countries. And those who know not the punishments which await them shall repent and grieve in vain; while those
who are faithful to me I will preserve eternally." . . . To these promises are added strange, fanatical, and quite unintelligible words, of
which no rational person can find the meaning: for so dark are they,
as to have no meaning at all; but they give occasion to every fool or
impostor to apply them to suit his own purposes.[22]

■ ■ ■

Jesus of Nazareth was a mostly traditional Jewish healer with a mostly
traditional eschatological prophecy. "Nation will rise against nation, and
kingdom against kingdom. There will be earthquakes in various places,
and famines. . . . Brother will betray brother to death, and a father his
child. Children will rebel against their parents and have them put to
death. . . . The sun will be darkened, and the moon will not give its light;
the stars will fall from the sky, and the heavenly bodies will be shaken."[23]
The "days of distress" will be followed by the kingdom of God, which is
described as a feast for those who have not feasted before. The only definite thing about the new order is that social roles will be reversed: "Blessed
are you who are poor, for yours is the kingdom of God. Blessed are you who
hunger now, for you will be satisfied. . . . But woe to you who are rich, for
you have already received your comfort. Woe to you who are well fed now,
for you will go hungry."[24]

None of this is meant for another world, another time, or another generation. In Mark's account, Jesus's first words are: "The time has come.
The kingdom of God is near. Repent and believe the good news!" And the
good news—the news that suffuses the prophet's message and his followers' lives—is that "this generation will certainly not pass away until all
these things have happened." "Some who are standing here will not taste
death before they see the kingdom of God."[25]

As in most prophecies, predestination and free will are finely balanced.
The End is ineluctable, but its nature and, possibly, its timing depend on
human actions. Jesus, human or not, is both the messenger and the agent,
and some of his listeners may still be able to affect the course of the divine
juggernaut. "If the Lord had not cut short those days, no one would survive. But for the sake of the elect, whom he has chosen, he has shortened

them." Nor is it too late now: "Make every effort to enter through the narrow door, because many, I tell you, will try to enter and will not be able to." Jesus's closest disciples, in particular, will be rewarded for their loyalty and sacrifice. Providence is, in part, the result of their efforts. "At the renewal of all things, when the Son of Man sits on his glorious throne, you who have followed me will also sit on twelve thrones, judging the twelve tribes of Israel. And everyone who has left houses or brothers or sisters or father or mother or children or fields for my sake will receive a hundred times as much and will inherit eternal life."[26]

What could one do in order to inherit eternal life? How was one to welcome, and perhaps help bring about, the days of distress and the kingdom of the Lord? First, one had to leave one's house and brothers and sisters and father and mother and children and fields—the way Jesus himself had done.

> Then Jesus' mother and brothers arrived. Standing outside, they sent someone in to call him. A crowd was sitting around him, and they told him, "Your mother and brothers are outside looking for you."
>
> "Who are my mother and my brothers?" he asked.
>
> Then he looked at those seated in a circle around him and said, "Here are my mother and my brothers! Whoever does God's will is my brother and sister and mother."[27]

To ensure salvation, one had to renounce one's family and join a new one. "If anyone comes to me and does not hate his father and mother, his wife and children, his brothers and sisters—yes, even his own life—he cannot be my disciple." Membership in the sect promised the ultimate reward in exchange for the ultimate sacrifice. It meant accepting a world in which all strangers were "neighbors"; all neighbors were brothers; and all brothers were the eternal children of one all-powerful Lord. According to Jesus, the two main commandments were: "Love the Lord your God with all your heart and with all your soul and with all your strength and with all your mind"; and, "Love your neighbor as yourself." The only people to be hated (at least at first, during the trial period for new members) were one's erstwhile father and mother, wife and children, brothers and sisters—and yes, even oneself.[28]

It was a universal message that allowed for multiple distinctions. Some—the weak, the meek, and the humble—were more likely to join and more deserving of membership ("I praise you, Father, Lord of heaven and earth, because you have hidden these things from the wise and learned, and revealed them to little children"). Those who did join were more deserving than those who did not. Ideally, all neighbors from among the chosen people were to become brothers (Jesus was not talking to Gentiles). In the meantime, the rich were trying to squeeze through the eye of the needle, while those who had abandoned their families were looking forward to judging the twelve tribes of Israel.[29]

"Repenting" meant "changing and becoming like little children." Changing and becoming like little children meant submitting fully and unreservedly to God the Father. God the Father was to become more consistent in his total claim on his people:[30]

> "You have heard that it was said to the people long ago, 'Do not murder, and anyone who murders will be subject to judgment.' But I tell you that anyone who is angry with his brother will be subject to judgment. . . ."
>
> "You have heard that it was said, 'Do not commit adultery.' But I tell you that anyone who looks at a woman lustfully has already committed adultery with her in his heart. . . ."
>
> "Again, you have heard that it was said to the people long ago, 'Do not break your oath, but keep the oaths you have made to the Lord.' But I tell you, Do not swear at all. . . . Simply let your 'Yes' be 'Yes,' and your 'No,' 'No.'"[31]

The Hebrew God tended to dilute his totalitarian claim—an absolute, undivided, unmediated, and randomly capricious domination of individuals in exchange for a guarantee of collective triumph—by multiplying legal regulations and occasionally emphasizing the contractual nature of his relationship with his subjects (some of whom might be excused for concluding that they were living in an ethical Rechtsstaat). Jesus would have none of that. He was a radical fundamentalist and a consistent enemy of the "Pharisees and the teachers of the law": "'You hypocrites!' [he railed at them for insisting on the observance of kosher rules.] 'For Isaiah was right when he prophesied about you: "These people honor me with their lips, but their hearts are far from me. They worship me in vain; their teachings are but rules taught by men."' Jesus called the crowd to him and said, 'Listen and understand. What goes into a man's mouth does not make him "unclean," but what comes out of his mouth, that is what makes him "unclean."'"[32]

It is not what you eat—it is what you say. It is not what you say—it is what you think (because your no is a no, and because "your Father knows what you need before you ask him"). It is not about your lips—it is about your heart. It is not about loving your "loved ones" ("are not even the tax collectors doing that?")—it is about loving the tax collectors. It is not about forgiving someone you are angry with—it is about not being allowed to be angry. It is not about not sleeping with your neighbor's wife—it is about not being allowed to have the desire. It is not between you and the law (as interpreted by the Pharisees and other would-be mediators)—it is between your Lord and your thoughts, all of them, all the time. "Do not be afraid of those who kill the body but cannot kill the soul. Rather, be afraid of the

One who can destroy both." The Big Father is watching you, and the only way to escape punishment is to be watching, too—and yes, even yourself. "Be perfect, therefore, as your heavenly Father is perfect."[33]

The fact that Jesus died before he got the chance "to drink of the fruit of the vine in the kingdom of God" was interpreted by his followers not as a failure of the prophecy but as an episode in the drama of divine rebirth, in the Osiris-Dionysus tradition—except that Jesus, in accordance with the Jewish eschatological expectation, was to come back only once—when "the time has come," this time truly for the last time. His resurrection was a preview of the coming resurrection for all.[34]

The orphaned members of the sect expected Jesus's return with the same degree of urgency and intensity with which Jesus himself had expected the original kingdom of the Lord. The Second Coming was to be a successful—and immediate—reenactment of the first one. As Paul wrote in First Corinthians, "What I mean, brothers, is that the time is short. From now on those who have wives should live as if they had none; those who mourn, as if they did not; those who are happy, as if they were not; those who buy something, as if it were not theirs to keep; those who use the things of the world, as if not engrossed in them. For this world in its present form is passing away." So quickly was the world in its present form passing away that Paul had to reassure his followers that their imminent redemption would not separate them forever from their dead brothers and sisters:

> We believe that Jesus died and rose again and so we believe that God will bring with Jesus those who have fallen asleep in him. According to the Lord's own word, we tell you that we who are still alive, who are left till the coming of the Lord, will certainly not precede those who have fallen asleep. For the Lord himself will come down from heaven, with a loud command, with the voice of the archangel and with the trumpet call of God, and the dead in Christ will rise first. After that, we who are still alive and are left will be caught up together with them in the clouds to meet the Lord in the air. And so we will be with the Lord forever.[35]

In the meantime, they were to take ritual baths, have common meals (any supper might be the last one), and be "alert and self-controlled" lest the day of the Lord surprise them "like a thief in the night." They should also make haste to welcome non-Jewish converts—because faith is above the law and because the failure of most Jews to recognize Jesus as the Messiah could mean only one thing: that God wanted his adopted sons to join the fold before his "natural" sons (the ones of Paul's "own race") could complete the fulfillment of the prophecy on Judgment Day.[36]

The description of the end days that made it into the Christian canon as the Book of Revelation uses images from the Jewish apocalyptic tradition but limits the ranks of the chosen to the followers of Jesus; 144,000 of them (still identified by membership in one of the twelve tribes of Israel) have seals put on their foreheads, so that the divine avengers do not slaughter them by mistake. (The concept of labeling and classifying is central to the Apocalypse: the minions of the beast are branded accordingly, and everyone is registered in a special book as belonging to either of the two categories. There are no abstentions, hesitations, or middle ground. "I know your deeds, that you are neither cold nor hot. I wish you were either one or the other! So, because you are lukewarm—neither hot nor cold—I am about to spit you out of my mouth.")[37]

Having returned to earth, Jesus "treads the winepress of the fury of the wrath of God Almighty" by destroying Babylon (the Roman Empire) and subjecting its agents to elaborate tortures. Their bodies are covered with "ugly and painful sores"; their rivers and springs are turned to blood; and their kingdom is plunged into darkness as they are "tormented with burning sulfur" and "gnaw their tongues in agony." (In keeping with the vision of two irreconcilable camps and the plot of violent retribution, none of the victims repents, reconsiders, or begs for mercy.) After the battle of Armageddon, Christ and those who have been martyred in his service rule the nations "with an iron scepter" for a thousand years. At the end of the "millennium," the dictatorship of virtue is attacked by the devil's armies, which are devoured by a fire from heaven. At the Last Judgment that follows, the dead are resurrected and "judged according to what they have done as recorded in the books." Those not found in the book of life are thrown into the lake of fire, to suffer for ever and ever; the rest are reunited with God, who wipes every tear from their eyes. "There will be no more death or mourning or crying or pain, for the old order of things has passed away." And the good news is the same as that proclaimed by Jesus at the beginning of his ministry: "The time is near. . . . I am coming soon."[38]

But time passed, and still he did not come. As Peter wrote to his flock, "You must understand that in the last days scoffers will come, scoffing and following their own evil desires. They will say, 'Where is this "coming" he promised? Ever since our fathers died, everything goes on as it has since the beginning of creation.'" And so it did. Generation after generation passed away, but the sun did not darken; the stars did not fall from the sky; children did not rebel against their parents; and perhaps most remarkably, scoffers did not come, scoffing and following their own evil desires. An exclusive millenarian sect formed in the expectation of a violent destruction of the world and a brutal humiliation of the proud and the arrogant grew into a universal church at peace with the state, family, property, priestly mediation, and a continued separation of humankind from God. The immediate salvation of a saintly community on earth turned into the eventual liberation of an individual soul in heaven. The thousand-year reign of Christ over the nations became, thanks to Augustine, a metaphor for the really-existing institution of the Christian Church.[39]

Jesus's solution to the "Axial" split between the real and the ideal (earth and heaven, the observable and the desirable) was a revolutionary transformation of the world through the imminent coming of the Lord. His disciples' solution to the Axial split was a revolutionary transformation of the world through the imminent return of Jesus. Christianity as a set of doctrines and institutions was an elaborate response to the failure of its two founding prophecies. Most scoffers seem to have been convinced by Peter's explanation. "Do not forget this one thing, dear friends: With the Lord a day is like a thousand years, and a thousand years are like a day. The Lord is not slow in keeping his promise, as some understand slowness. He is patient with you, not wanting anyone to perish, but everyone to come to repentance."[40]

■ ■ ■

Muhammad, like Jesus, was a radical renovator of the Hebrew scriptural tradition. He insisted, above all, on the unlimited and undivided nature of divine autocracy ("there is no god but God," who knows "how ye move about and how ye dwell in your homes"); accepted the legitimacy of Abrahamic succession; recognized Moses and Jesus as God's messengers; urged his followers to separate themselves from the nonmembers ("take not into your intimacy those outside your ranks: they will not fail to corrupt you"); and warned his audience of the approaching catastrophe, the return of Jesus, the resurrection of the dead, and the final Day of Judgment, when all humans would be divided into two clearly defined categories and dispatched accordingly. "Do they then only wait for the Hour—that it should come on them of a sudden? But already have come some tokens thereof, and when it (actually) is on them, how can they benefit then by their admonition?" The answer was the familiar combination of faith and works, action and intention, what goes into a man's mouth and what comes out of it.[41]

Both Jesus and Muhammad were apocalyptic millenarian prophets (in the broad sense of predicting an imminent and violent end of the world followed by a permanent solution to the real-ideal problem understood as a coming together of heaven and earth). The most important difference between them—in addition to the obvious ones of time, place, and audience—is the fact that Muhammad, whose ministry was much longer (about twenty-two years) and much more successful at attracting followers, found himself in charge of a growing state and a conquering army. Jesus never left the confines of a small egalitarian sect unencumbered by women, children, and property; never became king of the Jews by either popular acclaim or formal recognition; never got to rule the nations during his first stay on earth; never outlived the poised-on-the-brink intensity of the last days; never saw his disciples form a self-sufficient society; and never had a chance to explain what a complex polity should look like.

Muhammad, whatever his original intentions, had no choice but to do all these things. God was no longer a virtual Big Father with a monopoly on knowing "how ye move about and how ye dwell in your homes": thanks to Muhammad and his immediate successors, he became the uncontested legislator of a large empire, with the power to enforce his rules on how human beings should move and dwell, love and hate, live and die.[42]

Islam inherited a sacred beginning that was well-developed legally, politically, and militarily—and thus much more similar to the Jewish golden age of King David's reign than to the New Testament story of the ministry and martyrdom of a mendicant preacher. It is also much better documented than its two predecessors, providing a would-be fundamentalist renovator with a ready-made (if obviously contested) blueprint for a proper Islamic state. All human societies periodically recover and relive their sacred beginnings: the "traditional" ones do it through ritual; the Axial ones imagine—each in its own way—a total or partial resacralization of human existence. In Judaism, Christianity, and Islam, which represent the institutionalized embodiments of unfulfilled millenarian prophecies, such attempts at resacralization are associated with renewed expectations of imminent fulfillment. In post–Second Temple Judaism, episodes of intense messianic hope were not uncommon, but, in the absence of a Jewish polity to reform or liberate, were relatively muted. Indeed, the viability of the Mercurian ("middleman minority") specialization of diaspora Jews depended on their continued existence as strangers in Egypt/Babylon/Rome. After the collapse of that specialization, radical Jewish fundamentalism reemerged with great force (or was redirected into communism and other new dispensations). In Islam, renovation movements have been both frequent and diverse, but the political ideal rooted in visions of the Prophet's reign has remained stable and within reach. Most latter-day Islamic states are not fully legitimate because they do not live up to the Prophet's model; most restorations are political revolutions with explicit agendas; and most Muslim political "utopianism" is scrupulously historicist. The Abbasid and Safavid empires began as militant millenarian movements seeking divine justice. The possibility of nonpolitical politics, or of a perfectly just, this-worldly state composed of mortal men and women, is one of Islam's most fundamental assumptions.[43]

The founding act of political Judaism was an escape from slavery, and most of the Hebrew prophetic and apocalyptic tradition is about the imminent, violent destruction of "Babylon," real or symbolic. In Islam, foreign rule is worse than an abomination: it is not a part of the formative experience or the traditional conceptual repertoire (except when a bad Muslim ruler is the functional equivalent of an infidel, as argued by the Wahhabis, among others). Early Islam's Babylon was "Rum" (Byzantium), an evil empire to be conquered, not an evil conqueror to be destroyed. When, in the twentieth and twenty-first centuries, most Muslims found themselves in a world governed and defined by non-Muslims, the millenarian intensity of the response was reinforced by the sheer novelty of the experience. In the words of Osama bin Laden, "the *umma* is asked to unite itself in the face of this Crusaders' campaign, the strongest, most powerful, and most ferocious Crusaders' campaign to fall on the Islamic *umma* since the dawn of Islamic history."[44]

Christianity's sacred beginnings are limited to Jesus, his sect, and his teachings (the Old Testament tradition serving as a prophecy to be realized or prologue to be transcended). There is no guidance on how to run a state, an army, or a justice system, no clear indication of what life outside the sect should look like. The point, of course, is that there should be no state, no army, no justice system, and no life outside the sect. Or rather, the point is that there should be no state other than Jesus's millennial reign, no army other than the heavenly host of Armageddon, no justice other than the Last Judgment (salvation or damnation), and no life other than the eternal kind. All Christian societies are improvisations (concessions, inventions, perversions) to a much greater degree than their Judaic or Muslim—let alone Confucian—counterparts. Most earnest attempts at returning to the source of Christianity have led to a radical denial of nonsectarian (nontotalitarian) forms of human existence. At its sacred core, Christianity is incompatible with politics, but, unlike Hinduism or Buddhism, it foresees—and, in some sense, remembers—a redemption that is collective, violent, and this-worldly. Imitation of Christ suggests a sectarian or monastic existence (in the world but not of the world); faith in Christ's prophecy suggests the expectation of the imminent coming of the kingdom of God.

This congenital condition has three principal consequences. The first is the inbuilt tension—unique among Axial civilizations—between the City of God and the City of Man ("the church" separable from the state and the state separable from the church). The second is the variety and flexibility of political institutions with a potential claim to divine legitimacy. The third is the essential illegitimacy of all these institutions. The fact that Jesus did not envisage a just society before the End meant that, in the meantime, any society might qualify. Or none could. All avowedly Christian states have to mount a more or less unconvincing defense of their Christian credentials; all have to contend with more or less convincing millenarian challenges.

■　■　■

During the Middle Ages, such challenges bubbled up repeatedly and often violently, but the church managed to isolate and suppress them as heresies, incorporate and discipline them as monastic orders (that is, legalized and institutionalized sects), or contain and channel them into more acceptable activities, such as the extermination of Jews and Muslims (most prominently during the first two crusades).[45]

The Reformation was a massive revolt against the rites, symbols, and institutions that claimed to mediate between Jesus's prophecy and life in the world. Few were warranted and, ideally, none would remain. As Luther wrote to the Duke of Saxony, "If all the world were true Christians, that is, if everyone truly believed, there would be neither need nor use for princes, kings, lords, the Sword, or law." But all the world was not made up of true Christians—indeed, "scarcely one human being in a thousand is a true Christian." Accordingly, and on a strictly temporary basis, "God has ordained the two governments: the spiritual [government], which fashions true Christians and just persons through the Holy Spirit under Christ, and the secular government, which holds the Unchristian and wicked in check and forces them to keep the peace outwardly and be still, like it or not." Each had its own subjects, laws, and procedures. "Secular government has laws that extend no farther than the body, goods and outward, earthly matters. But where the soul is concerned, God neither can nor will allow anyone but himself to rule.[46]

The doctrine of a clear line separating the inward and outward inclined many of Luther's followers toward pietism and provided political liberalism with one of its most productive and enduring fictions. The separation of church and state was possible only if one assumed that the state could occupy itself with "the body, goods and outward, earthly matters" without ruling over the soul—or rather, that "taxes, duties, honor, and fear" (among many other things Luther mentions) had nothing to do with virtue.[47]

Calvin and the Puritans accepted the need for the distinction but argued that "Christ's spiritual rule establishes in us some beginnings of the celestial kingdom." Civil government could not yet be fully dissolved in the spiritual life of a Christian community, but it could—and should—be as godly as the saints' pursuit of righteousness would allow. Members could not be expected to abandon their "houses and brothers and sisters and fathers and mothers and children," but they could be asked to make their families as open, transparent, rule-bound, churchlike, and church-dependent as possible (ultimately constituting the primary unit of a godly commonwealth). They could not be counted on not to be angry with their brothers or commit adultery in their hearts, but they could be expected to demonstrate ceaseless self-restraint indicative of inner discipline. They could not be trusted not to let up occasionally in their efforts at self-observation, but they could be urged to monitor each other by means of formal surveillance and mutual admonition. Politics was a matter of public piety, which was a matter of laborious self-improvement, which was a matter of active participation in moral-political self-government (by means of attending endless meetings, sermons, votes, and debates, while also "keeping diligent watch, both by day and by night, each in his own place, of all comings and goings"). Official regulations reinforced self-generated activism: under Calvin's prodding, Geneva's magistrate not only banned gambling, dancing, begging, swearing, indecent singing, game-playing on

Sundays, and the owning of unlicensed books and popish objects of any kind, but also prescribed attendance at Sunday sermons, the religious instruction of children and servants, the number of courses at public banquets, the proper attire of artisans and their families, the number of rings to be worn on various occasions, and the kinds of ornaments and hairstyles compatible with Christian decorum (silver belts and buckles were permitted, but silver chains, bracelets, collars, embroidery, necklaces, and tiaras were not).[48]

Those who could not be reformed through participation or even excommunication were to be turned over to the secular authorities for appropriate punishment. Some might ask if magistrates could "be dutiful to God and shed blood at the same time." Calvin thought that they could. "If we understand that when magistrates inflict punishments, it is not any act of their own, but only the execution of God's [own] judgments, we will not be inhibited by any scruple on this score." Christians who steadfastly resisted sanctification had no place in a Christian commonwealth. As Calvin's friend Guillaume de Trie wrote of the antitrinitarian Miguel Servetus, Christendom should be "purged of such filth" (Servetus was burned at the stake). And as the Oxford Puritan Francis Cheynell told the House of Commons in May 1643, "these are purging times; let all the malignant humors be purged out of the ecclesiastical and political body."[49]

For most Calvinists, purging was a last resort and a sign of defeat. Their duty in an imperfect world was to do battle for the souls of the unrighteous, to touch their hearts with persuasive speech, and to teach self-discipline through godly discipline. But there were other reformers— "reformers" in the original sense of "going back to the source"—who stood for a universal purge, expected the Second Coming, and believed, on very good evidence, that Jesus had preached a life of sectarian equality and prophesied a violent apocalypse on the eve of a great feast for the hungry.

According to the radical German preacher Thomas Müntzer, the violent apocalypse and the great feast for the hungry were one and the same thing. Christ's warriors were the plowmen; the Antichrist's servants were the lords; and the end of time was now. The only way to receive the Holy Spirit was to follow Jesus along the path of poverty and suffering, and the only ones who understood the meaning of poverty and suffering were those who suffered on account of their poverty. "The stone, torn from the mountain without hands, has become mighty. The poor laymen and peasants see it more sharply than you do," he told the Duke of Saxony (the same one to whom Luther had addressed his letter on secular authority). The kingdom of heaven was for those with nothing but their chains to lose.[50]

There was but one way to enter. According to Jesus, the kingdom of heaven was prefigured in the story about a man who sowed good seed and told his servants to begin the harvest by burning the weeds:

"The one who sowed the good seed is the Son of Man. The field is the world, and the good seed stands for the sons of the kingdom. The weeds are the sons of the evil one, and the enemy who sows them is the devil. The harvest is the end of the age, and the harvesters are angels."

"As the weeds are pulled up and burned in the fire, so it will be at the end of the age. The Son of Man will send out his angels, and they will weed out of his kingdom everything that causes sin and all who do evil. They will throw them into the fiery furnace, where there will be weeping and gnashing of teeth. Then the righteous will shine like the sun in the kingdom of their Father. He who has ears, let him hear."[51]

Müntzer had ears, and he heard. "At the harvest-time one must pluck the weeds out of God's vineyard," he wrote, "but the angels who are sharpening their sickles for that work are no other than the earnest servants of God." The problem, as foretold in Jesus's parable, was that most servants of God had ears but did not hear. They were first by virtue of being last, but, like all the biblical proletarians from Moses's Israelites to Jesus's heavenly army, they needed to be awakened, instructed, and disciplined. "In truth, many of them will have to be roused, so that with the greatest possible zeal and with passionate earnestness they may sweep Christendom clean of ungodly rulers." Müntzer's role was to show the way. "The Living God is sharpening his scythe in me, so that later I can cut down the red poppies and the blue cornflowers." In May 1525, a large army of poor laymen and peasants followed him to Frankenhausen, where his promise to catch the enemy's cannonballs in the sleeves of his cloak seemed to be confirmed by the sudden appearance of a rainbow. In the ensuing massacre, about five thousand rebels were killed. Müntzer was found hiding in a cellar, forced to confess under torture, and beheaded in the camp of the princes. Luther found his confession to be "a piece of devilish, hardened, obduracy." [52]

Müntzer was the most articulate advocate of popular millenarianism since Jesus and the first popular millenarian to turn the fantasy of brutal retribution into an explicit and consistently argued program of class warfare. Like Jesus, however, he was not a successful proselytizer and never got the chance to live in a field free of red poppies and blue cornflowers. The first Christian millenarians to turn the City of Man into the City of God were the Anabaptists of Münster. Anabaptists ("re-baptizers") were programmatically radical because of their rejection of infant baptism. For the early Christians, baptism was a rite of induction into the sect—an act of purification symbolizing repentance of sins, acceptance of Christ, and entry into the community of believers. If the Protestants wanted to return to the days of the early Christians (and they all claimed they did), and if they believed, with Peter, that they were "a royal priesthood" (and therefore, according to Luther, "all equally priests")—then they could no longer acquiesce in the baptism of those who were incapable of understanding the Word. This sounded reasonable until one stopped to think of the implications, as most Protestants did. The prohibition of infant baptism meant that one could not be born into a community of faith—that there could be, in effect, no such thing as a church coterminous with society. Four hundred years later, Ernst Troeltsch would base his distinction between a church and a sect on this very point: a church is an institution one is born into. The Anabaptists were determined, above all else, to remain a sect—a group of believers radically opposed to the corrupt world, dedicated to the dispossessed, and composed of voluntary members who had undergone a personal conversion and shared a strong sense of chosenness, exclusiveness, ethical austerity, and social egalitarianism.[53]

In 1534–35, the Münster Anabaptists expelled all Lutherans and Catholics, burned all books except the Bible, destroyed altars and sculptures, renamed streets and days of the week (and named their city the New Jerusalem), abolished money and feast days, banned monogamy and private property, rationed food and clothing, enforced communal dining, decreed that all doors be kept open, and demolished all church towers ("all that is high shall be made low"). "Amongst us," they wrote to Anabaptist congregations in other towns, "God has restored community as it was in the beginning and as befits the Saints of God." Those unfit for saintliness were to be "swept from the face of the earth." Offenses punishable by death included envy, anger, avarice, lying, blasphemy, impurity, idle conversation, and attempts to flee.[54]

Monotheism had made the chosen people collectively guilty by attributing the perpetual postponement of salvation to their failure to obey the heavenly autocrat. Christianity had made all human beings guilty by emphasizing thoughts over actions and inner submission over outward obedience. Protestantism had made everyone permanently and inescapably guilty by instituting an austere god who could not be lobbied or bribed. The saints of the New Jerusalem made everyone guilty before the law by decreeing that true Christians should be "perfect as their heavenly Father is perfect." By the time government troops entered Münster in June 1535, two-hour court sessions followed by executions were being held twice daily.

In post–Civil War England, the saints came close to becoming the government. Inaugurating Barebone's Parliament (the Parliament of Saints) on July 4, 1653, Oliver Cromwell said: "Why should we be afraid to say or think, That *this* may be the door to usher in the Things that God had promised; which have been prophesied of; which he has set the hearts of his People to wait for and expect? . . . We are at the threshold;—and therefore it becomes us to lift up our heads, and encourage ourselves in the Lord. And we have thought, some of us, That it is our duties to *endeavor* this way; not merely to look at that Prophecy in Daniel, 'And the Kingdom shall not be delivered to another people,' and passively wait."[55]

Cromwell would eventually decide to wait, but some of the "Fifth Monarchists" (named after Daniel's last and everlasting kingdom) would not be deterred. As the "roaring" Puritan preacher John Rogers put it, "it is not enough to change some of these *Lawes*, and so to *reforme* them": the point was "to provide for the Fifth by bringing in the *Lawes of God*." Such work could not be entrusted to parliamentary majorities, for "how can the kingdom be the Saints' when the ungodly are electors, and elected to Govern?" The Saints were to bear witness themselves—"preaching, praying, fighting" (*praedicando, praecando, praeliando*), and, when necessary, bringing "terrour to them that do evil." Evil was as obdurate on the eve of the Second Coming as it had been during the First. "A Sword is as really the appointment of Christ as any other Ordinance in the Church, . . . and a man may as well go into the harvest without his Sickle, as to this work without . . . his Sword." Having failed in the Parliament of Saints, the Fifth Monarchists staged an armed rebellion, but were defeated by Babylon, perhaps because they did not wait until the year 1666.[56]

■ ■ ■

In Orthodox Christianity, millenarian outbursts tended to be less frequent because churches were either nationalized by local Christian kings or, after the Islamic conquests, maintained as nation-bearing institutions in more or less silent opposition to the mostly hands-off infidel rulers. The greatest "schism" occurred in Russia in the mid-seventeenth century, when the church and the rapidly expanding absolutist state launched a far-reaching overhaul of ritual practice. What began as a top-down reform in the interests of uniformity ended as a reformation in the sense of a broad-based revolt against the established political and ideological order. Both sides appealed to primeval purity but traced different genealogies: the original Greek in the case of the official church and the original Muscovite (and thus the original Greek) in the case of the "Old Believers." Both were traditionalists and innovators: the Old Believers, like Western Protestants, set out to correct abuses and impurities within the existing church but became radicalized by the momentum of confrontation. The rejection of the high priest led to the rejection of the whole priestly hierarchy, and the rejection of the whole priestly hierarchy posed the problem of how to consecrate a new clergy or what to do without any clergy at all. The Russian schismatics covered the entire Protestant spectrum, from the episcopalian "priestly" Old Believers, who built a new Orthodox Church without the patriarch, to the endlessly subdividing sects that abandoned all priestly mediation and kept debating the fate of the sacraments, especially marriage. The peculiarity of the Russian Reformation was the absence of alternative potentates to appeal to or foreign brethren to join; the remaining options included flight "to the desert," armed resistance, and mass suicide. The schismatics who believed that the last days had arrived saw all government officials as servants of the Antichrist and battled them accordingly. Salvation by way of martyrdom in the fire of Armageddon came in two varieties: at the hand of the Beast or through self-immolation. In the late seventeenth and early eighteenth centuries, more than eight thousand people burned themselves to death.[57]

The surviving Old Believers (about 10 percent of the empire's population at the turn of the twentieth century) continued to wait for the apocalypse in remote settlements around the edges of the empire or reached an accommodation with the state and applied themselves to money-making. Russia's most successful capitalists who were not Germans or Jews were Old Believers.[58]

The "spirit of capitalism" tends to thrive in communities of the chosen that separate themselves from the unclean world. There are two types of such communities: the Mercurians, or middleman minorities such as the Jews and Overseas Chinese, who cultivate inner cohesion and outward strangeness in the exercise of their mediating function; and the sectarians, who do it in the interest of exclusive salvation. The first are based on tribal unity, enhanced by the need for protection from polluting surroundings; the second, on the rejection of kin in favor of a community of faith. In the first, internal trust is based on blood ties renewed through ritual and endogamy; in the second, on constant self-discipline, mutual surveillance, and a suspicion of procreation as the nemesis of sectarian purity. Both value ceaseless toil: the first, because Mercurian occupations depend not on natural cycles but on the perpetual pursuit of gain through symbolic manipulation in a hostile human environment; the second, because sectarian commitments require constant struggle against worldly temptations. Mercurian tribes are protocapitalists by definition; "saints" have to beat plows into shares and earn salvation through accumulation. The point of connection is the prohibition of idleness and devotion to work as duty and virtue. Everything a sectarian (and his domesticated cousin, a monk) does—eating, drinking, mating, talking, reading, writing, listening, gardening, farming—is godly work for a heavenly wage. When the intensity of the expectation wanes, and the sectarian warily reenters the world, work as prayer may displace prayer as work, but aversion to leisure and the habit of vigilance and self-discipline remain constant—and turn lucrative. Meanwhile, ongoing procreation and the kinship bond it engenders continue to undermine the sectarian principle of a voluntary circle of the righteous, transforming metaphorical brothers into blood relatives, love of neighbors into nepotism, and saints into money changers. The chosen people of the second type join the chosen people of the first type. The Old Believers who continue to live "in the desert" and separate themselves from the world are among the first peasants to turn into farmers; the Old Believers who move to Moscow and engage in industry and philanthropy are among the first merchants to turn into capitalists. Those who abandon tribal and confessional exclusivity but retain a commitment to ceaseless work and vigilant self-discipline become "modern."

• • •

Having been defeated, tamed, or marginalized in Europe, Christian millenarianism moved to America, where it became a permanent feature of national life—as the raison d'être of the Puritan colonies, the wellspring of state messianism, a ready response to political and economic distress, and one of the ways to structure a national existence unprotected by a common folk or ecclesiastical tradition. In the absence of an ancien regime, an established church, or a claim to tribal cohesion, much of American communal life was built around Christian "denominations"; most outbursts of social and political creativity were accompanied by Christian revivals; and most Christian revivals ("awakenings") had to do with the expectation of the last days.[59]

The "First Great Awakening" of the 1740s saw the launching of "postmillenialism," or millenarianism without Armageddon (first proposed in England more than half a century earlier). Babylon was so far away, the army of Antichrist so small, and the "showers of grace" so plentiful that the new kingdom "must needs be approaching" (as Jonathan Edwards put it). There was no need for Jesus to bring perfection amidst trumpet calls and rivers of blood: it would be "gradually brought to pass" as the result of a natural spread of the Holy Spirit. The Methodist-influenced Second Great Awakening, from 1800 into the 1840s, effectively destroyed the Calvinist doctrine of predestination by making saving grace available to anyone determined to obtain it. As the prophet of new revivalism, Charles Finney, put it, "sin and holiness are voluntary acts of mind." And since sin equaled selfishness, and selfishness could be overcome by an act of conversion, it would be "a sad, dreadful mistake" to expect God to deliver redemption "chiefly without human agency."[60]

One consequence of salvation optimism was political millennialism and the reform activism associated with it. "I believe," said Andrew Jackson in 1828, "that man can be elevated; man can become more and more endowed with divinity; and as he does he becomes more God-like in his character and capable of governing himself. Let us go on elevating our people, perfecting our institutions, until democracy shall reach such a point of perfection that we can acclaim with truth that the voice of the people is the voice of God."[61]

Another was a series of attempts to hasten the return of Jesus by imitating the life of his sect. The key to saintliness was selflessness, and the key to selflessness was isolation from the world, regimentation of behavior, mutual surveillance, and strict control over reproduction. In the end, everything came down to control of reproduction, because nothing threatened selflessness as much as romantic love, exclusive sexual unions, parental and filial attachments, and inherited (private) property. The Harmonists and the Shakers enforced celibacy; the Oneida "Bible Communists" instituted "complex marriage," whereby all males were married to all females, all births were planned, and all children were raised communally.[62]

The largest, most original, and, in some sense, most successful American attempt to realize a Christ-inspired kingdom of God on earth was launched in the 1820s by Joseph Smith, a farmer's son from upstate New York. His original message was a conventional Christian apocalyptic revelation of an angel "glorious beyond description" informing him "of great judgments which were coming upon the earth, with great desolations by famine, sword, and pestilence; and that these grievous judgments would come on the earth in this generation."[63]

Smith went much further than other Christian prophets, however. He did to Christianity what Jesus had done to Judaism, but much more thoroughly and self-consciously. Indeed, he did to Judaism and Christianity what Muhammad had done to both of them, but even more thoroughly and self-consciously. Muhammad had accepted the Hebrew God and the sacrality of both testaments (including the prophecy of Jesus's imminent return and the ensuing slaughter) and added to them his own actions, instructions, and revelations. Smith accepted the Hebrew God and the sacrality of both testaments; added to them his own actions, instructions, and revelations; and discovered a new old testament containing a complete sacred history of his promised land. His scripture (the Book of Mormon, published in 1830) includes the original exodus, two new ones, and the promise of a third one, which he and his successors went on to fulfill. It also includes Jesus's preliminary Second Coming to America ("the prints of the nails in his hands and his feet") in preparation for his final Second Coming to America, and a limited continental holocaust as a prefigurement of the final universal one, which Smith was going to witness and perhaps help bring about.[64]

Americans had ears, and they heard. Within a few years, a small millenarian sect had become a complex society involving thousands of men, women, and children. For the first time since Münster, a Christian doomsday prophet faced the task of preserving apostolic communalism beyond a small band of brothers. In the absence of any guidance from Jesus, the only appropriate model was Moses. Moving around the Midwest, Smith founded two temples, attempted property redistribution, introduced "plural marriage" and the baptism of the dead, and created a complex hierarchy of lay priests. His successor, Brigham Young, led the "latter-day saints" across the desert to the New Jerusalem, where they established a state "under the immediate, constant, and direct superintendency of the Almighty." Within several decades, the expectation of an imminent collective redemption had been replaced by a belief in eventual individual perfection, and Utah territory had become a state under the indirect but steady superindentency of Washington, DC.[65]

Another farmer, William Miller in Massachusetts, was a much more conventional prophet of the last days and a consistent critic of "that doctrine which gives all power to man." He was also a rationalist who relied on demonstrable mathematical proof rather than divine revelation. According to his calculations, the world was going to end sometime in 1843. When it did not, he admitted his mistake, revised his timeline, and rescheduled doomsday for October 22, 1844. Thousands of sermons, lectures, and newspaper articles were dedicated to the event; thousands of Second Adventists (or "Millerites") sold their property, forgave their debts, abandoned their fields, and, on the appointed day, came out to be saved. What happened next is known as "the Great Disappointment." According to Hiram Edson,

> We confidently expected to see Jesus Christ and all the holy angels with him; and that his voice would call up Abraham, Isaac, and Jacob, and all the ancient worthies, and near and dear friends which had been torn from us by death, and that our trials and suffferings with our earthly pilgrimage would close, and we should be caught up to meet our coming Lord to be forever with him to inhabit the bright golden mansions in the golden home city, prepared for the redeemed. Our expectations were raised high, and thus we looked for our coming Lord until the clock tolled 12 at midnight. The day had then passed and our disappointment became a certainty. Our fondest hopes and expectations were blasted, and such a spirit of weeping came over us as I never experienced before. It seemed that the loss of all earthly friends could have been no comparison. We wept, and wept, until the day dawn.[66]

"The Great Disappointment" produced a variety of responses. Some returned to a life of permanent expectation, others accepted "the agency of man" and joined the Mormons or the Shakers. Yet others followed the example of the early Christians by claiming that the prophecy had, in fact, come true, but not quite as expected. The Seventh-Day Adventists, founded by the disappointed Hiram Edson, believed that Miller's calculations were accurate but that Jesus had not been able to return because of the practice of Sunday worship; instead, he had entered a special place in the heavenly sanctuary in order to go over the books and decide who deserved to be saved. The Jehovah's Witnesses moved the date to 1874 and then to 1914, arguing that Jesus did return as prophesied but remained invisible while he—along with some members of his "anointed class"—cleansed the temple in preparation for the coming bloodbath. The early Pentecostals returned to the idea of the imminent Second Coming but connected the event to the direct personal experience of God's presence. In April 1906, hundreds of people danced, screamed, moaned, prophesied, rolled on the floor, and sang in unknown languages on Azusa Street in Los Angeles. Among them were several Molokans, who had arrived from Russia a few months earlier. According to a report in the *Los Angeles Herald*, "there were all ages, sexes, colors, nationalities and previous conditions of servitude."[67]

They knew those were the last days because it had all happened before. After Jesus was taken up into heaven, his disciples gathered together in one room. "Suddenly a sound like the blowing of a violent wind came from heaven and filled the whole house where they were sitting. They saw what seemed to be tongues of fire that separated and came to rest on each of them. All of them were filled with the Holy Spirit and began to speak in other tongues as the Spirit enabled them." A large crowd assembled, and in that crowd were Jews out of every nation under heaven, and every one of them heard the sound of his own language, and some of them asked if the apostles were drunk. Then Peter stood up and said that they were not drunk, and quoted the prophet Joel: "In the last days, God says, I will pour out my Spirit on all people. Your sons and daughters will prophesy, your young men will see visions, your old men will dream dreams."[68]

Every disappointment was followed by an awakening. The greater the disappointment, the greater the awakening.

■ ■ ■

Millenarianism is the vengeful fantasy of the dispossessed, the hope for a great awakening in the midst of a great disappointment. Nowhere was Christianity-inspired apocalyptic millenarianism more common or more desperate than in the non-Christian societies that Christians had damaged or destroyed. As livelihoods were ruined, gods and ancestors humiliated, and symbolic worlds overturned or shattered, some of the explanations and solutions were provided by the people who had ushered in the calamity (and proved the power of their gods). Combined with local beliefs in the return of a Promethean hero or the journey to a land without evil, the biblical idea of cosmic retribution produced powerful social movements, many of them violent and self-sacrificial.[69]

The collapse of the Inca Empire was followed by an epidemic of "dancing sickness" (Taqui Onqoy), in the course of which the temporarily defeated local spirits moved from the rocks and trees into the bodies of the dancing humans in preparation for a flood that would obliterate the Spaniards and all memory of their existence. In North America, several Plains Indian groups (some of them familiar with Mormon and Shaker teachings) performed a special ghost dance in the expectation that the world of injustice would collapse, death and the whites would disappear, and the eternally young ancestors would return, driving before them thick herds of buffalo. The Lakota (Sioux), the last big group to have been defeated and confined to a reservation, danced the last dance before being massacred by the US Army at Wounded Knee on December 29, 1890. In northeastern Brazil, amidst the massive migrations and dislocations triggered by the abolition of slavery, the fall of the monarchy, and a series of severe droughts, several followers of an itinerant preacher known as "the Coun-selor" settled in the village of Canudos, renamed it "Belo Monte" (Beautiful Hill), renounced the republic, refused to pay taxes, rejected civil marriage, collectivized their animals, divided most of their possessions, and set about waiting for the End. Four years later, on the eve of being burned to the ground by the Brazilian army in October 1897, Belo Monte had thirty thousand inhabitants and 5,200 dwellings.[70]

In Latin America, most European settlers and their descendants be-came involved in various nation-building efforts. In Africa, where they almost never did, millenarianism became a permanent feature of political life. In southern Africa, the Xhosa were defeated in eight "Kaffir wars," driven from much of their land, and plagued by persistent droughts and cattle epidemics. In 1856, a teenage girl, whose uncle had been the first Xhosa to be confirmed as an Anglican, had a vision, in which the Xhosa ancestors ordered their people to destroy any remaining cattle, corn, tools, and other unclean possessions. In return, they were going to bring limitless supplies of everything, including health and youth, and drive the British beyond the seas. Helping them would be the "new people" known as "Russians." The Xhosa had recently heard that the much-hated former Cape governor, George Cathcart, had been killed in the Crimean War, and concluded that the people who had killed him were strong, black, and—since they were fighting the British—Xhosa ancestors, too. After two dates set for the resurrection passed without consequence, the believers blamed those who had refused to slaughter their cattle and embarked on a mas-sive campaign of killing and destruction. About four hundred thousand cattle were slaughtered and about forty thousand Xhosa starved to death. The British authorities provided famine relief in exchange for contract labor in the colony with no right of return. Xhosaland ceased to exist.[71]

More than half a century later, after more alienation of land and a great deal of missionary activity in what had become the eastern Cape, a former Methodist preacher by the name of Enoch Mgijima began prophesying an imminent Armageddon that would result in the annihilation of white peo-ple. His followers called themselves "Israelites," kept the Sabbath, cele-brated the Passover, believed that the New Testament was a forgery writ-ten by whites, and considered the exodus an allegorical foretelling of their own deliverance. In 1920, Mgijima's annual Passover celebration attracted more than a thousand converts who sold their possessions, built a com-munal settlement, and refused to pay taxes or register births or deaths. They founded their own Bible school and nursing station, maintained a security force, disciplined those who lapsed in their faith, and did a lot of praying and military drilling in the expectation of the apocalypse. "The whole world is going to sink in blood," wrote Mgijima to a local official, "the time of Jehovah has now arrived." On May 24, 1921, when a large police force surrounded the compound, the Israelites, armed with clubs and spears and protected by magic white robes, hurled themselves at machine guns. One hundred eighty-three of them were killed and about a hundred wounded. The tombstone erected by the survivors bears the inscription: "Because they chose the plan of God, the world did not have a place for them."[72]

A much larger and more successful millenarian sect that identified Africans with the biblical Israelites were the Jamaican Rastafarians, who believed that they were the true Hebrews exiled for their sins (long since forgiven), and that the coronation of Ras Tafari as Haile Selassie I, the emperor of Ethiopia, had ushered in the era of final liberation and the gathering of Israel. The Bible, originally written about the Africans, had been falsified by the whites in order to trick and enslave the chosen people. Haile Selassie was "the Ancient of Days" from Daniel and the "Lion of the tribe of Judah" from the Book of Revelation. His mission was to remake the world, punish the whites, and deliver his people from Babylon to the promised land of Zion in Ethiopia. "One bright morning when my work is over, Man will fly away home." In the meantime, "Rasta Man" was to withdraw from society, organize for immediate repatriation, or "get up, stand up, and fight." As the intensity of the expectation waned, "liberation before repatriation" became an increasingly common option.[73]

One of the starkest expressions of millenarian yearning were the so-called cargo cults, which arose in Melanesia after the arrival of the European missionaries and spread widely after the massive invasions and dislocations of World War II. In a society apparently overcome with self-doubt and a sense of the world's injustice, there appeared many men who, in Celsus's formula, "with the greatest facility and on the slightest occasion, assumed the motions and gestures of inspired persons." They disagreed on the particulars but agreed on the main claim—that the Europeans' wealth, known as "cargo" (after the term used by the newcomers to refer to the manufactured goods that kept arriving by sea or air) had been meant for the local communities but hijacked en route, and that very soon, and certainly in this generation, the ancestors were going to come back amid thunder and lightning and deliver the cargo—chocolates, radios, watches, mirrors, flashlights, bicycles, and countless other things, including eternal idleness and youth—to its rightful owners. The Book of Revelation brought by the newcomers revealed the source of their excessive luxuries: "cargoes of gold, silver, precious stones and pearls; fine linen, purple, silk and scarlet cloth; every sort of citron wood, and articles of every kind made of ivory, costly wood, bronze, iron and marble; cargoes of cinnamon and spice, of incense, myrrh and frankincense, of wine and olive oil, of fine flour and wheat; cattle and sheep; horses and carriages; and bodies and souls of men."[74]

All millenarianisms are cargo cults at heart. What the Melanesians lacked in metaphoric complexity they gained in the clarity of exposition. "We have nothing," said one group of believers to their prophet, "no aircraft, no ships, no jeeps, nothing at all. The Europeans steal our cargo. You will be sorry for us and see that we get something."[75]

There were many ways of getting something. Different sects—and some-times the same sect at different times—tried out different approaches: going back to the old ways or adopting new ones; mandating sexual pro-miscuity or abstaining from sex altogether; destroying property (to realize the metaphor of having "nothing at all") or stockpiling provisions (to wel-come the returning ancestors); organizing elaborate dancing rituals or asking for cargo directly (praying); speaking in tongues and foaming at the mouth or goose-stepping with wooden rifles and straw insignia; learning from the rich so as to discover their secrets or trying to take the cargo by getting up, standing up, and fighting. Some prophets claimed that the goods had already arrived; others blamed the failure of the prophecy on sinful individuals and staged public confessions and exemplary punish-ments. One of the doomsday prophecies in New Guinea came true when the Japanese bombed the area on the day of the predicted Second Coming (in 1942).[76]

The most successful doomsday movement inspired by Christianity took place in an area where biblical eschatology merged with the only powerful millenarian tradition born outside of Mediterranean monotheism. Chi-nese millenarianism had been mostly Taoist and Buddhist in inspiration. New challenges brought new prophets. Effective prophets are men or women whose personal madness resonates with the social turmoil around them and whose spiritual rebirth is equally convincing to the prophets themselves and those who believe they have "nothing at all." In 1837, a man by the name of Hong Xiuquan failed in his second attempt to pass the second-level Confucian examination, collapsed, went into a delirium, and had a vision about establishing the heavenly kingdom on earth. Another look at the Christian missionary tract that may or may not have inspired the vision in the first place convinced Hong that he was God's Chinese son and Jesus's younger brother. Having failed two more examinations, he fol-lowed his older brother's example by telling his parents that they were not his real parents and becoming an itinerant preacher of repentance and deliverance. Unlike his brother, however, he succeeded in attracting hun-dreds, later thousands, and eventually hundreds of thousands of converts and proceeded to battle Babylon on his own terms. His followers were the beleaguered Hakkas of southern China, and his ideologues were failed examination candidates, hired-out examination candidates, pharmacists' apprentices, and other marginal intellectuals. In March 1853, Hong's army of more than a million heavenly warriors captured Nanjing and declared it the heavenly capital of the heavenly kingdom (Taiping). As Hong, the heavenly king, wrote in a commentary on the Book of Revelation, "God's Heaven now exists among men. It is fulfilled. Respect this."[77]

Hong's solution to the sectarian problem—of having a complex society imitate thirteen or so unencumbered men—was to admit women but to keep the sexes strictly segregated and ban all "exchanges of personal af-fection," including "the casting of amorous glances and the harboring of lustful thoughts about others." Another way of maintaining equality among "brothers and sisters" was to abolish trade and private property. Taiping officials at various levels were to determine optimal subsistence levels and requisition the rest for communal needs. The same officials were to stage regular public recitations of Hong's commandments, enforce bans on selfishness and lustful thoughts, preside over a mutual surveillance network, lead troops into battle, burn false books (especially those by Confucius), and promote the reading of true ones. "The stupid, by reading these books, become intelligent; the disobedient, by reading these books, become good."[78]

Because those who would not become good and intelligent were "like men contaminated by sickness," Taiping's task was to cure them by all means necessary. "Wherever we pass we will concentrate on killing all civil and military officials, and soldiers and militiamen. People will not be harmed . . . , but if you assist the devils in the defense of a city and engage in fighting, you will definitely be completely annihilated." Within the heavenly kingdom, the same logic applied: "If we want you to perish, you will die, for no one's punishment will be postponed more than three days. Every one of you should sincerely follow the path of truth, and train yourselves in goodness, which will lead to happiness."[79]

In 1864, after about twenty million people had died in the war, the heavenly capital was besieged by government forces. When its residents began to starve, Hong ordered them to "eat manna," then picked some weeds in the palace courtyard, chewed on them by way of example, and died shortly thereafter. After the fall of the city, Hong's sixteen-year-old son told the interrogators that he had managed to read "thirty or more volumes" of ancient books forbidden by his father and that his only wish was to pass the Confucian examination that his father had failed. The government officials were not amused by the irony and had the "Young Monarch" executed.[80]

■ ■ ■

Jesus's Chinese brother was not destined for a Second Coming. But was Jesus? Back in the Christian world, Christianity was steadily losing its hold on human life. The retreat was slow and mostly dignified, with solid rearguard action on the American front, but the overall trend, especially among the elite, appeared irreversible. Fewer and fewer people referred to biblical precedents, interpreted life's events in terms of the Christian doctrine, or believed in the literal veracity of the scriptural accounts of creation, resurrection, and original sin, among many other things. The Christian solution to the Axial predicament was showing signs of age.[81]

But the predicament itself—the sense of standing back and looking beyond—was not going anywhere. God was not dead. Most lax, lapsed, and iconoclastic Christians seemed to assume that the hope for salvation would outlive the failure of the prophecy. The Second Temple Jews had rejected their would-be Messiahs (Theudas, John, and Jesus, among many others) and continued to wait—and wait, and wait. Those few who had accepted Jesus as the son of God did not lose hope even after he died without any of his predictions coming to pass. Millions of their followers, unmoved by the repeated postponement of the prophecy, had continued to wait for his return and the millennium of his rule. In the seventeenth, and especially in the eighteenth century, some of them had concluded that the millennium would happen by itself and that Jesus would not need to come except at the very end, to sum things up. In the late eighteenth, and especially in the nineteenth century, a new breed of prophets and lawgivers left Jesus out altogether without feeling compelled to change the plot. Providence had become history, progress, evolution, revolution, transcendence, laws of nature, or positive change, but the outcome remained the same. As the speculative geologist and William III's chaplain Thomas Burnet wrote in 1681, "If we would have a fair view and right apprehensions of Natural Providence, we must not cut the chains of it too short, by having recourse, without necessity, either to the First Cause, in explaining the origins of things, or to Miracles, in explaining particular effects." Through their own efforts, humans would find "the Scheme of all humane affairs lying before them: from the Chaos to the last period. . . . And this being the last Act and close of all humane affairs, it ought to be the more exquisite and elaborate: that it may crown the work, satisfie the Spectators, and end in a general applause."[82]

The Enlightenment (descended, like Burnet, from the marriage of the Protestant Reformation and the Scientific Revolution), produced several exquisite and elaborate drafts of the last act. Turgot proved the inevitability of human progress toward total perfection by demonstrating the historical consistency of technological and moral improvement, its obvious acceleration in recent years, its steady spread outside Europe, and its codification in the unimpeachable language of mathematics. The Christian theodicy problem was solved not so much by God's retirement from active duty as through the discovery of history's invisible hand: "The ambitious ones themselves in forming the great nations have contributed to the design of Providence, the progress of enlightenment, and consequently to the increase of the happiness of the human species, a thing which did not at all interest them. Their passions, their very rages, have led them without their knowing where they were going."[83]

Providence, like the wealth of nations, was the wondrous sum total of countless blind egoisms. Just as the apocalypse required the presence of the Antichrist and his demonic army, the "progress of enlightenment" required the passions and rages of ambitious humans. Once reason had triumphed, however, the passions and rages would become not only unnecessary but, by definition, impossible. Reason would reign supreme as the self-perpetuating cycle of self-understanding and self-improvement. Condorcet, Turgot's pupil and biographer, developed the scheme further by equating Providence with history, calling history a science, converting a godless theodicy into a historical dialectic (according to which every retrograde undertaking objectively produces its opposite), and arguing that the scientific inevitability of perfection did nothing to diminish the pleasure and duty of accelerating its approach.[84]

The Jacobins, who arrested Condorcet as he tried to flee Paris in 1794, believed that they could accelerate its approach all by themselves and that the present generation would not pass away until all these things had happened. The much abbreviated road to perfection lay through virtue, which, in Robespierre's formulation, stood for "the love of the fatherland and the high-minded devotion that resolves all private interests into the general interest." To attain virtue was "to tread underfoot vanity, envy, ambition, and all the weaknesses of petty souls," so that the only passions left would be "the horror of tyranny and the love of humanity" (fatherland and humanity being, in the final analysis, one and the same thing). "We wish, in a word, to fulfill the intentions of nature and the destiny of man, realize the promises of philosophy, and acquit providence of a long reign of crime and tyranny."[85]

It turned out, however, that most men were "dastardly egoists" with petty souls, and that the only way for morality to triumph over egoism was for the forces of morality to wage war on the forces of egoism. Virtue was to be "combined with terror": "virtue, without which terror is destructive; terror, without which virtue is impotent." In the Law of 22 Prairial (June 10, 1794), crimes punishable by death included most weaknesses of petty souls. In the forty-seven days that elapsed between the publication of this law and the execution of its chief sponsor, 1,376 people were guillotined in Paris. Condorcet had been found dead in his cell in March. "We know how to die, and we will all die," said Robespierre. And so they did.[86]

The Jacobins' self-immolation disillusioned some believers and inspired countless alternative visions, but it did little to discredit the faith itself. The Romantic "blue flower" was to Condorcet's redemption by progress what Christian mysticism had been to Thomas Aquinas's Summa theologica; in between lay most of nineteenth-century thought. Wordsworth, who lived to the age of eighty, moved his earthly paradise from the Jacobin "management of Nations" to "the discerning intellect of Man." The second version promised a consummation as noble as the first one; both dispelled "the sleep of Death"; and neither, according to Wordsworth, was any less heavenly than its Christian predecessor. Both were transcendental but not supernatural.[87]

The same was true of Faust's victory over Mephistopheles (who, as "part of that power which would the evil ever do, and ever does the good," represents Condorcet's self-defeating anti-Progress), of Hegel's Universal Spirit (which needs the Mephistophelean dialectic to reach full self-realization), and of the sundry "utopian" sectarians who fused the social and contemplative paradises in perfect communities of imperfect human beings (by combining needs, wants, and abilities in a harmonious balance). Robert Owen inherited the Harmonists' settlement of New Harmony; Charles Fourier provided the mold and the foil for the Oneida Bible Communists; and Claude de Saint-Simon proclaimed himself the new Messiah and told his disciples from his deathbed: "The pear is ripe, you must pick it. . . . The only thing that the attack on the religious system of the Middle Ages proved is that it was no longer in harmony with the progress of positive sciences. But it was wrong to conclude that religion was going to disappear; in fact, it simply needs to conform to the progress of the sciences. I repeat to you, the pear is ripe, you must pick it."[88]

They were all priests and prophets tending to whatever lay "beyond." In Christian societies, the tightly unified sacred realm was defined by priestly professionals, who manned the official paths to salvation, and self-appointed prophets, who policed priestly performance or proposed entirely new paths. In the post-Christian world, the universal church developed ever-widening cracks, and the sacred trickled out, attaching itself to human souls, bodies, products, and institutions. Access became more democratic but remained unequal, and most of the work of spiritual guardianship was taken up by the new entrepreneurs of the sacred, the "intellectuals." Some of them served as priests, creating legitimizing myths and rituals for newly reconstituted communities and imaginations; others offered themselves as prophets, ridiculing the "Pharisees and the teachers of the law" and discerning new heavens and a new earth. Human life was still felt to be inadequate; "salvation," in a variety of forms, was still the desired (expected) outcome; and prophets, as freelance guides to the sacred, were still in demand when full-time guides appeared lost.[89]

Depending on the nature and language of the message, nineteenth-century prophets could be divided into artists (of many different kinds, but mostly bards), scientists (of both the falsifiable and nonfalsifiable variety, but mostly the latter), and artists who drew on science as part of their creative repertoire. Depending on how ripe they thought the pear was, these prophets spanned the range between Jesus-style urgent millenarianism and various mystical and allegorical compromises. There were no two distinct liberal and totalitarian political traditions any more than there were two distinct Christian traditions of Augustinian liberalism and Anabaptist totalitarianism. Once the intensity of expectation subsided, the Anabaptists evolved into the meekly quiescent Mennonites. Everyone expected redemption; the question was how quickly and by what means; the answers were spread over a broad continuum.[90]

In other words, Christianity is inherently "totalitarian" in the sense of demanding unconditional moral submission (the coincidence of God's will and human desires) and emphasizing thought crimes over formal legality; the rest concerns the nature and intensity of enforcement and the degree of eschatological impatience. For most of Christian history, enforcement has been slack and the last days a metaphor. The modern state of more or less equal, interchangeable, and self-governing citizens has no founding injunctions to go back to, but its two main sources were uncompromisingly total in both practice and aspiration. The Puritan Revolution was a Christian revival that sought to eradicate impure thoughts by means of mutual surveillance ("brotherly admonition") and ostentatious self-control ("godliness"). The French Revolution was an Age of Reason revival that sought to eradicate impure thoughts by means of mutual surveillance ("vigilance") and ostentatious self-control ("virtue"). Both required universal participation and ceaseless activism while dividing the world into saints and reprobates (and the saints, into true and false ones). Both were defeated by the non-arrival of a New Jerusalem ("liberty") and the return of old regimes ("tyranny"), but both won in the long run by producing liberalism, the routinized version of godliness and virtue. The inquisitorial zeal and millenarian excitement were gone, but mutual surveillance, ostentatious self-control, universal participation, and ceaseless activism remained as virtues in their own right and essential prerequisites for democratic rule (the reduction of individual wills to a manageable uniformity of opinion). *Novus ordo seclorum* was overshadowed by *e pluribus unum*, and the expectation of imminent happiness was replaced by its endless pursuit.

The history of the new order, like that of the old one, is a story of routinization and compromise punctuated by sectarian attempts to restore the original promise. One can—with Augustine—rejoice in the permanence of the temporary and claim that compromise is all there is (and that the really existing nation is really indivisible, with liberty and justice for all), but faith in progress is just as basic to modernity as the Second Coming was to Christianity ("progressive" means "virtuous" and "change" means "hope"). "Totalitarianism" is not a mysterious mutation: it is a memory and a promise; an attempt to keep hope alive.

The relative ripeness of the pear is a matter of judgment. Millenarians are usually divided into quietists, who wait for the End in catacombs, real or symbolic, and activists, who believe that "the Deity does not cooperate in restoring liberty otherwise than by influencing man's decision." In fact, no one—not even a Calvinist—believes that man's decision is of no consequence whatever, and no millenarian does nothing at all in the face of the approaching End. Jesus had to say what he said and do what he did in order for the time to be fulfilled, and his disciples had to repent, become humble like children, and, if they really wanted to rule the nations, leave behind their houses and brothers and sisters and fathers and mothers and children and fields. The quietest of prayers is a mighty weapon in the hands of true believers, and all forms of salvation are both inevitable and dependent on man's decision. All millenarians—indeed, most human beings—believe in some combination of faith and works, fate and hope, predestination and free will, the inexorable tide of Providence and purposeful human action, the locomotive of history and the "party of a new type." As the end nears, some people pray, some sing, some starve, some make furniture, some study genealogy, some dance the ghost dance, some don't dance at all, some kill their cattle, some kill themselves, and some kill the forces of darkness variously defined as priests, lawyers, money-lenders, "lords and princes," and any number of Hittites, Girgashites, Amorites, Canaanites, Perizzites, Hivites, and Jebusites.

Post-Christian perfection, like the Christian kind, can manifest itself within particular human beings or in chosen communities. Individuals can be saved by therapies; communities can become indivisible through a combination of "national" and "social" emancipation. The Old Testament's chosen people were proletarians among nations, who were promised a tribal victory that was also a revolutionary transformation of slaves into masters. The New Testament equated the social revolution with the national one. Babylon (or Egypt, or Rome, or whatever imperial "whore" was oppressing the chosen people) was going to fall and receive "as much torture and grief as the glory and luxury she gave herself," but the same thing was going to happen to the Israelites who were too fat to squeeze through the eye of the needle. "Woe to you who are well fed now, for you will go hungry. Woe to you who laugh now, for you will mourn and weep." Jesus was not casting his pearls before the Gentiles, but he was not talking to all the Jews either.[91]

Depending on the nature of their "distress," both Christian and post-Christian millenarians could represent themselves as tribes facing other tribes (like Enoch Mgijima's "Israelites") or as the hungry facing the well-fed (like Thomas Müntzer's "League of the Elect"), but they were always a bit of both and usually represented themselves as such. The English Puritans' Holy Commonwealth was England (and later America), and Robespierre's universal happiness of free and equal men was equal to the hope "that France, once illustrious among enslaved nations, might, by eclipsing the glory of all free countries that ever existed, become a model to nations, a terror to oppressors, a consolation to the oppressed, an ornament of the universe." The liberal descendants of the two revolutions preserved the remnants of both the priesthood of all believers (the rights of man) and the holy commonwealth (the republic of virtue). Rights were guaranteed and enabled by nationalism, and the greater the insistence on the sacred immediacy of these rights (as in the self-admiring, Augustinian America), the more messianic the nationalism.[92]

The societies in which successful reformations had coincided with the defeat of old regimes (Britain, Holland, the United States, and, in a more muted form, Lutheran Scandinavia) could continue to enjoy the fruits of routinization by absorbing most forms of radical creativity into Protestant sectarianism, official nationalism, and franchise extension. The societies in which an unreformed church was subordinated to an infidel foreign state (Poland, Ireland, Serbia, Bulgaria, Greece) could continue to accommodate modern radicalism within biblical nationalism and its updated Romantic version (for as long as Babylon continued its depredations). Elsewhere, the ruins of Christendom were teeming with post-Christian prophets who, "although of no name, with the greatest facility and on the slightest occasion, whether within or without temples, assumed the motions and gestures of inspired persons." Germany, whose new and ambitious state could never quite discipline a society split by the Reformation or a Europe divided by old borders, produced a particularly large number of such prophets. So did France, Italy, Spain, Russia, and other societies in which relatively unreformed churches linked to old regimes, dead or alive, were confronted by new urban coalitions increasingly open to post-Christian millenarianism. Russia, whose unreformed church was most closely linked to the old regime and whose old regime was both politically alive and economically ambitious, gave birth to a particularly vibrant tradition of millenarian sectarianism, "the intelligentsia." Many of the new prophets, especially in Germany and Russia, were Jews, whose traditional legitimizing faith had collapsed along with their traditional economic role, and whose entry into nonmillenarian communities was often not welcome.[93]

As the French Revolution retreated into a recoverable past, apocalyptic prophecies tended to cluster at the poles of the national-to-socialist continuum. At the peak of millenarian hope and despair, the distance between tribal and social deliverance could grow as wide as the difference between Moses and Jesus. The chosen people constituted as tribes spoke the Old Testament language of escaping from Egypt and getting to the promised land by exterminating the internal enemies who threatened the indivisibility of the nation and the external Perizzites who threatened the purity of milk and honey. The chosen people constituted as those who wept and hungered spoke the New Testament language of toppling those who were cheerful and well-fed. Both were about a particular struggle leading to universal happiness, but the scale of the universal depended on the nature of the particular. Mazzini's prophecy that Italy was destined to hold "the high office of solemnly proclaiming European emancipation" primarily concerned the Italians, and Mickiewicz's prophecy that "a resurrected Poland would weld and fuse the nations in freedom" primarily concerned the Poles. Marx's prophecy of socialist revolution spoke to all those who had nothing to lose.[94]

■ ■ ■

Marx began in the same way as Mazzini and Mickiewicz. "The *emancipation of the German*," he wrote when he was twenty-five years old, "is the *emancipation of man*." Or rather, as he had written a month or two earlier, "emancipation from Judaism is the self-emancipation of our time." The emancipation of man was to proceed in stages.

The root of all evil was private property and money. "The view of nature attained under the domination of private property and money is a real contempt for, and practical debasement of, nature. . . . It is in this sense that Thomas Müntzer declares it intolerable 'that all creatures have been turned into property, the fishes in the water, the birds in the air, the plants on the earth; the creatures, too, must become free.'" To become free was to abolish private property and money. "Money degrades all the gods of man—and turns them into commodities." No one worships it more than the Jews, who are the living embodiment of egoism. "The god of the Jews has become secularized and has become the god of the world."

> What is the secular basis of Judaism? *Practical* need, *self-interest.*
> What is the worldly religion of the Jew? *Huckstering.*
>   What is his worldly God? *Money.*
>   Very well then! Emancipation from *huckstering* and *money*, consequently from practical, real Judaism, would be the self-emancipation of our time.[95]

Whether Marx wanted to abolish money by abolishing the Jews or abolish the Jews by abolishing money, the real question was how it would be done. Or, as it turned out, *where* it could be done. The answer was that the emancipation of man was the emancipation of Germany because Germany was "an anachronism, a flagrant contradiction of generally recognized axioms, the nothingness of the *ancien régime* exhibited to the world." And what was a modern ancien régime? "The *comedian* of a world order whose *true heroes* are dead"; "nothing but *wretchedness in office.*"

Fortunately for Germany, this was not all. "If . . . the *whole* German development did not exceed the German *political* development, a German could at the most have the share in the problems-of-the-present that a Russian has." But Germans were not Russians: their philosophical development did exceed their political development, as well as the philosophical development of the more advanced nations. "In politics, the Germans *th ought* what other nations *did.* Germany was their *theoretical conscience.* The abstraction and presumption of its thought was always in step with the one-sidedness and lowliness of its reality."

The more profound the wretchedness, the better for the final outcome. Marx's History was Faust's Mephistopheles—"part of that power which would the evil ever do, and ever does the good." The lowliness of German reality had sharpened its thought, and the sharpness of Germany's thought would help bring about the revolution, which would usher in the emancipation of man. The proliferation of people who, with the greatest facility and on the slightest occasion, assumed the motions and gestures of inspired persons and prophesied the approaching end, signified that the end was, indeed, approaching. The greatest achievement of German philosophy would be to dethrone religion (by which Marx meant Christianity): "The abolition of religion as the *illusory* happiness of the people is the demand for their *real* happiness. To call on them to give up their illusions about their condition is to call on them to *give up a condition that requires illusions*. The criticism of religion is, therefore, *in embryo, the criticism of that vale of tears* of which religion is the *halo*."

The performance of this task had begun—like most things in history—with an attempt to accomplish the opposite. It had begun in "Germany's revolutionary past," the Reformation:

> *Luther*, we grant, overcame bondage out of *devotion* by replacing it by bondage out of *conviction*. He shattered faith in authority because he restored the authority of faith. He turned priests into laymen because he turned laymen into priests. . . . But, if Protestantism was not the true solution of the problem, it was at least the true setting of it. . . . And if the Protestant transformation of the German layman into priests emancipated the lay popes, the *princes*, with the whole of their priestly clique, the privileged and philistines, the philosophical transformation of priestly Germans into men will emancipate the *people*.

Just "as the revolution then began in the brain of the *monk*, so now it begins in the brain of the *philosopher*." Much of the work had been done by Hegel; it was up to the twenty-five-year-old Marx to complete the task by bringing history and politics together. One of the two 1843 essays that launched Germany's—and the world's—ultimate philosopher was the introduction to *A Contribution to the Critique of Hegel's Philosophy of Right*.

The fundamental questions were clear:

> Can Germany attain a practice *à la hauteur des principes*—i.e., a *revolution* which will raise it not only to the *official level* of modern nations, but to the *height of humanity* which will be the near future of those nations? Will the monstrous discrepancy between the demands of German thought and the answers of German reality find a corresponding discrepancy between civil society and the state, and between civil society and itself? Will the theoretical needs be immediate practical needs? . . . Can [Germany] do a *somersault*, not only over its own limitations, but at the same time over the limitations of the modern nations?

The answer was, by now, familiar: it was precisely the monstrosity of the discrepancy that would allow Germany to rise to the height of humanity. "*Germany, as the deficiency of the political present constituted a world of its own*, will not be able to throw down the specific German limitations without throwing down the general limitation of the political present"—its own and everyone else's.

But how could it be done *politically*? "Where, then, is the *positive* possibility of a German emancipation?"

> *Answer*: In the formulation of a class with *radical chains*, a class of civil society which is not a class of civil society, an estate which is the dissolution of all estates, a sphere which has a universal character by its universal suffering and claims no *particular right* because no *particular wrong*, but *wrong generally*, is perpetuated against it; which can invoke no *historical*, but only *human*, title; which does not stand in any one-sided antithesis to the consequences but in all-round antithesis to the premises of German statehood; a sphere, finally, which cannot emancipate itself without emancipating itself from all other spheres of society and thereby emancipating all other spheres of society, which, in a word, is the *complete loss* of man and hence can win itself only through the *complete re-winning of man*. This dissolution of society as a particular estate is the *proletariat*.

Just as the Jewish spirit was embodied in capitalism, the spirit of Germany was embodied in the proletariat. Just as the Jews stood for unbridled acquisitiveness and self-interest, the Germans stood for the creativity of absence and innocence. "As philosophy finds its material weapon in the proletariat, so the proletariat finds its *spiritual* weapon in philosophy. Once the lightning of thought has squarely struck this ingenuous soil of the people, the emancipation of the *Germans* into *men* will be accomplished." And once the emancipation of Germans into men was accomplished, the emancipation of man would be assured:

> Let us sum up the result. The only liberation of Germany which is *practically* possible is liberation from the point of view of *that* theory which declares man to be the supreme being for man. Germany can emancipate itself from the Middle Ages only if it emancipates itself at the same time from the *partial* victories over the *Middle Ages*. In Germany, *no* form of bondage can be broken without breaking *all* forms of bondage. Germany, which is renowned for its *thoroughness*, cannot make a revolution unless it is a *thorough* one. The *emancipation of the German* is the *emancipation of man*. The *head* of this emancipation is *philosophy*, its *heart* the *proletariat*. Philosophy cannot realize itself without the transcendence of the proletariat, and the proletariat cannot transcend itself without the realization of philosophy.
> When all the inner conditions are met, the *day of the German resurrection* will be heralded by the *crowing of the cock of Gaul*.[96]

The solution to the German question followed from the solution to the Jewish question: "Once society has succeeded in abolishing the *empirical* essence of Judaism—huckstering and its preconditions—the Jew will have become *impossible*, because his consciousness no longer has an object, because the subjective basis of Judaism, practical need, has been humanized, and because the conflict between man's individual-sensuous existence and his species-existence has been abolished." On the one hand, "the *social* emancipation of the Jew is the *emancipation of society from Judaism*," and the emancipation of society from Judaism is the emancipation of mankind from oppression. On the other, the emancipation of the German from all forms of bondage is the alliance of German philosophy with the universal proletariat in the name of the emancipation of man. The emancipation of man ultimately depends on the reformation of the Jews and the resurrection of Germany.[97]

The entire edifice of Marxist theory—complete with its Mephistophelian frame and rich rhetorical ornamentation—was built on these foundations. Hegel's Preface to his *Philosophy of Right* ends with the owl of Minerva spreading its wings at the approach of dusk. Marx's introduction to his critique of Hegel's *Philosophy of Right* ends with the cock of Gaul (the gallus from Gallus) crowing at the dawn of a new day—the same one, presumably, that awoke the god of day and chased off the ghost of Hamlet's father. As Marx himself would explain, the philosophers had only interpreted the world in various ways; the point was to change it—through revolution and resurrection. Marx's discovery of the proletariat had accomplished this task.

The question of why Marx, of all the cocks heralding the German resurrection, ended up conquering much of the world is just as impossible and irresistible as the question of why Jesus, of all the Jewish prophets who assumed the motions and gestures of inspired persons, ended up founding one of the world's most owl-resistant civilizations. One possible answer is that they were, in fact, quite similar. Marx, like Jesus and unlike Mazzini or Mickiewicz, succeeded in translating a tribal prophecy into a language of universalism. He was his own Paul (in case Engels proved ineffective): the emancipation from Judaism and the resurrection of Germany were buried under the weight of the emancipation from capitalism and the resurrection of humankind.

Perhaps most remarkably, he succeeded in translating a prophecy of salvation into the language of science. As Celsus wrote about Jesus and other would-be messiahs and their visions, "To these promises are added strange, fanatical, and quite unintelligible words, of which no rational person can find the meaning: for so dark are they, as to have no meaning at all; but they give occasion to every fool or impostor to apply them to suit his own purposes." Marx, too, combined an extremely straightforward promise of deliverance with obscure oracular formulas that defied the comprehension of his future followers—much to their satisfaction, apparently. But Marx did not just alternate simplicity with complexity, clarity with obfuscation, striking metaphors with commodity-money-commodity equations; he expressed his eschatology in the form of a scientific forecast based on falsifiable claims and, most important, involving sociologically defined protagonists.

One of the greatest challenges for Christian millenarians trying to enact the New Testament apocalyptic scenario had been to distinguish between the saints and the reprobates and to understand the secret of Babylon's power and whoredom. Marx solved this problem by using categories—the "bourgeoisie" and the "proletariat," above all—that firmly bound the moral to the scientific, the subjective to the objective, and the individual to the collective. If society consisted of "classes" of people; if class belonging could be determined by a minimally trained believer; if conviction (inner righteousness) was directly related to membership; and if the new, non-illusory Armageddon was a class war, then the Anabaptist problem of lashing out at the Antichrist's self-regenerating "cunning army" (not to mention the Jacobin problem of trying to keep up with the hydra of counterrevolution) would be solved once and for all—by means of science. Jesus's "rich" and "poor" would be neatly classified, and Müntzer's descendants could "cut down the red poppies and the blue cornflowers" in the absolute certainty that, as originally predicted, all the participants would be color-coded and registered in special books. "Do not harm the land or the sea or the trees until we put a seal on the foreheads of the servants of our God." Marx, like Jesus, died a failed prophet, with few disciples and fewer signs of an imminent German resurrection. Like Jesus, he was rediscovered posthumously by barbarians who found his prophecy congenial (owing, at least in part, to "the problems-of-the-present that a Russian has.")[98]

The prophecy itself was utterly familiar. There was the prelapsarian fraternity of the innocent, the original sin of discovering distinctions, the division of the world into the hungry and the well-fed, the martyrdom and resurrection of a universal redeemer, the final battle between the forces of good and evil, the violent triumph of last over first; and the eventual overcoming of the futility, unpredictability, and contingency of human existence. The emotional center of the story was the contrast between the suffering of those with nothing but their chains to lose and the "wonders far surpassing Egyptian pyramids, Roman aqueducts, and Gothic cathedrals." The new Babylon, like the old, had reduced everything to the naked pursuit of cargoes of gold and "compelled all nations, on pain of extinction, to adopt the bourgeois mode of production"—by, among other things, forcing all women into "prostitution both public and private" and "stripping of its halo every occupation hitherto honoured and looked up to with reverent awe." Once again, "the kings of the earth committed adultery with her, and the merchants of the earth grew rich from her excessive luxuries."[99]

But the end was near. "In one day her plagues will overtake her," and "the great city of Babylon will be thrown down, never to be found again." The great conflagration was going to happen both because it was inevitable and because Marx's disciples—the Communists—"have over the great mass of the proletariat the advantage of clearly understanding the line of march, the conditions, and the ultimate general results of the proletarian movement." Like all millenarians, they would work hard to bring about the ineluctable. Free will and predestination were one and the same thing. "The theoretical conclusions of the Communists are in no way based on ideas or principles that have been invented, or discovered, by this or that would-be universal reformer. They merely express, in general terms, actual relations springing from an existing class struggle." Jesus had been both the messenger and the subject of the message; his disciples had had to both believe the message and help fulfill it by joining the messenger. The Communists merely expressed, in general terms, actual relations springing from an existing class struggle, but "they never ceased, for a single instant, to instill into the working class the clearest possible recognition of the hostile antagonism between bourgeoisie and proletariat" and never forgot that their practical mission consisted in the "formation of the proletariat into a class."[100]

The original mission was an internal German affair. The Communists, according to their Manifesto (written when Marx was thirty and Engels, twenty-eight), needed to spread the good news "in order that the German workers may straightway use, as so many weapons against the bourgeoisie, the social and political conditions that the bourgeoisie must necessarily introduce along with its supremacy, and in order that, after the fall of the reactionary classes in Germany, the fight against the bourgeoisie itself may immediately begin." But the German victory was everyone's victory, and the Communist Manifesto was—ultimately—addressed to the Gentiles, as well as the Germans: "The Communists turn their attention chiefly to Germany, because that country is on the eve of a bourgeois revolution that is bound to be carried out under more advanced conditions of European civilisation and with a much more developed proletariat than that of England was in the seventeenth, and France in the eighteenth century, and because the bourgeois revolution in Germany will be but the prelude to an immediately following proletarian revolution."[101]

The scheme was strictly trinitarian: the "childlike simplicity" of primitive communism was to be followed by the age of class struggle, which was to be followed by the kingdom of freedom. Likewise, the English Revolution of the seventeenth century had been followed by the French Revolution of the eighteenth century, which was to be followed by the German revolution of the last century of the world as we know it. Marxism itself, according to Lenin, had three sources and three main components: English political economy, French socialism, and German philosophy.[102]

Like most millenarian prophets, Marx and Engels acknowledged their predecessors as inspired but blinkered forerunners. They had all—from Thomas Müntzer to Robert Owen—represented "independent outbursts" of proletarian insight and realized the need for the abolition of private property and the family. Indeed, "the theory of the Communists," according to the Manifesto, "may be summed up in the single sentence: Abolition of private property." As for the family, it "will vanish as a matter of course when its complement [prostitution] vanishes, and both will vanish with the vanishing of capital." In the meantime, "all children, from the moment they can leave their mother's care," must be educated "in national establishments" that will combine instruction with production. Like most millenarian prophets (as well as millenarian sectarians and their institutionalized heirs, monks and nuns), Marx and Engels focused on the elimination of private property and the family as the most powerful and mutually reinforcing sources of inequality. Like most millenarian prophets, they wanted to turn the transitional, premillennial world into a sect—which is to say, to transform a complex, unequal society organized around property and procreation into a simple, fraternal society organized around common beliefs, possessions, and sexual partners (or sexual abstinence).[103]

Like most millenarian prophets, but unlike their acknowledged "utopian" predecessors (and many unacknowledged ones, including the Marquis de Sade and Restif de la Bretonne), Marx and Engels were extremely vague about what the kingdom of freedom would look like, with regard to either possessions or sex. As Engels wrote in *Anti-Dühring*,

> To the crude conditions of capitalist production and the crude class conditions corresponded crude theories. The solution of the social problems, which as yet lay hidden in undeveloped economic conditions, the utopians attempted to evolve out of the human brain. Society presented nothing but wrongs; to remove these was the task of reason. It was necessary, then, to discover a new and more perfect system of social order and to impose this upon society from without by propaganda, and, wherever it was possible, by the example of model experiments. These new social systems were foredoomed as utopian; the more completely they were worked out in detail, the more they could not avoid drifting off into pure fantasies.[104]

This is true. It makes perfect sense to apply the term "utopian" to those who discover a new and more perfect system of social order and try to impose it upon society from without by propaganda, and, wherever possible, by the example of model experiments. Marx and Engels were not utopians—they were prophets. They did not talk about what a perfect system of social order should be and how and why it should be adopted or tested; they knew with absolute certainty that it was coming—right now, all by itself, and thanks to their words and deeds. Unlike Saint-Simon, Fourier, and Owen, and like Jesus and his many descendants, they had a lot less to say about future perfection than about how it would arrive—and how soon. And, of course, it would arrive very soon and very violently, and it would be followed by the rule of the saints over the nations with an iron scepter, and then those who had overcome would inherit all, and the old order of things would pass away, and there would be a new earth, and the glory and honor of the nations would be brought into it, and nothing impure would ever enter it, nor would anyone who did what was shameful or deceitful.[105]

> In a higher phase of communist society, after the enslaving subordination of the individual to the division of labor, and therewith also the antithesis between mental and physical labor, has vanished; after labor has become not only a means of life but life's prime want; after the productive forces have also increased with the all-around development of the individual, and all the springs of co-operative wealth flow more abundantly—only then can the narrow horizon of bourgeois right be crossed in its entirety and society inscribe on its banners: From each according to his ability, to each according to his needs![106]

Unlike Fourier and Saint-Simon, Marx never explained how abilities were to be measured and what, besides unforced and undivided labor, constituted legitimate human needs. Marx's own sample list included the freedom "to hunt in the morning, fish in the afternoon, rear cattle in the evening, criticise after dinner, just as I have a mind, without ever becoming hunter, fisherman, herdsman or critic." Ultimately, it seems, needs were to coincide with desires, and desires were to reflect "natural necessity." The transition to Communism was "humanity's leap from the kingdom of necessity to the kingdom of freedom," and freedom, as Hegel had discovered, was "the insight into necessity." In Engels's formulation, "Freedom does not consist in any dreamt-of independence from natural laws, but in the knowledge of these laws, and in the possibility this gives of systematically making them work towards definite ends. . . . Freedom therefore consists in the control over ourselves and over external nature, a control founded on knowledge of natural necessity."[107]

Allowing for the customary substitution of "natural laws" for "God," this is a traditional Christian understanding of freedom as the coincidence of human will with the will of God. When Dante entered the lowest sphere of Paradise and met the spirits of inconstant nuns, he asked one of them if she longed for a higher place:

> Together with her fellow shades she smiled
> at first; then she replied to me with such
> gladness, like one who burns with love's first flame:
> Brother, the power of love appeases our
> will so we only long for what we have;
> we do not thirst for greater blessedness.
> Should we desire a higher sphere than ours,

then our desires would be discordant with
the will of Him who has assigned us here,
but you'll see no such discord in these spheres;
to live in love is here necessity,
if you think on love's nature carefully.
The essence of this blessed life consists
in keeping to the boundaries of God's will,
through which our wills become one single will;
so that, as we are ranged from step to step
throughout this kingdom, all this kingdom wills
that which will please the King whose will is rule.[108]

To quote from another divine comedy, "It was all right, everything was all right, the struggle was finished. He had won the victory over himself. He loved Big Brother."[109]

PART II
FULFILLMENT

4
THE REAL DAY

Few apocalyptic millenarians live to see the promised apocalypse, let alone the millennium. Isaiah, Jesus, Muhammad, Karl Marx, and most of their followers did not.

But some did. Indeed, most definitions of "revolution"—at least "real" or "great" revolutions, such as the Puritan, French, Russian, Chinese, and Iranian ones—refer to regime changes in which apocalyptic millenarians come to power or contribute substantially to the destruction of the old order. "Revolutions," in most contexts, are political and social transformations that affect the nature of the sacred and attempt to bridge the Axial gap separating the real from the ideal. As Edmund Burke wrote in 1791,

> There have been many internal revolutions in the government of countries. . . . The present revolution in France seems to me to be quite of another character and description; and to bear little resemblance or analogy to any of those which have been brought about in Europe, upon principles merely political. It is a revolution of doctrine and theoretic dogma. It has a much greater resemblance to those changes which have been made upon religious grounds in which a spirit of proselytism makes an essential part.
>
> The last revolution of doctrine and theory which has happened in Europe is the Reformation. . . . The principle of the Reformation was such as, by its essence, could not be local or confined to the country in which it had its origin.[1]

According to Crane Brinton, revolution is the assumption of power by the "delirious" idealists who expect the realization of "heavenly perfection." According to Martin Malia, it is a political transformation "perceived as the passage from a corrupt old world to a virtuous new one." And according to S. N. Eisenstadt, it is "the combination of change of regime with the crystallization of new cosmologies." Great revolutions (as opposed to Burke's internal ones) are "very similar to the institutionalization of the Great Religions and of the great Axial Civilizations." They are the best of times, they are the worst of times; everyone goes direct to heaven, everyone goes direct the other way.[2]

Revolution, in other words, is a mirror image of Reformation—or perhaps Revolution and Reformation are reflections of the same thing in different mirrors. The first refers to political reform that affects the cosmology; the second refers to cosmological reform that affects politics. The view that revolutions aspire to the creation of an entirely new world while reformations attempt to return to the purity of the original source is difficult to hold on to: Thomas Müntzer and the Münster Anabaptists were trying to bring about the fulfillment of a prophecy that had not yet been fulfilled. They believed that the way to perfection lay through the restoration of the Jesus sect, but they had no doubt that what they were building was "a new heaven and a new earth," not the old Garden of Eden. The new Jerusalem was to prelapsarian innocence what the kingdom of freedom was to "primitive communism." All reformations (as opposed to theological or ritual reforms) are revolutions insofar as they assume that "it is not enough to change some of these *Lawes*, and so to *reforme* them." All revolutions are "revolutions of the saints" insofar as they are serious about "insatiable utopias." As Thomas Case told the House of Commons in 1641, "Reformation must be Universall. *All the wives, with such as are born of them*, there must not be a wife or a child dispensed withall, in this pub-like Reformation. . . . Reform all places, all persons, all callings. Reform the Benches of Judgments, the inferior Magistrates. . . . Reform the Church, go into the *Temple*. . . , *overthrow the tables of these Money-changers, whip out them that buy and sell*. . . . Reform the Universities, . . . reform the Cities, reform the Countries, reform inferior Schools of Learning, reform the Sabbath, reform the Ordinances, the worship of God, etc."[3]

There was more to reform; there was nothing that did not need reforming. They had everything before them; they had nothing before them. They were all going direct to heaven, they were all going direct the other way. The key to salvation was firmness:

> You have more work to do than I can speak. . . . Give leave onely to present to you the *Epitome* and *compendium* of your great work, summ'd up by our Saviour, *Matthew* 15:13. *Every plant which my heavenly Father hath not planted, shall be rooted up.* Behold here a double *Universality* of *number* and *extent*.
>
> *Every plant*, be it what it will, though it be never so like a flower, though it seems as beautifull as the Lilly, which *Solomon* in all his *robes* could not outshine. *Every plant*, whether it be *thing*, or *person*, *order* or *ornament*, whether in *Church*, or in *Commonwealth*, where ever, what ever, if not planted of God, you must look to it, not to *prune it* onely, or *slip it*, or *cut it*. . . , but *pull'd up*. . . . *Not broken off*, then it may grow, and sprout again; but *pull'd up by the very roots*. If it be not a plant of Gods planting, what do's it in the Garden: out with it, *root and branch, every plant, and every whit of every plant*.[4]

And just as Jesus explained the meaning of his Parable of the Weeds ("the weeds are the sons of the evil one," who will be thrown "into the fiery furnace, where there will be weeping and gnashing of teeth"), so did

Thomas Case, to the same effect. The Puritan Reformation, like the one Jesus launched, had little to do with forgiveness:

> "I know men will crie out, *Mercie, Mercie*, but oh no *mercie* against poor souls; such *mercie* will be but *foul murder.* . . . Shew no mercie therefore, to pull guilt and bloud upon your own heads; now the guilt is theirs, if you let them goe, you will translate their guilt upon your own souls. You remember what the prophet told *Ahab*, I Kings 20:42. *Because thou hast let go out of thy hand, a man whom I appointed to utter destruction, therefore thy life shall go for his life, and thy people for his people.*"[5]

∎ ∎ ∎

Two days after the tsarist state collapsed and the Provisional Committee of the State Duma found itself in charge of what used to be the Russian Empire, nineteen-year-old Mikhail Fridliand went to the Duma headquarters in Tauride Palace, to bear witness to the revolution. The son of a Jewish cobbler from Kiev and later Bialystok, Fridliand was a student at the Institute of Psychiatry and Neurology and a regular contributor to the *Student Path* newspaper.[6] Three years later, he recorded his impressions in an essay titled "March in February," one of the first to be signed with the pen name "Mikhail Koltsov":

> I made my way to the palace through the menacing darkness, accompanied by the sound of random gunfire—now close at hand, then far away, then suddenly right next to my ear. The moon shone down in place of the streetlamps, which had long since been extinguished; the soft, warm snow fluttered down and tinted the streets a light blue. Trucks full of people kept rushing by every few minutes and then disappearing around the corner like screaming, rattling apparitions. The area in front of the palace, on Shpalernaia, was almost unbearably bright and noisy. Tauride had always been a quiet, old, cozy place, with silent doors and waxed floors, deputies strolling about arm in arm, and Duma marshals bobbing and gliding by. Now it was completely unrecognizable, with feverishly moving bright spots and a thousand sparkling lamps lighting up the darkness, exciting the city's mutinous blood and sucking it in with its pale tentacles. Directly in front of the main entrance, in the middle of the white, fluffy garden, a large, magnificent automobile lay on its side,

Mikhail Fridliand (Koltsov)
as a student
(Courtesy of M. B. Efimov)

like a wounded animal, its bruised nose and headlights buried in the snow. One of the doors was open, and large snowy footprints were visible on the stylish rug and tender leather of the seats. The entire courtyard around it was filled with motorcycles, carts, sacks, and people—a whole sea of people and movement breaking against the entrance in waves.

An old house invaded by the outside world was a familiar image. What was new was the claim that this was the very last old house (or, to an orthodox Marxist, the penultimate, feudal one). The "Nest of Gentryfolk" had become the House of Revolution:

> The sudden chaos of new creation had lifted up the ancient house, widened it, enlarged it, and made it enormous, capable of encompassing the revolution and all of Russia. Catherine Hall had become a barracks, parade ground, lecture hall, hospital, bedroom, theater, a cradle for the new country. Flooding in, all around me, were countless streams of soldiers, officers, students, schoolgirls, and janitors, but the hall never seemed to grow too full; it was enchanted; it could accommodate all the people who kept coming and coming. Chunks of alabaster from the walls crunched underfoot, amidst machinegun belts, scraps of paper, and soiled rags. Thousands of feet trampled over this trash as they moved about in a state of confused, joyous, incomprehensible bustle.

The swamp had turned into a sea. Some chroniclers and eyewitnesses, including Koltsov himself, occasionally resorted to other elements (fire, blizzards, volcanic lava), but the dominant image was the sea and the rivers that fed it—because they were readily associated with the chaos of new creation; because they were alive, as well as deadly; because they could be peaceful, as well as stormy; and because they could be turned back into a swamp—and then into a sea again. "In this elemental, volcanic explosion, there were no leaders. They bobbed along, like wooden chips, in the flooding stream, trying to rule, to direct, or at least to understand and participate. The waterfall flowed on dragging them with it, twirling them around, lifting them up, and then casting them down again, into the void."

The first to surface was Mikhail Rodzianko, the Speaker of the Duma, who stood up to welcome "the brave men of the Preobrazhensky Regiment" and left "in tired majesty, blowing his nose into a large handkerchief." Next, "the waves threw up Miliukov," the head of the liberal Kadet Party. He, too, wanted to speak to the sea, to rule over it:

> "Citizens, I greet you in this hall!"
> The sea listened to him and seemed to calm, while continuing to seethe and rumble below the surface with a deep, inextinguishable

roar. The diplomat's neatly packaged words dropped like pebbles into the water, leaving ripples on the turbulent surface before sinking without a trace. Another splash, and a new chip appeared on the crest of a wave. The Duma deputy, Kerensky, held up by strong arms, extended his lean torso upward and, straining his tired throat and screwing up his insomniac's face, cried out to the elements:

"Comrades!"

This word was warmer and more to the point than "brave men" or "citizens." The elements smiled on the responsive speaker, showered him with a waterfall of applause, enveloped him in the brass din of the Marseillaise.

Some speakers were more responsive than others. Tauride Palace had become the House of Revolution. The House of Revolution could encompass the world, but it could not—as Koltsov saw it after the fact—keep it whole. "Nearby, in a long, narrow room separated by a curtain, the Soviet of Workers' Deputies was holding a meeting. They, too, had been swept up and flung here by the spring flood waters coming from the factories, the army units, and the navy crews. This incredible meeting had been going on, with constant interruptions, for two days now. The excitement and the packed bodies made it hard to breathe. What were they saying, all these Mensheviks, SRs, and populists? They were not saying what they meant to say or needed to say because no one knew what was needed in this hour of deluge and fire."

And then there were the full-time prophets—those who had predicted the coming of the real day and could not believe it was here, at last:

Squeezed into a tiny room, labeled "Press Bureau," was the Russian intelligentsia. . . . They were just as bewildered and confused as everyone else. Free to say whatever they wanted, freed at last from censorship and prohibitions, and drunk with boundless rapture, they had not yet been able to find their voices, which were trapped deep within each man's breast.

German Lopatin pressed each passerby to his gray beard, mumbling tearfully: "Now lettest thou thy servant depart in peace."

"Yes, it's over! We've lived to see the end. . . ."

Leonid Andreev frowned, fiddling with his belt:

"The end? You think so? I think it's just the beginning."

And twirling a lock of hair around a finger on his left hand, he pointed with his right toward the window:

"Or rather, the beginning of the end."

Through the window, they could see the pale snow awakened by the early dawn.[7]

German Lopatin was a former member of the General Council of the First International, a legendary terrorist mastermind, the first translator of *Das Kapital* into Russian, and the survivor of several prison terms and one commuted death sentence. Leonid Andreev was the author of a celebrated short story about the last days of seven convicted terrorists and the curse of knowing the hour of one's end. Both wings of Russian post-Christian apocalypticism and both halves of Bukharin's Gymnasium No. 1 class were represented in the House of Revolution. "Now lettest thou thy servant depart in peace" (*nunc dimittis*) was not only the most recognizable Christian formula of fulfilled prophecy (uttered by Simeon after he had seen the baby Jesus); it was also the title of the best-known part of Rachmaninoff's *All-Night Vigil*, op. 37, written a year and a half earlier. Rachmaninoff himself was in town during those days, performing his most recent composition, the Études-Tableaux, op. 39. Immersed in the *Dies irae* theme, it opens with an image of a deluge drowning out all calls of distress, continues with a mournful scene of doomed expectation ("seagulls and the sea"), and culminates in a blood-curdling Last Judgment (no. 6). This was the flood from Pushkin's *The Bronze Horseman*—as seen by its victim, "poor Evgeny."[8]

■ ■ ■

Meanwhile, the Bolsheviks were returning from prison and exile. Sverdlov spent several days with Kira Egon-Besser and her parents before leaving for Ekaterinburg to run the Urals Party organization. His difficult housemate from his Kureika days, now called "Stalin," stayed on as one of the top Bolsheviks in Petrograd (as did Arosev's friend Skriabin, now commonly known as "Molotov"). Piatnitsky arrived in Moscow straight from Siberia and was put in charge of Party cells in the Railroad District. Bukharin traveled from his New York exile to San Francisco, then by ship to Japan, suffering greatly from seasickness on the way, and finally to Moscow, where he joined Osinsky (who had recently defected from the Southwestern Front) in the regional Party bureau. Trotsky took the less circuitous Atlantic route from New York to Petrograd's Finland Station, where he was greeted with solemn speeches. "Straight from the station," he wrote in his memoirs, "I plunged into the vortex, with people and episodes whirling by like wooden chips in a stream." Arosev interrupted his enforced journey to a penal battalion, reenrolled in the Moscow Warrant Officer School No. 4, from which he had been expelled, and went on to help found the Military Bureau of the Moscow City Party Committee. As he wrote five years later, "no sooner had the joyous spring sun of 1917 melted the winter snow with its golden rays than the whole expanse of Russia was touched by the purple wing of a rebellious angel. . . . From all of Moscow's squares, the soldiers, flushed with happy intoxication from the almost bloodless revolution, sent skyward a thousand 'hurrahs.'"[9]

Skobelev Square

One of those squares, named after General Skobelev and dominated by his huge equestrian statue, was, according to Arosev, the city's heart. "From this square, the red beams extended their rays along the streets and alleyways to the farthest ends of Moscow. At the base of Skobelev's mount, huge crowds would gather." Across Tverskaia from the Skobelev monument was Moscow's own House of Revolution: the former residence of the governor general and now home to the Provisional Government's Provincial Commissar and the Soviets of Workers' and Soldiers' Deputies. It was in front of its main entrance that "rallies lasted from early morning until late at night, with one speaker after another," and it was the soviets (councils), spreading steadily both inside and outside the building, that were, in Arosev's words, "a lighthouse in the midst of the stormy popular sea."[10]

In Arosev's account, the "Governor General's Building" was not only a metaphor for revolutionary politics—it was the main stage and perhaps the main point of the revolution. The "stormy popular sea" that had flooded the city needed a master; the equestrian General Skobelev had proven to be a false idol; the new, legitimate power (the true Bronze Horseman) had moved inside, whether he knew it or not: "The house on Tverskaia was not only the address of the social forces supported by the masses of workers and soldiers, but also the address of the institution that was preparing to take over power. When, at rallies and meetings, the workers proclaimed 'All power to the Soviets,' they knew perfectly well that it meant the power of the organization whose executive offices were located on Tverskaia Street."[11]

One Bolshevik who did not yet know the right address of the revolution was Voronsky, who, as a Zemstvo Union inspector and Bolshevik propagandist at the Western Front, found himself at the very source of the flood. His memoir of those days is called *The Eye of the Storm*:

Governor General's Building

Everywhere—at railway stations, in front of barracks and hospitals, in fields and on lawns, in courtyards and back alleys—soldiers were gathered together in tight groups, their irrepressible, boisterous speech, colorful and polyphonic, rising up and stirring the air. It was like a spring flood, when the river ice breaks up in the foggy haze of the night and predawn calm. The river begins to move, making mysterious rustling and gurgling noises, the ice floes crash into each other, their edges breaking off, and one huge ice block climbs on top of another, while somewhere far away the ice crumbles and dissolves into a deluge that spreads on and on, irrigating the flood plains and sweeping away winter debris.[12]

The main question was: "Will we be able to enter the main stream and direct its course, or will we drown in this new flood?" Voronsky's literary alter ego Valentin is overcome with doubt. "Visions of the northern forests under the spell of ancient dreams, the long and gloomy halls of the seminary, the summer nights on the Tsna, the attics of Trans-Moskva, and the straight avenues of Petrograd kept appearing and disappearing before his mind's eye.... What a strange feeling.... I spent the last ten years of my life as a wanderer, in prisons and exile, doing secret work, waiting for searches and arrests, losing friends. I used to be followed by traitors and spies. None of that exists anymore.... What will become of us all?" The answer was to enter the stream and take charge of its course by saying the "warmer words"—words that would not sink without a trace, words that would connect the Bolshevik truth to the happy intoxication of the crowd. The reward was omnipotence and, possibly, immortality.[13]

Arosev never slept. "The daily speeches in the streets and the barracks in front of the workers and soldiers, the heated arguments with those who were trying to betray our revolution, the feverish reading of leaflets and newspapers, of everything that screamed 'revolution' or smelled of revolution never seemed to tire me out, amazingly enough, but, instead, inspired me to work even harder." Voronsky's Valentin never slept, either: "He was warmed by the crowd, by its body, breath, movement, and murmur. These people . . . were now listening to him eagerly, their eyes glowing with the light of hope. They kept shaking Valentin's hand, watching out for him, warning those who accidentally jostled him, hurrying to offer him matches, asking if it was too cold or windy. This shared, solicitous human warmth absorbed him, subdued him, made him a part of itself, and he, as never before, found himself thinking its thoughts and feeling its feelings. . . . It was the highest happiness that one could have on earth."[14]

The most tireless and, by most accounts, most inspiring Bolshevik speaker was Trotsky, who seemed to talk continuously as he whirled around in the vortex of people and events:

I would make my way to the podium through a narrow trench of human bodies, occasionally being lifted above them and carried along. . . . Surrounded on all sides by tightly squeezed elbows, chests, and heads, I seemed to be speaking out of a warm cave of human bodies. Each time I made a broad gesture, I would brush against someone, and a grateful movement in response would intimate that I should not get upset or distracted, but should continue speaking. No exhaustion, no matter how great, could withstand the electric tension of that impassioned human throng. It wanted to know, to understand, to find its path. At certain moments it almost seemed I could feel on my lips the eager intensity of the crowd that had melded together to become one. At such moments, all the words and arguments prepared beforehand would wither and recede under the irresistible pressure of that sympathy, and other words and other arguments, new to the speaker but necessary to the masses, would emerge ready to do battle. It often felt as if I were standing a little to one side, listening to that speaker, unable to keep up with him and worried that he might fall off the edge of the roof, like a sleepwalker distracted by my promptings.[15]

Trotsky's self-consciousness was a version of Sverdlov's "habit of self-analysis" and Arosev's and Voronsky's attempts to reconcile their private selves with their Party-nicknamed doppelgängers. This could be a good thing—a form of "putting books to the test of life and putting life to the test of books"—but it could also be "intelligentsia weakness" leading to inaction. More pressing, in the spring of 1917, was another form of sectarian dialectic: free will versus predestination and the consciousness of historical necessity versus popular spontaneity. The Bolsheviks were the most exclusive and imminentist of the Russian millenarians, most suspicious of the swamp of daily routine and "appeasement," and most willing "to fight not only against the swamp, but also against those who are turning toward the swamp." The question now for all socialists, but especially for the Bolsheviks, was how much of the swamp had flowed into the sea. How close was life to the books? Was the stream clear enough, and was it flowing in the proper direction? Who was right—Trotsky the speaker, who threw away the script under the irresistible pressure of popular sympathy or Trotsky the prompter, who stuck to prepared arguments taken from books that put life to the test?

On the day Voronsky's Valentin experiences the highest human happiness of being absorbed by a shared human warmth, he is asked to talk to a crowd of soldiers who have surrounded the local police station with the intention of lynching everyone inside. On the way over, Valentin looks up at the stars and thinks: "We are walking toward our children's country, toward the faraway promised land. We are walking in the dark, without miraculous portents or burning bushes, with faith in ourselves only. Will we get there?" He does rescue the policemen (by arresting them "in the name of the revolution"), but is not happy with the speech he makes on the occasion.[16]

> This is not how he had imagined his first address to the people after their liberation from the autocracy. He had been dreaming endlessly about this incomparable moment in prisons, exile, and attics. This hour had appeared to him again and again in a wondrous revelation. He was going to find words that would burn with the flame of the true dawn. He would say all the things he had been forced to conceal. The powerful "hosanna" escaping his breast would merge with the shouts of victory. And now the hour had come, and he stood before the exhausted, disease-ravaged people who only yesterday had been sitting in the trenches, with death behind their backs. What better, more noble audience could a revolutionary hope for during the days of the first victories? And yet something was missing. What could it be?[17]

The answer came on Easter Monday, when Lenin entered Petrograd on a train and declared that the time had come; the prophecy had been fulfilled; and the present generation would not pass away until all these things had happened. Life had passed the test of books, and books had passed the test of life. As for those "appeasers" (*soglashateli*) who had ears but did not hear, Lenin knew that they were neither cold nor hot, and so, because they were lukewarm—neither hot nor cold—he was about to spit them out of his mouth. Any non-Bolshevik, anyone who compromised with Babylon, was an appeaser.

The challenge of organizing a welcoming reception in the midst of Easter celebrations fell to the head of the Bolshevik Military Organization, Nikolai Podvoisky, the son of a priest and a former seminarian. Podvoisky, who saw the event as "the end of the agonizing search for the right course of the revolution," managed to assemble a large crowd and procure an armored car. After being delivered to the Bolshevik headquarters in Krzesinska Palace, Lenin gave the good news to his bewildered followers. "It was so new to us," wrote one of Lenin's most loyal disciples and the secretary of the Central Committee, Elena Stasova, "that, at first, we simply could not get our minds around it." Some Bolsheviks, according to Podvoisky, "were frightened by Lenin's intolerance of the appeasers and the perspective of an immediate and complete split with them. Especially new and incomprehensible was his demand for the transfer of power to the soviets. There were those who were in total shock from Lenin's words."[18]

By the next morning, when Lenin unveiled his message to a packed joint meeting of all the Social Democrats in Tauride Palace, most Bolsheviks, according to Stasova, "perceived it as something absolutely sacrosanct and truly their own," the source of "a firm conviction that from now on [they] were walking down an unerring path." According to Podvoisky, "Vladimir Ilich began his speech by unmasking the appeasers as the lackeys of the bourgeoisie and its secret agents in the ranks of the working class. . . . Lenin's words drove the Mensheviks into a frenzy, provoking jeers, furious swearing, and threats. With each new comment by Lenin, the hostility grew. Lenin's statement that there could be no union between the Bolsheviks and Menshevik appeasers was met with rabid howling and roaring."

Finally, Lenin got to his main point, the immediate takeover of power. "The appeasers leapt out of their seats. They began to whistle, scream, bang madly on their desks, and stamp their feet. The noise rose to a deafening pitch. The Menshevik leaders—Chkheidze, Tsereteli, and other presidium members—became deathly frightened. In vain did they try to restore order, addressing their desperate pleas to the right, where their supporters were, and to the left, where the Bolsheviks sat. This continued for about ten minutes. Then the storm died down. It flared up again." And so it continued, in response to every one of Lenin's April Theses, until the end of the speech. "Amid all the raging elements, Lenin remained unperturbable. One had to see the incredible strength and serenity in his face, his whole figure, in order to understand Lenin's true role and significance at that crucial moment. . . . He stood there like the helmsman of a ship during a terrible storm—full of inner peace, clarity, simplicity, and majesty because he knew where to steer."[19]

Podvoisky's and Stasova's memoirs follow the Soviet hagiographic tradition, but there is no doubt that Lenin was the only socialist who knew where to steer. He was a true prophet who could both lead his people through the parting waves and attend, one way or another, to their every petulant complaint. "The agonizing search for the right course" was finally over.

■ ■ ■

"The peculiarity of the current situation in Russia," wrote Lenin in his April Theses, "consists in the transition from the first stage of the revolution, which has given power to the bourgeoisie owing to the insufficient consciousness and cohesion of the proletariat, to its second stage, which must give power to the proletariat and the poorest strata of the peasantry." The power, in other words, was to be handed to those who lacked sufficient consciousness or cohesion to recognize their inheritance. "I have seen these people," the Lord said to Moses, "and they are a stiff-necked people." "If only they were wise and would understand this and discern what their end will be!"[20]

The solution was to find the words that would align the people's wishes with the prophecy's fulfillment. According to Podvoisky,

> Vladimir Ilich explained to us the surest and fastest way to convince the soldiers who did not have much consciousness, found themselves under the influence of the agents of the bourgeoisie, or had a poor understanding of their complex environment.
>
> "They don't need long speeches," Lenin told us. "A long speech touches on too many things, and the soldier's attention dissipates. He can't absorb it all. You won't satisfy him, and he will be unhappy with you. You should talk to him about peace and about land, and there's not much you need to say about that: the soldier will know what you are talking about right away." . . .
>
> And who did Vladimir Ilich recommend as the best agitators among the soldiers? He said that during the February Revolution the sailors (along with the workers) had played one of the most prominent roles. And this meant that they should be the ones sent to the soldiers![21]

The strategy seemed to work. "Revolution" was universally understood to mean the end of the old world and the beginning of a new, just one. The longer the delay in the coming of the new world and the more acute the sense that the "provisional" government was becoming, in some sense, permanent, the greater the attraction of the Bolshevik message. And the message was, indeed, simple: the desirable and the inevitable were one and the same; all that was needed was for the exhausted and disease-ravaged to make one final push.

Later that same spring, Voronsky's Valentin went to a rally on the Western Front. The first speaker was Comrade Veretyev from the Socialist Revolutionary Party, who had spent the previous ten years in Siberian prisons. A pale man with a goatee, flaxen hair, a "high clear forehead," and "intelligent eyes," Veretyev talked about the sanctity of democratic freedoms, the special duty of the soldiers at the front, and the unrealistic promises made by irresponsible people. "He would sometimes pause and make a motion with his right hand; his nervous fingers fluttered, imparting a peculiar expressive mobility to his words and whole figure. The wind from the meadow ruffled his hair. One lock kept falling over his right eye, and Veretyev would throw it back with a quick, impatient movement."

The next to speak was a sailor from the Baltic Fleet, who said that soldiers covered in "piss, shit, dirt, and lice" do not care about rights and freedoms and that all they wanted was peace and bread and land, right away, as the Bolsheviks kept saying. He got some of his Bolshevik lines wrong, but he was saved by the "power of a newly converted zealot" and the "wild, passionate force" of his words. Veretyev stood next to the sailor, looking down at his feet and fumbling with his hat. "He looked like a man sentenced to death."

> What was happening was a tragedy for him. An old populist, he had worshipped the people and suffered for them. And now he was standing before the freed people, and they did not accept him and did not understand him. . . . And the person who reminded the soldiers of that was not an old political prisoner but a semi-literate sailor who had barely mastered the ABCs of revolutionary struggle. Verily, "you have hidden these things from the wise and learned, and revealed them to little children"! . . .
>
> According to the biblical legend, God showed Moses the Promised Land from a remote mountain in the Land of Moab. Moses was luckier than Veretyev. History brought him to Canaan, the Land of Abraham, Isaac, and Jacob, but Veretyev did not recognize it.[22]

Moses was luckier, but not by much: he was shown the promised land from a distance, but not allowed to cross the Jordan because he had broken faith with God in the presence of the Israelites at the waters of Meribah Kadesh in the Desert of Zin. After his death, the people he had led out of captivity were able to enter the land of their inheritance but did not find it flowing with milk and honey and "prostituted themselves to the foreign gods."[23]

The power of Lenin's conviction persuaded most Bolsheviks, and at the April Party conference his views prevailed. Some doubters continued to waver, but, as Podvoisky put it, "the party ship, guided firmly and confidently by its helmsman, set out on a new course." The person who did more than anyone to help Lenin with the practicalities of translating convictions into votes was Sverdlov, who returned to Petrograd as head of the Urals delegation and stayed on as Lenin's executive plenipotentiary. At the conference, (according to Stasova) "he called meetings if agreement was needed on a controversial issue, organized and put together commissions on various questions, and drew up lists of Central Committee members to be discussed, among other things. Whatever needed to be done, Yakov Mikhailovich was tireless in making sure it was taken care of. It was amazing how he managed to be everywhere at once and still chair all the countless meetings and conferences." One of the things he did was to remove Stasova's name from the Central Committee list and replace her as head of the Central Committee Secretariat, which she had been running with the help of Tatiana Slovatinskaia, Stalin's former friend and correspondent and Valentin Trifonov's wife.[24]

As the Party prepared for the coming revolution, it had two central tasks. One was administrative and organizational: objectives had to be defined, personnel assigned, weapons stockpiled, followers trained, contacts maintained, accounts kept, funds distributed, conferences organized, and meetings chaired (and manipulated). Sverdlov presided over most of these things, with the help of several women, including Polina Vinogradskaia, who remembered his notebook "filled with hieroglyphs that only he could understand. It was a magic notebook! With a quick glance, Sverdlov could tell you everything you needed to know about a comrade: where he was working, what kind of person he was, what he was good at, and what job he should be assigned to in the interests of the cause and for his benefit. Moreover, Sverdlov had a very precise impression of all the comrades: they were so firmly stamped in his memory that he could tell you all about the company each one kept. It is hard to believe, but true."[25]

Sverdlov continued to live with the Egon-Bessers. He got Kira a job in the editorial offices of the *Soldiers' Truth* newspaper, next to his secretariat in Smolny Palace (the new House of Revolution, as far as the Petrograd Bolsheviks were concerned). After a few weeks, however, Kira's parents insisted on moving her to the countryside for health reasons (her "protests notwithstanding"), and in early July, Sverdlov's wife and children arrived from Siberia. Novgorodtseva joined the Central Committee Secretariat, and the children were sent to their grandfather in Nizhny Novgorod. Some sections of the Secretariat and the Bolshevik publishing house, The Surf, were moved into the building of an Orthodox confraternity, with crosses over the main entrance and a back door leading into the church. It became known as "the place under the crosses."[26]

The Bolsheviks had always been good at administrative and "technical" work. The party's raison d'être was "fighting the enemy, not stumbling into the nearby swamp"; its self-description was "a fighting army, not a debating society"; and its organizational principle was "democratic centralism," not the other way around. Now, on the eve of the real day and under Sverdlov's supervision, they redoubled their efforts. "As the frequency and intensity of rallying subsided," wrote Arosev, "the center of gravity of the work of the soviets moved to their executive committees, and along with them, naturally enough, to record keeping." And when it came to record keeping, it was, naturally enough, the Bolsheviks who, "even during the most romantic revolutionary days, . . . distinguished themselves as 'apparatchiks.'" The Moscow Soviet of Workers' Deputies was run by its Bolshevik secretary, Arkady Rozengolts, and the only room assigned to the Soldiers' Soviet, which was dominated by the SRs, was occupied by its Bolshevik faction. "In those days, people acquired positions of power by being active and presenting the world with a fait accompli. The Bolsheviks, as the most active element, found themselves in almost all the administrative jobs."[27]

The Party's second task was "agitation," which consisted of making speeches at large rallies and writing articles in Party newspapers. The speeches revolved around concise slogans; the articles provided specific links between the changing slogans and the general prophecy. One of the most skillful and prolific Bolshevik "dialecticians" was Bukharin, who could offer instant sociological analysis in the light of both the foundational texts and immediate tactical objectives. "Because the proletarian masses proved insufficiently conscious and well-organized," he wrote in May 1917, echoing Lenin's April Theses, "they did not proceed immediately to the establishment of state power by the revolutionary lower classes." But, as they became more conscious and better organized, and as the true interests of the proletariat prevailed over those of its peasant allies, the soviets would take over power and clash openly with the imperialist bourgeoisie. The efforts of the enemy were both doomed and dangerous: "consequently, what was needed was feverish work everywhere without exception."[28]

As Cromwell had put it, "we are at the threshold;—and therefore it becomes us to lift up our heads, and . . . *endeavor* this way; not merely to look at that Prophecy . . . and passively wait." What was needed was the constant reading of the signs and feverish work everywhere without exception. "In the depths of the popular masses," wrote Bukharin on June 6, "there is a permanent process of fermentation, which, sooner or later, will manifest itself." The surest sign of the approaching end was the emergence of two clearly branded armies. "The bourgeoisie is emerging as a force bringing death and putrefaction; the proletariat, as the carrier of life-creating energy, is marching ahead." On July 30, at the Sixth Party Congress, Bukharin suggested that the peasant as property owner had entered into a temporary alliance with the bourgeoisie; his friend Osinsky (who, during the congress, was camped out next to him on the floor of a friend's apartment) responded by saying that the Communist Manifesto had predicted otherwise; but Stalin explained that there were different kinds of peasants and that the poor ones were "following the bourgeoisie because of their lack of consciousness." On October 17, one week after the Bolshevik Central Committee, chaired by Sverdlov, made the decision to stage an armed uprising, Bukharin wrote: "Society is inexorably splitting into two hostile camps. All intermediary groups are rapidly melting away." All that was needed was one last burst of feverish activity.[29]

"In the days of the last coalition," wrote the Menshevik N. N. Sukhanov, "the Bolsheviks demonstrated colossal energy and engaged in feverish activity throughout the country" (including his own apartment, where, secretly from him, his Bolshevik wife hosted the "uprising meeting" of the Central Committee). On October 21, Sukhanov listened to Trotsky speak about peace, land, and bread.[30]

The mood around me bordered on ecstasy. It seemed that, without any command or prior agreement, the crowd might suddenly burst into some kind of religious hymn. . . . At one point, Trotsky formulated a short general resolution or proclaimed a general formula to the effect that "we will defend the cause of the workers and peasants to the last drop of blood."

"Who's in favor?"

The crowd of thousands raised its hands as one man. I could see the raised hands and burning eyes of all the men, women, adolescents, workers, soldiers, peasants, and petit bourgeois. Were they in a state of spiritual fervor? Could they see, through the slightly raised curtain, a corner of that "holy land" they had been longing for?[31]

Two days earlier, after a different Trotsky speech, Sukhanov and his wife missed their streetcar. It was late at night, and the rain was pouring down; Sukhanov was in a bad mood because of the streetcar and the rain—and because Trotsky had said that the rumors of an imminent uprising were inaccurate insofar as they were not accurate. At last, they were able to catch a streetcar that would take them part of the way home.

I was extremely angry and sullen as I stood in the back of the streetcar. Next to us was a small, modest-looking man in glasses, with a black goatee and radiant Jewish eyes. Seeing my anger and sullenness, he seemed to want to try to cheer me up, comfort me, or distract me with some kind of advice about which route to take, but I responded curtly and monosyllabically.

"Who was that?" I asked my wife when we got off the streetcar.

"That was Sverdlov, one of our old Party men and a Duma member."

Despite my bad mood, I am sure I would have cheered up and had a good laugh if I had been told that within two weeks this man would become the official head of the Russian Republic.[32]

■ ■ ■

Most accounts of the October takeover in Petrograd center around Smolny Palace, former home to the Institute of Noble Maidens, which, since August, had housed the Petrograd Soviet and Bolshevik military headquarters. "The whole of the revolution was taking place in Smolny" (as well as, possibly, in the workers' suburbs), wrote Sukhanov. "Everywhere, armed groups of sailors, soldiers, and workers could be seen scurrying around. There was always a line of peasant emissaries and army unit delegates winding its way up the stairs to the third floor, where the Military-Revolutionary Committee was located."[33]

"The whole of Smolny was brightly lit up," wrote Lunacharsky, an old friend of Sukhanov's. "Excited crowds scurried up and down the halls. All the rooms bubbled over with life, but the highest human tide, a truly passionate blizzard, was raging in the corner of the upstairs hall, where, in the back room, the Military-Revolutionary Committee held its meetings. . . . Several completely exhausted girls were coping heroically with the indescribable upsurge of people with requests, complaints, and demands. If you got caught up in that whirlpool, you could see all the excited faces and the many hands reaching out for a directive or a written order."[34]

Mikhail Koltsov's "October" offers a faithful restaging of his "March in February":

> In the evening twilight, the heavy shape of Smolny, with its three rows of lit-up windows, could be seen from far away.
>
> Hurrying along the wide, hard, frost-covered road and dipping occasionally into potholes, soldiers and sailors, civilians with raised collars and squeaky galoshes, rattling automobiles and motorcycles all streamed toward the stone cavern of the main entrance.
>
> . . . Pressing forward in a nervous, jostling throng, they could not be contained within the walls of the building; they kept streaming in and then seething ponderously and eerily, before finally spilling over.
>
> It used to be quiet inside with schooldames walking solemnly by in soft kid shoes, quick-footed daughters of doomed rulers running up and down stairs, and, every so often, gold-embroidered old men with empty eyes floating by in clouds of reverent whispers.
>
> But now it was full of noise. Orders rang out and the hundred feet of a changing guard tramped by under the black arches. Patrols, crews, and pickets flowed out in thick gray streams.
>
> . . . Comrades! To the Winter Palace![35]

The canonical memory of the October Revolution, like that of its February precursor and French model, was about moving from one building to another—until such time as "the city of pure gold, like transparent glass," could be built. This time the flood swept into Smolny, surged up to the third floor, whirled around the entrance to the Military-Revolutionary Committee office, and then flowed, in orderly streams, toward the Winter Palace, where old men with empty eyes sat waiting. A member of the bureau of the Military-Revolutionary Committee, Nikolai Podvoisky, remembered guiding "the stormy stream" toward the palace and watching it "flood the porch, entrances, and stairways." Having sent the arrested government ministers to the Peter and Paul Fortress, he returned to headquarters and found Lenin writing a decree on land. "No

Nikolai Podvoisky

sooner had the reign of the bourgeoisie been toppled by armed people in the Winter Palace than Lenin began turning the first page of the emerging new world in Smolny."[36]

In Trotsky's account, around that time or perhaps a little later, Lenin looked at him "in a soft, friendly way and with an awkward shyness that suggested a desire for intimacy. 'You know,' he said hesitantly, 'after all the persecutions and a life underground, to come to power . . .'—he was searching for the right word, and suddenly switched to German, making a circular motion around his head: '*es schwindelt*' [it makes one's head spin]."[37]

According to Lunacharsky, who was also in Smolny in those days, some people were afraid that "the peasant sea was going to open up and swallow us," but "Lenin faced the enormous challenges with astonishing equanimity and took hold of them the way an experienced pilot would take hold of the helm of a giant ocean liner." Lunacharsky wrote this in 1918, on the first anniversary of what had already become "the October Revolution" and in the certainty that Smolny would be turned into "the temple of our spirit." But even in the midst of the revolution, on October 25, 1917, when he still had no idea what was happening around the Winter Palace, preferred a "democratic coalition" to a Bolshevik takeover, and thought the chances of victory were "dim and bleak," he had written to his wife, "These are frightening, frightening days on a knife-edge. They are full of suffering and worries and the threat of a premature death. And yet still it is wonderful to live in a time of great events, when history does not trot along lazily and sleepily, but flies like a bird into unknown territory. I wish you were here with me, but thank god you are not."[38]

In the event, nothing frightening actually happened. ("The ease with which the coup was carried out came as a surprise to me," wrote Lunacharsky two days later.) It was in Moscow, where the government forces put up some resistance, that the fate of the revolution was decided. According to Arosev, who, as one of the very few Bolsheviks with formal military training, had been put in charge of military headquarters, "that great uprising of the human mass in the name of humanity began simply

and without hesitation—exactly the way the old books describe the creation of the world." It began in a small room on the third floor of the Governor General's (Soviet) Building. "One might have thought that it was not a room but a stage represention of a room, in which a fierce battle of the cigarette butts had taken place the previous night." The secretary of the Military-Revolutionary Committee, Arkady Rozengolts, who could "make revolution with the same ease and inspiration with which a poet writes poetry," ordered Arosev to occupy the telegraph, telephone exchange, and post office, and then

Arkady Rozengolts

quietly disappeared. "It was as if he had inhabited those rooms for hundreds of years, like an eternal ghost, for he knew where everything was and seemed to move from one room to another through the walls."[39]

Arosev found the commander of the Moscow Red Guards, A. S. Vedernikov, and the two of them set off to carry out the order:

> Comrade Vedernikov and I emerged from the Soviet Building onto Skobelev Square. It felt strange: all the people in the square were scurrying about as usual, all rushing someplace and worried about something, just like the day before, or the day before that. Two newspaper boys were loitering near the Skobelev Monument, and a young lady was haggling with a cabby. Everything was just as it always was.
>
> "Do you have a revolver?" Vedernikov asked me.
>
> "No."
>
> "Me neither. We've got to find one. Let's go to the Dresden and see if one of the comrades can give us something."
>
> Everything all around was so peaceful, and we weren't being attacked by anyone. The uprising in Petrograd had already taken place, and half the ministers were in prison, so why did we need a revolver? Comrade Vedernikov's going off in search of a gun reminded me of a silly comedy in which the characters think they are more important than they actually are."[40]

Vedernikov found a gun, and the two of them went to the Pokrovsky Barracks, where Arosev made a short speech, and one company agreed to join them. Within two hours the telegraph, telephone exchange, and post office had all been occupied. The great uprising of the human mass in the name of humanity had begun.

In Moscow, the enemy were the students of Moscow's military schools, who had professional officers and a strong sense of duty, but no organized support, no single command, and—most important for Arosev—no address they could call their own. "While the Bolsheviks had one organization that was preparing to seize power—the Soviet of Workers' and Soldiers' Deputies with its executive offices in the right wing of the Soviet Building—the government, which was fighting for its existence, had several command centers . . . that vied with each other for supremacy." After the Bolsheviks formed the Military-Revolutionary Committee and demanded full power, the non-Bolshevik members of the Soviet moved out of the building and "found themselves without a territorial center." The great uprising of the human mass had acquired a home. "Its address had to be known to people in the districts, to regional commanders, scouts, and others."[41]

The military headquarters, headed by Arosev, moved into a small ground-floor room facing a side street (the Chernyshev/Voznesensky Alley); the Military-Revolutionary Committee moved in next door; and the adjoining room became the secretariat, where young women issued permits and screened visitors, and where, according to one of the women, there were always "thick throngs of people pushing and shoving." The rest of the building was "one long barracks." Or rather, "it was a soldiers' ant-hill," with detachments "in constant circulation: from the soviet to their positions at the battle sites and then back to the soviet to rest."[42]

The soviet building was Moscow's Smolny, but there was no Moscow Winter Palace. The Kremlin changed hands twice, but there was no one there to topple. There were no "White forces," either: groups of cadets at-tacked or defended various buildings looking for a tactical advantage but without any overall plan. There were times, wrote Arosev, when "it seemed as if the earth were shaking beneath our feet, our arms and feelings grow-ing numb, and we, along with our soldiers, sliding along a knife's edge, frightful and fateful, with victory on one side and death, on the other." Most of the fighting, however, took place far from the soviet building, closer to the river and especially around the bridges connecting the city center to Trans-Moskva.[43]

The Swamp was solidly pro-Bolshevik. The soldiers guarding the Main Electric Tram Power Station had handed their weapons over to the local Red Guards, who posted their detachments on the station towers, in the Salt Yard, and at the entrance to the Big Stone Bridge. The soldiers quar-tered at the Einem candy factory and Ivan Smirnov vodka distillery had given them a machine gun, which they placed on top of the bellfry of St. Nicholas. A field phone connected the station to the Gustav List plant, which provided the largest Red Guard detachment in the area (between forty and one hundred men). Some of the armed Gustav List workers were sent to guard the bridges; others converted the riverside bathhouse into a fortified bunker. "We used to shoot at the Kremlin through holes we had made in the stone wall, either from a standing or lying position, and some-times we had to take turns because there weren't enough guns to go around," remembered one of them. "It was even easier at night because we could aim at the different colored lantern flashes that must have been some kind of signals from the cadets who were running along the top of the wall to their lines below."[44]

After a week of fighting, the last loyalist bastion, the Alexander Military College, just up the street from the Big Stone Bridge, laid down its arms. In the small room occupied by the Military-Revolutionary Committee, Rozengoltz asked Arosev, who was sitting on the couch next to him, to write an order appointing Nikolai Muralov commissar of the Moscow Mili-tary District.

"Commissar or Commander?" I asked.
    "District Commissar—but it's the same as commander."
    "Commander," "Commissar," I thought, not really comprehending how such an important thing could be done so simply. All I needed to do was scribble down "hand over" and "appointed," put it to a

vote, and, lo and behold, you have a new government. It was hard to believe. . . .

But that is just what I did. I scribbled it down. A girl typed up the order. It was put to a vote, and Comrade Muralov became not simply Muralov, but District Commander. . . .

This is how the new military government was created—simply and naturally. Or rather, it was not created, but born, and, as with any natural birth, washed in blood.[45]

Arosev spent much of the rest of his life remembering that day. In the 1932 version of his memoir, he wrote:

During those nights when no one slept and each thought we might come out victorious or might all be slaughtered, it occurred to me that no matter what was written in literature or what was created by an author's imagination, nothing could be as powerful as this simple and austere reality. People were actually fighting for socialism. The socialism we used to dream and argue about was finally manifesting itself—in the flashing bayonets of the soldiers and raised collars of the workers swarming down Tverskaia, Arbat, and Lubianka Streets, gripping their Mausers and Parabellums and continuously advancing, tramping down harder and harder on the chest of the decaying, stinking bourgeoisie, that was infecting the weak ever so slightly with the smell of its decomposition. I have read almost everything lofty and solemn that we have in our old and new literature, looking in vain for something akin to the feeling we had on that cloudy morning when, in our trench coats smelling of rain and gunpowder, we climbed into an old, beat-up military car to be driven to headquarters as the new power.[46]

Meanwhile, Rachmaninoff was sitting in his apartment on Strastnoy (Christ's Passion) Boulevard, a short walk from Skobelev Square. According to his wife, "he was busy revising his First Piano Concerto and was concentrating on his work. Because it was dangerous to turn the light on, the curtains in his study, which faced the courtyard, were drawn, and he was working by the light of a single candle." As he told his biographer in 1933, "I sat at the writing-table or the piano all day without troubling about the rattle of machine-guns and rifle-shots. I would have greeted any intruder with the answer that Archimedes gave the conquerors of Syracuse." Many people around him "were hoping that each new day would, at last, bring them the promised heaven on earth," but he was not one of them. "I saw with terrible clearness that here was the beginning of the end—an end full of horrors the occurrence of which was merely a matter of time." Three weeks later, he and his family left for Petrograd. On December 20, he went to Smolny to request exit visas. On December 23, he and his wife and two daughters arrived at the Finland Station and boarded the Stockholm train (probably the same one that had brought Lenin to Russia). He died in Beverly Hills, California, on March 28, 1943. His wish to have *Nunc dimittis* ("Now lettest thou thy servant depart in peace," op. 37, no. 5) sung at his funeral could not be fulfilled. According to Rachmaninoff's biographer, who cites a letter from the composer's sister-in-law, "the choir was thought unable to cope and in any case the sheet music was not available at the time."[47]

■ ■ ■

A few days after Rachmaninoff's departure, the newly elected delegates of the All-Russian Constituent Assembly were gathered in Tauride Palace in Petrograd. According to Trotsky, Lenin had argued for postponing the elections indefinitely, but "Sverdlov, more closely connected to the provinces than the rest of us, protested vehemently against the postponement." Too much had been invested in the idea of a national legislative body, and too many promises had been made on its behalf (by the Bolsheviks, among others). The elections had been held; the SR's had won the majority of the seats, and Lenin had responded by saying that formal parliamentarism was a betrayal of the revolution. The leaders of the largest nonsocialist party had been arrested; martial law (to be enforced by Podvoisky) had been introduced, and a demonstration in support of the Constituent Assembly had been dispersed by gunfire. Late in the afternoon, the delegates were allowed to open the proceedings:[48]

> Constituent Assembly member Lordkipanidze (SR) states from his seat: "Comrades, it is 4 p.m., and we propose that the oldest member of the Constituent Assembly open the session. The oldest member of the SR faction is Sergei Petrovich Shvetsov . . . (*loud noise on the left, applause in the center and on the right, booing on the left . . . nothing can be heard; loud noise and booing on the left; applause in the center*). The oldest member of the Constituent Assembly, S. P. Shvetsov, mounts the platform.
>
> SHVETSOV (*rings the bell*). I declare the meeting of the Constituent Assembly open. (*Noise on the left. Voices:* Down with the usurper! *Prolonged noise and booing on the left; applause on the right.*) I declare an intermission. (*Sverdlov, the Bolshevik faction representative and chairman of the Central Executive Committee, mounts the platform.*)
> SVERDLOV. The Executive Committee of the Soviet of Workers' and Peasants' Deputies has directed me to open the meeting of the Constituent Assembly. (*Voices on the right and in the center:* Your hands are covered with blood! We've had enough blood! *Tumultu-*

ous applause on the left.) The Central Executive Committee of the Soviet of Workers' and Peasants' Deputies . . . (*Voice on the right:* It was rigged!) hopes that the Constituent Assembly will fully recognize all the decrees and resolutions of the Council of People's Commissars. The October Revolution has kindled the fire of the socialist revolution not only in Russia, but in all countries . . . (*laughter on the right and noise*). . . . We have no doubt that the sparks from our fire will spread all over the world . . . (*noise*) . . . and that the day is near when the working classes of all countries will rise up against their exploiters as the Russian working class rose up in October, followed by the Russian peasantry . . . (*tumultuous applause on the left*).[49]

This episode would enter the Soviet canon as the moment when the Bolsheviks made their final break with the Pharisees and the teachers of the law. According to Lunacharsky, all great revolutionaries were characterized by "[their] calm and absolute serenity at times when nerves should be overstrained and it seems impossible not to lose one's composure." No one could compare, however, to the "endlessly self-confident" Sverdlov, whose calm and serenity were "monumental and, at the same time, extraordinarily natural." On that occasion, the "tension had reached its highest point" when "Sverdlov suddenly appeared out of nowhere. In his usual unhurried, measured gait, he approached the platform and, as if not noticing the venerable SR elder, pushed him aside, rang the bell, and, in an icily calm voice that showed no sign of tension, declared the first meeting of the Constituent Assembly now open." According to Sverdlov's assistant, Elizaveta Drabkina, a sixteen-year-old Bolshevik who was sitting in the balcony booing the appeasers, "he walked up the stairs with steady, calm steps, as if there were no thousand-strong rabid mob raging behind his back, ready to tear him apart." And according to Sverdlov's own account, as reported by another young assistant,

> I came up behind the old man and snatched the bell from his trembling hand. Ringing the bell sharply, I called for silence and order in my lowest bass voice. Shvetsov was taken aback. He froze, with his hand suspended in midair and his mouth open in astonishment. His whole feeble body was like a question mark. Finally, he crawled down from the stage. Immediately, silence and order were restored. Many of those present were so dumbfounded that they were unable to speak. And I was able to read out the Declaration of the Rights of the Working and Exploited People that had been proposed by our Bolshevik faction.[50]

The Declaration proclaimed the Constituent Assembly illegitimate. In the exchange that followed, the main Bolshevik speech was delivered by

Bukharin, who said that no revolutionary change was possible for as long as the government included fainthearted appeasers, who were "the faithful lackeys and guard dogs of our oppressors and the exploiters of the working masses." The time was fulfilled, the real day had come, and this generation would certainly not pass away until all those things had happened:

> We are, indeed, facing a truly great moment. The watershed that divides this assembly into two irreconcilable—let's not kid ourselves and paste over the obvious with too many words—two irreconcilable camps—this watershed is about who is for socialism and who is against socialism. Citizen Chernov [the head of the SRs] has said that we need to manifest a will for socialism. But what kind of socialism does Citizen Chernov have in mind? The kind of socialism that will arrive in two hundred years, the kind that our grandchildren will be building—that kind? We, on the other hand, are talking about a living, active, creative socialism, the kind of socialism we want not only to talk about, but to implement . . . (*applause on the left*). . . .
>
> We are saying, comrades, right now, when the revolutionary fire is about to set the whole world aflame—we are declaring, from this podium, a war to the death against the bourgeois parliamentary republic . . . (*loud applause on the left, turning into an ovation*). . . . We Communists, we the Workers' Party, are striving to create, starting in Russia, a great Soviet workers' republic. We are proclaiming the slogan put forth by Marx half a century ago: let the ruling classes and their toadies tremble before the Communist revolution. The proletarians have nothing but their chains to lose, and a whole world to gain. Proletarians of all countries, unite! (*Ovation on the left. Voices:* Long live Soviet power!)[51]

Having declared civil war, the Bolsheviks left the hall. At 4:40 a.m., the remaining deputies were driven out of the building. When they came back the next day, the door was locked.[52]

Nikolai Bukharin

Trotsky claims that, after the takeover, Lenin once asked him: "If the White Guards kill you and me, do you think Sverdlov and Bukharin will be able to manage?" At the meeting of the Constituent Assembly, with Lenin among the spectators and Trotsky in Brest-Litovsk, they seemed to manage quite well. Bukharin was one of the most eloquent prophets of the coming conflagration; Sverdlov was, in Lunacharsky's account, a perfect "underground Bolshevik": "he had a lot of inner fire, of course, but outwardly, that man was made entirely of ice." Since November 1917, Sverdlov had been both the secretary of the Central Committee of the Party and the chairman of the Central Executive Committee of the Soviets.[53]

Two days after the Constituent Assembly was evicted, Sverdlov and Novgorodtseva moved into Tauride Palace. They shared a suite with Varlam Avanesov (Suren Martirosian), a former member of the Armenian Dashnak Party and now Sverdlov's second in command at the Central Executive Committee, and Vladimir Volodarsky (Moisei Goldstein), a former member of the Jewish Bund and now commissar of print, propaganda, and agitation. They lived as a commune, the way they had in exile. "All the residents of the apartment," wrote Novgorodtseva, "would get up at eight, gather around the table for breakfast, and leave by nine. The regime was very strict: no one could be late for breakfast, and no one was allowed to eat separately from the others. Breakfast did not last long: we would exchange a few jokes and run off, leaving any long conversations until later." Volodarsky would get back around midnight, Sverdlov and Avanesov, at 1:00 or 2:00 a.m., often accompanied by other people. Novgorodtseva, as the only woman, poured the tea. "Sitting around the table, we would discuss the events of the day, recount any amusing incidents, and exchange plans for the next day." The guests would usually stay for the night.[54]

While the house of failed parliamentarism was being downgraded and partially domesticated, the "temple of the Bolshevik spirit" was being transformed into a proper House of Revolution. In the words of Smolny's commandant, "though not right away and not without difficulty, we finally managed to rid Smolny of outsiders: all those schooldames, housemistresses, boarding school girls, servants, and others." Sverdlov's Central Executive Committee, Lenin's Council of Peoples' Commissars, and the Bolsheviks' Party Headquarters had all acquired their own rooms, secretaries, guards, and passes. There was a cafeteria (with mostly millet porridge on the menu), a basement jail, a commandant who answered directly to Podvoisky (now the commissar for military affairs), and about five hundred Latvian riflemen, who were thought to combine military discipline with a "proletarian spirit." (Latvia, along with the Caucasus and the Jewish Pale of Settlement, was one of the most radicalized parts of the Russian Empire; Latvian military units were a mainstay of Bolshevik power.)[55]

The transformation was never completed, however. In March 1918, as the German troops were approaching Petrograd, the new government moved its headquarters to Moscow (leaving behind Volodarsky, who was twenty-seven, single, and, according to Novgorodtseva, disconsolate). Most top offices and officials were housed in the Kremlin; those who did not fit were put up in several downtown hotels, renamed "Houses of Soviets" (the National became the First House of Soviets, the Metropol, the Second House of Soviets, and so on). Once again, "people whose presence was deemed unnecessary" had to be evicted (mostly monks and nuns, in the case of the Kremlin), a cafeteria set up, rooms assigned, icons and royal statues taken down, and Latvian riflemen armed and quartered.

Once again, Sverdlov took care of all these things by appointing officials who were capable of appointing other officials. "He seemed to have learned absolutely everything about the tens of thousands of people who made up our party," wrote Lunacharsky. "He kept in his memory a kind of biographical dictionary of Communists." In the words of Elizaveta Drabkina, who worked for him in the Kremlin, "for each more or less important Party official, he could say something like: 'This one is a good organizer; in 1905, he worked in Tula and after that, in Moscow; he spent time in the Orel central prison and was in exile in Yakutia. That one is not a great organizer but is an excellent public speaker.'"

Almost every more or less important party official owed his or her job to Sverdlov or one of his appointees—from Trotsky, the commissar of foreign affairs; to Bukharin, the chief editorial writer; to the sixteen-year-old Drabkina, who typed up the questionnaires he put together. Boris Ivanov, the "barely literate and politically underdeveloped baker" whom Sverdlov had tutored in Siberian exile, was made the head of the Main Directorate of the Flour Industry. Ivanov tried to refuse, saying that he was a baker, not a miller, and certainly not a manager, but Sverdlov allegedly responded: "You're a baker, and I'm a pharmacist, and an inexperienced one, at that. And here I am, sent by the party to do a job I never dreamed of." According to another memoirist, Sverdlov "viewed every matter, big and small, through the prism of particular people," and viewed particular people as both fallible and perfectible. "'The sun also has spots,' said Sverdlov [in March 1919]. 'People—even the best of them, the Bolsheviks—are made up of the old material, having grown up under the conditions of the old filth. Only the next generations will be free of the birthmarks of capitalism. What is important is to be able to pull a person up by playing on his strengths.'"[56]

Three years earlier, in a letter to Kira Egon-Besser from Siberia, he had written that, under capitalism, there could be no ideal individuals. "But already today you can see in some people certain traits that will outlive this life of antagonisms. The future harmonious person, as a type, can be discerned in these traits. The study of the history of human development leads to the certainty in the coming kingdom of such a person." Now that he was in charge of building that kingdom, he was following his own advice. All Bolsheviks assumed that present-day nonharmonious people could contribute to the destruction of the old economic "base," and that the new economic base would ensure the creation of future harmonious people. They also assumed, unlike the doubters and appeasers, that this could be done in their lifetimes. Their socialism, as Bukharin had explained, was not the kind that their grandchildren would still be building. According to Drabkina, Sverdlov's favorite stanza by his favorite poet, Heinrich Heine, was

A different song, a better song,
will get the subject straighter:

let's make heaven on earth, my friends,
instead of waiting till later.[57]

Meanwhile, they were settling into their new apartments and setting up house in familiar ways: sharing hallways, kitchens, and bathrooms; leaving doors unlocked and children unattended; and talking late into the night over tea that women poured. Osinsky left his wife and son and moved in with Anna Shaternikova, the recipient of his "Blacksmith" letter. The Sverdlovs brought their son, Andrei, and daughter, Vera, back from Nizhny Novgorod and moved to a larger apartment in the Kremlin. Their most frequent guest was Sverdlov's closest friend and Siberian housemate Filipp (Georges) Goloshchekin, the "regular Don Quixote." Most of the other visitors were also former coconspirators and fellow prisoners, too. When they got together, they would reenact their days of innocence by singing revolutionary songs and wrestling on the carpet.[58]

The only exception were various family members. Sverdlov's father visited regularly, accompanied by his two sons from a second marriage and once, by Yakov's eldest daughter, who lived with her mother in Ekaterinburg. Sverdlov's sisters had both become doctors. Sofia was married to a former entrepreneur, Leonid Averbakh, and had two children, Leopold and Ida. Sarra had briefly worked with Novgorodtseva in the Central Committee secretariat. Sverdlov's brother Veniamin had emigrated to America and become a banker but had recently returned at his brother's invitation to become the commissar of transportation—and the husband of Yakov's former lover, Vera Dilevskaia. The family, in Novgorodtseva's words, was "large, merry, and close-knit." Only Sverdlov's older brother, Zinovy, had left the fold for good. As the godson of Maxim Gorky, he had converted to Christianity; adopted Gorky's last name (Peshkov); studied at the Moscow Art Theater school; worked as a laborer in the United States, Canada, and New Zealand; interpreted for Gorky during his tour of the United States in 1906 (including the conversations he had with Mark Twain and John Dewey); lived with him on Capri (where he met Lenin, Bunin, and Lunacharsky, among others); joined the French Foreign Legion; lost his right arm during the fighting in France; returned to Russia in 1917 as a member of the French military mission; and left again after the Bolshevik Revolution, having failed in his efforts to keep Russia in the war. Zinovy and the rest of the Sverdlovs did not recognize each other's existence.[59]

The most important Sverdlovs of all were the children. The parents might have to sacrifice themselves to socialism; their grandchildren would be born too late to take part in the toil of creation. It was the children, "reared under the new, free social conditions," who would walk into the kingdom of freedom and "discard the entire lumber of the state" (as Lenin, quoting Engels, had written in State and Revolution). According to Novgorodtseva, when eight-year-old Andrei heard about the murder of Karl Liebknecht and Rosa Luxemburg, he asked:

"Daddy, wasn't Liebknecht a revolutionary and a Bolshevik?"

"Yes," answered Yakov Mikhailovich, "a real revolutionary."

"Was he killed by the bourgeoisie?"

"Yes, of course by the bourgeoisie."

"But Daddy, you are also a revolutionary. Does that mean they might kill you, too?"

Yakov Mikhailovich looked the boy in the eye, gently ruffled his hair, and said very seriously and very calmly:

"Of course they might, son. But you shouldn't be afraid of that. When I die, I will leave you an inheritance that is better than anything else in the world. I will leave you my name and my unblemished honor as a revolutionary."[60]

■ ■ ■

To be a revolutionary meant being both a herald and agent of the coming transfiguration. Voronsky, having been transferred from the Western Front to the Romanian Front before becoming a top Bolshevik propagandist in Odessa, prophesied the imminent consummation of the promise two weeks before the event. "The new and final wave of the revolution is coming. We are on the brink of a new revolutionary era, when, for the first time, the social element will pour into the revolution like a huge wave." The aquatic imagery, tempered by repeated references to "the revolution," accommodated both Christian and Marxist formulas (some of them identical). "The Russian Proletarian Revolution," he wrote when the hour finally struck, "will triumph as a world revolution no matter what trials await her because, for capitalist society, 'the time and all the prophecies are fulfilled.'" The apocalypse was the ultimate mixed metaphor:

> The Russian workers' and peasants' government represents the first buds that have appeared as a result of the coming proletarian socialist spring. The Russian Revolution has many enemies. Her paths are hazardous and thorny. . . . The frosts may damage the first buds, but they will never stop the triumphant march of spring. . . .
>
> Shrivelling, decaying bourgeois society is entering the New Year with, in one of the world's largest countries, a socialist workers' government allied with the poorest peasantry, a government whose every word is like a thunderous tocsin spreading the news of a worldwide revolutionary fire.[61]

The enemies were preparing for one last battle and weaving their "international cobweb," but "before an army ablaze with the enthusiasm of world liberation, the cannons would fall silent." The Third Congress of Soviets, which had legitimated the Bolshevik takeover and the dissolution of the

Assembly, was the focus of "that bubbling, seething, genuinely revolutionary ferment of existence, which was capable of igniting worlds and working miracles."[62]

Once in power, the Bolsheviks did what all millenarians do: waited for the inevitable while working to bring it about. The Marxist blueprint was no more specific than any other, but the basic goal of turning society into a sect was accepted by all true Bolsheviks (as Sverdlov understood the term). As usual, this included attacks on private property, trade, money, the family (especially inheritance, but ultimately all forms of kin loyalty), and "the rich" (determined according to an oft-revised table of social elements). The main principles were inherent in the Bolshevik version of Marxism; the disagreements over scale, timing, and sequence came down to the central question of any apocalyptic prophecy: they who have ears, will they hear?

As Voronsky wrote on the day the news of the uprising in Petrograd reached Odessa, "the achievement of the sacred goals of the revolution . . . is only possible with the cooperation and assistance of the masses themselves and their independent creativity." The Revolution was not the embodied creativity of the masses—it was a transcendental event that required their cooperation and assistance. "In this terrible hour of judgment, when the fate of the country is being decided, let us all, as one man, take the solemn oath of loyalty to the new revolutionary government." The government equaled the Revolution in the same way that Moses equaled the exodus. Loyalty to the prophet was the key to the fulfillment of the prophecy. Bolshevik eschatology was based on the assumption that the masses would stream toward the appropriate room in the appropriate building. In October 1917, the masses had acquitted themselves gloriously. The question was whether they would continue to do so.[63]

The answer was not always or perhaps not at all. When, during the German offensive of spring 1918, the time came to create an army ablaze with the enthusiasm of world liberation, the cannons did not fall silent. And when the government needed to "organize the whole economy on the lines of the postal service" (as Lenin had outlined in *The State and Revolution*), the sea turned back into a swamp. At the Einem Candy Factory, according to its early Soviet historian, "The attitude of the underdeveloped workers—and they were in the majority—toward the factory committee was so distrustful that some workers would come to the committee office during work hours to argue and curse over irrelevant things and insult the factory committee and its members. . . . During the most important and intense working hours, the members of the factory committee had to waste their time on explanations, arguments, and debates—all the more so because everyone felt that they had the right to abuse the committee, citing 'equal rights,' 'freedom of speech,' etc."[64]

Throughout 1918, the new state-sponsored factory committee struggled with the owner, the shareholders' board, and the workers as raw materials continued to disappear, production to drop, and other factories and shops around the Swamp to close down. "Against the background of the difficult economic situation, the discontent of the underdeveloped workers with low consciousness kept growing while work discipline kept falling; some workers would only show up in the morning and then again in the evening in order to punch their time cards. At the same time, drunkenness and the theft of both raw materials and finished products became rampant."[65]

With the introduction of rationing, what little sugar remained in circulation ended up in the hands of private traders and confectioners, and most mechanized candy factories went out of business. The state's war on private entrepreneurs drove them (and their sugar) farther underground or out of existence altogether; much of Einem's equipment broke down; and most of the sober workers left for their native villages. On December 4, 1918, the candy industry was nationalized. Einem became "State Candy Factory No. 1," run by the Main Candy Trust; the former owner, Vladimir Heuss, became a salaried "bourgeois specialist"; and the chairman of the board, Adolf Otto, left for Finland. Boris Ivanov, who had been appointed by Sverdlov to preside over the nationalization of the flour industry, was sent to the Astrakhan fisheries to work as an "agitator."[66]

All the debates and "oppositions" among the Bolsheviks were ultimately about whether the bubbling and seething ferment around them was a sea or a swamp. The most consistent optimists and imminentists among the Bolsheviks were the leaders of the Moscow distict party organization (and graduates of Moscow University): Bukharin, Osinsky, Osinsky's brother-in-law, Vladimir Smirnov, and a few of their friends and followers. Having defined themselves as "Left Communists," they lost to Lenin's appeasers on the question of the Brest-Litovsk Treaty, but won briefly on the factory-committee front. (Osinsky was the first chairman of the Supreme Council of the National Economy, with Bukharin and Smirnov on the board.) In 1919, as the "independent creativity of the masses" and the Bolshevik pursuit of the "goals of the revolution" continued to diverge, Osinsky and Smirnov led the "Democratic-Centralist" opposition to the "one-man rule principle." Since Communism was about spontaneously desiring the inevitable, trust in the independent creativity of the masses equaled confidence in the imminence of the millennium. As Osinsky wrote to Shaternikova on the day of the February Revolution, the shortest path to the "insatiable utopia" of natural morality lay through immersion in the "sacred fury" of the masses. At the time of the revolution, all Bolsheviks (officially renamed "Communists" in March 1918) believed that Communism would arrive very soon. The Left Communists believed that it would arrive even sooner.

On January 7, 1918, Lenin wrote that the triumph of the socialist revolution—beginning with a "period of ruin and chaos" and ending with a decisive victory over all forms of bourgeois resistance, was a matter of "several months." In early spring 1919, he wrote that "the first generation of fully trained Communists without blemish or reproach" would take over in about twenty years (and that, in the meantime, bourgeois specialists would have to keep working, whether Osinsky liked it or not). And in fall 1919, Bukharin argued that it might take "two to three generations formed under completely new conditions" for Communism to become fully developed, the state to wither away, and "all law and all punishments to disappear completely." There was, of course, room for argument about what constituted a complete victory of the socialist revolution, a Communist without blemish or reproach, or a fully developed Communist society, but, in the meantime, "very soon" had to keep moving, and the "Left" had to keep losing. Time, if nothing else, had to be appeased.[67]

One very large section of "the masses"—the peasantry—made too close an identification with popular creativity doctrinally suspect at the outset and practically impossible as the revolution unfolded. Osinsky's Left Communism collapsed over the peasants' unwillingness to give up their produce (as class solidarity would have dictated). In agriculture, he wrote in 1920, "the most important aspect of socialist construction is massive state coercion." Peasants were to be told when to sow, what to sow, and where to sow. They were to be forced to work wherever their work was needed. "The militarization of the economy and the implementation of universal labor conscription should begin in agriculture." Any attempts to shirk compulsory labor were to be met with "repressive measures" ranging from penal detachments to revolutionary tribunals. As Bukharin explained, violence against the peasants made good theoretical sense insofar as it represented a "struggle between proletarian state planning, which embodies socialized labor, and the peasant commodity anarchy and unbridled profiteering, which stands for fragmented property and market irrationality."[68]

Violence generally made good theoretical sense. All the Bolsheviks expected it as part of the revolution, and no one could possibly object to it in principle. Marxism was an apocalyptic movement that looked forward to the times of woe on the eve of the millennium, and the Bolsheviks, of all Marxists, defined themselves in opposition to appeasement. As Marx had written, in a passage made famous by Bukharin, "We say to the workers: 'You will have to go through 15, 20, 50 years of civil wars and national struggles not only to bring about a change in society but also to change yourselves.'" And as Bukharin wrote two and a half years into the age of civil wars and national struggles, "only such a class as the proletariat, the Promethean class, will be able to bear the terrible torments of the transition period in order, at the end, to light the torch of Communist society." Lenin had called for civil war long before October; warned of the "ruin and chaos associated with civil war" right after October; and, in June 1918, urged the workers to launch "that special war that has always accompanied not only great revolutions but every more or less significant revolution in history, a war that is uniquely legitimate and just, a holy war from the point of view of the interests of the toiling, oppressed, and exploited masses." In a July 1918 article titled "Prophetic Words," he cited Engels's prediction of a "world war of an extent and violence hitherto undreamt of. Eight to ten millions of soldiers will massacre one another and in doing so devour the whole of Europe until they have stripped it barer than any swarm of locusts has ever done."[69]

The Marxist version of the "iron scepter" rule of the saints was known as the "dictatorship of the proletariat." According to Lenin, Marx's formula was a summary of the "historic experience of all revolutions" in the matter of a "complete suppression of all the exploiters as well as all the agents of corruption." Every Bolshevik knew that the road to Communism must pass through dictatorship, "but," wrote Lenin in April 1918, "dictatorship is a big word, and big words should not be thrown about carelessly. Dictatorship means an iron rule, a rule that is revolutionarily bold, swift and ruthless in suppressing both exploiters and hooligans. But our rule is excessively mild, frequently resembling jelly more than iron."[70]

The opposition of hard iron to something resembling jelly was central to Bolshevism. The swamp could take many forms and seep into many spaces. The new rulers had to overcome "all manner of weakness, hesitation, and sentimentality" within themselves in order to win the war of an extent and violence hitherto undreamt of. Arosev's friend Skriabin had become "Molotov" (from "hammer"), Sverdlov's housemate Dzhugashvili had become "Stalin" (from "steel"), and Sverdlov himself, in Lunacharsky's words, "had found—probably instinctively—a costume that fit his appearance and inner character: he started going around clad from head to foot in leather." According to Trotsky, "from him, as the central organizing force, that costume, so befitting the temper of the age, spread very widely. The comrades who knew Sverdlov in the underground remember him differently, but in my memory, the figure of Sverdlov will always be covered in black armor."[71]

One comrade who remembered Sverdlov differently was Kira Egon-Besser, who wrote of his "mild humor," his "faith in people," and their embrace when he came back from exile. A year had passed since then.

Once, in the winter, on a gloomy, foggy St. Petersburg day, Yakov Mikhailovich came over to say goodbye before moving to Moscow. My mother and I were at home alone. Yakov Mikhailovich looked tired and thin. I noticed a change in his face. Later, when I looked at the last photographs of him (all photographs distorted his inimitable face, often lit up by a lovely smile), I understood: it was his lips that had changed. They had tightened somehow, and his expression had become stern and preoccupied. The leather jacket he was wearing imparted an unwonted hardness to his appearance. That was our last meeting.[72]

One of Sverdlov's housemates from those days, Varlam Avanesov, had accompanied Sverdlov to Moscow and become a top official of the secret police (among other things). The other, the young Vladimir Volodarsky, had become, according to Lunacharsky, the most hated Bolshevik in Petrograd—not because he was the new regime's chief censor but because he was ruthless. "He was suffused not only with the thunder of October, but also with the thunderous salvoes of the red terror that followed. We should not try to hide this fact: Volodarsky was a terrorist. He was absolutely convinced that if we hesitated to

Sverdlov in 1918

strike our steel blows to the head of the counterrevolutionary hydra, it would devour not only us but the hopes of the world awakened by October. He exulted in struggle and was ready to face any danger, but he was also ruthless. He had something of Marat in him."[73]

Volodarsky was assassinated on June 20, 1918. Sverdlov had arrived in Moscow the previous March, soon after saying goodbye to Kira. On one of his first evenings in the new capital, he appeared in the Moscow Soviet, which still thought of itself as the city's House of Revolution.

> The meeting of the presidium had ended, many of the members had left, and the Soviet had settled into its usual nighttime routine—with telephones ringing, typewriters clattering, executive committee members on duty sitting at their desks, and soldiers from the guard scurrying to and fro.
>
> Suddenly, a man clad from head to foot in a kind of black leather shell arrived on the scene. There was something efficient and vigorous in Sverdlov's trim figure. Small and slender, he looked very young. His gestures and movements were full of energy and vitality, and he had an impressive bass voice.
>
> It was not a very friendly meeting, however. With barely a hello, Yakov Mikhailovich began scolding everyone he found in the Soviet for not taking care of the new arrivals and for their poor choice of buildings and insufficient preparation. The comrades Sverdlov was dressing down were people he had known in exile and had continued to be friends with after October, but that was the kind of person Sverdlov was: business always came first.[74]

"That man," wrote Lunacharsky, "was like a diamond that had to be exceptionally hard because it was the pivot around which an intricate mechanism constantly rotated." That mechanism was the dictatorship of the proletariat, and dictatorship meant "iron rule, a rule that is revolutionarily bold, swift, and ruthless in suppressing both exploiters and hooligans." The exploiters and hooligans, by contrast, were always soft: the fat moneybags, the shuffling old men, the wavering appeasers, and the intellectuals who could not tell ends from beginnings. As Lenin wrote two months after the October takeover, "this sloppiness, carelessness, messiness, untidiness, fidgetiness, the tendency to substitute discussion for action and talk for work, and the tendency to take on everything and accomplish nothing are characteristics of 'the educated,'" most of whom are the "intelligentsia lackeys of yesterday's slaveowners." All these people—non-people, anti-people, enemies of the people—were creatures from under the "murky, dead film" of Voronsky's swamp. Lenin was at his most biblical and "Barebonian" when he talked about "those dregs of humanity, those hopelessly rotten and dead limbs, that contagion, that plague, those ulcers that socialism has inherited from capitalism." The revolution's "single common goal" was "to purge the Russian land of all harmful insects: fleas—thieves, bedbugs—the rich, and so on and so forth."[75]

The first step was to identify the two armies of Armageddon. Speaking at a meeting of the Central Executive Committee on May 20, 1918, Sverdlov said:

> When it comes to the cities, we can say that the Soviet revolutionary rule is strong enough to withstand the various attacks by the bourgeoisie. With regard to the villages, we cannot, by any means, say the same thing. That is why we should seriously consider the question of social differentiation in the village—the question of the creation of two opposing hostile forces; the objective of setting the poorest strata of the peasantry against the kulak elements. Only if we succeed in splitting the village into two irreconcilably hostile camps, only if we succeed in inciting the same civil war that was recently being waged in the cities, . . .—only then will we be able to say that we've done for the village what we've been able to do for the cities.[76]

The next step was to put special seals on their foreheads. In *The Economics of the Transition Period*, Bukharin singled out nine main groups to be subjected to "concentrated violence":

1) the parasitic strata (former landowners, rentiers of all kinds, bourgeois entrepreneurs not directly involved in production; trade capitalists, traders, brokers, bankers);
2) the unproductive administrative aristocracy recruited from the same strata (the top bureaucrats of the capitalist state, generals, archbishops, etc.);
3) the bourgeois entrepreneurs as the organizers and directors (managers of trusts and syndicats, the "operators" of the industrial world, the top engineers, the inventors directly connected to the capitalist world);
4) the skilled bureaucrats—civilian, military, and clerical;

5) the technical intelligentsia and intelligentsia in general (engineers, technicians, agronomists, veterinarians, doctors, professors, lawyers, journalists, most teachers, etc.);
6) the officers;
7) the well-off peasantry;
8) the middle and, in part, petty urban bourgeoisie;
9) the clergy, even the unskilled kind.[77]

"Concentrated violence" included arrests, searches, killings, censorship, forced labor, suppression of strikes, takeover of property, confiscation of produce, and confinement in concentration camps. The targets were identifiable by their marks of social status and defined according to a flexible class taxonomy ultimately derived from the kings who had committed adultery with the Whore of Babylon and the merchants who had grown rich from her excessive luxuries.[78]

One of the earliest mass executions carried out by the Bolsheviks was that of the tsar, his wife, son, four daughters, doctor, cook, maid, and valet on July 17 in a basement in Ekaterinburg. The killings were ordered by Sverdlov, presumably in consultation with Lenin, and supervised in Ekaterinburg by Goloshchekin, who had visited Moscow shortly before (staying with the Sverdlovs, as usual). According to the commander of the firing squad, Mikhail Yurovsky,

> The shooting lasted for a long time, and although I had hoped that the wooden wall would prevent ricocheting, the bullets kept bouncing off of it. For a long time I was unable to stop the shooting, which had become disorderly. But when I finally managed to stop it, I saw that many of them were still alive. For example, Doctor Botkin lay on his side, leaning on his right elbow, as if he were resting. I finished him off with a shot from my revolver. Aleksei, Tatiana, Anastasia, and Olga were still alive, too. Demidova was also alive. Comrade Ermakov tried to finish them off with his bayonet, but was not able to. Only later did the reason become clear (the daughters were wearing diamond breast plates, sort of like brassieres). I had to shoot them one by one.[79]

According to another executioner, "The last to fall was [Demidova], who tried to defend herself with a little pillow she had in her hands. The former heir continued to show signs of life for a very long time, even though he had been shot many times. The youngest daughter of the former tsar fell down on her back and pretended to be dead. When Comrade Ermakov noticed this, he killed her with a shot to the chest. He stood on her arms and shot her in the chest."[80]

A third member of the firing squad had run up to the attic to look out of the window. "Having come down from the attic to the place of execution, I told them that the shots and the howling of the dogs could be heard all over the city; that lights had gone on in the Mining Institute and in the house next to it; and that the shooting had to stop and the dogs, killed. After that, the shooting stopped, and three of the dogs were hanged, but the fourth, Jack, remained quiet, so he was not touched." Goloshchekin waited outside. According to another executioner, when the body of the tsar was brought out on a blanket, he leaned over to take a look. Then "a Red Army soldier brought out Anastasia's lapdog on his bayonet . . . and threw the dog's corpse next to the tsar's. 'Dogs deserve a dog's death,' said Goloshchekin contemptuously."[81]

The White Army investigators who arrived on the scene several days later inspected the blood-stained wallpaper in the basement and found the inscription:

> Belsatzar ward in selbiger Nacht
> Von seinen Knechten umgebracht.
> ["Belsatzar" was, that night,
> Killed by his own knights.]

The lines come from Heinrich Heine's poem "Belsazar" (Belsazar ward aber in selbiger nacht / Von seinen Knechten umgebracht). The person who left the inscription dropped the *aber* ("but"), presumably so the lines could stand on their own, and added the "t" in "Belsazar," perhaps to draw attention to the pun or, possibly, because German was not his native language. It is also possible that Goloshchekin, who was probably better read than the other participants, shared his friend's love of Heine. The poem is based on the biblical story of the Babylonian king Belshazzar (Balthazar), who had offended God by drinking wine from gold and silver goblets taken from the temple in Jerusalem. A disembodied human hand put an end to the feast by writing an inscription (the original "writing on the wall") prophesying the end of the king and his realm. Belshazzar was slain that night.[82]

In his diary, Trotsky claims to have heard about the execution after the fall of Ekaterinburg:

> In a conversation with Sverdlov, I asked in passing:
>   "So what about the tsar?"
>   "It's over," he said. "He's been shot."
>   "And the family?"
>   "The family, too."
>   "All of them?" I asked, probably with a note of surprise.
>   "All of them!" answered Sverdlov. "What of it?"[83]

Mikhail Koltsov's essay on the fate of the tsar begins with a reference to his essay on the fall of tsarism: "The spring flood is huge. It threatens to inundate an entire Moscow suburb. The rivers will rise mightily and carry the tired winter dirt toward the seas. Well-rested after many winters, having finally slept its fill, Russia is languidly stretching its limbs. . . . It was during just such a mighty and tempestuous spring that the snow melted one day in Petrograd and dissolved, without a trace, the 'most autocratic tsars of all Russia.'" Although, as Koltsov goes on to argue, there had been nothing left to dissolve. The vanquished evil had been everywhere and nowhere. "There was a regime. And besides the regime? Nothing. Nothing at all. Zero. Just like in Gogol's 'The Nose': 'a smooth, empty place.' It was not for nothing that the late historian M. N. Pokrovsky used to write the name 'Romanov' in quotation marks. . . . Quotation marks. Nothing in the quotation marks. An empty quote. Like a winter coat without a person inside."

The essay goes on to describe the late tsar as both winter dirt and nothing at all, both a cruel tyrant and a smooth, empty place. The conclusion, too, combines a victor's glee with an ironist's shrug:

> The Justice Minister of the Kolchak government, S. Starynkevich, sent a telegram to the allied council in Paris about the results of the investigation into the death of Nicholas and the location of his remains:
>
> "Eighteen versts from Ekaterinburg, some peasants uncovered a pile of ashes, which contained: a suspender buckle, four corset frames, and a finger, with regards to which doctors mentioned that the nail was very well groomed, and that it belonged to the hand of a well-bred person."
>
> That's it. All that's left. Of Nicholas. Of the Romanovs. Of the symbol that crowned a three-hundred-year-old order of unbearable oppression in a great country.
>
> In this early, powerful, and ardent spring, who in Russia will remember the pile of ashes outside Ekaterinburg? Who will give another thought to Nicholas?
>
> No one. Who would they remember? Someone who was not even there?[84]

In fact, 42 gold objects, 107 silver objects, 34 objects made of fur, and 65 other items classified as valuables were delivered to the Kremlin by Yurovsky, the commander of the execution squad. Some other property of the family was taken out of Ekaterinburg by train, in two special cars. When the Whites arrived, they found 88 items, including Alexei's diary and cross, in the apartment of one of the guards. The guard was discovered when someone recognized his dog as Alexei's spaniel Joy (not Jack), the dog that had not barked. Around 140 more items were found in other private apartments. Among the family things that no one had taken were sixty icons and about fifty books, mostly Christian devotional tracts. The finger found by the investigators was judged to have belonged to a middle-aged woman, and to have been cut off with a sharp blade.[85]

5

THE LAST BATTLE

On August 30, 1918, the head of the Petrograd Cheka, Moisei Uritsky, was assassinated. Later that day, Lenin was shot and wounded at a factory rally in Trans-Moskva. That same night, Sverdlov wrote an appeal "To all Soviets of Workers', Peasants', and Red Army Deputies, to all the armies, to all, all, all." The appeal, published in *Pravda* the next day, put the blame on the Right SRs and other "hirelings of the English and the French," and promised that the working class would respond to the attempts on the life of its leaders "with merciless mass terror against all the enemies of the revolution." On September 2, the Central Executive Committee adopted Sverdlov's resolution "On the Attempt on the Life of V. I. Lenin," which formally announced "mass red terror against the bourgeoisie and its agents."[1]

Sverdlov looked particularly "severe" during this period. According to Novgorodtseva, "he seemed even firmer, even more determined and focused than usual." He moved into Lenin's office in the Kremlin and took over the chairmanship of the Council of People's Commissars (while remaining in charge of the Central Executive Committee and the Party secretariat). He was present at the first interrogations of the accused shooter, Fannie Kaplan (conducted by Yurovsky, among others). The next day, Kaplan was moved from the Cheka headquarters to a basement room beneath the Sverdlovs' apartment in the Kremlin. The children were at the dacha in Kuntsevo at the time. On September 3, the commandant of the Kremlin, Pavel Malkov, was summoned by Sverdlov's deputy, Varlam Avanesov, and ordered to shoot Kaplan.[2]

"When?" I asked briskly.

In Varlam Aleksandrovich's face, usually so kind and friendly, not a muscle trembled.

"Today. Without delay."

Then, after a minute's silence:

"And where, do you think?"

I pondered for a moment and said:

"Perhaps in the courtyard of the Mechanized Detachment, in the blind alley."

"Good."

"Where do we bury her?"

Avanesov looked thoughtful.

"We hadn't considered that. We must ask Yakov Mikhailovich."

The two men walked over to Sverdlov's office, where Avanesov repeated Malkov's question.

Yakov Mikhailovich looked at Avanesov, then at me. He slowly rose and, resting his hands heavily on the desk as if crushing something beneath them, leaned forward a bit and said, firmly and distinctly:

"We are not going to bury Kaplan. The remains are to be destroyed without a trace."

Malkov went back to his office to fetch several "Latvian communists."

I ordered the commander of the Mechanized Detachment to roll out several trucks and start the engines and to park a car in the alley facing the gate. After placing two Latvians at the gate and ordering them not to let anybody in, I went to get Kaplan. Several minutes later I led her into the courtyard of the Mechanized Detachment.

. . . "[Walk over] to the car!" I ordered curtly, pointing toward the car parked in the alley.

Her shoulders twitching, Fannie Kaplan took one step, then another. . . . I raised my revolver.[3]

■ ■ ■

The killing of Fannie Kaplan, announced in the newspapers as an execution carried out "by Cheka decree," formally launched the Red Terror against the "bourgeoisie and its agents." As Malkov claims to have thought on his way out of Avanesov's office, "the Red Terror is not an empty word, not just a threat. There'll be no mercy for the enemies of the Revolution!" The main forms of "social defense" were mass executions, mostly of random hostages. The main selection criterion was class belonging, manifested (or not) in antigovernment actions and opinions. The main markers of class belonging were in the eye of the beheader: Bukharin had listed nine categories of external enemies, including the "intelligentsia in general," and one open-ended category of proletarians who required "coercive discipline" to the degree that they lacked "coercive self-discipline" ("the less voluntary inner discipline there is, the greater the coercion").[4]

There were no people in Russia who considered themselves to be "the bourgeoisie and its agents" and no armies or individuals who considered such a cause worth fighting for, but there was one group that combined a sense of social superiority with distinctive myths, uniforms, and institutions to allow for some coincidence of identification and self-identification: the Cossacks. The Cossacks were, traditionally, a self-governing estate of peasant warriors, who worked the land in the imperial borderlands and served in territorially raised cavalry units employed in frontier defense and regular war duty, as well as, during the last years of the empire, the suppression of internal unrest. At the time of the revolution, the Cossacks were divided into "hosts" that comprised nobles, priests, merchants, and rank-and-file Cossacks, some of whom had little or no land, had seen much service at the front, and were open to the message of millenarian egalitarianism. Most of the Bolsheviks, however, associated the Cossacks with pogroms and violent dispersals of anti-tsarist demonstrations and counted them among the plants that God had not planted. Stalin's 1919 formula seems to have been as reflective of Bolshevik fears and expectations as it was of their experiences: "Who else could become the bastion of the Denikin–Kolchak counterrevolution if not the Cossacks—that centuries-old tool of Russian imperialism, which enjoys special privileges, is organized into a martial estate, and has long exploited the non-Russian peoples of the borderlands?"[5]

The Bolshevik campaign against the Don Cossacks was the greatest single test of the Party's commitment to apocalyptic violence, the most radical application of Marxist class analysis to a named social group, and the most serious challenge to the categorical distinction between class and nation. The fate of the revolution, rhetorically and militarily, seemed to hang in the balance.

The Cossacks themselves were not sure. One of the first anti-Bolshevik uprisings, organized by the Don Cossack government of General Kaledin, failed for lack of popular support. As one of the founders of the White Volunteer Army, General M. Alekseev, wrote on January 27, 1918, "the Cossack regiments returning from the front are in a state of utter moral collapse. The ideas of Bolshevism enjoy wide popularity among the Cossack masses. They do not even want to fight to defend their own territory and property. They are absolutely convinced that Bolshevism is directed exclusively against the wealthy classes, the bourgeoisie, and the intelligentsia, and not against their region."[6] Two days earlier, the leader of the pro-Soviet frontline Cossacks, Lieutenant-Colonel Filipp Mironov, had written an appeal titled "Down with the Civil War on the Banks of the Don":

> *Socialism* believes that only because of private property are there people who have large fortunes. That is why *socialism*, in order to put an end to such things, demands the abolition of private property. . . .
>
> Citizen Cossacks! We are all socialists, except that we don't understand it and don't want to understand it out of obstinacy. Did not Christ, whose teaching we profess, think about the happiness of mankind? Was it not for the sake of this happiness that he died on the cross? . . .
>
> Socialists, like Christian believers, are divided into many schools and parties. . . . But remember one thing: *the ultimate goal of all*

these parties is the remaking of society in accordance with the princi-
ples of socialism.

It is toward this goal that various parties are taking different roads.

For example. The Party of Popular Socialists says: we will have given the people land and freedom and rights before 50 years have passed.

The Party of the Right Socialist Revolutionaries says: we will have given the people land and freedom and rights before 35 years have passed.

The Party of the Left Socialist Revolutionaries says: we will have given the people land and freedom and rights before 20 years have passed.

The Party of the Social-Democrats-Mensheviks says: we will have given the people land and freedom and rights before 10 years have passed.

But the Party of the Social-Democrats-Bolsheviks says: You can go to hell with your promises. The people should get the land, the freedom, the rights, and the power *right now*, not in 10, 20, 35 or 50 years!

Everything to the working people, everything at once![7]

After several months of socialism, the Cossacks rebelled again. This time (in the spring and summer of 1918), the Cossack elite was more uni-fied, outside help (from the advancing Germans) more effective, and forc-ible mass mobilization, more successful. The battle-cry of General Kras-nov's anti-Bolshevik "All-Great Don Host" was "the Don for the Don Cossacks." Don peasants who were not Cossacks were equated with the "Bolsheviks," and Don Cossacks who were pro-Bolshevik (about one-fifth of all Cossacks under arms) were considered non-Cossacks. Mass searches, executions, and expulsions were conducted accordingly. "Ter-ror" came in more than one color.[8]

Most participants in the Russian Civil War viewed political choices as expressions of social interests, identified social interests with "class" be-longing, consigned alien classes to history's trash heap, and saw local con-flicts as fronts of a single war. The Bolsheviks emerged victorious because their sociology was all-encompassing, their apocalypse inescapable, their leader infallible, their "address" unquestioned, their "record-keeping" un-matched, and their commitment to violence by numbers, absolute. Presid-ing over both the records and the violence was the man around whom "the intricate mechanism of the dictatorship of the proletariat constantly rotated."

On November 26, 1918, Sverdlov sent out a Central Committee circular letter to all the Party members: "Today, the Red Terror on the Southern Front is more necessary than it has ever been anywhere or anyplace—not only against direct traitors and saboteurs, but also against all cowards, self-seekers, aiders, and abetters. Not a single crime against the revolutionary military spirit and discipline will remain unpunished." The improvement in Red Army discipline coincided with the withdrawal of the German troops and the collapse of the All-Great Don Host. As entire Cossack units were surrendering, Sverdlov wrote to the head of the political department of the Southern Front, Iosif Khodorovsky, that the release of prisoners was "absolutely impermissible." "Organize concentration camps immediately. Make use of any mines or pits for the prisoners to work in, in their capacity as such." The next task was to dispose of the rest of the Cossack population. On January 24, 1919, Sverdlov's Orgburo issued a secret circular on how to proceed.[9]

> Considering the experience of the civil war against the Cossacks we must recognize that the only correct strategy is a merciless struggle against the whole Cossack elite by means of their total extermination. No compromises, no halfway measures are permissible. Therefore it is necessary:
>
> 1. To conduct mass terror against the rich Cossacks, exterminating them totally; to conduct merciless mass terror toward all the Cossacks who participated, directly or indirectly, in the struggle against Soviet power. With regard to the middle Cossacks, measures must be taken that would preclude any further attempts on their part to rise against Soviet power.[10]

Other mandated measures included the confiscation of grain and "all other agricultural products," the mass resettlement of non-Cossacks in Cossack areas, and the execution of all Cossacks found to possess weapons after the "total disarmament" deadline.

Interpretations varied. Given the Don Host's universal mobilization and requisitioning policies, the entire Cossack population had participated, directly or indirectly, in the struggle against the Soviet order. The determination of who was eligible for extermination was left to the local officials. The Revolutionary Council of the Southern Front, led by Khodorovsky, ordered the immediate execution of

(a) every single Cossack who has held a public office, either through election or appointment . . . ;
(b) every single officer of Krasnov's army;
(c) all the active participants in Krasnov's counterrevolution;
(d) every single agent of autocracy who has found refuge in the Don area, from ministers to policemen;
(e) all the active participants in the Russian counterrevolution who have gathered in the Don area;
(f) every single rich Cossack.[11]

At the same time, the Council recommended "intensive political work" among the "middle" Cossacks, "with the purpose of splitting this social group and attracting a part of it to the side of Soviet power." The less conciliatory Don Bureau of the Party's Central Committee advocated indiscriminate violence by means of mass hostage-taking and the execution of hostages along with the owners of hidden weapons. A member of the Revolutionary Council of the Eighth Army, Iona Yakir, ordered "the extermination of a certain percentage of the entire male population."[12]

Local officials tended to err on the side of more resolute action. According to a Trans-Moskva Bolshevik assigned to the Khoper District, members of the local revolutionary tribunal "were executing illiterate old men and women who could barely move their feet, Cossack corporals, and, of course, the officers, saying that they were following orders from the center. On some days, they killed groups of 50–60 people." The Morozov District chairman later claimed that, having received a telegram urging a "more energetic . . . implementation of the dictatorship of the proletariat," he "got drunk to dull the pain, walked over to the jailhouse, picked up a list of prisoners, summoned them by number one by one, and executed the first sixty-four of them."[13] According to another Moscow Bolshevik sent to the Khoper District,

> Executions were carried out during the daytime in plain view of the whole village. Groups of 30 to 40 people were led—with shouts, jeers, and insults—to the place of execution. At the place of execution, the convicted were stripped naked—and all this in plain sight of the villagers. When the women attempted to cover their nakedness, they were mocked and forbidden to do so. All the executed were buried in shallow graves by the mill, not far from the village. As a result, a pack of dogs formed by the mill, viciously attacking passers-by and carting off the arms and legs of the executed to various spots around the village.[14]

In mid-March, the Cossacks of the Upper Don rebelled again. According to a report sent to the Central Executive Committee, "the beginning of the uprising centered around one of the villages, which the revolutionary tribunal, consisting of Chairman Marchevsky, a machine gun, and twenty-five armed men, had entered sometime earlier, in order to as Marchevsky vividly put it, 'pass through this village like Carthage.'" On March 16, faced with a serious threat to the rear of the Southern Front, the Central Committee passed a resolution suspending the policy of extermination. "Considering the obvious split between the northern and southern Cossacks and the fact that the northern Cossacks can be of help to us, we are hereby halting the application of anti-Cossack measures and withdrawing our objections to the policy of stratification."[15]

■ ■ ■

The decision to suspend the "de-Cossackization" decree was made in the absence of its author and chief sponsor. In the first week of March, Sverdlov had traveled to Kharkov in order to supervise the election of the Ukrainian Communist Party's central committee. As one of his assistants put it, "by constantly reshuffling the 'left' and 'right,' like pieces on a chessboard, Sverdlov was trying to preserve the unity of the party." On the way back to Moscow, he began feeling sick. His wife, children, and brother Veniamin met him at the station and rushed him home. The Kremlin doctors diagnosed his illness as the Spanish flu. He continued to prepare for the Eighth Party Congress, but his fever kept getting worse and, on March 14, he lost consciousness. "In his delirium," wrote Novgorodtseva, "he kept talking about the Eighth Party Congress and attempting to get out of bed to look for a set of resolutions. He thought the resolutions had been stolen by certain 'Left Communists,' and kept asking us not to let them in, to take the resolutions away from them, to kick them out. He kept calling for our son, in order to tell him something." He died on March 16, the day the de-Cossackization decree was repealed. He was thirty-four years old.[16]

On March 18, Lenin made a speech at a special session of the Central Executive Committee. "In the course of our revolution and its victories," he said, "Comrade Sverdlov succeeded in expressing more fully and consistently than anybody else the most important and fundamental features of the proletarian revolution." Of those features, the most visible was the "resolute and ruthlessly determined annihilation of the exploiters and enemies of the working people," but the most profound and durable was "the organization of the proletarian masses" and total dedication to Party work. "Comrade Sverdlov stood before us as the most perfectly complete type of professional revolutionary, a man who had entirely given up his family and all the comforts and habits of the old bourgeois society, a man who had devoted himself heart and soul to the revolution. . . . The illegal circles, the revolutionary underground work, the illegal Party, which nobody personified or expressed more fully than Yakov Sverdlov—such was the practical school through which he had passed, the only path that could have allowed him to reach the position of the first man in the first socialist Soviet Republic."[17]

In the heat of revolutionary struggle, few things were as important as "absolutely unquestionable moral authority, the kind that derives its strength not from some abstract morality, of course, but from the morality of the revolutionary fighter." Sverdlov had such authority. "One word from him was enough to be sure, on his say-so alone, without any debates or formal votes, that a particular problem would be settled once and for all."

(Or, as Osinsky put it two days later in a speech on "bureaucratism," "the Central Committee did not, in fact, exist as a collegial organ.... Comrades Lenin and Sverdlov made all the decisions by talking to each other and to certain other comrades who represented particular branches of the Soviet apparatus.") Great revolutions, in Lenin's view,

> develop talents that would have been unthinkable before.... No one could have believed that from the school of illegal circles and under- ground work, the school of one small, persecuted Party and the Tu- rukhansk prison, would emerge an organizer of such absolutely un- challenged authority, the organizer of the whole Soviet order throughout Russia, the man, unique in his knowledge, who orga- nized the work of the Party that created the Soviets and established the Soviet government, which is embarking on its arduous, painful, bloody but triumphant procession to all nations, to all the countries of the world.[18]

A year later, Kira Egon-Besser and her parents visited Novgorodtseva in the Kremlin. "When she saw us, Klavdia Timofeevna, usually a very calm and reserved person, began to cry. For several minutes, we stood in silence in the room in which Yakov Mikhailovich had died, though in our memo- ries he would always be alive."[19]

Meanwhile, Sverdlov's legacy in "the Russian Vendée" was still in ques- tion. On the day the de-Cossackization decree was repealed, the Revolu- tionary Council of the Southern Front ordered "(a) the burning of all in- surgent villages; (b) the merciless execution of every single person who has taken a direct or indirect part in the uprising; (c) the execution of every fifth or tenth adult male resident in all rebellious villages; and (d) the mass taking of hostages in villages located near the rebellious ones" (among other things). The next day, Iona Yakir and Yakov Vesnik, on behalf of the Revolutionary Council of the Eighth Army, ordered the total anni- hilation of all those connected to the uprising, "including the extermina- tion of a certain percentage of the village population." Trotsky agreed. "The nests of these dishonest traitors and betrayers must be destroyed," he wrote in his May 25 order for a general counteroffensive. "These Cains must be exterminated."[20]

But the real question was what to do next. The Don Bureau, led by Ser- gei Syrtsov, argued consistently that "radical reprisals" (as Syrtsov put it in conversation with Yakir) should be followed by a final solution: "The complete, immediate, and decisive annihilation of the Cossacks as a spe- cific cultural and economic group, the destruction of its economic founda- tions; the physical elimination of all Cossack bureaucrats and officers, generally of the whole Cossack elite and any actively counterrevolutionary Cossacks, as well as the dispersal and neutralization of the rank-and-file Cossacks and the formal liquidation of the Cossackry."[21]

Another prominent member of the Don Bureau, Aron Frenkel, agreed with the overall goal but argued (in a report to the Eighth Party Congress in March 1919) that the timing and priorities would have to change:

The terrorist method of physical extermination of as many Cossacks as possible cannot be effective alone while there is still no iron Soviet rule in the Don Area because it will be impossible to annihilate all the Cossacks, and, under such conditions, the uprisings will continue. The solution is to accompany this method with more radical terrorist methods, indicated in the original Central Committee resolution but so far not implemented, such as: the expropriation of the Cossacks (de-Cossackization), their mass resettlement in the Russian hinterland, and the settlement of immigrant working elements in their place.[22]

By August 1919, when the Don area, along with the rest of southern Russia and Ukraine, was lost to the Whites, Frenkel broke with Syrtsov and abandoned the goal of physical extermination. "I consider correct the change in the Central Committee's Don policy. . . . The estate struggle between the Cossacks and the peasants (outlanders) in the Don area should, in my opinion, be conducted within the framework of class struggle, and not as an amorphous zoological struggle." No one argued against terror as such; no one could argue against terror and remain a Bolshevik. The debate was over the appropriate targets of terror—or, in this case, over the social nature of the Cossacks as a caste. The two options had been clearly formulated by Sverdlov: "inciting civil war" versus the "total extermination of the rich." The choice depended on whether some Don Cossacks were poor enough not to be considered rich.[23]

Valentin Trifonov, the commissar of the Special Expeditionary Corps for the suppression of the Upper-Don uprising, believed that they were. In a report sent to the Central Committee Orgburo on June 10 (and forwarded to Trotsky on July 5), he called the policy of indiscriminate terror "outrageously careless and criminally thoughtless." Every Marxist knew, he argued, that consciousness was determined by social being; the social being of the northerners was radically different from that of the southerners; ergo, "there was more than enough justification for the policy of splitting the Cossacks and fomenting the ancient hostility felt by the north toward the dominant south." Right now, what was needed for the conversion of all redeemable Cossacks was "skillful agitation and propaganda" that would "uncover all the dark aspects of Cossack life (there are many of them) and, through the practice of Soviet construction, demonstrate all the bright aspects of the new life." Finally, it was "absolutely imperative for the Don Area that it be governed by comrades with Russian names."[24]

Trifonov, who was thirty-one at the time, was born a Cossack (in a village in a southern district) but was orphaned at the age of seven and

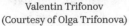

Valentin Trifonov   Filipp Mironov
(Courtesy of Olga Trifonova)   (Courtesy of Olga Trifonova)

worked in a railroad depot in Maikop before moving to Rostov and joining
the Bolsheviks at sixteen. Most of his prerevolutionary life was spent in
prisons and exile, including three years in the Turukhansk region. His
closest friend and mentor was Aron Solts, whom he met in exile when he
was nineteen and Solts was thirty-five. After his release, Trifonov moved
into the Petrograd apartment of Tatiana Slovatinskaia, where Stalin once
stayed before his own exile to Turukhansk. As a young conservatory student, Slovatinskaia was recruited into the Party by Solts. She was married
before (to Abram Lurye, Solts's cousin) and had two children, but it appears that the people she felt closest to were Solts, her old friend, and
Trifonov, her common-law husband. Trifonov was nine years younger than
Slovatinskaia. In February 1917, he was, according to his son, "in the whirlpool of Tauride Palace." During the October Revolution, he was one of the
commanders of the Red Guard in Petrograd.[25]

Trifonov's mention of "comrades with Russian names" referred to the
Cossack rebels' attempts to distinguish between "Soviet power" and "Jewish Communists." This was, in part, the tribal version of the "two hostile
camps," but it was also a reaction to what the Cossack socialist Filipp
Mironov called a regime "headed for the most part by young men of eighteen to twenty who can't even speak Russian properly." This was an exaggeration (the head of the local regime and the most persistent advocate
of indiscriminate terror against the Cossacks was Sergei Syrtsov, who
came from nearby Slavgorod), but it is true that many of the Bolshevik
commanders in the "Russian Vendée" were young men from the former
Jewish Pale of Settlement. Aron Frenkel and Yakov Vesnik were both
twenty-five, and Iona Yakir was twenty-three. Iosif Khodorovsky, at
thirty-five, was from the same generation as Sverdlov (as was Grigory
Sokolnikov, the most persistent opponent of indiscriminate terror against
the Cossacks).[26]

The government officials in Moscow were not sure whose advice to
follow. The Council of People's Commissars did order a mass transfer of

peasants to the Don Area, but the Whites continued to advance, and most of the settlers were stuck in overcrowded railway stations along the way. In early June 1919, when things at the front became desperate, Trotsky recalled Filipp Mironov from honorary exile in Serpukhov (where he had been sent at the request of the Don Bureau during the extermination campaign) and put him in charge of the Don Expeditionary Corps, with Valentin Trifonov as his commissar. Mironov issued several appeals ("Can Anti-Semitic and Pogrom Agitation Be Permitted in the First Socialist Republic in the World?"; "Should a Red Army Soldier, a Soldier of the People's Army, Be Allowed to Refuse an Order?"), but within a short time the Don Area had been lost, the Expeditionary Corps dissolved, and Mironov sent to Saransk to form a regular Cossack Corps. Trifonov refused to "participate in the creation of units that will conquer the Don Area in order to defend it later from Soviet Russia." In a letter to Solts, he called Trotsky a "completely inept organizer" and Mironov, an "adventurer."[27]

■   ■   ■

Filipp Mironov was an adventurer insofar as he was a prophet of a different revelation. The swamp and flood produced many who, "whether within or without temples, assumed the motions and gestures of inspired persons." When one of them proved his authenticity by moving into the house of government, all the others became adventurers. The choice they faced was to oust Lenin from the Kremlin, build their own house of government, or accept the truth of Bolshevism and renounce all claim to a separate prophetic vision.

Mironov tried all three possibilities. A forty-seven-year-old native of the Ust-Medveditskaia District and a much-decorated veteran of the Russo-Japanese and "imperialist" wars, he thought of himself as the voice and conscience of the "working Cossacks." The Bolsheviks thought of him in the same way—and treated him accordingly, depending on what they thought of the working Cossacks. Some believed that a Soviet Cossack corps was a necessary condition for reconquering the Don Area; others believed that the whole thing was an act of treason or gullibility. Meanwhile, Mironov sat in Saransk waiting for men and supplies, feuding with the local commissars (who kept warning Moscow of his unreliability), and trying to find out what had happened on the Don in his absence. Having been told about "Cain's work done in the name of the government," he wrote a letter to Lenin: "I cannot be silent anymore, for I cannot watch the people suffer for the sake of something abstract and remote. . . . The entire operation of the Communist Party over which you preside is aimed at the extermination of the Cossacks, the extermination of humanity as a whole."

He was still for the "social revolution," understood as "the transfer of power from one class to another." He was still awaiting the true "apostles of communism," who would bring to the people the gift of "the means of production." But the Communists had gotten it backward: "We haven't even built the foundation yet, . . . but here we are, in a hurry to build the house (communism). Our house is like the one Jesus spoke of when he said, 'the winds blew away the sand, the stilts fell down, and the house collapsed.' It collapsed because there was no foundation, just the stilts." "Building" had become the central metaphor for reaching communism. Communism, like government and revolution, was a house. The building of the house of communism, according to Mironov, required "many decades" of "patient and painstaking example-setting. . . . I will not give in to the insanity that has only now revealed itself to me, and I will fight against the annihilation of the Cossacks and middle peasants with whatever strength I have left. Only now have I come to understand the devilish plan of the Communists, and I curse the day when, out of naïveté, I defended their position."[28]

The next day, on August 1, 1919, Mironov wrote that his slogans were: "Down with the Autocracy of the Commissars and the Bureaucratism of the Communists!"; "Long Live the Soviets of Workers', Peasants', and Cossack Deputies, Elected on the Basis of Free Socialist Agitation!"; and "Down with the Ruthless Extermination of the Cossacks Proclaimed by the Jew Trotsky-Bronstein!" Then a week later, on August 8, he applied to join the Communist Party, citing his belief in Soviet power and the abolition of private property, as well as his desire to dispel "the atmosphere of slander that makes it difficult to breathe." A few days later, after his application had been rejected by his commissars, Mironov wrote the program of a new party he called the "Party of Workers, Peasants, and Cossacks":

Listen, all you Russian workers, rouse your conscience and let it tell you if you should continue to support the bloody Communists, who, having finished with the Cossacks, will move on to the middle peasants, because they consider real human beings merely a means to fulfill their program. For them there are no individuals, just class, and no human beings, just humanity, so go ahead and build your commune at the cost of loving your neighbor for the sake of loving the stranger. In short, exterminate present-day human beings for the happiness of the humanity of the future. . . .

If this is socialism, then anyone who still has some conscience should turn away from this horror.

Bent on provoking the Cossacks into counterrevolution by means of arbitrary violence and animated by sheer malice rather than compassion for their ignorance, the Communist Party, or rather, some of its leaders, have set themselves the goal of exterminating the Cossacks.

Having set two categories of people against each other, they are laughing at the Russian, the "goy" who is choking on his own blood.

Is this not why the Russian village has come to hate the Communists?

Is this not why there are so many deserters?

Free speech has died all over Russia.[29]

On August 15, one of Mironov's commissars wrote to the Central Committee and to the Southern Front that "the political backwardness and benighted consciousness" of the Cossacks, along with their privileged position before the Revolution, "makes it difficult for them to understand and desire progress toward a better world, toward communism." As a consequence, "Mironov's unrestrained agitation is making a big impression on the minds of the Cossacks." The only solution was to stop the formation of the Don Cossack Corps and "disperse the Cossacks among the other divisions."[30]

On the same day, Mironov wrote a personal letter to two friends fighting in the Red Army:

I don't know what to do. My soul cannot reconcile itself to the thought that if we reconquer the Don area, we will see them begin to exterminate our poor, ignorant Cossacks, who will be forced by the cruelty and ferocity of the new Vandals and new Oprichniks to burn their farms and villages. Will our hearts not break at the sight of this infernal vision? Will we ignore the curses of the tormented people?

On the other side are Denikin and the counterrevolution, who stand for the slavery of the working people, against which we have been fighting for a year and must go on fighting until their final destruction.

And so here I am, like the ancient Russian folk warrior, at the crossroads; if you ride to the left, you will lose your horse; if you ride to the right, you will lose your head; if you go straight, you will lose both your horse and your head.[31]

Waiting for her ancient Russian warrior, praying for him, and bearing his child was a twenty-one year-old village schoolteacher and Red Army nurse, Nadezhda Suetenkova. Her love poems dedicated to Mironov were modeled on folk poetry:

I love you like the sun
Looking down brightly
Through an open window.
I love you like the wind
Rustling the steppe grass,
Blowing softly on our faces.
I love you like the waves
Gurgling and frolicking
As they wash our feet.

I love you the way we love
Our brightest hopes:
More than happiness, more than life,
Brighter than the flowers in the forest.[32]

She wrote to him about their love; about his other terrible choice—between her and his wife of many years; and about his sacred mission as a folk warrior and a prophet. "Believe firmly in your destiny and wait patiently for your hour. It will strike."[33]

Your path may be arduous,
But for you it is joyous:
You are weary, and your breast is heavy,
But isn't human happiness the highest of rewards?[34]

On August 19, a special envoy of the Cossack Department of the Central Executive Committee sent a report to Moscow:

Because Mironov has absorbed all the thoughts, moods, and wishes of the popular and peasant masses at this time in the development of the revolution, one cannot help but see in his demands and wishes that Mironov is the anxious, restless soul of the enormous mass of middle peasants and Cossacks, and that, as a man devoted to the social revolution, he is capable, at this last dangerous moment, of inspiring the hesitating mass of peasants and Cossacks to wage a ruthless struggle against counterrevolution. . . .

On the other hand, . . . Comrade Mironov gives the impression of a hunted and desperate man. Fearing arrest or assassination, Mironov has started using bodyguards. The commissars are afraid of Mironov. The Red Army men are agitated and ready to defend Mironov with firepower against any attempt on his life by the commissars.[35]

Two days later, on August 21, one of Mironov's officers, Konstantin Bulatkin, wrote to his former commander, Semen Budennyi: "Comrade Mironov . . . is not only a great strategist and military commander, but also a great prophet. He is under political suspicion because he loves the truth. . . . If he were allowed to form his corps, I swear on my life that as soon as he appeared at the front, the morale would immediately improve and the advantage would be ours." The next day, Mironov ordered his men to get ready. "Remember, you are not alone. The true soul of the tormented people is with you. If you die on the battlefield, you will die for the truth. Jesus Christ has taught us to love the truth and to be ready to die for it."[36]

The following afternoon, Mironov received a call from a member of the Party Central Committee and the Revolutionary Military Council of the

Republic, Ivar Smilga. Smilga was twenty-six years old and the highest-ranking commissar in the Red Army. He was born and grew up in Latvia and joined the Party at the age of fourteen, after his father was executed by a government tribunal. He spent five years studying philosophy and political economy in Siberian exile, before presiding over the October military insurrection in Finland.[37] The call he made to Mironov was transcribed:

> SMILGA. I categorically insist that you not complicate the situation of our armies with your unauthorized actions. . . .
>
> MIRONOV. If you, Comrade Smilga, think as a true statesman, I also categorically insist that you not prevent my going to the front. Only there will I feel fulfilled. I ask you not to stir up tensions. I have made up my mind, seeing the agony of the revolution, and only death will stop me. I want to give my life to save the revolution, which needs my life right now. I repeat, if I am denied, I will lose all faith in the people in power.
>
> SMILGA. Comrade Mironov, nobody is trying to deny you . . . [Mironov interrupts]
>
> MIRONOV. But I will not lose my faith in the idea of the popular masses. I never wanted these things that are happening around me, and the atrocities perpetrated against the Urals Cossacks by the Communist Ermolenko and against the Don Cossacks, by the Don Bureau, have made a deep impression on me. . . .
>
> SMILGA. Moscow is calling about your action. In the name of the Revolutionary Military Council of the Republic, I order you not to send any units to the front without permission.
>
> MIRONOV. I am leaving by myself. I cannot live here because I am being badly insulted.
>
> SMILGA. Come to Penza. The Commander of the Special Group Shorin is here, as is Trifonov. We'll agree on a common plan. Don't create confusion.
>
> MIRONOV. I cannot go to Penza because I cannot be sure of my safety. I could bring my division.
>
> SMILGA. Nothing threatens your safety. I state this officially.
>
> MIRONOV. I ask for permission to bring 150 men as my escort.
>
> SMILGA. Fine. Take 150 men and come right away.
>
> MIRONOV. I ask that you inform the 23rd Division that I am being summoned to Penza, so they know what has happened to me. I entrust myself to you, Comrade Smilga, a man I have profound confidence in.
>
> SMILGA. Set out immediately. I am quite certain that we will sort out all the misunderstandings. I have to go answer a call. Good bye.[38]

Mironov seemed willing to set out immediately, but then changed his mind because someone, he would later claim, had warned him that he was going to be arrested. On August 24, he left for the front at the head of several thousand men, half of them unarmed. "All the so-called deserters are joining me," he wrote, "and will come together as a terrible force before which Denikin will tremble and the Communists will bow their heads." Smilga proclaimed him a traitor and called him "Denikin's lackey." Trotsky called on all "honest citizens" to "shoot him like a rabid dog" and accused him of spreading "a vile rumor that the Soviet government supposedly wants to exterminate the Cossacks." After three weeks of evasive maneuvers, minor skirmishes, and mass defections, Mironov and about five hundred of his men were surrounded by Red Army troops. On September 13, Konstantin Bulatkin wrote to the Red Cavalry Commander Budennyi that Mironov was "a true leader of the revolution" and that "the long-suffering, tormented soul of the people was with him." The next day, Mironov, Bulatkin, and their men surrendered to Budennyi without a fight. Budennyi ordered Mironov's execution, but Trotsky decided to stage a show trial for "educational" purposes. In a special *Pravda* article, he agreed with Bulatkin's characterization but revealed its true sociological meaning. There were the Cossack elites hostile to the proletariat, the Cossack proletarians loyal to the Soviet government, and "the broad intermediary stratum of middle Cossacks, politically still very backward." Mironov embodied "the confusions and waverings of the backward middle Cossack."[39]

One of the first things Mironov did after his capture was to ask the Extraordinary Investigative Commission to legalize his common-law marriage with Nadezhda Suetenkova, "in order to give a name to the child that she is expecting." In his prison diary, he wrote: "My spirit is floating in space, free; Nadezhda's free spirit is next to it."[40]

One of the first things that Konstantin Bulatkin did after his arrest was to deny his prophet. In a letter to Lenin and Trotsky, he wrote: "Great Leaders of the proletariat and Apostles of the world Commune, I am not a Mironovite, I am the knee over which Mironov tripped before falling, as he himself will confirm. Read my confession that I have submitted to the head of the Political Department of the Ninth Army, Comrade Poluian. For two years now, I have been an armed servant of Yours and of the Commune. I am boundlessly devoted to it and, in its name, beg You not to allow a fateful mistake that would doom my life." At the trial, according to a newspaper report, Bulatkin "tried to put all the blame on Mironov, whom he had allegedly followed with the only purpose of killing the traitor." According to the same report, Mironov "conducted himself calmly and with dignity."[41]

At Trotsky's request, the role of public prosecutor was given to Smilga, and that of presiding judge, to Smilga's brother-in-law, the Kuban Cossack, Dmitry Poluian. Mironov pleaded guilty and cited his state of mind as the reason for his words and actions:

> MIRONOV. When, after the October coup, I took the side of the Soviet government, Krasnov called me a traitor, while I, in the Don Area, was tirelessly explaining to the Cossacks the nature of the new order as an order in which all the working people would partici-

pate. Listening to me, the Cossacks agreed and eagerly joined the Soviet side. So when I saw all the crimes and atrocities being perpetrated by the Communists in the Don Area, I felt like a traitor to all those people I had talked into serving the Soviet government. I believed that Trotsky was the initiator of such a policy toward the Don Area, and I felt bad that the center viewed the Cossack question in that light, but, when I called Trotsky "Bronstein," I did not mean to stir up national hatred.

PRESIDING JUDGE. Did you attribute that policy to Trotsky as a political leader or a Jew?

MIRONOV. As a Jew, and I admit my mistake.

The defense of most of the accused was that they had followed Mironov. The defense of Mironov was that he had been blinded by emotion. "Of course I acted irrationally, but do understand my state of mind and the atmosphere that I was surrounded by for seven months. I feel bad that I did not fulfill your order and left for the front, but believe me that I had no ill intentions and that everything I did, I did in order to strengthen the Soviet order."[42]

In his speech, Smilga claimed that Mironov was a rooster, not an eagle or a folk hero. Mature leaders understood "the objectives of their class"; Mironov, on the other hand, was a "political runt" who had produced the "most confused and nebulous ideology" in the history of the revolution. Mironov's vision of the future state was a "semi-Tolstoyan, semi-sentimental melodrama" because he did not understand that "the path to socialism has to pass through a dictatorship of the oppressed over the oppressor." The meaning and essence of the revolution was "the struggle between two extremes: the working class, Communist Party, and Soviet Government on the one hand, and the bourgeois counterrevolution, on the other." Owing to the "inexorable iron logic of things," all attempts at appeasement and conciliation led to Denikin and counterrevolution. There was only one truth, one true evil, and one force that "would come out victorious from this terrible, colossal struggle." As for the Communist atrocities, they had, indeed, taken place, but most of those responsible had already been executed and, according to Communist teachings, atrocities as such meant nothing at all:

Recall the French Revolution and the struggle between the Vendée and the National Convention. You will see that the troops of the Convention committed terrible acts—terrible from the point of view of a particular human being. But the acts committed by the troops of the Convention can only be understood in the light of class analysis. They are justified by history because they were committed by a progressive class that was sweeping its path clean of the survivals of feudalism and popular ignorance. The same thing is happening today. You, too, should have understood this. You are talking about

Marx, but I dare say you have not read a single line by him. The quotations you use do you no credit. You should be more humble about quoting authors whose work you are not familiar with.

Smilga concluded by saying that "the litter of petit bourgeois ideology must be swept off the road of the Revolution" and that Mironov and his followers must be punished "without pity." He asked for the death sentence for Mironov and his officers and for the execution of every tenth soldier from Mironov's personal escort and every twentieth soldier from the rest of the rebel army.[43]

In his final statement, Mironov accepted the "student"-worker relationship suggested by Smilga and admitted to being "an experienced fighter, but a politically backward person incapable of understanding all the subtleties of politics and Party questions." He was, it is true, unfamiliar with the works of Marx, but in his prison cell he had read a book about "the social movement in France" and had found a scholarly name for people like him:

People who lack scientific knowledge but seek justice with their heart and their emotions are called "empirical socialists." That is exactly what I am, that is my undoing, and I ask the revolutionary tribunal to take that into account. . . . I am not even talking about how I grew up and what my childhood years were like. Wearing a uniform that was not my own and eating dinner from a kitchen that was not my own made me understand the misery and burden of poverty. You can see for yourselves that I spent my whole life trying to help the people, to ease their suffering. I came from the people myself and I understand their needs very well and have never abandoned the people from the first days of the revolution until now.

Mironov's last words were: "My life is a cross, and if I must carry it to Calvary, I will, and, whether you believe it or not, I will shout 'Long live the social revolution, long live the Commune and Communism!'"[44]

The court, in the person of Poluian and his two assistants, sentenced Mironov and ten of his officers to be shot within twenty-four hours. Mironov asked the court to allow the condemned to spend their last night together. He also asked for some paper and ink. Both wishes were granted.[45]

Back in prison, Mironov wrote a letter to his former wife, asking her to forgive him and to bless their children "for the hard life to come," and a long letter to Nadezhda, telling her that he had never betrayed the revolution; that he believed in the Commune and the Communists ("not the kind that spread bile through the body

Ivar Smilga

of the people, but the kind that are like a spring in the desert, for which the weary soul of the people is reaching out"); that she had made him "the happiest of mortals—even at the moment of death"; and that his only regret was that he would not get to see their child.[46]

In his diary, he wrote:

> At our request, they have brought us to a common cell, the same one in which we were interrogated. Those sentenced to death are gathered together. The psychology of the condemned has been described in Andreev's story about seven hanged men. But we have some stronger men among us. . . .
>
> Everyone has been trying to find something else to think about, to banish the thought of our imminent and, from the point of view of the crowd, inglorious end. We have sung songs, one man has danced, etc., but it is the walls that have taken most of the punishment: it is our attempt to justify ourselves in the eyes of the inevitable.
>
> "I have just finished talking to God . . ."—"Man, prepare yourself for death: in a few hours, you must die. Cleanse your soul and your conscience, and come to Me, so I can ask you—did you fulfill the mission that I gave you when I sent you down to earth?" 7/X-1919 (eight hours before the execution), F. Mironov.

Some time later, he wrote:

> This is not the kind of fear of death when, in the heat of the battle, amidst the rattling of machine guns, the buzzing of bullets, and the screeching of shells a man is playing with danger because he knows that his death is a matter of chance. He accepts death as a possibility. In battle, death is not frightening: one moment and it's over. What is terrible for the human soul is the awareness of an imminent, inescapable death, when there is no hope for another chance and when you know that nothing in the world can stop the approaching end, when there is less and less time before the terrible moment, and when finally they tell you: "your grave is ready."[47]

The verdict was read on October 7 at 3:00 a.m. Several hours later, Trotsky wrote to Smilga that, given Mironov's behavior at the trial, it might be expedient to pardon him. "The slowness of our advance into the Don Area requires concentrated political action with the objective of splitting up the Cossacks. In order to accomplish this mission, perhaps we could use Mironov, summoning him to Moscow after the sentencing and then pardoning him by a Central Executive Committee decision on condition that he go behind the lines and start a rebellion there." Trotsky had begun to reconsider the Party's Cossack policy around the time Mironov

Ivar Smilga and Valentin Trifonov (Courtesy of Olga Trifonova)

was captured in mid-September. It is impossible to know whether he staged the whole trial in order to pardon Mironov in the end, for "educational purposes."[48]

Smilga seemed happy to oblige. In a conversation with Trifonov the same day, he said that he "did not consider the killing of Mironov and his comrades useful." As he explained later, "the pardoning of a middle peasant—such was the political meaning of this trial." The Politburo promptly voted to stay the execution. On the night of October 8, Smilga entered the cell of the condemned and told them of the decision. According to Smilga's recollections, Mironov, whose hair had turned completely gray overnight, "sobbed like a child and solemnly vowed to dedicate the rest of his strength to fighting for the Soviet order."[49] On October 11, while still in prison, Mironov wrote an appeal to the Don Cossacks:

> Our old, silver-haired Don has lived through untold horrors.
> Because of the backwardness and ignorance of its sons, it is turning into a desert.
> Brother Cossacks! The killed, executed, and tortured people on both sides cannot be resurrected. It is beyond the ability of human beings. But the decision to stop more killings and executions is our decision to make. And we must do it, come what may. It is in our hands, it depends on us.
> I am appealing to you, the Cossacks of the Don, as someone who has, in a sense, returned from the other world.
> I am talking to you from beyond the grave, which, empty, has just been filled with earth behind me:
> Enough. *Enough!* Come to your senses, think hard before it is too late, before everything has been lost, while it is still possible to find a way toward peace with the working people of Russia. . . .
> I say this as a prophet. . . .
> The idea of Communism is sacred.[50]

Two days later, the Orgburo of the Central Committee ordered the Nizhny Novgorod Provincial Party Committee to release Nadezhda Suetenkova from prison, where she was being held as a hostage. Two weeks later, on October 26, 1919, the Politburo resolved to appoint Mironov a member of the Don Executive Committee, publish a revised version of his appeal to the Don Cossacks, and allow him to travel to Nizhny Novgorod "to be with his family." In January 1920, he was admitted to the Communist Party.[51]

In late August 1920, Trotsky appointed Mironov commander of the Second Cavalry Army, and Mironov's former judge, Dmitry Poluian, a member of his Revolutionary Military Council ("let bygones be bygones," he wrote in his telegram). The "Second Cavalry" distinguished itself in the fighting against Wrangel and played an important part in the occupation of Crimea. Mironov was awarded the Order of the Red Banner and, in January 1921, recalled to Moscow. The Civil War was over, the invading armies defeated, the false prophets gone, and the era of "coercive self-discipline" (as Bukharin put it) about to begin.[52]

Mironov and Nadezhda traveled by special train. Their infant daughter had died in the fall, and Nadezhda was pregnant again. At railway stations along the way, Mironov was greeted by large rallies and what he called "mass pilgrimages." In Rostov, he was visited by Smilga, who was then commander of the North Caucasus Front. Before setting off for Moscow, Mironov went to his hometown of Ust-Medveditskaia, where he heard stories of searches, arrests, starvation, food requisitioning, unhappiness among returning Red Army soldiers, and of an armed uprising led by one of his former officers. As Mironov wrote later, "what I heard from the villagers made a strong impression on me. At the front, amidst constant battles, I had no idea of how difficult our country's situation was, but now, having found myself away from the army and among the peasants, I felt great pity in my soul for their condition, because every single one of them had something to complain about." Mironov made several speeches against "false Communists," food requisitioning, and the continued ban on private trade and peasant markets. At a meeting in his house, several of his old friends and one new acquaintance agreed to keep him informed and send coded reports to him in Moscow. The new acquaintance was a secret police agent. On February 12, 1921, Mironov and Nadezhda were arrested and sent to the Butyrki prison in Moscow.[53]

According to Nadezhda, male and female inmates would be taken for walks in the same prison courtyard, but in separate circles. "During one of the walks, I suddenly saw him. We ran up to each other and embraced. I told him about my situation and asked him what I should do. He was pale and agitated, but he told me not to worry and to take care of myself and the baby, whatever happened to him. The guards yelled at us and told us to separate. I was greatly shocked by that meeting, and started having all kinds of terrible thoughts." They saw each other several more times. On March 31, Mironov gave Nadezhda a copy of a letter he had written to

Kalinin, Lenin, Trotsky, and Kamenev, in which he expressed his sense of vindication over the Party's decision, made two weeks earlier, to replace forcible requisitioning with the "new economic policy" (NEP) of legalizing trade. "I remember he asked me to be sure to come to the walk on April 2 because he was hoping to get an answer to his letter by then. But from what I remember, on April 2 the walk was cancelled."[54]

On April 2, the VChK Presidium ordered Mironov's execution. He was shot later that day in the prison courtyard during the scheduled walk in which only he participated. There was no trial and, apparently, no warning. He was spared "the awareness of an imminent, inescapable death, when there is no hope for another chance and when you know that nothing in the world can stop the approaching end." Nadezhda remained in prison for another four months. As one of the investigators put it, "Mironova is guilty insofar as she denies the guilt of her husband, considering his actions only from her point of view." She was never informed of Mironov's fate. On two occasions, she threatened to go on a hunger strike. It is not known whether she ever did. In late August or early September, she gave birth to a baby boy who died "several years later."[55]

6

THE NEW CITY

Most millenarian sects died as sects. Some survived as sects, but stopped being millenarian. Some remained millenarian until the end because the end came before they had a chance to create stable states. Christianity survived as a sect, stopped being millenarian, and was adopted by Babylon as an official creed. The Hebrews and Mormons survived their trek through the desert and traded milk and honey for stable states before being absorbed by larger empires. The Muslims created their own large empires bound by routinized millenarianism and threatened by repeated "fundamentalist" reformations. The Münster Anabaptists and the Jacobins took over existing polities and reformed them in the image of future perfection before losing out to more moderate reformers. Only the Bolsheviks destroyed the "prison of the peoples," vanquished the "appeasers," outlawed traditional marriage, banned private property, and found themselves firmly in charge of Babylon while still expecting the millennium in their lifetimes. Never before had an apocalyptic sect succeeded in taking control of an existing heathen empire (unless one counts the Safavids, whose millennial agenda seems to have been much less radical). It was as if the Fifth Monarchists had won the English Civil War, "reformed all places and all callings," contemplated an island overgrown with plants that the heavenly father had not planted, and stood poised to pull up every one of them, *"root and branch, every plant, and every whit of every plant."* The fact that Russia was not an island made the challenge all the more formidable.

There are two fundamental ways in which states relate to organized salvation professionals. The first is to assume a position of neutrality and treat various claims to a monopoly of the sacred with more or less equal condescension. This is characteristic of many traditional empires (including those ruled by nomadic warrior elites) and post-Christian liberal states "separate from the church." As Gibbon said of the Antonines, "the various modes of worship, which prevailed in the Roman world, were all considered by the people as equally true; by the philosopher, as equally false; and by the magistrate, as equally useful." This does not mean that such states are "secular" in the sense of being indifferent to sacred legitimacy; this means that they are self-confident enough about their own claim to sacred legitimacy not to need reinforcement from prophets unrelated to the divinity of the ruling lineage. The Western liberal states are no exception in this regard: by calling other would-be monopolies of the sacred "religions" and not calling their own anything in particular, they demonstrate the un-self-conscious strength of the official faith.[1]

There is no such thing as a "disenchanted" world or a profane polity. No state, however routinized, is fully divorced from its sacred origins, and no claim to legitimacy is purely "rational-instrumental." Particular governments may justify their right to rule in terms of due process, but the states they represent do not. Some laws may be proclaimed more "fundamental" than others, and some fundamental laws may be protected by priestly interpreters or Supreme Court justices whose mission is to sanctify changing practices in their light, but such constitutional traditions are much weaker than their rabbinical predecessors because of their more obvious circularity (all positive legislation is bound by a constitution, which is itself a piece of positive legislation). One solution is to root constitutional regimes in "natural law" and derive the rights of citizens from the "rights of man" and their heirs ("human rights"). Another, much more powerful, solution is to prop up legal-rational forms of authority with the sacred attributes of immortal nations. Monoethnic liberal states that can rely on existing tribal myths invest a great deal of effort in their elaboration and nationalization; those that cannot tend to equate nations with states and celebrate them accordingly. In the United States, the cult of national shrines, the ubiquity of the flag and the anthem, and the frequency of the ritualistic public praise of the warrior class are remarkable for their un-self-conscious ostentation. A state insulated by its own sacrality has no reason to worry about the flimsiness of its legal-rational scaffolding or the claims of a few self-doubting "denominations" (salvation monopolies that have lost the belief in their monopoly). Threatened by a serious challenge to the sacred center of its legitimacy and by the danger of mass conversions within the elite, the twentieth-century American state proclaimed its Communist subjects "un-American" and vigorously defended itself for as long as the threat remained serious. "The doctrine of tolerance" is reserved for the vanquished and the irrelevant.[2]

The other way for states to relate to competing salvation-granting institutions is to identify with one of them. Such monogamous states are usually classified according to the nature of the relationship between their political and ecclesiastical branches. At one end are the regimes in which the priestly bureaucracy is clearly subordinate to the political one, as was the case in the Russian Empire. At the other are what Weber calls "hierocracies" (the rule of the holy, otherwise known as "theocracies" or "ideocracies"), in which salvation specialists dominate the polity, as in some Tibetan, Judaic, or late Egyptian states; Calvin's Geneva; the Puritans' Massachusetts; and the Islamic Republic of Iran; among others.

States associated with a particular salvation-granting institution can be classified according to how they deal with alternative (unofficial) salvation providers on their territory. At one end are the unitary states (mostly hierocracies at the height of their salvation enthusiasm and strictly monogamous states such as Catholic Spain under Ferdinand and Isabella) that attempt to impose absolute uniformity of practice and conviction through expulsion, conversion, or extermination. Elsewhere along the spectrum are various forms of accommodation.[3]

The state that the Bolsheviks presided over at the end of the Civil War was a would-be hierocracy with serious unitary aspirations. All branches of rule—administrative, judicial, military, and economic—were controlled by the Communist Party, which remained a faith-based group with voluntary membership contingent on personal conversion. It remained a sect, in other words: the only requirements for entry and retention were scriptural competence and personal virtue as measured by senior members. It was not a priesthood ruling over a full-fledged hierocracy, insofar as most of the state's subjects were unconverted heathen. The head of the Party was the head of the state, whatever his formal title. The state itself was the Russian Empire run by a millenarian sect.

In regard to rival revelations, the NEP-era Bolsheviks were less consistently totalitarian than some of their predecessors: they violently attacked Christianity, Islam, and other keepers and vessels of false sacrality, but they did not ban them outright—partly because of the extraordinarily large number of the unconverted they had to deal with, but mostly because they considered beliefs that did not speak the language of social science as unworthy opponents. They viewed "religion" the way dominant Christian churches viewed "pagan" beliefs and practices: with scorn but without fear or a sense of immediacy. Such relative tolerance was not extended to the servants of the bourgeoisie or the appeasers from among their fellow sectarians.

All enemies of the Bolsheviks could be roughly divided into defenders of the old world or false prophets of the new. The latter consisted of various pseudo-Marxists, classified according to degree and method of appeasement; non-Marxist socialists, classified according to distance from Marxism; and integral nationalists, seen as unwitting representatives of the bourgeoisie (all non-Bolsheviks were seen as unwitting representatives of the bourgeoisie, but fascists and their kin were considered central to the pre-Armageddon phase of bourgeois false consciousness).

In fact, all early-twentieth-century revolutionaries, wherever they found themselves on the class-as-nation to nation-as-class continuum, shared a loathing for the world of old age, decay, effeminacy, corruption, selfishness, irony, artificiality, and cowardly compromise (including liberalism, parliamentarism, and democracy). Opposing them were the ideals of vengeance, violence, masculinity, simplicity, sincerity, certainty, self-sacrifice, brotherhood, and a faith in the coming renewal and necessity-as-freedom. Communists and integral nationalists were to the French and English revolutions what the Protestant Reformers had been to early Christianity: rebels against routinization and restorers of the original promise. Some of them were millenarians. But only the Bolsheviks were in power.

▪ ▪ ▪

The Soviet state rested on two pillars: specialized government ministries inherited from the old regime (as "People's Commissariats") and a hierarchy of regional Party committees culminating in the Central Committee and its various bureaus. The regional committees supervised all aspects of life in their jurisdictions; the Central Committee supervised everything without exception. All Party officials, including people's commissars and their key deputies, belonged to a universal system of appointments that emanated from the Central Committee Secretariat and radiated downward through various regional committees: the closer to the top, the greater the proportion of former students and the broader the expected area of expertise. The person at the very top had to be omniscient and irreplaceable. Sverdlov, who had "carried in his memory a biographical dictionary of Communists," was replaced by large administrative staffs and formal chains of command, but key appointments continued to be made on the basis of personal acquaintance that stretched back to the prerevolutionary underground and the Civil War revolutionary-military committees. A three-year interregnum at the top of the Central Committee Secretariat (filled, more or less ineptly, by Krestinsky and Molotov) was followed by the appointment of Stalin as general secretary in May 1922. Lenin had had Sverdlov; Sverdlov had had his "magic notebook." After Lenin's death, Stalin would become a perfect blend of Lenin and Sverdlov.[4]

The Party was surrounded by millions of unconverted "non-Party" outsiders who were now subject to Party rule. As a villain in Andrei Platonov's 1926 *The Town of Gradov* puts it, "So, like I was saying, what exactly is this Provincial Party Committee? Well, I'll tell you: the party secretary is the bishop, and the Provincial Party Committee is his—bishopric! Right? And the bishopric is wise and serious 'cause this is a new religion, and it's a lot stricter than the Orthodox kind. Just try skipping one of their meetings— or Vespers! 'Hand over your party card,' they'll say, 'so we can put a little mark in it.' Just four little marks, and they'll put you down as a pagan. And once you're a pagan, there'll be no more bread for you! So there!" The main difference was that there was no one above the Party secretary in his region, that the general secretary was the de facto head of state, that the lowliest priest could also be a judge and executioner, and that no priest had a permanent parish.[5]

No one except the leader had a permanent position (or street address). Bolshevik officials kept being transferred from one job to the next on the assumption that, as Sverdlov put it, a pharmacist, even "an inexperienced one," could run a state. Vasily Orekhov, the former shepherd who was exiled from Moscow in 1908 for "overturning a bowl of cabbage soup onto Kudelkin's head and boiling his whole head," served as a brigade commander in the Don Area, where he "received seven wounds, three of them severe," and then as a member of the Moscow revolutionary tribunal before becoming a deputy provincial prosecutor. Roman Terekhov, the Donbass miner who began his armed struggle by trying to kill a mechanic in his shop, organized underground Bolshevik cells in White-held territory, served as an "agitator" in the Red Army, and held various Party positions in his native Yuzovka before becoming director of the Ukrainian Central Control Commission. The calico printer, Pavel Postyshev, remained in Siberia after the February Revolution, became one of the top Bolshevik commanders in the Far East, and served as a Party official in Kiev before becoming secretary of the Ukrainian Central Committee. The "politically underdeveloped" baker, Boris Ivanov, was sent by his mentor Sverdlov to nationalize the flour industry, then worked as an agitator in the Astrakhan fisheries, before returning to Moscow to spend the rest of the 1920s as an official in the food workers' union. Sverdlov's friend and chief regicide, Filipp Goloshchekin, worked as director of the Iron Ore Trust, chairman of the Kostroma and Samara Provincial Executives, and, after 1924, secretary of the Kazakh Party Committee. Ivanov's fellow worker, Semen Kanatchikov (they had worked together as propagandists in the Petersburg Women's Mutual Aid Club in 1908, several years after Kanatchikov's apprenticeship at Gustav List in the Swamp), spent the Civil War in various Party posts in Siberia, the Urals, and Kazan before being assigned to the "culture front." He helped to found the Sverdlov Communist University in Moscow and served as rector of the Zinoviev Communist University in Petrograd, head of the Press Department of the Party's Central Committee, a TASS correspondent in Prague, and, after 1928, a member of the editorial boards of several journals and publishing houses.[6]

Kanatchikov's main competitor on the literature front was the former seminarian Aleksandr Voronsky, who was transferred from Odessa to Ivanovo, where he worked as secretary of the Party Committee and editor in chief of the *Worker's Path* newspaper; then to Kharkov, where he ran the Political Department of the Donetsk Railroad; and, in February 1921, to Moscow, where Lenin's wife, Nadezhda Krupskaia, put him in charge of the Publishing Department of the Main Committee for Political Enlightenment. Within weeks, he would become the head of the Modern Literature Department at the State Publishing House; editor in chief of the official literary journal, *Red Virgin Soil* (*Krasnaia nov'*); and the main judge, champion, and ideologue of new Soviet literature.[7]

One of Voronsky's literary protégés was Arosev, the conqueror of Moscow and a "memoirist of intra-Party emotional states" who thought of himself as a writer even as he continued to serve as deputy commander of the Moscow Military District, commissar of the Tenth Army, chairman of the Supreme Revolutionary Tribunal of Ukraine, deputy director of the Lenin Institute in Moscow, secretary at the Soviet embassies in Latvia, France, and Sweden, and then as ambassador to Lithuania and Czechoslovakia. Arosev's former commander Arkady Rozengolts, who had once seemed to "move from one room to another through the walls," now seemed to move—

with equal ease—through positions of political commissar of transportation (during which time he sent Voronsky to Kharkov), member of the Collegium of the People's Commissariat of Finance, head of the Main Directorate of the Air Force, Soviet ambassador to Great Britain, and people's commissar of foreign trade. Another participant in the Moscow uprising, Osip Piatnitsky, served as head of the Trade Union of Railroad Workers before becoming a member of the Comintern Executive Committee and one of the chief administrators of the international Communist movement. One of the leaders of the assault on the Winter Palace, the former seminarian Nikolai Podvoisky, had been named head of the Office of Supreme Military Inspection and was set on becoming the Revolution's "iron hand throughout the world," but Lenin disapproved of his subsequent performance as the people's commissar for military affairs of Ukraine, and had him transferred to the Supreme Council on Physical Culture and Sports International.[8]

Filipp Mironov's prosecutor, Ivar Smilga, served as head of the Main Fuel Directorate, deputy head of the Supreme Council of National Economy (VSNKh), deputy head of the State Planning Committee (Gosplan), and rector of the Plekhanov Institute of National Economy. Smilga's associate during the Filipp Mironov affair, Valentin Trifonov, worked as his deputy and then as head of the Oil Syndicate at the Fuel Directorate before becoming chairman of the Military Collegium of the Supreme Court of the USSR. In 1925, he was replaced by Vasily Ulrikh and sent abroad: first to China as deputy military attaché and then to Finland as head of the trade mission. One of Trifonov's successors in the Don area was Karl Lander, the son of Latvian day laborers who had lived with several Christian evangelical sects before converting to Bolshevism. As the special Cheka (secret police) plenipotentiary in the North Caucasus and Don region, Lander directed the executions of thousands of Cossacks in the fall of 1920. After the war, he served as head of the Agitprop Department of the Moscow Party Committee, Soviet representative at the foreign famine relief missions in 1922–23, and member of the Collegium of the People's Commissariat of Foreign Trade.[9]

Osinsky, the main ideologue of "War Communism" and the first chairman of both the State Bank and the VSNKh, went on to serve as chairman of the Tula Executive Committee, deputy people's commissar of agriculture, deputy director of VSNKh, member of the presidium of Gosplan and the Communist Academy, ambassador to Sweden, and head of the Central Directorate of Statistics. Osinsky's deputy in the Directorate of Statistics (and his predecessor as ambassador to Sweden) was Platon Kerzhentsev, who had converted him to Bolshevism twenty-five years earlier by defeating him in a debate about the Decembrists at Moscow Gymnasium No. 7. Kerzhentsev had also run the Russian Telegraphic Agency, the section of the Scientific Organization of Labor at the Worker-Peasant Inspection, and the Soviet embassy in Italy. After two years at the Directorate of

Statistics, he became deputy head of the Central Committee Agitprop and director of the Institute of Literature, Arts, and Language. Closest to the top of the pyramid—or so it seemed—was Osinsky's and Kerzhentsev's younger comrade from the early days of the Moscow Bolsheviks, Nikolai Bukharin. As he wrote in his official autobiography in 1925, "at present I am working as a member of the Central Committee and Politburo, member of the Presidium of the Executive Committee of the Comintern, as well as a writer, lecturer, party agitator, propagandist, etc."[10]

■ ■ ■

Most of those working in Moscow moved into the Kremlin or into one of several mansions and hotels designated as "Houses of Soviets" and administered by the Central Executive Committee's special Housekeeping Department. The old residents were expelled and their property confiscated, or, as Arosev put it, "all the old trash was shaken out." Lenin ordered the removal of all the icons and royal statues in the Kremlin. According to the Kremlin commandant, Malkov, "Vladimir Ilich could not stand the monuments to the tsars, grand dukes, and all those celebrated tsarist generals. He said on more than one occasion that the people, having been victorious, should tear down any such filth that reminded them of autocracy, and leave, by way of exception, only genuine works of art such as the monument to Peter in Petrograd." The "ruler of half the world" would remain on his steed (if not always on his pedestal) even after Petrograd became Leningrad; Moscow's most conspicuous horseman, General Skobelev, was replaced by the Liberty Obelisk. The building from which the ghostly Rozengolts ordered Arosev to go out and take over the city never fully recovered from the visit by the "man in the black-leather shell." The headquarters of the Revolution had moved down the street to where Lenin now lived and worked. Or, as Arosev put it, "for 'both now and ever, and unto the ages of ages,' the Kremlin has stopped being the crown on the head of 'all Russias' and turned into a stone engagement ring used to wed 'all the earth's nations in the name of peace, labor, and truth.'"[11]

Among the few old residents allowed to stay in the Kremlin were several palace doormen, retained in their previous capacity, but told not to wear liveries. According to Malkov and Novgorodtseva (who was now calling herself "Sverdlova"), the old men began by disapproving of the new masters but soon understood that their informality concealed real power and "became warmly and sincerely attached" to them. In 1918, Arosev wrote a short story about "an old servant of the old dead masters," left behind in an old empty palace. One day, soon after the Revolution, the old man revolts against the bronze statues of tsars and generals standing in niches along the palace's white stairway. The largest of all is a life-size Peter "wearing jackboots and wielding a sword," whom the old man accuses of having "stuck us all in a Petersburg swamp." Then, frightened by his own bravery, "the old man started and staggered back, grabbing onto the bannister and spitting over his left shoulder, before running as fast as he could down to the doorman's chamber, feeling a cold chill behind him all the way, as if he were being chased by a dead man."[12]

Malkov was not afraid of statues. Within a year of the introduction of the New Economic Policy, his Kremlin household had evolved into a vast real estate empire that included the Kremlin and eighteen Houses of Soviets with approximately 5,600 permanent residents and 1,200 dormitory beds. In 1922 alone, the Central Executive Committee (CEC) Housing Authority granted living space to 28,843 individuals—2,441 of them as permanent residents. The hierarchy of the buildings corresponded to the hierarchy of the officials. The Kremlin was reserved for the top Party leaders and their families. The First House of Soviets (formerly the National Hotel) housed the members of the Central Committee of the Party, Central Executive Committee, Central Control Commission, and governing boards ("collegia") of the People's Commissariats. The Second House of Soviets (the Metropol Hotel) was used for those who did not make it into the First House, as well as for the Central Committee and Central Executive Committee department heads and other "responsible officials" affiliated with the CEC. The Third House of Soviets (the former Orthodox Seminary on the corner of Sadovaia-Karetnaia and Bozhedomsky Alley) served as a dormitory for congress delegates and visiting high officials; the Fourth House (the Peterhof Hotel, on the corner of Vozdvizhenka and Mokhovaia) housed the CEC offices and staff members; and the Fifth House (Count Sheremetev's apartment building on Granovsky Street), which was added to the list later than the others, served as a respectable alternative to the first two. The remaining Houses of Soviets, which were less comfortable and farther away from the Kremlin, housed the lower officials and CEC staff and their families. Individual commissariats and other Soviet institutions had their own real estate, including residential housing.[13]

Over the course of the 1920s, the number of Houses of Soviets kept fluctuating (twenty nine in early 1924, then back down to eighteen the next year) as the need for housing clashed with a lack of funding. The greatest challenge for the Housekeeping Department was to keep up with the various transfers, promotions, and demotions by evicting some residents, installing others, and shifting the rest among rooms, floors, and houses. Rules connecting space to rank were undercut by countless complaints and demands citing special needs and patronage precedence. As the head of the housing authority wrote in the summer of 1921, "I was forced to make exceptions following requests and instructions from higher authorities, whom I was duty-bound to obey." Most of the claimants were higher authorities, and most of them objected to the strict ranking on personal or doctrinal grounds. The head of the Cheka Investigations Department, Grigory Moroz, who wanted to move to a lower floor in the First House of Soviets because he had TB, a small infant, a recalcitrant nanny, and a twenty-four-hour workday, enclosed a list of neighbors who did not have comparable qualifications (his request was approved). The head of the Archival Authority, David Riazanov, wrote that a certain comrade was "of proletarian origin, and consequently entitled to a room" (request denied). The residents of the Ninth, Tenth, and Eleventh Houses signed a petition arguing that they could not be taken off the budget just because they were service personnel, and thus proletarians (request approved but later ignored).[14]

In addition to being officials with secretaries and other employees, the residents were human, and consequently, mammals, who ate, drank, slept, procreated, grew hair, produced waste, got sick, and needed heating and lighting, among other things. All this required a vast and intricate infrastructure and a growing staff of service personnel (around two thousand in 1922–23). The Housekeeping Department's priorities were centralization, symmetry, transparency, cleanliness, accountability, and surveillance. All things and people were to be catalogued and, if possible, correlated. Doormen's chambers were to be free of "trash, cigarette butts, and spittle"; doormen were to accompany duly identified guests to their rooms; residents were to have passes corresponding to their status and location; and clerical staff were, in the interests of saving time, to drink tea at their desks. No one was to sleep with his boots on or eat on windowsills; everyone was to report all violations.[15]

Before 1921, all services and household items were free; after the introduction of private trade under NEP it was up to the management to set the prices. In January 1923, the head of the Housing Authority decreed that a regular male haircut should cost 3 rubles; a flat top, 3.75; a beard trim, 2.25; a head shave, 3.75; a beard shave, 3.75; a female haircut, 3.75; and a perm, 6. In August, after a currency reform, these prices rose sharply, but not all at the same rate (with head shaving emerging as the most expensive operation by a considerable margin). The same was true of the cost of firewood, laundry, and cafeteria meals. The drive for consistency (apartment rent was to vary according to house, floor, size, view, facilities, and so on) was partially thwarted by the demands of patronage and privilege (special conditions for those with greater responsibilities and their associates). The list of officials entitled to free use of Central Executive Comittee cars consisted of those who could transfer that right to others, those who could not transfer that right to others, and those who were not officials, but had certain unspecified rights. Stalin's wife, Nadezhda Allilueva, was on the list "by order of Comrade Stalin"; Sverdlov's widow, K. T. Sverdlova, was on the list "by order of Comrade Enukidze." Stalin and other top Party leaders rarely interfered, as various services were increasingly offered to them as "initiatives from below." Enukidze, as CEC secretary and one of Sverdlov's official successors, distributed favors from above as well as from below. Large and variously defined groups of officials and their dependents received special discounts.[16]

First House of Soviets (the National Hotel)

Second House of Soviets (the Metropol Hotel)

The extraordinary thing about the living conditions of high Soviet officials in the 1920s was how extraordinary they were by Soviet standards. As the head of the Housing Authority Food Supply Department wrote in 1920, the work of an organization "that serves the needs of the Kremlin, which is the political center of the country, as well as the needs of the Houses of Soviets, which contain the high officials who constitute the flower of not only the Russian, but also the world, revolution, must be considered of paramount importance, with all the consequences that that entails." There was no need for a special decree: the needs of the flower of the world revolution were considered paramount by all of the agencies charged with meeting them.[17]

All sects are, in theory and by definition, equal and fraternal. All are, in fact, hierarchical. Some consist of a teacher and several male disciples; some consist of a teacher and a commune including women and children (which may or may not belong to the teacher); and some grow large enough to contain ranked officials. The Kremlin and the most important Houses of Soviets had their own cafeterias as well as a bakery and kvass factory. During the famine of 1921–23, eleven special agents were sent to procure meat in the North Caucasus, Penza, and Saratov; grain and flour in Ukraine; vegetables in the Moscow and Vladimir Provinces; and rice in Turkestan. "In order to improve the quality of the food in the cafeterias, a special dietary office was created. A nutritional scientist with experience working abroad was invited to head it. In the cafeterias themselves, almost the entire staff was composed of individuals with special training in popular nutrition and the culinary arts." The dependents of CEC members received a special cafeteria discount irrespective of their place of residence; the dependents of CEC staff received the discount only if they lived in the Houses of Soviets. As few staff members as possible were to be assigned to the top five Houses of Soviets.[18]

The inhabitants of the top five Houses of Soviets had their own laundry services and a telephone station. They had their own club with sports, music, dance, and drama classes. They had their own "Kremlin" hospital, with outpatient clinics in the First, Third, and Fifth Houses and doctors available for home visits. They had their own school, day-care centers, kindergartens, and summer camps for about 850 children (with K. T. Sverdlova in charge). They had special passes "valid for free travel on all the railways and waterways of the Russian Socialist Federal Soviet Republic"—and, after 1922, of the Union of Soviet Socialist Republics. (Those who did not have such passes received free tickets to particular destinations, as Sverdlova did in September 1924 for a trip to Crimea with Andrei, Vera, and an unspecified fourth party, probably a nanny).[19]

They had special seats reserved for them in all the Moscow theaters, the circus, and State Movie Theater No. 1. In 1924, ad hoc demands for free admission were replaced by a formal obligation by the theaters to provide comfortable boxes to officials of certain ranks (more or less corresponding to residency in the Kremlin and the First, Second, and Fifth Houses of Soviets). Eligible officials could be accompanied by one adult or two children. Access to the CEC boxes was to be "regulated in such a way that only comrades with CEC tickets could enter them, while individuals with regular tickets could not." Enukidze, who wrote the decree, was famous for his love of opera and his appreciation of female beauty. In 1926, the women in the CEC Secretariat traded in their dark smocks for English suits with "elegant" shoes and blouses. According to one employee of the Statistics Department, the women decided to have two skirts made for each suit: one for everyday use and one for special occasions. They worked long hours, and often went to the theater straight from the office.[20]

After the first wave of housing requests had subsided, the most sought-after perquisites of high office were country houses (dachas) and stays at CEC "rest homes" and sanatoria. In 1920, Housing Authority agents began traveling around the country in search of appropriate gentry estates. In

1922, Enukidze created a special Department of Country Property. Later that year Prince Bariatinsky's estate in Maryino, Kursk Province, became Lenin Rest Home No. 1. The home included an 1816 palace "in the Italian style" for 150 guests; a twenty-seven-acre park; a large pond on a river with one motor boat and several rowboats; newly created courts for tennis, croquet, and skittles; gymnastics equipment; and a small library.[21]

By 1924, the Department of Country Property was overseeing a network of dachas outside Moscow and ten "rest homes" in the North Caucasus, the Caucasian and Crimean Rivieras, and central Russia (including several close to Moscow, used for weekend getaways). In 1925, at the suggestion of Rykov (Lenin's successor as chairman of the Council of People's Commissars), a special commission headed by Enukidze divided this rapidly growing "country property" into Group 1, for one hundred individuals and their families, and Group 2, for other eligible officials. All homes in both groups were further subdivided into three categories: general health spas, "balneological" spas (mostly around Kislovodsk and Sochi), and rest homes, "where medical treatment is provided on an individual basis." In Maryino, which belonged to the first category, guests were supposed to get up at 7:45, do calisthenics until breakfast at 9:00, receive various water and electrical treatments until lunch at 1:00, take a nap from 2:00 to 3:30, have tea at 4:30, receive more treatments or play games until dinner at 8:00; and take a compulsory constitutional until lights-out at 11:00. In 1927–28, most violations of the regimen "were of an innocent, inoffensive nature: missing afternoon naps, smoking in the rooms, and being out past bedtime."[22]

One of Lenin's close associates and, after Lenin's death, one of the deputy directors of the Lenin Institute, Vladimir Adoratsky, spent the summer of 1927 at a balneological spa in Essentuki. As he wrote to his daughter, who was in a different sanatorium, he was enjoying all his treatments: the "saline-alkaline baths with stray, tiny bubbles popping up in different places on your body"; the drinking water from Spring No. 4 and Spring No. 20; the "galvanization of the spine" ("tingles most delightfully as tiny ripples go down your body"); the electrical shower ("also a very pleasant invisible downpour"); the carbon dioxide baths ("bubbles all over your body" and "gas right up your nose"); the "circular shower" ("tiny little torrents raining down on you"); and the Charcot shower ("a ferocious pleasure—your body turns as red as our red flag"). He also enjoyed the billiards, the chess, the dominoes, the improvised concerts, the pleasant company, the attentions of his doctor, and the daily 5:00–7:00 p.m. musical performances, especially after the conductor, Brauer, from the Stanislavsky Studio had "simply transformed the orchestra." But most of all, he enjoyed the food:

Vladimir Adoratsky

Breakfast at half past eight: a chunk of butter about two inches long and as thick as your thumb, a dollop of caviar of approximately the same size, a couple of eggs, coffee, and as much cucumber and tomato salad as you want. The second breakfast at 11 a.m.: four fried eggs and a glass of milk or tea. A three-course lunch at 2 p.m. Tea with a bun at 5 p.m. (The buns are fresh!!) (I don't drink the tea.) Dinner at half past seven: a good-sized piece of schnitzel (or chicken) with cucumbers and tomatoes and a dessert (kompot, apple mousse with whipped cream, or simply fruit—apricots, pears, etc.) All four meals come with a cup of buttermilk.[23]

■ ■ ■

Having won the war, taken over the state, established stable administrative hierarchies, and rewarded themselves with a system of exclusive benefits and a good-size piece of schnitzel (or chicken), the Bolsheviks began to reflect on their past. Most memoirs of anticipation and fulfillment were written in the 1920s. Everyone was writing histories—to preserve the past, legitimize the present, and align personal experience with sacred time. Some did it spontaneously, as an affirmation of faith; some did it professionally, on behalf of special institutions; some did it as leaders of people and makers of events; some did it as followers of leaders and witnesses to events; some—such as the members of the Society of Old Bolsheviks—did it as a matter of institutional requirement; and most Soviets did it, in the form of official "autobiographies," as part of their regular interactions with the state—from college admissions and job applications to requests for apartments, services, and balneological treatments. Everything had to corroborate and constitute the story of fulfilled prophecy. Some parts of the story were more important than others.

Rituals that celebrate connections to sacred origins are acts of remembrance and reenactment. The most elaborate early Bolshevik eucharists were mass stagings of the storming of the Winter Palace. One of the main theorists of such celebrations—and of "people's theater" in general—was Platon Kerzhentsev. The point, he wrote in 1918, was not to "perform for the popular audience" but to "help that audience perform itself." The people were to perform by themselves, without professional or priestly mediation, and they were to perform (represent and celebrate) themselves, as both form and subject. Kerzhentsev took as his model the festivals of the French Revolution, especially the Fête de la Fédération of July 14, 1790, which, according to Kerzhentsev, centered on the swearing of the oath of allegiance to the constitution and the performance of musical and choral pieces. "The people expressed their joy by shouting and singing." But because the French Revolution had been a bourgeois revolution, such revolutionary festivals could not become permanent:

In today's France, nothing is left of those majestic revolutionary festivals. The famous "14 July" is a pathetic, gaudy fairground for the benefit of wine sellers and merry-go-round operators. . . . The same signs of decay and degradation are evident in the historic festival of another bourgeois revolution, the anniversary of the liberation of the United States from the yoke of absolutist England. In today's America, "the Fourth of July" has turned into a boring official celebration, at the center of which are fireworks that each year send hundreds of children and grown-ups to an early grave. When, two years ago, this dangerous entertainment was banned, the festival quickly wilted and lost all its color—so superficial and artificial had it become.[24]

Under socialism, the line separating sacred events from their ritual reenactment would be erased. Commemorations would dissolve "into those free expressions of joy that only become possible at a time of complete liberation from the heavy shackles of economic oppression."[25]

One of the earliest pieces of popular theater and the most consistent realization of the flood metaphor associated with the real day was Mayakovsky's *Mystery-Bouffe*, first performed on the first anniversary of the October Revolution ("sets by Malevich, directed by Mayakovsky and Meyerhold, acted by free actors"). After the deluge that destroys the old world, "seven pairs of the Clean" ("an Abyssinian Negus, Indian Raja, Turkish Pasha, Russian merchant, Chinaman, well-fed Persian, fat Frenchman, Australian and his wife, priest, German officer, Italian officer, American, and student") and "seven pairs of the Unclean" (a chimney sweep, lamplighter, driver, seamstress, miner, carpenter, day laborer, servant, cobbler, blacksmith, baker, washerwoman, and two Eskimos—one a fisherman, the other a hunter) escape in an ark. The Clean form an autocracy and later a bourgeois provisional government before being thrown overboard in the course of a proletarian revolution. Once the Unclean are left on their own, the plot changes from the flood to exodus. The Unclean suffer great privations but vow to withstand storms, heat, and hunger as they travel to the promised land. Suddenly they see Jesus, played by Mayakovsky. He walks on water and offers "a new Sermon on the Mount":

Come hither—
Those who have calmly plunged their knives
into enemy flesh
and walked away with a song.
Come, those who have not forgiven!
You'll be the first to enter
my heavenly kingdom.

The Unclean journey to hell, which looks like a gaudy fairground compared with the oppression they have suffered on earth; to heaven, which

they find populated by pompous windbags (including Rousseau and Tolstoy); and finally back to earth, which, in the absence of the Clean, is overflowing with milk, honey, and "Comrade things," eager to be possessed in
a never-ending orgy of unalienated labor.

> Day Laborer
> I'll take Saw. I'm young and ready.
> Saw
> Take me!
> Seamstress
> And I'll take Needle.
> Blacksmith
> I'm raring to go—give me Hammer!
> Hammer
> Take me! Caress me!
> The blacksmith leads the way.[26]

Mystery-Bouffe, "The Clean." Sketch by Mayakovsky

Mystery-Bouffe, "The Unclean." Sketch by Mayakovsky

Karl Lander, in his capacity as head of Moscow Agitprop, did not approve. *Mystery-Bouffe*, he wrote, "is some type of primitive, unconscious, unreal communism." Voronsky, from his position as supervisor of Soviet literature, did not approve, either. "Mayakovsky's socialism, which sees things as the only value and rejects everything 'spiritual,' is not our socialism." Mayakovsky's hero is huge and belligerent, but he is still too pale and abstract, "perhaps because Babylon has sucked too much of the blood and life's juices out of him." There were two major problems with *Mystery-Bouffe*, besides the lack of spirituality and life's juices. First, the flood metaphor had outlived its usefulness because the real day had been followed by the Civil War, and the Civil War required a more substantial (more mythic) representation of Babylon. And second, theatrical reenactments were too ephemeral to serve as history, let alone myth.[27]

The farther one moves from the sacred origins, the greater the ascendancy of narratives over participatory rituals (and their "people's theater" incarnations). As last suppers turn into regularly scheduled eucharists, written accounts of foundational events congeal into gospels (sutras, hadiths) that define the moral and aesthetic foundations of the founder's inheritance. The failure of the prophecy creates a world of expectation shaped by canonical stories of what once was and might yet be. The Bolsheviks took over the state before the past took over the present, and they made the writing of scripture a matter of state policy. History as Literature of Fact was too pedestrian to serve that purpose; Literature as Myth became a crucial part of "socialist construction." The New City's legitimacy depended on an army of fiction writers, with Voronsky in the lead. The winner's reward was immortality.

■ ■ ■

The main task of Bolshevik gospel-writers was to mythologize the Civil War. Most attempts to do so relied on the contrast between Babylon and the raging elements—winds, storms, blizzards, and inchoate human masses.

Babylon came in two varieties. One was the traditional biblical kind—drunk on the wine of her adulteries and overflowing with cinnamon and spice, myrrh and frankincense. In Aleksandr Malyshkin's corrupt city of Dair (*The Fall of Dair*, 1921), "yawning mouths pressed down on tender, oozing fruit flesh with hot palates; parched mouths slurped up delicate, fiery wine, shimmering jewel-like against the light; jaws, convulsed with lust, ingested, with loud smacking noises, all that was soft, fatty, or spiced." In Vsevolod Ivanov's *Armored Train 1469* (1921), Babylon's doomed bodies "oozed sweat, and hands became glued to walls and benches."[28]

The second, more "realistic" Beast was the provincial town of the intelligentsia tradition—a swamp where time stands still and dreams come to die. Yuri Libedinsky's *A Week* (1922) begins with a "heavy afternoon nap":

In every window of every house there is a geranium in bloom, its flowers perched on top like so many pink and blue flies. Oh, how many of these gray wooden boxes there are, stretching for street after street, and how cramped and suffocating it is inside each one of them! There is an icon shining dimly in the front corner and velvet-covered albums resting on small tables covered with lace doilies. In the dirty kitchens, there are cockroaches running up and down the walls and flies buzzing despondently against the windowpane.

The life led by the people living in these stifling houses resembles a gray September day, when a drizzling rain patters monotonously against the window, and through the glass covered with raindrops, you can just make out the gray fence and the red calf plodding through the mud. Every day, early in the morning, the woman of the house milks the cow before setting off with her basket to the market, and then, after lunch, she washes the greasy dishes in the kitchen.[29]

Andrei Platonov's "town of Gradov" (*Gorod Gradov* [Townstown], 1926) consisted of both huts and "more respectable dwellings," with "iron roofs, outhouses in the backyard, and flowerbeds in front. Some even had small gardens with apple and cherry trees. The cherries were used to make liqueur, and the apples were pickled. . . . On summer evenings, the town would fill with the sound of floating church bells and smoke from all the samovars. The townfolk existed without haste and did not worry about the so-called better life."[30]

The difference between a pastoral and the netherworld is mostly a matter of literary genre and police vigilance. Boris Pilnyak's town of Ordynin (*The Naked Year*, 1922) smells of mold and rotten pork; Isaak Babel's Jewish shtetl stinks of rotten herring and "sour feces"; and Voronsky's swamp swarms "with myriads of midges, soft, plump tadpoles, water spiders, red beetles, and frogs." Most of the residents are weeds planted by the devil. "Look at him," says Voronsky's Valentin: "Observe his excitement as he turns over and digs through the lumps of fat and lard! His eyes are oily; his lower lip hangs loose; his filthy, foul-smelling mouth fills with saliva." Babylon II has merged with Babylon I. "Seen from a hill," says Libedinsky's narrator, "all these little houses look so quiet and peaceful." But the local Chekist (secret police official) knows: "somewhere among them, our enemies are hiding."[31]

There are three main ways of representing the Civil War between the old world and the new: the apocalypse, the crucifixion, and the exodus.

The first is the story of mass slaughter: the storming of Babylon, the battle of Armageddon, or some combination of the two. The central theme—as in the original model—is merciless retribution through total violence against feminized evil: "Give her as much torture and grief as the glory and luxury she gave herself."[32] Such is the fate of Malyshkin's Dair:

Fire burst forth from the terrifying carts as they dashed and scampered about, cutting wide swaths with the invisible blades of their machine guns. Streams of bullets issued from the carts and raked through the cloud of men on horseback—slicing, pruning, cutting them down in full gallop, and mowing down whole columns; the unburdened horses, shrieking and twisting their heads, rushed wildly past and disappeared into the murk. Broken bones disintegrated; mouths, still bearing the imprint of a mistress' kiss from the night before, gaped darkly; and the streets, colored fountains, artistic elegance, and solemn hymns of dominion collapsed and were trampled into a bloody pulp.[33]

Every remnant of Babylon must be trampled into a bloody pulp. In Vsevolod Ivanov's *Colored Winds* (1921), the Red partisans attack a Siberian village defended by the Beast's branded servants: "The officer is at the head; the officer always stands at the head. . . . He gets an axe in the mouth. There are teeth on the axe. The officer lies on the ground. If you are going to kill, then kill. If you are going to burn, then burn. Kill everyone, burn everything. There is a slaughtered woman in every yard. A slaughtered woman in front of every gate. No men left? Then kill the women. The red flesh of their wombs lies exposed."[34]

Riding or walking at the head of the holy host is Jesus the Avenger. He is always at the head, leading his followers: "the eleven" (Boris Lavrenev), "the twelve" (Aleksandr Blok), "the nineteen" (Aleksandr Fadeev), or the countless armies of those who have inherited the earth. "With justice he judges and makes war. His eyes are like blazing fire, and on his head are many crowns. He has a name written on him that no one knows but he himself. He is dressed in a robe dipped in blood, and his name is the Word of God." In Lavrenev's comic answer to the Book of Revelation, Commissar Evsiukov wears a bright red leather jacket:

If one adds that Evsiukov is short, squat, and shaped like a perfect oval, then, in his bright red jacket and pants, he ends up looking like a dyed Easter egg.

And, on Evsiukov's back, the straps of his combat gear cross to form the letter "X," so when he turns to face you, you are expecting to see the letter "B."

Христос Воскресе! [Khristos voskrese!] Christ is risen!

But no, Evsiukov does not believe in Christ or Easter.

He believes in the Soviets, the "Internationale," the Cheka, and the heavy blue-steel revolver he holds clenched in his hard, knotty fist.[35]

All commissars are both saviors and avengers. Pilniak's "leather people" hold their executive committee meetings in a monastery. "And it's a good thing, too, that they wear leather jackets; you can't dampen them with the soda pop of psychology." Firmness comes at a price, especially for "the sluggish, unruly Russian people." Pilniak's head commissar, Arkhip Arkhipov, spends long nights thinking. "Once, daybreak found him bent over a sheet of paper, his brow pale, eyebrows knitted, and beard slightly disheveled, but the air around him clean and pure (not the way it usually was at the end of the night), for Arkhipov did not smoke. And when the comrades arrived and Arkhipov handed them his sheet of paper, the comrades read, among other words, the fearless phrase: '*to be shot.*'" As Jesus says in Mayakovsky's new Sermon on the Mount, "come hither—those who have calmly plunged their knives into enemy flesh and walked away with a song." To join the army of light, one had to learn what Babel's narrator in *Red Cavalry* (1924) calls "the simplest of skills—the ability to kill a man."[36]

In Arosev's *The Notes of Terenty the Forgotten* (1922), the Chekist Kleiner wears "the same leather jacket winter, summer, day, and night." He is full of a "hidden inner enthusiasm," and he kills people as a matter of personal vocation and historical inevitability. One of his ideas is to project the executions onto a large screen outside the Cheka building. "What is necessary does not corrupt," he says. "Try to understand. What is necessary does not corrupt." Arosev's literary patron, Aleksandr Voronsky, agrees: "Absolutely right is Arosev's Kleiner, who states that 'what is necessary does not corrupt.'" The trampling of arms and legs and the slaughtering of women is part of the providential plan, and therefore beyond morality. "There can be no justice, no categorical imperatives; everything is subordinated to necessity, which, at the moment, knows only one commandment: 'Kill!'"[37]

Some scriptural texts produced by the Bolshevik gospel-writers rival the Revelation of St. John in their exuberant sense of moral clarity and rhetorical elevation; others are, to varying degrees, touched by self-reflexivity and ambivalence. Andrei Platonov and Isaak Babel, in particular, struggled to produce myth but seemed unable to escape irony. As Bakhtin wrote about *Dead Souls*, "Gogol imagined the form of his epic as a Divine Comedy, but what came out was Menippean satire. Once having entered the sphere of familiar contact, he could not leave it, and could not transfer into that sphere his aloof positive characters." Platonov and Babel, too, kept imagining Paradiso, but getting stuck in Purgatorio, in full view of the Inferno. Their characters tend to be saintly simpletons: senile children (all of them orphans, one way or another) in the case of Platonov, and infantile warriors ("monstrously huge, dull-witted"), in the case of Babel. In Platonov's *Chevengur* (1928), the chief dragon slayer is a Soviet Don Quixote called Stepan Kopenkin. He rides a horse named Proletarian Power, worships the image of "the beautiful young maiden, Rosa Luxemburg," and fights the ghostly enemies of the Revolution as he rides toward Communism. "He did not understand and did not have any spiritual doubts, considering them a betrayal of the Revolution. Rosa Luxemburg had thought of everything on everyone's behalf—all that was left were the great deeds of the sword for the sake of the destruction of the visible and invisible enemy."[38]

By parodying medieval romance, Cervantes invented the novel; by parodying Cervantes, Platonov attempted to return to the innocence of medieval romance: "Unlike the way he lived, [Kopenkin] normally killed indifferently, though efficiently, as if moved by the force of simple calculation and household utility. In the White Guardists and bandits, Kopenkin saw unimportant enemies, unworthy of his personal fury, and he killed them with the same scrupulous thoroughness with which a peasant woman might remove weeds in her millet patch. He fought precisely, but hastily, on foot and on horseback, unconsciously saving his emotions for future hope and movement."

Platonov's problem as an orthodox gospel-writer was that he could not write the way Kopenkin killed. In the Communist town of Chevengur, Kopenkin's fellow Bolshevik orders the extermination of the town's bourgeoisie as part of the general plan for the end of the world. The Second Coming is scheduled for Thursday, because Wednesday is a day of fasting and the bourgeoisie will be able to prepare itself "more calmly." When the former exploiters (those who, in Luke 6:24, "have already received their comfort,") have assembled on the cathedral square, the head Chekist, Comrade Piusya, fires a bullet from his revolver into the skull of a nearby bourgeois, Zavyn-Duvailo. "Quiet steam rose from the bourgeois's head—and then a damp, maternal substance resembling candle wax oozed out into his hair; but instead of toppling over, Duvailo just sat down on his bundle of belongings." After shooting another member of the bourgeoisie, the Chekist returns to Zavyn-Duvailo.

> Piusya took hold of Duvailo's neck with his left hand, got a good, comfortable grip, and then pressed the muzzle of his revolver against it, just below the nape. But Duvailo's neck was itching, and he kept rubbing it against the cloth collar of his jacket.
>
> "Stop fidgeting, you fool. Wait—I'll really give you a good scratch!"
>
> Duvailo was still alive, and not afraid. "Take my head between your legs and squeeze it till I scream out loud. My woman's nearby and I want her to hear me!"
>
> Piusya smashed him on the cheek with his fist, so as to feel the body of this bourgeois for the last time, and Duvailo cried out plaintively: "Mashenka, they're hitting me!"
>
> Piusya waited till Duvailo had pronounced the last drawn-out syllables in full, and shot him twice through the neck. He then unclenched his gums, which had grown hot and dry.[39]

The district executive committee secretary and town intellectual (as well as hidden enemy), Prokofy Dvanov, expresses the official Soviet objection to such a representation of the apocalypse. "Prokofy had observed this solitary murder from a distance, and he reproached Piusya: 'Communists don't kill from behind, comrade Piusya!'" The Chekist's answer to Prokofy is Platonov's response to his critics: "Communists, Comrade Dvanov, need Communism—not officer-style heroics. So you'd better keep your mouth shut, or I'll pack you off to heaven after him! Nowadays every f——ing whore wants to plug herself up with a red banner—as if that'll make her empty hole heal over with virtue! Well, no banner's going to hide you from my bullet!" But Prokofy is right. By dispensing with the red banner and describing Armageddon as a solitary murder, Platonov undermines his identification with the "great deeds of the sword," dooms his attempt to write a great revolutionary epic, and consigns his narrator to the empty hole of ironic detachment. Once having entered the "sphere of familiar contact," he cannot leave it—much to the benefit of his posthumous (post-Communist) reputation.[40]

Babel, too, gains his share of immortality by failing to get a firm grip on the sacred. His *Red Cavalry* narrator, like Abraham, is ready but unwilling to sacrifice a human being and is given an animal instead: "A stern-looking goose was wandering about the yard, serenely preening its feathers. I caught up with it and pressed it to the ground; the goose's head cracked under my boot—cracked and spilled out. The white neck was spread out in the dung, and the wings flapped convulsively over the slaughtered bird. 'Mother of God upon my soul!' I said, poking around in the goose with my saber. 'I'll have this roasted, landlady.'"[41]

Babel's Cossacks, unlike Babel's evangelists, do not accept substitutes. They—like Comrade Piusya—slaughter humans with the same scrupulous thoroughness with which a peasant woman might remove weeds in her millet patch. They do to Abraham what Abraham was unwilling to do to Isaac:

> Right under my window several Cossacks were preparing to shoot a silver-bearded old Jew for spying. The old man was squealing and struggling to get away. Then Kudria from the machine-gun detachment took hold of the old man's head and tucked it under his arm. The Jew grew quiet and stood with his legs apart. With his right hand Kudria pulled out his dagger and carefully slit the old man's throat, without splashing any blood on himself. Then he knocked on the closed window.
>
> "If anyone's interested," he said, "They can come and get him. He's free for the taking."[42]

Voronsky, Babel's chief sponsor and publisher, admitted that "Babel's *Red Cavalry* never did any fighting" and that, in his stories, "there was no Red Cavalry as an entire mass—no thousands of armed men advancing like lava." Instead, there were solitary individuals and "what certain circles refer to as beastliness, brutality, animal stupidity, and savagery." The truth, however, was that those individuals were "almost all truth-seekers," and that Babel had a talent for seeing saintliness in savagery. Comrade Piusya was right: Communists could kill from behind as long as the killing was "for the benefit and victory of Communism." But Babel knew better (and could not help himself). As he would say at the First Congress of Soviet Writers, "Bad taste is no longer a personal defect; it is a crime. Even worse, bad taste is counterrevolution." For a true believer, to represent the guiltless mass murder of the apocalypse as solitary acts of ritual sacrifice was in bad taste.[43]

The apocalypse is a version of the myth about dragon slaying. Dragon slaying, when seen from the point of view of an individual dragon, is self-sacrifice (crucifixion). The second Civil War plot is about the death and rebirth of a martyr. Ivanov's *Partisans*, Libedinsky's *A Week*, Lavrenev's *The Forty-First*, Fadeev's *The Rout* (1926), Dmitry Furmanov's *Chapaev* (1923), and, in their "empty-hole" way, Platonov's *Chevengur* and Babel's *Red Cavalry* are partly or wholly about the death and resurrection of Bolshevik saints. The revolutionary commander Chapaev, like Moses, can see the promised land but is not allowed to cross the Ural River. He is killed mid-stream; most of his men—the rank-and-file as well as the Levites—are captured while still ashore: "Jews, Commissars, and Communists—come forward! And they did, hoping to keep the Red Army soldiers from being executed, though they could not always save them in this way. They stood before the ranks of their comrades, so proud and beautiful in their silent courage, their lips trembling and eyes shining with wrath, cursing the Cossack whip as they fell under the blows of sabers and hail of bullets."[44]

The counterrevolutionary uprising in Libedinsky's novella takes place during the Holy Week of the Christian calendar, and the slaughter of the town's Communists is followed by church bells announcing the beginning of the all-night Easter vigil. This completes the conversion of one of the central characters. "Listening to the chiming of the bells, Liza realized that she was here—not in church, not at Vespers, but at a Party meeting."[45]

The two plots—the apocalypse and the crucifixion—are either two ways of looking at the same event or one way of looking at cause and effect. In the Christian New Testament, the apocalypse is revenge for the crucifixion, and the permanent branding of the combatants is a way to keep the two armies separate (and, in the apocalyptic mode, anonymous). In the center of Malyshkin's Babylon can be found the reason for its destruction: "The night of the world was falling. In the murky doom of the squares, three figures hung on lampposts, with heads meekly bent and gaping black eye sockets gazing down at their chests." Calvary justifies the apocalypse. What follows the vision of the crucifixion is the dashing and scampering of terrifying carts, the raking of bullets through a cloud of men on horseback, and the trampling into a pulp of solemn hymns of dominion. But in describing the recent and still lingering Bolshevik past, as opposed to the sudden explosion of an imminent Christian future, it is difficult to end the story with countless armies of nameless and faceless enemies being thrown into a lake of fire. Even Malyshkin, who tries to avoid all "familiar contact," cannot help taking a closer look. In the novel's finale, the apocalypse reverts to the Passion of Christ as the last of Babylon's defenders are shot by a Red Army firing squad. "Pale, with eyes like still candle flames, they were silently and hastily lined up against the stone wall. Beyond the hush of the deserted alley, the rumble and noise that heralded the new dawn kept growing. Abruptly and eerily in the gloom, a truck rattled past the gate. With a sudden, muffled cry, unheard by anyone, Death passed on its way." The crucifixion is followed by the apocalypse, which is followed by the crucifixion. And so on.[46]

The main challenge of all salvation myths is to avoid falling into the trap of eternal return. Communism—like Judaism, Christianity, Islam, and their incalculable progeny—is a comedy, in which the world of youth rebels against the tyranny of corrupt old age and, after a series of trials and misrecognitions, expels or exterminates the incorrigible, converts the undecided, and celebrates its victory with a wedding or its happily-ever-after equivalent. A prophecy's promise is that the honeymoon will never end; the young lovers will never turn into old tyrants; and "there will be no more death or mourning or crying or pain."

For the Soviet gospel writers of the 1920s, one way to avoid ironic circularity is to focus on the journey separating the Passion from the apocalypse. The third and most important Civil War master plot is the exodus, or the story of the march from Egypt to the promised land, from suffering to redemption, and from a band of "stiff-necked people" to "a kingdom of priests and a holy nation." Most Civil War stories involve all three plots; the exodus chapter focuses on the hardships of the journey and the joy of homecoming, not on the original martyrdom or the eventual retribution.

In Lavrenev's *The Forty-First*, a Red Army unit wanders through the desert until it finds salvation in the waters of the Aral Sea (or so they think before the flood comes). In Furmanov's *Chapaev*, the "doomed Red regiments" embark on "the last exodus" that takes them to the shores of the Caspian Sea. In Malyshkin's *The Fall of Dair*, thirsty "hordes" march through the steppe and the swamp to the land of "milk, meat, and honey," where "summer never ends" and "evenings are like fields of golden rye."

In Ivanov's *Colored Winds*, the partisans emerge from the mountains and forests to find the spring fields of blue-green grass. "Baptize it with the plow! The pale golden wind is thrashing about—bleed it by sowing! It is your birth we're celebrating, earth, your birth!" And in Fadeev's *The Rout*, the partisans emerge from the swamp to find "the vast sky and the earth, which promised bread and rest."

The forest ended abruptly and a vast expanse of high, blue sky and bright russet fields, freshly mown and bathed in sunshine, stretched out on either side as far as the eye could see. On one side, beyond a knot of willows, through which the gleaming blue surface of a swollen river could be seen, lay a threshing-ground, resplendent with the golden crowns of the fat haystacks. . . . Beyond the river, propping up the sky and rooted in the yellow-tressed woods, loomed the blue mountain ranges, and through their toothed summits a transparent foam of pinkish-white clouds, salted by the sea, poured into the valley, as frothy and bubbly as milk fresh from the cow.[47]

Platonov would not write his own Soviet Exodus—*Dzhan*—until 1935. In the 1920s, he was still unable to escape the confines of the exodus's profane double—the knightly road quest. His Stepan Kopenkin was Don Quixote, not Moses: "Although it was warm in Chevengur, and smelled of comradely spirit, Kopenkin, perhaps from exhaustion, felt sad, and his heart yearned to ride on. He had not yet noticed in Chevengur a clear and obvious socialism—that touching but firm and edifying beauty in the midst of nature that would allow a second little Rosa Luxemburg to be born, or the first one, who had perished in a German bourgeois land, to be scientifically resurrected."[48]

In the original Exodus story, the failure to discover milk and honey remains outside the narrative, and the main characters are two larger-than-life questing heroes: Moses and the Israelites. The chosen people walk from slavery (a forced submission to false, transitory authority) to freedom (a voluntary submission to true, absolute authority); Moses must remain himself even as he represents God to the chosen people and the chosen people to God. He belongs to both and can play his role only if he remains in the middle: close enough to ultimate knowledge to know where to lead, and close enough to his people to know that he will be followed. It was a line too thin for anyone not fully divine to tread. The original Moses both succeeds and fails: he talks to God, but he is "slow of tongue and speech" and has difficulty talking to his people. He takes them to the edge of the promised land but is not allowed to enter because he had broken faith with God in the presence of the Israelites at the waters of Meribah Kadesh in the Desert of Zin.

What was needed in the Soviet version of Exodus, according to Voronsky, was "the life-giving spirit of the dialectic." All literary Bolsheviks were to combine "universalism and internationalism" with a "connection to our factories, our villages, and the revolutionary movement of past eras and decades." In the meantime, the Moses puzzle remained unsolved. Ivanov's Red commander, Vershinin, is a "rock and a cliff" (and his last name is derived from the word for "summit"), but he remains a Russian peasant, with few signs of universalism. Pilniak's leather men are "the best of the sluggish, unruly Russian people," but "none of them has ever read Karl Marx." Fadeev's Red commander, Levinson, has read Karl Marx, but he is not from the Russian folk at all, and Voronsky does not believe that Bolsheviks should appear as "foreign conquerors." The same is true of Malyshkin's "army commander," whose "stone profile" makes him "a stranger to the peaceful dusk of the peasant hut," and of Leonid Leonov's Comrade Arsen, whose eyes, words, veins, and scars are all blue "from iron." These people, according to Voronsky, are "strangers, who live by themselves." Even Libedinsky's Communists, led by the human-size Comrade Robeiko (who is slow of tongue and speech and says "exodus" instead of "escape"), are, in Voronsky's words, "a closed heroic caste that has almost no links to the surrounding world."[49]

One solution is to split Moses in two: a commissar who talks to History and a popular hero who leads the march through the desert (and becomes a crusader in the process). In Ivanov's *Colored Winds*, the wild, truth-seeking peasant, Kalistrat, is paired with the merciless Bolshevik, Nikitin, who explains their division of labor as follows:

> "Some need bread, and some need blood. I supply the blood."
> "And what about me? What am I supposed to supply?"
> "You'll supply the bread."
> "No I won't!"
> "Yes, you will."[50]

He does, of course. His job is to baptize the grass with the plow.

In *Chapaev*, the proletarian commissar Klychkov initiates the peasant warrior Chapaev into the secret knowledge of Communist prophecy. He molds him "like wax" until Chapaev is ready to embrace the "life-giving spirit of the dialectic." Chapaev's sacrifice by drowning means that Klychkov has learned how to mold the people, and the people have learned how to follow Klychkov.[51]

The twin dangers of straying too far in either direction are—as usual—represented by Platonov and Babel. Platonov's Communists are indistinguishable from other village idiots (he created folklore, not myth, whatever his original intentions). Babel's narrator, with glasses on his nose and autumn in his soul, never masters "the simplest of skills" and suffers silently from an unrequited longing and secret revulsion for his Cossack listeners.[52]

Platonov, Babel, and their characters strive to "pull heaven down to earth" but fail—and suffer for it. In the hands of an unbeliever, the exodus can become an eternal march through hell. Lev Lunts's short story, "In the Desert" (1921), has no beginning and no end. "It was frightening and boring. There was nothing to do—except walk on and on. To escape the burning boredom, hunger, and desert gloom and to give their hairy hands and dull fingers something to do, they would steal each other's utensils, skins, cattle, and women, and then kill the thieves. And then they would avenge the killings and kill the killers. There was no water, but plenty of blood. And before them lay the land flowing with milk and honey."[53]

.   .   .

The inferno, by most accounts, is Exodus without the promised land. The inferno justified by an eventual homecoming is a purposeful "tempering of steel," or Exodus the way it is meant to be. The most canonical Bolshevik representation of the Civil War is also the most complete Soviet version of the Exodus myth.

Aleksandr Serafimovich's *The Iron Flood*, published in 1924, was immediately hailed as a great accomplishment of the new Soviet literature and remained required reading in Soviet schools until the end of the Soviet Union. It is based on the story of the march of about sixty thousand Red Army soldiers and civilian refugees across the Caucasus Mountains in August–October 1918. Serafimovich, who was sixty-one at the time of publication, was a veteran radical writer and the official patriarch of "proletarian" literature. He was born into the family of a Don Cossack officer and raised in the Upper Don settlement of Ust-Medveditskaia (which was also the home of Filipp Mironov, who was nine years younger and several social rungs lower). Having been caught up in student "circle" life at the University of St. Petersburg in the 1880s, he had started writing in exile (on the White Sea, like Voronsky and Arosev) and later worked as a reporter, editor, and fiction writer in the Don Area and eventually in Moscow (for Leonid Andreev's *Moscow Courier*). During the Bolshevik uprising in Moscow, he had served as chief literary editor of the Moscow Soviet's *Izvestia*. In early summer 1919, he traveled to the southern front as a *Pravda* correspondent and wrote an article against de-Cossackization. "The victories blinded [the Red Army] to the local population, its hopes for the future, its needs, its prejudices, its expectations of a new life, its tremendous desire to know what the Red columns were bringing, and its unique economic and cultural traditions." One of Serafimovich's two sons served as a commissar in the Special Expeditionary Corps for the suppression of the Upper-Don uprising (with Valentin Trifonov) and was killed at the front in 1920 at the age of twenty.[54]

The Iron Flood begins with a scene of utter confusion: "From all sides came the din of voices, the barking of dogs, neighing of horses, and clanking of metal; the crying of children, rough swearing of men and shouting of women; and the raucous, drunken singing to the accompaniment of an accordion. It was as though a huge beehive had lost its queen, and its hum had become chaotic, frenzied, and discordant." The only force that can give shape to this chaos is the army commander, who makes his appearance as a nameless and motionless bearer of the revolutionary will. "Near the windmill stood a short, stocky man, with a firm, square jaw, who looked as though he were made of lead. His small, grey, gimlet eyes glittered under his low brows as he surveyed the scene, missing nothing. His squat shadow lay on the ground, its head trampled by the feet all around him."[55]

His name is Kozhukh, and he is slow of tongue and speech. "Comrades! What I mean to say is . . . well . . . our comrades are dead . . . and . . . we must honor them . . .'cause they died for us. . . . I mean . . . why did they have to die? Comrades, what I mean to say is that, Soviet Russia is not dead. It will live till the end of time.'" For the prophecy to come true, the people have to cross the wilderness. "The last station before the mountains looked like a scene from the Tower of Babel. Half an hour later Kozhukh's column set out and no one dared try to stop them. But the moment it set out thousands of panic-stricken soldiers and refugees took off behind them with their carts and cattle, jostling and blocking up the road, trying to pass one another and shoving into the ditches anyone who got in their way. And the long column began to creep up the mountain like a monstrous serpent."[56]

The first miracle they encounter after they reach the top is the sea, which "rose, unexpectedly, like an infinite blue wall, whose deep hue was reflected in their eyes."

"Look, the sea!"
"But why does it stand up like a wall?"
"We'll have to climb over it."
"Then why, when you stand on the shore, does it look flat all the way to the end?"
"Haven't you heard about how, when Moses led the Hebrews out of Egyptian slavery, like us now, the sea stood up like a wall and they passed over on dry land"?[57]

They do pass over on dry land, and keep going, on and on—a "dishevelled, ragged, blackened, naked, screeching horde, pursued by the sweltering heat, by hunger and despair." Enemy armies and "myriads of flies" stalk, attack, and lie in wait, but the column crawls on—"in order to reach the top of the range and then slither back down to the steppe where the food and forage are abundant and their own people await them."[58]

The other two Civil War plots—the crucifixion and the apocalypse— perform their usual functions. When all the heat, dust, flies, roar, and exhaustion become unbearable, Kozhukh orders a detour, so that the people may see both the heroic self-sacrifice made on their behalf and the reason for the slaughter they are about to unleash.

In the heavy silence, only the tramping of feet could be heard. All heads turned, and all eyes looked in one direction—toward the straight line of telegraph posts, dwindling into the distance like tiny pencils in the shimmering haze. From the four nearest posts, motionless, hung four naked men. The air around them was black with flies. Their heads were bent low, as if pressing down with their youthful chins on the nooses that held them. Their teeth were bared, and the sockets of their eyes, pecked out by the ravens, gaped emptily. From their bellies, also pecked and torn, hung green, slimy entrails. The sun beat down. Their skin, bruised black by the beatings, had burst open in places. The ravens flew up to the tops of the posts and watched with their heads cocked to one side.

Four men, and then a fifth . . . and on the fifth hung the blackened body of a girl, naked, with her breasts cut off.

"Regiment, ha-alt !"[59]

The violence visited on the poor and the hungry—back in Egypt, here in the desert, or anywhere since the beginning of time—is returned a thousandfold. They grind the Edomites, Moabites, Bashanites, and Amorites into the sand, raze their fortresses, and kill them all to the last man. "Neck-deep in the water, the Georgian soldiers stood with arms outstretched towards the vanishing steamers. They shouted and cursed, begging for mercy in the name of their children, but the swift sabers came down upon their necks, heads, and shoulders, staining the water with blood." The Cossacks did not beg for mercy. "When the sun rose above the hills and over the limitless steppe, one could see all the Cossacks with their long, black moustaches. There were no wounded, no prisoners among them—they all lay dead."[60]

Before entering one of the towns they come to, Kozhukh gives orders to two of his commanders. To the first he says: "Annihilate them all!"; to the second—"Exterminate them all!" And so they do: "The embankment, pier, streets, squares, courtyards, and highways were strewn with dead bodies. They lay in heaps in various poses. Some had their heads twisted round, and some were missing their heads. Brains were scattered over the pavement like lumps of jelly. As if in a slaughter-house, dark, clotted blood lay in pools along the houses and stone fences, and blood trickled through the cracks under the gates."[61]

Most of the violence is in the biblical mode of indiscriminate mass murder, but Serafimovich has enough faith and mythopoeic consistency to take a guiltless closer look. The scenes of individual sacrifice he pauses to describe do not substitute for Armageddon, the way they do in Platonov and Babel: they explain and illustrate it with the same scrupulous thoroughness with which Kopenkin killed:

From the priest's house they led out some people with ashen faces and golden epaulettes—part of the Cossack headquarters' staff had been taken. They cut off their heads by the priest's stable, and the blood soaked into the dung.

The din of the cries, gunshots, curses, and groans drowned out the sound of the river.

The house of the Ataman was searched from top to bottom, but he was nowhere to be found. He had fled. The soldiers began shouting:

"If you don't come out, we'll kill all your children!"

The Ataman did not come out.

They began to slaughter the children. Grovelling on her knees with her braids streaming down, the Ataman's wife clutched desperately at the soldiers' legs. One of them turned to her and said reproachfully:

"Why are you yelling like a stuck pig? I had a daughter just like yours—a three-year-old. We buried her up there in the mountains, but I didn't yell."

And he hacked down the little girl and then crushed the skull of the hysterically laughing mother.[62]

The Iron Flood became the canonical Book of the Civil War because it was the most complete realization of the flood metaphor, the most elaborate Soviet version of Exodus, and the most successful solution of the Moses puzzle—the "life-giving dialectic" between the transcendental and the local, the conscious and the spontaneous, predestination and free will. As the human mass turns into an iron flood, the Commander acquires a measure of humanity. By the time they arrive in the promised land, they come together for good.[63]

"Our father . . . lead us where you will! We will lay down our lives!"

A thousand hands reached out to him and pulled him off; a thousand hands lifted him over their heads and carried him. And the steppe shook for many versts, roused by countless voices:

"Hurrah -a-ah! Hurra-a-a-a-ah for Kozhukh!"

Kozhukh was carried to the place where the men stood in orderly ranks and then to the place where the artillery stood. He was carried past the horses of the squadrons—and the horsemen turned in their saddles and, with shining faces and mouths opened wide, let out a continuous roar.

He was carried among the refugees and among the carts, and the mothers held up their babies to him.

They carried him back again and set him down gently upon the cart. When Kozhukh opened his mouth to speak, they all gasped, as if seeing him for the first time.

"Look, his eyes are blue!"

No, they did not cry out because they could not put words to their emotions, but his eyes, when seen up close, really were blue and gentle, with a shy expression, like a child's. . . .

The orators spoke until nightfall, one after another. As they talked, everyone experienced the ever-growing, inexpressibly blissful feeling of being linked to the enormity that they knew and did not know, one that was called Soviet Russia.[64]

■ ■ ■

By the mid-1920s, the sacred foundations of the Soviet state had come to include the "October Revolution," which centered on the storming of the Winter Palace, and—much more prominently—the Civil War, which consisted of the Civil War proper (the war on the battlefield) and "War Communism" (the war on property, market, money, and the division of labor). War Communism was the murkiest part of the "glorious past": it represented the heart of Bolshevism (the transformation of a society into a sect), but it was scrapped in 1921 as unenforceable and later given its posthumous name, which suggested contingency and perhaps reluctance. The definitive Soviet text on its meaning and significance was written by one of its designers, the economist, Lev Kritsman. It was published in 1924 under the title *The Heroic Period of the Great Russian Revolution (An Analytical Essay on So-Called "War Communism")*.

Kritsman grew up in the family of a People's Will activist (who was also a dentist), attended Khaim Gokhman's Odessa Commercial Institute, joined his first reading circle at the age of fourteen, studied at the Odessa (New Russia) University before being expelled for revolutionary activity, graduated from the University of Zurich as a chemist, returned to Russia in a sealed train after the October Revolution, engineered (at the age of twenty-seven) the nationalization of the sugar industry, participated in the writing of the decree on the nationalization of all large industry, and, in 1924, became a member of the Communist Academy and a leading Bolshevik expert on rural economics and the "peasant question."[65]

According to Kritsman, the "Great Russian Revolution" (the term was modeled on the standard Bolshevik name for the French Revolution) made "the unthinkable *real*." It proved "the correctness of Marxism, which, decades earlier, had predicted the inevitability of everything that occurred in Russia after 1917: the collapse of capitalism, the proletarian revolution, the destruction of the capitalist state, the expropriation of capitalist property, and the onset of the epoch of the dictatorship of the proletariat." The Revolution's socioeconomic dimension, or "so-called War Communism," was "the proletarian organization of production and reproduction during the decisive period of the proletarian revolution; in general, therefore, it was not something that was imposed on the revolution from the outside." In fact, it was "the first grandiose experiment in building an autarkic proletarian economy—an experiment in taking *the first steps in the transition to socialism*. In its essence, it was not an error on the part of certain individuals or a certain class; it was—

although not in its pure form and not without certain perversions—*an anticipation of the future*, a breakthrough of that future into the present (now already past)."[66]

This "heroic" phase of the revolution rested, according to Kritsman, on five fundamental principles, all of them sacred, still relevant, and necessary for the transition to socialism. The first was the "economic principle," which meant that members' labor contributions were not distorted by "commercial, legal, and other considerations unrelated to production." Emancipated labor finally resolved the bourgeois contradiction "between the abstract, and therefore hypocritical, political system, in which individual citizens are seen as ideal, interchangeable atoms, and the economic system, in which real individuals coexist with other individuals in real life (and, most important, in relations of class domination and subjection.)" The state of the revolutionary proletariat was one of unprecedented transparency and consistency. It was a state without "politics" in the Babylonian sense.

The second was "the class principle," or "*the spirit of ruthless class exclusivity*." A member of the former ruling classes "was not simply deprived of his superior status—he was expelled from Soviet society and forced to huddle in dark corners, like barely tolerated dirt. A bourgeois was a contemptible outcast, a *pariah* devoid of not only property, but also honor." Proof of "untainted worker or peasant origins" replaced titles and money as a ticket to social advancement: "The stigma of belonging to the class of exploiters could guarantee a place in a concentration camp, prison or, at best, a hovel left behind by proletarians who had moved to better houses. Such ruthless class exclusivity, such social extermination of the exploiting class was a source of tremendous moral inspiration, of a *passionate enthusiasm* of the proletariat and all the exploited classes. It was a mighty call to the victims of domination, an assertion of their inner superiority over the dirty world of exploiters."

The third "organizing principle of the era" was the "labor principle," or the uncompromising adoption of St. Paul's motto, "He who does not work, neither shall he eat." In Kritsman's Marxist formulation, "the path to the realm of freedom passed through necessary labor." This involved forced labor for the former exploiters and more labor for the laborers. Contrary to the petit bourgeois view of production (rooted in unspecialized small-scale work), "modern productive labor is not an expression of man's free creative potential; it is not pleasurable as such. In this regard, the proletarian revolution does not bring about any fundamental change. On the contrary, because it presupposes a continued development of large-scale production, it leads to a further intensification of the necessary character of productive labor." What was different was the fact that, under the dictatorship of the proletariat, hard work would—eventually, lead to leisure, and leisure, under socialism, would become an expression of free human creativity. "The proletarian revolution returns necessary labor to its original purpose *of achieving leisure* by restoring the connection, severed by capitalism, between productive labor and leisure, thus creating a powerful incentive for a further intensification of labor." To conclude (in the style of the original scripture), "the emancipation of necessary labor from elements of free creativity means the emancipation of free creativity from the chains of necessary labor."

The fourth principle was collectivism, which manifested itself most forcefully in the nationalization of industry, but also in collective management (collegiality), barter, education, and housing, among many other things. "Probably nothing was more typical of that epoch than the desire to eradicate individualism and implant collectivism."

The fifth and final principle was "rationalization," or the rejection of tradition. "In revolutionary eras, the fact of the existence of a given social institution is not an argument in favor of its continued existence. . . . The motto of organic eras, 'it exists, therefore it is needed,' is replaced by a very different one: 'If it is needed, it exists, if it is not needed, it will be destroyed.'" In bourgeois revolutions, this principle had been applied to "religion, morality, law, domestic life, and political order," but not to the economy. During the proletarian revolution, the whole society was subject to reform, and the most important reform of all was "the destruction of fetishistic relations and the establishment of direct, open, and immediate connections among various parts of the Soviet economy." This meant, in the first place, "the destruction of the market, the destruction of commodity, cash, and credit relations."[67]

Most of Kritsman's book was about the destruction of the market as the central feature of the proletarian revolution ("a principle that enveloped all spheres of social life" and resulted in attempts to abolish law and religion, among other things). The predicted resistance of the enemies of the Revolution inevitably led to the Civil War, and the Civil War inevitably led to *"the forcible strangling of the market,"* "the suppression of money-commodity relations," "the total ban on trade," and "the expropriation of property owners." Unfolding "as an irresistible, all-destroying flood," this process inevitably went beyond economic rationality because only an all-destroying flood could deprive the counterrevolutionary capital of "the air of the market that it needed in order to survive." "This transcendence of immediate economic rationality was both the reason for the victory of the revolution and the root of the perversions that marked the autarkic proletarian economic order." This dialectic was the result of a pact between two mythic giants: the proletariat and the peasantry. The proletariat agreed to allow the peasantry to keep its land in exchange for military support from "the vast majority of the population"; the peasantry agreed to allow the proletariat to "strangle the market" in exchange for proletarian leadership in the war against the feudal order. Once victory over the feudal order was achieved, the peasantry withdrew its support for the strangling of the market. "Thus, the military and, most important, *political victory* of the proletariat inevitably led, under these conditions, to its *economic retreat.*"[68]

Under these conditions, the peasantry seemed to stand for "economic rationality," but Kritsman did not take the logic of his argument in that direction. "What was a retreat for the proletarian revolution," he argued, "was the *completion* of the antifeudal peasant revolution." NEP was to last for as long as necessary for this process to run its course. In 1924, it was clear that a new—"cautious and methodical"—offensive was getting under way. The point of this offensive was to prepare for "the coming world-historical battle between the proletariat and capital."[69]

.   .   .

Having won the war, taken over the state, established stable administrative hierarchies, rewarded themselves with a system of exclusive benefits, worked out a canon of foundation myths, and retreated temporarily in the expectation of the coming world-historical battle between the proletariat and capital, the Bolsheviks were about to face the most difficult moment in the history of any sect: the death of the leader-founder.

In March 1923, after Lenin suffered his second stroke and lost his ability to speak, Karl Radek wrote that the world proletariat's greatest wish was "that this Moses, who led the slaves out of the land of captivity, might enter the Promised Land along with us." On January 21, 1924, Lenin died. The next day, the Central Committee of the Party issued an official statement ("To the Party, to All Working People"), in which it summarized the main points of the new iconography of the Bolshevik leader.[70]

First, he was "the man who founded our party of steel, kept building it year after year, led it while under the blows of tsarism, taught and tempered it in the fierce struggle with the traitors of the working class—with the lukewarm, the undecided, the defectors." He was the man "under whose guidance our party, enveloped in powder-smoke, planted the banner of October throughout the land." As Bukharin wrote on the same day, "like a giant, he walked in front of the human flood, guiding the movement of countless human units, building a disciplined army of labor, sending it into battle, destroying the enemy, taming the elements, and lighting, with the searchlight of his powerful mind, both the straight avenues and the dark back alleys, through which the workers' detachments marched with their rebellious red flags."[71]

Lenin could be the founder and leader because he was a prophet. According to the official statement, "Lenin could, like no one else, see things great and small: foresee enormous historical shifts and, at the same time, notice and use every tiny detail. . . . He did not recognize frozen formulas; there were no blinders on his wise, all-seeing eyes." He could, in Bukharin's words, "hear the grass growing beneath the ground, the streams running and gurgling below, and the thoughts and ideas going through the minds of the countless toilers of the earth." As Koltsov wrote almost a year before Lenin's death, "He is a man from the future, a pioneer from over there—

from the world of fulfilled communism. . . . Treading firmly on the wreck-
age of the past and building the future with his own hands, he has moved
far above, into the joyous realm of the coming world."[72]

Like all true prophets, Lenin was as close to the earth as he was to the
world above, as close to his people as he was to the bright future. He was
both a teacher and a friend, a comrade and "a dictator in the best sense of
the word" (as Bukharin put it). "On the one hand," wrote Osinsky, "he is a
man of such 'common' and 'normal' appearance that, really, why couldn't he
get together with Lloyd George and chat with him peacefully about European affairs? But, on the other hand, that could result in both Lloyd George
and the entire Genoa conference being blown sky high! For, on the one
hand, he is Ulianov, but, on the other, he is Lenin." Or, in Koltsov's formulation, "There is Ulianov, who took care of those around him and was as nurturing as a father, as tender as a brother, and as simple and cheerful as a
friend. . . . And then there is Lenin, who caused Planet Earth unprecedented
trouble and stood at the head of history's most terrible, most devastatingly
bloody struggle against oppression, ignorance, backwardness, and superstition. Two faces—and only one man; not a duality but a synthesis."[73]

Lenin's synthesis went well beyond the unity of the Son of God and the
Son of Man. Lenin, in both his incarnations, was equal to his followers, and
his followers—in all their "countless units"—were equal to Lenin. On the
one hand, according to the Central Committee obituary, "everything truly
great and heroic that the proletariat possesses . . . finds its magnificent
embodiment in Lenin, whose name has become the symbol of the new
world from east to west and from north to south." On the other, "every
member of our Party is a small part of Lenin. Our whole Communist family
is a collective embodiment of Lenin." This meant that Lenin was, by definition, immortal:

> Lenin lives in the soul of every member of our party. . . .
> Lenin lives in the heart of every honest worker
> Lenin lives in the heart of every poor peasant.
> Lenin lives among the millions of colonial slaves.
> Lenin lives in the hatred that our enemies have for Leninism,
>   Communism, and Bolshevism.[74]

But Lenin was immortal in another sense, too. He was immortal because he had suffered and died for mankind in order to be resurrected
with the coming of Communism. "Comrade Lenin gave his whole life to the
working class, all of it from its conscious beginning to its last martyr's
breath." Or, in the words of Arosev's eulogy, "he accepted the enormous
and terrible burden—to think for 150 million people"—lifted the whole of
Russia, and, "having lifted it, lost his strength and broke down."[75]

The announcement of Lenin's death coincided with the nineteenth anniversary of Bloody Sunday, the massacre of a peaceful demonstration by

imperial troops in January 1905. According to Koltsov, "Lenin, the leader of the working people of the world, sacrificed himself to them nineteen years after those first bodies fell on Palace Square in Petersburg. . . . The date of January 21st, written in black to mark Lenin's death, says simply and firmly: "Don't be afraid of tomorrow's bloody-red date—the 22nd. That day of blood on the snow in Petersburg was the day of awakening. This awakening will come—albeit in blood, too—to the rest of the world." Lenin was the spring "of energy and faith" that Sverdlov had prophesied twenty years earlier—the "noisy and tempestuous" real day that was "sweeping away everything weak, feeble, and old." Lenin, according to Koltsov, "signi-fies a joyous and tempestuous awakening from a long sleep full of bloody nightmares to a new energy of struggle and work." The Easter egg commis-sar from Lavrenev's *The Forty-First* (published in 1924) was a miniature Lenin—as were all commissars, Party members, honest workers, poor peasants, and colonial slaves. Lenin was the chief Easter egg commissar and the original savior. His sacrality (immortality) resided in his "cause" and his disciples—but also in the icons, rituals, and myths that preserved his likeness. Ulianov was as immortal as Lenin—and so, it turned out, was their body.[76]

"Dear one! Unforgettable one! Great one!" wrote Bukharin, addressing "our common leader, our wise teacher, and our dear, precious comrade." Most of Lenin would live on through "his very own beloved child and heir—our Party," but the immediacy of physical affection might be gone forever. "Never again will we see that enormous brow, that marvelous head which used to radiate revolutionary energy, those vibrant, piercing, impressive eyes, those firm and imperious hands, that whole solid, robust figure that stood at the border of two epochs in the history of mankind." By switching from the physical "figure" to the metaphorical one within the same sen-tence, Bukharin suggests a solution. The images and personal objects of the dead help preserve the immediacy of physical affection for as long as live memories last; the icons and relics of sacred founders and heroes can preserve such immediacy for as long as the sacred universe they founded remains sacred. Most sacred objects associated with particular heroes—temples, icons, texts, meals, priests—acquire sacrality indirectly, by sym-bolic transfer; some are believed to be the hero's personal items (the closer to the body—tunics, cloaks, chains—the better); and some are actual bodies or bodily remains (the mummies of Christian and Buddhist saints, the tooth of the Buddha, the hair of the Prophet Muhammad, the head of Orpheus, the thumb of St. Catherine). The fact that Lenin's remains were sacred and would be venerated in some form was beyond doubt; the ques-tion was how. The answer was provided by the government Funeral Com-mission, which, in late March, was renamed the Commission for the Im-mortalization of the Memory of V. I. Ulianov (Lenin).[77]

The day after Lenin's death, an official delegation took a train to the Gorki estate outside of Moscow, where Lenin had been living. Mikhail

Koltsov, in his capacity as *Pravda* correspondent, traveled with them. "In the middle of the night, in the frozen mist, the elders of the great Bolshevik tribe set out for the place where they were to receive the still body of their departed chief: receive it, bring it back, and display it to the orphaned millions." From the station, a convoy of horse-drawn sleds took the delegates to the manor house. Sverdlov and Malkov had chosen it as Lenin's country residence in September 1918, soon after the assassination attempt. Its last prerevolutionary owner was Zinaida Morozova, the widow of the wealthy industrialist, Savva Morozov, who had financed the Bolshevik Party until his death in 1905.

> The tall white old house with slender columns is enclosed within a noble frame of silver forest and blue snow. The glass door opens easily to let us in. This small forest palace, the leader's final resting place, the place where an inimitable life and an unquenchable will for battle have ended, will always remain before the tired, expectant, and believing eyes of millions of oppressed people.
>
> The house is quiet, spacious, and comfortable. The carpets guard the silence. Every inch is history; every step leads to an object of devout reverence by future generations. Through these windows, patterned with frost, he, the giant who apprehended the whole world and was then cut down in his prime and forced to suffer the inexpressible torment of imposed powerlessness, peered into the future and saw, beyond the short forest path and overgrown village garden, the extended hands of the hundreds of millions of our brothers being crucified on the Golgotha of industrialism and roasted in the multi-storied capitalist hell of the entire world.

The delegates walked through the house and ascended the stairs to "the death room." "Here he is! He hasn't changed at all. He is just like himself! His face is calm, and he is almost—almost—smiling that inimitable, indescribable, sly childlike smile of his that is obvious only to those who knew him. His upper lip with its moustache is mischievously lifted and seems very much alive. It is as if he himself were puzzled by what has just happened. Going back down the stairs, a soldier—a Bolshevik—murmurs to himself: 'Ilich looks great—just the way he did when we last saw him.'"[78]

Lenin's heart and brain were handed over to Arosev, who was the "responsible custodian" at the Lenin Institute, created the year before. The rest of the body was transported to Moscow, placed in the Hall of Columns of the Trade Union House, where it lay in state for three days, and, after a solemn funeral ceremony, moved to a temporary crypt in Red Square. One of the members of the Funeral Commission, the commissar for foreign trade, Leonid Krasin, proposed preserving the body indefinitely by submerging it in embalming liquid and placing it in a metal box with a glass top. Krasin was a professional engineer who used to preside over the

St. Petersburg electric cable system and Savva Morozov's electrical power plant in Orekhovo-Zuevo—as well as Bolshevik bank "expropriations," bomb making, and fund-raising. (Most of the funds he raised came from Morozov, whose mysterious death in May 1905 had led to much inconclusive speculation about Krasin's involvement.) Krasin was the most consistent Bolshevik advocate of the technocratic path to human redemption (and, possibly, resurrection). In 1921, in his speech at the funeral of the director of the Chemical Institute and Old Bolshevik, Lev Yakovlevich Karpov, he had said: "I am certain that the time will come when science will become so powerful that it will be able to recreate a deceased organism. I am certain that the time will come when one will be able to use the elements of a person's life to recreate the physical person. And I am certain that when that time does come, when liberated mankind, using all the might of science and technology, whose power and scale we cannot now imagine, is able to resurrect the great historical figures, fighters for the liberation of mankind—I am certain that at that time, our comrade, Lev Yakovlevich, will be among those great figures."[79]

It was Lev Yakovlevich's friend and protégé, Boris Zbarsky, who beat Krasin out for the job of preserving Lenin's remains. Born in 1885 to a Jewish family in Kamenets-Podolsky, Zbarsky graduated from the University of Geneva and, in 1915–16, worked as an estate manager and director of two chemical plants in Vsevolodo-Vilva, in the northern Urals. The estate and the factories belonged to Zinaida Morozova (who also owned "the tall white old house with slender columns"). In 1916, Zbarsky invented a new method of purifying medical chloroform for frontline hospitals and launched, together with L. Ya. Karpov, its industrial production. After the Revolution, he moved to Moscow to become deputy director of the "Karpov Institute." When Zbarsky was consulted about the preservation of Lenin's body, he rejected Krasin's plan (along with various refrigeration alternatives) and proposed "moist embalming" as practiced in the anatomical museum of Professor Vladimir Vorobiev in Kharkov. In March 1924, after much lobbying and maneuvering and in the face of the body's steady deterioration, Zbarsky managed to persuade Feliks Dzerzhinsky (the head of the Immortalization Commission) to opt for the Vorobiev method and to persuade Vorobiev (a former White émigré) to agree to be involved.[80]

On March 25, 1924, the Funeral Commission announced that it had decided "to take measures available to modern science to preserve the body for as long as possible." On March 26, Vorobiev, Zbarsky, and their assistants began their round-the-clock working vigil in the freezing crypt. The goal was not simply to preserve the body but to preserve the likeness, thus creating an icon in the flesh. This ruled out traditional mummification, because, according to Zbarsky, "if you were shown the mummy of a loved one, you would be horrified." Moreover, that likeness had to look naturally uncorrupted, not visibly manipulated like body parts "in glass jars filled with antiseptic fluids." Soviet scientists, wrote Zbarsky later, "had been given a completely new task. The goal was to make sure that the body of Vladimir Ilich remained in the open air, at normal temperatures, accessible for daily viewing by many thousands of people—while preserving Lenin's appearance. Such an assignment was unprecedented in world science."[81]

Boris Zbarsky
(Courtesy of I. B. Zbarsky)

Zbarsky and Vorobiev had been asked to produce a miracle, and they did. On June 16, 1924, Dzerzhinsky inquired whether the body could be shown to the delegates of the Fifth Congress of the Comintern. Zbarsky went to see N. K. Krupskaia to ask for some clothes. Krupskaia told him she did not approve of the idea and did not believe it could possibly work, and, when she did bring "some shirts, long underwear, and socks, her hands were trembling." On June 18, the Comintern delegation and family members arrived at the newly built wooden mausoleum. According to Zbarsky, Krupskaia burst into tears. Lenin's brother Dmitry said: "I can't say much. I am very emotional. He looks exactly the way he did right after his death, perhaps even better." On July 26, exactly four months after the beginning of the work, a government delegation saw the body and approved its appearance. Enukidze said that "hundreds of thousands and perhaps millions of people would be extremely happy to see this man's image." On August 1, 1924, the mausoleum was opened to visitors. Vorobiev went back to Kharkov, and Zbarsky became the body's chief guardian.[82]

The chief guardian—"responsible custodian"—of Lenin's textual heritage was Arosev (who had transferred Lenin's heart to the mausoleum and Lenin's brain to the special Laboratory for the Study of V. I. Lenin's Brain). Arosev's main job at the Lenin Institute was to catalog Lenin's writings and compile the "calendar" of his life, but his most creative contribution to Leniniana was his short book *On Vladimir Ilich*, published in 1926. The book consists of several apparently unconnected episodes. In the first, two boys are having a race. The shorter, "light-haired" one, wins, and buys three birds in a cage. The boys go to a place called the Golden Crown to set them free, but one of the birds is sick and cannot fly. The tall boy is impatient, but the light-haired one cradles the bird in his hands, gives it water to drink, and insists on taking it to the bushes on the bank of the Volga, where it will be safe. "Now the tall one ran ahead because he wanted to get rid of the bird as quickly as possible, while the light-haired one lagged behind, blowing lightly on the bird and stroking it. He did not want to part with it."[83]

In the next scene, the light-haired little boy has become a ginger-haired university student "with the kind of brightness in his face that marks children who are developed beyond their years but have not lost their physical freshness." After he and his comrades are arrested for staging a student demonstration, one of the students asks him what he is going to do now:

> "What am I going to do?" he said, squinting toward the corner of the cell. "What can I do? My path has been set for me by my older brother." [Lenin's older brother had been hanged for attempted regicide when Lenin was seventeen.]
>
> He said this quietly, but everyone seemed to shudder. They looked at each other in silence.
>
> "So that was your brother?" asked someone quietly, as if Doubting Thomas had just thrust his fingers into the fresh wounds.
>
> The ginger-haired student continued to sit with his arms around his knees and left the question unanswered.[84]

In one of the later episodes, a balding young man reads a book (Hauptmann's *The Weavers*) to a circle of disciples. After the reading, he is approached by a worker named Grigoriev, who asks him many questions about meeting times and addresses. "For a moment, he looked hard at Grigoriev, as if trying to remember something deeply hidden. But Grigoriev could not look him in the eye. In the same way, Judas had not been able to look his teacher in the eyes at the last supper in Jerusalem, when the teacher said: 'One of you will betray me.'"[85]

In the next scene, a smiling, bald exile persuades a village storekeeper to take pity on a peasant who does not have enough money for an Easter present for his daughter. But when the peasant thanks him "from the bottom of his heart," the exile suddenly stops smiling. "The more 'kindness' we show toward the small producer (e.g., to the peasant) in the practical part of our program," he writes several months later, "the 'more strictly' must we treat these unreliable and double-faced social elements in the *theoretical* part of the program, without sacrificing one iota of *our* position. 'If you adopt our position,' we tell them, 'you can count on "indulgence" of every kind, but if you don't, well then, you've been warned! Under the "dictatorship," we will say about you: "there is no point in wasting words where the use of power is required."'"[86]

In the final episodes, only one man is prepared to use power when it is required. The meaning of the light-haired boy's Golden Crown has been revealed. Bukharin, Voronsky, and other Bolsheviks who grew up reading the Apocalypse, would have had no trouble recognizing Revelation 14: "I looked, and there before me was a white cloud, and seated on the cloud was one 'like the son of man' with a crown of gold on his head and a sharp sickle in his hand. Then another angel came out of the temple and called in a loud voice to him who was sitting on the cloud, 'Take your sickle and reap, because the time to reap has come, for the harvest of the earth is ripe.' So he who was seated on the cloud swung his sickle over the earth, and the earth was harvested."[87]

Arosev worked at the Lenin Institute for slightly more than a year before moving on to other things. (His next assignment was the press bureau of the Soviet embassy in Paris, under Ambassador Krasin.) A much more prolific writer on Lenin and Leninism was Platon Kerzhentsev (who continued to contribute to the canon throughout his life). But the most resonant words were Mayakovsky's. Several days after the Immortalization Commission announced its decision to preserve Lenin's body, he wrote the words that would later become the Soviet Union's motto: "Lenin lived, Lenin lives, Lenin will always live." By October, he had finished his poem about Lenin's life, death, and resurrection. "Lenin, even now, is more alive than the living" because he is both "a slayer, an avenger" and "the most humane of humans" ("the earthiest of those who have ever walked the Earth"). Above his mausoleum, "Red Square rises like a red banner,"

And from that banner,
    with every flutter,
Lenin,
  alive,
    beckons:
"Proletarians,
  prepare,
    for one last battle!
Slaves,
  stand straight
    and stiffen your backs![88]

Himself an avenger and savior, Mayakovsky first prophesied the last battle ("I'll rip out my soul . . . and hand it to you—all bloodied, for a banner") after his Gioconda was taken away from him. But of course no one took her away. She chose her own battles. After Mayakovsky left Odessa in 1914, Maria Denisova married an engineer, followed him to Switzerland, gave birth to a daughter, studied sculpture in Lausanne and Geneva, separated from her husband, left for the Civil War front, served as head of the Art Agitation Department in the First and Second Red Cavalry armies, and moved in with the famous Commissar Efim Shchadenko (who served in the Military Revolutionary Council under both Semen Budennyi and Filipp Mironov). In 1924, at the age of thirty, she enrolled at the Higher Art and Technology Studios in Moscow. For her graduation project, she submitted a marble sculpture of Lenin's head resting in his coffin.[89]

V. I. Lenin, by Maria Denisova

7

THE GREAT
DISAPPOINTMENT

Lenin's death was mostly about immortality. But it was also about sorrow and despair. "In 1924, after the death of the beloved leader of the Party, Comrade Lenin," wrote the shepherd-turned-public-prosecutor-turned-pensioner, Vasily Orekhov, "I could not bear his death and wept for about three months, resulting in traumatic nervosis."[1]

Moses had died, the promised land had been reached, but there was no milk and honey—presumably because the people had "prostituted themselves to foreign gods." Or, in the equally productive metaphor, the real day had come, but there was still death and mourning and crying and pain. As the founder of Seventh-Day Adventism, Hiram Edson, wrote after the "Great Disappointment" of October 22, 1844, "our fondest hopes and expectations were blasted, and such a spirit of weeping came over us as I never experienced before." And as a Xhosa peasant said after the world failed to come to an end on February 18, 1857, "I sat outside my hut and saw the sun rise, so did all the people. We watched until midday, yet the sun continued its course. We still watched until the afternoon and yet it did not return, and the people began to despair because they saw this thing was not true."[2]

Andrei Platonov's *Chevengur* is one of the most eloquent Bolshevik laments over the apparent nonarrival of Communism. Comrade Chepurny and his assistant, the Chekist, Piusya, have exterminated the bourgeoisie and expelled the "half-bourgeoisie" along with most of the animals. Only twelve people are left in the town: eleven Bolsheviks and a woman, who, "being the raw material of communal joy, was kept in a special house, away from the dangerous life of the masses." Chepurny "sat down on the ground by a wattle fence and softly, with two fingers, touched a burdock that was growing there; it too was alive—and now it was going to live under communism. Somehow dawn was a long time coming, though surely it must have been time for the new day. Chepurny went very still and began to feel afraid: would the sun rise in the morning, would morning ever come—now that the old world was no longer?"[3]

The Bolshevik spas and sanatoria of the 1920s were mostly about croquet, caviar, chess, concerts, billiards, boats, and "bubbles all over your body." But they were also about sickness and sorrow. At the time of Lenin's death, Voronsky was staying at a rest home (as was his friend and patron Trotsky, who was suffering from a mysterious melancholy). Smilga and Arosev had recently returned from sanatoria in Germany; Podvoisky was on his way to one there. Orekhov would never return to active work (he was forty when he started weeping); Lander would retire for health reasons within three years, at the age of forty-four; and Kritsman would be judged too sick to teach in 1929, when he was thirty-nine. Bukharin would remain active and energetic, but, in the words of his last wife, Anna Larina, "his emotional constitution was extraordinarily delicate, I would even say, morbidly frail." On the day Lenin died, most of the leader's disciples cried, "but no one sobbed as much as Bukharin." Indeed, "this trait—emotional fragility and acute sensitivity—would often send him into a state of hysteria. He wept easily."[4]

Orekhov and Bukharin were not alone. Of the 144 people who received medical treatment at the Central Executive Committee Rest Home in Tetkovo in the summer of 1928, 98 (or 68 percent) were diagnosed with emotional disorders: "Neurasthenia—18; Psycho-neurasthenia—6; Psychosis—1; Exhaustion—73." A year earlier, in 1927, the Lenin Rest Home in Maryino (the Central Executive Committee Rest Home No. 1) had received 1,266 guests. Of these, "six people (0.47 percent) were healthy, while the other 1,260 had various complaints." Almost one-half (598 of them) had "functional diseases of the nervous system"; 27 had "organic diseases of the nervous system"; 59 were diagnosed as "neurotics"; and 130, as "suffering from exhaustion." Altogether, 65 percent of the guests complained of some form of emotional distress. Neither of the homes was a specialized medical institution: both were vacation resorts designed for sociability and recreation, with one or two doctors sent over from the Kremlin Health Department.[5]

Rest and therapy produced the need for more rest and therapy. As Stalin's father-in-law, S. Ya. Alliluev, wrote to the head of the CEC Housing Authority in June 1930, "I would be very grateful if you could find it possible to place me in one of the CEC rest homes for a couple of weeks. Somewhere in the middle of a thick forest, where it's quiet. I recently returned from Matsesta [a balneological spa outside Sochi], where I was trying to cure my old man's ailments and my heart. The sulphur baths have made me quite weak, and I need to restore my health."[6]

At the height of the collectivization campaign (and three months before his son-in-law's "Dizzy from Success" article ordered a temporary halt to the mass violence), Alliluev may have had other reasons for wishing to be in the middle of a thick forest. Two years earlier, Olympiada Mitskevich's reasons seem to have been perfectly straightforward. The daughter of Siberian peasants, Olympiada had joined the revolutionaries at the age of sixteen when she married a prominent Bolshevik, Sergei Mitskevich (who had joined the revolutionaries at the age of fourteen when he read Turgenev's *The Virgin Soil*). By 1928, they had separated. He was working as the director of the Museum of the Revolution, and she was an employee of the Institute of Party History (and future employee of Adoratsky's Lenin Institute). Her main occupation, however, was to work on recovering from a life of self-deprivation that had begun when she dedicated herself to the future revolution and ended when she became a professional keeper of the past. In July 1928, she wrote from Czechoslovakia to the Society of Old Bolsheviks asking for help in moving from one resort to another. "After receiving treatment at Carlsbad, which always weakens me, I need rest. . . . I am not asking for financial assistance from you at this point. All I need is a ticket to Nizhny Novgorod and then down to Samara, and then another one, to return by the same route."[7]

The Society of Old Bolsheviks had been created soon after the Civil War for the purpose of preserving the common memory, passing it on to future generations, and attending to the welfare of its current members (all Bolsheviks with at least eighteen years of uninterrupted Party affiliation). The Society provided them with financial assistance, access to elite housing, and preferential college admissions for their children and grandchildren. The most frequent petitioners among the members were pensioners, who had plenty of time to convalesce and reminisce, and former workers, who did not have access to comparable benefits at their place of work. Since the salaries of Party members could not exceed a certain limit (the "Party Maximum"), and since even under NEP the supply of goods and services was uneven, most elite consumption took place through a highly stratified system of exclusive benefits. The Society of Old Bolsheviks mitigated the effects of this stratification among the original converts. The most common requests—even from the neediest members—were for rest and therapy.

On July 4, 1928, the baker-turned-trade-union-official, Boris Ivanov, reminded the Society of a request he had made in his previous letter.

I appealed to the society of old bolsheviks through a secretary with a request to be sent to a Kislovodsk spa for free treatment which request was denied due to the reason that I hadn't been a member for six months even though I was feeling bad and lay in bed sick for a whole month. I did get the treatment paid for by the central committee of the party so in that regard I am okay but they didn't include the railway ticket which means I'll have to pay my own way.

Although I receive the Party Maximum I am in very dire straits. Besides the family of four persons who are all my dependents of whom my wife is sick, I was on top of everything burgled about ten months ago which is to say that in my absence they robbed my apartment clean and took all our winter coats and some of our fall clothes and underwear of my whole family and of course they never found neither the theives nor the things. So I had to go into debt to get clothes for my children and will myself go around in a fall overcoat for the second winter in a row due to not having the necessary resources for the purchase. In this situation it's not so easy to add to your existing debts.[8]

Ivanov did not ask for money for a new coat; he asked for free train tickets to the spa. His request was granted.

The former shepherd, Vasily Orekhov, wrote to the Society in late 1927 asking for money. The board members received a typed version of the original letter.

In 1924 I got a bad case of traumatic nervosis for which I received treatment in Korsikov's sanatorium for three months. During this period I relatively rested and returned to work. Having worked until January 19, 1925, my illness came back, but in a more serious form. I lost the use of my tongue and legs. My physical condition was greatly affected by the cold. At the end of February the Moscow Committee sent me for treatment to Sevastopol, to the Institute of Physical Therapy, where I stayed for three months. At the end of the treatment my doctors suggested that I stay in the south. . . . In Simferopol, my apartment was broken into by some bandits, who killed my sixteen-year-old son, whose funeral cost 186 rubles. My family was so frightened by the attack that it entered into a mental condition, and my wife and daughter are still suffering from it. My wife fell very seriously ill, to whom was recommended by the Medical Commission to proceed to Evpatoria to take salt and mud baths, and, for the children, sea baths and electric treatments. I had to send my whole family to Evpatoria for two months. This treatment cost me 476 rubles. . . . Appealing to you with this request, I am asking you to lead me out of this vortex into which fate has thrown me.[9]

The Society arranged for him to receive a special pension of 175 roubles a month. In June 1930, his pension was raised to 200 roubles, but his financial situation and medical condition remained unsatisfactory, and he continued to request, and receive, free treatments at Crimean spas and free services not available at the Kremlin Hospital. In December 1930, he asked the Society to pay for "the replacement of two rows of teeth to the total amount of 26 teeth as well as the placement of two crowns on the two remaining teeth." The Society approved the request.[10]

Whatever the nature, symptoms, and etiology of the particular affliction, the 1920s were a time of deep malaise among those who believed that the real day would "sweep away everything weak, feeble, and old." The proclamation of the NEP retreat from Communism was followed by the onset of Lenin's illness, which was followed by the apparent rise of everything weak, feeble, and old. "After the death of the bourgeoisie, Chepurny had no idea, at first, how to live for happiness, and used to go off to distant meadows in order to concentrate and, there, alone in the living grass, to experience a premonition of communism." Or, as Aron Solts put it in a speech at the Sverdlov Communist University in 1925,

> We are going through a period when the nerves of a great number of people have suffered and experienced so much that they have no strength left to do what the Party requires of them. There are some young Party members who have gone through the Civil War, fought at all the fronts, worked in the punitive organs of the GPU [formerly Cheka], etc., and have become totally emotionally exhausted, because of the colossal self-control that has been demanded of them. The ones who lacked sufficient self-control thought that, after one last effort, they would enter the Communist paradise, but when they saw that things were more serious and required a longer period of work, they experienced a certain disappointment.[11]

One much-discussed problem was that the Party was too closed. A band of book-reading converts and dragon-slaying warriors had turned into a rigid hierarchy of state officials. Some concessions had been made to specialization, professionalization, and uniform regulations; some Party comrades had moved into exclusive apartment houses, dachas, and rest homes; and some had prostituted themselves to the gods of "bubbles all over your body." The "proletarian vanguard" had moved away from the proletariat and succumbed to "bureaucratism" and "degeneration." As Serafimovich, the author of *The Iron Flood*, wrote to a friend from the Trotsky Sanatorium in Kislovodsk in 1926, "the sanatorium is so beautifully appointed that I am afraid I might turn into a bourgeois myself (what? you say I already am one?!). In order to resist such a transformation, I have been spitting into all the corners and onto the floor, blowing my nose, and lying in bed with my shoes on and hair uncombed. It seems to be helping."[12]

The other much-discussed problem was that the Party was too open. The New Economic Policy engendered capitalism "continuously, daily, hourly, spontaneously, and on a massive scale." Or, as Chepurny noticed soon after he ordered the extermination of the "residual scum" of the half-bougeoisie, "the bourgeois are gone, but the wind continues to blow." Peasants were acting like peasants; traders were acting like traders; and some workers and even Bolsheviks were acting like peasants and traders, too— spontaneously and on a massive scale.[13]

The Houses of Soviets were being besieged by ragpickers, knife-grinders, "painted women and young ladies with ringlets," and street urchins guilty of "begging bordering on extortion, outrageous conduct (up to the baring of hidden parts of the body)," and assaults "involving the breaking of windows." Some of the contagion seeped into the Houses. Staff members were routinely exposed as drunks, prostitutes, speculators, counterrevolutionaries, and former exploiters. According to a 1920 report, the Second House of Soviets, which had been liberated "in the grievous torments of revolutionary struggle," had since become "a den of iniquity and greed." One employee was fired for saying that "Jews should be given a gold medal for revolutionary activity and then exiled to Palestine." Another had "uncovered drunkenness" on the part of three House administrators: "I am telling the truth and always will. Blood is being shed at the front, while here, in a Soviet house, bottles clink and people get drunk. I found wines from the Caucasus, some ashberry vodka, 3 bottles of champagne, a bottle of cognac, and another bottle of some really spicy stuff that tastes like pepper vodka and makes your mouth burn."[14]

Contagion was not only metaphorical. According to one of many such reports, "on the stairs and in the cafeteria, kitchen, and other areas there is a great deal of dirt; there are cigarette butts and paper everywhere. The employees see all this dirt and trash and pay absolutely no attention to it." The worst offenders, and an independent source of contagion in their own right, were the residents themselves. They chopped firewood and used primus stoves in their rooms, clogged the sinks and toilets with garbage, lay on their beds with their boots on, carried food and hot water up and down the stairs, hung up their wet clothes in the halls, brought in unauthorized guests, claimed to be someone they were not, and often behaved "in a rude and downright outrageous manner." On January 20, 1925, the director of the Third House of Soviets (which served as a dormitory for congress delegates and visiting officials) wrote a report about "one of those intolerable events that have been occurring on a daily basis for some time now." A "mentally disturbed" citizen had attempted to throw himself out of a third-floor window.

> Although a house employee arrested his downward fall, the glass in the big framed window was nevertheless broken. For a long time afterward, Citizen Volkov roamed the halls, cursing, whistling, and shouting, as a result of which, the war invalid, blind Citizen Tsibis, lost all patience and attempted to walk down the stairs, and fell and cracked his head. The comrades who live on that floor started a noisy fight, as a result of which, three of them simultaneously experienced severe seizures. Watching them thrash about and hearing their screams, blind Tsibis also suffered a severe seizure. The House doctor was summoned, and he ascertained that the House was in an intolerable condition. At present, the dormitory is populated by epileptics, brawlers, and the mentally ill, and it is hard to believe that the Third House of Soviets serves as a refuge for such comrades because it was originally intended for normal comrades. In its present state, it resembles a lunatic asylum and, if there are still any sane people left, their likeliest fate is to follow the example of blind Tsibis and end up crazy, too.[15]

One of the main reasons for both the distress and contagion was kinship and procreation. Lovers and relatives kept moving in and out, and children kept being born and growing bigger. Problems of space, services, and supplies were compounded by "problems of Communist everyday life." One report complained that there were "some unscrupulous comrades 'from the upper crust,' who live outside of the Second House of Soviets, but keep special rooms there for their 'second wives' or for their so-called retired wives." Another report, by the director of the Second House of Soviets, Comrade Rosfeldt, alleged that, on November 7, 1921, a non-Party woman without identification had attempted to enter the building with the intention of visiting Comrade Lander (who had just left his job as the Special Cheka Plenipotentiary in the North Caucasus and Don Region to become head of Moscow Agitprop, three years before his retirement for health reasons):

> When I stated that Comrade Lander, who resides in Room 408, must provide me with a note that he can vouch for her, she called Room 408, and Comrade Lander suggested that I let her in without further ado, to which I suggested that Comrade Lander make sure that his acquaintances carry their identification with them, to which he responded that she was his wife, however, considering the fact that Comrade Lander is registered with us as a single person and that I had seen various ladies leaving his room early in the morning, during the day, and late at night, a fact that can be confirmed by several of my staff members, and that on November 6, at about 11 p.m., after the pass bureau had closed, he had attempted to bring in two young ladies but had been prevented from doing so by Comrade Klaar—based on these and other considerations, I asked Comrade Lander, what wife, you must have at least half a dozen of them, and promised him an explanation at a later date. When, around 2 p.m. he showed up in my office and demanded an explanation, I promised to give him one after the end of my work day, but he was very unhappy and kept saying words to the effect that you are not my father, priest, or protector, and what do you want from me, to which I responded that what I want is for the Second House of Soviets not to be turned into a brothel, to which he said that you are being insolent, and so I told him that if in your opinion I am being insolent, then in my opinion you are ten times more insolent, and asked him to leave the office, after which he went away.

Rosfeldt concluded his letter by saying: "Perhaps my view of such things is too moral, but I was brought up in a country where the working class looked at family life from a different, more moral, point of view."[16]

■   ■   ■

Was there such a thing as a Communist moral point of view? According to Bukharin, there was not, because traditional morality was "fetishism," or "the submission of human behavior to an authority that comes from some unknown place and demands obedience for some unknown reason." What the building of socialism required was a conscious submission of human behavior to the needs of the building of socialism. Or, in Lenin's formulation, Communist morality was a system of ethics that rejected all "extra-human and extra-class concepts" in favor of the realization that all proletarian behavior should be "entirely subordinated to the interests of the proletariat's class struggle."[17]

The main Party expert on Party ethics was Aron Solts, otherwise known as "the Party's conscience." The central principle, he wrote, was simple enough: "At the foundations of our ethics are the requirements of our goal. Correct, ethical, and good is whatever helps us reach our goal, smash our class enemies, and learn to organize our economic life according to socialist principles. Incorrect, unethical, and inadmissible is whatever harms this. This is the point of view we must adopt when we try to determine whether a certain action by a Party member is ethical or not." The determination of whether a certain action by a Party member had helped or harmed the achievement of the Party's goal was the Party's job. "We, the government of the majority, can say openly and frankly: yes, we hold in prisons those who interfere with the establishment of our order, and we do not stop before other such actions, because we do not believe in the existence of abstractly unethical actions. Our objective is to institute a better life; this objective must be pursued, and all resistance to it must be crushed. This, in our view, is ethical."[18]

The Party was justified in pursuing its goal by any means necessary; individual Party members were to measure their behavior according to the requirements of the goal and the official Party strategies of its pursuit. The main principle of Communist morality was "usefulness to the Party" or "Party discipline"—that is, the submission of human behavior to an authority that comes from a known place and demands obedience for a known reason (which, in the case of Party members, was freely and voluntarily accepted). Obedience to the Party came before "one's own household, family, etc.," but obedience by itself was not enough. "Can there be free discipline in the absence of sufficiently good comradely relations? No, this would be barracks discipline." On the one hand, "only by looking at each other as comrades who have come together to reach a common practical goal can we have the kind of discipline that would help us overcome all kinds of difficulties." On the other, "the necessary comradely relations—love and friendship toward our

Aron Solts

comrades—are reinforced by the realization that they are my helpers and that it is only thanks to them that I have been able to preserve what is dear to me, what makes me a member of the Party in the first place."[19]

A mutually reinforcing unity of faith, obedience, and love for fellow believers is the central principle of all sectarian communities. According to Jesus of Nazareth, the two most important commandments were: "Love the Lord your God with all your heart" and "Love your neighbor as yourself." Loving God meant submitting to the inevitable; loving God with all your heart meant submitting absolutely and without qualification. Particular forms of submission were outlined in the scripture and revised by God's special representatives ("you have heard . . . , but I tell you"). As for "loving your neighbor," Jesus was not referring to those who were rich, those who had "already received their comfort," or anyone else who deserved to be thrown into the fiery furnace. He was referring to those who had followed him in abandoning their brothers and sisters and father and mother and children and fields, and those who were prepared to follow his followers at least part of the way. There could be no sufficiently good comradely relations in the absence of free discipline any more than there could be free discipline in the absence of sufficiently good comradely relations.

By the time the Christians finally became a ruling party, they had stopped being millenarian and arrived at a series of compromises between the sect they would have liked to remain and the society they had grown to be. The Bolsheviks took over a large heathen empire while still believing that "this generation will not pass away until all these things have happened." But before they could determine what to do with the millions of non-neighbors who had suddenly become would-be neighbors, they had to determine what to do with the thousands of certified neighbors they were expected to love as much as themselves. As Solts put it, "It is, of course, very difficult to preserve those close, intimate relations that we used to have when there were just a handful of us. The common fate and common persecutions of the comrades working in the tsarist underground drew us closer together and united us more than our current conditions do. There are many more of us now, and it is very difficult to have the same feelings of closeness toward every communist."[20]

But the biggest problem, as always, was not that there was not enough love for countless remote neighbors, but that there was too much love for a few close ones. Sects, by definition, transcend the bonds of kinship, friendship, and sexual love by dissolving them in the common devotion to a particular path of salvation (and, when available, to the prophets who represent it). The sects' greatest enemy, along with Babylon, is marriage—because of its centrality to all nonsectarian life and its traditional claim to primary loyalty. But marriage is not just a powerful source of alternative devotion; the reason it is central to all nonsectarian life is because it regulates reproduction, and reproduction is, by definition, at odds with sectarian life, which is based on a voluntary union of conscious (adult) converts. Sects are about brotherhood (and, as an afterthought, sister-hood), not about parents and children. This is why most end-of-the-world scenarios promise "all these things" within one generation; most radical Protestants object to infant baptism; and all millenarian sects, in their militant phase, attempt to reform marriage or abolish it altogether (by decreeing celibacy or promiscuity). Jesus's claim that his family was not his real family and his demand that his disciples hate their erstwhile fathers, mothers, wives, children, brothers, and sisters were as central to his ministry as they were impossible for his later followers to imitate (monastics being the rule-proving exception).

During the time of floods, massacres, and wanderings through the desert, the Bolsheviks assumed that marriage and the family would wither away along with private property, inequality, and the state. After the temporary postponement of Communism under NEP, it became clear that the Lander-Rosfeldt argument would have to be resolved, however provisionally, and that childbirth and childrearing would have to be supervised and regulated until the state could take them over completely. This meant that marriage as an institution had to be defined and, until further notice, consolidated. The former proved impossible; the latter, very difficult.

The main Bolshevik expert on the marriage problem was Yakov Brandenburgsky, an Old Bolshevik from the Pale of Settlement who had severed relations with his family as a gymnasium student radical, attended the Odessa (New Russia) University before being expelled for revolutionary activity, joined the Party in 1903, graduated from the Sorbonne law faculty in 1911, and served as a roving plenipotentiary in charge of food requisitioning during the Civil War. By 1925, he had become a member of the collegium of the People's Commissariat of Justice, first dean of the Department of Soviet Law at Moscow University, and chairman of the new family law commission.[21]

In bourgeois jurisprudence, wrote Brandenburgsky, what made matrimony different from cohabitation (concubinage) was its permanence. In the Soviet Union, because of the freedom of divorce, this distinction did not apply. The view that marriage was a cohabitation between two individuals who considered themselves husband and wife was, according to Brandenburgsky, circular and legally meaningless. Attempts to define marriage in terms of its goals (most commonly, child rearing) were not satisfactory, owing to the large number of exceptions. The argument that marriage was a legal contract could not be accepted because "some elements, conditions, and, especially, consequences of marriage depend on nature and not on the will of the parties." In the final analysis, definitions did not matter. "A legal definition will be found easily and effortlessly when the new forms of everyday life have established themselves." Or rather, the new forms of everyday life would obviate the need for a definition because there would be no marriage. In the meantime, cohabitation and reproduction would have to

Yakov Brandenburgsky

be regulated, whatever the terminology. "The family, which, in bourgeois countries, is based on marriage and creates certain rights and obligations for the spouses, parents, and children, will, of course, disappear and will be replaced by a state system of socialized child-rearing and social welfare. But until that happens, for as long as the individual family still exists, we impose certain mutual obligations, such as alimony, on family members."[22]

The early Soviet drive to destroy the family had been, in principle, appropriate, but "on the other hand, the population is justified in wishing that it not be destroyed so precipitously because this does not correspond to the current conditions of life." Under current conditions, there was no alternative to recognizing "de facto marriages" and "protecting the weak." Soviet legislation was based on realism, not moral "fetishism." In the case of family law, this meant—perhaps paradoxically—that it was based on biological kinship. "Abroad, in bourgeois countries, kinship is a relationship based on the legitimacy of marriage, so that, if I have a child out of wedlock, there is no family relationship—no kinship—between me and that child. We, on the other hand, have built our law on a different principle, according to which the relations between parents and their children are based on blood ties, on actual birth origins."[23]

The family was real and, for the time being, both useful and inescapable. But what was a new Bolshevik family? What did it mean for a Communist to be a good husband, wife, parent, or child? According to Solts, "the family of a Communist must be a prototype of a small Communist cell" or, to be more precise, "it must be a collectivity of comrades in which one lives in the family the same way as outside the family, and in which the members of the family must, in all their work and life, represent a unit of assistance to the Party." This was the Calvinist (Puritan) model of the family as a congregation in miniature or, insofar as the secular commonwealth managed to be separate-but-godly, a state in miniature. But what was the specific contribution of the family if one was to live inside it the same way as outside? In Brandenburgsky's formulation, the point was "for the relations between the spouses to be completely free of all prejudices, survivals, and preposterous conventions of bourgeois 'virtue,' for the woman to be fully emancipated from the power of the man, and for the wife to become economically independent from her husband."[24]

But what did it mean to be free of all prejudices? Had Lander gotten it right? According to the Presidium of the Party Control Commission, he had not—and neither had Rosfeldt. "In this matter, the Party can adopt neither the position of denying personal enjoyment, nor the position of priestly hypocrisy, nor the position of indifference toward unhealthy phenomena that arise in this sphere, provoking a strongly negative reaction among the toiling masses and producing socially damaging consequences." The reasoning, as usual, was purely pragmatic. As Solts put it,

> The fact that we advocate a total freedom of feelings does not mean that one can change partners according to random and temporary moods—that would be incorrect. There is no doubt that sexual promiscuity damages the organism, saps a person's strength, and weakens that person as a fighter and a Communist. Human capacity is limited: the more time and attention—emotional or any other kind—devoted to this aspect of life, legitimate and appropriate though it may be, the less strength remains for other functions that a Communist must perform. If a Communist seeks too much variety in the sexual sphere, then it will undoubtedly sap too much of his strength and will produce a flawed Communist.[25]

The same was true of masturbation, promiscuity, drunkenness, and other expressions of free feelings that might distract Communists from the task of building Communism. To the surprise and unease of many young Party members, the message seemed to be one of "moderation," which they associated with lukewarm appeasement and "bourgeois philistinism."[26]

Judging by repeated recitals of alarming statistics on moral laxity among Communists, the message was not being heard. As Bukharin put it, "our young people find themselves in the gap between the old norms that have already disappeared and the new ones that have not yet arisen. The result is a temporary anarchy in the rules of behavior and norms of personal relationships." Or, as Trotsky put it, "the family is shaking, disintegrating, collapsing, reemerging, and falling apart again. Everyday life is going through the trials of harsh and painful criticism. History is felling the old forest, and the chips are flying. But are elements of the new family being prepared?" The answer seemed lukewarm, if not philistine: "In the most important spheres, the revolutionary symbols of the workers' state are innovative, clear, and powerful: the red flag, the hammer and sickle, the red star, the worker and the peasant, "comrade," the "Internationale." But in the closed-off cells of family life, these new elements are almost nonexistent—or too few, at any rate. . . . That is why, in Communist circles, there are some signs of a desire to counter old rituals with new forms and symbols not only in the life of the state, where they are quite widespread, but in family life, too."[27]

Trotsky approved of the new revolutionary names such as Ilich and Oktiabrina, new Bolshevik baptisms involving "semi-facetious" induction-into-citizenship ceremonies, new rituals surrounding wedding registrations, and solemn "processions, speeches, marches, and fireworks" at Communist cremations. He spoke of such things "semi-facetiously," however, and had no specific suggestions to make or official policies to propose. Both he and Bukharin considered literature incomparably more important for "sentimental education" (as Bukharin put it). The "gap" remained.[28]

In a 1926 article called "My Crime," Mikhail Koltsov describes a visit by a group of peasants who want "a godless Soviet liturgy for deceased, honest, non-Party peasants, as well as a full schedule of Red Baptisms ('Octoberings') and a register of revolutionary saints' names for each day of the year for the naming of peasant infants." The narrator's reaction is predictable: "I tried to convince them that this was all nonsense and did not matter at all, and that what was important was not rituals but libraries, the liquidation of illiteracy, agricultural cooperatives, mutual aid committees, collective plowing, the fight against moonshine production, tractors, agronomists, newspapers, movies, and rural mail deliveries."

The visitors persist, however, and the narrator "commits an act of bourgeois philistinism and intellectual backwardness at the level of one village" by taking them to a stationary store and helping them buy "portraits of leaders, red lampshades, ribbons, slogans, and posters. . . . A cardboard poster 'Save Time: When Your Work Is Done, Go Home' may soon rustle above the head of a corpse. A fancy picture of airplanes and gas masks may well be displayed over the respectfully bent heads of newlyweds. A 'No Smoking' poster may hang before the tiny blue eyes of an unschooled newborn. . . . But none of this matters! I have committed a crime, but have yet to repent it."

Koltsov's conclusion is serious. "If laborers lost in the forests want to climb out of the pit of ignorance and superstition, we need to bring a stepladder or stretch out a helping hand—not simply order them to jump." But what awaited them outside the pit? What were those honest non-Party peasants and thousands of confused "young Communists" to do once they no longer needed cardboard posters and "semi-facetious" Octoberings? Koltsov's essay implies that he, "a progressive person free of prejudices," did not need any of those things. But what did he need? If he, Solts, and Bukharin were in "the vanguard," and if their own sentimental education was more or less complete, then the future of the Revolution might very well depend on what their own "family cells" looked like.[29]

■ ■ ■

In 1918, when he was twenty years old, Koltsov married an actress fifteen years his senior. In the early 1920s, he married another woman, but remained free of prejudices. As he wrote in one of his essays, "men and women live together without long and boring matchmaking, mediation by church or state, false witnesses, divorce trials, or the hypocrisy of forced cohabitation within marriage." He did not divorce his second wife when he moved in with another woman.[30]

Koltsov was famous for his good looks. According to another *Pravda* journalist, Sofia Vinogradskaia, he was "graceful, elegant, and neat," preferred suits to leather jackets and military tunics, and had a "slender, pale-ivory face shaven to an Egyptian blue, soft white forehead, perfectly chiselled lips, and an equally perfect shiny row of close-set teeth." Or, in the words of the director of the Moscow Children's Theater, Natalia Sats, "his wavy, dark-chestnut hair crowned a beautiful forehead, aquiline nose, and smiling, slightly capricious lips." He was famously short ("like a tiny penknife"), vain (gathering, like a bee, "the honey of impressions, praise, recognition, approval, and smiles"), and witty. "Little Koltsov with his beautiful sad eyes was full of jokes, funny stories, and bons mots. . . . He loved to pretend to be someone else, wear disguises, and write acrostics." Once, when he was in Natalia Sats's room, he suddenly asked her to dance. "But," she said, "if I sit down at the piano, how can I dance, and if I don't sit down at the piano, who will play for us?" Koltsov picked up the telephone, "called his brother Boris, asked him to hold the receiver next to his gramophone and turn on the song 'Valencia,' and we danced for three minutes, holding on to the telephone cord."[31]

Koltsov was famous for driving his own car, knowing all the cafés in Moscow, and being everywhere at once. He was famous as the founder of the journals *Ogonyok* (The little flame), *Za rulem* (At the wheel), *Krokodil* (Crocodile), *Za rubezhom* (Abroad), and *Zhenskii zhurnal* (The women's magazine), among other ventures. He was very famous and very powerful. In 1927, when Natalia Sats's theater was threatened with eviction, he published an essay arguing that a children's theater was no less useful than an orphanage. A *Pravda* article had the force of a government decree; the theater got its own building. (Natalia Sats was appointed head of the children's section of the Moscow Soviet's Theater and Music Department by Platon Kerzhentsev in 1918, when she was fifteen. Soon afterward she founded her own theater and, by the late 1920s, was already a celebrity. She married early, had a son, divorced, and married the director of the

Mikhail Koltsov

Natalia Sats
(Courtesy of Roksana Sats)

Moscow City Bank, who later became the Soviet trade representative in Warsaw and then in Berlin. She had a daughter, directed in various theaters in Europe and South America, collaborated with Max Reinhardt and Otto Klemperer, and, in 1935, left her second husband for the people's commissar of internal trade, Izrail Veitser. The following year, a special Party and government decree announced the creation of a much bigger Central Children's Theater on Sverdlov Square.)[32]

Koltsov had a dacha on the Kliazma, north of Moscow, where he often spent his weekends in the company of friends. According to one of them, the editor of *Za rulem*, N. Beliaev (Naum Beilin), "the hospitable host would spend the whole day on the volleyball court or playing forfeits or some other children's game, joking, telling stories, and entertaining his guests. Monday morning, everyone would go back to Moscow, and the dacha would grow silent again." In the early 1930s, four of the regular guests—the writers Boris Levin, Ilya Ilf, and Evgeny Petrov, and the artist Konstantin Rotov—bought the dacha from Koltsov and started using it as a common summer home. (Levin's former wife was Eva Rozengolts, the sister of the ghostly leader of the Moscow uprising, Arkady Rozengolts, now people's commissar of foreign trade. Eva studied painting under Robert Falk at the Higher Art and Technology Studios and graduated in 1925, the same year as Mayakovsky's La Gioconda, Maria Denisova. Her graduation painting, *Old People*, represented three elderly Jews, probably from her native town of Vitebsk. After the birth of their daughter, Elena, in 1928, Eva and Boris separated. Arkady remarried at about the same time, soon after his new appointment.)[33]

Koltsov's brother, Boris Efimov, was a political cartoonist. He married his first wife in 1919 when he was nineteen years old. He married his second wife in 1930, but without leaving the first one. He had sons by both women and spent the rest of his life sharing his time between the two families. The younger wife, Raisa Efimovna Fradkina, had three brothers and two sisters. One brother was a secret police interrogator, another a military intelligence agent, and a third, Boris Volin (Iosif Fradkin), had a distinguished Party career before becoming head of the press department of the Commissariat of Foreign Affairs and then, in 1931, of Glavlit (the central censorship office). Raisa's older sister died during the Civil War; her younger sister, Sofia, married a secret police interrogator, Leonid Chertok, and joined the service herself. According to Efimov, she had been required to seek permission for both her employment and marriage at a special interview with the OGPU (secret police) chief, Genrikh Yagoda, and his wife Ida. Ida Yagoda was Yakov Sverdlov's niece (the daughter of his sister Sofia). Her brother, Leopold Averbakh, a prominent proletarian literary critic, was married to the daughter of Lenin's closest friend and biographer, Vladimir Bonch-Bruevich.[34]

Yakov Sverdlov's son Andrei married one of the daughters of the commander of the assault on the Winter Palace, Nikolai Podvoisky. They first met as children and then again, for good, at the CEC resort of Foros in Crimea in 1932, when he was twenty-two and she was sixteen. Podvoisky and his wife, the Old Bolshevik Nina Didrikil (Diedrich-Kiel), had five daughters and one son. Their son, Lev, married Milena Lozovskaia, the daughter of Solomon Lozovsky (Dridzo), the head of the Red International of Labor Unions (Profintern); they, too, met in Foros. Milena's half-sister, Vera, Solomon Lozovsky's daughter from a previous marriage, was the secretary of Lenin's wife, Krupskaia. When Milena's mother died in 1926, she was adopted by the family of Gleb Krzhizhanovsky, the Old Bolshevik in charge of the "electrification of the whole country" and the first head of Gosplan. Milena's best friend was Elsa Brandeburgskaia (nicknamed Bryn-dia), the daughter of the author of the 1926 family code. One of Nina Did-rikil's sisters was married to the organizer of Red Terror in northern Rus-sia, Mikhail Kedrov; her nephew Artur Artuzov (Frauci) was Kedrov's protégé and collaborator in the Cheka Special Department before becom-ing head of Soviet foreign intelligence. The Bolsheviks were not just repro-ducing—they were reproducing themselves as a group.[35]

By all indications, the Podvoiskys were a happy family. As Nikolai wrote in a letter to his wife, Nina, "I don't know a wife, mother, friend, or comrade better, dearer, purer, stronger, or saintlier than you. . . . I stand before you as if gazing up at the warm sun, so high above." They took the task of pre-paring their children for life under Communism very seriously and often talked about it—to each other and to their children. Nikolai believed in education through industrial labor (two of their daughters, including An-drei's wife, worked as factory workers before becoming engineers); Nina put more emphasis on personal example. As she wrote in her diary on May 2, 1927, "I insist that parents (both of them) have a duty before mankind, for the sake of its progress, to teach their children and pass on to them the lessons of their own experience." This did not have to be an act of self-sacrifice. "I have a lot of fire in my soul," she wrote in July 1920, "and I feel guilty about not having given anything to mankind. Fire cannot be con-tained, it will burst forth, and I am certain that if it does not burst forth within me, it will do so through my children, who will make me immortal." The progress of mankind and immortality through one's children was one and the same thing—now that philistine domesticity was no more. As Nina wrote in an 1922 entry, "Now that the whirlwind of revolution has swept away the specter that was known in bourgeois society as 'the Family,' leav-ing nothing but the cloying and, sometimes, for our children and young people, nightmarish atmosphere of 'the hearth,' and since the emerging society has not yet grown a trunk that would be able to nurture and cher-ish its young leaves, we must be especially sensitive, especially loving to-ward the young shoots that are growing next to us."[36]

But what was a family that was not a family, and what was a home with-out a "hearth"? Could one pass on to one's children the lessons of one's own experience without reproducing philistine domesticity? And what if the new trunk turned out to be the same old tree of the knowledge of good and evil? The Podvoiskys' answer was the same as Solts's: the new biological family must become the primary cell of the Party family; life inside the family should be the same as life outside the family. As Nikolai wrote to his children, "if you want to love Vladimir Ilich [Lenin] deeply, diligently, and eagerly, you must be your mother's friends, you must talk to her about Lenin." And as Nina wrote to her daughter on her seventeenth birthday, months after she had said "yes" to Andrei Sverdlov,

> Congratulations, you are seventeen years old! Life at seventeen is like the sea in April: it changes colors in response to the spring wind, the sun, and the density of the air; it is like a young birch covered with tender leaves and adorned with little earrings; it is the most powerful and the most beckoning of springs. You are the spring, and life all around you is the spring. You are happy, and you will be even happier when you realize just how happy you are. And I think you already do, don't you? You are the youngest and the strongest, and the whole life of your society is young and strong. My wish for you, in your seventeenth spring, is that you continue to move closer and closer, in all your interests, feelings, and thoughts, to the camp of the youngest and strongest: to Marx, Engels, Lenin, all the true Bolsheviks.[37]

The task was to build socialism in one family within socialism in one country within the unfolding world revolution. The point of the pursuit was happiness, especially the happiness of the current generation of children. The most well-known take on children and the pursuit of happiness in the Soviet Union was Stanislavsky's production—to the music of Ilya Sats, Natalia's father—of Maurice Maeterlink's *The Blue Bird*, which premiered in 1908, quickly became a classic, and survived the Revolution to become a required rite of passage for elite Soviet children (and eventually the longest-running theater production of all time: in 2008 it celebrated its hundredth anniversary). In her evocation of the play on May 8, 1923, Nina Podvoiskaia seems to have been thinking about both the Soviet state and her own children. In the play, the little boy and girl, Tyltyl and Mytyl, find the bird of happiness and release it out into the world. In the diary entry, Podvoiskaia meets a German Comintern agent at a Black Sea resort and feels proud that she has

> held in [her] hands the magic "blue bird" that is flying over the sea to bring happiness to mankind. I want to work in the Comintern— that miracle-producing magic garden of communism, from where blue birds fly to every corner of the world, spreading the news of communist happiness. I want to caress and nurture those birds, breathe into them the strength that they need for their flight. . . . Oh

Podvoisky family

the enchantingly beautiful sea! The sea, the "magic garden," and, in that garden, the great magician Lenin and the fabulous "blue birds." There are lots of them, and there will be many many more. I love them with all my heart, I have boundless love for these "blue birds" that will overturn the world.[38]

Nina Podvoiskaia's actual job was to prepare Lenin's manuscripts for publication at the Lenin Institute, and, on the home front, to talk about Lenin to her children. Nikolai Podvoisky's job was to prepare Soviet bodies for future happiness. Having lost the fight to become the Revolution's "iron hand throughout the world," he became the head of the Supreme Council on Physical Culture, the founder and leader of Sports International, and the main champion of what he called "an alliance with the sun." His comparison of his wife to the "warm sun" was not entirely a metaphor. "Man, like all living things," argues his representative in a Platonic dialog he wrote in 1925, "is a piece of the sun, and this piece must be in constant contact with its whole, or it will fade away." The solution is to eliminate "artificial barriers between us, that is, our body, and the source of life, the sun."

"In other words," retorted Yuri, "just walk around in the nude. Right."
Well, aren't your hands bare, for god's sake? And your nose and the rest of your face? That's not a problem, is it? Not too scary? Almost all parts of the body could easily be left naked for most of the year. You don't catch a cold because your hands are wet, do you? But the minute you get your feet wet, you go straight to bed. That's your punishment for wrapping them up all the time, for hiding them from the sun. . . .
We can—and must—discard all the ballast that separates our body from the sun: coats, jackets, vests, shirts, women's fashions, socks, and boots. Nine times out of ten, people wear them not because they

need them, but because they want to show off or outdo others. Of course, in our climate we must protect ourselves from the elements for part of the year. But I am talking about an alliance with the sun, and when the sun is willing to enter into an alliance with us, we must not miss our chance."

Yuri the skeptic objects by saying that he cannot imagine the chairman of the Council of People's Commissars, Aleksei Ivanovich Rykov, showing up at an official reception in only his underwear. But the protagonist is ready for this objection. "It is very easy to imagine a perfectly natural setting in which a high-ranking official might appear in public in only his underwear. . . . The very fact of such an appearance would inspire the masses to debate the problem of developing and reinforcing the strength of the working people." Eventually, the masses would understand that "the sun is the best proletarian doctor." Yuri, for one, is persuaded.[39]

Podvoisky practiced what he preached—both in the matter of discarding the ballast and in making his family the primary cell of a larger transformation. In 1923, they received a dacha in Serebrianyi Bor (Silver Forest) on the Moskva River, next door to the Trifonovs. Yuri Trifonov describes the experiment in his novel *The Old Man*. The Burmins resemble the Podvoiskys, and Sanya—the author as a boy:

> Burmin, his wife, his wife's sisters and their husbands were devotees of "the naked body" and of the "down with modesty" society, and often used to walk around near their dacha in the garden—and sometimes even in the public vegetable plots where many people would assemble in the evenings—in an indecent state: that is, in the nude. The other residents were outraged—the professor wanted to write to the Moscow Council—but Sanya's mother just laughed and said it was an illustration of the tale of the emperor's new clothes. She once quarreled with his father, who forbade Sanya to go the vegetable plots while those "buffoons" were larking about. Father really had it in for Burmin because of that "down with modesty" business. Yet the others just laughed. Burmin was gaunt, tall, and bespectacled and reminded one more of Don Quixote than of Apollo; the Burmin women were no raving beauties, either. True enough, they were marvelously sunburned.

Sanya's father knows Burmin from their Civil War days. "Father thought Burmin was stupid (Sanya used to hear him say: 'That fool Semyon'), and adopted a skeptical attitude to his feats of military prowess and even to his decoration." As for discarding the ballast, some of the children talk others into imitating the grown-ups, and it all ends in a terrible scandal. "But was it really stupidity as his father said? Was he truly stupid, that land surveyor's son with the goatee, who was swept up onto the crest of a wave of monstrous force? Now, more than three decades later, what had seemed axiomatic then, Burmin's stupidity, seemed doubtful." (Valentin Trifonov and Nikolai Podvoisky had served together; Podvoisky's father was actually a priest, not a surveyor.)[40]

Valentin Trifonov was free of prejudices in a different way. After the Civil War, he moved back in with his common-law wife, Tatiana Slovatin-skaia, and her daughter from a previous marriage, Evgenia Lurye. Several years later, he left the mother for the daughter, and, in 1925, their son Yuri was born. At the time, Tatiana was fifty-six, Valentin, thirty-seven, and Evgenia, twenty-one. They continued to live together as one family. Tatiana worked as head of the visitors' office of the Party's Central Committee and director of the Politburo archive; Valentin was chairman of the Military Collegium of the Supreme Court; Evgenia postponed her studies at the Agricultural Academy to take care of the children (they had a daughter two years later). According to Yuri, Tatiana was a rigid, unsentimental true believer. "She is not a human being," says one of his characters, "she is some kind of an iron closet." Valentin seemed less orthodox but almost as impenetrable. "By temperament he was silent, reserved, even a little gloomy; he did not like to 'stick out,' so to speak."[41]

The Trifonovs' closest friend was Aron Solts, "the conscience of the Party," the cousin of Evgenia's father, and the mentor of both Tatiana and Valentin in matters of doctrine and Party ethics. Yuri remembered him as "a small man with a large, gray bumpy head. He had big lips and big, bulging eyes that looked at you shrewdly and sternly. I thought of him as very smart, very cross, and very sick: he always breathed heavily, with a loud wheeze. Also, I thought of him as an exceptional chess player. I always lost to him." Solts never married and lived with his sister Esfir. In the early 1930s, they were joined by their niece, Anna, who had been left by her husband, the Party boss of Uzbekistan, Isaak Zelensky. At about the same

Valentin Trifonov, Evgenia Lurye, Tatiana Slovatinskaia, and little Yuri

Tatiana Slovatinskaia, Anna Zelenskaia, Isaak Zelensky,
Aron Solts, and the Zelensky children, Elena and Andrei

time, they adopted a boy from an orphanage who, according to Anna's
daughter and Yuri Trifonov, was rude to the old people and talked of them
with contempt.[42]

It is not known what Solts thought of Valentin Trifonov's new living
arrangement or his own expanding household. At the height of his power
in the mid-1920s (when Koltsov's friends would restrain his playful imagination by threatening him with "a reprimand by Solts"), he believed that
the greatest danger for Communist families lay in unequal marriages with
class enemies. He considered such marriages to be in poor taste.

> This poor taste consists in the fact that such things should be con-
> sidered in the same way in which the old society considered a
> marriage between a count and a housemaid. The public would be
> scandalized: How dare he, he has abandoned our traditions, it is im-
> proper, he should be ashamed of himself! Such was the attitude in
> those days. Today, we are the ruling class, and we should have the
> same attitude. Intimacy with a member of the enemy camp when we
> are the ruling class—such a thing should meet with such public con-
> demnation that a person would think thirty times before making
> such a decision. Of course, every feeling is individual, and it is not
> always appropriate to interfere in a person's private life, but we can
> condemn such things the way the old society did when any of its
> members refused to obey its demands. We call this "prejudice," but
> when it comes to self-preservation, it is not prejudice at all. One
> should think long and hard before taking a wife from an alien class.[43]

Solts's warning came too late for Arosev. In 1916, he became engaged to
the sixteen-year-old daughter of a Kazan prosecutor and a housemaid.

Alexander Arosev   Olga Goppen

The father died early, and the daughter was educated at an institute for noble maidens. When Arosev was drafted into the army, she married another man, with whom she had a son. In 1918, Arosev returned to Kazan as a hero (he had just presided over the closure of all non-Bolshevik newspapers in Moscow) and took her away from her husband, apparently against her will. Her son soon died, but they had three daughters, born between 1919 and 1925. Her name was Olga Goppen; she spoke French, wrote poetry, liked to dress up, did not know how to cook, and prided herself on being "frivolous." Her mother, the former housemaid, treated her son-in-law with ironic forebearance and had all three girls secretly baptized. Soon after the birth of their third daughter, when Arosev was working at the Soviet embassy in Stockholm, Olga left him for his junior colleague and followed her new husband to Sakhalin, where he became regional Party secretary (having also left a wife and three children behind). Arosev refused to let Olga have any of the girls and raised all three with the help of a Swedish nanny, who accompanied them around Europe. In 1932, while serving as ambassador to Czechoslovakia, Arosev married his eldest daughter's dance teacher, Gertrude Freund. He was forty-two; she was twenty-two. Because she was a Czechoslovak citizen, he was not allowed to continue as ambassador and returned to Moscow to head the All-Union Society for Cultural Ties with Foreign Countries. The girls hated their stepmother "ferociously," as one of them put it. "She was the German version of a 'well-organized' European woman—cold, restrained, and very stingy." His comrades condemned him for once again marrying a member of the alien class.[44]

One of Arosev's comrades from the time of the Moscow uprising was Osip Piatnitsky. His first wife and fellow revolutionary, Nina Marshak, left him for Aleksei Rykov, and in 1920, at the age of thirty-nine, he married the twenty-one-year-old daughter of a priest (and widow of a general), Yulia Sokolova. She had partially redeemed her origins by serving as a Bolshevik spy in a White Army counterintelligence unit in Cheliabinsk. According to one fictionalized history of the Civil War, when her identity

Osip Piatnitsky   Yulia Sokolova

was discovered, she had hidden in a barrel of pickles and stayed there until the Red troops found her the next morning. Yulia and Osip met when she was convalescing in a Moscow hospital. Their first son, Igor, was born in 1921; the second, Vladimir, in 1925. Vladimir describes his father as taciturn and ascetic, and his mother, as "very emotional" with an "exposed conscience." Shortly before his birth, she left the Party because she considered herself unworthy.[45]

Boris Zbarsky only partly heeded Solts's warning. His first wife, Fani, was from his hometown of Kamenets-Podolsky in Ukraine. They got married in Geneva, where they were students together, and moved to the northern Urals in 1915, when their son, Ilya, was two years old. In January 1916, they were joined by Boris Pasternak and his friend, Evgeny Lundberg. Zbarsky knew Pasternak's father and gave Boris a job as a clerk in one of his factories. Fani had nothing to do and felt bored and lonely. According to her son, Ilya, "My father usually came home late. I used to spend whole days with my nanny or by myself while my mother sought consolation in the company of E. Lundberg and B. Pasternak. The latter played the piano, improvised, and wrote and recited poetry. My mother and Boris Pasternak must have had an affair, which later became one of the reasons for my parents' separation."

When the Zbarskys divorced in 1921, Ilya stayed with his father. Around 1927, Boris Zbarsky went to Berlin on business, met a college friend of Lydia Pasternak (Boris's younger sister), and eventually brought her to Moscow, first as his assistant and then, his wife. Her name was Evgenia Perelman. She was the daughter of a lawyer, granddaughter of a rabbi, and not a Communist herself. According to Ilya, she "turned out to be a mean, hysterical, miserly woman" who "constantly demonstrated her dislike of all things Russian and talked about her émigré past." She was also self-consciously and emphatically Jewish—something Ilya was not used to and found distasteful. Many people in his father's world, and the high Party elite in general, came from Jewish families, but they tended to assume that internationalism meant having no motherland and possibly no parents at

Vladimir Vorobiev and Boris Zbarsky with his son, Ilya
(Courtesy of I. B. Zbarsky)

all. Nationalism was the last resort of the enemy classes; "nationality" was
a remnant of the past tolerated in "laborers lost in the forests" but not in
"progressive people free of prejudices." The Russianness of Russian internationalism was taken for granted and noticed only when it was violated.
Ilya Zbarsky's stepmother fired his peasant nanny "and hired as a servant
an unpleasant Jewish woman who did not feed me and who brought into
the house an alien and unpleasant atmosphere. . . . The food was unfamiliar and did not taste good, and I had to listen to my stepmother's mocking
comments. Finally, I moved into my mother's communal apartment in the
Arbat, which she shared with twenty other people." Ilya went on to become
his father's assistant at the Lenin Mausoleum. Boris and Evgenia had two
sons; the first, Feliks-Lev, was named after the chemist Lev Karpov and the
Cheka head Feliks Dzerzhinsky.[46]

■ ■ ■

In the top ranks of the Bolshevik leadership, such violations of Solts's
injunction were rare. Most elite Communists socialized, one way or another, with other elite Communists—either because of shared loyalties or
because there were few other people in their offices, houses, clubs, dachas,
and resorts. In the 1920s, the most talked-about Party union was between
two of the most celebrated Party propagandists: Karl Radek and Larisa
Reisner. Radek's biographer described the couple as Quasimodo and Es-
meralda. One of Karl's high school classmates described him as "short,
skinny, and physically underdeveloped; from his earliest youth, he always
had a pair of glasses perched upon his nose. Yet in spite of his general ugli-
ness, he was very arrogant and self-confident. . . . His ugly nose, his gaping

mouth, and the teeth sticking out [from below] his upper lip marked him clearly. He was forever carrying a book or a newspaper. He was constantly reading—at home, on the street, during recess in the school—always reading, day and night, even during classes."[47]

He later abandoned Germanophilic Jewish enlightenment for Polish nationalism and then Bolshevism (although he continued to wear sideburns in honor of Mickiewicz). He was expelled from the Social Democratic Party of Poland-Lithuania, the Social Democratic Party of Germany, and, after the failure of the German revolution in 1923, from the Executive Committee of the Comintern and the Central Committee of the Party. He was known for his wit, sarcasm, slovenly bohemianism, self-deprecating buffoonery, ferocious personal attacks on ideological opponents, and eloquent defense of various causes in three different languages. Rosa Luxemburg had refused to sit at the same table with him, and Angelica Balabanoff "despised him personally and considered him a vulgar politician."

> He was—and is—a strange mixture of amorality, cynicism, and spontaneous appreciation for ideas, books, music, human beings. Just as there are people who have no perception of colors, so Radek had no perception of moral values. In politics, he would change his viewpoint overnight, appropriate for himself the most contradictory slogans. This quality, with his quick mind, his sardonic humor, his versatility and his vast reading, was probably the key to his journalistic success. . . .
>
> Because of his insensibility, he had no resentment about the way he was treated by other people. I have seen him attempt to go with people who refused to sit at the same table with him, or even put their signatures next to his on a document, or to shake hands with him. He would be delighted if he could merely divert these people with one of his innumerable anecdotes. Though a Jew himself, his anecdotes were almost exclusively those which dealt with Jews and which put them in a ridiculous or degrading light.[48]

He became a prominent Left Communist alongside Bukharin and Osinsky, a loyal Leninist after May 1918, and, after Lenin's stroke in March 1923, the chief promoter of "Leon Trotsky, the Organizer of Victory" (as he titled his programmatic article about Lenin's succession). According to a much-repeated anecdote, when Voroshilov accused Radek of being Leon's—or the lion's—tail, Radek responded that it was better to be Leon's tail than Stalin's ass. (A decade later his *Pravda* article, "The Architect of the Socialist Society," would become one of the cornerstones of the Stalin cult.) He was widely regarded to be the author of most anti-Soviet jokes. In the words of the journalist Louis Fischer, "he was a witty imp and an ugly Puck. He had dense, curly disheveled black hair which looked as if he never combed it with anything but a towel; laughing, nearsighted eyes behind very thick

Karl Radek   Larisa Reisner

glasses; prominent moist lips; sideburns that met under his chin; no moustache, and sickly sallow skin."[49]

Larisa Reisner was universally, almost ritualistically, acclaimed as the most beautiful woman of the Russian Revolution (or, in Nadezhda Mandelstam's words, "the Woman of the Russian Revolution"). Koltsov called her a "magnificent, rare, choice human specimen"; Mikhail Roshal, the secretary of the Helsingfors Bolshevik Committee in 1917, compared her to *La Gioconda*; the author of *The Week*, Yuri Libedinsky, wrote that she reminded him of "either a Greek Goddess or a Germanic Valkyrie"; and Trotsky called her "the Pallas Athena of the revolution." Vadim Andreev, the son of her literary mentor Leonid Andreev, claimed that "when she walked down the street, she carried her beauty like a torch, so that the coarsest objects seemed to acquire softness and tenderness at her approach. . . . Not a single man could walk by without noticing her, and every third one—a statistic I can vouch for, would stand rooted to the spot and look back until we had disappeared in the crowd."[50]

A law professor's daughter, poet, journalist, and, after 1919, commissar of the naval general staff, Reisner seems to have been the only person in Russia who appeared convincing as both a decadent writer and leather-clad Bolshevik, a "heavenly wagtail" and a "slayer and avenger." She had poems dedicated to her by Mandelstam, Pasternak, and Gumilev (with whom she had an affair while he was married to Akhmatova). Pasternak named his heroine in *Doctor Zhivago* after her, and Vsevolod Vishnevsky used her as the prototype for the "female commissar sent by the Party" in his canonical play, *An Optimistic Tragedy*. In 1918, she married Trotsky's deputy for naval affairs, Fedor Raskolnikov, who called her his "warrior goddess, Diana." She accompanied him to the Volga Fleet, the Baltic Fleet, and finally to Afghanistan, where he was sent as ambassador after the Kronstadt debacle. Sverdlov's assistant Elizaveta Drabkina saw her on the Volga in 1918: "In front, on a black stallion, rode a woman in a soldier's tunic and a wide, light-blue and navy checkered skirt. Sitting gracefully in her saddle, she galloped bravely across the ploughed field. Clods of black earth flew from under the horse's hooves. It was Larisa Reisner, Chief of Army Scouts. The rider's enchanting face glowed from the wind. She had light gray eyes, chestnut hair pulled back from her temples and coiled into a bun at the back of her head, and a high, clear brow intersected by a single tiny, stern crease."[51]

All millenarian sects committed to poverty and fraternity are men's movements. Bolshevism was aggressively and unabashedly masculine. Its hero was a blacksmith, *énorme et gourd*, and its most iconic war poster was *Beat the Whites with the Red Wedge*. Its main enemy was the swamp and everything "resembling jelly." Women produced children; women and children formed families; and families "engendered capitalism and the bourgeoisie continuously, daily, hourly, spontaneously, and on a massive scale." The only women who did not threaten the rule of the iron scepter were mothers of prophets or Amazons. Larisa Reisner was the Bolshevik Marianne in the flesh.

"Legends have enveloped her memory in a special aura, and it is difficult to think of her outside these semifictitious tales," wrote Vadim Andreev. "Stories have been told about how she was on the Aurora on the memorable night of October 25 and how she ordered the bombardment of the Winter Palace, or how she dressed up as a peasant woman, crossed the enemy lines, and started an uprising in the Kolchak Army." Most of these stories were not true, but she did seem to embody something Mayakovsky tried to create with words: the poetry of the Revolution. She was a living protest against the Great Disappointment, the divine bluebird of eternal revolution.[52] According to Voronsky,

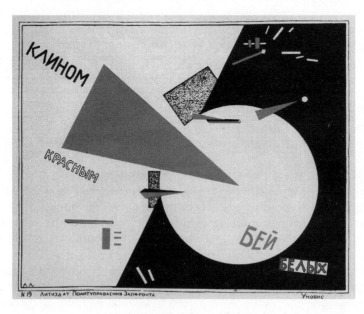

Lazar Lissitzky, *Beat the Whites with the Red Wedge*

During the decisive days of the revolution's bloody harvest, her noble, determined, feminine face, like that of a legendary Amazon with its halo of chestnut hair, and her nimble, self-confident figure could be seen in armored cars, on our Red warships, and among the rank-and-file soldiers. . . .

Larisa Reisner hated everyday philistinism, wherever it might be found. She did not know how to accumulate or settle down, did not like sinking into a quiet and dull everyday routine. In life's prose, she—an artist and fighter for the revolution—could always find the lofty, the gripping, the substantive, and the great.[53]

And according to Radek, who was not loved by anyone but the Woman of the Russian Revolution, "She knew that the petit bourgeois element was a swamp that could swallow up the grandest of buildings, and she could see the strange flowers blooming in that swamp. But, at the same time, she could see the path of struggle against the dangers that threatened the republic of labor: the dams that the proletariat and the Communist Party needed to erect in order to protect themselves."[54]

Karl Radek and Larisa Reisner got together in 1923, when she returned from Afghanistan and asked him to take her with him to witness the revolution in Germany. He obliged; she wrote about "the barricades of Hamburg"; and they became lovers. Larisa separated from her husband; Karl continued to live part-time with his wife, Rosa, and their four-year-old daughter, Sonia. The German revolution failed, Karl fell from grace, and three years later, at the age of thirty, Larisa died of typhoid fever in the Kremlin hospital. "This beautiful young woman has flashed across the revolutionary sky like a burning meteor, blinding many in her path," wrote Trotsky.[55]

Her coffin was carried by Isaak Babel, Boris Pilnyak, Vsevolod Ivanov, and Boris Volin (Boris Efimov's brother-in-law), "among others." Varlam Shalamov, who felt "purified and elevated" by his love for her, was there, too. As he wrote later, "Karl Radek was being supported on both sides as he followed the coffin," he wrote. "His face was dirty and had a greenish tinge, while a never-ending stream of tears blazed a trail down his cheeks lined with red sideburns." Boris Pasternak addressed the deceased directly ("Wander on, heroine, into the depths of legend), and one of Larisa's oldest friends wrote to the grieving father: "Many, many years ago, when I often used to visit, you once said that you lived and worked to serve a special religion—a Religion without God. All religions in the world, my dear M. A., serve as a refuge from sorrow. That, after all, is their ultimate purpose."[56]

The second-most-famous Bolshevik romance was between Bukharin and Anna Larina, the adopted daughter of the Old Bolshevik and radical anti-NEP economist, Yuri Larin (Mikhail Lurye). Bukharin was as commonly admired as Radek was despised (the two were close friends for a while). According to Ilya Ehrenburg, everyone loved "Bukharchik" for his

"contagious laughter" and "sense of fun" when he was a gymnasium student, and, according to Stalin's daughter, Svetlana, "everyone adored him"
when he visited her father's dacha when she was a little girl. "He used to
fill the whole house with animals, which he loved. There would be hedge-
hogs chasing each other across the balcony, garter snakes sunning themselves in jars, a tame fox racing through the park, and a crippled hawk
glaring from a cage. . . . He used to play with the children and tease my
nurse, whom he taught how to ride a bicycle and shoot an air rifle. Everyone always had a good time when he was around." Anna Larina claims to
have singled him out among her father's friends because of his "irrepressible love of life, his mischievousness, his passionate love of nature, and his
enthusiasm for painting."[57] They met the day Anna saw *The Blue Bird* for
the first time:

> I spent the whole day under the impression of the show, and when I
> went to sleep, dreamed of Bread and Milk and the Land of Memory,
> which was calm and serene and not at all scary. I could hear Ilya
> Sats's beautiful melody: "Here we come, to find the Blue Bird's
> home." And just as the Cat appeared, someone tweaked me on the
> nose. I was frightened—for on stage the Cat had been very big, as
> tall as a man, and I screamed: "Go away, Cat!" In my sleep, I could
> hear Mother saying: "Nikolai Ivanovich, why wake the child?" But I
> did wake up, and the Cat's face slowly dissolved into Bukharin's
> features. At that moment, I caught my own "Blue Bird"—not a fairy-
> tale one, but a flesh-and-blood one—one that I would pay a heavy
> price for.[58]

Bukharin had married his first cousin and fellow sectarian, Nadezhda
Lukina, when they were both very young. She had a serious back problem
and spent long periods of time in bed. "During such periods," wrote Lenin's
wife, Krupskaia, "Nikolai Ivanovich would run the household, put sugar
instead of salt into the soup, and talk animatedly to Ilich." In the early
1920s, he got together with Esfir Gurvich, who at the time was working at
Pravda, studying at the Institute of Red Professors, and living in Gorki
with Lenin's sister Maria (her boss at *Pravda*). In 1924, their daughter Svetlana was born; in 1927, Stalin asked Bukharin and Nadezhda to move into
the Kremlin; in 1929, Esfir left Bukharin. Soon afterward, he found himself
in a compartment of the Moscow-Leningrad train with a young woman
named Alexandra (Sasha) Travina. They started an affair, and a year and
a half later she told him she was a secret police agent. Seven years after
that, he wrote to Stalin "directly and openly about . . . what one doesn't
normally talk about":[59]

> In my life, I have been with only four women. N. was ill. We separated
> de facto back in 1920. When I got together with Esfir, she (N) almost

lost her mind. Ilich sent her abroad. To give N. time to recover, I temporarily separated from E. and then, fearing for N's health, kept my relationship with E. secret. Then our daughter was born, and the situation became unbearable. Sometimes I couldn't sleep for weeks on end. Objectively, I tormented E. by putting her in such a false situation. In the winter of 1929, she left me (perhaps partly because of my political problems at the time). I was in a terrible state because I loved her. She started another family. Then I got together (quite quickly and suddenly) with A. V. Travina, knowing that she was also close to some GPU circles. It didn't bother me at all since there was no reason for concern. We lived very well together, but soon the old problems returned, greatly magnified. That was when N. tried to poison herself, and Sasha began suffering from nervous paralysis. I rushed madly back and forth between the two sick ones, and, at one point, even thought about renouncing any kind of private life altogether. I had been living openly with Sasha. I went everywhere with her, including vacations, and everyone considered her to be my wife. But once again my soul was being devoured by all these growing torments, and there was a break-up. What made all of this even harder was that these women were kind, intelligent, and extraordinarily attached to me. . . . Meanwhile, Niusia [Anna] Larina had been in love with me for a long time (you were wrong about the "ten wives"—I was never with more than one woman at a time). And so what happened is that there was another horrible scene at Sasha's, and I didn't go "home" to sleep. I went to the Larins instead and stayed there. I am not going to go into all the details, but eventually Aniuta and I started living together. N. put up a partition in our apartment and calmed down. For the first time, a new life began for me in this regard.[60]

In the summer of 1930, when Anna was sixteen, she and her father had stayed at a government sanatorium in Mukhalatka, in Crimea. Bukharin was at his dacha in Gurzuf, down the coast. His "Right Opposition" to forced collectivization had been defeated and forced to apologize; the Sixteenth Party Congress was proceeding without him; he was forty-two years old. One day she came to visit. She was wearing a light blue calico dress with white daisies around the hem; her black braids (she reports in her memoirs) hung down, almost touching the daisies. They went down to the beach, and, having found a shady spot under a cliff, he started reading from Knut Hamsun's *Victoria*: "What is love? A wind whispering among the roses—no, a yellow phosphorescence in the blood. A *danse macabre* in which even the oldest and frailest hearts are obliged to join. It is like the marguerite which opens wide as night draws on, and like the anemone which closes at a breath and dies at a touch." He may or may not have read four more paragraphs of similes before getting to the last one: "Love was

God's first word, the first thought that sailed across his mind. He said, Let there be light, and there was love. And every thing that he had made was very good, and nothing thereof did he wish unmade again. And love was creation's source, creation's ruler; but all love's ways are strewn with blossoms and blood, blossoms and blood."[61]

Victoria had been required reading for the gymnasium students of Bukharin's generation. It was—perhaps appropriately—a modernist fairy tale about the doomed love of an Underground Man. Bukharin read two more passages: one about a woman who cut off her hair after her sick husband lost his, and the other about a man who threw acid in his face after his wife became "crippled and hideous." In the novel, both tales are the main character's fantasies about how his love might have ended, had it not been doomed. When he finished reading, Bukharin asked Anna if she could ever love a leper. She was about to respond (in the affirmative, she writes in her memoirs) when he stopped her and, still reenacting *Victoria*, said he feared an answer. A few days later she came to visit again. Bukharin had just received a letter from his fellow-"Rightist" Aleksei Rykov, who wrote that he had conducted himself with dignity at the Sixteenth Party Congress and that he loved Bukharin "the way even a woman passionately in love with you never could" (he, too, had read *Victoria*). This time, there was no ride back to Mukhalatka; Anna stayed overnight and "experienced a thrilling, romantic Crimean evening."[62]

A long and checkered courtship followed. Bukharin continued to "rush madly back and forth between the two sick ones"; Anna had an affair with Zhenia Sokolnikov, the son of Bukharin's childhood friend; both, according to Anna, suffered greatly from jealousy and uncertainty. Anna's father, Yuri Larin, seemed much more worried about Bukharin. "You should consider very carefully how serious your feelings for him are," he said once. "Nikolai Ivanovich loves you very much; he is a delicate, emotional person, and, if your feelings are not serious, you must step aside, or this will end badly for him." She asked if he meant suicide. "Not necessarily suicide," he

Nikolai Bukharin   Anna Larina

said, "but he certainly does not need any more suffering." In January 1932, as he lay dying, Larin told Anna that it would be "more interesting to live ten years with Nikolai Ivanovich than a lifetime with someone else."

These words of my father's became a sort of benediction. Then he gestured for me to bend down even closer because his voice was growing weaker and weaker, and barely managed to wheeze out:

"It is not enough to love Soviet power just because you live fairly comfortably as a result of its victory! You must be prepared to give your life for it, to shed your blood, if necessary!" . . . With great difficulty, he slightly raised his right fist, which quickly fell back down on his knee. "Swear that you will be willing to do this!"

And I did.[63]

Two years later, "after another horrible scene at Sasha's," Bukharin ran into Anna not far from where she was living in the Second House of Soviets. It was her twentieth birthday. She invited him over. Two years after that, their son Yuri was born. By then they were sharing a Kremlin apartment with Bukharin's father and Nadezhda Lukina-Bukharina (as she continued to sign her name). According to Anna, Nadezhda gave their family "all the warmth of her heart, and loved [their] son in a way that was deeply touching."[64]

The challenge of combining personal love with love for Soviet power—as prescribed by Solts and implied in Yuri Larin's blessing—was of immediate personal importance to Bukharin's former friend, cellmate, and fellow Left Communist, Valerian Osinsky. As Osinsky wrote to his own Victoria, Anna Shaternikova, in February 1917, love "over there" would "reveal without shame all of its profound tenderness and its charity without embellishment, without the tinkling bells of magnanimity and philanthropy." Life under Communism, he explained, quoting Victoria, would be "the kind of 'good time when any grief is easy to bear.'" Osinsky and Shaternikova had read Victoria aloud to each other in Yalta, where they had met a few months earlier. Several years later, he wrote to her that he had decided to reread a few passages—"to take a quick look, that's all, because I was sure I wouldn't like it this time. . . . I read 5–10 pages from the middle, went back to the beginning, read some more, then a little more, and by four in the morning had read it all. . . . What I find moving about Victoria (the ending) is not the sense of pity it evokes, but the enormous power of feeling. In its own way, it is comparable to revolutionary enthusiasm. It belongs to the same category. It has the same power, clarity, and purity. There is no doubt that Victoria is a novel of genius." [65]

Osinsky, like Bukharin, had married a comrade-in arms when he was a young man. In 1912, his wife, Ekaterina Smirnova, gave birth to a son, Vadim. In late 1916, he met Anna Shaternikova in a Yalta sanatorium. She was a volunteer nurse, a true believer, a would-be Party theoretician, and, as far as Osinsky was concerned, "young, tall, intelligent, and beautiful." They walked in the park and read *Victoria* by the sea. He left for the front and, on the eve of the February Revolution, wrote her the letter about "insatiable utopia." She joined the Party; he spent most of 1917 in Moscow with Bukharin and his wife's brother, Vladimir Smirnov, agitating for a military uprising. A few days before the October Revolution, he left for Kharkov—officially because he was frustrated by the old guard's foot-dragging and possibly because he wanted to be with Anna, who was there at the time. Soon afterward he left for Petrograd, where he was put in charge of the empire's economy (as director of the Central Bank and the first chairman of the Supreme Economic Council). In March 1918, as the chief ideologue of the defeated Left Communism, he resigned this position, and, after a stint in the provinces, became head of the People's Commissariat of Agriculture and the chief advocate of "massive state coercion" against peasants (in the form of forced labor and a variety of "repressive measures"). Love was on the verge of revealing without shame all of its profound tenderness and charity, and in September 1920 he told his wife that he was in love with another woman. As he wrote to Anna, "Ekaterina Mikhailovna, whom I told what needed to be told and who knows how to deal with it correctly, is digesting it with great effort and pain. It is very, very understandable for a person who has known and loved somebody for a very, very long time. She has asked me to leave her in peace and not talk to her about the situation until things have settled. . . . Don't worry, it will all get sorted out, because Ekaterina Mikhailovna is a good and intelligent person, but this is a delicate and tricky matter. It is not pleasant to be writing this, but one has to, of necessity."[66]

Valerian Osinsky and his wife, Ekaterina
(Courtesy of Elena Simakova)

Soon Ekaterina and their son Vadim ("Dima") left for Finland, where she found a job as a cryptographer at the Soviet embassy, and Anna moved into the Osinskys' Kremlin apartment. She was not happy there because, as she put it later, "everything smelled of another woman." He was not happy either; one day, Anna came home to find a note that he had left for Finland to rejoin his family. He was appointed ambassador to Sweden; he and Ekaterina had another son, who died as an infant, and then, in 1923, another, whom they named after his father but called "Valia." Two years later, they had a daughter, Svetlana. (Bukharin and Esfir Gurvich had started a trend: Stalin and Molotov would name their daughters "Svetlana," too.)[67]

In 1925, the Osinskys returned to Moscow and moved back into the Kremlin. At first they lived next to the Sverdlovs (Svetlana remembered Klavdia Novgorodtseva-Sverdlova as "taciturn, cold, dry, and colorless"), but then moved to a nine-room, two-story apartment (from which they could see Bukharin's pet squirrel and fox running around in their cages). At the beginning of 1926, Osinsky was made director of the Central Bureau of Statistics, but he still considered himself, above all, a scholar. "The most important thing we children knew about him was 'Father is working and cannot be disturbed,'" writes his daughter Svetlana. "Since he demanded absolute silence, his rooms in our second Kremlin apartment were separate from ours, across the stairway. His bed was covered with a white camelhair blanket. At the dacha his rooms were on the second floor—again, so that no one would disturb him. He was very irritable. Everyone was a little afraid of him."

He was tall and slim, wore a pince-nez with a gold rim, was always neat and clean-shaven, and preferred light suits. Their maid called him "the Master," or "Himself." According to Svetlana, "there was something cold and rational about him. I remember being shocked by something my mother once told me. When he was young, there were two women in love with him—both sisters of friends (and one of them my mother). As he later confessed, he chose as a wife the one who was healthier and more cheerful because that meant she would be a better mother for his children."

After his friend and brother-in-law, Vladimir Smirnov, was driven out of the Party (by his other friend, Bukharin), Osinsky no longer seemed to be close to anyone. According to Svetlana, "he almost never saw his brother and sisters, was for many years not on speaking terms with his mother, and did not even attend her funeral. None of this, however, prevented him from helping them in all sorts of ways." He liked to play Beethoven and Chopin on the piano and often read aloud to his children. After Vladimir Smirnov's arrest in 1927, he and Ekaterina adopted their four-year-old nephew, Rem ("Revolution, Engels, Marx"). As Osinsky had written earlier to Anna Shaternikova a propos of Victoria, "I have inherited my father's flaw: sentimentality. I don't know how to cry, but I get a catch in my throat during the emotional passages—even when I am reading silently to myself."[68]

In the meantime, Anna had married and given birth to a son, Vsemir (or "Worldwide," for the "Worldwide Revolution"). He had a congenital disorder, which had caused him to grow quickly to a gigantic size, and he was not expected to live long. In the late 1920s, Anna and Osinsky ran into each other at an official reception. She fainted, was taken to a hospital, and somehow lost her Party card. The only way to restore it was to have the original recommenders confirm the endorsements. Her original recommender was Osinsky. They met again and resumed their relationship. He wrote to her often—about his work, his children, his reading, and his feelings; about their secret meetings and their shared faith. He called her "dear Annushka," "darling comrade," and his "Caryatid," and kept assuring her that socialism—and, with it, the profound tenderness and charity of love without shame—would arrive "just as unexpectedly and just as quickly as when it first came to Russia." Any day—and any letter—might be the last one.[69]

■ ■ ■

But what if the power of love and the power of revolutionary enthusiasm pulled men and women in different directions? What if a Communist couple was, in fact, a cell of the Communist Party, and both the cell and the Party were torn by doubts and deviations? Could a difference of opinion destroy love? And if so, could a destroyed love create a difference of opinion?

Those were some of the questions that Mayakovsky's original Gioconda, Maria Denisova, and her husband, Efim Shchadenko, kept asking themselves. She was the "Maria" of the famous poem and, since 1925, a certified sculptor specializing in portraits (she did several of her husband and one of Mayakovsky). He was the son of a worker from the Don Cossack area and a high Red Army official known for his suspicion of "bourgeois specialists." He was twelve years her senior. He, too, wrote poetry, and believed he was close to finding his own voice. She was not convinced. He attributed her doubts to class difference and her impatience. "I don't know why you are accusing me of being a retrograde and reactionary in style and form and of backwardness," he wrote to her. "Yes I am backward like the working class as a whole is backward and right now we are trying to master knowledge but what does reactionary have to do with it? Simply as a new class while mastering the science and the arts which used to be a powerful weapon in the hands of the enemy class as a means of our exploitation naturally we are afraid to make fools of ourselves to go wrong and to become simply an educated intelligentsia no different from the old intelligentsia."

What Maria needed, he argued, was not poems "that are strong in form but meaningless in content," but a new monument by a genuinely new artist rooted in a genuinely new worldview—"that of Marx Engels Plekhanov Lenin and in part Trotsky."

It is not true that futurism is the new style of contemporary art which can be adopted wholesale by the proletariat no and a thousand times no because this style was taken not from the factories and plants and mines and shops, but from the street the in part rebellious hell-raising street from the cafés and restaurants and bawdy houses consequently it can't be proletarian it can only be rebellious it can delight by tickling the nerves of neurotic degenerates and in general the lovers of cheap thrills who look for strength and meaning not in content but in form because that whole crowd is empty of ideological content and it can't be otherwise because being determines the consciousness of the Briks and Co.

To Shchadenko, Mayakovsky's poem about Maria, *A Cloud in Pants*, was just that, a stuffed futurist blouse. "The Briks and Co." were Mayakovsky, his new muse, Lilya Brik, and her husband, Osip. Lilya was Moscow's most celebrated salonnière and an amateur sculptor. She, too, created portraits of both Mayakovsky and her husband. For several years, Lilya, Mayakovsky, and Osip Brik had been living together in the same apartment. *A Cloud in Pants* had been, ex post facto, dedicated to Lilya and published by Osip Brik. They had not stolen La Gioconda; they had stolen her portrait. But why should she care? And why should he? "My darling Marusia I can feel that I am growing day by day and there is no force that can stop my growth. . . . I just remembered what you wrote about how our difference of opinion had destroyed our love. It is necessary to create works that we would both like without reservation and not just like but absolutely love. I believe that in the end I'll be able to create a work (I am very close) that will meet the aesthetic demands of your capricious (but in many ways correct) artistic demands."[70]

When, in the late 1920s, the matter came to a head, it was no longer about whether he would be able to live up to her aesthetic demands; it was about whether she could live up to his political and personal ones:

Efim Shchadenko   Maria Denisova

Marusia! Our breakup is self-evident and I believe that it owes itself to the difference between our political views, our economic physical and moral interests.

Ever since you first felt over you the political economic and moral-physical oppression of a male fighter prepared by his whole prior experience of Party military and public struggle to be a part of an organized force you began to protest with your whole rebellious nature against the confines of our common living which limited and constrained your will. . . .

Very often you and I could not help considering each other sworn class enemies because in this time of intensifying class struggle there can be no other kinds of contradictions in public and family life.

As far as Shchadenko was concerned, NEP was over; the class struggle was inescapable; Bolshevism was identified with masculinity, and the new revolution might as well begin at home. He, as a man and proletarian, would no longer tolerate degeneracy. It was her turn to choose:

It's one or the other either there will be a radical shift in the direction of reconciliation with the existing new system and with the new relations of the submission of the bourgeois anarchic element to the communist i.e. organized element as a result of which comradely fraternal relations will establish themselves between two previously disagreeing elements of the same party, society or family or they should go their separate ways once and for all professing in their outlook two different philosophies of building social and family life.

It is obvious that we have chosen this last option and are going our separate ways in order to never meet again on the political, social and family road, we are becoming enemies in content even though it may not be obvious in form.[71]

Maria agreed. She asked Mayakovsky for money to pay for her studio materials, complained to him about "patriarchy, egoism, tyranny," and "moral murder" at home, and thanked him for "defending women from the domestic 'moods' of their Party husbands."[72]

The upshot seemed clear: if all contradictions in family life were class contradictions, and if one was to "live in the family the same way as outside the family," then a domestic enemy-in-content was to be treated the same way as any other enemy. The ultimate conclusion was provided by Shchadenko's fellow veteran of the First Cavalry Army, Sergei Mironov, when, around the same time, he was asked by his mistress, Agnessa Argiropulo, what he would do if she turned out to be an enemy:

I expected to hear him say that he would give up everything in this world for me, that he would defy everyone and everything. But without hesitating for a moment, his face frozen into a mask, he replied, "I'd have you shot."

I couldn't believe my ears.

"Me? You would have me shot? *Me*—shot??"

He repeated just as resolutely:

"Yes, shot."

I burst into tears.

Then he recollected himself, put his arms around me, and whispered, "I'd have you shot, and then I'd shoot myself." He covered my face with kisses.[73]

■ ■ ■

Sergei Mironov was born into a well-off Jewish family in Kiev. His real name was Miron Iosifovich Korol. He studied at the Kiev Commercial Institute but was drafted during World War I and later joined the Red Army. Once, in a hospital, he overheard some incriminating information in the ravings of a wounded soldier. He informed the head of the local "special department" and was recruited on the spot ("according to the classic rules of recruitment," as he said many years later). Having distinguished himself as an intelligence and sabotage specialist during the Polish War, he was made the head of the "active unit" of the Special Department of the First Cavalry Army. In the first half of the 1920s, he served as a top Cheka-OGPU official in the North Caucasus and the Kuban Cossack area, receiving two Red Banner decorations for anti-insurgent operations in Chechnya. He and Agnessa met in Rostov around 1924, when he was thirty and she was twenty-one. Agnessa was the daughter of a Greek entrepreneur from Maikop. After the Revolution, her father had left for Greece, and her sister had married first a White officer, who was shot by the Reds, and then an engineer, who was arrested for "wrecking" and exiled. Agnessa had married the chief of staff of the North Caucasus border troops. Sometime after moving with him to Rostov, she went to a Red Army Day rally. "The speakers, our local Rostov Party types, were poorly educated and uninteresting. Suddenly an unknown figure mounted the podium, a man in black leather, an army cap, a revolver at his waist. He was saying something about world revolution and about the interventionists, who had been chased away, but were raring to attack us again, but I wasn't listening—I was admiring his strong, handsome face. He had such beautiful brown eyes and amazing eyelashes—long and thick, like fans. His whole expression was nice—good-natured and appealing."[74]

Some time later the wives of the local military commanders were told to stop "thinking of nothing but dresses and housework, which was philistine behavior," and to start attending weekly political literacy classes. Agnessa's husband told her that she should not "compromise" him by playing hooky, so she went. The instructor was the speaker from the rally, who introduced himself as "Mironov." "He wasn't wearing his cap this time, so I was able to get a better look. He had a noble face with a high brow and arched eyebrows. His smiling eyes were unusual—the upper lids arched, the lower straight. And those amazing luxuriant eyelashes. He had dimples, a large, beautifully shaped mouth, straight white teeth, and thick wavy hair that framed his face. He was broad-shouldered and strong, with a thrusting, powerful gait. His smile was charming, and I could see that all the ladies were smitten."[75]

Agnessa applied herself to the study of Marxism-Leninism, beat the competition (with some help from her husband on her homework), and soon became Mironov's lover. He was also married and worked outside Rostov, so they met in hotel rooms and took walks together in the parks. "That's why I love rereading *Anna Karenina*," said Agnessa later. "I recognize my relationship with Mirosha in that book. No, I'm not speaking of what Anna subsequently suffered. I recognize the beginning of their romance. Those secret meetings, those quarrels, those violent reconciliations." He called her "Aga"; she called him "Mirosha." Parodying Party questionnaires, he called that period their "underground apprenticeship." It lasted six years.

In the summer of 1931, Mironov was transferred to Kazakhstan as deputy head of the republic's secret police (OGPU). Agnessa came to his train compartment to say goodbye. He asked her to come with him:

> I was wearing a light dress and jacket and carrying a small purse.
> "How can I go like this, with nothing?"
> That seemed like an irrefutable argument to me, but he rejected it right away:
> "Don't worry, we can buy it all. You'll have everything you need!"
> Suddenly the conductor came down the corridor saying:
> "The train is leaving in two minutes!"
> On the platform, the bell rang.

Sergei Mironov
(Courtesy of Rose Glickman)

Agnessa Argiropulo
(Courtesy of Rose Glickman)

"I won't let you go, Aga," Mironov said, laughing and gripping my hand.

"Hey," I laughed. "You're hurting me."

The bell rang twice, the train shuddered, and the railway buildings glided past the windows.

Agnessa considered getting off at the next station but did not. At the third station, they sent a telegram to her husband and mother. Mironov did not sleep at all that night, fearing she might run away. "In Moscow we stayed at the Metropol [the Second House of Soviets]. In those days couples didn't have to show their marriage certificate to get a room in a hotel. Marriages didn't even have to be officially registered. On the very first day we went to a store together. I picked out whatever I liked, and he paid for it. I wanted one thing, and then another—my desires kept growing. Sometimes I felt a little embarrassed, but he noticed what I liked and bought everything, although in those days there wasn't much to choose from."[76]

■ ■ ■

By marrying Agnessa, Mironov clearly violated Solts's "poor taste" injunction, but he does not seem to have worried much about "Party ethics" (his favorite activities outside of work were cards and billiards). For those who did worry about them, marriage loomed larger than other non-Party loyalties because it involved free choice but could not be reduced to it.

Or rather, there were three fundamental kinds of such loyalties. The first, friendship, was seen as a fully rational alliance based on shared convictions. Communists were not supposed to have non-Communist friends, and most of them did not. Solts did not have to say much on the subject because everyone seemed to agree and because compliance was taken for granted. Jesus did not have to mention friends among the loved ones to be hated, either. Committed sectarians can be trusted not to form strong, personal, nonsexual attachments to unrelated nonsectarians.

Erotic love was, of course, different insofar as it was widely acknowledged to be based on a feeling "comparable to revolutionary enthusiasm in power, clarity, and purity." One was free to resist and overcome that feeling if it interfered with revolutionary enthusiasm, but even Solts, who may never have experienced it himself, agreed that it was a serious challenge. Love and marriage are a problem for all sects because of their sect-destroying reproductive function (some try to limit all amorous activity to actual or symbolic sex with the leader, others fight long-term loyalties by prescribing promiscuity, and all worry a great deal about matrimony's non-coincidence with fraternity), but they are also a problem for all sects because they combine the realm of necessity and the realm of freedom in ways that seem compelling and mysterious in equal measure. Love is the law of life, Solts seemed to be saying, but a random meeting that leads to a particular attachment is not (especially if one considers the unpredictability of reciprocity). As Lev Kritsman, the advocate and theoretician of War Communism, wrote to his wife, Sarra, back in 1915, "I have always known that private life is a house of cards—too fragile to be reliable. I keep realizing that it is possible to know one thing and feel another. I cannot make myself accept that it is so."[77]

The third type of personal attachment, blood relationship, lay entirely in the realm of necessity: one did not choose one's father, mother, children, brothers, and sisters. One could, of course, leave them behind, as all sects prescribe and as the underground Bolsheviks did—permanently in the case of most of the proletarian members and almost permanently in the case of many of the "students." But the Party did not make it a formal requirement and, after the Revolution, seemed uncertain about how to proceed.

On the one hand, "class," the central category of Soviet life, was a heritable trait. As Kritsman wrote about War Communism, "Just as in a society built on exploitation anyone who wishes to gain 'public' respect tries to trace his origins to exploiters (titled feudal lords or capitalist magnates), so in this case anyone who wished to become a full-fledged member of Soviet society desperately tried to prove his undiluted proletarian or peasant origins by providing all sorts of documents and testimonies." In the 1920s, the intensity of violence subsided, but the centrality and heritability of "class" remained unchanged. Hirings and promotions, high school and college admissions, Party and Young Communist League (Komsomol) membership, access to housing and services, tax rates, and court decisions depended on class belonging, which depended on "origins" and occupation. In cases of doubt, origins trumped occupation: a top manager "of proletarian origin" was, for most practical purposes, a "worker"; a registry office clerk "of bourgeois origin" was always a potential hidden enemy. On the other hand, class heredity was Lamarckian, not Mendelian, and one could—by working in a factory, serving in the army, or renouncing one's parents—blunt the power of descent and hope to pass the newly acquired virtue on to one's children. More obviously, the heredity principle did not apply to the Bolshevik leaders, who were almost exclusively of nonproletarian origin, or to their close relatives, who qualified for elite privileges without tests of loyalty.[78]

The Kremlin and the Houses of Soviets were teeming with the fathers, mothers, children, brothers, and sisters of "the flower of the Russian Revolution." The conscience of the Party, Aron Solts, a wealthy merchant's son, lived with his sister and, later on, his niece and her children. Lenin, also of "bourgeois" origin, lived with his wife and sister. So did Arkady Rozengolts, who came from a family of wealthy Rostov merchants. The Krzhizhanovskys, both from the gentry, had taken in and were raising Milena Lozovskaia because she was their niece. (Milena's father, Solomon

Lozovsky, was the son of a melamed.) The Larins had adopted Anna for the same reason. Larin's own father had been a railroad engineer, his mother, the sister of the famous publishers, the Granat brothers (who financed Larin's revolutionary activities). Sergei Mironov and Agnessa Argiropulo would also adopt a niece and have Agnessa's mother, sister, and sister's sons come live with them for long periods of time. (Mironov had fond memories of his own grandmother Khaia, who had owned a dairy store on Kiev's central street, Kreshchatik.) Osinsky, of gentry background, who would later adopt his nephew, considered his son Valia "his best creation." Bukharin's father, a retired teacher of mathematics, lived in his son's Kremlin apartment. In *The Economics of the Transition Period*, Bukharin had singled out nine groups of people to be subjected to "concentrated violence": teachers were number five on the list (under "the technical intelligentsia and the intelligentsia in general"). Voronsky's and Podvoisky's fathers had both been priests (number nine on the list), and Podvoisky was surrounded by his wife's many sisters, clothed or not. (Their father had been an estate manager.) Lev Kritsman, who had written with approval that "belonging to the class of exploiters could guarantee a place in a concentration camp, prison or, at best, a shack left behind by proletarians who had moved to better houses," was the son of a dentist.[79]

Such relations and cohabitations were taken for granted and assumed to be theoretically unproblematic. There were, however, occasional exceptions. Kritsman's wife, Sarra Soskina, came from one of the wealthiest Jewish merchant clans in the Russian Empire (number one on Bukharin's list: "parasitic strata: bourgeois entrepreneurs not directly involved in production"). Unlike many others, the Soskins had not lost all of their wealth after the Revolution because an important part of their grain-exporting business was based in Manchuria, along the Eastern Chinese Railroad. (One of the brothers, Semen, had supplied the Imperial Army during the Russo-Japanese War.) In the 1920s, the Harbin-based "S. Soskin & Co., Limited" sold grain throughout the Far East, including the Soviet Union. Sarra's father, Lazar, was a minor member of the family, with no great fortune of his own, but he had been able to help Kritsman's father establish a dental practice outside Elisavetgrad and, in the early 1920s, to offer his daughter financial help.

In 1924, his wife came down with spinal tuberculosis, and he wrote to Sarra asking if "as the mother of Communists, she could be treated in a Soviet sanatorium at a discount." Sarra responded with indignation, and on April 8, 1926, Lazar wrote to her from Harbin, in imperfect Russian: "Sarra, let us talk heart to heart. For our relationship is not what a father-daughter relationship should be, and it is not my fault. . . . The fact that I supposed that you had the right to have your <u>relatives</u>, in the person of your mother, treated at a discount, is only natural, given my philistine mentality. And I wouldn't boast so much that you never ever accept

Lev Kritsman (Courtesy of   Sarra Soskina (Courtesy of
Irina of Shcherbakova)   Irina of Shcherbakova)

privileges, because that is no great act of heroism if privileges are a matter of mercy, not merit."

The Kritsmans were, of course, receiving privileges of every kind—from housing, food, and health care to Black Sea resorts and theater tickets—and their relatives were, indeed, eligible for special treatment, but the fact that Sarra's mother lived abroad and was married to a "bourgeois entrepreneur not directly involved in production" could very well make her stay at a CEC sanatorium impossible. It is not known whether Sarra made inquiries. She does not seem to have tried very hard to explain the workings of the system to her father, who was not amused, "There is no need to be so ironic in your letter about how it's not your fault that not everything in life complies with your father's wishes. Mother's illness came as a terrible blow to me, and the fear of losing her is too great. For better or worse, she and I have lived our lives together, and now, in our old age, we need each other too much. There is no one in the world closer to us, because you children have gone your own way, you have your own higher interests, and have no time for us."

There was nothing uniquely Soviet about Lazar Soskin's predicament, but of course the young Kritsmans did believe that "the parasitic strata" belonged "in a concentration camp, prison or, at best, a shack," and that any feelings that might interefere with revolutionary enthusiasm were to be extinguished ("If it is needed, it exists, if it is not needed, it will be destroyed"). Lazar addressed the matter directly—relying on both Dostoevsky and the traditional diaspora Jewish genre of parental lament:

> It seems that it is too much trouble for both of you to maintain family relations by writing an occasional short letter. Well, I am not asking for that, either. In your view, it is all a philistine prejudice not worthy of you, so please feel free to act toward us in accordance with your views and convictions about life in general and family re-

lations in particular. After all, Lev Natanovich doesn't seem troubled and, since you arrived back in Russia, hasn't once deigned to add even a few words as an attachment to your letters. Who are we, really, to seek to be in touch with such a pillar of the great movement as our Lev Natanovich. He has more important things to do, and of course we are not complaining. . . . Far be it from us. . . . Well, enough of this, or God knows where this will lead me. But I dare say that I am no less a communist in the profound sense of the word than you are, except that I don't have communist conceit. So don't worry, Sarra. Mother is not going anywhere, and we don't need any help from you.

"Communist conceit" was a term coined by Lenin to refer to members of the Communist Party "who have not been purged yet and who imagine that they can resolve all problems by issuing Communist decrees." But the point was not Lenin; the point was King Lear.

But, daughter dear, let's not fight. I am writing this letter in a hospital, waiting for an operation, which is scheduled for tomorrow. They say it's quite serious, something to do with my bladder. It's been five days since they started preparing me, but the operation itself is tomorrow. Mother can't come to visit because she is not allowed to go out yet. Thank you for ending your letter by saying that you kiss us <u>both</u>. . . . Mother has not yet learned how to write lying down, so I allowed myself to write you one more letter. Well, take care of yourself, I kiss you many many times, my darling little girl. Forgive me if I was too harsh in this letter.

　　Take care, yours, L. Soskin[80]

Four days later, Sarra's brother Grisha, a Red Army officer, received the following telegram: "Father died yesterday after prostate operation. Tell Sarra. Mother." Grisha, who was living in a small apartment in Kiev at the time, decided to bring his mother to live with him. "The only thing that has me a bit worried," he wrote to Sarra on April 12, 1926, "is the terrible dampness of our apartment (the walls leak). I think dampness is dangerous for Mother's health, but I hope to get her a place in a sanatorium as my dependent." Grisha did arrange for his mother to move in with him. But later, in 1929, when he was expecting a transfer in advance of an imminent war with Poland, he wrote again to Sarra to ask if their mother could come live with her. Sarra responded that it was not possible.[81]

Sarra's own son, Yuri, died of scarlet fever in 1920 at the age of nine (Bukharin had arranged a special car to take him to the hospital, but it was too late). Kritsman's classic, *The Heroic Period of the Great Russian Revolution*, opens with a picture of Yuri in a sailor suit and the following dedication:

Title page of Lev Kritsman's *The Heroic Period of the Great Russian Revolution*

To the memory of little Yurochka,
my only child,
To the memory of countless children,
Who fell victim to the intervention
of world capitalism,
And to all those who have not perished
and have now become
the cheerful young pioneers of the wonderful country
of the happy children of the future.[82]

■ ■ ■

In Party discussions and private conversations, the connection between the remnants of the family and the postponement of the prophecy was drawn repeatedly but inconclusively, and often defensively. In Bolshevik fiction, it was at the center of the plot. Bolshevik fiction, unlike Party discussions and private conversation, dealt in "types" and reached for the myth. It strove to express the universal in the particular and to understand the present by appealing to the eternal. It put the Revolution to the test of love and marriage.

Arosev's story "The White Stairway," about the old doorman in the former imperial palace haunted by the Bronze Horseman, was published in 1923 by Voronsky's Krug (Circle) Press. Another story included in that collection, "A Ruined House," is about a young woman named Masha, who lives in a small provincial town but traces her lineage "to a worker's family from the Obukhov Works in St. Petersburg." Masha is nineteen years old, "slender, not very tall, with bright red lips and firm breasts." She is married to a phlegmatic Latvian by the name of Karl but feels a powerful attraction to the Chekist Petr, who wears black leather and talks in short "imperious" sentences.

Masha works in the local army unit's secret police department but feels unfulfilled and wants to move to Moscow; Karl "does not seek anything" and is "perfectly happy to have served two years without a break as commissar in various army regiments." They live "in a small hotel in a tiny, filthy room suffused with the smell of mice and rotten food." One day, when Karl is away, Petr stops by and tells Masha to come out with him. They walk through the dark, snowbound town until they reach the ruins of a large mansion.

It used to contain human life—petty, stupid life, not amusing but meaningless and cruel, like a rock. Even love here used to be stiff and puffed up, like a paper rose.

There was "she," a medalist from some local school, wrapping her shawl around her shoulders and trying to stay warm by the fireplace or fingering the keys of a piano and summoning the hopeless sounds of a maudlin romance.

And there was "he," sitting beside her, smoking cigarettes, stroking her hands, or reciting poetry. It wasn't clear what he wanted: her, her dowry locked away in iron-bound coffers, both at once, or neither—or whether he was simply going through the motions inherited from the inertia of successive generations.

The walls of that house had witnessed many unnecessary tears—and soaked them all up. Its corners had absorbed the warmth of human blood. The doors in all the rooms had learned to imitate human sighs. The sofas, like loyal, sleeping dogs, had been able to tell the difference between strangers and masters and used to squeak in different ways under their soft human behinds. The mirrors had had their favorites, whom they reflected in true portrait style. Porcelain cats, clay cats, painted cats, and live cats had served as household gods and were used by the owners to perfect their Christian love of their neighbor.

Masha and Petr feel the warmth of this vanished life and submit to "blind instinct, as old as the earth." On the way back, Masha tells Petr that she does not even know his last name. He says that it is better that way. She asks what he means. He says: "An apple can only be eaten once." She asks whether they are going to see each other again. He says yes, once she has rid herself of the "old yeast" and they have built a new life in which there are neither husbands nor wives. She asks whether it will be death, not life. He says it will be "better than life"—a Shrovetide festival.[83]

The Communist literature of the 1920s came out of "The Ruined House." The proletarian Adam and Eve had joined the secret police and tasted their apple. What followed was both a new beginning and the Fall; the acquisition of knowledge and, for that very reason, an expulsion from paradise; the promise of a Shrovetide festival and, in the meantime, the curse of having to earn their food by the sweat of their brow, give birth to children with painful labor, and return to the ground from which they had been taken, for dust they were, and to dust they would return. NEP literature retained the memory and the hope of the last days, but it was, more than anything else, a literature of the great disappointment, of unquenchable weeping, of the realization that the sun had not stopped at its zenith and that the serpent (the blind instinct as old as the earth) had not been forced to crawl on its belly, after all.

At the center of NEP laments was the ruined house, at the center of the house was the hearth, and next to the hearth were "she," "he," their reflections, and the inertia of successive generations. In 1921, Comrade Rosfeldt had offered to resign from his post as director of the Second House of Soviets because he could no longer preside over a brothel. Milk and honey, mixed together, had reproduced a "bubbling, rumbling, rotting, and gurgling" swamp. The New City had turned out to be the old one. "What can be done?" asked Lenin as early as 1919. "We must fight against this scum over and over again, and, if this scum crawls back in, clean it out over and over again, chase it out and watch over it."[84]

There were two main ways of representing the profaned Houses of Soviets. One was the ruined mansion with its sighing doors, squeaking sofas, and shimmering mirrors; the other, Karl and Masha's room, suffused with the smell of mice and rotten food. One was the old imperial palace transformed into a House of Soviets; the other, a gray wooden box with blooming geraniums in the windows. One was a stage for gothic horror; the other, a swamp of deadly domesticity. One was descended from the myth about a town sacrificing its young brides to a dragon; the other, from the story of Samson in Delilah's arms and Odysseus on Calypso's island. One was about rape; the other, about castration.[85]

In Arosev's *The Notes of Terenty the Forgotten* (1922), the Old Bolshevik Derevtsov, a former carpenter, comes to see his comrade Terenty, who works in a former governor's mansion:

> Derevtsov was sitting in a large, oaken armchair with lion-paw feet. His pale face stood out against the back of the chair, like the portrait of a knight. The deep, sunken eyes, ringed by dark circles, glowed on that immobile face. Derevtsov stared at the round dark-green tile stove, standing in the corner like a forgotten, moldy servant left behind by his previous owners, a silent witness. . . . It seemed as if someone had smeared blood over the transparent blue sky: the sunset was nearing extinction. Its dark-purple reflections flickered on

the white windowsill and the white door. This produced a slight drowsiness and a desire to listen to medieval tales about mysterious castles and parks with old ponds. It was as if there were traces of former life nestled behind every square inch of silk wallpaper.

Like most Bolsheviks, Derevtsov is suffering from postclimactic melancholy. Unlike most, he also writes poetry. "He's like a saint or small child; his eyes are light blue, like a monk's." Late one evening, Terenty is sitting alone in the palace, writing an appeal to the peasants about grain requisitioning. "Suddenly, my eye fell on the armchair in which Derevtsov had been sitting. What the devil! How absurd! I thought I saw Derevtsov's pale face shining whitely against the back of the chair. Shuddering, I threw down my pen and leapt up. How ridiculous. It was only the bright, white door throwing its reflection on the back of the chair." In the middle of the night, the telephone rings. The Chekist, Kleiner (who wears leather, conducts mass executions, and believes that what is necessary does not corrupt), informs Terenty that Derevtsov shot himself earlier that evening. He left a suicide note that said: "I'm tired, and, in any case, it's all in vain."[86]

Infants, saints, monks, and poets are commonly used as surrogates, but the sacrificial lamb par excellence, especially in gothic tales, is a maiden. In Arosev's *Nikita Shornev* (1926), a young woman named Sonia, a peasant (Shornev), and a student (Ozerovsky) all meet in the Moscow Soviet building during the October uprising. At one point, Shornev embraces Sonia, but an exploding shell interrupts their kiss. Several years later, she comes to see the two men in their separate rooms in one of the Houses of Soviets. The student Ozerovsky is now a coldly articulate Chekist executioner. The peasant Shornev is a high Party official. He tries to kiss Sonia, but she pushes him away.

"But Sonia," he said, "back then, it was the struggle that got in the way."

"You don't understand," she said, also using the intimate form of the pronoun. "It is still the struggle getting in the way."

"How?"

"Because it doesn't provide an answer about how we—you and I—are supposed to live."

Unable to decide between the Chekist's "lies that contain truth" and the true believer's "truth that contains lies," Sonia leaves Moscow on a Party assignment. Some time later, during a May 1 rally on Red Square, in front of the Chapel of the Virgin Mary of Iveron, Ozerovsky tells Shornev that Sonia has committed suicide by throwing herself out of a window. "Because Ozerovsky's words seemed impossible to him, their meeting also seemed impossible. And for that reason, everything—the crowd and the May 1 celebration—suddenly became impossible. It was all a dream."[87]

NEP was a gothic nightmare, and Masha's suspicion that Petr was a messenger of death, not life, might prove accurate, after all. In Gladkov's *Cement*, an idealistic young woman who suffers from "leftist infantilism" and has recurrent dreams about Babylon is raped in her House of Soviets room by a "strong and imperious" Party official. "On one of those sultry, sleepless nights, something she had long expected as inevitable had happened." She cries uncontrollably, spends time in a sanatorium, and is "purged" from the Party. A purge was a symbolic death with the possibility of resurrection. In V. Kirshon and A. Uspenskii's *Korenkovshchina*, the violated heroine kills herself for good; in Malashkin's *Moon from the Right Side*, she attempts suicide, recovers, "leads a maidenly life" in the woods, and rejoins the struggle.[88]

A virgin fearing and anticipating "the inevitable" represented the loss of revolutionary innocence. A self-confident woman to whom the inevitable has already happened was NEP incarnate. One of the main reasons for Derevtsov's emasculation was a certain Comrade Sheptunovskaia ("Whisperer"), who had "small, mousy eyes," collected things out of "spontaneous greed," communicated by "chirping" or "rattling," had burrowed her way into the Party, become a Women's Department activist, and secretly married Derevtsov, who "followed her around like a trained animal." Not all predators were equal, it seems. The greatest danger was not that Petr the Chekist might turn out to be a vampire—it was that Masha, with her "bright red lips and firm breasts," might turn out to be a witch. The greatest danger was not the haunted House of Soviets—it was the small room containing an emasculated commissar who "does not seek anything." In the 1920s, nothing seemed more frightening and more inevitable.[89]

In Arosev's *Recent Days* (1926), a Chekist of proletarian origin, Andronnikov, remembers how, as an exile on the White Sea, he used to take German and math lessons from a young Socialist Revolutionary by the name of Palina ("Scorched"). As they sat by the hot stove, one of her eyes would look directly at him, the other, "somewhere into the corner." One night, Andronnikov tosses his book down and embraces her, but she "threw back her head, her eyes sparkling with a devilish mischievousness, and, still facing his burning gaze and flushed lips, stuck out her tongue." Suddenly, a fellow exile runs into the cabin crying that there is a wolf outside. They rush out, but "the wolf, of course, runs away." And so, of course, does Palina. Several years later, during the Civil War, they meet at a Red Army headquarters on the Volga. Palina is in the kitchen mixing batter for blini, "looking like a young witch stirring her brew." Andronnikov recognizes her, realizes that she is "the enemy," and shoots her in the back. "She fell backward into the gaping black jaws of the Russian stove. . . . She flopped into those jaws on top of the soft blini, hot as blood, which splattered under her."

The she-devil had gone back to where she came from, but was the spell broken? Was there more to milk and honey than the hot, soft, splattering blini? Back in NEP Moscow, in his room "under a glass dome," Andronnikov suffers from doubts, headaches, "the murky stream flowing in the narrow ditch of half-gossip," and terrible nightmares in which Palina's crossed eyes seem to beckon him on. "And just a few steps away, all around the Second House of Soviets, huge, multicolored Moscow is teeming with noises and people." Tsarist generals, speculators, spies, and prostitutes go about their business, and, in the middle of Theater Square, an old Jew plays his violin.[90]

Andronnikov lives alone in his room, but of course most people in the Second House of Soviets did not. The most widely debated NEP-era book about the NEP era was Yuri Libedinsky's *The Birth of a Hero*. An Old Bolshevik and Party judge, Stepan Shorokhov, lives in one of the Houses of Soviets with his two sons and his late wife's younger sister, Liuba (short for Liubov, or "love"). One day he sees her naked, loses his peace of mind, and, after a short and inconclusive inner struggle, marries her. His older son, a teenager named Boris, calls him an "appeaser" and her, "a bitch." Boris is right: Liuba reveals herself to be a mindless philistine and sexual predator, and Stepan grows listless and irritable from sleeplessness and remorse. He moves out of her bed, but she pursues him with reproaches and caresses until he flees to Turkestan on a Party assignment. His coworker is a soulless bureaucrat by the name of Eidkunen ("Eydtkuhnen" was the East Prussian town closest to the Russian imperial border); the case he is investigating involves a Communist who shot his "class-alien" wife.

Meanwhile, Boris realizes that all the evil in the world comes from the fact that grown-ups are always busy dealing with "that shameful, important, and not really comprehensible thing that leads to the birth of children." The father of one of his friends leaves his wife for a typist; the father of another beats his wife because he suspects that his son is not his own; and the father of a sweet girl named Berta kills Berta's stepfather and drives her mother to insanity. Worst of all, Boris notices that his moustache is beginning to grow, and that some girls in his class seem to enjoy being touched. In an attempt to break the cycle, he proposes the creation of Children's Cities, or Houses of Soviets the way they were meant to be— truly fraternal. He imagines "grandiose games by thousands of children without any nannies, under the supervision of some intelligent people, and completely free from the grown-ups, from all those Moms and Dads."

While Stepan is away, Liuba moves in with a fellow philistine and gives birth to Stepan's son. Suddenly free, as if awakened from a nightmare, he realizes that the two dangers—Eidkunen's dry bureaucratism and Liuba's lush domesticity, are two faces of the same evil. He returns to confront Liuba:

> Liuba was pacing up and down the room, cradling the baby in her arms and singing the eternal mother's lullaby, and there was an instinctive, protective, predatory power in her supple movements and the husky, almost moist tones of her cooing, low voice. . . . Next to

her, Stepan suddenly felt brand new, as if he were the one who had just been born and still had his whole life ahead of him. And in the emptiness and desolation of that large room, he could see the barely visible signs of Liuba's domestic little world: the colorful embroidery on the window sill, the new meatgrinder glistening in the corner, and her cozy, worn little slippers under the bed. And he saw all these things, which used to be so dear to him, as a reappearance of the old enemy, the spontaneously regenerating perennial and loathsome forms of life.

Liuba tells Shorokhov that she will not give up the baby, but Stepan says that all he wants is to make sure the child is not corrupted by her influence. At the end of the novel, they stand "on either side of the cradle, intense in their hostility toward each other and ready for new struggles."[91]

The hero of the title has been born. Or rather, two heroes have been born. Or rather, two protagonists have been born, a father and a son. Revolutions do not devour their children; revolutions, like all millenarian experiments, are devoured by the children of the revolutionaries. Stepan feels truly free for the first time when he realizes that he is past the age of unreason; to use Osinsky's formula, "revolutionary enthusiasm" can finally prevail over "the enormous power of feeling." But what was Boris to do? Revolutions, Boris's nascent moustache seems to suggest, begin as a tragedy and end at home.

For Platonov, this was the greatest tragedy. Platonov's Communism is an eternal Children's City for orphans of all ages, but Platonov's Communists do not know how to build it and what to protect it from:

Prokofy wanted to say that wives were also working people and that there was no ban on their living in Chevengur, so why not let the proletariat go take by the hand and bring back wives from other settlements, but then he remembered that Chepurny wanted women who were thin and exhausted, so they would not distract people from mutual communism, and he said to Yakov Titych:

"You'll set up families here and give birth to all kinds of petty bourgeoisie."

"What's there to be afraid of, if it's petty?" asked Yakov Titych with some surprise. "Petty means weak."[92]

Petty meant weak, and weak meant strong. Nothing was more dangerous than women, even the exhausted kind, and nothing was more justified than worrying about the cozy, worn little slippers under the bed. In an article defending Arosev from accusations of faintheartedness, Voronsky writes that "Terenty's hamletizing may be harmful for some people, but it prevents self-satisfaction and, for the Party as a whole, represents 'the water of life' and 'the God of a living person.'" It proves that the faith is still

strong—because "it is not Hamlet's spirit, it is the spirit of Faust: that irrepressible, indestructible, active element of the human soul that is not
satisfied with what has been achieved, but seeks new untrodden paths, so
the heart is rejuvenated and the mind always remains engaged." This was
not an easy argument to make. Goethe's Faust is saved in the end; Arosev's
Derevtsov loses his faith and commits suicide, while his comrade, Terenty,
dies of typhus (and is, of course, forgotten). As Platonov's Prokofy puts it,
earnestly and hopefully, "Everyone is dead, now the future can begin."[93]

The future was best described by Mayakovsky. In his 1929 play, *The Bedbug*, the young Communist, Ivan Prisypkin, leaves his loyal, proletarian
girlfriend, Zoia Berezkina, for a rich hairdresser's daughter. Zoia shoots
herself. Ivan celebrates his wedding in a hair salon, amidst bottles and
mirrors. ("On the left side of the stage is a grand piano, its jaws wide open,
on the right, a stove, its pipes snaking around the room.") The party ends
in a fight, which leads to a fire. Everyone dies, but one body is missing. Fifty
years later, Ivan's frozen corpse turns up in a flooded cellar in the "former
Tambov." The director of the Institute of Human Resurrections and his
assistant, Zoia Berezkina, who, as it turns out, has survived her suicide
attempt, bring Ivan back to life. He reveals his foreignness to his Communist surroundings by demanding beer and pulp fiction (both long extinct)
and is placed in a special cage at the zoo. The bedbug, defrosted along with
him, is placed next to him. As the zoo's director explains, "there are two of
them, of different sizes, but identical in essence. They are the famous 'bedbugus normalis' and 'philistinius vulgaris.' Both live in the musty mattresses of time. 'Bedbugus normalis' gets fat drinking the blood of one
person and falls under the bed. 'Philistinius vulgaris' gets fat drinking the
blood of mankind and falls on top of the bed. That's the only difference!"

Lenin's metaphor would soon be realized: the Russian land would be
purged of bugs. In a poem from the same period, Mayakovsky writes about
hearing, through the noise of "domestic mooing," "the rumble of the approaching battle." The Revolution's last act was about to begin. The
"hearth's family smoke" would soon be extinguished. Maria Denisova, his
stolen Gioconda, had sent him a note thanking him for protecting women
from the "domestic moods of their Party husbands."

But there was another possible interpretation. Ivan, his bedbug, and
the world of sour-smelling "soups and diapers" they represented might be
indestructible, after all. Having survived the fire, the flood, and the freeze,
they would reenter the world of the future. On April 14, 1930, four months
after receiving Maria's letter, Mayakovsky shot himself. His suicide note
ends with a poem, which begins with a pun.

"The case has been revolved,"
as they say.
The boat of love
has crashed on domesticity."[94]

8

THE PARTY LINE

Different millenarian sects have different ways of bringing about the inevitable, from praying and fasting to self-mutilation and mass murder, but they all have one thing in common: the inevitable never comes. The world does not end; the blue bird does not return; love does not reveal itself in all of its profound tenderness and charity; and death and mourning and crying and pain do not disappear. As of this writing, all millenarian prophecies have failed.

There are various ways of dealing with the great disappointment. One is to point to failures in the implementation. Hiram Edson founded Seventh-day Adventism on the assumption that the millennium had to be postponed because of the continued practice of Sunday worship. For the Bolsheviks, the most popular early explanation of the apparent nonfulfillment of the prophecy was the failure of the world outside Russia to carry out its share of the world revolution. As Arosev wrote in 1924, "the young, northern country flashed its red fire, through the wilderness of its forests, at European life, and then fell silent, expecting an answer from the west." The fact that the answer was slow in coming had to do with tactical miscalculations, not the original prediction, and large numbers of Old Bolsheviks spent much of the 1920s abroad ushering in the world revolution. The most durable success came in Mongolia, where Boris Shumiatsky helped create a nominally independent Soviet state. (The son of a Jewish bookbinder exiled to Siberia, Shumiatsky was a lifelong revolutionary and top Bolshevik official in Siberia and the Far East. Having supervised the Mongolian Revolution of 1921–22, he became ambassador to Persia, and, in 1925, rector of the Communist University of the Toilers of the East. In 1930, he was made head of the Soviet film industry.)[1]

Other commonly cited reasons for the postponement of the end were the recalcitrance of evil (which, according to Kritsman, was both foreseen and excessive); the peculiarity of the Russian situation (especially the size of the predictably unwieldy peasantry); and the tendency of the proletariat to prostitute itself to foreign gods, especially those of soups and diapers. In theory, the Bolsheviks subscribed to the strong version of the circular mythological conception of fate, in which every freely chosen departure from the oracular prophecy is a part of that prophecy; in practice, they followed the Hebrew god's practice of blaming the nonfulfillment of the promise on the chosen people's lack of proletarian consciousness. The fact that immaturity was part of the original design was no excuse for immaturity.

The next, more radical step in dealing with the great disappointment is to adjust the prophecy itself. Augustine turned the millennium into a metaphor; Miller moved the end of the world from 1843 to 1844; Stalin and Bukharin proclaimed that socialism could first be built in one country. A particularly productive subset of this strategy is to proclaim that the prophecy has been fulfilled and that the remainder of human history is a mopping-up epilogue. Among the disappointed Millerites and their descendants, the Seventh-Day Adventists believed that Jesus had been briefly detained in a special antechamber, while the Jehovah's Witnesses argued that he had returned as prophesied but remained invisible so as to allow the faithful to make their final preparations. Christianity as a whole is based on a similar claim: the failure of the founder's prophecy about the imminent coming of the last days became the main confirmation of the truth of that prophecy. Jesus's arrest and execution before any of "those things" could happen became both an act of fulfillment and a sacrifice needed for the future fulfillment. NEP-era Bolsheviks were in a similar position: there was much weeping, of course, but the fact that the revolution had begun was the best indication that it would end.

In the meantime, they had to learn how to wait. All millenarians who do not burn in the fire of their own making adjust themselves to a life of permanent expectation in a world that has not been fully redeemed. Special texts, rituals, and institutions are created in an attempt to mediate between the original prophecy and the fact that it has not been fulfilled and that nobody lives in accordance with its precepts. The millennium is postponed indefinitely, claimed to have been realized in the current unity of the faithful (as in Augustine's new orthodoxy in Christianity), and either transformed into an individual mystical experience or transferred to another world altogether. Promises become allegories, and disciples who have abandoned their old families start new ones. Zoroastrianism, Christianity, Islam, Mormonism, and the Commonwealth of Massachusetts are all examples of successfully routinized, bureaucratized millenarianisms—and so, to all appearances, was the Stalin-Bukharin Party line of the 1920s. As the new regime settled down to wait, its most immediate tasks were to suppress the enemy, convert the heathen, and discipline the faithful.

Money changers had to be allowed into the temples and "bourgeois specialists" had to be used as their own gravediggers, but the policy of "ruthless class exclusivity" (as Kritsman put it) remained the main guarantee of final liberation. It was easier for a camel to go through the eye of a needle than for a former rich man or his children to enter a high-status Soviet institution (not counting all the special exceptions for the "flower" of the world revolution). As a matter of self-conscious, self-fulfilling prophecy, class aliens were continually being unmasked as active enemies. As Koltsov wrote in a 1927 essay,

> The Cheka has become the GPU, but the only things that have changed are the outward conditions and methods of work.
>
> In the old days, the chairman of a provincial Cheka, a worker, would sit down on the remnants of a chair and, fully armed with his sense of class righteousness, jot down an order in pencil on a scrap of paper: "Milnichenko—to be shot—as a vermin of the international bourgeoisie. Also the seven men in the cell with him." Now, the GPU works in collaboration with the courts, worker-peasant inspection, and control commissions, under the supervision of the Procuracy. The methods and rules of the struggle have become more complex, but the dangers and number of enemies have not diminished.

One thing that had not changed, according to Koltsov, was the pride that the revolutionary state took in its commitment to violence. The Soviet secret police possessed the same advantage as its predecessor, the Jacobin Committee of Public Safety: it was not secret. The agents of the ancien regime had snooped around in dark alleys and hidden their victims in dungeons. The Jacobins had nothing to hide. "On the Place de Grève, the glittering blade of the guillotine worked day and night, and all could see the fate that awaited the enemies of the people. The Jacobin police did not conceal its work. It carried out its activities openly and in public view. Armed with the righteousness of an ascending class, it relied on a vast number of supporters, voluntary helpers, and collaborators."

The GPU (Soviet secret police) was in an even better position. Unlike the Jacobin police, it represented the last class in history and could rely on total, unconditional support. Koltsov asked his readers to imagine what would happen if a White Guardist spy were to come to the Soviet Union and stay in the apartment of a coconspirator.

> If the White guest appears, in any way, suspicious, the alarmed Party cell of the building will take a special interest in him. He will be noticed by the Komsomol member who comes to fix the plumbing. The maid, upon returning home from a meeting of household employees where she has just heard a lecture on the external and internal enemies of the dictatorship of the proletariat, will begin to examine this strange new tenant more closely. Finally, the neighbor's daughter, a Young Pioneer, will lie awake at night feverishly trying to make sense of a conversation she had overheard in the corridor. And, suspecting a counterrevolutionary, a spy, or a White terrorist, they will all—together and separately—refuse to wait for someone to come question them, but will go to the GPU and recount what they have seen and heard in great detail, and with great feeling and certainty. They will lead the Chekists to the White Guardist; they will help capture him; and they will join in the fight if the White Guardist tries to resist.[2]

To make sure this was the case, the Soviet state had to fulfill its second fundamental task: to convert the majority of the population to the official faith. It was an enormous task: the Bolsheviks had taken over the world's largest empire. NEP represented a "retreat," but most Bolsheviks, including Arosev, continued to hope that the present generation—or today's young children, at the very latest—would live under Communism. Christians had not become the ruling party in the Roman Empire until more than three centuries after the death of the sect's founder; the NEP-era Bolsheviks counted sacred time in years and clearly assumed, as had Paul, that "the world in its present form is passing away." As Kritsman put it at the end of *The Heroic Period of the Russian Revolution*, NEP's function was to prepare for "the coming world-historical battle between the proletariat and capital." Such hope and expectation clashed with the fact that most of the Party's subjects were not proletarians, and most proletarians were not fully "conscious." NEP was the time of fomenting world revolution outside the Soviet Union and educating the revolution's beneficiaries within. The second task had a much higher ratio of free will to predestination. The numbers were huge, and the time was short. The point, as the Puritan Richard Baxter said of a similar commonwealth, was to force all men "to learn the word of God and to walk orderly and quietly . . . till they are brought to a voluntary, personal profession" of the true faith. Fulfillment had been postponed and some "hamletizing" was natural, but the faith remained strong and the faithful remained a sect.[3]

The main Bolshevik conversion strategy was to transform all stable face-to-face communities—peasant villages, factory shopfloors, school classes, kindergarten "groups," university departments, white-collar offices, and apartment building associations—into would-be congregations of fellow believers collectively contributing to the building of Communism. This was achieved by having every one of such units (known, after the mid-1930s, as "collectives") house a Party "cell." There were Komsomol cells for young people, Young Pioneer "stars" (or primary units of five members, each representing a point on the Red Army star) for children between the ages of ten and fourteen, and "Octobrist detachments" for schoolchildren under the age of ten. With the Party as their guide, communities of classmates, neighbors, and colleagues were to become cohesive units with their own elected officials responsible for discipline, hygiene, literacy, "physical culture," political education, and in-house newspaper. Koltsov knew what he was talking about: in 1927, every resident of his hypothetical apartment would have been a member of a "collective" and, as such, a regular participant in meetings, rallies, "volunteer Saturdays," and other Party-sponsored activities. The overall structure was a combination of the Calvinist-style network of self-disciplining congregations and Catholic-style supervision by licensed ideology professionals, with the not insignificant difference that the Soviet rank and file were mostly pagan. Eventually, all Soviets would become Communists; in the meantime, some members of the "collective" needed to be told what Communism meant. No one could refuse to participate, but not everyone was assumed to be a believer. The Party was a hierarchy of licensed ideology professionals; the "collectives" were not yet full-fledged congregations of fellow believers.[4]

The process of conversion consisted of three main elements. One was doctrinal training—through classroom instruction, "political education" seminars (modeled on prerevolutionary "reading circles"), public lectures, speeches at rallies, and newspaper reading, among other things. Participation in most of these activities was compulsory for "collective" members, from the neighbor's Young Pioneer daughter to the maid registered by the building residents' council. Study of the "classics" was rare; most people learned about Marxism-Leninism from school textbooks, popular summaries (such as Bukharin and Preobrazhensky's *The ABC of Communism* or Kerzhentsev's *Leninism, The Dictatorship of the Proletariat,* and *The Bolshevik's Handbook*), and lectures similar to those delivered by Sergei Mironov to the wives of the Rostov military commanders. Most of the instruction focused on Party policy, not Communist theory.

Another important element of the makeover was mandatory participation in collective activities. Like most comprehensive faiths, Bolshevism was a communal affair that required attendance at public rituals and disapproved of individualism; like most missionaries, the Bolshevik mass-education ideologues insisted that the initiates spend as much time together as possible; like the Calvinists, whose congregation model the Soviet "collectives" most closely resembled, the Bolsheviks demanded constant mutual surveilance and public transparency from their members.

The third and largest part of the Bolshevik conversion effort was the "civilizing process." Missionary work involves more than the transfer of belief and the creation of new communities. The message of salvation comes accompanied by words, gestures, stories, rituals, and routines associated with the original prophecy and its journey toward the present. All conversions involve some degree of "civilizing"; the Bolshevik kind, because of Marx's identification of universal salvation with European urban modernity, was forcefully and self-consciously civilizational. Becoming Soviet meant becoming modern; becoming modern meant internalizing a new regimen of neatness, cleanliness, propriety, sobriety, punctuality, and rationality.[5]

Podvoisky's "alliance with the sun" was but a small part of the massive NEP-era campaign for hygiene, "physical culture," "the culture of everyday life," "rational nutrition," and other measures aimed at creating clean, trim, healthy, and—as a consequence—beautiful bodies. Young people were to be "tempered" and disciplined through exercise; women, in particular, were to be liberated from the stifling confines of home life (the "gray wooden boxes"). According to the head of the Committee on People's Nutrition, Artashes ("Artemy") Khalatov, family kitchens were dark, filthy caves "where the female worker was forced to spend much of her time," undermining her own health and tormenting her "hungry, tired proletarian husband" with unbalanced and unappetizing meals. The answer was to create "factory kitchens" stocked with "mechanical meat grinders, potato peelers, root cutters, bread slicers, knife cleaners, and dishwashers." As Andrei Babichev from Yuri Olesha's *Envy* wants to say to Soviet women (but does not), "We will give you back all the hours stolen from you by the kitchen; one-half of your life will be returned to you." (Khalatov himself came from a middle-class Armenian family in Baku. He joined the Party in 1917, when he was a student at the Moscow Commercial Institute and a member of the presidium of the Trans-Moskva Military-Revolutionary Committee.)[6]

What were Soviet families to do with so much leisure? The challenge, according to Podvoisky, was to institute "an organized, healthy, sober, and cheerful full-day regimen; games in a healthy environment involving movements that would expand your chest, fill your lungs with fresh air, stimulate your heart, make your blood flow faster and spread vital forces everywhere, fuel an appetite for healthy food—bread, fruit, and vegetables—improve your mood, and enhance the state of your whole being." Thus invigorated, human beings would respond more readily to guidance and instruction. Three minutes of purposeful activity by specially trained organizers—and a festive "crowd of many thousands" would be transformed into "a rigid framework of two single-file formations; those left behind would run up to see what was happening and end up joining the ranks." The goal was "political propaganda in an entertaining form: through joking, singing, dancing, and staged speeches and meetings, people would imbibe the ideas of international proletarian solidarity."[7]

Platon Kerzhentsev, the main ideologue of the Soviet self-disciplining campaign, started out as a theorist of mass theatrical performances that would "help audiences perform themselves." By 1923, he had concluded that spontaneity required consciousness. Russian workers had to learn how to work and dream "according to a plan and a system." They were to "organize themselves," internalize social discipline, and develop a "love of responsibility." The Bolshevik work ethic, like its Puritan predecessor, consisted of "regarding one's work, no matter how petty it might be at any given moment, as important, significant work on whose success the common great cause depended."[8]

It also depended on "developing a sense of time." Peasants and noblemen had regarded time as "an elemental force that operated according to arbitrary, incomprehensible laws." The intelligentsia, too, "bore the same stamp of sluggish somnolence and disdain for time." Capitalism "taught everyone to carry around a watch so you can't help seeing it several hundred times a day." Communism was about conquering the kingdom of necessity by submitting to it. It was "embodied harmony, where everything happens with accuracy, precision, and correctness, and where the sense of time is so deeply ingrained that there is no need to look at a watch because the proper flow of life will endow all things with a distinct temporal form." In the meantime, according to Kerzhentsev, the task was to imitate and overtake capitalist modernity by reversing, cargo-cult-style, its causes and consequences. "All Englishmen, with the exception of a tiny handful of people, go to bed at 11 or 12. They all get up at a certain time, too—between 7 and 8 a.m. During the day, rest periods are rigidly fixed: between noon and 1 p.m., the English, irrespective of social status, have lunch; at 4:30 they all drink tea, and at 7 p.m. they all have dinner. Such scheduling norms have entered the flesh and blood of members of every class because the industrial way of life requires the creation of orderliness, with the correct alternation of periods of work and rest."[9]

Well-ordered time required well-ordered space. Soviet work and rest were to unfold amidst properly arranged objects whose aesthetic appeal was in direct proportion to their functional utility. In a 1926 article devoted to the "Worker's Home" exhibition at the State Department Store, Koltsov listed spotless "cupboards, shower stalls, iceboxes, and wardrobes"; "blindingly bright pots, tea kettles, coffeemakers, and pans"; and "splendid enamel bathtubs, sinks, and even urinals." But wasn't this bourgeois philistinism? Was not an Englishman who ate his porridge at 9:00 a.m. and shaved over his enameled sink the epitome of middle-class vacuousness? Didn't Kerzhentsev, who liked to read Dickens aloud to his daughter, remember the pompous Mr. Podsnap from *Our Mutual Friend* and his "notions of the Arts in their integrity"?

> Literature; large print, respectfully descriptive of getting up at eight, shaving close at a quarter past, breakfasting at nine, going to the City at ten, coming home at half-past five, and dining at seven. Painting and Sculpture; models and portraits representing Professors of getting up at eight, shaving close at a quarter past, breakfasting at nine, going to the City at ten, coming home at half-past five, and dining at seven. Music; a respectable performance (without variations) on stringed and wind instruments, sedately expressive of getting up at eight, shaving close at a quarter past, breakfasting at nine, going to the City at ten, coming home at half-past five, and dining at seven.[10]

"This is not the worst of it," wrote Koltsov. "Answering the call of nature and taking daily baths are not necessarily signs of philistinism. But what would you say after seeing the model three-room proletarian apartment on exhibit at the State Department Store? Rugs! A china cabinet!! Curtains on the windows!!! A lampshade embroidered with little flowers!" What you would say, it turns out, is that "the revolution has come into contact with the rug and the curtain, but the Soviet order is not dying—it is getting stronger, along with the worker and peasant who are getting stronger in their material well-being and their enjoyment of life." The proletarian revolution required bourgeois civilization, and bourgeois civilization required rugs and curtains. "It would be silly and criminal to grab the proletarian by the sleeve and try to convince him to despise rugs and not to wear ties or use cologne. In our present circumstances, this would be the worst kind of bourgeois philistinism." Koltsov himself, after all, wore suits and spent weekends at his dacha. "If laborers lost in the forests want to climb out of the pit of ignorance and superstition, we need to bring a step-ladder or stretch out a helping hand."[11]

■ ■ ■

There were many ways for the Soviet state to stretch out a helping hand. NEP was about creating the Revolution's preconditions: modern industrial development and proletarian self-awareness. Industrialization was going to take some time; conversion—officially known as "enlightenment," "agitation-propaganda," or the need to "learn, learn, and learn,"—was NEP's primary task in the meantime. Besides formal schooling and a variety of lectures, study groups, and literacy campaigns, the state could reach the masses by means of posters, newspapers, movies, radio broadcasts, and books. Different educational tools could be effective in different contexts, but for most Old Bolsheviks presiding over the Soviet state, none was of greater importance or personal interest than literature. Reading had been central to their own conversion and their early efforts to convert others; reading imaginative literature was of special significance because of the "enormous power of feeling" that it could generate. As Osinsky wrote to Shaternikova, it was "comparable to revolutionary enthusiasm" in its "power, clarity, and purity," and it could fan or temper that enthusiasm, if directed accordingly. He himself could not think of a better representation of the "psychology of future times" than Verhaeren's poem, "The Black-smith"; Bukharin attributed his discovery of love without God to Dostoevsky's *The Adolescent*; Voronsky had found the best portrait of a ruthless revolutionary in Ibsen's Brand; Sverdlov's favorite prophecy of future perfection came from Heine's "Germany"; and Sverdlov's (and Voronsky's) friend Filipp Goloshchekin, who oversaw the massacre of the tsar's family, had left behind an epitaph from Heine's "Belsazar." Fiction had structured, nuanced, and illustrated the Bolshevik experience. The new Soviet fiction was going to immortalize it.

The task of organizing and guiding Soviet literature fell to Aleksandr Voronsky. In February 1921, the Central Committee appointed him editor in chief of the new "thick" journal, *Red Virgin Soil*, and, after a brief stint as a volunteer, helping to put down the Kronstadt uprising, he set to work. "He is a good, decent person, even though he doesn't seem to know much about the arts," said Gorky. "But, judging by his temperament, he'll learn. He is extremely tenacious."[12]

Voronsky agreed that he owed everything in life to his love of hard work and did his best to maintain the "self-discipline, punctuality, and rigid daily schedule" that he had perfected in prison. In 1921, Russian literary life consisted mostly of writers reading their work to each other in private seminars. According to Vsevolod Ivanov,

> Voronsky would go from one seminar to another, listen to the discussions, and then ask the participants which of the young writers they considered the most talented. The writer who got the largest number of votes would receive an invitation to publish in *Red Virgin Soil*.
>
> At first, Voronsky was suspicious of the writers. Their extreme sensitivity struck him as odd, and the low level of their political consciousness often exasperated him. Sometimes, having read a manuscript and discussed it with the author, he would throw up his hands in indignation and say, while blinking rapidly:
>
> "I am not sure he has ever heard of the October Revolution!"[13]

He persevered, however, and found most of them open to direction. The talented young writers had all heard of the October Revolution, and many of them had participated on the right side, if not always at the appropriate level of political consciousness. Ivanov continues: "His manner was informal, and he preferred to talk about literature in his own home or the writers' rather than in the editorial offices. 'It is easier for us to understand each other this way,' he would say. Most conversations were about the manuscripts he was planning to publish. It seems to me that those conversations took the place of an editorial board, which *Red Virgin Soil* did not have for a while. He gradually developed his own taste and eventually began to write decent fiction himself. It was not for nothing that Gorky had called him 'tenacious.'"[14]

In the 1920s, Voronsky lived in a two-room apartment in the First House of Soviets with his mother, Feodosia Gavrilovna, a priest's widow; his wife, Sima Solomonovna, whom he had met in exile and whose eyes, as he put it, projected "the soft, ancient Jewish sorrow"; and their daughter, Galina, born in 1916. After a while, Feodosia Gavrilovna moved into a room of her own in the Fourth House of Soviets, but she continued to spend much of her time in her son's apartment, cooking on the primus stove and taking care of her granddaughter. During the day, Voronsky wrote at his desk, often stopping to answer the phone or "talk with some comrade from another floor who stopped by to ask for a cigarette or a book, or just to share some impressions about a trip or a newspaper article." In the evenings, he used to talk to writers and anyone else who showed up. "We often got together at Voronsky's," wrote Ivanov. "We used to bring a bottle of red wine and sit over that bottle all night, talking expansively and reverently about literature. Esenin read his poems, Pilnyak—*The Naked Year*, Babel—*Red Cavalry*, Leonov—*The Badgers*, Fedin—*The Garden*, and Zoshchenko and

Nikitin—their short stories. Voronsky's friends, the Old Bolsheviks and Red Army Commanders Frunze, Ordzhonikidze, Eideman, and Griaznov, used to come, too." Ivanov himself read his *Partisans* and *Armored Train 1469*. Among other frequent visitors, according to Galina Voronskaia, were Arosev, Boris Pasternak, "the ugly and very witty Karl Radek, in his heavy horn-rimmed glasses," and the close family friend, Filipp Goloshchekin, whom Voronsky affectionately called "Philip the Fair."[15]

For about two years, Voronsky was the supreme and uncontested discoverer, promoter, publisher, censor, and dictator of the new Soviet literature. His job was to separate the weeds from the good seed and to champion the very best of the good. "Political censorship in literature," he wrote a propos of the first task, "is a complex, important, and very difficult endeavor that requires great firmness but also flexibility, caution, and understanding." As he explained to the author of *We*, Evgeny Zamiatin, "We have paid for this right with blood, exiles, prisons, and victories. There was a time . . . when we had to keep silent. Now it is *their* turn." As for finding "the most talented," Voronsky may have been influenced by those he was guiding (as Vsevolod Ivanov claimed), but his general sense of what constituted good literature was derived from his prison reading, which—like that of all "student" revolutionaries—was centered on the "classics." His particular favorites were Pushkin, Tolstoy, Gogol, Chekhov, Homer, Goethe, Dickens, Flaubert, and Ibsen. His most prized protégés were Babel, Esenin, Ivanov, Leonov, Seifullina, and Pilnyak.[16]

In 1923, Voronsky's monopoly began to be challenged by a small but vocal group of "proletarian" critics, who argued that all literature that was not militantly and self-consciously revolutionary was counterrevolutionary, and that Voronsky was, "objectively" and perhaps deliberately, advancing the cause of the proletariat's class enemies. None of the proletarian ideologues was a proletarian. Most of them were young men from Jewish families (at the time of the formation of the "October" group of proletarian writers in 1922, Semen Rodov was twenty-nine; Aleksandr Bezymensky and Yuri Libedinsky, twenty-four; G. Lelevich, twenty-one, and Sverdlov's nephew Leopold Averbakh, seventeen). They were all Party members, however, and believed that the job of leading the Bolshevik artistic production should be transferred from the lukewarm Voronsky to a true "Party cell." Which of the feuding "proletarians" should receive the commisson was a matter of dispute, but everyone agreed that Voronsky and his "fellow-travelers" had to go.[17]

Voronsky responded by describing his detractors as false prophets of the apocalypse (and caricatures of his underground alter ego, Valentin): "Those righteous and steadfast men

Aleksandr Voronsky

ate locusts and wild honey, did not drink alcohol, walked not in the counsel of the ungodly nor stood in the way of sinners, but did unceasingly
rebuke the men of little faith and of no faith in public squares, and whenever the prophetic trumpet failed them, they would, by all accounts, apply
themselves sullenly and noisily to shattering glass, smashing window
frames, and breaking down doors." More important, he responded by formulating a theory of literature that added Freud and Bergson to Belinsky
and Plekhanov to produce a synthesis he believed to be genuinely Marxist.
Literature, according to Voronsky, was not a weapon in the class struggle
but a method of discovering the world. "Art, like science, apprehends life.
Art and science have the same object: reality. But science analyzes, art
synthesizes; science is abstract, art is concrete; science is aimed at man's
reason, art, at his sensual nature."[18]

Artistic process was about neither class nor "technique": it was about
"intuition" (formerly known as "inspiration"). Intuition was a way of getting at the truth "by going beyond conscious, analytic thought." Every true
artist was Pushkin's "seeing and perceiving" prophet. "He steps aside from
the daily routine, the petty joys and disappointments, and the clichéd
views and opinions, and becomes suffused with a special sympathetic
sense, a feeling for the life of others that exists separately and independently from him. Beauty is revealed in objects, events, and people irrespective of how the artist would like to interpret them; the world separates
itself from man, frees itself from the self and its impressions, and appears
resplendent in its original beauty." The whole of human life was organized
around the memory of that beauty and the hope of recovering it:

> Surrounded by the world distorted by his impressions, man pre-
> serves in his memory, if only as a faint, distant dream, the unspoilt,
> genuine images of the world. They make themselves known to man
> in spite of all the obstructions. He knows about them from his child-
> hood and his youth; they reveal themselves to him in special, excep-
> tional moments, or during the periods of public upheavals. Man
> yearns for those pristine, bright images, and creates sagas, legends,
> songs, novels and novellas about them. Sometimes consciously but
> mostly unconsciously, genuine art has always sought to restore,
> find, discover these images of the world. This is the true meaning of
> art and its true function.[19]

Art, in other words, had "the same goal as religion." But "religion" (by
which Voronsky meant the latter-day Christianity he had learned in the
seminary), sought pristine beauty in another, ultimately false, world,
whereas art "seeks, finds, and creates 'paradise' in living reality." Religion
competed with art on its territory (Tolstoy and Gogol lost their gift of clairvoyance when they turned toward religion), but art, as true revelation, had
nothing to fear in the end. "The more successful an artist is at *surrendering*

to the power of his immediate perceptions and the less he insists on correcting those impressions by imposing general rational categories, the more concrete and independent his world becomes."[20]

The dictatorship of the proletariat had nothing to fear, either. Lenin was, in a sense, "possessed," and had "the prophetic sight given by nature and life to geniuses." "Such 'possessed' men look at everything from the same angle and see only those things that their main idea, feeling, and mood force them to see. The keenness of their sight, hearing, and powers of observation are superhuman. But to be possessed by one great idea does not mean to miss the details." The best illustration of this was Lenin's relationship with his early disciples, the Old Bolsheviks—"those special human beings 'who are looking for the city that is to come.'" On the one hand, he "unites, organizes, disciplines, and welds people together into one collective, one cohort of steel." On the other, he judges them on the basis of passion, intuition, and "the immediate perception of the very core of their beings." He was both an Old Testament prophet and an artist who surrendered to the power of his gift with the "almost feminine tenderness toward the human being." Bolshevism as a whole was both about science (the Law) and art (the intuitive recovery of the original beauty of the world). It was exactly like religion except that it was true.[21]

True art, and especially great literature, had "the same goal" as Bolshevism. Voronsky's "proletarian critics" were like Gogol's doomed seminarian haunted by a flying witch: "They are drawing a magic circle around themselves lest the bourgeois Viy give the Russian Revolution over to the unclean and the undead. This is, of course, praiseworthy, but it should be done with some sense: the circle should have a radius." The true artists from the past did not just belong on the inside—they had helped reveal the sacred realm that, under Communism, would encompass the world. "In order to find the new Adam, who yearns for his new, very own paradise, . . . we must keep fighting tirelessly against the old Adam within us and without. In this struggle, the classical literature of past epochs is one of our most loyal friends." Without the classics, one could neither vanquish the undead nor locate the new paradise—"discovered, in spite of everything, in spite of logic and intelligence, in spite of all things evil and unjust by Homer, Pushkin, Tolstoy, Dostoevsky, Gogol, Lermontov, and Flaubert, among others. They love such happy and rare revelations and seem to want to exclaim, along with Faust: 'Oh moment, stay a while—you are so fair!'"[22]

The response of Voronsky's critics amounted to a reminder that Faust's words were part of his bargain with the devil and that he had never uttered them, anyway. Voronsky's quest for "exceptional moments" was a fool's errand; Voronsky's "Circle" (the name of the publishing house he had founded) was filled with the unclean and the undead. To counter the political support that Voronsky was receiving from Trotsky, Osinsky, Radek, and Mikhail Frunze, the proletarians recruited several patrons of their

own, including the ideologue of the Bolshevik "sense of time," Platon Kerzhentsev, and the only Old Bolshevik proletarian taking part in the literary
debate, Semen Kanatchikov. According to Voronsky's November 11, 1924,
letter to Stalin, Kanatchikov, in his capacity as head of the Central Committee's Press Section, was "creating the impression that the Communist
Party does not need literature except as a form of *blunt and narrowly conceived* propaganda and that the Central Committee supports the vulgar
and aggressive position of Rodov and company."[23]

Among the established writers, the main supporter of the "proletarians"
was the author of *The Iron Flood*, Aleksandr Serafimovich, whose Moscow
apartment served as the headquarters of the anti-Voronsky forces. "How
many evenings did we spend in that small, warm, cozy apartment!" wrote
one of its members, Aleksandr Isbakh. "We used to sit around a large table
under a bright lamp, a samovar hissing noisily before us." The young writers
would read their works and argue "for hours" about literature. Serafimovich
always presided, occasionally "rubbing his bald head and straightening his
signature white shirt collar, which he wore pulled out over his suit jacket. . . .
He liked to joke and to laugh at our jokes. Whenever a new guest arrived,
he would squint slyly, introduce him formally to his wife, Fekla Rodionovna,
invite him to the table, and begin the 'interrogation.' 'Well, young man, I can
see by your eyes that you have written something extraordinary. Don't try
to hide it, my dear man, don't try to hide it.'"[24]

Fekla (Fekola) Rodionovna Belousova was Serafimovich's second wife.
A peasant from the Tula province, she had worked for several years in his
house before marrying him in 1922, when he was fifty-nine years old and
she was thirty. They lived with Fekla's mother, whom everyone called
"Grandma," in the First House of Soviets in the apartment next to the
Voronskys, and later in a small house in Presnia. Serafimovich's favorite
pastime was singing folk songs. According to one of his proletarian protégés, "His voice was rather mediocre, but he sang with great feeling,
waving his arms about like a choir conductor. Our most devoted listener

was Serafimovich's mother-in-law, who was a
great admirer of his singing. As we sat together,
singing, she would sit with her hand on her
cheek, looking at him with awe and repeating
over and over again: 'What a voice! What a
voice!' He would be flattered, of course, and say,
with feigned indifference and a bit of bravado:
'Wait till you hear what I can really do, Mother-
in-law, dear!'"[25]

But literature came first. According to Isbakh,
the most memorable gathering of their reading
group was the evening Serafimovich read his
manuscript of *The Iron Flood*:

Aleksandr Serafimovich

It was a remarkably solemn evening. The brightly polished samovar gleamed festively; the table was laden with all sorts of delicacies. Fekla Rodionovna had baked some exceptionally good, absolutely delicious pies.

Seated around the table were the writers of the older generation: Fedor Gladkov, Aleksandr Neverov, and Aleksei Silych Novikov-Priboi. We youngsters stood modestly in the rear.

Serafimovich was wearing a blindingly white shirt collar.

Fekla Rodionovna was serving out wine and pie.

Serafimovich winked at us, his other eye squinting, as usual.

"I'm a sly fox. . . . My plan is get you all drunk, so you'll be a little kinder. And then you can criticize all you want."

He read well, not too fast, and with feeling.

He did not stop until midnight.

Oh how proud we were of our old man![26]

The old man was proud of them, too. "Go after them!" he used to say, according to Gladkov. "You're sure to win. Why are you coddling these types? They may be wreckers, for all we know." "The most important public discussions usually took place in the Press House. Serafimovich would sit in the presidium like a patriarch, surrounded by Komsomol members. When making one of our tough, aggressive speeches, we would look back at him, see his encouraging smile and slyly squinted eye, and reenter the fray with renewed confidence."[27]

In June 1925, the Politburo ordered a ceasefire. A special decree on Party policy toward literature, written by Bukharin, declared: "In a class society, there can be no such thing as neutral art," but "the class nature of the arts in general and of literature, in particular, is expressed in forms that are infinitely more diverse than, for instance, in politics." On the one hand, the Party considered proletarian writers to be "the future ideological leaders of Soviet literature" and wanted to "support them and their organizations." On the other, it was determined to struggle against "any careless or dismissive attitude toward the old cultural heritage" and "all forms of pretentious, semiliterate, and self-satisfied Communist conceit." In literature, as in many other spheres of life involving the mysteries of human emotion, there were limits to how far and how fast the Party could go. "While directing literature in general, the Party cannot support *one* particular literary faction (classified according to its views on style and form), any more than it can issue decrees on the proper form of the family, even though it obviously does direct the construction of a new everyday life."[28]

Both sides felt vindicated, and, after a short lull, hostilities resumed. Leopold Averbakh, who had emerged as the uncontested leader of the Russian Association of Proletarian Writers (RAPP), proclaimed that "Voronsky's Carthage must be destroyed." Voronsky responded with a generalization and a warning: "The Averbakhs of the world don't appear by accident. They may be young, but they are going places. We have seen our share of such clever, successful, irrepressible, everywhere-at-once young men. Self-confident and self-satisfied to the point of self-abandonment, they harbor no doubts and make no mistakes. Naturally they swear by Leninism and naturally they never depart from official directives. But in our complex, multicolored world, their cleverness can sometimes turn downright sinister."[29]

It could turn particularly sinister when supported by official directives. On October 31, 1925, Voronsky's old prison comrade and main Central Committee patron, the people's commissar for military and naval affairs, Mikhail Frunze, died of chloroform poisoning during a routine stomach ulcer operation. Three months later, Boris Pilniak wrote a novella called *The Tale of the Unextinguished Moon*, which opens with a dedication to Voronsky ("in friendship") and a disclaimer that any resemblance to the circumstances of Frunze's death is coincidental, and goes on to tell the story of how a famous Red Army commander dies of chloroform poisoning during a routine stomach ulcer operation. In the "Tale," Commander Gavrilov does not want to have an operation, but "the unbending man," whose movements are "rectangular and formulaic" and "whose every sentence is a formula," tells him that the operation, and the risks associated with it, are in the interests of the Revolution. "The wheel of history, and especially the wheel of the revolution—regrettably, I suppose—are mostly moved by death and blood. You and I know this only too well." The night before the operation, Gavrilov goes to one of the Houses of Soviets to see his old comrade, Popov, who tells him that his wife has left him for an engineer and "a pair of silk stockings" and that he now lives alone with his little daughter. "Popov related the petty details of the separation, which are always so painful precisely because of their pettiness—the kind of detail, the kind of pettiness that obscures the important things." Gavrilov responds by telling Popov about his own wife, "who has grown old but is still the only one for him."

Finally, late at night, he gets up to leave. "Give me something to read, but, you know, something simple, about good people, a good love, simple relations, a simple life, the sun, human beings and simple human joys." Popov did not have such a book. "That's revolutionary literature for you," says Gavrilov, as a joke. "Oh well, I'll reread some Tolstoy, then." He does reread Tolstoy's "Youth" and, the next morning, dies during the operation. The operation reveals that the ulcer has healed. Popov receives a letter with Gavrilov's last testament: "I knew I was going to die. Forgive me, I realize you're no longer young, but I was rocking your little girl, and I thought: my wife is growing old, too, and you've known her for twenty years. I've written to her. You should also write to her. Why don't you move in together, get married, perhaps, and raise the kids. Please forgive me."

There is the kind of pettiness that obscures the important things, and there is the all-important revolutionary necessity that ends up being a mistake. And then, perhaps somewhere in between, there are the good people, good love, simple relations, simple life, sun, human beings and simple human joys, including the most important ones—getting married and "raising kids." Only Commander Gavrilov—"a man who has the right and the will to send other men to kill and die"—understands this—and only because it is now his turn to die. "Revolutionary literature" cannot provide either solace or understanding. Tolstoy can.[30]

Voronsky's antiproletarian stance ended up being a Faustian bargain, after all. Within days of the publication of the *Tale* (in the May issue of *Novyi mir*), the Politburo issued a decree calling it "a malicious, counter-revolutionary, and slanderous attack on the Central Committee of the Party," and ordering an immediate confiscation of the entire print run. "It is obvious that the whole plot and certain elements of Pilniak's *Tale of the Unextinguished Moon* could only have been made possible as a result of the slanderous conversations that some Communists were having about Comrade Frunze's death, and that Comrade Voronsky bears partial responsibility for this. Comrade Voronsky is to be reprimanded for this." He was also to write a letter to the editor of *Novyi mir*, "rejecting the dedication with an appropriate explanation approved by the CC Secretariat."[31]

In a written explanation to the chief censor (head of Glavlit) I. I. Lebedev-Poliansky, Pilniak claimed that the novella was based on a conversation he and Voronsky had had once—"about how an individual . . . always follows the wheel of the collective and sometimes dies under that wheel"—and that it was during the same conversation that Voronsky had told him "about the death and various habits of Comrade Frunze." In his letter to the editor approved by the CC Secretariat, Voronsky wrote that Pilniak's dedication was "highly offensive" to him as a Communist, and that he rejected it "with indignation."[32]

The proletarian writers were triumphant: the destruction of "Voronsky's Carthage" was now a matter of time (and method). Writing in the May issue of *Red Virgin Soil*, Voronsky addressed his official boss, People's Commissar of Enlightenment Anatoly Lunacharsky: "I love life, and it is hard for my soul to part with my body. But if it is fated that I accept the end, then let it not be from the hand of Averbakh. It would not be dignified to die that way. It is hard but honorable to die on the battlefield from a frontal attack—'there is joy in battle'—but to suffocate from Averbakh's 'literary gases'—let this cup pass from me."[33]

Voronsky's wish was partially granted. The attack was not frontal, but it came from Bukharin, not Averbakh. On January 12, 1927, *Pravda* published Bukharin's "Angry Notes," in which he attacked Voronsky by attacking some of Voronsky's protégés. The "peasant poets" that *Red Virgin Soil* was championing, and especially Voronsky's favorite, Sergei Esenin, were, according to Bukharin, guilty of "*blini* nationalism" and "chauvinistic swinishness."

"Eseninism" was a "disgustingly powdered and gaudily painted Russian obscenity," and the "broad Russian nature" that Esenin stood for was nothing but "internal sloppiness and lack of culture." "If in the old days the traditional intelligentsia admiration for its own mawkishness, impotence, and pathetic flabbiness was disgusting enough, it has become absolutely *intolerable* in our own day, when we need energetic and resolute characters, not the rubbish that should have been thrown out a long time ago."[34]

The attack was, in a sense, justified. Voronsky did admire peasant poets and published them regularly in his journal, and his memoirs, which he had recently begun writing, did represent "*blini* Russia" as an aesthetic and perhaps moral value to be reckoned with. ("The light-colored river lay tranquil, its gentle curves gleaming with copper flashes. Behind the river, fields stretched into the distance. Little hamlets dotted the hills. Behind them was the silent, solemn pine forest. The cadenced tones of distant church bells floated slowly through the air.")

More to the point, the "broad Russian nature" as understood by Voronsky was but a special case of "intuition," which represented a way of getting at the truth "by going beyond conscious, analytic thought." Lenin, in his clairvoyance, was "Russian from head to toe." He had had "something of the roundness, nimbleness, and lightness of [Tolstoy's] Platon Karataev, of the spontaneity of the muzhik stock, of Vladimir and Kostroma, of the Volga region and our insatiable fields." The "broad Russian nature" was, of course, about "hooliganism, drunkenness, gratuitous mischievousness, idleness, and indifference to organized work and culture," but it was also about "the huge reserves of fresh, unspent strength and powerful vital instincts; the blooming health; the wealth and variety of thoughts and emotions." Both Tolstoy and Lenin had possessed it, and both had been the greater for it.[35]

This view was unacceptable to the rationalist (Calvinist) wing of the Party. According to one of Voronsky's most consistent opponents, Platon Kerzhentsev, what the Party needed was "healthy literature," and what proletarian readers needed to learn was English-style "love of responsibility." And according to the concluding paragraph of Bukharin's "Angry Notes,"

> What we need is literature for healthy people who march in the midst of real life: brave builders who know life and are disgusted by the rot, mold, morbidity, drunken tears, sloppiness, self-importance, and saintly idiocy. The greatest figures of the bourgeoisie were not drunken geniuses like Verlain, but such giants as Goethe, Hegel, and Beethoven, who knew how to *work*. The greatest geniuses of the proletariat—Marx, Engels, and Lenin—were great *workers*, with extraordinary work *ethic*. Let us stay away from the martyred "poor in spirit," the holy fools for Christ's sake, and the café "geniuses for an

hour"! Let us stick closer to the wonderful life that is flourishing all around us, closer to the masses remaking the world![36]

The rest was up to Averbakh's RAPP and the Press Section of the Central Committee, headed at the time by Sergei Gusev (Yakov Drabkin, the father of Sverdlov's last secretary, Elizaveta Drabkina). In April 1927, Voronsky lost influence over the editorial policy of *Red Virgin Soil*, and on October 13, 1927, the Politburo removed him from the board. His friendship with Trotsky had contributed to the outcome.[37]

■ ■ ■

Of the Party's three main tasks of the 1920s—suppressing the enemy, converting the heathen, and disciplining the faithful—the third was by far the most important. As Bukharin reminded the Party in 1922, soon after the introduction of NEP and the banning of internal "factions," "unity of will" had always been the key to Bolshevism:

> What the Philistines of opportunism considered "antidemocratic," "conspiratorial," "personal dictatorship," "stupid intolerance," and so on, was, in fact, the best possible organizing principle. The selection of a group of like-minded people burning with the same revolutionary passion while being totally united in their views was the first and most necessary condition for a successful struggle. This condition was fulfilled by means of a merciless persecution of all deviations from orthodox Bolshevism. This merciless persecution and constant self-purging welded the core party group into a clenched fist that no force in the world could pry open.

The core group of leaders was surrounded by a wide circle of disciplined "cadres":

> The harsh discipline of Bolshevism, the Spartan unity of its ranks, its "factional cohesion" even during the moments of temporary cohabitation with the Mensheviks, the extreme uniformity of its views, and the centralization of all its ranks have always been the most characteristic features of our Party. All the Party members were extremely faithful to the Party: "Party patriotism," the extraordinary passion with which Party directives were carried out, and the ferocious struggle against enemy groups wherever they could be found—in the factories, at rallies, in clubs, even in prisons—made our Party into a sort of revolutionary monastic order. This is why the Bolshevik type was so unsympathetic to all the liberal and reformist groups, to everything "leaderless," "soft," "generous," and "tolerant."

And this is why Christ, according to the Revelation of St. John, was going to spit the lukewarm—neither hot nor cold—out of his mouth. Growing up on Bolshaia Ordynka, across the Drainage Canal from the Swamp, Bukharin had read the Apocalypse "carefully, from cover to cover." His article on Party discipline ends with the following words: "Having survived a terrible civil war, famine, and pestilence, this great Red country is getting on its feet, and the trumpet of victory is sounding its call for the working class of the entire world, and the colonial slaves and coolies to rise up for the mortal battle against capital. And at the head of that countless army, under glorious flags cut through by bullets and bayonets, there marches the courageous phalanx of battle-scarred warriors. It marches in front of everyone, it calls on everyone, it directs everyone. Its name is: the Iron Cohort of the Proletarian Revolution, the Russian Communist Party."[38]

At a time when the Party was gathering strength before the final battle, the challenge was all the greater. "The more our Party grows," wrote the "Party's Conscience," Aron Solts, in 1924, "the harder it is to preserve the comradely relations that were formed during the common struggle, but also the more necessary, and the comrades must feel and understand all the more strongly what is needed in order to maintain such voluntary discipline. It is easier to preserve good, comradely relations when there are twenty of us than when we are a group of eighty thousand, as is the case in the Moscow party organization." Sects in power tend to become churches, and churches tend to become more hierarchical and less exclusive (or, as the Bolsheviks put it, "bureaucratized"), especially at a time when the swamp "engenders capitalism and the bourgeoisie continuously, daily, hourly, spontaneously, and on a massive scale." In order to remain an iron cohort, the Party had to heed Lenin's call: "Fight against this scum over and over again, and, if this scum crawls back in, clean it out over and over again, chase it out and watch over it."[39]

The first precondition for internal unity was a strict membership policy. The Bolshevik rites of admission were similar to those of the Puritans. A preliminary screening by the Party cell's bureau (the congregation's elders) was followed by a public confession before a general assembly. Candidates presented their spiritual histories and answered questions from the audience. The point was to demonstrate the genuineness of the conversion by presenting a detailed account of one's earthly career as well as the inner doubts, comforts, temptations, and blessings attendant on the process of regeneration. Witnesses vouched for the candidates' character and corroborated certain parts of their accounts; the interrogation centered on errors, omissions, and inconsistencies. The principal innovation introduced by the Bolsheviks was the division of all candidates into three categories according to social origin: "proletarians" were more naturally virtuous than "peasants," who were more naturally virtuous than "others." The principal innovation introduced by the New Bolsheviks, as distinct from the Old ones, was the relatively low priority given to scriptural knowledge. Before the Revolution, proletarian Party members had needed to become intellectuals; under the dictatorship of the proletariat, most Party intellectuals had to become proletarians of one sort or another (or "Averbakhs," as Voronsky put it). The only exceptions were the original Old Bolsheviks, who presided, at least nominally, over the dictatorship of the proletariat.[40]

Within the Party, discipline was maintained by means of regular "check-ups" or purges by special committees and constant mutual surveillance by rank-and-file members. As Walzer wrote of the Puritans who had passed various tests of godliness, "Those who remained were drawn into the strange, time-consuming activities of the Puritan congregation: diligently taking notes at sermons, attending endless meetings, associating intimately and continously with men and women who were after all not relatives and, above all, submitting to the discipline and zealous watchfulness of the godly. Puritanism required not only a pitch of piety, but a pitch of activism and involvement."[41]

Bolshevism required the same thing—or, as Gusev, Voronsky's nemesis, put it at the Fourteenth Party Congress in December 1925, "Lenin used to teach us that every Party member should be a Cheka agent—that is, that he should watch and inform." But Bolshevism was in a difficult position: "If we suffer from one thing," continued Gusev, "it is that we do not do enough informing." The Party ruled over a vast empire, most residents of which knew little of Bolshevism; it believed that the entry into the first circle of the kingdom of freedom ("socialism in one country") was possible only after most of those residents had converted to Bolshevism; and it assumed that the most promising converts were workers and peasants, who combined the purity of Jesus's target audience ("I praise you, Father, Lord of heaven and earth, because you have hidden these things from the wise and learned, and revealed them to little children") with the "backwardness" that made them susceptible to "that contagion, that plague, those ulcers that socialism had inherited from capitalism." The Bolsheviks had to keep expanding their missionary work, keep producing new missionaries, and keep recruiting new untutored members, who did not do enough informing and did not have enough resistance to contagion.[42]

Bolshevism required a pitch of activism and involvement, but it also required strict top-down policing. It could not afford to rely solely on the daily public confessions and mutual criticism sessions common among coresidential sectarians (such as the Shakers, Harmonists, and Oneida Communists), or on the mutual "instruction and admonition" practiced by the New England Puritan congregations (whose salvation did not depend on the conversion of other settlers, let alone the Indians). The Party was a large bureaucracy with a monopoly on state power and special access to scarce goods, which tried to remain cohesive and exclusive even as it continued to offer substantial material benefits to potential proletarian recruits. Increasingly, Solts's "voluntary discipline" had to be manufactured and monitored by special agencies, not least by the Party Control Commission over which Solts presided.

Party "purges" were periodic restagings of admissions rituals with the purpose of cleaning out the scum that had crawled back in or had been missed at the time of joining. Most of those reprimanded or excommunicated were new members, and most infractions had to do with character flaws and lack of self-discipline: "squabbling," "excessive consumption," sexual license, drunkenness, violations of Party discipline ("in the form of nonattendance at Party meetings, nonpayment of membership fees, etc."), nepotism, careerism, embezzlement, indebtedness, and "bureaucratism." Related to them was "participation in religious rites," which was common among peasant members and considered a sign of backwardness, not genuine apostasy. More serious were "links with alien elements" (especially by marriage). The least common, and by far the most dangerous, were acts of willful heterodoxy.[43]

Within sects, different interpretations of revealed truth may lead to schisms and the formation of new sects. Every orthodoxy presupposes the possibility of heresies ("choice" in the original Greek), and all true prophets must warn of false ones ("for false messiahs and false prophets will appear and perform great signs and wonders to deceive, if possible, even the elect"). When one sect acquires the monopoly on political power—by building its own state, as in the case of Islam and Taiping, or taking over an existing polity, as in the case of Christianity, Bolshevism, and the Taliban—heresy can finally be suppressed. The intensity of persecution depends on the state of the orthodoxy: the greater the millenarian expectation and the more beleaguered the elect, the greater the need to expose the deceivers and spit out the lukewarm.[44]

The Bolshevik equivalent of the First Council of Nicaea (the banning of factions at the Tenth Party Congress) coincided with the postponement of the final fulfillment. The politics of NEP consisted of the Central Committee's defense of the reconciled, routinized, and bureaucratized status quo from a variety of reformations that urged the return to the original millenarian maximalism and sectarian egalitarianism. The Left (the Trotsky opposition, Kamenev-Zinoviev opposition, and United Trotsky-Kamenev-Zinoviev Opposition, among others) kept returning to Lenin's warning about small-scale production engendering capitalism "daily, hourly, spontaneously, and on a massive scale," and urging the immediate uprooting of every whit of every plant while inveighing against "the division of the Party into the secretarial hierarchy and the 'laity.'" Names, members, and arguments of various oppositions kept changing, but the core claims remained the same: NEP as a retreat from socialism had to end, and the Party as the locomotive of history had to stop being "bureaucratic."[45]

Substantively, "the question of questions" (as NEP's Grand Inquisitor, Bukharin, put it) was what to do with the peasants. Bukharin kept warning against a return to "War Communism" and the desire, on the part of some "eccentrics," "to declare a St. Bartholomew's Night against the peasant bourgeoisie." The opposition kept accusing "the Stalin-Bukharin group" of "denying the capitalist elements in the development of the contemporary village and minimizing the class differentiation among the peasantry."[46]

Both sides used statistics produced by Soviet agrarian economists, who were themselves divided into two factions analogous to the Voronsky and Averbakh camps in literary criticism. The Organization-Production school, rooted in prerevolutionary agronomy and led by the director of the Institute of Agricultural Economics at the Timiriazev Academy, A. V. Chayanov (whose father had been born a serf), argued that the Russian peasant household was not capitalist in nature; that its purpose was not to maximize profit but to satisfy its members' subsistence needs; that the main cause of rural differentiation was the ratio of workers to consumers (which varied according to family composition); and that the development of capitalism in the Russian village was both unlikely and undesirable. The Agrarian-Marxist school, composed of young Party members and led by the director of the Agrarian Section of the Communist Academy, Lev Kritsman (who had never lived in a village), argued that rural differentiation was caused by unequal access to the means of production; that the Soviet peasantry was becoming increasingly polarized between rural capitalists and agricultural wage laborers; that, given the Party's monopoly on power, this polarization was a good thing (but probably not as good as the opposition claimed); and that the solution to the "question of questions" consisted of either the victory of socialism as a result of the growth of the cooperative movement (as Lenin predicted in 1923), or the victory of socialism as a result of the victory of capitalism (as Lenin predicted in 1899).[47]

The key to the answers to all questions (as Lenin taught) was who had state power. All the Bolsheviks—the various oppositions and the orthodox—agreed that there was only one truth based on the one true revelation, and that any deviation from that truth was by definition "bourgeois." All the Bolsheviks agreed—and kept repeating on every occasion—that there was nothing more important than Party unity, and that Party unity was never more important than on that particular occasion. As Radek wrote on behalf of United ("Bolshevik-Leninist") Opposition in August 1926, "the opposition cannot possibly defend the existence of factions: in fact, it is their most resolute opponent."

How was one to know which views were true and which were factional? One measure was the doctrinal orthodoxy of one's views. According to Radek, "every step away from the class position of the proletariat toward the position of the petty bourgeoisie engenders and must engender resistance on the part of the proletarian elements within the Party." The only reliable way to determine the class position of the proletariat was to determine what Lenin's position would have been. Bukharin, who had recovered from his own "infantile leftism" a few years earlier, accused the opposition of trying to restore War Communism, from which Lenin had "retreated" in the direction of NEP.[48]

What was to be done? In Lenin's absence, who could tell what Lenin would have said? Who was, in fact, fighting "not only against the swamp, but also against those who were turning toward the swamp"? At the Fourteenth Party Congress, Filipp Goloshchekin offered a summary of what provincial Party officials expected from their Central Committee. "Comrade Lenin has died, and none of you can pretend to fill his place. Every one of you has his flaws, but every one of you also has many qualities that make you a leader. Only together can you stand in for Lenin: we demand that you work together in leading our Party."[49]

The leaders could not work together because they continued to disagree about where they should be leading the Party—and who should be leading the leaders. Claims of loyalty to Lenin's ideas could be reinforced by claims of previous physical proximity to Lenin, but because Lenin had not appointed a successor and had said disparaging things about all of his close associates, most arguments about original discipleship turned back into arguments about ideas. Three months after signing "the Letter of the Forty-Six" (which objected to "the division of the Party into the secretarial hierarchy and the 'laity'") and one week before Lenin's death, Osinsky had defended Trotsky against the Kamenev-Zinoviev-Stalin Central Committee: "Comrade Trotsky was absolutely right in telling these sinless apostles of Leninism, who have proclaimed themselves to be Lenin's apostles and have turned Lenin's words into holy writ, that 'no apostleship can guarantee the correctness of the political line. If you truly follow Comrade Lenin's line, then you are Leninists. But the fact that you are his disciples does not mean anything in and of itself. Marx had disciples who later vanished. You, too, may end up vanishing.'"[50]

Another way to ensure legitimate succession and determine the correctness of the political line was to hold a vote. "Bolshevik" meant "majority"; the principle of "democratic centralism" consisted of the submission of the minority to the majority; and the most common argument against oppositions was that they did not represent the majority of the Party. Ultimately, however, the majority had to be obeyed only if it was on the path of struggle and not the path of conciliation. At the Fourteenth Party Congress in late 1925, Lenin's widow, Krupskaia (who had been told repeatedly that physical proximity to the founder did not mean anything in and of itself), reminded the delegates that they were not "English jurists": "For us, Marxists, truth is what corresponds to reality. Vladimir Ilich used to say: 'Marx's teaching is invincible because it is true.' Our Congress must occupy itself with the search for a correct line. Such is its task. We cannot comfort ourselves by saying that the majority is always right. In the history of our Party there have been congresses when the majority was not right. Think of the Stockholm congress. The majority should not bask in the glory of being the majority; it should be impartial in its search for the correct solution. If it is correct, it will set our party on the right path." Party congresses were not about voting: they were about a higher truth emerging from a series of public confessions. In Krupskaia's formulation, "everyone should tell the congress as a matter of conscience what has been perturbing and tormenting them lately." Bukharin, for one, had compounded the damage done by his conciliatory policies by "denying them three times."[51]

Two years later, at the Fifteenth Party Congress, Krupskaia rejoined the majority and attributed the existence of opposition to the fact that some people had lost their class "intuition." The Party represented "what the masses were feeling"; the Party was represented by its Central Committee; any refusal to obey the Central Committee was a betrayal of what the masses were feeling. In the final analysis, the only way to stay on the right path was to follow the leaders. As Bukharin explained, one of the most fundamental principles of the Bolshevik Party was "absolute loyalty to its leading institutions." This was, of course, true of many institutionalized sectarian communities: bishops have the monopoly on the correct interpretation of the original revelation because they are bishops. The charisma of office does not depend on the method of investiture: the pope does not owe his role as St. Peter's rightful successor to the fact of having been elected. Nor is St. Peter disqualified from his position as Jesus's rightful successor by the fact that he has denied him three times.[52]

The general recognition of the legitimacy of official succession must lead to "absolute loyalty to leading institutions." As Bukharin put it on October 26, 1927, at the height of his struggle with the United Opposition (which brought together the leaders of various previous oppositions, including Trotsky, Radek, Kamenev, and Zinoviev), "it is either one or the other. Let the comrades from the opposition come out and say openly: we do not believe that what we have in this country is a proletarian dictatorship! But let them not get angry with us, then, if we tell them that their statement that they wish to defend such a country from an external enemy is vile hypocrisy."[53]

Party members who opposed the Party leadership became indistinguishable from non-Party members; non-Party members might include former Party members; former Party members were expelled Party members; "and an expelled Party member," as Goloshchekin put it, "is someone spat out by the Party, and thus an enemy of the Party." Any disagreement with the Central Committee was, objectively, an alliance with the enemy. As Bukharin put it, "all kinds of scum is grasping at the opposition's coattails, trying to sneak through the cracks and proclaim itself their allies. . . . That is why Comrade Kamenev was absolutely right with regard to today's situation when, in January 1925, he said that the Trotsky opposition had become "the symbol of all the anti-Communist forces."[54]

Bukharin was absolutely right with regard to Kamenev and all the other oppositionists: they, too, were against "factions." The fact that they thought that the Stalin-Bukharin orthodoxy was heresy did not change the consensus that all heresies were treason. As Bukharin's closest associate, Aleksei Rykov, said at the Fifteenth Party Congress in December 1927, "Comrade Kamenev ended his speech by saying that he does not separate himself from those oppositionists who are now in prison. I must begin my speech by saying that I do not separate myself from those revolutionaries who have put some supporters of the opposition in prison for their anti-Party and anti-Soviet activities. (*Tumultuous, prolonged applause. Shouts of "hurray." The delegates rise.*)" It was the Party's tradition to "forbid the defense of certain views"; the only way for an oppositionist to remain in the Party was to formally "recant the views" rejected by the Party. As for those who did not, the congress, in the words of the secretary of the Moscow Control Commission and former head of the Cheka Investigations Department, Grigory Moroz, "would have to snip off the heads of the arrogant oppositionist noblemen who are taunting the Party."[55]

On November 7, 1927, on the tenth anniversary of the Revolution, Moroz presided over the dispersal of an opposition demonstration organized by Ivar Smilga (who had remained a close associate of Trotsky since the trial of the Cossack commander Filipp Mironov). Smilga; his wife, Nadezhda Smilga-Poluian; and their two daughters, aged five and eight, were living in a large four-room apartment in the Fourth House of Soviets, four stories above the Central Executive Committee Visitor's Office and just across Mokhovaia from the Kremlin. On the morning of the 7th, Smilga, Kamenev, and Muralov (Arosev's commander during the 1917 Moscow uprising) had hung a banner "Let's Fulfill Lenin's Testament" and portraits of Lenin, Trotsky, and Zinoviev from the apartment windows. As the three described the events later that day in a letter to the Politburo, "Comrade Smilga's wife, a Party member, refused to let a group of strangers, who wanted to pull down the 'criminal' banners, into the apartment. Several individuals sent to the roof for the purpose attempted to tear the banners down with long hooks. The women inside the apartment thwarted their heroic efforts with mops.... Eventually, about fifteen to twenty Central Committee school officers and Military Academy cadets broke down the door of Comrade Smilga's apartment, smashing it to bits, and forcibly entered the rooms."[56]

Nadezhda Poluian then took the two girls to the apartment of her brother Yan, who lived in the same house (but was not on speaking terms with Smilga for doctrinal reasons). Smilga and several other opposition leaders walked two blocks down the street and attempted to address the crowds from the balcony of the Twenty-Seventh House of Soviets, on the corner of Tverskaia and Okhotnyi Riad (the former Paris Hotel). Soon, cars arrived, bringing Moroz, the secretary of the Red Presnia district Riutin, and several other officials. As Smilga wrote three days later, "Under the direction of the newly arrived authorities, the crowd that had assembled under the balcony began to whistle, cry 'Down with them!' and 'Beat the opposition!' and throw rocks, sticks, cucumbers, tomatoes, etc. at comrades Smilga, Preobrazhensky, and the others. At the same time, some people standing on the balcony of Comrade Podvoisky's apartment, located across the street in the First House of Soviets, attacked comrades Smilga and Preobrazhensky by throwing ice, potatoes, and firewood."[57]

District Secretary Riutin ordered the militia man on duty to unlock the street door, and several dozen people broke into the apartment and began beating up the opposition. At the head of the crowd, according to Trotsky, was "the notorious Boris Volin, whose moral character needs no introduction." Smilga claimed to have appealed to Moroz, who allegedly responded: "Shut up, or it'll get worse." The oppositionists were locked up in one of the rooms of the house, where they were guarded by Boris Shumiatsky, the liberator of Mongolia. A little while later, they escaped from their guard, ran across the street, and disappeared into the Second House of Soviets.[58]

At the Fifteenth Party Congress in December 1927, the United Opposition was formally defeated. Ninety-eight oppositionists, including Radek and Smilga, were expelled from the Party. Some, including Voronsky, were expelled a bit later; many, including Radek, Smilga, and, a year later, Voronsky, were sent into exile. The secret police official in charge of the operation was Yakov Agranov, a member of the Brik-Mayakovsky salon. One of the expelled oppositionists (and one of Voronsky's closest friends), Sergei Zorin, wrote to Bukharin: "Be careful, Comrade Bukharin! You have had many arguments in our Party. You will probably have more. Watch out, or, courtesy of your current comrades, you too will get Comrade Agranov as an arbiter. Some examples are contagious."[59]

■ ■ ■

Zorin's warning would come true much sooner than he (or Bukharin) might have imagined. Within months of the defeat of the United Opposition, Stalin would emerge from Bukharin's shadow, adopt a radical version of the opposition's program, and usher in a second "heroic period" of the Russian Revolution. Lenin had described NEP as a "retreat" followed by "a most determined offensive." The time for that offensive had come. Lenin had predicted that "some day, this movement will accelerate at the pace we can only dream of now." That day—the real real day—had finally arrived.[60]

Early signs of the return of the apocalypse, in 1927, would include the massacre of the Chinese Communists in Shanghai, the police raid on the Soviet trade mission in London, the assassination of the Soviet ambassador in Poland, the grain procurement crisis in the villages, and the "uniting" of former oppositionists into a secret army of false prophets. Over the next two years, the movement toward the final fulfillment would accelerate at the kind of pace that Lenin could only dream of. All true prophecies are self-fulfilling: "Ask and it will be given to you; seek and you will find" (or, in the words of a Soviet song, "those who desire will receive; those who seek will always find"). On closer inspection, recalcitrant grain producers would turn out to be kulaks; skeptical bourgeois experts would turn out to be wreckers; and foreign Socialists would turn out to be Social-Fascists. By "the year of the great breakthrough," 1929, it would become clear that the last battle would be won within a decade or two. In 1931, Stalin would be able to say: "There are no fortresses that the Bolsheviks cannot take. We have achieved a number of difficult goals. We have defeated capitalism. We have taken power. We have built a large socialist industry. We have set the middle peasant along the path of socialism. We have finished the most important part of our construction plan. There is not much left to do: just to study technology and master science. When we have done that, we will achieve the kind of acceleration we can only dream of now."[61]

The great breakthrough was not War Communism because what was appropriate now had been premature then, but it was a war, and it was the last stop before Communism (which Kerzhentsev, in his *The Bolshevik's Pamphlet* of 1931, defined as "the only way for mankind to save itself from death, degeneracy, and decline"). The great breakthrough was about the simultaneous violent fulfillment of two different prophecies: the long-overdue one concerning the creation of socialism's economic base and the medium-range one concerning the complete abolition of private property and total destruction of all class enemies. On the eve of the last war against capitalism, the steel and concrete foundations of socialism were to be laid, the wreckers and bureaucrats were to be routed, the rural kulaks were to be "liquidated," the rural non-kulaks were to join the workers, the workers were to become "conscious," and all consciousness was to become socialist. "Either we do it or we will be crushed."[62]

Bukharin and Rykov, having just presided over the humiliation and expulsion of the Leftists, were caught off guard. The orthodoxy they represented had suddenly become heresy; hard realism had become "appeasement"; and the center had become the "Right." Forming an opposition was out of the question, especially at a time when—everyone agreed—war was imminent and enemies were everywhere. As Bukharin said to a hostile Central Committee audience on April 18, 1929 (after the whole point had become moot): "The old forms of resolving intra-Party disagreements by means of quasi-factional struggle are currently *unacceptable* and objectively *impossible*." The "Rightists" argued and schemed behind closed doors and wrote scholarly articles about Lenin's views on the worker-peasant alliance, but they kept silent in public because they had just defeated the United Opposition by arguing that any disagreement with Party leadership was tantamount to treason. As Bukharin explained, after the fact, "we kept silent because, had we appeared at some conference, rally, or Party cell meeting, a discussion would have started, and we would have been accused of initiating it. We were in the position of people who are hounded for *not* explaining and *not* justifying themselves, but who

would be hounded *even more* for *attempting* to explain, *attempting* to justify themselves."[63]

In July 1928, soon after the magnitude of the coming breakthrough had
become clear, Bukharin went to see the disgraced Kamenev and told
him, confidentially, that Stalin was intent on imposing "tribute" on the
peasantry, unleashing a civil war, and "drowning uprisings in blood." As
Kamenev wrote later that day, "[Bukharin] looks extremely agitated and
exhausted. . . . His tone is one of absolute hatred toward Stalin and of a
total breakup. At the same time, he is agonizing, wondering whether to
speak openly or not. If he does, they will cut him down based on the schism
provision. If he does not, they will cut him down with their petty chess
game. . . . He is extraordinarily shaken. His lips keep trembling from nervousness. Sometimes he looks like a man who knows he is doomed."[64]

Stalin won the chess game. While Bukharin was agonizing, Bukharin's
allies in the Trade Union Council and Moscow Party organization (including the organizers of the "Beat the Opposition" raid from the previous year,
Riutin and Moroz) were removed and reassigned. Bukharin's would-be allies from among the former oppositionists were neither able nor willing to
offer support. Kamenev's notes of their secret meeting soon reached the
recently exiled Trotsky, who had them published as a leaflet. The text was
edited by the recently retired Voronsky.[65]

Stalin won the argument, too. In a sect that defined itself in opposition
to "appeasement," prided itself on its readiness for violence, and looked
forward to an imminent universal slaughter, Bukharin's "Notes of an Economist" (as he called his September 1928 amillennial manifesto) did not
generate much enthusiasm. Many Party members—both Old Bolsheviks
and young Civil War veterans—had spent the NEP years suffering from
"neurasthenia," "degeneration," gothic nightmares, "crawling scum," spilt
milk and honey, and "cozy, worn little slippers under the bed." Most were
ready for the last and decisive battle.

Different reformations hark back to different sacred origins. Christian
reformers have nothing but a small egalitarian sect to go back to; radicals
insist on replicating the original design; others improvise temporary solutions until such time as "there is neither need nor use for princes, kings,
lords, the sword, or law" (as Martin Luther put it). Muslim reformers have
a sprawling state to go back to: the question is how faithful to Mohammed's caliphate that state should be. Lenin, like Mohammed, left behind
a sprawling state, but he had called that state a profane compromise in
need of future acceleration at a pace he could only dream of. The Bolshevik reformers of 1928–29 (including Bukharin, who did not doubt the need
for acceleration) had nothing but Lenin's state to go back to: the radicals
yearned for the "heroic period of the Great Russian Revolution" and urged
a better, fuller War Communism; the moderates stuck to "Lenin's Political
Testament" and called for a readjustment of the NEP compromise. The
argument was about what Lenin had really meant; the mood of the faithful
and most of Lenin's legacy favored the radicals. On November 26, 1929,

after the Central Committee vowed to annihilate peasant agriculture within a matter of months, Bukharin, Rykov, and their ally Tomsky published a formal recantation. "Admitting our mistakes," they wrote, "we pledge to make every effort to conduct, along with the rest of the Party, a resolute struggle against all deviations from the general Party line, above all the Right deviation and appeasement, in order to overcome all difficulties and bring about the complete and earliest possible victory of socialist construction."[66]

At the Sixteenth Party Congress, in June–July 1930, the Rightists were asked to repent properly. As Postyshev said, in the very first speech of the discussion session, "prove, through your actions, the sincerity of your admission of mistakes, the sincerity of your declaration. Prove that it was not a maneuver similar to what the Trotskyites do. The Party has asked a very tough question, and comrades Rykov, Tomsky, and Bukharin must give the Congress an unambiguous answer (*applause*)." "The Trotskyites" had become shorthand for persistent apostates. Bukharin claimed to be sick and stayed at his dacha in Crimea. Rykov admitted his own mistakes but refused to renounce Bukharin. "I am responsible for what I have done, for the mistakes I have made, and I am not going to use Bukharin as a scapegoat. You cannot ask that of me. I, not Bukharin, should be punished for the mistakes I have made." Several hours before Bukharin and Anna Larina spent their "thrilling, romantic Crimean evening" together, Bukharin received a postcard from Rykov. The last paragraph, according to Larina, said: "Come back healthy. At the congress, we talked about you with dignity. Know that I love you the way even a woman passionately in love with you never could. Yours, Aleksei."[67]

Tomsky made a full confession, stating that his main errors had been, first, to assume that the reconstruction of "the whole life of the country" was a matter of mere "technical and industrial reconstruction," and, second, to forget that "any more or less long-term opposition against the Party line and its leadership inevitably leads, and will lead, to an opposition against the Party as such." The audience did not seem convinced. Tomsky persevered:

> The Party has the right to ask us: how sincere are our admissions of mistakes? Isn't this a maneuver? (*Artiukhina:* "That's right!") Isn't there a danger of a relapse? Some people even say: We don't believe words, words are meaningless, ephemeral, hot air, didn't Lenin once say, "do not take their word for it," and so on? But if we interpret Lenin as crudely as some comrades have been doing here at the congress, then we must stop talking altogether. What is the point of talking? (*laughter*) . . .
>
> At a certain point, I, along with Zinoviev, told Trotsky: "Bow your head before the Party." Later, I said the same to Zinoviev, who was with Trotsky, "Bow your head before the Party, Grigory." I have made my share of mistakes, I am not ashamed of that, and I am in no way

ashamed of bowing my head before the Party. I think that, in my speech, I have admitted my mistakes with all the necessary sincerity and frankness. But it seems to me, comrades, that it is rather difficult to be in the role of a permanent penitent. Some comrades seem to be saying: repent, repent without end, do nothing but repent (*laughter*).[68]

Tomsky's difficulty was resolved by the Leningrad Party Secretary (and new Politburo member) Sergei Kirov, who said that true repentance consisted in acknowledging that any disagreement with the Party leadership was tantamount to enemy sabotage. "What we needed to hear from comrades Rykov and Tomsky is not just the admission of their mistakes and the renunciation of their platform, but the admission that it was, as I said, a kulak program, which, in the final analysis, would have led to the death of socialist construction." But could one admit something like that and be forgiven? And what about the Left, whose sin had consisted in struggling against the Right when the Right was still the center?[69]

Most of the original Leftists were already in exile when they learned of the victory of their long-held views. Trotsky admitted that Stalin's policies were "undoubtedly, an attempt to approach our position," but argued that "in politics, what matters is not only what is being done, but also who does it and how." Stalin may have had something similar in mind when he sent Trotsky to Alma-Ata (and later to Turkey), Radek to Tobolsk, Smilga to Narym, and Vladimir Smirnov, a veteran oppositionist and Osinsky's brother-in-law, to the northern Urals. At the Ninth Party Congress in 1920, Osinsky and Smirnov had still been leading the "Democratic Centralist" opposition against centralization, "bureaucratization," and the employment of bourgeois experts; Osinsky later rejoined the general line (if not without his usual irritable reservations), but Smirnov remained an irreconcilable proletarian purist and was punished accordingly. On January 1, 1928, Osinsky wrote a letter to Stalin:

Dear Comrade Stalin:

Yesterday I learned that V. M. Smirnov was being exiled for three years to a place in the Urals (apparently, to the Cherdyn district), and today I ran into Sapronov, who told me that he was being sent to the Arkhangelsk Province for the same period of time. It seems they are required to leave as early as Tuesday, but Smirnov just had half his teeth removed, in the expectation of having them replaced with false ones, so now he will be going to the northern Urals without his teeth.

When Lenin kicked Martov out of the country, he made sure he had everything he needed and even worried whether he had his fur coat and galoshes with him. And that was because Martov had once been a revolutionary. Our former Party comrades, who are now being sent into exile, have committed a grave political error, but they have never stopped being revolutionaries—this cannot be denied. Not only will they be able to return to the Party some day (despite the silly nonsense they have been spouting about a new party and about the old party having outlived its usefulness), but, if hard times come, they will be able to serve it as well as they did in October.

The question arises, therefore: is it really necessary to send them to the North—adopting, in effect, a policy of their spiritual and physical annihilation? I do not think so. I do not understand why they cannot either be 1) sent abroad, as Lenin did in the case of Martov, or 2) settled in the interior, in places with a warmer climate, where Smirnov, for example, would be able to write a good book about credit.

This policy of exile produces nothing but unnecessary resentment among people who cannot yet be considered lost and for whom the Party has sometimes been more of a stepmother, than a mother. It lends credence to the mutterings that the present regime is similar to the old police state, and that "those who made the revolution are now all in prison and exile, while power rests in the hands of different people." Such mutterings are very bad for us, so why give them extra ammunition? All the more so because our attitude toward our political opponents from the camp we call "socialist" has so far been characterized by an effort to weaken the influence of their activity, not punish them for that activity.

I do not know whether these measures are being taken with your knowledge and consent, and so I thought it was important to inform you and offer my view. I am writing on my own initiative, without their knowledge.

With comradely greetings, Osinsky.

The letter was returned to Osinsky, with an accompanying note from Stalin.

Comrade Osinsky,

If you stop to think, you will probably understand that you have no right, moral or otherwise, to censure the Party or take upon yourself the role of an arbiter between the Party and the opposition. I am returning your letter, as offensive to the Party. As for your concern about Smirnov and other oppositionists, you have no reason to doubt that the Party will do everything possible and necessary in that regard. J. Stalin, 3 January 1928.

The following day, Osinsky responded.

Comrade Stalin. I do not need any time to think about whether I
can be the arbiter between the Party and the opposition, or anyone
else. Your interpretation of my point of view and my general
position is fundamentally wrong.

I did not realize that the decision about the exile had been taken
by a Party agency and honestly assumed otherwise. I did not find it
among the Politburo protocols. Perhaps it was classified. My letter
to you was entirely personal. I wrote it (as I am writing this one) on
my portable typewriter, and I personally delivered it to the Central
Committee. I would have dropped it at your home address, but,
when I tried to do that in 1924, I was told to go to your secretariat,
even though the matter was top secret. I wrote "personal" on this
letter, on the assumption that your personal letters were not read
by your secretaries.

My general position is that I consider it within my rights to have
independent opinions on some issues, and occasionally to express
those opinions (sometimes—in the most sensitive cases—only
personally, to you or to you and Rykov, as I did during the
congress, as you will recall).

In recent days, I have been taught two lessons in this regard. In
connection with the grain procurement, Rykov told me that I ought
to have lead poured down my throat, and now you have returned
my letter. Well, if that, too, is unacceptable, I will have to bear it in
mind.

Wouldn't it be much simpler to let me go abroad to work on my
book for a year and be relieved of my bothersome presence
entirely?

With comradely greetings, Osinsky.[70]

Osinsky may have been within his rights to have independent opinions
"on some issues," but he was not within his rights to have independent
opinions on matters of Party policy. As he had written in 1917, there was
no greater pleasure or duty for a Bolshevik than to dissolve his personality
in the "sacred fury" of the proletariat's collective will. That will—then and
now—was embodied in the Party, and the will of the Party—despite the silly
nonsense the oppositionists were spouting—was embodied in the decisions taken by its leaders. Ultimately, only the Party's leaders could tell
where "some issues" ended and Party policy began. Ultimately, according
to Osinsky's own logic, he had no right to have independent opinons about
anything—any more than he had the right, moral or otherwise, to make
distinctions between Stalin the person and Stalin the general secretary of
the Party's Central Committee. Such distinctions, common among cornered oppositionists and their sympathizers, were obviously offensive to
the Party (and any other sectarian or priestly institution). If Osinsky had
stopped to think, he would have understood that a letter about how to deal

with oppositionists could not possibly be personal. He would have understood that no letter to Stalin could possibly be personal. As Bukharin's
disgraced ally, Tomsky, would later say in his confession to the Sixteenth
Party Congress,

> We have seen how, in conditions of fierce class struggle, in a large
> Party intimately connected to the broad masses, the *particular* can
> sometimes become the *general*, and the *personal* can become the
> *political*. We have seen how ostensibly private conversations of poli-
> ticians become political facts, so that if two people, one of whom is
> a member of the top leadership and the other one is, too, get to-
> gether and talk about political matters, even in the course of a pri-
> vate conversation, then those are *no longer private conversations*.
> When people standing at the helm of power in the greatest country
> in a difficult, politically charged moment have private conversa-
> tions, these private conversations—no matter how many times you
> say that they are private—become political, not private. . . . When we
> fight, we do not fight the way liberals do. They are the ones who sep-
> arate the personal from the political. Among us, it does not work
> that way: if your politics are lousy, then you are a lousy, good-for-
> nothing person, and if your politics are wonderful, then you are a
> wonderful person.[71]

Smirnov was duly sent into exile. Osinsky and his wife, Ekaterina
Smirnova, adopted their four-year-old nephew, Rem (Revolution-Engels-
Marx). At the time, the Osinskys' oldest son, Vadim, known as "Dima," was
fifteen and best friends with Sverdlov's son, Andrei. Both were friendly
with Anna Larina. Two and a half years later, when Bukharin returned to
Moscow after the Sixteeth Party Congress, he went to visit some of his
former allies. Among those present were Andrei Sverdlov and Dima Osinsky. According to another young man who was there: "Still under the impression of what Bukharin had been saying about Stalin, Andrei Sverdlov
proclaimed: 'Koba [Stalin] must be bumped off.'"[72]

Smilga was exiled at the same time as Smirnov. Smilga's older daughter,
Tatiana, who was eight at the time, remembered a lot of people at the station, her own warm scarf and woolen tights, her father's massive fur coat
and hat, Radek's words "Farewell, Bear," and her father's prickly moustache
(he had never kissed her before). Smilga was taken to Narym, but was
soon—thanks to Ordzhonikidze—transferred to the less remote Minusinsk,
not far from where Lenin had once been exiled. The following summer,
Nadezhda and the two girls joined him there. Tatiana remembered intense
heat, bouts of dysentery, and frequent dust storms ("when dust whirls
around in towers and columns"). Twice she had to run to the local planning office where her father worked: once, to bring him home because he
wore glasses and could not see in the dust; and then again, when her

Ivar Smilga in Minusinsk   Nadezhda Smilga-Poluian
                                    with the children

mother started crying and could not stop. "He came to see Mother, and they talked about something for a long time. Maybe they reached the conclusion that they should try to do something, rather than just dying quietly like that." Soon afterward, Nadezhda took the sick girls back to Moscow. Nadezhda's brother Dmitry Poluian, a high official at the People's Commissariat of Transportation (and the presiding judge at the trial of Filipp Mironov in 1919), provided a separate train compartment. The following summer, Smilga came down with acute appendicitis and was brought back to the Kremlin hospital for an operation. On July 13, 1929, *Pravda* published a statement by Smilga, Radek, and Preobrazhensky (the original champion of the "tribute on the peasantry"), in which they announced the abandonment of their opposition and their "full solidarity with the general Party line," most particularly the policy of industrialization, the creation of collective farms, and the struggle against the kulak, the bureaucracy, Social-Democracy, and the Right ("which, objectively, reflects the unhappiness of the country's capitalist elements and petty bourgeoisie with the policy of the socialist offensive conducted by the Party").[73]

Voronsky was arrested on January 10, 1929. After a month-long investigation (conducted by Agranov, whom Voronsky had met at various literary events), he was sentenced to five years in a "political isolation unit," but Rykov and Ordzhonikidze interfered, and he was sent into exile in Lipetsk instead. He lived there with his mother and was occasionally visited by his wife, daughter, and former literary protégés, including Babel and Pilniak. In one of his letters home, he complained of loneliness and asked for a dog; a friend lent him a "furry, pale-yellow husky with black eyes." He enjoyed skating, but fell down awkwardly once and damaged his kidney. He continued to work on his memoirs: the first part had been published in *Novyi mir*; the second part was banned. His wife, Sima Solomonovna, managed to find out that the ban "concerned *Novyi mir* as a central and widely circulating publication," and wrote to Molotov asking for a small-print separate edition. Molotov requested the opinion of the

head of Agitprop (and one of Voronsky's most influential "proletarian" opponents), Platon Kerzhentsev. Kerzhentsev wrote that much of the book
had been published before "without raising any objections" and that "the
Agitation, Propaganda, and Press Department considers it possible to
allow a separate printing of Voronsky's book with the run not to exceed
five thousand copies, under the supervision of the chairman of the editorial board of Federatsia Press, Comrade Kanatchikov."

Kanatchikov, the former Gustav List worker and the only former proletarian among Voronsky's "proletarian" critics, had since gotten caught up
in the Zinoviev opposition, spent a year and a half in exile as a TASS correspondent in Prague, proclaimed his loyalty to Stalin after the Fifteenth
Party Congress, been reinstated as a top literary administrator, and published, to great acclaim, the first part of his own autobiography. Kanatchikov did not only comply with Kerzhentsev's request—he became the
main champion of Voronsky's new work, sponsoring the second printing
of *In Search of the Water of Life* and publishing the short stories and fictionalized memoirs about seminary life that Voronsky wrote in exile. Another former "proletarian" critic of Voronsky, G. Lelevich (Labori Gilelevich
Kalmanson), who had also been arrested for opposition activities, wrote
to Voronsky—from one place of exile to another—proposing a coauthored
Marxist history of Russian literature. Voronsky agreed to write the chapters about Pushkin, Gogol, Lermontov, Tiutchev, Tolstoy, Uspensky, Chekhov, Andreev, and "a few of our contemporaries." In the fall of 1929, he returned to Moscow for medical consultations, signed a letter renouncing
his opposition views, and was pardoned on the spot.[74]

There were many reasons to renounce opposition views—loneliness,
boredom, dust storms, small children, ill health—but one of the most important was the desire to rejoin the Party. For lifelong Bolsheviks, there
was no truth or meaning outside the Party, and, for most of those expelled,
there could be no other party, despite the silly nonsense the handful of
remaining apostates continued to spout. The Party was the ontological
foundation of the true believer's universe, the vessel of sacrality on the
eve of the end, the only point of support in a world where everything outside the building of socialism was a "fetish" (as Bukharin, following Lenin,
put it in 1925). In 1929 and 1930, most Bolsheviks, orthodox and nonortho-
dox, believed that socialism was finally being built and that the end was
near. Trotsky, who shared that belief but could not rejoin the ranks,
claimed that "in politics, what matters is not only what is being done, but
also who does it and how." Sometimes, however, what matters in politics
is not only who and how, but also what. And sometimes, politics do not
matter at all. As Tomsky would tell his confessors at the Sixteenth Party
Congress, Bolshevik politics were different from liberal politics in that
they left no room for the personal.[75]

On March 7, 1930, three months after his recantation, Bukharin wrote
a response to Pope Pius XI's protest against the persecution of Christian-

ity in the Soviet Union. Bukharin did not claim that the Soviet Union valued "tolerance, freedom of conscience and other good things": he claimed that the pope did not value them either—or rather, that the pope's newfound liberalism was a symptom of old age. Quoting from Thomas Aquinas's *Summa theologica* to the effect that heretics, that is, those who disagree with church authorities, "deserve not only to be separated from the Church by excommunication, but also to be severed from the world by death," he wrote: "Of course, the popes' reach is not what it used to be: their former grandeur has faded, and their peacock's tail has been plucked rather thoroughly by old Dame History. But when this shriveled vampire attempts to spread its claws, when it relies on the still powerful force of imperialist murderers, when it puts on the mask of tolerance, we *must remember* its executioner's commandment: a heretic (i.e., anyone who is not a slave of the pope) should be *'severed from the world by death'*"![76]

The problem for Pius XI was not who and how but what, and the problem for Christianity in general was not that it was a prophecy but that it was a false one, and thus "spiritual prostitution, the ideology of perfidious castrati and pederasts, *sheer filth*." The shriveled beast was preparing for one last battle, wrapping itself in "papal robes," and issuing calls "meant to sound like the trumpet of the apocalyptic archangel." But the "heroic proletarian army" would not be deceived. "This counterrevolutionary cancan, this cannibalistic howling of lay and church hyenas, accompanied by the jingling of spurs, the rattling of sabers, and the fuming of censers is a 'moral' preparation for *an attack* on the USSR." In the USSR, meanwhile, "superhuman efforts are being made to lay down, for eternity, the strongest possible, steel-and-concrete foundation for the immense and perfectly shaped house of communism."[77]

There is little doubt that Bukharin did not believe in the existence of a third, lukewarm, force and that he knew which side he was on. The first thing Voronsky did when he came back from exile was to meet with Stalin and propose the creation of a new literary journal called *War*. (Stalin agreed: the journal appeared first as the *Literary Section of the Red Army and Navy* and then as *The Banner* [*Znamya*]). In January 1928, when NEP still seemed unshakeable, Osinsky had sulked behind the tall fence of his dacha; in June 1931, he was trying to determine whether, by the end of the second Five-Year Plan, "the proletariat as a class will complete its development, arrive at the realization of its tasks and interests . . . , master its own power, and, having become a class *an und für sich*, turn into its own negation." (His answer was that it was a complicated matter and that he needed to devote himself "to the revelation, for everyone, of the dialectic method, which is hardly much less important than the building of 518 factories.") In a private letter to his lover and fellow true believer, Anna Shaternikova, he wrote that the growth of Soviet factories gave him as much personal pleasure as the thought that his son Dima would soon become an engineer:[78]

I am saying that it gives me <u>personal pleasure</u> not because I am an individualist, but because I think that the launching of these factories is a <u>personal</u> pleasure for <u>everyone</u>, just like the pleasure of seeing <u>our children</u> grow up. Because, confound it, we have grown up together with all these real, existing factories—the Stalingrad Tractor Plant (100 tractors per day), the Putilov (80 tractors per day), the Kharkov Tractor Plant (will start producing 100 tractors a day very soon), the Moscow Automobile Plant (will produce 100 automobiles a day <u>very soon</u>, because that sly fox Likhachev requested a postponement precisely so he would be able to present spectacular statistics right away, and, of course, everyone at that plant knows how to work), the Nizhny Automobile Plant (100 cars by the summer), Kuznetsk (a thousand tons of rails a day as soon as January), Magnitogorsk (same thing by spring), Berezniki (will be producing thousands of tons of nitrogen), etc.—and it (all) happened practically overnight! There we were, waiting and waiting, and suddenly, we woke up in a totally transformed country, <u>unimaginable without</u> automobiles, tractors, fertilizer, well-equipped railroads, electric power stations, thousands of new houses etc., etc. They can't help appearing because the wheels have started turning. It's fantastic![79]

A few weeks earlier, he had attended a discussion about the second Five-Year Plan at the Communist Academy. "The arguments," he wrote to Shaternikova, "were about whether classes would still exist—because the kulaks have already been liquidated; 100% of the farms will have been collectivized; the majority of the population will be working in factories; and the rural population will be employed by agro-industrial combines." They would find out soon enough. "Dear Annushka, socialism everywhere is much closer than we could ever imagine, and it will appear just as unexpectedly and just as soon as when it first came to Russia."[80]

The words about "socialism everywhere" were written in August 1931 in Amsterdam, where Osinsky was serving as head of the Soviet delegation at the International Congress of Planned Economy. His topic was "The Premises, Nature, and Forms of Social Economic Planning," and his main thesis (in the official English translation) was the same as in his letters to Shaternikova. "The plan is the expression and the weapon of that last struggle of human history, which the working class is waging for the destruction of classes and for the building up of socialism. . . . Millions [of people] draw it up, carry it out, and closely watch the course of its fulfillment. This is the basis of the success of planned economy, this is the fundamental advantage of the Soviet system of economy. This is the source of the unprecedented rate of development in the USSR."[81]

The other members of the delegation were Osinsky's colleagues from the governing boards of the State Planning Committee (Gosplan) and Supreme Council of the National Economy: the thirty-two-year-old Aron

Gaister, thirty-four-year-old Ivan Kraval (Jānis Kravalis), and thirty-six-year-old Solomon Ronin. Gaister, Kritsman's closest collaborator among the "Agrarian Marxists" and, after 1932, the deputy head of Gosplan, had been criticized in 1929 for insufficient optimism. In Amsterdam, he claimed that the Five-Year Plan had fulfilled Engels's prediction about the efficiency of collectivized agriculture and laid the foundations for "the liquidation of the contradiction between town and village." According to his daughter, he worshipped his boss, the head of Gosplan, Valerian Kuibyshev, and named his youngest daughter Valeria after him. Kraval, the deputy people's commissar of labor and, after 1933, Osinsky's deputy (and later successor) at the Central Directory of Economic Statistics, had belonged to the Right Opposition and, at about the same time, violated Solts's "poor taste" principle by marrying the daughter of a wealthy Jewish-Latvian cattle trader. His topic was "Labor in the Planned Economy of the USSR," and his main thesis was that labor, according to Stalin's declaration at the Sixteenth Party Congress, had been transformed "from a shameful and heavy burden into a matter of glory, valor and heroism." He, too, worshipped Kuibyshev. Ronin, a high-ranking Planning Agency official and a former member of the Marxist-Zionist "Poale Zion" Party, had gotten into trouble in 1921 when his father, a former rabbi, had his son Anatoly circumcised (Ronin's wife was expelled from the Party as a consequence). In Amsterdam, he argued that the First Five-Year Plan would "make it possible to move forward at a still higher speed and to write a new and still more brilliant socialist page in the history of human society." After the conference, he asked to be allowed to participate in the construction of the Magnitogorsk Steel Mill. Instead, he was given a choice between serving in the new Soviet consulate in San Francisco or supervising collectivization in the Azov–Black Sea territory. He chose the latter.[82]

■ ■ ■

One of Voronsky's correspondents when he was still in exile in Lipetsk was Tania Miagkova, the daughter of Voronsky's closest Tambov friend and revolutionary mentor, Feoktista Yakovlevna Miagkova—the same earnest, all-or-nothing, Brand-like, "olive-skinned Tania" who used to dismiss his tall tales as frivolous when she was twelve years old.

Tania had since joined the Party, graduated from the Kharkov Institute of Economics and Sverdlov Communist University in Moscow, married the head of the Ukrainian Planning Agency, Mikhail Poloz, had a daughter, Rada (in

Tania Miagkova

1924), joined the opposition, and, in 1927, been expelled from the Party and exiled to Astrakhan. In Astrakhan she collected money for unemployed exiles, organized opposition meetings, and distributed leaflets accusing the Party leadership of betraying the working class and appeasing the NEP-men and kulaks. In February 1929, she was deported to Chelkar (Shalkar), in Kazakhstan, where she, along with two other exiles, Sonia Smirnova and Mirra Varshavskaia, rented a room in the house of a local railroad engineer. At thirty-one, Tania was the oldest of the three. She had lost most of her teeth and wore dentures, which she kept in a special glass at night. She was reserved and had, according to Mirra, "great inner delicacy, tact, and integrity." She was responsible for assigning communal responsibilities and heating up the stove. As she wrote to her husband, Mikhail, on March 15, 1929,

> I use thorny brush, or "chagor," instead of logs. I usually bring two huge bundles and sit for a couple of hours in front of the stove, tossing in the thorny branches, one at a time. They crackle and burn, my hands are full of cuts and splinters, and I can think about anything I want. . . . After that, we make millet porridge or fry potatoes on the stove. I do all that, too (or rather, I, too, do all that), and yesterday I made a wonderful potato soup. So you see, my friend, you should not have complained about my impracticality: all you needed to do was send me into exile early in our life together. So far, I must say, these household chores don't really feel like a burden to me. I've decided to master the mechanics of all this, and it's not so bad to have to switch my attention from my books to the poker or the well for a change.
>
> It's pleasant to walk to the well. It's at the very edge of the settlement (we ourselves are pretty close to the edge). The steppe is beautiful—even here, in Chelkar. And far away, on the road, you can often see camels walking off into the distance, one after another. . . . In the evenings, we sometimes sit on a bench in the yard, listening to the barking of dogs and the clanking of wheels whenever a train passes by.[83]

She did not have a job, and there was not much to do in Chelkar. The OGPU (former Cheka) provided the exiles with thirty (later fifteen) rubles a month, but Mikhail, who had been appointed the Ukrainian people's commissar of finance, was in a position to help. She spent much of her time writing letters—mostly to Voronsky and her family. (Her mother, Feoktista Yakovlevna, had since moved to Kharkov to live with Mikhail and Rada). Her "chief obsession" was the fear that Rada, now five years old, would forget her, or that she would "miss out on" Rada's development. She sent Rada stories (first fairy tales and then funny scenes from her own life), picture books, shirts that she sewed herself, and once she made a large appliqué for the wall over her bed. She kept asking Mikhail to send Rada out for a visit, but he never did, perhaps because "the living conditions, as well as the climate and the medical care" in Chelkar were "too difficult." She promised not to indoctrinate her daughter: "Regarding my 'dogmatism,' I am, first of all, quite certain that I won't pass it on to Rada, and, second, it can't be done, in any case (according to my ideas about education, this is not the time to talk to a child about these things, and of course she won't see any of my supposed 'dogmatism' herself)."[84]

Her other obsession was the Five-Year Plan. She asked for the *Soviet Trade* and *Problems of Trade* journals, subscribed to *Kazakh Economics*, "mastered" a two-volume publication of the Kazakh State Planning Commission on "regionalization," started learning the Kazakh language and history (because of Kazakhstan's "great potential and great scale"), worried about the Ukrainian harvest, and kept asking for a book about the Five-Year Plan. "I need the Five-Year Plan so much, so very much," she wrote on May 20, 1929. "Generally all I need are the Five-Year Plan and a pair of size-37 sandals." In early June, it finally started to rain. "I am so happy to see the rain," she wrote, "not only for the usual reason that it is good for the Soviet state, but also because I have missed it so much."[85]

She missed Mikhail, too. "It's been raining for five days now, sometimes a fall drizzle, sometimes a hard rain alternating with suffocating humidity. One night was beautiful: all around me were flashes of distant lightening and the dizzyingly bitter smell of wormwood. It was, of course, my turn to

Tania Miagkova (*standing*) in Kazakhstan

go get the water (for some reason, I always have to do it at night), and I wanted very much to keep walking far into the steppe, but . . . with you." She wrote about her love for him, wondered if he missed her kisses, and offered to help him with his work. She wrote about the joy of dropping her letters in the mail car of the Moscow train and "watching them set out on their long journey," and then, two months later, about "the terrible trag-edy" that had befallen the Chelkar exiles: "the fast train that we have been using to send our mail now passes by at 2 a.m." She kept asking for more letters, postcards, and photographs. "My darling, my dear Mikhailik. I am holding you very, very tight. Where are you now? Oh how I wish I could curl up on your sofa, when it's dark outside, and it smells of acacia. And here all we have is wormwood, the bitter grass."[86]

Finally he came to visit. According to Tania's roommate, Mirra Var-shavskaia, "he and Tania would walk in the steppe for many hours and come back late, with Tania looking exhausted and depressed. I thought he had come to convince her to renounce the opposition, and, to my distress, he seemed to be succeeding. I also thought that he had brought some secret arguments and information that Tania was not sharing with us. After his departure, Tania was quieter and even more reserved." When a new collective letter of recantation was circulated among the exiles, Tania signed it. Mirra felt betrayed: "Tania's stellar moral qualities excluded the possibility of mercenary reasons for deviating from the correct line," so it must have been her daughter (a reason Mirra, "not knowing a mother's heart from personal experience," considered "not good enough to betray a common cause"). Another possibility was the fact that the Party leader-ship was no longer appeasing the NEP-men and kulaks, and thus no longer betraying the working class. Soon Tania left—"without urging anyone to follow her example, without proselytizing, without words." As their land-lady put it, "she left the same person as she came." Some time later Mirra received a letter, in which Tania wrote: "Don't let life pass you by." She didn't say if she meant motherhood or the Five-Year Plan.[87]

Tania Miagkova and her husband, Mikhail Poloz

BOOK TWO
AT HOME

PART III
THE SECOND COMING

9
THE ETERNAL HOUSE

In September 1929, the "proletarian" literary journal *October* published Andrei Platonov's story "Doubting Makar." Makar is a peasant who, like all peasants, "does not know how to think because he has an empty head over clever hands." Makar's village chairman, Comrade Lev Chumovoi, on the other hand, does a lot of thinking because he has "a clever head, but empty hands." One day Makar makes iron ore out of mud, but soon forgets how he did it. Comrade Chumovoi punishes him with a large fine, and Makar sets off for Moscow "to earn himself a living under the golden heads of all the temples and leaders":

"Just where exactly is the center around here?" Makar asked the militiaman.

The militiaman pointed downhill and informed him:

"Next to the Bolshoi Theater, in that gully down there."

Makar descended the hill and found himself between two flower beds. On one side of the square was a wall, on the other, a building with pillars. These pillars were holding up four harnessed iron horses, but they could have been a lot thinner since the horses were not very heavy.

Makar looked around the square searching for some kind of pole with a red flag, which would indicate the middle of the central city and the center of the entire state, but instead of a pole there was a stone with an inscription on it. Makar propped himself against the stone in order to stand at the very center and experience a feeling of respect for himself and his state. Makar sighed happily and began to feel hungry. He walked down to the river where he saw an amazing apartment building being built.

"What are they building here?" he asked a passerby.

"An eternal house of iron, concrete, steel, and clear glass!" responded the passerby.

Makar decided to drop by in order to do a bit of work and get something to eat.

There was a guard at the door. The guard asked:

"What do you want, blockhead?"

"I'm a bit on the hollow side, so I'd like to do a little work," declared Makar.

"How can you work here when you don't have a single permit?" said the guard sadly.

At this point a bricklayer came up and started listening eagerly to Makar.

"Come to the communal pot in our barracks—the boys there will feed you," said the bricklayer to Makar helpfully. "But you can't sign up with us right away because you live on your own, which means you're a nobody. You've got to join the workers' union first, and then undergo class surveillance.

And so Makar went to the barracks to eat from the common pot in order to nurture himself for the sake of a better future fate.[1]

The eternal house they were building was officially called the House of the Central Executive Committee and the Council of People's Commissars, commonly known as the House of Government. It was designated for leaders with golden heads and designed by a man named Boris Iofan.

For most of the 1920s, top-ranking Soviet officials had been camping out in hotels and palaces converted into dormitories (Houses of Soviets). Everyone knew that the arrangement was temporary: the Left expected the imminent death of all domesticity; the Right looked forward to turning the Houses of Soviets into proper homes; and the growing contingent of foreign visitors required "large, well-appointed hotels with large comfortable suites of two to three rooms, with a bath, etc." (The most desirable were the First and Second Houses of Soviets, formerly the National and the Metropol Hotels.)[2]

In January 1927, when the Right was still on the rise, Rykov, in his capacity as head of government, formed a Commission for the Construction of the House of the Central Executive Comittee and Council of People's Commissars and appointed Boris Iofan head architect. Iofan was born in an Odessa Jewish family in 1891, received an Odessa Art School diploma in 1911, worked as an assistant architect in St. Petersburg, and, in 1914, emigrated to Italy, where he graduated from the Higher Institute of the Fine Arts in Rome and started practicing as an architect. In 1921 he joined the Italian Communist Party and, in 1924, acted as cicerone to the visiting Rykov family. Later that year, he had accepted Rykov's invitation to return to Russia. His first two projects were a garden city for the workers at the Shterovskaia Hydroelectric Dam in Ukraine (1924) and a communal workers' settlement on Rusakov Street in Moscow (1925). No other architect was considered for the House of Government commission.[3]

At its first meeting on January 20, 1927, the commission, chaired by Central Committee Secretary Avel Enukidze, decided to build the House of Government between the Nikitskie Gates and Kudrinskaia Square. It was to be seven stories: the ground floor was to be occupied by shops, the rest to be divided into two wings: one with three-room apartments, the other, with five-room apartments (two hundred apartments in all). The

House was to be "open from all four sides" and to
possess "high-quality" facilities, including central heating, parquet floors, hot water, and gas
stoves. It was to be built of reinforced concrete,
with brick walls and a metal roof; the construction was to be completed by the fall of 1928; the
total cost was to be three million rubles.[4]

A month later, the commission decided to double the overall number of apartments, add some
four-room apartments, supply the five-room
apartments with special rooms for servants, double the total cost, and move the location to Star-
ovagankovsky Alley, next to the Central Archive

Boris Iofan

(the site of the future Lenin Library). Three weeks later, the commission
decided to tear down the Central Archive. Two and a half months later, on
June 24, 1927, it made "the final decision" to build the House of Government
in the Swamp.[5]

The new location had some serious disadvantages. Building a large
structure in the Swamp meant that the ground level had be raised (by at
least half a meter above the level of the 1908 flood, or about 10.57 meters
overall), the embankment reinforced, and the building itself supported (by
about three thousand reinforced concrete piles, sunk into the bedrock five
to fifteen meters below). The extra cost and effort were deemed justifiable,
however, because of the site's proximity to government offices and its relatively low density of development. The clearing of the area involved the
closure of the Wine and Salt Yard, the relocation of the Regional Courthouse (the former Assembly of the Justices of the Peace), the tearing down
of three residential buildings and more than twenty warehouses, the eviction of approximately one hundred permanent residents, and the transfer
of the lumber yard belonging to the Electric Tram Power Station to the
territory of the former Smirnov Vodka Factory.

A few months later, the Construction Commission also decided to
straighten All Saints Street and demolish the Swamp Market (beginning
with the stone and metal warehouses and the public toilet). At the same
time, Iofan asked Enukidze's permission to tear down the Church of St.
Nicholas the Miracle Worker in order to build a detached kindergarten and
day-care center. The State Historical Preservation Workshop, which was
housed inside St. Nicholas, put up a strong resistance, claiming that the
church was a part of the seventeenth-century Averky Kirillov Residence,
and thus a much needed reminder of "the mutually advantageous proximity of religion and the ruling class" under the old regime. More to the point,
they argued that the territory of the church was not large enough for a
proper House of Government children's facility complete with sunlit gardens and playgrounds. The Central Executive Committee ordered the Historical Preservation Workshop to vacate the premises, but then concurred

with the size argument and decided to incorporate the children's facility into the House of Government No. 2, to be built on the site of the former Swamp Market. The church was spared (and the second House of Government was never built).[6]

On April 29, 1928, the Moscow Regional Engineering Bureau issued a permit authorizing construction. The building was to be made of reinforced concrete with outer walls of brick. The bureau "considered it possible to allow, by way of exception, the construction of residential buildings ten stories high, instead of six, as prescribed by a binding regulation of the presidium of the Moscow City Soviet, with each stairway serving twenty apartments, instead of twelve, as prescribed by the same regulation." The proposed complex consisted of seven attached residential buildings varying in height from eight to eleven stories, a movie theater for 1,500 people, a grocery store, and a club for 1,000 people, containing a theater, cafeteria, and various sports facilities. It stretched the length of All Saints Street from the Drainage Canal to the Bersenev Embankment, and was centered on three landscaped courtyards connected by tall archways.[7]

The residential wings were to include 440 three-, four-, and five-room apartments, not counting the special rooms set aside for the janitors and guards. Each apartment was to have a kitchen with gas stove and icebox, a toilet, a bathroom with hot water and shower, a ventilation system, a garbage chute, hot water radiators in special niches under the windows, and a large entrance hall that could be partitioned into two separate spaces, one of which "could serve as a place where servants could rest." All garbage was to be burned in basement incinerators, "liquids and feces" evacuated into the municipal sewage system, and snow melted in special concrete pits and drained into the river. The laundry was to be located in a separate building.[8]

Bersenev Embankment. The building on the right is being torn down in preparation for the construction work.

House of Government construction site
(facing the Kremlin)

The sinking of the piles began on March 24, 1928. The piles (3,520 altogether) were delivered to the site by three traveling cranes and lifted onto eight pile-driving rigs by electric winches; the same winches were used for hoisting the steam pile hammers, which ranged from two thousand to twelve thousand kilograms in weight. Cement mixers were placed in special carts and transported as needed. Sand and gravel were sorted and washed on the other side of the Ditch and delivered to the site by means of an aerial tramway. Much of the equipment had been transferred to the Swamp from the newly completed Volkhov Hydroelectric Dam. The workers came from the Moscow Employment Office or just wandered in.[9]

Makar settled into the life of the building of the house the passerby had called eternal. First he ate his fill of nutritious, black kasha in the workers' barracks, and then went to look at the construction work. All around, the earth was scarred with pits, people were scurrying about, and machines of unknown name were driving piles into the soil. Cement gruel was pouring from spouts, and other productive events were also taking place before one's eyes. It was obvious that a house was being built, but not clear for whom. But Makar was not interested in who was going to get what: he was interested in technology as a future boon for all the people. Makar's commander from his native village, Comrade Lev Chumovoi, would, on the contrary, have become interested in the distribution of apartments in the future house, and not in the steam pile hammers, but only Makar's hands were literate, and not his head; therefore, all he could think about was what he could make.[10]

Most workers were like Makar: seasonal laborers who came to Moscow to get away from Comrade Lev Chumovoi and to "nurture themselves for

House of Government construction site (facing the power station)

the sake of a better future fate." This called for special vigilance: the brick-layer who tells Makar that he will have to join the workers' union first, and then undergo class surveillance knows what he is talking about. The Construction Workers' Union warned repeatedly that "the presence, among the unemployed, of a significant number of people who are alien to the Soviet order, do not truly need work, have a permanent income from temporary jobs including petty trade and artisanship, retain close links to the peasant way of life, and possess skills that have not yet been classified, ... presents the Moscow Employment Office with the task of carefully checking all the unemployed." Sixty percent of all union members were seasonal laborers who had to be "watched more closely at the time of hiring and then again in their day-to-day work." In March 1928, when work on the House of Government was just getting under way, the Trans-Moskva District Party Committee declared that "the most common diseases" among the district's workers were "(a) vulgar egalitarianism with regard to the city and the countryside, different kinds of workers, workers and specialists, etc.; (b) peasant attitudes (in particular, in connection with grain requisitioning); (c) trade loyalties; (d) mistrust regarding the rationality or feasibility of various campaigns (e.g., the rationalization of work, seven-hour workday, etc.); (e) anti-Semitism; (f) religious beliefs, etc."[11]

One way to change the workers' consciousness was to change their "social being": the construction commission kept asking for mittens, jackets, pants, guards' uniforms, "permits for goods in particularly high demand," and, most urgently, living space. (As of late 1927, "the actual average living space of 5.57 square meters per person" in the Trans-Moskva district "continued to decline owing to the growth of the population and the deterioration of the existing living space.") More important was the direct work on consciousness in the form of rallies, lectures, question-and-answer sessions, "construction workers' congresses," "production conferences," lit-

House of Government construction site (facing the river)

eracy campaigns, newspaper subscriptions, the establishment of Lenin shrines ("little red corners" in workers' barracks, analogous to the "red," or icon corners in Orthodox Christian dwellings), and, in particular, repeated acts of public denunciation and confession known as "criticism and self-criticism" ("a powerful tool aimed at mobilizing the masses for the implementation of Party decisions"). Workers were to become "activists," and activists were to expose evil by exposing its human agents. As one member of the Construction Workers' Union said at a meeting of the Commission for Assistance to Worker-Peasant Inspection: "All the activists, as soon as they notice a parasite, must report to the commission right away. Only in this way will we be able to fulfill Lenin's commandments." Platonov's Makar is determined to fulfill Lenin's commandments. When the parasites with clever heads and empty hands ignore his invention of a special hose for pumping cement, he takes his case to the Worker-Peasant Inspection ("they like complainers and all kinds of aggrieved people over there"). His main sources of inspiration are Lenin's deathbed articles, faithfully paraphrased for him by his friend Petr. "'Our institutions are shit,' read Petr from Lenin, while Makar listened, marveling at the precision of Lenin's mind. 'Our laws are shit. We know how to prescribe, but not how to execute. Our institutions are full of people who are hostile to us, and some of our comrades have become pompous bureaucrats and work like fools.'"[12]

In November 1927, as the site for the new House of Government was being cleared, the head of the Moscow Trade Union Council, Vasily Mikhailov, told the Trans-Moskva Party conference that improving the quality of the workers' cafeterias was one of the Moscow Party Committee's highest priorities—"because the workers have been telling us that there are one or two flies floating in every bowl, probably to enhance the flavor." Three years later, the bureau of the Trans-Moskva Party

House of Government construction site
(facing the Cathedral of Christ the Savior)

Committee found that the quality of the cafeteria food at the district's construction sites had not improved. "In some cases, the poor quality of the food exceeds all limits: in Cafeteria No. 43, seasonal workers were served spoiled food with maggots in it." In September 1932, the House of Government construction site was housing six hundred people in six barracks with leaky roofs. According to the district's control commission, "the barracks are in an unsanitary condition. There is not enough light. There are 8–10 workers for every 6–7 meters of space. There is no fuel for the winter. Party, state, and union officials never come to the dorm; cultural work is organized poorly." According to the Moscow branch of the Construction Workers' Union, this was true throughout the city. "Not all construction sites have boxes for complaints; articles from various newspapers are not being clipped and sorted; elements engaged in bureaucratic perversions of the class line in practical work are not being unmasked."[13]

One of the most obvious consequences of poor supervision was drunkenness and other forms of "degeneration." As one activist and foreman-in-training by the name of Oleander told the Extraordinary Congress of Construction Workers in February 1929, "the workers at my construction site tell me: Comrade Oleander, how can you lead if your own Communists spend our last kopeks carousing with young ladies?" Makar, too, notices that among the clever people with empty hands are "a great variety of women dressed in tight clothing indicating that they wish to be naked," and that the parasite in charge of the trade union office "had read Makar's note through the mediation of his assistant—a rather good-looking and progressive girl with a thick braid." But the real danger, pointed out by Lenin in his testament, was that the people in charge of the union parasites were themselves parasites. The 1929 Extraordinary Congress of the Construction Workers' Union was extraordinary because "the degeneration within the top tier of the provincial hierarchy had led to the dismissal of the whole governing board." When Makar and Petr finally make it to the Worker-Peasant Inspection, they find two rooms. "Having opened the first

 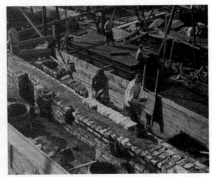

Workers at the construction site

door in the upstairs corridor, they saw an absence of people. Over the second door hung the terse slogan 'Who, whom?' and Petr and Makar went in. There was no one in the room except for Comrade Lev Chumovoi, who was busy presiding over something, having left his village at the mercy of the landless peasants."[14]

In June 1929, the Trans-Moskva Party Committee and Control Commission conducted an investigation into the construction of the House of Government and found "a series of outrages" involving "gross mismanagement" and violations of labor discipline. "Workers loitered around the construction site, and the situation with technical personnel was so terrible that the house seemed left to its own devices." Boris Iofan was reprimanded for going abroad "at the height of the construction work" and leaving the project in the care of his non-Party brother, as well as for failing to adequately explain to the workers the policy (endorsed by the Construction Workers' Union) of requiring two hours of overtime each day. The site supervisor and his deputy were fired for incompetence; the deputy head of construction, for "not promptly informing the District Party Committee of the problems on the site"; and the secretary of the Party cell, for "a lack of proper firmness" and "elements of infighting and degeneration." The governing board of the Construction Workers' Union had, of course, already been dismissed for degeneration; the head of the Moscow Trade Union Council, Vasily Mikhailov, had been fired for "vacillations" and "conciliatory tendencies" and transferred to the Dnieper Hydroelectric Dam, as deputy head of construction. The new Party cell was told to "exercise great caution in hiring new workers" and to "conduct systematic purges of construction workers in order to eliminate self-serving and hostile elements who cause degeneration among the workers." The new secretary of the Party cell, Mikhail Tuchin, was a thirty-three-year-old Red Cavalry veteran who had studied construction in a technical school and served as a member of the Party Committee in Tarusa; his non-Party wife, whom he had met in his native village in the Smolensk Province, had

Workers at the construction site

graduated from library school (and, according to their daughter, used to make delicious kulich and paskha for Easter). The new site supervisor, Comrade Nikitina, was fired when it was discovered that her father had been a priest in the Tambov Province. On February 8, 1930, the heated enclosure of Building No. 1 (closest to the bridge) caught fire. Parts of the brick wall were seriously damaged; a new investigation was launched; and new outrages were uncovered.[15]

For Makar, the quixotic journey from one outrage to another ends according to Lenin's *State and Revolution*:

Makar was not frightened by Chumovoi and said to Petr:
"Since it says, 'Who, whom?', then let's get him?"
"No," countered the more experienced Petr, "We're dealing with a state here, not a bunch of noodles. We should go higher."
They were received higher up where there was a great longing for real people and authentic rank-and-file intelligence.
"We are class struggle members," said Petr to the highest official. "We have accumulated intelligence. Give us power over the oppressive scribbling scum. . . ."
"Take it, it's yours," said the highest one, and handed over the power to them.
After that, Makar and Petr sat down at some desks in front of Lev Chumovoi and began to talk with the visiting poor people, deciding everything in their heads on the basis of their compassion for the have-nots. But soon the people stopped coming to that de-

partment because Makar and Petr thought so simply that the poor were able to think and make decisions in the same way, and so the toilers began to think for themselves inside their own apartments.

Lev Chumovoi was left all alone in the office because he was never recalled from there in writing. And he remained there until the state liquidation commission was formed. Comrade Chumovoi worked in that commission for forty-four years and died in the midst of oblivion and the files which contained his institutional state intelligence.[16]

Back in the Swamp, the eternal house was still being built. The initial reaction of the Trans-Moskva District Party Committee was to welcome the construction of the House as "the first step in the creation of an important cultural center in the area," but the scale of the project and the uncertainty of its form and function provoked some puzzlement. The newspaper *Construction* wondered if the House was being built without any plan at all, while the journal *Building of Moscow* complained that, contrary to Soviet legislation, the plan was being kept secret. "The design was produced without an open competition, in a nontransparent, unacceptable way. Was the completed design discussed by the wider public? Unfortunately, *it was not*. Was the design published anywhere? No, *it was not*. The editors tried to obtain a copy for publication, but their efforts proved unsuccessful. Someone, somewhere, somehow, produced and approved a 14-million-ruble project that the Soviet public knows *nothing* about."

Iofan responded by saying that the design had been considered by fourteen professional experts, approved by a special government commission, and discussed by the Moscow Regional Engineering Bureau, with the participation of "all departments concerned." He ignored the question about the required open competition and public oversight, but agreed to publish a detailed description of the project. Doubts regarding the wisdom of building an eternal house in the middle of the Swamp persisted for a while before dissipating in the face of the inevitable. When one of the delegates to the Trans-Moskva District Party Conference of January 1929 said that the project could easily "wait another five years, thus saving tens of millions of rubles that could be used for, say, steel production," the committee secretary responded: "What can we do? Building on the house has begun; the foundation has been laid; and construction is going forward. In the future, we should probably learn from this experience and make sure that there are no more big, showy projects like this one." In September 1929, in the wake of the discovery of the "outrages," the head of the district Control Commission restated the obvious: "We cannot interfere, because the government has made its decision, and the higher authorities have given their approval. In other words, where to build and how to build—these things do not depend on us."[17]

Iofan (*third from the left*) at the construction site

In November 1928, the State Office for Financial Control wrote to Rykov that, since the decision to build the House in an "unfit" location could "no longer be reversed," some parts of the project would have to be scaled down in order to keep down the costs. Rykov disagreed and in his capacity as chairman of the Council of People's Commissars forced the People's Commissariat of Finance and the State Bank to make up the difference. The government, he made clear to all departments concerned, could build its own house by lending itself money as needed. The chairman of the State Bank, Georgy Piatakov, pointed out that "it is very awkward when the debtor, namely the Council of People's Commissars . . . , issues a decree extending its own payment deadline," but complied without further objection. Between February and November 1928, the estimated cost of construction rose from 6.5 to 18.5 million rubles. Within two years, it would reach 24 million. The final cost would exceed 30 million (ten times the original projection). A special review committee appointed by the Council of People's Commissars in May 1931 concluded that, in the foreseeable future, the Soviet Union could not afford another residential building of comparable size and cost.[18]

The main reason for the high construction costs, according to Iofan, were the "heightened quality requirements" demanded by the government for a project of "government importance." "When it comes to the use of materials, the construction of the House of Government cannot possibly be compared to <u>ordinary wood-framed residential construction</u> because of the presence, in this case, of <u>public buildings with reinforced concrete frames</u> (a movie theater, theater, club, grocery store, etc.), which make up about 50% of the cubic capacity of the residential wings, and the <u>heightened requirements</u> concerning the structure of the residential wings and living conditions within them (passenger and cargo elevators, garbage chutes, etc.)."[19]

The use of reinforced concrete frames throughout the complex, and not just in the public areas, was dictated by considerations of hygiene and fire safety. The extra high (3.4 meters) ceilings were a matter of residents' convenience; terrazzo window panes and granite paneling were choices made for aesthetic reasons. Marble steps were preferred to concrete ones because of their durability; the same was true of ceramic, as opposed to cement, tiles in the kitchens and bathrooms. The more expensive flat roofs were used because of the "necessity" to have solariums. Extra floors were needed in order to accommodate more apartments (505, instead of the projected 440), which were needed in order to accommodate more residents and service personnel. Some other expenses not listed in the original plan included the building of a post office, bank, and shooting gallery; the laying of radio and telephone cables, including a direct line to the Kremlin; the furnishing of all the apartments (at a cost of about 1.5 million rubles); the use of "special military guards and special fire brigades"; and the fighting of the 1930 fire and several floods. The effort to complete the work by the thirteenth anniversary of the October Revolution in November 1930 required paying more workers to do more work. In April 1930, the construction committee decided to switch to two and possibly three shifts and employ two hundred to three hundred additional plasterers. In September, the committee introduced a ten-hour work day and asked for new technical personnel, as well as five hundred more plasterers, three hundred carpenters, and fifty roofers. The House was still not finished by November 1930. The first residents began to move into the wings closest to the Ditch in the spring of 1931. The wings facing the river, including the theater, were not completed until the fall of 1932. The work in the courtyards and on the embankment continued into 1933.[20]

View of Trans-Moskva from the cathedral. In the foreground is
the Church of St. Nicholas the Miracle Worker. Behind it is the
power station. The construction site is on the left.

Construction of the theater and club. In the background on the right is the Big Stone Bridge.

View of construction from the Kremlin

View of construction from the cathedral

Construction of the movie theater. A view from the Trans-Moskva side.

View of the nearly completed House of Government
and movie theater from the Drainage Canal

Reconstruction of the Bersenev Embankment, with the Big Stone Bridge
and Kremlin in the background and the theater facade on the right

House of Government construction nearly complete. Festive illumination marking
the fourteenth anniversary of the Revolution in November 1931.

■ ■ ■

The fact that socialism was inevitable meant that it needed to be built. The
USSR had no choice but to become "a gigantic construction site." The new
structure was eternal but mysterious. "It was obvious that a house was
being built, but not clear for whom." Or rather, it was obvious that the
House would contain socialism, but not clear what it was going to look like.
In the process of fulfilling the Five-Year Plan, the Bolsheviks, according to
Krupskaia, "had run up against the challenge, unforeseen by many, of
building a residential shell for the socialist society of the future." Or, as one
architect put it, "we are giving shape to a new everyday life, but where is
this life? It does not exist. It has not yet been created. We know it must
exist, we can say what it should look like, but it does not yet exist, nor does
any assignment that would correspond to it." The task was to "design for
the future, even if such designs are not feasible or even appropriate at
present."[21]

"The task of the architect of the coming era," wrote the Gosplan economist, M. Okhitovich, "is not to build a house, but to 'build,' or shape, social
relations and productive functions in the form of buildings." This meant
that "the only architect prepared for the current conditions is Karl Marx,
whose 'client' is the general interest and whose 'employer' is today's proletariat and tomorrow's classless society. Up until now it has been impossible to build without capital. From now on it will be impossible to build

without *Das Kapital*." The fact that *Das Kapital* offered little guidance on how to "shape social relations in the form of buildings" was not a serious challenge because Karl Marx's representative in socialist society was Comrade Stalin, and Comrade Stalin was, by (Radek's) definition, "the architect of socialist society." The fact that Comrade Stalin offered little guidance on how to shape social relations in the form of buildings meant that ordinary Soviet architects would have to do it themselves.[22]

The most popular plan envisioned "agro-industrial cities" encircling "production centers" and consisting of several "communal houses" or "residential combines" with twenty thousand to thirty thousand adult residents each. According to one much-discussed project, the "city of the near future" (five to fifteen years hence, according to different projections) would be covered by a large, green park crisscrossed by avenues lined with trees and bicycle paths and with a sidewalk along the perimeter.

Large residential buildings, their facades broken up by the wide, glass panels of windows and balconies, will be set off from the sidewalk by green lawns. The flat roofs of the buildings will be covered with terraces decorated with flowers and gazebos for shade. The buildings will be painted in light, joyous colors: white, pink, blue, and red—not in dull gray or black, but in harmonious, carefully chosen color schemes.

The first thing you will see when you enter a building is a large vestibule. To the left and right will be washrooms, shower rooms, and gymnasiums, in which residents, tired after a day's work, can shower, change, and hang up their work clothes in special lockers if, for some reason, they were not able do so at their place of work or in the fields. Of course, each place of employment must guarantee total cleanliness.

Beyond the vestibule will be a reception area with an information desk, a kiosk for selling small items, a hair salon, and a room for shining shoes and washing and repairing clothes. Also here, tucked away in large alcoves, there will be comfortable furniture, to be used by residents for socializing or by the "welcoming committee" for receiving visitors from near and far. Farther along will be various rooms dedicated to cultural activities, including billiards, chess, photography, music, and many others, as well as larger rooms to be used for collective discussions and musical rehearsals and shops and labs for amateur radio technicians, electricians, and dressmakers to hone their skills while serving the needs of the residents.

An easy passage across a beautiful archway leading out to the park will bring you into a large American-style cafeteria. On the long counter, in pans and on electric burners, will be a great variety of dishes that can be served out in portions of different sizes. Visitors will be able to help themselves to any combination of dishes.

Past the dining hall, or perhaps on the third floor, will be a large reading room with an adjoining rooftop veranda. The selection will not be large, but it will be possible to request any book from the central library by telephone. Next to the reading room will be small carrels for people who need to write reports for production meetings or speeches for rallies, or simply need a place to concentrate.

The upper part of the building will contain small rooms for each of the residents. In this compact, but comfortable space will be everything an individual needs: a bed or couch, a closet for clothes and other things, a convenient desk, a couple of comfortable chairs, some bookshelves, space for pictures and flowers, and, if possible, a door leading onto a balcony. The room should be around 7 to 9 square meters.[23]

As Lunacharsky put it, communal houses must "express their inner essence clearly, albeit in a variety of ways, with individual dwellings grouped around a common core: cultural clubs and other public spaces."[24]

The idea was not novel. Most Russians, according to Krupskaia, were familiar with similar arrangements. "In conditions of exile and emigration, the need for cheaper and more rational meals led to the creation of consumers' communes. Among workers, seasonal laborers often had communal eating arrangements, as did various rural work crews." Those were not proper communes, however. "A dormitory becomes a commune only when the residents are united by a common idea, a common goal." But this was not enough, either. "Monasteries used to be, in essence, communes," but monks and nuns were united by the wrong idea and the wrong goal. Most important, their "religion-fueled intensity of effort" and "well thought-through organization of labor" were fueled by the practice of celibacy. The challenge was to create a true-believing, hardworking, coeducational monastery that permitted procreation and incorporated a day-care center. A common sectarian solution of having the leader monopolize or regulate access to all females was not acceptable. Fourier's phalansteries were often cited as appropriate residential shells, but his ideas about matching residents by temperament were rejected as silly (individual psychology being, for orthodox Marxists, irrelevant to future harmony).[25]

The answer was contained in *The Communist Manifesto*:

On what foundation is the present family, the bourgeois family, based? On capital, on private gain. In its completely developed form, this family exists only among the bourgeoisie. But this state of things finds its complement in the practical absence of the family among the proletarians, and in public prostitution.

The bourgeois family will vanish as a matter of course when its complement vanishes, and both will vanish with the vanishing of capital. . . .

Bourgeois marriage is, in reality, a system of wives in common and thus, at the most, what the Communists might possibly be reproached with is that they desire to introduce, in substitution for a hypocritically concealed, an openly legalised community of women. For the rest, it is self-evident that the abolition of the present system of production must bring with it the abolition of the community of women springing from that system, *i.e.*, of prostitution both public and private.[26]

According to N. A. Miliutin's widely read commentary on this passage, "it is difficult to imagine a better answer to all the crusaders against the new forms of everyday life and against the creation of the material preconditions for the destruction of the family. It is amazing that the bourgeois ideology is still so strong among some Party members that they keep inventing, with a zeal worthy of a better cause, new arguments for the preservation of the double bed as a permanent, obligatory fixture of a worker's dwelling." As *The Communist Manifesto* made clear, the abolition of private property would make permanent bonds based on mating and child rearing unnecessary. "By creating public cafeterias, nurseries, kindergartens, boarding schools, laundries, and sewing shops, we will achieve a genuine radical break with the existing property relations within the family, thus creating the economic preconditions for the abolition of the family as an economic institution."[27]

But was there anything else to the family? According to another communal house theorist, L. M. Sabsovich, "the question of a 'natural,' biological bond between parents and children, the question of 'maternal affection,' the possible loss of an incentive for women to have children, etc.—all these questions are usually raised not by workers or peasants, but by certain circles within our intelligentsia, strongly infected with petit bourgeois, intelligentsia prejudices. Exclusive love for one's own children is, of course, based not so much on 'natural,' biological factors, as on socioeconomic ones." Accordingly, "the principle of providing each worker with a separate room must be followed without deviation." Any attempt to distinguish between single and married residents was "totally unjustified opportunism":[28]

It is obvious that in the socialist way of life each worker can be considered both "single" and "married" at the same time because any of today's "single" people may become "married" tomorrow, and any of today's couples may tomorrow become two single individuals, and because those elements of compulsion, most particularly the shortage of housing and common raising of children, that today often force men and women to continue their relationship and cohabitation even when the inner bond between them is broken and nothing else keeps them together, will become increasingly irrelevant with the provision of communal satisfaction of private needs and public education for children.[29]

This did not mean that couples could not choose to live together for as long as mutual affection persisted:

> All rooms in a residential combine should be connected with internal doors or movable partitions (which are much more expensive, but also much better). If a husband and wife wish to live together, they can receive two contiguous rooms connected by a door, i.e., something resembling a small apartment, or open the partition and transform the two rooms into one. But if one of the parties decides to have a separate room or end the relationship completely, the door or partition can be shut. If a worker's family wishes to keep their children at first (although this is definitely irrational and can last for only a very short period of time), the children may be assigned to a third room, in which case the family will receive something like a three-room apartment.[30]

The period of time would have to be very short. Today's children were tomorrow's "new men and women." "Children who are now five or six will enter what we currently call 'middle school' (at the age of around twelve) under completely new conditions—conditions of a totally or almost totally fulfilled socialism." Under these conditions, "children will no longer be 'the property' of their parents: they will be 'the property' of the state, which will take upon itself the solution of all problems involved in child rearing." Not everyone accepted Sabsovich's timetable or his idea of separate "children's towns" (along the lines of young Boris's dream in Libedinsky's *The Birth of a Hero*), but every Bolshevik assumed that, in the "near future," the state would take upon itself the solution of all problems involved in child rearing.[31]

Sabsovich's main opponents were the "disurbanists," who believed that communal houses were too similar to prerevolutionary workers' barracks. According to the architect Aleksandr Pasternak (brother of Boris, friend of Zbarsky, and, thanks to the latter, one of the designers of the first Lenin Mausoleum and the Karpov Biochemistry Institute),

> Will a large army of people accidentally assembled in one building become a true commune? And, even if they do, will it be able to live normally in a communal house, whose most characteristic features (we have now seen some graphic renditions of the theoretical concept) are extremely long corridors lined with tiny cells, long lines to the most basic facilities (sinks, toilets, coat racks), and equally long lines to the cafeteria, where people have to gulp down their meals with the speed of a visitor to a railway-station café who is late for

his train (you can't detain a comrade who is waiting for his plate, fork, and knife, can you?).[32]

Sabsovich had compared capitalist urbanism to "life in stone cages." Would not such "enormous, heavy, monumental, and permanent" communal houses produce more of the same? According to the main ideologue of disurbanism, Mikhail Okhitovich, all modern cities and their illegitimate "communal" offspring were Babylons and Carthages that "must be destroyed." Under primitive communism, common labor had required common living. Modern communism was different. "Modern communism must unite, through a common production process, hundreds of millions of people, at the very least. If collective labor were always accompanied by collective living arrangements, it would mean building one house for several hundred million." This would, of course, be absurd—as would the idea that "our whole planet should be equipped with one laundry and one cafeteria."[33]

Human beings, according to Okhitovich, had always lived where they worked. The nomads' herds moved around, and so did the nomads. The peasants' fields were stationary, and so were the peasants. Cities were an aberration, "the result of the separation of artisanship from agriculture, the separation of processing from extraction." The task of socialism was to overcome the inequality and irrationality of urban life, which inevitably resulted from the inequality and irrationality of capitalism. In Pasternak's formulation, "the fulfillment of the ideas of Marx, Engels, and Lenin—the elimination of the gap between the city (excessive concentration) and the countryside (idiocy and isolation) and the creation, in their place, of new forms of settlement that would be the same for everybody (i.e., the socialist, uniform distribution of working populations)—is the unique historical role that has fallen to our country, our Union."[34]

The main hurdle, as usual, was the coresidential family. According to Okhitovich, the rural patriarchal dwelling housed four generations; the burgher's dwelling, two generations; and the modern capitalist dwelling (a cottage or an apartment), one generation. Under socialism, all housing would be individual. Why does this not happen under capitalism?

Because husband and wife cannot end the division of labor between them, just as the capitalist is connected by the division of labor to his hired labor. Husband and wife are connected by common economic interests, common investments, and the inheritance of property. In the same way, the proletarian family is brought together by the common interest in reproducing its labor and by the hope that their children would support them in their old age.

Only socialism will allow society to confront the human producer directly, while allowing the human producer to confront social relations directly, without mediation.

For it will put an end to the division of labor between a man and a woman.[35]

The fact that Communism stood for the abolition of the division of labor meant that it stood for the abolition of the family and, ultimately, for the freedom of the individual "to hunt in the morning, fish in the afternoon, rear cattle in the evening, criticise after dinner, just as I have a mind, without ever becoming hunter, fisherman, herdsman or critic" (as Marx had put it). Collectivism did not represent monotony or anonymity. "Celebrating the collective while ignoring the individual is like praising the Russian language while banning particular Russian words." In fact, wrote Okhitovich, "the stronger the collective bonds, the stronger the individuals composing that collective." Private property would be gone,

> but human beings will continue to be born separately, not collectively. They will always eat, drink, and sleep—i.e., *consume*—separately. . . . The disappearance of private property will be followed by the disappearance of the bourgeois, capitalist property and the bourgeois, capitalist individual, but personal property, personal consumption, personal initiative, personal level of development, personal hands, personal legs, personal heads, and personal brains will not only not disappear, but will, for the first time, become accessible to everyone, and not only to the privileged few, as was the case before socialism.[36]

Sabsovich was right that workers were entitled to their own separate rooms, argued the disurbanists, but surely there was no need to confine those rooms to awkward, inflexible, immovable buildings. The only dwelling fit for Communism was the kind that "could be improved, like clothing, by augmenting width and height, increasing size of windows, etc. But is this thinkable with the old technology? No, only prefabricated houses, easy to assemble, dismantle, and enlarge, will be able to meet the needs of each developing individual." Such houses would be light, mobile, and connected to the world by radio, telephone, and constantly improving means of transportation, terrestrial or otherwise. And they would certainly fit the social needs of developing individuals much better than Sabsovich's doors and partitions. As Pasternak explained, "No one will object if husband and wife, or two close buddies, or even several good friends place their houses next to each other and link them up; each unit will remain autonomous, with its own separate entrance and access to the garden. But if the couple separates, or friends have an argument, or one of them gets married, there will be no complications with 'living space,' since the units can, at any moment, be decoupled, enlarged, or reduced, or even dismantled entirely and moved to a different location."[37]

Both the urbanists and disurbanists were disurbanists. The main point of contention was whether modern cities were to be broken up into economic and residential nodes consisting of a few communal houses surrounded by "green zones," or "decentered" and "destationized" completely. No one wished to preserve city streets and blocks; the question was whether the individual "cells" were to be attached to long corridors in mul-tistory communal houses or to endless roads traversing the newly decen-tered landscape (or not attached to anything at all: Bukharin's father-in-law, Yuri Larin, envisioned flying, floating, and rolling individual dwellings, with each human being behaving "like a snail carrying its own shell").[38]

Both the urbanists and disurbanists were collectivists. Most human activities, with the exception of urination, defecation, and procreation, were to be conducted in public. Sleep was a matter of debate. Konstantin Melnikov designed giant "sleep laboratories" with mechanically produced fresh scents and soothing sounds. N. Kuzmin proposed two classes of bed-rooms: "group bedrooms" for six people and double bedrooms "for former 'husbands' and 'wives.'" Most planners preferred individual cells. The main question was how many people to assign to each shower room, laundry, or cafeteria or where to position oneself between the two poles of countless mobile cafeterias, on the one hand, and a single planetwide "factory-kitchen, on the other."[39]

Both the urbanists and disurbanists were individualists. "In place of the old bourgeois society, with its classes and class antagonisms," pro-claimed one of the most oft-quoted passages of the *Communist Manifesto*, "we shall have an association, in which the free development of each is the condition for the free development of all." "The stronger the individual," wrote Okhitovich, perfectly uncontroversially, "the stronger the collective served by that individual." Bourgeois individualism was a bad thing; the socialist individual was the measure of all things. In the absence of classes, any association of randomly assembled Soviet citizens could be-come a collective. Some Soviets were better prepared than others, but, except for the unmasked enemies who needed to be "reforged" before being reincorporated, all Soviets were ultimately interchangeable. A per-son was a member of a residential-building collective by virtue of residing in a building, a member of a kindergarten collective by virtue of being a kindergartner, and a member of an office collective by virtue of being an office clerk. Starting with the Stalin Revolution (the "great breakthrough"), most Soviets were assumed faithful until proven guilty. If a commune was a coresidential community of people "united by a common goal," and if all Soviets, except for a handful of increasingly desperate enemies, were united by the common goal of building socialism, then the Soviet Union was one very large commune. Because there were no "antagonistic" differ-ences within Soviet society, and no stronger commitments than the one to socialism, it did not matter which collective a particular Soviet belonged to. "Collectivism" stood for a direct connection between the individual and the state (Soviet universalism), or a willingness to see any group of Soviets as a community united by the common goal of building socialism.

"Bourgeois individualism" represented an attempt to surround the in-dividual with an extra protective layer; a desire to belong to an untrans-parent community. Each Soviet belonged in his own cell, or shell. "This room," wrote Lunacharsky, "is not only a place for sleeping. . . . Here begins the absolute right of the individual, which no one is allowed to violate." Where the Soviet did not belong was in a "bourgeois-family" apartment, or "an autonomous, isolated unit that normally includes a separate entrance, one to three rooms, a kitchen, and other auxiliary spaces." "It makes no difference," wrote Kuzmin on behalf of all the architects of the future, "what the number or quality of such apartments is, or whether they are built as separate cottages or as units within multistory apartment buildings or so-called communal houses (called so in order to discredit a revolutionary idea), for what kind of 'communal house' is it, if it consists of apartments?"[40]

Bourgeois individualism, in other words, was "family individualism." Soviet collectivism consisted of individuals; bourgeois individualism resided in families. Emancipation—primarily of women, but also of children and eventually of all—meant freedom from the family. The "residential cells" of emancipated men, women, and children would be homes free of bourgeois domesticity (*meshchanstvo*). As one instruction manual put it, "dwellings in which people spend most of their lives from birth to death must be hygienic, i.e., spacious, light, warm, and dry. They must not contain stale air, dampness, or dirt." They must, in other words, be free of the swamp and everything associated with it: greasy dishes, primus stoves, and dark corners on the one hand, and "muslin curtains, potted geraniums, and caged canaries," on the other. The Revolution's last and decisive battle was to be against "velvet-covered albums resting on small tables covered with lace doilies." Softness threatened suffocation: nothing was more dangerous than the down pillow and double bed. Functional furniture was to be provided by the state (so as to liberate the workers from enslavement to things); as many pieces as possible—desks, beds, trays, stools, closets, bookshelves, and ironing boards—were to be folded away into special niches. Rooms were to resemble ships' cabins or train compartments. Everyone quoted Le Corbusier to the effect that "whatever is not necessary must be discarded" (or, in Mayakovsky's version, "rid your room of all useless stuff: it will get cleaner and be big enough"). As Kritsman wrote in *The Heroic Period of the Great Russian Revolution*, "the motto of organic eras, 'it exists, therefore it is needed,' is replaced by a very different one: 'If it is needed, it exists, if it is not needed, it will be destroyed.'" What Kritsman had in mind was "the destruction of fetishistic relations and the establishment of direct, open, and immediate connections among various parts of the Soviet economy." What the architects of the future were attempting to accomplish was the establishment of direct, open, and immediate connections among Soviet individuals—connections undisturbed by "useless stuff" or durable affections.[41]

Most of the architects of the future were not architects. Those who were did not get a chance to build very much. The disurbanists, in particular, had to wait for the decentralization of production, "destationization" of

the population, and the "electrification of the whole country." M. Ya. Ginzburg and M. O. Barshch designed a "Green City" on stilts to be built outside
of Moscow, and two large teams proposed long "ribbons" of stackable
dwellings for Magnitogorsk, but none materialized since there was no infrastructure. Communal houses were easier to create—by converting existing dormitories or building one house at a time. One such structure in
Moscow was Ivan Nikolaev's communal house for students, built in 1929–
30. It was based on five fundamental principles: "The expulsion of the
primus stove is the first step. Domestic collectivization and the organization of the learning process is the second step. The third step is the hy-
gienization and sanitation of everyday life. The fourth step is the transition to full self-service and the mechanization of the cleaning operations.
The fifth step is the collectivization of the children's sector." The building
consisted of two parallel units connected by a "sanitary block." The three-
story day-use section included a cafeteria, gym, health center, solarium,
children's sector, library with a large study area, and multiple rooms for
club activities. Passing through the sanitary block at the end of the day,
residents were required to take a shower and change into different clothes.
The eight-story nighttime section contained one thousand six-by-six-
meter "sleeping cubicles," organized along narrow two-hundred–meter
corridors. Each cubicle contained two bunks, two stools, and a concrete
windowsill that served as a desk. In the mornings, students would exercise
on the balconies of the sanitary block before proceeding to their study
areas. During the day, the sleeping unit was closed to residents for ventilation and "sanitation" purposes.[42]

What might work for university students did not—yet—work for workers' families ("although this was definitely irrational and could last for

Ivan Nikolaev's communal house

only a very short period of time"). Most experimental housing built during the First Five-Year Plan was of the "transitional type," in which residents were provided with collective services but allowed—for the time being—to live in family apartments. The most celebrated such building was M. Ya. Ginzburg's and I. F. Milinis's House of the Commissariat of Finance (Narkomfin) on Novinsky Boulevard in Moscow (1928–30). According to a report on the project's completion,

> The huge building is 82 meters long; in place of a ground floor are columns—slim, graceful columns that carry the heavy weight of the gray stone. If not for these columns, which endow the building with a certain lightness, it might be taken for an ocean liner. The same flat roof, terrace-style balconies, radio masts, and continuous horizontal windows. The tall ventilation chimney enhances the resemblance. . . .
>
> The building is traversed by well-lighted corridors, from which small stairways lead up and down to the residential cells. Each apartment consists of a tall, double-lighted room for daytime activities and low sleeping lofts which are an integral part of the interior space.
>
> The only "problem" with all the apartments in the new building is that they have no room for that broad, solid chest of drawers and absolutely no space for a primus stove.
>
> Every apartment has clothes closets, a tiny anteroom for changing, and solid, sliding windows. The so-called "kitchen element" is in a separate corner. This "unhealthy element" consists of a small cabinet with an exhaust fan, several gas burners, a small refrigerator, a cabinet for dishes, and a sink.
>
> For the sake of fairness, it must be noted that this bow in the direction of the old domestic arrangements is moderated by the fact that, if desired, the whole kitchen element may be tossed out in favor of public nutrition.
>
> The communal "barge" is attached to the residential unit by a heated bridgeway. It has an engine room (kitchen) below, a cafeteria for two hundred people with windows on the opposite walls on the floor above, and a library, reading room, and pool hall on the third floor. Next to the cafeteria is a well-equipped gym and shower rooms. . . .
>
> "A good house," says an elderly seasonal worker, while planing a board. "Except you can't live in it just any old way. . . ."
>
> Indeed, one must know how to live in it. The trick is to be able to leave all kinds of domestic junk behind in the old house in order not to smuggle the spirit of the old stone boxes into the new apartment.[43]

The Narkomfin house was routinely represented as a prototype for the mass-produced—and, with a few adjustments, communal—housing of the

Narkomfin house

future. The "ocean liner" was a common metaphor combining the two main attributes of the age: mobility and monumentality. Another one was the airplane (a new interpretation of the cross), with long and narrow residential wings attached to oval or square service units by perpendicular bridges or walkways. Ginzburg's design, and the constructivist aesthetic in general, combated the dampness and softness of domesticity with light, air, transparency, and the pure lines of elementary ("industrial") geometric forms. Each significant social function was encased within its own, rigidly articulated, but not self-contained, "volume." Life inside consisted of "processes" that involved synchronized movements of people analogous to Podvoisky's mass games. The dominant indoor theme was the assembly line (Miliutin's "functional-flow principle"): furniture served as equipment; human flows obeyed specific "schedules of motion"; and the entire "residential shell" was characterized by what one architect called "plastic Puritanism and austere nakedness."[44]

Human life began with work, could not be separated from work, and needed to be organized accordingly. Kerzhentsev's "love of responsibility" was to be applied to the "process of everyday life" to produce Communism as "embodied harmony, where everything happens with accuracy, precision, and correctness." Kerzhentsev's "sense of time" was to be combined with the architect's sense of space to produce harmonious men and women who love what they cannot escape. As Kuzmin put it, "There is no such thing as absolute rest. Human beings work all the time (even when they are asleep). Architecture influences human work with all of its material elements. The scientific organization of the material elements of architecture (light, color, form, ventilation, etc.), or rather, the scientific organization of work, is, at the same time, the organization of human emotions, which are a direct consequence of labor productivity." The question was whether the workers could be trusted "not to smuggle into a new apartment the spirit of the old stone boxes." Speaking on behalf of Ginzburg's "transitional" approach, the head of the Art Department of the Commissariat of Enlightenment, Alfred Kurella, argued that they could not. "If we build houses with only a communal kitchen, the worker is going to set up a primus stove in his room." Citing the success of forced collectivization, Kuzmin argued that they could—and that Ginzburg's not-quite communal "communal houses" were "an insult" to both Lenin's ideas and the unfolding "socialist reconstruction."[45]

It soon turned out that the question was not whether they could be trusted, but whether they should. The answer, according to a preview of the official position, written by Koltsov, was that they should not. In a *Pravda* article published on May 1, 1930, two months after Stalin's "Dizzy with Success," he hinted that the primus stove might be redeemable, that leftism might, once again, be infantile, and that the end of the socialist offensive might be in sight. Soviet architects, he wrote, were suffering from "intoxicating dizziness." The urbanists were preaching the creation of "enormous barracks, where the children are totally isolated from their parents, all aspects of a worker's life are strictly regimented, everything is done on command, and where the greatest virtue is visibility and the greatest sin is solitude, even for the purpose of reflection and intellectual work." The disurbanists, meanwhile, were proposing to settle the worker and his wife in two separate cabins on stilts, with an automobile underneath. "When the welder Kuzma wants to see his Praskovia, he must climb down his ladder, get into his automobile, and drive down a highway built especially for the purpose." These absurd projects discredited socialist ideas, provoked the legitimate indignation of the workers, and amounted to wrecking. "No one has the right, whatever the justification, to fight against the basic needs of human nature, including the desire to spend some time by oneself or the desire to be close to one's child."[46]

Within three weeks, Koltsov's elaboration of the official position had been reformulated as the Central Committee decree "On Work toward Transforming Everyday Life":

> The Central Committee notes that, simultaneously with the growth of the movement for a socialist way of life, certain comrades (Sabsovich, and to some degree, Yu. Larin and others) are engaging in totally unjustified, semifantastical, and therefore extremely harmful attempts to surmount "in one leap" those hurdles along the path toward a socialist transformation of everyday life that are rooted, on the one hand, in the country's economic and cultural backwardness, and, on the other, in the need, at the present moment, to mobilize all available resources for the fastest possible industrialization of the country, which alone is capable of creating the true material conditions for the radical transformation of everyday life.[47]

The argument was consistent with the spring 1930 respite from the "dizziness" of collectivization. The utopian schemes of certain comrades were harmful because they cost too much money, put the cart before the industrial base, advocated things for which the culturally backward population was not ready, contradicted natural human desires, and discredited the project of a genuine and radical transformation of those desires.

The House of Government was lucky. By May 1930, its shape and structure had long been determined, its budget exceeded, and its walls completed. It had often been accused of being elitist and wasteful. The architect A. L. Pasternak had written:

> A large residential complex for the employees of the Central Executive Committee and the Council of People's Commissars is being built in Moscow right now. It has a club, theater, cafeteria, laundry, grocery store, day-care center, and even a walk-in clinic. Here, one would have thought, is a model for a new socialist dwelling. However, the residential sector of the complex consists exclusively of *apartments* made to accommodate the family economy and the individual servicing of family needs, i.e., *circumscribed, autonomous family life* (the apartments have *their own* kitchens, bathtubs, etc.).
>
> Here we find two *negative* facts of our housing policy: on the one hand, the spread of individual apartments, which predetermine the nature of our dwellings and, consequently, our urban life for a long time to come (in the case of stone buildings, no less than 60 to 70 years); and, on the other hand, an incorrect interpretation of the idea of a communal house, which results in the postponement, and perhaps the discrediting, of the introduction of new social relations into the masses.[48]

In May 1930, however, it turned out that it was Pasternak and his fellow utopians who were guilty of discrediting new social relations, and that the House of Government was a model building "of the transitional type." Luck may not have been the only reason for Iofan's vindication: some of the people involved in the writing of the decree were the House's sponsors, and most were its future residents (including Koltsov, who had launched the attack). It is possible that they were not quite ready to part with their children or live in individual cells; it is certain that most of them, as good Marxists, believed that "industrialization alone was capable of creating the true material conditions for a radical transformation of everyday life."[49]

The House was, indeed, "transitional" in Ginzburg's terms: the public sector was designed to cover a wide variety of needs, while the residential block allowed for a "circumscribed, autonomous family life." The club (still referred to as the "Rykov Club" in 1930 but soon to be renamed after Kalinin) included a cafeteria capable of serving all House residents, a theater for 1,300 spectators, a library, several dozen rooms for various activities (from playing billiards to symphony orchestra rehearsals), and, above the theater, both tennis and basketball courts, two gyms, and several shower rooms. There was also a bank, laundry, telegraph, post office, day-care center, walk-in clinic, hairdresser's salon, grocery store, department store, and movie theater for 1,500 spectators (the Shock Worker) with a café, reading room, and band stage. The residential part consisted of seven ten- to eleven-story units, with a total of twenty-four entryways (numbered, for unknown reasons, 1–10 and 12–25), two apartments per floor, 505 apartments altogether. Each apartment had three, four, or more furnished rooms with large windows; a kitchen with gas stove, garbage chute, exhaust fan, and fold-away bunk for the maid; a bathroom with bathtub and sink; a separate toilet, telephone, and both hot and cold running water. All apartments had cross ventilation and windows on both sides (including in the kitchen, bathroom, and toilet). Some apartments, particularly those facing the river (Entryways 1 and 12) were much larger than others. Some entryways had cargo, as well as passenger, elevators.

The "utopians" (both urbanists and disurbanists) seemed justified in arguing that the House of Government was functionally similar to bourgeois apartment buildings. As early as 1878, a New York court had formally distinguished between tenements, which housed several families living independently under one roof, and apartment buildings, which provided collective services to its residents. Most luxury apartment buildings in New York had public kitchens, restaurants, and laundries; some had play areas and dining rooms for children. The Dakota, on Central Park West between Seventy-Second and Seventy-Third Streets, had all those things plus croquet lawns and tennis courts. Expensive apartment-hotels were closer to communal houses in that they were designed for bachelors and did not have private kitchens.[50]

The House of Government was transitional in another sense: stylistically, it was both constructivist and neoclassical. The whole complex was in the shape of a triangle, with the base (the club) facing the river, the truncated tip (the movie theater) abutting the Drainage Canal, and the store and laundry buildings centering the east and west sides, respectively. Plain, rectangular residential blocks of uneven height connected these public units, which served as the nodes of the composition and flaunted their functions in their design. The continuous horizontal windows above the club entrance mirrored the length of the gymnasium; the semicircular rear of the club repeated the shape of both the theater auditorium and dining room; the commercial unit (which included the two stores and hairdresser's salon) stood out for its relatively small size and large windows; while the movie theater, with its huge semicone sitting atop a square base, resembled a giant flashlight pointing toward the island's Arrowhead.

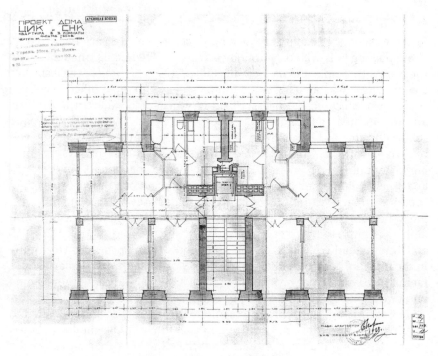

Three-room apartment floor plan

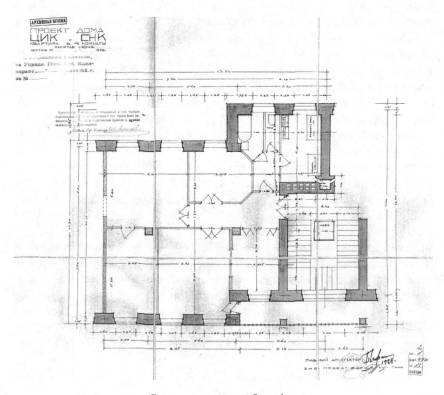

Four-room apartment floor plan

Interior view of one of the
stairway entrances

Apartment door on one of the floors.
On the left is the elevator door.

Cafeteria

Movie theater foyer

Movie theater stairway

Movie theater reading room

Club stairway

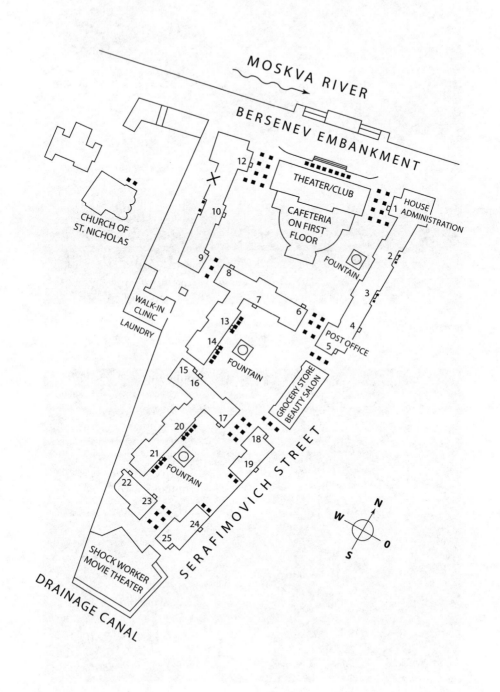

MOSKVA RIVER

BERSENEV EMBANKMENT

CHURCH OF ST. NICHOLAS

12

10

9

X

THEATER/CLUB

CAFETERIA ON FIRST FLOOR

FOUNTAIN

HOUSE ADMINISTRATION

1

2

3

4

5

WALK-IN CLINIC

LAUNDRY

8

7

6

POST OFFICE

13

14

FOUNTAIN

15

16

17

GROCERY STORE

BEAUTY SALON

20

21

FOUNTAIN

18

19

22

23

24

25

SHOCK WORKER MOVIE THEATER

SERAFIMOVICH STREET

DRAINAGE CANAL

N
W   O
S

The constructivist elements did not add up to a constructivist whole, however. Because of the domination of massive, bottom-heavy rectangular blocks squeezed into a small area bounded by water, the overall impression was of immobile, fortresslike solidity. The three thousand piles connecting the building to the Swamp's bedrock were hidden from view, and the newly raised and reinforced embankment was clothed in granite. The island location suggested a continued use of the ship metaphor, but it was not easy to imagine the House of Government staying afloat. Most dramatically, the side bordering the embankment was designed as a solemn, palatial facade. Flat, grand, and symmetrical, with its three colonnades flanked by the huge towers of Entryways 1 and 12, it looked out across the river toward the Museum of Fine Arts, whose Ionic portico it attempted, in rough outline, to reflect.[51]

As Lunacharsky wrote, against fashion, while the House of Government was still being built, classicism was not one architectural style among many—it was a universal "language of architecture that fit many different epochs. Just as some geometric forms—the square, the cube, the circle, and the sphere—represent something essentially rational, subject to modifications that render them vital and flexible but always remaining the eternal elements of our formal language, so most classical architectural forms are qualitatively different from all others because they are correct irrespective of time periods."[52]

The epoch of the First Five-Year Plan and great breakthrough, known to contemporaries as the "period of reconstruction" or the "period of transition," was embodied in two iconic buildings completed at about the same time: the Lenin Mausoleum and the House of Government. One contained the leader-founder; the other his successors. One was a small structure designed to dominate a historic square; the other a huge fortress meant to fill a swamp. One represented the center of New Jerusalem; the other the first in a series of endlessly reproducible dwellings for its inhabitants. Both attempted to combine, and perhaps identify, the avant-garde's search for the "eternal elements of our formal language" with the "classical architectural forms." The mausoleum consisted of a massive cube supporting a stepped pyramid crowned with a portico. The House of Government resembled a Timurid mausoleum, with a tall, flat facade both shielding and advertising the tomb's sacred contents.[53]

The mausoleum was carefully inserted into the hallowed space of Red Square. The House of Government resembled an island within an island. The tall archways leading into the inner courtyards were blocked by heavy gates; the two embankments framing the building from the north and south were Siamese dead ends conjoined at the Arrowhead; the Big Stone Bridge would soon be elevated, turning All Saints Street into another dead end; and the western side, mostly invisible to pedestrians, overlooked the Einem (now Red October) Candy Factory, with St. Nicholas and a few other remnants of the Swamp cowering in perpetual shadow in between.

View from the bridge

View from the Kremlin

View from the cathedral

View from All Saints Street

View from the Drainage Canal (Ditch)

Relocation of the Big Stone Bridge (for the purpose of improving traffic access)

• • •

The House of Government was not going to remain an island for very long: a second House of Government was to be built on Bolotnaia (Swamp) Square, and a third one, across the river, in Zariadye (a crowded artisans' quarter east of the Kremlin). But the task was not to fight the Swamp one building at a time: the task was to rebuild the capital along with the rest of the country. As Koltsov had written after the introduction of NEP in 1921, old Moscow, "bareheaded and unkempt," had "crept out from under the rubble and poked her head up, grinning her old hag's grin." Malevolent and apparently immortal, she "looked the new world in the eye and bared her teeth, wishing to live on and to get fat again."[54]

It would take the great breakthrough to finish her off. In the words of a 1930 article, "The disorganized Moscow street has no face of its own, no perspective, no hint of any consistency of growth: from an eight-story 'sky-scraper,' your eye slips down, with a sick feeling, into the gap of one-storyness; the street looks like a jaw with rotten, uneven, chipped teeth. Old Moscow—the way it is now—will inevitably, and very soon, become a serious brake on our advance. Socialism cannot be squeezed into an old, ill-fitting, worn-out shell." Socialism required a new capital, and the new capital required a proper plan. "In this regard, we are lagging behind the capitals of bourgeois Europe. For several decades now, Paris has been built and rebuilt according to the so-called Haussmann plan. Australia has announced an international competition for the best design of its capital. But here, in the land of the plan, in the country that created the five-year plan, our capital, Moscow, continues to grow and develop spontaneously, according to the wishes of particular developers and without any regulation."[55]

The construction of the mausoleum and the House of Government was a good beginning, but it was the Palace of Soviets—the site of national congresses and mass processions, the official stage for the House's residents, and the ultimate public building of all time—that was going to provide the center around which the new world would be built. On February 6, 1931, while still working on the House of Government, Boris Iofan submitted a proposal and a timetable for the design competition; in spring 1931, a preliminary competition was held (Iofan was both a contestant and the chief architect within the Construction Administration); and on July 13, 1931, the presidium of the Central Executive Committee issued a decree "on the construction of the Palace of Soviets on the square of the Cathedral of Christ the Savior and the demolition of the latter." The palace was to contain a main auditorium for 15,000 people, a second auditorium for 5,900 people, two additional halls for 200 people each, and an administrative area. By the December 1 deadline, 272 projects, including 160 professional designs, had been submitted to the Construction Council chaired by Molotov. On December 5, the Cathedral of Christ the Savior was dynamited. On February 28, 1932, the commission announced that the three

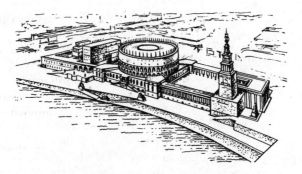

Zholtovsky's 1931 design for the Palace of Soviets

Iofan's 1931 design

Hamilton's 1931 design

first prizes would be awarded to Ivan Zholtovsky, Boris Iofan, and an American, Hector Hamilton. Zholtovsky's design included a tower that resembled a Kremlin tower and an auditorium that resembled the Colosseum in Rome. Iofan's design was similar to Zholtovsky's except that the tower and the colosseum were stripped of overt classical references. Hamilton's massive rectangular fortress resembled Iofan's House of Government (which was to serve as its shadow on the other side of the river).[56]

None of the three winning designs was perfect, however (Iofan's was considered "not organic enough"). According to the Construction Council, "the monumentality, simplicity, integrity, and grace of the architectural interpretation of the Palace of Soviets associated with the greatness of our socialist construction have not received their full expression in any of the submitted projects." The announcement for a new, closed contest called for one monumental building of "a boldly tall composition" devoid of "temple motifs" and located on a large square not delimited "by colonnades or other structures that might interfere with the impression of openness."[57]

By the spring of 1933, two closed competitions (for twenty invited participants and then, separately, for five finalists) resulted in a victory for Iofan, whose design represented a massive rectangular platform, with an elaborate facade resembling the Great Altar at Pergamon, supporting a three-tiered cylindrical tower and an eighteen-meter statue placed off-center above the portico. "This bold, firm, articulated ascent," wrote Lunacharsky, "is not an imploring gaze toward heaven, but, rather, a storming of the heights from below." On May 10, 1933, the Construction Council adopted Iofan's design as the project's "baseline," but mandated that the building "culminate in a massive statue of Lenin 50 to 75 meters high, so that the entire Palace of Soviets would serve as a pedestal for the figure of Lenin." On June 4, 1933, the Council appointed V. A. Shchuko and V. G. Gelfreikh, who had recently won the Lenin Library competition and whose own Palace of Soviets submission was a variation on the theme of the Doge's Palace in Venice, as Iofan's "coauthors." The compromise version, with the Lenin statue centered at the top and the upper cylinder elongated in order to accommodate its size, was officially accepted in 1934. Iofan was appointed chief architect.[58]

According to a book about the final version of the design, the Palace of Soviets was to be 416 meters (1,365 feet) high. "It will be the highest structure on earth: higher than the Egyptian pyramids, higher than the Eiffel Tower, higher than the American skyscrapers." It would also be the biggest: "In order to equal the internal space of the future Palace in Moscow, one would have to add up the volumes of the six largest American skyscrapers." The statue of Lenin would weigh six thousand tons and reach a height of one hundred meters. "It will be three times as high and two-and-a-half times as heavy as the famous Statue of Liberty." It would soar above the clouds, and, on clear days, be visible seventy kilometers from Moscow. "At night, the brightly lit-up shape of the statue of Ilich would be seen . . . even farther away: a majestic lighthouse marking the spot of the socialist capital of the world."[59]

The building was to house the world's first genuine parliament—the Supreme Soviet, its presidium, and its administrative apparatus—as well as the central state archive and countless museums, winter gardens, cafeterias, and reception halls.[60]

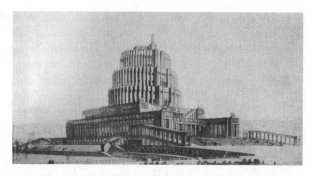

Iofan's 1933 design

Gelfreikh and Shchuko's 1933 design

Iofan, Gelfreikh, and Shchuko's 1933 design

Palace of Soviets

The six columns of the Main Entrance to the Palace of Soviets will bear the engravings of the six commandments from the oath that Comrade Stalin took after Lenin's death. These commandments will also be represented in sculptures.

Beyond the colonnade and loggias will be the Hall of the Stalin Constitution, which will seat 1,500 people, and, finally, the Great Hall. Figures are powerless in this case, so perhaps a comparison will help: the space of the Great Hall will be almost twice as great as the entire space of the House of Government, complete with all its residential buildings and theaters.[61]

The Palace of Soviets was going to be the ultimate wonder of the world: a tower that reached unto heaven not out of pride, but in triumph; a tower that gathered the scattered languages of the earth and made them one; Jacob's ladder in stone and concrete:

There was once the Lighthouse of Alexandria, which stood at the mouth of the Nile and helped ships find their way into that trading port of the ancient world.

There were the Hanging Gardens of Babylon. There were the great works of religious art: the Temple of Artemis at Ephesus and Phidias's gold and ivory statue of Zeus at Olympia.

In later years, mankind created even more grandiose structures: the Panama and Suez canals connected oceans; the St. Gotthard and Simplon tunnels cut through the rock of the Alps; the Eiffel Tower rose over Paris.[62]

All of these structures were great masterpieces, but they were built by slaves in the service of false gods. In the Soviet Union, people would be free to build an indestructible monument to their own future:

> State borders will vanish from the map of the world. The earth's very landscape will change. Communist settlements, completely different from the old cities, will rise up. Man will defeat space. Electricity will plow the fields of Australia, China, and Africa. But the Palace of Soviets, crowned with the statue of Ilich, will still stand on the bank of the Moskva River. People—generation after generation—will be born, live happy lives, and gradually grow old, but the Palace of Soviets, familiar to them from their favorite children's books, will remain the same as we will see it in a few years. Centuries will leave no traces on it, for we will build it in such a way that it will stand for eternity. It is a monument to Lenin![63]

The new center of Moscow was to be formed by three linked squares. The mausoleum containing Lenin's body and the Palace of Soviets supporting the Lenin statue would be connected to a third rectangular square named after Lenin's patronymic (Ilich, or the son of Elijah). Radiating out from them would be straight, broad avenues, including "the ceremonial thoroughfare of Greater Moscow, Lenin Avenue." The House of Government was the first in a series of new buildings meant to frame the city's core. None of them, however, was to look like the House of Government. As Kaganovich said in September 1934, some buildings "overwhelm the individual with their stone blocks, their heavy mass. . . . The House of Government, designed by Iofan, is not a success in this regard because its top is heavier than its bottom. We are proud of this house as the biggest, most important, and most cultured house we have built, but its composition is a bit too heavy and cannot serve as a model for future construction."[64]

■ ■ ■

The literature of the epoch of great construction sites was mostly about great construction sites. To take the best known, Yuri Olesha's *Envy* (1927, a part of the movement's advance detachment) is about the building of a giant public kitchen; Ilya Ilf and Evgeny Petrov's *The Golden Calf* (1931) is,

Palace of Soviets and the new Moscow

in part, about the building of the Turkestan-Siberia Railway; Valentin Kataev's *Time, Forward!* (1932) is about the building of the Magnitogorsk Steel Mill; Ilya Ehrenburg's *The Second Day* (1933) is about the building of the Kuznetsk Steel Mill; Boris Pilniak's *The Volga Flows into the Caspian Sea* (1930), Marietta Shaginian's *Hydrocentral* (1931), Bruno Jasienski's *Man Changes His Skin* (1932), and Fedor Gladkov's *Energy* (1933) are about the building of river dams; Leonid Leonov's *The Sot'* (1929) is about the building of a paper mill (on the River Sot'); the multiauthored *The White Sea–Baltic Canal* (1934) is about the building of the White Sea–Baltic Canal; and Andrei Platonov's "Doubting Makar" (1929) and *The Foundation Pit* (1930) are each about the building of an eternal house.[65]

Most of them would later be classified as "production novels," but none of them truly is one, because no actual production—of steel, paper, electricity, or sausages—ever takes place. They are, rather, construction stories—

or, since human souls are also under construction—construction-cum-conversion stories. What matters is the act of building—a new world, a new Jerusalem, a new tower that will reach the heavens. "You've got a proper Socialist International here," says a visiting foreign correspondent in Jasienski's *Man Changes His Skin*. "Yes, we've got a real Tower of Babel" responds the head of construction, and he begins to count:

> Hold on, let me see: the Tajiks, make one, the Uzbeks, two, the Kazakhs, three, the Kyrgyz, four, the Russians, five, the Ukrainians, six, the Lezgians, seven, the Ossetians, eight, the Persians, nine, the Indians, ten—that's right, we've got Indians, too, émigrés. The Afghans make eleven: there are several Afghan crews, right here and in Sector Three. Twenty percent of the drivers are Tatars—that's twelve. In the repair shop, there are some Germans and Poles—that's fourteen. Among the engineers there are Georgians, Armenians, and Jews—that's already seventeen. There are also two American engineers, one of whom is the head of this sector—that's eighteen. Did I forget anybody?
> "There are some Turks, too, Comrade Commander."
> "That's right: there are some Turks, and also some Turkmen."[66]

In Kataev's Magnitogorsk, there are "the men of Kostroma with their finely distended nostrils, Kazan Tatars, Caucasians (Georgians and Chechens), Bashkirs, Germans, Muscovites, Leningraders in coats and Tolstoy shirts, Ukrainians, Jews, and Belorussians." In Ehrenburg's Kuznetsk, there are "Ukrainians and Tatars, Buriats, Cheremis, Kalmyks, peasants from Perm and Kaluga, coal miners from Yuzovka, turners from Kolomna, bearded road pavers from Riazan, Komsomols, exiled kulaks, unemployed miners from Westphalia and Silesia, street traders from the Sukharevka flea market, embezzlers sentenced to forced labor, enthusiasts, swindlers, and even sectarian preachers." And in Leonov's *The Sot'*, there are sawyers and glaziers from Ryazan, stonemasons and stove fitters from Vyatka and Tver, plasterers from Vologda, painters from Kostroma, diggers from Smolensk, and carpenters from Vladimir. "From Perm they came, and from Vyatka, and from all the provinces where the old peasant ways passed down from their forefathers were no longer possible, but new ones had not yet arrived." One of the carpenters offers to send for the young women, too, but the head of construction shakes his head: "We're building a paper mill—not Babylon!"[67]

It is Babylon, of course (as the head of construction realizes toward the end of the novel)—only in reverse: from dispersion to unity. As Platonov's Chiklin puts it, "Heard of Mount Ararat, have you? Well, if I heaped all the earth I have dug into a single heap, that's how high it would reach." And as Platonov's engineer Prushevsky thinks to himself, "It was he who had thought up a single all-proletarian home in place of the old town where to this day people lived by fencing themselves off into households; in a year's time the entire local class of the proletariat would leave the petty-proprietorial town and take possession for life of this monumental new home. And after ten or twenty years, another engineer would construct a tower in the middle of the world, and the laborers of the entire terrestrial globe would be settled there for a happy eternity."[68]

All construction stories are stories of creation; the epigraph to Ehrenburg's *The Second Day* is an epigraph to them all: "And God said, Let there be a firmament in the midst of the waters. And it was so. And the evening and the morning were the second day." The most common cosmogonic myths are creation ex nihilo and creation from chaos. Platonov's "all-proletarian house" is to be built on a "vacant lot" (*pustyr'*, from *pustoi*, "empty"); Jasienski's dam and Ilf and Petrov's railroad are to be built in the desert (*pustynia*, from *pustoi*, "empty"); and Kataev's Magnitogorsk is in the middle of nowhere. "There was no way of telling what it was—neither steppe nor city." In Gladkov's *Energy*, "the gray-brown clay hills, the granite boulders wrested from the earth, and the river squeezed between its high rocky banks slept sadly and soundly." Only at night, with the coming of searchlights, did "the chaos of rocks, cliffs, quarries, and concrete structures come alive in bright contrasts of light and shadow, like a moonscape."[69]

Another word for "chaos" is "wilderness," and another word for "wilderness" is "Asia." In the creation tales of Kataev, Jasienski, Ehrenburg, and Ilf and Petrov, the departure from Europe is marked as a prologue to genesis. In *Man Changes His Skin*, the traveling American engineer, James Clark, notices that "the endless plain, which began long before Orenburg, was becoming more and more yellow and monotonous." At the gate of Asia, he breaks his journey in Chelkar, the place of Tania Miagkova's exile. She had probably left by then, having reconciled with her husband, mother, and the Party line.[70]

But by far the most popular form of chaos is the swamp: partly because it is a familiar interpretation of the biblical "waters," but mostly because all Soviet creation novels come out of Pushkin's *The Bronze Horseman* ("from the darkness of the forests and the quagmires of the swamps"). Gladkov's "precipice" smells of "swampy rot"; Ehrenburg's builders work, "sinking into the yellow mud"; Leonov's mill drowns in a boggy forest "choked with old-growth timber"; and the White Sea–Baltic Canal makes its way, just barely, through the "strips of mud" left behind by the glaciers. When one of Leonov's young engineers says that Peter the Great "drained the vast Russian marsh in almost identical style," the head of construction responds that he had done so without the benefit of a "Marxist approach."[71]

True to both Testaments—the Christian and the Pushkinian—most Soviet creation tales include a flood that wipes out the wicked along with the innocent: "the man and beast, and the creeping thing, and the fowls of the air." The few construction sites that are not on the water have to make do with fires and storms. Kataev's Magnitogorsk has both. The storm destroys the old circus, which stands for Babylon.

> The circus posts come loose, topple and sprawl on the ground. The parrots scream as they are crushed by the falling timbers.
> The canvas roof swells and flies off, only to get caught up in the wires.
> Feathers of every hue—red, yellow, blue—fill the air.
> The elephant stands with his massive forehead against the storm. He spreads his fan-shaped ears and raises his trunk.
> His ears inflate like sails in the wind.
> The elephant fights off the dust with his trunk. His eyes look crazed, diabolical.
> The wind compels him to retreat. He backs away. He is completely enveloped in the black whirlwind of dust. His body steams. He wants to escape, but the chain holds him fast. He lets out a dreadful, spine-chilling elemental scream.
> It is the trumpet call of the Last Judgment.[72]

The world of silt, mud, rot, and dust contains countless things that need to be swept away, from Platonov's "petty and unfortunate scraps of nature" to the Cathedral of Christ the Savior. Every construction project of the era of the First Five-Year Plan is a future Palace of Soviets. When the Magnitogorsk engineer Margulies calls his sister in Moscow, she supplies the script in the form of local news:

> And the dome of Christ the Savior . . . Can you hear me? I was just saying that the dome of Christ the Savior . . . half of it has been dismantled. I never realized it was so huge . . .
> "Good," Margulies muttered.
> "Every section of the cupola was over two meters wide. And, from a distance, it looked just like an empty melon rind. . . . Are you listening?
> "Goo-ood!," Margulies roared. "Go on, go on!"[73]

The most rotten scraps of the old world come from bourgeois apartments. The villainous Bezdetov (Childless) brothers from Pilniak's *The Volga Flows into the Caspian Sea* make their living buying up antique furniture. The pregnant proletarian girl from *Time, Forward!* looks out her train window and sees "an old kitchen table, a disassembled wooden bed with head and footboards tied back to back, a chair, and a badly scorched stool." "They're bringing their bedbugs with them!" says the conductor.[74]

At the center of the old home stands Odysseus's bed—the "terrifying bed" from Olesha's *Envy*, "made of precious wood covered with dark cherry varnish with scrolled mirrors on the inside of the head and footboards." It belongs to a false Penelope by the name of Anechka Prokopovich. "She was

Dismantling of the dome of the Cathedral of Christ the Savior

sleeping with her mouth open, gurgling, the way old women do when they sleep. The rustling of the bedbugs sounded as if someone were tearing at the wallpaper. Their hiding places, unknown to daylight, were revealing themselves. The bed-tree grew and swelled. The window-sill turned pink. Gloom gathered around the bed. The night's secrets were creeping out of corners and down the walls, washing over the sleeping pair, and crawling under the bed." One of the bed's main accessories is a blanket ("I boiled under it and squirmed, jiggling in the warmth like a plate of aspic."). Another one—more compact both as object and metaphor—is a pillow. The Soviet creation novel's most eloquent defender of everything resembling jelly is Ivan Babichev, a "modest Soviet magician" and the crafty serpent who guides the questing hero into Anechka's Eden. Ivan is a short, "tubby" man who goes around "dangling a large pillow in a yellowed pillow case behind his back. It keeps bumping against the back of his knee, making a hollow appear and disappear."[75]

Ivan Babichev looks like a pillow. Shaginian's "Philistines" look like beasts of Babylon: "I saw something that looked like a stairway from the Apocalypse, a stairway overflowing with rams and goats in tailcoats. The men and women were making bleating noises, and the women had sprouted fat sheep's tails. They wagged their tails and diamond earrings, their round eyes bulging obscenely."[76]

But most swamp creatures look like swamp creatures. In Leonov's *The Sot'*, a young Soviet woman is walking through the woods and comes upon a cave filled with monstrous monks. Deep inside, ringed by "gaping nostrils," "dangling earlobes," and "huge, scurvy-stricken mouths torn by silent screams," is a pit containing "the monastery's treasure," the hermit Eusebius. "It took her a moment to get used to the putrescent warmth emanating from the hole and swirling the flame before she could look in. There, in a nest of filthy rags, rolled a small human face overgrown with fur that looked like moss to her. The earth itself seemed to be shining through the translucent skin of the forehead. The lower lip was stuck out fretfully, but the eyes were closed. The holy man was blinded by the light, and his wild, bushy eyebrows trembled with tension."[77]

Pilniak's patriarch, Yakov Karpovich Skudrin, drips slime on the living room floor and cradles his hernia through a slit in his pants. "His eyes watering with his eighty-five years, the old man swelled up, putrid and happy, like a boil full of pus." He is an aged, but defiant Smerdiakov offering his services to a despondent Ivan Karamazov (the engineer Poltorak). "There's always some deadwood in the swamp: the mud sucks it in; the leeches cling to it; the crawfish grab onto it; the minnows swarm round it; and the cows piss in the midst of all this filth and stench—while I live on, playing the fool, fouling the earth, seeing and understanding everything. We don't mind killing. Just give me a name."[78]

True "wreckers" are selflessly and uncompromisingly devoted to the devil. "I can do anything," says Skudrin, "but I wish only evil, and only evil makes me happy." Their purpose is to sabotage the work of creation. They may take on various disguises, but their true nature is duly noted by the narrator and discovered—eventually, if not always simultaneously—by the reader and the secret police investigator. Skudrin has to cradle his hernia; Poltorak's teeth are "disfigured by gold"; Gladkov's Khablo has "blind eyes" and a "hideously scarred arm"; and of the three main villains in *Man Changes His Skin*, one is left-handed, one has a misshapen finger, and the third is missing an eye. All of them plan to unleash a flood. During the era of construction, a flood is the devil's work. The devil's work is, ultimately, God's will. Skudrin is part of "that power which would the evil ever do, and ever does the good."[79]

Leading the charge against the swamp and treading the winepress of the fury of historical necessity are the Bolshevik commanders of the army of builders. Some construction heads, chief engineers, and Party secretaries are young enough, or timeless enough, to serve as the Adams of the new world. Kataev's David Margulies, Jasienski's Ivan Morozov, and Shag-inian's Arno Arevyan find young socialist brides and give every indication of being fruitful and multiplying. Others cannot "jump out of time" (as Kataev puts it). In Gladkov's *Energy*, the head of the site's Party organiza-tion, the Old Bolshevik and Civil War hero Miron Vatagin, goes for a swim, gets caught up in a whirlpool, and is pulled ashore by a young girl named Fenia. Both are naked. "'Why is he being so shy?' thought Fenia in amaze-ment. She thought it was funny—funny and pleasant. Up until then, it would never have occurred to her that Miron could possibly be shy in her presence—timid and confused because of such a trifle, just because he was naked in front of her. After all, she was also naked—and did not feel any shame at all." Miron, it turns out, has seen too much good and evil to be admitted into paradise. He comes to terms with his mortality, adopts a paternal role, and watches Fenia fall in love with someone her own age.[80]

In *The Sot'*, the head of the project, Uvadyev, and his chief engineer, Burago, are both in love with their protégée, Suzanna. She chooses a younger man, and they console themselves by listening to "The March of the Trolls" from Grieg's *Peer Gynt*. "In my view," says Burago, who stands for intelligentsia self-reflectivity next to Uvadyev's Bolshevik action, "a new Adam will come and name all the creatures that predated him. And he will rejoice." Suzanna will inherit the earth because she is as innocent as a child. "But I am an old man. I still remember the French Revolution, the Tower of Babel, Icarus's unfortunate escapade, and the vertebra of a Neanderthal in some French museum."[81]

What is their role in the creation myth, then? Pilniak's engineer Laszlo, who knows he is not God, goes back to what all "fathers" keep going back to: the exodus. "Turn your attention to Comrade Moses who led the Jews out of Egypt. He was no fool. He journeyed across the bottom of the sea, made heavenly manna out of nothing, lost his way in the desert, and or-ganized meetings on Mount Sinai. For forty years he searched and fought for a decent living space. But he never reached the Promised Land, leaving it to Joshua the son of Nun to cause the sun to stand still. His children reached it in his stead. People who have known Sodom cannot enter Ca-naan—they are not fit for the Promised Land."[82]

The Old Bolshevik in *The Sot'* is dying from leukemia; the Old Bolshevik in *The Second Day* is dying from heart disease; and the Old Bolshevik in *Energy* is dying from tuberculosis. In Platonov's *The Foundation Pit*, all the builders of the eternal house are their own grave diggers. Only Kozlov "still believed in the life to come after the construction of the big buildings," but Kozlov masturbates under his blanket, has a weak chest, and is eventually killed by the kulaks. The others know that the big houses are for "tomor-row's people," take in a little orphan girl, and observe "the sleep of this small being who one day would have dominion over their graves and live on a pacified earth packed with their bones." Those who did not die in the normal course of events would have to be killed. The war invalid Zhachev, who represents unquenchable proletarian wrath, "had made up his mind that, once this little girl and other children like her had matured a bit, he would put an end to all the big shots of his district. He alone knew that the USSR was inhabited by all-out enemies of socialism, egotists, and the blood-suckers of the bright future world, and he secretly consoled himself with the thought that sometime soon he would kill the entire mass of them, leaving alive only proletarian infancy and pure orphanhood."[83]

Ehrenburg's Old Bolshevik, Grigory Markovich Shor, is forty-eight years old, but his young disciple, Kolka, calls him an old man. Shor's life resembles "a completed questionnaire from the Party archive." The son of a shopkeeper, Shor joins the Party while it still feels "like a tiny reading circle." He spends time in prisons, exile, and Paris. After the revolution he makes speeches "in circus tents, in barracks, on trucks, and on the steps of Imperial monuments." During collectivization he is beaten by the kulaks. In Kuznetsk, he studies bricks and concrete the way he used to study political economy, agriculture, and the "prison ABCs." "But behind that harsh, rigid life was a stooped man, short-sighted and genial, with a poorly-knotted tie, who could rapturously smell a flower in a railway station garden and then ask a little girl, 'What kind of flower is this, or rather, what is its name?'" Shor lives next to the blast furnace. Once he hears a fire alarm and races over, but the alarm proves false. He feels unwell, returns home, and dies in the arms of young Kolka.[84]

In Pilniak's *The Volga Flows into the Caspian Sea*, the Old Bolsheviks live right next to the furnace, but they belong to the swamp as much as they do to the fire. They are spent men "for whom time stopped at the end of War Communism," and their leader is Ivan Ozhogov ("Burnt"), first head of the local executive committee, brother of the slime-dripping wrecker, Yakov Skudrin, and descendant of Leonov's underground monks. "Ivan Ozhogov plunged into the depths near the factory furnace, into the dark, stifling heat, and crawled toward the mouth. . . . The heavy air smelled of smoke, tar, stale humanity, and fish—like the crew's quarters on a ship. Ragged men with long, matted hair and beards lay in the dark on the clay floor around the mouth of the furnace." They are Left Deviationists—the fire-and-brimstone radical Puritans of the Bolshevik Revolution who have spent the years of the great disappointment weeping next to the mouth of the furnace. They know that the coming flood will be the second act of creation. "The year 1919 is coming back!" says Ozhogov. Or, as the Bolshevik Sadykov responds to the tale of Moses's demise just short of the promised land: "It is true that he never got there, but he did write the Commandments."[85]

Gladkov's Old Bolshevik, Baikalov, is an orthodox Party official whose life is the proletarian version of Shor's "student" (Jewish) biography, but he, too, is "burning with an inner fire." He, too, was present at the Battle of Dair, "when there was nothing in the dark of night but a hurricane of flames, as if the whole world were exploding amidst the rumble, fire, and smoke of an earthquake." He, too, realizes that the coming flood is the beginning of eternity. "It is true that soon he will be no more and that the world will disappear for him. And yet, he is immortal." As he tells another Bolshevik Moses, "I declare with the greatest conviction, that death, in its old, obsolete sense, cannot exist for us."[86]

When the flood finally comes, Ivan Ozhogov's cave fills "with green, slow-moving swamp water." Ivan—"a splendid man from the splendid era of 1917–21"—dies next to his furnace. A little boy named Mishka is watching the flood. "The creation of the new river signaled Mishka's genesis, just as the factory whistle had for Ozhogov and Sadykov." Peopling the newly cleansed earth will be today's children: Petka, Kolka, Mishka, and the two Fenias, among others. Some of them have reached the age of fruitfulness (every construction story contains at least one pregnant woman, and Olesha's Valia and Volodia plan to get married on the day construction is completed), but most are innocent representatives of proletarian infancy and pure orphanhood. Platonov's diggers keep digging for the sake of a little girl named Nastia, who will have dominion over their graves and live on a pacified earth packed with their bones. Leonov's Uvadyev imagines a little girl "somewhere over there on the radiant border, beneath the rainbows of a vanquished future." "Her name was Katya, and she was no more than ten years old. It was for her and her happiness that he fought and suffered and imposed suffering on all around him. She had not yet been born, but she could not fail to appear, since untold sacrifices had already been made on her behalf." And in Shaginian's *Hydrocentral*, the artist Arshak is thundering against rams and goats in tailcoats when he suddenly has an epiphany. "It came from a pair of eyes, the dark brown and wide open eyes of an eight-year-old girl, the house's Cinderella. With her chin resting on the edge of the table and her little head tilted back, she listened to him with her mouth open, with all the seriousness of her mysterious child's being."[87]

Standing between the dying Bolsheviks and pure orphanhood are thousands of builders being tested by the act of building. Some are doomed from the start by illegitimate birth and branded with the seal of the beast; others, the *intelligenty*, spawn spiritual sickness and plebeian wreckers with their delirious speech. Ehrenburg's Volodia Safonov cannot stop reading Dostoevsky. "Feeling guilty but unable to help himself," he keeps plunging "into the thicket of absurd scenes, hysterical crying fits, and hot, clammy pain." One day, he meets the embodiment of his faithlessness (a boy named Tolia), talks to him of freedom, and forces him to repeat a version of Smerdiakov's refrain ("It's always interesting to talk to an intelligent person"). The following morning Tolia wrecks an important piece of equipment.[88]

But most builders pass the test: reforge themselves, achieve full conversion, submit to baptism (often in a river), and join the Bolsheviks in building the eternal house. In one of the central scenes in the quasi-documentary history of the White Sea–Baltic Canal, "a Ford comes roaring" into a labor camp.

> The car made a sharp turn. Dust flew from under the braking wheels. A shaggy head popped out of the window and looked around.
>
> On the opposite bank was a human anthill. The foundation pit reached to the horizon. Dusty wheelbarrows could be seen surging toward the crest. On the right stood the scaffolding of an unfinished structure. That was the lock.
>
> A foreman ran up to the car and saluted. The shaggy-headed one put out his hand: "I'm Solts."

He walks through the crowd "as if he were in Moscow in his own apartment." He knows they have been reborn and baptizes them with the word "comrades." They respond by shedding their "socially unhealthy" pasts and promise to work harder. "That same day they christened themselves the Five-Year Plan Crew and dug up eight hundred cubic meters of soil instead of the usual two hundred."[89]

The new world is born in a labor camp. Or did it give birth to a labor camp? Few Five-Year Plan creation stories are free of irony. All come out of *The Bronze Horseman*, and all belong to the continuum between a paean to the New City and a lament to its victim, who perishes in the flood.

> There were young Communists working at the construction site. They knew what they were doing—they were building Leviathan. Working alongside them were some expropriated kulaks. They had been brought here from far away: peasants from Riazan and Tula. They had been brought here together with their families, but they did not know why. They had traveled for ten days. Then the train stopped. There was a hill above a river. They were told that they would live there. The babies cried, and the women gave them their shrunken, bluish breasts to suckle.
>
> They looked like survivors after a fire. They were called "special settlers." They began to dig in the earth—to build earthen barracks. The barracks were crowded and dark. In the morning the people went to work. In the evening they returned. The children cried, and the exhausted women muttered, "Hush!"
>
> There were prisoners working at the Osinov mines, digging coal. Ore and coal together produced iron. Among the prisoners was Nikolai Izvekov ["from time immemorial"], the priest who administered the last sacrament to Kolka Rzhanov's mother. After Izvekov was purged from the Sanitation Trust, he began to preach "the Last Days." He copied the epistles of St. Paul and sold the copies for five rubles each. He also performed secret requiem services for the deceased Tsar. He was sentenced to three years in a concentration

camp. Now he loaded coal in a pit. By his side worked Shurka-the-Turk. Shurka used to sell cocaine. Izvekov would say to Shurka: "The impious will be cast into the lake of fire and brimstone."[90]

Socialist construction sites were also labor camps, and possibly gateways to hell. On the Dnieper, "workers with shovels and crowbars, singly and in groups, swarmed among the rocks, next to the cables, trolleys, and iron boxes." On the Sot', "the number of diggers kept shrinking, and the last thirty had only seven square feet or so to maneuver in." And on the Mizinka, "the scoop bucket rose, the gravel poured drily into the open mouth of the cement mixer, and from above, at automatic intervals, a thin stream of water squirted down on the gravel like a spray of saliva. . . . Rising again, the scoop bucket overturned the dripping mass into the concrete mixer, and the its jaws chewed on the gravel mixed with sand."[91]

"This is like the creation of the world," writes one of Ehrenburg's Communist brides to the doubting Volodia Safonov. "Everything at once: heroism, greed, cruelty, generosity." The creation of the world demands great sacrifice; great sacrifice involves great suffering, and great suffering produces doubt: the same doubt that Sverdlov and Voronsky struggled with in their own prerevolutionary catacombs. Volodia Safonov's torment is not his alone: "At meetings everyone knows beforehand what each person will say. All you have to do is remember a few formulas and a few figures. But to speak like a real human being, that is, tripping up, stammering, and with passion, to speak about something personal—that they cannot do. . . . And yet they are the builders of a new life, the apostles called upon to make prophecies, the dialecticians incapable of error." When the engineer Burago says that he cannot enter the new world because he remembers Icarus and the Tower of Babel, is he saying that he is too old or is he saying that the "new Adam" will have to learn about hubris?[92]

Burago is an honest tower-builder, but even the dishonest and ill-intentioned ones manage to speak with considerable power and conviction. The oily American in Kataev's *Time Forward!* surveys the Magnitogorsk panorama and then looks down at an old baste shoe lying in the grass before him:

"On the one hand, Babylon, and on the other, a baste shoe. That is a paradox."

Nalbandov repeated stubbornly: "Here there will be a socialist city for a hundred and fifty thousand workers and service employees."

"Yes, but will humanity be any happier because of that? And is this presumed happiness worthy of such effort?"

"He is right," Nalbandov thought.

"You are wrong," he said, looking coldly at the American. "You lack imagination. We shall conquer nature, and we shall give humanity back its lost paradise."[93]

The smooth German riding on the train in Ilf and Petrov's *The Golden Calf* makes the same point by telling the story of a Communist Adam and Eve who go to Gorky Park, sit down under a tree, pluck off a small branch, and suddenly realize that they are made for each other. Three years later they already have two sons.

"So what's the point?" asked Lavoisian.

"The point is," answered Heinrich emphatically, "that one son was called Cain, the other Abel, and that in due course Cain would slay Abel, Abraham would beget Isaac, Isaac would beget Jacob, and the whole story would start anew, and neither Marxism nor anything else will ever be able to change that. Everything will repeat itself. There will be a flood, there will be Noah with his three sons, and Ham will insult Noah. There will be the Tower of Babel, gentlemen, which will never be completed. And on and on and on. There won't be anything new in the world. So don't get too excited about your new life. . . . Everything, everything will repeat itself! And the Wandering Jew will continue to wander the earth."[94]

The only person to respond with a story of his own is the "Great Operator" and one the most popular characters in Soviet literature, Ostap Bender. The Wandering Jew will never wander again, he says, because in 1919 he decided to leave Rio de Janeiro, where he had been strolling under the palm trees in his white pants, in order to see the Dnieper River. "He had seen them all: the Rhine, the Ganges, the Mississippi, the Yangtze, the Niger, the Volga, but not the Dnieper." He crossed the Romanian border with some contraband, and was caught by Petliura's men and sentenced to death. "'But I am supposed to be eternal!' cried the old man. He had yearned for death for two thousand years, but at that moment he desperately wanted to live. 'Shut up, you dirty kike,' yelled the forelocked commander cheerfully. 'Finish him off, boys!' And the eternal wanderer was no more."[95]

Ostap Bender wins the argument. The wandering Jew is supposed to stop wandering on the eve of the millennium; the millennium is scheduled to begin at the great construction site in the desert; and the train they are on is leaving the world of eternal return behind. Or is it? A short time later Ostap crosses the Romanian border with some contraband. His plan is to go to Rio de Janeiro and stroll under the palm trees in his white pants. The border guards catch him and beat him up, but they do not kill him. The Wandering Jew is on the loose again. "Hold the applause! As the Count of Monte Cristo, I am a failure. I'll have to go into apartment management instead."[96]

Ostap may be difficult to destroy (he had been killed and resurrected before), but he is a homeless stranger in search of a mirage. Olesha's Ivan Babichev, the god of the bed and brother of the chief tower-builder, Andrei

Babichev, is much more dangerous because he sits at the very source of eternal return. "Keep your hands off our pillows!" he says to his brother on behalf of humanity. "Our fledgling heads, covered with soft reddish down, lay on these pillows; our kisses fell on them in a night of love, we died on them—and people we killed died on them, too. Don't touch our pillows! Don't call us! Don't lure us, don't tempt us! What can you offer in place of our ability to love, hate, hope, cry, regret and forgive?"[97]

Ivan is "a magician," however—and possibly a fraud. His own pillow is homeless, and the bed he ends up in is the bedbug-ridden realm of the snoring Anechka. But there is one test of the legitimacy of doubt that every Russian reader knows to be unimpeachable. What if the child who is to live in the New City and for whom "untold sacrifices" have been made dies before the work is done?

Platonov's Nastia, "the fact of socialism," catches a cold during the "ordeal of the kulaks," dies, and is buried in the foundation pit of the eternal house. But *The Foundation Pit*—closest to *The Bronze Horseman* in its degree of ambivalence—was not published at the time. Much more striking is the death of the little girl in Leonov's *The Sot'*, which was praised as a flawed but timely account of socialist construction at the Sixteenth Party Congress. "The engineers felt a strange, guilty sorrow because the corpse was that of a little girl, and, judging from her size, she could not have been more than eleven. Her bare knees were covered with mud. In its senselessness, the accident resembled murder." Uvadyev, the chief of contruction, imagines that "he has recognized in the dead girl the one who had been so closely bound up with his own fate. Driven by a strange need, he asked her name and was told it was Polia."[98]

In the end, however, it always turns out that the sacrifice has not been in vain and that Dostoevsky's absurd scenes and hysterical crying fits are but a passing sickness. Doubt is natural, and the suffering terrible, but the work of creation cannot be tainted by the loss of innocence. (Even in *The Bronze Horseman*, the death of Evgeny does not seem to doom "Peter's creation." And, of course, the most popular of all Soviet construction novels is Aleksei Tolstoy's *Peter I*, which depicts the prologue to the First Five-Year Plan as a joyfully violent event.) In *The Sot'*, Uvadyev reaches a conclusion "that would not make sense to anyone else and was possible only on such a terrible night: she was the sister of the one for whom he had suffered and caused others to suffer so much." In the novel's final paragraph, he sits down on a bench above the river:

Having scraped off some of the icy crust, Uvadyev perched on the edge of the wooden plank and continued sitting there with his hands resting on his knees until the lights at the construction site began to glow. Half an hour later, the wet snow had partially covered the man sitting on the bench. His shoulders and knees were white; the snow on his hands was melting, but still he did not move, although it had already grown dark. Staring out into the March gloom with a barbed, dispassionate gaze, he could probably make out the cities that were to rise from those inconceivable expanses and feel the fragrant breeze that would blow through them and tousle the locks of a little girl whose face he knew so well.[99]

Even in *The Foundation Pit*, the work goes on. Voshchev, victim of "a vain mind's troubled longing" and the collector of "petty and unfortunate scraps of nature," finds, thanks to Nastia, true knowledge, hope, and his place as the head of the purged peasants. And of course "Nastia" comes from "Anastasia," which means "resurrection." The engineer Prushevsky sees past his own approaching death, and perhaps that of Nastia, too. "Prushevsky looked quietly into all of nature's misty old age and saw at its end some peaceful white buildings that shone with more light than there was in the air around them. Prushevsky did not know a name for this completed construction, nor did he know its purpose, although it was clear that these distant buildings had been arranged not only for use but also for joy. With the surprise of a man accustomed to sadness, Prushevsky observed the precise tenderness and the chilled, comprised strength of the remote monuments."[100]

10

THE NEW TENANTS

In spring 1931, the chief builders of the new world began moving into their own, as yet incomplete, eternal house. Apartments were distributed among members of the Party's Central Committee, the Central Executive Committees of the Soviet Union and the Russian Federation, the Executive Committee of the Comintern, the People's Commissariats of the Soviet Union and the Russian Federation, the Central Control Commission and Worker-Peasant Inspectorate, the Supreme Council of the Economy, the State Planning Agency, the Trade Union Council, the Trade Union International, the Unified Main Political Administration (OGPU, the new name for secret police), the Moscow City Soviet and Party Committee, the Lenin Institute, the Society of Old Bolsheviks, the editorial board of *Izvestia*, the families of late heroes and high officials, assorted fiction writers, and "the House of Government's administrative and maintenance personnel." The apartments varied in size and status: the largest and most prestigious faced the river and had views of the Kremlin and the Cathedral of Christ the Savior (Entryways 1 and 12). Most leaseholders (eligible individuals in whose name the apartments were registered) held positions that entitled them to extra "living space." After 1930, each government agency kept a list of such positions. Not everyone who qualified for extra living space could receive an apartment in the House of Government. Each position within the Party and state hierarchy entitled its holder and an indeterminate number of his or her relatives to a wide range of goods and services. Any move within the hierarchy was accompanied by numerous other moves, including those within the House of Government.[1]

Arkady Rozengolts, the leader of the Bolshevik insurrection in Moscow and now people's commissar of foreign trade, who used to move through the walls like a ghost (and was described by his niece Elena as "gloomy and morose"), moved into a large apartment on the eleventh floor with a long balcony overlooking the river (Apt. 237, in Entryway 12). His first wife and their two children stayed behind in the Fifth House of Soviets on Granovsky Street. His House of Government family included his new wife; their two daughters, born in 1932 and 1934; his wife's mother and brother; one of his brothers; his sister Eva (the painter who had recently separated from her husband, the *Pravda* journalist Boris Levin); Eva's daughter, Elena, born in 1928; and the maid, "Duniasha."[2]

Rozengolts, his second wife, and one of their daughters   Eva Levina-Rozengolts with
her daughter, Elena

Eva's Higher Art and Technology Studios classmate, Maria Denisova, and her "proletarian" husband, Efim Shchadenko (now a member of the Central Control Commission), received two separate apartments: a very large one on the sixth floor of Entryway 1 (Apt. 10) with a view of the river, and a smaller one at the opposite end of the complex, in Entryway 25 (Apt. 505, probably meant to serve as her studio). According to their neighbors, however, Maria tended to live in the first one, and Efim, in the second. In her December 1928 letter to Mayakovsky, she wrote that she had returned to her husband because he threatened to shoot himself. In May 1930, less than a month after Mayakovsky's suicide and about a year before they moved into the House, she was diagnosed as a "psychopath with schizophrenic and cyclical traits."[3]

Maria Denisova working on a
bust of Efim Shchadenko

Rozengolts's deputy during the Moscow insurrection, now head of the All-Union Society for Cultural Ties with Foreign Countries, and still a writer, Aleksandr Arosev, was also given two apartments: a four-room one on the tenth floor for his three daughters, a nanny, and a governess (Apt. 104, in Entryway 5), and a one-room one on the same floor (Apt. 103), for his new wife and their newborn son Dmitry. At the time of the move, he was planning "a large work based partly on personal recollections and partly on written sources about how, in the course of revolutionary work, first illegal and later legal and state-directed, the threads of human connections, sympathies, friendship, and love come together and then get torn apart; how individuals enter the revolutionary movement and sometimes move away from it, and how all of this is, in the final analysis, only a ripple on the surface of the epic class struggle, which has produced such a 'Great Rebellion' in our country." The projected novel was to consist of "pictures of that rebellion that would resemble pictures of a river flowing partially underground and partially on the surface, just like now."[4]

Aleksandr Arosev

Arosev's old comrade and now top Comintern official in charge of finances and foreign agents, the famously "taciturn" Osip Piatnitsky, moved into a five-room apartment (Apt. 400) with his wife Yulia, their two sons (ten and six in 1931), and Yulia's father, the former priest, with his new wife and daughter. Another famously taciturn veteran of the Moscow uprising, and now the chairman of the Main Committee on Foreign Concessions at the Council of People's Commissars, Valentin Trifonov, moved into a four-room apartment (Apt. 137, in Entryway 7) with his wife Evgenia (an economist in the People's Commissariat of Agriculture); their two children, Yuri (1925) and Tatiana (1927); Evgenia's mother (and Valentin's former revolutionary comrade and wife) Tatiana Slovatinskaia; a Chuvash boy nicknamed Undik, whom Slovatinskaia adopted during the Volga famine in 1921, when he was four years old; and a maid.[5]

The Trifonovs' friend and author of the proposition that the family was "a small Communist cell," Aron Solts, moved into Apt. 393 with his sister, Esfir; a young boy they had recently taken in, Evgeny; and their niece, Anna, who was separated from her husband, Isaak Zelensky. (Their marriage had been arranged by Aron and Esfir, who met him in Siberian exile in 1912.) In 1931, Zelensky was transferred from Uzbekistan, where he was serving as head of the Central Asian Bureau, to Moscow to become chairman of the Central Union of Consumer Cooperatives. He moved into Apt. 54 with his new wife, their daughter, and his and Anna's two children, Elena and Andrei (named after one of Solts's Party pseudonyms).[6]

Solts's coauthor, Supreme Court colleague, and fellow expert on the family, Yakov Brandenburgsky, moved into Apt. 25 with his wife, Anna, whom he met in their native town of Balta, north of Odessa, and their daughter Elsa, born in 1913. In July 1929, Brandenburgsky was relieved of his duties as legal theorist and sent to Saratov to supervise collectivization (as deputy chairman of the Lower Volga Province Executive Committee and member of the Provincial Party bureau). In March 1931, he was fired for "dizziness from success" and transferred to the Commissariat of Labor as an expert on labor legislation. In 1934, after several months in the Kremlin hospital, he was appointed to the USSR Supreme Court.[7]

Yakov and Anna Brandenburgsky

Dizziness and domesticity were at the center of the literary work of Aleksandr Serafimovich, who moved into Apt. 82 with his wife (and former maid) Fekla Rodionovna, his son by a previous marriage, and the son's wife and daughter (named after Lenin's newspaper, *Iskra* [Spark]). After finishing *The Iron Flood*, Serafimovich embarked on a novel set in a large apartment building ("House No. 93"). According to the outline of one chapter draft, "The family is falling apart: (1) Sergei and Olga Yakovlevna; (2) Pania and Sakharov; (3) Petr Ivanovich Puchkov—pulling himself together, crying; (4) sitting around, talking about the people they know: mostly men changing wives, sometimes women changing husbands." In 1930, Serafimovich's former wife died in a mental institution. In 1931, he abandoned the "House" idea in favor of a novel about collectivization. In January 1933, the day before his seventieth birthday, he received a telephone call from People's Commissar of the Army and Navy Kliment Voroshilov, who told him that members of the government had decided to name the city of Novocherkassk after him. Serafimovich, according to his

Serafimovich with his
granddaughter, Iskra

own account, proposed his hometown of Ust-Medveditskaia instead. Voroshilov objected that Ust-Medveditskaia was not a city, but then called back to say that the problem had been resolved: Ust-Medveditskaia would first be reclassified as a city, and then renamed. All Saints Street (which formed the eastern boundary of the House of Government and connected the Big Stone Bridge to the Small Stone Bridge) also received a new name at that time. The House of Government's official address became "2, Serafimovich Street."[8]

Serafimovich's key ally in the struggle for proletarian literature against "Voronskyism," Platon Kerzhentsev, moved into a five-room apartment on the tenth floor (Apt. 206, in Entryway 10) with his second wife, Maria; their daughter, Natalia (born in 1925); and maid, Agafia. Kerzhentsev met Maria in Sweden when he was Soviet ambassador and she was Aleksandra Kollontai's secretary. After that, he became chief theoretician of the Bolshevik "sense of time," while serving as ambassador to Italy (where Natalia was born), president of the editorial board of the State Publishing House, deputy head of the Central Statistics Directory (under Osinsky), director of the Institute of Literature, Arts, and Language at the Communist Academy, and deputy head of Agitprop (in which capacity he first helped defeat Voronsky and then allowed his memoirs to be published). Shortly before his move

Kerzhentsev with
daughter Natalia

to the House of Government, he was appointed chief administrator of the Council of People's Commissars.[9]

Kerzhentsev suffered from a heart condition, and around 1935 (after he became head of the Radio Committee), the family moved down to the third floor to Apt. 197. Their next-door neighbors in 198 (a five-room apartment) were the Old Bolshevik and Kerzhentsev's predecessor as head of the Radio Committee, Feliks Kon, who was seventy years old at the time, and his wife Khristiana (Kristina, or Khasia) Grinberg, who was seventy-seven. ("Khristiana" was the name she received when she formally converted to Orthodox Christianity in order to get married officially when they were in exile in Siberia). Kon's new assignment was to head the Museum Section of the People's Commissariat of Enlightenment.[10]

Kon and Grinberg's daughter, Elena Usievich (born in Siberia in 1893), lived in the same entryway, but on the first floor in Apt. 194. Elena and her daughter, Iskra-Marina (b. 1926), shared the apartment with the Old Bolshevik Mark Abramovich Braginsky and his wife (three rooms for Elena, Iskra-Marina, their nanny and maid, and two for the Braginskys and their maid). As Iskra-Marina put it many years later, "It never occurred to either my mother or my grandparents that it might be better for us to live with them rather than some old people we weren't even related to." (The Braginskys' children had an apartment in a different entryway.) Elena and her first husband, Grigory Usievich, returned to Russia from Swiss exile in Lenin's "sealed car" in April 1917. After Grigory's death in the Civil War at the age of twenty-seven, Elena worked in the Cheka, the Economic Council (under Yuri Larin), and the Crimean Theater Repertory Censorship Committee, before graduating from the Institute of Red Professors in 1932. Her second husband, a Far Eastern Bolshevik and later second secretary of the Crimean Party Committee, Aleksandr Takser (Iskra-Marina's father), died in 1931, soon after they moved into the House. Elena's first child (Grigory's

Elena Usievich

son) died in 1934 in his grandparents' apartment at the age of seventeen. By then, Elena was already a well-known literary critic and prominent fighter against the Association of Proletarian Writers and was serving as deputy director of the Institute of Literature and the Arts at the Communist Academy (under Kerzhentsev's successor, Lunacharsky).[11]

Elena Usievich's closest friend and Institute colleague was Lunacharsky's secretary and brother-in-law, Igor Sats. Igor's niece and director of the Central Children's Theater, Natalia Sats, moved into the House of Government (Apt. 159) in 1935, when she married Commissar of Internal Trade Izrail Veitser. Natalia's patron, admirer, and onetime dance partner, Mikhail Koltsov, lived close by, in a large four-room apartment on the eighth floor (Apt. 143). Still formally married to his second wife, Elizaveta Ratmanova, he had been living since 1932 with the German writer and journalist Maria Gresshöner (who changed her name to "Osten" and broke with her "bourgeois" family soon after her arrival in Moscow, when she was twenty-four years old).[12]

One of Koltsov's closest collaborators and head of the Association of State Book and Magazine Publishers (OGIZ), Artemy Khalatov, moved into a large, six-room apartment on the seventh floor of Entryway 12 (four floors below Rozengolts). His family consisted of his mother (head of collections at the Lenin Library), wife (a graphic artist), cousin (an actress at the Moscow Art Theater), daughter Svetlana (born in 1926, after Svetlana Stalina and Svetlana Bukharina but before Svetlana Molotova), and their maid, Shura. Khalatov (thirty-five at the time of the move) was famous among the Bolsheviks for his long curly hair, full beard, and Astrakhan hat, which he rarely took off. Before being put in charge of nationalizing and centralizing the publishing industry, he supervised rationing in War Com-

Artemy Khalatov

Khalatov's wife, Tatiana

munism Moscow, chaired the Commission for the Improvement of Scholars' Living Conditions, founded the State Puppet Theater, and, as head
of People's Nutrition ("Down with kitchen slavery! Long live communal
food consumption!"), inspired Yuri Olesha's *Envy*. According to Khalatov's
daughter, Svetlana, Koltsov used to amuse her by riding her tricycle up
and down the hall, shouting, "Time for tea!"[13]

One of Khalatov's employees at OGIZ was K. T. Sverdlova (Novgorodtseva), who headed the department of children's literature and school
textbooks. She and her family did not move from the Kremlin to the House
of Government until 1937, but in 1932, her son Andrei married Nina Podvoiskaia and joined the Podvoisky-Didrikil patriarchs in Apt. 280, in Entryway 14. The apartment residents included the senior Podvoiskys, three
(but later just one) of their daughters, and, on and off, their son Lev with
his wife, Milena (whose father, the head of Trade Union International,
Solomon Lozovsky, was living in Apt. 16 with his new wife, young daughter,
and in-laws). The Didrikil sister who was married to the Chekist Mikhail
Kedrov lived in Apt. 409. The Sverdlovs, including Nina Podvoiskaia, would
eventually move into Apt. 319. Andrei Sverdlov sided with the Trostkyists
as a high school student in 1927, studied foreign languages in Argentina in
1928–29, conspired with Bukharin and other rightists in 1930 (proclaiming,
according to an eyewitness account and his own later confession, that
"Koba [Stalin] must be bumped off"), studied briefly at Moscow University
and the Moscow Tractor Institute, and graduated from the Military Academy of Mechanized Forces in 1935, at the age of twenty-four.[14]

Yakov Sverdlov's (and Voronsky's) close friend, Filipp Goloshchekin,
moved in permanently in 1933, after he was dismissed as Party boss of
Kazakhstan and appointed head of the State Arbitrage Court. He lived in
Apt. 228 with his second wife, her mother, and her son from a previous
marriage. Sverdlov's and Goloshchekin's proletarian protégé, the "baker,"
Boris Ivanov, moved into Apt. 372 on the fifth floor (Entryway 19). Before
that, he had been serving as chairman of the Crimean Trade Union of Food
Industry Workers and was still relying on the Society of Old Bolsheviks for

Podvoisky family

basic assistance a year after the family's clothes were stolen: "I have a family of four dependents including a nonworking wife and three children between the ages of 3 and 11 of which two children go to school and the absence of warm clothes for the children makes their school-going impossible during the period of winter besides which my wife and I are unclothed too in the absence of winter coats but these funds are being asked for the children only."[15]

In May 1930, Ivanov was appointed deputy chairman of the Main Administration of the Canned Food Industry and transferred from Crimea to Moscow. Because the approval process at the Party's Central Committee took several months "due to Wrecking in the abovementioned organization and the now occurring personnel purge," he asked for a grant of two hundred rubles, citing the fact that his wife suffered "from nervous fits." Ivanov's wife, Elena Zlatkina, came from a large family of Yiddish-speaking tailors-turned-revolutionaries. One of her brothers, Ilya Zlatkin, distinguished himself as a Red Army commander during the Civil War and later served as head of political departments in various armies. In spring 1931, Ilya left for his new posting in the Soviet legation in Urumqi, China, and the Ivanov family moved into their three-room apartment in the House of Government. "Since during the move several more related expenses took place (horse-cart movers and so on) along with the necessity to purchase several household items namely a table and some chairs I request to render financial assistance in the amount of 150 rubles if not possible as a grant then payable within three months." Ivanov's request was granted, as were most of the requests he submitted over the next few years (several a year, mostly for free tickets to Black Sea resorts and northern Caucasus spas). After being officially diagnosed with "neurasthenia" in May 1931, Elena Zlatkina stopped working. The Ivanovs (Boris, forty-four; Elena, thirty-four; two sons, ages eleven and ten; and a daughter, age eight) decided to rent out one of their three rooms.[16]

Despite their reduced circumstances, the Ivanovs, like most residents of the House of Government, had a maid ("domestic employee"). Her name

Boris Ivanov   E. Ia. Ivanova (Zlatkina)

was Niura, and she was sixteen or seventeen at the time of the move. One day, while walking with the children in the courtyard, she met Vladimir Orekhov from Apt. 384, who was in his early twenties. Soon afterward, they got married, and Niura moved into his apartment. Vladimir was the son of Vasily Orekhov, the former shepherd and public prosecutor who had succumbed to "traumatic nevrosis" as a result of Lenin's death in 1924. By 1931, he had turned forty-seven, retired, and received "two rows of teeth to the total amount of 26 teeth," but continued to suffer from poor health and spent much of his time at Black Sea resorts.[17]

Orekhov and the Ivanovs were not the only Old Bolsheviks having difficulty recovering from the Civil War and the great disappointment. The director of the Marx-Engels-Lenin Institute, Vladimir Adoratsky, continued his program of balneological treatment. Several months before moving into the House of Government (Apt. 93) at the age of fifty-three, he wrote to his wife from Gurzuf, on the Black Sea, that "the food here continues to be of the highest caliber. The vegetarian soups (borscht) are of excellent quality, and the roasts with fried potatoes are always delicious and so abundant that Varia cannot eat it all." (Varia, Adoratsky's daughter and a translator at his institute, was twenty-six at the time. She also suffered from poor health and often accompanied her father on his trips.) Several months after moving into the House, Adoratsky and Varia went to a spa in Kislovodsk. There were no oxygen treatments, but the mountain air was so good "you could get it even without all those special gadgets." In Moscow, he had access to a special "dietetic cafeteria," where he ate "vegetables, fruit, and meat, but no bread," and a clinic for regular "ultraviolet" treatments.[18]

Adoratsky's colleague at the Marx-Engels-Lenin Institute and the first director of the Health-Care Department of the Resort Administration in Crimea, Olympiada Mitskevich, retired within a year of moving into the House (Apt. 140), at the age of fifty. Her preferred place of residence, she wrote to the Society of Old Bolsheviks, was a sanatorium; her first trip after the move was to the Borzhomi Mineral Spa, in Georgia. The former "Christian Socialist," organizer of mass executions in the Don Area, and curfew violator at the Second House of Soviets, Karl Lander, retired four years before moving into the House (Apt. 307), "following a severe nervous illness and a series of severe emotional shocks." As a "personal pensioner" since the age of forty-four, he devoted himself to scholarly work on "the history of the Party, Leninism (theory and practice), history of the revolutionary movement, and historical questions in general." Another long-term invalid, the theoretician of War Communism and chief agrarian economist, Lev Kritsman, stopped teaching for health reasons in 1929, when he was thirty-nine years old. In 1931, when he and his wife Sarra moved into Apt. 186, in Entryway 9, he was made deputy head of Gosplan, but, in 1933, he retired from "operational work" and became a full-time scholar, editing Russian translations of Marx for the Marx-Engels-Lenin

Institute, contributing to the first volume of the *History of the Civil War*, and working on a book titled *The First World Imperialist War and the Disintegration of Capitalism in Russia.*[19]

Kritsman's closest ally on the agrarian front and his successor at Gosplan, Aron Gaister, moved into Apt. 167 with his wife, Rakhil (an economist at the People's Commissariat of Heavy Industry); their two daughters; and their maid, Natalia Ovchinnikova. A third daughter, named after Kuibyshev, was born in 1936. Gaister's fellow delegates to the Planned Economy Conference in Amsterdam and fellow Kritsman protégés, Ivan Kraval and Solomon Ronin, moved in at the same time (into Apts. 190 and 55, respectively).[20]

Kritsman, as he wrote in one of his letters to Stalin, had been "an opponent of all oppositions and deviations within our Party since the middle of 1918." The recently repentant deviationists were also made welcome. Karl Radek resumed his role as a propagandist and diplomatic negotiator (visiting his mother during a trip to Poland in 1933) and moved into Apt. 20 with his wife, daughter, a poodle named Devil, and Larisa Reisner's portrait. The first book he published after the move was about engineers accused of wrecking ("they could not struggle against us face to face, they could only do it by hiding in our institutions and attacking us from behind, like vipers").[21]

Radek's fellow oppositionist (and prosecutor at Filipp Mironov's trial), Ivar Smilga, was readmitted to the Party, appointed deputy chairman of the State Planning Agency (as head of planning coordination), and given a six-room apartment (Apt. 230) in the House of Government, where he lived with his wife; two daughters; the daughters' nanny; Nina Delibash, the wife of his exiled friend Aleksandr Ioselevich; and an Estonian woman, who, according to Smilga's daughter Tatiana, had nowhere else to live.[22]

Another repentant exile, Aleksandr Voronsky, was put in charge of the Russian and Foreign Classics Section of the newly created State Fiction Publishers (within Khalatov's OGIZ monopoly). He lived in Apt. 357 with his wife, Sima Solomonovna, and their daughter, Galina. According to Ga-

Aron Gaister
(Courtesy of Inna Gaister)

Rakhil Gaister with daughter Inna
(Courtesy of Inna Gaister)

Aleksandr Voronsky with his mother and daughter

Sima Solomonovna
Voronskaia

lina, "after his return from Lipetsk, Father kept to himself and refused not only to speak publicly on literary matters, but even to attend literary conferences and seminars." After being readmitted to the Party, he chose to join a "primary cell" at the print shop, not the publishing house. His friend Goloshchekin suggested that he attempt to improve his position by publishing (or ghostwriting) an attack on Trotsky's autobiography, but he declined. He continued to work on various versions of his memoirs, a biography of the revolutionary terrorist, Zheliabov, and a book about Gogol.[23]

Voronsky's friends from the days of his revolutionary youth in Tambov, Feoktista Yakovlevna Miagkova and her daughter Tania, moved into one of the first completed apartments (next to the Shock Worker Movie Theater) in 1930, after Tania was released from Kazakhstan and Tania's husband, Mikhail Poloz, was transferred from Kharkov to Moscow as deputy chairman of the Central Executive Committee's Budget Commission. After the House was finished, they moved to a larger and quieter apartment (Apt. 199, in Entryway 10). The family also included their daughter Rada, who was six at the time; their maid; and Tania's sister Lelia and her son Volia (Vladimir). Tania got a job as an economist at a ball bearing factory.[24]

Some of the most resolute crusaders against "factionalism" lived next door. Boris Volin, who had led the "beat the opposition" raid in November 1927, moved into Apt. 276 with his wife, Dina Davydovna (a former gynecologist and now editor at the Music Publishing House); their daughter Victoria, born in 1920; and their maid, Katia, who had been with the family since Victoria's birth. Volin had been as tough on the Right Opposition as he had been on the Left. As head of the Press Department of the Commissariat of Foreign Affairs, he had written several confidential letters unmasking his colleague, Deputy Commissar Maksim Litvinov, as "one of the worst Right opportunists in our Party" ("Litvinov <u>hates</u> the OGPU. He can't talk about it without extreme, savage loathing."). Within two years, Litvinov (Apt. 14) would become commissar of foreign affairs; and Volin, chairman of the Central Censorship Office (Glavlit).[25]

Grigory Moroz with his mother and sons

Another leader of the raid against the Left Oppositionists, the former Chekist Grigory Moroz (who warned Smilga that things would get worse and then, at the Fifteenth Party Congress, promised to "snip off the heads of the arrogant oppositionist noblemen") had since fallen into right deviationism, recanted, become a trade union official in charge of trade, and moved into Apt. 39, in Entryway 2, with his wife, Fanni Lvovna Kreindel, who was a pharmacist, and their three sons, Samuil (eleven), Vladimir (nine), and Aleksandr (three). According to Samuil, his father was "short, hollow-chested, and stooped," with a moustache that "at first used to cover the whole space between his nose and upper lip, and later just the little furrow between his mouth and nose." His eyes "were always half closed—from exhaustion, anger, or, very rarely, when he smiled." He was able to maintain "a remarkable balance between reason and will, and hence a perfect conformity of word and deed. . . . He was not known for unquestioning obedience, but when a certain name was associated with an idea, he had his faith—a faith in the infallibility of Lenin and Dzerzhinsky and the correctness of the Party line as defined by Stalin."[26]

■ ■ ■

Upon moving in, residents had to sign detailed inspection checklists. Podvoisky's consisted of fifty-four items, including ceilings, walls, wallpaper, tile floors (in the kitchen, bathroom, and toilet), parquet floors (in the rest of the apartment), closets, windows, hinges, lampshades, doors (French and regular), locks (two kinds) doorknobs (three kinds), nickel-plated doorstops, an electric doorbell, enamel bathtub with overflow drain and nickel-plated plug, nickel-plated shower, wall-mounted porcelain sink, water heater, cold and hot water faucets, a porcelain toilet, raisable oak toilet seat, mounted toilet water tank with porcelain pull chain, gas stove with four burners and two vents, a samovar vent, wall-mounted cast-iron enamel kitchen sink with hot and cold water faucets and chain plug, an icebox, a garbage chute with flap doors, and an extra cargo elevator with a metal door and call button (and garbage pail that a special attendant emptied out twice a day). Apartment regulations urged residents not to hang objects on electric plugs and switches; not to place paper and rugs over heaters; not to hit water pipes with heavy objects; not to clog sinks with matches, cigarette butts, and other small items; and not to throw bones, rags, and boxes into the toilet. Furniture—heavy, rectilinear oak pieces designed by Iofan—could be leased from the carpentry shop located in the basement. All the residents requested some furniture, supplementing it with pieces of their own they did not want to part with. Arosev brought a Venetian armchair inlaid with mother-of-pearl; Volin—a desk; Khalatov—a desk, couch, armchairs, and weapons collection; Podvoisky—a tall bookcase; Kerzhentsev—most of his furniture and a large German radio set; and the Ivanovs—a chandelier and a wardrobe.[27]

The first residents moved into apartments next to the movie theater and Ditch (but some, like Tania Miagkova and her family, would later move to more prestigious parts of the house). In the spring and summer of 1931, children played in the furniture warehouse, on the wooden walkways placed over the mud, among the piles of earth and bricks in the courtyards, on the volleyball court by the laundry, and around the Church of St. Nicholas the Miracle Worker (known as *tserkovka* or *tserkvushka*: "the little church").[28]

The church's most recent tenants—the State Historical Preservation Workshop and the Institute of the Peoples of the East—took a long time to move out. The only available alternatives were other churches, for which there was intense competition despite the many problems involved in converting them to secular uses. After much acrimony (and several conflicting claims to the Church of St. Nicholas in the Armenian Alley, Trinity Church in Nikitniki, and the nearby Church of the Resurrection in Kadashi), the Historical Preservation Workshop was assigned to the Assumption Church on Herzen Street, and the Institute of the Peoples of the East, to the Church of St. Martin the Confessor on Big Communist Street (in the Taganka District). In April 1932, permission to tear down "the little church" was officially withdrawn; in July 1932, most of the premises were forcibly taken over by the House of Government's largest tenant, the New Theater; in March 1934, both the church and the Averky Kirillov residence were formally, though inconclusively, transferred to the jurisdiction of the House of Government.[29]

By this time, the area around the House had changed considerably. The Swamp's shops and stalls were gone, as were most of the tenements. The Maria Women's College was now School No. 19; the Einem Candy Factory became State Candy Factory No. 1, and, in 1922, the Red October; the Gustav List Metal Works became Plant No. 5, Hydrofilter, and, later, the Red Torch; and the Kharitonenko mansion was first turned into a guest-house of the People's Commissariat of Foreign Affairs and then, in 1929, taken over by the British embassy. The most dramatic change was the disappearance of the Cathedral of Christ the Savior, which was blown up on December 5, 1931, to make way for the Palace of Soviets. According to Mikhail Korshunov from Apt. 445, who was seven at the time, "salvos of rock, marble, and brick shot straight up and spread out over a large area. The ice on the river must have cracked: in any case, a loud, lingering boom sounded over the river—and in the courtyard wells. The beacons along the fence flashed on and off, and, after straining to find its voice, the siren began screaming." Korshunov's neighbor from Apt. 424, Elina Kisis, who was six at the time, remembered how the river "became covered with dust and smoke," and how her grandmother "stood in the corner of the kitchen, praying and crossing herself." Four construction foremen and their families living in Apt. 4 (which they had received as a prize from the Construction Committee), heard the sound of the explosion and ran out onto the balcony facing the river. According to the daughter of one of them, Zinaida Tuchina, "the grown-ups were very upset, and some even cried."[30]

It took several months to remove the rubble (referred to in official documents as "the pile"). According to Korshunov, "the workers brought to remove the pile worked in three shifts, with no days off. The site was lit up at night, and the shadows cast by the ruins seemed to move—as if the cathedral were still alive." On April 14, 1932, Adoratsky wrote to his daughter, who was staying at a Crimean resort, that the Cathedral of Christ the Savior "has disappeared for good: the brick-and-mortar Easter bread [*kulich*] has been completely liquidated." The only part of the neighborhood that remained untouched was the western corner of the Swamp between the candy factory and the Arrowhead. In the words of Inna Gaister from Apt. 167, "the conditions there were terrible: two-story buildings densely packed with large families and crawling with bedbugs."[31]

Final demolition of the Cathedral of Christ the Savior

After the explosion. The sign on the fence surrounding the
site says: "The source of opium is now a palace."
The House of Government can be seen in the background.

The House of Government was well protected from encroachment. As
of November 1, 1932, the number of officially registered residents was 2,745
(838 men, 1,311 women, 276 children under the age of six, and 320 children
ages six and older). They were shielded by 128 guards, 34 firefighters, 15
janitors (23 in the winter), 7 pest-control experts, a cedar hedge consisting
of three hundred trees (though many died the first year), and an unspecified number of bloodhounds (fed on specially ordered meat and cared for
by a full-time trainer). The guards manned all the gates and a desk in each
entryway. They wore military-style black uniforms with green insignia and
lived in ground-floor communal apartments.[32]

One of the head guards, Emelian Ivchenko, was the son of a peasant in
Briansk Province and a former Donbass miner. According to family tradition, one day in 1932, as a twenty-seven-year-old Central OGPU School
cadet patrolling the platform of Moscow's Leningrad Railway Station, he
had spotted a young girl crying. She told him that her name was Anna; that
she was seventeen years old; that she was originally from Borisoglebsk,
outside of Voronezh; that she had been working in the port of Leningrad
and been rewarded for her excellent work with a trip to Moscow; and that
on the train from Leningrad someone had stolen her wallet with all her
money and documents. He told her playfully that her only option was to
marry him and be registered as an OGPU officer's wife, but she chose instead to follow a young man in civilian clothes, who invited her to a party
at his dorm and promised to find her a place to stay. (She was, according
to her daughter, "a tough woman—she had been working as a stevedor,
after all! So, naturally, she drank, smoked, swore, and all that.") At the
party, Anna discovered that the dorm belonged to the Central OGPU

School, that the civilian young man was actually a plain-clothes agent, and that the cadet who had proposed to her was also there. After two weeks of futile attempts to get a job and be registered in a dorm, Anna agreed to marry Emelian because, as an OGPU's officer's wife, she could travel back home to Borisoglebsk for free; because he did not have any cash and could not help her in any other way; and because he struck her as a "very good, . . . very decent sort of person." She did not think that she was in love with him ("she felt too scared and too confused") but decided to return to him after her trip home anyway. Within a year, Emelian received an assignment to the House of Government and a three-room apartment there (Apt. 107). Anna got a job as a cashier at the post office. They went on to have five children: Vladimir (in 1935), Elsa (1937), Boris (1939), Viacheslav (1941), and Aleksandr (1943). Elsa got her name after a German woman whom Anna had met in the Kremlin maternity ward lost her baby daughter Elsa. Anna promised to name her daughter in her honor, and did.[33]

The House administrative staff occupied the first two floors of Entryway 1 and consisted of twenty-one employees including the manager, commandant, staff supervisor, and head of the registration desk, as well as various accountants, secretaries, cashiers, and couriers. Immediately above them, serving as a cushion between the House and the Government, was the apartment shared by the four prize-winning construction foremen, including the former Party secretary of the House of Government Construction Committee, Mikhail Tuchin. Eight adults and nine children shared nine rooms, two bathrooms, and two kitchens, and—after years of living in overcrowded dorms like most construction workers—considered themselves lucky and got along well. Mikhail Tuchin found a job as an inspector at nearby Gorky Park; his wife Tatiana (née Chizhikova) worked as a salesclerk in the accessories department of the House of Government store.[34]

Anna (*front, center*) and Emelian Ivchenko (*on her left*)

| Mikhail Tuchin | Tatiana Tuchina with Zinaida and Vova |

Other members of the staff were divided into service personnel (thirty-three employees, including the janitors, dog trainer, and various warehouse attendants), cleaning personnel (fifteen cleaning women and seven garbage collectors), and maintenance workers (fifty-eight carpenters, electricians, blacksmiths, metal workers, house painters, elevator technicians, and floor polishers, among others), who were joined by twenty-four heating technicians, three ventilation technicians, and sixty-nine repairmen. The House dining room had 154 employees; the laundry, 107; and the café in the movie theater, 34.[35]

Besides staff salaries, the highest expenses involved in the early running of the House of Government were heating (which proved much more costly than expected), elevator maintenance (forty-nine elevators and five permanent employees), water and sewage, restocking, supplies, current repairs, ventilation, and snow disposal. The House was supposed to pay for itself, and, during the first two years, it did. A substantial portion of the income came from the residents' rent and utilities payments, but the main contributors were the institutional tenants, particularly the theater, the movie theater, the department store, and the club.[36]

The House of Government club, or "The Club of the Employees of the Central Executive Committee of the USSR, the Central Executive Committee of the Russian Federation, and the Councils of People's Commissars of the USSR and the RSFSR," was a new and expanded version of the Rykov Club, formerly located in the Second House of Soviets (the Metropol). The new patron's name was Kalinin, and the new location was the space above the theater, or, as Adoratsky wrote to his daughter in March 1932, "the block with the uninterrupted line of glass windows facing the river. Tikhomirnov says that it is wonderful: there is a tennis court and different rooms where you can do whatever you like: play chess, music, etc." Besides tennis and chess, the club offered classes in fencing, painting, skating, skiing, singing, sewing, boxing, theater, volleyball, basketball, photography, stenography, target shooting, radio building, and various foreign

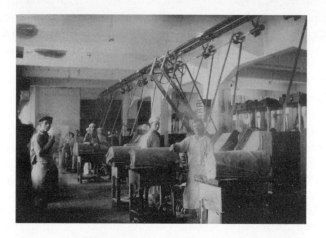

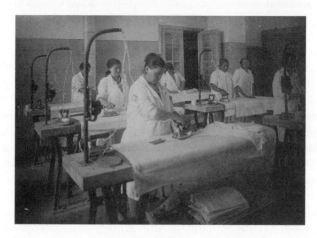

Laundry

Tennis court

languages. It opened a library and planned to organize three orchestras (symphony, wind, and domra) and to acquire fields for soccer and bandy ("Russian hockey") teams.[37]

. . .

The House of Government's most visible tenant was the New Theater, whose massive classical entrance served as the building's facade. Its company had been formed in 1925 by graduates of the Maly Theater School and was known, up until the move to the House of Government, as the Maly Theater Studio. It enjoyed the patronage of Avel Enukidze and the reputation, in the words of one contemporary critic, of a "mischievous, cheerful, and sunny" ensemble committed to a "highly individual style of light irony and life-affirming vitality."[38]

The theater's artistic director, Fedor Nikolaevich Kaverin, joined the Maly Theater School in 1918, when he was twenty-one years old. "Left behind," he wrote in his memoirs, were

> the gymnasium with its classical curriculum and unofficial student groups, one devoted to self-education and one, to Shakespeare; the three years in the Philology Department of Moscow University; the hard work in the military hospitals during the Imperialist War; the peripatetic life as a private tutor; the first ardent—and, for several years, unrequited—love; the accelerated graduation—as a junior officer—from the Alexander Military School during the February Revolution; the fever of the company, regiment, and garrison committees of the Kerensky era; the encounter with simple Russian soldiers and life and work among them; the friendship with the Bolsheviks at the front, and, finally, the return to Moscow.[39]

The "journey through the bubbling, flooding Motherland" ended. Kaverin discovered his true home in the theater and his life's hero in Gennady Neschastlivtsev, the tragic actor from A. N. Ostrovsky's *The Forest*:

> Neither my mind nor my heart could keep up with the wonderful chaos that, like a flood, came pouring down from the stage and completely enveloped me: Neschastlivtsev is an actor; the person playing Neschastlivtsev is also an actor; and this Aksiusha, whom he is initiating into the acting profession, is also a well-known actress. They are talking about the stage, about a life devoted to fame and art. That stage is right here in front of me. And then, suddenly, it is no longer a stage: the theater platform is transformed into an old garden, and the round flashlight behind the canvas sky looks like a real moon to me. But for Neschastlivtsev, on this great night of his initiation, both the garden and the moon are part of a stage setting. It is all intermingled: my swirling feelings, impressions, and thoughts raise me to dizzying heights. I want to run onto the stage, push the hesitating Aksiusha out of the way, kneel before the great madman, kiss his hand, take the oath, and, without thought or hesitation, accept initiation into the pure, knightly order of theater actors.[40]

According to his friend, the playwright Aleksandr Kron, Kaverin was faithful to his oath. "He was a jolly ascetic, a cheerful saint, a normal person fully possessed. . . . He was never coy, unless one counts the innocent desire to surprise and confound. He loved mystification. . . . He was always excited about something, and not just excited, but enraptured to the point of ecstasy, of delirious infatuation." He always smiled, "happily when he was understood and sadly and compassionately when he was not." He walked "with his hands pressed to his sides, treading carefully on his toes and bobbing to the rhythm of his steps, as if he were always bowing." Ruben Simonov, of the Vakhtangov Theater, claimed to have realized that he could play Don Quixote when he thought of Kaverin: "He wasn't tall, but he always looked over the heads of the people around him."

He was not a smooth speaker. "When excited, he often gave his actors impossible instructions such as: 'you should walk quickly past him with slow steps.' But the actors did not mind. They understood him." And he was a famously inept administrator. "Outside of work, he was soft and trusting, like a child. He had no practical sense, no shrewdness, and no toughness. . . . But in rehearsals, he was truly daring." Kaverin was always on-stage—or backstage. According to Kron, he walked the way he did because "he always walked as if he were backstage during a performance, trying not to make any noise, stumble over a cable, or run into a piece of scenery—as if he were saying: 'Hush! There's a show going on.' He loved the magic of the theater, its ability to transform nondescript rags and cheap baubles into fabulous garments and sparkling ornaments; he was intoxi-

cated by the rattling of wooden swords and the
clinking of cups wrapped in gold paper. What he
loved about theater was its theatricality."[41]

Kaverin objected to revolutionary theater (of
the *Mystery-Bouffe* variety) and, with his friends
from the Maly Theater School, used to boo during Meyerhold's speeches because he believed
that the avant-garde was destroying the magic
of theater. "You cannot search with your mind,
or search with only one of the senses," he wrote
in his diary in 1924, "because whatever is new for
the eye (constructivism) or for the ear (jazz) will
only offend the eye or the ear and never manage

Fedor Kaverin, 1928

to get it right." Theater "must be the nerve of its time and place." It must
"engage the audience."[42]

But Kaverin's main enemy was Stanislavsky's Moscow Art Theater,
which epitomized "the victory of prose, the triumph of the petty over the
sublime":

"Forget that you are in a theater!," its walls, chairs, and hidden stage
lights seem to be saying.

"Quiet! In just a second, I'll move discreetly out of the way, and
you, from your hiding place, will be able to spy on the lives of simple
and ordinary people just like you," the noble curtain—so modest yet
oh so boring—seems to be whispering.

"Look, we've banished theater from the stage," the whole production seems to be suggesting. "Don't you appreciate how well, how
intimately we know your life? At home, you have the same walls, the
same chairs, and the same steam rising from the samovar and soup
bowl."

"Can't you hear how we're speaking?" the actors seem to be asking. "Do we look like actors? Have you noticed the silences? You, too,
remain silent more often than you speak. It's true, this play, for
some reason, was written in verse, but we destroy that verse, we
break it up with our prosaic coughing, grunting, and wheezing."[43]

And what was the result? The result was that "our stages are haunted
by the dignified, tasteful ghosts of actors, who pause more than they
speak, . . . but lack the most important thing: creativity, Sturm und Drang.
In the best cases, such acting can amount to solid professionalism. But in
fact, it is the worst kind of formalism dressed up, like a wolf in sheep's
clothing, in the garments of verisimilitude."[44]

"Real theater" was like the Maly, or the way the Maly was meant to be.
"Long live Geltser's curtain with its gaily decorated drapery and golden
tassels, festive stage lights and bright strip of light peeking out from

underneath the curtain, sudden sunrises and nightfalls, elevated speech and expressive gestures"! Theater was a temple, no matter how "banal and cliché" the expression might be: "a temple of humanity, which reveals to humans what is great about them and what they do not see in the tedium of their daily routine."[45]

Kaverin's first independent production, in 1925, was *Kinoroman*, based on Georg Kaiser's 1924 *Kolportage*, a comedy of errors involving a large inheritance, a stolen baby, and a collection of scheming beggars, industrialists, and aristocrats. The idea, according to Kaverin, was to create "a parody of the kind of movie melodrama that continued to attract a large audience." Scenes were staged like a montage of film shots lit up by spotlights. "Platforms on casters moved actors from one end of the stage to the other, creating the impression of a motion picture. Black velvet curtains revealed and concealed shots as needed." During pauses, one could hear the clicking sound of the movie projector. A very large window and portraits of aristocratic ancestors with only their legs visible to the audience made the very small stage (the Sretenka Theater, with 320 seats, of which 20 were reserved for government officials) resemble a room in a large castle. The five-person orchestra "understood the humor of the concept" and brought it into "the tired old tunes they were playing."[46]

Kinoroman became a huge success and the studio's signature production. Another popular favorite from the mid-1920s was V. V. Shkvarkin's *Harmful Elements*, a comedy about gamblers and NEP-men that Kaverin staged as a vaudeville featuring dueling guitars, ringing alarm clocks,

Kinoroman (1925)

Harmful Elements (1927)

dancing curtains, jumping briefcases, swaying columns, and, most famously, a scene in prison, in which a group of gamblers, arranged around
a table like the Cossacks in Repin's painting, compose a letter to the prosecutor. Another big hit was Shakespeare's *All's Well That Ends Well*, which
began as "a boring comedy in verse" (with handkerchiefs falling from the
ceiling to help the grieving courtiers wipe away their tears), continued in
pantomime (with Helena, in typical NEP-era fashion, rejuvenating the king
by means of magic surgery), and ended well, with a wedding. One of
Kaverin's teachers from the Maly Theater, N. A. Smirnova, praised the "ostentatious theatricality and exaggerated characterization of the comic
figures and situations, combined with the tremendous lightness, simplicity, and sincerity in the depiction of the play's poetic moments."[47]

With the launching of the First Five-Year Plan and the rise of the Creation plot, tremendous lightness was no longer appropriate. Kaverin responded by producing D. Shcheglov's *The Recasting*, about a steelworker
who invents a machine that makes his own labor redundant. What follows,
in the words of one reviewer, is "the overcoming of narrow personal and
guild interests, their recasting in the interests of the whole plant and the
whole state." The new invention is adopted, the wrecker is slain, and the
doubting workers are born again. "By remaking the world, the proletariat
remakes itself." By staging this play, wrote Kaverin, the theater had
achieved "a genuine recasting." The principles of "nonliteral realism" had
found a proletarian content. The workers from the Hammer and Sickle
Plant who saw a special preview were greatly impressed, as were the critics. "Has the theater passed the test of modernity?" asked *Smena*. "It most
certainly has." The Maly Theater Studio, wrote the *Voronezh Commune* on
June 18, 1930, "has demonstrated its ability to move on to Soviet subject
matter."[48]

The work of recasting did not come easily to Kaverin. As he wrote in
his diary in the fall of 1928, "I reject art for art's sake, but sometimes I
have trouble resisting its lure and have to struggle mightily in order to

The Recasting (1929)

overcome it. I want to work with modern material, but all my dreams are about classical poetry and painting. I want to work for the new public, but I find the Theater of the Moscow Trade Union Council [MGSPS] disgusting and would be lying publicly if I were to accept what goes on there as art."[49]

He was against MGSPS's proletarian accessibility, "prescribed by the law and the authorities as a fixed ideal"; against the literal realists from the Association of Artists of Revolutionary Russia (AKhRR), who "speculate on the 'backwardness of the masses' in order to hide their own backwardness"; against arts administrators such as Kerzhentsev, "who introduce Cheka methods from the War Communism period into the politics of art"; and against every other attempt to "drive all discussions about art out of the art world." He was "no reactionary," of course: he wanted to "work in a cultured way," and he greatly admired his censor, Nikolai Ravich, who himself admired some of the plays he was censoring. "He is a cultured, broad-minded person and he probably has more right than most to inflict the terrible pain I have to endure as I make all these changes."[50]

According to Ravich, the workers in *The Recasting* suffered from too much doubt, and, according to the *Vecherniaia Moskva* (Evening Moscow) reviewer, the wrecker in the play was "too much of a Hamlet." Both seemed to be talking about Kaverin himself. As he wrote in his diary on September 3, 1928, "I love theater so much that life without it is like a desert. Yet sometimes I agonize to the point of believing that theater is like a silly and totally useless piece of candy and that only totally useless people can take it seriously, and so I start making perfectly fantastic plans about my future life outside the theater. I love theater, and I hate it. I love actors and I despise them." The key, he wrote on December 7, was "to keep on working as conscience dictates."[51]

Within two years, Kaverin's studio had passed the test of modernity and was invited to move into the future House of Government. After two more years, on April 23, 1932, a special Central Committee decree ordered the dissolution of the Russian Association of Proletarian Writers and "a similar change in other forms of art." On November 13, 1932, the newly renamed State New Theater (117 employees, including 60 actors) inaugurated its new 1,300-seat auditorium. The *Prologue*, which included characters from some of the troupe's best-known productions, was followed by the seven hundredth performance of *Kinoroman* and an official welcome ceremony featuring addresses by the deputy commissar of enlightenment, Comrade Epstein; deputy chairman of the Moscow City Soviet, Comrade Melbart; director of Odessa's January Uprising Factory, Comrade Ershov; spokesman from the Zhukovsky Air Force Academy, Comrade Lass; and head of the All-Russian Theater Society and celebrated Maly Theater actress, A. A. Yablochkina.[52]

Kaverin, who had just turned thirty-five, was awarded the title of "Distinguished Artist of the Republic." He was still subject to doubt: one month after the inaugural performance in the House of Government, he "accidentally came across" Trotsky's *My Life*. "The book is filled with such passion and conviction that sometimes you can't help having doubts: and what if all this is true? But no, it cannot be." It could not. Following the Party's rejection of the "Cheka methods" in the arts and owing to his own hard work of self-improvement, Kaverin had largely succeeded in recasting himself. Over the course of the summer and fall of 1932, while the theater was moving into the House, he had read Adoratsky's *On the Significance of Marxist-Leninist Theory*; Lenin's *Selected Articles on the National Question* ("copying out quotations chapter by chapter"), and, with particular diligence, Engels's *Origins of the Family, Private Property, and the State* ("this one is particularly useful for the theater; I should get to know it well; I've taken notes on the whole book, and will proceed this way with my classics"). The old classics looked different in light of the new ones: *Anna Karenina* "left a completely different impression after studying Marxism. Levin's utterly tendentious gentry point of view really sticks out in places." *Les misérables* was not appropriate for the stage either: "I don't see much point in it because I am wary of abstract romanticism and humanism." Nothing, in the end, could compare to Lenin as depicted in N. K. Krupskaia's memoirs. "The book touched me greatly. It forces you to think about such endless, unswerving self-abnegation in the service of an idea. As a human being, Lenin seems to be, in this sense, an ideal, . . . an amazing union of philosophical thought and daily activity."[53]

The first season in the House did not go well. According to Smirnova (who, as the studio's founder, also became a Distinguished Artist on November 13), "in the [old] small theater, the audience was able to see and hear everything. The actors were used to speaking in normal voices, applying light makeup, acting intimately, and conveying slight nuances by means of gestures and facial expressions. Neither the directors nor the actors took this into account when they pushed for moving from a crowded space into a large theater." In the new building, *Kinoroman*, in the words of Kaverin's friend and student, B. G. Golubovsky, "got lost in the vast expanse of the never-ending stage. The barely audible dialogue did not reach the audience; the only people laughing were those who had seen the show many times before." Kaverin called the opening night a bad omen. "The old shows did not take off on the enormous new stage; removed from the intimate space in Gnezdnikovsky Alley, they lost their charm."[54]

The new show, *The Other Side of the Heart*, did not take off either. Based on a Ukrainian-language novel by Yuri Smolich, it was a tale of doubles: two men who share the name Klim Shestipalyi. One "resembles a wolf, but a cunning wolf. His distinguishing characteristic is the degenerate's low forehead, with the hairline beginning almost at the eyebrows." The stage directions refer to him by his last name, "Shestipalyi" or "Sixfingers," which, according to a popular construction-plot convention, indicates the stamp of the beast. The other Klim—known simply as "Klim"—is "lanky, awkward, and absent-minded. His distinguishing features are his eyes: huge, with long eyelashes, radiant, naive, and ever ready to light up with joy, excitement, and enthusiasm."

The action begins shortly before the Revolution and ends during the Five-Year Plan. Sixfingers follows Klim everywhere, the way a last name follows a first. His job is to tempt, and possibly to reveal. Klim is a peasant who "parts with his pigs, breaks with his family, and leaves for the city to study and become a doctor." Once there, he continues to study while his friends join the Revolution. During the Civil War, he (still shadowed by Sixfingers) goes to fight—briefly and absentmindedly—on the side of the Reds. Arrested by the Whites for speculation, he saves his Bolshevik fiancée by claiming that she, too, is merely a trader. After the war, he lives abroad for a time among Cossack émigrés, who beat him up. Back in the Soviet Union, he reunites with his friends and fiancée and resumes his studies.

The last act begins in Kharkov: "In the background is the scaffolding of socialist construction. Then, before the eyes of the audience, the scaffolding disappears and the socialist city takes shape behind it." When Klim has only one exam left before graduation, he, his friends, his fiancée, and Sixfingers (who has been posing as a Soviet activist) decide to hire a maid. The old peasant woman who answers the ad turns out to be Klim's mother. "Angry, threatening, her arms akimbo," she tells him that their pigs have been collectivized and that his father has been sent to the Solovki concentration camp for attempting to burn down the house of the "whore" who presided over their ruin. Once inside the apartment, they realize that the "whore" is Klim's fiancée and that her acolytes are his friends and roommates. Stunned, Klim drops his mask and reveals what he has been hiding "on the other side of his heart." "The revolution has kept me from making something of myself!" he screams. "It has taken everything away from me! It has destroyed my life!"[55]

By the time he pulls himself together, it is too late: he has shown himself to be the enemy. His fiancée tells their friend, the undoubting Bolshevik, Makar Tverdokhleb ("Hardbread"): "Only yesterday I was urging our comrades to be vigilant, and look at me now." Sixfingers calls the secret police and reports on Klim's "brazen counterrevolutionary display." Makar Tverdokhleb orders Sixfingers to sit down and wait for the secret police. Curtain.[56]

The censor ordered Kaverin to "tone down the kulak hysterics" in the final act. Even after the revisions, however, most critics were not convinced. At a special discussion in the Theater Department of the Commissariat of Enlightenment on December 17, 1933, one of them, a Comrade Vinogradov, called the whole premise erroneous. "You would like to show Klim as a class enemy under the mask of romanticism and realism. The audience likes Klim, the audience believes in him and sympathizes with him when he makes mistakes. It feels sorry for Klim and thinks that his mistakes are the result of his weakness. And then, suddenly, in the last act, in the starkest—I would even say, RAPPist—way possible, you proclaim him to be a class enemy. Who will believe it? No one will believe it because the dramatic material does not plant a single seed for such a transformation." In fact, said another participant, "what stands out in the minds of the spectators who have seen the three previous acts is not the biological connection to the mother, which you try to demonstrate, but the development of the character that they have been observing for three hours. The spectators know Klim as someone who has been wavering for three hours, but is always on the side of the Reds, and then, suddenly, his mother comes and he is reborn. The spectators do not believe it." The trust between the theater and the audience had been broken. "This is not theatrical deception," argued another critic, "this is a swindle. Deception is achieved by more complex means, but if you try to swindle your audience, all it is left with at the end of the show is a sense of disappointment." According to a certain Comrade Uspensky, "a story has been making the rounds about an old Jew, who happened to be sitting next to a Party member. At the beginning of the fourth act, he suddenly says: 'There's something fishy going on here' [laughter]." "So why does the Fourth Act feel false? Because every morning, our spectator reads in the newspapers about the White Sea–Baltic Canal and the construction of the Volga–Don Canal, and reads various letters from former wreckers, . . . and so this spectator knows that, in our epoch, human regeneration is an everyday occurrence. But in this show, he sees the opposite: he sees that, in spite of everything, he cannot be reborn, cannot become a useful member of society. It is no wonder the spectator feels that the ending is false."[57]

Creation stories included conversion stories; conversion stories—successful or not—had to be psychologically motivated. According to the majority opinion, Klim's character "cannot be considered from the point of view of social categories. He is a pathological character, not a social category." There were some obvious enemies, like Sixfingers; there were some obvious paragons, "who do not oppose the personal to the collective." And then, "lost in between these two sets of characters, is a blue-eyed boy named Klim." He was the only nontransparent character, the only candidate for conversion, the only protagonist whose motivations needed to be understood. He might yet be saved (like those "Canal Army Fighters" baptized by Aron Solts), or he might be damned (like Ehrenburg's Volodia Safonov in *The Second Day*)—but he could not simply switch masks. Vigilance was about psychological insight, not relentless paranoia.[58]

Kaverin defended his creation along two interconnected lines. One had to do with his theatrical credo, his desire "to work with a text that has an edge to it, that rises somewhat above the pedestrian realism and naturalism that reigns in most other theaters and that we consider unacceptable and refuse to make our own." The audience was shocked because the theater had done its job. "When the old Jew mentioned by Uspensky says, 'there's something fishy going on here,' he is saying exactly what we want him to say. We know that when the fourth act starts, the spectator has to say to himself: 'this makes no sense.' There are moments on stage when we say: 'pause.' This pause should make the spectator believe that the actors have forgotten their lines." The idea, it is true, is "to deceive the spectator," but "only at a certain moment in the show, as a way of breaking with existing theatrical conventions."[59]

Kaverin's other argument had to do with the ideological concept of the enemy and with his own efforts at self-recasting. Most of those present were of nonproletarian origin. None mentioned, and perhaps none thought relevant, that Fedor Kaverin, an intelligentsia fellow traveler, was "soft and trusting, like a child"; that he had "no practical sense, no shrewdness, and no toughness"; and that he was "always excited about something, and not just excited, but enraptured to the point of ecstasy, of delirious infatuation." There was a special reason why he wanted to stage *The Other Side of the Heart*:

> This Klim—this soft, trusting Klim who is so quick to fall under the influence of others and so quick to escape it—this Klim struck us all, including the actors, as a particularly familiar enemy because this Klim, lit up by the suns of his eyes, still lives in many of us. This Klim may be a greater enemy than Sixfingers because Sixfingers is an obvious enemy, whereas Klim is someone we still feel within ourselves, someone we are still trying very hard to completely strangle within ourselves, but have not been able to completely strangle yet. We realize that this Klim still lives in our attitudes toward our roles, toward each other, and toward our work. This Klim deserves more of our hatred and our anger.[60]

A few speakers supported Kaverin. The actress Maria Boichevskaia (herself the daughter of a high tsarist official) said that she had realized right away that Klim would turn out to be an enemy. A Comrade Garbuzov said that Klim had not been executed yet and might still be reborn ("I can foresee a whole story of inner struggle, a whole history of regeneration," an "Act Five"). But it was Kaverin's colleague, S. I. Amaglobeli, the recently arrived and soon-to-be-retired administrative director of New State Theater, who spelled out the implications of Kaverin's position:

> Politically, this show is done correctly because none of us has a fully transparent soul. If we take a transverse section of our souls, including that of Comrade Vinogradov, we would find positive and negative traits—not good and evil in the general sense, but, as part of the complex creation of the socialist era, some enduring elements of individualism. . . .
>
> We can see that each part of the show plays with the spectator the way a cat plays with a mouse. The cat lets the mouse loose, and then pounces on it again. Our theater does the same thing. In this show, it offers a story, then grabs the spectator, confounds that story, and proclaims that it is nothing but bourgeois individualism. It is a good device, but it is painful for those who find themselves in the role of the mouse.
>
> Yes, there is the White Sea–Baltic Canal construction. And from that we can conclude that wreckers are being reborn because our Soviet reality is so bounteous that even our enemies can be reborn. . . . But does that mean that we will not be watching every move they make? Of course not. It would be a mistake to say that we should not be extra vigilant toward those who engage not in deception, like Klim Sixfingers, but in self-deception, like the other Klim.[61]

The general Bolshevik conception of sin was identical to St. Augustine's ("a thought, words and deed against the Eternal Law"). The key Marxist innovation consisted of the discovery that original sin (derived from the primeval division of labor and perpetuated through class exploitation) applied in different degrees to different social groups. Various nonproletarian categories were to be subjected to "concentrated violence," close surveillance, and special requirements concerning the "inner struggle" in "act five." This did not mean, however, that proletarians were free of the "enduring elements of individualism." The difference was one of degree: no one's soul was fully transparent, and no one's thoughts adhered unswervingly to the Eternal Law. As Bukharin put it, "even some relatively wide circles of the working class bear the seal of commodity capitalism. This inevitably leads to the need for *coercive discipline*. . . . Even the proletarian avant-garde, consolidated in the party of the insurrection, must establish such *coercive self-discipline* in its own ranks; it is not strongly felt by many elements of this avant-garde because it coincides with internal motives, but it exists nonetheless."[62]

No one's internal motives, including Bukharin's, coincided with the Eternal Law; everyone, with the possible exception of the Eternal Law's ex officio representative, was a mouse. Bolshevik soteriology, like its Christian rival and predecessor, assumed that full perfection in this world was impossible. Only with the coming of Communism would the seal of commodity capitalism be wiped off, the enduring elements of individualism, eliminated, and the cycle of eternal return, broken forever. The real question—for all theories of salvation—is what happens in the meantime. How can one prepare oneself and help others prepare? Amaglobeli's (perfectly Christian) answer was that everyone—to varying degrees—was to submit, and subject others, to permanent surveillance and relentless repentance. This was obviously correct in the abstract, but what did it mean for literary plots, theater performances, and individual lives? As Bukharin's fellow-Rightist, Mikhail Tomsky, said at the Sixteenth Party Congress, "it seems to me, comrades, that it is a little difficult to be in the role of a permanent penitent." Sixfingers could not be trusted; the other Klim could not be trusted; Tomsky could not be trusted; and, since no one's soul was fully transparent, the undoubting Bolshevik Makar Hardbread could not be trusted, either. If "words are meaningless," concluded Tomsky, "then we must stop talking altogether. What is the point of talking?"

Most of the participants in the discussion of *The Other Side of the Heart* in December 1933 did not stop talking. A solution, of sorts, was provided by the deputy head of the Theater Department of the Commissariat of Enlightenment, Pavel Ivanovich Novitsky, who presided over the conference. "The question of the class enemy, the double-dealer, the traitor, the timeserver . . . must be addressed," he said in his concluding remarks, "but I insist that the question of the class enemy is not the same question as that of the remnants of bourgeois and petit bourgeois mentality in each one of us." There was a difference between defeating the class enemy and overcoming the enduring elements of individualism, a difference that was not directly related to class origins. "If the theater wanted to show the class enemy in each of us, in our morals and everyday behavior, if it wanted to unmask many of us, it went about it the wrong way."[63]

Novitsky was proposing a version of Thomas Aquinas's distinction between mortal sins, which involve a deliberate rejection of the Eternal Law, and venial sins, which are a matter of carelessness and disorder. The story of Klim falls into the second category. "I insist that the blue-eyed Klim, as a dramatic character, is evolving in the direction of Soviet reality. For me, this is a fact. . . . And if he is evolving in the direction of Soviet reality, then the theme of the class enemy has been replaced by another theme, that of the possibility of class rebirth." The play's denouement betrayed the spectator by betraying its own "aesthetic texture":

> At issue is not whether it feels false or not; it is that the spectator does not agree with you. Why? Because this is the most important

question for us, the central question of socialist construction, of a new attitude toward labor, toward work, toward the state, and toward your comrades: the question of overcoming, within each one of us, the survivals of petit bourgeois mentality, property-centered selfish mentality, self-interested mentality. Our task is to give a new, socialist birth to the whole immense mass of petit bourgeois, proletarian, and semiproletarian working people of our country, and even to all the remnants of the capitalist classes, and turn them into useful members of a classless socialist society. Not only every employee, every intelligentsia member, and every actor, but every Communist, too, should think of nothing else, as we all engage in the inner struggle aimed at the reeducation of human beings.[64]

The Other Side of the Heart was not appropriate because the whole point of the reconstruction period was that even the remnants of the capitalist classes were capable of being reborn. The show was dropped until further notice.

Entrance to the theater

11

THE ECONOMIC FOUNDATIONS

The Stalin revolution, launched in 1927, is also known as the great break-through, the revolution from above, the period of transition, the period of reconstruction, and, most commonly, the era of the First Five-Year Plan. The First Five-Year Plan was inaugurated in 1928 and completed in 1932, one year ahead of schedule. Its purpose was to bring about the fulfillment of the original prophecy by creating the Revolution's economic preconditions. The Revolution was supposed to have taken place in an industrialized society. The First Five-Year Plan, insofar as it was a plan, consisted of industrializing the Soviet Union ten years after the Revolution and, according to Stalin, fifty to a hundred years after the "advanced countries" had reached this state. Industrialization was to be accompanied by its presumed consequences: the abolition of private property and the destruction of class enemies. Different parts of the original prophecy were to come true simultaneously, inevitably, and as the result of deliberate effort. The effort was to come from "Ukrainians and Tatars, Buriats, Cheremis, Kalmyks, peasants from Perm and Kaluga, coal miners from Yuzovka, turners from Kolomna, bearded road pavers from Riazan, Komsomols, exiled kulaks," and everyone else involved in the building of the house of socialism. The Stalin revolution was about adding an industrial foundation to the already solid political roof. The work of industrialization was to be carried out at "great construction sites" that rivaled the second day of creation: the Magnitogorsk and Kuznetsk steel mills, the Kharkov and Stalingrad tractor plants, the Nizhny and Moscow automobile plants, the Dnieper Hydroelectric Dam, the White Sea–Baltic Canal, the Turkestan–Siberia Railway, and the Berezniki chemical plant, among others.[1]

One of the first construction projects to be completed was the House of Government, which served as the Moscow home for most of the top industrial managers. The House's chief architect, Boris Iofan, lived in a large penthouse apartment on the top floor of Entryway 21 with his wife Olga and her two children by a previous marriage. Olga and Boris had met in Italy, as fellow members of the Communist Party. Olga was the daughter of Duke Fabrizio Sasso-Ruffo and Princess Natalia Meshcherskaia. Her first husband was Boris Ogarev, a cavalry officer. The Iofans' apartment overlooked Iofan's next—and the world's last—public building, the Palace of Soviets.

The head of construction of the Palace of Soviets was Vasily Mikhailov, a former stitcher at
the Sytin printshop, one of the leaders of the
October insurrection in Moscow, head of the
Moscow Trade Union Council in the early days of
the House of Government construction, fighter
against flies in workers' soup bowls, a "vacillat-
ing" Right deviationist, and, by way of punishment, deputy head of construction of the Dnieper
Hydroelectric Dam (where he became one of the
prototypes of the Bolshevik Moses in Fedor Gladkov's *Energy*). Brought back to Moscow for a job

Vasily Mikhailov

he, according to his daughter, did not want, he
shared his apartment (Apt. 52, in Entryway 3) with his wife Nadezhda Ushakova, a fellow Old Bolshevik and the daughter of a forestry professor at
the Timiriazev Academy; their daughter Margarita; Vasily's two daughters
by a previous marriage; and Nadezhda's daughter by her first husband,
Johann Kuhlmann, a Soviet secret agent in Germany.[2]

The man in charge of all Moscow construction was Nikita Khrushchev,
who had interrupted his career as a Party official in Ukraine in order to
study at the Industrial Academy, where he had received the double good
fortune of prevailing over the Right Opposition and meeting Stalin's wife,
Nadezhda Allilueva. Within three years of arriving in the capital, he had
become head of the Moscow Party Committee (de facto, under Kaganovich,
in January 1932, and officially in January 1934). His main job was to rebuild
Moscow; his most important assignment was to create its idealized reflection underground. The Moscow Metro was an upside-down version of the
Bronze Horseman's (Peter the Great's) imperial capital: functional and
palatial in equal measure, it grew downward through the swamp. As
Khrushchev wrote in his memoirs, the work of construction "had to be
carried out in the conditions of underground Moscow—in Moscow's soil,
full of quicksand and saturated with water." He claims to have spent 80
percent of his time underground. "I would go to work at the Party Committee and back from work through the subway shafts." His home above
ground was a five-room apartment in the House of Government (Apt. 206),
where he lived with his parents; his two children from a previous marriage; his wife, Nina Petrovna Kukharchuk; and their three young children
(Rada, born in Kiev in 1929, and Sergei and Elena, born in Moscow in 1935
and 1937).[3]

The Metro's most immediate sacred prototype was the Lenin Mausoleum (the "first-phase" stations tended to imitate its combination of a
modest, symmetrical above-ground temple with a granite-and-marble
netherworld). On December 31, 1925, Lenin's embalmers, Boris Zbarsky
and Vladimir Vorobiev, had written to the Commission for the Im-
mortalization of Lenin's Memory, urging the government to replace the

temporary mausoleum with a permanent one. "Continued preservation of the body in the temporary mausoleum is intolerable," they wrote. "Fungi have been detected on the padding of the walls, the flag of the Paris Commune, and even on the clothes, one hand, behind the right ear, and on the forehead. Disinfection of the entire building is impossible." The stone version of the mausoleum was built at the same time as the other foundations of socialism—and just as quickly. Construction work began in the spring of 1929 and was completed by October 1930, in time for the thirteenth anniversary of the Revolution. The following year, the body's chief guardian, Boris Zbarsky, moved into Apt. 26, which he shared with his son by a previous marriage, Ilya; his new wife, Evgenia; and their infant son, Lev-Feliks (born in 1931). In 1934, ten years after the initial embalming, a special government commission concluded that "the work of preserving the body of Vladimir Ilich Lenin for an extended period of time must be considered a brilliant success. . . . The commission finds it necessary to emphasize that the preservation of the body of V. I. Lenin is a scientific achievement without precedent in history." At the same time, the twenty-one-year-old Ilya Zbarsky, who had recently graduated from Moscow University, was made his father's assistant. As he wrote in his memoirs, "I was taken by the mystique of the priests' solemn performance. The word 'paraschite,' in particular, fascinated me: there was something mystical and bewitching about it." ("Paraschites," he explained elsewhere, were members of the Egyptian caste of embalmers who "lived in special city quarters away from the rest of society" and specialized in "making cuts in the chest and abdominal cavities on the left side of the corpse.") "At first I imagined myself a paraschite and compared our little group to Egyptian priests officiating at a sacred ritual. I even thought about writing a novel called 'The Paraschites,' with Vorobiev and my father, under fictitious names, as the main characters." Soon, however, the work on Lenin's body "became a habitual routine":

> [We] would come to the Mausoleum two or three times a week, closely inspect the exposed parts of the body—the face and the hands—and moisten them with the embalming solution in order to prevent desiccation and parchmentization. At the same time, we would remove various small defects: the darkening of certain sections of the skin, small spots, the appearance of new pigments or changes of color. Sometimes it would prove necessary to correct an occasional change in shape. In such cases, we resorted to injections of a paraffin-vaseline fusion. The most alarming development, however, was the appearance of patches of mold: we had to carefully clean and disinfect those areas. . . . Particularly important was the preservation of natural coloring and the prevention of the appearance of the grayish-brown pigmentation caused by formalin.[4]

■ ■ ■

The chemicals used in the preservation of Lenin's body (as well as in curing the sick, fertilizing the soil, refining fuel, and exterminating pests, among many other things) were to be produced in the Soviet Union. One of the top construction projects of the First Five-Year Plan—mentioned by Osinsky in his letter to Shaternikova as one of his "favorite children"—was the chemical plant in Berezniki, in the northern Urals, next to Zinaida Morozova's estate, where Boris Zbarsky invented the new method of purifying medical chloroform (while Ilya watched Boris Pasternak court his mother). Launched in 1929 and known as "the City of Light," it was a miraculous realization of Leonid Leonov's *The Sot'*, which was written at the same time. Built on the left bank of the Kama, not far from several seventeenth-century saltworks, a soda plant, and vast newly discovered potash deposits, the Berezniki Chemical Works was to produce ammonia and ammonia-based nitrogen fertilizers for the new Soviet industry. According to a special report of the Committee on Location, "the low, swampy river bank was subject to annual spring floods. This problem could be solved . . . by building a protective dam and filling the area with imported soil two to four meters high, as well as by installing special foundations capable of ensuring the stability of structures on swampy land and weak soil filling."[5]

The man in charge—as head of construction and then director of the chemical works—was Mikhail Aleksandrovich Granovsky. According to one of his deputies, Z. Kh. Tsukerman,

> Granovsky was a typical economic manager of the tempestuous, exceptionally tense period of the First Five-Year Plan. An enormous capacity for work, harsh temperament, native intelligence, mercilessness toward himself and others, tremendous willpower, determination, an ability to sort out every detail of the most complicated question, courage, relentless drive, intolerance toward formalism and hypocrisy, an ability to set specific tasks—these were the traits that I saw in him during our work together. He was a strong manager, a take-charge commander. Unfortunately, his positive qualities could occasionally turn into negative ones, such as rudeness and curtness. He paid no attention to time: he could work night and day, and he demanded the same of his workers. . . . Of course, in the

Site of the Berezniki Chemical Plant, 1929

Mikhail Granovsky

difficult struggle for the fulfillment of the plan, there were cases of dictatorial excess. But, as they say, a pike lives in the lake to keep all the fish awake.[6]

Granovsky was born in 1893 in Zvenigorodka, Ukraine, in the family of a Jewish merchant. At the age of fifteen, he became a revolutionary. From 1913 to 1917, he studied chemical engineering at the Moscow Commercial Institute. After participating in the Moscow insurrection, he served as head of the Chernigov Economic Council, the Ukrainian Wine and Spirits Commission, and the All-Union Syndicate of the Glass and Ceramics Industry. In the fall of 1929, he took command of the Berezniki project. His family—wife Zinaida and two sons, Anatoly and Valentin—joined him the following spring, when the weather was warmer and the director's house had been built. Their five-room apartment in the House of Government (Apt. 418) was to remain vacant until their return. Anatoly was eight at the time. As he wrote (in English) in his memoirs,

We went by rail as far as Perm in comfortable Pullman coaches, and from there by river boat to Berezniki. It was a delightful journey. From the windows of the train Valentin and I looked entranced at the scene changing before us—the glistening early morning frost on the ground, the little farms with their untidy yards mostly empty of animals; here a cow, there a goat, maybe a couple of geese. And then the little villages, huddles of log houses with thatched or boarded roofs. It took us altogether four days.

My father was at the quayside to meet us, together with a large delegation of the district notables. The welcome was effusive as befitted the wife and children of the most important man for miles around.

We were driven in a Ford car to our new home, the top floor of a large wooden house, and all those who had met us followed to drink a toast in vodka to our homecoming. There was much talking and laughing and our heads were patted avuncularly by a number of burly men. The house had been liberally warmed by fires that must have been burning half the day, and there was a smell of new paint and a freshness that came from the pine forests not far off.

I was vaguely excited and it seemed like the beginning of a new era for me. I did not know that it was also, to some extent, the end of innocence.[7]

After the floods, quicksand, the cold, and two major fires, Mikhail Granovsky's greatest trial was the labor shortage. According to Tsukerman, "the man's character was certainly difficult and often unpleasant, but in order to judge him fairly, one must have a clear sense of the enormity of the task and the conditions in which the work of construction was being carried out. These conditions were exceptionally difficult. Just to take one example, when it came to personnel, besides a certain number of people who were ready to dedicate all their abilities to the great cause, besides the genuine enthusiasts of the project, there were plenty of people who were there for a variety of other reasons." About two hundred of them were foreigners, who came for the good pay, out of genuine enthusiasm, to escape unemployment at home, or—the majority—because their firms had sent them over to install and service equipment (the largest were Nitrogen, Babcock & Wilcox, and Cemico from the United States; Power Gas from Britain; Brown-Bovary from Switzerland; and Sulzer, Borzig, Hannomag, Zimmerman, Kerstner, Siemens-Schuckert, Ergart Semer, Leine Werke, and Krupp from Germany). They lived in a separate settlement and ate in a special restaurant. Granovsky called them "the Capitalist International."[8]

At first, the preparatory work of filling the swamp was done by local villagers, who transported the sand in horse-drawn carts. They were reinforced by genuine enthusiasts sent by the Komsomol Central Committee from Moscow and Leningrad (about two hundred in April 1930, when Granovsky's family arrived), and, in more significant numbers, by contract laborers, mostly refugees from collectivization. Some skilled workers were transferred by the People's Commissariat of Labor from other, less strategically important sites. According to a crew leader from Kazan, "workers were coming from all over the Soviet Union. There were all kinds: Muscovites, Leningraders, Siberians, lots of our people from Kazan, and up to a thousand diggers with their horse carts from somewhere beyond Kurgan. They built a whole city of dugouts along the banks of the Zyrianka and the Talycha. They drank water from the river and slept under their carts and wagons." Few of them stayed for long. As Granovsky wrote on January 1, 1931, "the workers sent to the construction site as contract laborers or transfers from other enterprises tend to arrive in Berezniki without any warm clothing. With the coming of cold weather, they demand warm clothing, but such demands cannot be fully met. We have received only 350 of the 3,960 pairs of felt boots we had ordered and only 300 of the 2,500 winter jackets." At the time Granovsky wrote this letter, the number of workers leaving Berezniki exceeded the number of new arrivals.[9]

One solution was to have whole villages—or rather, newly created collective farms—assigned to the project. The construction management would sign a contract with a rural district pledging to deliver agricultural equipment and telephone lines in exchange for labor by peasant crews. Enforcement proved difficult, however: according to an official report, "during a period of nine months in 1933–34, 1,263 collective farmers from the [Elovo] district were recruited to work in the construction of the

Work on the Berezniki site

Berezniki Works. Of those, 493 left the site without having worked a single day." A more effective strategy was to use the labor of peasant deportees ("special settlers"). In 1930–31, 571,355 "dekulakized" peasants were exiled to the Urals, 4,437 of them, to the Berezniki District. Those who were assigned to construction work were settled in barracks not far from the site. On any given day, about five hundred to six hundred "special settlers" were employed in the work of filling the swamp. The question of who, if anyone, should provide food rations for nonworking family members remained a matter of debate and improvisation for a number of years.[10]

Despite these measures, the labor shortage at the site remained acute. In the fall of 1929, the People's Commissariat of Labor called the situation "catastrophic"; in late 1930, Granovsky admitted that "the supply of labor has fallen short of the plan by a considerable margin" (at least 3,500 workers). The solution proved both obvious and innovative: Berezniki and the neighboring Vishera Paper Mill in Vizhaikha became pioneers in the large-scale use of convict labor. Before 1929, the only labor camp in the Soviet Union was the Solovki Special Purpose Camp, which included the White Sea–Baltic Canal site and had a branch on the Vishera, north of Berezniki. In 1926–27, a Solovki inmate, N. A. Frenkel, proposed, and later administered, the use of prisoners on construction projects outside the camp. On June 27, 1929, the deputy head of the OGPU, G. Yagoda (Yakov Sverdlov's second cousin, also married to his niece, Ida), and the head of the OGPU's Special Department, G. I. Bokii, ordered that the Vishera camp be expanded from five thousand to eight thousand inmates, and that they "pay the full cost of their upkeep by being employed in work that does not involve the use of state funding." Two weeks later, on July 11, the Council of People's Commissars issued a decree "On the Use of Criminal Inmate Labor," which prescribed the creation of a new network of labor camps charged with developing sparsely populated northern territories and "exploiting mineral resources by using prison labor." The Vishera branch of the Solovki camp was transformed into a separate Vishera Special Purpose Camp and expanded to accommodate additional inmates. Industrialization was to rely on forced labor as much as it did on "genuine enthusiasts."[11]

G. G. Yagoda

∎ ∎ ∎

The new policy and the new wave of prisoners solved Granovsky's labor problem. A few weeks after the publication of the decree, a group of Vishera prisoners was sent down to Berezniki. Among them was Varlam Shalamov. "In the fall of 1929, in the company of Angelsky, a former officer who had run away from Perm that same year, and fifty other prisoners, I set out by boat from Vizhaikha to the settlement of Lenva, near Usolye, in order to found a new branch of the Vishera camp, thus inaugurating the giant of the First Five-Year Plan, Berezniki."[12] The branch became a transit point, and then a camp.

> The inmates spent the winter of 1929–30 "warming up" the stone boxes erected by the contract laborers in Churtan, the City of Light. There were thousands, tens of thousands of people sleeping on the damp planks or heaped together on the floor and spending their days building the City of Light, working at the chemical plant, or building a new camp for themselves a little closer by, on Adam's Mountain. . . . As soon as the new camp on Adam's Mountain was finished, the construction workers were moved over there. They found forty barracks, built according to the two-level Solovki model, and the camp service personnel waiting for them.[13]

Only the best workers from each convoy were selected to work at the site. The camp commander, M. V. Stukov, and head of personnel (and convicted "wrecker"), P. P. Miller, prided themselves on being able to see the other side of the heart:

> Huge convoys passing through on their way to the camp headquarters would stand in formation at the Berezniki station. Stukov, the head of the Berezniki branch, would walk down the line and simply point his finger, without asking anything and almost without looking—"this one, this one, this one,"—selecting, without fail, the hardworking peasants, who had been arrested under Article 58.
> "But they're all kulaks, Citizen Commander!"
> "You're still young and eager. The kulaks are the very best workers."
> And he would grin.[14]

Over the course of a year (from the summer of 1929 to the summer of 1930), the overall number of inmates in OGPU camps increased from 22,848 to about 155,000 (in addition to the about 250,000–300,000 being held in republic-level NKVD camps). The prison population of the Vishera camp, which included both Berezniki and the Vizhaikha paper mill, grew from 7,363 in 1929 to about 39,000 in April 1931. On April 25, 1930, a new OGPU camp administration was formed. After November, it became known as the Main Camp Administration, or GULAG.[15]

In Berezniki, according to Shalamov, matters had come to a head in the fall of 1929, around the time of his—and Granovsky's—arrival:

> Granovsky, the head of construction or some Moscow commission— it's all the same—discovered that the first stage of the Berezniki Works, for which millions of rubles had already been spent, simply did not exist. . . .
>
> Granovsky and his deputy, Omelianovich, and later Chistiakov, had a noose hanging over their heads. Both the engineer and the administrator had run away from Berezniki in fear, but Granovsky, the boss who had been sent down by the Central Committee, could not escape. It was at this moment that a brilliant solution was suggested to him—to get the camp involved in the construction.[16]

After three months of work by the carefully selected Berezniki inmates and many more unaccounted-for transit prisoners, "the honor of the project was saved, and the territory was connected to a real railroad with real train cars and filled with real sand procured in a real forest quarry."[17]

In the summer of 1930, a special OGPU commission came to inspect the new camp. The head of the commission was the thirty-two-year-old deputy head of the GULAG, Matvei Berman. The son of a brick factory owner and graduate of Chita Commercial College, Berman had been in the Cheka/OGPU since the Civil War. He had recently received an apartment in the House of Government, but, like Granovsky, was hardly ever in Moscow. According to the history of the White Sea–Baltic Canal (written after Berman became head of GULAG),

> It took this man very little time to answer the personnel-form question concerning his occupation since 1917.
>
> What did cause some difficulty was the question concerning his permanent address. To save time, he would have preferred to write nothing and simply attach the map of the Soviet Union. But this did not prove possible. What could he do? In the personnel office they always told him there was no such place of registration. And this was said to a person who, over the course of twelve years, had changed only his place of residence—never his occupation. . . .

He could spot an engineer, tsarist army officer, dentist, manufacturer, railroad worker,
or apartment building manager as easily as if
each one were openly wearing a badge of his
profession. In fact, many were concealing it
and surviving by passing themselves off as
other people.

He knew the dialects of the Urals, Siberia,
Ivanovo-Voznesensk, and the docks. And although many people lacked such powers of
recognition, Berman did not think it was anything special. It was a common trait among
the breed of people to whom he belonged.

Matvei Berman

Berman was a Chekist. He lived with the clear knowledge that he
was responsible for the Party each day of his life.

He was permanently engaged in the creative intellectual process
of generalization. A casual word, unexpected intonation, unconscious gesture, stiff gait, accidental occurrence, or odd error would
imprint themselves on his memory.

A railroad official's cap glimpsed through the window of an international train car at the Tashkent Station might become linked
to an automobile parked in front of a famous professor's house in
Leningrad.

What all these capriciously scattered details had in common was
an absolute hostility and mendacity.

The counterrevolution no longer liked to speak openly or look
one in the eye. It had learned to detect and distinguish voices by the
movement of the lips alone; to interpret a look by the tension in the
eyelids or the slight trembling of the eyelashes.

Berman's perspicacity, the counterrevolution's hostility, and the needs
of industrialization came together in the "Vishera experiment." According
to the same history,

A convict costs the state more than 500 rubles per year. Why on
earth should workers and peasants feed this army of parasites,
swindlers, wreckers, and counterrevolutionaries? Let's send them
to the camps and say: "Here are your means of production. Work, if
you want to eat. Such is the principle of existence in our country. We
will make no exception for you."

The camps should be run by an organization that will be able to
carry out the important economic assignments and initiatives of
the Soviet state and to colonize a number of new territories.

"Such was the direct order of the Party and government," remembered Berman.[18]

In the summer of 1930, he had just begun the work of building the GULAG. According to Shalamov,

> Berman arrived with a large retinue, all wearing trench coats with two or three stars on the collars. Berzin, the Vishera camp commander, a man of impressive height with a dark goatee and wearing a long cavalry coat with three stars, loomed over the other members of the commission. Accordingly, Stof—the army medic, inmate, and head of the medical section who was supposed to report to the commission—leapt off the porch and, goose-stepping straight up to Berzin, directed the full poetry of his camp report at him.
>
> Berzin stepped to one side and, with the words "This is the Commander," gave way to a short, stocky man with a pale prison face, wearing a worn black leather jacket—the obligatory Cheka uniform of the first days of the revolution.
>
> In an attempt to aid the bewildered medic, the GULAG boss unbuttoned his jacket to reveal the four stars on his collar. But Stof was struck dumb. Berman shrugged, and the commission moved on.
>
> The brand-new camp territory glistened in the sun. Every piece of barbed wire shone and glittered blindingly. Inside were forty barracks—250 two-level, continuous bunks each, according to the Solovki standard of the 1920s; a bathhouse with an asphalt floor for 600 wooden tubs with hot and cold water; a theater with a projection booth and a large stage; an excellent new disinfection chamber; and a stable for 300 horses.[19]

The inspection went well. The head of camp personnel and convicted wrecker, P. P. Miller, took advantage of the good mood and asked Berman for an audience. His account of the meeting was recorded by Shalamov: "Berman was sitting behind the desk when I entered the room and stood to attention, as required. 'So tell me, Miller, what exactly did you wreck?' asked the head of the GULAG, clearly enunciating each word. 'I did not wreck anything, Citizen Commander,' I said, and felt my mouth go dry. 'Then why did you ask for a meeting? I thought you wished to make an important confession. Berzin!' the head of the GULAG called out loudly. Berzin stepped inside the office. 'Yes, Comrade Commander.' 'Take Miller away.' 'Yes, Comrade Commander.'"[20]

■ ■ ■

The brick factory was ready by August 1930; most of the auxiliary shops (foundry, smithy, welding shop), by early 1931; the oxygen plant, by May 1931; the sulphuric acid factory, by December 1931. On April 25, 1932, *Pravda* wrote: "The ammonia factory of the Berezniki Chemical Works has started production. It is a great day not only for the Soviet chemical industry, but for the whole country."[21]

Berezniki Chemical Plant, 1932

Towering over the cranes, chimneys, and masts was the figure of Granovsky, whom his deputies depicted as the reincarnation of Peter the Great during the building of St. Petersburg. "Every day on the site you could see the head of construction, M. A. Granovsky, doing the rounds of the shops or rushing by in a carriage. The bay stallion, the carriage, and the coachman—everything looked solid, as solid as their passenger." (According to his son Anatoly, he also had a car and a motorboat; according to a complaint by a disgruntled German Communist, the carriage was also used to take his sons to school; according to Shalamov, his boots and overcoat had been made by prisoners.) "Dark legends were being told about this man. People hated and feared him, but no one dared disobey or ignore his orders. . . . Mikhail Aleksandrovich went into every technological detail himself and issued orders that, as I said, no one would think of contradicting for fear of rousing his wrath. In effect, he played the role of chief engineer—quite justifiably, in my view, because he did not want to entrust his favorite child to a handful of timeservers." In Tsukerman's summary, "Granovsky acted as if he were on the frontline of a battle: he did not spare himself and was ruthless in his demands toward those who worked under him."[22]

In 1933, he received the Order of Lenin (Berman did, too). In January–February 1934, he attended the Seventeenth Party Congress. In November 1934, on the seventeenth anniversary of the Revolution, the Granovsky

Granovsky (*left*) accompanying People's Commissar of Heavy Industry G. K. Ordzhonikidze, on his visit to Berezniki, 1934 (Courtesy of I. T. Sidorova)

Granovsky with his youngest
son, Vladimir, 1936
(Courtesy of I. T. Sidorova)

family moved into a new two-story house. According to Anatoly's memoirs, written in English: "The grounds were soon full of the cars and horse-drawn coaches of all the leading officials and authorities for many miles around and a gay party was held lasting well into the night. The building was presented to us fully furnished and most splendidly decorated. The interior walls were paneled up to about five feet from the floor and above that were painted with a mural design. All the finest chinaware, silver, linen and everything needed to make a princely home had been provided at not a kopec's cost to my father."[23]

A woman who, as a little girl, had lived in a small room off the kitchen of the Granovsky house recalled: "From the outside, it was nothing special, but the interior decorations were impressive. On the first floor was the technical library and a large tiled kitchen. On the second floor was the study and some other rooms. The house had solid furniture, a chandelier, and many large potted palms." Anatoly's fondest memories were of being at home with his father. "I remember the warmth of warm, dark bedrooms, the flutter and soft padding of snow on windows as I lay open-eyed just before sleep under thick, smooth blankets and on soft, receiving mattresses. I remember the awe I felt for my father, the fearful love I bore him and the feeling of safety and assurance that he inspired—when I was good."[24]

Five months later, in April 1935, Granovsky was made director of the Central Administration of Railroad Construction, and the family moved permanently into the House of Government. According to Anatoly,

> The Berezniki we left was very different from that which we had encountered when we arrived five years before. Then it had been a little town surrounded by forest and marsh and boasting three stone houses, the rest being of wood. Now it was a thriving industrial hive in which lived 75,000 workers and their families.
>
> Many people came to see us off at the station as we prepared to leave in our special coaches, all smiling and wishing us well. Some of the workers too came out of curiosity and stood staring at us from a little way off. Their faces were blank and expressionless.[25]

According to the head of the Planning Department, Fedorovich, "the employees of the Chemical Works reacted to this change in different ways. Some breathed a sigh of relief—finally, they were free of Granovsky's despotic power; others were sorry he was leaving; yet others felt at a crossroads and wondered what would come next."[26]

12

THE VIRGIN LANDS

The First Five-Year Plan was about construction: "installing special foundations capable of ensuring the stability of structures on swampy land" and building eternal houses "that shone with more light than there was in the air around them." But it was also about destruction: draining the bubbling, rumbling swamps and slaying the wreckers who lived there. The real revolution—the most radical of Stalin's "revolutions from above"—was to take place in the damp, rural shadow of the cranes, chimneys, and masts. The goal was to do what Peter the Great, in his "small-artisan way," had not considered, and what no state in history had ever attempted: to turn all rural dwellers—peasants, shepherds, trappers, reindeer breeders—into full-time laborers for the state.

Industrialization could not be accomplished without foreign equipment; foreign equipment had to be bought for cash; cash could only be raised by selling grain; grain had to be procured from the peasants in the form of "tribute" (as Stalin put it). Because a steady flow of tribute from traditional peasant households could not be counted on (as the grain crisis of 1927 clearly demonstrated), traditional peasant households were to be destroyed once and for all.

In a millenarian world, whatever is necessary is also inevitable, and whatever is inevitable is also desirable. "Collectivization" had been predicted (mandated) by Marx, Engels, and Lenin; the fact that its fulfillment was urgently needed meant that it was about to begin, and the fact that it was about to begin meant that those who had ears were ready to hear. The policy of wholesale collectivization was launched on November 7, 1929, by Stalin's speech, "The Year of the Great Breakthrough," which revolved around a series of Lenin's predictions and proclaimed, contrary to what most eyes could see, that the majority of the peasants had decided to give up the old ways and, "in the face of desperate resistance by all manner of dark forces, from kulaks and priests to philistines and right opportunists," follow the Party on the path to a "radical breakthrough."[1]

The Central Committee plenum of November 1929 made the new policy official. On December 27, 1929, Stalin told Kritsman's Conference of Agrarian Marxists that, since the countryside was not going to follow the city of its own free will, "the socialist city can *lead* the small-peasant village only by *imposing* collective and state farms upon it." And, since the peasants who were not kulaks were now ready to have the collective and state farms imposed upon them, the Party could move on to the policy of the "liquidation of the kulaks as a class." On January 6, 1930, the Central Committee formalized the new policy, and on January 30, the Politburo issued a "strictly confidential" decree "On Measures Regarding the Liquidation of Kulak Households in the Areas of Wholesale Collectivization."[2]

All rural residents in the Soviet Union were divided into three categories: poor, middle, and rich (*kulaks*). Selection criteria varied considerably and tended to be improvised by local officials, most of whom were specially mobilized urbanites. The poor peasants were expected to welcome the imposition of state and collective enterprises (the collectives, or *kolkhozes*, were also run by the state). The middle peasants were expected to be persuaded by the success of the poor ones and the fate of the kulaks. The kulaks were to have "their backs broken once and for all" before they had a chance to reveal their intentions. According to the January 6 decree, they were to be deprived of their possessions and subdivided into three categories. The first group was to be "immediately liquidated by means of imprisonment in concentration camps, not hesitating to use the death penalty with regard to the organizers of terrorist acts, counterrevolutionary actions, and insurrectionary organizations." The second was to be exiled to "uninhabited and sparsely populated areas" in "remote regions of the USSR," for use as forced laborers. The third group was to be resettled in specially designated locations within their native districts.

According to approximate quotas, the Middle Volga OGPU was to arrest and execute 3,000–4,000 people and deport 8,000–10,000; the North Caucasus and Dagestan OGPU, 6,000–8,000 and 20,000; the Ukrainian OGPU, 15,000 and 30,000–35,000, and so on, for a total of 49,000–60,000 people to be imprisoned or executed and 129,000–154,000 people to be deported. The OGPU order of February 2, 1930, made it clear that family members of first-category individuals were to be treated as second-category, and that quotas for the second and third categories referred to families, not individuals. "The measures" as a whole, therefore, targeted about a million

Boris Bak
(Courtesy of Nikita Petrov)

people (based on the standard average of five persons per family), but the numbers were subject to negotiation among various deporting officials interested in overfulfilling the plan, bosses of "uninhabited and sparsely populated areas" interested in receiving fewer starving and homeless charges, and industrial managers like Granovsky interested in obtaining free labor. The head of the Middle Volga OGPU, Boris Bak, proposed the deportation of 6,250 families but added that, if necessary, "this number can, of course, always be increased." A week later, on January 20, 1930, he reported that he was about to launch "a mass operation involving the extraction from the countryside of active counterrevolutionary and kulak–White Guardist elements" numbering ten thousand families (Bak was a relative of the head of the Gulag, Matvei Berman, and his neighbor in the House of Government.) During the most intense period of collectivization, 1930–33, about two million second-category exiles were deported to uninhabited and sparsely populated areas. Those who did not die en route built their own "special settlements."[3]

The kulaks, "subkulaks," and would-be kulaks who were not deported left their villages to become the Tower of Babel of Berezniki, Kuznetsk, and Magnitogorsk. "From Perm they came, and from Vyatka, and from all the provinces where the old peasant ways passed down from their forefathers were no longer possible, but new ones had not yet arrived." Those who stayed behind were searched, beaten, robbed, and starved until they joined the collectives. According to a March 1930 report on "excesses" in one rural district in Boris Bak's Middle-Volga Territory,

> In the village of Galtsovka, Lunin District, the middle peasant Mishin was dekulakized because he spoke out against collective farms at a village assembly. All his possessions, including soup spoons, children's skis, and toys, were confiscated. Mishin had worked for forty years as a day laborer and railroad patrolman, paid ten rubles' worth of agricultural tax, and was an activist. His children had received a present from N. K. Krupskaia: a little library of books.
>
> In the village of Ust-Inza, Lunin District, during the dekulakization of the kulak Imagulov, the entire family was evicted at 1 a.m. and forced out into the winter cold. The baby froze to death and Imagulov's sick daughter-in-law was badly frostbitten. (She had given birth two days previously.)[4]

Once inside the collectives, the peasants, herders, hunters, gatherers, and fishermen were given production plans calculated on the basis of yield forecasts and the need for urban food supplies and export revenues. A failure to fulfill the plan resulted in more searches and beatings. According to Bak's report of June 28, 1932, the most common peasant response was to try to leave the collectives. "Usually, after submitting their resignations, collective farmers attempt to repossess their horses, which must then be retaken by force—and stop reporting for work, thus sabotaging such important activities as weeding, mowing, and silaging, as well as fallow preparation and fall plowing." Other common practices included flight, the slaughtering of animals, and the killing of local activists. Bak's response was to restrain the local activists guilty of "excesses" while also "arresting anti-Soviet elements, improving the dissemination of political information, and taking preventive measures through our agent network." The central government's response was the decree of August 7, 1932, which equated newly collectivized household possessions to state property and punished theft (attempts at repossession) by applying "the ultimate method of social defense in the form of execution, accompanied by the confiscation of all possessions." The determined enforcement of ambitious production plans resulted in a famine that killed between 4.6 and 8 million people.[5]

Collectivizers at all levels were to demonstrate Bolshevik firmness without committing excesses or suffering from "dizziness from success" (decried by Stalin in March 1930). The line between firmness and excess was both mobile and invisible. Roman Terekhov, who joined the revolutionary movement because of his "great hatred for those who did not work and lived well, especially the bosses" (and began his armed struggle by trying to kill a mechanic in his shop), had since become the Party secretary of Kharkov Province and a member of the Ukrainian Central Committee. In December 1932 he inspected the Kobeliaky District and found "an orgy of brazen deception of the state." Local officials, he wrote in his report to the Ukrainian Party secretary, had abetted the "plundering and wasting of grain" by violating the Party's directives on "discontinuing the supply of grain for communal consumption," allowing the farmers to "cut off individual ears of grain," distributing bread "to the lazy and the greedy," and setting aside emergency funds for the teachers and the disabled. On Terekhov's recommendation, all those responsible were arrested and put on trial. The district officials were sentenced to ten years of forced labor "in remote areas of the Union." A large number of kolkhoz employees (accountants, millers, warehouse guards, and beehive keepers), were unmasked as kulaks. "In addition to that," concluded the report, "we have taken measures to restore the health of the local Party organization and cleanse it of degenerate elements and kulak agents."[6]

Roman Terekhov with his daughter, Victoria

Within days of writing this, Terekhov traveled to Moscow and told Stalin that the plan was unrealistic and that the collective farmers were starving. Stalin's response, according to Terekhov, was: "We have been told, Comrade Terekhov, that you are a good speaker, but it turns out that you are a good storyteller. You came up with this fairy tale about a famine, thinking to scare us. But it won't work! Wouldn't it be better for you to resign your posts of provincial Party secretary and Ukrainian Central Committee member and join the Writers' Union? Then you can write fairy tales, and fools can read them." On January 24, 1933, Terekhov was relieved of his duties, transferred to the Committee of Soviet Control in Moscow, and given an apartment in the House of Government, which he shared with his wife, Efrosinia Artemovna (who was made deputy director of Clinic No. 2 of the Kremlin Health Service), and their two children, nine-year-old Victoria and two-year-old Gennady.[7]

Terekhov was replaced in Kharkov by the first secretary of the Kiev Provincial Party Committee, Nikolai Demchenko, who was firmer in his struggle against sabotage and wiser in not approaching Stalin directly. According to Khrushchev, who worked under Demchenko in Kiev and greatly admired his loyalty to the Party, he approached People's Commissar of Supplies Anastas Mikoyan instead. In Khrushchev's version of Mikoyan's account,

> One day Comrade Demchenko came to Moscow and stopped by my place. "Anastas Ivanovich," he said, "does Stalin know, does the Politburo know what the situation in Ukraine is like?" (Demchenko was the secretary of the Kiev Provincial Committee at the time, and provinces were very large back then.) Some train cars had arrived in Kiev, and when opened, turned out to be full of dead bodies. The train was on its way from Kharkov to Kiev via Poltava, and somewhere between Poltava and Kiev, someone had loaded up all those corpses. "The situation is very difficult," said Demchenko, "but Stalin probably doesn't know about it. Do you mind, now that you know about it, letting Comrade Stalin know, too?"[8]

Demchenko remained in Ukraine until September 1936, when he became the deputy people's commissar of agriculture and moved into the House of Government with his wife, Mirra Abramovna (who was made head of the Department of Colleges in the People's Commissariat of Transportation), and their two sons—Nikolai (seventeen) and Feliks (eight, born the year Feliks Dzerzhinsky died).

Another high-ranking Ukrainian official who combined public firmness with private pleas for mercy was the chairman of the Ukrainian Central Executive Committee, Grigory Petrovsky. "Another reason for providing help," he wrote to Molotov on June 10, 1932, "is that starving peasants will harvest unripe grain, much of which may perish in vain." As co-chairman of the All-Union Central Executive Committee and candidate member of the Politburo, Petrovsky had received a permanent apartment in the House of Government—as had his son Leonid, a division commander and an Old Bolshevik in his own right. Petrovsky's other son, Petr, was in prison as an unrepentant Right Oppositionist.[9]

Terekhov, Demchenko, and Petrovsky were all Ukrainians open to accusations of softness on

Grigory Petrovsky and his son Leonid

account of local commitments, but even the republican and territorial viceroys (none of whom was a native of the area he was collectivizing) were often accused of writing fairy tales. Their main job was to fulfill the plan; famines and unrealistic plans made fulfillment less likely. At the October 1931 Central Committee plenum, Molotov had to rebuke the normally firm Filipp Goloshchekin, who called the quotas for Kazakhstan "impossible."[10]

The most obvious remedy for softness born of nepotism, vested interests, and participant observation was to send central officials out on short-term missions. Yakov Brandenburgsky, the family law expert, was sent to the Lower Volga; Solomon Ronin, the planning economist, to the Black Sea–Azov Territory; and Osinsky, still head of the Main Directory of Statistics, to Tatarstan. Boris Shumiatsky, the founder of the People's Republic of Mongolia and president of the Communist University for the Toilers of the East, was put on the Moscow Province Dekulakization Committee. But they, too, proved unreliable. Brandenburgsky, according to his daughter, cried "so much that, had I not been a witness to those scenes, I would never have believed it." (He was brought back home in disgrace in March 1931, before the famine had begun to spread.) Ronin, according to his daughter, was shocked by the violence of collectivization and came home in time for the Congress of Victors in January 1934. Osinsky, according to Anna Larina, was among those friends of her father who "were not in opposition to Stalin's collectivization policy, but reacted with horror to the news of the situation in the countryside." In May 1933, more than three years after his own stint on the grain procurement front, he wrote to Shaternikova from Ronin's territory: "During my trip, I saw all those things the local plenipotentiaries had been telling me about, and that I told you about. They can be seen in all their glory all over the western part of the North Caucasus from the Sea of Azov to the mountains." Shumiatsky, for reasons unknown, was transferred from the dekulakization commission to the chairmanship of the Soviet film industry after seven months. Even Sergei Syrtsov, a strong proponent of the extermination of the Don Cossacks in 1919 and one of the organizers of the anti-peasant violence in Siberia in 1928, had his career end over his objection to the "inflated plans" and the "solution of difficult economic problems with GPU methods."[11]

The method of last resort was the formation of emergency commissions headed by members of the inner sanctum known for their firmness, most particularly Andreev, Kaganovich, Molotov, and Postyshev. Pavel Postyshev, the former "calico printer" from Ivanovo-Voznesensk and a member of the commission charged with the "supervision and overall direction of the deportation and resettlement of the kulaks," was sent to two of the most important, and most challenging, grain-producing regions: the Lower Volga and Ukraine. Soon after his arrival in the Lower Volga, he received a telegram from Stalin and Molotov about the arrests of two local officials accused of halting grain procurement. "We propose, first, that all such criminals from all the districts be arrested, and, second, that they be put on trial immediately and given five or, better, ten years in prison. Sentences and the reasons for them should be published in the press. Send report upon fulfillment." The goal of the campaign was, as Postyshev put it at a meeting in Balashov in December 1932, "to fulfill the grain-procurement plan by any means possible." According to a local official present at the meeting, one of the district Party secretaries said: "'Comrade Postyshev, we won't be able to fulfill

Pavel Postyshev

the plan because we have winnowed the chaff and threshed a lot of straw, but are still a long way from fulfillment. We have nothing left to winnow or thresh.'—'Is this really a district Party secretary?' asked Postyshev, addressing the room. 'I propose relieving him of his post.' And they did."[12]

Postyshev did veto some local initiatives by "dizzy" activists, but his job was to ensure plan fulfillment by any means possible. District prosecutors and people's courts were told to "proceed to the immediate extraction of all uncovered grain" and "apply a maximum level of repression . . . to all the malicious non-fulfillers of the grain procurement plan." On June 12, 1933, the territorial Party secretary reported that, "if not for the help of the Central Committee secretary, Comrade Postyshev, the Lower-Volga Territory would not have managed to fulfill the grain procurement plan." Over the next year and a half, the population of the area (split between the Saratov and Stalingrad territories) fell by about a million people. By then, Postyshev had received his next assignment. In late December 1932, he, along with Kaganovich, had been told to "leave immediately for Ukraine in order to help the Ukrainian Central Committee and Council of People's Commissars" and "take all the necessary organizational and administrative measures needed for the fulfillment of the grain procurement plan." The Central Committee decree of January 24, 1933 (which also announced the firing of Roman Terekhov), appointed him second secretary of the Ukrainian Central Committee. He, along with his wife, a fellow Old Bolshevik, T. S. Postolovskaia; their three sons (Valentin, eighteen; Leonid, twelve; and Vladimir, ten); and his wife's sister and mother moved from the House of Government to Kharkov and, shortly afterward, to Kiev. (A different—smaller—apartment in the House of Government was reserved for their visits to Moscow.) According to Leonid, Valentin accompanied their father on his first trip to the countryside and was so distressed by what he saw that Postyshev had to assemble the family and tell them not to conduct anti-Party conversations at home.[13]

■ ■ ■

Filipp Goloshchekin

The Lower Volga and Ukraine, along with the North Caucasus, accounted for the largest total number of famine deaths, but, per capita, the most affected area was Kazakhstan, where, according to estimates based on official statistics, 2,330,000 rural residents (39 percent of the whole rural population) were lost to death and emigration between 1929 and 1933. The ethnic Kazakh population was reduced by about 50 percent: between 1.2 million and 1.5 million died of starvation, and about 615,000 emigrated abroad or to other Soviet republics.[14]

The man in charge of Kazakhstan during those years was Sverdlov's friend, the "regular Don Quixote," chief regicide, and former dentist, Filipp Goloshchekin. According to the head of the Central Committee Information Section at that time, "F. I. Goloshchekin was a rather strongly built, gray-haired man of about fifty, animated and extraordinarily mobile. His blue, expressive eyes seemed to follow everyone and notice everything. While thinking, he would stroke his pointed beard with his left hand. On formal occasions, he was a lively, fluid, energetic speaker whose gestures merely enhanced his already expressive voice." In an apparent imitation of Stalin, he liked to pace with his pipe in his mouth.[15]

In principle, the "revolution from above" was the completion of the October Revolution and the fulfillment of Lenin's prophecy (at a pace Lenin could only dream of). In Kazakhstan, it was also a restaging of the entire course of the Bolshevik Revolution and much of human history. "Right now, comrades," said Goloshchekin at the Sixteenth Party Congress, "we are living through a time when the backward national republics are undergoing the transition from semifeudal to socialist relations, bypassing capitalism."[16]

The transition began in 1928 with the confiscation of the property of all "semifeudal" nomads. In the Aktiubinsk District, for example, the expropriation of sixty households yielded 14,839 head of livestock, as well as "16 yurts, 11 earth dugouts, 6 haymowers, 4 horse rakes, 7 self-rake reapers, 3 bunkers, 26 carpets, 26 felt mats, etc." "One thing that makes this experiment interesting," wrote Goloshchekin in December, 1928, "is that, for the first time in history, we are carrying out the confiscation of livestock, which is considerably more difficult and complicated than the confiscation of land." Despite the additional difficulties, Kazakhstan was to be in the forefront of collectivization. "I have heard the view," said Goloshchekin in December 1929, "that the kolkhoz movement will proceed more slowly in our republic than in other regions of the USSR. I consider such a view incorrect." Collectivization, "sedentarization," and the final abolition of "feudal, patriarchal, and clan relations" were to proceed all at the same time and without delay. This achievement was going to be, "literally, of global importance."[17]

On March 2, 1930, Stalin accused overzealous collectivizers throughout the Soviet Union of "dizziness from success." At a Party conference held in Alma Ata in June, Goloshchekin accused his employees of "misunderstanding the Party line." "In Alma-Ata province," he told the delegates, the rate of collectivization was "17% in January and 63.7% in April (*laughter*); in Petropavlovsk, 38% in January and 73.6% in April; and in Semipalatinsk, 18 and 40%, respectively (here the approach was a bit more god-fearing) (*laughter*)." The highest rates had been recorded in areas of nomadic pastoralism. In Chelkar (where Tania Miagkova had spent time in exile), 85 percent of all households had been collectivized. "We, the Bolsheviks, are seriously alarmed," said Goloshchekin in his concluding speech (according to the minutes of the conference). "Alarmed, but not panicked." The conference resolved "to publish Goloshchekin's complete works in Russian and Kazakh (*applause*)" and "to name the new Communist university being built in Alma-Ata 'The Comrade Goloshchekin Kazakh Communist University' (*applause*)." Goloshchekin joked that he might get dizzy, but "voices from the audience" assured him that he would not.[18]

The campaign resumed at the end of the summer and did not let up until most of the surviving peasants and pastoralists had been collectivized. In February 1931, Goloshchekin announced a new phase of the transition from semifeudal to socialist relations: "In our discussions of Kazakhstan, we often wrote: 'given the special conditions of Kazakhstan.' In other words, the achievement of the objectives set by the Party only partially concerned us. But now? Now the situation is different. Now Party decisions concern Kazakhstan absolutely, fully, and completely, and not only partially. Do we still have peculiarities and backwardness? Yes, we do, but they are no longer the ones that prevail and dominate."[19]

Some local officials were slow to respond. "In this procurement season," wrote Goloshchekin in the fall, "we face a new phenomenon: the fear of excesses." A special telegram from the Kazakhstan Party Committee ordered provincial Party officials to rehabilitate all those previously reprimanded for dizziness. "The provincial Party committees must be able to guarantee the total fulfillment of the plan without having to fear the consequences." The most obvious consequence was famine. According to a report by the Secret-Political Department of the OGPU, "based on obviously incomplete data, between December, 1931 and March 10, 1932, there were 1,219 officially registered cases of death from starvation and 4,304 cases of swelling due to starvation."[20]

The agency responsible for collecting this information—as well as for arresting and deporting kulaks, suppressing rebellions, and assisting collectivizers with force of arms—was the OGPU Plenipotentiary Office in Kazakhstan. The formal head of the office was V. A. Karutsky, but the man doing most of the work was his first deputy, Sergei Mironov (Korol), who

V. A. Karutsky
(Courtesy of A. G. Teplyakov)

had arrived in August 1931 in the company of his mistress Agnessa Argiropulo (after their elopement from Rostov and shopping spree in Moscow). According to Agnessa,

> Karutsky—paunchy, swollen—was a big drinker. His wife had been married to a White officer and had a son by him. People began to throw this in Karutsky's face. So he said to his wife: "I think it would be better if the boy lived with your mother." They sent him away, but Karutsky's wife missed him terribly and not long after we arrived she killed herself.

Karutsky had a dacha outside of Alma-Ata where he used to throw bachelor parties. Soon after we arrived, he invited us over. There I saw some pornographic pictures done by a very good French artist, but I don't remember who. I still remember one of them. It was of a church in Bulgaria. Some Turks had forced their way in and were raping the nuns.

Karutsky loved women. He had an assistant, Abrashka, who used to procure them for him. He would pick them out, butter them up, and then hand them over. This same Abrashka started dropping in on me every morning as soon as Mironov left for work. And each time he would bring me something different: grapes, melons, pheasants—all sorts of things.[21]

Afraid to leave Agnessa in Alma-Ata by herself, Mironov took her with him on his inspection trip around Kazakhstan. As she recalled,

We traveled in a Pullman car that was built in the days of Nicholas II. The salon was upholstered in green velvet, the bedroom in red. There were two large sofas. The conductors, who doubled as cooks, fed us magnificently. Besides me, there was only one other woman— a typist.

It was late fall, but in northern Kazakhstan it was already winter with fierce winds, freezing temperatures, and snowstorms. The car was well heated, but it was impossible to go out anywhere. Being from the south, I was always cold. So they found me a coat that was lined with fur as thick as your hand. I could wrap myself up in it and go out wherever I wanted—even in a snowstorm or the freezing cold—and still be warm.

Everything was fine, except that for some reason, Mirosha was becoming gloomier and more withdrawn with each passing day, and even I could not always shake him out of it.

One day we arrived at a way station completely buried in snow.

"This," we were told, "is the village of Karaganda. It is still under construction."

Our car was uncoupled, and some of the staff went to see what kind of place Karaganda was. I wanted to go with them, but Mirosha wouldn't let me. They were gone a long time, and Mirosha and I went into the bedroom. Mirosha lay down on the couch, was silent for a while, and then fell asleep. I got bored and went to look for the others again. They were all squeezed into one compartment. The ones who had gone to the village had come back and were talking about it.

"This Karaganda" they were saying, "is just a word. It's only some temporary huts built by exiled kulaks. The store has nothing but empty shelves. The saleswoman told us, 'I have nothing to do because there's nothing to sell. We've forgotten what bread even looks like. But you say you don't need any bread? What can I offer you then? I think there may be a tiny bottle of liqueur somewhere. Would you like to buy that?'" They bought it and got into a conversation with her, and she told them:

"Some exiled kulaks were sent here in special trains, but they're all dying off because there's nothing to eat. Do you see that hut over there? The mother and father died, leaving three small children behind. The youngest, a two-year-old, died soon after. The older boy took a knife and started cutting pieces off and eating them and giving some to his sister until there was nothing left."

When Mironov woke up, Agnessa told him about what she had heard, "thinking to shock him." He said he knew all about it and had himself seen a hut filled with corpses. "He was very upset, I could tell. But he was already trying not to think about such things and to brush them aside. He always believed everything the Party did was right, he was so loyal."[22]

A few weeks or possibly days earlier, on October 7, 1931, Mironov had written the following memo: "According to the information at our disposal, owing to a lack of housing, inadequate health care, and insufficient food provision, large numbers of the special settlers distributed among the hamlets of the Chilikskii District New-Hemp-Trust State Farm No. 1 are suffering from contagious diseases, namely typhus, dysentery, etc. Those sick with typhus have not been isolated and continue to live in the general barracks. As a result, there has been some flight and high mortality among the special settlers."[23]

The northernmost point of Mironov's and Agnessa's inspection trip was Petropavlovsk. It was a real city, and Agnessa was happy for the chance to socialize:

As soon as we arrived, the head of the Petropavlovsk OGPU came to see Mirosha. Mirosha was supposed to inspect the work of these officials, but he didn't act the part of the dreaded inspector-general— just the opposite.

"We'll start working tomorrow," he said in a friendly way, "but why don't you and your wife come over for dinner today? We're having roast suckling pig."

They did come. His wife, Anya, was pretty, but really fat. And her dress! Why on earth would you wear something like that if you are overweight? A pleated skirt always makes you look even fatter! I remember her trying to make excuses: "The reason I've gained so much weight is because we were in Central Asia, where it's really hot in the summer, so I drank water all the time."

The table in the salon was set unimaginatively, but sumptuously. Our cook came in carrying a huge platter with the suckling pig, cut into pieces and covered in gravy. As he was passing by and probably trying to avoid Anya's extravagant hairdo, he slightly tilted the platter—and some of the gravy splashed out onto her dress! She jumped up screaming, "This is simply outrageous!" and then began cursing.

The cook froze, and his face turned white as a sheet. What would happen to him now?!

I tried to calm her down and told her to sprinkle salt on the stain, but the dinner was ruined. Mirosha turned to her and said:

"Surely you're not going to let a dress keep you from sampling this suckling pig?"

Her husband frowned at her, as if to say—"that's enough!" but she didn't calm down for the rest of the dinner.

The next day we were invited to their house. Now that was a feast! All kinds of flunkies and servants and various types of toadies and bootlickers serving every kind of fresh fruit imaginable—even oranges. And I'm not even talking about all the different kinds of ice cream and grapes![24]

On January 11, possibly on the return leg of the same trip, Mironov wrote a report on the situation in the Pavlodar District:

Recently, according to the data collected by our Pavlodar district network, 30 secret grain pits have been discovered. Animal theft and the mass slaughter of animals have increased.

Grain procurement is being conducted in an atmosphere of sheer coercion. The following instructions have been issued by the procurement plenipotentiaries to the Party cells and local soviets: "during procurement, confiscate all grain and use all possible measures except beatings," as a result of which there have been reports of flight by kolkhoz members.

The District Party Committee's plenipotentiary in Settlement No. 1, Matveenko, conducted full-scale searches of kulak families deported from their home districts and confiscated all personal-consumption grain, as a result of which 40 cases of mortality, mostly among children, have been reported. Others feed themselves by consuming cats, dogs, and other carrion.[25]

Such numbered settlements had been built for the newly "sedentarized" nomads. In a long "Short Memo" written four days after the Pavlodar one, Mironov described the "unplanned, slow, and criminally wasteful" way in which the campaign was being implemented. Most settlements, according to him, had no water; some were too far from their pastures; some were organized "according to the clan principle"; some had been built on sand and were sinking; and some consisted of buildings that "had begun to collapse after the rains." The officials responsible for this state of affairs were "great-power chauvinists" who believed that Kazakhs were not ready for settled life, and Kazakh nationalists, who agreed with the great-power chauvinists. Both revealed their hostile intentions by blaming the Party for what they called "hunger and misery." By spring, the "difficulties with food provision" had, according to Mironov's report of August 4, "acquired extremely acute forms." In the Atbassar District, "as a result of starvation, numerous cases of swelling and death have been reported. Between April 1 and July 25, there were 111 registered deaths, 43 of them in July. During this period, there were five reports of cannibalism. In this context, there have been reports of the spread of provocative rumors."[26]

In October 1932, a prominent Kazakh journalist and fiction writer, Gabit Musrepov, traveled to the Turgai District. He was accompanied by a territorial Party Committee official, a coachman, and an armed guard ("or else they might eat you," said the local executive committee chairman, himself a deportee). In the steppe, they lost their way in a blizzard, but then came upon rows of dead bodies stacked up like firewood. "Thanks to them, we found the road: the corpses were lined up along both sides." According to a later version of Musrepov's original account,

They dug themselves out of the snowdrifts and set off down this road of the dead. They kept passing villages that were completely empty. The coachman, who was from the area, called out the names of these settlements—known only by number. There was not a soul in sight. Finally, they arrived in a yurt town that appeared strange to Kazakh eyes. Since the beginning of collectivization, a great many of these had sprung up in the steppe. For some reason, the yurts were laid out in rows, and each one had a number as if it were a city house on a city street. The white felt yurts were spacious and new. The coachman explained that they had recently been confiscated from the local kulaks. Two or three months ago, he added, there were a lot of people here. Now the place was deathly still. The absolute silence was broken only by the sound of the wind-driven snow: a dead city of white yurts in the white snow.

They walked into one yurt, and then another. All the household items were there, but there were no people.

In one yurt, the mats and carpets were frozen, and snow was coming in through an opening at the top. In the middle of the floor lay a large pile with a small hole at the bottom.

Suddenly, they heard a shrill, thin sound that made their flesh crawl—like the squealing of a dog or the shrieking of a cat, followed by a low growl.

From a tiny hole in the pile, some sort of small creature darted out and rushed toward the men. It was covered in blood. Its long hair had frozen into bloody icicles that stuck out at all angles. Its legs were skinny and black, like a crow's. Its eyes were wild, and its face covered with clotted blood and streaks of fresh blood. Its teeth were bared, and its mouth dripped with red foam.

All four men recoiled and fled in fear. When they turned to look back, the creature was no longer there.[27]

Goloshchekin was bombarded with letters. Stalin and Molotov wanted to know what was being done to stem the flow of Kazakh refugees to China; the Party boss of West Siberia, Robert Eikhe, complained about the invasion of starving Kazakhs and asked, sarcastically, whether it was the kulaks who had uprooted "thousands of poor and middle-income households"; Gabit Musrepov accused the Party Committee of "being afraid of Bolshevik self-criticism when it comes to the catastrophic reduction in livestock population and famine"; Mironov and his colleagues reported regularly on the many "cases of mortality" and how they were being used for hostile propaganda; and an unknown number of people wrote to beg for food and mercy.[28]

In August 1932, the chairman of the territorial Council of People's Commissars and second-most-important official in Kazakhstan, Uraz Isaev, wrote a letter to Stalin in which he accused Goloshchekin of blaming his own "sins" on the kulaks and low-level officials; believing his own myth "that every single Kazakh had decided to join the kolkhozes"; engaging in "ritual curses and incantations" against the kulaks instead of correcting his own mistakes; and trying to solve every problem by transferring the same—and sometimes "totally corrupt"—Party activists from one place to another.[29]

Goloshchekin defended himself by arguing that, "slanderous claims" and real excesses notwithstanding, the fact remained that, in accordance with Comrade Stalin's prediction, the poor and middle Kazakhs had "voluntarily, in powerful waves, turned toward socialism." The new campaign of violence unleashed by Moscow in the fall of 1932 seemed to vindicate his approach. On November 11, 1932, Goloshchekin and Isaev ordered mass arrests, deportations, and a goods blockade in all kolkhozes accused of "artificially slowing down grain collection." ("The task," wrote Stalin in a telegram praising the order, "is, first and foremost, to hit the communists at the district and below-district level, who are wholly infected by petit bourgeois mentality and have taken up the kulak cause of sabotaging the grain procurement campaign. It stands to reason that, in such conditions, the territorial Council of People's Commissars and Party Committee would have no choice but to engage in repression.") In October and November 1932, when top-level emergency commissions were being sent to all the important grain-producing areas, Goloshchekin remained his own emergency commission. In early January, speaking at a joint plenum of the Central Committee and Central Control Commission, he said: "The enormous successes achieved by the implementation of the Five-Year Plan in Kazakhstan . . . are the best argument against the opportunists and nationalists and their counterrevolutionary slander, which exaggerates certain negative phenomena that are inevitable given the very complicated processes that are taking place in Kazakhstan."[30]

A few days after the plenum, Goloshchekin was dismissed from his post and sent to Moscow as head of the State Arbitrage Court. He, his second wife, Elizaveta Arsenievna Vinogradova, her mother, and her son from a previous marriage moved into the House of Government, Apt. 228. According to Voronsky's daughter Galina, who saw a great deal of them, Elizaveta Arsenievna was "broad-faced, very lively, and, despite her plainness, extremely charming." She was also relatively young (twenty years younger than Goloshchekin) and a strict disciplinarian: when her son started getting bad grades in school, she forced him to work at a factory and live in a workers' dorm for a year before allowing him to come back home. According to Galina,

> She was just as strict with her husband. At one time F. I. Goloshchekin had been a first district party secretary. For some sins, real or imagined, Stalin had dismissed him from that position. Filipp Isaevich was very depressed and kept moping about, talking of suicide all the time.
>
> "I had completely had it with his 'I'm going to shoot myself' talk," Elizaveta Arsenievna once told us, "so the next time he made one of those speeches, I walked up to his desk, pulled out the drawer where he keeps his gun, and said: 'Go ahead then, shoot yourself!'"
>
> "Stop it, stop it," Filipp Isaevich cried, throwing up his hands.
>
> "Fine, you don't want to shoot yourself. So don't let me hear any more of this suicide talk. I'm sick of it."
>
> And the subject never came up again.[31]

■   ■   ■

Mironov and Agnessa remained in Kazakhstan until September. Once, Agnessa wrote to her sister Lena in Rostov, asking if she would like her to send some stockings, dresses, and silk. Lena asked for food instead.

> Later Lena told me: "I was giving everything to Boria (her son), everything I could get with my ration coupons, and wasting away myself. The streets and doorways were full of corpses, and I kept thinking—I'll be one of them soon. . . . Then suddenly a car stopped in front of the house, and a soldier unloaded some sacks. He rang the doorbell and said, with a shy smile: 'This is for you . . . from your sister, I think.'
>
> I couldn't believe my eyes. I opened one of the sacks—millet! I poured out a bit for him, of course, then quickly ran inside to make some porridge. I tossed some millet into a pot, added some water, and started cooking it, but then couldn't wait till it was done and began gobbling it down raw."[32]

Soon afterward, Agnessa went to Rostov with a large food parcel herself. What struck her most was the behavior of Lena's son, Boria, "who was just a little boy then. Somber, joyless, silent—all he did was eat. He ate his way through everything I had brought." When Agnessa got back to Alma-Ata, she heard that one of Mironov's employees—"pretty, with a delicate porcelain face, black shoulder-length hair, and bangs"—had been flirting with Mironov at an office picnic.

> I was immediately on my guard!
>
> "Did they go off alone? So, what did they do?"
>
> "She offered him a pastry from her basket."
>
> I wasn't too happy about that either. It was right before the holidays, and we were planning a party.
>
> I always watched my figure. If I let myself go and started eating everything I wanted, I'd get fat in no time! But I didn't and was always half starved because I was so careful about my diet. Everyone was amazed at how slender I was. I decided to have a dress made for the party and designed it myself. Just imagine—black silk (black is very slimming) with multicolored sparkles, close fitting around the waist and hips, and diagonal pleats. . . . Here, let me draw it for you. I've never seen anything like it since. It had these pleats flowing down from the top, and then, at the bottom, just below the knees, it widened out into a flounce skirt—as light and airy as a spring fog at dusk. And here, on the side, there was a large buckle, which shimmered with color, just like the sparkles on the fabric.
>
> We had several servants: Maria Nikolaevna, who cooked for us and went everywhere with us just like a member of the family (I couldn't possibly have managed without her); Irina, who used to

Agnessa Argiropulo, 1932
(Courtesy of Rose Glickman)

bring us our meals and whatever we were entitled to from the special stores and cafeterias; a housemaid, who cleaned and served at table; and a laundress, who did the washing and ironing and helped the others when there wasn't any laundry to do. And then my mother came to live with us as well.

They all loved to dress me. They'd pull here and tug there and fasten me up—and then just stand and marvel. On the evening of the party even my mother, who was more restrained than the servants, couldn't help saying:

"You'll outshine them all tonight!"

And that's exactly what I intended to do. To outshine them all! To outshine and sweep away like a grain of dust any who dared to rival me.

And so I appeared among the guests in that dress, and all eyes turned to me, while she, that employee with the black bangs and little porcelain face, in her plain white blouse and skirt, stood arm-in-arm with a girlfriend. . . . How could she think she could compete with me? She ceased to exist the moment I walked into the room. Mirosha was able to see with his own eyes the kind of woman I was, and the kind she was.[33]

In September 1933, Mironov was transferred to Ukraine as the OGPU's plenipotentiary in Dnepropetrovsk Province. (Ekaterinoslav had been renamed in 1926 in honor of Grigory Petrovsky.) It was an important promotion. They moved into a large house and sent for both of Lena's boys, Boria and Lyova. (Agnessa's brother's daughter, Aga, was already living with them.) "I remember an old two-story mansion," wrote Lyova. "On the second floor there were dozens of rooms for family and guests, a viewing room for movies, a billiard room, and a toilet and bathroom in each wing. My uncle's chauffeur and his family lived on the first floor, where there was also a huge study that opened out onto a glassed-in terrace. I had been brought to Dnepropetrovsk and enrolled in the kindergarten. As soon as I began to boast that Mironov was my uncle, everyone—the teachers, my playmates' parents, and even my playmates—started fawning all over me and trying to curry favor. Everyone knew I was special: after all, I was the nephew of a very powerful man, Mironov himself!"[34]

Mironov's job remained the same: enforcing collectivization, "repressing" its enemies, and dealing with its consequences. In March, before they arrived, the Dnepropetrovsk OGPU office had reported the death from starvation of 1,700 people and the swelling from hunger of 16,000. Over the next two years, the province lost about 16 percent of its rural population.[35]

When not working, Mironov played cards and billiards with his friends or spent time with Agnessa:

> Mirosha had two lives. One was with me. That's the one I knew and that's the one I'm telling you about—because I knew nothing about his other life, his working life. He made it very clear that he was determined to keep it separate.
>
> When he came home, he would cast off his official cares like a suit of armor and not want to think about anything except having fun together. Though he was eight years older, I never felt the difference in age between us. We were friends and used to fool around and play our game of love without ever growing tired of it.
>
> Sometimes we went on long hikes together. We really loved those walks. Or we might go to the theater or take a trip and "live it up" somewhere like Tbilisi, Leningrad, or Odessa.[36]

Every fall, they went to the Black Sea resorts (in Sochi, Gagra, or Khosta), and in the summer, to Berdiansk on the Sea of Azov, where the OGPU (renamed the NKVD in 1934) had its own sanatorium.

> Three times a day a policeman would bring us food from a special sanatorium. For dessert after lunch we sometimes got a whole bucket of ice cream.
>
> Once, the woman who worked for us there asked, "Is it okay if I take the leftovers home? I have three children . . ."
>
> "Of course!" my mother exclaimed.
>
> Two days later the same woman asked, "Is it okay if I bring my children to play with yours?"

Sergei Mironov and Agnessa Argiropulo
(Courtesy of Rose Glickman)

She brought them—a little boy and two girls. We were shocked at how thin her children were. The little boy, Vasia, had ribs that stuck out like a skeleton's. He looked like a picture of death next to our Boria, who had grown quite chubby. Someone had photographed them side by side. I said, "Remember that old advertisement for rice flour? Showing someone very skinny before he began eating rice flour and very fat afterward? This photo is exactly like that ad—with Vasia before the flour, and Boria after it."

Then, this woman, our servant, could see that we felt sorry for them, and she brought her fourteen-year-old niece from Kharkov to live with us, too. When she arrived, she was so weak the wind could have blown her over.

We were now up to nine (including Boria and Lyova). The sanatorium started providing lunches for all of us. They didn't dare refuse. We were a tiny island in a sea of hunger.[37]

. . .

The House of Government was and was not an island. Among the residents who helped shape collectivization and determine its course were the head of the Kolkhoz Center and one of the most radical advocates of antipeasant violence, Grigory Kaminsky (Apt. 225); the head of the Grain Trust and Kaminsky's close collaborator and personal friend, Mark Belenky (Apt. 338); the head of the Center of Consumer Cooperatives (and the former husband of Solts's niece), Isaak Zelensky (Apt. 54); and the head of the Grain and Fodder Department at the People's Commissariat of Internal Trade (and Natalia Sats's husband), Israel Veitser (Apt. 159).[38]

Some residents—including Postyshev, Terekhov, Demchenko, Goloshchekin, and Zelensky (in his dual capacity as head of the Central Asian

Bureau and Party boss of Uzbekistan)—enforced collectivization as high-ranking regional officials; some—including Ronin, Shumiatsky, and Brandenburgsky—assisted the enforcers as special emissaries; and some—including Gaister, Kritsman, Kraval (and Osinsky, who was still living in the Kremlin)—drew up plans and collected procurement statistics (while also serving as occasional special emissaries). Some top OGPU/NKVD officers, including Matvei Berman and his brother-in-law, Boris Bak, presided over arrests, deportations, executions, surveillance, and forced labor. (Sergei Mironov did not become eligible for a House of Government apartment until 1936, when his old comrade, M. P. Frinovsky, was appointed deputy head of the NKVD.) Some top industrial managers, including Granovsky, employed the forced labor supplied by the NKVD.

The Central Executive Committee's Housekeeping Department, to which the House of Government belonged, ran several farms that provided the House cafeteria and various nearby resorts with food. On November 13, 1932, the director of the Maryino State Farm and Resort wrote to the head of the CEC Housekeeping Department, N. I. Pakhomov:

> Dear Nikolai Ivanych!
>
> During my absence, several more people were picked up, so now there have been eighteen arrested, of whom twelve were released. Just now, they brought a warrant for the arrest of our agronomist-zootechnician, Zelenin, and our veterinarian, Zhiltsov, but then relented and allowed them to remain under their own recognizance. Our best workers keep leaving—for fear of being arrested themselves. The same phenomenon can be observed among our technicians. The local OGPU organs are on a rampage looking for hidden theft and wrecking—but what can a laundress or a mute cowherd possibly wreck? Therefore, Nikolai Ivanych, I ask you to inform Mikhail Ivanovich and Avel Sofronovich that measures must be taken to set up an inquiry into the correctness of the arrests and further threats. We need to create a normal working environment. With these abnormal and incorrect arrests, we may find ourselves in the kind of situation and the kind of conditions where we have no one left here to do the work.[39]

Most Soviet institutions adopted one or more kolkhozes as the recipients of moral, intellectual, physical, and, if possible, financial assistance. The House of Government Party cell had become the official sponsor of the "Lenin's Path" collective farm north of Moscow. On December 7, 1933, during a respite on the collectivization front, it received a reprimand from the Party Committee of Moscow's Lenin District (where the House was located) for an "unacceptably formal approach" to its responsibilities. "Having been sent by the cell, the Communists Ivanchuk and Tarasov committed a gross distortion of Party policy and violations of revolutionary legality at the sponsored kolkhoz by engaging in coercion and by initiating and carrying out criminal acts of abuse against a group of adolescents (intimidation, beatings, etc.)." Most members of the House of Government Party cell were House employees; the leaseholders and their family members tended to register at work and travel to their own adopted kolkhozes.[40]

Some House residents encountered collectivization indirectly. Nikolai Maltsev (Apt. 116), Molotov's and Arosev's childhood friend and a member of the Central Control Commission, was asked to respond to a letter sent to Stalin by a peasant named Nikulin. "The heads of the benighted and undeveloped collective farmers and proletarians," wrote Nikulin, echoing Doubting Makar, "are being laid down like bricks in the foundation of socialism, but it's the careerists, curly-haired intellectuals, and worker aristocracy who will get to live under socialism." Maltsev replied: "Your letter addressed to Comrade Stalin is not a good letter at all. In it, you are thinking in a non-Party way." The Zbarskys' encounter was more substantial. "In the 1930s," wrote Ilya Zbarsky, "a collective farmer named Nikitin attempted to shoot at Lenin's body, was apprehended, but managed to kill himself. In a letter found in his pocket, he wrote that he was avenging the terrible conditions of life in the Russian village. The mausoleum guard was increased; the sarcophagus was provided with bullet-proof glass; and a metal detector was installed."[41]

Some House residents had friends and relatives in the countryside. Olga Avgustovna Kedrova–Didrikil (Apt. 409), Andrei Sverdlov's aunt by marriage and the wife, mother, and aunt of three prominent secret police officials (Mikhail Kedrov, Igor Kedrov, and Artur Artuzov), interceded, at the request of a friend, in behalf of two dekulakized peasants. A subsequent investigation established that the two peasants, Efim and Konstantin Prokhorov, had been dekulakized correctly (for owning four houses, two horses, two cows, six sheep, a threshing machine, and thirteen beehives); that both had been sentenced to one year in prison, but that one of them, Efim, "had, on account of poor health, been released from prison and, while at large, been conducting anti-Soviet propaganda in the following cunning way: after dekulakization, he had begun walking door to door in rags not only in his own village but also in neighboring villages asking for testimonies that would support the return of his property and vouch for the fact that he had never hired labor." The investigation concluded that "in this matter, Comrade Kedrova does not have a clear sense of the class struggle in the countryside and the Party line, which circumstance we find it absolutely necessary to convey to the Party bureau of the Society of Old Bolsheviks."[42]

Kedrova's brother-in-law, Nikolai Podvoisky, kept up a vast correspondence with former comrades-in-arms, who wrote asking for character references, various favors, and help getting out of prison. Podvoisky's former "personal orderly, the cavalryman Kolbasov, Stefan Matveevich," had been fired from his position as chairman of his village soviet and secretary of the Party cell for what he claimed was embezzlement perpetrated by his subordinates. According to a letter from Kolbasov's brother, "while carrying out, from 1929 until the present, the Party's hard-line policy on the liquidation of the kulaks as a class, all the kulaks and subkulaks, having become openly hostile toward him and, in connection with his arrest, keep concocting false accusations." Another old comrade wrote from the Vishera camp (in Granovsky's Berezniki or in nearby Vizhaikha). "I was so distressed by the wholesale collectivization campaign of February–March, 1930, before the Party directives were issued, that I kept grumbling and complaining—probably not in the best manner, but for the best of reasons." A third letter writer, the Civil War veteran Tit Aleksandrovich Kolpakov, understood that good intentions were no excuse for weakness but confessed to feeling "like a pencil without lead." He asked for Podvoisky's help in obtaining release from prison and saving his family from starvation:

> From September 3 to October 26, 1932 I worked in the Kuban Grain Council as head of a department in charge of 10,000 hectares, but I was unable to overcome the difficulties that stood in our way, gave in to weakness, and quit my supervisory position. . . .
>
> I fully realize my mistake and sincerely repent for giving in to weakness on the labor front—something I never did on the bloody battlefronts. Dear Nikolai Ilich! On behalf of my children and their sick mother, on behalf of my Red-Partisan soul, I am not just asking, I am begging you. . . .
>
> How is the health of your family? Your boy must be quite big by now. How is the health of your better half, your spouse, Nina Avgustovna?[43]

Efim Shchadenko was at the center of his own large patronage network. One of his correspondents, a Civil War hero and now collectivization official in Kalach-on-the-Don, A. Travianov, wrote about the difficulties and rewards of rural activism:

> You'd die of laughter if you knew how we live next to them and them next to us we taught them many political and economic words for example they now know bourgeoisie exploitation speculation contractation wholesale collectivization and so on and so forth etcetera. I apologize for not writing for a long time because I was mobilized by the district committee for all the grain procurement campaigns, my throat is sore from making speeches and ordering up whatever is needed and necessary, like let's do the five-year plan in four years if we fulfill all the plans drawn up by our Soviet government then things will get good for you peasants and workers in all

things and we won't want for anything we just need to endure a little bit longer and gather our strength to improve the sowing and improve animal breeding and so on more faith in socialist construction—be selfless firm well-organized united friendly loving united all together workers peasants day laborers poor and middle on the economic front. And now dear Comrade to the most important thing the campaigns are going not too badly and not too well so far nothing to brag about and nothing to complain about the fulfillment is getting close to 100% the kolkhozes exceeding and the individual peasants still having some difficulties.

In other news, according to Travianov, the harvest had been bad in fourteen rural soviets on the left bank of the Don, and twenty people had been arrested for conspiring against the Soviet state. "And they all confessed and testified against each other and for this thing they got ten years each from the GPU collegium but in my own opinion I would bite off their noses and ears with my own teeth."[44]

The writer A. S. Serafimovich went home to Ust-Medveditskaia every summer—to see his friends and relatives, ride in his motorboat, and do research for his novel about collectivization. Throughout the rest of the year, he stayed in touch by writing letters. One of his regular correspondents was his wife's friend, Sonia Gavrilova, who spent parts of 1931, 1932, and 1933 on grain-procuring missions. On the whole, she wrote on December 3, 1931, the situation was "nightmarish":

> All this squeezing out of grain, hay, flax, and other crops is taking place under difficult circumstances. They whine and whimper that there's nothing left, but when you grab them by the throat, they deliver both grain and hay, and whatever else they're required to. My nerves are always on edge. You have to be on guard or else they might bash you on the head, but I've gotten used to it by now, and I can walk from one village to another at night. I'm still alive, but who knows what will happen next. And yet, in spite of all the hurdles and difficulties, we have emerged as victors, met our grain and hay targets 100%, and managed to kolkhozify this whole petty, private-property peasant mass.[45]

A few years later she got her reward: "Please congratulate me on my new Party card. I received it today at 1 p.m. My heart was overcome with incredible joy, like I'd never felt before. When the district committee secretary handed me my new card and said, 'Take it, Comrade Gavrilova, you have worked hard for it,' and firmly shook my hand, I almost cried with joy, but somehow managed to keep my composure."[46]

Another one of Serafimovich's frequent correspondents was his elderly relative, Anna Mikhailovna Popova (Serafimovich's real name was

"Popov"). On January 18, 1932, she wrote that her grandson, Serafim, had moved away and not been in touch with her since. "I live in very difficult conditions. I have no money or bread. I wish he would send me something, anything at all. Other people feed me sometimes, I have nothing left to sell." She asked for some dried bread cubes and a little money. "I don't know what to do. I have nothing left but debts. I wait for death to bring salvation. Please forgive a poor wretch and invalid for bothering you. I pray for you all every day and thank you for your help and kindness, my dear ones! I never thought I'd live to such a state. . . . My friend has asked me to move out, what else can she do? She is in need herself, we are now eating cakes made of grass."

On March 3, 1933, she heard of the renaming of Ust-Medveditskaia and sent her best wishes—from the new town of Serafimovich to: Aleksandr Serafimovich Serafimovich, No. 2 Serafimovich Street, Apartment No. 82. "Dear Aleksandr Serafimovich: Congratulations on your 70th jubilee and the cross you received and the renaming of our town in your honor as a fighter for the people's freedom, such merit as yours will live on for many generations." She had still not heard from her grandson, Serafim. "I am now all on my own. Please take pity on me and send some dried bread cubes. I've been waiting for them all this time and am sending you my very best regards and wishes for good health. . . . For food, I have oak bark mixed with chaff. For over a month I've had no bread, and no death either. You're the only person, who, I hope, will not abandon me."

Her last letter was sent twelve days later. "Dear Aleksandr Serafimovich: I am dying, I beg you please send 70 rubles for my burial, I owe Agafia Aleksandrovna 11 rubles that need to be returned. She fed me the best she could, I was a burden to her but she never abandoned me, if you cannot send this money tell Serafim to send this money right away to Agafia Aleksandrovna Kozmina. This is my last request of you. You treated me like a true relative, you and your whole family. Anna Mikhailovna Popova March 15, 1933, town of Serafimovich."[47]

Several months later, Serafimovich arrived in "his own" (as he put it) town to witness the final scene from his own Iron Flood. He described it in a letter to one of his proletarian-writer protégés, V. P. Ilyenkov:

It was, you might say, a triumphal entry on a white horse: the bridge on the other side of the Don (the meadow, forest, devilish sun)—the flags, the glistening brass, and the thunderous, unimaginable roar. The band roared; the kids, eyes popping and red cheeks puffed out, roared into their long trumpets; it was utter madness; the drums—of the 900 young pioneers, both local and those brought in from Stalingrad (where they have a summer camp)—roared; and the district Party committee, district executive committee, trade unions, cooperative officials, fishermen, grape growers, cobblers, goldsmiths, outhouse cleaners, old men, women, and infants (drowning out everyone else) all roared. Then I puffed up like a rooster and began roaring, too. I made speeches at them, and they made speeches at me, and then they bent my head down, placed a young-pioneer scarf around my neck, and presented me with some ears of grain, as a symbol of the harvest.[48]

Sometimes collectivization arrived in the flesh, close enough for some House of Government residents to see. Tatiana Belenkaia, the daughter of one of the architects of collectivization, Mark Belenky, was five years old in the winter of 1933. Every day around noon, her nanny, Aniuta, would put her on a sled, and the two of them would cross the river to a government take-out cafeteria on Granovsky Street. "Once," writes Tatiana, "I heard Father tell Aniuta (and made a note to myself): 'Don't throw away a single crumb. Take any leftover food to the bridge.' There, under the Big Stone Bridge, is where the beggars stood: grown-ups and children, who looked like little skeletons, with their hands stretched out." Elina Kisis from Apt. 424 was three years older. Her school was on Yakimanka, south of the Ditch. "Grandma would wrap up some sandwiches for me, but I never got to eat them because every morning I used to run into some boys by the Small Stone Bridge, and they would open my bag, pull out my breakfast, and eat it right on the spot. They often used to fight over a piece of bread."[49]

Bridges, large and small, were traditional shelters for outcasts and breeding grounds for swamp creatures. Sometimes, however, the "documentary proof of the planless creation of the world" made it as far as the gate. According to Kisis, "during the first years of the existence of the House of Government, security was very strict, but skinny children from the nearby houses would slide through the bars of the metal gates and fences, hide beneath the columns, and beg for food. This continued until ration cards were abolished" (in January 1935).[50]

There were also those who did not need to hide, those who were not seen as documentary proof of anything: the various guards, painters, gardeners, carpenters, janitors, laundresses, floor polishers, and cafeteria servers, most of them former peasants. And then there were the domestics. Every apartment had a maid, and most maids were refugees from the countryside. Belenkaia's nanny Aniuta was one, and so was Kisis's Dunia. Dunia went on to marry one of the House guards, but most nannies never married. Some residents knew about the families of their "home workers" (Nadezhda Smilga-Poluian sent food packages to the starving relatives of her children's nanny). Others did not. The House of Government was and was not an island. One of the consequences of collectivization was that almost every child raised in the House of Government was raised by one of its casualties.[51]

∎ ∎ ∎

Another casualty of collectivization was its fictional representation. Se-rafimovich never finished his novel, *The Kolkhoz Fields*, and what he did write about the transformation of Ust-Medveditskaia was entirely within the industrial framework of the creation/construction myth. "You can-not imagine how unrecognizable the Ust-Medveditskaia landscape will be," he wrote to his brother in August 1933. "In Kalach-on-the-Don, a 35-meter-high dam is going to be built. In Ust-Medveditskaia, the water will rise by 25–28 meters and flood the lower part of the town of Serafi-movich, as well as Berezki, the meadow, the forests, the sands, Novo-Aleksandrovka, and perhaps Podolkhovskie, too. The land will remain on the horizon. It will all become a large bay. I can't help feeling sorry for the forests, the meadow, and the lakes I know so well, but it is better this way, it will be magnificent." As for the surviving settlement, "it is going to be a garden city, a city of schools, study, and rest."[52]

But what about "the kolkhoz fields"? And who would be left on them after the flood? "Who," asked Mikhail Koltsov in a 1931 *Pravda* essay, "will tell us about the march of one hundred thousand people from the south to the north of the Central Black-Earth Region during the cold winter of 1930–1931?"

> It was with astonished incredulity that the people—individual households—entered the unheard-of world of common labor and economy. Everything terrified them. Everything seemed—and was—amazing, stupefying, topsy-turvy, contrary to everything they knew about the way the world worked. But this old way, which had been protected for a thousand years by their oppressors—this powerful, gray-haired way covered with the moss of centuries—turned out to be foolish and feeble-minded compared to the young and vigorously intelligent Bolshevik way.
>
> Every individual owner who has been drawn into the collective by the masses or has joined it himself must experience a moment when the new truths, imposed from the outside, enter the head through the ears, clash with the old truths, and come out on top. The kol-khoz propaganda becomes the individual's personal conviction. It is this decisive battle inside the peasant's head that marks the true, actual—not just on paper—registration of a new kolkhoz member.[53]

One of the earliest attempts to give shape to this story was Andrei Pla-tonov's "For Future Use: A Poor Peasant's Chronicle" (1931). While traveling through the Central Black-Earth Region in March 1930, "a certain soulful poor peasant"—innocent, like Makar, of "both selfishness and self-respect"—comes across a large assortment of melancholy enemies: left deviationists, who "take their own individual mood for universal enthusi-asm"; right opportunists, who want to postpone the building of socialism "until the distant time of a lofty universal consensus"; and unmasked wreckers, who are "marched to the district center and left there for eternity." Arrayed against them are conscious kolkhozniks, who "have no need for any urging coercion," and honest activists, who "have the courage of gloomily telling the kolkhozniks that what awaits them in the near future is the grief of unruliness, incompetence, unreliability, and want." One particularly "indomitable" collectivizer watches his family "become extinct" from hunger and tells the people "in the words of the Gospel because he did not know the Marxist words yet": "these are my wives and fathers and children and mothers: I don't have anyone but the indigent masses." After many trials, he finally realizes that spirit alone is not enough for those who are looking for the city that is to come: "what we need is a live person—but the same as Lenin. As soon as I finish the sowing, I'll go looking for Stalin. I feel my source in him."[54]

The story seemed right, but it was not. Once again, Platonov had reached for a myth but written a picaresque folk tale; imagined a Divine Comedy but produced Menippean satire; celebrated the indigent masses by representing lone eccentrics. Igor Sats (Lunacharsky's brother-in-law, Natalia Sats's uncle, and Elena Usievich's friend and colleague) wrote in his reader's report for *Red Virgin Soil* that the novella was very well written and full of "hatred for all things that damage the socialist construction," but that it could not be published in its current form because the author "did not understand the true meaning of the reconstruction as a mass movement." Fadeev, the new editor of *Red Virgin Soil*, published it anyway— perhaps because there were no other manuscripts about collectivization. Stalin read it, called it "a story by an agent of our enemies," and ordered Fadeev to apologize in print. Fadeev apologized, called it "an attack by an agent of the class enemy," and wrote that, "in order to falsify the true picture of kolkhoz construction and struggle," Platonov "turns all the kolkhoz builders into idiots and holy fools. On Platonov's instructions, these idiots and holy fools do everything they can to embarrass themselves in front of the peasantry, so as to benefit the kulaks, while Platonov, pretending to be an idiot and holy fool himself, sneers at the reader by rhapsodizing over their actions. Saintly simplicity, indeed!"[55]

Platonov wrote to *Pravda* and *Literaturnaia gazeta*, renouncing all his "previous creative work" as non-Party and "therefore in poor taste," and to Maksim Gorky, assuring him that he was not a class enemy. "No matter how much I suffer as a result of my mistakes, such as 'For Future Use,' I cannot become a class enemy, and it is impossible to reduce me to that condition because the working class is my motherland, and my future is connected to the proletariat." His other response might be hidden in the text of "For Future Use": "The rich peasants, after becoming the bureaucratic leaders of the village, taught the people to think and talk in such an officially tongue-tied way, that many a poor peasant's phrase, though expressing a sincere emotion, sounded almost ironic. A listener might suppose that the village was inhabited by sneering subkulaks, while in fact these were poor peasants, tomorrow's builders of a great new history, expressing their thoughts in an alien, ambiguous, kulak-bureaucratic language."[56]

The task was to demonstrate the true meaning of the reconstruction as a mass movement while having the masses speak their own language; to show how the new truths, imposed from the outside, enter the head through the ears, clash with the old truths, and come out on top. It was fulfilled almost a year after Platonov's fiasco, by Mikhail Sholokhov's *Virgin Soil Upturned*. One of the novel's central characters, Makar Nagulnov, is Platonovian in more than first name. During the Civil War he "hacks at the vermin" until he begins having epileptic fits; during collectivization he "hunkers down and drags everyone into the kolkhoz, closer and closer to the world revolution"; and in a rare moment of quiet reflection, he confesses that he does not need a wife because he is "all sharpened up for the world revolution: it's her, my sweetheart, I'm waiting for." But Makar Nagulnov—unlike Platonov's Makars—eventually figures out the true meaning of the reconstruction as a mass movement. The plot is propelled by the confrontation between Bolshevik collectivizers (who have their own maturing to do) and kulak and White Guardist wreckers (whose opposition has psychological, as well as political, motivation), but the novel's true center is the "decisive battle inside the peasant's head." *Virgin Soil Upturned* is centered on the conversion episode from the canonical construction plot—without the construction. In the kolkhoz fields, the work of creation was mostly invisible.[57]

No other novel about collectivization would enter the Soviet canon. (F. Panferov's *Bruski* was warmly acclaimed on arrival but irreparably damaged—Serafimovich's defense notwithstanding—by Gorky's 1934 attack on its literary quality.) One reason may have been the long shadow cast by Sholokhov. (Serafimovich, the first and most forceful champion and publisher of *The Quiet Don*, seemed unable, in the drafts of his *The Kolkhoz Fields*, to escape the influence of *Virgin Soil Upturned*.) But the main reason was the much longer shadow cast by the cranes, chimneys, and masts of the great construction sites. The true meaning of the reconstruction as a mass movement was the building of the eternal house, not the decisive battle inside the peasant's head. The real reason for Serafimovich's barrenness was not the success of *Virgin Soil Upturned*, but the irresistible image of the purifying flood washing up against the brand new city of Serafimovich.[58]

■ ■ ■

The greatest exceptions to the reign of urbanism were "the backward national republics undergoing the transition from semifeudal to socialist relations, bypassing capitalism." In central Asia and Kazakhstan, the greatest effort was directed at "feudal, patriarchal, and clan relations," and

Koltsov's appeal for more descriptions of how the gray-haired way turned out to be foolish compared to the vigorously intelligent Bolshevik way applied all the more. Some necessary plot twists related to backwardness included a starker contrast between the two ways (separated as they were by most of human history) and the centrality of young women and children as positive characters (given the association of backwardness with immaturity). One of the pioneers of what would become the "long journey" literature was the proletarian writer and member of Serafimovich's circle, Fedor Kallistratovich Fedotov.[59]

Fedotov was born in 1887 in a peasant family. He joined a socialist circle as a young man, spent time in prison for distributing leaflets, and, around 1914, emigrated to America. In New York he met his future wife, Roza Lazarevna Markus (who had arrived from Nikolaev by way of a Paris millinery shop). According to an interview she gave many years later, the only time he ever kissed her was in 1917, when he heard the news of the Russian Revolution. According to a personnel form he filled out in 1931, he stayed in the United States for about five years. "Worker (a miner), but employed as a turner and stevedore. In 1914 joined the Bolshevik section in New York. In 1915–16 president of the dockworkers' union. One of the organizers of the Communist Party of the United States. Arrested and sentenced to ten years in prison. Spent one year in Trenton Prison before escaping to the Soviet Union." In the 1920s and early 1930s, he served as secretary of the Semirech'e Provincial Party Committee (based in Alma-Ata), member of the Central Committee of the Communist Party of Turkestan (based in Tashkent), and head of the organizational department of the Osh District Party Committee in the Kyrgyz Autonomous Republic.[60]

Fedor Fedotov and Roza Markus

During collectivization, Fedotov was in the Bazar-Kurgan District in the Fergana Valley. He kept a diary, which may or may not have been edited by his biographer.

> The situation is as follows. Here in the Bazar-Kurgan District, where we have been conducting wholesale collectivization, there is an emergency situation.
>
> On March 7th, at 10 a.m., we received the news: In Bazar-Kurgan, armed kulaks had incited a peasant rebellion.
>
> I jumped on my horse and rode to Kokand-Kishlak, from where I called the Andijan OGPU and requested help. Then I mobilized the local militia, which sent fifteen men to Bazar-Kurgan.
>
> Our Machine-Tractor station was in danger. When I got back with the militia men, I discovered that in Bazar-Kurgan, the kulaks who were demanding the release of all arrested kulaks, had organized an uprising by the local population. In the melee, three people—a militia man and two local activists—were killed, and one, the secretary of the district committee, injured. At the same time, a crowd of peasants led by the kulaks and religious leaders were demanding the dissolution of the kolkhozes.[61]

Help arrived; the siege was lifted; and wholesale collectivization continued in accordance with Party policy. But Fedotov's real ambition was to become a fiction writer. His first attempt had been a play written in 1916 for the dockworkers' union in Erie, Pennsylvania. "I am yet to write my big book," he wrote fifteen years later in his diary, "a book that will be about life and still be a piece of life: full of passion, risk, and adventures."[62]

In 1930, the year of the Bazar-Kurgan uprising, he published a fictionalized memoir about the adventures of five unemployed workers in America. Frank is a dark, hot-tempered, Italian anarchist; Red is a red-haired Irish union organizer; "Negro Willie" dreams of getting rich and moving to Africa; "Punch, the American" has big fists, but no principles or convictions; and Fred, the narrator, is a Russian revolutionary. They wander around the country doing odd jobs and often going hungry. A mining executive wants to employ them as scabs, but they refuse. An insurance company official offers them money for burning down uninsured houses, but only Frank, Punch, and Willy agree. Fred and Red get hired as sailors, discover that the ship they are on is transporting weapons to the anti-Bolshevik forces in Murmansk, organize a mutiny, and are sentenced to ten years in Trenton Prison. According to Aleksandr Isbakh's review, the book was "interesting, but artistically weak." In 1931, Fedotov was admitted to the literary seminar at the Institute of Red Professors in Moscow. On March 12, he, Roza, and their eight-year-old son Lyova moved from the First House of Soviets to the House of Government, Apt. 262.[63]

Fedor, Roza, and their son, Lyova

According to Isbakh, who was in the same seminar, "learning did not come very easily for him. At first he was too hard on the classics, inveighing against Gogol's reactionary views, deflating Turgenev, and making sarcastic remarks about Hugo. . . . At Party meetings and during seminars on the international situation, Fedor liked to talk about America. On this subject, of course, he knew a lot more than the rest of us—and not just about America: he had crossed two oceans and knew Mongolia well."[64]

He did publish two books. One was an illustrated children's book about two Mongol orphans, a boy and a girl, who stop fearing "the lamas, rich people, and Chinese and Japanese generals," join the young pioneers, and start singing the song of the Soviet drummer-boy with new lyrics:

Puntsuk the Mongol hunter,
Puntsuk the Mongol hunter,
Puntsuk the Mongol hunter
   Got himself a gun.
Did a little jumping,
Did a little shouting,
Made the greedy lamas
   Turn and run.

Both plan on going to Moscow to study. The boy will learn how to build "not yurts, but houses, factories, and railroads"; the girl will become a schoolteacher.[65]

The second, more grown-up book was set in the Bazar-Kurgan District during wholesale collectivization. The main character is a Kyrgyz cotton-procurement plenipotentiary named Galim Isakeev, and the central scene (soon to become common in long journey narratives) is a meeting of poor peasants who begin by denying that there are any kulaks in their village, but then, as new truths, skillfully conveyed by Isakeev, enter their heads through the ears and come out on top, draw up a list of forty-two households to be liquidated as a class. Surrounding the decisive battle is a traditional hero's quest narrative, as Isakeev, with the help of some children and young women, searches for the hidden cotton, which is being guarded by a giant bandit, a rich trader, and a two-faced innkeeper.[66]

In January 1933, at the height of the famine, the Party's Central Committee created political departments in rural machine-tractor stations. Their responsibilities included plan-fulfillment, political supervision, and secret-police work. They were to be independent from local Party and state control. The chairmen were to be experienced Party functionaries selected by the Central Committee (seventeen thousand in all), and their deputies would be OGPU officers appointed by provincial plenipotentiaries and confirmed by OGPU head, G. Yagoda. In March 1933, Fedotov was summoned to the Central Committee but, according to Isbakh, was not selected because his big book had not been finished yet. He protested and received an appointment as head of the political department of the Altai State Farm. He got there by mid-April.[67]

Fedotov's first brief letter to Isbakh was followed by a long silence. "I couldn't write earlier," he explained in his next letter, "because there was no time for letter writing. Can you imagine a situation in which all the state farm officials (with a few exceptions) have turned out to be wreckers? They had an organization of up to fifty members and needed to be rooted out." He mentioned the hard work and the "incredible tension," but he did not complain ("there is no difficulty a Bolshevik cannot overcome"). He described the steppe and the harvest; promised to write an article about his experiences; and asked for a printing press and a women's organizer. His department was headquartered in the houses of the deported peasants.[68]

You ask what my life is like. It's a wonderful life: I'm absorbed in my work, enjoy it immensely, and do it easily (despite the great difficulties) and with the kind of desire that I did not, to be honest, feel in Moscow. The only thing that sometimes ruins my mood is that I don't have any time to read or do literary work. I keep up with my diary, but the book—the book, my dear Sasha, is exactly where it was when I left off. And that pains me. I sometimes feel the absence of a literary environment and of you, Sasha, our songwriter-poet ("off to the political department, you rush at full speed"), and I miss my son.[69]

Fedor Fedotov with his son, Lyova

On September 4, 1933, Fedotov's OGPU deputy sent the following telegram to Moscow:

On August 29, at around 5 or 6 p.m., Fedotov, the director of the garage (political officer Kliushkin), and company commander, Kirillov, left to go hunting in the area of meadows that is located 10 to 12 kilometers northwest of the farm headquarters. The meadows are dotted with lakes, marshes, brush, grass, and so on.

Upon arrival, Fedotov left the others and went on ahead. In the meadows, on one of the lake shores, Fedotov had an epileptic seizure, fell into the shallow water, and, apparently, drowned. At said time and place, he was alone and of sound mind.

The next day (August 30th), around 6 or 7 p.m., I personally discovered Fedotov's body and pulled it out of the water, but did not find any signs of violence. The medical specialists who performed the autopsy did not detect any signs of physical violence, either.[70]

13

THE IDEOLOGICAL
SUBSTANCE

The canonical Soviet histories of the First Five-Year Plan consisted, like Marxism in Lenin's definition, of three components: industrialization, which stood for the construction of the economic foundations of socialism; collectivization, which stood for the destruction of the force that "engenders capitalism and the bourgeoisie continuously, daily, hourly, spontaneously, and on a massive scale"; and the cultural revolution, which represented the conversion of all nominal Soviets to genuine Marxism-Leninism. As a proletarian judge in Platonov's "For Future Use" says of a former fool named Pashka (little Paul), "Capitalism gave birth to fools as well as to the poor. We can handle the poor just fine, but what are we to do with the fools? And this, Comrades, is where we come to the Cultural Revolution. So therefore I propose that this comrade, entitled Pashka, must be thrown into the cauldron of the Cultural Revolution so we can burn away the skin of ignorance, get at the very bones of slavery, crawl into the skull of psychology, and fill every nook and cranny with our ideological substance."[1]

The goal of the cultural revolution was to fill every nook and cranny with the Bolshevik ideological substance. The most visible part of the campaign was the remaking of the arts and sciences. When in the summer of 1931, Ilya Zbarsky was admitted to Moscow University (his father's Order of the Red Banner of Labor for preserving Lenin's body was officially equated with proletarian origin), he wanted to enroll in the department of organic chemistry, but was told there was no such specialization:

"Perhaps physical chemistry then?"
"We do not have that specialization either."
"So what specializations do you have?"
"'Engineer specializing in the production of sulphuric acid,' 'engineer specializing in the production of aniline dyes,' 'engineer specializing in the production of plastic materials,' 'engineer . . .'"
"I'm sorry, but I was actually thinking of studying chemistry."
"We need specialists, who are essential for socialist industry, not desk-bound scholars."

Zbarsky wanted to follow in his father's footsteps, but he was not sure which engineering specialization would be appropriate.

> I walked over to the Biology Department, but it turned out that there was no such thing. Instead there were botany and zoology departments. When I said I wanted to study biochemistry, I was told that there was no such specialization, but that there was hunting science (formerly "zoology of the vertebrates"), fishing science (formerly "ichthyology"), physiology of labor (formerly "physiology of animals"), and so on, including "physicochemical biology." They probably could not think of a way to rename it. It sounded like the only department in which science had survived, and I applied and was accepted.[2]

Ilya Zbarsky's job after graduation was exempt from Marxist exegesis. (He liked to call himself a "paraschite," but his official title was "Lenin Mausoleum employee.") In other arts and sciences, young proletarian true believers of mostly nonproletarian origin were trying to oust their former teachers while fighting among themselves over Party patronage and definitions of orthodoxy. Urbanists, disurbanists, constructivists, RAPPists, AKhRRists, and sulphuric acid engineers were planning a new world in the ruins of the old. The only criterion of success was endorsement by the Party. The most conclusive revolutions took place in agrarian economics (because Stalin intervened directly) and literature (because it meant so much to the Bolsheviks and because Stalin intervened directly).[3]

The Party's turn toward the policy of forced collectivization had formalized the triumph of Kritsman's Agrarian Marxists (who were studying the spread of capitalist class relations in the countryside) over Chayanov's "neopopulists" (who had insisted on the traditional nonmarket specificity of peasant agriculture). Chayanov had lost his institute, renounced his views, and abandoned the study of peasant households in favor of the study of large state farms. On the last day of the First All-Union Conference of Agrarian Marxists in December 1929, Stalin was expected to congratulate the delegates and set the goals for future work. ("Given the complete contamination of virtually all agricultural experts with Chayanovism," wrote Aron Gaister in a private letter to Kritsman, "the struggle against it by means of daily agitation and Marxist propaganda is a huge and important task.") Instead, Stalin used the occasion to proclaim the policy of the liquidation of the kulaks as a class, rendering Kritsman's and Gaister's work on social differentiation meaningless and possibly harmful.[4]

Ilya Zbarsky as a student
(Courtesy of I. B. Zbarsky)

On June 21, 1930, Chayanov was arrested for membership in a Peasant Labor Party, allegedly led by his colleague, Professor N. D. Kondtratiev. The party was an OGPU fiction, but, as is often the case in thought-crime inquisitions, the fiction had been of Chayanov's own making. According to his 1920 novella, *My Brother Alexei's Journey into the Country of Peasant Utopia*, peasant representatives were going to enter the government around 1930, become the majority party in 1932, and embark on the wholesale destruction of the cities in 1934. Now, in real-life 1930, the ten-year-old fantasy had become a plausible reaction to the wholesale destruction of the peasantry. On September 2, 1930, Stalin wrote to Molotov: "Might the accused gentlemen be prepared to admit their *mistakes* and publicly drag themselves and their politics through the mud, while at the same time admitting the strength of the Soviet state and the correctness of our collectivization strategy? That would be nice." In the end, the alleged members of the Peasant Labor Party were not asked to do this (unlike the alleged members of the Industrial Party, who were, and did). "Wait before turning the Kondratiev 'case' over to the courts," wrote Stalin to Molotov on September 30. "It is not entirely risk free." On January 26, 1932, the OGPU Collegium sentenced Chayanov to five years in a labor camp.[5]

At the time of Chayanov's arrest, Kritsman was being publicly criticized for having incurred Stalin's criticism. On July 12, 1930, he wrote to Stalin asking whether his (Stalin's) speech at the Conference of Agrarian Marxists should be interpreted as criticism of his (Kritsman's) work. In January 1931, Stalin told Kritsman that he disapproved of the press campaign being waged against him. In April 1931, he pointed out certain faults in Kritsman's speech at the international agrarian conference in Rome. In his response, Kritsman wrote that his words had been misrepresented, and that he had followed Stalin's instructions to the letter not only because he considered them "compulsory in general," but because they corresponded with his own "understanding of these things." The cultural revolution on the agrarian front ended with the victory of Kritsman's "understanding" to the extent that it corresponded with Comrade Stalin's instructions.[6]

In literature, the monopoly of Leopold Averbakh's Russian Association of Proletarian Writers (RAPP) survived until April 1932. The role of Chayanov had been played first by Voronsky, and then, after his fall, by his shadow. "Voronskyism" stood for neopopulism, "*blini* nationalism," and "abstract humanism." One of the latter-day representatives of Voronskyism was Andrei Platonov, who seemed to oppose his holy fools to those who "only thought of the big picture, and not of the private Makar." As Averbakh wrote in his review of "Doubting Makar,"

It is well-known that both Marx and Lenin often compared the building of socialism to childbirth, i.e., to a painful, difficult, and excruciating process. We are "giving birth" to a new society. We need to muster all our strength, strain all our muscles, concentrate totally on our goal. But then some people come along with a sermon about easing up! They want to evoke our pity! And they come to us with their propaganda of humanism! As if, in this world, there were something more genuinely human than the class hatred of the proletariat; as if it were possible to demonstrate one's love for the "Makars" other than by building new houses, in which the heart of the socialist human being will beat![7]

Platonov's story was ambiguous, concluded Averbakh, but "our time does not tolerate ambiguity." The Party was "making it impossible to oppose 'private Makars' to 'the big picture.'"[8]

Of the many proletarian groups contesting RAPP's monopoly on Marxism in literature, the most serious was the circle of Serafimovich's protégés, which included Isbakh, Parfenov, and Ilyenkov. On the day of the publication of the Politburo decree of April 22, 1932, which put an end to the search for orthodoxy (and Averbakh's rule) by abolishing all proletarian writers' groups in favor of an all-encompassing writer's union, they gathered in Serafimovich's apartment in the House of Government. "What has happened, has happened," said Serafimovich, according to Isbakh. "It's as if we had finally recovered from a terrible fever. But now let's think ahead, about how we will work from now on. So, young men, what are your plans? What can you say in your defense?"[9]

The cultural revolution in literature ended with the victory of private Makar to the degree that he fit into the big picture. Helping the writers with their plans and occasionally calling on them to say something in their defense was the greatly expanded central censorship office (the Main Directorate for Literary and Publishing Affairs, or Glavlit) under its new head, Boris Volin (himself a former RAPP activist). Upon taking over, Volin announced "a decisive turn toward extreme class vigilance," and, two years later, on April 9, 1933, promised the creation of an "integral censorship" and the use of "repression" against errant censors.[10]

Another institution that had been designed to discipline literary production was the Association of State Book and Magazine Publishers (OGIZ). On August 5, 1931, the head of OGIZ, Artemy Khalatov, was scheduled to report to the Politburo. The editor of *Izvestia*, Ivan Gronsky (who lived in Entryway 1, on the other side of the State New Theater from Khalatov's Entryway 12), described the proceedings in his memoirs:

On the agenda was the work of OGIZ. The presenter was Khalatov. He entered the room and stood, not where he was supposed to, but at the other end of the table, closer to Stalin. Just as Khalatov was about to begin, Stalin suddenly asked:
"Why are you wearing a hat?"
Khalatov looked lost.

"But you know I always wear this hat."

"It shows a lack of respect for the Politburo! Take off your hat!"

"But, Iosif Vissarionovich, why?"

I had never seen Stalin in such a state. Usually he was polite and spoke softly, but now he was absolutely furious. Khalatov still did not remove his ill-fated hat. Stalin jumped up and ran out of the room. We all began to reason with Khalatov in semi-facetious terms: "Artem, don't be silly . . ." Khalatov relented, and began his report. Stalin came back, sat down, and raised his hand. Molotov, as usual, said: "Comrade Stalin has the floor."

The General Secretary's brief intervention can be summarized as follows: "The political situation in the country has changed, but we have not drawn the appropriate conclusions. It seems to me that OGIZ should be split up. I propose taking five publishing houses out of OGIZ."

The proposal was accepted. Khalatov left the meeting as a nobody.[11]

In fact, only two publishing houses were taken out of OGIZ (the State Science and Technology Publishers and the Party Press), and Khalatov was not formally dismissed until April 1932. Bureaucratic politics seem to have been at least as important as Khalatov's hat. One of the initiators of the removal of the Party Press from OGIZ was Aleksei Stetsky, the head of the Central Committee's Cultural-Propaganda Department and a close friend of Gronsky. (Soon after moving into the House of Government, Stetsky and Gronsky had switched apartments: Stetsky moved into Apt. 144, Gronsky's original assignment, and Gronsky, who had a larger family, moved into

Artemy Khalatov (*left*) with Maxim Gorky. Khalatov had led the effort to persuade Gorky to return to the Soviet Union

Apt. 18, in Entryway 1, under Radek, who often wrote for Gronsky's *Izvestia* and sometimes walked home with him.) Khalatov became Head of Personnel at the People's Commissariat of Transportation and, three years later, chairman of the All-Union Society of Inventors. He continued to live in the House of Government and to wear his hat.[12]

∎ ∎ ∎

The transformation of the arts and sciences and the creation of an integral censorship system provided the necessary conditions for the cultural revolution's principal goal: the penetration of the skull of Comrade Pashka's psychology and the filling of every nook and cranny of his mind with the Bolshevik ideological substance.

The best kind of surgery was a purge, or a public confession before a general assembly of the congregation, and the best possible purge subject was the prototypical underground Bolshevik, Aleksandr Voronsky. Voronsky's purge took place at the State Fiction Publishing House on October 21, 1933, four years after his readmission to the Party and a year and a half after the banishment of all Averbakhs. Asked "what Voronsky had done to root out 'Voronskyism,'" he said: "Very little. I think that 'Voronskyism' is, in essence, correct." Not everyone was happy with this answer, but he insisted that his political mistakes were distinct from his literary opinions. "I do not think these questions are connected to the opposition. I do not understand what the theory of immediate impressions has to do with Trotskyism. . . . And, as I said before, I have the same view of the psychology of literary creativity now as I did then, and consider it the only correct theory for Soviet art."[13]

Voronsky was not saying that he had the right to have views contrary to those of the Party: he was saying that the Party—unlike Averbakh—did not have an official view on the psychology of literary creativity. Ultimately, there was only one correct theory of anything, the correctness of any theory depended on what was good for the building of socialism, and the determination of what was good for the building of socialism was the job of the Party leadership. But when the Party leadership was silent, and Averbakhs were in power, it was better to give up altogether. "In the end, I arrived at the conviction that the right thing for me to do was to break my critic's pen in two. And that is what I did."[14]

According to the purge commission, he had no right to do so. "You say that you broke your pen," said one of the interrogators. "But that is not your decision to make. The Party must say to you: 'No, do not break your pen, you must disavow your position on politics and literature, because, with your pen, you did great damage to the whole proletarian revolution, the Party and Soviet literature.'" But this was just the beginning. Since the Party made no distinction between private Makars and the big picture, making things right with the Party meant remaking oneself in its image.

"Personally, I don't doubt Aleksandr Konstantinovich's sincerity," said the director of the State Fiction Publishing House, Nikolai Nakoriakov. "But this admission of his errors took so much out of him that he has become inactive. . . . His breaking of his pen, which was a political weapon handed to him by the Party, will certainly be followed by the breaking of many other weapons and, ultimately, himself." Voronsky needed to return to the ranks as a Party soldier, and he needed to do so sincerely.[15]

Voronsky was willing, but he kept repeating that he could not say things he did not believe, while also claiming (unconvincingly, according to several inquisitors) that his beliefs would change by themselves if the Party issued a formal decree to that effect. While offering a full confession of his fall into heresy and subsequent reawakening, he proposed a general theory of the cultural revolution. "I have thought long and hard about what happened to me," he said. "My answer is this: the central objective of our opposition was to struggle against the Central Committee and the Soviet apparatus. . . . And now I ask myself: how did it happen that I set such an objective? My answer to this question is as follows: I gave an incorrect answer to the question of the relationship between the mass movement . . . and the apparatus, democracy and centralism, democracy and the Party, the Party and its leaders." This was, he argued, an old question. Bakunin had proposed mass struggle; the People's Will had proposed conspiracies by the leaders; and Lenin had provided the answer by demonstrating that the leaders were the embodiment of the masses. Lenin's early disciples (he went on) had constituted an organic body of believers:

It was based on a certain mutual trust. No one told you that you had to do something in a certain way. You did it yourself, without any need for formal rules. And then after the revolution happened, in the early days, as you well know, spontaneity prevailed. . . . And then the Civil War ended, and the question of building arose. I saw that a large state apparatus was being built. I also saw that a mass, well-organized, and inclusive Party was being built. And so, the same questions regarding the relationship between mass struggle and the leaders, the class and the Party, the Party and the leaders—those questions arose again, and in this case I was not able to resolve them. It seemed to me that we were being weighed down by domesticity. It seemed to me that our apparatus, both the Party and state branches, was becoming too top-heavy. It seemed to me that the leaders were prevailing over democracy and centralism was prevailing over democracy—and from that everything else flowed.

Everything else included his joining the opposition, signing various appeals, and taking an active part in the events of 1927:

You see how things could unfold logically. If the apparatus is this way, if it is weighed down, if it is becoming alien, if it is becoming overly bureaucratic, then the building of socialism is out of the question, serious industrialization is out of the question, the real victory of the dictatorship of the proletariat is out of the question. That is how matters looked to me then, and I made my decision. . . .

So what happened next? Next, I realized that I had made a mistake. And what was my mistake? What made me realize my mistake? The thing that made me realize my mistake was collectivization and industrialization. When the industrialization and collectivization plan began to be implemented, I asked myself: okay, so if our apparatus is so very bad and so very bureaucratic, if Party leadership prevails over work with the masses and mass initiative, then how can this same apparatus move such a huge thing off the ground? It's one or the other: either this whole thing fails, or my criticism is wrong.[16]

In Voronsky's telling, Stalin's "revolution from above" was, indeed, from above, insofar as it was launched by the apparatus. It was also, indeed, a revolution, insofar as the apparatus managed to move such a huge thing off the ground. The second coming of the real day was significantly different from the first, but it was accomplishing the same goals: the building of socialism and the real victory of the dictatorship of the proletariat. The same was true of personal conversion: spontaneous "mutual trust" had been replaced by formal institutional obedience, but the commitment to organic wholeness (intolerance of ambivalence) remained the same. The point of the cultural revolution was to restore and universalize the original spontaneity by decree: to transform a sect into a church without losing innocence. Voronsky, who had once served as a volunteer in the suppression of the Kronstadt uprising, was again free of doubt and ready to serve.

The success of the general enterprise—as suggested by the construction/conversion plot—was assured. But was this possible in the case of Voronsky? Was he, in fact, ready to serve again? Most members of the purge commission seemed impressed by his sincerity (and perhaps by his proximity to Stalin), but no one accepted his distinction between the political and the literary. "As for my literary views," he said at the end of his confession, "I said before, and will say again, that I still consider my theoretical views correct, and cannot, at this time, renounce them. If someone were to come to me and say: 'One way or the other, you must renounce them,' I, to be absolutely frank with you, would not be able to do it."

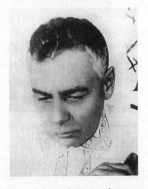

Aleksandr Voronsky

Did this mean that his confession was incomplete? And if so, was it incomplete because he had not fully "disarmed" or because, "at this time," the Party had no clear position on Voronskyism? And what if the person coming to him were Stalin himself? The chairman of the purge commission (the Old Bolshevik, head of the printers' union, and Central Committee member, Boris Magidov) saved his best question for last:

CHAIRMAN. What is the role of Comrade Stalin in our Party?

VORONSKY. There is no need for you to ask this question, because, personally, Comrade Stalin and I have always been on the best of terms. Our differences of opinion were exclusively about matters of principle. I, like the Party as a whole, consider him our Party's best leader and ideologue.

CHAIRMAN. With this, let us conclude today's session.[17]

Voronsky had passed his purge trial and was retained in the Party.

■   ■   ■

Fedor Kaverin had "passed the test of modernity" and earned his place in the House of Government by staging *The Recasting* (about the conversion of the redeemable). His subsequent attempt to tackle "the other side of the heart" had proved premature and resulted in a serious financial and creative crisis. His theater's survival now depended on a new treatment of conversion. His last hope was Mikhail Romm's *The Champion of the World*. As he wrote in his diary in May 1932, "I have to do everything possible to make sure this play takes off in the new building." And as he wrote to the theater's administrative director, Yakov Leontiev, "in this atmosphere of uncertainty, occasional general hostility, unwanted loneliness, and my own prickliness, the only breath of fresh air is my copy of 'The Champion.'"[18]

Mikhail Davidovich Romm (no relation to the film director) was one of Russia's first soccer players, a member of the 1911–12 national team, Tuscany's champion as a defender for Firenze in 1913, coach of the Moscow all-stars at the first "Spartakiad of the Peoples" in 1928, and a close collaborator of N. I. Podvoisky at Sports International. *The Champion of the World* was his first literary effort. It is set in the United States. A magnate named Ferguson sponsors an amateur boxer named Bob, who is training for a championship fight. Bob is a miner; his opponent, Crawford, is black. Ferguson's plan is to use the fight in his campaign for governor. Crawford is the better boxer, but he receives anonymous threats and throws the fight so as to avoid "Negro pogroms." Bob finds out about the plot and exposes Ferguson. Ferguson loses the election, blacks and miners find a common language, and the Communist Party gets more votes than usual. According to the censor's memo, "the play shows the ugly chauvinism of the Americans, the plight of the oppressed Negroes, and the shameless political machinations of American capitalists."[19]

Most important, it showed a doctrinally unimpeachable conversion in an exotic setting perfectly suited for "nonliteral realism." Kaverin was enraptured to the point of ecstasy, of delirious infatuation. As part of his preparation, he read Theodor Dreiser, Jack London, John Dos Passos, several brochures about sports and racism, and Lenin's articles on the national question. He designed an important scene in a black club where Negro proletarians in bright clothes get together to sing "Deep River," drink Coca-Cola, and eat corn and watermelon. As he wrote in his notes for the production, "culturally, the Negro population lags far behind the average level in America. Only the sailor, Strang, is able to establish contact with them by pointing to a way out of slavery in simple language. Strang shows them Soviet illustrated magazines, and when the whole crowd gathers around him, the political leaders who have been arguing with each other—the Zionist Almers, the chauvinist Hollis, and the appeaser Forrest—find themselves together, in one hostile group." The culmination of the show was to be the fight scene as glimpsed from the locker room to the accompaniment of drums, whistles, loudspeakers, megaphones, and banging doors. During the intermission, the "noisy sensationalism" of the election campaign and championship fight was to follow the spectators to the foyer, café, and back to their seats. The singing of the "Internationale," by contrast, was to be done with "convincing simplicity." "Of help here should be the conspiratorial atmosphere in which the Negro workers listen to the new song, and the uncertain performance by Strang, who does not just strike up the tune, but slowly tries to figure it out." The goal was to depict spiritual awakening by means of "good theatricality" and "forceful expressiveness."[20]

Romm was worried. "I am afraid that the stress on dancing is, on the whole, wrong," he wrote to Kaverin on July 2, 1932, "and so is the stress on primitiveness, because American Negroes have left primitiveness behind, but have not yet arrived at urbanism." What was needed was less theatricality and more simplicity. "Sport is about the vast expanse and clean lines of a stadium. Sport is about a simple movement, beautiful in its rationality and devoid of anything superfluous, cumbersome, or ineffective. Sport is about a simple, comfortable costume, a simple, healthy psyche, and simple, healthy relations between men and women." The theater's administrative director, Yakov Leontiev, was worried, too. After months of disagreement over the move to the House of Government, the need for a new aesthetic, and the new play, he had decided to resign. In his last letter to Kaverin, he wrote that his excitement about Romm's play was not warranted "either by the general circumstances or by the quality of the play." He warned Kaverin about the danger of misguided enthusiasms, but offered his continued affection and sympathy. "I am very sad about the state you are in."[21]

Kaverin persevered. By spring 1933, the production had been completed, and the censor's approval was secured. The last remaining hurdle was a special review by the People's Commissariat of Foreign Affairs. On March 4, 1933, Kaverin wrote in his diary:

> Very soon, in three hours or so, some very serious and important people will come here, to our theater: Stetsky, Bubnov, Litvinov, Krestinsky, Karakhan, Shvernik, Kamenev, Kiselev, and many others. They will come in order to see the dress rehearsal of "The Champion of the World" and decide whether we will be allowed to go ahead with the production. The show has no great sins, either political or artistic. The issue is America, about which the show has some tough things to say. In this tense moment on the world scene, diplomatic relations with it may require the removal of that toughness—or, simply put, the banning of the show for an indefinite period of time.
>
> My conscience is clear. And yet, I am very nervous. I am nervous because the plan for the year, derailed by the construction of the stage, which is still not quite finished, is unraveling and slipping through my hands. I feel awful about the seven months of work by the whole troupe (and, in my own case, almost a year). I am afraid that before such an audience, the actors will feel unsure of themselves, and the show will lose its vitality for reasons that have nothing to do with substance. Such important, but nontheatrical, people will not take this into account, and the accidental casualty will be the fate of the show that was supposed to be the start of our new life.[22]

According to Aleksandr Kron's version of Fedor Kaverin's favorite dinner-table story, the important people came, "sat stone-faced through the whole show, and, when it was over, whispered for a long time among themselves and left with hardly a word of goodbye." The show was put on hold, but Kaverin did not lose hope, and he eventually managed to reach the people's commissar of foreign affairs, Litvinov, who lived upstairs in Apt. 14. Litvinov promised to come to a private performance:

> Several days later, a middle-aged man with extraordinarily intelligent and mischievous eyes in a broad face was sitting in the fifth or sixth row of the cold and empty theater with a winter coat draped around his shoulders. The performance was meant for him alone. There were no more than ten people in the auditorium, all theater employees or friends. They had received no instructions from Kaverin, but it was understood that they would not be looking only at the stage.
>
> The famous diplomat turned out to be a remarkably responsive spectator. He laughed, gasped, slapped his knees, and even wiped his

eyes with his handkerchief several times. It was a joy to watch him. With each new act, hope grew.

After the viewing, Fedor Nikolaevich walked over to the people's commissar in his usual bobbing way and, smiling shyly, asked what he thought of the show. Maksim Maksimovich shook Kaverin's hand warmly and repeatedly:

"Thank you for getting me out. With my awful schedule, I hardly ever make it to the theater. And, in this case, it was both business and pleasure—work-related and fun."

"Did you like it?"

"Very much. You know, I knew almost nothing about your theater. It's been a while since I got so caught up in a performance."

"So, you think that we have succeeded in conveying, to some degree . . ."

"More than some. It's very accurate. That's exactly how it works."

Fedor Nikolaevich beamed:

"So, the show can be released?"

Litvinov's expression changed abruptly.

"Absolutely not. Don't you know, my dear fellow? Oh well, I guess you don't. No, this is the worst possible timing."

"Maksim Maksimovich, but this is a catastrophe. So much work, so much money! We've used a whole train car's worth of plywood . . ."

Livinov burst out laughing. He could not stop for a long time. The train car's worth of plywood had amused and touched him.

"My dear man . . . A train car's worth of plywood . . ."

Suddenly, he turned serious, took Kaverin by the arm, and walked toward the exit.

When Fedor Nikolaevich came back, he looked so happy that everyone thought there was still hope.

"What a man! If only everyone talked to me this way . . ."

The show was banned.[23]

On November 16, the Soviet Union and the United States established diplomatic relations. On December 19, the Politburo issued a secret decision on the desirability of joining the League of Nations.[24]

All millenarian eruptions—from Jesus to Jim Jones—take place in hostile surroundings, real or imagined. The Stalin revolution had been framed by the "war scare" in 1927, the Comintern's turn against appeasement in 1928, the Wall Street crash in 1929, and the launching of Litvinov's "collective security" policy in 1933–34. The immediate threat from Germany had resulted in the postponement of the potential threat from the rest of the capitalist world. The siege had been lifted, and the Stalin revolution was coming to an end. Fedor Kaverin had failed his test by the House of Government. *The Champion of the World* came too late.

∎ ∎ ∎

The Stalin revolution began to slow down in early 1933 (with the lowering of production plans, reduction in the number of forced laborers, cessation of mass deportations, and promise to help each peasant household purchase a cow). But the solemn inauguration of a new age and final redefinition of the ideological substance took place in 1934 at the Seventeenth Party Congress, also known as the "Congress of Victors," where it was officially announced that the prophecy had been fulfilled, the old world destroyed, and the new one founded and reinforced. In the words of the head of the Central Control Commission, Yan Rudzutak (Jānis Rudzutaks),

> Whereas Marx provided the general, theoretical guidelines for the historical development of society, the inevitability of the demise of capitalism, and the inevitability of the creation of the dictatorship of the proletariat, which represents a transition toward a classless society; and whereas Lenin further developed Marx's teachings relative to the age of imperialism and the dictatorship of the proletariat; Stalin provided both the theoretical framework and practical methods for applying the theory of Marx-Lenin to certain historical and economic conditions in order to guide the whole society toward socialism by way of the dictatorship of the proletariat. Under the guidance of Comrade Stalin, our Party, in fulfilling its plan of great construction, has created a firm foundation for socialism.[25]

This steel-and-concrete foundation rested on solid bedrock, permanently drained of the idiocy of rural life. In the words of the Leningrad Party boss and Politburo member, Sergei Kirov, "the socialist transformation of the petit bourgeois peasant economy was the hardest, most difficult, and most complicated problem for the dictatorship of the proletariat in its struggle for a new socialist society. It is this problem, this so-called peasant question, that engendered, in the minds of the oppositionists, doubt in the possibility of a victorious construction of socialism in our country. This central question of the proletarian revolution has now been solved completely and irreversibly in favor of socialism."[26]

It had not been easy ("one must say candidly and completely unequivocally," said Postyshev, referring to Ukraine, "that, in those difficult years, repressions were the main form of 'governance'"), but the victory had been won, the victors could only be judged by history, and history's whole point consisted of that victory's inevitability. The task for the next five years included "the final liquidation of capitalist elements and classes in general, the complete elimination of the causes of class differences and exploitation, the overcoming of the survivals of capitalism in economic life and in people's consciousness, and the transformation of all the working

Pavel Postyshev (*right*) and G. K. Ordzhonikidze
at the Seventeenth Party Congress

people of the country into conscious and active builders of a class-free socialist society."[27]

Some of the repentant oppositionists were allowed to join in the celebration by making public confessions. All claimed to have been born again. "If I have the courage to present to you, from this podium, my chronicle of defeats, my chronicle of errors and crimes," said Kamenev, "it is because I feel within myself the realization that this page of my life has been turned, that it is gone, that it is a corpse that I can perform an autopsy on with the same equanimity and personal detachment with which I dissected, and hope to be able to dissect again, the political corpses of the enemies of the working class, the Mensheviks and Trotskyites."[28]

All echoed Voronsky by claiming that they had been born again by witnessing the miracle of universal rebirth. Evgeny Preobrazhensky, who had stood next to Smilga during the opposition's protest on November 7, 1927, was now a new man filled with the right ideological substance. "I remember that sad date in my biography. For a long time, I stood on the balcony of the France Hotel shouting in a hoarse voice at the passing columns of demonstrators: 'Long live the international leader of the world revolution, Trotsky!' (*laughter*). It was a moment, comrades, that I am ashamed to remember, ashamed not in the everyday sense, but in the political sense, which is much worse." The reason he was not ashamed in the everyday sense was that the non-Party part of him was now dead, and the reason it was dead was "the miracle of the fast revolutionary transformation of the millions of small-peasant households along collective lines. It was something, comrades, that none of us had foreseen, it was something done by the Party under the leadership of Comrade Stalin."[29]

This was the crux of the matter and the main theme of the congress. The miracle performed by the Party had been performed by Comrade Stalin. There was no other way to define the Bolshevik ideological substance. Everyone understood this, but it was the former oppositionists who, as part of their confessions, attempted to reflect on what it meant. "As far as Comrade Stalin is concerned, I feel the most profound sense of shame—not in the personal sense, but in the political sense, because here I probably erred more than in any other matter," said Preobrazhensky.

> You know that neither Marx nor Engels, who wrote a great deal about the question of socialism in the countryside, knew the specifics of how the rural transformation was going to occur. You know that Engels tended to think that it would be a fairly long evolutionary process. It has been Comrade Stalin's tremendous insight, his tremendous courage in setting new goals, his tremendous firmness in accomplishing them, his profoundest understanding of the age and of the correlation of class forces that have made it possible to achieve this great task in the way in which the Party, under the leadership of Comrade Stalin, has done it. It has been the greatest transformation in the history of the world.[30]

Rykov—who had fought against Preobrazhensky when Preobrazhensky was on the left while he was on the right but thought he was at the center—felt the same way. His opposition to Comrade Stalin filled him with "an enormous sense of guilt before the Party," a guilt he would "try to expiate, come what may. I would like to stress that the main guarantee that the cause of the working class will prevail is the leadership of our Party. I state with absolute sincerity and with the profoundest conviction based on what I have lived through during these years, that this guarantee is the present leadership and the unswerving defense of Marxism-Leninism that this leadership ensures. I state that this guarantee is Comrade Stalin's contribution to the practical application and theoretical development of the teaching of Marx, Engels, and Lenin."[31]

Stalin had become, as Bukharin put it, "the personal embodiment of the mind and will of the Party." The mind and will of the Bolshevik Party had been formed around Lenin. Lenin's death and the NEP retreat had produced great disappointment, dissention, and doubt. The revolution from above had restored faith and unity by performing the miracle of rebirth. The man who had presided over that revolution was a new Lenin—a reincarnation of what Koltsov had called "not a duality, but a synthesis," a human being who embodied the fulfillment of the prophecy. As Zinoviev said at the congress, "we can see how the best representatives of the advanced collectivized peasantry yearn to come to Moscow, to the Kremlin, yearn to see Comrade Stalin, to touch him with their eyes and perhaps with their hands, yearn to receive from his mouth direct instructions that they can pass on to the masses. Doesn't this remind you of pictures of Smolny in 1917 and early 1918, when the best people from among the peasants . . . would show up at Smolny Palace in order to touch Vladimir Ilich with their eyes, and perhaps with their hands, and hear from his mouth about the future course of the peasant revolution in the village, about how things will be?"[32]

Stalin was even greater than Lenin—not only because Lenin was "more alive than the living," whereas Stalin was both more alive than the living and actually alive—but because Stalin was at the center of a society where peasants had been collectivized and souls had been recast: a society that had become a sect. The most important outcome of the Stalin revolution was the expectation of absolute unity and cohesion beyond the Party; the assumption that all Soviet citizens—with the exception of various enemies to be redeemed or cast aside—were Bolsheviks by definition (Party or "non-Party"). Stalin represented that unity, guaranteed its permanence, and stood for its cause and effect. It had been Stalin's leadership, according to Preobrazhensky, that had made it possible to achieve the great victory in the way in which the Party, under Stalin's leadership, had done it; and it would be Stalin's leadership, according to Rykov, that would guarantee the unswerving defense of Marxism-Leninism that his leadership guaranteed. Stalin had become fully sacralized.[33]

This gave greater urgency and consistency to the traditional sectarian belief that any internal sectarianism was a form of blasphemy. As Tomsky explained in his speech, not only did any attack against Stalin constitute an attack against the Party, but—even worse—any attack against the Party constituted an attack against Stalin, "who personified the Party's unity, provided the Party majority with its strength, and led the rest of the Central Committee and the whole Party." Rykov called his former self a "secret agent" of the enemy, and Bukharin said that the success of their opposition would have led to foreign intervention and the restoration of capitalism. What was needed now was "cohesion, cohesion, and more cohesion . . . under the leadership of the glorious field marshal of the proletarian forces, the best of the best, Comrade Stalin."[34]

But how could more cohesion be achieved? How could one resist doubt, heterodoxy, and subsequent perdition? Preobrazhensky's solution was a stripped-down version of Voronsky's (the fact that both were priests' sons may or may not be a coincidence):

What should I have done if I had returned to the Party? I should have done what the workers used to do when Lenin was still alive. Not all of them understood the complicated theoretical arguments with which we, the "clever ones," used to oppose Lenin. Sometimes you'd see a friend voting for Lenin on one of these points of theory, and you'd ask him: "Why are you voting for Lenin?" And he would say: "Always vote with Ilich, and you can't go wrong" (*laughter*). It is this proletarian wisdom, which conceals great modesty and a capacity for disciplined fight—for you cannot win otherwise—it was this that I did not understand in the beginning, after I had rejoined the Party. . . .

I must say that at this moment I feel more than ever before and understand more than ever before the wisdom of that worker who told me: "even if you don't understand everything, go with the Party, vote with Ilich." And so today, comrades, now that I understand everything and can see everything clearly and have realized all my mistakes, I often repeat that worker's words to myself, only now in a different stage of the revolution, saying: "vote with Comrade Stalin, and you can't go wrong."[35]

Not everyone agreed. One delegate interrupted Preobrazhensky, saying: "we don't need someone who thinks one thing but says another," while another (Ivan Kabakov, head of the Urals Party Committee and peasant's son who never made it beyond the parish school) said: "It is not true that the program set forth by Lenin and Stalin has ever been accepted blindly by the workers who have voted for them. Then and now, the workers have voted for the Lenin-Stalin theses with great enthusiasm and conviction; they accept the program outlined by Comrade Stalin at the Seventeenth Congress because it is a proletarian program, which expresses the hopes and desires of the working class of the entire world." Toward the end of the proceedings, Radek congratulated the audience on rejecting his "friend" Preobrazhensky's remarks. "For if having been taught for a number of years, we still cannot come to the Congress and tell the Party, 'thank you for teaching us a lesson; we have learned it very well and will never sin again' (*laughter*), then things really do look bad. I am going to hope that this was just a slip of the tongue on Preobrazhensky's part."[36]

But was it? And how did things look for Radek, his friend Preobrazhensky, the rest of the former oppositionists, and all those who might sin in the future? The delegates knew that the lesson Radek had learned was a harsh one. "I was sent by the Party, a little involuntarily (*laughter*), to relearn Leninism in some not-too-distant parts. . . . And, sadly, I have to admit that whatever did not enter my brain through the head had to enter it from the other direction (*burst of laughter*)." The Party's way of making sure that lost members thought what they said and said what they should might have to begin with an act of blind obedience.[37]

Finally, there was the question of whether the hard-won cohesion was genuine and whether Radek and the people he called his "fellow sinners" actually meant what they said. "Comrade Zinoviev spoke with sufficient enthusiasm," said Solts's former son-in-law, Isaak Zelensky, "but whether he spoke sincerely is, I think you will all agree with me, something that only time will tell." Kirov devoted a whole section of his speech to an extended metaphor of a disciplined army waging a mortal battle, while a few cowards and doubters, some of them former commanders, fall behind, hide in the supply train, sow indiscipline and confusion, and enter increasingly into the enemy's calculations:

And now imagine the following scene. The army has won several decisive battles against the enemy and taken some key positions; the war is not over, far from it, but there is something like a brief breathing space, if I can put it that way, and the whole great victorious warrior host is singing its powerful victory song. At this point, what are all the ones who have been back in the supply train all this time supposed to do? (*applause, laughter*).

They come out, comrades, and try to insert themselves into the general celebration, they try to march in step, to the same music, and participate in our festivities.

Take Bukharin, for example. He sang according to the score, from what I could tell, but he was a bit off key (*laughter, applause*). And I haven't even mentioned Comrade Rykov and Comrade Tomsky.

ROIZENMAN. Yes! Yes!

KIROV. In their case, even the tune was wrong (*laughter, applause*).
     They sing out of key and can't keep step either.

I must admit, comrades, that, in human terms, it is not easy; we can appreciate the plight of these people who have spent long years, the decisive years of the toughest battles waged by the Party and the working class, sitting in the supply train.

ROIZENMAN. Supply-train warriors, supply-train warriors.

KIROV. It is hard for them to identify with the Party's platform. And
     it seems to me—I do not want to be a prophet, but it seems to me
     that it will take some time before this supply-train army fully
     joins the ranks of our victorious Communist host (*applause*).

ROIZENMAN. Bravo, bravo.[38]

Words of repentance were "meaningless, ephemeral, hot air." Six-fingers could not be trusted; the other Klim could not be trusted; Tomsky could not be trusted; and, since no one's soul was fully transparent, the undoubting Bolshevik Makar Hardbread could not be trusted, either. Four years after Tomsky first asked whether his lot was to "repent, repent without end, do nothing but repent," the answer still seemed to be "yes." Words had to continue to be spoken, for there were few other windows to thoughts. To become meaningful, they had to be backed up by virtuous acts. Virtue—Bolshevik or any other—is obedience to the Eternal Law. To make sure that obedience arose spontaneously, it had to be cultivated and, if necessary, enforced. Kirov's chorus, Boris Roizenman, received one of the first Orders of Lenin ever awarded for his achievements "in carrying out sensitive assignments of special state importance concerning the purge of the state apparatus in the foreign legations of the USSR."[39]

But "enough about them, already," as one delegate shouted during Zelensky's speech. The supply-train army was marginal, and, as Kirov put it, "the Congress had listened to those comrades' speeches without particular attention." What mattered was the celebration of the great victory, the continued cohesion of the glorious host, and the "implementation of the program designed for us by Comrade Stalin." Rather than passing a formal resolution, the Congress of Victors, on Kirov's suggestion, pledged "to fulfill, as Party law, all the theses and conclusions contained in Comrade Stalin's report. (*Voices:* That's right! *Prolonged, tumultuous applause. Everyone rises, while continuing to applaud.*)"[40]

■ ■ ■

The task of reflecting on the implications of the theses and conclusions of the Congress of Victors fell to the first All-Union Congress of Soviet Writers, which opened on August 17, 1934, more than a year behind schedule. The Congress of Victors had announced the victory of the Stalin revolution and formally identified the Bolshevik ideological substance with the person of Stalin. The job of the writers' congress was to explain what this meant on the cultural front.

The original head of the organizing committee and secretary of its Party cell was the editor in chief of *Izvestia* and *Novyi mir*, Ivan Gronsky (Fedulov). The son of a peasant migrant to St. Petersburg, Gronsky went through the usual stages of proletarian awakening, from the reading of *Oliver Twist* to apprenticeship in prisons and underground circles and work as an itinerant propagandist. After the Revolution, Gronsky served as a Party official in Yaroslavl, Kursk, and Moscow, and, in 1921–25, studied at the Institute of Red Professors (while working at the Karl Liebknecht Pedagogical Institute and, as part of the "Lenin mobilization" of 1924, secretary of the Kolomna District Party Committee). After graduating, he joined *Izvestia* as head of the economics department and married Lydia Vialova, an amateur actress and painter and the daughter of an expropriated drugstore owner. Before proposing, he asked her whether she wanted to have more children (she had a two-year-old son by a previous marriage)

Ivan Gronsky

and what she thought about the relative merits of work and family. Her answers proved satisfactory, and they moved in together. She had two more children (Vadim, born in 1927, and Irina, born in 1934) and stayed at home, taking painting lessons. In 1931, they moved into the House of Government, first into Apt. 144 and then into Stetsky's Apt. 18, with a large dining room and a view of the river.[41]

By 1932, when the thirty-eight-year-old Gronsky was appointed head of the organizing committee of the first All-Union Congress of Soviet Writers, he (along with Postyshev and Stetsky) had become Stalin's personal liaison to "creative workers." His formal assignment from the Central Committee was "to guide the work of the Soviet and foreign intelligentsia." He had a direct telephone line to Stalin, but Stalin was not always available. "Not infrequently," he wrote later, "I had to take risks by making important decisions of a political nature not knowing in advance what Stalin would say." Regular meetings held in the Gronskys' large dining room involved thirty to fifty people and a great deal of drinking, singing, and poetry reading. The challenge was to overcome "factionalism," create comfortable conditions for creative work, and agree on the general principles of representing a world free of both kulaks and Averbakhs. Most writers appreciated the support. As the writer Georgy Nikiforov put it, "if the Party keeps us alive, no Averbakh will eat us alive."[42]

The solution proved elusive. Gronsky suspected the "honorary chairman" of the organizing committee, Maxim Gorky, of factionalism and self-promotion, and found Radek's and Bukharin's congress speeches (submitted in advance and approved by Gorky), as "more than reprehensible both politically and aesthetically." Stalin listened to everyone but backed Gorky. Gronsky resigned; Gorky became the sole organizer; and Radek and Bukharin delivered their speeches. As for the general principles of representing the new world, Stalin's guidelines were general enough to force the delegates to take risks by making important decisions of a political nature not knowing in advance what Stalin would say. "The artist must show life the way it is," Stalin had said. "And if he shows our life the way it is, he cannot help noticing, and showing, the forces that are leading it toward socialism. This is what we call 'socialist realism.'"[43]

The point of departure was the fact of the great victory. "Your congress is meeting at a time," said Andrei Zhdanov, opening the proceedings, "when, under the leadership of the Communist Party and under the guidance of our great leader and teacher, Comrade Stalin (*tumultuous applause*), the socialist mode of production has triumphed fully and irreversibly in our country." The fears that the miracle of total transformation might take a long time, said Aleksandr Serafimovich, have proved unfounded. "The first layer of scaffolding," said Isaak Babel, "is being taken down from the house of socialism. Even the most nearsighted people can see this house's shape, its beauty. We are all witnesses to the fact that our country has been gripped by a powerful feeling of pure, physical joy." The Soviet people, said Leonid Leonov, "are standing guard at the gate of a new world full of buildings of the most perfect social architecture." The Soviet present was "the morning of a new era," "the most heroic pe-

Leonid Leonov
(N. A. of Makarov)

riod of world history," "the most capacious historical age of all those experienced by humankind."[44]

Leonov's *The Sot'* was the most widely acclaimed Soviet construction novel. Like all such novels, it ended just short of fulfillment, with a faint vision of the city that was to come. The new—postconstruction—challenge was to show its shape, its beauty—and its Adam. This was an enormously difficult undertaking—"as difficult as tracing the shadow of a thunder cloud on a huge meadow." But it had to be done, and done by writers who had been shaped by the old world. (Leonov was the grandson of a Zariadie grocer, the son of a proletarian poet, the son-in-law of a famous publisher, and a veteran of both the Red and, unbeknownst to the delegates, White armies.) "Our mirror is too small for the central hero of our time. And yet, we all know full well that he has come into the world—its new master, the great planner, the future geometer of our planet."[45]

There were two ways of representing a hero this large. The first was "to step back a century, so as to reduce a bit the angle of vision from which we, his contemporaries, view him." The second, and the only one acceptable to a Soviet writer, was "to become equal to his character in size and, above all, in creative fervor." The writer was to become his own hero:

> This means that we must rise to the height from which we can see most clearly the barbarity of yesterday's stone age and understand more deeply the historical force of the new truths, whose philosophical depth and social greatness consist in their very simplicity; become, at last, an inalienable part of the Soviet order, which has taken upon itself Atlas's task of building a society on the basis of the highest humanity, the socialist kind. If we do, comrades, we will not have to waste time on technical gimmicks, which fill our books, or on scholastic discussions, which often do nothing but corrupt the living matter of literature; we will not have to worry about the longevity of our books, because the hormone of immortality will be contained in their very material. If we do, we will have every reason to say that we are worthy of being Stalin's contemporaries.[46]

Babel took the argument further. The Soviet writer, as an "engineer of souls," was a central participant in the work of construction; the writer's tools were words; the building of socialism required few words, "but they must be good words, because contrived, hackneyed, and stilted words are bound to play into the hands of our enemies." Bad writers, or good writers who used bad words, were wreckers because, "in our day, bad taste is no longer a personal defect; it is a crime. Even worse, bad taste is counterrevolution." Good writers who used good words would bring about the victory of good taste. "It will not be an insignificant political victory because, fortunately for us, we have no such thing as a nonpolitical victory." Writers' words must be as big as the writers themselves, and the writers themselves must be as big as their heroes. "Who should we model ourselves after? Speaking of words, I would like to mention a man who does not deal with words professionally: just look at the way Stalin forges his speech, how chiselled his spare words are, how full of muscular strength." As Babel had written on a different occasion: "Benia says little, but he says it with gusto. He says little, but you wish he would say more."[47]

Arosev added to Babel's formula by referring to a moment of comic relief in Stalin's report to the Congress of Victors six months earlier: "You all know that at the Seventeenth Congress Comrade Stalin gave us two types of characters: the conceited grandee and the honest windbag. The form in which Comrade Stalin expressed this was highly accomplished aesthetically, especially in the part about the windbag. The dialogue he cited was of great artistic quality. The previous speaker, Comrade Babel, said that we should learn from Comrade Stalin how to handle words. I would like to amend his statement: we must learn from Comrade Stalin how to identify new literary types."[48]

All this made good sense given Stalin's uncontested place at the center of the victorious new world. But what should texts worthy of the time—worthy of being Stalin's contemporaries—actually look like? In the central speech of the congress, Bukharin defined socialist realism in opposition to "old realism" or "simply-realism." The literature of an emerging world could not be reduced to "objectivism," which "claimed to represent reality 'the way it actually is.'" This meant that it could not be divorced from romanticism, which implied a revolutionary transformation. "If socialist realism is characterized by its activism and efficacy; if it offers more than a simple photograph of the historical process; if it projects the whole world of struggle and emotions into the future; and if it places the heroic on the throne of history, then revolutionary romanticism is its inalienable part." Unlike traditional revolutionary romanticism, however, socialist realism was "not anti-lyrical." The fact that socialism opposed individualism did not mean that it opposed the individual. On the contrary, socialism, and therefore socialist realism, stood for "the flourishing of the individual, the enrichment of his inner world, the growth of his self-awareness." Socialist realism, like the struggle for socialism that it represented, combined realism and heroic romanticism, collectivism and lyricism, monumentalism and 'the entire world of emotions of the emerging new man, including the 'new eroticism.'"[49]

There were two reasons, according to Bukharin, why such an art was possible, even for writers shaped by the old world. One was implicit in the congress's mandate: if the victory of socialism was both a reality and a promise, so was its artistic reflection. The other, more specific reason was that it had been done before. "Opposed to the old realism in the conventional sense is the kind of poetic work that depicts the most general and universal features of a particular epoch, representing them through unique characters that are both specific and abstract, characters that combine the greatest possible generalizability with enormous inner richness. Such, for example, is Goethe's *Faust*."[50]

There were other models as well. Samuil Marshak began his discussion of children's literature with *The Song of Roland*; Bukharin ended his speech by referring to Pushkin; Fadeev called on F. Panferov to write a Soviet *Don Quixote* (about a peasant who travels through the country in search of a noncollectivized village); and Leonov compared the central hero of the age to the "international constellation of human types whose members include Robinson Crusoe, Don Quixote, Figaro, Hamlet, Pierre Bezukhov, Oedipus, Foma Gordeev, and Raphael de Valentin." The main task of Soviet literature was to capture "the new Gulliver" by learning from Jonathan Swift. Abulkasim Lakhuti (Abulqosim Lohuti), a Persian poet representing Tajik literature, called for the mastery of the work of Daqiqi, Rudaki, Avicenna, Ferdowsi, Saadi, Havez, Omar Khayyam, "and dozens more brilliant craftsmen of the word."[51]

Ehrenburg agreed (his examples were *War and Peace* and the novels of Balzac), but cautioned against eclectic imitation, citing the plight of Soviet architecture:

> We used to build American-style buildings. They were good for factories and offices. But it is difficult to live in them. The eyes of the workers demand a great deal more joyousness, intimacy, and individuality from a residential building. The workers are justified in protesting against barracks-like housing. All this is true. But does this mean that it is okay to take a quasi-classical portal, add a bit of Empire, a bit of Baroque, a bit of old Trans-Moskva (*laughter, applause*) and represent the whole thing as the architectural style of the great new class? . . .
>
> The main character of our novel is not fully formed yet. Our life is changing so fast that a writer sits down to write his novel and by the time he is finished, he realizes that his hero has already changed. That is why the form of the classic novel, transferred to our time, creates false assumptions and, most important, false endings.[52]

Ehrenburg was defending the documentary style of his *The Second Day*, but Ehrenburg, like his novel, was still in the creation/construction mode. As Bukharin suggested, echoing many other speakers and demonstrating his mastery of Hegelian dialectics, the history of Soviet poetry consisted of three periods. The first was "cosmic" and "abstract-heroic"; the second, associated with the "feverish, practical work of construction," was analytical and discrete; and the third, the one the congress was meant to inaugurate, was "synthetic." The central character of the new Soviet literature was, *pace* Ehrenburg, mostly formed. The shadow of a thundercloud on a huge meadow could, in principle, be traced: Goethe, among others, had done it before. *Faust* was "not about a particular historical process": it was about both "the struggle of the human spirit" and the "poetic-philosophical self-affirmation of the bourgeois era." Socialism was but the final chapter in the story of historical materialism. "Poetry such as *Faust*, with a different content and, consequently, different form, but with the same extreme degree of generalization, is an integral part of socialist realism." Or, as Gronsky put it on another occasion, "socialist realism in painting is Rembrandt, Rubens, and Repin in the service of the working class and socialism."[53]

What all these names had in common was that they represented "golden ages," or what Bukharin (quoting Briusov) called "the Pamirs": no longer the miracle of birth and early growth and certainly not the skepticism and rigidity of old age, but the strength, dignity, and self-confidence of young adulthood. Socialist realism was to socialism what *Faust* had been to the bourgeois era. As Stalin said two years earlier, "it is no accident that, early in its history, the bourgeois class produced the greatest geniuses in drama: Shakespeare and Molière. At that time, the bourgeoisie was closer to the national spirit than the feudal lords and the gentry." And as Radek said at the first writers' congress,

> In the heyday of the slaveholding era, when it produced ancient culture, Aeschylus, Sophocles, and Aristotle did not see any cracks in the foundation of the slaveholding society. They believed that it was the only possible and the only rational society, and so they could do creative work without any sense of doubt. . . .
>
> In the heyday of capitalism, when it was the carrier of progress, capitalism could produce bards who knew and believed that their works would find a response from hundreds of thousands of people who considered capitalism a good thing.
>
> We must ask ourselves: Why did Shakespeare appear in the sixteenth century, and why is the bourgeoisie incapable of producing a Shakespeare now? Why were there great writers in the eighteenth and early nineteenth centuries? Why are there no writers as great as Goethe, Schiller, Byron, Heine, or even Victor Hugo today? . . .
>
> It is enough to read *Coriolanus* or *Richard III* to see the enormous passion and tension depicted by the author. It is enough to read *Hamlet* to understand that the author was confronted by the big question: where is the world going? The author grappled with this question, he said, "alas, I have to set right the world that is out of joint," but those great questions were his life.
>
> When, in the eighteenth century, Germany was recovering from a period of total exhaustion, when it kept asking itself what the solution was—and the solution was unification—it gave birth to Goethe and Schiller.
>
> When a writer can affirm reality, he can produce an accurate representation of that reality.

Dickens produced an unvarnished picture of the birth of English industrial capitalism, but Dickens was convinced that industry was a good thing, and that industrial capital would propel England to a higher level, and so Dickens was able to show the approximate truth of that reality. He softened it with his sentimentality, but in *David Copperfield* and other works he painted a picture that today's reader can still use to see how modern England was born.[54]

The art of the newly constructed socialism was an art that affirmed the reality of socialism. It was an art produced by artists who did not see any cracks in the foundation of socialism and believed that socialism was the only possible and the only rational society. The fact that they happened to be right was, contrary to the avant-garde's discredited claims, not relevant to how socialism was to be represented. What mattered was that genuine socialist art affirmed reality, and an art that affirmed reality was realist art by definition—in the sense in which the works of Aeschylus, Sophocles, and Aristotle were realist. As Lunacharsky had said about classical architecture, it was "essentially rational" and "correct irrespective of time periods." "Having died during the Romanesque era, which was replaced by the Gothic, it was resurrected as the self-evident style of reason and joy during the Renaissance, adapting itself to new conditions. Having been preserved at the core of the baroque and rococo, which were but peculiar versions of classicism, it was reborn again in the Louis XVI style, grew stronger during the revolutionary age, and then spread all over Europe as the empire style." And as Aleksei Tolstoy had put it, also a propos of architecture, the art of victorious socialism was the "reinterpretation of the culture of antiquity" by means of a "proletarian renaissance." It was more mature than the abstract-heroic art of the real day and incomparably more vigorous than the corrupt art of the bourgeoisie, which was dominated by impotent irony (in the sense of producing one underground man after another and believing that cracks were inescapable, youth doomed, and time cyclical). There was no definition of socialist realism that did not apply to *Faust*. Now that the first layer of scaffolding had been taken down from the house of socialism, Soviet artists, gripped by a powerful feeling of pure, physical joy, were to describe its shape and beauty in ways that were correct irrespective of time periods. *Alles Vergängliche ist nur ein Gleichnis*. Everything transient was but a likeness.[55]

PART IV
THE REIGN OF THE SAINTS

14

THE NEW LIFE

In the First Five-Year Plan creation story, most Old Bolsheviks presiding over the work of construction had been doomed to martyrdom. Their job was to build the eternal house and leave it for "proletarian infancy and pure orphanhood." As one of Pilniak's dam engineers explains (deliberately invoking a Civil War image), "Comrade Moses . . . searched and fought for a decent living space. But he never reached the Promised Land, leaving it to Joshua the son of Nun to cause the sun to stand still. His children reached it in his stead. People who have known Sodom cannot enter Canaan—they are not fit for the Promised Land."

The two great congresses of 1934 had revised the script—or rather, moved the action forward in time, all the way to the end. The eternal house was to become a refuge where Moses could make his home and raise a family until the wolf moved in with the lamb and the leopard lay down with the goat. During the Stalin revolution, the original Bolshevik eschatology had been expanded to include a second great tribulation preceded by a managed retreat. The new creed adopted in 1934 followed St. Augustine and most institutionalized Christianity in proclaiming the millennium to be a spiritual and political allegory. Of the three fundamental solutions to the nonfulfillment of a millenarian prophecy—the extension of the violence of the last days, the indefinite postponement of the final redemption, and the claim that the millenarian prophecy had, in fact, been fulfilled—the Stalin revolutionaries, like most of their predecessors, chose a combination of the last two. The coming of Communism was imminent but beyond anyone's capacity to schedule; "socialism" as a prelude to eternity was, "in essence," already there. As Sergei Kirov put it, "the central question of the proletarian revolution has now been solved completely and irreversibly in favor of socialism."[1]

There was no cause for disappointment or need for resignation. There were no cracks in the foundation of socialism and no obstacles large enough to block the future. One could not live in that era and not see the shape and beauty of the house of socialism. It was a time of both fulfillment and expectation, dignity and enthusiasm, discipline and merriment, proletarian infancy and Old Bolshevik wisdom. It was a "synthetic" era that, like Goethe's *Faust*, combined the Sturm und Drang with the "essentially rational" classical antiquity, the Renaissance, and the Empire style.

It was an epoch of heroic domesticity in the House of Government. It was an age without old age, and possibly without death.

. . .

For some residents of the House of Government, the announcement of the coming of eternity came too late. Karl Lander and Lev Kritsman were too ill to work outside the home, while many others, including Vladimir Adoratsky and Olympiada Mitskevich, continued to require regular treatments at various Black Sea and North Caucasus resorts. Vasily Orekhov never recovered from his wounds and persistent melancholy. In April 1934, he went to Foros, in Crimea, for the last time. On December 10, 1934, at the age of fifty, he died in the Kremlin Hospital. Two days later, his body was cremated. The Society of Old Bolsheviks paid for a niche in the columbarium, an urn, and a plaque that identified the deceased as a "member of the VKP(b) since 1913" and "member of the Society of Old Bolsheviks."[2]

But the vast majority of the original revolutionaries were ready for a new beginning. Rejuvenated by a powerful feeling of pure, physical joy, they moved in, made themselves comfortable, and settled for a long stay.

In 1935, the House of Government had 2,655 registered tenants living in 507 apartments. Seven hundred residents were leaseholders assigned to particular apartments; the rest were servants and dependents, including 588 children. There were more leaseholders than apartments because some apartments (such as the Ivanovs', the Tuchins', and the Usievichs') contained more than one family. Altogether, there were 24 one-room apartments, 27 two-room apartments, 127 three-room apartments, 179 four-room apartments, 120 five-room apartments, 25 six-room apartments, and one seven-room apartment. (The four remaining ones were taken up by the kindergarten, which, despite repeated requests, never received a building of its own.) Residential areas accounted for 42,205 square meters of space within the House; the movie theater, store, club, and theater took up 11,608 square meters; the rest belonged to the Central Executive Committee Secretariat (2,665 sq m); House administrative offices (500 sq m); and the Committee for the Settlement of Toiling Jews on the Land (365 sq m).[3]

All leaseholders were divided into "nomenklatura members" (high officials entitled to certain goods and services appropriate to their place in the Party/state hierarchy); "personal pensioners" (retired nomenklatura members still entitled to certain goods and services); and "non-nomenklatura members" (House personnel, prize-winning builders, Central Executive Committee administrators, demoted nomenklatura members, and relatives of nomenklatura members with apartments of their own, such as Arosev's second wife and Stalin's in-laws). Those who lost the right to reside in the House of Government as a result of demotion or dismissal were to be evicted; those promoted to higher positions had the right to move to larger apartments. Both tasks were difficult to accomplish because of resistance on the part of the losers. Such resistance could be effective because the classification of officials was not directly related to the classification of apartments and because all classifications were subject to exceptions based on formal exemptions and personal patronage.[4]

Attempts to overcome such resistance had to be based on even stronger personal patronage. The Persian poet and revolutionary, Abulkasim Lakhuti (Abulqosim Lohuti), who emigrated to the Soviet Union in 1921 and served as a high Soviet official in Tajikistan, received a one-room apartment with a large balcony in 1931, when he became a correspondent of both *Pravda* and *Izvestia*. The following year, at the age of forty-four, he married Tsetsilia Bentsionovna Bakaleishchik, a twenty-year-old student of Oriental languages from Kiev. By 1934, they had two children, and he had a new job as a "responsible secretary" of the Writers' Union. In August 1934, he represented Tajik literature at the first All-Union Congress of Soviet Writers. Soon after the congress, the Central Committee Secretary, Lazar Kaganovich, ordered the Housekeeping Department to move the family to a bigger apartment.

The move was delayed because of the existence of more urgent claims (one large apartment was being prepared for the hero of the Reichstag Fire Trial, Georgi Dimitrov, who had recently arrived from Germany) and because of "great resistance on the part of those being evicted." On October 22, 1934, Lakhuti wrote to Molotov that "the unbearable noise of the streetcars outside the apartment and the commotion and crying of an infant inside" made productive literary work impossible. "For many months now, I have been deprived of the most basic rest and sleep at night that I need after doing volunteer work outside the house. As a result, my health and nervous system are deteriorating. My children are weak and often sick. My work, which the Party seems to consider useful, suffers accordingly. I am unable to receive the collective farmers, students, and young writers from Central Asia, who, on their visits to Moscow, wish to meet with me." Any further postponement of the move threatened "to turn a toiler for the Party and literature into a uselss invalid." This would be a tragedy for everyone involved, he concluded. "One can patiently wait to be rescued when a leaky ship is just beginning to go down. One can wait when the ship is halfway under water. But when the waves begin to cover the deck, every second's delay may be lethal." It took another year and Stalin's personal intercession for the family to move to a larger apartment (Apt. 110). Several months later, Lakhuti sent Stalin a traditional ruba'i:

Stalin, you are greater than greatness,
You know the hearts of men and the soul of beauty.
My soul is singing, and my heart is proclaiming
That Lenin's path and Sign were given to me by you.[5]

Abulkasim Lakhuti and his wife, Tsetsilia Banu

The poem was translated by Lakhuti's wife, who, under the pen name Banu ("Lady" in Farsi), had become a professional translator of Persian poetry—her husband's and that of the "brilliant craftsmen of the word" that he listed in his writers' congress speech. Three years and one child later, the family moved to an even better apartment.

The government portion of the house accounted for about 60 percent, or, if one includes personal pensioners, 70 percent of all apartments. Most nomenklatura leaseholders had been sect members since before the real day (new arrivals, such as Lakhuti and Dimitrov, and newly promoted young officials, such as Khrushchev, were a small minority). They were almost all men: in keeping with the original sectarian practice, female members were rarely promoted to positions of power outside the Women's Section (most female leaseholders—about 10 percent of the total in 1935—were personal pensioners, not active state and Party officials). The original distinction between "workers" (including peasants and artisans) and "students" (intelligentsia members and Jews of all backgrounds) remained crucially important and readily obvious in speech, gestures, writing proficiency, home furnishings, and family celebrations, among other things. Former workers were a minority among leaseholders. They might feel more comfortable around the House guards and gardeners than around the former students (Orekhov's son had married Ivanov's maid); rarely rose very high within the nomenklatura hierarchy; and tended to be overrepresented among the sick, the needy, and the prematurely retired. Their hard-won privilege required constant protection and reinforcement.[6]

One such former worker (peasant, machinist, and railroad engineer, among other things) was Pavel Gerasimovich Murzin, who was given a job as an inspector in the People's Commissariat of Transportation, but spent most of his time treating his angina, gout, rheumatism, inflammation of the gall bladder, and, as he wrote in an official request, "malignantgastritis of the stomach," "calitis of the intestines," and "miasthenia of the heart." In 1930, at the age of forty-three, he "received the consent of a professor of Kremlin consultation at the Kremlin Hospital of the Council of People's Commissars" that he be allowed to perform only "work not at all resulting in fatigue and nervous stress." His wife, Maria Stepanovna, aged forty-five, was, according to Murzin, "totally unfit for work because she shared all of the privations of the prerevolutionary period, as well as during the revolution." Both required frequent stays at resorts and sanatoria and various forms of material assistance from the Society of Old Bolsheviks. The Society showed a great deal of understanding, but the symptoms persisted—"exclusively because of the apartment," which was small, full of children, and offered "neither peace nor quiet." Murzin's repeated requests for better accommodations met with "foolishness and slander" on the part of various officials, who thought they could do whatever they liked "while Old Bolshevik workers languish in basements." The situation was made worse by bad news from Murzin's native village Stary Buian, in Samara Province, where his sister Polia and her husband Markel had been forced to harness themselves to the plow but were being paid "not a penny" by the kolkhoz. After another of Murzin's in-laws was killed "by the kulaks," Polia's and Markel's daughter, Nina, came to live with the Murzins, adding considerably to their difficulties.[7]

In 1931, Murzin received a small apartment (Apt. 130) in the House of Government. Later that year, he wrote to the Society of Old Bolsheviks:

I have received an insult as a result of a brazen act of hooliganism on October 27 at 4 p.m. on the front platform of streetcar No. 10 between theater square where I got in and the house of government. First while mounting the car a certain citizen acted rudely toward a woman with child "where the hell are you going can't you see its crowded" and sat down both of them in the front engine area as soon as the streetcar started to move this citizen crossed his legs and leaned against my side so I stated to him citizen I am not a wall and it's hard for me to hold you up, to which he turned around and responded with rude contemptuousness toward me it's okay you can handle it fatface I thought that the fellow was drunk and without saying anything I asked him to let me pass and walked inside the car no sooner had I entered the car than he in the presence of the driver, two militiamen, and one man of his ilk who was with him, in a similar act of rudeness stated in a loud voice "see I have liquidated him as a class from the engine platform" and both of them giggled gleefully. Then I proceeded to ask the militiamen to find out the identity of this citizen according to his ID and showed the militiamen and the citizen who had twice insulted me my society of old bolsheviks document.

The citizen and his companion refused to comply. Murzin and the two militiamen rode with them to the end of the line, enlisted the help of a third militiaman, and eventually discovered that the hooligans were pleni-potentiaries of the Moscow Criminal Investigation Unit, Citizen Pashkin and Citizen Kochkin. Murzin "got into the streetcar with difficulty because of chest pains and went back home completely chilled to the bone."[8]

Even those former workers who had risen high in the Party hierarchy tended to preserve a sense of separateness and perhaps the memory of an incomplete apprenticeship. Efim Shchadenko's struggle against the tastes and friends of his wife, the sculptor Maria Denisova, reflected the Party's fight against the opposition. It was not quite right to suppose (he wrote to an old friend, probably with Mayakovsky's circle in mind), "that the point of the argument consists of the fact that the workers . . . can't stand the intelligentsia in general and the Jewish intelligentsia in particu-lar." The point (he wrote to another friend), was that "the intelligentsia monopolists of theoretical knowledge can't help noticing that the workers are beginning to master that knowledge, combining it with huge practical experience, which not every intelligentsia member may have." The war had been won, but unity and equality remained precarious. The former print-shop stitcher Vasily Mikhailov was still only second in command to former "students" on both the Dnieper Hydroelectric Dam and the Palace of So-viets construction sites. The former metal worker Ivan Gronsky found himself directly under Stalin but continued—like his predecessor Semen Kanatchikov—to play the role of proletarian watchdog over unreliable in-tellectuals. Even Pavel Postyshev, the former calico printer who had joined Stalin's inner sanctum and was a quick learner and capable writer, kept a low profile around his former social superiors (including the ones he for-mally supervised). According to the chronicler of an informal meeting of Politburo members with about fifty Soviet writers in Gorky's house on October 26, 1932, "Postyshev is amazingly modest. He does not seem to have uttered a single word the whole evening and just tried to stay in the background." As Postyshev had written to his intelligentsia patron in 1913, when he was twenty-six years old, "the evil, inescapable fate of the prole-tarian will never leave me in peace." Most of the proletarians with success-ful careers (including Shchadenko, Mikhailov, Gronsky, and Postyshev) were married to women with more formal education.[9]

The majority of government officials residing in the House of Govern-ment were former "students" (provincial intellectuals "of various ranks" who had joined socialist sects while still in school). By far the largest sin-gle group among them were Jews, who constituted 23 percent of all lease-holders and about 33 percent of the nomenklatura ones (counting "per-sonal pensioners"). If one includes family members, the proportion was even higher: Jewish women were more strongly overrepresented among socialist sectarians than Jewish men (partly filling in for the absence of "workers" among female sectarians), and many non-Jewish officials, including Arosev, Bukharin, Ivanov, Rykov, and Voronsky, were married to Jewish women. During the second wave of informal marriages, in the 1920s, female Party members of proletarian background became available but remained unrepresented at the top: most second and third marriages by high Soviet officials were to upper-class and Jewish women. The Jews who lived in the House came from a variety of social backgrounds, but almost none—including those from families of small artisans—fit the "worker" category. Of the many millenarian rebellions that comprised the eventual "October Revolution," the Jewish one had been the most massive and radical. Of the many residents of the House of Government, the Jewish ones were the most millenarian and cosmopolitan. The modernization of late imperial Russia had destroyed the traditional Jewish monopoly on a broad range of service-sector occupations in the empire's western border-lands. The Jewish revolution against the tsarist state had been insepara-ble from the Jewish revolution against traditional Jewish life. A minority of Jewish rebels chose Zionism; most of those who chose cosmopolitanism did so with an intensity and consistency unparalleled among socialists with traditional national homelands. Polish, Latvian, and Georgian resi-dents of the House of Government seemed to assume that proletarian internationalism was compatible with their native tongues, songs, and foods. The Jewish ones equated socialism with "pure orphanhood" and made the point of not speaking Yiddish at home or passing on anything they thought of as Jewish to their children. Their children were going to live under socialism. In the meantime, they continued to list themselves as "Jews by nationality" in various forms and seemed to recognize each other as belonging to the same tribe and the same revolution.[10]

Some of the other groups of residents who thought of themselves as sharing a common pre-Bolshevik origins were Latvians, Poles, priests' sons, and natives of the same regions of the Russian Empire, but such distinctions seemed minor compared with those based on position within the nomenklatura, duration of Party membership, and shared experiences in prison, exile, and the Civil War. What mattered most to the residents of the House of Government was whatever distinguished them from all the nonresidents of the House of Government.

∎ ∎ ∎

Inside the House of Government, what mattered most to the residents was the size and shape of their apartments. Apartment geography reflected family hierarchy. The symbolic center—and largest room—of most apart-ments was "father's study." The walls of most studies were covered with floor-to-ceiling dark oak bookcases with "barrister" glass doors that could be lifted by a little knob and pushed back. Most bookcases were built to order by House carpenters, with niches carved out for a desk and couch. The most frequently mentioned books were the gold-lettered, multivolume

Abulkasim Lakhuti's study. The photographs
are of Taras Shevchenko and Maxim Gorky.

editions of the *Brockhaus and Efron Encyclopedia*, Alfred Brehm's *Lives of Animals*, and the Treasures of World Literature series from Academia Publishers. (Nomenklatura residents periodically received Academia catalogs in which they could mark the books they wanted to be delivered free of charge.) Arosev also collected rare books of different types; Volin collected first editions of Pushkin and Lermontov; and the secretary of the Council of Nationalities of the Central Executive Committee (and a permanent representative of Belorussia in Moscow), A. I. Khatskevich, liked to collect the complete works of classical authors.[11]

The rest of the office furniture could be ordered from the House factory (such pieces remained government property, as indicated by the metal tags with numbers) or brought in by residents. Arosev was attached to his Venetian armchair with mother-of-pearl inlay; Volin, to his enormous desk; and Osinsky, to his enormous couch. Mikhailov brought his father-in-law's dark-green armchair, and Khalatov his stepfather's armchairs, couch, and enormous desk. The former trade representative in Great Britain, A. V. Ozersky, ordered all his furniture from London. According to his son, V. A. Ozersky, "there was a Mr. Trivers, who came to Moscow with my father. Father showed him the apartment. He made all the measurements and suggested a design. Father was given the required sum, and the furniture was shipped over."[12]

Most desks had lamps with green glass shades. Mikhailov's also had an etching of Lenin sitting at his desk. Smilga had a marble bust of Dante on his desk and a needlepoint portrait of Lenin above it. Stalin's father-in-

Boris Iofan's study

law, S. Ya. Alliluev, had four portraits on the walls of his study: a silk one of Lenin; an oil one of his late daughter, Nadezhda (by S. V. Gerasimov); and two watercolor portraits by P. E. Bendel: one of Stalin and one of Dzerzhinsky. Above Arosev's desk hung a portrait of his daughter, Olga, by V. S. Svarog. Khalatov had a portrait of his daughter, Svetlana, also by V. S. Svarog, several paintings by S. V. Gerasimov (including a portrait of Khalatov himself), and, on one of the walls, a carpet covered with a collection of sabers and daggers. Gronsky, who had defined socialist realism as "Rembrandt, Rubens, and Repin in the service of the working class and socialism," had paintings by I. I. Brodsky, E. A. Katsman, and P. A. Radimov. The head of the Ship-Building Directorate, Romuald Muklevich (Muklewicz), had portraits of sailors by F. S. Bogorodsky and, on the floor, the skin of a polar bear that had been killed (according to Muklevich's daughter, Irina) by members of the Chelyuskin Arctic expedition. The study of Malkov's successor as commandant of the Kremlin, Rudolf Peterson, contained a saber with his name engraved on it, a pair of field binoculars, map case, shoulder belt, and several hunting rifles. In Yuri Trifonov's fictional version of his father's study, the wall was decorated with "an English carbine, a small Winchester with a polished green stock, a double-barreled Belgian hunting rifle, a saber in an antique scabbard, a plaited Cossack whip, soft and flexible, with a little tail at the tip, and a broad Chinese sword with two silk ribbons, scarlet and dark green."[13]

Boris Iofan had a large studio on the eleventh floor with large windows and a skylight. His downstairs neighbor, Elina Kisis (the daughter of a Soviet Control Committee official, who turned ten in 1935), enjoyed visiting him there. "During the day, Boris Mikhailovich liked to work in his studio, and I would often go visit him there. He grew fond of me and used to show me beautiful picture books and postcards, give me apples, and pat me on the head. There, for the first time, I saw many things that we, and others, did not have. There were some dark, shiny figures and figurines (probably

Iofan's studio

bronze, but also a few white marble ones) on tall stands. There were lots of paintings and other mysterious things. In the middle of the studio, on tripods, were some huge drawing boards with pictures of a tall building that looked like a Kremlin tower with a man on top ("That's Lenin," he said) and a blue sky above."[14]

In smaller apartments, the father's study might also serve as a dining room and the parents' bedroom, but most nomenklatura apartments had a separate "dining room" (also known as the "living room" or simply as the "big room"), which was used for festive meals and large gatherings. At the center would be a large table surrounded by chairs and with a burnt-orange silk-fringed lampshade hanging over it. The other required piece was a piano. (Most of the girls and some of the boys had private music tutors.) The rest was a matter of conviction and improvisation. Vasily Mikhailov's wife, Nadezhda—a professor's daughter, Bestuzhev Women's University graduate, and Old Bolshevik retired in 1929 at the age of forty—felt strongly about proper living room furniture. In addition to the table and piano, they had a redwood glass cabinet, "full of various

Yuri Trifonov, drawing of the family's dining room
(Courtesy of Olga Trifonova)

charming, antique knickknacks," with vases on top; a couch with velvet cushions embroidered by Nadezhda and her mother; two small arm-chairs; a special table for the telephone; a long settee; another armchair with an ottoman; fresh flowers on the windowsills; and, next to the French doors leading into the hall, a small table with an embroidered towel and a shiny samovar.[15]

Children usually lived in a small "children's room," which tended to have a desk for homework, one or more beds, and a wardrobe. Kerzhentsev's daughter, Natalia, hung up magazine reproductions of classical paintings (different ones, depending on her changing enthusiasms); many adolescents, including Natalia, put up maps. Maids, most of whom doubled as nannies, might sleep next to small children or in their own rooms, but the great majority slept in a little nook at the entrance to the kitchen, usually behind a curtain. The rest of the rooms were occupied by grown children and other relatives and dependents.[16]

The place of the mother (normally the leaseholder's wife) was not pre-determined. The Podvoiskys, who cultivated an exemplary relationship of mutual devotion and respect for each other's Party work, had two studies: "Father's" (which also served as a dining room) and "Mother's" (Nina Av-gustovna worked in the Lenin Department of the Marx-Engels-Lenin In-stitute). Some apartments had a "parents' bedroom," which might serve as the mother's private space during the day. (The Petersons' bedroom had a polar-bear skin on the floor, but most were sparsely furnished and deco-rated.) In families where fathers slept in their studies, the women might have their own room, known as "Mother's bedroom" (small walk-through ones in the case of Ekaterina Smirnova-Osinskaia and Tania Miagkova-Poloz). Nadezhda Smilga-Poluian's had a desk, bookcase, and vanity table with her perfumes, three-way mirror and photograph of her little daugh-ters in their underwear. Nadezhda Mikhailova shared her bedroom with her daughter Margarita. It contained Nadezhda's large, antique bed ("with some kind of drawings on it," according to Margarita's recollections), an antique chest-of-drawers with linen (and dried flowers for fragrance), a night table with a lamp and a pile of French novels, and Margarita's corner with her bed, tiny desk, and toy chest. (Mikhailov's two daughters by a previous marriage had a separate "children's room," and Nadezhda's much older first daughter had a room of her own.)[17]

The former workers who did not pursue elite fashion and did not rise to the top of the government hierarchy did not usually have studies. The Ivanovs had three rooms, one of which they rented out. The remaining two were divided between the adults and their three children, and the maid slept in the kitchen nook (before marrying Orekhov's son and becoming a family friend). All of their furniture, except for one wardrobe and a chandelier, was government property. Vasily Shuniakov, another former Petrograd worker associated with the food industry (as a Central Control Commission member specializing in purges), kept all three of his rooms: the "parents' room" (Shuniakov, like Ivanov, was married to a Jewish seamstress); the "children's room" (the Shuniakovs had three children, two of whom died young); and a dining room (which also served as the bedroom of Shuniakov's mother-in-law). The maid slept in the kitchen nook. Much of the furniture was built by Shuniakov himself, who, like most former workers, suffered from "nervous exhaustion" and spent long periods of time at home and in various sanatoria.

The family of the prize-winning construction foreman, Mikhail Tuchin, had two connecting rooms (in a nine-room apartment that also housed the families of three other prize-winning construction foremen). The parents' room had a bed, vanity table with three-way mirror, and desk, which was also used by the children when doing their homework (although, according to the Tuchin's daughter, Zinaida, who was twelve in 1935, her younger brother Vova never did his). The "children's" room contained Zinaida's sofa bed and Vova's tiny cot, a small wardrobe, a large china cabinet and dinner table, and a framed picture depicting a fox in the snow.[18]

In the fall of 1937, the first secretary of the City of Kolomna Komsomol Committee, Serafim Bogachev, was transferred to the Komsomol Central Committee in Moscow and assigned to a recently vacated apartment (Apt. 65) in the House of Government. Serafim was newly married. He and his wife, Lydia, were both twenty-eight years old, and both were from peasant families. According to Lydia,

[Serafim's mother] was a very religious old woman—and couldn't read or write. He was her only son. How she loved him! She absolutely adored him. He was a kind, good man. So considerate—and funny sometimes, too. He loved life. His dream was to live in the forest and work outdoors as a warden. Once, while we were still courting, he asked me: "Would you be willing to live in the forest, in a little lodge?" And I said: "Yes, I would. I love nature, too." "That's my dream," he said. "But perhaps when this is all over. . . . I can't do it now. You can see what the situation is like in the country. The Komsomol still needs us. But afterwards I'll go live in the forest."

They moved in with their three-month-old baby girl, Natasha. Serafim was often gone. ("The struggle against the enemies of the people was just getting under way, or rather, it was reaching its peak, so they were all terribly overworked. There were only three secretaries then: Kosarev, Bogachev, and Pikina.") Lydia was preparing for her university entrance exams and had to go to a preparatory class each morning (in a special room at the Lenin Library, just across the Big Stone Bridge). She had graduated from a factory school in Kolomna, but had never been to high school. They were assigned a nanny, whom Lydia did not like. The apartment consisted of two furnished rooms.

Everything had been arranged. In the bedroom, there were two beds and a little crib in a niche, which, I think, we bought ourselves. No, we brought it from Kolomna. . . .

But I didn't see any of that until later. When I came into the apartment, he set out a chair for me. I sat down, with my baby in my arms, and then I just sat there and cried . . . and cried. . . . And when he came home, he found me in the same spot. I had not gotten up or done anything, except breastfeed the baby (she was still very small). I hadn't even changed her diapers. It was so rare for me to cry like that. . . .

He walked in and looked confused. "What's wrong?" he asked. "I can't do it," I said. "I don't want to live here. Everything here depresses me." After our old apartment, and now with the baby, I felt some kind of chill. . . . It all seemed gloomy somehow. . . .

I didn't know any of the neighbors. One day I went to the people below or perhaps on the same floor to ask about something, and I saw (I can still remember it) a huge vase of flowers, but they weren't real—they must have been some kind of artificial ones.

After a while, they settled in. They brought her dowry things and an extra-large table (by using the cargo elevator in the kitchen). Lydia's mother came up from Kolomna, fired the nanny, and hired a new, much better one. The House guards recognized them as equals. "I always felt their sympathy toward me. They would hold the baby, or help get the carriage ready. They were kind and attentive. You could tell they were simple people. And they could see that we didn't put on airs or anything like that." They bought two carpets, one green, the other with a picture of a falcon hunt. They put them down on the parquet floor, so the baby could crawl. But they did not put up any pictures, leaving the walls "bare and dry." Lydia did not shop or cook, either. She was too busy studying. She was also an athlete: she played volleyball and had to go to practice.[19]

Serafim Bogachev

Many House residents found Iofan's straight lines and large windows too "bare and dry." Most did something about it: brought in old beds and chests, hung up swords and photographs, or laid down carpets and bearskins. Some took great care to cover up as much of the constructivist frame as possible—by painting flower patterns on the walls or covering them with "silklike" wallpaper or hanging up thick curtains on the large windows (which were very drafty in the winter). Nadezhda Mikhailova attempted to recreate her parents' Victorian domesticity. Stalin's sister-in-law, Evgenia Allilueva (the wife of Nadezhda's brother, Pavel, and the daughter and granddaughter of Novgorod priests), possessed, according to her daughter, Kira, "a remarkable talent for making everything around her cozy with the help of a few simple things—a bright tablecloth, some pictures. . . . Everyone in our house loved flowers. There were always some on the table in the big room. Dad preferred lilies of the valley, and Mom, forget-me-nots. On my birthday, people would bring roses or peonies—and, in the spring, a branch of mimosa. And there were some charming, delicate watercolors—of landscapes and barefooted ballerinas—hanging on the walls of the big room."[20]

In 1935, no one seemed entirely sure whether this was good taste for new times or the "spontaneous regeneration of the perennial and loathsome forms of life." Some House of Government residents insisted on leaving the walls bare and dry. Some drew the line at curtains, the great disappointment's symbol of philistine domesticity. The head of the Directorate of the Alcoholic Beverages Industry, Abram Gilinsky, did not mind a carpet on the wall, a large china cabinet with a collection of playing cards inside (he was a tireless Preferans player), or an exhibit of miniature liqueur bottles on top of his daughter's piano, but when his mother-in-law hung up some curtains, he ordered them removed. Ivan Kraval (who, in 1935, replaced Osinsky as head of the Central Directory of Economic Statistics) compromised by allowing narrow green curtains that framed—but did not cover—his study window.[21]

In spring 1936, Adoratsky, Arosev, and Bukharin were in Europe buying documents and memorabilia for the Marx-Engels Lenin Institute (of which Adoratsky was director). Adoratsky was, as usual, accompanied by his daughter, Varvara. On April 5, he wrote to his wife from Paris: "I have bought a medallion with Marx's portrait and hair, which used to belong to his daughter, Jenny Longuet. . . . I am also going to buy the armchair in which Marx died and a wooden armchair from his study, which he sat on while writing *Das Kapital*." Five days later, he visited the studio of the sculptor Naum Aronson, where he admired a bust of Lenin ("his energy, will, and deep intelligence are rendered very well"), and picked up a suit made for him by a Parisian tailor ("it's gray, well tailored, and made of Cheviot wool"). But nothing impressed him as much as the interiors of the homes he saw. In one house in Holland, in particular, everything was "exceptionally solid and comfortable. All the rooms are paneled: the dining-room, in dark oak; the study, in walnut; and the living room, in maple or birch; the bedroom is painted with white oil-based paint; and there are many walk-in closets. The kitchen is in the middle of the house, between the dining room and the bedroom. All the rooms are large and spacious, and there is lots of storage space." Most of the Marx-Engels archive had been moved from Hitler's Germany to Copenhagen. The delegation arrived there on March 16. "We have been put up in a terrific hotel. I have never lived in a hotel like this. Everything is solid and full of all kinds of handy contraptions. For example, there's a blue sack in the closet where you can put your dirty clothes, and they'll wash them for you. The tub and other things are very clean, and there's this amazing magnifying mirror in which you can see your whole face almost doubled in size—for when you're shaving."[22]

The House of Government did not have special blue bags for dirty linen or magnifying mirrors for shaving, but it did offer laundry services (in a separate building between the House and St. Nicholas Church), and it did provide a large number of accessories, including lampshades, doorbells, and raisable oak toilet seats. For apartments that had cargo elevators, special attendants came twice a day to pick up trash (other apartments had garbage chutes, and some had both cargo elevators and garbage chutes). Mail carriers came twice a day to drop letters and newspapers through mail slots in the doors. Repair work and cleaning services, including floor polishing and window cleaning, could be requested from the House management by telephone. The hairdressing salon (located above the grocery store) offered home appointments. Dogs could be left in a special pen in the basement. There was a shooting range under Entryway 1, a kindergarten on the top floor of Entryway 7, a children's club on the first floor of Entryway 3, and a walk-in clinic with on-duty nurses and doctors next to the laundry. And, of course, there was the large club located above the theater, which, as Adoratsky wrote in another letter, "has a tennis court and different rooms where you can do whatever you like: play chess, music, etc." Virtually none of the residents ate in the House cafeteria (which was used by House employees and occasional conference delegates). Nor did they do much cooking: prepared food in special stackable containers could be brought up (by the maids) from the cafeteria or delivered (by personal chauffeurs, sometimes accompanied by the maids) from exclusive food distribution centers (most frequently the one in the Fifth House of Soviets on Granovsky Street, a short distance away). There were three kinds of "food receipt cards": "employee" (issued to nomenklatura members), "dependent," and "child." The selection and quality were widely seen as satisfactory; one list of ingredients bought by the cafeteria included a wide variety of meats (beef, pork, lamb, chicken, tongue, liver, and several kinds of sausage), fish (including smoked fish and herring), dairy products, vegetables, eggs, grains, flour, pasta, rice, potatoes, bread, beer, fruit, dried fruit, nuts, tea, coffee, jams, and spices (pepper, ginger, vanilla, cardamom, cinnamon, and cloves).[23]

The material contents of the House were protected by several layers of security. According to Nadezhda Mikhailova's elder daughter, M. N. Kulman,

> each entryway of the House of Government had its own guard, with a desk, chair, and telephone mounted on the wall. This was all near the entrance door, by the stairway. When a person entered, the guard would ask for their last name and who they were going to see and then call the resident the person had named and ask if it was okay to let them in. The guards worked around the clock, and there were always three for each entryway. They took turns working twenty-four-hour shifts and also rotated on the weekends. The guards were very strict about making sure that nonresidents did not take anything out of the building: if a person wanted to leave an apartment with a suitcase or bundle, the official resident would either have to escort that person out or call the guard to escort them. The guards knew all the residents by sight and could even distinguish them by their voices. Once, a woman tried to leave our apartment with a bundle . . . , but the guard would not let her pass, saying, "There are no grown-ups at home, and a child cannot be expected to know what may or may not be taken from the home." So she had to return to our apartment and wait for my mother. When my mother finally arrived, he told her: "There's a woman here, who was trying to leave your apartment with a bundle."[24]

■ ■ ■

Most of the men rarely spent time at home. As Khrushchev put it, "in those days, we were all engrossed in our work; we worked with tremendous passion and excitement, depriving ourselves of virtually everything." And, as Natalia Sats described her third husband, People's Commissar of Internal Trade Izrail Veitser, "He did not like to be seen in public and paid no attention to his personal appearance. His fanaticism about his work was the stuff of legends. He considered it perfectly natural to leave for work at 9 a.m. and not come back until 4 a.m. the following morning." After their marriage in 1935, Veitser's deputy and House of Government neighbor, Lev (Lazar) Khinchuk, sent them a line from *Eugene Onegin*: "They came together: waves and stone, poems and prose, flames and ice." Sats was not so sure: "'If he is prose,' I thought to myself, 'then that prose is worth all the poetry in the world.' . . . They used to say 'Soviet trade is our personal,

Bolshevik cause.' For Veitser, it truly was personal. He was the poet of Soviet trade."[25]

Veitser had two explanations for his "fantasy and fanaticism." One was his love for the Party (according to Sats, he was "an ideal Bolshevik-Leninist"). The other was his Pale-of-Settlement childhood. "Most of all I feared the Sabbath. My mother, Hannah, used to put the three of us—my brother Iosif, my brother Naum, and me—all together in one tub and scrub us all with the same sponge. Mother was always in a hurry; we would be wriggling around; soap would get into our eyes; and shrieks and slaps on the head would

Izrail Veitser

follow. We were little boys and always getting dirty—we used to run barefoot through the puddles—and there was only one tub. Once, I remember saying: 'God, if you exist, make the Sabbath go away.'"[26]

"We knew no rest," wrote Khrushchev. "On our days off (when there still were days off—later they disappeared), we would usually hold meetings, conferences, and rallies." When asked about Stalin, Artem Sergeev, who grew up in Stalin's household, said: "What was his most characteristic trait? He seemed to work all the time. . . . He worked constantly, always and everywhere." Most top nomenklatura members had schedules similar to Veitser's. Mikhail Poloz and Mark Belenky worked until 2:00 a.m.; Aron Gaister, until 5:00 or 6:00 a.m. Ivan Gronsky describes his schedule as follows:

> I usually got up at 8 a.m., did my exercises, took a cold shower, and ate breakfast. I had to be at the Kremlin by 9. On most days, various state and Party commissions would begin working at that time. Every ten days, at 11 a.m., there would be a meeting of the Politburo, which I was required to attend. Those meetings usually lasted until 7 p.m., with one 15–20 minute break. On other days, the Council of People's Commissars and the Council of Labor and Defense would hold their meetings, in which I also participated. I usually arrived at Izvestia after 7 p.m. The newspaper came out in the morning. . . . I normally did not get home before 3 a.m.[27]

Those who worked at home tended to have a similar schedule. Osinsky and the literary critic Elena Usievich usually worked for most of the night and never ate with their children. No one was allowed to disturb them while they were in their studies writing. According to Osinsky's daughter, Svetlana, "'Father is working and cannot be disturbed' was the most important thing we children knew about him." Koltsov, according to his colleague and friend, N. Beliaev (Naum Beilin), "did not write, but dictated his works. His secretary, Nina Pavlovna Prokofieva, or simply Ninochka, used to report to work at 11:00 a.m. "At that time, Koltsov, still groggy after three or four hours of sleep, and having quickly gulped down a cup of strong coffee and taken an aspirin for his headache, would begin dictating another chapter."[28] As she tells it, "In the mornings, I used to go to his home, first on Bolshaia Dmitrovka and then to the House of Government on the Bersenev Embankment, where he lived in a four-room apartment on the eighth floor and where he had a large study with a balcony. He always walked about when dictating; he couldn't dictate sitting down." Her job required both speed and patience.

> I would arrive, take off my coat in the hall, and then enter the study. He would greet me warmly, but I would know by the look on his face—concentrated, serious, remote—that he was ready to start dictating. I would set out both regular and carbon paper, insert two sheets into the typewriter, and sit quietly at the desk with my back to the window. The light would fall on the typewriter, leaving me in the shadow. Mikhail Efimovich, wearing slippers and an old jacket or a dark-blue knitted vest over a light-blue shirt, would pace up and down the room, stopping occasionally in front of the balcony, where he would reach up and grab the top of the door frame and stare pensively into the distance—or, as it seemed to me at the time, at the clock that used to hang in the gateway arch of the house. Then he would sit down next to the desk, cup his chin in his hand, and examine a pack of Kazbek cigarettes. Or he might rest his cheek on his hand and look off into space until I began to think he had completely forgotten about me, my typewriter, and the essay.
>
> But then he would suddenly jump up and begin slowly dictating the first sentence, as if he were trying it out. Sometimes he would have the title ready, but more often it came only after the last word had been dictated.[29]

Mikhail Koltsov dictating

Outside the home, Koltsov wore suits. He had always worn suits. A *Pravda* journalist remembered his first appearance in the editorial offices, soon after the Civil War. "There were tunics, blouses, uniforms, folk shirts, Tolstoy-shirts, field jackets, leather jackets, and trench coats—and then, suddenly, amidst all that uniformity of diversity, I spotted a real suit." By 1935, almost everyone had switched to a real suit. Even Veitser, who was famous for always wearing the same overcoat (which also served as a blanket when he slept in his office), got himself a new black suit. Osinsky wore light suits; Rozengolts wore hats (to go with his suits); Rozengolts's friend Arosev wore bowties and tuxedoes (and used expensive English soaps and colognes, which he brought back in bulk from his foreign trips). The head of the Trade Union International (Profintern), Solomon Abramovich Lozovsky, wore suits made by his father-in-law, the famous tailor Abram Solomonovich Shamberg (who was living in his apartment, Apt. 16). Lozovsky's daughter by a previous marriage, Milena (named after Marx and Lenin and married to Podvoisky's son, Lev), believed that her father "would be easy to imagine on a Parisian boulevard," but that it was his friend, the deputy head of the Supreme

Vladimir Adoratsky

Court, Petr Krasikov, who looked like the "real boulevardier." Krasikov's adopted daughter, Lydia Shatunovskaia, thought he looked like "a Russian nobleman." Adoratsky bought his suit in a Parisian shop, the day he saw Aronson's bust of Lenin.[30]

The ones primarily responsible for the elegance of both the suits and interior decorations were the wives. Some did not work because they were invalids (as in the case of the wives of the "proletarians" Boris Ivanov and Vasily Orekhov); some because they were committed housewives (as in the case of the wives of Mark Belenky and Ivan Gronsky); and some because they were both invalids and committed housewives (as in the case of Nadezhda Mikhailova and Maria Peterson). But most of the women had professional jobs (as editors, accountants, statisticians, economists, pharmacists, doctors, and engineers), worked regular daytime hours, and rarely saw their husbands or spent much time with their children during the week. Some of them continued to favor the severe style of sectarian asceticism (gray or black suit, white blouse, and hair pulled into a tight bun at the back of the head), but most had discovered "elegance." According to Inna Gaister, around 1934–35 her mother, Rakhil Izrailevna Kaplan, "suddenly remembered that she was a beautiful woman." She had graduated from the Plekhanov Institute in 1932 and was working in the People's Commissariat of Heavy Industry. "At some point she began having dresses made for her, and I remember feeling very indignant: 'look at her, she is having two dresses made, no three!'" (Rakhil was thirty-two at the time, and Inna ten.) According to Irina Muklevich (born 1923), "after around 1935, things began to change quite a bit. You could already see it: all those beautiful wives." Irina's thirty-five-year-old mother, a Party member and section head at the State Planning Directorate, suddenly took to wearing evening dresses. The forty-year-old Nadezhda Smilga-Poluian, also a Party member and one of the editors of the *Short Soviet Encyclopedia*, alternated suits with black silk dresses, which she accented with a cameo brooch bought for her in Italy by her husband. Elena Usievich, the literary critic and former Chekist, developed a passion for hats. Most of the women

cut their hair short and wore perfume. (Nadezhda Smilga-Poluian preferred Quelques Fleurs.) The cosmetic equivalent of curtains (as the symbol of philistine vulgarity) was lipstick. A manicure was acceptable, but
lipstick was not.[31]

The women who did not work tended to cultivate domestic femininity.
The night Lydia Gronskaia's sister Elena met her husband, the poet Pavel
Vasiliev, the two sisters were "perched on the couch" in the Gronsky's dining room "engaged in the usual female tasks: sewing and embroidering."
Nadezhda Mikhailova embroidered cushions and, according to her daughter, "was a good singer and an excellent pianist, and loved to dance. Toward
the end, she put on quite a bit of weight, but she still danced beautifully,
and loved doing it." She did not have many outfits, but those she did have
were "in good taste," including "a very beautiful cameo brooch." Lydia
Khatskevich liked to have her female friends over for tea. Maria (Mirra)
Ozerskaia preferred to shop (a taste she had developed in London, where
her husband was a Soviet trade representative). Maria Peterson spent
much of her time presiding over her large household. According to one of
her daughters, "Mother had a real talent for running the house and for
making it cozy and efficient. She had good taste and a sense of beauty,
which she imparted to our home. This beauty could be felt in the things she
made herself and in the way she furnished the rooms. She passed on her
talent for drawing and needlework to us. She was in charge of various
maids, nannies, and even some visiting German governesses at one time.
She knew how to give orders and take command. . . . Mother was very pretty
in her youth: small and fragile with long thick dark hair down to her knees.
That hair caused Mother so much trouble and was such a burden that, in
the mid-1920s, she cut off her thick braid and got one of those short perms
that were the fashion then. . . . By the time I came along, Mother had put on
weight, but she was still light on her feet and always wore high heels."[32]

Evgenia Allilueva (Zemlianitsyna), according to her daughter (and
Stalin's niece) Kira, "wasn't particularly political and wasn't too crazy

about the whole high society thing. It was all
these Bolshevik women, and Mom wasn't one of
them. Mom was more feminine, more flirta-
tious." She loved music and dancing, opera and
ballet. "At that time, it was fashionable to wear
your hair cut short and permed into waves.
Mom had her hair cut, too. But she saved her
braid, which she kept in a special box and would
'wear' on special occasions." According to Kira,
most House of Government women had their
clothes made to order—"not only dresses and
suits, but even overcoats and fur coats. There
weren't any Soviet fashion magazines. So it was
only if someone brought them from abroad.

Evgenia Allilueva
(Courtesy of Kira Allilueva)

Mom would borrow and look through them and then work some magic with the help of her dressmaker, Evdokia Semenovna. She would bring a French fashion magazine, point out a dress or a suit, and ask Evdokia Semenovna: 'Could you make this?' To which Evdokia Semenovna would always reply: 'Evgenia Aleksandrovna, it won't be easy, but I'll try.' And then she'd do it."[33]

In 1936, there was a special event in the Kremlin on the occasion of the adoption of the new constitution, and Evgenia decided to wear a new dress. As Kira tells it,

Almost overnight, Evdokia Semenovna had to create something extraordinary: a dark dress with a white lace insert in the bodice. That insert was a masterpiece of needlework. It had tiny ruffles—very intricate and beautiful! There was only one problem: Evdokia Semenovna wasn't able to finish in time. She was still putting in a few last-minute stitches, even after Mom already had the dress on.

That day the radio in our apartment was turned up full blast. It was a historic moment; you couldn't miss it. It was being broadcast live. Stalin had already started speaking, and Mom was still home, getting dressed. A car with a driver was waiting for her downstairs. Dad, of course, was already in the Kremlin, waiting nervously.

Mom entered the hall in the middle of Stalin's speech and, crouching down low (as low as she could), she made her way to her seat. When the official session ended, many of the guests walked over to St. George's Hall, where a lavish banquet was laid out.

People were lining up to talk to Stalin, and to offer their congratulations. When Mom's turn came, he says to her: "So, Zhenia, why were you late?!" Mom was amazed: "How did you spot me?"—"I'm farsighted," he said with a chuckle. "I can see for miles. You were crouching down as you were walking. Who else would do something like that? Only Zhenya!"[34]

Several months later, a large Soviet delegation went to Paris to participate in the International Art and Technology Exposition. Evgenia's husband, Pavel Alliluev, was appointed the delegation's commissar (Party supervisor):

When Mom found out about it, she ran over to talk to Stalin. "Iosif, I've never asked you for anything. I'm dying to go to Paris! I've heard so much about it, and I took French in school . . ." He looked at her, and then at Ezhov, who happened to be in his office at the time, and said, smiling under his moustache: "What do you think, should we let her go?" . . .

She spent twelve days in Paris. According to her, she never slept more than four hours a night. She wanted to see everything. She

Pavel Alliluev and Evgenia Allilueva at the
Paris Exposition (Courtesy of Kira Allilueva)

loved the city. She was amazed at the way the cars yielded to pedestrians because that was the custom in France.

She seems to have felt at home in Paris. She went to the Opera, a
Josephine Baker show (she had seen her in Berlin once before), and
the Louvre. She was absolutely captivated by the famous Venus of
Milo. "I went around to take a look at 'Venus' from the back, and she
was breathing!" . . .

She and Dad went to a restaurant and tried the famous onion
soup and some oysters. She explained to us later that you were supposed to eat them with a slice of lemon, and that they even squeak.[35]

At the exposition, the Soviet pavilion, designed by Iofan, and the German pavilion, designed by Albert Speer, both received gold medals. The two
structures faced each other across a boulevard in the Trocadero. The facade of the German pavilion was a tower crowned with an eagle. The
facade of the Soviet pavilion was a tower crowned with Vera Mukhina's
Worker and Kolkhoz Woman. According to Elina Kisis from Apt. 424, an early
model of the Kolkhoz Woman had appeared in the House of Government
courtyard around 1934 or 1935. "The model was slightly larger than life size
and made of plaster or clay. In any case, it was gray, and Mukhina had it
installed in the fountain in front of Entryway 21, where I lived. When the
workers were removing the boards, a piece of the 'Kolkhoz Woman' broke
off." The Paris version was brought back to the Soviet Union and installed,
along with the Worker, at the main entrance to the All-Union Agricultural

Soviet and German pavilions at the Paris Expo, 1937

Soviet pavilion at the 1937 Paris Expo

Exhibition. Evgenia Allilueva came back with "presents for everyone," including "an elegant little pipe" for Stalin.[36]

The most renowned connoisseurs of beautiful things were the wives of
provincial Party officials and industrial managers. Before moving to the
House of Government, the Granovskys lived in a "splendidly decorated"
house in Berezniki with "all the finest chinaware, silver, linen and everything needed to make a princely home." Sofia Butenko, the wife of the

director of the Kuznetsk Steel Plant, Konstantin Butenko, was one of the leaders of a nationwide women's volunteer movement (which urged the wives of top industrial managers to see to the cleanliness, beauty, and "cultured domesticity" in the lives of their husbands' workers). On her regular trips to Moscow, she would visit an exclusive dressmaker's atelier, look at samples, and usually order several suits and dresses (paying about 140 rubles for a three and a half–meter length of the best dress material and about 350 rubles for the labor, or about twice the average RSFSR monthly salary per dress).[37]

Another source of beauty—employed in a variety of ways—was the theater. When Natalia Sats's daughter, Roksana, was in the second grade at Exemplary School No. 25, she once hit a girl named Dashenka (but only after Dashenka had pushed her off her gym stool and then bragged that no one dared touch her because of her powerful grandfather who was driven around everywhere in a chauffeured limousine). Roksana was publicly reprimanded by the principal and sent home. The next morning before school, she complained to her mother.

It must have been difficult to make sense of my confused, inarticulate mumblings, but Mom understood perfectly. She stood up, called the theater to let them know she would be late for rehearsal, and began to get dressed. It was never a simple process, but this time she dressed as if she were on her way to a diplomatic reception instead of an elementary school. And when she threw her leopard fur coat into the arms of the school cleaning lady, who suddenly appeared out of nowhere, and walked down the school corridor in her silver lacquered pumps and her bright red dress with the wide sleeves lined with white silk, the effect was truly spectacular. The long break was just beginning, and kids were streaming out of the classrooms. At the sight of Mom, however, even the wildest boys, who were already racing headlong toward the cafeteria, suddenly stopped, changed course, and ran after her, staring in amazement.

The principal was in the gym, presiding over a young pioneer induction ceremony. My mom's sudden appearance with her large entourage in tow put an abrupt end to the proceedings. The pioneer leader forgot why she was holding a red scarf and stepped aside, letting Mom pass. The forgotten inductee craned his neck in utter bewilderment, made a 180-degree turn, and ducked back into the column of not-yet-pioneers. Mom marched straight up to the principal.

"Where is this other girl?" she demanded.

Dashenka was in the gym, too.

"I want you to tell me exactly what happened yesterday," Mom ordered.

Dashenka began, slowly: "She was sitting . . . I came up . . . I said . . ."

Natalia Sats with the Children's Theater
conductor and composer, Leonid Polovinkin
(Courtesy of Roksana Sats)

Not daring to repeat what she had said before, Dashenka hung her head and was silent. Mom finished her story for her.

"So is that what happened? Or did I get something wrong?" she asked at the end.

"No," mumbled Dashenka, completely embarrassed.

"Roksana, come here," ordered Mom.

I walked to the middle of the gym and stood between the column of young pioneers and the rapidly growing crowd of onlookers. Mom's words rang out in the total silence:

"Even the greatest accomplishments of those closest to us do not justify arrogance. You did the right thing yesterday. Never allow anyone to humiliate you."

She nodded to me, said goodbye to the principal, and walked out. Almost the whole school followed after her. They stood and watched as she put on her fur coat, got into her car, and shut the door. And then, when she rolled down the window and waved mischievously to the kids, they all waved back and shouted:

"Goodbye!"[38]

Another group known for its well-dressed women and well-furnished apartments were the high-ranking military officers (especially aviators) and NKVD (secret police) officials. When they were living in Dneprope-trovsk, Sergei Mironov and Agnessa Argiropulo used to throw lavish parties for Mironov's colleagues and their wives. Once, one of the wives, Nadia Reznik, began flirting with Mironov. As Agnessa tells the story,

> Nadia, I have to admit, also knew how to rise to the occasion. She was blonde, and the cornflower blue dress she was wearing really suited her. That was too much for me. Blue was my color. It complemented my chestnut brown hair perfectly. A clerk at the hard-currency store helped me exchange my coffee-colored, crepe georgette fabric for—no, not a cornflower blue—but a very pale shade of blue that looked even better on me.
>
> My Dnepropetrovsk seamstress was a magician. The design she came up with was a masterpiece. It had two soft folds from the waist that streamed out when you walked, like Nike's, the Greek goddess of victory.
>
> The table was elegantly set, with flowers at each place setting. At the table I reigned supreme, but after the meal I suddenly noticed that Mirosha and Nadia had moved to a couch in another room and appeared to be engrossed in lively conversation. I walked by once, twice, the folds in my skirt flowing like the wind, or a pale blue breeze, almost as if I were flying like Nike. But Mirosha didn't seem to notice.[39]

Agnessa asked her maid to call Nadia on the phone and tell her that she was wanted at home on an urgent matter. Nadia left in a hurry. When she called a few minutes later and asked what the point of the joke was, Agnessa replied that "one should know how to behave in someone else's house" and hung up the phone. When she told Mironov what she had done, he "burst out laughing in delight."[40]

Managing the home front was relatively easy. Agnessa's biggest challenges were the vacations at large sea resorts in the Caucasus.

> Before leaving for the sanatorium I would go to Kiev to buy fabric at the foreign-currency store and then have outfits made in Kiev or by my seamstress magician in Dnepropetrovsk.
>
> Mironov kept telling me to dress more modestly, saying that my extravagant outfits embarrassed him, but I continued to have glamorous gowns made as well as modest ones—and it's a good thing I did.
>
> When we arrived at the Ukrainian Central Committee sanatorium in Khosta that fall, all the young women were competing with each other to be the best dressed. I said to Mirosha: "See? It's a good thing I didn't listen to you!"[41]

One of Mironov's oldest colleagues (they had served in the Caucasus together) was the commander of the Border Security Forces, the former seminarian, Mikhail Frinovsky.

We used to run into them at the sanatoriums in the Caucasus. Frinovsky had an arrogant, fat face. His wife Nina was terribly vulgar—plain, pug-nosed, and wore way too much gaudy makeup. Mirosha and I used to make fun of her. Mirosha once told me, howling with laughter:

Mikhail Frinovsky
(Courtesy of A. G. Teplyakov)

"I was sitting across from her at the restaurant. It was hot, and she was sweating, and suddenly I saw two black streaks run down from her eyes and mix with the rouge on her cheeks, then roll down her chin and drip slowly onto her plate."

But when we arrived in Sochi in the fall of 1936, Mirosha said to me: "Take a look at Nina! She used to dress like a prostitute, but now she's really something!"

I saw her and couldn't believe my eyes. She was like a different person! It turned out that she had just gotten back from Paris, where they had given her a "make-over": found her style, taught her how to do her hair, and picked out the right makeup and clothes for her. I remember she was wearing a blue gingham dress and a blue ribbon in her hair that were so flattering you could hardly tell it was the same person. She knew it, too, and was very proud.

That fall Yagoda was dismissed (it was the beginning of his downfall), and Ezhov was appointed Commissar of Internal Affairs. As soon as the news reached us, Nina really came into her own. She didn't try to hide her hopes from me: "This is excellent," she said, "Ezhov is a big friend of ours."

They had spent some holidays together somewhere, and the two families had become friends.

And sure enough, some time later I read in the paper that Frinovsky had been appointed Deputy People's Commissar.

You should have seen the reaction at the sanatorium! All the toadies came running up to Nina and started fawning all over her.

She left the next day. I remember walking her over to the car. She was wearing a black hat, an elegant, close-fitting black suit, and white gloves. As she was saying her goodbyes, she singled me and Mirosha out, hugged me, and gave me a meaningful look. . . .

Our hopes came true. Mirosha received an order to wind up his affairs in Dnepropetrovsk and go to Novosibirsk as head of the NKVD Directorate for all of West Siberia.[42]

15

THE DAYS OFF

When the House of Government was being built, most Soviet institutions were on the so-called uninterrupted production schedule. The seven-day week had been abolished. The year now consisted of 360 working days organized into seventy-two five-day weeks and five common holidays. All workers and employees were divided into five groups, each with its own work schedule. In keeping with the First Five-Year Plan ethos of ceaseless work by autonomous individuals organized into random but seamlessly cohesive production "collectives," factories and construction sites never shut down, and members of the same family might have different days off. The demand for individualized spaces coincided with the drive for individualized schedules. The chief promoter of both was Bukharin's future father-in-law, Yuri Larin, who liked to imagine the future producer as "a snail carrying its shell." Rational collectivism was about extreme individualism.[1]

The House of Government had been built as a structure "of transitional type" combining extended communal services with a concession to family longevity. On December 1, 1931, soon after most House residents moved into their apartments and a whole year before the First Five-Year Plan was pronounced to have been fulfilled "ahead of schedule," the uninterrupted five-day calendar was replaced by a uniform six-day week, with universal days off falling on the 6th, 12th, 18th, 24th, and 30th of each month. All Soviets, including those forming affective and reproductive units within more or less insulated separate spaces, were to synchronize their lives.[2]

For top nomenklatura officials and their families, however, weekday schedules remained uncoordinated. A continued attachment to the ethic of ceaseless work in an age of proliferating "parks of culture and rest" meant that those who never slept had to sleep while others worked. In the House of Government, maids, nannies, grandmothers, and female poor relations would get up early, make breakfast for the children (hot cereal, sandwiches, or both), see the young ones off to school (help them across the streetcar tracks on Serafimovich Street or hand them over to their fathers' chauffeurs), and then do things around the house. Some did their own cooking; most relied on prepared meals from the House cafeteria and other exclusive food distribution points, supplemented (usually at dinner) with homemade dishes made from ingredients picked up at various distribution points or purchased at the House grocery store. Working mothers might eat breakfast with their children or a bit later. Nonworking mothers (a minority in the House) might get up before their husbands and engage in a variety of activities (volunteer work, dressmaking, shopping, sewing, conversing with visiting friends or live-in relatives) or get up and have breakfast with their husbands in either the kitchen or the dining room. Most men did not linger over breakfast and might or might not have time to read through *Pravda* (everyone did eventually—at work if not at home); their chauffeurs might come up or wait outside. Soon after the men's departure, the schoolchildren would come home and have lunch (usually by themselves, served by the nannies). Tutors normally came in the late afternoon. Some working mothers might have dinner with their children and other live-in relatives; others would come home late and eat by themselves, usually quickly and with little ceremony. The men might or might not have dinner at home. Most would come home when all the other apartment residents were asleep. The only permanent presence in the home—the fixed axis of the weekday schedule and the only person vitally connected to every other member of the household—was the nanny or maid (assisted, and occasionally replaced, by the grandmother or another resident female relative).[3]

The sixth day of the six-day week was the "day off." It was not called "Sunday," but it was a common holiday officially dedicated to rest and unofficially serving as the chronological pivot of family life. After the first layer of scaffolding was taken down from the house of socialism, the Sabbath was gradually returning (even for Veitser, who was now happily married). Once every six days, the maids and nannies would step into the shadows and cede the space and schedule to their "masters."

Most families woke up to the sound of the radio. Each apartment had a radio cable connected to a round black loudspeaker (or "dish") mounted on the wall, usually in the kitchen or dining room. Radios were always on, but on holiday mornings they were turned up and actively listened to. "Day-off" programming usually included children's shows, music shows (Soviet songs and classical music), and, later in the day, live broadcasts of concerts, operas, and theater performances. The man responsible for both the programming and the nationwide cable and relay network was the expert on rational time-keeping and work ethic, Platon Kerzhentsev, who served as head of the All-Union Radiofication and Broadcasting Committee between 1933 and 1936. Like many other men in the House, Kerzhentsev also owned a German valve radio set, which he kept in his study.[4]

All the men read newspapers (which meant a lot of articles written by Koltsov, among others). Some recuperated from their work week by working on themselves. Osinsky studied Hegel and mathematics; Arosev wrote fiction and kept a diary. Almost everyone read for pleasure. The most popular books remained the same as in prison and exile, with the exception of both the Russian radical tradition (Chernyshevsky, Kravchinsky, Gorky) and fin-de-siècle Belgian and Scandinavian modernism, which did not seem to fit the age of Augustinian fulfillment and gradually dropped out of the high culture canon. Still compulsory were "the Pamirs" of European literature (Dante, Cervantes, Shakespeare, Goethe); the Russian classics (with Pushkin and Tolstoy at the top); and the nineteenth-century European standards (especially romantic and early realist works, headed by Dickens and Balzac). Another large category included the adventure stories the House of Government men had enjoyed as boys. It consisted of two overlapping sets of texts: early-nineteenth-century historical novels reimagined as literature for adolescents (Walter Scott, James Fenimore Cooper, Alexandre Dumas) and books of imperial exploration, whose popularity had coincided with their Old Bolshevik youth (Thomas Mayne Reid, Robert Louis Stevenson, Jules Verne, Louis Henri Boussenard, Jack London, and O. Henry). Of contemporary writers, the most popular was Romain Rolland, who was seen as a reincarnation of heroic realism (and perhaps of his—and his readers'—great heroes, Beethoven and Tolstoy). Soviet literature was read by few people who were not directly involved in producing or supervising it. The great exceptions were children's books (including Nikolai Ostrovsky's *How Steel Was Tempered*, which was popular among adolescents) and, of the adult novels produced in the 1930s, Aleksei Tolstoy's *Peter I* (a construction/creation story in the form of a realist historical epic).

Other popular forms of home entertainment for men were photography and chess. Cameras (along with gramophones and clothes) were among the most important items brought home from foreign trips, and many men spent hours developing photographs. (Ivan Kraval created a fully enclosed photo lab inside his dining room.) Chess complemented reading as a form of relaxation that combined high-culture credentials with entertainment. Kerzhentsev clipped match reports from newspapers, classified the matches in various ways, and then analyzed and replayed them himself. The added value of chess was social. Some men had permanent partners. (Yakov Brandenburgsky played with N. V. Krylenko, the people's commissar of justice and head of the Soviet Chess Federation; Romuald Muklevich played with Iosif Unshlikht [Józef Unszlicht], the chairman of the Civil Aviation Directorate and a fellow Pole.) Most fathers played regularly with their sons. Kerzhentsev's son (from a previous marriage) had died young, so he played with his daughter, Natalia, who was not particularly interested. The Komsomol Central Committee secretary, Serafim Bogachev, played with his young wife, Lydia. "Sima really loved chess," she remembered, "and in the evenings, when we had some free time, we would often sit down and play. He would say: 'Stop doing your math; let's play chess instead.'"[5]

Many parents, particularly fathers, devoted their days off to their children: playing with them, reading to them, and taking them to the theater, the movies (usually the Shock Worker and, in the late 1930s, the First Children's Movie Theater, located in the New Theater auditorium), the Tretyakov Art Gallery (a short walk away on the other side of the Ditch), the Museum of Fine Arts (a short walk away on the other side of the river), and Gorky Park (a slightly longer walk, first along the Ditch and then along the river). Gorky Park was a particularly popular destination. In 1935, Koltsov's new wife, Maria Osten, published a book on behalf of a ten-year-old German boy she and Koltsov had adopted in the Saar and brought to their House of Government apartment. The book was called *Hubert in Wonderland*, and one of the greatest wonders Hubert had seen in the USSR was Gorky Park, which he visited in the winter of 1934, soon after his arrival: "I went to the Park of Culture and Rest. Even in winter, there were plenty of fun things to do. The squares, avenues, and paths were turned into mirror-smooth skating rinks. There were rinks for beginners and for regular and figure skaters and special areas for games and rides. In the evenings, they were all lit up, with Red Army bands playing. At the far end of the Park was a ski area that stretched all the way to the Lenin Hills. I spent many wonderful hours in the winter in the Park of Culture and Rest, skating, skiing, and sledding." His next visit was in the spring:

> Everywhere you look, someone is painting or building something, or a banner is being put up. The circus is open, and the Swing Boats are ready. Posters announcing the new season have been displayed in front of the theater and the cinema. There is a Ferris wheel, a parachute jumping tower, a roller-skating rink. . . . I don't know where to go or where to begin.
>
> I run around, as if in a maze: to the house of mirrors, reading room, restaurant, children's village, and boat rental. . . . An orchestra is playing in one of the pavilions. A little farther on, someone is playing an accordion. In one place couples are dancing a foxtrot. In another, they are learning folk dances. I look at the people around me, and each one seems to be headed toward a specific goal. Only I run back and forth, confused. That is because it is all so new to me.
>
> I spent many fun days at the Park of Culture and Rest. I was seldom alone there. I met new friends and often went with my classmates. We used to swim, take out rowboats, exercise, ride on the Zero Gravity, roller-skate, and go to the theater, cinema, or circus. Unfortunately, we were not allowed to parachute because we were still too small, but we used to stand for hours watching others do it.[6]

Hubert in Wonderland was a political work published by Koltsov as a special issue of his illustrated weekly, *Ogonyok*. If Soviet children wanted to be like the Reichstag-trial hero, Georgi Dimitrov, wrote Georgi Dimitrov in his introduction to the book, they must read about Hubert's travels. "To be like Dimitrov," wrote Dimitrov, "means to be a consistent proletarian fighter," and to be a consistent proletarian fighter meant knowing the difference "between the joyful and truthful world of socialism and the mean,

Hubert L'Hoste in Gorky Park

lying, and bloodthirsty world of fascism." Most of Hubert's (and Dimitrov's) neighbors in the House of Government did know the difference, did want to be like Dimitrov, and, whether or not they thought much about such things, did enjoy going to Gorky Park. Boris Volin's daughter, Viktoria, who was fourteen in 1935, remembered going there to watch movies, dress up for "carnivals," eat ice cream, skate, and walk. "We used to walk and walk and walk. We'd kiss and we'd walk. We did all kinds of things." In 1935, the official things to do included twenty amusement rides that were open from noon to 11:00 p.m. In addition to those mentioned by Hubert, there were different kinds of carousels, a bumper-car rink, an "upside-down room," and a "Magic Chamber." The "Music and Song" part of the entertainment included daily symphony concerts, no fewer than ten other orchestras and bands playing on any given day, mass chorus singing on two different stages, and a music center consisting of a "room for musical games," a "gramophone-record listening room," and "a room for individual music lovers" with free tutoring sessions. Theater options included an open-air ("green") theater for 20,000 spectators, an indoor theater for 1,270 spectators, a music theater for 1,500 spectators, a small drama theater, a circus (two shows daily), and a children's theater.[7]

Theater was everywhere: in kindergartens, schools, parks, and family apartments, as well as in theaters. Actors and directors from prominent Moscow theaters were objects of adoration, subjects of gossip, and constant recipients of dinner invitations from those prominent enough to hope for a response. "Going out" at night usually meant going to the Bolshoi, Maly, Art, Vakhtangov, or, less commonly, to the Chamber or New theaters. Most preferred the nineteenth-century repertoire; few cared for Meyerhold; and almost all considered it a duty, as well as pleasure, to go to the ballet (at the Bolshoi, top nomenklatura members and their families were entitled to seats in the royal box).

On September 24, 1934, Arosev had a day off that included both Gorky Park and the ballet, among other things:

> Sent children off to Gorky Park. Dressed, washed, and played with son.
>
> Picked up children and took to theater (*Carmen*). Left children there—then went to bookstores. Bought lots of interesting books. Especially happy about Petrarch.
>
> Went to CPC [Council of People's Commissars] cafeteria. Telephoned Kaganovich, but he'd already left for work. Called the Kremlin, but he hadn't arrived yet.
>
> Picked up girls. Took them to CPC cafeteria. Read Al. Tolstoy's *Peter I* in cafeteria library.
>
> Went home.
>
> Read some Petrarch. There's absolutely no one who doesn't grapple with the question of death!
>
> Went to ballet at Conservatory. Duncan Studio's Maria Borisova especially good. Very impressive woman.
>
> Read more Petrarch.[8]

At home, Arosev liked to direct his younger daughters, Olga and Elena, in home plays they produced together. (His eldest daughter, Natalia, lived with her mother and her new family in a communal apartment in a different building; Olga and Elena lived with him and their governess and maid; his son, Dima, lived with his mother in the apartment next door; Arosev split his time between his younger daughters and his new wife and son.) Feliks Kon liked to play charades with his wife and grown children; Osinsky's wife, Ekaterina Smirnova, and her children played "literary games."[9] Literary games came in a variety of forms. Arosev's daughters had a special bookshelf.

> He would put some books on the shelf, quite a few, and we were supposed to read them all by the end of the week. And not only that—we also had to report, either orally or in writing, on what we had read. That was to make sure we hadn't cheated by claiming to have read something we hadn't. But we didn't need to be forced. We loved to read and often read into the night. We used to go to bed late because we always waited up for Dad—and he often had receptions in the evening at VOKS. We used to listen for the elevator, try to figure out which floor it was stopping on, and then, when we heard his key in the lock, quickly jump into bed and pretend to be asleep. Dad would

come in thinking we were sleeping, give us a kiss, and then go over to Apartment 103 or straight to bed.[10]

Most fathers closely monitored their children's reading, which included the same books they had read themselves in prison and exile (and continued to reread), in a particular order. Osinsky, according to his daughter, Svetlana, "was very strict about it, and did not allow us to take books off the shelves without his permission. Only once, I remember, I . . . there was no one in his study, and he wasn't supposed to be coming back, so I got Dante down and was looking through the *Divine Comedy* with those scary pictures by Doré. And just at that moment, he walked in. But instead of yelling, he said, well . . . when the time comes, we'll read Dante."[11]

"We'll read Dante" might mean either "I'll tell you when the time comes to read Dante," or "I'll read Dante to you when the time comes." Reading aloud was an old form of noble—and, later, intelligentsia—sociability, an important way of establishing and maintaining spiritual intimacy between friends and lovers and within families. It had also been a part of the Old Bolshevik prison and exile experience. Osinsky had first listened to his father reading aloud and then read aloud to his fellow reading-circle members and later to his lover, Anna Shaternikova (their relationship had continued into the 1930s). Now it was his children's turn:

> Not too frequently, but not so infrequently either, he would read aloud to us. We had our own special ritual. We would sit down on the couch, and the three of us took turns sitting next to him. He would prepare a special drink, which we called "wine" (I think it was probably watered-down fruit syrup), and give each of us a little glass. He would open the book, and total bliss followed. Afterward, we would always beg: "Keep reading, Dad!" and Dad never ignored our pleas. . . . I remember reading Jules Verne. Huge, heavy atlases in leather bindings would be opened up before us so that we could trace the routes of the ships and look for the places where the Mysterious Island might be or where Captain Grant's children had come ashore. Dad read Dickens to us. We particularly loved *Great Expectations* with its funny beginning, and Joe Gargery's famous words to young Pip, "WOT LARX," became a household saying.[12]

The Osinskys also read Pushkin, Gogol, Nekrasov, Turgenev, Tolstoy, Dostoevsky, Chekhov, Korolenko, Longfellow, Victor Hugo, Alphonse Daudet, E.T.A. Hoffmann, Heine, Oscar Wilde, and Kipling, among others. Kerzhentsev, who had debated Osinsky at Moscow Gymnasium No. 7 in 1905, read Dickens, Pushkin, and Gogol to his daughter, Natalia. Arosev read Gogol's *Dead Souls* to his daughters the day before taking them to see the Art Theater's adaptation of the novel on May 30, 1935, which was a day off. The director of the Archive of the People's Commissariat of Foreign Affairs and former Soviet trade representative in Turkey, Akim Yuriev (Apt. 467), read Gibbon to his daughter.[13] He may have gotten the idea from everyone's favorite writer:

> "Bought him at a sale," said Mr Boffin. "Eight wollumes. Red and gold. Purple ribbon in every wollume, to keep the place where you leave off. Do you know him?"
>
> "The book's name, sir?" inquired Silas.
>
> "I thought you might have know'd him without it," said Mr Boffin slightly disappointed. "His name is Decline-And-Fall-Off-The-Rooshan-Empire." (Mr Boffin went over these stones slowly and with much caution.)
>
> "Ay indeed!" said Mr Wegg, nodding his head with an air of friendly recognition.
>
> "You know him, Wegg?"
>
> "I haven't been not to say right slap through him, very lately," Mr Wegg made answer, "having been otherways employed, Mr Boffin. But know him? Old familiar declining and falling off the Rooshan? Rather, sir!"[14]

■ ■ ■

Having guests over for dinner was not common practice. Chess partners might come over in the evenings, but they tended to stay in the study. So would card (mostly Preferans) players, who were more numerous and usually stayed longer. The head of the Alcoholic Beverages Directorate, Abram Gilinsky, used to play with his deputies; the head of the Bookselling Directorate, David Shvarts, played with his brother, brother-in-law, and best friend, Aleksandr Kon (Feliks's son). While the men were playing, the women might go off to the theater or talk in the dining room. Card playing was particularly popular among NKVD officials. On his visits to Kiev, Sergei Mironov used to play with the deputy head of the Ukrainian NKVD, Z. B. Katsnelson. Agnessa, who liked going to Kiev to shop, normally came with him.[15]

> We went over to Balitsky's deputy's house every day. Mirosha really enjoyed those visits and would sit up half the night playing cards for money. The three of them—Balitsky's deputy, Mirosha, and another high official—played for high stakes. Balitsky didn't take part in the game and didn't even know about it. They would sit in the study, while we wives sat in the living room and gossiped about everyone we knew for lack of anything better to do.

Sometimes, late in the evening, Mirosha would rush in:

"Aga, give me some money!"

That meant he was losing. I would give it to him—what else could I do? But I'd be furious. There went all my big shopping plans! Sometimes he'd gamble all our money away in one night. We'd leave, and I'd start in on him:

"How could you lose so much?!"

But he would just chuckle:

"Don't worry, you'll get it all back."

And, amazingly enough, I would. The next day Mirosha would bring me money—lots of money.

It turned out that Mironov had been losing on purpose and that, soon after each loss, he would receive a special reward from Katsnelson for good service.[16]

But then Ezhov became the people's commissar of internal affairs, his friend Frinovsky became his deputy, and *his* friend Mironov became the head of the NKVD Directorate of West Siberia, where the local Party boss, Robert Eikhe (Roberts Eihe), was afraid of him. Neither Mironov, nor Agnessa, had to lose to anyone anymore.

In Novosibirsk we were given the former governor-general's mansion. A guard was posted at the gate to protect us.

We had a huge garden with a stage, where local actors used to perform for us. There was also a separate little house for billiards, and, inside the mansion itself, a film screening room that had been built especially for us. As the first lady of the city, I got to choose from a list which film I wanted to see that day.

I had my own "court" and was surrounded by "ladies-in-waiting"—the wives of the top brass. Who to invite and who not to invite was my decision, and they all competed for my favor. And though I might ask for their opinion, I was the one who chose the films.

Sometimes, as we sat in the viewing room watching a film, the "toadies" would come in with fruit and cakes. Of course, you're right, that's not the right word. "Servants" would be more accurate, but I used to call them "toadies"—they always tried so hard to please and anticipate our every wish. They were constantly hovering around. These days they're called the "help" (rather than "servants," like in the old days).

They would sometimes bring in these cakes—do you know them? They had ice cream inside and were covered in flaming alcohol, but you could eat them without getting burned. Just imagine all those little blue lights glowing in the darkened room. Of course I didn't eat them very often myself. I was always watching my weight and mostly ate only oranges.[17]

In the House of Government, such displays were physically impossible and socially unacceptable; even simple dinner parties were rare. There were some exceptions, however. The Shvarts and the Gaisters were friends and frequently invited each other for dinner. Both families, with similar lower-class Pale of Settlement roots, were large, loud, successful, and sociable. At one point, the Gaisters' maid got tired of having to deal with so many last-minute dinner invitations and left them to work for the commander of the Soviet Air Force, Yakov (Jēkabs) Alksnis, who lived in Apt. 100, one floor above Aron Gaister's brother, Semen (Siunia). She returned one month later, probably because she missed the Gaister children, whom she had raised. Another frequent host was Karl Radek, who was known for his eccentricity and, according to Elina Kisis, his poodle, Devil, who used to greet all the visitors to his apartment. "If the guests did not immediately remove their hats, Devil would jump up from behind and come down with a hat between his teeth. He was always given a seat at the dinner table and a plate of food that he would carefully munch on." According to Elina Kisis, Radek's daughter Sofia "was a glamorous girl. She had all kinds of admirers, mostly pilots. Sometimes they got drunk and threw up in the bathroom."[18]

Writers liked to stage large gatherings complete with public readings. They were also—along with famous actors and artists—in constant demand as celebrity guests at government receptions and birthday parties for nomenklatura officials. Koltsov was a regular at many of them, often several in one evening. Arosev, who could not stand Koltsov, was, too—both as a fiction writer and as head of the All-Union Society for Cultural Ties with Foreign Countries (VOKS). October 24, 1934, exactly one month after Arosev bought his volume of Petrarch, was another day off:

> Went to see Dimitrov. Raskolnikov also there. Dimitrov serious, charming, and dressed in military uniform that doesn't suit him. He has beautiful hands, truly beautiful. Discussed Bulgarian affairs. Went home. Barbusse and Gosset already there.
>
> The Raskolnikovs arrived. Had warm and friendly conversation about fascist atrocities. Barbusse cited many facts. About last days of our own Russian Revolution, I took lead. Mentioned so many interesting facts, our French visitors demanded I write it all up and have it translated.
>
> Wouldn't mind—except editors illiterate and have blunted sense of beauty.
>
> At 9 p.m., after Barbusse and Gosset left, wife and I went to Tarasov-Rodionov's. Usual crowd there. Also Kamenev, wonderful pianist named Lugovskoy, and Comrade Chinenov (former soldier, wonderful fellow, and sensitive revolutionary—very modest), who's leaving for Far East and came to say goodbye to me. Pianist played well. Especially Liszt piece dedicated to "Lyon Weavers' Revolt." I did

dramatic readings of Chekhov and Zoshchenko and made such an impression that Kamenev began reciting Voloshin's poetry (in usual monotone, but with some embellishments).[19]

Dimitrov, the star of the Reichstag Fire Trial, had recently arrived to a hero's welcome and embarked on a campaign against Piatnitsky's "Third Period" policy of restoring sectarian purity within the Comintern. His wife had committed suicide in Moscow the year before, while he was still in prison in Berlin. Two weeks after Arosev came to see him, he was joined by Rosa Fleischmann, a Viennese journalist (originally from Moravia) whom he had met in 1927. She stayed on to become his second wife, Roza Yulievna Dimitrova (in Apt. 249 and later Apt. 235). Fedor Raskolnikov (Larisa Reisner's first husband) had just been named Soviet ambassador to Bulgaria. The novelist Henri Barbusse was writing a biography of Stalin; the journalist Hélène Gosset was trying to get an interview with Stalin; the writer Tarasov-Rodionov had been a literary ally of Arosev's in the 1920s (his much-debated 1922 novella, "Chocolate," was about the emasculation of Chekists by the feminine sweetness of NEP).[20]

Arosev had long wanted to be an actor, as well as a writer, and often performed in front of his friends and colleagues. On March 10, 1937, after a long day at work, he came home, signed a life insurance policy, discussed his daughter Olga's cold with her doctor, and then walked over to Serafi-movich's apartment. Other guests included the Spanish ambassador, the Spanish poet Rafael Alberti, the painter Petr Konchalovsky, and the writer Stepan Skitalets. "We sang, danced, and performed dramatic readings. Came home at 2 a.m. Only positive thing, I think, was that I recited Maya-kovsky and Chekhov. That always makes me feel brave and honest about myself. Skitalets told me I read more expressively than a professional actor. Especially 'The Thinker.' My 'Thinker' is not funny, but frightening.

Aleksandr Arosev reciting Chekhov

'Chekhov himself had no idea he'd created such a devil,' Skitalets said. 'It's the devil who tempts his "interlocutor."'"[21]

Serafimovich continued to run his circle for former proletarian writers and amateur singers. "I have known few people," wrote Fedor Gladkov, "with the same passion for friendly gatherings and the same need for constant human companionship. When friends were over, he would always be the one to start singing. He sang with pleasure and abandon—and would get very annoyed if anyone sat silently off to the side. 'Sing, by god, sing! All together now!' he would bellow, and start waving his arms around like a conductor." Elena Usievich, who once made common cause with Serafimovich against Leopold Averbakh, liked to host regular late-night poetry readings. One of her discoveries was Pavel Vasiliev, who was married to Gronsky's sister-in-law and often stayed in Gronsky's apartment, where some of the largest gatherings took place. Gronsky's job was "to guide the work of the Soviet and foreign intelligentsia" on Stalin's behalf. His most frequent guests were the realist (AKhRR) painters Isaak Brodsky, Boris Ioganson, Evgeny Katsman, Viktor Perelman, Vasily Svarog, and Pavel Radimov (who was also a poet) and the poets Sergei Gorodetsky, Aleksandr Zharov, and Pavel Vasiliev. Another frequent guest and one of the top Soviet officials was Valerian Kuibyshev. According to Gronsky's wife Lydia,

He would come over not only to converse with artists and poets, but also just to relax. He particularly enjoyed hearing the Svarogs sing.

The painter Vasily Semenovich Svarog and his wife Larisa were frequent guests at our place. He would bring his guitar or banjo, and they would sing Neapolitan songs. Later he presented Valerian Vladimirovich with a knee-length portrait of Larisa, beautifully painted in a broad style—with Larisa in a dark dress with a bright shawl over her shoulders. The Svarogs' visits were like holidays for me: with singing, conversations about socialist realism, and the rejection of everything alien: formalism, naturalism, etc.[22]

Another one of Lydia's favorites was Pavel Radimov. Once she visited him in his studio behind the altar of a church on Nikolskaia Street, near Red Square. He almost ruined the experience by offering to get a bottle of wine, but she did not hold it against him—so "sunny and joyous" was his art. She remembered his first meeting with Kuibyshev in their apartment:

All three painter friends—Radimov, Katsman, and Perelman—were sitting around the table, as usual. Kuibyshev asked Radimov:

"What's your job? What do you do?"

"I'm a poet," Radimov answered.

"What kind of poet?"

"The peasant kind."

Kuibyshev filled a glass of vodka and handed it to Radimov, who, without hesitating, knocked it back with a satisfied grunt.

"Now I can see you really are the peasant kind," said Kuibyshev, with a laugh.[23]

Radimov was a priest's son; Kuibyshev, an officer's. In May 1933, Stalin wrote to Gronsky accusing him of abetting Kuibyshev's drinking. Gronsky responded by saying that the purpose of the parties at his place was "to use the conversations between Communists and non-Party people in order to recruit the non-Party ones and draw them into the Party." The result was that "a large number of undecided non-Party people have been drawn to our side, the proof of which, in the case of the writers, can be found in their published works." As for Kuibyshev, continued Gronsky, he did not come over as often as he used to. "I used to see Comrade Kuibyshev more often, but after I noticed that he was drinking heavily, I decided to see less of him and, when I did see him, to discourage him from drinking so much. For example, if I went to his dacha, I would try to distract him from drinking by getting him involved in volleyball games. At my place (especially if he was already tipsy when he arrived), I would ask some of the comrades (his close friends) to keep him from drinking, and we would often succeed in getting him to switch to 'Napereuli' [Georgian wine] or tea."[24]

The problem was that many of Kuibyshev's friends, especially the painter, Svarog, were heavy drinkers themselves, and Gronsky was not sure he could be successful in the long run. More to the point, he was not sure he was the right man "to guide the work of the Soviet and foreign intelligentsia." His letter to Stalin ended with a confession and a plea:

I have established contacts with hundreds of people from the intelligentsia milieu. Many of them come to visit me, I visit many of them, and they all approach me with various requests, ask for advice, call me on the phone, write letters, etc., etc. It is a unique, important aspect of Party work that no one notices, but one that literally wears me out. Once I counted all the telephone calls I received, and it turned out that I was answering 100 to 200 calls a day. I could ignore them, but these people are extremely quick to take offense. If you miss a call, don't visit, or fail to invite them over from time to time, these people get their feelings hurt, and these feelings, unfortunately, can easily be transferred to the Party and the Soviet state, not to mention the literary organizations. Besides, they all squabble, scheme, gossip, flatter each other, and try to cobble together all kinds of opportunistic groups and caucuses. I need to delve into every aspect, keep track of all the petty intrigues, and continue to push my line, without antagonizing any of the writers or painters, but without making any concessions, either. I have never had a job that was so difficult and so devilishly complicated.

Valerian Kuibyshev   Ivan Gronsky, 1931

Even Voronsky and the RAPPists, "who had been specializing in literature and the arts for a number of years," had failed at it. He, a former
worker, had to master high culture even as he was supervising its fractious
practitioners. "Perhaps I am not suited for this job," he concluded. "If so, I
should be replaced by another comrade, but the work itself must go on
because it is, in effect, a struggle for the intelligentsia. If we do not lead
the intelligentsia, our enemies will. I can see it at every step."[25]

Gronsky kept his job for another year or so (before being replaced by
several comrades, including Stetsky and Kerzhentsev on the domestic
front and Arosev on the foreign one). Lydia Gronskaia's favorite memories
of the time they spent guiding the work of the Soviet and foreign intelligentsia were Sergei Obraztsov's puppet show in their apartment ("I remember a basso profundo doll with an endlessly stretchable neck, but the
real sensation was a song 'We're Just Friends,' performed by two little
dogs"); a party for about thirty guests at which Tolstoy's granddaughter,
Anna Ilinichna, played the guitar and sang romances ("melancholy yearning and wild abandon flowed freely, enchanting the grateful audience");
and a small soiree in Petr Konchalovsky's studio:

> We were drinking cognac. The dinner-table conversation was very
> interesting. It was about art. It was easy to follow and interesting.
> Not like the political discussions, which bored me. Gorodetsky's
> wife, Nympha Alekseevna—a beautiful, statuesque woman—did not
> join in the conversation, as I recall. I watched these people with
> wide-eyed awe. If I remember correctly, Petr Petrovich began sing-
> ing "Don't Tempt Me in Vain," and I got up the courage to sing along.
> He looked surprised, gave me a big smile, and walked over and sat
> down at the piano. The two of us (I was shy at first, but then grew
> more confident) sang the entire romance.[26]

There were other House residents with artistic connections and bohemian inclinations. Khalatov, the former head of the publishing directorate,
and Yakov Doletsky (Jakób Dolecki/Fenigstein), the head of the Soviet

Vasily Svarog, *I. V. Stalin and the Members of Politburo in
Gorky Park, Surrounded by Children*

Telegraph Agency (TASS), were, according to Gronsky, old drinking partners of Kuibyshev and Svarog. (Svarog painted portraits of Khalatov's and
Arosev's daughters, as well as Kuibyshev and other Party leaders. His best-
known painting was *I. V. Stalin and the Members of Politburo in Gorky Park,
Surrounded by Children*.) Khalatov's cousin, who had a room in his House
apartment, was an Art Theater actress and later a radio announcer. Doletsky's friend, Romuald Muklevich, liked to entertain artists and hung
their paintings on his walls. All of them, and many others, had friends
among the theater actors.[27]

■ ■ ■

Most adult House residents led quiet lives within their families, with
guests coming over a few times a year, on special occasions. The most
common special occasions were birthdays, celebrated by most adults and
all children. The other rites of passage—weddings and funerals, as well as
Pioneer, Komsomol, and Party induction ceremonies—were normally conducted outside the home, although the Gaisters did organize a wedding
party for Aron's brother-in-law, Veniamin Kaplan (Rakhil's brother). Perhaps the only ones to have had a "proper" wedding with elements of the
traditional East Slavic rural ceremony were Sergei Mironov and Agnessa
Argiropulo, (neither of whom came from a rural East Slavic background).
The reason they could do it was that they were not yet living in the House
of Government.

> For several years after Mirosha and I left Rostov, my husband, Zar-
> nitsky, waited for me, believing that I would return. But after five
> years he asked for a divorce because he wanted to remarry.
>   All the marriage registry offices in Dnepropetrovsk Province
> were under Mirosha's control, so one day he summoned a registry

office employee to our house. That employee dissolved my marriage to Zarnitsky and Mirosha's to his wife Gusta (in those days both spouses did not have to be present) and then married Mirosha and me. The whole thing—two divorces and one marriage—took half an hour to complete.

V. A. Balitsky
(Courtesy of Nikita Petrov)

Soon afterwards Mirosha had to go to Kiev, and I always tried to accompany him. We arrived in Kiev, but news of our marriage had arrived before us, and everyone kept congratulating us. V. A. Balitsky, the People's Commissar of Internal Affairs of Ukraine, kept laughing and demanding a wedding.

It all happened so quickly I didn't even have time to order a white dress. Balitsky gave us some money for the wedding—government money, of course, what else? They used to hand it out in envelopes in those days, you know. The place they picked out for the wedding was an NKVD dacha on the bank of the Dnieper. They thought of everything! Their people did a brilliant job organizing it all—everyone wanted to have a good time.

There was still the problem of the dress . . . One woman offered me her wedding dress, but it had already been worn! So I politely refused.

I ended up wearing a light green dress trimmed with gold buttons, but nobody seemed to mind. Everyone was having a great time. They wanted us to kiss, but when Mirosha told them we'd been married for twelve years—six years of living together without a license and six years of "underground apprenticeship," they all started shouting at once: "To hell with the underground apprenticeship! We don't want to hear about it! We want the rest of your life to begin now. And for you to be newlyweds!"

Everyone really wanted it to be like the real thing.

I had to carry around a tray with a glass of vodka while everyone sang: "Whose turn is it to empty the glass?" I would go up to each man in turn, and he would drink the vodka, kiss me, and place some money on the tray.

When I got to Balitsky—a handsome man, tall, strapping, blond, a regular Siegfried—they sang their song and waited. What would happen next? I knew that Balitsky liked me, but his wife was sitting right beside him. She was a pathetic, mean little thing and never took her eyes off him for a moment. He downed the vodka in one gulp, but with her glaring at him, he didn't dare kiss me—though he did put a silver ruble on the tray. At that time, they were very rare.

After the banquet everyone started shouting: "Lock them in the bedroom"—and they did. But I begged them to let me out, saying that Mironov would fall asleep as soon as his head hit the pillow (he used to get very tired), and that I wanted to go on having fun with the rest of them. So they let me out.

That's how, in the summer of 1936, I became Mironov's legal wife.[28]

The next-most-common special occasion—and by far the most popular public holiday—was New Year's Eve. German-style Christmas celebrations had spread in Russia in the 1840s and quickly become the center of the annual cycle for urban families and a life-defining experience for noble and bourgeois children. The Orthodox Church had protested repeatedly, and traditional peasant celebrations remained largely unaffected, but most turn-of-the-century urbanites had grown up with the regular rite of midnight magic associated with the domesticated version of the *axis mundi*. (Tchaikovsky's *Nutcracker*, which premiered in St. Petersburg in 1892, followed a well-established mythic pattern.) Bolshevism, like all new faiths, viewed competing sacred calendars as pagan superstitions and campaigned vigorously against them. During the reconstruction period of the late 1920s, the Christmas tree was, in effect, banned, although some true-believer families, including the Kerzhentsevs and the Mikhailovs, continued to decorate fir trees for their children (correctly assuming, one suspects, that the E.T.A. Hoffmann and Hans Christian Andersen versions they had grown up with had little to do with the cult of baby Jesus). The official position was clarified in late 1935. According to Khrushchev (who lived in Apt. 206),

One day Stalin called me and said: "Get over to the Kremlin. The Ukrainians are here. I want you to take them around Moscow and show them the city." I immediately went over there. Kosior, Posty-shev, and Liubchenko were with Stalin.... "They want to see Moscow," said Stalin. "Let's go." We walked out and climbed into Stalin's car. We all managed to squeeze in. We talked as we drove around.... At some point, Postyshev asked: "Comrade Stalin, wouldn't a Christmas tree celebration be a good tradition, one that would appeal to the people and bring joy, especially to the children? We've been condemning it, but why not give the tree back to the children?" Stalin agreed: "Take the initiative, publish your suggestion to give the tree back to the children in the press, and we'll support you."[29]

On December 28, 1935, *Pravda* published Postyshev's letter, itself based on a familiar Hans Christian Andersen image, but substituting "New Year" for Christmas:

In prerevolutionary times, the bourgeoisie and their officials always staged New Year Tree celebrations for their children. The children of the workers would look on with envy through the windows at the tree ablaze with gaily colored lights and the rich men's children making merry around it.

Why do our schools, orphanages, kindergartens, children's clubs, and palaces of young pioneers deprive the children of the Soviet working class of this wonderful joy? Some deviationists, probably of the "left" variety, have labeled this children's entertainment a bourgeois invention.

It is time we put an end to this improper condemnation of the New Year Tree, which is a wonderful entertainment for children. Komsomol members and Young Pioneer instructors should stage mass New Year Tree celebrations for children. Children's New Year Tree celebrations must take place everywhere—in schools, orphanages, palaces of young pioneers, children's clubs, and children's theaters and movie theaters. There should not be a single kolkhoz where the governing board, together with the Komsomol members, does not organize a New Year's Eve party for its children. Municipal councils, heads of district executive committees, rural soviets, and local public education offices must help stage New Year Tree celebrations for the children of our great socialist Motherland.[30]

The celebrations were duly held in all the towns and kolkhozes. As Maia Peterson wrote to her father, who had recently been removed from his position as commandant of the Kremlin and transferred to Kiev: "Comrade Postyshev ordered all the children to decorate a New Year tree." (Maia's brother Igor had made a red star with a little light bulb inside to put on top of their tree.)[31]

New Year's Eve quickly became the most popular Soviet holiday—an elaborate, state-managed public production reflected and replicated in every home. For most Russian intelligentsia members and their peers from rich men's families, it was, indeed, a return. For most Jewish Bolsheviks, it was a welcome substitute for the rejected family traditions. For most ordinary Soviets, it was a "Christmas" miracle. (The Little Match Girl lit a match—and "there she was sitting under the most magnificent Christmas tree: it was still larger, and more decorated than the one which she had seen through the glass door in the rich merchant's house. Thousands of lights were burning on the green branches, and gaily-colored pictures, such as she had seen in the shop-windows, looked down upon her.") The only House residents who did not celebrate New Year's Eve were those former workers who had remained workers in taste and habit. Among them were the families of the prize-winning foreman Mikhail Tuchin (who now worked in Gorky Park and often came home drunk or not at all) and the "barely literate and politically underdeveloped baker," Boris Ivanov. Ivanov's wife, Elena Zlatkina, was perhaps unique among the House of Government Jewish residents in showing little interest in upward mobility by way of cultural imitation. One of her brothers, Ilya Zlatkin, became a diplomat, and later, a prominent historian of Mongolia; she, even in retirement, remained a seamstress alongside her husband, who was still a baker. Tuchin's and Ivanov's daughters were close friends; Zinaida Tuchina, whose parents were never home during the day, often ate with the Ivanovs.[32]

One year after Postyshev's decree was issued, People's Commissar of Internal Trade Izrail Veitser organized a New Year tree bazaar in downtown Moscow. He asked his wife, Natalia Sats, to direct the festivities:

> It was the winter holidays at the end of December 1936. There were New Year trees everywhere—in shop windows, in the arms of passers-by, red-cheeked from the cold—and everyone was preparing for a joyful New Year's Eve celebration. But it was at its most joyful on Manege Square, near the Kremlin, where, right before your eyes, a fairytale town emerged: huts on chicken legs, a gingerbread house, the house of the puppet girl Malvina, a fir-tree forest, an open-air zoo, a children's "airport" with hot-air balloons taking off with their little passengers, and a huge, twenty-meter-high New Year tree decorated with wonderful ornaments. You could pick out Buratino in his bright cap, the Swan-Princess, the Golden Fish, and other characters from popular children's theater shows. They were not hard to spot: these ornaments were the size of small children, and they stood out gaily among the glittering decorations and bright lights of the New Year tree, so resplendent in its green velvet robe.[33]

Buratino and Malvina were both characters from Aleksei Tolstoy's deliberately unfaithful 1935 adaptation of *The Adventures of Pinocchio*. True to the new amusement park image of Soviet childhood, Tolstoy's *The Golden Key* tried to be more entertaining and less moralistic: the new hero Buratino was to Pinocchio what Huck Finn had been to Tom Sawyer (two other Soviet childhood favorites). At the end of the story, Buratino does not become human: he redefines himself as a puppet in his own theater. Natalia Sats's first production in her theater's new building on Sverdlov Square was a show based on *The Golden Key*. She had spent several months trying to persuade Tolstoy to adapt it for her theater and finally succeeded by supplying his new wife (and former secretary) with foreign fashion magazines. Natalia Sats's Children's Theater (saved by Koltsov, renamed the "Central," and reborn next to the Bolshoi on the spot where Doubting Makar begins his journey through Moscow) represented the end of Buratino's quest: a theater of free, self-directed puppets. The text was serialized in *Pionerskaia Pravda*, and some critics compared the adventures of Buratino to Hubert's travels in Wonderland. The show premiered on December 10, 1936, about two weeks before the opening of the first New Year's Eve Bazaar and about a two-minute walk away.[34]

On December 31, Veitser, as usual, worked all day. Natalia waited for him in their House apartment. "He came home late—and froze in amazement. I had bought and decorated a little New Year tree and lit the candles. What happiness it is to do something for a man who can appreciate even the smallest sign of attention!"[35]

■ ■ ■

The most public of Soviet public holidays were the May 1 International Workers' Day and the November 7 Day of the Great October Socialist Revolution. On May 2, 1932, Adoratsky wrote to his daughter, Varia:

> On one side of the House of Government, at the top, we have Lenin's portrait, and on the other, Stalin is gazing out over the Moscow River. . . . The Stone Bridge has been decorated to look like one of the steamships that will arrive in Moscow after they finish the Moscow–Volga Canal, which will be 140 kilometers long and have 9 locks and four power stations (according to the inscription on the bridge).
>
> The street decorations and signs carried by the parade participants suggest that the whole production has been carefully planned and they make an extremely good impression with their perfect symmetry.[36]

The whole production had, indeed, been carefully planned. Preparations usually began about two months in advance. Plans were fulfilled, workers rewarded, rallies organized, streets cleaned, speeches scripted, signs painted, and parade marchers selected and instructed. According to the special "May Day" instructions issued in 1933 by the Party committee of Moscow's Lenin District, which included the House of Government, "all drafts of all decorations of all enterprises, offices, and educational institutions, streets, large shop windows, artistic installations, posters, photo exhibits etc., as well as everything to be carried by parade participants, their performances, floats, etc. must be approved by the district's Artistic Subcommittee." The House of Government was to decorate itself and the Big Stone Bridge; the theme of the bridge decoration was to be "Moscow's municipal economy." In preparation for the November 7 celebration in 1934, the House of Government administration spent 351.76 rubles on the repair, upholstering, and mounting of the three-meter-high wooden letters in "Long Live," and 403.49 rubles on the manufacture, upholstering, and mounting of the illuminated letters in "Worldwide October." The total for all the decoration work, not counting materials and including the construction of scaffolding, restoration of the portraits of Comrades Stalin and Kalinin, painting of new portraits of Comrades Lenin and Kaganovich, painting of 150 slogans and their placement on balconies, mounting of a ten-meter star on the club balcony, and hoisting of two flags on top of the building and 150 flags above the club, was 10,287.25 rubles (based on a special hardship rate "given the building's height and the particular inconvenience of having to carry out the work in a hanging position"). The overall decoration budget was 20,000 rubles; the shock worker bonus budget, 12,000 rubles.[37]

Shock workers were workers who consistently overfulfilled the plan. In the House of Government, it paid to be a shock worker: the average holiday bonus was approximately equal to a month's salary. In November 1935, the stairway cleaner Smorchkova and floor-polisher Barbosov received 80 rubles each, the painter Apollonov and laundress Kartoshkina, 100 rubles, and the "administrative-technical" employee Mokeev, 300 rubles. Mokeev's colleague, Mosienko, received only a diploma because he was just back from a free trip to a Crimean resort; the senior guard Emelian Ivchenko, who talked the lost Leningrad port employee, Anna, into a marriage of convenience, received 200 rubles (they had just had their first child, and Anna's mother had moved in to help). Altogether, out of the ninety-five people proposed by the various departments within the building, eighty-nine were approved by the "socialist competition committee." The six rejected candidates were replaced by those whose "commitment to the cause has brought great benefits to our House." (Between October 1934 and September 1935, the proportion of shock workers among House staff members had increased from 34.1 percent to 43.9 percent. About one-third of them received holiday bonuses.) The House Party Committee Secretary M. A. Znot, Trade Union Committee Chairman K. I. Zhiltsov, and House Commandant V. A. Irbe and his two deputies could only be rewarded by the Central Executive Committee Housekeeping Department on the recommendation of the House Socialist Competition Committee. The committee duly recommended that, "taking into account their extraordinary management of a complex enterprise and large staff," they be rewarded "as our very best shock workers, who have achieved high marks in their management of the House."[38]

The festivities usually began the night before. According to Hubert's memoir of Wonderland,

> On the eve of May 1st [1934] on the streets of Moscow, one could hear the sound of hammers late into the night. The last nails were being driven in, wires suspended, and floodlights connected. At night the red cloth of the banners looked especially beautiful, illuminated by the white light. A forest of flags filled several squares.
>
> When it grew dark, long, multicolored beams of light from the floodlights appeared in the sky and lit up the city for much of the night. Factories, power stations, workers' clubs, and offices had been decorated with brightly colored electric lights. There were huge portraits of Lenin and Stalin hanging everywhere.

May First demonstration in front of the
Lenin Mausoleum on Red Square

Festive crowds swarmed through the streets to the sound of loud music, which was being transmitted over the radio at every corner and intersection. The whole city was taking part in the joyous celebration.[39]

Early the next morning, most House residents would go watch the parade. High nomenklatura members would have passes to Red Square (the higher the rank, the closer to Stalin); the rest would line up along the route or stroll around listening to the music and enjoying the festive decorations and celebrating crowds. Those who stayed behind (various guards, servants, old people, and some wives) would listen to the live radio broadcast. Adoratsky, who did have a pass, described the 1932 May Day parade in his May 2 letter to his daughter:

This year's parade was wonderful. It began, as usual, with Voroshilov, on a beautiful stallion, inspecting the troops (not only on Red Square but also on Resurrection Square and, I believe, the right side of Theater Square, as well). Next, he made a fifteen-minute speech and read the text of the oath, with each phrase being repeated by everyone standing in the square in a thousand vibrant voices. Then the cannons on Tainitskaia Tower fired their salutes (a lot of them— at least thirty salvoes), which sounded like thunder. After that, the marching columns appeared. First came the cadets from the Military Academy of the Red Army Command and the Central Executive

Committee School, Navy pilots, various infantry units, cavalrymen on foot, and even militiamen in their gray helmets and white gloves. Then came the student battalions in civilian dress with rifles slung over their backs and partisan units, which included some gray-beards. Next came the Komsomol battalions in gray tunics and Komsomol girls wearing the red scarves of the communications services. Then came the units with German shepherds (they serve, too). Next came the horse-drawn artillery, then artillery on trucks, then APCs, tanks of different kinds, and radio stations that looked like carriages with radio transmitters mounted on the roof. Above the tanks more than a hundred airplanes, including some five-engine giants, were flying in neat formations.[40]

The Bolshevik public holidays marked key moments in the Bolsheviks' private lives. The history of the Party and the biographies of faithful Party members were, in theory and in personal recollections, one and the same thing. Bolsheviks who were also close friends were Bolsheviks who had experienced key moments in Party history at the same time and in the same way. The May Day celebrations in forest clearings on the eve of the real day had been celebrations of shared faith as shared youth ("we are the young spring's messengers, she has sent us on ahead"); the October Revolution was to be the birth of the new world and the rebirth of its messengers.

Nikolai Podvoisky and his wife Nina Didrikil had met at a May Day celebration in 1905, when he was twenty-five and she was twenty-three. By October 1917, when he, as the chairman of the Petrograd Military-Revolutionary Committee, was guiding "the stormy stream" toward the Winter Palace, they already had three children. On April 28, 1933, Nikolai wrote to his wife from the House of Government:

> My darling, darling, darling Ninochka, pride of my heart and our mighty fortress! I am sending you a great big hug from home (the biggest possible), kisses, and, once again, congratulations on our military parade day.... It is with great pride that I will stand on Red Square on May 1, sensing your presence, your shoulder next to mine, and our two Bolshevik hearts beating in unison. I will rejoice in the knowledge that, since May 1, 1905, you and I have always stood together and cut through the elements and through the waves aligned against the proletariat: by force of arms, when necessary; when not, with words, by example, or through study.[41]

All successfully routinized new faiths graft their sacred chronology onto the natural cycle of eternal return and the personal life cycle of individual believers. The Bolsheviks had done well on the first score: the two great revolutionary holidays—November 7 and May 1—invoked traditional harvest (Thanksgiving, Pokrov, Sukkot) and spring rebirth (Easter, Passover, Nowruz) festivals, with New Year's Eve joining them later as Postyshev's winter equinox miracle. The second requirement—the extension of the universal chronology into the home and the transformation of family rites into state-regulated sacraments—remained unfulfilled. As Trotsky had written in 1926, "in the most important spheres, the revolutionary symbols of the workers' state are innovative, clear, and powerful. . . . But in the closed-off cells of family life, these new elements are almost nonexistent—or too few, at any rate." Ten years later, they were still too few or nonexistent: what had changed was that no one worried about them anymore. In 1926, Koltsov had written that whereas he, "a progressive person free of prejudices," did not need home reinforcement for his revolutionary faith, the "laborers lost in the forests" might benefit from dressing up their baptisms, weddings, and funerals in new Soviet garb. But with the triumph of the First Five-Year Plan and the inauguration of Bolshevik Augustinianism, no one was lost in the forests anymore, and no one tried to connect family rites of passage to the official canon (the way Jews and Christians do). The socialist "base" had been laid; the appropriate "superstructure" would arise by itself. Marxism had left the Party with no instructions concerning the "closed-off cells of family life," and the Party offered no guidance to the cells. Everyone was lost in the forests, but on the threshold of a new era, it did not matter.

In the House of Government, as elsewhere, virtuous home behavior had to be improvised. No one knew what to do after the May Day military parade was over. Osinsky, for one, did nothing at all: he used to bring his children home from Red Square and then resume his usual study routine (or sneak out to see Shaternikova). Neither, at the other end of the class spectrum, did the prize-winning foreman Mikhail Tuchin and his wife, Tatiana. The biggest day of the year for them was Tatiana's saint's day. Relatives (but not friends or apartment neighbors) would come over, drink a lot of vodka, and eat Tatiana's pies, *vatrushki* (pastries with sweet cheese), jellied meat and fish, and assorted pickles (which she made herself). Another—much smaller—holiday was Easter, complete with the traditional Easter breads (*kulichi*) and sweet cheese dessert (*paskha*). On regular days off, Tuchin read newspapers, books about Cossacks, and adventure stories, while Tatiana made pies and read *Health* and *Female Worker* magazines. It is not known whether the stairway cleaner Smorchkova, floor-polisher Barbosov, painter Apollonov, or laundress Kartoshkina celebrated any of the three great Soviet holidays.[42]

The Rykovs followed the turning-Christmas-into-New Year's model by moving Easter to May Day. Their maid, Anna Matveevna (an experienced domestic who had, as she put it, "worked in good homes," including Zinaida Morozova's) would use eighty egg yolks to make a large batch of *kulichi*: a huge one for the entire family, a large one for the father, a medium-size one for the mother, and small ones for each of the children. "It was, as they say, a sacred ritual in our home," according to Natalia Rykova. "We were not allowed to run or to bang doors for any reason, or else the dough might fall." The Ivanovs celebrated May 1 by combining Easter, Soroki (the traditional rural spring festival), and Passover meals: Boris did the baking, while Elena made gefilte fish. The same dishes, except for the special spring "lark" cookies, were served on Revolution Day.[43]

But most House residents found "religious" trappings inappropriate and potentially polluting. They either did nothing at all or staged generic feasts without ritual references to the nature of the occasion (except for a toast or two). Kira Allilueva describes the special feasts her mother (and Stalin's sister-in-law) Evgenia used to prepare:

> We did not make a cult of food in our household, but we did enjoy eating. Mother used to bake Novgorod meat and cabbage pies to go with the chicken soup. They were huge, almost half the size of the table. She would put the dough and the yeast in an enamel bucket and cover it with a cloth napkin. We children would watch, and when it began creeping up trying to escape, we would shout excitedly: "Mommy, the dough is rising! It's getting out!"
>
> The appetizers always included herring with green onions. And my mother used to make a delicious tomato and onion salad: she would squeeze a lemon over it or add some sunflower oil and vinegar and pepper. And we always had mushrooms—ones we had gathered ourselves at our dacha in Zubalovo.
>
> Of the drinks, I remember light wines, Armenian brandy, vodka, liqueurs, and a sweet vodka infusion called "Zapekanka." There was also a punch that my mother made by mixing white wine with pineapple and sour-cherry juice.
>
> Afterward, they would take their time drinking tea from cups and saucers. A samovar heated with pine cones would stand on a tray with a little teapot on top. For dessert my mother used to make delicious, sweet saffron pretzels. The dough would turn an incredible yellowish-green color because of the nutmeg and vanilla she added. Good cakes were sold in the stores, too, but I did not eat them because of the icing. And, besides, why would I want them if I could have my mother's sweet pretzels?
>
> After the meal, they would usually dance. The rooms in our apartment were so big we did not even have to move the table. They danced to a phonograph. We had brought a lot of records from Germany with tangos, fox trots, the Boston Waltz, and the Charleston. In those days, everyone knew how to dance. It was the fashion.
>
> My father never danced, though, and neither did Stalin. On such occasions, Iosif Vissarionovich always urged Redens: "Stakh, dance with Zhenia. You dance so beautifully together!"[44]

Stanislav (Stanislaw) Redens, the son of a Polish cobbler and the husband of Anna Allilueva (the sister of Stalin's wife Nadezhda and Evgenia's husband, Pavel), was a top-ranking secret police official: head of the Ukrainian OGPU/GPU in 1931–33 (during collectivization and the famine) and head of the Moscow Province NKVD since 1934. According to his son, Vladimir, he was "an outgoing, friendly person, easy to get along with. He had a pleasant appearance: soft facial features, curly hair, and a trim, athletic physique. He was charming and popular, especially with women."[45]

Stanislav Redens
(Courtesy of Nikita Petrov)

The Alliluev holiday feasts seem to have been typical of what high-nomenklatura House residents did on special occasions. Food was plentiful but simple, prepared mostly by peasant maids according to peasant recipes: beet, cabbage, and chicken soups and, as the standard festive dish, meat, mushroom, and cabbage pies. Osinsky liked kasha; Arosev and Kraval liked Siberian dumplings; and Romuald Muklevich (a Pole from Suprasl, outside of Bialystok) liked potato pancakes, fried pork, and boiled potatoes sprinkled with bacon cracklings and fried onions. The most popular salad was the traditional Russian "vinegret" (made of boiled beets, carrots, eggs, and potatoes with pickles, onions, and sauerkraut), but some cooks experimented with newer recipes. (Nadezhda Smilga-Poluian's culinary mentor was her longtime admirer, the famous Art Theater actor, Nikolai Khmelev.) Vodka was always around (Rykov prepared a special orange-peel infusion known as "Rykovka" and had a shot before lunch every day), but most people preferred Crimean and, less frequently, Georgian wines (wines tended to be sweet, and it was increasingly common to be a connoisseur). Dessert consisted of tea with cakes and chocolates and, occasionally, liqueurs. (Muklevich and his Polish friends drank coffee.) Most men and some of the women smoked a great deal—as a sign of both harried self-denial at work and bodily pleasure at the dinner table. The most popular cigarette brand was Herzegovina Flor, which Stalin favored. Ivan Kraval followed Stalin's example of unrolling the cigarettes and using the tobacco to fill his pipe.[46]

Dancing the tango and foxtrot to phonograph records brought from abroad was, indeed, the fashion. (Everyone's favorite performers were the Russian émigrés Vertinsky and Leshchenko.) Also common were more or less formal recitals by amateur and professional musicians, but the most popular conclusion to a festive dinner was the general singing of revolutionary hymns and Russian and Ukrainian folk songs. Osinsky, like Serafimovich, liked to conduct. (The "choir" usually consisted of his eldest son, Dima, and Dima's friends.) His favorite songs were "In Chains" and

"Martyred by Hard Servitude." Ivanov liked "Bravely, Comrades, March in Step"; Arosev liked "Twelve Bandits"; and Podvoisky (who used to be the choirmaster of the Chernigov Theological Seminary) liked traditional Ukrainian songs. The head of the Bookselling Directorate, David Shvarts, also liked Ukrainian songs. Once, when Shvarts was still living in the First House of Soviets, he and about ten of his friends and relatives went for an after-dinner walk through Manege Square. It was midnight, and they were singing Ukrainian songs. According to Shvarts's son, Vladimir, "they were all from Ukraine, after all. All Jews, all from Ukraine. They may even have been singing in Ukrainian. And then a militiaman came up to them and said: 'Citizens, you are disturbing the peace. You are being too loud.' Next to them was a row of coachmen waiting for passengers (there were no taxis then). So those coachmen intervened: 'Come on, let them sing. They are singing so well. Let them sing.'"[47]

16

THE HOUSES OF REST

An option not available to the Tuchins was to spend regular days off in "one-day rest homes" outside of Moscow. In 1935, the Housekeeping Department of the Central Executive Committee had about a dozen such homes, all of them prerevolutionary gentry and merchant estates. The usual practice was to arrive in the afternoon before the day off, spend the night, and leave on the following afternoon. This created obvious problems for the staff. According to the director of one of the most popular one-day rest homes, Morozovka, "it was not a regular rest home, some rooms were reserved for certain people, but we had no idea who would arrive, and when. A comrade might arrive at 2 in the morning. If his room was occupied, you couldn't send him back to Moscow, and then he would have a fit because his room was occupied."[1]

One such unhappy visitor to Morozovka was Arosev, who, in March 1935, complained to the Housekeeping Department. The head of the Section of Out-of-Town Properties, A. Chevardin, responded that, "in accordance with the established procedure, all comrades go there with the advance permission of the Housekeeping Department, depending on room availability." Arosev responded by forwarding "Chevardin's vacuous reply, which contains elements of rudeness and inaccuracy," to the department head, pointing out that established procedures varied by rank. "The comrades of my category, i.e., Old Bolsheviks and high officials, are included in the list of those who have permanent access to the Central Executive Committee rest homes and need no additional case-by-case permissions. I would appreciate not being discriminated against in this matter and being put on the appropriate list." Several weeks later, on May 17, 1935, Arosev arrived in Morozovka with his four children (to read *Dead Souls* to them and work on his diary) and was given a room, but "slept badly because the people who arrived at 2 in the morning banged their doors unceremoniously and talked loudly between the bathroom and their room, as if they were at home. Where does this shameless Russian parasitism come from?"[2]

For the most part, however, the staff were helpful; the rooms were ready; the house was quiet; and the food was good (although Adoratsky disapproved of the coffee). Located on the bank of the Kliazma River right off the Leningrad Highway, Morozovka—like Lenin's last refuge and Zbarsky's first house—used to belong to the Morozov merchant clan. The main building was an art nouveau version of a medieval gingerbread castle.

Morozovka

Lydia Gronskaia, like most House residents, used to enjoy going there: "Morozov's old house was tastefully appointed and cozy. I especially liked the library, with its stained-oak paneling, dark wooden ceilings, bookcases, and soft leather furniture. It was so cozy to curl up in a corner of the couch with a book! The billiard room was wonderful, too. I practiced a lot, and could even beat Ivan sometimes." Billiards was the most popular pastime for guests of all ages. The House of Government boys would learn how to play there, mostly from the servants, who had little else to do on weekdays, and then show off, and perhaps make some money, in the pool halls of the best Moscow hotels. Other pastimes included chess, Preferans (the card table, covered with green cloth, was on a round balcony, so no one could stand behind the players' backs), and various outdoor activities. Valerian Kuibyshev (according to his sister, Elena), liked to do certain tasks himself when he was there. He "planted trees, worked in the vegetable garden, took care of the rabbits, and cleaned the volleyball court." Winter was the high season, and the most popular activities were skiing and skating. The son of the deputy chairman (and, after 1938, chairman) of Intourist, Mikhail Korshunov, remembered one winter evening in Morozovka:

It was growing dark. The housekeeper had sounded the dinner gong. My father, mother, and I were sitting at one end of the long dining table, surrounded by chairs with high, carved backs. No one else had arrived—yet. Through the huge windows that reached almost to the floor, you could see the deepening shadows in the park and hear the knocking sound coming from the water tank. The water tank was down at the edge of the park, and the sound of the knocking emphasized the surrounding silence. The Schooner House seemed to float along in this silence. That was the name we had given to the house because it used to creak slightly in the wind: wooden, partially draped in canvas, and with its tiny towers, intricately curved balco-

Nikolai Podvoisky

nies, and decks, it resembled a sailing ship on the waves. At night, you would lie awake, listening, and dream of being at sea.[3]

Winter was high season in Morozovka (and other nearby rest homes) because in warmer seasons House residents could travel farther and stay away longer. The most popular destinations were the Black Sea resorts and the North Caucasus mineral spas. The most difficult problem—as in Morozovka, the House of Government, and throughout the Soviet Party-state—was to match ranked officials with ranked destinations amid fluid schedules, inconsistent hierarchies, and competing patronage claims. Only a few top officials close to Stalin had personal cottages reserved for them; all others had to hope for the best vacancy appropriate to their rank, connections, and persistence. On July 30, 1932, the head of the Sochi Group of CEC Rest Homes, Ivan Stepanovich Korzhikov (an experienced administrator and former director of the Second House of Soviets), wrote a routine report to the head of the CEC Housekeeping Department, Nikolai Ivanovich Pakhomov:

The other day Comrade Vlasik told me that Valery Ivanovich Mezhlauk had left Sochi in a huff, and that this news had reached the vacationer in Cottage 9. I already wrote to you once about this matter. This is basically what happened: on July 13, Comrade Mezhlauk's wife, Ekaterina Mikhailovna, arrived in Sochi. I personally met her at the railway station and told her that a room in Cottage 8 was ready for them, but she absolutely refused to go there. She refused to go to the "Riviera" as well, so I finally took her to Cottage 4, which happened to have a small room available. Two days later I transferred her to a larger room in the same cottage. For the next three days or so, she and some military man kept coming to see me, asking for a room in Cottage 2, but there was nothing I could do since there was not a single free room left. On July 19, Valery Ivanovich Mezhlauk himself arrived from Mukhalatka [another CEC resort in Crimea]. I saw him when he arrived, and he told me that he had come to pick up Ekaterina Mikhailovna and that they would both be leaving for Mukhalatka in two days. And that is exactly what they did: on July 21 they both left for Mukhalatka. . . . Ekaterina Mikhailovna was very unhappy—she felt insulted and complained bitterly to Valery Ivanovich. On their return to Moscow she will probably complain to you. She made a lot of threats to me here, but I did not say anything particularly rude back to her, as I think you will understand.[4]

Valery Ivanovich Mezhlauk (Mežlauks, in Latvian) was the first deputy chairman of the State Planning Agency. (He and Ekaterina Mikhailovna soon separated, but both remained in the House of Government: he and his new wife, Charna Markovna, in Apt. 276; Ekaterina Mikhailovna in Apt. 382.) Nikolai Sidorovich Vlasik was the personal bodyguard of the vacationer in Cottage 9. The vacationer in Cottage 9 was, as Bukharin once said, "the personal embodiment of the mind and will of the Party." Korzhikov's next letter to Pakhomov was sent two days later:

Last night the vacationer in Cottage 9 ordered me to come by with a list of all the guests in all of our cottages. The results of our conversation are as follows:

(1) People have been calling him on the phone with all sorts of complaints. I personally believe that most of the complaints have reached him through Ekaterina Davydovna Voroshilova.
(2) The Boss asked me how things were going. I told him that everything was going fine. His questions mostly concerned the accommodation of Comrades Kabakov, Rukhimovich, and Mezhlauk. Why didn't Comrade Kabakov get a room immediately upon request? Why didn't Comrade Mezhlauk get a room in "Blinovka"? Why was Comrade Rukhimovich put up in the Riviera Hotel, and not in a separate cottage?

I responded: Comrade Rukhimovich has been staying at the Riviera and never approached me about this. Comrade Mezhlauk (the wife) did not receive a room in "Blinovka" because when she arrived, there was not a single free room left, and when a room did open up, they turned it down. Comrade Kabakov could not be given a room because, again, I did not have any available at the time, but when Comrade Ter-Gabrielian's room in Zenzinovka became free, Comrade Kabakov moved in without waiting for authorization.

(3) The Boss asked about the criteria I use to assign rooms in our cottages. He asked: On what basis did I give rooms in Zenzinovka to the wives of Comrades Yusis and Vlasik? Why do the wives of Comrades Kork, Mogilny, and Semushkin live in separate cottages?

He also asked why we had closed down Cottage 3 and converted it into a walk-in clinic. And then he told me, jokingly: "As you can see, I know everything about your affairs."

In the end, the Boss suggested that I always keep one or two rooms in reserve, just in case—for such comrades as Comrade Kabakov and the like.

He also said that he would talk to Comrade Enukidze, to make sure that separate vacation cottages are not to be given to people who do not belong there.[5]

Ivan Kabakov was the Party boss of the Urals; Saak Ter-Gabrielian—the chairman of the Council of People's Commissars of Armenia; Moisei Rukhimovich—the general manager of the Kuzbass Coal Trust. Ivan Yusis was Vlasik's fellow bodygard. Comrades A. D. Semushkin (the People's Commisariat of Heavy Industry) and A. M. Mogilny (Molotov's secretariat) were mid-level functionaries. The commander of the Moscow Military District (and House of Government resident, Apt. 389), August Kork, was an intermediary case. His unaccompanied wife was not.

The director of the Berezniki Chemical Works, Mikhail Granovsky, was the equal of Rukhimovich, if not quite of Kabakov and Ter-Gabrielian. When he and his family arrived in Sochi a month later (when the first stage of construction at Berezniki was nearly complete), they found everything to their liking. According to Mikhail's son, Anatoly,

The main gates give out onto the Caucasian Riviera and there a sentry checks your papers and salutes as you enter. Immediately beyond is the area reserved for sports, with tennis courts, croquet lawns, basketball courts and so on neatly laid out and separated by wide beds of well-kept flowers and neatly tended footpaths. Then comes the area devoted to night life and indoor entertainments. There is a large dance hall, an open air and an indoor cinema, billiards saloons and a number of rooms for card games, chess and draughts. There is also a spacious restaurant beyond which is the communal kitchen. The residential area that follows comprises some thirty-two four- to five-bedroom houses, each set in a plot of ground some four hundred yards square and screened off one from the other by lines of trees, their lawns and gardens meticulously cared for by a small regiment of gardeners. The most remarkable feature about the houses is that none of them has a kitchen. No cooking is done in the houses at all as all meals are ordered from the communal kitchens. At any time of the day or night a servant may be sent to get piping hot food which is delivered on a tray under a gleaming insulating cupola. There is never, of course, any question of payment or signing of bills for anything ordered.[6]

It is not clear whether the Granovskys received a whole cottage to themselves; most people of their rank did not. It is also not clear whether they had their food delivered to their rooms; most people of their rank used the dining room. The food was, by all accounts, plentiful; most Central Executive Committee sanatoria had their own "auxiliary farms." According to a 1935 report on the Foros resort in Crimea, "the livestock provided whole milk and dairy products; the pig farm offered a regular supply of sausages and smoked meats; the sheep farm made up for any shortages in the meat supply; and the chicken farm provided fresh eggs, so that, as a result of the work of the auxiliary farm, the rest home had no interruptions in supplies." The farm also produced its own fruits and vegetables and made its own wine (Mourvèdre, Madeira, Muscat, Aligoté, and Riesling, among others).[7]

There were three separate categories of diners, each with its own dining room ration. In 1933, the nomenklatura guests and resort managerial personnel were entitled to (per day): 50 grams of caviar, smoked fish, ham, or sausage; 400 grams of meat (or 500 grams of fish); 3 eggs; 200 grams of milk; 40 grams of cheese; 50 grams of butter; 40 grams of "cow's" butter; 40 grams of other dairy products; 1,000 grams of vegetables; 400 grams of fruit; 100 grams of assorted grains; 300 grams of white bread; 200 grams of black bread; 15 grams of vegetable oil; 4 grams of coffee; 2 grams of tea; and 150 grams of sugar, among other things. Mid-level resort managers and skilled workers, including drivers, received smaller and less varied meals; unskilled workers received even less. Only the salt ration—20 grams per day—was the same for all three categories.[8]

Sergei Mironov and Agnessa Argiropulo used to arrive in Sochi in the fall, "when it was overflowing with fruit":

Just imagine, it's October, beginning of November—the autumn season, when it is no longer hot and humid, but the sea is still warm. There are grapes of every kind, persimmons, mandarins—not to mention all the imported exotic fruits they plied us with. They used to put huge bowls of fruit on every table. Once Mirosha and I bought some nuts, but by the time we got back, the same nuts—hazelnuts and walnuts—had appeared on all the tables. Mirosha said jokingly to the manager:

"See what you have done to us? You have deprived us of the last opportunity to spend our own money!"

The manager laughed: "Forgive me, but the fact that you had to spend your own money means that I have been remiss in my duties."

Oh, the chefs they had and the dishes they created for us! If only we could have eaten as much as we wanted. . . . Mirosha tended to put on weight, too, but, following my example, he tried to watch what he ate and stay in shape. The doctor ordered fasting days of only milk and dry toast for him. For each one of those days Mirosha lost over a pound. And no siestas either! Every day, right after lunch, we would head straight for the billiard room. Several hours of billiards each day kept us in good shape. I was the one who kept urging Mirosha to follow this exercise regimen, and he agreed, knowing I was right and that otherwise we would burst from all those fabulous sanatoria meals.[9]

The Gaisters, according to their daughter, Inna, "did a lot of hiking, because they thought they were too fat and needed to hike." The Muklewichs combined walking and fasting. In Foros, they went on daylong hikes every other day. Romuald led the way, and his wife, Anna, followed. They did not bring any food with them. According to Irina, "my mother was a bit worried about my father's health, because he was, in spite of it all, still rather stout."[10]

David Shvarts and his wife,
Revekka Felinzat, at a resort

Postyshevs at a resort

The Shvartses used to play a lot of volleyball, chess, and billiards. Adoratsky and his daughter went for walks, read, and played the piano (although the one in Mukhalatka had "a tinny sound" and was "not particularly pleasant to play on"). They did not have a weight problem and enjoyed good food (the Gurzuf breakfast eggs were "perfect and done just right"), but their favorite part, as always, were the bubbling mineral baths, which they took both morning and afternoon. "After the baths," he wrote to his wife from Kislovodsk, "I lie down and rest, and then we are brought back to our rooms by car or on horseback, and I lie down and rest again. This allows us to pass the time and provides us with an illusion of activity." Osinsky also preferred Kislovodsk to the beach resorts, but spent most of his time studying. In October 1931, however, he was so exhausted from constant travel and collectivization-related worry that he allowed himself a little vacation. "I thought of nothing," he wrote in a letter to Shaternikova, "did nothing, and did not write to you; instead I slept, ate, and read whatever substitutes for fiction for me. I also walked, but not very far: only to the "Blue Rocks" and "The Little Saddle" (once). After vegetating for five days, I suddenly pulled myself together and thought: What about Hegel?! I've been wasting precious time! So I jumped into harness and started reading Hegel, though not terribly quickly. Up to now, I've only been rereading my notes, comparing them with Lenin's, and then rereading Hegel in the original. I've managed to get through 105 pages this way, and, starting tomorrow, I'll begin reading <u>new</u> material." His goal was "to understand everything, in order to be

Terekhovs at a resort

Gronskys and the Belenkys
at a spa in Essentuki, 1933

able to launch the universal mastery of the dialectical method in its profoundest and most developed form." His first (Hegelian) phase was
mostly complete by 1934, after several more stays in Kislovodsk. While
there, he normally worked for much of the day, while most of the other
guests played billiards.[11]

Besides billiards, the most popular evening entertainment at the sea
resorts was cards. One of the oldest Party members, Elena Dmitrievna
Stasova (sixty-two in 1935, from Apt. 245), played every evening on a terrace next to the main building in Mukhalatka (in much the same way as
her gentry aunts and grandmothers once did). According to Aleksei
Rykov's daughter, Natalia,

> With Elena Dmitrievna, one had to play Clubs. It was a card game—
> rather simple, but not too. . . . Whenever my father played with her,
> it would turn into a complete farce—because ten minutes into the
> game, she would always say: "Alesha, you're cheating again!"—"Who,
> me? Elena Dmitrievna, surely you don't think me capable of such a
> thing?" And then he would do something outrageous again. And they
> would repeat the same scene day after day. . . . But the main attrac-
> tion was when they all played Podkidnoi Durak [Throw-in Fool] with
> two decks. Now that was a circus, a real circus. Then the cards could
> end up under the table, under the players, or just about anywhere—
> because everyone cheated. They would all be joking and laughing. It
> was so much fun![12]

While the older people played cards, the younger ones danced. In 1935,
Agnessa Argiropulo was thirty-two, and her husband, Sergei Mironov,
forty-one. His boss, the "regular Siegfried" Vsevolod Apollonovich Balitsky,
and the representative of the People's Commissariat of Heavy Industry in
the Ukrainian SSR, Daniil Ivanovich Petrovsky, were in their early forties.
Once, around that time, they were all staying in the Ukrainian Central
Committee rest home in Khosta, outside of Sochi. They danced on many
occasions, but November 7 was special:

> The manager said to us, "I've ordered some cars for you. You can go
> to the mountains for a picnic, and we'll have everything ready for
> you when you get back."
> We climbed into the open cars, already loaded with baskets of
> wine and other delicacies. We drove to the market in Adler, then for
> a swim—and then up into the mountains for a walk. We had a won-
> derful time and came back crowned with garlands of cypress.
> The banquet tables had already been set. There was a vase of
> flowers at each place setting and a bouquet of flowers under each
> fork and knife.

Sergei Mironov and Agnessa Argiropulo at a resort
(Courtesy of Rose Glickman)

We rested a bit, then changed for dinner. I wore a white dress with a large white bow with blue polka dots in front and white shoes. (Nobody wore sandals back then.)

Postyshev, Chubar, Balitsky, Petrovsky, and Uborevich were all there that evening, and Mikoyan came later from Zenzinovka, where Stalin was staying.

Balitsky was master of ceremonies. As I said before, he was slender, lively, fun, and very amusing. Pretending to be angry, he shouted: "What's going on here? Why are the ladies sitting together and not with the men? Up! Everybody up!"

He grabbed one lady by the hand, and then a man, and sat them down next to each other; then the next pair. . . . When he got to me, I acted coy. "I don't want to sit next to just anyone. I first want to know who you are going to put me with."

He paused, hesitated for a moment, then raised his eyebrows and said softly, "You'll sit next to me."

And he ran off to seat the others. He got everyone seated, including me, but still did not sit down himself. His wife was looking at me across the table, her eyes narrowed contemptuously. Suddenly everyone burst out laughing because Mirosha had brought a chair and squeezed in between me and Balitsky.

Balitsky said, "This will not do."

He whispered to two of the waiters, and they picked up the chair with Mirosha in it and carried him back to the lady who'd been chosen for him. Everyone laughed until tears ran down their faces.

Finally, Balitsky sat down and began talking to me and serving me with food and drink, but not for long: as master of ceremonies he had to make toasts and keep things moving.... Meanwhile, I tried to ignore his wife's dirty looks.

After dinner the dancing began. I think I must have danced with them all! My first partner was Balitsky, and others danced, too—but when Daniil Petrovsky and I began doing the tango, a circle formed around us, and they all stepped back to watch. We really laid it on—he would dip me, and I would lean backwards over his arm, then he'd pull me up, and we'd walk sideways, cheek to cheek, with our arms outstretched. These days no one knows how to dance a real tango. But Daniil did, and we understood each other without words. Postyshev was sitting in his chair, dying with laughter, and his wife was laughing, too. When we were done, they all applauded until their hands hurt.[13]

■ ■ ■

Besides the one-day rest homes (frequented mostly in the winter) and several-week sanatoria (frequented—following Stalin's lead—mostly in the fall), there were permanent country houses (dachas) outside of Moscow, where some women and most of the children and old people lived all summer long (and, in the case of the better heated and insulated dachas, during winter vacations, as well). The men usually came on their days off and whenever else they could. Most dachas belonged to the state and were

Trifonovs in Serebrianyi Bor

Mikhailovs in Serebrianyi Bor

distributed according to rank, although, starting in the early 1930s, the top officials started buying their own "cooperative" (de facto private) country houses. The largest concentration of Central Executive Committee state dachas was in Serebrianyi Bor, on the western edge of the city. The Podvoiskys, Trifonovs, Sverdlovs, Khalatovs, Mikhailovs, Volins, Larins, Morozes, and Zbarskys, among many others, lived in close proximity to each other (usually several families per dacha), swam in the Moskva River, gathered mushrooms, rode bicycles, played tennis and volleyball, and grew fruit, vegetables, and flowers. On August 6, 1937, Yuri Trifonov, who was not quite twelve at the time, wrote a lyrical entry in his diary: "The sun and the trees. The smell of pine. All the greenery. A light breeze coming through the open window and stirring the pages of my diary. . . . The phlox and dahlias under my window perfuming the air. Bushes and trees and other greenery all around. Greenery, greenery, everywhere. . . . And the sun turning it all emerald green."[14]

The most desirable dachas were farther west, along the high bank of the Moskva River, upstream from the city. Some were rest homes with rooms permanently reserved for particular families. The aviator Yakov Smushkevich (commander of Madrid's air defenses during the Spanish Civil War and, since 1937, deputy commander of the Soviet Air Force, from Apt. 96 in the House of Government) used to spend summers with his family in one such communal dacha in Barvikha. According to his daughter, Rosa,

> He was a lifelong, passionate fisherman. He used to sit by the pond with his fishing rod. But the famous Maly Theater actor, Ostuzhev, would pace back and forth behind him memorizing his and other people's roles in a loud voice. (He was hard of hearing, you know.) Ostuzhev adored my father. He loved being near him. So my father would come home with an empty bucket, grumbling jokingly: "Ostu-

zhev chased all the fish away..." I remember a lot of people in Barvikha—Ezhov's wife, a red-haired Jewish woman, who used to call very loudly: "Ko-o-olia!" The Berias lived there, too. Beria himself didn't come very often, but his very nice wife, Nina, did, and their son, Sergei—a wonderful young man, and Beria's sister—a good, kind woman. They used to play with me. Among the guests in the nearby sanatorium were [the famous theater actors] Vasily Ivanovich Kachalov, Ruben Simonov (young and very handsome), Varvara Osipovna Massalitinova, Prov Mikhailovich Sadovsky, and Ekaterina Pavlovna Korchagina-Aleksandrovskaia. They loved spending time with my father. They were affectionate with me and gave me their photographs.[15]

In another former manor house, the Old Bolsheviks Feliks Kon, Petr Krasikov, Gleb Krzhizhanovsky, Nadezhda Krupskaia, the German Communist Clara Zetkin, and the former head of the Department of Female Workers in the Party's Central Committee, Klavdia Nikolaeva, all ate in the same "Gothic" dining-room, walked in the woods, and—especially Krasikov and Krzhizhanovsky—hunted for mushrooms.[16]

But most dachas were separate houses custom built for individual families on large plots of land within "dacha settlements." According to Osinsky's daughter, Svetlana,

> During the construction of our dacha in Barvikha (state-provided, of course), my father had a tall fence built around the huge lot so that nothing and no one could disturb him. Inside, a tennis court, volleyball court and croquet lawn were set up. A long, long stairway was built from the high bank down to the river. One whole area was planted with strawberries, fruit trees, and berry bushes. There was also a small wooded grove where mushrooms grew, a ravine, lots of hiding places, and, away from the main building, the so-called "gazebo," which was actually a small wooden cottage where my father used to work. And what a main building it was! Wooden, with two stories and ten rooms, a deck, glassed-in veranda, running water, septic tank, and bathroom. And a grand piano in the dining room.

Most dachas had tall wooden fences, usually painted green. The Osinskys also had a guard dog, "a ferocious Caucasian shepherd named Choba":

> Everyone except my brother Valia and [the maid] Nastia was scared to death of her. My father had her put on a chain, and she used to run back and forth along a wire by the gate, greeting all our visitors with a low, fierce growl. Choba hated my father—and with good reason. For training purposes, in order to get her accustomed to loud noises and I don't know what else, he used to fire his pistol into the

Valerian Osinsky at his dacha next to the corn
he planted (Courtesy of Elena Simakova)

fence behind her wire. I remember how Valia once brought Choba on a leash to the tennis court. When she saw my father behind the high wire fence, she started barking madly, standing on her hind legs and throwing herself at the fence, while he stood on the other side in his white slacks and tennis shoes, with his racket practically poking her in the nose. Later they took the dog back to the kennel.[17]

The Gaisters' dacha was a bit further upstream, in Nikolina Gora. Aron Gaister did some of the work himself: planting apple, pear, and cherry trees; starting a vegetable garden; and building a special shed for the white Leghorn chickens he brought back from one of his trips. As his daughter, Inna, remembers it,

The lot was right above the river, on the high side. The dacha was a large, two-story building with six rooms. There were three large rooms downstairs, three upstairs, and a huge veranda. My mother's brother Veniamin, not without secret envy, liked to refer to it as our "villa."

The rooms were always full of people. Some of my father's and mother's numerous relatives, especially my cousins Elochka, Nina, Igor, and Vitia, used to stay there regularly. My parents' friends usually came from Moscow on their days off. The poet Bezymensky, who was a close friend of my father, came a lot. Next door were the dachas of the parents of Irina and Andrei Vorobiev and the large Broido clan. I hung out with the kids from the dachas closest to ours: Vera Tolmachevskaia, Natasha Kerzhentseva, the Broido girls. To make it easier for Grandma to get down to the river, my father built a stairway with at least a hundred steps; it was called "the Gaister stairway" for many years after that. It was built as a serpentine because the bank was very steep. Some dachas had wooden piers for swimming. By our pier, the river was deep, and I only swam there when my father was around. Most of the girls liked to gather by the Kerzhentsevs' pier, where it was shallow and great for swimming.[18]

Aron Gaister
(Courtesy of Inna Gaister)

Platon Kerzhentsev's dacha was built according to his own design. It had a veranda with sliding glass walls and retractable partitions inside. Next door was a dacha that Elena Usievich used to rent for the summer; she had been offered one in the writers' settlement in Peredelkino, but, according to her daughter Iskra-Marina, preferred not to have to worry about her own "cooperative" property. She usually came on her days off in her father Feliks Kon's car; Iskra-Marina spent most of her days with Inna Gaister and Natasha Kerzhentseva. The Rozengolts' dacha in nearby Gorki-10 was designed by his sister, the painter Eva Levina-Rozengolts. Downstairs was a large hall, a study with its own veranda, Eva's studio, a dining-room with a long table for up to fifty people and an adjacent veranda, a kitchen, and, next to it, the servants' quarters (including a room mostly used as a waiting area by the chauffeurs); upstairs there were two bedrooms, a living room, a bathroom, a toilet, and a billiard room, separated from the living room by a covered walkway. According to the US ambassador, Joseph E. Davies, who visited on February 10, 1937, "the winding approach from the road to the dacha was attractive. The house was large and comfortable and commanded a beautiful view of the snow-covered landscape on all sides. It was well and attractively furnished after the rather heavy modern German type." Efim Shchadenko and Maria Denisova had a six-room, two-story dacha in Kraskovo 4, to the east of Moscow. One of the largest dachas (Bakovka-111, 241.2 cubic feet, not far from the Osinskys) belonged to Shchadenko's former Red Cavalry commander, Semen Budennyi. In December 1937, it included some large apple, pear, plum, and cherry orchards, 40 gooseberry and 207 raspberry bushes, and, among many other things, a workhorse named Maruska, a black cow named Willow, a red cow named War, and a pig with no name weighing 550 pounds.[19]

For Arosev, nothing seemed to come easily. (He was not admitted to the Society of Old Bolsheviks until the summer of 1933 because of concerns

Aleksandr Arosev and one of his daughters at Molotov's dacha

regarding his overly detailed description of his youthful enthusiasm for SR terrorism.) In 1934, he picked out a spot for a dacha in the writers' settlement in Peredelkino, went there a few times to oversee the construction, and talked at length to the engineer in charge, but, in 1935, was removed from the list by A. S. Shcherbakov, Gronsky's successor as the Central Committee overseer of the Writers' Union. He then chose a place in Troitse-Lykovo just west of Serebrianyi Bor, but was told not to bother because it was a restricted area close to Kaganovich's dacha. He applied anyway, was turned down, applied again, this time directly to Stanislav Redens (head of the Moscow Province NKVD), and finally, on May 28, 1935, received a permit. While waiting for construction to begin, he rented various cottages (also in restricted areas), traveled unannounced to one-day rest-homes, and often visited his friend Molotov ("Viacha"), whose dacha was in Sosny, next to Nikolina Gora. On July 12, 1936, he was visiting with his daughters, Olga and Elena. Two of Molotov's and Arosev's friends from their Kazan days, German Tikhomirnov (now an official in Molotov's secretariat) and Nikolai Maltsev (now head of the Central Archival Directory), were also there. As Arosev wrote in his diary, "Viacha was, as usual, playful and in a great mood. We went for a swim. He wanted to push me into the water in my clothes. I was the only one who didn't want to swim, but I had no choice. At least he let me get undressed first."[20]

Meanwhile, Olga, who was ten at the time, was playing around a bend in the river, next to Molotov's wife, Polina Semenovna Zhemchuzhina:

Floating on round, glossy green leaves next to the bank of the Moskva River were water lilies of such snow-white purity they seemed to glow a pale pink. I swam over and picked a whole bunch of these lilies. Polina Semenovna wove them into a wreath and placed it on my head. She admired me for a moment and, after saying that with these flowers and stems I was the very image of Undine

Polina Semenovna Zhemchuzhina; her daughter, Svetlana
Molotova; and Aleksandr Arosev at the Molotovs' dacha

herself, told me to swim over to the men's bathing area to show myself to my father and the other guests. What I saw there shocked me.

Molotov had always been an extremely quiet and reserved man.
Newspapers often printed his photographs: old-fashioned pince-
nez and a pug-nosed face, seemingly good-natured, but generally
unremarkable and rather closed and expressionless. My father, despite his excitability at home, also came across in public as a man of
European cultivation and reserve. But here, in the bathing area,
they were fighting, dunking and grabbing on to each other's legs and
shoulders, tearing off any remaining clothes, and raising a fountain
of splashes every time they climbed out onto the bank and crashed
into the water again. They were acting wild and ferocious, like little
boys, I thought, reproachfully, at the time. And I was right. For a few
moments on that peaceful summer day at the dacha, on the grassy
bank and in the water, they were transformed from statesmen into
regular, spontaneous people. Could it be that they—these former
swimmers, brawlers, and athletes—had suddenly recollected their
Volga childhood?[21]

According to Arosev's diary, they spent the rest of the day inside. "We
watched a movie and talked about literature—about Gorky and Dostoevsky.
Viacheslav loves literature and really understands it. He had some scathing
things to say about Chukovsky and quoted Lenin well and very appropriately, to the effect that socialism as an ideology enters the working class
from the outside and may be poisoned by bourgeois influences."[22]

17

THE NEXT OF KIN

Socializing—particularly of the ferocious and wild variety—was limited to dachas, rest homes, and sanatoria. In Moscow, Arosev, Molotov, Maltsev, and Tikhomirnov rarely visited each other, even though all except Molotov were neighbors in the House of Government. For nomenklatura men, Moscow life was about work, and House of Government apartments were for sleeping or work. With the exception of those professionally involved in "guiding the work of the Soviet and foreign intelligentsia" and a few irrepressibly gregarious men such as Radek and Kuibyshev, most people rarely received guests outside the four annual feast days (birthdays and the three Soviet holidays), and some never received them at all. Nomenklatura men had no friends, in the sense of surrogate siblings with a claim to unconditional loyalty, and no neighbors, in the sense of next-door residents with rumors or household items to exchange. They had special comrades and more or less close relatives.

All Bolsheviks belonged to the same family and referred to each other as "comrades," but not all Bolsheviks were welcome in each other's apartments. As Solts wrote in the 1920s, "it is, of course, very difficult to preserve those close, intimate relations that we used to have when there were just a handful of us. The common fate and common persecutions of the comrades who worked in the tsarist underground drew us closer together and united us more than our current conditions do. There are many more of us now, and it is very difficult to have the same feelings of closeness toward each communist." This had been true in the days of the tsarist underground, as well (Arosev had been closer to Molotov, Maltsev, and Tikhomirnov than to other Kazan Social-Democrats, not to mention those he did not know personally), but it was particularly true now, when the economic foundations of socialism had been laid and the sect had become a church. Or rather, a fraternal, faith-based group radically opposed to a corrupt world had become a bureaucratic, hierarchical, world-accepting institution with weak horizontal bonds and porous boundaries. The post-1934 Soviet Union was no longer a heathen empire ruled by a millenarian sect: it was an ideocratic (theocratic, hierocratic) state composed of nominal believers and run by a priestly hierarchy. All Soviets were assumed to be more or less observant Communists (adherents of Christianity, Judaism, and Islam were analogous to "pagans" in Christian states: awaiting remedial conversion but posing no existential danger to ideocratic monopoly). The Bolshevik priestly elite consisted of two layers: the rank-and-file Party members recruited from the general population on the basis of scriptural competence and personal virtue and retained as potential no-menklatura members; and, above them, active nomenklatura members recruited from rank-and-file Party population and assigned to positions of responsibility in the administrative, judicial, military, and economic spheres. The nomenklatura members were divided into those who tended toward professional specialization (especially in industrial management) and those who remained interchangeable universal supervisors, from the Party's "general secretary" at the center to republican, provincial, and district secretaries throughout the Soviet Union.

The original sectarians had to adjust socially and emotionally, as well as politically. Friendship without comradeship was still inconceivable, but the fact that most comrades were now strangers made it obvious that some comrades were also friends (in the sense of having close, intimate relations rooted in a shared sacred past). As the Old Bolshevik Fridrikh Lengnik (Fridrihs Lengniks, in Latvian), from Apt. 200, wrote in his Society of Old Bolsheviks questionnaire, "I have no requests. I would like to have the warmth of comradely relationships that we used to have, but I realize that, in a Party of a million members, that is impossible." To emphasize the point, he attached a "list of personal friends," specifying the number of people involved and the origin of the relationship:

1.	The Lepeshinskys	2: exile and emigration
2.	N. K. Krupskaia	1: ditto
3.	M. I. Ulianova	1: Cental Control Commission
4.	The Krzhizhanovskys	2: exile and illegal work
5.	A. S. Shapovalov	1: exile and emigration
6.	N. N. Panin	1: exile
7.	G. I. Okulova	1: Sverdlovsk
8.	E. I. Okulova	1: exile and emigration
9.	P. A. Krasikov	1: emigration
10.	Fotieva	1: emigration
11.	M. N. Liadov	1: emigration
12.	M. M. Essen	1: ditto
13.	I. I. Radchenko	1: illegal work
14.	Lezhava	1: Dep. Comm. of Agr.
15.	Shotman	
16.	Enukidze	
17.	Stasova	
18.	Rubinshtein[1]	

The warmth of comradely relations was not what it used to be even for the original sectarians (one of Lengnik's jobs as deputy head of the Society of Old Bolsheviks was to settle conflicts among members), but some of them, especially those in their sixties like Lengnik and his personal friends, did get together regularly on Bolshevik feast days in order to reminisce and sing revolutionary songs. Most of their favorite recollections were about courtships, friendships, and homemade dumplings in Siberian exile, when spring was on its way.[2]

But the most common strategy for dealing with the affective consequences of sectarian dissolution was to revert back to the family. The most frequent, and often the only, guests at special holiday dinners were family members. Some House of Government residents favored the husband's side, some favored the wife's, and some embraced both, but virtually every apartment served as the center of an extended kinship-based patronage network. Charity began at home: in addition to the leaseholder's wife, children, and servants, most apartments contained some combination of parents, siblings, and poor relations. Compared to the House leaseholders, most relations were poor: helping them move to Moscow and get jobs, apartments, and places in colleges and children's camps was an important part of life for most adult House residents. Even the famously misanthropic Osinsky helped his brother with promotions and, according to his daughter, Svetlana, got his sister a job as an actress at the Vakhtangov Theater, "even though she was, of course, totally talentless."[3]

Some families—the Sverdlovs, Gaisters, Kuibyshevs, Arosevs, Podvoiskys, Lozovskys, Zelenskys, and Alliluevs, among many others—received more than one apartment within the House. Some, including the ever-expanding Sverdlov-Kedrov-Podvoisky-Lozovsky-Krzhizhanovsky-Yagoda-Artuzov clan, extended their reach and welfare through in-House and out-of-House marriages. Arosev's comrades and neighbors Maltsev and Tikhomirnov both married cousins of his second wife (before he married for the third time and received two House of Government apartments). The collectivizer of the Middle-Volga peasants, Boris Bak, moved into the House in March 1935, when he was made deputy head of the Moscow Province NKVD (under Redens); his sister, also a secret police official, was married to Boris Berman, the brother of the head of the Gulag, Matvei Berman, and a high-ranking secret police official in his own right. Boris's brother Solomon did not live in the House because he was, at that time, head of the Karaganda Province NKVD in Kazakhstan.[4]

■   ■   ■

Comrades and relatives who lived or traveled outside of Moscow stayed in touch by writing letters. Most adult House residents—like most literate Soviets—were active participants in the thick web of correspondence that defined and held together social circles, family networks, patronage rankings, and, ultimately, the "Soviet people" (all the more so because foreign correspondence slowed to a trickle after the house of socialism was built).

At work, high officials governed the state by means of letters and tele-grams (while Aleksei Rykov governed all private and official letters and telegrams as the people's commissar of post and telegraph); at home, they maintained personal ties by writing letters, telegrams, and postcards—to old comrades, clients requesting favors (many of them old comrades), va-cationing household members, and an assortment of relatives, mobile and stationary.

If old family connections did not provide "feelings of closeness," new (or old) loves could. A separate category of personal correspondence con-sisted of letters to more or less secret lovers: letters that, because of their assumption of utmost privacy, intimacy, immediacy, and emotional au-thenticity, were similar to diaries and prison confessions (two other popu-lar Bolshevik genres). Osinsky continued his relationship with Anna Shat-ernikova, writing regularly about his health, children, life at work, and life's work: mostly Hegel and mathematics, but also Gogol, Heine, and the Soviet automobile industry. After the first few years, he stopped writing about the freedom of relationships. He and Anna had a special address in Moscow to which they sent their letters. He kept offering her money: for sanatorium stays and—his fondest wish—for her to be able to go to univer-sity and take up the formal study of Marxism-Leninism. She kept refusing, but seems to have accepted some help, possibly to allow her to take care of her son, Vsemir, who was not expected to live long.[5]

Around 1937, the Old Bolshevik Feliks Kon, who was seventy-three at the time, started an affair with Maria ("Mara") Filippovna Komarova, an employee of the All-Union Radio Committee (which he had headed until 1933, when Kerzhentsev took over). (It is possible their liaison started ear-lier, but the surviving correspondence begins in 1937.) They met regularly, although it appears that he was not always up to the physical challenge. She suffered from jealousy and suspected him of being unfaithful. His best defense was his reputation as a Party veteran. "I am sorry, my dear Mara, but there is one question I cannot help asking you: is it possible to love someone and not trust him, not to trust in him? You are a Bolshevik. You will understand the full horror of this question. All my life, I have consid-ered myself, and have been considered by others, an honest man. But you have cast doubt on this. . . . It is killing me." His loyalty as a Bolshevik and faithfulness as a lover were one and the same thing.[6] That still left the question of what should be done in a situation both found painful, as well as rewarding:

You are young. You have decades left to live. And me?! I do believe that it would be natural for you to become involved with somebody else and start living in a way that is different from the way you live now, from one meeting to the next. Would it be painful for me? Very much so, but . . . And there is one more thing, besides old women's

Feliks Kon

gossip. There is Khr. G. [Khristina Grigorievna Grinberg]. . . . One way or another, I have lived with her for 45 years. How could I leave her now? . . . How could I even think of leaving Khr. G., an 80-year-old invalid, who has given me the best years of her life? She would not be jealous, but it would cause her great pain. You keep bringing up the A. Karenina analogy. It simply doesn't apply.[7]

Things would eventually change because the Revolution had won, but change took time—probably more than they had. Anna Karenina's—and Khristina Grigorievna Grinberg's—pain had not yet become unimaginable. As he wrote to Komarova, "The modern family has many, many deficiencies. But these are growing pains. The old forms of marriage involving buying and selling ('you've got the goods, we've got the merchant'), business contracts between the parties, the wife's adulteries and the husband's open debauchery both before and after the wedding ('boys will be boys'), as well as the peculiar division of labor, with the husband earning a living while his wife runs the household, are rotted through and through, but the miasma of decay is still poisoning today's spouses."[8]

What mattered, in the meantime, was that Feliks and Maria had each other. "I keep remembering," he wrote in a letter devoted mostly to Khristina Grigorievna's illness, "how I kissed my little girl for the first time. . . . It was so wonderful, and it brought us so close together for the rest of our lives!"[9] That closeness, like all true closeness between a man and a woman, was spiritual, as well as physical:

> As you can see, my dear girl, we are thinking about the same things, and that is the best part of our relationship. Because, no matter what I do, I am spiritually connected to you. In everything I write, there is a little part of you, and in every one of your feelings, there is more than a little of mine. In spite of everything, our lives have become inextricably linked. As I write this, I think of all the things that have tied us so closely together. There you are, my darling Mara! Please always remember how much you mean to me, and how I wish you were free of all this . . . anxiety, so that you could live, for as long as possible, a full personal, spiritual, and public life.[10]

Aleksandr Serafimovich's soulmate was Nadezhda Petriaevskaia (Nadia). In 1931, when they began to correspond, he was sixty-eight and she was twenty. As he wrote on August 20, 1932, from his native Ust-Medveditskaia (a few months before it became Serafimovich),

Nadia, it is amazing to what extent we complement each other. My mind is slow and heavy;
it moves laboriously, like a millstone, always
lagging behind. Your mind is exceptionally
quick; it sparkles as it apprehends everything
it touches. What saves me is my ability to
reach a certain depth, to synthesize. You are
brilliant at analyzing, subtly and exhaustively.
(I am writing to you from the steppe: on my
right is a glittering wall of rain; on my left is
the mountain called the Pyramid, on top of
which is a tower made of criss-crossing beams,
a survey marker, the beginnings of a railroad,

Aleksandr Serafimovich

and the graves of some Whites killed in 1919 with secret flowers on
them.) It looks like I'll be whipped by the rain. I'm hiding here, reading
[Engels's] *Anti-Dühring*. At home people are always getting in the way.
That is your doing. You have gotten under my skin. I have just finished
Lenin's *Materialism and Empiriocriticism*.[11]

The flip side of long-distance spiritual intimacy is loneliness at home.
"Write to me, my dear Nadia: I am alone. There is no one I want to share
my thoughts or anything else with. When I come, I'll bring a whole pile of
work plans I want to discuss with you." He needed her in order to do his
writing: "your fresh eye can see things that escape me, and your mind is
fresh, sharp, searching, and active."[12] He measured time by counting her
letters; he measured distance by how far away she was. She was a student
of science at Leningrad University; in the summer of 1932, she was doing
field work in Goloshchekin's Kazakhstan:

> Your letter has just arrived, about your trip to some deserted place
> with a nice description of your journey and of the student Kerbalai.
> And I know it's silly, but I can't get rid of a deep-seated suspicion
> that Kerbalai is an agent provocateur. I have no idea where it came
> from. My first gut reaction was: "Does she have a gun?" I can't sleep.
> I go to bed with the chickens and fall into a mute, all-enveloping
> blackness. And then two or three hours later, I wake up and can't go
> back to sleep again. The whole house is asleep, while I, full of an-
> guish, climb out the window, so as not to disturb anyone, and wan-
> der around the garden. I am losing weight. I know this isn't helping
> anyone, but there is nothing I can do.[13]

Reading her letters from Kazakhstan, he discovered that she was a talented writer. They shared a bond, a faith, and, as it turned out, a gift. The
best analogy for their relationship could be found in the life of one of the
Soviet Union's most popular writers.

Have you read Jack London's biography? A glorious writer, really close to my heart. Sasha [Serafimovich's secretary and daughter-in-law] and I have been reading him. And what about his second wife, Charmian? She is like you: an excellent swimmer, diver, horse rider, shooter, and mountain climber. They did everything together. They crossed the ocean in a little sailboat from San Francisco to Hawaii in twenty-five days. He called her his "Mate Woman." When she got sick, he said: "If she dies, I'll kill myself." But, with all these similarities, there is one crucial difference between you two: she did not have your mental sharpness and intensity, even though she and London worked together, and she wrote a book of her own. Most important, she did not have the feeling of collectivism that you are suffused with. That is understandable: you find yourselves in totally different social circumstances—profoundly bourgeois ones in her case, the revolution and socialist construction, in yours.[14]

There was another difference: he and Nadia were not married. (Serafimovich's wife, Fekla Rodionovna, was a peasant woman famous for her pies, with no apparent interest in science or literature.) Nadia was his "Mate Woman," but in a way that appeared incomplete or temporarily split. In one of his letters, Aleksandr Serafimovich Serafimovich (or simply Aleksandr) writes to the public Nadezhda about the private Nadia. In social circumstances totally different from those of the Londons, the "Mate" has become a comrade. Or rather, "Nadezhda" is a comrade, whereas "Nadia" is a "Comrade Woman" who is all the more beautiful as a woman for being a true collectivist comrade:

Ask her [Nadezhda] to look me in the eye with her own deep eyes filled with the resolute preparedness for struggle and readiness to forge her will. . . . Tell her (confidentially, so she won't laugh) that I won't use bleach to treat myself anymore (at least not foolishly), that I am working on my publication, that I have finished one important task, about which more when we meet, and I wait for her letters here at my rest home. And tell her how my heart fluttered when she mentioned in one of her letters that "life without a *collective* is impossible." She is made of healthy, firm substance, no matter which way the wind blows outside. And tell her, do tell her, that I am not idealizing her, that romanticism is a lie, that I keep adding up all the debit and credit entries, and that the total, fixing me with its cold eyes, is slowly telling me: "You will never, ever, meet another Nadia like this."—"Oh, shut up; I don't need you to tell me." No, don't tell her that—I can see the tiniest snake of a smile wrinkling the corner of her mouth. Just tell her that I firmly grasp her hand in mine, and that I am—Aleksandr.[15]

The former Chekist and Right Oppositionist (and, in the 1930s, head of the Union of State Trade and Consumer Employees), Grigory Moroz, liked to tease his wife by playing Aleksandr Vertinsky's "A Song about My Wife" ("to be able to forgive my regular infatuations, one has to know a thing or two about life"). She suffered from jealousy and confided her fears to her son, Samuil.[16]

Yakov Smushkevich

Roza Smushkevich was eleven years old in 1937 when her father, the Air Force commander Yakov Smushkevich, returned from Spain (where he became known as "General Duglas"). Fifty-three years later she talked about her father in an interview for a documentary:

One day I was walking home from school through the little park that was across from the house. . . . Suddenly, a woman came up to me and asked: "Are you Roza?" Surprised, I answered, "Yes, I am." Then she said, "Let's sit down on a bench and talk." That surprised me even more. We sat down, and she pulled out a large box of chocolates. . . . There used to be some chocolates called "Deer" in those days. She opened the box and offered me some. I took one piece. She said that her name was Aunt Tamara and that she used to be my father's interpreter in Spain. And that she was madly in love with him, and he with her, and let's live together, and some other things along those lines. . . . I completely lost control, threw her chocolate in her face, and started yelling something. When I got home, I flung my briefcase into the corner. My father was home. He asked: "What's the matter?" And I screamed: "Leave me alone! Go back to your Aunt Tamara!" My father walked out of the room, and I could hear my mother say: "See, I've been trying to keep it hidden from Roza, but now she knows, too." Without a word, my father walked over to the telephone, dialed a number, and said: "Please leave me and my family alone." Then he took me on his lap and said: "My dear, sweet girl, there is no one who means more to me than your mother and you." . . . Of course, I hated her. But then . . . the years passed . . . and I started feeling sorry for her. I heard that she loved him very, very much. I believe she even had a son by him, but I think he died."[17]

Bolshevism was a men's movement. Before the Revolution, women were junior partners in the struggle and the embodiment of a time when "any grief is easy to bear." After the Revolution, they served as a symbol of both the dream's vulnerability and the old world's tenacity. In the House of Government, they stood for the preservation and renewal of sectarian intimacy.

Most high officials who left their old comrade women for new ones did it during the time of the great disappointment: a midlife crisis for both the Revolution and the revolutionaries. In the 1930s, even those who did not conceal their new liaisons seemed reluctant to abandon the women who had given them the best years of their lives (and had shared with them the best years of the Revolution). Koltsov got together with Maria Osten without breaking up with Elizaveta Ratmanova; his brother Boris Efimov openly shared his time between his two wives and their children; Ivan Kraval moved his third wife in without parting from his second (who continued to live in their House of Government apartment along with her sister and her sister's husband and son, as well as Kraval's daughter from his first marriage). Kuibyshev's first, second, and fourth wives (P. A. Stiazhkina, E. S. Kogan, and O. A. Lezhava) lived in separate apartments in the House of Government, apparently on good terms with each other. His death in 1935 produced two widows with claims to benefits: O. A. Lezhava and A. N. Klushina. The Gorky Park inspector, Mikhail Tuchin, left his wife, Tatiana Chizhikova, for another woman, but continued to live in their House of Government apartment.[18]

What all genuinely close relationships had in common—whether among comrade friends, comrade men and women, or various family members— was the construction of socialism. This was not true of the former construction worker, Mikhail Tuchin, who was often drunk, belligerent toward his family, and, apparently, indifferent toward socialism, but it was true of many, perhaps most, nomenklatura households. Watching Soviet factories grow gave Osinsky as much "<u>personal pleasure</u>" as watching his own children grow; studying Marxist dialectics was "no less important than the building of 518 factories"; and one of the greatest personal pleasures in his relationship with Anna Shaternikova was the thought of her devoting herself full time to the study of Marxist dialectics. Feliks Kon reassured his distraught lover by referring to their common Party membership, and Serafimovich exiled himself to the steppe in order to read Engels and Lenin and write to Nadia about Bolshevik collectivism as the key to an exclusive reciprocal relationship (and a rival who might be an agent provocateur). On January 22, 1935, Arosev wrote a testament to his children, in which he asked them to be resolute in pursuing their dreams. "Don't be afraid of criticism and don't resent it. Trust the collective and test yourself through the collective. But, of course, you will be living in an age when the collective will be playing a much greater role than it does in our day." In the same year, Podvoisky wrote to his children urging them never to forget how much their mother had done for them. "Remember it in order to nurture, develop, and strengthen your sense of duty toward not only each other and your loved ones, but also toward those who are far away, toward the entire working class."[19] Izrail Veitser had two true loves: Natalia Sats and, as the primary loyalty on which everything else depended, the Party. Natalia Sats reciprocated—on both counts:

More than anything else in the world, Veitser treasured and safe-guarded the confidence of the Party. Each time he was about to leave on one of his foreign trips, he would hand me the keys to our safe deposit box, and we would always have the same conversation.

"I leave everything to you."

"But what do you have to leave??"

He looks at me with reproach and surprise.

"My Party card and my medals."

Abroad, he had what they called a "blank check": all his expenses were government expenses. How dear this trust was to him, and how cheap his blank check was for the state!

For me, he was the ideal Bolshevik-Leninist.[20]

Serafimovich's friend, Sonia Gavrilova, "almost cried from joy" when, on July 2, 1936, she received her new Party card (as part of the Party card verification and exchange campaign of 1935–36). Another friend, Mirra Gotfrid, wrote to him in a private letter: "Are there any fortresses the Bol-sheviks cannot overcome? No, none and never will be. That is true happi-ness. . . . A person who is honest and who truly loves his motherland and the Party of Lenin-Stalin cannot die." Efim Shchadenko wrote to his "dar-ling, sweet little Maria" to congratulate her on the "Great holiday of the October Socialist Revolution" and to his old friend, Arkady, to tell him what was going on in his life: "As far as work is concerned, I have nothing to write: in our wonderful country, all is well: everything keeps growing, ma-turing, and developing in the direction required by the Party and the peo-ple. Obviously you have been reading our newspapers and rejoicing in our successes and achievements as much as we have. So that's about it then." And as Khrushchev remembered many years later (a propos of his close friendship with Beria in the 1930s), "In those days, I looked at things as an idealist: if a person had a Party card and was a true communist, he was like a brother, and even more than a brother, to me. I believed that we were all connected by the invisible threads of a common struggle for ideas—the ideas of the building of socialism, something lofty and sacred. To speak the language of religious believers, every participant in our movement was, for me, a kind of apostle, who, for the sake of our idea, was prepared for any sacrifice."[21]

Sofia Butenko, the wife of the director of the Kuznetsk Steel Plant, Kon-stantin Butenko, and one of the leaders of the nationwide women's volun-teer movement, was thirty-three years old when Sergo Ordzhonikidze, her husband's boss and the patron of the women's volunteer movement, died on February 18, 1937. She still remembered how she felt sixty-one years later: "When they took away my husband . . . I sobbed and cried. But the way I cried when Ordzhonikidze died, I never . . . my eyes were all swol-len. . . . I couldn't even open them. The secretary of our city Party commit-tee even told me: 'This has to stop.' And he put me in his car and said, 'Let

At the All-Union Congress of Wives of Managers and Engineers
Working in Heavy Industry, May 1936. Sofia Butenko is on the right.

me take you out for a bit of fresh air." You can't imagine how I sobbed. I just couldn't stop."[22]

When Agnessa Argiropulo was told by Sergei Mironov that he would have her shot if she turned out to be a hidden enemy, but would then shoot himself, she "accepted the compromise." He loved her as much as the cause; for as long as the two did not clash, life could go on.[23]

■   ■   ■

Agnessa Argiropulo was not a hidden enemy, but Tania Miagkova was—or may have been. Agnessa was never a Communist; Tania was, and felt strongly about it. Agnessa's role in the building of socialism was to make her husband happy; Tania thought of socialism as a cause she shared with her family and her country. Agnessa's question about a possible conflict between two kinds of love was a playful test of her husband's devotion; Tania's commitment to both her family and socialism was tested continuously. Her mother and husband followed the Party line; she followed her heart and her Bolshevik conscience. When she was leaving Kazakhstan, her fellow exiles were not sure if she had found inner reconciliation or chosen one over the other.

After her return to Moscow in 1931, she continued to see her friends from the former opposition and, according to her OGPU investigator, appeared to believe that total collectivization threatened the country's productive forces and that the Party suffered from insufficient rank-and-file activism. In January 1933, two years after the family moved into the House of Government and two months after her thirty-fifth birthday, she was arrested, tried as part of the "counterrevolutionary Trotskyite group of I. N. Smirnov, V. A. Ter-Vaganian, E. A. Preobrazhensky, and others," and sentenced to three years in the Verkhneuralsk "political isolator," fifty kilometers from Magnitogorsk.[24]

According to a former inmate, "the Verkhneuralsk political isolator was a huge building standing all by itself on the bank of the Ural, three kilometers from Verkhneuralsk. During the day, it made a strong impression because of its enormous bulk; at night, because it was lit up with blindingly bright electric lights amid the silent steppe darkness. They started building it during World War I as a military penitentiary, but never finished, so it was the Bolsheviks who completed it to house their own political opponents. The building was subdivided into separate blocks, with long corridors interrupted by a succession of iron doors. The corridors were wide, so prisoners from opposite sides could not hear each other tapping. There were different kinds of cells: for four, three, or two people. . . . The worst were the solitary cells in the east wing: they had a complex system of passageways; the cells were small; the windows were high, just under the ceiling; and the whole wing was isolated from all the others."[25]

Judging from her letters home, Tania had several cellmates and a window with a beautiful view: "the faraway horizons, black and green ploughed fields, and mountains off in the distance." She liked to stand by the window at dusk: "In the evening air, I can sometimes hear the rattling of horse carts from somewhere far away, or a song (probably from a kolkhoz shepherds' encampment): a slow, sad Russian song. The horses graze nearby, and sometimes the herd approaches. Far, far away on the left, I can see the edge of the setting sun and the bright, rapidly changing colors of the clouds over the pale-blue mist of the mountains. Every evening, some kind of night bird monotonously repeats its call."[26]

After several weeks of uncertainty, dejection, and waiting for parcels from home, she transformed her corner of the cell into an "illusion of home" (complete with dictionaries, sugar tongs, family photographs, an apron, calendar, inkwell, teapot, medicine kit, Swiss Army knife, tiny mirror, cushion for the stool, small tablecloth for the bedside table, carpet for the wall next to the bed, and a reproduction of *La Gioconda*) and settled into the traditional political-prisoner routine of study, exercise, reading, drawing, and writing letters home:

> We now walk from 8 to 9 and 12 to 1. I begin by tackling *Das Kapital*. I usually manage 5–7 pages in 2–3 hours (including note-taking, of course). I read and am horrified that I understand everything. Don't get me wrong—I'm not being coy, but I've been told (and it does seem to be true) that if the first chapters come easily, it means you're skimming the surface and not truly comprehending what you're reading. Besides, I've had very few thoughts of my own about the text so far and, to be honest, even those have not been terribly profound. Well, the first step is always the hardest! Intelligent thoughts are bound to come sooner or later! After *Das Kapital*, lunch, and the walk—it's math's turn. I'm almost done with trigonometry. . . . I've been working on it with long breaks in between, but am now determined to push

through. After the second lunch (or dinner, officially), I lie down to rest, though every so often some newspapers arrive, and I glance through them in bed. Then comes English—followed by a second reading of *The Elements of Machines*, journals, serious newspaper reading, and sleep. The next day, I start all over again.[27]

The rigidity and intensity of the schedule did not vary much, but the program of study did. In addition to *Das Kapital*, English, and trigonometry, Tania worked on her specialty of industrial economics ("with an emphasis on machine-building and technology"), as well as algebra, French, German, physics, statistics, accounting, draftsmanship, economic geography, analytical geometry (a particular favorite), the history of Greece, and the history of the French Revolution (using Mathiez, Kropotkin, and a collection of Robespierre's letters).[28] Her plan to study art history proved unrealistic because of the lack of material:

> As for *Das Kapital* [she wrote to her husband on January 12, 1934], it did turn out ("just as I, poor me, knew it would!") that I missed some very important things. I now have a new method: I take copious notes and then write out all my questions, confusions, and "revelations" (when they occur) in the margins. After that, I hand my notebook over to a very intelligent person who really knows *Das Kapital* well. This person then writes out his own comments, explanations, and confusions concerning my "revelations," accompanied by exclamation marks (lots of them!). I receive a great deal of benefit and pleasure from this (he, probably, less so), and I strongly hope that by the end of my third year here, I will begin to understand some of it.[29]

Before bedtime, she usually read fiction: Balzac, Stendhal, Zola, Flaubert, Goethe, Pushkin, Lermontov, Tolstoy, and various Soviet writers. (She especially liked Bagritsky's poems and Aleksei Tolstoy's *Peter I*.) Sometimes she and her cellmates read aloud to each other: she mentions Blok, Hasek's *The Good Soldier Svejk*, and Pushkin's *Boris Godunov*. Of special significance to her were Voronsky's *The Seminary* (a memoir of his student days) and *Zheliabov* (a biography of one of the leaders of the People's Will executed in 1881 for the assassination of Alexander II). When Tania was still a little girl with a "critical frame of mind," and Voronsky was her mother's apprentice as an underground socialist, she used to dismiss his stories as fiction. Now she read them "with enormous pleasure" but remained critical: *The Seminary* was good, but not as good as *In Search of the Water of Life*, and *Zheliabov*, while "very exciting," showed signs "of having been written hastily."[30]

Zheliabov was about the birth of Bolshevik morality, as Voronsky understood it. Whereas Dostoevsky's Raskolnikov believed that, in a world without God, "everything was permitted," Voronsky's Zheliabov understood that, in true Christianity, everything was permitted, but only outside the army of light. Zheliabov the terrorist did what Jesus had taught and what his Bolshevik successors would finally accomplish. "Like the mythological hero," writes Voronsky in the book's conclusion, "Zheliabov sowed the dragon's teeth. From them sprouted a forest of thick-necked warriors clad in armor—the invincible proletarians." Voronsky was not mixing archetypes: his Jesus, like Zheliabov's, came from the Book of Revelation and belonged in the same category as Cadmus, Jason, and countless other dragon-slayers. It is not clear whether Voronsky remembered that the warriors who sprouted from the dragon's teeth ended up killing each other. Nor is it known which part of his argument Tania found unconvincing. She could not write to him directly because she was only allowed to correspond with her husband, mother, and daughter (at their House of Government address).[31]

The main difference between Tania's "political isolation" in the Soviet Union and Voronsky's (and Zheliabov's) "prison and exile" in tsarist Russia was that Tania had been jailed by a state she considered her own. "How do I feel?" she wrote in her first letter home. "I can't say I feel good. I find myself in an extremely difficult situation because my position (I immediately announced my unconditional support for the Party's general line) provoked a certain reaction on the part of my cellmates. I asked the administration to transfer me to a cell with comrades who, like me, support the Party line, but the matter has not been resolved yet, and I don't know if it will be resolved favorably." It was. About two weeks later, she was transferred to a different cell, where she was able to "feel calm" among like-minded comrades. Still, one had to be vigilant. As she wrote to her husband, the deputy chairman of the Central Executive Committee's Budget Commission, Mikhail (Mikhas) Poloz, "you don't have to worry: even in these conditions, just as in any other, I am able to isolate myself politically from my surroundings. You know me; you know that the fact that I am here is the result of a misunderstanding. It will be cleared up, I think. In the meantime, I have to wait patiently and use my time here for studying."[32]

The main difference between Tania's and Voronsky's prison study programs, besides her professional interest in economics and mathematics, was her "serious and detailed," "pencil-in-hand" reading of newspapers: especially *Pravda* and *For Industrialization*, but also *Izvestia*, the *Literary Gazette*, and the *Pioneer Pravda*. She read official speeches (including her husband's), took down plan fulfillment numbers, worried about the harvest, rejoiced in "Litvinov's victory" (the recognition of the Soviet Union by the United States), and was "very much taken by the romance of Arctic exploration." The main themes of her letters reflected the recently introduced main themes of Soviet public life: the love of life, the richness of everyday experience, the joy of being a witness to history. The newspapers and the letters from home conveyed and communicated the "powerful feeling of pure, physical joy" that reigned throughout the country. Tania was particularly touched by the autobiography of the head of the Dnieper Hydroelectric Dam construction project, A. V. Vinter, published in the almanac *Year Sixteen*. Its title was "My Happy Life," and its concluding sentence was: "My life has been happier than what a human being is probably entitled to."[33]

Tania could not say that about herself, but her "love of life and curiosity about life" were "as strong as ever," and her perception of happiness seemed all the more intense for being postponed. "I cannot say that I am not sad at all, but the main reason for this sadness is that I have to sit on the sidelines while such a wonderful life passes me by," she wrote to her mother soon after reading about the *USSR-1* high-altitude balloon, the Moscow–Kara Kum–Moscow auto rally, and the First Nuclear Conference in Leningrad. "But I am preparing myself for it much better now, studying a lot, and waiting. . . . I don't know how long I'll have to wait, but the day will come. . . . The balloon, the Kara Kum rally, and the nucleus of the atom have provoked in me the same thoughts and feelings they have provoked in you. You probably know it from my letter to Mikhas. It is so good to be a citizen of the USSR, even if you are temporarily confined to an isolator. . . . I am also very happy that the children have taken so much interest in the balloon. I hope they, too, will develop a strong sense of pride in the achievements of the Soviet state. I know you will be able to instill it in them." Her mother, Feoktista Yakovlevna, did her best. According to Tania's daughter, Rada, her grandmother "lived on newspapers and the latest news on the radio" and raised both her and her cousin Volia as fervently patriotic Soviets. (The cooking was done by the maid.)[34]

True happiness consisted of taking "personal pleasure" in the launching of the *USSR-1* balloon: in loving all good Soviets as much as one's close relatives and loving one's close relatives to the degree that they were good Soviets. The adults, weighed down by sins voluntary and involuntary, might not be redeemed; their children were born pure and reared within the sect. The Soviet world of happiness was, like its Gorky Park reenactment, centered on childhood—because future Communism was designed for today's children and because Communist redemption was, like the Christian kind, about becoming a child. As Tania wrote to her mother on October 23, 1933 (with her sister Lelia in mind),

> Today I read an issue of the *Literaturnaia gazeta* [Literary gazette] devoted entirely to children's books. Right now, kids are at the top of our country's agenda, and I think that the Central Committee decision on children's book publishing is, in its own way, no less significant than the flight of a high-altitude balloon. I am very happy that both Rada and Volia will still be children when this work gets fully under way, but still, it is absolutely imperative that both Lelia and I have one more child each: she, a girl, and I, a boy, so that they will be able to take full advantage of everything (that's one of the

reasons I wouldn't mind getting out of the isolator sooner rather
than later). . . . I want our children to feel that they belong not only
to our family, but also to the Soviet Republic. Last week was international children's week. Did their school do anything special? (Oh,
how happy I would be to be working at their school right now!)
That's why I would like Rada to spend next summer in a pioneer
camp.[35]

She urged Rada (who was nine at the time) to read the latest appeal of
the Central Committee of the Komsomol to young Octobrists, to prepare
her home library for the national "inspection of the young Octobrist's
bookshelf," and to work hard in order "to enter the broad arena of the organized Soviet child." Her engagement seems to have been sincere, but it
was up to the OGPU to decide, and, in early December 1933, the OGPU
decided not to reconsider her case (originally prepared by Interrogator
Rutkovsky in Moscow). As she wrote to Mikhail on December 30,

Apparently, they did not believe my application was sincere this
time. I sometimes feel like writing a letter to a particular person (for
example to Rutkovsky) instead of an official request. I think the opportunity to write not in the official style, but more freely would
make it easier to express the sincerity of my thoughts and attitudes.
I will write again, but I believe that it would be better to do it in two
or three months so the matter can be reconsidered. Of course, my
dear sweet Mikhailik, it is very hard for me to put it off for such a
relatively long time and continue my life in this isolator apart from
the real life, which keeps getting better and more amazing. I think
that if I were in a concentration camp and if I were working, my true
attitude toward the policies of the Party and my own past would
become clear very soon. . . . So, my dear, this is my sad news. But
don't be sad, my love. I think—and really truly want to believe—that
before long my case will change for the better. It can't be otherwise.
And so I'll cheerfully wait for that time, while following from afar all
the miracles you are performing in the USSR. I will leave here with
an enormous reserve of energy and a slightly greater store of
knowledge.[36]

There was more bad news: she had lost three teeth (in addition to the
ones she had lost in Kazakhstan) and was having difficulty chewing. The
two teeth that might still be used for a bridge were also in poor condition,
but there was no gold to be had in the isolator, and the hope of being taken
to Sverdlovsk or Moscow for dental work was slight, in any case. Her hair,
on the other hand, had suddenly stopped falling out (just as she "had gotten used to the idea of becoming completely bald within six months")—
probably because of the arsenic and cod liver oil treatment that she had

devised. But what she really wanted to talk about, she insisted, were the "happy subjects": the triumph of the Communists at the Reichstag Fire Trial in Leipzig, the planned publication of the Large Soviet World Atlas, her desire to learn more about Trofim Lysenko's "vernalization," her reading of *Das Kapital*, and, on the home front, Mikhail taking Rada to Gorky Park to skate, Mikhail taking Rada to the Bolshoi to see *The Barber of Seville*, Mikhail and Rada reading *The Jungle Book* together, and Mikhail's name being mentioned in the newspapers in connection with a meeting of the Central Executive Committee.[37]

Mikhail was very busy at work and in his Party cell. Tania was keenly interested ("Tell me more about your purge session. What theory questions did they ask you? I am dying of curiosity")—but also understanding: "I won't worry at all if you don't write for some time. In general, I hope that during all these meetings you won't be spending any of your physical or emotional energy on me. I regret having written to you about the rejection a while back. If I had only known that you hadn't heard, I would never have done it. And please, my darling, try not to miss me too much—in spite of everything, I really am perfectly cheerful, and I trust and hope that we will see each other soon."[38] But it was hard to be perfectly cheerful—especially on New Year's Eve:

> It's a beautiful, moonlit, snowy night! Such a perfect pale blue . . . Oh, to be walking around on such a night, making the snow squeak underfoot . . . But to be walking with you, dear Mikhailik. . . . I stayed up until midnight. For some reason this evening was especially sad, even though I enjoyed all sorts of pleasures: went to the bath house, washed my hair, put on a completely fresh set of clothes, but felt bad that I didn't have my "Lily" or "Acacia" perfume; their fragrance brings back a lot of good memories. . . . And when I was all ready to "greet" the New Year, I sat down at my desk and read through several newspapers, then looked out the window at the pale-blue plains, thinking of all of you and knowing that you must be thinking of me—when the lights went out, which meant that it was midnight. So it's now 1934 . . . What will it bring? I feel somewhat curious, and my breath catches a little when I think of all the good things it might bring . . . It is odd how you feel the flow of time so acutely at such moments, as if the constant and varied stream of life were passing right through you—whereas, in fact, it is passing you by, far, far away.[39]

It was even harder not to miss him too much and not to worry about not hearing from him. On January 12, when the Central Executive Committee session was over, she wrote to tease him about his portrait in the newspaper, to ask for the original photograph, and to mark the first anniversary of her arrest: "I've been remembering how badly I wanted to see you before being taken away, and how happy I was when you came. And how in jail I have been reading the reports about the Central Executive Committee

Mikhail Poloz with his daughter Rada,
with her hair shaved off for the summer

meeting. Yes, my dear Mikhasik, it's already been a year. How much longer? It is comforting, of course, to think that had I not ended up here, I would never have learned trigonometry, and my knowledge of *Das Kapital* would have remained at its previous, fairly modest level. But still, even these serious advantages do not fill me with very much joy. It's been a year since I've seen our little Rada! She must have changed so much."[40]

Five days later, she wrote again:

17 January

Mikhasik, my darling, my very own, beloved Mikhasik! Oh how I want to see you, to hold you, to talk to you, to be silent together in your room at dusk. Over the last several days, I have been overcome by such profound sadness, such a desire to be with you and our Rada, such boundless love for you both. Oh Mikhasik, if only I could be sure that I would get to see you this year . . . My dears, I love you both with all my heart, and right now my heart is aching with all this love . . .

My mother writes that you are very, very tired, my love, and that you need lots of care and attention. Oh how happy I would be to give it to you—like back in those days when I would come to Moscow to see you in that big, empty apartment. And as always in such cases, I can't help thinking with acute and painful regret of all those times when I could have given you joy, but didn't, and perhaps even made you suffer instead. It is not good to remember such things in an isolator, when you can't <u>actively</u> express your feelings of love and your desire to make your loved one happy.

I am waiting for your letter, waiting patiently . . . It may arrive soon—tomorrow or maybe the day after tomorrow. Yesterday I received my mother's letter of January 1; it took 17 days. The mail broke down for a while, but now everything seems to be okay, and my most recent letter to you was sent on its way at the normal time. I hope your letters will start arriving more quickly, too.

Mikhasik, my darling, if you have a free moment, please remember how I wait for your letters.

Oh well, I won't add anything to what just got written. Don't feel bad for me, my darling: such boundless love is a great happiness in and of itself, even in an isolator . . . I hope you were able to get some pleasure from my letter, too. I want you to be happy. If you are all happy, I, too, am happy and calm, even if far away.

18 January

Dear Mikhasik, a day has passed, but the intensity hasn't diminished. I feel good and sad, and I love you and everyone there. It makes me so happy to read my mother's descriptions of your conversations with Rada. The day will come, won't it, when we can all be together and have such conversations? And in the meantime, I think I can allow myself to feel a little sad between *Das Kapital* and trigonometry.

Well, that's all for now. I kiss you very, very tenderly, my love . . .

She continued to correspond with her mother: about her teeth, her shoes, her need for more cod liver oil, her disappointment with *Pionerskaia Pravda*, her opposition to wallpaper for their apartment ("it will only attract bedbugs"), and her worries about Rada's winter vacation in the country. On January 24, she had still not received anything from Mikhail.

24 January

Mikhas, my darling! I thought for a long time about whether or not I should write to you what I am about to write or exercise restraint and not show my true weakness. Especially since this weakness and the way I express it will affect not only you. Still, I have decided "to react" . . . I do not know if it will make things better or make me feel better afterward, but I do know how hard it is for me right now . . . And so, after this solemn introduction, which might lead one to expect some extraordinary revelations, it's actually something simple that should not be hard for you to understand: I am quite ill without your letters, dear Mikhas. I don't mean this as a metaphor. I have grown much weaker physically over the last several weeks due to extreme stress. I can't eat; I can't sleep; and study is impossible. When I wake up at night or in the morning, I feel a heavy weight on my chest, and I think: here comes another day with nothing in the mail. I keep asking myself: why is this happening? Have I really failed to make you understand what your letters mean to me here (and not only here)? Don't you want to write to me yourself? When I think about what kinds of letters you have been receiving recently, with what kinds of news and questions (I really do need your answers), I simply cannot understand your silence. Perhaps you have written? Perhaps I simply did not receive your letter? Or are you so tired and exhausted that you can't write a serious letter? But surely it wouldn't be hard to add a line to my mother's letters (such a line could be written at any moment on any sheet or scrap of paper, so as not to tie yourself to the timing of my mother's letters) . . . In the state I am now in, whatever lies ahead (for me personally) looks very gloomy. I know that I have gotten caught up in "personal emotions" . . . I do understand, my dear Mikhas, that this is completely unjustified weakness . . . It seems that this past year has left its mark on me as far as my emotional state is concerned. It is very sad. What will happen by the end of my third year? Please bear this weakness of mine in mind, my darling. No one else will help me in my moment of weakness, and that's the way it should be. But surely I can count on you for help? All the more so because I am not asking for much: just enough for me to feel the thread that continually connects us. Really, my darling, I don't need much for that . . .

She went on to talk about Rada's upbringing. Then, after addressing several questions to her mother, she added a postscript:

Mikhas, darling, I have reread my letter and decided not to mail it, but there was no time to write another, so I only crossed out one passage and am sending the rest. I cannot say I am calm now: I am calm on the outside, but it takes a lot of effort. I am still in complete suspense. Please don't judge my letter harshly, and try to understand. Reach out your hand to me. Tania.[41]

■ ■ ■

Mikhail did not respond because on January 12, the day Tania wrote the first of her "sad" letters, he had been arrested as a Ukrainian nationalist (a former member of the Ukrainian Left-SR "Borotbist" Party). According to the report submitted by the arresting officer, Edelman, to the commander of the OGPU Secret-Political Department, Molchanov, the attempt to enter the apartment without warning failed because both doors had been bolted. Mikhail opened the door in his pajamas:

After we initiated the search, we immediately became aware that Poloz had been preparing for it, since the contents of his cupboard lay in complete disarray: books, medicine, and personal items were scattered about at random, in no apparent order. All the drawers in his desk had been completely cleaned out, and only on top of the desk were a few budget committee documents that he had been using to prepare his report for the meeting. He had not set aside any extra clothing or shoes.

He spent a long time saying goodbye to his mother-in-law, the mother of the Trotskyite, Miagkova, emphasizing the parting, but also feeling compelled to say out loud: "Well, I hope things get cleared up, and we see each other again, even if it takes a little while."

Thirty rubles (the ones we found in his wallet) was all the money he had, and he took it with him, leaving Miagkova nothing but a receipt for a suit that could be sold and a special-store pass, which he handed to her.

Also notable was the total absence of the collected works of Lenin and Stalin, except for a copy of the most recent edition of *Problems of Leninism* with no marginal comments, while, at the same time, there was other literature such as Bukharin and some brochures written by Rykov that had been read thoroughly.

Notable, too, was the absence of any portrait of Comrade Stalin, while at the same time there were a large number of photographs of Ukraine's nationalist leaders, a portrait of Skrypnik (a personal gift), and several books by Voronsky with a personal dedication to Miagkova. There was nothing at all on the walls. It gave the impression of a temporary camp.[42]

Mikhail had, indeed, "been preparing for it" (many of the former "Borotbists" had already been arrested). Rada had been sent out of town to make sure she did not witness her father's arrest. Tania heard the news in late January, but was not allowed to write to him directly.[43]

You must have many worries and cares, so please don't worry about me at all, Mommy dearest, except to send news as regularly as you can (you understand, of course, how important this is for me). I am calm, dear, and not expecting anything bad. In any case, all bad things eventually pass. Try not to overwork yourself, my dear, and take care of Lelia [Tania's sister]. Don't forget to feed yourselves as well as the children. Lelia should remember that this is also for the sake of the kids. . . .

So, my darlings, goodbye for now and please don't be angry about the short letter. After I receive your letter, Mommy, dearest, I'll write lots and lots. As for Mikhasik, my own darling Mikhasik, whom I love more than ever, please send him a very, very tender kiss from me, Mommy, dear. And kiss dear sweet Rada, too. . . .

> That is all, my darlings.
> I send kisses to you all,
> Your Tania

My darling, beloved Mikhasik, sun of my world and joy of my life, I am sending you a big, big, big hug and a kiss.

Dearest Mommy, I don't have to tell you how much I look forward to your letters, do I? My teeth are not so bad and can still wait a bit longer, so please don't worry about them, my dear.[44]

During the first few days after Mikhail's arrest Tania could only manage to read fiction (mostly Tolstoy's *Resurrection* and *Anna Karenina*), but by February 12, she had resumed her studies (although *Das Kapital* was still too difficult, "maybe because my work on it, and on mathematics, was associated with a whole series of thoughts, feelings, and emotions that are a little difficult to return to right now"). She had also regained her desire for a full life understood as a seamless connection between her, her family, and the building of socialism. "That reminds me," she wrote to her mother on February 18, "why didn't you write about how the plan was approved, and about Lelia's health? As for Rada, you have made me happy. That's the kind of mood I'd like to see her in. Let her think about me and dream about a life together even less often. I am absolutely sure, for some reason, that I won't lose her affection. I would not want for her childhood to end now." The family members remaining in Moscow—Feoktista Yakovlevna, Rada, Tania's sister Lelia, and Lelia's son Volia (the maid had left soon after Mikhail's arrest)—were evicted from their House of Government apartment and chose a new one in Orphan Alley, next to the Comintern radio station. (They were offered a choice of several apartments and given some House of Government furniture, complete with numbered tags.) Lelia became Rada's official guardian. Both Lelia and Feoktista Yakovlevna committed themselves to making sure that Rada's—and, to the extent possible, their own—childhood would not end. According to Feoktista Yakovlevna's letters, and Rada's own recollections, they largely succeeded. Tania seemed grateful and relieved. "In analyzing the

Volia, Lelia, and Rada Poloz, with Feoktista Yakovlevna Miagkova.
A photo taken for Tania Miagkova.

work of one of our poets," she wrote on June 4, "the *Literaturnaia gazeta* cites his description of young pine trees. They frolic in the breeze, like a circle of kids, who don't know grief, and whose parents are near. The reason Rada 'doesn't know grief,' even though her parents are, alas, very far away, is your doing. Yours and Lelia's. Because one of my most painful thoughts after the news about Mikhailik was: 'So Rada's childhood has come to an end.'"[45]

Tania did her best to participate in the effort. When she heard that Rada and Volia had made a lot of new friends in Orphan Alley, she wrote: "I am very happy that the kids like their new apartment. What kind of families do all those children come from? What is the population of the building in general? I hope it's mostly workers' families (are there factories nearby?). The kids would benefit from finding themselves in such an environment." When she decided that Rada might have literary abilities, she wrote: "I would hope that Rada would want not only to write about life, but, even more important, to create life. But it's still very early: she can always change direction. All that is needed now is for her to march in step with our life, to feel the romance of the machine, the factory, and construction (of our Soviet machines and construction), and to fall in love with technology, or at least to become interested in it." And when she heard that Rada had not been in Moscow for the May Day celebrations (the ones Hubert described), she wrote: "What a pity Rada missed out on the demonstration! If only I had been there with all of you to see Budenny's Red Cavalry. This year the demonstration must have been especially rousing. It gives me so much pleasure to look at the wonderful photographs in *Izvestia*: the group of laughing leaders on the podium and the group of Schutzbund members, also laughing, on the same podium. Such wonderful faces! It's a shame that the Chelyuskinites could not make it in time."[46]

The *Chelyuskin* was a steamship that had attempted to travel the Northern Maritime Route from Murmansk to Vladivostok in a single navigation season. It had made it to the Bering Straits, but was then crushed by ice in the Chukchi Sea on February 13, 1934. The "Chelyuskinites" set up camp on an ice floe, built an airstrip, and were eventually evacuated by Soviet polar aviators during the second week of April as part of a massive rescue operation directed by Kuibyshev. Tania repeatedly mentioned the Chelyuskinites amid news and worries about her own life and kept asking her mother, who seemed similarly engaged, about Rada's involvement. The June 5 welcome home parade on Red Square in honor of the Chelyuskinites was the biggest Soviet public event of 1934. Tania wrote about it on June 24. Or rather, she began by writing about her own hope of delivery (referring mostly to a continued uncertainty about Mikhail's fate): "I have certainly had more than enough practice in patience and fortitude recently. There are occasional lapses: periods of depression when I can't do any math and generally don't feel like dealing with the world. But, first, I used to go through similar cycles even on the outside, and, second, I tend to pull myself out of such states (they are not frequent) quite quickly." In the next paragraph, she moved on to the Chelyuskinites:

> That was some welcome you all organized! I can imagine what it must have been like! Have you been reading the articles about the Chelyuskinites and their reminiscences in the newspapers? If not, get all the *Pravda* issues and read them. There are a lot of articles that the kids should read. What a wonderful "episode," which has now turned into a political event of exceptional importance. The cost of the steamship has been repaid a thousand times over. And it is not just Bolshevik fortitude that is important, but rather Bolshevik fortitude imbued, at the most difficult moments, with the spark of joyous communal living, laughter, and good cheer. Now the world has truly seen what the Bolsheviks are capable of![47]

Her next letter began with the Chelyuskinites (before moving on to Rada's and Volia's upbringing, her "mathematically organized way of life," her "socialist experimental garden," and her struggles with fraying stockings, bras, and nightshirts):

> So, let us sum up the lessons of the Chelyuskin saga (I'll write special "Chelyuskin" letters to the kids, too).... The Chelyuskin saga has given the whole country a shot of heroism, united "one and all" around the general staff (the Party and Politburo), and helped every single person realize what it means to be a Soviet citizen, how precious each human being is for the country, and how precious the Soviet country is for its people—and this is all steeped in powerful emotion, a common, all-encompassing burst of enthusiasm, and a desire to be a hero of the Soviet Union along with a desire to excel at one's routine daily tasks, based on the understanding that those tasks are connected to the common cause and to what the Chelyuskinites and the aviators have done.... It's been a dizzying year! Dimitrov ("hurray!"), the Schutzbundists ("hurray!"), and the Chelyuskinites ("hurra-a-a-a-ay!")....
>
> You are right, mommy, dearest: the Chelyuskin saga is a test of the achievements of the revolution—above all, its achievements in the countryside, in the matter of the rebirth of the peasant. The kolkhozes have won, and the "idiocy of rural life" is disappearing. Has not the Chelyuskin saga demonstrated its disappearance?...
>
> I have a secret confession: while reading the newspaper issues devoted to the welcome parade (and all of them from cover to cover, of course), I—like those who had assembled at the railway station to greet them—couldn't help crying (just a little).[48]

Tania's letters were not proper confessions, and they were not confidential. They were addressed to her mother, who expected Party orthodoxy; her daughter, whose happy childhood was to be preserved; her own self, which seemed to yearn for a reconciliation with life ("I discipline myself in every way possible"); and her censors, who were responsible for helping in all these endeavors as well as—presumably—determining the degree of their success. The Bolsheviks—like most priests, historians, and the participants in the discussion of the State New Theater's production of *The Other Side of the Heart*—had no clear doctrine on how to judge the sincerity of contrition. It was—and is—impossible to be sure on what occasions Tania resorted to *mentalis restrictio*, but it does appear likely that, for the most part, she tried her best to erase the distinction between her yearnings on the one hand and her mother's Party-minded expectations, her daughter's happy-childhood entitlements, and her censors' inscrutable ways, on the other. As Dante's nuns, who were assigned to the lowest sphere of paradise, put it, "Should we desire a higher sphere than ours, / then our desires would be discordant with / the will of Him who has assigned us here."[49]

The greatest test of Tania's fortitude—in her letters if not in her soul—came in late July, when she received the news that Mikhail had been sentenced to ten years in a labor camp.

> My dear, sweet, darling mom, you are so wonderful, and I don't know where we would be without you! Thank you and thank Lelia. You two make it possible for me to be courageous and determined and able to endure such hardships. I received your letter yesterday and marveled at myself after I read it: no depression (let alone despair) and not even much sadness. What has given me this strength at such a difficult time? It was the news of Mikhailik's high spirits, his active desire to grab his fate by the horns and turn it back onto the right path, and his firm belief that it can be done. Mommy dear, I know Mikhas better than anyone else. I do not know what he has been accused of, but I do know Mikhas, and I know that he can and must be rehabilitated. A concentration camp? So be it! Over a period of several years? So be it! Long, difficult years? So be it! Mikhas must be accepted back into the Party. Whatever I can do to help him, I will. Above all, I must be with him for the rest of my term, wherever he may be and no matter what the conditions. I have already written a short application to the Secret Political Department, and now I must wait. I have tremendous hope that I will see Mikhailik soon—and that is the second reason why I was in an almost exultant mood after reading your letter.[50]

Being together, even if in prison, was better than being apart; being involved in labor, even if forced, was better than being isolated; and being exultant over such news was proof, if proof were needed, that both Tania and her mother had passed another test.

To be honest with you, I still don't know what constitutes a harsher punishment, an isolator or a concentration camp, but I think that, in the case of a ten-year sentence, a concentration camp is much better: first, it means working and therefore participating in the life of the country; second, it means the possibility of a shortened term. Ten years in an isolator, on the other hand, has an air of hopelessness about it. One of the many reasons we love the Soviet order is because it has no prison term fetishism, and ten years is not really ten years, but only what you manage to make of them. There is no place for hopelessness in our—very tough—system . . . One thing continues to make me feel good about my reaction to all this. A comrade with whom I shared some of my news and feelings in this regard asked me half seriously and half jokingly, "But you're not angry with the Soviet order, are you, Tania?" I was silent for a while, and then gave a totally serious answer to what was probably an equally serious question, despite the jocular tone: "No, I'm not angry at all." I needed to be silent because I wanted to test myself once more to see if all these difficult personal experiences (and not my own this time) had affected what I might call my emotional-political feelings (sorry for the clumsy word). And that's the third reason your letter gave me such a shot of energy: your own reaction to what has been happening. I was afraid for you, mommy dear. I was afraid that these unexpected blows, and such heavy ones, too, might undermine you physically and morally and destroy your view of things, but now I see that there is not even a hint of that. So this means that, generally, everything is fine, though Mikhailik is in a concentration camp, and I am in an isolator. There is nothing to fear, "as long as we have the Soviet order and our mutual love for each other."[51]

In her letter, Feoktista Yakovlevna seems to have mentioned that Mikhail's interrogators in Kiev had made some favorable remarks about Tania's letters. "I won't lie to you," Tania responded, "such an assessment from such an institution—indeed, especially from such an institution, is far from being disagreeable to me. But I'm afraid the Moscow GPU does not share this opinion of my honesty and sincerity. Say what you will, but I did receive three years in an isolator after being accused of duplicity." And this was the final and most important benefit of the news about Mikhail:

Yes, the advantage you write about, mommy dearest—the "conclusiveness and irreversibility" and the "getting rid of all the birthmarks" is a huge thing. My comments to you on this subject have been short and dry, though I could have written much more, and in greater detail. It's just that I am somewhat inhibited by the possibility that my letters on this topic might be regarded as a duplicitous move, and that is very unpleasant, as you can imagine . . . I used to be extremely skeptical of prison conversions, but now I can see what an inaccurate and superficial view that was. I can't help thinking that, had I been sent into exile, my development would have been much slower. Sometimes it is useful to hit a person over the head with a club (at least it has been in my case). Of course that does not mean that I am very happy to have ended up in an isolator. Still, if I were faced with the dilemma: the isolator and a genuine break with Trotskyism or Moscow and my prior semi-Trotskyite views, I would not hesitate to choose the former.[52]

There was nothing Tania could do about the obvious danger that claims of sincerity might be interpreted as proof of duplicity. All she could do was wait. "Waiting without the slightest possibility of doing anything about it ought to have been included as a separate punishment for sinners in one of the rings of Dante's inferno . . . At the same time, even in the rings of Dante's inferno, life clearly goes on." She rearranged her belongings ("so the only thing left to do would be to put them in suitcases"), resolved to work even harder, and devoted the rest of her time to imagining the future. "My dream," she wrote to her mother on August 12, "is for the concentration camp to be in a forest and for me to arrive in the fall when the birches and aspens are yellow and red . . . (But that's just a dream: I would take the concentration camp even without the birches and aspens)."[53]

I want to think about <u>our</u> future, [she wrote to Mikhail on the same day], at first tough and difficult, perhaps, but then (definitely!) sunny and joyful.

I really want to hear from you that you are also sure about our good future together . . . But first I want you to rest alongside me.

Because being together is a form of rest, isn't it, my dear? I am also tired after all this time and want to lay my head on your chest . . .

Oh how I long for our meeting, Mikhasik, my love . . .

I kiss you and love you.

Don't be angry with me for writing the same thing over and over again. It's just that I always feel the same thing. And so strongly![54]

Mikhail responded by saying that he was, indeed, sure about their good future together, that he was on his way to Kem, on the White Sea, and that Kem was a "lovely" place. Tania could finally make concrete plans for their life together. "Let us adopt the slogan, 'a ten-year plan in four years (and preferably less),'" she wrote on August 17, "and let us work toward that together (in case your sentence is not overturned). Together . . . Mikhas dear, I am a little worried about being so sure that I'll be with you. I can't think of any possible reason for a denial, but I've gotten so used to the idea of coming to live with you (I have even determined the time: I'll arrive in

September, when the forest is red and gold) that it will be very hard if there is a delay of some kind." She agreed that Kem sounded good but worried about whether it was possible "to grow flowers and start a vegetable garden there." She was still not sure if he was going to Kem, or via Kem, to Solovki. "The latter may be even better, because the camp up there is very well run and the nature is beautiful."[55]

Two weeks later, Tania was told that Mikhail had been sent to a timber-rafting camp within the White Sea–Baltic Canal camp system. "The fact that Mikhas is in the White Sea–Baltic Canal camp made me happy," she wrote to her mother on August 30. "After all, it is one of the best camps, very well run, and the construction itself is interesting. But the timber rafting part has me a bit worried. Is it possible that instead of working as an agronomist or surveyor, Mikhas is wielding a pole? That would not be ideal, although, if that is the case, we should probably think of it as a period of 'production startup costs.' After all, even in timber rafting there are lots of jobs appropriate to his specialty, perhaps even some surveying work." While waiting to find out, she followed the newspaper reports about the first Congress of Soviet Writers ("it's too bad the kids did not send Gorky their letter about which books they like and what sort of books they wish writers would write") and read a lot of poetry. One of her old favorites was Walt Whitman. "What enormous strength! What an extraordinary joy of living! What a powerful interpretation of my favorite quotation: 'I love life equally whether I am on a horse or under it. Life is equally beautiful in joy and in sorrow.'"[56]

Ten days later, Tania was informed that her application had been turned down. "I cannot say, of course, that this decision was not a blow to me," she wrote to her mother, "but I seem to have gotten used to them over the years, so please don't worry about my mood. I worry more about Mikhas, about how he will take this news in the first months of his 'new life,' especially without our letters." Her own new life required some tightening up, but no major revisions:

Tomorrow I'll put together a precise schedule for the remaining year and four months. Nothing came of the concentration camp idea, so we'll try a different tack. In addition to higher mathematics, I plan to get through mechanics and draftsmanship (as well as descriptive geometry). This is the main thing, and if I can pull it off, I'll consider it a huge achievement. I also want to finish *Das Kapital* and work on my languages. These last few weeks have shaken me somewhat. My self-discipline faltered a bit, though I never abandoned my studies for more than the briefest of periods. But now I will pull myself together . . . As for my undershirts, three are in decent shape, and the rest are all worn and thin the way Lelia likes them, but they should last through the winter just fine. My blouses are also worn and frayed, including even—you won't believe it—the lilac gingham one (the one just like yours). For the winter, I'm planning to make a blouse out of that tangerine flannel you sent me. Also, I wonder if I shouldn't make a white blouse with long sleeves from that linen sheet that was too wide. What do you think? I did a brilliant job washing the black wool dress in mustard, but the seams are coming apart at the armpits. The lace, on the other hand, which had faded in the wash, is now a metallic steel color and looks very festive. It would be nice to have some gloves (women's knit ones), but only if you happen to run across them. There's no need to go out and look for them specially: I can get by with my mittens. The same goes for felt boots. Mine are still fine, but I am writing in advance, just in case. As for shoes, the gray canvas and black leather ones are completely worn out, but both the yellow and black pairs of walking shoes are still in good shape. So, the winter and spring are taken care of (and summers here you can get by with cloth slippers)... Mommy dear, perhaps sometime you could send me photos instead of a parcel? It's been a whole year since I've seen Rada (since her last photograph).[57]

Almost two months later (on November 5 and November 10) she received two letters from Mikhail. He was in Solovki, and the letters had taken about a month to arrive. He was not allowed to write to Moscow, so Tania would now become the center of the family's delicate epistolary web. "He writes that the situation there is more difficult than here. It must be true, and I have never doubted it. Besides, I think that he generally finds it much harder than I do to adapt to unfavorable circumstances. But don't be afraid for him, my dear, and don't worry too much. Solovki is no worse, and may be even better, than any other camp. Mikhas has inner strength. He will 'settle in,' and we will help him in every way we can." In the meantime, his main worry was about the children. (Tania was very happy that he considered Volia one of his own.)[58] Now that he was gone (and along with him the maid, special passes, and House of Government services) the children needed to grow up—without leaving their happy childhoods behind:

The most efficient method, in his opinion [wrote Tania to her mother], would be to draw up a familywide socialist contract, which would list all the responsibilities of the children (cleaning their room, setting and clearing the table, helping with the dishes, doing homework, calisthenics, etc.) alongside all the duties of the grown-ups, including nondomestic ones. This would show how much more extensive the adult duties were and introduce elements of equality. Such institutionalization of the "family code" would allow the kids to regard it as a part of a larger system. We could also consider incorporating certain incentives (including those of a nonmaterial nature). The very act of drawing up such a contract would be of great pedagogical significance.[59]

Tania voted for introducing the system gradually, so as not to overwhelm the children with detail and her mother with extra work, but, on the whole, she approved of the initiative. A few days later, she read a newspaper article titled "Our Children," about a school in Moscow that had adopted a "student daily schedule" ("for the whole day, not just the school day"). "In that school," she wrote to her mother, "every student used the model template to work out an individualized schedule adapted to the family's schedule. Our kids need to do that, too (in the form of a socialist contract as suggested by Mikhas), so that they can become, through the pioneer organization, the initiators of this campaign in their own classes (at first only for the pioneers)."[60]

The task was for the children to become responsible members of the family, and for the family to become a functioning part of the state. The family was to become a formalized institution bound by contractual obligations; the state was to become a family in which all children (and factories) were "our children." Neither transformation was to be complete, however: no one envisioned an imminent dissolution of kinship ties and no one imagined the state as a patriarchal institution unmediated by legal codes enforced by strangers. The governing assumption—and the necessary condition for the victory of socialism—was the inherent compatibility and mutual attraction between the two.

But what if the state spurned some members of a particular family? Could Rada's happy childhood and her parents' possible apostasy be reconciled? "It is with tremendous sadness," wrote Mikhail to Tania, "that I think of how Rada will find out about my current reality. I would like for it to happen after your release, so that you can explain to her about your past and my present. That would make it easier for her to absorb. The main thing I am asking for is that the children have the same understanding about you and me and that Rada still love me."[61]

Could Rada still love her parents if the state was right to distrust them? Could Tania and Mikhail still love each other if one of them was irredeemably duplicitous? For as long as Tania's answer was "no," her love of the high-altitude balloon had to be as great as her love for her mother, Rada, and Mikhail. "I knew that the crash of the *Maksim Gorky* airplane would be a huge shock to you," she wrote to her mother on May 30, 1935. "The common experience of joy and grief in our USSR is extremely precious."[62]

18

THE CENTER OF
THE WORLD

The USSR was structured as a series of concentric circles. Tania and Mikhail found themselves in the outer layers (rings of purgatory). The House of Government, from which they had been exiled, was connected to the sacred center by the Big Stone Bridge. The sacred center included the Kremlin, where Comrade Stalin worked, and the Lenin Mausoleum, where Lenin's body lay in state. On Soviet holy days, the two came together (with Stalin standing directly above Lenin's tomb). Both were part of an ensemble centered on the Palace of Soviets (with Lenin on top). The Palace of Soviets served as the *axis mundi* connecting heaven and earth. The first circle around the Palace was the city of Moscow.

After the Congress of Victors and the first Writers' Congress of 1934 had ushered in the last golden age, harkening back to previous golden ages, the idea of constructing a brand new city was abandoned in favor of reconstructing the old one. The General Plan for the Reconstruction of Moscow, adopted on July 10, 1935, proposed to "radically regularize the network of streets and squares" while preserving the traditional radial-concentric structure of old Moscow. The new "parks, wide avenues, fountains and statues, and, in the immediate vicinity of the Palace of Soviets, gigantic squares covered with colored asphalt," were to be built along the lines of the city's "rings."[1]

Perfect human communities tend to be represented as either pastoral or urban. Pastorals are poorly disciplined; ideal cities are symmetrical and rigidly centralized. The Heavenly Jerusalem "had a great, high wall with twelve gates, and with twelve angels at the gates. On the gates were written the names of the twelve tribes of Israel. There were three gates on the east, three on the north, three on the south and three on the west. The wall of the city had twelve foundations, and on them were the names of the twelve apostles of the Lamb. . . . The city was laid out like a square, as long as it was wide." The capital of Thomas More's Utopia was also in the form of a square. It was divided into four parts, with a marketplace in the middle. All the streets were of the same width, all the buildings were "so uniform that a whole side of a street looks like one house," every house had two doors, and all doors had two leaves. All the other cities were identical to the capital, so that "he that knows one of their towns knows them all."

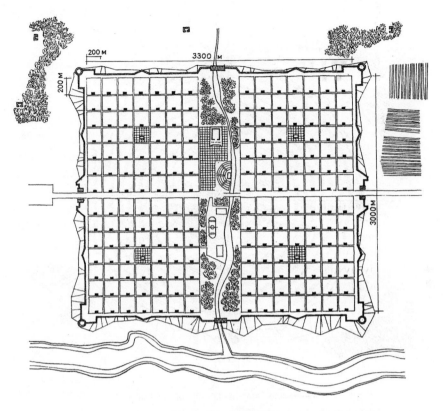

Thomas More's Amaurot

Albrecht Dürer's ideal city, Johann Valentin Andreae's Christianopolis, and Robert Owen's harmonious settlement all had the same square or rectangular shape.[2]

The other matrix of urban perfection is the circle. Plato's Atlantis consisted of a hill surrounded by five concentric circles, "two of land and three of water"; Vitruvius's city was radial (for defense purposes, he claimed). The ideal cities of the Renaissance repeated the classical formula: Bartolommeo Delbene's City of Truth was a cartwheel with five spokes representing roads of virtue emanating from the central tower and cutting through the swamps of vice; Tommaso Campanella's City of the Sun was "built upon a high hill" and "divided into seven rings or huge circles named from the seven planets, and the way from one to the other of these is by four streets and through four gates, that look toward the four points of the compass." The design of the City of the Sun was based on Copernicus's diagram of the planets revolving around the sun (as well as on St. John's Jerusalem); its shape resembled the pictorial allegories of Dante's purgatory as a terraced mountain with seven concentric rings. Ebenezer Howard's 1902 Garden City was a circle divided into six equal sectors.[3]

Tommaso Campanella's City of the Sun

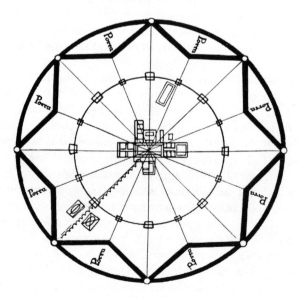

Sforzinda

The circle could be squared in a variety of ways. Filarete's ideal city of Sforzinda, designed for Francesco Sforza in 1464, derived from two super-imposed squares, forming an eight-point star inscribed into a circle; the center (a public square or, in the original design, a tower) was connected to the points of the star by canals and to the inner angles, by roads. Iofan's Palace of Soviets was a stepped cone resembling Augustine's earthly city or Dante's Purgatorio placed centrally on top of a square.[4]

Ideal cities are not simply spatial representations of the cosmic order: they are more or less elaborate diagrams of traditional human habitations—which tend to be spatial representations of the cosmic order. Most traditional dwellings are organized around two axes intersecting at the center to form a cross. Whether the points of the cross are connected by straight lines or a circle is secondary: the round Mongol yurt and the Russian peasant hut with its "corners" are both divided into four quarters with different practical and symbolic functions. The center is the vertical *axis mundi* that connects this world to its higher and lower counterparts.[5]

Some new settlements follow the same pattern: at the moment of founding, the creation of the world is reenacted; the cosmic waters are divided; the axes of the settlement aligned with those of the universe (one following the sun, the other forming the axis around which the world turns); and the center marked with a stone, tree, temple, fountain, forum, or tomb of the hero-founder. Not all cities are elaborations of traditional settlements or deliberate new creations, and not all those that *are* pre-serve their original diagrams, but no city is entirely divorced from the cosmic order, and some make the point of making the connection explicit. Prominent among the latter are holy cities (which often double as admin-istrative centers) and administrative centers (which attempt to project holiness), including Roma quadrata ("Square Rome") and its countless clones, the squares and rectangles of Chinese imperial centers, and the

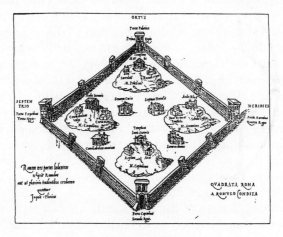

Roma quadrata

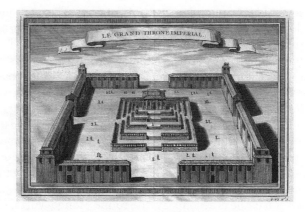

Forbidden City in Beijing

perfect circles of Median, Parthian, and Sassanian capitals (and their Muslim successor, Baghdad).[6]

Cities impose order on the world. As time goes on, swamp waters seep through, migrants and money-lenders pour in, sheds and shortcuts proliferate, circles abandon their regularity, and right angles lose their sharpness. The original vision can be restored symbolically, through ritual, or physically, by means of demolition and new construction. In post-Reformation Europe, Rome set the standard for cutting through urban flesh; and Versailles, for starting anew. Both, along with Versailles's monumental successor, St. Petersburg, were organized around a trivium, or three streets radiating from a common center (and suggesting—at least in diagram form—the rays of the sun). All embodied the restored symmetry of heavenly and earthly power; all spawned multiple progeny (including the tridental replicas of Russia's imperial capital in Tver and Kostroma).[7]

The next Age of Empire began in the second half of the nineteenth century. Emperor Napoleon III replaced old Paris with a network of avenues, boulevards, and star-shaped squares centered on the cross formed by the Rue Rivoli and Boulevard Sebastopol/St. Michel (but leaving the Swamp— Le Marais—intact in the northeastern quarter). Emperor Franz Josef I ordered the replacement of Vienna's city walls with the world's most spectacular boulevard. The British Empire did in New Delhi what it could not do in London: build a Rome "one size larger than life." As one reporter wrote approvingly at the time, "Not a hint of utilitarianism interpolates upon the monumental affirmation of temporal power."[8]

Other colonial capitals within the empire strove for the same combination of symmetry and legibility. The two towers, two wings, and the connecting semicircular colonnade of Pretoria's Union Buildings symbolized the unbreakable alliance of the two South African races (Briton and Boer). Canberra was designed as a "Parliamentary Triangle" superimposed on a cross formed by the "Land Axis" and "Water Axis." The Secre-

Versailles

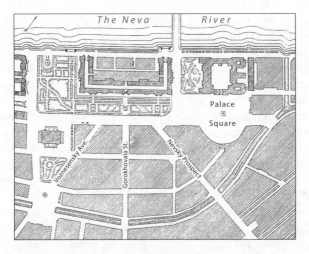

St. Petersburg

tary for Home Affairs who approved of the site claimed to have felt like "Moses, thousands of years ago, as he gazed down on the promised land." Ottawa, by way of exception, tended toward the Gothic and the picturesque, and never quite lived up to the 1897 vision of John Galbraith, who described "the city of Ottawa in 1999" as a collection of monumental buildings and "immense skeleton towers," with "mottoes formed of electric lights stretched between them."[9]

The capitals of the newly restored European empires were to be firmly neoclassical. According to Mussolini's reconstruction plan, formally promulgated in 1931, "Rome must appear marvellous to all the people of the world—vast, orderly, powerful, as in the time of the empire of Augustus." The theater of Marcellus, the Capitoline Hill, and the Pantheon were to be surrounded by vast spaces and connected by straight avenues; "all that has grown around them in the centuries of decadence must disappear." Hitler, himself a student of architecture, admired Paris and Vienna and was determined to transform Berlin from an "unregulated accumulation of buildings" into a proper capital aligned along two cosmic axes. The plan's main feature was the north-south avenue two and a half times as long as the Champs Elysées, lined with government buildings as well as, according to Albert Speer, "a luxurious movie house, for premieres, another cinema for the masses accommodating two thousand persons, a new opera house, three theaters, a new concert hall, a building for congresses, the so-called House of the Nations, a hotel of twenty-nine stories, variety theaters, mass and luxury restaurants, and even an indoor swimming pool, built in Roman style and as large as the baths of Imperial Rome." The House of the Nations was "a huge meeting hall, a domed structure into which St. Peter's Cathedral in Rome would have fitted several times over." The inspiration, according to Speer, was provided by the large buildings of Greek antiquity in Sicily and Asia Minor. "Even in Periclean Athens," he wrote, "the statue of Athena Parthenos by Phidias was forty feet high. Moreover, most of the Seven Wonders of the World won their repute by their excessive size: the Temple of Diana at Ephesus, the Mausoleum at Halicarnassus, the Colossus of Rhodes, and the Olympian Zeus of Phidias."[10]

Other reborn national capitals had their own dreams of Augustan and Parisian grandeur (Athens and Helsinki, in particular, entertained comprehensive reconstruction plans on a monumental scale), but, when it came to both ambition and execution, none could compete with the United States. A preview of things to come had been provided by the magical "white city" of the Chicago World's Fair, which rose out of a swamp in 1893 before being swallowed up again (only the Palace of Fine Arts survived—as the Museum of Science and Industry). Among its legacies were the song "America the Beautiful" and the City Beautiful urban renewal movement, which transplanted the beaux arts version of the baroque city to the United States. The movement's accomplishments included the large domes, open vistas, civic centers, landscaped parks, axial avenues, and ceremonial malls of many American cities and universities, but it was Washington, DC—the original "Versailles on the Potomac"—that benefited the most. L'Enfant's palatial plan of 1791 ("proportional to the greatness which . . . the Capital of a powerful Empire ought to manifest") was revived in 1902 and mostly implemented over the next three decades—in a way that combined symmetrical consistency with an openness to later additions along preexisting lines.[11]

Central Washington was organized around the east-west axis of the National Mall and the north-south axis of the White House, with the *axis mundi* monument to the founder at the point of intersection. As *National Geographic* put it in 1915, "the Washington Monument seems to link heaven and earth in the darkness, to pierce the sky in the light, and to stand an

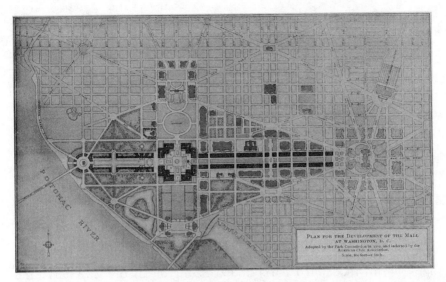

National Mall, Washington, DC

immovable mountain peak as the mists of every storm go driving by." The overall composition, according to one of the designers, was "a crusader's shield, emblazoned with a cross." The base of the cross was the Capitol, the two arms were the Jefferson Memorial and the White House, and the top was the Lincoln Memorial, beyond which, according to another member of the original team, lay "the low bridge spanning the Potomac (symbol of the Union of North and South as foretold by Andrew Jackson and Daniel Webster) leading both to the heights of Arlington where Lincoln's soldiers rest in eternal peace, and also to Mount Vernon, shrine of the American people. Washington the founder, Lincoln the saviour of the nation, standing on the same axis with the Capitol whence emanates the spirit of democracy." The Capitol was directly connected to the White House by the diagonal of Pennsylvania Avenue, which formed the Federal Triangle and symbolized the signing of both the Declaration of Independence and the Constitution. New ministries and sacred memorials were placed symmetrically along the main axes. No variety theaters, movie houses, restaurants, baths, or cafés were allowed to interfere with the solemn monumentality of the ensemble.[12]

The General Plan for the Reconstruction of Moscow was not as ambitious, or as consistently implemented, as the plans for New Delhi or Washington. The Palace of Soviets, the city's vertical axis, was modeled after American skyscrapers, which were themselves patterned on classical columns and tended to serve as either corporate temples (each one its own "empire state") or state capitols (such as the ones built in Louisiana in 1929 and Nebraska in 1932). No Soviet public building came close to the scale and symbolic legibility of the Pentagon, built in 1941–43 next to the Arlington Cemetery, where Lincoln's soldiers rest in eternal peace.[13]

Pentagon, Washington, DC

There is no such thing as "totalitarian," let alone "socialist-realist," architecture—but there are degrees of "the monumental affirmation of temporal power" as a reflection of the cosmic plan. Stalin's Moscow and Hitler's Berlin resembled Paris and Washington in the way Paris and Washington resembled Rome and Versailles and in the way Jesus's Heavenly Jerusalem resembled Babylon the Great: they served similar purposes and strove to supersede their corrupt predecessors by imitating their original designs. As the architect and city planner Arnold W. Brunner said in 1923 about the neoclassical "civic centers" at the heart of American cities, "the civic center is the most anti-Bolshevik manifestation possible, for here civic pride is born." Within a decade, Bolshevik civic centers had become neoclassical, too—because neoclassicism was "essentially rational" and thus "correct irrespective of time periods." In a 1936 article, Iofan praised the Lincoln Memorial (1922) and Folger Shakespeare Library (1932), but argued (anticipating Cold War criticism of his own work) that most other government buildings in Washington, DC, were absurdly oversized caricatures of their Greek and Roman models. As pompous as empire style buildings, but much less accomplished, "these soulless copies fail to evoke the solemnity and monumentality to which they aspire. . . . Overall, the

Folger Shakespeare Library, Washington, DC

architecture of US government buildings is a monumental decoration aimed at persuading the ordinary American of the permanence of the existing political order."[14]

Soviet neoclassicism was to be both monumental and "essentially rational." In the former Russian Empire, this meant that the new Soviet capital was to rival the old imperial one. According to a 1940 manual on urban planning, "the general plan of St. Petersburg is a well-thought-out and complete architectural composition, with justified street directions and well-placed squares—a monumental composition rich in detail and worthy of a capital of an immense and powerful state." Built in a swamp and organized around semicircular canals and three radial avenues emanating from the vertical axis of the Admiralty Spire, it was superior to its contemporaries, including Paris, with its "agglomerations of haphazardly built houses amidst narrow lanes and blind alleys," and London, which, "in spite of Wren's brilliant efforts, would always remain an undisciplined city." The General Plan of the Reconstruction of Moscow prescribed a well-thought-out and complete architectural composition, with justified street directions, well-placed squares, and ceremonial waterways. Thanks to the new

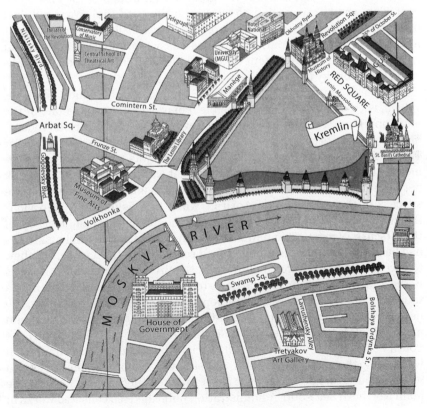

Intourist map of Moscow, 1938

Moskva–Volga Canal (1933–37), the city was to become "a port of five seas." In the words of the plan, "the Moskva embankments, clothed in granite and supporting wide avenues with uninterrupted traffic, must become the city's main thoroughfares."[15]

Socialist-realist art was "Rembrandt, Rubens, and Repin in the service of the working class and socialism." Socialist-realist literature was Goethe's *Faust* for a new age ("but with the same extreme degree of generalization"). The new Moscow was "the capital of an immense and powerful state," and thus an heir to Rome and St. Petersburg, ready to overtake Paris and Washington.

■   ■   ■

By virtue of being the capital of the Soviet Union, Moscow was the center of the world. Like all ontological centers, Moscow lay at the intersection of the east-west/north-south spatial axes and the vertical *axis mundi* representing the tree of time, with roots deep underground and the trunk pointing upward, toward a heavenly future. The expectant present was preceded, most memorably, by the great breakthrough of the First Five-Year Plan, the heroic period of the Revolution and Civil War, and, just below the surface, the sacred unity of prison and exile. The thickest roots included the history of Marxism and the Russian prophetic tradition that culminated in the martyrdom of the People's Will (described and explicated by Voronsky in his *Zheliabov*).[16]

The north-south axis was just that—an axis around which Earth revolved, with only the two poles visible. Polar exploration was one of the most popular spectator sports in the Soviet Union, with various record-breaking contests covered ceaselessly in newspapers and on the radio. For Tania Miagkova's mother, the "*Chelyuskin* saga" was "a test of the achievements of the revolution"; for Tania herself, it was the most emotional link between her isolator and the building of socialism. Arosev learned of the success of the operation on April 13, while he was at the Nemirovich-Danchenko theater for a performance of Shostakovich's *Lady Macbeth of the Mtsensk District*. "The news arrived that twenty-two Chelyuskinites had been rescued, and that only six had remained on the ice floe, but they, too, were eventually saved. Before Act 1, Nemirovich-Danchenko, who was in the audience, announced the news to the spectators, and led them in a touching, humane 'hurray.' The audience gave him, and through him, the heroic aviators, an ovation." (Two of the heroic aviators, Nikolai Kamanin and Mikhail Vodopyanov, soon moved into the House of Government.) The South Pole was less visible but still crucially important: Roald Amundsen was among the most popular non-Soviet Soviet celebrities; his books and other accounts of his travels were constantly reissued, and, in 1935–39, the Main Northern Sea Route Administration published his collected works in five volumes.[17]

The world between the two poles stretched along the east-west axis. The best way to represent it in its entirety was to follow the sun. At the first Congress of the Soviet Writers' Union in 1934, Gorky issued the following challenge to the foreign delegates: "Why don't you try to create a book that would depict one day in the life of the bourgeois world? It doesn't matter what day—September 25, October 7, or December 5. What you need is any weekday as it is reflected in the pages of the world press. What you need is to show the colorful chaos of modern life in Paris and Grenoble, London and Shanghai, San Francisco, Geneva, Rome, Dublin, and so on, and so forth, in the cities and in the countryside, on water and on land."[18]

The foreign writers did not have the means to produce such a book, but Koltsov's Newspaper and Magazine Alliance did. "Friends of the Soviet Union" throughout the world were asked to send in newspaper clippings, calendar pages, announcements, cartoons, photographs, posters, "and all kinds of other curious social, cultural, and human documents." The chosen day was September 27, 1935—"the third day of the six-day week" in the Soviet Union and "Friday" in most of the rest of the world. The ultimate goal, as Gorky wrote to Koltsov, was "to show to our reader what a philistine day is filled with, and to juxtapose that picture with the content of our Soviet day." The Soviet press wrote a great deal about the decay of the bourgeois world. The challenge was "to give a vivid, clear sense of exactly how" it was decaying.[19]

The work took a long time because of the inherent difficulty of collecting material from around the world; the disappearance—and subsequent removal from the text—of many of the Soviet protagonists; Gorky's last-minute demand for starker contrasts ("they have to jump out at you from every line"); and Gorky's death on June 18, 1936, at the age of sixty-eight. On August, 10, 1936, the galleys were sent to the print shop; about a year later, The Day of the World saw the light of day. It was a large-format, richly illustrated, six hundred–page volume. The print run was 20,250 copies; the price, 50 rubles (about 60 percent of the monthly salary of the stairway cleaner Smorchkova and the floor-polisher Barbosov).[20]

The book was organized around the world's most "dangerous flashpoints": first, the countries involved in the Abyssinian conflict, including England; then the visit by Hungarian Prime Minister Gömbös to East Prussia and the three parties immediately concerned; then all the countries threatened by German aggression (fanning to the east, south, west, and north); Japan and its victims, past and future; the rest of the colonial world; "the countries of the Near, Middle, and Far East, which have succeeded, after a desperate struggle, in preserving their independence from imperialist domination"; the Americas; and, finally, "a different world, which represents the exact opposite of the other five-sixths of the globe—the world of liberated labor and joyously creative life, the world of socialism, the USSR."

Of the non-Soviet five-sixths of the globe, the largest entries were on France, Germany, the United States, and Britain ("England"). There was much on war preparations, rising prices, class struggles, and unemployment, but the emphasis was on the "colorful chaos" and boundless foolishness of daily life under capitalism: palm readers, Bible preachers, drunk drivers, cat collars, gossip columns, beauty contests, prayer meetings, spitting records, and lonely hearts advertisements. The Soviet Union (at one hundred pages, one-sixth of the book) represented the "exact opposite." There was much on border security, labor productivity, plan fulfillment, and full employment, but the emphasis was on the small joys and satisfactions of daily life: participants in the Lake Baikal–Moscow kayak marathon approaching Moscow; children in the "crawlers' group" at the Kalinin Factory nursery learning how to walk; housewives from the Residential Cooperative No. 1 in Podolsk forming a choir; a six-month-old calf by the name of Ataman weighing in at 313 kilograms; Professor Nevsky from Leningrad State University working on a dictionary of the extinct language Si-Sia; shock worker D. N. Antonov from the Molotov Automobile Factory receiving a free automobile; miners from the Far North arriving at the Red Krivoi Rog sanatorium in Alushta, Crimea; and E. M. Katolikova from the Molotov collective farm announcing at a tailors' conference in Kaluga that "female kolkhoz workers are demanding new fashionable dresses." On the day of the world, residents of Moscow purchased 156.6 tons of sugar, 51 tons of butter, 236 tons of meat and sausage items, 137 tons of fish products, 96 tons of confectionary items, 205,000 eggs, 2,709 tons of bread, 200,000 liters of milk, 1,700 tons of potatoes, 100 tons of pickles, 300 tons of tomatoes, and 300 tons of apples and pears, among many other food items. The list concluded with a comment by the editors: "In the future, Moscow plans to eat even better."[21]

Soviet life on the eve of full socialism was about peace, prosperity, creative labor, and "cultured rest." The French writer André Gide, who, on closer inspection, decided that he did not agree, was struck by the apparently universal Soviet conviction "that everything abroad in every department is far less prosperous than in the USSR." The most obvious consequence of that conviction was the look of contentment on the faces of Soviet children. "Their eyes are frank and trustful; their laughter has nothing spiteful or malicious in it; they might well have thought us foreigners rather ridiculous; not for a moment did I catch in any of them the slightest trace of mockery." But the most remarkable thing was that "this same look of open-hearted happiness is often to be seen too among their elders, who are as handsome, as vigorous, as the children." Even in the Gorky Park of Culture and Rest, which was meant for games and entertainment, "crowds of young men and women behaved with propriety, with decency; not the slightest trace of stupid or vulgar foolery, of rowdiness, of licentiousness, or even of flirtation. The whole place is pervaded with a kind of joyous ardour."[22]

Gorky Park

Gide found this spectacle of contentment to be both genuine and staged, simple and contrived, pleasing to the eye and strangely frightening. Ultimately, he concluded, it was the result of the inescapable propaganda and "an extraordinary state of ignorance concerning foreign countries." Lion Feuchtwanger, who visited the USSR a year later and wrote a rebuttal called *Moscow 1937*, attributed it to realism and justifiable pride: "I cannot take offense at the Soviet people's love of their country, even though it is expressed in always the same, often very naïve, forms. Rather must I confess that their childlike patriotic vanity is rather pleasing to me than otherwise. A young nation has, with enormous sacrifices, accomplished something really great, and now stands before its achievement and cannot itself quite believe in it. It is overjoyed at what it has achieved, and is eager that the foreigner, too, should never cease to confirm how great and fine the achievement is." Feuchtwanger was happy to oblige, and there is good reason to believe that most House of Government leaseholders were as pleased with his book (which was translated and widely publicized) as they were displeased with Gide's (which only they had access to). Some of them, most prominently Koltsov and Arosev, had been specifically charged with courting foreign celebrities and shaping their impressions, and all of them, including Koltsov and Arosev, upheld the fundamental principles of Communism, shared a common love of the Soviet Union, and believed that in the near future the Soviet Union would be the happiest and most powerful country on earth.[23]

Aleksandr Serafimovich traveled to Paris about a month after the chosen Day of the World and several months before André Gide arrived in the USSR. On November 6, 1935, he wrote to his wife:

> The weather in Paris is like ours in early fall: around 5–6 degrees, on the damp side, the ground cold, and the walls inside cold, although there is some heating. It is (usually) either foggy or raining. They do get snow in the winter sometimes, but it doesn't stay on the ground and melts right away. The river Seine is cold and leaden, but it doesn't freeze. It's that way all winter long.
>
> The buildings are high: 5–6–7 stories. They are dark and gloomy. Some of them are hundreds of years old. At night everything is lit up.
>
> There are different kinds of streets: some are so wide they look like squares that have been elongated, and some are so narrow they are scary to walk on: at any moment a car or a bus might hit you and run you over. The sidewalks are so tiny and narrow, you have to press yourself against the wall (as hard as you can). But in other places they are huge—even wider than our streets.
>
> The crowds are huge. There are lots of people. They don't walk or run—they scurry. When you look down from your window, it's like an anthill. And what tense faces, worn out by need and anxiety! The women look emaciated, but each tries her best to dress up, i.e., to dress like the bourgeoisie. Most have crudely painted lips, and on Sundays they plaster their faces with makeup.
>
> The air outside is so vile you can hardly breathe. When you get home, you find soot in the corners of your eyes, and on your handkerchief. A huge mass of cars flows by in an unending stream; the smell of burnt gasoline is everywhere. It is killing people. The bourgeoisie feel fine: they regularly go on trips to the beach, the mountains, or the woods, while the workers suffocate. The exploitation is expert, relentless, unceasing.[24]

It was about four months later that the Soviet delegation consisting of Arosev, Bukharin, and Adoratsky traveled to western Europe to inspect and purchase the Marx-Engels archive. In early April, Bukharin was joined in Paris by Anna Larina, who was pregnant with their son. According to Larina, she was met at the railway station by Bukharin and Arosev. Arosev handed her some carnations, saying that Bukharin was too shy to do it himself. Bukharin blushed, and they all got into a car and drove around Paris for a while before arriving at their hotel. "The members of the delegation lived in neighboring rooms. Adoratsky used to come to Bukharin's room only when business required it, but Arosev often stopped by. He liked to discuss things, or simply chat lightheartedly with N. I. Unlike the dry, dogmatic Adoratsky, he was a charismatic, talented person." Before Larina's arrival, Bukharin and Arosev "spent a lot of time together, walking around Paris. They had been to the Louvre more than once. They were both in a good mood and joked a lot." Once, when Arosev, Bukharin, and Larina were on Montmartre, Bukharin saw some couples kissing. Saying he would do them one better, he "did a handstand and started walking on his hands, to the delight of the passers-by."[25]

At some point during their time in Paris, Larina witnessed a conversation between Bukharin and the exiled Menshevik (and priest's son) Boris Nicolaevsky, who was representing the Marx-Engels archive (and had recently written a Marx biography):

> Nicolaevsky asked: "So, how is life over there, in the Soviet Union?"
> "Life is wonderful," responded Nikolai Ivanovich.
> He talked about the Soviet Union with genuine excitement, in my presence. The only difference between his words and his most recent newspaper articles was that he did not keep mentioning Stalin's name—something he had to do in the Soviet Union. He talked about the rapid growth of industry and the development of electrification, and shared his impression of the Dnieper Hydroelectric Dam, which he had visited along with Sergo Ordzhonikidze. Citing numbers from memory, he described the huge steel plants built in the eastern part of the country and the accelerated development of science.
> "You wouldn't recognize Russia now," he concluded.[26]

When Larina was not around, he may have had other things to say, but all his fears, doubts, and criticisms had to do with Stalin's personality, not the rapid growth of industry, the development of electrification, or the accelerated development of science, let alone the overall superiority of the Soviet Union over the capitalist world.[27]

Overall superiority did not mean superiority in all things. Soviet modernization consisted in overcoming backwardness, which Stalin defined as a "50–100 year lag behind the advanced countries." The Five-Year Plans' greatest achievement had been to replicate Western achievement. The results were spectacular, but not consistent or uniform. While Bukharin was talking to Nicolaevsky, Adoratsky was writing his letters home about the oak-paneled rooms, walk-in closets, magnifying mirrors for shaving, and his new custom-tailored Cheviot-wool suit. Bukharin was wearing a tailor-made suit, too. (According to Larina, a few days before his departure, Stalin had told him: "Your suit is frayed, Nikolai. You can't go looking like that. Have a new one made quickly. Times have changed. We need to dress well now.") Bukharin worried about his French; Arosev was proud of his and dismissive of Osinsky's. House of Government children were learning German, and House of Government adults traveling in the West were buying clothes, cameras, radios, gramophones, refrigerators, and fashion magazines. A bad foreigner in the Soviet Union was usually described as arrogant and condescending (as well as fearful); a bad Soviet abroad was usually described as ingratiating or uncouth (as well as belligerent).[28]

Arosev, whose job was to preside over "cultural ties with foreign countries," suffered from both bad foreigners and bad Soviets. Western diplomats "projected mockery and cowardice at the same time"; André Gide combined arrogance with treachery; and Lady Astor's guests, including George Bernard Shaw, raised arrogance to the heights of innocence ("it seems that if one of them were to unbutton his pants and urinate on the carpet, no one would pay any attention, and the servants, without having to be told, would simply remove the soiled carpet as quickly as possible"). Bad Soviets were more detrimental to the cause and more personally aggravating. On November 2, 1932, while Arosev was still ambassador to Czechoslovakia, he passed through Germany and then into Poland on his way to Moscow. "After the Polish border, the train became dirtier and the staff, less disciplined and more confused. It was as if everything gradually began to lose meaning. Such is the terrible difference between a European and the resident of the Russo-Polish Plain. The latter does not seem quite sure why he was born or what his place in the world should be, while the European, by the age of seventeen, knows all this, as well as when he will die and how much capital he will leave behind."[29]

Aleksandr Arosev and his wife,
Gertrude Freund, in Berlin

Not much had changed when, in 1935, he crossed into Poland from the other direction on his way from the Soviet Union to Paris:

19 June.
Travel impressions. Moscow-Negoreloe. Dining car.

Walked in, sat down, and for at least half an hour, no one has paid any attention to me. The two tables by the entrance are occupied: one, by a waiter, counting money and looking despondently at the abacus sitting in front of him; the other, by a man in civilian clothes, stretching his arms and looking bored. He could pass the time by reading or writing, but, like all Russians, he is lazy and does not appreciate the value of fast-flowing time. He appears to be some kind of supervisor or commissar.

Two young Englishmen walked in just now. The waiter came up to them, but couldn't understand anything. So a second came up, but he couldn't understand them, either. Then the idle supervisor himself came up. All three suspended their melancholy faces over the Englishmen, and all three failed to understand a single word. Then, with a slow, grudging motion, the supervisor summoned a fourth, whom he recommended as a German speaker. The waiter asked [also in Russian]:

"Roll, tea?"

At last hearing a Russian word they recognized, the two Englishmen cried in unison:

"Tea!"[30]

The Soviet cultural celebrities engaged in establishing cultural ties were, as far as Arosev was concerned, not much better than dining-car waiters. According to his diary, at a 1932 Kremlin reception for foreign diplomats, Boris Pilniak had "loitered next to the food tables" while Leonid Leonov had "acted like a shopkeeper made a bit reckless by the sound of an accordion on a Sunday." At a VOKS reception on October 17, 1934, the invited Soviet writers had "distinguished themselves by their bad manners and complete cluelessness about what to do or say." In June 1935, at the Congress for the Defense of Culture in Paris, the Soviet delegates had "made the French blush." In July 1935, some Soviet dancers touring England had shown themselves to be "enthusiasts and narcissists at the same time." And in December 1935, in Paris, four visiting Soviet poets (Kirsanov, Lugovskoi, Selvinsky, and that "jug-eared, snub-nosed 'genius,'" Bezymensky) had arrived "with faces frozen with self-importance." On the day of their departure, the physiologist A. D. Speransky, who happened to be in town on an official visit, had gotten drunk and "at the railway station, babbled incoherently and kept looking for women."[31]

∎ ∎ ∎

Lev Kritsman (Courtesy of
Irina Shcherbakova)

Arosev did not like his job. But the reason he did not like his job was that the cause of the Revolution was being represented "by complete idiots and ignoramuses," not because he ever doubted the cause itself. He did not want to do "the work of a maître d'hôtel" because he believed that he himself was at the top of his creative powers. "I want," he wrote to Stalin on July 21, 1936, "to work more intensely and with greater responsibility for socialism, which is being built under your direction." He would prefer an assignment in the People's Commissariat of People's Enlightenment or a full-time job as a writer, working on his "historical-psychological" tetralogy about the Russian Revolution (*Spring*, covering 1905–13, *Summer*, on the immediate prerevolutionary years, *Fall*, from the October Revolution to Lenin's death, and *Winter*, about "our Party's work on the economic building of socialism under your direction and the falling off of the de facto alien elements more interested in the process of the revolution than in its results.") Ultimately—no matter who waited on tables or who shuttled back and forth as a maître d'hôtel—crossing into the USSR stood for "entering the country that is the source of all the strongest human impressions, emotions, and ideas." The best people in the West understood that too, idiots and ignoramuses notwithstanding. "Many very honest, loyal, and heroic human beings are drawn toward us."[32]

One such human being was Lev Kritsman's childhood friend Senia, who had emigrated to America around 1913, settled in Los Angeles, gotten a job as a cobbler in a shoe shop, and become Sam Izeckman (also known as Itzikman or Eisman). He and his wife, Betia, had never liked America. It was bad enough to be a "deaf mute" immigrant, he wrote in his letters to Kritsman, but the worst part was the "atmosphere of greed and wealth" that permeated everything. People in America worked day and night and talked of nothing but material things: "here even a hungry person thinks less about getting food than buying a house of his own." Los Angeles (he wrote in Yiddish-inflected Russian) "is a lousy boring little town a European could even die here from boredom." There was nothing to describe and an awful lot to regret, even before he heard about the Russian Revolution. "I absolutely do not like America and do not want to write anything about it."[33]

In 1930, Kritsman visited the United States as part of a delegation of Soviet agrarian economists and met with Senia. Shortly afterward, Senia (who by then had started mixing up his Roman and Cyrillic alphabets) wrote to describe the effect the meeting had had on him. "I am seriously considering moving back to Russia and so I ask you to please let me know (1) what I have to submit in order to enter the U.S.S.R. in terms of paperwork and (2) whether it is possible to stay there upon arrival? Without securing a visa in advance? And also if possible write what things are like in our line of work and do they need people of my caliber there? I know you are very busy but I hope you won't refuse." Three months later, he was still trying to get a visa. "Now that you're back home you must be busy like bee, but in the name of our good old days I ask you to steal your precious moments and write to me. . . . How do you feel when it comes to health? Busy day and night I imagine but Lyonia what supreme joy it is to be working in such conditions for better future and toward such wonderful goal I wish that future the best possible success. Yours forever Senia." In April 1936, he was still hoping to move, working for the cause, and had much improved writing skills in Russian. "My son sends his comradely greetings. He lives permanently in San Francisco. He has joined the ranks and is working actively for the establishment of a Soviet government here in America. I subscribe to and read all of this year's enormous achievements and am very interested to know what is being done in the field of mechanical shoe repair if you write let me know what progress has been made in that particular area of industrial production. Betty sends her best to Shura. I hope to receive your reply. Yours, Senya."[34]

Senia never made it to the Soviet Union, but many people did, and some of them stayed. The largest political émigré community was German: in 1936, there were about 4,600 German-speaking refugees living in the Soviet Union, most of them in Moscow. The top Soviet expert on German politics was Karl Radek, who was responsible for the official manifestos announcing a new pro-Versailles policy, secret negotiations suggesting a continued Soviet willingness to cooperate, and the public and private statements aimed at Communists and fellow-travelers. During the first Congress of Soviet Writers in 1934, he made two speeches: a formal one—in which he called on foreign writers to face the choice between obedience to Party discipline and "dismissal from the struggle for which their soul yearns"—and an improvised one at Gorky's dacha, in the presence of Molotov, Bukharin, and a select group of foreign visitors. One of those visitors was the German writer Gustav Regler, who described the occasion in his memoirs (which he wrote when he was no longer a Communist):

> Radek spoke first in Russian. Since he spoke several languages fluently I suspected that his words were intended more for his own Government than for ourselves. I asked Koltsov to interpret, which he did.
>
> It was a Dostoevsky speech, an act of ecstatic confession and self-flagellation. "We must look more deeply into our hearts and scatter the eggshells of our self-deception!" he cried. "We must seek our own private peace of mind." . . .
>
> He spread his shirt wider apart. There was now no stopping him. I found him terrifying, with his gleaming eyes and the little, ugly

fringe of beard on his chin that served only to emphasize the thinness of his lips. He was certainly drunk, but this had loosened his tongue without impairing his wits. "He's talking too much!" Koltsov whispered to me, and glanced anxiously towards the Government people. I noted Molotov's tense mouth and Gorky's wrinkled forehead. "He is in a mood to throw everything overboard," said Koltsov, and craned his neck to see whom Radek was now facing. But what was there for Radek to throw overboard? All sound in the room had died down.

"We are still far from the objective," said Radek in his high-pitched voice. "We thought the child had come of age, and we have invited the whole world to admire it. But it is self-knowledge, not admiration, that we need." . . .

With his shirt hanging over his belt he paced up and down amid the cigarette-smoke and the clinking glasses, but always keeping at a certain distance from Molotov, and suddenly he directed his attack at the Germans. He upbraided them, talking of his bitter disappointment at their swift betrayal of the Revolution, the way the workers had adapted themselves to Hitler, and the ease with which the literary calling had been *gleichgeschaltet*, brought into line. It must be said that not many had fallen upon fruitful ground!

He was now speaking in German, but not out of courtesy. His purpose was to insult and offend. . . .

Then, beneath the basilisk gaze of Molotov, he returned to self-accusation, and in the end his discourse became a mere mumbling, the firework display petered out amid the hubbub of talk and the general indifference which finally he seemed to share. He picked up glasses as he passed, perhaps finding comedy in his own pathos. . . .

Finally, he faded away through the tobacco-smoke and vanished like a ghost into some other part of the house, and I heard Koltsov breathe a sigh of relief.

"The party is over," he said in an exhausted voice.[35]

Karl Radek

Koltsov was more cautious, more polished, more influential, and more directly responsible for relations with writers. Koltsov's House of Government apartment served as the headquarters of German cultural life in Moscow, and his common-law wife, Maria Osten, served as its principal coordinator. She worked in the Soviet Union's main German-language newspaper, *Deutsche Zentral-Zeitung*; founded and managed the international German literary journal, *Das Wort* (financed by Koltsov's Magazine-and-Newspaper Alliance and edited—after Osten's unsuccessful courtship of Heinrich and Thomas Mann—by Berthold Brecht, Willi Bredel, and Lion Feuchtwanger); and arranged Soviet tours for German cultural celebrities, including Brecht and Feuchtwanger. According to Bredel (who also lived in Moscow), "Maria Osten had a poor reputation among virtually all the German writers in Moscow. It was her own fault. In spite of her relatively modest literary abilities, she, as Koltsov's friend, played an undeservedly major role in German literature, corresponded with Heinrich Mann, Lion Feuchtwanger, and Bert Brecht, and, still as Koltsov's friend and confidante, exercised all kinds of power and presented herself as a grande dame, so to speak. It seemed that she aspired to be the hostess of a literary salon."[36]

Maria Osten

The daughter of a Westphalian landowner, Maria Gresshöner (Osten) had become a visible presence in Berlin's bohemian café life in 1926, when, as an eighteen-year-old, she got a job at the radical Malik Press, became the mistress of the co-owner, Wieland Herzfelde (who was married at the time), and joined the Communist Party. In 1929, she followed the Leningrad film director Evgeny Cherviakov to the Soviet Union, but, after discovering he was also married, returned to Berlin. In the same year, she wrote her first short story and started publishing sketches about rural day-laborers in the *Rote Post* Communist newspaper (under the rubric of "rural agitation"). In 1930, her photograph appeared on the cover of the Malik-produced translation of Ilya Ehrenburg's *The Love of Jeanne Ney*. In 1932, she met Koltsov and followed him to Moscow. In the fall of 1933, Koltsov and Maria spent some time in Paris in the company of Boris Efimov, the writers Ilya Ilf and Evgeny Petrov, and Koltsov's official wife, Elizaveta Ratmanova. From Paris they traveled to Saar to report on the preparations for the referendum on whether the territory should rejoin Germany. In December, in the town of Oberlinxweiler, they met Hubert L'Hoste, the ten-year-old son of a local Communist.[37] Hubert describes the occasion in Maria's book, *Hubert in Wonderland*:

> The time flew by very quickly. We were all terribly sorry when Mikhail said that he could not stay for the night because he had to return to Saarbrücken.
> But the most wonderful memory that I have of that evening were his words that kept ringing in my ears:
> "Why don't we take him with us?"
> Mikhail put me on his lap and patted my head.
> "But only on one condition," he said, having thought for a minute.
> "What condition?"

Terribly disappointed ("were they making fun of me?"), I climbed down off his lap. Now he was sure to say: "We will take you with us only if you've read Marx's *Communist Manifesto* or *Das Kapital*. In my mind, I was blaming my father for not bringing me these books, even though I had asked him to many times. In response, he would always say that I should wait a little before reading them.

Mikhail put me back on his lap.

"Our condition," he said, "is that you will write one page each day about what you have seen."

"I will, I will, of course I will!" I said, clapping my hands, and everyone laughed.

"And, perhaps, we'll even use what you write in a book we'll put together for the young pioneers of the entire world."[38]

Hubert's father approved of the plan. On the way to Moscow, Hubert and Maria stopped over in Paris, where Gustav Regler showed Hubert around. On the Paris–Vienna train, Hubert read the Belgian novelist Charles de Coster's *The Legend of the Glorious Adventures of Thyl Ulenspiegel in the Land of Flanders and Elsewhere* (because it was one of the most popular children's books in the Soviet Union and because the story of a wandering trickster's rebirth as a revolutionary hero seemed to presage Hubert's own life's journey). In Moscow, Hubert received a hero's welcome, made a radio address, met Marshal Budennyi, and saw Lenin in his mausoleum. In Maria's version of Hubert's account, Lenin made a strong impression on him: "He is wearing a khaki jacket, and his hands are resting on a red cloth, which covers him up to his chest. I do not want to leave. Lenin seems to be asleep. His little beard casts a shadow over his cheeks and enlivens his face."[39]

Hubert liked everything in the Soviet Union, especially Gorky Park and Natalia Sats's children's theater. Even his own new home was special. It

Hubert L'Hoste with Natalia Sats

had "not one courtyard, but several. A survey of the whole huge territory revealed that there were three of them. Small fences indicated where the hedges, now mostly covered in deep snow, were hidden. Only the soft green tops of the fir trees could be seen above the huge snowdrifts. The pathways leading to the numerous entryways were completely free of snow. In the middle courtyard was a grocery store, whose shop windows faced the street. It was a cooperative building for workers." In fact, it was the House of Government, but Hubert's—and Maria's—job was to describe the typical, not the particular (what is becoming, not what is).[40]

Hubert was enrolled in Moscow's Karl Liebknecht German school (which Arosev's daughters also attended). In the summer, he and his classmates went to the Ernst Thälmann pioneer camp, where he learned "to submit to discipline and live within a collective." When he came back in August, he saw Gustav Regler, who was in town for the Writer's Congress, and returned the favor by showing him around Moscow. Hubert was proud to be able to show him things that "did not exist in the entire world or were inaccessible to us in the capitalist countries." Regler particularly liked Gorky Park. On his first visit there, he never made it to the Children's Technical Station, where children built their own radios, turbines, and trolleybuses, because he could not stop doing the parachute jump. Another guest of the Writers' Congress was Thomas Mann's son Klaus, who wrote in his diary that the "all-powerful Maria" had shown him a department store, the Metro, and some specialty stores.[41] Mann's traveling companion, Marianne Schwarzenbach, liked both Koltsov and Maria:

He has such wit and such a lively mind, and has grown so much in his position, that one is tempted to assume that he can do anything. Besides, he is warmhearted and friendly, and Maria loves him with a solicitous sweetness out of keeping with her usual aggressive manner. In his presence, she seems smaller and a bit quieter than

Mikhail Koltsov and Maria Osten in Moscow

usual. Actually, she is an extraordinary girl, with a very feminine, not entirely self-conscious, intelligence, extremely frank and open, a bit devious, and affectionate in an impetuous, feline, never-to-be-trusted sort of way. In short, it would be dangerous and painful to be in love with her, for it would be impossible to fully possess her or pin her down.[42]

In January 1935, the Saar plebiscite was won by the pro-German party. Hubert's parents emigrated to France, and he stayed on in the Soviet Union indefinitely. In spring 1936, Maria started an affair with the German Communist singer, Ernst Busch. A year later, she and Koltsov separated but remained close friends and collaborators.[43]

■   ■   ■

Germany was by far the most important country in the world. But Germany (as Radek kept saying) had betrayed the Revolution. The country that had recently fallen in love with the Revolution, and was ardently loved in return, was Republican Spain. Germany had always been present in the House of Government apartments in the shape of books, tutors, gadgets, and governesses. Most of what the House residents came to learn about Spain came from Koltsov's dispatches from the Civil War, reissued in 1938 as *The Spanish Diary*.

The *Diary*'s overall plot corresponded to Soviet policy toward the Spanish Republic, which corresponded to the standard exodus and construction stories about the transformation of a motley crowd into a holy army. In one of the *Diary*'s early entries, a group of Aragonese peasants in a tiny movie theater recognize themselves in the film *Chapaev*, about the Red Army Civil War hero; in another, members of the Madrid government are watching *We Are from Kronstadt*, about the White Army general Yudenich's assault on revolutionary Petrograd, when someone suddenly rushes in:

> "Bad news! Illescas has been taken! Our troops are retreating. Seseña may have been taken, too."
> The spectator sitting next to me asks, without taking his eyes off the screen: "How many kilometers away are they?"
> "They, who? Do you mean Yudenich or Franco? And how many kilometers from where—Petrograd or Madrid?"[44]

In the background, once again, is Babylon: mostly diplomats and spies posing as "representatives of arms manufacturers, correspondents of large telegraph agencies, and movie producers," but also "bootleggers from Al Capone's detachments, adventure-seekers from Indochina, and a disappointed Italian terrorist who is trying his hand at poetry." "In the whole of the enormous Florida hotel, the only guest left is the writer Hemingway.

He is warming up his sandwiches on an electric stove and writing a comedy." (In *For Whom the Bell Tolls*, Robert Jordan says that "Karkov" had "more brains and more inner dignity and outer insolence and humor than any man that he had ever known.")[45]

In the foreground is a Spanish version of the Magnitogorsk melting pot. "The rough features of the Castilians and Aragonese alternate with the swarthy, feminine roundness of the Andalusians. The sturdy, heavyset Basques follow the bony, slender, fair-haired Galicians. But it is the emaciated, gloomy, destitute Estremadurans that predominate in this long, motley peasant procession." The Spaniards, taken together, are "a colorful, full-blooded, distinctive, and spontaneous nation, and, most remarkable of all, strikingly similar to some of the peoples of the Soviet Union." They, too, will overcome their spontaneity. Some of them already have: "Now one can say with certainty that these are brave, resolute, battle-tested detachments. When visiting units you have seen before, you cannot help being amazed by how much the men and officers have changed. One anarchist battalion is fighting courageously in Villaverde. Over the past four days, they have lost twenty dead and fifteen wounded. And this is the same battalion that caused so much trouble and had so many desertions in Aranjuez, when they tried to hijack a train in order to run away from the front!"[46]

Koltsov's job as Soviet ambassador to Spanish Petrograd was to describe and inspire the Spanish exodus. Koltsov's charge as a post-1934 Soviet writer was to celebrate the land of red capes, black berets, roadside inns, and exotic names ("marching along the Estremadura highway, the rebels took Navalcarnero, an important transportation hub, as well as Quijorna and Brunete"). Koltsov's young House of Government readers drew them in their albums, marked them on their wall maps, and recognized them from the translated adventure books they had been raised on. Koltsov brought Spain home by making it recognizably remote:

> We have never known this nation; it was distant and strange; we have never fought or traded with it, never taught it or learned from it.
> Only loners, eccentrics, and lovers of spicy, slightly bitter exoticism ever traveled from Russia to Spain.
> Even in the minds of educated Russians, the Spanish shelf was dusty and almost empty. All one could find there was Don Quixote and Don Juan (pronounced the French way), Seville and seguedilla, Carmen and her toreador, [Pushkin's] "the raucous, quick Guadalquivir," and perhaps *The Mysteries of the Madrid Court*.[47]

It was not quantity that mattered most, however. The age of socialist realism had descended from the "Pamirs" of classical heritage. One of the peaks, as Koltsov's narrator suddenly realizes, is still in Toledo—"the tragic Toledo of inquisitors, rakes with swords, beautiful ladies, licenciates, and Jewish martyrs at the stake, the repository of the most mysterious works of art he knew of—the hauntingly powerful, elongated and ever so slightly puffy faces on the canvases of El Greco."[48]

The other "peak" was one of the highest. Responding to Koltsov's demand for greater firmness in dealing with some rebels holed up in the city's Alcazar, the governor of Toledo urges magnanimity. "You are in Spain, señor," he says, "in the country of Don Quixote." Some French journalists, who are present at the scene, speak in the governor's defense:

> "For Koltsov, he is simply a traitor. Whenever something goes wrong, the Bolsheviks immediately suspect wrecking and treason."
> "And Don Quixote, according to them, is nothing but a dangerous liberal . . ."
> "Subject to expulsion from the ranks of conscious Marxists . . ."
> I retorted:
> "Don't talk to me about Don Quixote! We are on better terms with him than you are. In the Soviet Union, there have been eleven editions of *Don Quixote*. And in France? You cry over Don Quixote, but you leave him all alone in his hour of need. We criticize him and help him at the same time."
> "But when you criticize, you also have to consider his nature . . ."
> "What do you know about his nature? Cervantes loved his Quixote, but he made Sancho Panza governor, not him. Good old Sancho never claimed to possess his master's high virtues. As for this bastard, he's neither a Quixote nor a Sancho. The phone in his office still works, after all, and it has a direct line to the Alcazar!"[49]

To prove his point, the narrator asks his driver, Dorado, to take him to El Toboso, where he finds a Potemkin collective farm and a "very young, very tall, and very sad" Dulcinea begging the devious local alcalde for an extra meat ration for her sick father. By the time he has inspected the last point on his itinerary, a horse stable full of mules, it has grown dark.

> It was pitch black outside. In such darkness, you didn't need to be a daydreamer or a Quixote to mistake the howling wind for the battle cry of the enemy hosts or the slamming of a gate for a shot fired by the perfidious enemy. Small groups and gangs of homeless fascists haunted the roads of the Republican rear: during the day, they hid in caves and ravines; at night, they crept into villages seeking loot and revenge. . . .
> The alcalde took us to an inn. Our car was already sheltered under an awning, next to a hollowed-out stone trough from which Rocinante must have once drunk. Inside the tavern, in the faint glow of an oil lamp, a hungry Dorado could be discerned, reclining next to a cold stove, a sour expression on his face. But the alcalde called the innkeeper aside and whispered something in his ear that

produced a magic transformation in the cold, dismal hovel. Suddenly a bright fire was burning in the stove and an appetizing leg of lamb was browning over the coals. It appeared that in El Toboso one could get meat without a doctor's prescription, and in amounts hazardous to your health, too.[50]

At this point, no doubt remains: it is Koltsov who is the real Don Quixote, and Dorado is his Sancho Panza. The howling wind is the battle cry of the enemy hosts; the slamming of a gate is a shot fired by the perfidious enemy; and the very tall and very sad peasant girl is the beautiful Dulcinea. As Leonid Leonov put it at the Writers' Congress, "The central hero of our time does not fit in a mirror as small as ours. And yet, we all know full well that he has entered the world." It was not just Koltsov who was Don Quixote: it was his readers, too. They were all heroes, but their idealism had been disciplined by unblinking realism, and their enemies were real. In the kingdom of giants, there were no windmills.

19

THE PETTINESS
OF EXISTENCE

Most of the House of Government's nomenklatura residents read Koltsov. As giants living in an eternal house, they could see the Pamirs, as well as the Kremlin and the Palace of Soviets foundation pit, from their apartment windows. All former "students" (and some of their former proletarian students) would have read *Don Quixote*, perhaps more than once. The same was true of such other "peaks" as Dante, Shakespeare, and Goethe, the nineteenth-century romantic and realist canon, and the full complement of Russian classics, with a universal preference for Tolstoy over Dostoevsky. Few people read Soviet literature, and those who did, did not read much. As Leonov said in his Writers' Congress speech, the heroes of the new age would eventually join the "international constellation of human types whose members include Robinson Crusoe, Don Quixote, Figaro, Hamlet, Pierre Bezukhov, Oedipus, Foma Gordeev, and Raphael de Valentin." But until that time—until the artists had adjusted and polished their mirrors so as to produce a Soviet *Robinson Crusoe* or *Don Quixote*—the heroes of the new age had no choice but to keep rereading the originals. Their favorite theaters were the Bolshoi, which staged classical operas and ballets; the Maly, which Fedor Kaverin described as "a temple of humanity that reveals to humans what is great about them"; and the Moscow Art Theater, whose pursuit of psychological realism would culminate in the 1937 production of *Anna Karenina*. Their favorite museums were the State Museum of Fine Arts and the Tretyakov Gallery (both within easy walking distance); their favorite composer was Beethoven; and their favorite living writer was Romain Rolland, celebrated as a twentieth-century Tolstoy (as well as Beethoven's biographer). The art that had sustained the early Bolsheviks in the catacombs had become the official art of the state they built. When Yakov Sverdlov learned in March 1911 that his wife had given birth to a boy, he wrote to her from prison about Natasha Rostova from *War and Peace*. When, a year later, Voronsky found himself in a "semi-dungeon" with "damp corners crawling with wood lice," he abandoned his usual study routine in favor of Homer, Dickens, Ibsen, Tolstoy, and Leskov. When, the night before the operation he knows will probably kill him, Commander Gavrilov from Pilniak's *Tale of the Unextinguished Moon* asks his friend for a book about "simple human joys," his friend tells him that he does not have such a book. "That's revolutionary literature for you," says Gavrilov, as a joke. "Oh well, I'll reread some Tolstoy, then." When, six years and another revolution later, Tania Miagkova heard of her husband's arrest, she switched from *Das Kapital* to *Anna Karenina* and *Resurrection*, and when she found out that she would not be allowed to join him in So-lovki, she went on a "poetry binge." "I read Briusov for a while, then Bag-ritsky, then Mayakovsky and Blok . . . , and all this richness of harmony put together is a true feast. But then you pick up Pushkin, and it is clear that he towers above them all." The socialist realism that the heroes of the new age designed and demanded was not a kitschy appropriation of all the "greatest achievements of world culture"—it was a deliberate attempt to build on the previous Augustinian—and Augustan—ages of heroic fulfill-ment and dignified maturity. Some degree of youthful ardor was accept-able; "chaos instead of music" was not.[1]

In March 1935, when Stalin's adopted son Artem Sergeev (Apt. 380), turned seven, Stalin gave him a copy of *Robinson Crusoe*, with the following inscription: "To my little friend, Tomik, with the wish that he grow up to be a conscious, steadfast, and fearless Bolshevik." The implied comparison to the hero of Puritan industriousness was probably unintentional; the belief that one must climb the Pamirs to become a conscious, steadfast, and fearless Bolshevik was both self-conscious and common.[2]

But it was also dangerous. Not every giant recognized his neighbor as such, and not every windmill was convincing as a giant. Seen from the Pamirs—of either socialism or *Don Quixote*—most people and things looked small. "Cervantes loved his Quixote, but he made Sancho Panza governor, not him. Good old Sancho never claimed to possess his master's high vir-tues," as Koltsov's narrator says to the skeptical French reporters. But what did this mean? Was it irony or resignation? And was Sancho Panza a symbol of realism and loyalty or philistinism and stupidity, as Arosev sus-pected? "I should start writing books like *Don Quixote*," he wrote in his diary on April 24, 1937, "only the other way around: a modern Sancho Panza, and next to him, Don Quixote."[3]

Heroes kept slaying monsters, but socialism had not grown much be-yond its "economic foundations." The House of Government had been built, but the Palace of Soviets was still a hole in the ground. The former Party secretary of the House of Government Construction Committee, Mikhail Tuchin, had become a Gorky Park inspector, found himself a mis-tress, and started drinking; the head of construction of the Palace of So-viets, Vasily Mikhailov, was a former Right Oppositionist.

As far as Arosev was concerned, Sanchos were everywhere and, if not for Stalin and his closest associates, the building of socialism would have been sabotaged a long time ago. Kerzhentsev was not the only one "swell-ing up with stupidity the way one swells up with fat," and Soviet tourists in Paris were not the only idiots and ignoramuses. According to Arosev's diary, Molotov's speech at the Seventeenth Party Congress in January 1934 had been delivered "from the heart and with passion," but few delegates seemed to care. Arosev's and Molotov's friend from the Kazan days, Nikolai Maltsev, "sat listening with his face all screwed up, trying desperately not to yawn." Three years later, the participants at a Party meeting at VOKS included several Old Bolsheviks who kept recycling the same happy memories, some time-serving clerks who had no idea why they were there, and a few activists "who had never taken part in revolutionary battles and therefore looked upon revolutionary strategy as a kind of magic."[4]

On April 4, 1935, Arosev and his deputy, N. Kuliabko, had gone over to see the deputy head of the Central Committee's Department of Culture and the Propaganda of Leninism (Kultprop), Pavel Yudin. Later that day, Arosev reported in his diary:

> Having left his office, as always, in a depressed and gallows-humor mood, Kuliabko and I shared our impressions. He said, with his usual sarcasm,
>
> "It's almost as if they had been trying to shove some of those heavy office inkwells up our butts. They huffed and puffed and sweated without any success until the ink spilled all over our pants. . . . What we told Yudin amounted to 'wait, let us take off our pants first, it will make it easier for you.' To which Yudin replied: 'Don't worry, we'll just see if we can screw them in through your pants.'"
>
> Our only consolation was that Stalin was planning to give a speech and there were rumors going around that Kultprop might be closed down soon. That would be a good thing. It's a ridiculous institution, especially if one considers the responsibility it is charged with.[5]

Within five weeks, Kultprop had been closed down. For Arosev the diarist, Stalin remained the principal defense against the Sancho Panzas, the ultimate guarantor of the triumph of Communism, and the addressee of his most intimate letters and poems. But Stalin would not respond, and the question remained. Communism was going to triumph, but what about Arosev? What was he to do in the meantime? Kuliabko soon turned out to be "just one more petty devil in our dusty chancelleries," and so did the head of the Foreign Ties Commission of the Writers' Union, the "eunuch" Mikhail Apletin. "He loathes me, my wife, and everything that has to do with me. He's no more than a calligraphy teacher. The tragedy for him is that uniforms and funeral masses have been abolished."[6]

The tragedy for Arosev was that he, too, loathed his wife and "the petit bourgeois atmosphere and greedy little hen's world with its hen-and-rooster problems" that she represented. "I have never once seen my wife happy about anything. The minute I appear, she starts in on her demands: why haven't I found a new maid yet or looked for vegetables for our son Mitia or procured a ticket for her friend or some such thing. She also has a lethal talent for nagging on and on, and always about the same thing: how bad it is to live here, how it puts her on a completely different footing with me, and so on." Arosev had, of course, broken Solts's injunction against marrying class aliens, especially foreign ones, but the frightening thing was that everyone else seemed to be languishing in the same stifling embrace. "I think Molotov is afraid of extending a more definite invitation because he is under the influence of his wife Polina, who is herself under the influence of my former wife Olga Viacheslavovna, and who, moreover, is jealous of her husband's relationship with me, as well as his relationship with my wife, and, in general, wants to have a great deal of influence over her husband."[7]

But Arosev's greatest tragedy was that he was unhappy with his own life: his "maître d'hôtel job," his "tragically diminishing taste for life," and his losing battle against "the pettiness of existence." "We are living in our new apartment, and each day brings new progress on the bourgeois domesticity front: today it's a prettier tablecloth; tomorrow, after much effort, we'll manage to find a worker, who will spend a lot of time doing something to improve our apartment." Molotov, his oldest and closest friend, had called him a "petit bourgeois" when he asked for help in getting a room at the "Pines" rest home. Stalin, his savior and confessor, was not answering his letters. When he wrote in his diary that "every woman is, in some sense, Madame Bovary, and every man is, from a certain point of view, Don Quixote," he did not mean that he and his wife were giants too large to be represented. Perhaps—his diary seems to suggest—it was not the mirror that was crooked: perhaps it was the face.[8]

In 1932 *Pravda* published a short story by Ilf and Petrov, titled "How Robinson Was Created," about a magazine editor who commissions a Soviet *Robinson Crusoe* from a writer named Moldavantsev. The writer submits a manuscript about a Soviet young man triumphing over nature on a desert island. The editor likes the story, but says that a Soviet Robinson would be unthinkable without a trade union committee consisting of a chairman, two permanent members, and a female activist to collect membership dues. The committee, in its turn, would be unthinkable without a safe deposit box, a chairman's bell, a pitcher of water, and a tablecloth ("red or green, it doesn't matter; I don't want to limit your artistic imagination"), and broad masses of working people. The author objects by saying that so many people could not possibly be washed ashore by a single ocean wave:

"Why a wave?" asked the editor, suddenly surprised.

"How else would the masses end up on the island? It is a desert island, after all!"

"Who said it was a desert island? You're getting me confused. Okay, so there's an island, or, even better, a peninsula. It's safer that way. And that's where a series of amusing, original, and interesting adventures will take place. There'll be some trade union work going on, but not enough. The female activist will expose certain deficiences—in the area of dues collection, for example. She'll be supported by the broad masses. And then there'll be the repentant chairman. At the end you could have a general meeting. That would be quite effective artistically. I guess that's about it."

"But—what about Robinson?" stammered Moldavantsev.

"Oh yeah . . . , thanks for reminding me. I'm not wild about Robinson. Just drop him. He's a silly, whiny, totally unnecessary character.[9]

The era of socialist realism was separated from the era of the great disapppointment by the epoch of great construction sites. It was different from the great disappointment because the most labor-intensive part of the construction work had been completed. The foundations had been laid, the first layer of scaffolding had been taken down, and the shape and beauty of the house of socialism could be seen by all those who had eyes. Or, as Kirov put it at the Seventeenth Party Congress (using another key Bolshevik metaphor), "the army has won several decisive battles against the enemy and taken some key positions; the war is not over, far from over, but there is something like a brief breathing space, if I may say so, and the whole great victorious warrior host is singing its powerful victory song." At the Seventeenth Party Congress and at the writers' congress that followed, the delegates' main job was to compose, rehearse, and start performing that victory song. Back at work and at home, they had to keep waging the war. Everyone who had ears had heard Stalin's words first uttered in 1928 and invoked repeatedly and emphatically through the mid-1930s:

> The more we advance, the greater will be the resistance of the capitalist elements and the sharper the class struggle, while the Soviet Government, whose strength will steadily increase, will pursue a policy of isolating these elements, a policy of demoralising the enemies of the working class, a policy, lastly, of crushing the resistance of the exploiters, thereby creating a basis for the further advance of the working class and the main mass of the peasantry.
>
> It must not be imagined that the socialist forms will develop, squeezing out the enemies of the working class, while our enemies retreat in silence and make way for our advance, that then we shall again advance and they will again retreat until "unexpectedly" all the social groups without exception, both kulaks and poor peasants, both workers and capitalists, find themselves "suddenly" and "imperceptibly," without struggle or commotion, in the lap of a socialist society. Such fairy-tales do not and cannot happen in general, and in the conditions of the dictatorship of the proletariat in particular.

It never has been and never will be the case that a dying class surrenders its positions voluntarily without attempting to organise resistance. It never has been and never will be the case that the working class could advance towards socialism in a class society without struggle or commotion. On the contrary, the advance towards socialism cannot but cause the exploiting elements to resist the advance, and the resistance of the exploiters cannot but lead to the inevitable sharpening of the class struggle.[10]

Some enemies bleated like goats, dripped slime over the living room floor, and had gaping nostrils, dangling earlobes, and scurvy-stricken mouths torn by silent screams. Others, like Tania Miagkova, looked unremarkable but were found guilty of duplicity and might not be sincere in their recantations. Yet others, including Smilga, Radek, and Voronsky, continued to live in the House of Government but seemed to be singing out of tune and might yet be found guilty of duplicity. And then there were all those who resisted the advance by refusing to retreat: the petty devils in dusty chancelleries, the hens with their hen-and-rooster problems, the Sancho Panzas on trade union committees, the authors and editors of the absurd pseudo-Soviet *Robinson Crusoe*, and possibly Robinson Crusoe himself, if it turned out that he had, in fact, spent several years on a desert island without a trade union committee. Class enemies were being engendered daily, hourly, spontaneously, and on a massive scale. Eventual victory over them was both assured and difficult: like all millenarian prophecies, the guarantee of the coming of Communism made predestination dependent on free will. As Arosev wrote in his diary on September 28, 1934, less than a month after the writers' congress, "Moscow is being transformed heroically. There are new tall buildings and wide squares. Will all this remain socialist? Yes, it definitely will, but it will have to be defended!"[11]

■ ■ ■

The home front was the least well defined and therefore the most dangerous. The House of Government, designed as a "transitional type" building dominated by straight lines, right angles, and wide windows, was swelling up with fat. Various commissions and inspections complained repeatedly about the bloated staff, inflated costs, growing debts, and opaque accounting practices. The first casualties were the Kalinin Club and the State New Theater. The club was stripped of its property and employees and converted to a much more modest "cultural center" for the members of the Central Executive Committee's trade union organization; the tennis court was rented out to the All-Russian Artists' Cooperative (Vsekokhudozhnik). The theater never fully recovered after the banning of *The Champion of the World*. Most of the season-ticket holders asked for their money back; the old productions did not work on the new stage; the remaining new productions were widely seen as failures; the administrative director, S. I. Amoglobeli, left for the Maly Theater; and the House of Government administration never agreed to lower the rent (which, at 160,000 rubles, was 2,000 percent higher than what the theater used to pay for its previous venue). The theater made some money by going on tours, selling the *Champion*'s costumes, and firing thirty employees, but the situation remained bleak. Meanwhile, the introduction of socialist realism had put into question Fedor Kaverin's choice of material and the legitimacy of his "nonliteral realism." The new administrative director, G. G. Aleksandrov, announced that the theater's task was to fulfill Party directives, that Party directives reflected the demands of the proletariat, and that the proletarian demanded "the kind of art that measures up to the times we are living in." The art that measured up consisted of the classics (most prominently represented in 1934 by "Ostrovsky, Gogol, and Griboedov among the Russians and Shakespeare, Schiller, Goldoni, and others among the foreigners") and all the "first-rate" Soviet plays that measured up to the classics. The fact that none—except for Gorky's—did was not an excuse for not staging them. On the "artistic personality" front, the State New Theater was to continue to produce "striking, theatrical, rhythmic shows based on the creativity of the actors and the use of stage convention," while combating "inventiveness for the sake of inventiveness" and "elements of eclecticism."[12]

Kaverin responded by saying that nonliteral realism was perfectly compatible with the socialist kind and that "the Art Theater's anti-theater" would not be allowed onto his stage. The theater briefly considered producing Mikhail Levidov's *A House on Prechistenka* (in which, according to Aleksandrov, class enemies provoked "not feelings of compassion, as in Bulgakov's *The Days of the Turbins*, but those of hatred"), but it was Karl Gutzkow's 1847 romantic tragedy, *Uriel Acosta*, that was going to prove that the State New Theater was capable of combining artistic integrity with financial solvency, striking theatricality with high moral seriousness, and the greatest possible generalizability with enormous inner richness. The plan almost worked: *Uriel Acosta* premiered in the spring of 1934 and was playing to full houses and getting enthusiastic reviews when, on November 3, 1934, the Central Executive Committee ordered the theater's eviction from the House of Government. According to Kaverin's diary, he reached Stalin's secretary, A. N. Poskrebyshev by phone several days later. Kaverin's student, B. G. Golubovsky, offers an account of what happened:

Kaverin did the impossible: he reached Poskrebyshev, Stalin's secretary, and said that he was speaking on behalf of the theater's collective that had been created by the revolution and had always faithfully served the Party's cause, and that they were all indignant, shocked, and confused by such a devastating decision. Poskrebyshev asked Kaverin to wait on the line and then disappeared for about fifteen minutes. When he returned, he told Fedor Nikolaevich not to hang up and to wait by the phone no matter how long it took.

Kaverin and the actors, who had all managed to squeeze into his office, waited. Occasionally someone would replace him for several
minutes, holding the receiver until he came rushing back. Finally,
Poskrebyshev came on the line: "The order must be carried out. It is
a matter of state importance. I am to convey Comrade Stalin's assurance that you will soon receive a building at least as good as the
previous one. That is all." And the line went dead.[13]

They did get a magnificent new building (which had formerly belonged
to the newly disbanded Society of Former Political Prisoners and Exiles),
but soon lost it, too, along with their "State New" name. Kaverin's hopes
for another breakthrough and another new building became focused on
Faust, The Merchant of Venice, and a "peak" that was not usually mentioned
as part of the Pamirs: *The Communist Manifesto*. (According to Golubovsky,
Kaverin always believed that the real reason for his theater's expulsion
from the House of Government was the rumored existence of an underground passage that began under the stage and ended in the Kremlin.)
After the theater's departure, the building was given over to The First Children's Movie Theater. In February 1935, the head of the Central Executive
Committee's Housekeeping Department, N. I. Pakhomov (Apt. 204), complained to Enukidze that the theater had not yet removed some of its
property stored in the "former church." But the following October, when
the head of the Theater Directorate finally asked to have it back, Pakhomov wrote that "none of the property belonging to the theater remains in
the House."[14]

The "New Theater" sign above the facade has been replaced
by one saying "First Children's Movie Theater."

At that point, Pakhomov's Housekeeping Department had other things to worry about. The eviction of the club and the theater, along with several other budget-cutting measures, had resulted in a reduction of House of Government personnel from 831 in October 1934 to 612 in October 1935, but a special Central Executive Committee inspection found the gains to be insufficient or illusory. The cost of maintaining the House of Government exceeded the Moscow norm by 670 percent (6.47 rubles as compared with 0.84 rubles per square meter per month). The main reason, according to the inspection report, was the still unacceptably large staff (one employee for every four residents, including fifty-seven administrators and forty-three plumbers and electricians). Another reason was the profligate spending: most of the savings were revealed to have been "not savings but the difference between actual expenses and those anticipated by inflated plan estimates." The cafeteria, with eighty-six employees, and the laundry, with ninety-four, were used by the House staff and Housekeeping Department employees, but almost never by the House residents. The quality of service was poor ("low-quality lunches" and "torn linen with rust stains"); the cafeteria, in particular, was a serious financial liability. Also troubling was the large number of cars in the courtyards and the survival of the old Swamp in the form of various affiliated "wooden residential houses that have fallen into disrepair."[15]

One obvious remedy was to increase the supervision, financial discipline, and labor productivity. Another was to improve the quality of personnel. According to a November 4, 1935, joint report by the House commandant, Party committee secretary, and trade union committee chair, the introduction of additional screening for job applicants and repeated purges among current employees had reduced the danger of enemy infiltration. Guards were being recruited "exclusively from the ranks of the Red Army, Red Navy, and border troops, with the goal of maximizing the number of Party members"; their political knowledge and combat readiness were being tested on a regular basis and with "100 percent involvement." The staff Party organization consisted of sixty-four individuals: forty-five members and nineteen candidate members. In addition to attending regular meetings, all Party members engaged in specialized study: some outside the House (at evening schools for workers, district schools for Soviet work, courses on Marxism-Leninism, the Communist Higher School of Propagandists, and the Communist Higher School for Party Organizers), and the rest, in the locally run reading groups devoted to Party candidate training, general education, and the study of Leninism and Party history. Attendance was kept by group leaders and Party organizers; all reading notes were checked before class; truants were summoned to Party bureau meetings; and stronger students were assigned to weaker ones as tutors. Komsomol activities (for forty-three members) were organized the same way. Non-Party members were reached by means of lunch-break newspaper readings, regular rallies, lectures on Party and government decisions, monthly in-house newspapers, and political education classes. Thirty activists from among the nonworking wives of staff members were involved in running a children's club, located on the administrative floor. There was a kindergarten for thirty-five children of staff members with its own summer camp, a library with 320 books, and various clubs (including theater, music, sewing, and foreign languages). Over the course of 1935, the trade union committee issued 205 discounted passes to rest homes and organized an unspecified number of picnics and collective trips to theaters and museums. The residents' maids were to be included in as many of these activities as possible. Twenty-four of them were organized into an activists' group.[16]

It is not known how many of these claims were exaggerated or inaccurate: the Central Executive Committee inspection report did not address staff matters beyond recommending the firing of "no less than 25 percent of service personnel" and the tearing down of "wooden residential houses that have fallen into disrepair." The report did not specify which houses the inspectors had in mind, but it is likely that some of them were dorms for House staff members. There were three altogether: one, the "Wooden Barrack No. 17," in the village of Nizhnie Kotly (absorbed into southern Moscow in 1932), and two others right next to the House of Government—the exemplary one reserved for the guards, with its own refrigerator; and, as described in the administrative report, "the dorm at Bersenev Embankment, No. 20, for janitors, porters, and unskilled laborers, with a fluid population of mostly temporary workers, such as janitors, whose numbers grow to 30 in the winter and fall to 16 in the summer. Despite such impermanence, the management has been able to maintain good order and cleanliness. A radio has been installed. The dorm has been painted with oil paint and has a good, cultured appearance. There is a stove for cooking and boiling water."[17]

. . .

The swamp was still there: in the wooden shacks next to the House, the forgotten warehouse inside the former Church of Nicholas the Miracle Worker, the abandoned backstage area (and perhaps an underground passage) inside the former theater, the soon-to-be-evicted Artists' Cooperative inside the former club, the storage rooms filled with unused "copper pipes" in the basement, and the overcrowded administrative offices on the first floor of Entryway 1.[18]

But the most opaque, remote, and vulnerable parts of the House were the residents' apartments. The House of Government was "transitional" by design: some entryways were more prestigious than others; some apartments were more spacious than others; and some nomenklatura members belonged in some apartments and not in others. Some people who moved into the apartments proved unworthy and had to move out.

But what about those who remained? How many of them were unworthy, and how could one tell? Arosev, who kept trying to reassure himself that the new socialist buildings would be defended from hen-and-rooster problems, seemed unable to defend his own two apartments. Comrade Stalin was silent, and no one else seemed to know what to do.

One of the central tenets of Marxism as a millenarian doctrine was that the key to salvation lay in the sphere of production. One of the central features of Bolshevism as a life-structuring web of institutions was that Soviets were made in school and at work, not at home. The Party committees that supervised every aspect of Soviet life were territorially based (from the district to the republic), but the primary Party cells were in schools and in workplaces. Members of the Party and various auxiliary institutions (from the Octobrists, Pioneers, and Komsomols to the Young Naturalists and Voroshilov Sharpshooters) were inducted, examined, rewarded, and mobilized in school and at work, but not at home. Home life did come up at purge meetings and in connection with admissions and promotions, but only insofar as the person in question admitted certain shortcomings in his or her autobiographical statements or if a neighbor, friend, or relative volunteered a written denunciation. In theory and iconography, family life was an integral part of socialist construction; in practice—including the practice of such self-reflexive Communists as Aron Solts and Nikolai Podvoisky—the family remained autonomous and largely hidden from view. The communal experiments of the 1920s had never altered the Party's institutional setup, had affected the lives of few families, and had mostly run out of steam by the time the House of Government was built. When Arosev and Lydia Bogacheva suspected their maids of spying on them, they fired them and found new ones without having to explain their actions to anyone. And when inspection committees arrived in the House of Government, they headed for the basement, the cafeteria, and the administrative offices on the first floor, without ever venturing upstairs. Dorm activists might organize room inspections, and schoolteachers might send children's delegations to the homes of failing students, but the idea of a Party committee visiting Arosev's apartment in an effort to help him combat hens and roosters was alien to 1930s Bolshevism.

One reason was the unquestioned centrality of the workplace in the teachings of the Party; the other was the fact that, in the mid-1930s, no one seemed to know what a good Communist home—or even a good Communist—looked like. No one talked about Bolshevik baptisms or weddings anymore, and no one knew whether curtains and tablecloths represented "a good, cultured appearance" or the "perennial and loathsome forms of life." Bolshevik theory seemed to assume that heroic tall buildings (the base) would produce heroic apartment residents (the superstructure). The Bolshevik family was subjected to much less pastoral guidance and communal surveillance than most of its Christian counterparts (particularly the Puritans, whom the Bolsheviks tried to imitate in the matter of efficiency, "love of responsibility," and "sense of time"). The only Party, Komsomol, "mass-cultural," and "mass-political" work conducted in the House of Government was conducted by—and for—the staff members who worked there. The only self-organizing done by the residents as residents was done by the housewives concerned with the state of the courtyards or the work of the kindergarten. The women's volunteer movement was probably a good thing (especially after the movement's first nationwide congress in May 1936, at which Sofia Butenko, the wife of the director of the Kuznetsk Steel Plant and a part-time resident in the House of Government, Apt. 141, delivered one of the central speeches), but could Arosev be sure that it did not belong to the hen-and-rooster category? And could Sofia Butenko be sure? Her own efforts to make the Kuznetsk Engineers' Club "cozy" and to encourage young workers to wear suits focused on her husband's steel mill, not either of the houses in which she lived.[19]

Meanwhile, the House of Government (where she lived whenever she was in Moscow on one of her dressmaking expeditions) was filling up with desks, chests, busts, swords, carpets, curtains, portraits, bearskins, lampshades, pillows, tablecloths, forget-me-nots, and the *Treasures of World Literature*. Chests were swelling up with toys, sheets, pajamas, and ironed handkerchiefs. Residents were swelling up with suits, skirts, scarves, shawls, and black silk dresses. Apartments were swelling up with children, parents, siblings, uncles, aunts, cousins, nieces, nephews, in-laws, children from previous marriages, children of starving or exiled relatives, former spouses, and poor relations. No one listed, counted, or cataloged these people and things; no one checked their histories and associations. The House of Government leaseholders were selected, transferred, and removed according to their place within the government hierarchy; the House of Government staff members were subjected to a "thorough filtration" that included both a month-long background check and month-long initial probation period. The people who lived alongside the Government leaseholders in their apartments and who—as a majority of the House population, made the greatest claims on the House personnel's labor—remained invisible to Party scrutiny and absent from most discussions on the sharpening of class struggle.

In the meantime, Osip Piatnitsky and Pavel Alliluev were sharing their apartments with their wives' fathers, both former priests. Serafim Bogachev and his wife, Lydia, were relying on Serafim's mother, an illiterate, devoutly Orthodox woman, to help around the house. The Central Committee Women's Department head's sister, Maria Shaburova, was also illiterate (but so helpful around the house that the Shaburovs decided not to hire a maid). In Vasily Mikhailov's apartment, the main helper was his eldest daughter's godmother, an Orthodox Old Believer who begged Vasily not to take charge of whatever was going to replace the Cathedral of Christ the Savior; the mother-in-law of the head of the Soviet gold industry, Aleksandr Serebrovsky, was so distraught by the demolition of the cathedral that the whole family had to move to the Fifth House of Soviets, from which the hole in the ground could not be seen. Arkady Rozengolts's mother-in-law, a Russian gentry woman, had his children baptized; A. V. Ozersky's father-in-law, a former Pale of Settlement shopkeeper, recited Hebrew prayers. Aron Gaister's mother, who came for a visit from Poland, wore wigs and kept kosher; Solomon Ronin's father, a former rabbi, had his grandson circumcised; and Gronsky's brother-in-law, the Siberian poet Pavel Vasiliev, was arrested for "hooliganism and anti-Semitism." The Smilgas took in the wife of their arrested friend, Aleksandr Ioselevich; Osinsky adopted the son of his arrested brother-in-law, Vladimir Smirnov; and both Agnessa Argiropulo and Sofia Butenko adopted the daughters of their starving sisters.

Most of the House residents who came from rural areas had relatives who starved during the famine; most of the Jewish residents had relatives abroad; and most of the maids were refugees from collectivization. Inside the apartments' inner sanctum, the class-alien wives (Arosev's, Mikhailov's, Zbarsky's, Gronsky's, Kraval's, Alliluev's, and Rozengolts's, among others) were "making progress on the front of bourgeois domesticity"; the nonworking "wives of industrial managers and engineers," presided over by Sofia Butenko, seemed to be doing the same thing in their husbands' domains; and the fully employed, Party-minded House wives had "suddenly remembered that they were beautiful women." The most prominent Soviet wife, Polina Zhemchuzhina (Molotova), was head of the Soviet perfume and cosmetics industry.[20]

20

THE THOUGHT
OF DEATH

The swamp was back. The "juice of the old life" from Arosev's "Ruined House" had seeped into the house of socialism. But there was no reason for panic—because the Bolsheviks never panicked and because the new steel foundations ensured the essential soundness of life inside the building. As Voronsky wrote in 1934 (while sitting in his study in Apt. 357), it is private property "that makes 'material things' suspect and the spirit, sick":

> It is obvious that, with the disappearance of such property, the body-spirit dualism must lose its absolute character.
>
> *The "transformation" of the flesh and the spirit and a more organic—earthly and not supernatural—connection between them will result not in the resurrection of the dead, as Gogol hoped, but in a fully developed Communist society.* Man will see in things not a temptation and not a dangerous snare that breeds greed and self-interest and deadens the human soul, but [Gogol's] "lovely sensuality" and "our beautiful earth"—not an oppressor, but a friend, which will help him develop his best capabilities ad infinitum.
>
> Things will once again become the source of joy that they are in Homer's *The Odyssey*, but they will be richer, more varied, and not only a source of pleasure but also a means to the resounding victory of man over the elemental forces of nature and over himself.[1]

Was this hubris? Was it true, as Adoratsky's "prayerful" mother wrote to her son, that "people had rejected God, taken over God's dignity, and become lost in arrogance and corruption"? Voronsky's answer was consistent with the doctrine of historical materialism. The Communist transformation was not a rejection of God insofar as "God" stood for Eternal Law. In fact, it was Gogol's modern followers who, in their talk of changing the world by way of moral self-improvement, had rejected Providence in favor of rootless individualism:

> Those who fight for the social transformation of life cannot be, and have never been, indifferent to the human soul. Every revolutionary, and certainly every Marxist revolutionary, every Bolshevik, goes, in

the course of his struggle, through a hard school of inner reforging, sometimes agonizing and always very intense. He has his own "spiritual work" to do, but he cultivates in himself traits that are very different from—indeed, the opposite of, those of a Christian ascetic. In any case, it can never be said about a Marxist revolutionary that he is indifferent to his inner enlightenment. What makes him different from Gogol's followers is not an indifference to spiritual work, but his conception of that work, a conception that rests on the conviction that *man transforms the outside world and himself not arbitrarily, but in obedience to certain laws that guide that transformation.*[2]

Voronsky's answer, in other words, was consistent with what he had learned in the seminary and what both Gogol and Adoratsky's mother believed to be true. Human salvation depended on the marriage of predestination and free will—or, in Voronsky's terms, of "historical inevitability" and conscious human action, both social and spiritual. The difference between Bolshevik and Christian spiritual work was not apparent (the emphasis on violence was neither exceptional by apocalyptic standards nor central to the 1934 Bolshevik self-portrait), and the final goal—the aligning of one's thoughts and desires with eternal truth—was the same. The tools employed in such work included the study of sacred texts, the production of accurate autobiographical statements, full participation in the life of the "collective," regular purge confessions, and routine self-scrutiny. The latter, known as "psychology," included injunctions to "work on the self" and perhaps to keep a diary, but no specific instructions or recommended exercises comparable to monastic or Puritan self-monitoring techniques. Arosev described his diary as his "thought laboratory," "an imperfect sketch of the human soul," "an attempt to live on after death," and a "frightening report to oneself and nobody." His private spiritual work was a series of improvisations. As he wrote on November 12, 1935, "I was looking at Lenin's portrait, thinking: human life is primarily about psychology. Man is all about psychology. Psychology is our life. But, up until now, psychology has not been able to stand on firm scientific legs, i.e., our understanding of the essence of life is still quite weak. And so, consequently, is our understanding of death."[3]

Death—as self-sacrificial martyrdom or "traumatic nervosis"—had always been central to Bolshevism. After the foundations of the eternal house had been laid, it became a problem. As the Old Bolsheviks entered their fifties, they required better health care and longer stays in hospitals and sanatoria. (In the summer of 1934, the veteran of the Decossakization campaign and high-ranking trade and education official, Iosif Khodorovsky, from Apt. 365, was appointed head of the Kremlin Health and Sanitation Department with a mandate to dramatically expand its budget and range of services. In 1936, the House of Government outpatient clinic, a branch of the Kremlin Department, had about twenty-five employees, including three physicians, three pediatricians, one neurologist, one half-time ophthalmologist, and the famously cheerful otolaryngologist, David Yakovlevich Kuperman, who addressed everyone as "my dear.") The longer they convalesced, the more they thought about their own mortality and about the central problem of all millenarian movements—that of succession (the transition from sect to church and the legitimacy of infant baptism, or automatic conversion). But the challenge was much greater. Death from torture, wounds, labor, and tears had a clear meaning repeatedly explicated in word and image. But what did it mean to die peacefully in the eternal house?[4]

Insofar as Arosev's diary was his "thought laboratory," his "thought of thoughts" was "the thought of death." "It dictates my diary entries. It writes my stories and novels. It rules my imagination. I want to penetrate the mystery of nonbeing. My consciousness is more durable than my body. It endeavors to lift the body up to its own level. But instead of doing this great mental work, I am caught up in the 'vermicelli strands' of petty and unnecessary chores." One way to break free was to live each day as if it would last a lifetime. "If one day equals life, then only those who die on that day are mortal, and everyone else is immortal. That means that deaths are accidents, and most people are immortal." Another was to concentrate on overcoming the fear of death. "Fear turns man into beast; fearlessness, into God. My mother, who was shot by the Whites on September 18, 1918, ten versts from the town of Spassk, Kazan Province . . . was terrified of death. Her motto had always been: death is a small word, but knowing how to die is the greatest deed." She did know, or had learned, when the time came. But the times had changed. Immortality was both closer and farther away.[5]

In Yuri Trifonov's *The Disappearance* (which remained incomplete at the time of his death in 1981), "Nikolay Grigorievich" is based on his father, Valentin, and "Liza," on his mother (and his father's second wife), Evgenia Lurye. "Grandma" is based on Yuri's own grandmother—his father's first wife and his mother's mother.

> Before going to bed, Nikolai Grigorievich stood at the window in his study—it was a moment of quiet, the guests had left, Liza was in the bathroom, Grandma was asleep in her room behind the curtain—and after turning out the light, leaving only the reading lamp by the couch, he looked out over the courtyard, at the thousands of windows, still filled with evening bustle, lit up by orange, yellow, or red lampshades—green ones appeared only rarely—and in one window out of a thousand was a bluish light, and he thought, confusingly, about several things at once. His thoughts formed layers, were made of glass, each one showing through the other: he thought about all the houses he had lived in, beginning with Temernik, Saratov, Yekaterinburg, then in Osypki, in St. Petersburg on the Fourteenth Line,

in Moscow in the Metropole, in sleeping compartments, in Helsingfors on Albertsgatan, in Dairen, and God knows where, but nowhere
had he been at home, everything had been ephemeral, rushing
along somewhere, an eternal sleeping compartment. That feeling
had only arisen here, with Liza and the children, of life running out,
it had to happen sometime, it was for the sake of that, for the sake
of *that*, after all, that revolutions were made, but suddenly it occurred to him, with immediate and devastating force, that this pyramid of coziness, glowing in the night, this Tower of Babel made of
lampshades, was also temporary, was also flying, like dust in the
wind—deputy people's commissars, central board heads, public
prosecutors, army commanders, former political prisoners, presidium members, directors, and prize winners, turning out the lights in
their rooms and enjoying the darkness, flying off somewhere into an
even greater darkness. That's what occurred to Nikolai Grigorievich
for a second just before bedtime, as he stood at the window.[6]

■ ■ ■

In August 1936, the journal *Literaturnyi kritik* (Literary critic) printed Andrei Platonov's short story, "Immortality." A special editorial introduction
(probably written by Platonov's main supporter on the board, Elena Usievich) explained the unusual decision to publish a work of fiction by arguing
that the author had overcome "the grave creative errors" of "Doubting
Makar" and "For Future Use," produced new stories of "great artistic value,"
and was being treated unfairly by the literary journals, which refused to
publish his work out of "a bureaucratic fear of consequences" masquerad-
ing as Bolshevik vigilance. The story's main character, Emmanuel Semenovich Levin, is a stationmaster at a junction called the Red Line. He
hardly ever sleeps or eats, and does not talk much. His wife and daughter
live far away, and his soul, scarred by anti-Semitism, had "anticipated its
distant death" when he was still a little boy. "He had pushed aside the
hands of his wife and friends so he could leave for the station at midnight
whenever he felt there was any grief or worry down there. The train cars
contained cargo: the flesh, soul, and labor of millions of people living beyond the horizon. He could feel them more strongly than the loyalty of
friends or the love of a woman. Love must be the first service and aid in
his worry about all the unknown but dear people living beyond the faraway terminals of the tracks running from the Red Line."[7]

He does not spare himself and wants "to live out his life as quickly as
possible," but he is different from a Christian ascetic and from his own
former self because he has heard Stalin's 1935 speech about the "cadres
deciding everything," understood the importance of a complete human
being at the gate of the new world, and seen the "hen-and-rooster problems" his workers were suffering from for what they were: "not a danger-

ous snare," but a "lovely sensuality" and "our beautiful earth." "It had become clear to him long ago that, in essence, transport was a simple, straightforward thing. So why did it demand, sometimes, not ordinary, regular work, but anguished effort? The dead or hostile human being—that was the difficulty! That was why you needed to warm another person with your breath constantly and without ceasing and to hold him close, so that he would not die, and so that he would feel his importance and would give back, if only out of shame and gratitude, the warmth of help and comfort he had received in the shape of honest work and honest living."[8]

One day, an employee named Polutorny tells Levin that he needs a "suitable, worthy rooster" for his wife's special hens. "Levin looked quietly at Polutorny's face: the things a person could live for—even hens and roosters could feed his soul and even in a backyard chicken coop could his heart find consolation! 'I understand,' said Levin quietly. 'I know a chicken breeder in Izium. He's a friend of mine. . . . I'll give you a note for him, and you can go see him on your day off.'" There is also Polutorny's wife, who wants to study French; a young clerk and his wife who need a babysitter; a tired worker who needs help with his sleeping schedule; and various other "small accidents and minor injuries" that need attention. "Levin understood that little glitches were major catastrophes that only by chance died in infancy." He is needed everywhere, by everyone, all the time.[9]

Love for others demands self-sacrifice. Levin does not preach asceticism: he practices it quietly because someone must. (He has a maid who worries about his bodily comfort, but she understands his mission and shares his wisdom.) His job is to ensure the salvation of others. "At night, after a short rest, Levin went back to the station. There was nothing dangerous happening, but Levin felt bored at home. He believed that for a transitory, temporary person there was no point in living for himself. The real, future people may already have been born, but he did not count himself among them. He needed to be away from himself day and night in order to understand others. . . . In order to hear all voices, one has to become almost mute oneself."[10]

Levin is "a lonely man," but he is not alone. Shortly before dawn, the station telephone rings:

"Hello, Red Line stationmaster speaking."

"And this is Kaganovich speaking. How are you, Comrade Levin? And why did you pick up the phone so quickly? How did you manage to get dressed? Weren't you asleep?"

"No, Lazar Moiseevich, I was just about to go to bed."

"Just about! Most people go to bed at night, not in the morning. . . . Listen, Emmanuel Semenovich, if you ruin your health down there at the Red Line, I'll charge you for the loss of a thousand locomotives. I'm going to be checking on your sleep, but don't make me be your nurse."

The remote, kind, deep voice fell silent for a while. Levin also stood silently: he had long loved his Moscow interlocutor, but could never, under any circumstances, express his feelings directly: there was no way to do it without being tactless and indelicate.

"It must be night in Moscow, too, Lazar Moiseevich," said Levin quietly. "Most people don't go to bed in the morning there, either."

Kaganovich understood and burst out laughing.[11]

Levin is not alone. Kaganovich is to him what he is to Polutorny; he is to Kaganovich what his maid is to him; and Kaganovich is prepared to be his nurse, if need be. Such is the immortality of the people bound together by the tracks running from the Red Line. Such, in particular, is the immortality of those who do not sleep when others do. The following night, an hour after Levin goes to bed ("not for the pleasure of repose, but for the sake of the morrow"), he is awakened by a call from the station office: "They just contacted us from Moscow to ask about your health and whether you were asleep. As if you were a great, immortal being!" A midnight call to see if Levin is asleep is not just foolishness: it is a reminder, as well as a confirmation, that Levin is a great, immortal being. "Levin sat on his bed for a while, got dressed, and went back to the station."[12]

Platonov and Elena Usievich (in whose House of Government apartment he was a frequent guest) seemed to believe that he had finally grasped the true spirit of the Revolution and perhaps even solved the mystery of Bolshevik immortality. They were wrong. A year later, *Red Virgin Soil* published an essay by the influential critic, A. S. Gurvich, in which he argued that Platonov's new work was as "profoundly erroneous" as his "Doubting Makar" and "For Future Use." "Whatever we may have been told about the socialist content of the story 'Immortality,' we see in its protagonist an ascetic, a self-denying penitent." Platonov's Bolshevik was another one of his beggars and holy fools, and Platonov's vision of immortality was "an absurdity, dead end, and slander." "Does he realize that his 'love' can only benefit those who hate, and that his mournful, sorrowful pose can attract

Andrei Platonov

only those who try to 'grow into socialism' in the guise of little jesuses?" Platonov's characters, according to Gurvich, were divided into those who wanted to abolish the state, like Makar, and those who wanted to merge with the state, like Levin. They were either "poor Evgenys" or the bronze from which the Galloping Horseman was made. In reality, however—and especially in the new reality of unfolding socialism—the great work of construction and the simple human joys were inseparable. "More than that, they presuppose each other." Socialism brings life, and life's "miracle-working sources" include, in equal measure, "the Bronze Horseman and poor Evgeny, the big picture and private Makar, the roar of the train and the quiet birdsong."[13]

Platonov, Usievich, and the editorial board of the *Literaturnaia gazeta* objected to the harshness of Gurvich's criticism and pointed to signs of conversion and rebirth, but Platonov's career never recovered. In Gurvich's view, the problem was not his criticism, but Platonov's lukewarmness. "His popularity is limited to a narrow circle of literary specialists" because he is "anti-national," and he is anti-national because he lacks "power, depth, and breadth in the depiction of human emotion." In Russia, the most national of poets was Pushkin. Platonov had represented him as "our comrade." Gurvich represented him as a reproach to Platonov: "Platonov understands Pushkin's great dream, which makes him 'our comrade'—a dream about a time 'when nothing will prevent a man from releasing the sacred energy of his art, feelings, and intelligence.' Pushkin believes, writes Platonov rapturously, that '*a brief, ordinary human life is quite sufficient for the accomplishment of all conceivable goals and a full enjoyment of all the passions.* Those who are not able to do it will not be able to do it even if they become immortal.' Do not these words spell the death sentence for the 'immortal' Levin?"[14]

■ ■ ■

A much more serious attempt to tackle the problem of Bolshevik immortality was Leonid Leonov's *The Road to Ocean*. Leonov was the same age as Platonov (both turned thirty-six in 1935, when *The Road to Ocean* was published), but his career had been moving in the opposite direction: from unsound (merchant) social roots and "fellow-traveler" literary beginnings to the vanguard of socialist realism following the acclaim of *The Sot'* and the effect of his speech at the writers' congress about the "great planner" and the small mirror. *The Road to Ocean* was meant to mark the culmination of his professional and spiritual journey and the appearance of the great planner as a literary hero commensurate with Faust (in a mirror commensurate with the great planner). As Leonov said many years later, "that novel is the pinnacle of my faith": "I wrote *The Road to Ocean* in a state of spiritual exaltation, with an almost physical sensation of the grandeur of our accomplishments and aspirations." In the opinion of Voronsky, his patron in the 1920s, "Leonov creates and sees types. In this sense, he has preserved more of the sacred fire of the classics than his contemporaries. He is in a position to connect modern literature to the classics by a strong, straight thread." After 1934, nothing was more important than the thread

Leonid Leonov
(Courtesy of N. A. Makarov)

connecting modern literature to the classics, and no one seemed in a better position to create and see the new hero than Leonid Leonov. The challenge was to move into the new era by returning to the most classic of genres. "Only a genuine tragedy," wrote Leonov, "can stake out a place for the new man in the gallery of world characters."[15]

The Road to Ocean is about a railway line from Moscow to the Pacific—and, at the same time, "a road to the future, the dream, the ideal, to Communism." What makes *The Road to Ocean* a tragedy is that its central character (the railroad's political commissar and an Old Bolshevik) Aleksei Kurilov, learns that he has cancer. The figure of an Old Bolshevik dying in peacetime had appeared, inauspiciously, in Pilniak's *Tale of the Unextinguished Moon*, and then again in various construction novels, in the secondary but structurally important role of Moses on the bank of the Jordan. Now the time had come to move him to the center of the plot and organize the world around his approaching demise and presumed immortality.[16]

The person Leonov had in mind when writing the novel ("to some degree, a prototype")—the person he interviewed, accompanied on inspection tours, and eventually became close to—was the director of the Moscow–Kazan Railroad, Ivan Kuchmin. Born in 1891 to a peasant family in the Volga Region, Kuchmin enrolled in a teachers' college, joined a Marxist reading group, discovered Ernest Renan's *Life of Jesus*, and taught for two years in a village school before becoming a full-time revolutionary. During the Civil War he distinguished himself as the organizer of the defense of Uralsk in May–June 1919 and as a commissar in Ukraine, Turkestan, and Poland. During the First Five-Year Plan, he served as chair of the Stalingrad District Executive Committee and then first secretary of the Stalingrad Party Committee. In August 1931, he was transferred to Moscow, first as deputy chair of the Moscow Province Executive Committee and then, in August 1933, as political commissar and then director of the Moscow–Kazan Railway. Kuchmin's wife, Stefania Arkhipovna, also of Volga Region peasant background, taught biology at the Institute of Chemical Engineering and presided over the Moscow–Kazan Railroad's Women's Council. The

Ivan Kuchmin

Kuchmins lived in a five-room apartment in the House of Government (Apt. 226, in the prestigious Entryway 12, facing the river) with their two children (Oleg, born in 1922, and Elena, in 1926) and Stefania's sister Ania, who did all the housework. Ivan's study and the large dining room were rarely used; the other rooms included the parents' bedroom, Oleg's room, and the room shared by Ania and Elena. During the famine in the Volga Region, many of the Kuchmins' relatives came to stay with them for long periods of time; Stefania's (and Ania's) younger brother, Shura, came to stay for good, but a few months later accidentally killed himself playing with Ivan's revolver. Elena, who had been the one to discover Shura's bleeding body, was taken to the Leonovs' apartment on Gorky Street, where she spent three days. The Kuchmins and the Leonovs were also dacha neighbors (in Barvikha, across a small ravine from the Osinskys). It was at the dacha that Leonid and Ivan first met and where they used to go on long walks and talk about *The Road to Ocean*.[17]

In the novel, Aleksei Kurilov is immediately recognizable as an Old Bolshevik and a reflection of the iconic Stalin. "He was a large and somber man; only rarely was his greying, waterfall moustache disturbed by a smile." He has "the shoulders of a stevedore and the forehead of Socrates," and his eyes, at closer inspection, appear "not unfriendly." His past and thoughts explain his appearance—two sacred images are "merged" in his mind: that of Lenin and that of his former teacher, the metal caster Arsentyich (a double of Osinsky's "Blacksmith" who, in an extra reference to Hephaestus, walks with a cane). Kurilov's last name ("Smoker") and his ever-present pipe reinforce, and further merge, the Stalinist, Promethean, and proletarian allusions. His early Bolshevik education has included both Pushkin and Shakespeare.[18]

He lives on the top floor of the House of Government. One morning, the narrator comes over for one of their regular conversations. "We are at the window looking out. The house is tall. If you press your cheek to the frame, you can just see a corner of the Kremlin from Kurilov's window. Today it appears stooped and a bit diminished. The sky is overcast, although it was below freezing last night. There is a gigantic plume of black smoke stretching from the nearby power station to the faded gold of the Kremlin. Snowflakes hover in the air, slowly looking for a place to land."[19]

Kurilov embodies the landscape—the Kremlin, the House of Government, the Big Stone Bridge—and looms over it. He is a "man-mountain, from whose summit the future can be seen," "a bridge over which people pass into the future," and "an enormous planet" in whose orbit others circle, like so many "insignificant satellites." Among them are his quiet wife, Katerinka, who is bound to him by a relationship of "honest and sober friendship," and whose death early in the novel presages Kurilov's own passing; his sister Klavdia, a "dry, self-willed, straightforward" Party inquisitor who has "no personal biography" beyond "public anniversaries"; another sister, Frosia, who marries the industrialist, Omelichev, and is punished for it with a deaf-mute son; Omelichev himself, whose function is to provide "malicious and intelligent criticism," but whose mirror is "too small to reflect Kurilov's entire expanse"; and Kurilov's prey, double, and antagonist, Gleb Protoklitov ("First-Named"), who has three doubles of his own: a secret one in Leonid Leonov, whose biography he has partially appropriated, and two obvious ones, including his redeemable self and brother, Ilya Protoklitov. Ilya is a surgeon married to a theater actress named Liza, who aborts his child; Liza has an uncle, a former Latin teacher

Eva Levina-Rozengolts, *The Power Station in Winter* (1930–31)
View from Apt. 237 (Courtesy of E. B. Levina)

named Pokhvisnev, who prophesies the end of the world; Pokhivsnev has his own double, the former director of Ilya's gymnasium, who lives in an "old-regime catacomb" amidst the rotting leftovers of the human past. And so on.[20]

Kurilov's planet has many more satellites, which have their own satellites, which tend to travel in pairs along intersecting orbits and clash occasionally, producing minor and major catastrophes. But Kurilov's most important relationship is with his own mortality. The novel begins at the scene of a train wreck. In the confusion, one of the surviving passengers, the former Latin teacher, Pokhvisnev, drops his book, which Kurilov picks up. It is a history of world religions.

> The gods were fashioned from fear, hatred, flattery, and despair; the material at hand determined the face of the god. There was a winged one with an all-seeing eye in the back of its head so no man could attack from behind; another in the image of an aloof woman decorated with armored breasts another in the shape of a hairy nostril inhaling sacrificial smoke, and yet another in the form of a misty sphere full of slanted eyes in perpetual motion. There was a god with thirty hands, according to the number of human trades, a dog-headed god, a bull, a Cyclops, an elephant with a sacred spot on its

forehead (and it will be amusing to see what shape this image will take in Kurilov's mind over the course of the next few months), a she-wolf, a many-headed hydra, a prickly African Euphorbia with poisonous milky sap, and finally, a simple block of wood painted in sacrificial blood with narrow Ostyak eyes and a greedy mouth big enough to devour itself.

Next comes Hellas. "Rosy-heeled goddesses cavorted in laurel groves; uncouth giants, Homer's playthings, drunkard gods, swindler gods, and gods of the military profession feasted in the company of assorted relatives and upwardly mobile proletarians on a tall mountain in the middle of the world." But it is Charon, the ferryman of the dead, whom Kurilov finds most interesting: "Out of the luxuriant animal chaos came the first sad glimpse of self-knowledge. Having learned the smile, humanity learned to fear its absence. Not being familiar with the living conditions in antiquity, Kurilov imagined Charon after the Russian fashion. Round-faced and pock-marked, his legs wrapped in soldier's puttees, Charon sat in the stern of his leaky boat on sackcloth he had spread for himself, rolling cheap cigarettes and fouling the air; a worn army canteen—to bail out water that seeped through the cracks—lay at his feet."[21]

What had happened to mankind happens to Kurilov, too. Out of the luxuriant animal chaos comes the first glimpse of self-knowledge. "I have lost faith in my body," he tells a doctor, who has a photograph of Chekhov in his study. "I'm afraid something is rusted inside." The doctor confirms the presence of rust, telling him that he has a cancerous tumor in his kidney. Kurilov's pains continue to grow worse until, one day, he loses consciousness and then discovers that his pipe—his manhood, divine attribute, and human essence—has been stolen. "'What do you need a pipe for, now, brother?!' the soldier Charon from Pokhvisnev's book seems to be saying to Kurilov."[22]

There are several possible paths to immortality. The most obvious one is through formal memorialization: the deputy editor of the railroad newspaper, Alesha Peresypkin, researches the road's prerevolutionary origins; a "regional patriot" writes a history of the Omelichev family fortune; a young woman named Marina, who works for the railroad propaganda department, writes Kurilov's biography; and the narrator, who is also a character, playfully and self-consciously writes a history of them all. Pokhvisnev, the Latin teacher, walks around with a history of world religions; Ilya Protoklitov, the surgeon, collects clocks; and his former teacher, the professional historian, collects everything.

All things end up in the "shimmering, ever-wakeful Ocean." Those who find their historians live longer and perhaps fuller lives. Kurilov, a human mountain and bridge to Ocean, will have a posthumous existence worthy of his size. The problem is that histories, including Leonid Leonov's own *The Road to Ocean*, cannot be trusted. Marina, whom Kurilov calls his "Plutarch," wants heroic deeds, not a life he would recognize as his own. He mocks her by reciting "an edifying tale" she might or might not recognize as quasi-sacred: "I was born fifty years ago of honest and pious parents."[23]

Much more reliable are Kurilov's old comrades: the living monuments to their common struggle. "When I look at your faces," he tells them at his fiftieth birthday party, "those dear old funny faces of yours, I see myself reflected in them many times over. . . . And if I fall out of this circle, your friendship will remain unchanged. It binds you by an iron and rational discipline; it does not spoil or decay." It does not decay, but it may end. One difficulty with this kind of immortality is that there is (as Kurilov's iron sister, Klavdia, keeps reminding them) no guarantee against betrayal; another is the fact that Kurilov and his friends belong to a particular generation, and that none of them will outlive Kurilov for long. The biggest question is not whether they will continue to live in each other's memories, but whether those who come after them will keep their memory from being turned into "edifying tales." Their successors will have their own memories to worry about. "We may be self-taught," says one of Kurilov's comrades, "but we know this much of Hegel and Heraclitus: the stream does not stop, and it carries with it whatever is needed for life to continue." Kurilov is not convinced, but the conversation is interrupted by a telephone call. Kurilov is needed at another crash site, but his back pain is so severe, he cannot move.[24]

The most obvious, but also most treacherous, path to immortality is love. Most of Leonov's House of Government readers would have read Goethe's *Faust*, and would remember that the temptation of friendship is followed by the greatest temptation of all (at least as far as the devil was concerned). They would also remember that before Faust can meet Margaret, he has to drink the witch's magic potion and become young again. Kurilov finds true love soon after turning fifty. "Here, at the sunset of his life, love was becoming a powerful and as yet unexplored means of physiotherapy. At any other time he would have thought it was magic. For two days in a row, it seemed to him that he had completely forgotten about his attacks. He was now counting the symptoms of his rejuvenation by the dozen."[25]

This, of course, is the wrong kind of immortality. When his closest friend, Tyutchev, tells him that it is "precisely at this biological crossroads between old age and a woman" that "the final boundary can be seen," Kurilov objects vehemently. "Not true! It was not death he feared, but dying: losing the chance to influence the world and becoming an object of ridicule for his enemies and a burden and object of pity for his friends!" Immortality is not about his own eternal youth—it is about the "renewal of our planet." Tyutchev, who believes otherwise (and is named after the poet-author of "The Last Love," as well as "Spring Is on Its Way"), is a theater director and famous wit who turns Kurilov's birthday celebration into a magic show (and Kurilov's House of Government apartment, into Auersbach's cellar).[26]

Kurilov thwarts the devil by making a speech about "iron and rational discipline." In due course, his speech is interrupted by a summons from the Road; his journey to the Road is interrupted by an attack of pain; his pain is cured by love; and love seems, by its very nature, incompatible with iron and rational discipline. Faced with a choice between two young women—Marina, his simple-minded proletarian biographer, and Liza, a talentless theater actress anxious for access to the all-powerful Tyutchev—Kurilov chooses the latter. Love proves redemptive, as well as blind, and Liza grows more mature as Kurilov grows younger. "What she needed now to be happy was not the coveted interview with Tyutchev, but just a little approval from Kurilov." She tells him that she would like to have his son, and just as they are about to consummate their love, he is incapacitated by another attack and loses his pipe for good. The test of love ends in the same way as the test of friendship.[27]

Liza cannot give Kurilov a son, but Marina, whose name suggests a connection to Ocean, already has a son named Ziamka, to whom Kurilov has become attached. "Ziamka" is short for "Izmail" (Ishmael), which suggests illegitimacy, but that may be the point: true immortality is not about your own children or even your adopted children (Kurilov has taken in two homeless boys): it is about all the children, all those who will travel down the Road he is building.

Once, on a moonlit night, Kurilov opens the window of his office, looks down at the garden below, and sees a whispering young couple under a snakelike tree branch. "At this point it might be nice to whistle (fingers in mouth) just as the Lord once did when faced with two such organisms. The famous exile would be repeated; the spell of the garden would be broken; and not they, but Kurilov himself would be that much poorer." The couple keeps reappearing in various guises; the day before his operation, Kurilov runs into them again. "Every time he thought of them, he ran into them—everywhere—at all the great construction projects . . . or at the May First demonstrations (walking hand in hand past the reviewing stands) . . . or at his railway station (perhaps on their way to the mysterious city of Komsomolsk, halfway to Ocean). There was a peculiar regularity to their appearance."[28]

In one of the novel's central episodes, Kurilov and the industrialist Omelichev reproduce the dialogue between Father Nikolai and the young revolutionary in Voronsky's *In Search of the Water of Life*. The conversation takes place during the Civil War. Omelichev, who is married to Kurilov's sister, Frosia, shelters him from the Whites, but accuses him of blindness:

"You don't understand the people. Take everything away from me, but leave me a tiny plot, a tiny plot of land . . . and I'll grow a miracle on it. You'll see a tree and birds building their nests amidst golden apples. But this plot must belong to me, my son, my grandson, my great-grandsons."

"You seek immortality, Omelichev... but property is a flimsy stairway to it. And you don't even have a son yet."

Omelichev ignored his mockery. "I know man as well as you do. He becomes a magician when he takes charge of his own life. No one will give him and his whelps anything when they go hungry, and he knows it, the son of a bitch. And so he looks around, racks his brains, comes up with solutions, and rejoices."[29]

Both are proven wrong. Omelichev cannot conceal his tenderness toward other people's children (even before his first son dies and his second, Luka, is born deaf and mute). Kurilov "loses faith in his body" and hears the call of kinship. When Frosia asks for permission to stay for a few days in his House of Government apartment, he tells her that she should be ashamed of herself. "We're family, after all," he says. Iron Klavdia warns him that Frosia's husband, now a fugitive from Soviet justice, might show up unexpectedly to visit his child. "He might," answers Kurilov. "The revolution did not abolish the rights of fathers."[30]

Omelichev does show up unexpectedly, and he and Kurilov have another version of their first conversation. Their roles are reversed, but the arguments are the same. Meanwhile, Kurilov is being domesticated, and even Klavdia, who lives seven floors below, is beginning to show signs of sisterly love:

Frosia's vigorous housekeeping had affected Kurilov's whole apartment. The furniture stood solidly where it belonged, the scrubbed windows admitted twice as much light as before, and on top of the bookcases, where the sickly Katerinka never looked, not a speck of dust remained. Dinner was ready at a fixed hour, and Frosia scolded her brother whenever he was late. Klavdia came to see him more often, but each time it would appear to be only a chance visit. Walking slowly through the rooms, she could see all the little signs of what had been going on in her absence. Opening the sideboard, she would find new things instead of the old broken, ill-matched pieces of china; glancing into the bathroom, she would see a clean, shiny floor. Life was returning to this uninhabited barn.[31]

Could it be that paradise was hidden in plain sight—in the garden outside Kurilov's office window or even in his own House of Government apartment? Kurilov does not think so. Young couples on their way to Ocean must pass through Komsomolsk, and his job is to prepare the tracks. The key to true immortality is faith in the coming of Communism. Through a thousand different channels, the flood of the Revolution is flowing into the shimmering, ever-wakeful Ocean. Kurilov is justified by faith alone: nothing on earth is stronger than death—except his dream of Ocean: "A man of his time, Kurilov always tried to visualize the distant lodestar toward which his Party was moving. This was Kurilov's only form of leisure. Of course, he could fantasize only within the narrow confines of the books for which he managed to steal time from work or sleep. And this imaginary world, more material and more adapted to human needs than the Christian paradise, was, in his view, crowned by the outer limit of knowledge—non-death."[32]

Four times over the course of the novel—three times after suffering bouts of pain and, finally, after dying—Kurilov ("the statesman"), accompanied by the author ("the poet"), travels to the Ocean of his imagination. The rust inside his body can deprive him of love, friendship, and fatherhood, but it cannot take away his Party's lodestar or his ability to visualize it. "When our eyes failed, and the insight of the poet equaled the perspicacity of the statesman, we also resorted to fiction. It served as a wobbly bridge across the abyss, where torrents rush—in an unknown direction."[33]

The future consists of two ages. First comes the "indescribable slaughter," borrowed, in equal measure, from "the poet from the little island of Patmos" and from Kurilov's favorite stories about South Sea pirates. "I followed with interest the evolution of characters from an old childhood book," comments the narrator in a footnote. "I recognized the words 'Pernambuco,' 'Fortaleza,' and 'Aracajú,' which sounded like birds calling to one another in a tropical forest at noon." The statesman concocts a future apocalypse out of the colonial adventure books he has read, and the poet can reproduce that apocalypse because he has read the same books. If the surgeon, Ilya Protoklitov, were to join them, he, too, would feel at home in Pernambuco. The stamps he collected as a child represented "giraffes, coral islands with horseshoe-shaped lagoons, palm trees, black-mustachioed South American generals, pyramids, and sailboats. All these were pictures from the boys' world of James Fenimore Cooper, Louis Jacolliot, and Louis Henri Boussenard." Most of Leonov's readers and Kurilov's neighbors among the House of Government leaseholders had grown up in this boys' world, and so had their sons (and so would their sons' sons). Jacolliot would go out of fashion, but Cooper and Boussenard (of Le Capitaine Casse-Cou fame) could be found in every apartment, next to new Soviet editions of Jules Verne, Mayne Reid, Jack London, Rider Haggard, Robert Louis Stevenson, and O. Henry.[34]

Beyond Armageddon and Aracajú lies Ocean, which, on closer inspection (and not unexpectedly, given the original blueprints), turns out to be a city. "We gave this city the generic name of Ocean because this capacious word contains a maternal sense with regard to the seas of all ranks, which, in turn, are united by the brotherly ties of the rivers and canals." From the center of the city, "if you walk from the embankment down Stalin and Yangtze Streets past Academy Square," you can see Unity Hill with its huge fountain called "The Tree of Water." The narrator mentions a few science-fiction staples, including winged canoes and multi-level streets ("the ancient tendency of architecture to concern itself with the view from above has finally received its definitive, harmonious expression"), but keeps the list relatively short ("reports sent by early explorers are always sketchy and inaccurate"). The real question is how different life in Ocean is from life in the House of Government. The poet finds "the usual proportion of loafers, fools, and malcontents." The statesman "emphatically denies the existence in this city of the future of any dust, flies, or accidents—or even the various minor evils that are inevitable in any human community." The poet is proven right when the two are "sucked into a gigantic magnetic dust collector" and attacked by a swarm of "unbearable boys." Kurilov later claims that this episode never happened, but it is the narrator who has the last word. The future belongs to the poet. Mayakovsky's question has been resolved and Lenin, quietly, proven wrong. Bedbugs are indestructible, after all.[35]

But what about Kurilov? His roommate in the Kremlin hospital hears the stories he tells Ziamka and accuses him of not being a true atheist. "Atheism is ignorance of God," he says. "But you reject him, pick fights with him, try to wrest the universe away from him. . . . You can't be angry at something that does not exist, can you?" Kurilov tells him that he should talk to his sister Klavdia, who loves such conversations. He needs more time to think about it. Back when he was reading about world religions, it had occurred to him "that someday this book might include pages written about him."[36]

The next morning Kurilov is taken to the operating room. The surgeon is the father of Liza's aborted child and former clock collector, Ilya Protoklitov. The operation is successful, but two days later Kurilov dies of a hemorrhage. His death coincides with the coming of spring. "Storm clouds accumulated, thickened, and broke apart, but each new one appeared darker and more threatening than the ones before (making it that much easier for the mind's eye to perceive behind them the blue, sorrowless sky of the future)."[37]

Kurilov's satellites, chastened by his bodily disappearance, drift in the same direction. Frosia and her deaf-mute child leave for Siberia to start a new life; the iron Klavdia begins her speech at the next plenum with the words "we are called to work in a joyous and beautiful time, my dear comrades"; and Liza says no to Tyutchev's offer of a job in the theater. One of Kurilov's adopted sons, the deputy editor of the Road newspaper and amateur Road historian, Alesha Peresypkin, comes to see the narrator, and they travel to Ocean together. "Actually, there were three of us: Kurilov was there, too, because, once we had left the present, his reality became equal to ours. . . . We passed hundreds of indistinct events, barely sketched on the surface of the future; we visited dozens of cities, remarkable for their history, that did not yet exist. Frolicking like little boys, Alesha and I romped through the immense expanse of the universe, and Kurilov's shadow loomed over us, like a mountain." Then the rain comes. They take cover under some trees and suddenly see a whispering young couple. Just as suddenly, the couple disappears. "Lovers have always had that magic ability to hide from a stranger's curiosity by dissolving into the rustle of trees, the moonlight, and the fragrance of nocturnal flowers. . . . And although our Moscow Textile Factory coats were soaked right through at the shoulders, we left our shelter and silently set off down the road that must be taken by anyone who leaves home in stormy weather." The End. The Soviet Faust had ascended to a heaven of his own making. *Alles Vergängliche / Ist nur ein Gleichnis; / Das Unzulängliche, / Hier wird's Ereignis.* ("Everything transient is but a likeness; the unattainable is here the past.")[38]

The publication of *The Road to Ocean* became a great literary event. *Novyi mir* organized a two-day conference on the novel in November 1935, while it was still being serialized, and in May 1936, the presidium of the governing board of the Writers' Union staged a formal discussion (the first such discussion in the board's history). On both occasions, the *Literaturnaia gazeta* proclaimed that *The Road to Ocean* was "a great victory not only for Leonov, but for Soviet literature as a whole." The book was widely praised for its scale, range, courage, literary quality, and sincere commitment to socialism. Ultimately, however, most reviewers agreed that the novel had failed to fulfill its two monumental ambitions: to paint a worthy portrait of the hero of the age and to write a novel worthy of the classics.[39]

"The theme of love and family, etc., etc., can, of course, be a central, not a marginal theme," wrote Ivan Vinogradov, "but then one should find a typical conflict and show here, too, the principal theme of our age, the theme of the struggle for the socialist way of thinking and feeling, for socialist human relations." If Kurilov is truly a human mountain, then everything about him must be big, whatever his physical condition. His love, argued Elena Usievich, must be worthy of a life-loving Bolshevik; his hatred, argued Aleksei Selivanovsky, must be worthy of an ever-vigilant Bolshevik. Instead, argued V. Pertsov, "Kurilov ends up being a very lonely, sad widower, a mortally sick man with an unfulfilled love." Everyone agreed with Gorky that "Dostoevsky's gloomy and spiteful shadow" had darkened much of the text. Socialist realism was about a return to the classics, and a return to the classics meant, in Vinogradov's formulation, "an orientation not toward decadent, externally complex but internally impoverished art, but toward the art of the golden age, classical art." Dostoevsky was not a classic in this sense, and *The Road to Ocean* was too indebted to Dostoevsky to be truly Faustian.[40]

In the final analysis, the novel's fatal flaw was that it had been designed as a tragedy. Leonov's assumption that "in the arts, the social maturity of a class expressed itself in tragedy" might be correct with regard to other ruling classes, but it could not possibly be correct in the case of the proletariat. The critic I. Grinberg concludes his discussion of *The Road to Ocean* by siding with Kurilov against Leonov: "The works of art of past centuries were full of pictures of suffering and unhappiness. Now, the time has come for a great change in the life of mankind. We are witnessing the destruction of the social order that dooms people to suffering and torment. On one-sixth of the earth's surface, a happy and beautiful life has already been created. Therefore, the time has come for a great change in the arts. Soviet artists have a lofty task: to depict people who are destroying suffering and unhappiness, people who are creators of happiness."[41]

This was the key to solving the book's central problem—the problem of death and immortality. "The revolution has transformed the question of death," said Viktor Shklovsky at the Writers' Union discussion in May 1936. "The novel fails because, as has been said before, it resolves new situations with old methods." Mikhail Levidov agreed: "Any decent person can die well. But only in our age and in our social environment are the objective conditions being created that will facilitate a good death."[42]

■ ■ ■

The Road to Ocean failed as a novel because it failed to represent a good death. It failed all the more obviously because, shortly before it came out, everyone was shown what a good death—and a good book about death—ought to look like. On March 17, 1935, Koltsov published an essay in *Pravda* called "Courage," about an unknown thirty-year-old writer.

Nikolai Ostrovsky is lying flat on his back, completely immobile. A blanket is wrapped around the long, thin, straight pillar of his body, like a permanent, irremovable case. A mummy.

But inside that mummy, something is alive. Yes, the thin hands—only the hands—move slightly. They feel damp to the touch. One of them clutches weakly at a thin stick with a rag tied to the end of it. With a weak movement, the fingers direct the stick toward the face. The rag chases away the flies that have boldly assembled on the ridges of the white face.

The face is also alive. Suffering has wizened its features, dulled its colors, and sharpened its contours. But the lips are open, and two rows of youthful teeth make the mouth beautiful. Those lips speak, and that voice is soft but steady, only occasionally trembling with exhaustion.

"Of course, the threat of war in the Far East is great. If we sell the Eastern Chinese Railway, the border will be a little quieter. But don't they understand that it is too late to fight with us? We are strong now and getting stronger all the time. Our power builds and grows with every day. Just recently someone read a piece out of *Pravda* to me . . ."

At this point we suddenly make a terrifying new discovery. Not everything—no, not quite everything—in that man's head is alive!

The two large eyes with their dull, glassy glow do not respond to sunlight, an interlocutor's face, or newsprint. On top of everything else—the man is also blind.[43]

Koltsov goes on to describe the life of Ostrovsky the writer, merging it with the life of Ostrovsky's literary creation, Pavel Korchagin: rebellious youth, Civil War heroism, railroad construction, Komsomol activism, and, finally, sickness, paralysis, blindness, and testimony through writing. Ostrovsky's—and Korchagin's—life is extraordinary, and therefore typical. "The attraction of the struggle is so great," concludes Koltsov, "and the power of persuasion of our common work is so irresistible that blind, paralyzed, and incurably sick warriors are joining the march and vying heroically for a spot at the head."[44]

Ostrovsky's novel, *How the Steel Was Tempered*, had been slowly growing in popularity amidst silence from literary critics and government officials. (Serafimovich, who had made it his vocation to nurture young proletarian writers, had visited him in his little room in Sochi and made several editorial recommendations, but never suggested that he had discovered anything extraordinary.) After the publication of Koltsov's essay about Ostrovsky, *How the Steel Was Tempered* eclipsed *The Iron Flood* and everything else ever written by any Soviet writer. Ostrovsky was presented with the Order of Lenin, a new apartment in Moscow, and a big house in Sochi. He received thousands of letters. Pilgrims came to see him and be touched by him. One of them was André Gide. "If I were not in the USSR," he wrote, "I should say he was a saint. . . . During the whole hour our visit lasted, his thin fingers never ceased caressing mine, entwining them and transmitting to me the effluvia of his quivering sensibility." He died on December 22, 1936, with the whole country looking on. *How the Steel Was Tempered* would become the most widely read, translated, reprinted, and, from what one can tell, beloved book by a Soviet writer in the history of the Soviet Union and the Communist world as a whole.[45]

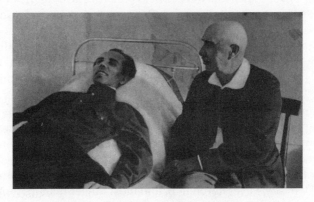

Aleksandr Serafimovich by Nikolai Ostrovsky's bedside

One reason for the book's success seems to have been the near total fusion of the author with his main character (suggested by Ostrovsky himself and designed forcefully and deliberately by Koltsov in his essay). The mythic hero was there in the flesh, embodying the reality of the age of heroes and serving as the "bridge over which people pass into the future." Another reason—and the guarantee that the hero could appear in the flesh without risking desacralization—was the fact that he had no flesh left: that he was a "mummy," or a living relic. He was there and not there at the same time: he embodied sainthood by appearing in spirit only.

The greatest virtue of the text itself was that it represented the sacred story of the Revolution as a straightforward bildungsroman: the education of a Bolshevik from innocence to knowledge. Each chapter in the history of Bolshevism corresponds to a stage in Pavel's (Paul's) journey: the early apprenticeship culminating in conversion; the "battle of unheard-of ferocity" leading to the "crushing of the beast's head"; the struggle against the philistines at the time of the great disappointment; the construction of a railroad in the "sticky mud" of a boundless swamp; and, finally, the office work as an "apparatchik" (as Pavel refers to himself ironically at the end of the book). Each major episode ends with the hero's symbolic death followed by resurrection. (The construction chapter concludes with a formal announcement of Pavel's death and his subsequent "resurrection in the organization's rolls.") At each stage, Pavel loses the use of one or more parts of his body, so that by the end of the story he has attained full knowledge at the cost of complete immobility and blindness. As one female character, tortured and raped by the servants of the beast, says to her fellow martyrs on the eve of their execution: "Comrades, remember, we must die a good death."[46]

Most readers would have recognized the hero's quest (or warrior-saint's life) resulting in a good death and subsequent immortality. They would also have recognized and appreciated the novel's style, which had a great deal in common with the books that both the hero and his creator grew up reading. Pavel's favorites were Ethel Voinich's *The Gadfly*, Raffaello Giovagnoli's *Spartacus*, James Fenimore Cooper's frontier novels, and, in particular, the anonymous chapbooks serializing the adventures of Giuseppe Garibaldi. Ostrovsky himself also admired Jules Verne, Walter Scott, Conan Doyle, Alexandre Dumas, Robert Louis Stevenson, and Edgar Allan Poe. Those were, of course, the same books that Kurilov read on the road to Ocean. The difference is that Kurilov set *The Three Musketeers* aside in order to read about the history of world religions, and when his proletarian biographer, Marina, asked him whether he was personally acquainted with the author of *Spartacus*, he only smiled at her naïveté. Romantic adventure books were good for fantasies about future wars, not for "Kurilov's life in all of its complexity," which could barely be fit within Leonov's epic. Nikolai Ostrovsky, Pavel Korchagin, and most Soviet readers took a different view. *How the Steel Was Tempered* was Kurilov's life written by a Kurilov never touched by "Dostoevsky's gloomy and spiteful shadow." It was a spiritual autobiography inside a five-kopeck chapbook. Early in the novel, Pavel falls in love with a girl named Tonya, who seems to reciprocate his feeling. Soon afterward Victor, the son of a local notable, asks Tonya if she has read the romance novel he lent her: "'No, I have started a new romance, more interesting than the one you gave me.' 'Is that so?' muttered Viktor, annoyed. 'Who is the author?' Tonia looked at him with her shining, mocking eyes: 'No one.'"[47]

Tonia's romance is an event in her life, not a novel written by someone else. *How the Steel Was Tempered* was written by its hero, not by an author, and it was read by everyone, not just those touched by Dostoevsky's shadow. As Samuel Johnson said of John Bunyan's *The Pilgrim's Progress*, "this is the great merit of the book, that the most cultivated man cannot find anything to praise more highly, and the child knows nothing more amusing." There were only two other books that Johnson considered the equal of *The Pilgrim's Progress* as books "written by mere men that were wished longer by their readers." One, of course, was *Don Quixote*; the other was *Robinson Crusoe*, the *Pilgrim*'s successor as the Puritan gospel that even children (including the young Stalin and his adopted son, Artem) find amusing. Leonov's Soviet *Faust* (or was it *Hamlet?*) may have failed, but Ostrovsky's *Pilgrim's Progress* proved a great success. The magazine editor from Ilf and Petrov's *Pravda* essay had been right, after all: one could write a *Robinson Crusoe* that was "amusing, original, and full of interesting adventures" while also taking place on a peninsula that contained a trade union committee with a safe deposit box, a chairman's bell, a pitcher of water, a tablecloth, and broad masses of working people.[48]

One way in which the original Robinson Crusoe attains true knowledge is by writing down the story of his discoveries (both spiritual and material). In *How the Steel Was Tempered*, this is a central theme: when Pavel realizes that he is too weak to serve in any other way, he devotes himself to writing. His last symbolic death comes when the only copy of his manuscript gets lost in the mail, but then he starts over, and the story is born again. Ostrovsky's book about Pavel ends with the publisher's acceptance of Pavel's book about himself. "The iron ring was broken. Armed with a new weapon, he was returning to the ranks and to life."[49]

But there was also another path—one mostly ignored by critics, but crucially important to Kon, Kurilov, Arosev, Osinsky, Serafimovich, and other Old Bolsheviks from the House of Government. After Pavel is given his pension and "labor invalid" certificate and can no longer walk without crutches, he briefly considers suicide, but rejects the idea as "too cowardly and easy." Instead, he offers his "friendship and love" to Taya Kyutsam, the eighteen-year-old daughter of his philistine landlord. "I can give you a lot of what you need," he tells her, "and vice versa." What she needs is his help in becoming a Party member; what he needs is not made explicit, but the reader knows that "her firm young breasts are bursting out of her striped worker's blouse."[50]

Before becoming an invalid, Pavel has been celibate. He has had a number of temptations, but he has resisted them all in the same way he has forced himself to stop swearing and smoking. His model is the Gadfly—"a revolutionary for whom the personal was nothing compared to the collective." Once, when Pavel's mother asks him if he has found a girl, he says, "Mother, I have taken a vow not to make love to any girls until we have exterminated the bourgeoisie all over the world." When he meets Taya, the bourgeoisie has not yet been exterminated, but two things have changed: his flesh has been mostly mortified, and socialism seems more secure. After Taya accepts his proposal, he repays her "tender caresses" with a "profound tenderness" of his own and sees the "glow of barely concealed joy" in her shining eyes. Several weeks later, he loses the use of his legs and left arm, and then, finally, his eyesight. He offers Taya her freedom, but she stays with him, as his partner at home and his equal within the Party. Both are rewarded with the publication of his book and, eventually, immortality. Ostrovsky's widow, R. P. Ostrovskaya (née Raya Matsyuk), would publish her husband's biography in Gorky's The Lives of Extraordinary People series. Platonov's Levin, Leonov's Kurilov, and young Pavel Korchagin were justified in their asceticism during the time of wars, cease-fires, and dam building. But now that the foundations of socialism had been laid and the revolutionaries' bodies had been tamed, they were entitled to some tenderness and family immortality. Christian the Pilgrim and his wife had found knowledge and salvation; Robinson Crusoe had found knowledge and wealth; Pavel Korchagin found knowledge and a wife.[51]

21

THE HAPPY CHILDHOOD

Most House of Government leaseholders were assured of collective immortality by virtue of being high priests of the Revolution (as confirmed by their assignment to the House of Government). Of the more personal strategies, the most obvious one was having one's name attached to a more lasting object. Serafimovich, who doubled his (heavenly) name by making his pen name identical to his patronymic (resulting in "Aleksandr Serafimovich Serafimovich"), divided his time between Serafimovich Street in Moscow and the town of Serafimovich on the Don. A closely related approach (central to the plots of both *The Road to Ocean* and *How the Steel Was Tempered*) was to publish one's life story—either as a memoir or as a biography produced by someone else. For those unwilling to wait (or trust in the future), the best hope for a Faustian "time, stay!" moment was a "last love," as proposed to Kurilov by his Mephistopheles. "I have revived, I have become younger," wrote the seventy-four-year-old Feliks Kon about the effect that his relationship with Maria Komarova had had on his life and on his ability to record it.[1]

Arosev, whose diary was suffused with his "thought of thoughts" about conquering death, was unhappy in his last love, but persistent on other fronts. He asked his children to inter his ashes in the Kremlin Wall (as a "fighter of the October days and a revolutionary who has devoted his whole life to the struggle for Communism"); considered commissioning a statue of himself from the sculptor Merkurov (who specialized in death masks and Lenin and Stalin images); wrote a series of memoirs (and some drafts of an autobiographical epic); and was planning a novel with a wide cast of characters (including a Bolshevik, Trotskyite, "honest legalist," and fascist who sides with the Trotskyite and "those who defy Stalin and our regime"). He shared his ideas with Stalin, who represented the Revolution, and kept a diary, which represented "an attempt to continue life after death." According to an entry written three weeks after the Writers' Congress, the idea of recording all his "encounters, conversations, and observations" had been inspired by the Persian poet Ferdowsi's *Shahnameh* (*The Book of Kings*), "as well as Stendhal and the chroniclers." Stendhal represented a strategy of combining historical novels, heroic biographies, multiple autobiographies, and private diaries in a successful effort to immortalize the Revolution along with its chronicler.[2]

But the main path to salvation lay in the children. When the new world was still being born, Nina Podvoiskaia once wrote in her diary that if the sacred fire of the Revolution did not burst forth within her, it would do so through her children, "who will make me immortal." In 1935, Nikolai Podvoisky wrote to their children that they owed their membership in the Soviet community to their mother's effort to "nurture, raise, and educate" them. When the eternal houses were being built, Osinsky wrote to Anna Shaternikova that Soviet factories were as dear to him as his own children. In 1934, he wrote that his "best creation" was his youngest son, Valia. And Arosev, in his search for the keys to his own immortality, concluded that "the truest and most beautiful ones" were his children. "The question of death, which has tormented me for many years and prevented me from writing, working, and living straight, without wavering, seems to be coming to a resolution. Death is inevitable. I am not to blame for it any more than I am for my birth. I must simply look it straight in the eye and prepare to leave—not meekly and haphazardly, caught unawares—but having fully prepared and taken care of the children. . . . Once I have taken care of them—by all means!—I will not fear death and decay."[3]

This looked like surrender—a return to the "ruined house" and the "loathsome forms of life." The Revolution, according to Nina Podvoiskaia, was the blue bird of universal happiness, but Maeterlinck's play from which she had borrowed the symbol—the play with which her children and all the other House of Government children had begun their journey of self-discovery—was about the eternal return and the circuitous road home. As the main characters, the boy Tyltyl and the girl Mytyl, discover at the end of the play (and at the beginning of their self-aware lives), the truth they seek has been with them all along: indeed, they are that truth. This was also the story of Peer Gynt, which Sverdlov and Voronsky had admired in their Siberian exile, and the most persistent theme of the "world culture" with which socialist realism had become identified. The "creation" of St. Petersburg is, like its divine predecessor, followed by a flood; Faust wins his bet partly because he loses it; Don Quixote and Sancho Panza return home, at least temporarily; and Robinson Crusoe finds nothing new in the new world. And then there was *War and Peace*. If seeing the Art Theater's production of *The Blue Bird* at the age of six or seven was the rite of passage that ushered in the age of reason, reading *War and Peace* at puberty was the ticket to adulthood. And *War and Peace* seemed to suggest that truth and happiness were hidden in plain sight and that any attempt to build, or even plan, the eternal house was a folly best represented by Napoleon's vanity and the German generals' pedantry.[4]

To the House of Government dialecticians, however, the apparent surrender was the antithesis leading to the synthesis. The focus on children was not about reproducing oneself or passing on accumulated wealth, material or otherwise: it was about "nurturing, raising, and educating" the citizens of a redeemed world. The Augustinian era of Soviet history was the "happy childhood" on the eve of eternity. Children were at the center of life not because children were always at the center of life or because the Bolsheviks had to start over, but because the Soviet Union was a country where Tyltyl and Mytyl did not have to grow up. Tania Miagkova, who had been expelled from the House, discovered that her hope of return was coterminous with her daughter's childhood. Those who still lived in the House knew this by virtue of being good Soviet citizens.

■   ■   ■

The nomenklatura families within the House represented a great variety of traditions with very different kinship systems, divisions of labor, rules of inheritance, and patterns of cohabitation. Once inside the House, all of them tended toward the nineteenth-century Russian model as represented in "golden age" Russian literature (which, unlike most of its western European counterparts, was aristocratic, not bourgeois): the remote, admired, feared and usually absent father; the less remote, less admired, less feared and frequently absent mother; the more or less pitied German governess; the more or less dreaded piano teacher; and the beloved peasant nanny, who did most of the child rearing until it was time to see *The Blue Bird* and go to school.

Fathers were associated with festive day-off activities: trips to theaters and fine arts museums, stays in one-day rest homes, Sunday dinners at the dacha, book reading and chess playing in the evenings, and occasional summer vacations on the Black Sea. (Most parents traveled to resorts by themselves, leaving their children in Moscow or at the dacha in the care of nannies and female relatives.) Mothers were not associated with anything out of the ordinary, except perhaps trips to the theater in early childhood. Some families had live-in German governesses; the rest had them come every day to give German lessons. Many small children belonged to "playground groups" supervised by German teachers (who doubled as governesses with particular families). Besides language instruction, "the German women" (most of them middle-aged political émigrés, refugees from the Baltic states, or professional governesses with prerevolutionary experience) were responsible for teaching good manners and correct posture. They tended not to develop a strong rapport with their charges and were greatly resented by the Russian nannies jealous of their prerogatives. The Terekhovs (the family of Roman Terekhov, the former Donbass miner and Ukrainian Party official transferred to Moscow after Stalin called him "a writer of fairy tales") fired their children's governess after the nanny complained that she was cruel to the children. The Kuchmins (the family of Ivan Kuchmin, the son of Volga peasants and the prototype for Leonid Leonov's Kurilov) fired the first of their three German governesses after repeated pleas from the children. The Belenkys (the family of Mark Belenky, the son of a Baku industrialist and head of the Grain Trust) fired their daughter's nanny after she pummeled the German governess. The director of the Party Publishing House and the Lenin Museum (and Kerzhentsev's deputy at the Committee for the Arts), Naum Rabichev, forbade his mother to teach his son German because of her Yiddish accent.[5]

Most girls and some of the boys took piano classes; a few attended music schools, but most studied with teachers at home. For children under seven, there were several "playground groups" and a "children's facility" on the top floor of Entryway 7. The facility consisted of a nursery for fifteen to twenty children under the age of two and a boarding kindergarten for fifty to ninety children between the ages of two and seven, with a staff of about twenty-five employees, including a doctor, nurse, two "teaching nurses," a German teacher, music teacher, eight regular teachers, and a "seamstress/tailor." In addition to toys, meals, sheets, diapers, towels, and chamber pots, the kindergarten provided a large assortment of children's clothing, including socks, trunks, mittens, slippers, dresses, garters, galoshes, "day shirts," nightshirts, undershirts, camisoles, sailor suits, felt boots, winter coats, and masquerade costumes. On days when there was no rain or snow, the children, wrapped in wool blankets, would take their afternoon naps on the roof above Entryway 7. Every summer, the kindergarten was moved to a camp ("colony") outside of Moscow. All the children received character references that described their "work habits" and status within the group ("she is liked by the collective").[6]

School-age children took chess, tennis, and music classes in the Kalinin Club above the theater. After the club's closure in 1934, two ground-floor apartments in Entryway 3 were converted into a club for children between the ages of eight and seventeen. It had a billiards room, a small stage with a piano, several classrooms, and a photo lab. The classes included photography, choir, drawing, knitting, sewing, "rhythmic dance," theater, and "navy." Most were very crowded; those that grew too large were divided into different age groups. The most popular ones were theater (with regular productions and intense competition for the lead parts) and navy, in which boys and girls were given sailor collars to wear and were taught how to row, march, sing sea chanteys, use flags for signaling, and identify different types of ships. Adolescents staged frequent dance parties, and several boys knew how to play the tango and foxtrot on the piano.[7]

Other places where the House children liked to congregate were the shooting gallery in the basement and the "Little Church" vacant lot, also known as the "stinkhole" (*voniuchka*). But the most important playgrounds and focal points of the House's collective life were the three courtyards. Or rather, the focal points of the House's collective life were the children, and the children were mostly in the courtyards. The House of Government was designed as a transitional building that retained old-fashioned family

Children by the gate of Courtyard No. 1

Members of the children's club in Entryway 3

Tamara Matiukhina (daughter of the award-winning construction foreman, G. A. Matiukhin, from Apt. 4, where the Tuchins also lived) and Tolia Ronin (Solomon Ronin's son, from Apt. 55), in the club's production of *La farce de Maître Pathelin*

Courtyard at the House of Government

apartments within a growing network of innovative collective services. In practice, and possibly as a sign of things to come, the historical axis (from the individual to the collective) coincided with the generational one (from the old to the young). The adults ignored the collective services almost entirely (especially after the closure of the club)—indeed, they rarely visited each other's apartments and almost never engaged in traditional neighborly practices such as exchanging gossip and borrowing small household items. The maids, who presided over family economies, tended to be protective of their realms and did not cooperate with each other. The availability of food items and repair services within the building made last-resort appeals to neighbors unnecessary, as well as undesirable. The dominant form of socializing consisted of exchanging greetings on stairs, in elevators, and on paths connecting entryways to outside gates.

To the extent that the House of Government was a common home and not a random collection of individual family cells, it was the children who made it so. And to the extent that the House of Government, like the rest of the Soviet Union, was a children's world, it was the three courtyards, and not the surrounding apartments, that served as its structural and social pivots. Seen from above and below, the House of Government ensemble consisted of three unequal rectangular spaces bounded by thick protective walls. The boundary was broken in several places (the courtyards were connected to each other and to the street), but, for children under fifteen or so, they represented different worlds. Infantile collectivism was limited by age, gender, and courtyard, with the latter almost as important as the first two. Outside the neutral territory of the club and the Little Church (which also served as a soccer field, volleyball court, and skating rink), most preadolescents played with "their own kind," or "kids from their courtyard" (that is, from all the entryways that led out into that courtyard). Some games were gender specific: hopscotch, "good-

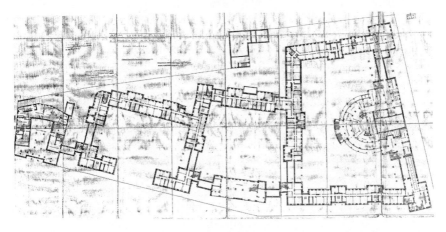

Floor plan of the basement

luck rocks," and various jump-rope and small-ball games for girls and soccer and "war" for boys; others were common to both boys and girls, but
usually played separately: tag, hide-and-seek, lapta (a traditional Russian
bat-and-ball game), "twelve sticks" (a version of hide-and-seek with a
home base the "it" player had to protect while searching), and *shtander* (a
version of dodgeball). One of the most popular games was "Cossacks and
Robbers," in which the object of the robbers was to overrun the Cossacks'
headquarters, while the object of the Cossacks was to find out the robbers'
password by torturing their captives, more or less symbolically. Perhaps
for the latter reason, it was normally played by boys and girls together.

School-age children (seven and older) were usually allowed to walk to
school and around the neighborhood by themselves. The most popular
destinations included the House movie theaters (the Shock Worker and,
after 1934, the First Children's, with jazz bands playing in both) and Gorky
Park, especially in the winter, when many of the alleys were turned into a
labyrinthine skating rink, and loudspeakers played dance music. Also
popular was skiing along the Ditch and down the snowbound steps leading
from the embankment to the river. Groups of girls often walked along the
embankment, holding hands and talking.

All children were defined by their courtyard origin and, as they grew
older, their class in school. The primary units were groups of two-to-four
close friends, who spent most of their out-of-school time together. Some
individuals might migrate, but core members tended to stay together
throughout their school years and beyond. They would join the same
classes in the club, team up in courtyard games and on city exploration
trips, sit together in school (unless broken up deliberately by the teachers),
and spend much of the remaining time in each other's apartments (with a
preference for those with absent or welcoming grown-ups and high-status
books and toys)—talking, drawing, developing photographs, listening to the

Skiing on the embankment
(from *Hubert in Wonderland*)

gramophone, reenacting popular books or movies, and doing homework. Teenage girls often went to the theater and opera to watch celebrity performers. The most famous were the Bolshoi tenors Sergei Lemeshev and Ivan Kozlovsky, who had large and well-organized groups of female followers. As fourteen- and fifteen-year-olds, Elena Kraval and her girlfriends would try to catch a glimpse of Lemeshev as he was leaving the theater after his death in the duel in the second act of *Eugene Onegin*.[8]

Age, gender, and courtyard identity could be reinforced or complicated by school alliances. Most groups of friends were informally affiliated with one or two same-age groups of the opposite sex, usually from the same courtyard and school class. Common activities included *shtander*, skating, Cossacks and Robbers, volleyball at the Little Church, theater productions in the club, and, in later adolescence, dancing and joint trips to movies, art museums, Gorky Park, and beyond. Toward the end of high school, two to four such groups could merge into one *kompaniia* and eventually split into couples, but that did not usually happen until college, when new *kompanii* were formed. Until marriage, duos or trios of "best friends" remained the primary cell of social organization. New college friends might quickly supplant high school ones, lose out to them in the end, or coexist with them as two related clusters or as one merged threesome or foursome.

Children living in various dorms and tenements in the old Swamp were collectively known as "Tatars." Girls from these "bedbug hotels" (as Inna Gaister called them) could be incorporated into House of Government social networks via school friendships, but rarely became full-fledged members—because of their visible awe at the wealth they observed, their status as recipients of hand-me-down clothes, and their unwillingness to invite House children to their homes (single rooms in barracks or communal apartments). When such visits did take place, girls from the House tended to express shock at the squalor they found and no wish to see it again.

Valia and Svetlana Osinsky (*center and right*) at the dacha

Boys were usually kept apart by the strongly felt need to protect territorial integrity and to prevent dating across the House-Swamp boundary. House boys on their way home from school risked being ambushed and beaten up.[9]

Dacha life temporarily rearranged some of the children's social networks without undermining them. Most House of Government families had their dachas along the high (Kremlin) bank of the Moskva, from Serebrianyi Bor in the east (where Yuri and Tania Trifonov lived next to the Podvoiskys, Sverdlovs, Khalatovs, and Morozes, among others) to Nikolina Gora in the west (where House and school friends Inna Gaister, Natasha Kerzhentseva, and Marina Usievich would reunite for the summer). Dacha life was at the sacred center of the House of Government version of the Soviet happy childhood. Like so much else, it was modeled—more or less consciously—on the pastoral descriptions of noble estate life from a previous golden age.[10] The Osinsky children—Dima, Svetlana, and Valia—spent their summers in Barvikha, about halfway between Serebrianyi Bor and Nikolina Gora. The future family chronicler was Svetlana:

> The long, happy days of summer. Sometimes you might go outside early, while everyone was still asleep, and the air was chilly, but with the promise of a glorious day ahead. The house was surrounded by sweet-smelling flowers. I might stand by the small bench near the entrance to the woods pondering where to go—down the steep stairway to the river or past the arbor to the far end of our lot where you could play in the sand above the ravine. The thought of the long day ahead that I would invariably spend playing with my brothers and their friends would fill me with a sense of joy. . . .
>
> We often went to visit our friends in what we called the "Plywood Settlement" near the Razdory train station. We'd form a large group and gather pine cones and play war, tossing them and sometimes painfully hitting the mark (I was actually scared of that game) or play

Svetlana Osinskaia at the dacha
(Courtesy of Elena Simakova)

twelve sticks or hide-and-seek. Or the three of us would play by ourselves, not really needing anyone else. We rode our bikes or played in the sand at the edge of the huge ravine on the other side of the fence, building not castles, but entire cities. On Sundays we used to walk in the forest with our mother, who loved gathering huge bouquets of flowers, and never thought she had enough. We would climb tall pine trees and play Indian. Valia used to carve boats and all kinds of small figures out of pine bark. But he liked reading best of all, and most of the time he could be found curled up in some cozy corner devouring his book.[11]

■ ■ ■

In her memoirs, Svetlana described herself as spoiled and endlessly indulged—in part deliberately ("it was evident that my parents loved Valia more and could not help showing it, so my mother, realizing that I knew and sensing the injustice, tried to make up for it by giving me everything I wanted") and in part because such was the life of the Party elite as it appeared to her in hindsight. She liked sweets and expensive toys, was driven from Barvikha to school in her father's limo, took exotic foreign paints to her drawing class, and "believed, from an early age, that all people moved around in cars and that public transport existed for fun." Inna Gaister remembered demanding expensive presents and making the point of wearing her watch to school; Anatoly Granovsky (the son of Mikhail Granovsky, the director of the Berezniki Chemical Works) described his friends as "the heirs of the universe" who exuded the "conviction of personal power as though they had been suckled to it"; and Irina Muklevich remembered sitting at her school desk and looking at her father's portrait on the wall (while her best friend, Svetlana Tukhachevskaia, was looking at *her* father's). According to Irina, she and Svetlana took care to climb out of their fathers' limos a block or two away from school, but both knew that everyone knew: the portraits were there to prove it, and they did not seem to mind. (Their school, the Moscow Exemplary, was a fifteen-minute walk from the House.) Some House children were not shy about displaying their wealth: Roza Smushkevich, Sonia Radek, and Lelia Kobulova (the daughter of the secret police official, B. Z. Kobulov, who moved into Apt. 8 in Entryway 1 after being transferred to Moscow from Georgia in September 1938) were famous for their dresses and fur coats. According to the award-winning construction foreman's daughter, Zinaida Tuchina, Rosa was also famous for her mother's hospitality, which included "both kinds of caviar sandwiches [red and black], all sorts of piroshki and sweet pastry, and apples or some kind of fruit."[12]

In a tacked-on comment at the bottom of a 1935 diary entry, a teacher from School No. 19 on the Sophia Embankment, Vera Shtrom, mentioned that some of the children from the House of Government suffered from "a sense of belonging to the elite and, considering how utterly and unremittingly busy their parents are at work, from total parental neglect." At a District Party Committee plenum on February 11, 1940, the head of the committee's education department described the problem as "a great evil": "The parents spoil their children, free them from all chores at home, and cultivate great selfishness and a great sense of entitlement among their children. Some parents worship their children. For example, in School No. 19, one high official put a car and other luxuries at the disposal of his child. Obviously, the picture that emerges is not a pretty one." At the same plenum, the director of the First Children's Movie Theater (the heir to the State New Theater) said that one of his employees had been found guilty of trading tickets for leather gloves, and that some of the children involved "had elements of criminality."[13]

Samuil Moroz, the son of the former Chekist, Grigory Moroz, got into trouble for selling his father's books and robbing their neighbors' apartments. Anatoly Ivanov, the son of Boris Ivanov, "the Baker," was a "hooligan" often detained by the police. Vladimir Rabichev, the son of the director of the Lenin Museum, remembered being "neglected" and "difficult," learning how to steal, fighting often, and not doing any homework until the eighth grade. And Aron Solts's adopted son, Zhenia, preferred the company of the "Tatars" to that of the House children and, according to the daughter of Solts's niece who lived in the same apartment, treated his father "as nothing but a sick old man and a source of income."[14]

Zhenia dropped out of school and soon vanished. But he had always been an outsider. Most House of Government children were not spoiled and difficult, or not spoiled and difficult for very long. Samuil Moroz discovered the joys of reading and mathematics; Anatoly Ivanov went on to Moscow's most prestigious engineering college (the Bauman Institute); and Vladimir Rabichev started doing his homework, graduated with distinction (with a "red diploma"), and would have become a historian if his father had not persuaded him to become a military journalist. All three were saved by other children: Moroz's friends spent most of their time talking "about literature, history, and the country's future," and Rabichev's friends demonstrated to him "that studying math and solving geometry problems could be interesting." (He had always known that history and literature were interesting.) The teacher from School No. 19, Vera Shtrom, made it clear in her diary that most of the children from the House of Government were "talented and interesting," and that it was "a pleasure working with them."[15]

Most of the children from the House of Government were happy dwellers in the land of happy childhood. They admired their fathers, respected
their seniors, loved their country, and looked forward to improving themselves for the sake of socialism and to building socialism as a means of
self-improvement. They were children of the Revolution because they were
their fathers' children, because they were born after the Revolution, and
because they were proud of their paternity and determined to carry on
what was at once their father's "profession," their country's mission, and
history's secret purpose. (Most of the women assigned to the House of
Government because of their own, as opposed to their husbands', revolutionary service, were childless. Most female Old Bolsheviks had to choose
between family and revolution. Most House families were as patrilineal
and patriarchal as the Soviet state of which they were a part.)

But, above all, they were children of the Revolution because they were
children of the great construction. Born in the 1920s, they came of age
along with socialist realism and Soviet Augustianism. While waiting to
grow as big as the age—and waiting for Soviet literature to come of age at
the same time—they read *Don Quixote, Faust, Robinson Crusoe*, and other
"treasures of world literature" that combined lyricism and monumentalism, realism and romanticism, and the greatest possible generalizability
with enormous inner richness. Growing up amidst this "international constellation of human types," they measured themselves against them and
thought of them as their heroic predecessors and eternal contemporaries.
What Faust, the character, had been to the bourgeois age, they, the first
truly self-aware generation in history, would be to the age of socialism.
And socialism—as well as, by extension, socialist realism—was about "the
flourishing of the individual, the enrichment of his inner world, the growth
of his self-awareness."

The heart of socialist realism, argued Bukharin at the first Writers'
Congress, was romanticism. "The soul" of "most of the young people of that
time," wrote Svetlana Osinskaia, who turned ten in 1935, was "romantic"—
romantic in the sense of being exalted, vibrant, hopeful, and vulnerable,
and romantic in the sense of seeking transcendence in the here and now:
in nature and, above all, within itself. The fathers' generation had been
shaped by the expectation of the apocalypse; the children's generation
was "religious" about the heavenly city they inhabited. The fathers had
comrades: fellow sectarians bound together by a common cause. The children had friends and lovers: unique individuals whom they loved for reasons they felt compelled to discuss but were never supposed to exhaust.
The fathers' first loyalty was to the Party and, through the Party, to history; the children's first loyalty was to each other and, by extension, to the
Party. The fathers' "classical" reading was tempered by symbolism and
disciplined by the study of Marx, Lenin, and economics. The children were
bored by modernism, entirely innocent of economics, and only indirectly
acquainted with Marxism-Leninism through speeches, quotations, and

history-book summaries. *How the Steel Was Tempered* appeared as a natural sequel to the adventure books that both Pavel Korchagin and Nikolai Ostrovsky read growing up. No one ever read *Das Kapital*.

Schools propagated and institutionalized the new faith. After 1932, and especially after 1934, the "leftist excesses" and "harmful experiments" left over from the previous age were systematically removed in favor of massively reinforced and transparently hierarchical educational institutions charged with the organized transfer of a well-defined body of knowledge to individually graded "schoolchildren." At the center of the new system, which closely followed the old imperial one, were standard curricula, stable textbooks, structured lessons, and professionally trained teachers—assisted, in a subordinate capacity, by parents. Exams, abolished after the Revolution, came back as "testing trials" and later as "exams"; class preceptors (responsible for good conduct, morals, and teacher-parent relations) came back as "group leaders" and, later, "class mentors." "Pedology," a branch of child psychology committed to intelligence testing and present in most Moscow schools in the form of special labs, was banned in 1936 (on the initiative of Boris Volin, recently transferred from the central censorship office to the Central Committee's School Department) for "abandoning the study of a particular living child," preaching the concept of "the fatal dependence of a child's development on biological and social factors," and spreading "the most harmful and ridiculous nonsense" about the impending disappearance of the family.[16]

School subjects were to reflect the most important branches of human knowledge, including, in particular, history, geography, physics, chemistry, and biology. Laying the foundation for everything else and taking up the bulk of class time were mathematics and the newly acclaimed queen of all subjects, language and literature. By far the largest public campaign conducted by the Moscow schools in the 1930s was the celebration of the one hundredth anniversary of Pushkin's death, which culminated in a week-long series of events beginning on the anniversary day of February 10, 1937, and involving concerts, contests, readings, meetings, rallies, lectures, shows, tours, and parades.[17]

Some House of Government children attended the Moscow Exemplary School, located directly across the river and named after the Old Bolshevik, Panteleimon Lepeshinsky (who lived in Apt. 212 with his wife, a specialist in human rejuvenation and the leading proponent of the theory of spontaneous generation of life from inanimate matter). Hubert L'Hoste and the Arosev sisters went to the Karl Liebknecht German school; Vladimir Ozersky, the son of the former Soviet trade representative in Great Britain, A. V. Ozersky, went to the Anglo-American school; but the great majority of House children went to School No. 19, formerly the Maria Women's College, on the Sophia Embankment. Rachmaninoff's piano (a Julius Blüthner) was still there; the ground floor still contained the administrative office and the dining hall. According to Georgy Lesskis, who was a student there in the mid-1930s, "a sweeping staircase led up to the second floor and the huge assembly hall with its high ceiling. The recreation hall was slightly smaller and on the wall was an enormous clock with a pendulum that was almost the size of a small first-grader. Its chimes, which could be heard throughout the school, seemed to echo the Kremlin's Spasskaya Tower ones, which could also be heard quite clearly. Along both sides of the assembly hall were doors leading into bright, spacious classrooms with high ceilings and windows that looked out over the tops of the small trees growing in the school yard." The larger assembly hall had a huge aquarium flanked by two potted palm trees. According to Mikhail Korshunov (the son of the Intourist director, P. S. Korshunov, from Apt. 445), there were also some "ancient mirrors in which our girls used to admire themselves a hundred times a day," "tall white doors with ornamental reliefs and thick glass," tiled stoves in the corridors, and, "in the administrative office, a huge leather couch that looked like a carriage without a top." A narrow stairway led up to the third floor with its low ceilings and small classrooms converted from young ladies' bedrooms. The most popular one was a physics lab with two small windows leading out onto the roof.[18]

Some teachers had taught in prerevolutionary gymnasia, but most were the young beneficiaries of accelerated reconstruction-era training programs. The Moscow City Education Department worried about the level of preparation of some new recruits but seemed to have no complaints about School No. 19. The House of Government parents had neither the time nor the inclination to ask questions, and the children themselves loved their principal (who turned twenty-nine in 1935); their principal's successor, whom Gaister described as "a quiet, cultured person"; their vice principal for academic affairs (who lived on the ground floor of the school with his

School No. 19

son, Mikhail Korshunov's classmate); and most of their teachers, who seemed to share their hopes, their enthusiasms, and their assumption that school was, in some crucial sense, an extension of the courtyard. Everyone's favorite was the literature teacher, David Yakovlevich Raikhin, who turned twenty-seven in 1935, lived on the ground floor, next to the vice principal, and was, according to Korshunov, "a genius and an innovator." "His obvious erudition was combined with an extraordinary narrative skill," wrote Moroz. "His literature classes were pure joy. No one noticed how the forty-five minutes flew by, and no one wanted to leave when the class was over. But he was also strict and demanding, would punish the lazy, and occasionally (extremely rarely!) get angry and kick people out." Of Lesskis's eighth-grade class of sixty students, only twenty-six remained at the time of graduation. "For three years," he writes, "all twenty-six of us were immersed in literature (although only two of us—Ira Bunina and I—went on to major in literature). We went with David Yakovlevich to the Tretyakov Gallery, attended theater performances he recommended, ran a literary society, and published a literary journal." There were also physics and mathematics societies, citywide "school Olympics" (in mathematics and later in physics and chemistry), concerts, excursions, and newspapers. "Since we lived so close to the school, we often hung around there till late in the evening," wrote Inna Gaister. "Even if we ran home to have lunch, we often went back afterward. It was interesting at the school: there were a lot of clubs and different activities. I really loved our school."[19]

What was interesting in school was also what was interesting at home and in the courtyard: friendship and learning. The children learned from their teachers, from each other, occasionally from their parents, and—continually and religiously—from books. Samuil Moroz thought of himself as a late developer:

> I learned to read before I was five. The first book I ever read was called *Great Love Stories*. All I remember from that book were the names: Abelard and Heloise, Dante and Beatrice, Petrarch and Laura. It was not until much later that I found out who they were: back then I was, like Gogol's Petrushka, more interested in the actual process of reading.
>
> After that, I read nonstop. By the time I was sixteen, I had read virtually everything by Jules Verne, Mayne Reid, and Cooper, and a great deal by Boussenard, Jacolliot, and Burroughs. I read Burroughs's *Tarzan* several times.
>
> Later I started reading serious books. Around the age of twelve, I read Tolstoy's *War and Peace* and at fourteen or so, Dostoevsky's *Crime and Punishment*. At sixteen I fell in love with foreign literature: Romain Rolland, Stefan Zweig, Maupassant. I cannot possibly list them all.[20]

Inna Gaister in fourth grade
(Courtesy of Inna Gaister)

Elena Kraval, who turned fourteen in 1935, remembered her father (Osinsky's successor as the head of the Central Statistics Bureau) coming home to find her reading Maupassant, and first saying that it was too early, but then allowing her to go on. Among her childhood favorites were "the marvelous" academic edition of Pushkin, "Scheherazade's tales," *Robinson Crusoe, The Count of Monte Cristo*, and *War and Peace*, which she read at the age of twelve, "skipping all the war parts." Tatiana Smilga (sixteen in 1935) read "indiscriminately, everything from Maupassant to Turgenev and on." She did not remember any Soviet books. "I remember mostly reading the classics. Balzac, Byron, Shakespeare, and the Russians, of course: Turgenev, Tolstoy, Chekhov, and my true love, Pushkin." (As she put it in 1998, "I consider Russian literature to be incredibly beautiful and wonderful. I think that without the Russian literary classics, the whole world would collapse.") Inna Gaister (ten in 1935) "read a lot: at home, in class, at every free moment; read nonstop, indiscriminately: Turgenev, Gogol, Pushkin, Balzac, Zola." Postyshev's son Leonid (fifteen in 1935) remembered "reading a lot, nonstop, and without much discrimination." Gaister's cousin, Igor, who lived in Apt. 98, had to be searched before going into the bathroom, to make sure he did not lock himself in with a book. In 1935, Mikhail Koltsov spent a week as a ninth-grade teacher in School No. 27, not far from the House of Government. The most popular writer among his students was Jules Verne: none of the thirty-five students had read fewer than three of his novels, and half the class had read between eight and ten.[21]

Most of the House children read more or less "nonstop" (the same Russian term is used for "binge drinking"), but they did not read "indiscriminately." The "classics" were by definition extraordinary, and even the adventure books constituted a tight, mostly nineteenth-century, canon that the children had inherited from their parents (and could explore "indiscriminately" at home). They read—and went to the theater, opera, concerts, museums, and exhibitions—for pleasure, but also as a matter of social obligation and personal self-improvement. They made lists, filled gaps, set goals, took lessons, designed projects, and made informal presentations on a variety of artistic and academic topics. They thought of the world as something to be known and joyfully possessed, and of knowledge, as a finite collection of cultural achievements and scientific disciplines to be mastered and put to use. They were animated by Faust's passion to "understand whatever / Binds the world's innermost core together, / See all its workings, and its seeds." They loved atlases and encyclopedias, memorized flags and capitals, and collected coins and stamps (preferably from the "colonies"). They were all Chelyuskinites and "Captain Grant's children": knowledge and adventure were one and the same thing. The song that defined the decade came from the movie version of Jules Verne's *The Children of Captain Grant (In Search of the Castaways)*, released by Mosfilm in 1936. It was called (and addressed to) "The Jolly Wind," and sang "about wild mountains, the deep mysteries of the seas, bird conversations, blue horizons, and brave and great people." The refrain was: "Those who are jolly will laugh, Those who desire will receive, Those who seek will always find." The biblical references would not have been noticed by the House of Government children; the Promethean ones would.

True knowledge was inseparable from self-knowledge; the mastery of the world both presupposed and generated self-mastery. The House children prepared themselves for the journey by strengthening their bodies (Leonid Postyshev, Vladimir Kuibyshev, and Vladimir Rabichev all took up boxing, with Jack London in mind), exercising their willpower, and fine-tuning their emotions. As Faust put it, "Whatever is the lot of humankind / I want to taste within my deepest self." Some wrote poetry, novels, or short stories; many kept diaries, in which they probed their deepest selves. The effort of careful introspection in the service of learning and self-improvement was known as "working on oneself." The overall goal was the pursuit of truth and knowledge understood as one and the same thing. The ultimate reward was socialism understood as universal harmony.

The House of Government children admired their fathers and saw themselves as their true heirs—the legitimate children of the Revolution—but their greatest heroes came from the "international constellation of human types" that they found in literature. Most of these heroes were, in some sense, rebels, but only a few of them—the Gadfly, Spartacus, Pavel Korchagin—happened to be proper revolutionaries. What mattered was the larger romantic rebellion, the Promethean defiance of the jealous gods. Not all great heroes were lone individuals (great love—Abelard and Heloise, Dante and Beatrice, Petrarch and Laura—and great friendship, from Herzen and Ogarev to the three musketeers, were crucial parts of the quest), but they were all individuals, not party members. When asked to identify nonliterary heroes, the House of Government children, encouraged by their schoolteachers, tended to name the greatest officially celebrated individual martyrs for truth and knowledge, Galileo and Giordano Bruno.

■ ■ ■

Fedor Kaverin's last production before the State New Theater was expelled from the House of Government was *Uriel Acosta*, based on the 1847 Romantic play by Karl Gutzkow. A staple of Russian and Yiddish theater, it had been staged by Kaverin's nemesis, Konstantin Stanislavsky, and Kaverin's close friend, Solomon Mikhoels (both had played the lead role). The action takes place in the Jewish community of Amsterdam in the seventeenth century. Uriel Acosta is excommunicated for writing a rationalist treatise questioning rabbinical dogma. His only supporter is the beautiful Judith, who is engaged to a rich merchant, Ben Jochai. Uriel and Judith persist in their defiance until Uriel, with a heavy heart, decides to recant in order to save Judith and his elderly mother from dishonor. While he is held incommunicado, preparing for the ceremony of public confession, his mother dies and Judith agrees to marry Ben Jochai, who blackmails her by ruining her father. Uriel recants his views and is about to be subjected to the ritual trampling at the synagogue's threshold (with the triumphant Ben Jochai first in line) when he learns that his sacrifice has been in vain. He reasserts the truth of his convictions, utters Galileo's "and yet it moves," and condemns his judges for their blindness and hypocrisy. Judith drinks poison, and Uriel shoots himself offstage, leaving behind his disciple, the young Baruch Spinoza.[22]

Kaverin had finally found his hero. On the one side, according to his conception of the show, are "the oppressive power of the Torah and the Talmud, connected with the power of money; the deadening, leaden traditions with no room for hesitation or doubt; the place of death." On the other is Uriel Acosta, "young, ardent, in love with life and with his Judith, accepting life and not the letter of the law, the author of a treatise that undermines the foundations of the stock exchange and the synagogue, the spring wind that bursts into the grim vault and sends the thousand-year-old scrolls of the dead law flying in all directions." Uriel and Judith stand for youth and good books: the manifestos of free thought that Uriel has written and the original book of love—the Song of Songs—that they read to each other. One of the central episodes in Kaverin's production is a ceremony that suggests both the historical depth and contemporary relevance of Uriel's struggle. "On a dais, the heretical books of a true scholar are piled up high. In vain does Uriel try to pull out at least one; the flames rise up and, amidst general rejoicing, the fire burns and precious, thought-provoking pages, perish." But, of course, they do not. As one of the most articulate spokesmen for Soviet Faustianism put it (at about the same time), "manuscripts do not burn." In the play's final scene, the young Spinoza falls on Uriel's body and says his last farewell. "In his teacher's cloak he finds a book, the only one that Judith rescued from the flames and handed to Uriel before she died. The boy presses the book to his chest and walks through the frozen crowd, carrying it into real life, into the future."[23]

The response was universally enthusiastic. The censor from the Main Repertory Committee cut a few lines from Uriel's monologue in which he praises Christianity for serving as a stage on his journey to inner freedom, and, after the pre-release discussion in the Commissariat of Enlightenment, Kaverin promised to eliminate any suggestion that there was anything specifically Jewish about "talmudism," but the consensus was that the overall conception was a triumph. The deputy head of the Theater

Uriel Acosta at the State New Theater (Courtesy of the State Central Theater Museum)

Fedor Kaverin, 1937

Department of the Commissariat of Enlightenment, Pavel Ivanovich Novitsky, concluded the discussion by congratulating Kaverin on capturing the spirit of the age. The confrontation was between dogmatism of all stripes and the tradition of free thought represented "by a number of great men from Galileo, Bruno, and Spinoza all the way to Marx, Lenin, and Stalin." It was a tradition of spring, wind, and eager learning, and Kaverin's best insight was to stress Uriel's youth. "Acosta must be young, temperamental, impetuous, and, at the same time, in his everyday behavior, he must be a person who loves life, who is filled with joy and a special feeling for life. He absolutely must be young." And so he was. "Instead of an antiquarian philosopher and wise scribe," wrote Em. Beskin in *Literaturnaia gazeta*, "we have a vibrant, exciting, and excitable young enthusiast, full of the spring flowering of his feelings for his beloved Judith and of his faith in the social cause that he fights and dies for."[24]

The play's achievement—and the mythology of the House of Government children—is summed up in the *Pravda* review: "Uriel is not a heroic titan who brings down the temple's columns like the legendary Samson. He is a pure and exuberant youth who courageously enters into an unequal struggle against talmudic scholasticism and religious fanaticism. . . . The real historic Uriel may have been much older (at the time of his excommunication, he was fifty-seven), but the young one is better, more convincing. He fully 'fits' his passionate monologues, which contain much more romantic rebellion than mature but cold wisdom." The fathers were the titans, ruling the world during the golden age, and possibly Samsons, succumbing to the seduction of hen-and-rooster problems. The children were both romantic Uriels and his youthful disciples, carrying his books "into real life, into the future." Kaverin arrived at this realization too late: within five months of the publication of the *Pravda* review, his theater was expelled from the House of Government for not being pure and exuberant enough. The author of the exuberant *Pravda* review was a prominent theater critic, Osaf Litovsky (Kagan). His other pseudonym, going back more than ten years, was "Uriel."[25]

22

THE NEW MEN

The House of Government children were pure and exuberant Uriels with no old world to confront. They had inherited a happy childhood; their job was to read nonstop and "work on themselves" as they—and their country—grew into adulthood-as-immortality. They did spontaneously and together what Tania Miagkova was attempting to do in her "political isolator" (except that they had no more need for *Das Kapital*).

Boris Ivanov, "the Baker," and his wife, Elena Yakovlevna Zlatkina, had three children: a daughter, Galina, and two sons, the "hooligan" Anatoly and the eldest, Volodia, whom Galina described as "good-looking, intelligent, and self-disciplined." Volodia liked acting and kept a diary (a task he found difficult but necessary). In an entry from April 14, 1937, when he was seventeen years old, he described his morning's activities: looking out the window to see how the reconstruction of the Big Stone Bridge was going, "washing up" in the bathroom (probably bending over the bathtub, splashing water over his back and shoulders, and rubbing himself dry with a towel, as was the custom), making his bed, and reading the newspaper over breakfast, "beginning with the events in Spain," which he summed up in his diary: "Today the Republicans have once again pushed back the rebels and the German and Italian interventionists on all fronts. On the central front, in the Casa de Campo Park, the Republicans have taken some of the rebel positions, and the commander of the defense of Madrid, General Miaja, has called on the rebels in the University City to surrender. The Republicans are doing a great job beating the interventionists! After that I read about other events happening abroad and in our country."[1]

After graduating from school, Volodia went to work at the Research Institute of the Fishing Industry. In early 1938, he responded to the Party's appeal for more Komsomol volunteers in the Far East, and in July 1938, set out for Kamchatka. The trip took three months: outside of Blagoveshchensk, the Trans-Siberian Railway was shut down for four days because of flooding on the Zeya, and in Vladivostok, there was a month-long wait for a ship to Petropavlovsk-Kamchatsky. As Volodia wrote in a letter home, "You must know from the newspapers about the provocation of the Japanese militarists, and here, in Vladivostok, the indignation that our people feel toward the Japanese aggressors can be felt very strongly. And so, in connection with these events, the steamers, which have to pass by the Japanese Islands, are being detained in Vladivostok until further notice."

Volodia Ivanov, drawing of the view from his apartment   Volodia Ivanov, 1936

(Another reason for the delay may have been the arrival of large numbers of new prisoners, who needed to be shipped to labor camps in Kolyma.) After another month of waiting in Petropavlovsk, he caught a steamer to the Kikhchik Fishery on the west coast of Kamchatka, where he was going to work in the chemistry lab.

> For a very, very long time, we traveled with no water and no bread. I was elected by all the passengers as their representative, which meant that I had the following responsibilities: first, to try to get water, and, second, to procure bread and, in general, deal with all the problems, of which there were many on that ship because it was designed to transport cargo and not passengers. But the worst part was the storm. You cannot even begin to imagine what a terrible sight it was with the ship rocking, the waves washing over it and carrying into the sea whatever had not been attached or tied down in advance, the passengers all sick—but don't think that I was sick, too. No, I held up bravely, and the sea had no effect on me whatso-ever. And so we arrived in Kikhchik with the storm.[2]

Life in Kikhchik was hard. "It's not so nice here in Kamchatka because it's cold and there's nothing to eat," he wrote to his parents. "It keeps snowing, and the wind blows with such force that the roofs of some of the buildings fly off, and when you step outside, it takes a lot of strength and energy just to walk a few steps." He suffered from colds, boils, fevers, toothaches, and exhaustion, and his eyes hurt from the bright sun. His salary was high, but he did not receive it regularly, and whatever he did receive he spent on food. His parents kept asking for money, and he gave them his "word as a Komsomol" that he would start sending it as soon as he could. "I feel terrible when I think that Mother and Galya do not have coats, but I can't send the money now because my salary has been delayed, so I don't have a coat either and have been walking around in a leather jacket." The trick was to remain optimistic. "Right now, our store is as empty as a desert. There are no suits, no coats, no socks, and no under-wear, but I don't get depressed because I know that soon we'll have every-thing." He continued to keep a diary and practice self-restraint. "What do the local people do?" he wrote in a letter, apparently in response to a ques-tion from his parents. "The local residents, although of course not all of them, are mostly engaged in drinking. They drink pure alcohol, which costs 50 rubles a liter, or make moonshine, but not the kind of moonshine you have in Moscow; it's a much stronger brew. You probably think that I have learned to drink alcohol and moonshine here, but I swear on my Komsomol honor that I have not had a single drop of either alcohol or moonshine."[3]

No one had said it was going to be easy. "Overcoming difficulties" and "conquering nature" was at the heart of the Bolshevik ethos and of Volo-dia's own education, in and out of school. What mattered was that "the fishery workers are showing unprecedented rates of labor productivity and that Kamchatka as a whole is growing and getting stronger: new work-ers' settlements are being built, new refrigerators are being set up, and, in the not too distant future, Kamchatka will be connected to the 'Mainland' by a railroad from Petropavlovsk to Khabarovsk." His own life, with or without a coat, had to be measured against the life of the entire Soviet Union and in conjunction with the lives of his fellow volunteers, his fishery coworkers, and his family, which had contributed to his education and served as a microcosm of Soviet society: "Listen, Mom [he wrote on Octo-ber 3, 1939], Galya tells me that you're worried about me. I ask you not to be anxious about this, for I am living and working well and cheerfully, and I'm glad to be working here in Kamchatka because I can feel the eyes of the whole country on the Far East and that makes me glad and fills me with joy, so you shouldn't worry, but instead be proud that your son is liv-ing and working on Kamchatka for the good of the USSR."[4]

His younger brother was also doing his part as a future scientist: "Let Anatoly study, and when he finishes his studies, let him build airplanes that will be capable of flying from Moscow to our remote but beloved Kamchatka." His sister was working on the music front: "Galya must have become a true piano virtuoso by now, playing day and night. That is very good!" His own contribution had proceeded along several lines at once. He had completed a three-month political agitator's course, become a candi-date member of the Party, worked hard at the fishery (even when "the blizzard howls, the snow keeps falling, and it's scary to step outside"), and continued to "work assiduously on himself" by reading the Short Course of the History of the Party. He also continued to write regularly to his fam-ily and to act in the local theater, hoping to reach the "Artistic Olympics" in Petropavlovsk and Vladivostok.[5]

His family was as firmly attached to his country as Kamchatka was to Moscow (the eight-hour time difference notwithstanding). As he wrote to his parents on March 10, 1939, "Today, when the whole country is rejoicing on the day of the opening of the Eighteenth Congress of the VKP(b), I write to you, my loved ones. . . . As a gift to the Eighteenth Congress of the VKP(b), our Young Workers' Theater has prepared Furmanov's play *Mutiny*, and so, today, at 8 p.m. local time and noon Moscow time, we will walk out on stage in order to represent, before the eyes of our spectators, the struggle of the Red Army in 1920."[6]

Another important date that year had not been foreseen by Volodia and his family. On September 17, 1939, they learned of the Red Army's entry into Poland. "All the people of Kamchatka, who are an inalienable part of the Soviet people, have met Comrade Molotov's speech with such enthusiasm that the rallies that have been taking place at all the fisheries have been full of devotion to our government, with the residents of Kamchatka saying that, if necessary, they will give their lives in defense of their country and expressing their support for the policy of the Soviet government, which has taken under its protection our class brothers, the Ukrainians and Belorussians."[7]

Molotov had spoken of "blood brothers," not "class brothers," but Volodia, raised in the faith that had brought his Russian-peasant father and Jewish-seamstress mother together, does not seem to have noticed. Shortly before, he had received an offer to become a full-time Komsomol official (the assistant political secretary for the Komsomol in the political department of the Kamchatka Corporation), but he had a more exciting prospect. "First of all, I can give you some very good news: I am going to serve in the Red Army, this year's draft has assigned me to the armored troops of the Workers' and Peasants' Red Army until further notice, and it gives me great pleasure to know that I am fit and that I am going to join the ranks of our glorious Red Army."[8]

■　■　■

As the oldest of three children, Volodia Ivanov had important family responsibilities. He wrote to Galina and Anatoly with advice, encouragement, and an occasional reprimand, and knew that he was expected to help his "barely literate and politically underdeveloped" parents in matters practical, political, and ideological. Valia Osinsky's role in his family was quite different. According to his sister, Svetlana, "our parents adored him, especially our father, who did not conceal his preference for his youngest son, never regretted spending time with him, did a lot to educate him, and took him along on his trips around the country." The Osinskys were not just much better off than the Ivanovs—as former "students," they subscribed to the intelligentsia belief that child rearing was primarily about passing on "cultural achievements" and intellectual passions (along with the faith, which they shared with the Ivanovs but increasingly left up to the schools). In June 1934, Osinsky took Valia, who was eleven at the time, to a rest home with him. On June 22, he wrote to Anna Shaternikova:

It's good that I have brought little Valia here with me because I have to spend time with him instead of working, and he helps me relax without ever getting in the way—he's such a sweet, well-read, and smart little boy. I like him very much. We have been reading Belinsky together, in the following way: first I assign him an article to read, then we read it together, then he takes notes on the article (naive and a bit clumsy, but he is just <u>learning</u> how to write). After that he reads the next article. Also, every night before his bedtime, I read one chapter from Heine's *Deutschland* to him (the only thing by Heine that we could find in German here). He likes Heine very much (some of the poems he has read here in Russian), and once, when I mentioned something about Heine's old age and death, he said: "I think Heine could never be old," thus characterizing Heine very accurately. He, of course especially liked this demand:

> Yes, fresh peas for everyone
> as soon as the pods have burst.
> Heaven we'll leave to the angels, and
> the sparrows, who had it first. . . .

I had thought that he read plays without much critical discernment (here he's read Goethe, Schiller, Byron, Molière, Hauptmann, and Ibsen's *An Enemy of the People* and *The Pillars of Society*—he's a fast reader, but, amazingly enough, seems to remember everything), but no: while reading Belinsky's article on *Woe from Wit*, which has a negative reference to Molière as an overly cerebral writer who gives us unconvincing, tendentiously caricatured types and droning bores, Valia suddenly grew animated and began agreeing with Belinsky, citing examples and elaborating on his argument. Actually, I don't like Molière either and have never been able to read him.

You understand, of course, that I am reading with him in the secret hope of making him a writer, something he will probably end up becoming in any case, of his own volition. But I want him to be my successor in the family business, or "N. O. II," as he'll need to sign his work. That's why we've been reading Belinsky—my spiritual father, and Heinrich Heine—the friend and comrade of my ideological grandparents, Dr. Marx and General Engels.[9]

Valia's favorite part from Heine's *Deutschland* came shortly after the stanza about building heaven on earth, which Sverdlov liked to sing. "N.O." was the way Osinsky signed his own work. Marx and Engels were Valia's and Volodia's ideological grandparents whose work was almost always too early to read. (Just a few months earlier, Hubert L'Hoste, who was the same age as Valia, had finally confessed to Maria Osten that he had never read Marx because his father would not let him. "'He was absolutely right!' said Maria. 'It is too early for you to read Marx.'") Osinsky's plan was to introduce Valia to his ideological grandparents in three or four years. Meanwhile, he wondered if Valia had enough intensity ("I mean lyrical intensity of a very particular kind: the lyricism of the beautiful in man's best strivings") and whether he was "acerbic enough." N.O.II was "more good-natured" than N.O.I, according to the latter. He shared his father's romantic intellectualism, but not his "uncompromising, red justice."[10]

Valia's sister, Svetlana, described Valia as a "pure soul," a "kind, sweet boy," and "a tender son and brother." They had an older brother, Dima (Vadim), born in 1912, and a cousin, Rem Smirnov, who was the same age as Valia and had been living with them since his father's arrest in 1927. According to Svetlana,

> All of our relatives loved Valia, and he loved all of them: Grandma and all of our aunts. When we were little, we used to fight terribly, and he would hurl himself at me, fists flailing and crying with frustration. I liked to tease him—for his absentmindedness and his stutter. Poor Valia! He had developed a stutter after having scarlet fever as a baby, and no one had been able to cure him. For some reason, his agonizing attempts—he would lower his head and splutter and gesticulate wildly—used to irritate me, even later, after we became friends, and our childhood fights were a thing of the past.
>
> Valia's absolutely favorite pastime was reading. Rem and I also liked to read, but no one could compare to him. He would wrap himself up in some kind of incredible rags—such as an old, tattered blanket, for instance—and curl up in some remote corner, and just read and read.[11]

Valia Osinsky at the dacha
(Courtesy of Elena Simakova)

. . .

Yuri Trifonov, the son of Valentin Trifonov and Evgenia Lurye, was a writer as well as a reader. He wrote his first short story on October 11, 1934, when he was nine years old.

The Aero-Elephant.

It took place in America, in the city of Denver. Jim was walking to the tavern. He was walking and daydreaming. Suddenly the earth gave way under his feet and he fell into the land of the aero-elephant.

To be continued.[12]

The story's style and location came from the adventure stories in Valentin Trifonov's library. A flying elephant machine must have seemed fitting three months after the world's heaviest airplane, the *Maksim Gorky*, beat a world record by lifting a fifteen-ton load. (It is not likely that Yuri would have read Kataev's *Time Forward!* before the age of nine, and neither *The Road to Ocean* nor Disney's *Dumbo* had been released yet.) The next installment came on December 29:

The Aero-Elephant. Part 2.

. . . As soon as he felt his feet touch the ground, he looked up and saw 20 men standing near him and one of them had a revolver and was aiming it at him. Jim looked coolly at the revolver, but then one of them asked:
    "Who are you?"
    "I'm Jim—from Philadelphia."
    "How did you get here?"
    "I fell in."
    "We're not going to let you out of here."
    "Why not?"
    "You'll find out later, but now follow me."
    He led Jim down the long corridors until he finally brought him to a room with some kind of metal contraption in it (this was the aero-elephant).[13]

Yuri, according to a classmate, Artem Yaroslav (the nephew of the Soviet Control Committee official and former "Rightist," A. I. Dogadov), "reminded me a bit of a bear cub: thick and stocky with shaggy brown hair, he looked like a forest creature. . . . He always wore some kind of velvet or corduroy jacket, knickers, and had large glasses, which was fairly unusual for the time." He kept a diary, collected coins and stamps, ranked writers

Yuri Trifonov

and characters ("D'Artagnan's got nothing on Edmond Dantès!!!"), dreamed of running away to South America, acted in school theater productions, went to movies ("Saw *Lenin in October*. A wonderful movie! Excellent! Magnificent! Ideal! Superb! Terrific! Very good! Exceptional!"), worked on himself by lifting his father's weights, and, of course, "read nonstop." In January 1938, when he was twelve, he spent ten days at the dacha, skiing with his friends (as he later wrote in his diary). "While at the dacha, I read *Thyl Ulenspiegel*, Hugo's *Hans of Iceland*, Celine's *Journey to the End of the Night*, and Gautier's *Captain Fracasse*. It would have been nice to spend another ten days at the dacha." He could not stay at the dacha because he had to go back to school. Three weeks later, he wrote:

> Nothing special happened at school except for getting punched in the eye during a fight. A whole ton of blood came out! I couldn't open my eye for two days and didn't go to school. It's still black and not completely healed. But I did manage to read Sholokhov's *Quiet Flows the Don* and *Virgin Soil Upturned*, Hugo's *Les misérables*, Daniel's "Yulis," Gogol's "The Nose" and "Rome," and Ernest von Hesse's scholarly work, *China and the Chinese*. Very interesting.
>
> On the 23rd I saw *A Little Negro and a Monkey* at the Children's Theater—a ridiculous piece of melodrama! Disgusting!
>
> Right now I am writing "A Cro-Magnon Icarus," a story about life in the Aurignacian period.[14]

"Yulis," by the Yiddish writer Mark Daniel, was a story about the Civil War in Vilnius. It was probably given to Yuri by his grandmother, Tatiana Slovatinskaia, who had grown up and converted to Bolshevism there. *A Little Negro and a Monkey* was a play that Natalia Sats cowrote with her first husband, S. G. Rozanov, and directed in her theater, to great acclaim. It was the story of an African boy and his friend, a monkey, who gets sold to a European circus. With help from some sailors with red stars on their caps, they become reunited in Leningrad and are finally able to return to Africa, where they organize young-pioneer detachments. The Cro-Magnon story was one of four that Yuri wrote about prehistory; the three others were "Diplodocus," "Dukhalli," and "Toxodon Platensis." He also wrote richly illustrated papers about history and geography (for school and for his own pleasure and edification). His most ambitious school project was a Pushkin album, which he, with his mother's help, prepared for the Pushkin anniversary celebrations in January 1937 (at the age of eleven).[15] A version of this episode appears in Trifonov's novel, *Disappearance*:

Yuri Trifonov

Gorik spent his evenings putting together an album: as a gift to the school literature society and an item for the Pushkin exhibition (and in the desperate hope of taking first prize for it). Into a large "Spiral-bound Sketchbook" he pasted portraits, pictures, illustrations clipped from magazines, newspapers, and even, when his mother wasn't looking, several books and carefully copied out, in India ink and block letters, the best-known poems. For instance: "I have erected to myself a monument not of human making"—and right next to it a picture depicting the Pushkin monument on Tverskoy Boulevard clipped from the newspaper *For Industrialization*, which his father subscribed to. Unfortunately, all the newspaper clippings had yellowed from the glue, which had seeped through.[16]

According to his sister, Tania, Yuri's album did win a school prize and was included in the citywide exhibition of the best work devoted to Pushkin. In the novel, however, what mattered most to the main character and made him feel so bad was that he was not among the top three. "The first prize had gone to a boy from the eighth grade for a clay figurine entitled 'Young Comrade Stalin Reading Pushkin,' the second prize had been awarded to a girl who had used silver threads to embroider a pillow cover with a picture inspired by 'The Tale of Tsar Saltan,' and the third prize had been taken by Lyonia Karas—a fine friend, working on the sly and concealing it from everybody!—for a portrait in colored pencil of Pushkin's friend, Küchelbecker (it's true, though, the portrait was amazing, the best at the exhibit)."[17]

Yuri and Tania Trifonov

But Yuri's greatest passion was writing. When he was twelve, he joined Moscow's House of Pioneers, which had opened a year earlier in the building of the recently disbanded Society of Old Bolsheviks. In the diary entry for November 2, 1938, he remembered the previous year. "That House was so interesting that I was ready to go there every day. First I joined the geography club and then switched to literature. Those were wonderful evenings sitting around the large table discussing one of our stories and being transported to the heavens by our conversations. We quoted thousands of writers, from Homer to Kataev. Our teacher, the editor in chief of the *Young Pioneer* magazine, Comrade Ivanter, used to explain our mistakes to us in such an interesting way that it was truly a school where you could learn a great deal."[18]

Perhaps as a result of what he learned in the House of Pioneers, Yuri became dissatisfied with his prehistoric fiction. "I want to write a simple, funny story, not some rubbish about Diplodocus, Cro-Magnon man, Dukhalli, and other monsters. A simple story—that's what I'm aiming for!" His first such story was disguised as a diary entry for November 2, 1938. His closest House of Government friends were Lyova Fedotov, Misha Korshunov, and Oleg Salkovsky. Oleg (who lived in Apt. 443, right under the Korshunovs) had once told Yuri that Misha and Lyova were secretly working on a short story "about an Italian engineer who invents a special device and goes to Spain to join the Republicans, but is seduced by a fascist singer from Milan's La Scala opera theater, who steals the device." Yuri and Oleg decided to retaliate by writing a story of their own. Yuri came up with a "devilishly simple" plot in the manner of Jules Verne, "about a young man who goes on vacation to a collective farm in the Altai Mountains and hears about a forest spirit. I am not going to describe it all, but I will tell you that the forest spirit turns out to be a gigantic bat." After several early drafts, they ran out of steam and watched helplessly as their rivals locked themselves up in Misha's apartment until 10:00 or 11:00 p.m. each night. Finally, Yuri had an idea:

"Oleg!' I yelled at the top of my voice and grabbed him by the sleeve. "Eureka! I have an idea! Let's make this into a story the young man tells his fellow engineers sometime later. We'll call it "Gray Hair." Someone will ask him "so, why is your hair gray?" and then he'll tell the story. At the end, no one will believe him, but just at that moment the gigantic bat will fly overhead."

"Perfect!" exclaimed Oleg.

They wrote some more—together, separately, and together again, with little success—until one day Yuri's telephone rang. It was Lyova, who revealed that he and Misha had had a falling out over the role of the Italian opera singer. Relieved, Yuri called Oleg, but he was not home: he had gone over to Misha's. "Thus ended that particular literary rivalry. Everything returned to normal. Lyova would come to my place and look at butterflies and different kinds of bugs and insects, while Oleg went to Misha's, and they would talk about the pleasant weather, two fools named Yuri and Lyova, and Nadia Kretova's face in the window."

Yuri had graduated from scientific-adventure stories to framed scientific-adventure stories to an elaborately designed "simple" story about boys writing scientific-adventure stories, framed and unframed. The narrator was Yuri Trifonov, who was also a thirteen-year-old diary keeper: "This story just happened to me, of its own accord. I decided to call it 'The Rivals.' If I were to read it to the characters themselves, they would find a few details added by me. And they would be right: I have added some details. But the core idea, the actual events did take place on Planet Earth, in the Solar System, Eastern Hemisphere, Europe, USSR, Moscow, No. 2 Serafimovich Street, also known as the House of Government, to four unnamed youth. They all harbored literary ambitions, and still do." They were literary creations twice over—as Yuri's characters and as four binge readers from the House of Government, on Serafimovich Street.[19]

Drawing of a desk by Yuri Trifonov
(Courtesy of Olga Trifonova)

■ ■ ■

By all accounts, the most extraordinary, and thus the most typical, of Yuri's House of Government contemporaries was his friend and fellow author, Lyova Fedotov, the son of the Russian peasant, American worker, Trenton Prison inmate, Central Asian collectivizer, proletarian writer, and machine-tractor-station political chairman, Fedor Fedotov. In 1933, when Fedor's body was found in a marsh not far from the state farm he was managing, Lyova was ten years old. He was living in a small first-floor apartment (Apt. 262) with his mother, Roza Lazarevna Markus, a costume maker at the Moscow Youth Theater. Lyova, according to Yuri Trifonov, "was short and swarthy, with a slightly Mongol face and golden Slavic hair":

> From boyhood on he strove passionately and eagerly to improve himself in every possible way, quickly devouring all the sciences, all the arts, all books, all music, and all the world—as if he were afraid of running out of time. At the age of twelve, he seemed to live with the sense of having very little time and an awful lot to accomplish. . . .
>
> He was interested in many sciences, especially mineralogy, pale-ontology, and oceanography; drew very well—his watercolors were exhibited at art shows and published in the *Young Pioneer* magazine; loved classical music and wrote novels in thick, cloth-bound note-books. I first got into this tedious business of novel writing because of Lyova. He also tried to toughen himself physically: walking around in shorts and no coat in the winter, learning judo holds, and, despite various congenital defects—bad eyesight, minor deafness, and flat feet—working hard to prepare himself for distant travels and geographical discoveries.[20]

Once, Yuri and Lyova had a contest to see who could draw a better elephant. Oleg, who served as referee, decided in Lyova's favor. (Yuri was

Lyova Fedotov

better at chess, though. "We were excited by the players' extraordinary names," he wrote. "Elis-cases, Lilienthal, Levenfish . . . They sounded as exotically beautiful as ones like Honduras or Salvador, for example.") When Lyova was eleven, he won second prize at the Moscow Schoolchil-dren's Art Exhibition (and received an easel with oil paints and a palette). One of the judges, a woman from the Tretyakov Gallery, became a lifelong friend and patron. He studied art at the House of Pioneers (where Yuri studied litera-ture) and at the Central House for the Artistic Education of Children (where he met his close

Lyova Fedotov's drawings

friend Zhenia Gurov). He drew pictures for the school newspaper and sketches for the House of Government's Children's Club theater decorations, but he preferred the thematic "series" and "albums" he prepared as part of his school assignments or as independent projects based on his reading. Included among them were "Italy," "Ukraine," "Zoology, "Mineralogy," "Oceanography," "Marine Animals," and "The Ice Age." "Once," wrote Mikhail (Misha) Korshunov, "he showed up with a roll of white wallpaper. That was certainly a first: a roll of wallpaper instead of the usual briefcase. He rolled it out the full length of the hall and then ordered me to stand on one end, so it wouldn't curl up, while he stood on the other. Painted all along it were prehistoric animals moving through ancient forests, seas, and swamps, under the title 'The Earth's Chronicle.' 'What a monster I've created!' he said with satisfaction."[21]

His collection of "series" (he distinguished between albums with illustrated text and series made up of single drawings) included one on dinosaurs, one on "the little church," one "on the growth of the Palace of Soviets, beginning with the Cathedral of Christ the Savior that once stood there, through the completed Palace" (as Lyova put it in his diary), and one portrait gallery of great musicians. Lyova had demonstrated his musical talent very early, in 1925, during the October Revolution celebration, when he was still living with both his parents, Fedor and Roza, in the First House of Soviets (the National Hotel) in a room facing Tverskaia. "We were sitting on the balcony," Roza remembered, "and down below people were singing and dancing, and the accordion was playing . . . and, suddenly,

Lyova repeated it all exactly: 'We Are Blacksmiths' and 'When My Mother Was Seeing Me off to the Red Army.' He was two years old, and hadn't really started talking yet, but he sang it all perfectly." Ten years later, she managed to buy him a piano. "After Fedor's death, things were financially very difficult for Lyova and me, very difficult. But I decided to buy him a piano, come what may. I began selling my husband's things through a consignment store and putting the money into a bank account. When I had saved five thousand rubles, I found a Rönisch concert piano through a newspaper ad, so he could practice at home." Lyova took private lessons from the composer Modest Nikolaevich Rober, whom he greatly admired and, in his diary, referred to as "my teacher." He practiced regularly at home, but tried not to do it in his mother's presence because she suspected that he preferred improvisation to homework. She need not have worried: he did spend some time picking out his favorite opera arias, but his goal was accuracy, not ornamentation. "You should have seen his desk," she said fifty years later, conceding the point and addressing a different age:

> You would never have guessed it was a child's desk. It was like the desk of . . . of some kind of professor. There were always lots of books . . . and each book had a bookmark. He would sit there and write. He had a herbarium . . . you should have seen it . . . he would make a tiny cut in the page and carefully insert the stem . . . so the flower would lie nice and flat . . . and he'd write out its name in Latin. And the stamps? He didn't glue them in . . . he had these tiny tweezers . . . and he'd use the tweezers . . . never his fingers . . . to pick up each stamp and place it very carefully into a special album. He also collected minerals. . . . He had a box with niches . . . each little niche was lined with cotton . . . and in each one was a mineral. Right next to it would be a cardboard label with the mineral's name . . . and not just the name, but also the type, cleavage and fracture, hardness . . . that's how particular he was.[22]

Lyova Fedotov's drawings

He worked on himself by not wearing gloves in the winter, not wasting time playing cards, and not drinking wine or champagne (even on New Year's Eve). He worked on his spelling and literary style by copying out *War and Peace* by hand. He tried to embrace the world by regimenting his life as much as possible. In the same diary entry in which he complained about his mother's expectations, he attempted to manage his own. "What have I accomplished this summer? Drawn the Little Church series, but even that is not finished. Did not travel incognito to Zvenigorod, did not finish my papers . . . That's a shame!" He listed only special projects (Zvenigorod was famous for its monastery and cathedral founded in the fourteenth century), not any of the things he did as a matter of course. "He was capable of sitting at his desk from morning till night and staying occupied," according to his mother. "Writing. Or drawing. Or arranging his stamps. Or with his herbariums, or other things."[23]

I never saw him just sitting and doing nothing. If he was sitting, he was reading. His father was the same way—wherever he went, he always had a book with him. When they put him in Trenton Prison in America in 1917—he was sentenced to ten years—in his cell there, he said, there was one narrow beam of sunlight coming down from above. He used to follow that beam around with his book and read. Lyova read all the time, too. Whenever we took the streetcar, he would always read standing up. You know that little area up at the front right behind the driver? That's where Lyova always used to stand. He never sat down. Let others who find it hard to stand sit down, he used to say.[24]

Lyova vowed to accomplish more the following summer and sealed his pledge with a reference to Giovagnioli's *Spartacus*: "May Jupiter favor me in this undertaking!" As he wrote a few weeks later, after coming home from the first day of his last year in school (1940),

When I got home I immediately remembered the plan of action I had devised last year and decided to renew it on paper straight away in order to have the pleasure of renewing it in practice as soon as possible. . . .

First, I included homework, then my walks, Little Church series, Ukraine album, music, short story, and diary. I jotted it all down on a clean sheet of paper. The homework, of course, would always get fit in, and the walks, whenever possible; I could finish the series when school quit piling up on me, and when I did finish, I'd replace it in the plan with my "Italy" presentation; I'd be working on "Ukraine" along with the series; music would always be there, and I'd start working on my short story again as soon as I finished my letter to Raya, which I needed to do as quickly as possible (I'd have done it right away, if school weren't poisoning my existence); and finally, the diary, too, would always get written. I preserved the old plan along with the new one.

In order to test myself, I decided to spend today, the first day of school, according to my plan. So that's what I did. I managed to make progress on the Little Church drawing and redo the cover of "Ukraine" to make it easier for me to color in later. I wasn't able to get any writing done on my short story today—there was no point in spending only a few moments on it. To write, I need both inspiration and concentration.[25]

In his earlier lament about his lack of productivity over the summer, Lyova did not mention his diary. In fact, that entry (August 29, 1940) was at the beginning of Notebook XIII. (He wrote his diary entries in numbered notebooks.) The previous surviving notebook, Notebook V, ends on December 8. That means that over the course of nine months, including the unproductive summer, Lyova had completed seven notebooks (in tiny script and with no margins or blank spaces, judging by the appearance of nos. V and XIII). He wrote as he read, and he read as he wrote, and he lived through what he read and wrote in an ever-tightening dog-chase-tail race for the fullness of time and limitless self-awareness. He embodied the age of "great planners and future geometers" in which, as Leonid Leonov suggested at the first Writers' Congress, every hero was his own author and every event was its own chronicle. For two years, Lyova had been dreaming of going to Leningrad, the city of perfect architecture. On December 5, 1939, he and his mother finally talked about buying the tickets:

"I'll have to record this conversation in my diary," I said. "It is precisely these kinds of details that make up an event such as my trip to Leningrad. Yes, I'll definitely write it all down. And I'll also write down what I just said . . . That would be original. And I'll write down what I just said as well!"

"Enough," my mother interrupted me. "Or it will never end."

"You're wrong: the end has come," I said. And with that, the day ceased to exist.[26]

A month earlier, he had written a one hundred–page entry, in which he attempted to provide a complete record of November 5, 1939. He called it "A Day in My Life" and wanted to read it aloud to his music teacher, Modest Nikolaevich, but there was not enough time, so he read the November 6 entry instead. He probably did not know of Tolstoy's similar undertaking eighty-eight years earlier (or he would have said so: he was a scrupulous observer of scholarly conventions); either way, Lyova seems to have been more insistent on the circularity of the action-reflection process. According to his friend from the Central House for the Artistic Education of Children, Zhenia Gurov, every time they met, Lyova would play the triumphal march from Verdi's *Aida*, read aloud a new chapter from his novel, *The*

Underground Treasure ("Jules Verne's influence was obvious"), "and then read out the diary entry about our previous meeting."[27]

The idea was to compress cause and effect into a single present. Two days after the conversation with his mother about how writing follows events, Lyova had a different conversation about how events follow writing. "Salo" was Oleg Salkovsky's nickname, and "Mishka" (also known as "Mikhikus") was Misha Korshunov:

> Today during history in our crowded little classroom, Salo leaned over and whispered conspiratorially:
>
> "Would you like to join Mishka and me? Only you have to promise not to tell anyone."
>
> "Okay, okay! What's up?"
>
> "You know the church near our building? The Maliuta Skuratov one?
>
> "Yeah?"
>
> "Mishka and I discovered a vault there, which leads into some underground passages . . . some really narrow ones! We've already been in them. You're in the middle of writing *The Underground Treasure*, so you should find it very interesting."[28]

Misha and Oleg described their previous trip to the dungeon, which had ended prematurely because they did not have a flashlight or the right clothes. "As I listened," Lyova continues, "my curiosity grew . . . as I pictured the dark, gloomy tunnels—damp and low, the sinister rooms with mold-covered walls, the underground passages and wells . . . until my patience and imagination were exhausted. I could hardly believe that I would soon get to see it all in real life. In short, I reached a point of extreme tension. Mere words cannot begin to express what I felt."[29] But he was, above all, a scholar and chronicler. He pulled himself together and had Misha and Oleg draw maps of the dungeon independently of each other, to make sure they were telling the truth. Then he took charge:

> "You know, Mishka," I said. "I think we should introduce a few changes to this underground expedition. You and Oleg went there the first time just out of curiosity, but now I'd like to propose bringing along a pencil and notebook in order to sketch some things down there, record our route, as well as all of our conversations, and to make an accurate map of the passages. This may all prove useful later from a scientific point of view.
>
> "That sounds good," agreed Mikhikus. "Since you keep a diary, you can record all of our observations. And since you know how to draw, you can be in charge of that, too, okay?"
>
> "Sure, I can do that. And you know what else?" I said. "We should definitely record our first words after we enter the vault. That will be both interesting for us later on and very original. Is that clear?

Our exact words say as soon as we find ourselves underground? We'll need to record them all afterward, so we don't forget. We'll find some kind of little room or alcove where we can sit and record them all. But probably first, you'll ask me—either you or Salo: "So, Lyova, what do you think?" And I'll probably answer: "Hmm, not bad at all!"

"You're right, that would be interesting to record," said Mikhikus. "Our very first words down there! That's perfect!"

"I'll record that in my diary, too," I said.

"What do you mean?"

"All the things we've just been saying. It's precisely on such conversations that this expedition of ours is based, so I'll record them all. And these words just now—I'll record them, too! And these! And the next . . . and the next!"

"You could keep going on like that forever," said Mishka. "And these . . . and the next!"

"I'm not a fool," I said. "I'm definitely going to record the words you just said in my diary, and I'm not kidding either."

"And will you record what you just said to me?"

"You can't spoil kasha with butter. And words can't hurt you," I said. And I'll record that, too!"[30]

And he did. On the day of the expedition (December 8, 1939), his equipment included his notebook, a pencil, a pair of compasses, and a flashlight. Victoria (Tora) Terekhova, the daughter of Roman Terekhov, was supposed to provide the batteries, but did not, so they had to use candles, which were more appropriate to the occasion, in any case. They also brought some matches, rope, and, on Lyova's insistence, a weighted string to measure the depth of the wells. They made it through two interconnected vaults and into a winding underground tunnel, but had to turn back after several turns because the passage became too narrow. Lyova, who went first because he was the thinnest and most determined, had to be pulled back out with the rope. His step-by-step account ends at the entrance to the last tunnel. The next notebook has been lost, but the story is familiar: "I didn't see no di'monds, and I told Tom Sawyer so. He said there was loads of them there, anyway; and he said there was A-rabs there, too, and elephants and things. I said, why couldn't we see them, then? He said if I warn't so ignorant, but had read a book called Don Quixote, I would know without asking."[31]

One of the two sacred objects Lyova kept in memory of his father was the "American watch" with the engraving "to Fred from Red" (his father's friend, fellow tramp, and revolutionary, "Red" Williams). The other was a copy of *Huckleberry Finn* his father had given him on his tenth birthday, with the inscription, "To my little lion cub from the wild man. F. 10.1.33." ("Lyova" is the diminutive for "Lev," the Russian version of Leo, or "lion"). What Don Quixote was to chivalry romances, Tom Sawyer and Huckleberry Finn were to Don Quixote, and what Tom and Huck were to Don Quixote,

Lyova and his friends were to Tom and Huck. In Mark Twain's story, Sancho takes over as both the narrator and central character (and, for a while, turns into Don Quixote). In Kafka's parable, "The Truth about Sancho Panza," Don Quixote becomes Sancho's dream. In Lunacharsky's 1922 play, *Don Quixote Unbound*, he is banned from the "Promised Land" because of his refusal to kill for the Revolution. In Platonov's *Chevengur*, he kills "precisely but hastily" until he is killed himself (when he charges the four enemy horsemen). In Lyova's diary, Don Quixote is back in charge (because he has learned how to make dreams a reality). Misha Korshunov is a joker and a trickster; Oleg's Salkovsky is Salo ("Lard"); Lyova leads the way and tells the story. "My candle flared up just in time: at that moment Salo put his hand with the burning candle through the small opening of the door and, grunting, managed to squeeze through. His massive bulk took up the entire space of the door, so that all we could see was the lower part of his body and his feet sliding helplessly on the floor."[32]

Once, Lyova's cousin Raya asked him if he knew what he wanted to do when he grew up. "I told her that at one point, as she well knew, I had taken up—and even now would never forget—history, astronomy, biology, geology, and geography, but that gradually some of these subjects had begun to capture my interest more than others, and that two had now taken the lead: geology, in the form of mineralogy and paleontology, and biology, in the form of zoology. 'And now it remains to be seen,' I said, 'which will prevail in the end.'" The final decision depended on a combination of inspiration (which could not be hurried) and rational choice. Lyova was greatly impressed by his Uncle Isaak's idea that "in nature, there are no devious stratagems: everything in it is simple, as long as you know how to discover and decipher its laws." Also, as Lyova explained to Zhenia Gurov's mother, "A painter can't have a lab on the side just to do some science every once in a while, but for drawing, all a scientist who works in a lab needs is some paper, paints, and brushes."[33]

Cousin Raya, Uncle Isaak, and Zhenia Gurov's mother were not the only adults with whom Lyova discussed his future and his scholarly interests. He had close personal and intellectual relations with his teachers (prin-

Lyova Fedotov, *To the Memory of Lyova Fedotov and Some Joint Underground Adventures*

Lyova Fedotov, *The Entrance to the Dungeon Was Walled Up with Bricks*

cipally Modest Nikolaevich Rober, but also David Yakovlevich Raikhin and two other teachers from School No. 19), his friends' mothers (the fathers were usually not around), and, in particular, his many relatives, with whom he corresponded regularly and whose visits he awaited anxiously and documented religiously. His decision to record his life as fully as possible was inspired by a visit, in August 1939, from his Leningrad relatives: Cousin Raya (Raisa Samoilovna Fishman), her husband Monya (Emmanuil Grigorievich Fishman, a cellist and professor at the Leningrad Conservatory), and their daughter Nora, whom Lyova called Trovatore, after Verdi's opera. "Those were some of the happiest days of my life, but I was foolish enough not to record them in my diary. So now they have vanished without a trace. It was that summer that Raya invited me to visit them in Leningrad during the winter break. How I regret now that I did not record everything about their stay in Moscow!"[34]

Emmanuil had asked him then if he was going to describe their visit in his diary, but Lyova had answered that it was not remarkable enough. "Oh what a monstrous mistake that was! Today I blame myself bitterly for not having recorded such beautiful hours of my life as our Leningrad relatives' visit. But not to worry! When I go to Leningrad in the winter, I'll describe the entire trip in great detail. I can already picture the train compartment, the dim lamps, the darkness outside, the reflection of the berths in the window, and the sound of the wheels carrying me to Leningrad. Yes, there will be some happy moments in the future—though still a long way off."[35]

Lyova's mother's large, close, upwardly mobile Jewish family provided, along with teachers and friends, a vital link between Apt. 262 and the wider world of history, discovery, and socialism. Raya, Emmanuil, and Trovatore had come to Moscow to attend the opening of the All-Union Agricultural Exhibition. The exhibition's function was to demonstrate the achievements of collectivized agriculture and—through the arrangement and appearance of its visitors, buildings, and statues—the achievement of an All-Union Gemeinschaft. What was a hope and a work in progress for Tania Miagkova was a reality for Lyova Fedotov. "Hail to the Exhibition!" he wrote on November 27. "Thanks to it, we have an extra opportunity to see our relatives, who are scattered across the many cities of the European part of the USSR."[36]

The USSR was one large House of Government that brought families together. All Soviets were part of one large family. Lyova's next diary entry was for November 28, 1939: "Tonight I listened with great interest to a radio show about the Kirov Museum in Leningrad. It described the museum's objects, which tell the story of the complex and beautiful life of our unforgettable Sergei Mironovich Kirov. It is clear that it is a very valuable and interesting museum. In short, that show made me think, and I decided that I would definitely visit that museum during my trip to Leningrad. I will be sure to share with my reader my impressions of this manifestation of the life of one of the most important revolutionaries of our era."[37]

"The reader" was Lyova's omnipresent contemporary and constant interlocutor. So was the voice of the radio, which Lyova never turned off:[38]

After that I was fortunate to hear a newscast about the official note from the Soviet Government to the Government of Finland protesting the provocative firing on Soviet troops. I found the Finnish Government's response outrageous. It turns out that the Finns are denying their crime. Who ever heard of a country's troops staging target practice in full view of the troops of a bordering state? And yet, that is exactly what the Finns are saying. . . . Their arrogance has no limits! It's monstrous! And they even dare to threaten our Leningrad! Leningrad is a major port and has always belonged to us, so, therefore, we will be the ones to decide how to ensure its security, and we will not allow these Finnish oafs to interfere in our internal affairs! Let them take a look at their own country first. They will see some truly awful things. But they refuse to do this. Concerned with their own pockets and the interests of England and France, they ignore the suffering of their own people. But they will pay for it soon enough! Yes, they will! With their unwise and extraordinarily foolish policy of preparing for war with the USSR, they are hastening the arrival of the day of reckoning. The Finnish people will not allow them to threaten the USSR—the only hope and defender of the exploited masses of the world.

I was very glad to hear the response of our wise Government, which unmasked the whole pathetic gang of Finnish scoundrels and executioners. Let justice prevail!

After that I began working on my next "Italy" drawing, while listening to Verdi's opera *Un ballo in maschera*. I cannot add anything to my previous reflections on this opera at present, so I will wait and do it the next time. In my drawing I depicted the Mediterranean seabed covered with corals, which the Italians harvest in large quantities and use to make jewelry and small decorative pieces.

And that is how the day ended.[39]

The ever-present radio brought news, pleasure, and instruction while bringing people closer together. The next day Lyova and Modest Nikolaevich had a long discussion about Verdi. After that Lyova read him the previous day's entry from his diary and asked:

"So, what do you think of Finland's latest antics?"

"They'll live to regret it," said M.N. "It's too bad the people have to suffer, but we'll teach those wolves a lesson!"

"They certainly deserve one," I said.

"We'll give them one they won't soon forget," added M.N.

Then I began playing for him.[40]

The next morning the Soviet Union attacked Finland. In school, Lyova ran into his friend, Izia Bortian.

> "I know," he said. "Our planes have already destroyed two Finnish airports, one in Helsinki and one in Viipuri."
>
> "I look at the map," I said, "and think about how small but feisty Finland is. It must be counting on England."
>
> "But how can England help?" said Izia. "The best route is through the Baltic Sea, but that route is closed off because of Germany. England is at war with Germany, so they won't allow them through."
>
> "That's true!" I exclaimed. "Actually England can't handle Germany even with France, and here they are talking about attacking us through Finland. They're clearly biting off more than they can chew. Just look at the antiwar movement there. It will double in strength if England starts a war against the USSR because the English exploited masses won't allow their country to turn against the only socialist country in the world."
>
> "That's exactly right," confirmed Izia.[41]

At home that afternoon, Lyova read the *Pravda* editorial about the fifth anniversary of the assassination of S. M. Kirov:

> It has now been exactly five years since the vile, cowardly hand of an enemy treacherously pointed the barrel of a gun at our comrade and pulled the trigger. What a good person Kirov was! A very good person! Yes, I will definitely visit his museum when I go to Leningrad!
>
> Today's paper also included the text of a radio intercept: "The Appeal of the Communist Party of Finland to the Finnish Workers." I read it straight through. Very well said! Very plainly and clearly! I hope that it will be understood by every worker, every peasant, every intellectual, and every soldier. I believe that after reading the appeal, the Finnish soldiers must immediately rise up against their dim-witted rulers, who are leading them to certain death in the war against the Soviet Union.[42]

Lyova Fedotov, drawing of troops in battle

Lyova Fedotov, *Venice*

He spent the rest of the day working on the chapter on the Italian colonies for his "Italy" report.

> No sooner had I sketched a view of the Libyan desert than, at exactly 6 p.m., the newscast came on. I put the radio receiver on my desk and began listening with my mother. I won't go into great detail here, but will summarize what we heard. We heard about how the mutton-headed government of White Guardist Finland, after hearing that the Soviet troops had crossed the border, had panicked and all its members resigned. Serves you right, you scoundrels! And whose fault is it? Your own! Whatever possessed you to embark on such a nefarious adventure? Oh, that's it! The English! Right, now it's clear to me as two plus two equals four. Of course! And to top it off, many of the soldiers in the Finnish army, having understood the appeal of the Communist Party, have risen up against their hapless government. The working people have also risen up in revolt and are refusing to fight against the Soviet Union. In the town of Terijoki, in eastern Finland, a people's government of a new Democratic Republic of Finland has already been formed, headed by Otto Kuusinen. The war against the USSR is over! It began this morning at 3 a.m. and ended this afternoon. So now it's a war inside Finland, a civil war, a war between two governments—the new government of a free Finland and the dark, scary "government" of Tanner, who replaced Cajander and Erkko after they fled. It seems to have been the most remarkably short war in history, for it lasted for no more than half a day![43]

The war lasted three and a half months. After the signing of the peace treaty between the Soviet Union and Finland in March 1940, Otto Kuusinen's government was disbanded, and he was made chairman of the newly formed Karelo-Finnish Soviet Socialist Republic. His permanent address was Apt. 19 in the House of Government, on the tenth floor of Entryway 1. For Lyova, the greatest casualty of the war was his long-awaited trip to

Lyova Fedotov's drawings

Leningrad. He had been there before, but not by himself. He kept hoping that the hostilities would end before the school vacations, but they did not, so he postponed the trip until the next winter break and spent the year of 1940 preparing for it.

His other passion was Verdi's *Aida*. He knew it by heart, played it regularly, and discussed it repeatedly with his mother, friends, and teachers. On August 27, 1940, he went to see it at the Bolshoi Theater Annex:

> The conductor, Melik-Pashaev, a short, dark-haired man with a round head, receding chin, and squinting eyes behind glasses, gently stepped up onto the podium and lifted his arms. . . .
>
> From the moment I heard the first notes of the violin, I felt as if I were in a fever dream. The overture was wonderful. Melik elicited a warm, lush sound with bright overtones from his orchestra. The prayer was very well conducted. The priests sang almost inaudibly, barely opening their mouths, creating a sense of majesty that made a tremendous impression on me. I listened to Ramfis's arioso, of course, with eyes wide open.
>
> In short, I spent most of the time just watching the orchestra and the conductor! The arrival of the prisoners, the aria of the imprisoned Amonasro, and the funereal chorus of the priests worked their magic on me, as always. I tried hard to grasp the rhythm and tempo of the chorus so I could learn to play it better. . . . The Chorus of the People didn't actually live up to its name because that melody was sung more by the priests surrounding Radames and Amneris, and not by the crowd. I have to give those bloodthirsty priests their due: the best choruses certainly belong to them.[44]

He had a great deal more to say—about the work as a whole and about particular arias, choruses, duets, instruments, and performers. On the whole, he found Melik-Pashaev's version superior to Lev Shteinberg's ("the orchestra sounded mellower and more together"). *Aida* was his "music school," especially with regard to orchestration. But it was its emotional effect that mattered the most: "It's impossible to describe the state I was in this evening after the performance. First, for some reason, I took the sugar bowl back to the bathroom instead of the kitchen. Then I turned off the light as I was leaving the room, even though Lilya and my mother were still sitting at the table. At one point, I spent a long time vigorously stirring my tea, forgetting that I hadn't put a single grain of sugar into it. And, finally, to top it all off, instead of making my bed as usual, I dragged the whole pile of sheets and blankets over to the couch and spread them out there!"[45]

Lyova Fedotov, *Giuseppe Verdi*

A week later he went to see Glinka's *Ruslan and Ludmila* at the Bolshoi, but, contrary to Modest Nikolaevich's prediction, was not able to forget *Aida*, except "for a moment" during Chernomor's march. The following week, on September 10, *Aida* was broadcast on the radio. "Channel 2" on Lyova's radio receiver was not working, so he went over to Misha Korshunov's apartment:

It is hard for me to describe my emotions when I am listening to or watching the scene in which the Ethiopian prisoners are led in. When I hear this passage, I begin to shiver all over like a poor little puppy caught out in the rain. I cannot listen calmly to that scene. Is it not a heartrending moment when the humiliated, chained prisoners appear before the pharaoh, and Aida, seeing her father, the Ethiopian ruler Amonasro, among them, rushes toward him, lamenting her orphaned Fatherland? And Amonasro roughly grabs her and whispers to her not to give him away! Yes, that is one of the best scenes in the opera.[46]

On October 10, many months of study, reflection, and careful listening resulted in an unexpected triumph:

Something extraordinary happened today! I'm not sure why, but when I got home from school, I was consumed by the overwhelming desire to play the march from *Aida*. I generally like to play it only when I'm in the right mood and try never to sit down to play it without desire or emotion. There was no one else at home, and I felt completely uninhibited. I put all my emotions into the march and played it the way it should be played, with all of its numerous complex shades and so forth. Normally it seems to come out sounding rather monotonous and shapeless when I play, but today I can honestly say that, because of the extraordinary desire I had to play it, it did not sound bad. I wish I could always play it like that.[47]

On November 3, *Aida* was broadcast again. On November 9, Lyova told his friend Zhenia, who was also going to Leningrad, that he had conceived the extraordinary idea of combining his two dreams into one: to conduct the entire opera in his mind on the train. "Just remember," I said. "No matter what the conditions—whether we stand the whole way, sit, or lie down—I am going to conduct the whole of *Aida* from beginning to end. Won't that be interesting? Isn't it an amazing idea?"[48]

He spent the next month and a half reading about the "former Petersburg," talking to Zhenia "about the upcoming blissful days in Leningrad," and rehearsing different parts of the opera. "Scene after scene kept flowing through my mind, and no one could tell that I was now rehearsing the scene by the Nile where the furious Amonasro curses his daughter, Radames unwittingly betrays his country, as well as some other heartrending moments since I was lying quietly on the couch, as if taking a nap."[49]

The plan, as he explained to Zhenia, was to take the night train and spend the first four hours conducting *Aida*. Zhenia worried that it might be too long, but Lyova explained that he wanted to conduct the entire opera because he had never done it before, and he wanted to combine his personal premiere with "such a wonderful event as a trip to Leningrad."[50]

> "The main thing is that it won't be hard for me at all! Playing or singing is actually a lot harder! For those, you need to move your hands or strain your vocal cords, but for this you can be completely still—you can sit without moving, and the piece, since you know it well, just flows through your head, and all you have to do is listen. Besides, the rhythmic sound of the train will make it even easier to imagine the sound of the singers and the orchestra. And there will be no one to prevent me from seeing the opera in my mind and picturing all the scenes and characters, which means that I'll get to experience *Aida* one more time in all its glory, and I'll get to experience it the way I interpret it, since this time, I'll be directing it myself. I'll finally be able to correct all the defects introduced by our theaters in the Annex production!"
>
> "I see what you mean!," said Zhenia. "That will be very interesting for you!"[51]

Lyova and Zhenia were not able to get tickets for the same train. Lyova's (no. 22, smoking car no. 12) was departing on December 31, at 1:00 a.m.

Finally, the day had come.

That evening I collected all the things on my list. Next to my suitcase, I put a pack of white drawing cards (I didn't have a proper sketchbook), some color pencils, my diary notebooks with descriptions of our adventures under the Little Church and summer break, my notes and textbook for German, the finished drawings from the

Little Church series, and even the game the reader knows as "To the Moon," in order to play it occasionally with Nora. True, in my absence, my mother had already managed to stuff a huge pile of shirts and underwear into my tiny suitcase, but nevertheless, I decided that my diary and drawing things should have priority.[52]

Lyova's mother came home from work around 9:00 p.m. "The time was ticking away." She packed his suitcase. He wrote about his day in his diary. Finally, he put on his light fall coat (he refused to wear winter clothes), galoshes, and fur hat (a concession to his mother), and they walked out the door. "I almost hesitate to describe the feelings that were churning around inside me at that moment. The reader, I hope, will know what I mean. The courtyard was empty and, since it was close to midnight, one of the street lights had been turned off. The darkened windows of the buildings made the walls of the house appear gloomy and blank. It was a beautiful winter night. The stars seemed to shimmer in the black-blue sky. The snow that covered the lawns and sidewalks looked like shiny white sugar frosting in the dark. The crisp air filled my lungs, invigorating my soul."[53]

They walked across the bridge to the Metro station and rode to Railway Station Square. "On the square the winter night seemed even colder: the lights of the cars and streetcars intersected across the snowy carpet, and the station buildings looked like bright steamships tied up at the dock." They walked past the "crowds of people scurrying to and fro and groups of porters standing by, chatting and waiting patiently," found the right train, and walked down the platform to his car. He showed his ticket to the conductor, who was holding a flashlight, and climbed in. "The passageway was full of people trying to shove their bags onto the upper bunks, so it was not easy to get through. Blue ribbons of tobacco smoke swirled around the flickering orange ceiling lights." His seat was occupied, but he found a better one in the corner by the door, across from the service compartment, ran out to say good-bye to his mother, rushed back to his spot, "which, fortunately, hadn't been taken," and sank "into the deep, dark shadow" thrown by the overhanging bunk. "I sat calmly watching the crowds of people passing by with their heavy loads—screaming, cursing, swearing, and calling each other names. Among them were some choice exhibits from the 'Museum of Curses,' which, fortunately, does not actually exist. I could also hear muffled laughter, conversations, and instructions as people settled into their places with their luggage. There were so many smokers in the car that everything was soon half hidden behind a ghostly blue veil."[54]

Suddenly "there was a jerk and a clank, and then, a soft knocking sound accompanied by a slow, even rocking motion." Someone said that the train was moving. "The knocking grew faster, and soon the train picked up speed." The conductors went into the service room and closed the door behind them.

I sat motionless in my dark corner, convinced there was no better spot in the entire car.

Thoughts kept running through my head. It's hard to even say what I was thinking. I could scarcely believe I was on my way to Leningrad, having become so used to only dreaming about it. It felt as if the train were heading somewhere into the unknown rather than to the city I had been longing to see all this time. The people around me were traveling to Leningrad, that I knew for certain, but I was traveling to some other place. My destination seemed divine, otherworldly. I simply could not comprehend that tomorrow I would be seeing the streets of Leningrad, the Neva, and St. Isaac's, as well as my dear relations, Raya, Monya, and Trovatore. "Yes, all these people on the train are traveling to Leningrad," I thought, "but I—I am traveling into the unknown!" And yet some strange, new, solemn feeling kept telling me that it was all a reality. It's true, I swear! I felt as if I were caught up in a dream or reverie.[55]

Most of the passengers had settled in. A large man who had been standing in the aisle talking to Lyova's neighbor returned to his seat.

Finally, the moment had arrived when I could begin to fulfill my dream—to perform *Aida*. At first, I could hear only the march in my head, then I repeated it, but I wasn't up for doing it a third time. In order to become accustomed to my surroundings, I went through both marches from *Il Trovatore* and then stopped there. The rhythmic knocking of the wheels helped tremendously in achieving a clear and correct sound from my imaginary singers and orchestra. I kept postponing the beginning of the opera because I wanted to savor this moment of bliss and could not quite yet bring myself to commence with the prelude to *Aida*.[56]

Then one of his neighbors began to eat, and he decided to follow suit. When he was finished, he pulled out the postcard his mother had given him and, using his suitcase as a desk, wrote that the train had just passed Klin and that he was doing well and would describe the rest of the journey when he got to Leningrad. He put the postcard in his coat pocket and prepared to begin.

The car was finally quiet. The voices had faded, the tumult long subsided, and the air was filled with nothing but clouds of blue smoke.

"Time to begin," I thought. In my mind's eye I pictured the opera house, the rows of armchairs, the curtain.... The lights went out, and *Aida* began. Musical themes followed one upon another.... It was true theater, which even the company of such sad characters couldn't ruin. At the end of act 1, I knew that an hour and five minutes or so had already gone by since the beginning of the performance.

Most of the people in the car were asleep, and the service door opened only during infrequent stops. My neighbor was already asleep, and I was not far behind. I propped my suitcase against the wall and decided to take a little nap before the opera's second act.

It didn't take long to fall asleep. My thoughts grew hazy, and I didn't wake up until the train jolted, and I heard the railwayman telling someone that this was Bologoe. The conductor took his flashlight and went into the vestibule. I was so exhausted that I entered the world of dreams once more without waiting for the train's departure. I heard someone saying it was very late, someone else agreeing, a door slamming somewhere, someone whistling in his sleep. . . . Time passed, and I once more fell sound asleep.

When I woke up, I saw that it was still dark and that the inside of the train looked the same. Everyone around me was still sleeping. I could see the first rays of the winter dawn through the frosted patterns on the windows. The sun was beginning to rise! Along with the sun, a new feeling was rising within me. Before that moment, I had grown used to the haze, shadows, and pale lamplight inside the car, but the new day's rays penetrating the frozen windows reminded me again that I was on my way to the long-awaited city of Leningrad.[57]

He conducted the second act, "with its march, dances, and scenes of captive Ethiopians"; ate breakfast in his corner; watched "a bunch of peasant women with screaming five-year-olds" get on at Malaia Vishera; and, "to the accompaniment of chit-chatting women and kids jumping up and down and getting in the way of standing passengers," finished the opera.

Suddenly, people were beginning to move. I looked around me. Outside my window I could see the flickering tracks, pillars of smoke, red walls of the train sheds, some green and blue train cars, and a line of locomotives. We were approaching Leningrad. Everyone was already packed, and, standing next to us, near the door to the vestibule, was a small cluster of heavily-laden people. The train began to slow down . . .

"Oh my goodness!" I thought, standing up at the same time as the village gossips. "Can it really be true? I can't believe it!" I could feel a terrifying wave of happiness rising up inside of me.

I heard the wheels clank and the sound of metal, a blast of freezing air hit my face . . . and the train stopped![58]

BOOK THREE
ON TRIAL

PART V
THE LAST JUDGMENT

23

THE TELEPHONE CALL

On December 1, 1934, Khrushchev was in his office in the Moscow City Party Committee when the telephone rang. "It was Kaganovich. 'I am calling from the Politburo, please come immediately.' I arrived at the Kremlin and walked into the hall. I was met by Kaganovich. He had a terrible, frightening look on his face, seemed badly shaken, and had tears in his eyes. He said: 'Something awful has happened. Kirov has been murdered in Leningrad.'"[1]

The deputy head of the Military Chemical Trust and former representative of the Communist Party of Poland at the Comintern, Vatslav Bogutsky (Waclaw Bogucki), was in his House of Government apartment (Apt. 342) that evening. With him were his wife, a librarian at the Lenin Institute; Mikhalina (Michalina) Iosifovna; and their nine-year-old son, Vladimir, who later wrote about it:

> One evening my father received a telephone call. He answered in the usual way. But suddenly, the expression on his face changed dramatically. In a voice filled with emotion he asked several quick questions. We could not hear the answers, but the tone of the conversation and the expression on his face frightened my mother and me. When he hung up the phone, he had tears in his eyes. My mother asked in alarm who it was and what had happened. He named the caller (it was someone he knew from the Comintern or the Central Committee apparatus, I don't remember anymore) and said quietly: "Kirov has been killed." Never again did I see such an expression of grief on my father's face.[2]

According to Inna Gaister, who was also nine at the time, her parents found it strange that their next-door neighbors in Apt. 166, the director of the construction of the Agricultural Exhibition, Isaak Korostoshevsky, and his wife did not seem to grieve as much as they did. "My mother said they were less upset because they did not have any children." The death of Kirov was a personal tragedy that different members of the Soviet family experienced to the best of their emotional ability and moral imagination, but everyone seemed to know that, as Khrushchev put it, "everything had changed."[3]

Agnessa Argiropulo and Sergei Mironov were still in Dnepropetrovsk, where Mironov was head of the provincial NKVD office. On December 1, Agnessa came home and was surprised to see his hat in the hall.

I ran to his study. I found him sitting, still in his overcoat, with a strange look on his face and his thoughts far away. I knew then: something had happened.

"What's wrong?" I asked, in alarm.

He answered simply:

"Kirov has been killed."

"Who's Kirov?"

"Remember, I pointed him out to you at the railway station in Leningrad."

I did remember. I have an excellent visual memory. Though it's true, I'd only seen Kirov very briefly in Leningrad that time.

Mirosha had a few days off once and we'd decided to splurge on a quick trip to Leningrad from Moscow: the "Red Arrow" there and back, and one day there to "live it up." At the station Mirosha pointed to a man and whispered:

"Kirov, the Provincial Party secretary."

Not very tall, with a pleasant face, he greeted us warmly and said:

"So, you've decided to come see our Leningrad?"

The head of the NKVD Directorate in Leningrad was Medved, and then Zaporozhets joined him there. We knew them both well from the sanatorium in Sochi. Filipp Medved was large and burly. Zaporozhets was tall and slender, became famous during the Civil War, was wounded in the leg, and so he walked with a limp. His wife Roza was a real beauty. They'd never been able to have kids, but there'd been a rumor that she was, finally, already in her fourth month. Every day she'd go on long walks in different directions— seven or eight kilometers one way and then seven or eight back—to get in shape and get strong for the birth.

"Killed?" I asked, astonished. "By whom?"

"The killer has been arrested. His name is Nikolaev." And then he added, with a harsh laugh: "The Leningrad Chekists haven't been doing their job too well, have they?"—as if to suggest that on his watch such a thing would never have happened. But he also seemed relieved that it had not happened in his district.[4]

According to Stalin's adopted son, Artem Sergeev (who lived with his mother in Apt. 380 and turned thirteen in 1934), "nothing was ever the same again." According to Sergeev's close friend, Anatoly Granovsky (the son of the director of Berezniki Chemical Works, Mikhail Granovsky), "the news made a subtle change in everything. People suddenly started to act as though they had been told by their doctors that they suffered from a malignant growth which might, or might not be cancer. There was a general suspension of opinion and speculation. Men just waited. But it was soon established that the Trotskyites had done it. It was a name I was not very familiar with, except to know it indicated something despicable. I accepted what I was told and was prepared to forget the whole incident, little knowing what had been started by that single shot."[5]

■ ■ ■

The scapegoat is a central figure in human life. A community that feels threatened identifies groups or individuals responsible for the crisis, casts them out by killing or expelling them, comes together healed and renewed, and attempts to forestall the next crisis by restaging the original event in ritual or else by wondering how it could have punished an innocent lamb (and trying to identify groups or individuals responsible for the delusion). Both the term and the practice seem to originate in sacrifice:

> And Aaron shall offer his bullock of the sin offering, which is for himself, and make an atonement for himself, and for his house. And he shall take the two goats, and present them before the Lord at the door of the tabernacle of the congregation. And Aaron shall cast lots upon the two goats; one lot for the Lord, and the other lot for the scapegoat. And Aaron shall bring the goat upon which the Lord's lot fell, and offer him for a sin offering. But the goat, on which the lot fell to be the scapegoat, shall be presented alive before the Lord, to make an atonement with him, and to let him go for a scapegoat into the wilderness.[6]

Both goats are scapegoats: both suffer for our sins and both serve as ransom to jealous gods and redemption for those who stay behind ("ransom" and "redemption" have the same root). In the Greek *pharmakos* ritual, maidens, children, or—more commonly—low-status men were, in times of crisis, given figs to eat and then driven out or killed. Many creation myths begin with the expulsion of the devil (or his trickster associates). Many heroic quests (including those of Adam, Moses, Paris, and Oedipus) begin as tales of ritual expulsion or infant exposure. For farming to take hold, Abel has to die. For Rome to be built, Remus and Romulus have to be abandoned and Remus has to be killed.[7]

Whichever came first—the act or the myth—human sacrifice is one of history's oldest locomotives. Much of literature is about scapegoats: comedy is the story of expulsion from the point of view of society; tragedy is the same story from the point of view of the outcast. Comedy is about social reintegration: a temporary or illusory exclusion of the protagonists (by prigs, snobs, mobs, clowns, monsters, impostors, unjust laws, unseeing peers, and obdurate fathers) and their eventual redemption, accompanied by the conversion of some wreckers and the expulsion or execution of others. For David Copperfield to mature and for Mr. Micawber (the descendant of supernatural helpers and trickster-servants) to live "in a perfectly new manner," Uriah Heep must go. A relatively recent—and particularly popular—variation on the scapegoat theme is the detective story, which Northrop Frye describes as "a ritual drama around a corpse in which a wavering finger of social condemnation passes over a group of 'suspects' and finally settles on one. The sense of a victim chosen by lot is very strong, for the case against him is only plausibly manipulated." In the less optimistic version of the story, the hero gives up on society, reverses the meaning of the sacrifice, and chooses to exile himself (literally, like Chatsky in Aleksandr Griboedov's *Woe from Wit*, or metaphorically, like the good soldier Svejk). In the cases of Noah, Lot, and Aeneas, the renewal of the world requires two sacrifices: one genocide and one exile.[8]

Tragedy (from the Greek for "goat") focuses on the act of sacrifice and the figure of the scapegoat. Some tragic heroes—Oedipus, Macbeth, Anna Karenina—may be guilty; some—Joan of Arc, Tess of the D'Urbervilles, Joseph K—may be innocent, at least in the eyes of the reader; and some—Iphigenia, Jesus, Romeo and Juliet—are programmatically innocent as well as willingly self-sacrificial, but that is not the point (as Job is told by the best authority on the subject). The plot of tragedy is much less concerned with the nature of the transgression than with the inexorability of the fall: goats and lambs go to the altar together, and Jesus was crucified next to two thieves, one penitent and one impenitent. Lambs and goats are ultimately interchangeable (Sophocles would have had no difficulty pointing to Jesus's hubris). All outcasts are, by definition, redeemers, and vice versa. The villains of comedy—"Heeps of infamy"—may come back as tragic heroes, and tragic heroes may turn out to be innocent. Oedipus begins his life as an exposed infant and ends it as an outcast king. And so, in his own way, does Moses. Harper Lee's *To Kill a Mockingbird* is about the traditional American scapegoating ritual: the trial of a black man accused of raping a white woman. But the interesting thing is that the alternative suspect and the main accuser are also traditional scapegoat figures: the mysterious recluse and the town drunk. The black man remains an innocent victim, the alternative suspect becomes a dragon-slaying hero, and the accuser is killed as an impenitent thief. All look familiar; the most famous town drunk in America is Huck Finn's father.[9]

Flesh-and-blood scapegoats are associated with crises—from family disputes and boarding school fights to the Final Solution and the Global War on Terror. The victims tend to be deviants, outsiders, and possessors of dangerous knowledge: twins, priests, monks, cripples, healers, strangers, traders, moneylenders, noblemen, and old women, among others.

They are accused of causing the crisis in general and of committing particular acts that threaten the sacred center of social life: rape, incest, arson, bestiality, cannibalism, iconoclasm, infanticide, contagion, blood sacrifice, food poisoning, and gratuitous murder. If the crisis persists, the accusations tend to snowball, as more communities and officials join the search for culprits. In the case of judicial persecutions, they snowball further, as creative interrogations and serial confessions help uncover large conspiracies by implicating the kinsmen and associates of the original suspects. In the late 1620s and early 1630s, amid crop failures and continuing "wars of religion," the witch trials in Bamberg, Bavaria, resulted in the burning of several hundred people, including most of the town elite.[10] One of them, according to the minutes of the proceedings, was the town's top official, Johannes Junius:

> On Wednesday, June 28, 1628, was examined without torture Johannes Junius, Burgomaster at Bamberg, on the charge of witchcraft: how and in what fashion he had fallen into that vice. Is fifty-five years old, and was born at Niederwaysich in the Wetterau. Says he is wholly innocent, knows nothing of the crime has never in his life renounced God: says that he is wronged before God and the world, would like to hear of a single human being who has seen him at such gatherings [as the witch-sabbaths].
>
> Confrontation of Dr. Georg Adam Haan. Tells him to his face he will stake his life on it [er wolle darauf leben und sterben], that he saw him, Junius, a year and a half ago at a witch-gathering in the electoral council-room where they ate and drank. Accused denies the same wholly.
>
> Confronted with Hopffens Elsse. Tells him likewise that he was on Haupts-moor at a witch-dance; but first the holy wafer was desecrated. Junius denies. Hereupon he was told that his accomplices had confessed against him and was given time for thought.
>
> On Friday, June 30, 1628, the aforesaid Junius was again without torture exhorted to confess, but again confessed nothing, whereupon, . . . since he would confess nothing, he was put to the torture.[11]

After five days of torture and "urgent persuasions," Junius confessed to having been seduced by the she-devil, renouncing God, joining a large conspiracy, participating in witch dances, desecrating a holy wafer, and trying to kill his son and daughter (but killing his brown horse instead). On July 24, 1628, he wrote a secret letter to his daughter:

> Many hundred thousand good-nights, dearly beloved daughter Veronica. Innocent have I come into prison, innocent have I been tortured, innocent must I die. For whoever comes into the witch prison must become a witch or be tortured until he invents something out

of his head and—God pity him—bethinks him of something. I will tell you how it has gone with me. When I was the first time put to the torture, Dr. Braun, Dr. Kotzendorffer, and two strange doctors were there. Then Dr. Braun asks me, "Kinsman, how come you here?" I answer, "Through falsehood, through misfortune." "Hear, you," he says, "you are a witch; will you confess it voluntarily? If not, we'll bring in witnesses and the executioner for you." I said "I am no witch, I have a pure conscience in the matter; if there are a thousand witnesses, I am not anxious, but I'll gladly hear the witnesses." Now the chancellor's son was set before me . . . and afterward Hoppfen Elss. She had seen me dance on Haupts-moor. . . . I answered: "I have never renounced God, and will never do it—God graciously keep me from it. I'll rather bear whatever I must." And then came also—God in highest Heaven have mercy—the executioner, and put the thumb-screws on me, both hands bound together, so that the blood ran out at the nails and everywhere, so that for four weeks I could not use my hands, as you can see from the writing. . . . Thereafter they first stripped me, bound my hands behind me, and drew me up in the torture. Then I thought heaven and earth were at an end; eight times did they draw me up and let me fall again, so that I suffered terrible agony. . . .

And this happened on Friday, June 30, and with God's help I had to bear the torture. . . . When at last the executioner led me back into the prison, he said to me: "Sir, I beg you, for God's sake confess something, whether it be true or not. Invent something, for you cannot endure the torture which you will be put to; and, even if you bear it all, yet you will not escape, not even if you were an earl, but one torture will follow after another until you say you are a witch. Not before that," he said, "will they let you go, as you may see by all their trials, for one is just like another." . . .

And so I begged, since I was in wretched plight, to be given one day for thought and a priest. The priest was refused me, but the time for thought was given. Now, my dear child, see in what hazard I stood and still stand. I must say that I am a witch, though I am not—must now renounce God, though I have never done it before. Day and night I was deeply troubled, but at last there came to me a new idea. I would not be anxious, but, since I had been given no priest with whom I could take counsel, I would myself think of something and say it. It were surely better that I just say it with mouth and words, even though I had not really done it; and afterwards I would confess it to the priest, and let those answer for it who compel me to do it. . . . And so I made my confession, as follows; but it was all a lie. . . .

Then I had to tell what people I had seen [at the witch-sabbath]. I said that I had not recognized them. "You old rascal, I must set the executioner at you. Say—was not the Chancellor there?" So I said yes.

"Who besides?" I had not recognized anybody. So he said: "Take one street after another; begin at the market, go out on one street and back on the next." I had to name several persons there. Then came the long street. I knew nobody. Had to name eight persons there. Then the Zinkenwert—one person more. Then over the upper bridge to the Georgthor, on both sides. Knew nobody again. Did I know nobody in the castle—whoever it might be, I should speak without fear. And thus continuously they asked me on all the streets, though I could not and would not say more. So they gave me to the executioner, told him to strip me, shave me all over, and put me to the torture. "The rascal knows one on the market-place, is with him daily, and yet won't name him." By that they meant Dietmeyer: so I had to name him too.

Then I had to tell what crimes I had committed. I said nothing.

. . . "Draw the rascal up!" So I said that I was to kill my children, but I had killed a horse instead. It did not help. I had also taken a sacred wafer, and had desecrated it. When I had said this, they left me in peace.

Now, dear child, here you have all my confession, for which I must die. And they are sheer lies and made-up things, so help me God. . . .[12]

In the margins, he added: "Dear child, six have confessed against me at once: the Chancellor, his son, Neudecker, Zaner, Hoffmaisters Ursel, and Hoppfen Els—all false, through compulsion, as they have all told me, and begged my forgiveness in God's name before they were executed. . . . They know nothing but good of me. They were forced to say it, just as I myself was."[13]

■ ■ ■

In the 1980s and early 1990s in the United States, amid the "culture wars" that centered on procreation, abortion, homosexuality, and the nature of the family, thousands of people were accused of raping and torturing small children. In 1983, in Kern County, California, two couples were sentenced to 240 years for tying up, chaining, and raping their children and selling them for sex. The following summer, several more people in the same county were sentenced to 273 to 405 years for drugging their children, hanging them from boards, and raping them repeatedly in the presence of strangers. In March 1984, seven teachers from the McMartin Preschool in Manhattan Beach, Los Angeles County, were arrested for sexually abusing 360 children over the course of ten years. The accusations included drinking blood, eating feces, cutting babies into little pieces, and staging orgies in underground tunnels, graveyards, and air balloons. Over the next ten years, hundreds of child-care centers throughout the United States were accused of "ritual abuse." Most cases began with an allegation by one parent and evolved into large campaigns involving multiple agencies. The only evidence was the children's testimony and, in a few cases, the defendants' confessions; no scars, films, graves, tunnels, bodies, or witnesses were ever produced. Most defendants never saw their accusers and were presumed guilty by the judges.[14]

As the day-care campaign unfolded, hundreds of adults began to accuse their parents of having abused them when they were children. In August 1988, the twenty-one- and eighteen-year-old daughters of the deputy sheriff and Republican Party chairman of Thurston County, Washington, Paul Ingram, suddenly remembered that their father had been regularly raping them since they were little girls. Confronted by his colleagues in the police department, Ingram denied his guilt but added that, since his daughters would not lie about such things, "there must be a dark side of me that I don't know about." Several hours into his first interrogation, he confessed to having sexually abused both of them for many years. By May 1989, when his trial got under way, he had confessed to belonging to a large satanic cult whose members routinely murdered babies, drank blood, and raped humans and animals. By June 1993, more than four thousand US parents had been accused by their adult children of having molested them in the more or less remote past. About 17 percent of the accusations involved satanic-ritual abuse. A report by a prison official in Idaho, circulated to police workshops around the country, estimated that satanic cults sacrificed fifty thousand to sixty thousand people each year. In a speech delivered in 1988, the psychiatrist Benett G. Braun, who believed that about two hundred thousand Americans suffered from "multiple personality disorder" and that about one-fourth of them were victims of ritual abuse, described the satanic conspiracy as "a national-international type organization that's got a structure somewhat similar to the communist cell structure."[15]

The judicial campaign was accompanied by media reports about poisoned Halloween candy, child pornography networks, battered-women shelters, brainwashed cult members, secretly encoded rock songs, and thousands of missing children (depicted on milk cartons in every grocery store). Christian fundamentalists, anxious to protect home and family from the devil, and radical feminists, anxious to protect women and children from patriarchy, joined forces against an enemy that was both demonically possessed and legally liable.[16] When Frank Fuster, the owner of a babysitting center in a Miami suburb, was convicted on fourteen charges of sexual abuse and sentenced to at least 165 years in prison, the *Miami Herald* editorial attempted to express its readers' sentiments:

> Few criminals in South Florida history have deserved a genuinely life-long prison sentence more than Frank Fuster Escalona. The man lurked at his Country Walk Babysitting Service like a venomous spider that has built a web to bring his victims near. He practiced gross sexual acts on small children entrusted by their parents to his

care. He violated them systematically and over time, as a life style, not as a momentary aberration. . . . If these horrors had to be visited upon these tiny innocents, then the maximum positive results have been realized. Laws have been changed, victims comforted, parents emboldened, prosecutors strengthened, public consciousness raised. And the monster Fuster is destined to spend the remainder of his unnatural life deservedly caged.[17]

Most experts, investigators, and interrogators were therapists acting as policemen and policemen trained as therapists. The result was an inquisitorial regime dedicated to a search for both lost memories and hidden enemies. The number of memories and enemies grew in direct proportion to the investment of effort. One of the pioneers of abuse archaeology, the psychiatrist Lawrence Pazder, claimed that sexual abusers were organized into a powerful coven of "normal-looking" monsters, who had deliberately infiltrated all strata of society and posed as "doctors, ministers, professionals of every kind." According to a 1991 poll, about one-half of California social workers "accepted the idea that SRA [satanic ritual abuse] involved a national conspiracy of multigenerational abusers and baby-killers and that many of these people were prominent in their communities and appeared to live completely exemplary lives. A majority of those polled believed that victims of such extreme abuse were likely to have repressed the memories of it."[18]

The form of "repression" theory that enabled the therapeutic terror of the 1980s posited (as had Freud in his pre-Oedipal period) that what was repressed was not forbidden wishes but actual abuse by elders. The memories of such events were banished as soon as the acts of abuse had occurred; therapy consisted in "recovering" those memories for the purpose of healing the victim and punishing the perpetrators. Confessions were obtained and interpreted by counselors not bound by any confirmation or verification requirements. Deputy Sheriff Paul Ingram was both a Pentecostal Christian used to speaking in tongues and a police officer trained in recovered-memory cases. After several hours of questioning, he told his interrogators: "I really believe that the allegations did occur and that I did violate them and probably for a long period of time. I've repressed it." Three days later, he asked Pastor John Bratun, of the Church of Living Water, to exorcise the demon that had taken possession of him. The combined efforts of the police interrogator and the exorcist, both practicing counselors, produced immediate results: "Ingram began seeing people in robes kneeling around the fire. He thought he saw a corpse. There was a person on his left in a red robe who was wearing a helmet of cloth. 'Maybe the Devil,' he suggested. People were wailing. Ingram remembered standing on a platform and looking down into the fire. He had been given a large knife and was expected to sacrifice a live black cat. He cut out the beating heart and held it aloft on the tip of the knife."[19]

Another method of extracting confessions was plea bargaining (the suspension of a show trial in exchange for an admission of guilt). The twenty-five-year-old Gina Miller, seen as the least culpable defendant in one of the Kern County cases, was offered immunity, a new identity, financial assistance, and custody of her four children if she confessed to engaging in ritualistic sex abuse and testified against her codefendants. She refused, insisting on her innocence, and was sentenced to 405 years in prison—several decades more than the alleged cult leaders. In a Freudianized (inquisitorial) criminal justice system, denying one's guilt was further evidence (symptom) of guilt; not an act of self-defense but a "defense mechanism." On July 7, 1995, nine years after his conviction for sexual abuse at a day-care center in Pennsylvania where he was a substitute janitor, Thomas McMeachin wrote a letter to the journalist Mark Pendergrast: "I'm one of them people that was falsely accused. . . . I've went up for parole 3 times since 1992 and each time I was turned down because I didn't finish the sex offender program. Well now that I completed the program the psychologist told me that he could not recommend me for parole because I'm in denial of my crime because I won't admit to it."[20]

When the Paul Ingram case began to collapse under the weight of the Boschian detail the defendant kept providing, the investigators invited an expert on "cults" (Richard Ofshe, of the University of California, Berkeley, Sociology Department), who concluded that the memories had been manufactured and urged Ingram to withdraw his guilty plea. After two months of reflection (he kept a log of his memories, classified by degree of certainty), Ingram wrote "Died to Self" in his Bible and petitioned to change his plea. His request was denied. At the sentencing hearing, he said: "I stand before you, I stand before God. I have never sexually abused my daughters. I am not guilty of these crimes." He was sentenced to twenty years in prison, with the possibility of parole in twelve years. He served fifteen.[21]

Frank Fuster, a thirty-five-year-old immigrant from Cuba, and his seventeen-year-old Honduran wife, Ileana Flores, were arrested in August 1984 for ritually abusing twenty children in a "gated" Miami suburb. The Dade County state attorney and head prosecutor, Janet Reno (who had an election coming up), promised to do "everything humanly possible to see that justice is done." Ileana spent six months in solitary confinement with the light permanently on. As she said later in an interview, "I was there alone in a very small cell with a bed and a toilet. But the thing is that they would switch me from cell to cell. There was this other cell—I'll never forget. It was called 3A1. I'll never forget that, because most of the people that were there, it was like a big room with little cells next to each other. And most of the people—well, all the people that were there were suicide or suicide watch or they were crazy. Everybody was naked." Ileana's defense attorney told her that her only hope was to plead guilty and testify against her husband. Two psychologists, who ran a business called Behavior

Changers Inc., visited her on at least thirty-five occasions. "It's kind of a manipulation," one of them, Dr. Michael Rappaport, explained. "You could make them feel very happy, then segue into the hard things." Several times, she was visited by Janet Reno. According to Ileana, "She was like, 'Hi, how are you? I'm Janet Reno, the State Attorney.' And I would tell her, 'I am innocent.' And she said, 'I'm sorry, but you are not. You're going to have to help us.' . . . I'd been in jail already a year or so; I'm not sure. I wanted her to help me. But I was afraid of her after she told me—she was very clear—if I didn't help, she was going to make sure I was never going to get out of there."[22]

On August 22, 1985, Ileana agreed to plead guilty. "Judge," she said in court, "I would like you to know that I'm pleading guilty not because I feel guilty, but because I think—I think it's the best interest . . . for my own interest and for the children and for the court and all the people that are working on the case. But I am not pleading guilty because I feel guilty. . . . I am innocent of all those charges."[23]

Sitting between Rappaport, who hugged her from time to time, and Janet Reno, who held her hand, she told the court that Frank had raped her, put a crucifix up her rectum, put a gun and a snake in her vagina, poured acid on her in the shower, and forced her to have oral sex with the children she was babysitting. When she could not recall a certain incident, Rappaport would request a break; after a few minutes in private, they would return to the courtroom, and she would continue her testimony. Frank was sentenced to six life terms and 165 years in prison. Ileana was sentenced to ten years in prison and ten years' probation, served three and a half years in a youthful offender program, and was deported to Honduras. In March 1993, Janet Reno was appointed US attorney general (after two previous appointees had withdrawn because they had employed illegal immigrants as nannies). One month later, she ordered an assault on the Branch Davidian compound outside Waco, Texas. The Branch Davidians (offshoot of Seventh-Day Adventists) were an apocalyptic millenarian sect led by the last days prophet David Koresh (Vernon Howell, who renamed himself after King David and the liberator of the Jews from the Babylonian captivity, Cyrus the Great). The assault resulted in a fire, in which seventy-six sect members, including David Koresh, died. Reno's official reason for ordering the assault was the allegation that the children within the compound were being abused.[24]

In the summer of 2001, Ileana contacted the PBS documentary program, *Frontline*, and requested an interview. The reporter asked her if the events she had described in her testimony actually occurred.

A. No, they didn't.
Q. Frank Fuster—aside from how you feel about him as a husband or as a man—was he guilty of the things that he was accused of and convicted and is serving prison time for?

A. No, he's not guilty, sir.
Q. Did he do these things? Did you witness any of these acts of which he was accused, those children you all brought into your home?
A. I never witnessed it.
Q. Did any of this nightmarish scenario that came to be known as the Country Walk child abuse case—did any of this happen?
A. No, sir. None of that happened. . . . I never hurt any children specifically or anybody. Country Walk just didn't happen.[25]

In July 1998, the same reporter interviewed Frank Fuster, who was serving the first of his six life sentences:

Q. Frank, did the state ever offer you a deal?
A. Oh yes. They insisted. They offered me 15 years, regular 15 years. And if I had taken those, I would have been home 10 years ago.
Q. Why didn't you take it?
A. Because I am innocent. I went to trial not only for me. I went to trial also for the children. I went to trial for Ileana. I went to trial for everyone involved. Someone had to say the truth. I decided to do it, and I did it.[26]

As of this writing, Frank Fuster has been in prison for thirty years.[27]

■ ■ ■

Scapegoats are sacrificed everywhere, all the time: symbolically (in myths, films, tales, and temples) and in the flesh (at the same time that the devil worshippers were being hunted down in the United States, hundreds of "traitors," many of them accused of witchcraft, were being burned alive in South Africa, and hundreds of thousands of people were being "ethnically cleansed" in the former Yugoslavia). Some societies succeed in limiting sacrificial offerings to special occasions; others have to improvise acts of atonement in response to unexpected catastrophes. Sects, or "faith-based groups radically opposed to a corrupt world," are besieged fortresses by definition. Millenarian sects, or sects living on the eve of the apocalypse, are in the grip of a permanent moral panic. The more intense the expectation, the more implacable the enemies; the more implacable the enemies, the greater the need for internal cohesion; the greater the need for internal cohesion, the more urgent the search for scapegoats.[28]

The Münster Anabaptists began by expelling Catholics and Lutherans, went on to mandate universal adult baptism (compulsory sect membership for all citizens), and ended up discovering that none of the apparently faithful were "as perfect as their heavenly father is perfect." The Taiping warriors found it increasingly difficult to distinguish between the Manchu barbarians outside the heavenly capital and the hidden enemies within.

Robespierre argued that the true "enemies of the people" were not the foreigners and aristocrats assembled at the border, but the citizens who sought "to deprave morals and to corrupt the public conscience." Every Armageddon requires a witch hunt.[29]

Egypt could be struck with many plagues, but when contagion began to spread to the chosen people, Moses stood at the entrance to the camp and said: "'Whoever is for the LORD, come to me.' And all the Levites rallied to him. Then he said to them, 'This is what the LORD, the God of Israel, says: "Each man strap a sword to his side. Go back and forth through the camp from one end to the other, each killing his brother and friend and neighbor."' The Levites did as Moses commanded, and that day about three thousand of the people died. Then Moses said, 'You have been set apart to the LORD today, for you were against your own sons and brothers, and he has blessed you this day.'"[30]

Apostates are not simply allied with the outside enemy; they are worse than the outside enemy because they have seen the truth. As Peter wrote in his Second Epistle, "It would have been better for them not to have known the way of righteousness, than to have known it and then to turn their backs on the sacred command that was passed on to them. Of them the proverbs are true: 'A dog returns to its vomit,' and, 'a sow that is washed returns to her wallowing in the mud.'"[31]

On the eve of the End, all enemies are connected to each other (and to impure thoughts). Those who are free to choose are more dangerous than those who have never heard the sacred command. Hidden enemies are more dangerous than the clearly branded ones. Within a millenarian sect (and in unitary states with serious sectarian aspirations, such as Aragon and Castile under the "Catholic Monarchs"), all enemies are both deliberate and hidden, and no enemies are as dangerous as those closest to the inner sanctum.

Satan is a fallen angel; Antichrist is pseudo-Christ; and Jesus had Judas. Korah, who challenged Moses's monopoly on virtue by saying "the whole community is holy, . . . why then do you set yourselves above the LORD's assembly?" was himself a Levite, set by God above the assembly. Aaron, who corrupted the public conscience by making the Golden Calf, was Moses's brother and the assembly's head priest. And Miriam, who joined Aaron in saying "has the LORD spoken only through Moses? Hasn't he also spoken through us?" was their older sister who had saved the baby Moses from Pharaoh's spies. The Hebrew God could afford to be a nepotist (Korah was swallowed by the earth; Miriam was affected with leprosy for seven days; and Aaron was spared at his brother's request), but his more consistent successors could not. As Calvin told his Geneva audience in a sermon on the Levites' massacre, "you shall show yourselves rightly zealous of God's service in that you kill your own brethren without sparing, so as in this case the order of nature be put under foot, to show that God is above all."[32]

All millenarians practice self-monitoring and mutual surveillance with the purpose of identifying and punishing heterodoxy. What makes them both more anxious and more hopeful than other besieged fortresses is that the current set of enemies is going to be the last one. For, as Peter argued in his Second Epistle, against his own evidence,

> If God did not spare angels when they sinned, but sent them to hell, putting them in chains of darkness to be held for judgment; if he did not spare the ancient world when he brought the flood on its ungodly people, but protected Noah, a preacher of righteousness, and seven others; if he condemned the cities of Sodom and Gomorrah by burning them to ashes, and made them an example of what is going to happen to the ungodly; and if he rescued Lot, a righteous man, who was distressed by the depraved conduct of the lawless (for that righteous man, living among them day after day, was tormented in his righteous soul by the lawless deeds he saw and heard)—if this is so, then the Lord knows how to rescue the godly from trials and to hold the unrighteous for punishment on the day of judgment.[33]

The fact that it happened before is the best guarantee that it will never—after the coming day of judgment—happen again. The unrighteous are like animals, "born only to be caught and destroyed," and "like animals they too will perish"—this time for good.[34]

■　■　■

The Bolsheviks lived in a besieged fortress. The Revolution and Civil War involved the use of "concentrated violence" against the easily classifiable enemies from the top of Bukharin's list ("parasitic strata," "unproductive administrative aristocracy," "bourgeois entrepreneurs as organizers and directors," and "skilled bureaucrats") and their properly uniformed and color-coded defenders. The purges of the 1920s confronted the revolutionaries' great disappointment (as Peter did in his Second Epistle, whose main subject was the apparent nonfulfillment of the prophecy). The third and final battle was the Stalin revolution against the remaining targets from Bukharin's list, including "technical intelligentsia," "well-off peasantry," "middle and, in part, petty urban bourgeoisie," and "clergy, even the unskilled kind." The Seventeenth Party Congress of 1934 had then proclaimed victory, provisionally pardoned the doubters, and inaugurated the reign of the saints.[35]

There were no open enemies left. One of the most important and least discussed consequences of the proclamation of victory in 1934 was the assumption that most Soviets were now "non-Party Communists." There was no act of collective baptism accompanied by the expulsion of nominal unbelievers, as in the case of the Münster Anabaptists or fully "reconquered" Spain, but the outcome was the same: all subjects were by definition believers, and all remaining corruption was a matter of heresy and apostasy, not enemy resistance. The Party's main instrument of maintaining internal cohesion was no longer concentrated violence but the "transverse section of the soul" (as the administrative director of the State New Theater put it, apropos of *The Other Side of the Heart*). Bukharin called it "coercive discipline": "The less voluntary inner discipline there is, . . . the greater the coercion. Even the proletarian avant-garde, consolidated in the party of the insurrection, must establish such *coercive self-discipline* in its own ranks; it is not strongly felt by many elements of this avantgarde because it coincides with internal motives, but it exists nonetheless." Since 1920, when he wrote this, Bukharin had experienced several occasions on which to feel it; now, in the wake of the victory celebration that he had joined as part of the "supply train," every Soviet citizen was, theoretically, in his position.[36]

How effective were coercive discipline and self-discipline? On the one hand, family apartments were filling up with nephews and tablecloths; Don Quixotes were being replaced by Sancho Panzas; and Izrail Veitser was marrying Natalia Sats and buying himself a suit. On the other—and much more consequentially, according to Arosev's diary—a combination of schooling, newspaper reading, and "work on the self" was producing such "non-Party Bolsheviks" as Volodia Ivanov and Lyova Fedotov. Socialism was a matter of time, and time was apparently elusive but ultimately predictable. As Peter wrote in that same epistle, "do not forget this one thing, dear friends: With the Lord a day is like a thousand years, and a thousand years are like a day. The Lord is not slow in keeping his promise, as some understand slowness. Instead he is patient with you, not wanting anyone to perish, but everyone to come to repentance."[37]

The same was true of history, which took its time while economic and social preconditions sorted themselves out and Volodia Ivanov and Lyova Fedotov "worked on themselves." The enemy was still at the gate, and henand-rooster problems continued to get in the way, but, in the annus mirabilis of 1934, most signs seemed to indicate that the Bolsheviks were going to heed Peter's warning and be steadfast and patient lest they be led away with the error of the wicked. And then, on December 1, the telephone rang.

■ ■ ■

There are two reasons why the assassination of a prominent but undistinguished Party official resulted in a vast moral panic that "changed everything."

The first was domestic. The House of Government was as much a besieged fortress inside the Soviet Union as the Soviet Union was in the wider world. The assumption that most Soviets were now converts to Communism implied that some open enemies were now hidden; that coercive discipline might require additional scrutiny; and that Fedor Ka-verin's production of *The Other Side of the Heart* (which had suggested that friend and foe might be twin brothers) may have been correct, after all. At the same time, Party officials were as much under siege in their House of Government apartments as the House of Government was inside the Soviet Union. While Volodia Ivanov and Lyova Fedotov were working on themselves, hens and roosters were doing what hens and roosters do—at a pace that the builders of eternal houses could only dream of. The saints were reigning over a swamp.

The second reason was international. The Soviet Union had always been a besieged fortress, but just as victory was being proclaimed at the Seventeenth Party Congress, an effective metaphor was becoming geopolitical reality. In the east, Japan had occupied Manchuria and approached the Soviet border. In the west, the birthplace of Marxism and Russia's traditional model and antipode had been taken over by a hostile apocalyptic sect. Fascism, long seen by the Bolsheviks as the ultimate expression of capitalist aggression, was a modern version of nativist *ressentiment* of the Old Testament variety. The scorned chosen tribes of a degraded Europe were to rise up against Babylon and restore their wholeness, one at a time. Some were trying, with varying degrees of conviction, but only in Germany would the movement reach millenarian proportions, take over the state, proclaim the third and final Reich, and set out to fulfill its own prophecy by preparing for one final battle. What Edom and the "tall Sabeans" had been to the biblical Hebrews and what the white people were to Enoch Mgijima's and Ras Tafari's Israelites, the international Jewry was to the German Führer. As Hitler would say to the Reichstag on January 30, 1939, "Should the international Jewry of finance succeed, both within and beyond Europe, in plunging mankind into yet another world war, then the result will not be a bolshevization of the earth and the victory of Jewry, but the annihilation of the Jewish race in Europe."[38]

Like the Bolsheviks (but unlike most millenarians), Hitler was in a position to bring about what he had prophesied. Like the Bolsheviks (and many other millenarians), he led his people against an enemy whose power was largely esoteric. It was the same enemy—but whereas the Bolsheviks thought of it as a class, the Nazis thought of it as a tribe. Each considered the other a blind instrument in the service of Babylon. Both followed Marx, but Hitler did not know it (and the Bolsheviks did not know it about Hitler and did not usually read Marx's *Contribution to the Critique of Hegel's Philosophy of Right* and "On the Jewish Question"). The final battle (*Endkampf*, or the *poslednii i reshitel'nyi boi* of the "Internationale") would reveal who was the beast and who treaded the winepress of divine wrath. The key to victory was the draining of the swamp.

24

THE ADMISSION
OF GUILT

The search for Kirov's assassins started at the top and aimed at the fallen angels. On December 3, the Politburo approved the "Central Executive Committee and Council of People's Commissars Decree of December 1." According to the decree, cases involving "terrorist organizations and terrorist acts" were to be completed within ten days and with no right to appeal. Death sentences were to be carried out immediately. As N. I. Ezhov, who was put in charge of the campaign, said two years later, "it was Comrade Stalin who started it. I remember very clearly how he summoned me and Kosarev and said: 'Look for the murderers among the Zinovievites.'" And that is what they did. On December 16, Zinoviev and Kamenev (Lenin's closest associates and, after Trotsky's expulsion, the most prominent former Left Oppositionists) were arrested. On December 29, the assassin, Leonid Nikolaev, and thirteen other people, some of whom had worked under Zinoviev, were executed. On January 16, seventy-seven former oppositionists in Leningrad and nineteen in Moscow (including Kamenev and Zinoviev) were sentenced to various terms in prison and exile. According to one of the lead investigators, G. S. Liushkov, who escaped arrest by defecting to Japan in June 1938, "I can state with absolute confidence before the whole world that none of these conspiracies ever existed and that they were all deliberately fabricated. Nikolaev definitely never belonged to Zinoviev's circle. He was an abnormal person who suffered from megalomania. He was determined to die in order to enter history as a hero. It is obvious from his diary."[1]

Kamenev and Zinoviev at first denied their guilt but then understood that the affair was, as Kamenev put it at the trial, "political, not legal." Or, as Zinoviev realized by the end of the investigation, it was about the soul, not politics. Two days before the trial, he wrote a letter to his inquisitors (led by the veteran opposition expert, Yakov Agranov):

> Comrade Agranov has pointed out to me that the testimony I have provided so far does not impress the investigation team as full and candid repentance and does not reveal everything about what took place.

The investigation is coming to an end. The confrontations with witnesses have also had an effect on me. I must tell the investigators everything without exception.

It is true that what I had to say in my previous testimony had more to do with what I could say in my defense than what I must say in full expiation of my guilt. There is much that I have truly forgotten, but there is much that I did not want to think through to the end, let alone tell the investigators.

Now I would like to disarm myself completely.

The point, he had finally realized, was not whether he had had anything to do with Kirov's murder. The point was the continued existence of the other side of his heart:

I was sincere in my speech to the Seventeenth Party Congress, and I thought that I was "adapting myself" to the majority in the way in which I expressed myself. But, in fact, two different souls continued to live within me.

In the main group of former "Zinovievites," there were stronger personalities than I. But the problem is that, because we were unable to properly submit to the Party, merge with it completely, become imbued with the same feelings of absolute acceptance toward Stalin that the Party and the whole country have become imbued with, but instead continued to look backward and to live our separate, stifling lives—because of all that, we were doomed to the kind of political dualism that produces double-dealing.

The reason he had not disarmed himself earlier was that he had been "afraid of history"—afraid of finding himself "in the position of a man who is, in effect, promoting terrorism against the leaders of the Party and the Soviet state." Now he understood that the only way to stop promoting terrorism was to admit to having been its spiritual leader. "Let my sad example serve as a lesson to others, let them see what it means to stray from the Party's path and where it may lead."[2]

He was sentenced to ten years in the Verkhneuralsk Political Isolator (it had been a year since Tania Miagkova first arrived there). In a secret letter to Party organizations issued two days after the trial, the Central Committee reiterated that "the stronger the USSR becomes and the more hopeless the position of its enemies, the faster those enemies—precisely because of the hopelessness of their position—may sink into the swamp of terror." The Zinovievites were the first Party members to have done so. They were, "in effect, a White Guard organization in disguise, worthy of being treated like White Guards." Others might follow. "Party members must know not only how the Party fought and overcame the Kadets, SRs, Mensheviks, and Anarchists, but also how the Party fought and overcame the Trotskyites, "Democratic Centralists," "Workers' Opposition," Zinovievites, Right deviationists, Rightist-Leftist freaks, etc."[3]

Accordingly, 3,447 former oppositionists were arrested in 1935 and 23,279 in 1936. Between May and December 1935, a verification of Party documents, conducted jointly by the Party Control Commission (headed by Ezhov) and the People's Commissariat of Internal Affairs (NKVD), resulted in the expulsion of about 250,000 Party members and the arrest of about 15,000. In spring 1935, an investigation of Kremlin guards, doormen, secretaries, librarians, and telephone operators began by suggesting that slanderous rumors (mostly regarding the suicide of Stalin's wife, Nadezhda Allilueva, and the murder of Kirov) "might generate terrorist intentions against the leaders of the Party and government" and ended by uncovering a conspiracy to assassinate Stalin and other leaders of the Party and government. Two people were sentenced to death and 108 others, to various terms in prison and exile. Avel Enukidze, the secretary of the Central Executive Committee and the chief supervisor of the government (and the House of Government) patronage system, was accused of corruption and expelled from the Party.[4]

"Degeneracy" and treason within the Party were presumed to be connected to the survival of certain social groups that might feel threatened by the coming of socialism and heartened by the prospect of foreign intervention. In February–March 1935, 11,072 "remnants of the defeated bourgeoisie" (4,833 heads of families and 6,239 family members) were deported from Leningrad, mostly to "special settlements" in northern Russia. In the summer and fall, Soviet cities were "cleansed" of 122,726 "criminal and declassé elements" and 160,000 homeless children. About sixty-two thousand children were placed in NKVD "children's reception points" and about ten thousand were transferred to the criminal justice system. On April 20, 1935, minors over twelve became eligible for the death penalty. These and similar operations (including screenings and firings of enterprise employees) were conducted on the basis of NKVD "watchlists," which included people associated with former privileged classes, former members of non-Bolshevik political parties and Bolshevik oppositions, former kulaks, expelled Party members, and all those conducting "counterrevolutionary conversations" and engaging in acts "discrediting Party leadership."[5]

Prominent on the watch lists were people with reported or presumed connections to foreign countries. The Kirov murder coincided with a growing hostility toward the Soviet Union on the part of Japan, Germany, and, as far as Stalin and his top associates were concerned, all those who attempted to appease, engage, or accommodate them (with Poland particularly prominent in the wake of the Polish-German nonaggression treaty of August 1934). In the winter and spring of 1935, the border regions of Ukraine, Karelia, and Leningrad Province were "cleansed" of thousands of ethnic Germans, Poles, Finns, Latvians, and Estonians. At the same time, thousands of kulaks and "anti-Soviet elements" were deported from Azerbaijan and the "national republics" of the North Caucasus. As the "enemy encirclement" continued to tighten and the watch lists of internal suspects continued to grow, all foreign citizens (including political émigrés and Comintern members) became potential spies, and all Soviet citizens with links ("subjective or objective") to hostile states became potential traitors. It did not take long to realize that all states bordering the USSR were hostile, and all potential spies and traitors were, or could quickly become, real. The Soviet experience in the Spanish Civil War reinforced the foundational Bolshevik preoccupation with internal dissension and provided a new productive term to describe it. A significant, and rapidly growing, proportion of Soviets became "the Fifth Column" of the approaching invaders. In 1935–36, 9,965 people were arrested for spying (among them, 3,528 for Poland, 2,275 for Japan, and 1,322 for Germany). As Robespierre had said under similar circumstances, "is not this dreadful contest, which liberty maintains against tyranny, indivisible? Are not the internal enemies the allies of those in the exterior?"[6]

In early 1936, Ezhov—on Stalin's instructions and with Agranov's assistance—established that the Zinovievites had conspired with the Trotskyites and that both were guilty of "terror." More former Zinovievites and 508 former Trotskyites were arrested and sent to remote camps, sentenced to death, or used as sources of further revelations. As the interrogator A. P. Radzivilovsky reported to Ezhov, "three weeks of exceptionally hard work with [the former Trotskyite E. A.] Dreitser and [the former Zinovievite R. V.] Pickel resulted in the fact that they have begun to testify." "Hard work" included threats, sleep deprivation, and appeals to Party solidarity. As the former Trotskyite, V. P. Olberg, wrote to his interrogator, "after your most recent interrogation of January 25, I was, for some reason, gripped by a terrible, excruciating fear of death. But today I am a bit calmer. I am ready to incriminate myself and do anything in order to put an end to this torment."[7]

Zinoviev was brought back for more interrogations. On April 14, 1936, he wrote to Stalin:

Whatever happens, I have very little time left to live: perhaps an inch or two of life, at most.

There is only one thing left for me to do: to make sure that people say about these few remaining inches that I understood the full horror of what happened, repented to the end, told the Soviet state absolutely everything I knew, turned my back on everyone and everything that was against the Party, and was ready to do anything and everything in order to prove my sincerity.

There is only one desire in my soul: to prove to you that I am not an enemy anymore. There is no demand that I would not fulfill in order to prove this. . . . I reached the point where I spend long periods of time looking intently at your portrait and the portraits of the other members of the Politburo in the newspapers with one thought only: my dear ones, please look into my soul, can it be that you do not see that I am not your enemy anymore, that I am yours body and soul, that I have understood everything, and that I am ready to do anything to deserve forgiveness and mercy?[8]

On July 29, 1936, the Central Committee of the Party sent out a secret letter to local Party committees. The letter, drafted by Ezhov and edited by Stalin, stated that "the Trotsky-Zinoviev Counterrevolutionary Center and its leaders, Trotsky, Zinoviev, and Kamenev," had "sunk definitively into the swamp of White Guardism" and "merged with the most notorious and embittered enemies of the Soviet state." In the process, they had "not only become the organizing force behind the remnants of the defeated classes in the USSR, but also the vanguard of the counterrevolutionary bourgeoisie outside the Union, the transmitter of its wishes and expectations." The lesson to be learned was clear: "Under current conditions, the most important quality of every Bolshevik ought to be his ability to recognize an enemy of the Party, no matter how well disguised he may be."[9]

The public trial followed within three weeks. All sixteen defendants, including Zinoviev, Kamenev, Dreitser, Pickel, and Olberg, confessed to having engaged in terrorism and were sentenced to death. The sentences were carried out on August 25, one day after the verdicts were read. Trotsky and his son, Lev Sedov, were sentenced in absentia. Radek wrote in *Izvestia*: "Taking advantage of what was left of the Old Bolshevik trust in them, they feigned remorse and, counting on the Party's nobility, created a system of lies and deceit unprecedented in the history of the world. . . . They became fascists, and they worked for Polish, German, and Japanese fascism. Such is the historic truth. And it would be a historic truth even if there were no proof of their links with fascist intelligence services."[10]

In the wake of the trial, 160 people were executed on charges related to the "Anti-Soviet United Trotskyite-Zinovievite Center." Thousands more former oppositionists were arrested. On September 26, 1936, Ezhov was appointed people's commissar of internal affairs. Three days later, the Politburo issued a decree ordering "the annihilation of the Trotskyite-Zinovievite scoundrels" who had been arrested or sentenced earlier. On October 4, the Politburo (with Kaganovich, Molotov, Postyshev, Andreev, Voroshilov, and Ezhov present) voted to condemn "585 active members of the Trotskyite-Zinovievite counterrevolutionary terrorist organization as a single list" (that is, without considering individual cases). New arrests led to new confessions, which led to new arrests. Some of the former oppositionists were economic managers; their arrests led to the arrests of economic managers who were not former oppositionists.[11]

. . .

During the August trial, Kamenev and Zinoviev had named Radek and the former Rightists (Bukharin, Rykov, and Tomsky) as their coconspirators. Tomsky shot himself at his dacha on August 22. Bukharin, who was hunting and painting in the Pamirs, heard the news on the 24th and sent Stalin a telegram: "Have just read scoundrels' slanderous testimony. Utterly outraged. Leaving Tashkent by plane morning 25th." Anna Larina, who had recently given birth to their son, Yuri, met him at the airport. "N. I. was sitting on a bench, huddled in the corner. He looked sick and lost. He had asked me to meet him, fearing that he might be arrested at the airport." Two days later he wrote a long letter to the Politburo, in which he proclaimed his innocence and discussed the possible motives of his executed accusers. The letter ends with a plea:

> I am shaken to the very core by the tragic absurdity of what is going on. After thirty years in the Party, and despite my most sincere devotion to it and so much work done (I have done some good things, after all), I am about to be added (and am already being added) to the enemy list. And what enemies they are! To end my biological life is to commit a political crime. Life after political death is not life. It is a complete dead end, unless the Central Committee exonerates me. I know how difficult it is to trust someone after the stinking, bloody abyss that opened up at the trial, when humans stopped being human. But here, too, there is a limit: not all former oppositionists are double-dealers.
>
> I am writing to you, comrades, while I still have some emotional strength left. Do not cross the line in your distrust! And—please—do not drag out the case of the defendant Nikolai Bukharin. Right now, my life is a terrible, deadly torment; I cannot bear the fact that even passers-by are afraid of me—especially since I am not guilty.
>
> It is excellent that the scoundrels were shot. It cleared the air immediately. The trial will have tremendous international importance. It will drive an ash stake through the corpse of a bloodstained peacock whose arrogance has led him into the fascist secret police. In fact, we tend to underestimate its international importance, it seems to me. In general, it is good to be alive, but not in my sitation now. In 1928–9 I was criminally foolish, not realizing the consequences of my mistakes or the high price I would have to pay.
>
> My best to you all. Remember that there are people who have truly left their past sins behind and whose whole heart (while it still beats) and soul will always be with you, no matter what happens.[12]

On August 31, he wrote a separate letter to People's Commissar of Defense Voroshilov, asking whether he and the others truly believed that he had been insincere in what he had written about Kirov. He was addressing the Politburo, and ultimately the Party as a whole (and using the second-person plural):

Nikolai Bukharin meeting with shock workers during a
mountaineering trip to the Caucasus

You must face the question honestly. If I was insincere, I should be
arrested and destroyed immediately, for such scoundrels must not
be tolerated.

If you think I was insincere, but leave me at large, then you are
cowards, unworthy of respect.

But if you yourselves do not believe the lies told by that cynical
murderer, vilest of human beings, and human carrion Kamenev, then
why do you allow resolutions (like the one in Kiev), where it is stated
that I "knew" about the-devil-knows-what?

What, then, is the point of the investigation, the legality, and so
on?[13]

The problem was that the point of the investigation and revolutionary
legality was to determine whether he was sincere. And the only way for
him to prove that he was sincere was to keep saying that he was. As his
friend Tomsky had put it at the Sixteenth Party Congress in 1930, the peni-
tents had nothing but words, and words, according to some comrades,
were meaningless. "Repent, repent without end, do nothing but repent."
The Central Committee notice on Tomsky's suicide, published in *Pravda*
on August 23, 1936, stated that he had killed himself, "having become ensnared in his relationships with the counterrevolutionary Trotskyite-
Zinovievist terrorists." Bukharin did not want to commit suicide. His strategy was to produce more words: words addressed to the Party leadership
as a whole and to particular individuals who were both Party leaders and
intimate friends. The second half of his letter to Voroshilov is in the intimate—second-person singular—key:

It was good to be flying above the clouds the other day: the minus 8
degree (Celsius) temperature, the crystal clarity, the air of serene
majesty.

Perhaps what I wrote to you made no sense. Please don't be angry with me. In this climate, it might be unpleasant for you to receive a letter from me—God knows, anything is possible.

But, "just in case," I assure you (as someone who has always been like a friend to me): your conscience can be completely clear; I have never let you down by betraying your trust in me; I truly am not guilty of anything, and sooner or later it will become clear, no matter how hard some people are trying to sully my name. . . .

Take my advice: read Romain Rolland's plays about the French Revolution some day.

Forgive me for such a confused letter. I have thousands of thoughts galloping like crazed horses, and no strong reins to hold them back.

I embrace you, for I am pure.

Nikolai Bukharin
31 August, 1936.[14]

Three days later, the letter was returned.

To Comrade Bukharin:

I am returning your letter, in which you allowed yourself vile attacks against the Party leadership. If by writing this letter you wanted to convince me of your total innocence, you have convinced me of one thing only: that I should stay away from you irrespective of the outcome of the investigation into your case. If you do not retract in writing the foul epithets you directed at the Party leadership, I will also consider you a scoundrel.

K. Voroshilov
3 September, 1936

Bukharin wrote back immediately.

To Comrade Voroshilov:

I have received your *terrible* letter.
My letter ended with "embrace."
Yours ends with "scoundrel."
What can I possibly write after that?
But I would like to clear up one political misunderstanding.
My letter was a *personal* one (something I now deeply regret). Tormented and feeling persecuted, I simply wrote to a generous human being. I was losing my mind at the thought that someone might actually believe in my guilt.[15]

Bukharin made the same mistake that Osinsky had made in January 1928, when he attempted to distinguish between Stalin the person and

Stalin the Party leader. Party leadership—and Party membership, in general—was not a job one could come home from.

Less than a week later, on September 8, Bukharin was summoned to the Central Committee building to participate in a direct confrontation with his childhood friend (and the father of his rival for the hand of Anna Larina), Grigory Sokolnikov. Sokolnikov had recently been arrested and was now claiming that the Rightists might have had secret dealings with Kamenev and Zinoviev. Kaganovich, who was present at the confrontation, wrote to Stalin (who was in Sochi): "After Sokolnikov's departure, Bukharin shed a few tears and kept asking to be believed. I got the impression that even if they did not have a direct organizational connection to the Trotskyi-Zinoviev Bloc, they knew about Trotskyite activities in 1932–33, and possibly later. . . . In any case, it is necessary to keep looking for a Rightist underground organization. It definitely exists. It seems to me that the role of Rykov, Bukharin, and Tomsky is yet to be revealed."[16]

In the meantime, the prosecutor general's office announced that there was not enough evidence to proceed with the investigation of Rykov and Bukharin. There was no mention of the Radek investigation. According to Anna Larina, Radek called Bukharin and asked for a meeting (they were dacha neighbors). Bukharin refused, but Radek came anyway, assured Bukharin of his innocence, and asked him to write to Stalin in his behalf. "Before leaving, he said again: 'Nikolai, please believe me! Whatever happens, I am not guilty of anything!' Karl Berngardovich spoke with great emotion. He walked up to N. I. [Bukharin], said goodbye, kissed him on the forehead, and left the room." Several days later Bukharin wrote to Stalin:

> Radek's wife rushed in to say that he had been arrested. I implore you, on his and my behalf, to become involved. She asked me to tell you that Radek is willing to shed all his blood to the last drop for our country.
>
> I am also stunned by this unexpected development and, despite all the "buts," my excessive trust in people, and my past mistakes in this regard, my Party conscience obliges me to say that *my own* impressions of Radek (on the big issues, not the minor ones) are only positive. I may be mistaken. But all the inner voices of my soul tell me that it is my duty to write to you about this. What a terrible business![17]

The guarantors of Radek's sincerity were the admittedly unreliable inner voices of Bukharin's soul. The only guarantor of Bukharin's own sincerity was Stalin, who was both "the personal embodiment of the mind and will of the Party" (as Bukharin had said at the Seventeenth Party Congress) and an old friend nicknamed Koba (as Bukharin kept stressing in his letters). "Only you can cure me," he wrote to Stalin on September 24. "I did not ask you to receive me before the end of the investigation because I thought it would be politically awkward for you. But now I am asking you with my whole being. Do not refuse me. Interrogate me, turn my skin inside out, but dot the 'i' in such a way that no one will ever dare kick me and poison my existence, thereby driving me to the madhouse."[18]

The Stalin/Koba distinction was based on the Lenin/Ulianov and Lenin/Ilich pairings that Bukharin had helped formulate. In Koltsov's version, there was Ulianov, "who took care of those around him and was as nurturing as a father, as tender as a brother, and as simple and cheerful as a friend," and then there was Lenin, "who caused unprecedented trouble to the Planet Earth and stood at the head of history's most terrible, most devastatingly bloody struggle against oppression, ignorance, backwardness, and superstition." Over time, "Ilich" had replaced "Ulianov" as Lenin's human incarnation, but the two-in-one doctrine remained. Both "Lenin" and "Ilich" were public symbols used to name streets, cities, and collective farms, all of them ultimately connected to the mausoleum. According to Koltsov's summary: "Two faces—and only one man; not a duality but a synthesis."

The founder of Bolshevism was a Moses equidistant from God (history) and the people. His successor was much closer to history because history was now much closer to its final fulfillment. After the victory proclaimed at the Seventeenth Party Congress, that victory's architect (as Radek called him) became wholly indivisible. Nothing could be named after "Iosif Vissarionovich Dzhugashvili," in any combination, and "Koba" (which had never been public) was no longer in use. Since all oppositions disappeared and all enemies became invisible, heresy was replaced by insincerity and the two-in-one leader was replaced by one Comrade Stalin. Only Bukharin kept trying to prove himself to history by appealing to an old personal connection. "Dear Koba," he wrote on October 19:

> Forgive me once more for daring to write to you. I know how busy you are, as well as what and who you are. But, heaven knows, you are the only one I can write to, as a dear friend, whom I can appeal to, knowing that I won't get a kick in the teeth for it. In the name of all that is holy, please do not think that I am trying to be familiar with you. I believe I understand your significance better than most people. But I am writing to you the way I used to write to Ilich, as a truly dear person, whom I see even in my dreams, the way I used to see Ilich. It may seem strange, but that's the way it is. . . . If only you possessed an instrument that would allow you to see what was going on inside my poor head.[19]

On December 4, 1936, Bukharin and Rykov were summoned to a Central Committee plenum devoted in part to their case (the other part concerned the approval of the new constitution, which Bukharin had helped draft). Ezhov made a speech accusing the former Rightists of involvement in terrorist activity. Bukharin maintained his innocence by countering specific claims made by imprisoned oppositionists and appealing to the Central Committee for trust and understanding. Stalin explained the difficulty. "Bukharin has no idea what is happening here. None whatsoever. He does not understand the position he is in, or why the plenum is discussing his case. He does not understand anything. He talks about sincerity and demands trust. Okay then, let's talk about sincerity and trust." Kamenev and Zinoviev, said Stalin, had claimed sincerity and then betrayed the Party's trust. Other former oppositionists had claimed sincerity and then betrayed the Party's trust.

Nikolai Bukharin

The recently arrested first deputy of the people's commissar of heavy industry, Georgy Piatakov, had offered to prove his sincerity by personally executing the convicted terrorists, including his own wife, and then betrayed the Party's trust.

> So you see what a hellish situation we find ourselves in. Just try believing in the sincerity of the former oppositionists after this! We cannot believe what the former oppositionists say even when they volunteer to personally execute their friends.
>   . . . So, that's the situation we're in, Comrade Bukharin. (*Bukharin:* I will never admit to anything—not today, or tomorrow, or the day after tomorrow. *Noise in the hall.*) I am not saying anything about you personally. You may be right—and you may not. But you cannot stand here and complain that people do not trust or have faith in your, Bukharin's, sincerity. That is old hat. The events of the last two years have demonstrated convincingly that sincerity is a relative concept.[20]

Tomsky had been right: words were meaningless. But Tomsky had drawn the wrong conclusion: suicide, according to Stalin, was "a means used by former oppositionists, the Party's enemies, to confuse the Party, to evade its vigilance, to deceive it one last time by means of suicide and to put it in an awkward position." Suicide was worse than meaningless: it was proof of insincerity. "I would urge you, Comrade Bukharin, to think about why Tomsky resorted to suicide and left behind a letter saying that he was 'pure.' You can see clearly that he was far from being pure. Indeed, if I were clean, then—as a man, a human being, and not a weakling, let alone as a Communist—I would shout at the top of my voice that I was right."[21]

Bukharin kept shouting, but words were meaningless. And so, in the end, were facts. Bukharin's and Rykov's attempts to point to contradictions and absurdities in the accusations were dismissed by their Central

Committee comrades as irrelevant. What mattered was not whether they had done or said certain things; what mattered was that they had betrayed the Party once before and were, therefore, likely to do it again. And if they were likely to do it, they probably had. And the more loudly Bukharin shouted, the more entangled he seemed to become. What was the most important task on the eve of the last war? To make sure (as he admitted in his speech at the plenum) "that all the Party members from top to bottom become imbued with a sense of vigilance and help the appropriate services exterminate the scum that engages in acts of sabotage and so on." Where was the scum to be found? Among the nine targets of "concentrated violence" that he had identified sixteen years ago plus those former oppositionists who had turned out to be scum. Could Kamenev and Zinoviev be trusted? No, they could not (their execution had "cleared the air"). Could Bukharin be trusted?[22]

This question was obviously important to Bukharin and possibly interesting to Koba, but it was irrelevant to history and to Comrade Stalin. As Bukharin wrote in his letter to Voroshilov, "it sometimes happens in history that remarkable people and excellent politicians make fateful mistakes in 'particular cases': what I will become is a mathematical coefficient of your particular mistake. Sub specie historiae (from the point of view of history), this is a trifle, a mere literary detail." The general principle was shared by all; whether Bukharin's particular case was a mistake remained an open question. The plenum resolved "to accept Comrade Stalin's suggestion to consider the case of Rykov and Bukharin unfinished, continue the investigation, and postpone the solution until the next Central Committee plenum."[23]

■　■　■

The Rykovs—Rykov himself; his wife, Nina Semenovna Marshak (formerly married to Piatnitsky); their twenty-year-old daughter Natalia, who taught literature at the Border Guard Academy; and their companion of many years, Glikeria Flegontovna Rodiukova, or "Lusha" (a native of Narym, where they had been in exile when Natalia was born)—were told to move from the Kremlin to the House of Government. They moved into Apt. 18, which had been vacant since Radek's arrest (Radek and Gronsky had recently exchanged apartments: Gronsky had moved to the eleventh floor, and Radek, who did not need as much room, had moved down to the tenth, next to Kuusinen). It had been exactly ten years since Rykov formed the Commission for the Construction of the House of the Central Executive Committee and the Council of People's Commissars (of which he was then chairman) and appointed Boris Iofan as head architect. According to Natalia, the only people who visited them in the House of Government were Nina Semenovna's sister and one of Rykov's nieces. The near-complete

Aleksei Rykov and Nina Marshak

isolation, she wrote, "broke Rykov morally." "He became withdrawn, stopped talking, ate almost nothing, and paced silently from one corner of the room to the other. Or he lay in bed for hours, thinking just as intensely. Strange as it may seem, he smoked less than usual during those days. He seemed almost to forget about that old habit of his. He had aged a great deal, his hair had thinned and was always disheveled looking, and his face was haggard with dark bluish circles under his eyes. I don't think he ever slept. He never talked. He just kept thinking and thinking."[24]

Bukharin, Anna Larina, their son Yuri, Bukharin's father, Ivan Gavrilovich, and Bukharin's disabled first wife, Nadezhda Mikhailovna Lukina, all continued to live in Stalin's old apartment in the Kremlin. (They had switched apartments at Stalin's request after the suicide of his wife.) According to Larina,

> The furniture in our room was more than modest: two beds with a bedside table between them, a rickety couch with springs showing through the dirty upholstery, and a small table. A dark gray radio speaker was hanging on the wall. N.I. liked this room because it had a sink with a faucet and, next to it, a door leading into the toilet. So N.I. installed himself in this room and rarely left it. . . .
>
> He became isolated even within the family. He did not want his father to come in and see him suffering. "Go away, Pops," he would say in a weak voice. Once Nadezhda Mikhailovna literally crawled in to see the latest testimony and then barely made it back to her bed, with my help.
>
> N.I. grew thin and aged, and his red goatee turned gray. (It was my job to serve as barber; otherwise N.I. would have grown a huge beard over the course of six months).[25]

On December 15, *Pravda* published an article accusing the former Rightists of working hand in hand with "Trotskyite-Zinovievite spies, murderers, and saboteurs, as well as Gestapo agents." Bukharin wrote a formal letter of complaint to the Politburo and a personal one to Stalin. "What am I to do? I am hiding in my room, can't see anyone, never go out. My family is desperate. I am desperate, too, for I am powerless against the slander that is suffocating me. I was counting on the fact that you had the extra advantage of knowing me well. I thought you knew me better than the others and that, despite the correctness of the general mood of distrust, that circumstance would have been an important component in your over-all assessment." Stalin sent a memo to *Pravda*'s editor in chief, Lev Mekh-lis: "The case of the former Rightists (Rykov, Bukharin) has been post-poned until the next Plenum of the Central Committee. Consequently, attacks against Bukharin (and Rykov) must be stopped until the matter has been resolved. It does not take great intelligence to understand such a basic truth."[26]

Meanwhile, Ezhov, on Stalin's instructions, was working on the resolu-tion. Former oppositionists and their associates were being arrested or brought back from the camps and forced to incriminate Rykov and Bukharin (as well as themselves and others). According to M. N. Riutin's letter to Stalin, "at each interrogation, they threaten me, yell at me, as if I were an animal, insult me, and don't even allow me to submit a reasoned refusal to testify." According to L. A. Shatskin's letter to Stalin, false tes-timony was being demanded "in the interests of the Party." Those who wrote to complain wrote to Stalin, who stood for the interests of the Party. Stalin—in the interests of the Party (sub specie historiae)—supervised the operation, edited the confessions, and suggested new names and general directions.[27]

After three months of interrogations by Boris Berman (the brother of the head of the Gulag, Matvei Berman, and the brother-in-law of the Mid-dle Volga collectivizer and currently deputy head of the Moscow Province NKVD, Boris Bak), Radek began to incriminate Bukharin. On January 13, 1937, they confronted each other at a hearing attended by Stalin, Voroshi-lov, Ezhov, Kaganovich, Molotov, and Ordzhonikidze. Radek accused Bukharin of involvement in terrorist activity. Bukharin asked him why he was lying. Radek said that he would explain. Several minutes later, he did. "I would like to say that no one physically coerced me into testifying. No one threatened me with anything before I began testifying. Comrade Ber-man told me: 'I am not telling you that you will be shot if you refuse, and I am not telling you that you will not be shot if you provide the testimony we consider correct.' Besides, I am old enough not to believe any promises made when you are in prison."

He was not out to save his skin, he claimed, because he had given up on it long ago. The hardest part was testifying against Bukharin, "as com-rades will confirm." "At first I did not consider the overall political signifi-cance of this whole thing at the trial and so on, but then I said to myself:

any attempt to deny this thing at the trial will only serve to reinforce it, so it is necessary to put an end to all this, primarily because there is a war going on. And then I said to myself that personal friendship should not be allowed to prevent me from revealing the fact that, in addition to the Zinovievite-Trotskyite organization, there is an organization of Rightists." Radek's statements combined the needed confessions with an explanation of why they were needed. Some seemed preliminary and needed to be reformulated. In the typed minutes of the confrontation, Stalin crossed out the self-reflexive introduction up to the colon and substituted "will only serve to reinforce the terrorist organizations" for "will only serve to reinforce it."[28]

Three days later Bukharin wrote to "dear Koba," asking whether it might be possible that some nameless group within the Party "understands its Party duty in such a way that I need to be destroyed a priori." He was willing to die for the Party, but not as the Party's enemy. "I can't think of a more monstrously tragic situation than my own. It is a profound tragedy, and I am crumbling from exhaustion. Comrade Ezhov says, in all innocence: Radek also protested at first, and then . . . and so on. But I am not Radek: I know I am innocent. And nothing and no one will ever force me to say 'yes' if the truth is actually 'no.'"

But what if a yes was required by the Party? Could he still say no? "If I am to be removed from the Central Committee, a political motive will have to be given. In any Party cell, I will have to admit my guilt in a way that I refused to do in front of you. That is impossible. The consequence is expulsion from the Party, which means death." The only way out was to convince the Party, or at least Koba, that the whole thing was a deliberate campaign by the "Trotskyite protobeasts." "When Radek was shedding tears and lying about me, I looked into his clouded, depraved eyes and saw all that Dostoyevskian perversion and depth of human vileness that has left me half dead, wounded by his slander."[29]

He never mailed that letter to Koba. Instead, he wrote one to Comrade Stalin, with copies to the other participants in the confrontation. It made the same points in a less confessional mode and ended with the words: "I am for the Party, for the USSR, and for our victory, whatever they may say about me on the basis of slander spread by wicked and cunning people. This is not a newspaper article ending, but my profoundest conviction and the very core of my existence."[30]

At the trial of the "Anti-Soviet Trotskyite center," which opened on January 23 (one week after Bukharin mailed his letter), Radek said that it had taken him two and a half months to understand what was required of him. "In case someone has raised the question of whether we were tortured during the investigation, I must state that it was not the investigators who tortured me, but I who tortured my investigators."[31] The passage about Bukharin had been revised in accordance with Stalin's suggestions:

I knew that Bukharin's situation was as hopeless as my own, because our guilt—if not de jure, then de facto—was the same. But he and I are close friends, and intellectual friendships are closer than other kinds of friendship. I knew that Bukharin was in the same state of shock as I was, and I was convinced that he would provide honest testimony to the Soviet state. For that reason, I did not want to have him brought in handcuffs to the Commissariat of Internal Affairs. I wanted him to do what I wanted our other associates to do: to disarm himself. This explains why it was only at the very end, when the trial was upon us, that I realized that I could not appear in court, having concealed the existence of another terrorist organization.[32]

He could now do publicly what he had rehearsed in his confrontation with Bukharin: incriminate himself and others and explain his reasons for doing so. The prosecution's entire case, he said in his last word, was based on his testimony and the testimony of his co-defendant, Piatakov ("all the other testimony by all the accused rests on our testimony"). He did not have to admit his guilt, but he did, anyway: "I admitted my guilt and testified exhaustively about it not from a simple need to repent—repentance may be an inner realization that does not have to be shared or demonstrated—and not from a general love of truth—the truth in my case is very bitter and, as I said before, I would rather be shot three times over than admit it. I must admit my guilt because of how I understand the general benefit that would be produced by that truth."[33]

That benefit was the realization by all those whose hearts were not wholly devoted to the Party that, on the eve of the last war, even the slightest doubt meant siding with the beast. Active terrorists could easily be handled by the police ("on that score we, based on our own fate, have not the slightest doubt"). The real danger came from the "half-Trotskyites, quarter-Trotskyites, and one-eighth-Trotskyites," who might, through pride, carelessness, or "liberalism," encourage the active terrorists. "We find ourselves in a period of utmost tension, on the brink of war. Speaking before the court and facing our hour of judgment, we say to those people: if there is the slightest crack in your relationship with the Party, be forewarned that tomorrow you may become a saboteur and a traitor, unless you carefully repair that crack by means of full sincerity before the Party."[34]

Lion Feuchtwanger, who was present at the trial, wrote that he would not "easily forget" Radek's performance:

How he sat there in his brown suit, his ugly fleshless face framed by a chestnut-colored old-fashioned beard; how he looked over to the public, a great many of whom he knew, or at the other prisoners, often smiling, very composed, often studiedly ironical; how he laid his arm with a light and easy gesture round the shoulders of this or that prisoner as he came in; how, when he spoke, he would pose a little, laugh a little at the other prisoners, show his superiority; arrogant, skeptical, adroit, literary. Somewhat brusquely, he pushed Piatakov away from the microphone and himself took up his position there; often he smote the barrier with his newspaper, or took up his glass of tea, threw a piece of lemon in, stirred it up, and, whilst he uttered the most atrocious things, drank it in little sips. Nevertheless, he was quite free from pose whilst he spoke his concluding words, in which he admitted why he had confessed, and, despite his apparent imperturbability and the finished perfection of his wording, this admission gave the impression of being the self-revelation of a man in great distress, and it was very affecting. But most startling of all, and difficult to explain, was the gesture with which Radek left the court after the conclusion of the proceedings. It was towards four o'clock in the morning, and everyone—judges, accused, and public—was exhausted. Of the seventeen prisoners, thirteen, amongst whom were close friends of Radek, had been condemned to death, while he himself and three others had been sentenced only to imprisonment. The judge had read the verdict, and all of us had listened to it standing up—prisoners and public motionless, in deep silence. Immediately after the reading the judges retired and soldiers appeared, and first of all approached the four who had not been condemned to death. One of them laid his hand on Radek's shoulder, evidently with an order to follow him. And Radek followed him. He turned round, raised a hand in greeting, shrugged his shoulders very slightly, nodded to the others, his friends who were condemned to death, and smiled. Yes, he smiled.[35]

Radek offered himself—along with Bukharin, among other friends—as a scapegoat, a metaphor of unopposed temptation, the embodiment of forbidden thought. He may not have murdered anybody, or even conspired with any murderers, but in Bolshevism, as in Christianity or any other ideology of undivided devotion, it was the thought that counted. "You have heard that it was said, 'You shall not commit adultery.' But I tell you that anyone who looks at a woman lustfully has already committed adultery with her in his heart." The interchangeability of acts and thoughts was the main theme of Radek's exchange with the state prosecutor, A. Ia. Vyshinsky. The fact of having had sinful thoughts was proof of the reality of criminal actions, whether they occurred or not. All criminal actions were emanations of sinful thoughts—and, therefore, premeditated:

Karl Radek

VYSHINSKY: Were you for the defeat or victory of the USSR?

RADEK: All my actions during those years testify to the fact that I was helping to bring about its defeat.

VYSHINSKY: Were they conscious actions on your part?

RADEK: I have never committed an unconscious act in my life, except for sleeping (*laughter*).[36]

Bukharin, who had discovered the world without God by reading *The Adolescent*, was not the only one to think of Dostoevsky. The following morning, *Pravda* published an article by the head of its arts and literature section, I. Lezhnev (Isai Altshuler), titled "Smerdiakovs": "Sitting in the dock are the monstrous offspring of fascism, traitors to the motherland, wreckers, spies, and saboteurs—the most evil and perfidious enemies of the people. They appeared before the court in all their loathsome nakedness, and we saw a new edition of Smerdiakov, a disgusting image become flesh and blood. The Smerdiakovs of our day provoke combined feelings of indignation and revulsion. They are not just the ideologues of the restoration of capitalism, they are the moral incarnation of the fascist bourgeoisie, the product of its senile dementia, mad ravings, and creeping putrefaction."[37]

The image of nakedness was borrowed from Radek's article about the previous show trial. As Vyshinsky said in the courtroom: "Radek thought that he was writing about Kamenev and Zinoviev. But he made a slight miscalculation! This trial will correct this mistake of his: he was writing about himself!" What the nakedness revealed was that Radek, like the traitors he had helped expose, was the incarnation of a disgusting image that was the incarnation of Ivan Karamazov's thoughts. He was not what he appeared to be because he was a metaphor, a thought become flesh and blood, Mephistopheles who had betrayed himself even as he was trying to betray others. As Vyshinsky said at the trial, "he puffed away on his pipe everywhere, blowing smoke in the faces of not only his interlocutors." And as Lezhnev wrote in his *Pravda* article,

How this Jesuit, this puny, sanctimonious hypocrite with his theatrically affected Onegin persona must have been cackling to himself as he let loose his verbal fireworks and bravely fenced on the newspaper stage with his cardboard sword!

This foul, prostituted creature, spat upon and soiled by the dregs of imperialist kitchens, reeking of the stench of the diplomatic backstage—this male courtesan actually had the gall to lecture Soviet journalists and writers about high morals and class loyalty. How many millions of false words this creature has uttered, how often he has inveighed against venal bourgeois journalists! How many false praises this vilest of vile traitors has sung as he offered up his loose, streetwalker's lips for a kiss! Before the ink on his articles had a chance to dry, he would scurry over to diplomatic receptions at foreign embassies, where he had his second, real job as a lackey to his imperialist masters, and would whisper in their ears about the best way to ruin the very socialist democracy he had been praising an hour earlier.

But if, shocked by all this, you were to stop and ask yourself if such duplicity and such depth of moral depravity were indeed possible, Dostoevsky would answer you in the words of Smerdiakov:

"Pretending, sir, is not very difficult for an experienced person."[38]

Was Radek pretending during his trial? According to Lion Feuchtwanger, many of his friends in the West thought so:

And to me also, as long as I was in Western Europe, the indictment of the Zinoviev trial seemed utterly incredible. The hysterical confessions of the accused seemed to have been extorted by some mysterious means, and the whole proceedings appeared like a play staged with consummate, strange, and frightful artistry.

But when I attended the second trial in Moscow, when I saw Piatakov, Radek, and his friends, and heard what they said and how they said it, I was forced to accept the evidence of my senses, and my doubts melted away as naturally as salt dissolves in water. If that was lying or prearranged, then I don't know what truth is.[39]

Two days after Radek's verdict was announced, A. K. Voronsky, the foremost theorist of the Bolshevik as an underground man, was arrested in his House of Government apartment.[40]

■ ■ ■

On February 18, People's Commissar of Heavy Industry Sergo Ordzhonikidze committed suicide (the official announcement described the cause of death as "heart failure"). On February 20, Bukharin wrote to the Politburo announcing a hunger strike until all the accusations were lifted. "I swear to you one more time on the last breath of Ilich, who died in my arms, on my ardent love for Sergo, on everything that I hold sacred, that all this terrorism, wrecking, and alliances with Trotskyites, etc., is, in my case, vile, unprecedented slander." On the same day, he sent a letter to "dear Koba," asking him not to be angry and apologizing for having disagreed with him in the past:

As I have written before, I am guilty before you for the past. But I have expiated my guilt many times over. I truly love you now, belatedly, but deeply. I know that you are suspicious and that you are often wise in being suspicious. I also know that events have demonstrated that the level of suspicion must be increased considerably. But what about me? I am, after all, a flesh-and-blood person, entombed alive and spat on from all sides.

Above all, I wish you health. You do not age. You have iron self-control. You are a born general, destined to play the role of the victorious leader of our armies. Those will be even greater times. I wish you, dear Koba, quick and decisive victories. Hegel says somewhere that philistines judge great men based on trivialities. But even their passions are the instruments of what he calls the "World Spirit." Napoleon was the "World Spirit" on horseback. Let people see world events that are even more interesting.

Accept my greetings, my handshake, my "forgive me." In my heart I am with you all, with the Party, with my dear comrades. In my mind, I am at the graveside of Sergo, who was a marvelous, true human being.[41]

Bukharin's last hope was to reconcile the laws of history with the "flesh-and-blood person" by addressing the World Spirit as "dear Koba." According to Larina, he sat "trapped" in his room, refusing to bathe and avoiding being seen by his father. "His birds—two African lovebirds—lay dead in their cage. The ivy he planted had wilted; the stuffed birds and pictures on the walls were covered with dust." As he was writing his two letters, or perhaps soon after he finished writing them, three men walked into the apartment and ordered the family to move out of the Kremlin. At just that moment, according to Larina, the telephone rang. It was Stalin, who lived nearby.

"What's going on over there, Nikolai?" asked Koba.

"Some people are telling me to move out of the Kremlin. I don't care about staying in the Kremlin, I am only asking for some place where I could fit my library."

"Tell them to go to the devil," said Stalin and hung up.

The three man were standing near the phone, heard Stalin's words, and ran off "to the devil."[42]

Meanwhile, Rykov, according to his daughter, "kept thinking and thinking": "One day I entered the room and was startled by my father's appearance. He was sitting by the window, his back to it, in a strange, unnatural pose—with his head tilted back, his hands crossed and pressed between his crossed legs, and a tear rolling down his cheek. I don't think he even saw me, he was so engrossed in his thoughts. I could hear him saying, in a kind of drawn-out half whisper: 'Surely Nikolai couldn't really be mixed up with them, could he?' I knew that 'Nikolai' stood for 'Bukharin,' and 'they,' for those whose trial had recently ended."[43]

On February 21, Bukharin stopped eating. According to Larina, within two days he had "turned pale and gaunt, with hollow cheeks and huge dark circles under his eyes."

Finally, he gave up and asked for a sip of water. This was a great moral blow to him: a full hunger strike meant abstaining not only from food, but also from water. I was so worried about N.I.'s condition that, to give him some strength, I secretly squeezed some orange juice into the water. N.I. took the glass from my hand, got a whiff of the orange juice, and flew into a rage. The glass with the life-giving liquid flew into the corner and broke.

"You are trying to make me deceive the plenum! I won't deceive the Party!" he shouted furiously. He had never talked to me that way.

I poured him another glass of water, this time without the juice, but N.I. flatly refused to drink it.

"I want to die! Let me die here, beside you!" he added in a weak voice.[44]

He composed a letter "To the Future Generation of Party Leaders," asked Anna to memorize it, and tested her several times to make sure she had it right. He was "lowering his head," he wrote, "not before the proletarian sword, which must be ruthless but chaste," but before "an infernal machine, which, probably employing medieval methods, had acquired enormous power." The NKVD had become degenerate and could transform any Party member into a traitor. "If Stalin doubted himself for a second, the confirmation would follow immediately." History, however, was on his side. Sooner or later, it was going to "wash the dirt" off his head. "Know, comrades, that on the banner that you will be carrying on your victorious march toward Communism, there is a drop of my blood!"[45]

On the evening of February, 23 Bukharin and Rykov arrived at the Central Committee plenum devoted, in part, to the discussion of their case. According to Larina, Bukharin felt dizzy when he entered the room and sat down on the floor in the aisle. Ezhov opened the proceedings by announcing that Bukharin's and Rykov's participation in the counterrevolutionary terrorist conspiracy had been confirmed. The discussion that followed was a four-day scapegoating (*pharmakos*) ritual, in which the participants jeered, taunted, and ridiculed the selected victims, shouted and pointed fingers at them, called them "scum," "fiends," "beasts," "snakes," "vipers," "fascists," "renegades," "vile cowards," "spiteful cats," and "puffed-up little frogs," and demanded their immediate destruction and the cutting off of their "tentacles." (In Russian, *vreditel'*, or "wrecker," refers to pests and vermin, as well as saboteurs.) As the chairman of the Bashkirian Party Committee, Yakov Bykin (Berkovich), put it, "They must receive the same retribution as their accomplices, their friends from the first and second trials of the Trotskyites and Zinovievites. They must be destroyed in the same way as the Trotskyites, and those who are left alive should be kept in cages under lock and key rather than sent into exile. (*Voice from the floor:* That's right.)"[46]

Bukharin and Rykov responded in two different ways. One was to refute specific charges by providing alibis, pointing to inconsistencies, and denying knowledge of certain events and individuals. Such arguments—analogous to Bukharin's "Comrade Stalin" letters—were rejected as irrelevant: the Central Committee plenum was not a tribunal and "lawyerly behavior" was not appropriate. "But what does it mean that this is not a tribunal?" asked Bukharin. "What is the meaning of such a statement? Aren't people interpreting specific facts? Haven't eyewitness accounts and factual testimonies been circulated? Yes, they have. Aren't these factual testimonies influencing the minds of the comrades entrusted with judging and drawing conclusions? Yes, they are. (*Voice from the floor:* This is not a tribunal, this is the Party's Central Committee.) I know that this is the Party's Central Committee and not a revolutionary tribunal. But if the difference is only in name, then this is a tautology. What is the difference?" The difference, his judges told him, over and over again, was that his guilt was assumed and his job was to confess and repent, not to argue.[47]

The second line of defense was the "dear Koba" appeal to the accusers' humanity. As Bukharin said by way of explaining his hunger strike and his letter to the Politburo,

Of course, if I am not a human being, then there is nothing to understand. But I believe that I am a human being, and I believe that I have the right to my psychological state, at this extremely difficult and painful moment in my life (*Voices from the floor:* What else did you expect?), at this extremely difficult time, of which I wrote. So there was no element of intimidation or ultimatum on my part. (*Stalin:* And your hunger strike?) I have not eaten (anything) for four days. I told you and wrote to you why, in desperation, I had resorted to this. I wrote to a narrow circle of people because, with such accusations as these being leveled at me, I cannot go on living.

I cannot shoot myself with a revolver—because then people will say that I have killed myself in order to harm the Party, but if I die as if from a disease, then what do you have to lose? (*Laughter. Voices from the floor:* That's blackmail! *Voroshilov:* What disgusting behavior! How can you say such a thing? It's disgusting. Think about what you are saying.) But you must understand—it is hard for me to go on living. (*Stalin:* And for us, it's easy? And it's easy for us? *Voroshilov:* How do you like that: "I won't shoot myself, but I'll die"?) It is easy for you to talk about me this way. What do you have to lose? Because, if I am a wrecker, a son of a bitch, and so on, then why feel sorry for me? I am not asking for anything; I am simply giving you an idea of what I am thinking and feeling. If this causes any political harm, however miniscule, I will, of course, do whatever you tell me to (*laughter*). Why are you laughing? There is absolutely nothing funny about any of this.[48]

According to Larina, "he came down from the podium and sat down on the floor again, this time not because he felt weak, but because he felt like an outcast." When he came home that evening, he ate dinner—"out of respect for the plenum."[49]

The next session began with a special request from Bukharin:

BUKHARIN. Comrades, I have a very short statement to make of the following nature. I would like to apologize to the Central Committee plenum for my ill-considered and politically harmful act of declaring a hunger strike.

STALIN. That's not enough!

BUKHARIN. I can explain. I ask the plenum of the Central Committee to accept my apology because it is true that I did, in effect, present the Central Committee with a kind of ultimatum, and that ultimatum took the shape of this unusual step.

KAGANOVICH. An anti-Soviet step.

BUKHARIN. By doing this, I committed a very serious political error, which can only partially be mitigated by the fact that I found myself in an extremely agitated state. I am asking the Central Committee to excuse me and apologize sincerely for this truly unacceptable political step.

STALIN. Excuse and forgive.

BUKHARIN. Yes, yes, and forgive.

STALIN. That's better!

MOLOTOV. Don't you think that your so-called hunger strike may be seen by some comrades as an anti-Soviet act?

KAMINSKY. That's right, Bukharin, it has to be said.

BUKHARIN. If some comrades see it that way ... (*Noise in the room. Voices from the floor:* How else can it be seen? That's the only way to see it.) But, comrades, this was not my subjective intention ... .

KAGANOVICH. According to Marxism, there is no wall separating the subjective from the objective.[50]

Kaganovich was right, and Bukharin knew it (and had argued the same point himself many times before). A sinful thought was a criminal act, and a criminal act was the embodiment of a sinful thought. Bukharin did not question that; what he was trying to do (because of his exceptionally difficult situation) was to preserve a distinction between himself as a human being and himself as a politician who had committed some very serious political errors—a distinction that corresponded to the one between Comrade Stalin and dear Koba:

> I was told that I was using some kind of cunning maneuver when I wrote to the Politburo and then to Comrade Stalin, in order to appeal to his kindness. (*Stalin.* I am not complaining.) I am saying this because this question has been raised and because I have heard many reproaches or semi-reproaches about the fact that I write to Comrade Stalin a little differently from the way I write to the Politburo. But, comrades, I do not think that it is a legitimate reproach and that I should be suspected of any particular cunning.... It seems to me that this practice began under Lenin. Whenever one of us wrote to Ilich, he would ask certain questions that he would not address to the Politburo, write about his doubts and hesitations, and so on. And no one ever saw this as any kind of clever ruse.[51]

They did now. Lenin had been a two-in-one "synthesis," and the person Bukharin used to share his hesitations with had been "Ilich," not "Lenin." Comrade Stalin was indivisible, and Bukharin admitted as much by not publicly mentioning the true addressee of his personal letters. There was no "Koba" anymore, and no "human understanding" distinct from Party vigilance. As Kaganovich put it, "at first glance it may appear simple: these are just people trying to defend themselves, Bukharin and Rykov are appealing to our human understanding—'you must understand, as human beings, the position we are in,' and so on, and so forth, but in fact, comrades, this constitutes—and I would like to stress this, in particular—this constitutes a new move by the enemy. (*Voices from the floor:* Exactly!)"[52]

The chairman of the Sverdlovsk Party Committee, Ivan Kabakov, addressed Bukharin and Rykov directly:

> You have committed vile counterrevolutionary acts. You should have been in the dock answering for those acts long ago. And yet you come here with your soft little voices and tears in your eyes, weeping. For example, last night, Bukharin kept making comments and squeaking just like a mouse caught in a trap (*laughter*). His voice changed, and his expression changed, too, as if he had just emerged from a cave. Take a good look at him, members of the Central Committee, and see what a miserable person he is. (*Postyshev:* They really did live in caves at one point. Like some kind of monks!)[53]

The plenum was not a tribunal. It was a ritual performance, and Bukharin was playing the wrong part—badly. As Molotov put it,

> He knows that Tomsky's last card has been played (and lost), that everyone has understood the meaning of his suicide, and that no

one feels sorry about Tomsky's suicide. He sees that this isn't going to work, so he comes up with a new trick. He's like a tiny Jesus. Just look at him bobbing his head up and down, but then he forgets, and quits bobbing. He kept forgetting, and then he'd quit bobbing and be just fine, but whenever he'd remember, he'd start bobbing away again. (*Postyshev.* Like some kind of martyr.) . . .

Two days had passed since he declared a hunger strike, but he gave a speech here saying: "I have been fasting for four days." Didn't he even read his own letter? What a comedian he is! Bukharin, the actor. A small-time provincial actor. Who is he trying to impress? It's just a petty acting ploy. A comedy of a hunger strike. Is this the way real revolutionaries fast? This is the counterrevolutionary, Bukharin, after all. (*Stalin.* Do we have a record of how long *he* fasted?) They say he fasted for forty days and forty nights on the first day, for forty days and forty nights on the second day, and for forty days and forty nights on each day after that. This is the comedy of Bukharin's hunger strike. We were all terrified, in complete despair. And now his hunger strike is over. He is not a hunger striker at all, but simply an actor, a small-time bit player, certainly, but an actor for all that. (*Stalin.* Why did he begin his hunger strike at midnight?) I think it's because no one eats before bedtime: doctors don't recommend it.

Comrades, this whole hunger strike is a comical episode in our Party. Afterward, people will say: "That was a funny episode in the Party with Bukharin's hunger strike." Such is Bukharin's role, a role to which he has sunk. But this is not art for art's sake; this is part of the struggle against the Party. (*Voices from the floor:* Exactly!)[54]

Anything that Bukharin and Rykov said or did short of a full confession was a struggle against the Party. As Yagoda, who had stage-managed the Zinoviev trial (and who used to be Rykov's close friend), told them, "You have no more than two minutes to realize that you have been unmasked and that the only way out for you is to tell the plenum—right here, right now, and in great detail—about all of your criminal terrorist activity against the Party. But you cannot do this, since you continue to fight against us as enemies of the Party."[55]

They could not do it because they did not consider themselves guilty of criminal terrorist activity against the Party. Or rather, they considered themselves guilty objectively, in the sense of being politically responsible for the criminal terrorist activity carried out against the Party, but not subjectively, in the sense of participating in an attempt on the life of Comrade Stalin or the sale of Ukraine to Germany. One reason this line of defense did not work was that there was no wall separating the objective from the subjective. The other was that, according to the logic everyone seems to have accepted, Bukharin and Rykov had to be lying. They were not fighting for their lives yet (that would happen later, in the NKVD interrogation rooms); they were fighting for their Party membership. Party membership entailed the unconditional acceptance of Party decrees. The Party had decreed that the testimony of convicted terrorists was truthful:

> MOLOTOV. Is the testimony of the Trotskyites plausible? . . .
> BUKHARIN. When it comes to their accusations against me, it is not (*laughter, noise in the hall*). Why are you laughing, there is nothing funny about this.
> MOLOTOV, When it comes to their testimony against themselves, is it plausible?
> BUKHARIN. Yes, it is.[56]

If all the testimony was truthful by definition, how could Bukharin and Rykov be the only exception? Or, as Rykov put it, "How can I prove anything? It is clear that my political confession cannot be relied upon. How else, by what other means, can I prove anything?"[57]

The answer was that the plenum was not a tribunal. The choice, as Stalin presented it, was clear. "There are people who give truthful testimony, even when it is terrible testimony, in order to completely wash off the dirt that has stuck to them. And then there are those people who do not give truthful testimony because they have become attached to the dirt that has stuck to them and do not want to part with it." Did this mean that Rykov had no choice but to confess to something he had not done? "It is completely clear to me now," he said, "that I will be treated better if I just confess, it is clear to me, and that all my sufferings will be over, at whatever cost, as long as there is some sort of resolution."[58]

No, he did not have that choice. "What is clear?" asked Postyshev from the floor. "What sufferings? He is posing as a martyr now." The real martyrs were the people who had to put up with Bukharin's and Rykov's recalcitrance. "Radek, that scum of the earth," said the Gosplan chairman, Valery Mezhlauk, "had found the courage to say that it was he who was torturing his interrogator, not the other way around. I would like to say that no one is torturing you, but you are torturing us in the most unacceptable, despicable way. (*Voices from the floor:* That's right! That's right!) For many, many years, you have been torturing the Party, and it is only because of Comrade Stalin's angelic patience that we have not torn you apart politically for your vile terrorist activity." Comrade Stalin had been wise to let the investigation run its course, but now that there was no doubt about Bukharin's and Rykov's guilt, all they had to say was: "I am a viper, and I ask the Soviet state to destroy me as a viper. (*Voice from the floor:* That's right!)"[59]

■ ■ ■

How many more vipers were there in the Central Committee? The peculiar feature of the plenum's logic was that it applied to everyone. As Bukharin had written in his "Letter to the Future Generation of Party Leaders," "if Stalin doubted himself for a second, confirmation would follow immediately." He was wrong about Stalin: Stalin was the sacred foundation on which the entire logic was built. He was also wrong about "immediately": Bykin, Postyshev, and Mezhlauk, among others, would not be revealed as vipers for almost a year. But he was right about the connection between self-doubt and confirmation: the fact that everyone, except for Comrade Stalin, had sinned against the Party at some point, in thought or in deed, meant that everyone, except for Comrade Stalin, was objectively responsible for the criminal terrorist activity against the Party (and doomed irreparably as a result of any publicly issued accusation). One of the most prominent accusers, the former NKVD chief Genrikh Yagoda, became the accused four days later, as part of the fifth item on the plenum's agenda ("The Lessons of the Wrecking, Sabotage, and Espionage of the Japanese-German-Trotskyite Agents within the NKVD"). Another person who found himself drifting from one category to the other was Osinsky. Toward the end of the evening session on February 25, Molotov, who chaired the event, was introducing the next speaker when he was suddenly interrupted by First Secretary of Ukraine Stanislav Kosior:

MOLOTOV. The next speaker is Comrade Zhukov.
KOSIOR. Hasn't Osinsky signed up to speak?
VOICES FROM THE FLOOR. Is Osinsky going to speak?
KOSIOR. Comrade Molotov, people would like to know. Is Osinsky going to speak?
MOLOTOV. He hasn't signed up yet.
POSTYSHEV. He has been silent for a long time.
KOSIOR. Yes, for many years.[60]

The next morning, Osinsky was the first to take the floor. He had turned fifty the previous day.

OSINSKY. Comrades, I was not going to speak on this question for the following two reasons . . . (*Voices from the floor:* You're speaking now. We'll see why soon enough.) that I would like to elaborate on at the outset. (*Voices from the floor:* Interesting.) In general, I tend to speak on questions that, as it were, inspire and captivate me (*Voice from the floor:* And the struggle against the Rightists does not captivate you? *Laughter, noise*) and to which I can add something that has not been said before, something that is new to the listeners and contains something that may be significant and useful, at least from my perspective, for the Central Committee (*noise, laughter*). My dear comrades, surely you do not consider me a Rightist? Why do you start interrupting me right away? (*Shkiriatov:* Can't we simply ask you some things? *Kosior:* We don't hear from you very often.) And if you don't hear from me

Valerian Osinsky
(Courtesy of Elena Simakova)

very often, then allow me to add that the third reason I was not going to speak is that, at the previous plenum, I was the thirteenth person to sign up to speak on the agricultural question, which interests me, but my turn never came, even though thirty people spoke. (*Voices from the floor:* He feels hurt, mistreated. *Noise, laughter.*)

Anyway, this particular question not only does not inspire or captivate me, it provokes in me a feeling of utter revulsion. (*Voice from the floor:* Toward whom?) The case that is being considered is, to put it mildly, extremely unappetizing and, therefore, difficult and unpleasant to talk about, so that I have very few subjective incentives to speak on this question. . . . But since I was, so to speak, called up to the podium on the initiative of Comrades Beria, Postyshev, and others, and since I am flattered by such attention from the Central Committee, I have decided to speak. Perhaps it will be of some use.[61]

Osinsky was called up to the podium because he and Bukharin had once opposed Lenin as leaders of Left Communism. He had apologized for opposing Lenin many times before. Now he needed to apologize for doing so jointly with Bukharin:

Bukharin and I ended up as leaders of Left Communism because we had been great friends since before the Revolution. We started our Party work at the same time, did a lot together within the Party (*Voice from the floor:* Was that the only reason?), spent time in prison together, and, by the way, were very close in our political views, because, before the Revolution, I was, to use the term that has recently come into use, a Leftist, and so was Bukharin. Then, when the Revolution happened, and after a fairly long break in our relationship (Bukharin had been living in emigration, and I had been wandering around Russian provinces, in various exiles), we met again, and our friendship was renewed. Indeed, at first I had great hopes for it. It interested me and I thought that something good might come of it. But what did come of it, during the first year and a half, was our common participation in Left Communism: nothing good, in other words, as I can state now quite clearly and very sincerely (*laughter*). It was, as Lenin charitably put it in those days, "a childhood disease within Communism." For me, it was Childhood Disease No. 1, because my Childhood Disease No. 2 was Democratic Centralism.

It was a very charitable definition because there is no doubt that those "infantile disorders" of ours caused considerable damage to the working class. Our "childhood diseases" had incurred some very serious costs. In addition, they gave support to such people as Trotsky and reinforced and promoted petit bourgeois elements within the working class. (*Vareikis:* Lenin called you a petit bourgeois gone mad.) That is true, but didn't he call you the same thing, Comrade Vareikis? (*laughter*). (*Vareikis:* I was not one of them at that time. In any case, everyone knows that I was for the Brest Treaty, the whole of Ukraine knows that.) Okay, then you went mad a little later, during Democratic Centralism (*laughter*).[62]

Everyone had suffered from one or more childhood diseases, and each disease had caused considerable damage to the working class. Everyone was objectively responsible for criminal terrorist activity against the Party. Who still belonged in the Party (and why)? Osinsky had held various administrative posts in his career as a Bolshevik, but his heart "lay then, and lies now, in scholarly pursuits, and not in such work (*laughter*)." Accordingly, his defense at the plenum focused on his disagreements with Bukharin on theological matters. Once, around 1931–32, or perhaps 1933, he was walking in the Kremlin and ran into Bukharin, who asked him what he had been up to lately. When he responded that he had been studying philosophy, Bukharin told him that he had been studying philosophy, too, and that he was having difficulty understanding the concepts "objective contradiction" and "quantity becoming quality." Osinsky found Bukharin's difficulty to be "bourgeois-positivist" in nature and, when he got home that night, wrote an essay on the subject. He was going to send it to Bukharin, but then he changed his mind. "I thought to myself: 'Should I really send it if the man has such a profound and persistent misunderstanding of the most basic things about the dialectical method? After all, our views on the subject have nothing in common, so there is no point in talking, especially since we don't have anything in common in political matters, either. And someone might even think: they started by talking about theoretical matters and then moved on to joint political activities.'"[63]

The speech ended with the words: "All logical and legal prerequisites for bringing Bukharin and Rykov to trial have been met." The implication seemed to be that what had started out as a misunderstanding of Marxist dialectics had inevitably led to terrorism. Did this mean that Marxist dialectic was more important than Left Communism, so that Osinsky's and Bukharin's childhood diseases were trivial cases of measles compared to Bukharin's bourgeois-positivist cancer? Or did this mean that one did not have to be an open oppositionist to cause significant damage to the Party, so that everyone who had ever had difficulty with Marxist dialectics, which is to say, everyone with the exception of Comrade Stalin, could be brought to trial? The plenum did not rule on the matter.

On February 26, during the morning session, Bukharin and Rykov were allowed to respond. Both argued that they were human beings, as well as former oppositionists, and that there was, in fact, a wall separating the subjective from the objective:

> RYKOV. I don't know—of course it's okay to mock me. I'm finished, no doubt about it, but why mock me for no good reason? (*Postyshev.* We are not mocking you, but we do need to establish the facts.) It's terrible. (*Postyshev.* There's no need to mock you. You have yourself to blame.) I am about to finish, and I fully understand that this is my last speech at a Central Committee plenum and possibly in my whole life. But I will say once more that to confess to something I did not do or represent myself as the kind of scoundrel people here say I am, for my own or someone else's benefit, this I will never do.
>
> STALIN. Who's asking you to?
>
> RYKOV. But for God's sake, that is surely what follows? I have never been a member of any bloc, never belonged to any Rightist Center, and never engaged in any wrecking, espionage, sabotage, terror, or any other filth. And I will keep saying this for as long as I live.[64]

The mockery was not gratuitous. The point of the ritual was to prepare the victims for sacrifice. Laughter was the most effective way of making sure that the former oppositionist was no longer a human being:

> BUKHARIN. My sins before the Party are very grave. My sins were particularly grave during socialism's decisive offensive, when our group became a de facto brake and caused a great deal of damage. I confessed those sins: I confessed that between 1930 and 1932 I still had some unresolved issues that I have since recognized. But with the same force with which I admit my real guilt I deny the guilt that is being imposed on me. I will always deny it—not only because it is important to me personally, but also because I believe that one should never take on extra responsibilities, especially if neither the Party, nor the country, nor I personally need it (*noise in the room, laughter*). . . .
>
> The tragedy of my situation is that Piatakov and the rest have poisoned the atmosphere to such an extent that no one believes human emotions any more: feelings, passions, tears (*laughter*). Human behaviors that used to serve as proof, and there was nothing shameful about it, have lost their power. (*Kaganovich:* There's been too much hypocrisy!)[65]

Human emotions had always been at the heart of Bolshevism. For Sverdlov, the real day arrived when he kissed Kira Egon-Besser; for Mayakovsky, the world ended when his Gioconda was stolen; and for Postyshev and Voronsky (as well as for Sverdlov and Mayakovsky), the key to "the gates of a new kingdom" was the sheer power of hatred. For Osinsky, Hamsun's *Victoria* brought together his luminous faith, his love for Anna Shaternikova, and his friendship with Nikolai Bukharin. For Bukharin, it stood for his sacrifice for the Revolution, his love for Anna Larina, and his friendship with Aleksei Rykov. For Rykov, the "dignity" with which he conducted himself at the Sixteenth Party Congress (where the Rightists were being pilloried while Bukharin was in Crimea with Anna) had something to do with the fact that he loved Bukharin "the way even a woman who was passionately in love with [him] never could." The telephone call on December 1, 1934, changed everything. No one believed human emotions any more. Words were as powerless at expressing feelings as they were at making legal arguments.

At home in the House of Government, Rykov stopped talking almost completely. His wife had a stroke the day she heard about the death of Ordzhonikidze (whom she considered their protector) and lay in bed motionless, unable to speak. Natalia was fired from her job at the Border Guard Academy in early January and rarely left the apartment. According to her memoirs,

> During the last days of the plenum, my father would come home and walk straight into my mother's room because she was sick in bed. I remember him once saying (I remember it well—he was taking off his shoes, his face turned up, tense, the skin bluish and hanging in folds, his hands untying and loosening the shoelaces: "They want to lock me up." And then, on another occasion, "They're going to lock me up. They're going to lock me up." But this was not addressed to those present (my mother and me), the way people usually speak, but into space, without looking at us directly. In those days, he did not seem to live on Earth, among other human beings, but in some world of his own, from which a few words and thoughts would occasionally reach us.[66]

He had stopped seeing his two closest associates, Tomsky and Bukharin, after the fall of the Right Opposition. In his speech at the plenum, he said that he now believed in Tomsky's guilt. He had asked his other friend, Boris Iofan (who had recently renovated his dacha for him), not to call or come by anymore. Another friend, Yagoda, had stopped coming himself.[67] On his last day at the plenum, Rykov came home while it was still light outside:

> This time he walked straight to his room without answering any of my questions. I remember asking if the session was over or if he had left early, but he did not answer. At a loss and realizing that he was not quite himself and therefore capable of doing the wrong thing, I

called Poskrebyshev, told him that my father had come home, and asked if he was needed and if I should send him back. Poskrebyshev told me not for now, but, if necessary, he'd call. At dusk he called and said: "Go ahead and send him over now." I helped my father dress and walked him to his car, although I did not think then that he would never return. He did not go in to see my mother and did not utter a single sound the whole time. He got dressed and walked mechanically.

We spent several hours anxiously awaiting his return. At eleven the doorbell rang, and I opened the door, but it was not my father, but instead, about ten NKVD men, who spread out through the apartment and began their search. We realized that my father had been arrested. It was February 27, 1937.[68]

Bukharin, Anna, their nine-month-old son Yuri, and Bukharin's father and first wife were waiting in their Kremlin apartment. In the evening, Stalin's secretary, Poskrebyshev, called and told Bukharin that he must report to the plenum.

We said our farewells.

It is difficult to describe Ivan Gavrilovich's state. Exhausted with worry for his son, the old man had mostly kept to his bed. When the time came to say goodbye, he started having convulsions: his legs kept flying up uncontrollably and then falling back on the bed, his hands shook, and his face turned blue. He seemed on the verge of death. But then the attack passed, and he asked his son in a weak voice:

"What's happening, Nikolai? What's happening? Please explain to me!"

Before N.I. had a chance to answer, the phone rang again.

"You are delaying the plenum," said Poskrebyshev, at his Master's bidding. "Everyone is waiting for you."

I cannot say that N.I. was in a particular hurry. He said goodbye to Nadezhda Mikhailovna. Then my turn came.

It is impossible to describe the tragic moment of that terrible farewell or the pain that still lives on in my soul. N.I. fell on his knees before me and, with tears in his eyes, asked me to forgive him for ruining my life, to raise our son a Bolshevik ("definitely a Bolshevik!"), to fight for his exoneration, not to forget a single line of his letter, and to hand the text to the Central Committee when the situation improves. "Because it will definitely improve," he said. "You are young and will live to see that day. Swear to me that you will do it!" And I swore.

He rose from his knees, hugged and kissed me, and said, with great emotion:

"Whatever, you do, don't hold a grudge, Anna dear. History has occasional misprints, but truth will prevail!"

I started shaking with emotion, and I could feel my lips trembling. We knew that we were parting forever.

N.I. put on his leather jacket and his fur hat with the ear flaps, and headed for the door.

"Make sure you don't tell any lies about yourself, Nikolai!" was all I could say in farewell.

No sooner had I seen him off to purgatory and lain down for a bit than they came to search the apartment. There was no longer any doubt: N.I. had been arrested.[69]

The group of about a dozen NKVD men was led by Boris Berman, who, according to Larina, "came dressed as if to a banquet, wearing an expensive black suit and white shirt with a ring and a long nail on his little finger." The procedure, including body searches, lasted a long time. "Closer to midnight, I heard some noise coming from the kitchen and went to see what was going on. The picture I witnessed startled me. The agents had gotten hungry and were having a feast. There was not enough room around the kitchen table, so they were sitting on the floor. On the newspaper that was serving as a tablecloth, I saw a huge piece of ham and some sausage. Eggs were frying on the stove. I could hear their merry laughter."[70]

■ ■ ■

Two months later, Anna, Yuri, Ivan Gavrilovich, Nadezhda Mikhailovna, and their maid Pasha (Praskovia Ivanovna Ivanova) moved to the House of Government. They did not have to pay rent, and Pasha worked for free. Ivan Gavrilovich, who had taught math at a women's gymnasium before the Revolution, spent his days "filling sheet after sheet with algebraic formulas."[71]

Natalia Rykova, her mother, Nina Semenovna Marshak, and Glikeria Flegontovna (Lusha) Rodiukova stayed on in their large apartment (Apt. 18) on the tenth floor of Entryway 1. Since their move from the Kremlin in late fall, they had not had a chance to hang up curtains or unpack most of their books. After Rykov's arrest, Nina Semenovna regained her ability to speak and asked Natalia to read *The Brothers Karamazov* to her. Soon afterward, she went back to work in the People's Commissariat of Health (the people's commissar, Grigory Kaminsky, from Apt. 225, had been one of Rykov's accusers at the February–March Plenum). In July, two NKVD agents came with a warrant for Nina Semenovna's arrest. Natalia took out the little suitcase she used for carrying her skates and wool socks to the Gorky Park skating rink and packed her mother's nightshirt, a toothbrush, some soap, an extra summer dress ("white, with black dots"), and probably a change of underwear (she was not sure many years later). Before leaving, Nina Semenovna stopped at the door "and told me, really firmly: 'Go on living . . .' She probably wanted to say 'honestly,' that's what seemed to be coming, but stopped short and said 'the best you can.' We said goodbye and kissed. And then she left. Not a tear was shed, of course. . . . It was just the two of us, Lusha and I, left. We talked a little. I said: 'What are we going to do, Glikeria Flegontovna?' And she said: 'What are the two of us going to do here?'"[72]

They asked for permission to move and were given a room in an apartment above the Shock Worker movie theater, at the opposite end of the building. The former renter had been arrested, but his wife and two small children were still living there. Natalia and Lusha brought with them some sheets and pillowcases, a few dishes, and a small cupboard. Before leaving their old apartment, Natalia broke a plaster bust of her father and smashed it into little pieces, so strangers would not desecrate it. The carpet with her father's portrait (a present from some textile workers) was too large and heavy, so she left it behind.[73]

The Rykovs' old apartment on the tenth floor was then occupied by the Osinskys. In June 1937, Osinsky had been removed from the Central Committee and asked to move from the Kremlin to the House of Government. Following the arrests of a group of top Red Army commanders in April and May, many apartments had become vacant. The Osinskys first moved into the apartment of the commander and commissar of the Military Academy, August Kork, and then, after Natalia's and Lusha's departure, into the much bigger Rykov (formerly Radek, formerly Gronsky) apartment. When they arrived, they found Rykov's study still sealed with brown sealing wax. On the kitchen table stood a teapot with the inscription: "To Dear Aleksei Ivanovich Rykov from the Workers of Lysva."[74]

Unlike Rykov, Osinsky had all his books unpacked, sorted, and shelved. Since there was not enough space for them all, he had additional bookcases built in the middle of the room, perpendicular to one of the walls. His

wife, Ekaterina Mikhailovna Smirnova, moved into a small walk-through room. The children's former nanny, Anna Petrovna, got a room of her own. Another bedroom was given over to the children—Svetlana, who was twelve, and Valia and Rem, who were fourteen. Svetlana slept on Kork's mahogany bed, which they had brought from their previous apartment. The maid, Nastia, slept in the children's room. (Rem's father and Ekaterina's brother, the former "Democratic Centralist" Vladimir Smirnov, had been brought back from exile after Kirov's murder, sentenced to three years in prison, retried on May 26, 1937, and executed later that day, about the same time

Dima Osinsky
(Courtesy of Elena Simakova)

Dima Osinsky (*left*) and Andrei Sverdlov (*right*) with friends
(Courtesy of Elena Simakova)

the Osinskys moved into the House of Government.) The sixth and final room—counting Rykov's sealed study—belonged to the Osinskys' eldest son, Vadim ("Dima"), and his pregnant wife, Dina. Dima was a military engineer. "He loved my mother and was very close to her," wrote Svetlana, who was thirteen years younger. "As for me, I remember very little about him, except how he would half-jokingly, half-seriously call me a little bourgeois girl, rock me on his knee, where I would get a delicious whiff of his military boot, and scare me by talking about how much I loved going to the Bolshoi and how the Bolshoi chandelier had once fallen straight into the audience and probably would again."[75]

Osinsky's favorite pastime, when Dima's friends came over, was to conduct them in the singing of "In Chains" and "Martyred by Hard Servitude." One of Dima's closest friends and most frequent guests was Yakov Sverdlov's son, Andrei. Dima and Andrei had grown up as next-door neighbors in the Kremlin and studied together at the Academy. In March 1935, when Dima was twenty-three and Andrei was twenty-four, both had been arrested as part of the "Kremlin affair" investigation (after one of the suspects, D. S. Azbel, had testified that, following a 1930 meeting between Bukharin and some of his youthful supporters, Andrei had said, in Dima's and Azbel's presence: "Koba must be bumped off"). Osinsky had written to Stalin vouching for Dima; Bukharin had called Stalin pleading on behalf of Andrei (for his father's sake). Both had been promptly released.[76]

On February 2, three weeks before the February–March plenum, Osinsky had mailed his last letter to Anna Mikhailovna Shaternikova ("A.M."). Their relationship had been deteriorating along with his position within the Party leadership (which had begun to slide after Dima's arrest in March 1935). The reason, in both cases, was the apparent loss of the original wholeness, the persistent search for the guilty party, and the growing inability to trust words and feelings:

You're a strange person, A.M, above all, in the sense that we cannot have a single conversation. And the strangest thing is that you don't understand that this is, in fact, the main reason why things have not worked out between us. . . .

All our conversations invariably turn to how I am <u>guilty</u> before you for one reason or another. But this whole approach is beside the point. Human closeness is based—and can only be based—on mutual affection, on the fact that it (human closeness) brings joy and satisfaction, that people, together, do something positive for each other. This is precisely what has not been working.

Why has it not been working? Probably because both you and I have been badly damaged by adversity. For myself, I can say that, when it comes to <u>personal</u> relations with people, I have become a recluse. I live by myself, slave away at higher mathematics and think mostly about getting through it as quickly as possible (the end is in sight—only a month to a month and a half left), then getting through Hegel, and finally starting to write books again. You, too, have been damaged, by your relationship <u>with me</u>, among other things. But you don't seem to realize that that is not the only reason, and that much else has contributed to the damage. As a result, you have been taking out all of your bitterness on me and keep presenting me with demands for a reckoning.[77]

Human closeness—between lovers, as well as among Party comrades—was not a matter of moral accounting. Human closeness was a prerequisite for "insatiable utopia," which still—twenty years after he had first written to Anna—stood for "tenderness without shame" and "charity without embellishment." The problem was that twenty years earlier, it had seemed to come naturally, and now it was a matter of duty and, increasingly, guilt and innocence:

I consider mutual help among friends not a duty, but a natural thing. There is really nothing to discuss here, it is perfectly obvious. There is no such thing, nor can there be, as <u>psychological</u> duty, or duty in the realm of <u>emotion</u>, otherwise there is nothing left but boredom and frustration. In fact, the main difference between the old and the new type of marriage is that the former was a constraining duty, whereas the latter is a free union (obviously, accompanied by material obligations associated with the birth of children). But when the latter reverts to the former, it becomes clear that things are not working, and the situation is truly bad.[78]

The answer was to withdraw. In his personal life, he had become a recluse. In his Party work, he had managed to relinquish most of his administrative duties. "My continued employment in a position for which I feel an irresistible, profound, and ever growing revulsion," he wrote to Molotov on May 15, 1935, in regard to his job as head of the Main Directory of Statistics, "may have bad consequences not only for me personally, but also for the institutions in which I work." Molotov gave in, and Osinsky was transferred to the much less demanding and, for him, much more congenial directorship of the Institute of the History of Science and Technology of the Academy of Sciences.[79]

He could not hide, however, and he did not seem to want to. The "luminous faith" he had described in his 1917 letter to Anna was still there, and the reason he was studying Hegel and higher mathematics was to grasp the inner dialectic of the "insatiable utopia." He still thought of Soviet construction projects as his own children and tried to raise his children as conscious participants in the great work of construction. In the Central Committee, he voiced and defended his views about agriculture, the car industry, and other subjects that inspired and captivated him. And if Anna wanted to know why he had not broken off their relationship if he thought things were not working (or why he had not really become a recluse), he would give two answers:

> First, I kept thinking that things would work out in the end, when things got easier for you; second, because you are a good person, the kind one does not meet often in this world, and so one tries, in spite of oneself, to prolong the relationship in some form.
>
> It is really quite simple. I am not a bad person either; the problem is that I have a very difficult personality. It hasn't always been difficult—on the contrary, it used to be cheerful, sociable, and lively. But because of the circumstances, it has become difficult and unpleasant—I know it myself. But do bear in mind: your personality is just as bad. You probably weren't born this way either, but have, in fact, become this way. This is something you would do well to remember. And yet, in spite of this, you are—I am saying this truthfully and sincerely—a decent, interesting person.
>
> And since it is generally natural to want to maintain a relationship with a good, albeit difficult, person, I kept "procrastinating and muddling through," as you, I suppose, would choose to call it. But if, as we can see now, nothing is working, then, alas, nothing can be done.[80]

Nothing was working because of their difficult personalities, and their personalities had become difficult because of the times. The times—for unexplained reasons—were bad, and the worst thing about them was that conversations had become impossible.

> But as soon as I point that out, you immediately begin to ask: "Whose fault is it?" Why can't you understand the obvious—that

nothing shows more clearly that things are bad, that they're not working, than <u>that very question</u>? Against this background, every conversation becomes a legal battle—something I prefer not to engage in. In the course of this litigation, I could also argue that it's <u>your fault</u>, but I don't want to, and I'm not going to because that's not the point, and who needs it anyway. So should I try to argue that it's <u>not my fault</u>? I don't want to do that either because it would mean going back to the old, boring, "it's-your-duty" routine. The only thing left is to stop talking altogether.[81]

The letter ended with a plea to Anna not to return the money he had given her for her Marxist-Leninist education:

First become a professor of philosophy and then you can return it. And even then, there's no need. I have always felt that any money that leaves my hands is no longer mine; I live day to day; I have no use for any kind of savings, reserves, or accumulation: I am truly a Communist.

I suppose that is all. I wish you all the best possible.

V.[82]

25

THE VALLEY OF THE DEAD

The search for enemies started at the top and spread outward, from the former leaders of the world revolution to vaguely defined social and ethnic categories consisting of anonymous, interchangeable individuals. After the February–March plenum of 1937, the people's commissars were given one month to draw up detailed plans for the "liquidation of the consequences of the destructive work of saboteurs, spies, and wreckers." The people's commissar of external trade (and Arosev's former commander, from Apt. 237), Arkady Rozengolts, needed more time to "carefully consider and study the proposals concerning measures aimed at the unmasking and prevention of espionage activities." The people's commissar of internal trade (and Natalia Sats's husband, from Apt. 159), Izrail Veitser, found that the enemies of the people were responsible for shortages and lines for bread, sugar, and salt. The chairman of the Central Union of Consumer Cooperatives (and Solts's former son-in-law, from Apt. 54), Isaak Zelensky, discovered that the cooperatives he presided over had been causing supply problems and cheating customers in grocery stores. There was no longer such a thing as a mistake, accident, or natural disaster. According to the campaign's logic, any deviation from virtue—not only in human thought and deed, but in the world at large—was the result of deliberate sabotage by well-organized agents of evil.

It was the logic of magic; the logic of "traditional societies," in which misfortune is attributed to spirits or witches; the logic of all witch hunts, which return to tradition by promoting healing through acts of scapegoat sacrifice. Forces of darkness are, by definition, legion, and the darker the darkness and greater the fear, the more numerous, dangerous, and ubiquitous they are. As one of the principal promoters of the American ritual-abuse panic of the 1980s, the psychiatrist Lawrence Pazder, put it, "any position of societal power or influence should be seen as a target of infiltration." All such infiltrators are connected to each other in what another prominent ritual-abuse doctor compared to a "communist cell structure." In seventeenth-century Bamberg, the witches who had infiltrated every street and institution had the same structure. In April 1937, when the struggle against the consequences of the destructive work of saboteurs, spies, and wreckers was just beginning to gather strength, the director of the Lenin Museum and Kerzhentsev's deputy in the Committee for the Arts, Naum Rabichev, wrote a programmatic article about the persistence of evil. "All mixed together in one dirty, bloody pile are the counterrevolutionary dregs of the Trotskyites, Rightists, SRs, professional spies, White Guardists, and fugitive kulaks. This frenzied gang of capital's mercenaries tries to penetrate the most important, the most sensitive parts of the state organism of the Soviet land in order to spy, harm, and soil." Rabichev (Zaidenshner) lived in Apt. 417 with his wife (the Party secretary of the Izvestia Publishing House), his mother (whom he had forbade to teach his son German because of her Yiddish accent), his son, Vladimir (who had been "difficult" until his friends persuaded him of the value of formal education), and their maid. He had six fingers on his left hand.[1]

The Bamberg witches had served the she-devil and her associates. The Soviet wreckers worked for foreign intelligence services. "Their masters have given them the assignment to hide until the hour of the decisive battle," wrote Rabichev. "Every so often, the fascist masters check on their hirelings' whereabouts and test their ability to harm by ordering them to carry out exploratory acts of sabotage, wrecking, and murder, so that, undetected, they can continue to remain in hiding until the hour of decisive battle." Accordingly, the main targets of the police investigations were foreigners, especially Poles, Germans, and Japanese, as well as all Soviet citizens who had spent time abroad, had ethnic links to foreign countries, or had reasons to harbor resentments against the Soviet order. By the time of the Central Committee Plenum of June 23–29, Ezhov had uncovered an enormous spy network that had been operating in several regional Party organizations and People's Commissariats (including his own) and culminated in the "Center of Centers," run by Rykov, Bukharin, and other former oppositionists.

By then, Rykov, who had been in prison for four months, had begun to name names. New arrests led to new confessions and more arrests. Stalin regularly read the interrogation transcripts sent to him by Ezhov and suggested new lines of investigation. Ezhov complied with Stalin's requests and produced new suspects and new evidence. Stalin circulated some of the interrogation transcripts among the Central Committee members, including those accused of treason. On June 17, the people's commissar of health and former head of the Kolkhoz Center, Grigory Kaminsky (Apt. 225), wrote to Stalin dismissing new testimony against him and describing the suspicious behavior of the deputy commissar of health of the Russian Federation, Valentin Kangelari (Apt. 141). Kangelari was arrested on June 17. On June 25, Stalin circled Kaminsky's name (along with Khalatov's and Zelensky's) in the text of the interrogation of the deputy commissar of communications, Ivan Zhukov (who, at the February–March plenum, had called for the speedy execution of his former boss, Rykov). On the same day, Kaminsky spoke at the plenum, accusing Beria and Budenny. Later that day, Kaminsky was arrested. Khalatov and Zelensky were also arrested (but Beria and Budenny were not). By the end of the summer, most of the participants in the February–March Central Committee plenum had been jailed.[2]

The fate of arrested high officials was decided by Stalin and his closest associates. The NKVD prepared lists of those to be sentenced, dividing them into Category 1 (execution), Category 2 (ten years in prison), and Category 3 (five to eight years in prison). Category 3 disappeared after July 1937; Category 2 appeared infrequently. The lists were signed by a handful of Politburo members (who might move some names from one category to another, cross them out altogether, or make marginal comments or recommendations), returned to the NKVD, and then sent down to the Supreme Court's Military Collegium, which staged five-to-ten-minute individual trials and issued formal sentences. This procedure had been pioneered in the fall of 1936, when 585 people were condemned as a single list in the wake of the Zinoviev trial, but it did not become a regular sentencing method until the opening day of the February–March plenum, when 479 people, including Aleksandr Tivel-Levit, Radek's deputy in the Central Committee's International Information Bureau and the official Comintern historian, were marked for execution. Altogether, in 1936–38, 43,768 individuals organized into 383 lists were sentenced in this fashion, most of them to death. Of these lists, 372 were signed by Molotov, 357 by Stalin, 188 by Kaganovich, 185 by Voroshilov, 176 by Zhdanov, 8 by Mikoyan, and 5 by Kosior. Kosior himself was executed in February 1939, when the lists had been mostly discontinued.

The chairman of the Military Collegium of the Supreme Court, Vasily Ulrikh, did not live in the House of Government, but he knew many of the people he formally sentenced. His former wife's sister, Marta (Matla) Dimanshtein, an Old Bolshevik and chief editor of Moscow's Radio Committee, lived in Apt. 279, next door to the Podvoiskys, with her two children and maid. Her former husband, Semen Dimanshtein, had served as chairman of the Central Committee's Nationalities Section, director of the Institute of Nationalities, and head of the Committee for the Settlement of Toiling Jews on the Land. Both couples had separated in the 1920s but remained close and saw each other regularly. Semen was arrested on February 21, 1938, included in the "List of Individuals to Be Tried by the Military Collegium of the Supreme Court" (313 names, all Category 1) by the head of the NKVD's First Special Section, Isaak Shapiro; approved for execution by Stalin and Molotov on August 20, 1938; sentenced by Ulrikh's Collegium on August 25, 1938; and shot on the same day.[3]

∎ ∎ ∎

Sergei Mironov (Korol) had taken up his new job as head of the NKVD Directorate of West Siberia in late December 1936, two months after Frinovsky's appointment as Ezhov's deputy. He and Agnessa were accompanied by her sister Elena, her nephew Boria (Elena's son), and her niece Agulia (her brother's daughter), whom they had adopted and were raising as their own. They moved into what Agnessa described as the former governor-general's mansion. Their first visit was to West Siberian Party Secretary Robert Eikhe.

And now, picture this: Siberia, dead of winter, minus forty, and forest all around—spruces, pines, and larches. It's the middle of nowhere, the taiga, and suddenly, in the midst of all this cold and snow, a clearing, a gate, and behind it, glittering with lights from top to bottom—a palace!

We mount the stairs, are met by the doorman, who bows respectfully and opens the door for us, and then dive straight from the cold into tropical warmth. The "lackeys"—I beg your pardon—the "attendants" help us take off our coats, and it's warm, as warm as summer. We are in a huge, brightly lit antechamber. Before us is a staircase covered with soft carpet; on the left and right of each stair are vases of fresh blooming lilies. I had never seen such luxury before! Even our governor's mansion could not compare.

We walk into the hall. The walls are covered in reddish-brown silk, and then there are drapes and a table . . . Just like in a fairytale!

Eikhe himself came out to greet us. He was tall, lean, stern-looking, and said to be honest and well-educated, but too much of a courtier. He shook Mirosha's hand, but barely glanced at me. I was beautifully and tastefully dressed, but all I got was a passing glance and a rather scornful greeting. I felt the scorn immediately, and still can't quite forget it. In the hall, the table was set as it might have been in one of the Tsar's palaces. There were several women there, all "bluestockings," dressed very somberly and without a hint of makeup. Eikhe introduced us to them and to his wife, Elena Evseevna, who was wearing a conservative, but extremely well-tailored English suit. I already knew she was a highly educated woman with two academic degrees. And there I was in my lavender dress shot with gold, my neck and shoulders bare (I always thought a woman should not hide her body, but show as much as decency allowed—because it's beautiful!), and in my high heels and tasteful makeup. My god, what a contrast! In their eyes, of course, I was just an empty-headed, dressed-up doll. No wonder Eikhe had looked at me with such scorn.

At the table, though, he tried to be nice, handing me the menu first and asking what I would like to have. I had no idea, there were so many things to choose from. I admitted that I didn't know . . . So he spoke to me as if to a child, indulgently, even tenderly:

"But I do. Why don't you order the veal shank fricassee? . . .

At the table we talked about this and that—the usual banalities. How do you like Siberia? What do you think of our winter? It's very dry here, so the cold is easier to take—all the things people usually say about Siberia.

Then the men walked over to the next room to play billiards. Mirosha—thick-set, burly, broad-shouldered and Eikhe—tall, dry, and lean.[4]

Robert Eikhe

Several days later, Eikhe went on an inspection tour of Siberia's industrial region. The new director of the Kuznetsk Steel Plant, Konstantin Butenko (whose wife, Sofia, had recently distinguished herself at the first nationwide conference of the women's volunteer movement) reported that, "thanks to the direct assistance of Comrade Eikhe and the appropriate organs," various previously undiscovered enemies of the people had finally been unmasked. Typical in this respect was the case of the Novosibirsk water supply system. As Eikhe explained, "When we asked the comrades who are supposed to be in charge of these things why the water supply was not working properly, they sent us piles of paper with all sorts of general explanations. I asked them to provide more detailed explanations. They explained once, twice, but it made no sense. They explained a third time. And it still made no sense. It made no sense because people look for general explanations instead of going to the heart of the matter. . . . And when we looked into the heart of the matter, it turned out that the water supply system had become infiltrated by our sworn enemies."[5]

In the logic of magic that dominates scapegoating campaigns, the general and the particular change places. Explanations having to do with the specifics of faulty pumps and rusty pipes become general, while general claims regarding enemy infiltration become specific. In West Siberia, the inquisitor-in-chief responsible for identifying masked witches was Mironov. Upon arrival in Novosibirsk, he accelerated his predecessor's operation against the Trotskyites and extracted several important confessions. One former Red Partisan admitted that he was "a scoundrel" and a terrorist after interrogations conducted personally by both Mironov and Eikhe.[6]

That was not good enough. The head of the Central NKVD Secretariat, Yakov Deich, kept telling Mironov about the "brilliant cases" that were being sent in by other regional chiefs and warning him about Ezhov's growing impatience. According to Agnessa, Mironov "would come home late, exhausted, and I began to notice how tense he was. Up until then, he had been good at hiding his feelings about his problems at work, but now, something had started to give."[7]

Sergei Mironov
(Courtesy of Rose Glickman)

At the February–March plenum, Mironov, according to his own later claim, complained to Ezhov about the large numbers of fictitious cases he had inherited from his predecessor, V. M. Kursky. Ezhov's recommendation was to have "stronger nerves." On the same occasion, Mironov's old friend Frinovsky (now Ezhov's first deputy) allegedly told him that Ezhov was "understandably unhappy" about the slow case turnover. Upon their return to Novosibirsk, Eikhe and Mironov spoke at the regional Party meeting, which took place on March 16–18. Eikhe said that it was a disgrace that none of the economic managers had informed the NKVD of specific acts of wrecking at their enterprises. (Konstantin Butenko shouted from his seat that he had, in fact, done so on one occasion.) Mironov admitted that, during the years of collectivization, his organization had gotten used to general, as opposed to particular, methods of repression. "In those days, we had a term 'to trim,' and so we kept 'trimming' the counterrevolution and neglecting, even back then, its deep roots."[8]

As a place of exile, West Siberia was, by definition, filled with former enemies. Former enemies were, by definition, present-day terrorists. Over the course of the spring, Mironov uncovered several large terrorist networks, including the "Rightist-Trotskyite" conspiracy within the Party apparatus, the "Military-Fascist" conspiracy within the Siberian Military District, the "Russian All-Military Union" involving the remaining representatives of the tsarist privileged classes, and secret organizations among former Red Partisans, Christian "sectarians," and Menshevik and SR exiles. Some of the prisoners were interrogated by Mironov himself. One of them, the head of construction of the Turkestan-Siberia Railway, Vladimir Shatov, had known Mironov and Agnessa well from their days in Kazakhstan. According to Agnessa, "Once some prisoners had arrived, and he was informed that one of them had asked for a meeting with 'Mironov.' Mironov agreed to see him. Shatov never let on that they were acquainted. Mirosha didn't tell me what they talked about, but afterwards he was terribly upset and nervous. He couldn't sleep, kept smoking and thinking, and wouldn't answer any of my questions." Shatov had been accused of being a Japanese spy, but he persisted in denying his guilt and was not executed until October.[9]

On May 14, one day before launching a massive campaign of arrests among military commanders, Mironov addressed the members of the Fifth (Special) Section of his department:

Our task is to purge the Army of all those under our investigation. There will be more than 50 of them, maybe 100–150, or maybe more. . . . It will be a hard fight. You'll have almost no time for lunch. And when we arrest these 50–100 people, you will have to sit in your offices day and night. You will have to forget about your families, drop everything personal. There will be some whose nerves will prove too weak. Everyone will be tested. This is a battlefield. Any hesitation is tantamount to treason. . . .

I am sure we will get it done quickly. . . . Comrades, your life as a true Chekist is about to begin.[10]

By the end of 1937, the number of arrested "members of counterrevolutionary units within the Siberian Military District" had exceeded 1,100. The nerves of some of the employees of the Special Section, including its head, did prove too weak, and most of the work had to be done by the Secret Political Section. Some investigators were expelled for questionable social origins and "moral corruption" (mostly drunkenness), and some were arrested as spies and "double-dealers." Meanwhile, in Moscow and across the country, top NKVD officials who had worked under Yagoda were being exposed as traitors and replaced by Ezhov appointees. On June 6, Mironov's former boss and the sponsor and organizer of his wedding, V. A. Balitsky, received a secret order to arrest the head of the NKVD's Counterintelligence Department, Lev Mironov (Kagan), who was touring Siberia and the Far East. Within days, Balitsky and Lev Mironov arrived in Novosibirsk. According to Agnessa,

He arrived with a whole retinue: charming officers who kissed all the ladies' hands and danced beautifully. Mirosha threw a party for them. It was winter, but we had fresh vegetables from special greenhouses in Novosibirsk. They could not get enough of those vegetables—or the fruits, of course.

Mironov-the-Guest had been placed in the seat of honor. He caught sight of our Agulia (she was four at the time) and could not keep his eyes off her. He took her on his lap, gently stroked her head, and spoke softly to her as she nestled up against him. It seemed strange to me somehow: rather than flirting with the women or drinking and talking with the men, he'd turned to the child for some tenderness.

Later I said to Mirosha:

"This Mironov of yours seemed sad."

Mirosha started and said angrily:

"What gave you that idea? Why would he be sad? He was received with great respect.[11]

Several days later Lev Mironov and his entire delegation were arrested, put on a special train, and sent to Moscow. Balitsky, who had presided over the operation, had a long conversation with Eikhe and Sergei Mironov (who had helped stage it). Soon afterward, Mironov wrote to Ezhov that in the course of that conversation, Balitsky had expressed surprise at the arrest of the former head of the Kiev Military District (and one of the main proponents of the "extermination of a certain percentage" of the Cossack population in 1919), Iona Yakir, and had then gone on to say that, in the prevailing atmosphere, anyone could be arrested for any reason and confess to anything at all. On June 19, Ezhov sent Balitsky excerpts from Mironov's letter and ordered him to report to Moscow immediately. Balitsky appealed to Stalin ("I have no feelings of pity for the enemy and have personally used the most acute forms of repression efficiently and on more than one occasion"), but complied with the order and was arrested on July 7 and shot four months later.[12]

Meanwhile, Mironov, encouraged by Ezhov and Frinovsky, had been rapidly expanding the case of the Russian All-Military Union. On June 9, he reported that Japanese agents in Mongolia were stockpiling weapons and arming Buddhist lamas as part of preparations for a military rebellion centered in Siberia. On June 17, three days after the arrest of Lev Mironov, he sent Ezhov (with a copy to Eikhe) a memo describing a vast conspiracy that brought together former SRs, White officers, "and Kadet-Monarchist elements from among old regime people and reactionary circles within the professoriate and research scholars." An elaborate network of terrorist cells based in several West Siberian cities had, according to Mironov, been organized into a giant army commanded by White émigrés in Prague and Harbin and Japanese diplomats stationed in the Soviet Union. The manpower was being provided by exiled kulaks. "If one bears in mind that, on the territory of Narym District and Kuznetsk Basin, there are 280,400 exiled kulaks and 5,350 former White officers, members of punitive expeditions, and active bandits, it becomes clear how broad the foundation was upon which the insurgent work was based." So far, the arrest of 382 people had resulted in the unmasking of 1,317 members of the organization, but there was little doubt that the overall number of potential targets was going to "exceed significantly the number of participants identified up to this point." Prisons were full, the transportation of prisoners difficult, and access to Narym by boat impossible after September. The only solution, according to Mironov, was for Moscow to send down a special delegation of the military tribunal or "to give us the right to issue death sentences on SR and All-Military-Union cases by means of a simplified procedure through a special collegium of the provincial court or a special troika." ("Troikas" were the extrajudicial three-member tribunals first instituted in 1918 and widely used during collectivization for issuing death sentences to kulaks.)[13]

On June 22, Ezhov forwarded Mironov's memo to Stalin, proposing the creation, in West Siberia, of a "troika charged with the extrajudicial adjudication of cases involving liquidated anti-Soviet insurgent organizations." Six days later, the Politburo issued a decree ordering the execution of "all activists of the insurgent organization among exiled kulaks" and announcing the creation of a troika consisting of Mironov (chair), Eikhe, and the West Siberian prosecutor, I. I. Barkov. The next day, on June 29, the head of the NKVD Secretariat, Yakov Deich, sent Mironov a telegram informing him of the Politburo's decision.[14]

On July 2, the Politburo applied Mironov's West Siberian model to the Soviet Union as a whole (and launched what would become known as the Great Terror) by issuing the resolution "On Anti-Soviet Elements." On July 3, it was sent to all the local Party secretaries and NKVD chiefs:

> It has been observed that a large number of former kulaks and criminals who were deported at one time from various regions to the North and to Siberian districts and then, at the expiration of their period of exile, returned to their native provinces are the chief instigators of all sorts of anti-Soviet crimes, including sabotage, in both kolkhozes and sovkhozes, as well as in transportation and in certain branches of industry.
>
> The Central Committee of the Communist Party (Bolsheviks) directs all secretaries of provincial and territorial Party committees and all provincial and republican NKVD representatives to register all kulaks and criminals who have returned home, so that the most hostile of them may be arrested without delay and executed pursuant to an administrative decision by a troika, while the remaining, less active but nevertheless hostile elements may be listed and exiled to districts as indicated by the NKVD.[15]

On the same day, Ezhov sent a telegram to the local NKVD chiefs ordering them to divide the registered kulaks and criminals into Category 1 (execution) and Category 2 (exile) and to submit the results by July 8. Mironov was ready. On the appointed day, he reported that in 110 towns and 20 stations of his territory, the NKVD had registered 25,960 people, consisting of 6,642 kulaks and 4,282 criminals marked for execution and 8,201 kulaks and 6,835 criminals marked for exile. "Despite the large number of people subject to extraction," he wrote, "we guarantee the operational and political success of the operation." The preparations included the opening of ten new prisons for nine thousand people. (Two weeks earlier, the head of the Gulag, Matvei Berman, had ordered the clearing out of prisons by means of transferring prisoners to camps; Berman's brother-in-law, House of Government neighbor, and, since March, the NKVD chief of the Northern Province, Boris Bak, proposed to solve the problem of prison availability by registering large numbers of prisoners as enemies subject to "extraction"). Two days later, Mironov asked Ezhov for permission to pass sentences "not only on kulaks but also on all the old regime people and White Guardist and SR activists."[16]

On July 16, the local NKVD chiefs were summoned to Moscow for instructions. According to Mironov, "Ezhov gave a general political and operational directive, and Frinovsky elaborated on it and worked with each head of directorate on operational quotas." The "operational quotas" referred to the Category 1 and Category 2 targets assigned to each area. Mironov later claimed that he had told Ezhov that some prisoners were providing "highly unconvincing" testimony about their accomplices and that Ezhov had responded by saying: "Arrest them and then see; those against whom there is no evidence can be weeded out later." He also, according to Mironov, authorized the use of "physical interrogation techniques."[17]

Back in Novosibirsk, Mironov convened a meeting of the regional NKVD commanders of West Siberia and issued instructions concerning the conduct of the operation: "This operation should be considered a state secret with all the consequences that entails. As I acquaint you with the plan for the territory as a whole, any numbers you hear must, as far as possible, perish inside your head. Those who can must banish those numbers from their minds, while those who cannot must force themselves to do it anyway because anyone found guilty of divulging the overall numbers will be subject to a military tribunal."

There was no need for more than two or three interrogations per person. Confrontations with witnesses could be dispensed with. All that was required was a confession ("a single record should suffice"). The goal was "to send the troika a ready draft of the troika's resolution." The choice of particular enemies and the decision on whether to execute or imprison them was up to the regional offices: "For the first operation, the quota is 11,000 people, which means that on July 28 you must arrest 11,000 people. Or you can arrest 12,000 or 13,000, or even 15,000. Don't worry, I'm not holding you to that number. You can even arrest 20,000 under Category 1, so that later you can select the ones that are appropriate for Category 1 and the ones that need to be moved to Category 2. For Category 1 the quota we have been given is 10,800. I repeat, you can arrest as many as 20,000, so that later you can select the ones that are of particular interest."

Mironov concluded with "some technical matters." Killing large numbers of people and disposing of their bodies required careful preparation. Some "operational sectors" had to be prepared to carry out "about 1,000 and in some cases 2,000 death sentences each. So what must each operational sector head do as soon as he returns? He must find one place for carrying out the death sentence and another for burying the corpses. If it is in the forest, the turf must be cut in advance and then put back over the spot so that the place where the death sentences are carried out remains secret and does not become a place of religious fanaticism for various counterrevolutionaries and priests."[18]

According to one NKVD officer present at the meeting, Mironov's speech was met "with noisy approval from everyone in attendance, because those measures were long overdue, since our organs had not done anything substantial up to that point because of the enemy sabotage on the part of Yagoda and his accomplices." Any surprise or bewilderment would have been reflected in subsequent conversations in the hall, "the way it usually happens when something new is introduced in the way people work, but there were no such conversations."[19]

■ ■ ■

On July 30, Ezhov issued the "Operational Order of the People's Commissar of Internal Affairs of the USSR No. 00447 Concerning the Repression of Former Kulaks, Criminals, and Other Anti-Soviet Elements." The next day it was approved by the Politburo and sent out to local NKVD chiefs. Partly in response to input from local officials, including Mironov, the list of "contingents subject to repression" had been expanded beyond "former kulaks and criminals" to include members of non-Bolshevik political parties, Whites, priests, and active believers. Those placed in Category 1 were "subject to immediate arrest and, upon consideration of their cases by troikas, execution"; those placed in Category 2 were to be sentenced to eight to ten years in camps or ("the most persistent and socially dangerous among them") in prison. The troikas, modeled on the original one in West Siberia, were to consist of the local NKVD chief, Party secretary, and prosecutor. The highest quotas were assigned to Redens's Moscow Province (five thousand under Category 1; thirty thousand under Category 2) and Mironov's West Siberian Territory (five thousand under Category 1; twelve thousand under Category 2). The NKVD camps were to execute ten thousand inmates. The total for arrests was 268,950 people, 75,950 of them under Category 1. The official in charge of the operation was Mironov's old friend, the former seminarian Mikhail Frinovsky. On August 8, he sent out a special addendum to Order No. 00447: "The troikas' sentences should be announced only to Category 2 prisoners. Sentences to Category 1 prisoners are not to be announced. I repeat—not to be announced."[20]

Quotas could only be raised by permission from Ezhov. According to one campaign participant, they were "the subject of a kind of competition among many of the local NKVD commanders. The atmosphere in the commissariat was such that those regional commanders who had been able to quickly exhaust their quotas and receive new quotas from the people's commissar were considered top performers." Mironov seems to have performed well. By October 5, 1937, the West Siberian troika had sentenced 19,421 people, 13,216 of them to death. Another top performer, the head of the Moscow Province NKVD directorate (and Stalin's brother-in-law), Stanislav Redens, reported to Ezhov in mid-August that the "extraction of kulak and criminal elements" had greatly improved labor discipline and productivity in rural districts.[21]

According to Order No. 00447, the operation's purpose was "to destroy the whole gang of anti-Soviet elements in the most ruthless manner, de-

fend the working people of the Soviet Union from their counterrevolutionary schemes, and put an end, once and for all, to their vile work of sabotage against the foundations of the Soviet state." According to Frinovsky,
who knew about the importance of referring to *Don Quixote* but had not
had a chance to read it, "without such an operation, any talk about being
able to prevail over this counterrevolutionary work would have been like
tilting at watermills."[22]

Kulaks, "old regime people," and various former oppositionists were not
the only potential saboteurs. Simultaneously with the "anti-kulak" campaign, the NKVD, following Stalin's orders, conducted a series of "national
operations" directed at individuals with links to hostile neighboring
states. Most neighboring states were hostile: accordingly—and reflecting
Stalin's foreign policy preoccupations—the national operations began, on
July 25, with the German operation; continued, on August 11, with the Polish one, and went on to include, over the course of 1937 and 1938, Romanian, Latvian, Greek, Estonian, Lithuanian, Finnish, Iranian, Bulgarian,
Macedonian, Afghan, and Chinese operations, as well as a related one
against the employees of the Chinese Eastern Railway ("Harbiners"), who
had returned to the Soviet Union after the railway's sale to the Manchu-
kuo government.

Candidates for arrest were selected on the basis of ethnic belonging
(determined, in the absence of formal ascription, by a variety of means) or
any other sign of susceptibility to enticements from abroad (fluency in the
language, history of travel, correspondence with foreigners). There were
no quotas, but the lists of Category 1 and 2 prisoners (known as "albums")
were subject to approval by Ezhov and Vyshinsky or their deputies. On
March 21, 1938, Frinovsky complained to the head of the Sverdlovsk Provincial NKVD that, according to the albums received by Moscow, the 4,142
people arrested in Sverdlovsk as part of the German operation included
only 390 Germans, and that the same was true of the other national operations: 390 Poles out of a total of 4,218 arrested Polish spies; 12 Latvians out
of a total of 237 arrested Latvian spies; 42 Harbin returnees out of a total
of 1,249 arrested "Harbiners"; 1 Romanian and 96 Russians as part of the
Romanian operation; and, "with regard to the Finnish operation, not one
single Finn, but five Russians, eight Jews, and two others." The Polish operation was the largest (with 139,835 people sentenced, 111,091 executed);
the Finnish, one of the most lethal (with an execution rate of more than
80 percent); and the Latvian, the most politically and operationally sensitive because of the large number of ethnic Latvians in the security apparatus. At the same time, all borderland populations considered unreliable
were deported to the interior. The largest such operation involved the
deportation of more than 170,000 Koreans from the Far East to Kazakhstan and central Asia in September and October 1937.[23]

Overall, according to the incomplete and continually revised statistics,
between August 1937 and November 1938, when the mass operations were

halted, the operation against kulaks and anti-Soviet elements resulted in 767,397 sentences, 386,798 of them under Category 1 (as compared to the original quotas of 268,950 and 75,950, respectively). The national operations resulted in 335,513 sentences, 247,157 of them under Category 1.[24]

The key to good work on the part of NKVD officials was "ruthlessness toward the enemy." Mironov's predecessor as head of the West Siberian NKVD, V. M. Kursky, declared that what a Chekist needed was "Bolshevik fury against the Zinovievite-Kamenevist scoundrels." The head of Mironov's Secret Political Department reported that every one of his employees was "imbued with fury and hatred for the counterrevolutionary Trotskyite-Zinovievite gang." Mironov himself set the example by conducting interrogations, attending executions, arresting unreliable Chekists, and continuing to unmask enemies among high-ranking Party officials (including Eikhe's second-in-command, V. P. Shubrikov, and the chairman of the West Siberian territorial Executive Committee, F. P. Griadinsky). When, on July 31, 1937, the deputy chairman of the Secret Political Department proved insufficiently imbued with fury and shot himself in his office, an emergency Party meeting approved Mironov's report expressing "contempt for this treacherous and foul deed." And when one of the interrogators proved unable to obtain the required number of confessions, Mironov said (at a special Party meeting): "Did Kuznetsov fight against the enemies of the people? Yes, he did, but in this struggle, his legs were shaky. When an enemy makes himself out to be an innocent lamb, Kuznetsov, who is unsteady on his feet, begins to vacillate." Kuznetsov received a reprimand for "opportunist vacillation, which manifested itself in a relative lack of faith in the guilt of the enemies of the people," and was asked to retire on account of ill health.[25]

Mironov's fury was occasionally accompanied by another key Chekist trait: "Party sensitivity." Kuznetsov's mild punishment was the result of his past achievements and a sincere willingness to overcome his vacillations. And when another employee of the Secret Political Department, K. K. Pastanogov, was denounced by his colleagues for having refrained, back in 1930, from participating in the execution of his uncle, Mironov told the Party meeting: "Not every Chekist can carry out a death sentence—sometimes for health reasons, for example. Therefore, citing this episode as a reason for a direct political accusation is not quite correct, it seems to me, especially considering the fact that Pastanogov was not assigned to that firing squad. Comrade Pastanogov is the one who provided the first information about his uncle's counterrevolutionary activity. And even if Pastanogov had stated that it would be awkward for him to execute his uncle, it would not have been a violation of Party ethics, it seems to me." The Party meeting proclaimed Pastanogov "rehabilitated" and noted that, in this case, his comrades had lacked Party sensitivity.[26]

In Mironov's own case, the only person in a position to show sensitivity was his wife, Agnessa:

He had a huge billiard room at work. Sometimes I would go to his office, and if he had a free hour, we would play a game or two. Once, we were playing, and it was his turn, but he suddenly froze with the cue in his hand and turned pale. I followed his gaze. Through the enormous window of the billiard room, I could see three soldiers in service caps with red bands.

"Mirosha," I whispered. "What's wrong?"

And then I understood. "Mirosha, it's only the changing of the guard."

And, sure enough, the corporal of the guard had brought two soldiers to replace the ones in the sentry box. It was just that, for some reason, they had momentarily entered the courtyard.[27]

One of Mironov's concerns was Eikhe. The conduct of the mass operations was their joint responsibility, but the Party and NKVD jurisdictions were not clearly differentiated, and the two men's survival strategies did not always coincide. Mironov complained about Eikhe's unauthorized arrest orders, while Eikhe lobbied in behalf of his close associates, whose arrests by Mironov seemed to expose his lack of vigilance. Mironov controlled the content of the confessions produced by his office (including a number of alleged assassination attempts against Eikhe), but Eikhe had the last word on all important decisions and a direct line to Stalin. Ezhov's response when Mironov complained was that Eikhe knew what he was doing and that maintaining a good relationship with him was part of Mironov's job. Eikhe seemed to agree. The two men regularly met outside of work, sometimes in the company of their wives.[28] According to Agnessa, the Eikhes also had a smaller dacha, as "luxurious" as the palace they had first received them in, "but cozier and nicer":

Once, Mirosha and I went there, just the two of us. Eikhe and his wife were alone at the dacha (not counting the servants). She had on bright pink lounging pajamas, very informal. (I also wore pajamas at home, only they were light blue.) We had a great time, the four of us. They were a close couple, and Mirosha and I were, too.

It was not at all like the first time—very simple, unpretentious—although Eikhe's attitude toward me hadn't changed. He was probably saying to himself, "All she cares about are her outfits, unlike my wife, who has two degrees and does important Party work." He was very proud of her. . . .

They gave us a luxurious room on the second floor. True, it was a bit cold, but there were some bearskins, and we piled them on top of the covers and could have slept beautifully—it's so nice to sleep in a cold room under warm covers . . . But I woke at dawn sensing that Mirosha was awake. I was right. It was very quiet, but I listened to his breathing, and sure enough, he was awake.

"What's the matter?"

He whispered: "You know, I think my secretary is spying on me."

"Osipov? What nonsense!"

"He must have been assigned to spy on me . . ."

"Oh, Mirosha, there you go again, just like that time with the guard commander!"

I tried to cheer him up and distract him with caresses.[29]

He continued to do his job well. By August 9, he and Eikhe, assisted by the prosecutor Barkov, had sentenced 1,487 people, 1,254 of them to death. By mid-August—within three weeks of the beginning of the operation—Mironov's directorate had arrested 13,650 people. Ezhov praised West Siberia for being second in the countrywide race for the speediest destruction of the enemy underground. (The first was probably Redens's Moscow Province.) On August 15, Mironov was appointed Soviet ambassador to Mongolia.[30]

> Eikhe was impossible to recognize. This was not the same man who had received us with such pomp and circumstance in his country palace or so informally, with such affectionate condescension, in the intimate atmosphere of his forest retreat. I saw an obsequious, ingratiating man stripped of all his pride. He became extremely attentive and courteous to me. He sat beside me at the table and started talking to me about politics, China, and Chiang Kai-shek. When I confessed to him that all those Chinese-Japanese names sounded the same to me (thereby admitting my total ignorance), there was no hint of contempt or condescension in his face. He immediately changed the subject and began asking my opinion of a film he knew I'd seen. He was desperate to find some point of contact or common ground with me and, hoping I would tell Mirosha, kept repeating how sorry he was to see us go, how we had become such dear friends, how he and Mirosha had worked so well together.[31]

■ ■ ■

Three days after hearing of the new appointment, the Mironovs joined Frinovsky on a special train bound for Ulan Ude. (The rest of the journey to Ulaanbaatar had to be made by car.) The Eikhes came to the railway station to say goodbye, but Mironov, according to Agnessa, was busy talking to Frinovsky and did not even bother to respond:

> Mirosha had cheered up visibly as soon as he got wind of his coming promotion. Now all his old ambition, self-confidence, proud bearing, and reckless decisiveness were back. His eyes seemed different: they sparkled with the light of success, as if he were back in the

days of his youth doing "real work" in the struggle against counter-revolutionaries in Rostov.

All the way to Mongolia, Mirosha and Frinovsky, both former border guards, spent hours poring over maps, thinking and planning. Here's Outer Mongolia, there's Inner Mongolia, and over there is Manchuria, now occupied by the Japanese, whose goal is to pounce on Lake Baikal and separate the Far East from the rest of the Soviet Union. The Japanese had already shown their true colors: after the execution of Tukhachevsky and other high-ranking officers, they had provoked a skirmish on the Amur and occupied the Bolshoi Island.

Meanwhile, I had completely forgotten all my fears and begun to breathe more easily and to have fun again. I eagerly studied the Rules of Behavior for Soviet Plenipotentiaries Abroad, about how to dress for receptions: tuxedos, shirt fronts, cuff links made of mother-of-pearl as opposed to imitation pearl. The foreign diplomats wore diamonds; we couldn't, of course—they were too expensive—but fake pearls were tasteless and vulgar, and bound to provoke ridicule. Mother-of-pearl, now that is elegant and modest.[32]

During a stop in Irkutsk, Mironov and Frinovsky visited the local NKVD office. According to Agnessa, Mironov came back very upset. She asked him what happened:

So he told me. He and Frinovsky walked into the office of the local NKVD boss and saw a man being interrogated. He didn't say who. They were interrogating him, but he wouldn't confess. Suddenly Frinovsky punched him hard in the ear! And then started beating him! He knocked him to the floor and kicked him over and over again. Mirosha couldn't believe his eyes. As they were leaving, Frinovsky was red in the face and breathing heavily, and could barely pull himself together. Seeing Mirosha's amazement, he grinned:

"What, you don't know yet? There's been a secret order from Comrade Stalin—if the bastard doesn't confess, beat him till he does."

Remember I told you once that I sometimes ask myself: was Mirosha really an executioner? Of course, I want to believe that he was not. The incident I've just described—the impression that brutal beating made on him—that speaks in his favor, doesn't it? That must mean that up to that point, he had not used torture himself, right?[33]

It is possible that Mironov did not participate in the beatings of prisoners—or had not, up to that point. The fact of the beating in Irkutsk is confirmed by the local interrogator, I. F. Kotin, who described the scene a year and a half later: "In Irkutsk, Frinovsky listened to the reports of the department heads about the cases under investigation—and then offered to interrogate the prisoner Korshunov. In my presence and in the presence of S. N. Mironov, he began to reinterrogate him about his testimony concerning Zirnis and the other NKVD officials. Korshunov confirmed it, but then began wavering. Frinovsky started beating him—and Korshunov stated that he had falsely accused Zirnis and the other officials." Yan (Jānis) Zirnis had been the head of the East Siberian NKVD and a close colleague of Mironov's. The news of his fate may have contributed to Mironov's distress.[34]

The same fate (at about the same time) had befallen Mironov's predecessor as Soviet ambassador to Mongolia, Vladimir Tairov (Vagarshak Ter-Grigorian). Agnessa knew that Mironov owed his promotion to Tairov's arrest:

> Once, when the train stopped, Agulia and I went for a walk along the platform. We were both wearing our blue fox stoles, and I had on a wonderful little hat. It was completely empty with no one around, just one little building off to the side. Suddenly we heard a bloodcurdling shriek, a terrifying, almost inhuman howl of anguish and despair. And then, utter silence.
>
> "Agulia, did you hear that? Where did it come from?"
>
> Agulia started fantasizing about how an airplane had just flown by and how the howl must have come from there.
>
> In the train I asked Mirosha about it.
>
> "It must have been Tairov," he said, stone-faced.[35]

On August 24, 1937, Mironov and Frinovsky arrived in Ulaanbaatar. Their mission was to secure an official invitation for the Soviet Army (which had already entered the country) and to supervise the extermination of the enemies of the Mongolian people. The invitation was issued the following day. The extermination campaign began on September 10 with the arrest of sixty-five top state, Party, and military officials. On October 2, Frinovsky formed a troika chaired by Mongolian Minister of Internal Affairs Khorloogiin Choibalsan. On October 18–20, a show trial of fourteen top officials was held in Ulaanbaatar's Central Theater. Thirteen of them were sentenced to death. According to the historian Baabar, "before the sentences were pronounced, the accused were bathed and fed." Over the course of the campaign, thirty-six of the fifty-one Central Committee members elected at the most recent Party Congress were executed. Choibalsan was the only member of the Central Committee Presidium to survive Mironov's scrutiny.[36]

In accordance with the Soviet model, the purge of top officials was followed by two mass operations: the national one, directed at the Buriats, Barga Mongols, Kazakhs, and Chinese, and the social one, directed at the "feudals" and, above all, "counterrevolutionary Buddhist lamas." In 1932, Fedor Fedotov, Lyova Fedotov's father, had written a book for children about Mongolia:

> Puntsuk the Mongol hunter,
> Puntsuk the Mongol hunter,
> Puntsuk the Mongol hunter
>   Got himself a gun.
> Did a little jumping,
> Did a little shouting,
> Made the greedy lamas
>   Turn around and run.

Sergei Mironov's job was to finish what Puntsuk and Fedotov had started. On October 18, 1937, he wrote to Frinovsky (who had left for Moscow once Mironov was firmly installed and the troika had begun to function) about the "discovery of a large counterrevolutionary organization in the Ministry of Internal Affairs"; on February 13, 1938, he asked Ezhov for permission to arrest the Mongolian Trotskyites and the "Japanophile wing of the Panmongols" (among others); and on February 22, he reported on the confessions of highly placed "Khalkha nationalists" involved in the creation of a "Japanophile Altai State." By March 30, he had ordered the arrest of 10,728 people (including 7,814 lamas, 1,555 Buriats, 408 Chinese, 322 feudals, 300 ministerial officials, and 180 top military commanders) and the execution of 6,311 of them. Next on the agenda was the arrest of 6,000 lamas, 900 Buriats, 200 Chinese, and 86 ministerial officials. By April 1939, Choibalsan's troika had sentenced 20,099 people to death.[37]

As in Novosibirsk, the territory's two top officials socialized outside of work. Agnessa was a regular participant:

As head of the government, Choibalsan had a European house, where he held receptions. But in the courtyard there were two yurts, where he and his wife lived.

At one reception, I remember, they served sausage. I was trying to watch my weight and not eat any fat, so I was picking out the bits of fat and eating only the meat. Suddenly, I noticed that all the Mongolian women had started picking out their bits of fat, too. Good heavens, I thought: that's just because I'm doing it!

Choibolsan's wife was very young. I gave the hem of her robe a slight tug, shook my head, and pointed to myself, as if to say: why are you in a robe—you ought to be in a dress. So she pulled back the sleeve of her robe and stuck out her wrist, as if to say: see how thin my arms are—much too thin, and I told her: but that's a good thing—and looks pretty!

My hair was cut in the latest style that evening, and I was wearing a long cornflower blue dress. Choibalsan's wife had a gorgeous braid, with real strings of pearl woven in.

Then, at the very next reception, she shows up with her hair cut exactly like mine, in a blue evening gown! True, not of Crêpe-Georgette—you couldn't get it there—but silk. And all the other ladies had on the same blue dresses.[38]

Choibalsan personally directed the executions that followed the October show trial. Agnessa, who "was trying to introduce culture" by promoting the use of outhouses and other hygienic practices, went on an excursion to the local "Valley of the Dead":

The Mongols are Buddhists. Buddha forbade them to dig in the earth. They are herders, so they don't need to till the soil for food. Fish and dogs are holy animals to them. They are allowed to eat sheep and cows. They do not bury their dead. They wrap them in shrouds and take them to the Valley of the Dead. The sun and wind dry out the bodies. I went there once in a car with Mirosha and Frinovsky.

It was a large valley, and the field there was littered with skulls and bones. Savage wild dogs, with brightly-colored bits of cloth hanging all over them, lived on the edge of the field. When people came to dispose of a corpse, they would call these dogs (already trained for the purpose) and hang strips of cloth from their necks. Some had too many of these strips to count—which meant that they had eaten a lot of corpses. . . .

The Russians had decreed that the dead be buried in the ground. They had even dug some deep pits in the valley. But no one followed the decree.[39]

Mironov did not get a chance to finish arresting six thousand lamas (his successor, Mikhail Iosifovich Golubchik, whom he brought from Novosibirsk, did). Soon after he wrote his April 3 report on the arrests and executions, he was summoned to Moscow. Agulia had scarlet fever at the time, so she and Agnessa had to join him later:

We arrived at the Yaroslavl Station in Moscow. Agulia saw Mirosha from the window and started jumping up and down, yelling "Papa, Papa." When he entered the train, she threw herself into his arms. She was such a pale little thing, her skin looking almost transparent after her illness.

Mirosha had these wonderfully expressive, large, light-brown eyes. I had learned to read most of his feelings in them. So when our eyes met that day, I could see that he was happy, and not only because we were together again. I was dying to know what it was about, but he didn't say a word and kept smiling mysteriously. I did notice that he was wearing a beautiful, imported Chesterfield coat instead of his NKVD uniform.

There was a lot of bustle over how to unload and deliver our luggage, but none of it concerned us: it was the "lackeys'" job. We came out of the station to find a huge, luxurious car waiting for us. We got in and were whisked off through the streets of Moscow. After Ulaanbaatar, it felt like the Tower of Babel. First we passed Myasnitskaya (already renamed Kirov Street), then Dzerzhinsky Square, then Sverdlov Square. I was sure we would turn into a hotel, but no! We kept going—past Okhotny Ryad, Mokhovaia, the university, the Manege, the Big Stone Bridge . . . Where could we be going?

At last we drove into the courtyard of the House of Government, where we took an elevator to the seventh floor to a fabulous six-room apartment—and with such furnishings! Fresh flowers and fresh fruit! I looked at Mirosha, who, laughing and happy that he had pulled off the surprise, hugged me and whispered in my ear:

"Are you surprised? Don't be. I am now the Deputy Commissar of Foreign Affairs for the Far East. Take a closer look at me!"

I did, and there it was—the Lenin Medal on his chest. His eyes were shining. How well I knew that sparkle of success![40]

26

THE KNOCK ON
THE DOOR

By the time Mironov and Agnessa moved into the House of Government, about four hundred of the original residents had moved out or been moved out. Among the first to go, in early 1934, was the recently forgiven Trotskyite (and former top Civil War commissar and prosecutor at the Filipp Mironov trial), Ivar Smilga. He had lost his job in the State Planning Commission, and the family—Smilga, his wife Nadezhda Poluian, their two daughters, the daughters' nanny, and Nadezhda's friend Nina Delibash (the wife of the exiled oppositionist, Aleksandr Ioselevich)—had been asked to move across the river to a four-room apartment in 26 Gorky Street (behind the Art Theater). Smilga was still formally affiliated with the Central Committee and worked for the Academia Publishing House. Shortly before the move, he had published an introduction to a new translation of Dickens's *The Pickwick Papers*. "Our country's youth," he wrote, "will embrace everything that is useful and exciting in Dickens, while criticizing his weak points. The pedagogical role of Dickens as an artist is far from being exhausted. Our descendants will be reading him with profit and pleasure."[1]

Then, on the evening of December 1, 1934, when Smilga, Nadezhda, and the girls (fifteen-year-old Tatiana and twelve-year-old Natalia) were about to leave for a walk, the telephone rang. According to Tatiana, "Dad picked up the phone and said in an awful voice: 'Oh no! Of course. I'll be right over.' He came up to us—we were all three standing in our coats. 'My friends,' he said in a strange voice, 'Kirov has been assassinated in Leningrad.'" It was Bukharin calling from *Izvestia*; he wanted Smilga's Civil War reminiscences about Kirov for the memorial issue.[2]

A month later, on the evening of January 1, 1935, Tatiana and Natalia were in bed after a sleepless New Year's night when Smilga walked into their room and said: "Kids, I don't want you to worry, they're just picking up some of us old oppositionists." He was taken away in the morning, after a search that lasted many hours. According to Tatiana, his parting words were, "You do know you are saying goodbye to an honest man, don't you?" He was sentenced to five years in the Verkheuralsk Political Isolator (around the time Tania Miagkova was about to be released). He spent his time there studying philosophy and political economy and reading Racine and Corneille in an effort to improve his French. Nadezhda was allowed to come visit him. She asked him to swear that he had not participated in any conspiracies, but, as she later told Tatiana, he gave her such a look that she felt ashamed of herself. She was arrested herself on July 1, 1936, soon after her return to Moscow. Tatiana, Natalia, and their nanny stayed in one room; the other three were occupied by other families. Nina Delibash was also arrested, as were Smilga's brother, Pavel, and Nadezhda's brothers, Yan and Dmitry. Dmitry had been the presiding judge at Filipp Mironov's trial.

As Smilga said at the time, while arguing for the death sentence, the "terrible acts" committed by the Convention in the Vendée were "terrible from the point of view of a particular human being" but "justified by history." The other top Bolsheviks who had been involved in the de-Cossackization campaign, but were now serving in different capacities—Iona Yakir (commander of the Kiev Military District), Yakov Vesnik (director of the Krivoi Rog Steel Combine), Iosif Khodorovsky (director of the Kremlin Health and Sanitation Department), Aron Frenkel (member of the Central Committee's Control Commission), and Sergei Syrtsov (director of Chemical Plant No. 12, after being dismissed as chairman of the Council of People's Commissars of the Russian Republic in 1930) were all arrested and executed within two years of Smilga's arrest. The former commander of Trotsky's armored train, Rudolf Peterson, who was dismissed as commandant of the Kremlin after the Kremlin affair of 1935 and employed by Yakir as his deputy for supplies, was arrested a month before Yakir (on April 27, 1937). In a note to his children from prison, he wrote: "Forgive me for everything" and "It has to be this way."[3]

Smilga's closest collaborator from the time of the Mironov affair (as a fellow member of the Revolutionary Military Council of the Special Group of the Southern Front in 1919), Valentin Trifonov, was arrested on June 21, 1937. One of the accusations was his continued relationship with Smilga. Since 1932, Trifonov had been chairman of the Main Committee on Foreign Concessions, but his chief preoccupation was Soviet readiness for an imminent enemy attack. Shortly before his arrest, he had sent his new manuscript, "The Outlines of the Coming War," to Stalin and several other Politburo members but received no reply. His son Yuri was eleven at the time. He had recently passed his fifth-grade exams and was reading *The Count of Monte Cristo*, writing a short story, "Diplodocus," and planning his escape to South America. The family was living at their dacha in Serebrianyi Bor.[4]

22 June, 1937.

This morning Mom woke me up and said:
  "Yura, get up, there's something I have to tell you."
  I rubbed my eyes. Tanya sat up in her bed.

Ivar Smilga's arrest photographs

Nadezhda Smilga-Poluian and her daughters,
Natalia and Tatiana, after Smilga's arrest

Nadezhda Smilga-Poluian's arrest photographs

"Last night," Mom said, her voice trembling, "something terrible happened. Dad was arrested." And she almost started crying.

We were completely dazed.

I have no doubt that Dad will be released soon. Dad is the most honest person in the world.

Today has been the worst day of my life.[5]

During the next two months, he played a lot of tennis and read "non-stop." In early August, a new pier for passenger boats, with a café and ticket office, was opened on the Moskva not far from their dacha. On August 18, he saw a big air show and "balloons with portraits of Stalin, Molotov, Kalinin, Voroshilov and other Politburo members." On August 28, he turned twelve. His mother and grandmother gave him two sets of French colonial stamps, an album for drawing, and a thick notebook for his short stories. In the fall, he saw *A White Sail Gleams* at the Children's Theater, was elected chairman of the school literary club, finished "Diplodocus," and wrote "Dukhalli," "Toxodon Platensis," and a "purely academic paper on France" (while Lyova Fedotov was working on his "Italy" album). On September 14, his uncle, Pavel Lurye, was arrested. On December 19, his other uncle, Evgeny Trifonov, died of a heart attack. It was on January 1, 1938, that he saw *Lenin in October* ("A wonderful movie! Excellent! Magnificent! Ideal! Superb! Terrific! Very good! Exceptional!"). And in early February, he teamed up with Oleg Salkovsky (Salo) in order to challenge the Lyova Fedotov–Misha Korshunov writing duo, but ended up—somehow—writing his first realistic story, "The Rivals."

Trifonovs after Valentin Trifonov's arrest. *Left to right:* Yuri's grandmother Tatiana Slovatinskaia, Ania Vasilieva (the wife of Yuri's uncle Pavel Lurye), Yuri, his mother, his sister, his stepbrother Undik.

3 April, 1938

Last night NKVD agents came and took Mommy away. They woke
us up. Mommy was very brave. They took her away in the morning.
Today I did not go to school. Now it's only Tania and me with
Grandma, Ania, and Undik.

On the 7th we'll go with Ania to try to find out which prison
Mommy is in. This is awful.

Ania, Pavel Lurye's wife, had been living with them since her husband's
arrest. Undik was Yuri's twenty-year-old adopted brother, who had recently taken up smoking and started working in a chemistry lab.

April 8, 1938.

"Misfortunes never come singly."

My days have become completely empty. But someday this must
end. On the 6th Tania, Ania, and I went to the Fine Arts Museum.
We did not have time to see everything because Ania was in a
hurry to feed her daughter, Katia. Grandma suggested that I write
everything down, to let Mommy know how we are getting along
without her.

Today, right after school, Tania, Ania, and I went to Kuznetsky
Bridge to try to find out where Mommy is. It was a small room
with around 20 people in it. For about 30 minutes we waited for
the little window to open. All the faces were sad, mournful, and
streaked with tears. Soon the window opened, and I got into
line. When my turn came, I showed them my number, 1861, and
my school ID. They told me that Mommy was in the Butyrki
prison. On the 11th I'll go leave some money for both Mom and
Dad. At school nobody knows yet. Yesterday Tania and I went to
Natasha's birthday [Natasha was Yuri's half-sister, Valentin
Trifonov's daughter from his first marriage]. We spent about an
hour and a half there and left. Now I'm reading Tolstoy's *War
and Peace*.

I've finished my homework for tomorrow. My whole body feels
tired. And no wonder, after two hours standing up. Ania and Tania
could sit down, although Tania only did at the very end. Exams are
coming up soon, but I'll manage somehow.

Oh, I'm so-o-o-o depressed!!!

Mommy-y-y-y-y-!!!!yy!! I can't stop cr . . .

9 April, 1938

I must be strong and wait.

16 April, 1938

Yesterday I got a C in Geometry. This won't do! I need to be an even better student while Mom is away. I'm going to study a lot, I swear.

21 April, 1938

It's evening now. Grandma went out to buy some bread. Tania, Ania, and I are at home. I feel sick at heart. Mommy! I am sending you my greetings, wherever you are. Today we received a letter from Pavel. He is in Ufa, on his way to Camp Freedom. It's so depressing!
    Mommy-y-y-y-y-y-y-y!!!![6]

■ ■ ■

Aleksandr Voronsky, who, in 1927, had joined with Smilga and the other active oppositionists, had continued to serve as head of the Classics Section at State Fiction Publishers. Between mid-1932 and late 1934 (when Smilga was working on his essay on Dickens), he had published the collected works of Goethe, Balzac, Flaubert, Griboedov, Pushkin, Lermontov, A. Koltsov (no relation), Saltykov-Shchedrin, Tolstoy, Ostrovsky, and Chekhov. According to his daughter, he had "kept to himself and refused not only to speak publicly about literature, but even to attend literary meetings and conferences." He spent most of his time reading philosophy and writing fiction. As his boss put it during his purge meeting on October 21, 1933, "Aleksandr Konstantinovich has lost something in his life as a Communist, and he cannot quite find it to this day. . . . The breaking of his pen, which is a political weapon handed to him by the Party, will certainly be followed by the breaking of many other weapons and, ultimately, himself."[7]

Right after Kirov's death, he had been expelled from the Party—"for helping to organize aid for the writer Mirov, who had been exiled for anti-Soviet propaganda," for failing to mention that fact at the purge meeting of 1933, and "for concealing his ties with Zorin, who had been arrested in connection with the murder of Comrade Kirov." In May 1935, he appealed the decision to the Central Committee's Party Control Commission, claiming that his relationship with Sergei Zorin (Aleksandr Gombarg, the former secretary of the Petrograd and Briansk Party committees) had been "of a purely domestic and literary nature" and that his compassion for Mirov had been a momentary lapse:

It is true that in 1931 I gave material help to the beginning writer and anarchist Mirov. I admitted and continue to admit that I did commit that crime, having been influenced by reports that his family was in need, but I ask you to bear in mind that this help, given four years ago, was a one-time act. I have never given any help to any other exiles. Nor can I accept the accusation that I deliberately concealed my help to Mirov at my purge meeting. I simply forgot about it. When, in February this year, I was asked if I had ever given financial assistance to an exile, it was not until I got home that I, with the help of my family, remembered this fact and immediately reported it to the Party committee secretary.[8]

The Bolshevik inquisitorial procedure, like its numerous Christian, Buddhist, and post-Freudian counterparts, assumed that a wholly virtuous life was impossible, but that partial reconciliation could be achieved through confession and that an unconfessed sin could be forgiven if it was honestly forgotten, not deliberately concealed. The difference between honest forgetfulness and deliberate concealment, apparent to God, history, and perhaps an experienced interrogator, was, in most human interactions, a matter of trust. But, as Stalin would tell Bukharin at the December 1936 Central Committee plenum, after Kirov's murder, no one, even those who "volunteer to personally execute their friends," could be trusted. It was a "hellish situation": sincerity, as the events of the previous two years had demonstrated convincingly, had become a relative, and therefore irrelevant, concept.[9]

Voronsky's defense was to confess again (by recapitulating the story of his fall, first formulated at his purge meeting) and to point out that he had never made any "political mistakes" in his work as a publisher of classic literature, and that no one had ever questioned the sincerity of the "very necessary" work he was doing in crafting the literary image of the underground Bolshevik:

I have decisively broken with the opposition. The Party is dear to me. Its past, present, and future are dear to me. I am certain that, under the leadership of its Leninist Central Committee and of Comrade Stalin, the Land of the Soviets will continue its steady march toward the establishment of a socialist society.

In conclusion, I would like to say that whatever decision the Control Commission of the Central Committee reaches in my case, I will continue to think of my life as being inseparable from the Party. Unconditional obedience to Party decisions and to the Party leadership headed by its Central Committee and Comrade Stalin will remain an absolute requirement for me.[10]

The response from the Party Control Commission did not arrive for more than a year. It was negative. Voronsky was formally expelled from the Party and the Writers' Union and removed from his job at Fiction Publishers. At an interrogation conducted on January 25, 1935 (by Boris Volin's and Boris Efimov's brother-in-law, the investigator Leonid Chertok), Sergei Zorin had admitted that, "by virtue of maintaining, in 1930,

1931, and 1932, political ties with Zinoviev and Kamenev and being, on some questions, in agreement with their political views," he had acted as a "double-dealer." Since, for Party members, there was no such thing as a "domestic and literary" relationship distinct from a political one, it followed that, by virtue of maintaining, all the way through December 1934, domestic and literary ties with Sergei Zorin, Voronsky, too, had acted as a double-dealer.[11]

Voronsky did not entirely disagree. His fictionalized autobiography was about doubles: Brands and Peer Gynts, Don Quixotes and underground men, the self-doubting first-person narrator and his embodied Party nickname. The literary character of the Bolshevik Moses he had championed in the 1920s was either one character with two natures or two characters with one mission. His Lenin was both a thundering Moses and an artist with an "almost feminine tenderness toward the human being." "Double-dealing" is what had happened to Koltsov's "two faces—and only one man; not a duality but a synthesis."[12]

Around the time of Kirov's murder, Voronsky had received the proofs of his new book about Gogol. According to his daughter, Galina,

> My father became completely engrossed in that work. For a while, he could speak of nothing but Gogol. At home, on walks, and visiting friends, he would talk excitedly about various episodes from Gogol's life and work. Once, on a cold winter day, when he and I were walking around the Arbat, we stopped in front of Gogol's statue, and he said:
> "Gogol was a mysterious and strange man. There was something of the devil in him. I think I have managed to lift the curtain on his work just a little and say something new about him. But I cannot escape the feeling that he will not let me say what I want to."[13]

The key to Gogol's genius, according to Voronsky, was his dual nature, and the greatest turning point in Gogol's life was the novella "Viy," in which the "philosopher" seminarian, Khoma Brut, is assailed by the forces of darkness while he is in church in the middle of the night. "The doors tore from their hinges, and a numberless host of monsters flew into God's church. A terrible noise of wings and scratching claws filled the whole church. Everything flew and rushed about, seeking the philosopher everywhere." Khoma is protected by the circle he has drawn around himself until he is identified by the monstrous Viy with his iron face.

> "Don't look!" some inner voice whispered to the philosopher. He could not help himself and looked.
> "There he is!" Viy cried and fixed an iron finger on him. And all that were there fell upon the philosopher. Breathless, he crashed to the ground and straightaway the spirit flew out of him in terror.
> A cockcrow rang out. This was already the second cockcrow; the gnomes had missed the first. The frightened spirits rushed pell-mell

for the windows and doors in order to fly out quickly, but nothing doing: and so they stayed there, stuck in the doors and windows. When the priest came in, he stopped at the sight of such a disgrace in God's sanctuary and did not dare serve a memorial service in such a place. So the church remained forever with monsters stuck in its doors and windows, overgrown with forest, roots, weeds, wild blackthorn; and no one now can find the path to it.[14]

In the midst of the literary battles of the 1920s, Voronsky had compared his proletarian critics to "those righteous and steadfast men" who, like Gogol's philosopher seminarian, "had drawn a magic circle around themselves lest the bourgeois Viy give the Russian Revolution over to the unclean and the undead." Or had he meant to compare himself to the philosopher seminarian, and his proletarian critics, to the unclean and the undead? He was a former seminarian, after all, and they were those "everywhere-at-once young men," whose "cleverness could sometimes turn downright sinister." Or were both he and his proletarian critics doomed seminarians, assailed by the same monster? And was it not Bukharin who had first broken Voronsky's pen and then chased away the Averbakhs? And wasn't Bukharin later revealed as a double-dealer?[15]

According to Voronsky, Gogol had two natures and lived in two worlds.

The two worlds—the real world and the world of terrifying nightmares and evil spirits—struggle against each other in Gogol's work, becoming ever more vivid and drawing closer together. In *Evenings on a Farm near Dikanka* reality gets the upper hand: monsters, witches, and vile snouts enter ordinary life, but are ultimately defeated by it. Even the sorcerer in "A Terrible Vengeance" perishes in the end. In *Viy* the dead, undead, and unutterable triumph over reality and become an integral part of it. The Christian writer does not even spare the "holy place," the church. The undead get stuck in its windows.

What makes Gogol different from the philosopher seminarian is that his circle protects him even when he does look. And so he is able to stay inside it and bear witness. "The vile snouts burst in and come alive. After that, the artist's gaze is drawn inexorably toward them—for he cannot resist the temptation and looks, and sees his native land crawling with smirking monsters, and knows that there is nowhere the philosopher poet can hide." He tries to read the psalms, like Khoma Brut, but all he can see is the apocalypse. "He is like the priest who no longer dares celebrate the mass, and when he does, his words come out powerless and lifeless, and the images and characters meant to represent the sacred and reconciliation appear artificial and unconvincing. The artist's brush is strong only when it paints the devil's legions in all their picturesque and hideous monstrosity. Such is the artist's curse."[16]

In Voronsky's literary theory, all true artists are prophets with "the special gift of clairvoyance." Gogol's gift was to live in a world in which the dead souls had won—and not to give in.[17]

> The reader who pores over these glorious pages and wonders about the terrible fate of their creator may think of any number of images and comparisons. But the most terrifying of them all comes from Gogol's unfinished novel about two captives in a dungeon, a man and a woman. The smell of decay takes one's breath away; an enormous toad stares with bulging eyes; thick clumps of cobweb hang from the ceiling; human bones are strewn about. "A bat or an owl would be a beauty here." When they begin to torture the female captive, a dark, frightening voice can be heard saying: "Don't give in, Hannah!" Suddenly, a man appears: "he was alive, but had no skin. His skin had been torn from his body. He consisted entirely of boiling blood. Only the blue branches of his veins spread throughout his body. The blood was dripping from him. A mandolin on a rusty leather strap hung over his shoulder. His eyes blinked hideously in his bloody face." Gogol was that bard with the mandolin, with the eyes that had seen too much. He is the one who, in spite of himself, screamed in a dark voice, for all of Russia to hear: "Don't give in, Hannah!"
>
> For that, they skinned him alive.[18]

Who are "they"? And what happened to the "real world" in which the priest was supposed to celebrate his mass?

Voronsky spent the year 1936 waiting to be arrested. Most of his friends quit coming to see him; his daughter Galina was expelled from the Young Communist League; and the typeset of *Gogol* was destroyed at the print shop. He prepared a stack of books on philosophy to take to prison with him. According to Galina, "Father spent a lot of time writing and a lot reading, living an almost full life, and trying not to see or call even those few friends who had not deserted him." The Voronskys celebrated New Year's Eve at home. Galina remembered decorating a small New Year's tree with Mandarin oranges and listening to Jules Massenet's Élégie on the radio. At the end of January, Radek and several other defendants at the Second Moscow Show Trial confessed to having led double lives. According to Galina, Voronsky "did not doubt the truthfulness of the defendants' testimony." Two days after the verdict was announced, on February 1, 1937, Voronsky worked in the morning, went on his usual walk to Red Square before lunch, took an afternoon nap, and sat down to work again. In the evening Galina and Sima Solomonovna went down to the Shock Worker to see the last showing of Protazanov's *Without a Dowry*. They got back to their entryway around midnight:

> The guard opened the elevator door for us and gave us a long, strangely stern, searching look, but didn't say anything. From the

stairway we could see the windows of my father's study. He usually kept only his desk lamp on because he didn't like bright light. But this time the windows were brightly lit and that made me feel nervous somehow, but I didn't have time to think why. My mother opened the door with her key. A short, fat man in military uniform was standing just inside the door holding a saber, for some reason. Five or six men in uniform were conducting a search. My father was sitting on the couch. My mother and I were not allowed to sit next to him or speak to him, but we spoke anyway, despite the constant screaming of the NKVD men. It was a very thorough search, especially when it came to the books. We had an anniversary edition of Goethe's collected works, in gray leather bindings. They sliced into each binding and carefully examined it, with the NKVD man even making a pretence of asking our permission first. . . .

My father calmly and deliberately went about his preparations. Ignoring the NKVD men's objections, he took quite a few things. . . . Before leaving he asked to be allowed to drink a cup of hot, strong tea.

When we were saying goodbye, I burst into tears.

He tried to comfort me: "Make sure to finish college. If they send me into exile, you can come visit me in the summer."

I will never forget that scene: the dark hall, my father wearing his overcoat and fur hat with the ear flaps hanging down, and the large bundle in his arms.[19]

His manuscripts and books, including the proofs of *Gogol*, were arrested along with him. The arrest warrant was signed by Yakov Agranov, who was arrested himself five months later. Galina and Sima Solomonovna were moved from the House of Government to a communal apartment on 2nd Izvoznaia (Studencheskaia) Street. Galina was arrested almost immediately, in mid-March; Sima Solomonovna, in August. One of Galina's interrogators was "a very nice guy":

This young man turned out to be a huge fan of Esenin, and when he found out—this was during the interrogation—that Esenin was one of the writers I knew personally, he actually jumped in his seat: "No! Really?" Our subsequent interaction (as investigator and prisoner) consisted in our reciting to each other the verses of this forbidden, seditious poet (whom my father also liked very much) and correcting each other if either made a mistake, but whenever a third person (i.e., another NKVD officer) walked into the room,

Aleksandr Voronsky's arrest photograph

my K. (we'll call him that here) would quickly readjust his manner and shout: "Voronskaia, you'd better start testifying!"[20]

Providing testimony at about the same time were Voronsky's "proletarian" adversary but later friend and coauthor, G. Lelevich (a former Trotskyite), and the Party patron of the anti-Voronsky forces but later publisher and defender of his autobiographical writings, Semen Kanatchikov (a former Zinovievite). Just as Voronsky's memoirs represented the canonical life of the Bolshevik "student," Kanatchikov's represented that of the Bolshevik worker. Both books were proscribed after their authors' arrests. The head proletarian critic, Leopold Averbakh, was arrested on April 4, 1937. His sister, Moscow's deputy prosecutor Ida Averbakh, was arrested along with her husband, the former NKVD chief, Genrikh Yagoda. (Her book on "reforming the consciousness" of the prisoners employed in the building of the Moscow–Volga Canal had been published a year earlier.) Their mother, Yakov Sverdlov's sister Sofia, was also arrested, as was Yakov Sverdlov's brother and former deputy people's commissar of transportation, Veniamin Sverdlov. Yakov Sverdlov's son Andrei, who had been briefly arrested in 1935, was rearrested in January 1938. Sergei Zorin's interrogator, Leonid Chertok, jumped out of an eighth-floor window when his colleagues came to arrest him. His wife, Sofia Fradkina, an NKVD employee and the sister of Boris Volin and of Boris Efimov's wife, was, according to Efimov, much happier in her next marriage.[21]

∎ ∎ ∎

In January 1936, Voronsky's old friend, Tania Miagkova (Poloz), had finished her three-year term in the Verkhneuralsk Political Isolator and been sentenced to three years' exile in Kazakhstan. She had traveled to Alma Ata, where she had been told to go to Uralsk. She wrote to her mother that although Alma Ata was more interesting, Uralsk was a better option because it was closer to Moscow. She had found a job as an economist in a mechanical spare parts warehouse and rented a room in a "nondescript" house with no roof (the landlady had promised to put one on by spring), a piglet and roosters in the entryway (the landlady "had bought a rooster and a hen, but the hen had turned out to be a rooster, too") and a "dilapidated" outhouse, also with no roof. The room was "clean and pleasant," but "very petit bourgeois" (with a crystal cabinet, lace curtains, and a carpet on the wall). The windows did not open, and there were lots of wood lice. Tania was sick a lot and asked her mother to send her more clothes:[22]

Oh yes, I also wanted to let you know how I reacted to my shabby appearance when I finally crawled out of my hole into the light of day. In general, my reaction was (and still is to some extent) very subdued because of my exhaustion and my cold and also because I have been directing all my energies into achieving some essential and very practical goals. Still, my appearance did cause me some distress. My winter coat was wrinkled and stained, my boots were dirty, with patches on top of patches, and my gloves were completely worn through. My dress was also covered with patches and had a hole in the elbow, so I ended up putting on a green knit sweater that was stretched out and hung on me like a sack. It was awful! And just then some women walked by in the train in their sables, fancy shoes, cute little berets at an angle, and waves of perfume. . . . I even felt a little jealous. I had only a small, stained handmade purse for my money and a plain knotted rag for my coins. I have to confess that the first thing I bought here was a wallet. In general, I think it's better to wait and buy good quality things, but during a transition period such as the one I'm in now, one should not stand on principle, so I bought myself an oilcloth wallet for 2 rubles and 5 kopeks. I also managed to buy a cheap belt and some simple stockings for a little over two rubles. My shopping spree came to an end with the purchase of a sponge for the bathhouse, at least until I find a permanent job. Still, I believe I am much more elegant now.[23]

She still had not fixed her false front tooth. "The tooth is just there for show. When I talk or laugh, it more or less stays in place and there's no gap, but when I eat, I have to take it out. In general, my teeth are in need of major repair. I clearly need bridges in at least two different places. I am not planning on doing everything at once, but I would like to fix the front tooth as soon as possible." She wanted "to join, in that sense, the ranks of normal people (and, if possible, even a tiny bit higher than the average)." She asked her mother to knit a small beret for her. It could be dark blue, light blue, red, or black ("colors in order of preference"). In late March, her mother came to visit for two weeks. After her departure, Tania felt she had somehow lost her "taste for loneliness" ("I keep trying to convince myself, and coming up with all kinds of Herzen quotes to help, that a true human being should know how to live alone, but it isn't really working.") She also kept hoping that her daughter, Rada, would be able to come visit and perhaps stay permanently.[24]

Then, in early April, she was told to go back to Alma Ata. At first she was upset about having to look once more for a room and a job, but then she decided that whereas Uralsk was a better option because it was closer to Moscow, Alma Ata was more interesting and much more beautiful. She marveled at her own buoyancy. "I suddenly grew a bit frightened of this trait of mine: might it not lead to conforming to circumstances, rather than triumphing over them? I decided to watch myself very carefully. But, actually, come to think of it, there's no reason for panic. I simply do everything in my power to improve my circumstances and to see the good side of things when I have no control over them."[25]

The trip from Uralsk to Alma Ata took over a week, mostly by slow trains through the desert. "Such surroundings," she wrote on the fourth day, "are trying very hard to provoke in me a feeling of melancholy, but I am standing firm and sticking resolutely to the rule I use in all kinds of trials: 'Sufficient unto the day is the evil thereof.'" She was a priest's grand-daughter. The phrase came from the Sermon on the Mount, Matthew 6 (in the Old Church Slavic version):

> Therefore take no thought, saying, What shall we eat? or, What shall we drink? or, Wherewithal shall we be clothed?
>
> For after all these things do the Gentiles seek: for your heavenly Father knoweth that ye have need of all these things.
>
> But seek ye first the kingdom of God, and his righteousness; and all these things shall be added unto you.
>
> Take therefore no thought for the morrow: for the morrow shall take thought for the things of itself. Sufficient unto the day is the evil thereof.[26]

In Alma Ata, after about three weeks of searching, she found a job as an economist in the provincial Department of Internal Trade. Finding a room proved much more difficult. After several days in a hotel, she moved in with an old classmate from the Sverdlov Communist University who was also a fellow exile: "He is a very good person and in complete agreement with me when it comes to politics: firmly and unconditionally for the Party line and absolutely committed to his work, no matter how much time or effort it takes." About three weeks later, he found her another temporary room with a roommate. The room was cluttered with old books, suitcases, fur coats, and empty bottles, but she embarked on a major "reform program" and was happy with the early results. "What is remarkable is that I find things interesting and, despite the difficult circumstances, eagerly confront life in all its manifestations." She continued to read newspapers, worry about the situation in Mongolia, and enjoy walks in the Park of Culture and Rest. "Spring in Alma Ata is absolutely wonderful! The rains have ended, but it still hasn't gotten hot. The blackthorn and cherry trees are already in bloom, and the apple trees are just about to bloom. The air smells as sweet as the air in Crimea in the spring. We're surrounded by snow-covered mountains and trees. Even as I was running around wildly looking for a job, I was able to enjoy the coming of spring. I saw the movie *We Are from Kronstadt*. It's extraordinary. It held me in suspense the whole time. It is excellent and very profound. Now I dream of seeing *Chapaev*!"[27]

The biggest question was whether Rada (who was turning twelve in June) would join her at the end of the school year or two months later, after pioneer camp, and whether Tania would be able to find a permanent room for the two of them. The prospects were not very good, but, as she wrote to her mother, "I steadfastly *credo quia absurdum* [believe because it is impossible]." Meanwhile, she was developing "a taste for life outside." "Did I write to you that I have some perfume now? One bottle of 'Glorious Lilac' and one of 'Jasmine.' I love the 'Glorious Lilac,' even though it's half the price, but I'm not sure about the 'Jasmine.' I have to confess that it was not me who bought them. Do send me the crepe de Chine, Mommy dear, with Rada or by mail, although I think I'll be able to get some clothes here. The comrade I'm living with right now enjoys making dresses and is very good at it. So my Ukrainian shirt is bound to be turned into a dress at some point."[28]

Finally, everything was ready. According to Rada, "in June 1936, they bought me a ticket to Alma Ata, found some people to accompany me, packed my things, and sent a telegram with my itinerary. When they received no reply, they sent an urgent telegram with a prepaid response. The response came back immediately: 'The addressee no longer resides at this address.'" They heard from Tania about a month later. Rada remembered waking up at night when her grandmother and aunt turned on the light so they could see the map of the Soviet Union hanging over her bed. They were trying to find Nagaeva Bay.[29]

Tania had been arrested on June 14 and sentenced to five years in a labor camp. She had been sent by train to Vladivostok and from there, by boat, to Magadan, in Nagaeva Bay. Her first telegram arrived sometime in July:

My dear ones: My journey is over. I am told that it has never taken place under better weather conditions. I have now sailed on the Pacific Ocean. I spent the whole time on deck—as if I were on a nice tourist excursion, with no hint of seasickness. There were some magic moments—for example, the moonlit night on a barge in Vladivostok Bay (when we were being taken to our ship). Whatever may have happened before and after that night, I will never forget it. Nagaeva Bay is large. It is surrounded by fog-covered mountains. Everything is fine. I can see the city, too. I kiss you, my darlings. Don't worry about me, everything will be all right. Love, Tania.[30]

The first letter was sent on July 18, 1936:

I have been here for several days, not sure how many: I seem to have lost my ability to count the days. Everything is still temporary and unsettled. We will be living in the club building of the so-called Women's Detachment until we are moved to the barracks (which are not bad and do not have "alien elements"). I don't have work yet. The food is not any worse than what I've been getting over the last three years, but very monotonous: there are no vegetables at all here. If you are going to send something, send garlic, onions, and, if available, some kind of vitamins, but don't send a lot until I can start sending money (which I hope to be able to do soon). There's no scurvy here, the health care is good, and the air is wonderful. In the Women's Detachment area, we can move around freely. I have not been outside yet, but it is probably a matter of time and work. Right now I am catching up on my sleep after Alma Ata and the trip over here. I always sleep badly when I travel. The trip was good and interesting; I wish it had not ended so soon. To be honest with you, I still haven't recovered from the shock, and the atmosphere around here is not conducive to concentrated reflection. . . . But you know I am indestructible, and quite soon I'll be in good shape again.[31]

The second letter, mailed on July 29, was about the continuing uncertainty. She was hoping to get a job as a planning specialist at an auto repair plant. It seemed likely that she would stay in Magadan, the "capital" of Kolyma. This was a very good thing because Magadan had better connection to Moscow and more reliable mail service.

I don't know much about life and work in Kolyma yet. In any case, it is not an ordinary camp. In many ways, it is better, freer than most— if only it weren't so far away. . . . Mommy dear, from the tone of my letter, so different from my usual letters, you can probably tell that I am still not quite "back to normal." I won't lie to you: in spite of the fact that this camp is much freer than most, I am not overjoyed at being here and not exactly moved to repeat my favorite lines:

I'll greet the coming days as cups
Filled to the brim with milk and honey.

To be honest, I am not so sure about the milk and honey. But I'll wait and let my natural optimism take over again. It's bound to somehow, isn't it, and I'll be afloat again.[32]

The lines are from "Thyl Ulenspiegel," by Eduard Bagritsky. The poem, about one of the most popular heroes of Soviet happy childhood, ends with the epitaph: "Here lies, in peace, the jolly wanderer, who never learned to cry."

In Kolyma, Tania was reunited with Mirra Varshavskaia, her roommate from her exile in Chelkar in 1929. They had been together at the Verkhneuralsk Political Isolator, too, but they had not been on speaking terms there because Mirra had remained in opposition while Tania had embraced the Party line. In Kolyma, those differences had lost their significance.[33]

■   ■   ■

In the House of Government, disagreements over orthodoxy had lost their significance several years earlier, when open opposition became impossible. Anyone already in prison was guilty irrespective of his or her particular beliefs, past or present. Anyone still in the House of Government was suspect because no one could be trusted. Former oppositionists were guilty by virtue of having been oppositionists. The arrest of Smilga and the other former participants in the 1927 demonstration was followed by the arrest of those who had suppressed that demonstration. Grigory Moroz, who had promised to "snip off the heads" of the Leftists before being unmasked as a Rightist, was arrested on July 3, 1937, at his dacha in Serebrianyi Bor. According to his son, Samuil, who was seventeen at the time, he told his family that it was a misunderstanding and that he would be released once the facts had been established. Two months later, his wife, Fanni Lvovna Kreindel, was arrested, and his two younger sons, the fourteen-year-old Vladimir and eight-year-old Aleksandr, sent to an orphanage. Samuil was moved from Apt. 39 to Apt. 402, where he was joined by the nineteen-year-old Kolia Demchenko, the son of the people's commissar of state farms and former Party secretary of Kiev and Kharkov provinces, Nikolai Nesterovich Demchenko (who had been arrested on July 23). Kolia's eleven-year-old brother, Feliks, had been sent to an orphanage. Kolia and his wife, Tatiana, were still celebrating their honeymoon, provoking "desperate envy" on the part of Samuil. On January 28, 1938, both Samuil and Kolia were arrested.[34]

Ten days earlier, Boris Shumiatsky, who had helped Moroz disperse Smilga's demonstration (and had, since 1930, presided over the Soviet film industry), had been arrested in his House of Government apartment along with his wife, Leah Isaevna. Among his belongings listed by the arresting officers were an eight-cylinder 1936 Ford, a Schröder piano, a General Electric refrigerator, a Latin-script Royal typewriter, a Cyrillic-script Mercedes typewriter, 1,040 books, and portraits of Marx and Lenin. Yakov Agranov, who had presided over the interrogations of both the Left and Right Oppositionists, had been executed ten days earlier.[35]

Grigory Moroz with his son Samuil

The "extraction" campaign had begun to accelerate during the Central Committee plenum of June 1937. On June 17, Sergei Mironov had written to Ezhov asking for the right to issue death sentences "by means of a simplified procedure" and had proposed the creation of special troikas. On June 22, Ezhov had endorsed Mironov's proposal in a memo to Stalin. On June 23, he had opened the plenum with a report on the total infestation of Soviet institutions with terrorists and spies. Three days later, while the plenum was still in session, the NKVD arrested Deputy People's Commissar of Agriculture Aron Gaister. According to his secretary, he was summoned to the office of his boss, People's Commissar Mikhail Chernov, and was never seen again. (Chernov lived in Apt. 190, not far from the Gaister's Apt. 167.) Gaister's wife, Rakhil Kaplan, was at work in the People's Commissariat of Heavy Industry when her husband's secretary called to say that their apartment was being searched. Later that night, two NKVD agents drove over to the Gaisters' dacha in Nikolina Gora to conduct another search. Rakhil accompanied them. Inna Gaister, who was eleven at the time, woke up when two men in military uniforms walked into her bedroom and started breaking the lock on her desk. Several days later, the Gaisters' dacha and House of Government apartment were sealed. Rakhil was told to move to a four-room apartment on the fourth floor of Entryway 4, which had to be shared with the wife and three children of the recently arrested member of the Committee of Soviet Control, Viktor Karpov. The Gaisters' children—Inna, seven-year-old Natalia ("Natalka"), and one-year-old Valeria ("Valiushka")—went to their grandmother's dacha. On August 30, they moved back to Moscow in time for the beginning of the school year. They were accompanied by their nanny, Natasha. Inna turned twelve that day.

> That night they came for my mother. I woke up right away. Natasha and Valiusha woke up, too. Natalka was still asleep. Mother kept walking through the rooms with me following behind her in my nightshirt. And Natasha followed after me with Valiushka in her arms. We just kept walking like that in single file around the apartment. At some point, Mother needed to go to the bathroom. In the Karpov apartment, the door to the bathroom had a glass window, with a curtain covering it. When Mother went into the bathroom, the NKVD officer told her to open the curtain and stood watching her. When she came out, we resumed our single-file motion.
>
> I was sobbing the whole time. Mother kept saying: "Don't worry, sweetie, we're not guilty of anything. Daddy and I are not guilty of anything. I'll be back soon." At about 5 a.m. they took her away. I remember hearing some kind of noises on the stairs the whole time. My mother must not have been the only one to be picked up that night.[36]

Inna's friend, Svetlana Khalatova, returned to Moscow at about the same time. Her father, the former director of the State Publishing House

Rakhil Kaplan's arrest photographs (Courtesy of Inna Gaister)

Inna, Valeria (Valiushka), and Natalia (Natalka) Gaister after
their parents' arrest (photograph they had made to
send to their mother in the camp) (Courtesy of Inna Gaister)

and most recently chairman of the All-Union Society of Inventors, Artemy Khalatov, had been arrested on the same day as Aron Gaister. His wife (Svetlana's mother) was arrested shortly afterward. Svetlana had been in the Artek Young Pioneer Camp in Crimea. When she came back to Moscow, her grandmother told her that her parents had gone to Leningrad, but when they arrived at the House of Government, Inna Gaister, who was playing hopscotch outside, ran up to Svetlana and said: "The same thing happened to you as to us!" Svetlana and her grandmother were transferred to a three-room apartment that they had to share with the younger brother and two children of the head of the Mobilization Department of the People's Commissariat of Heavy Industry, Ivan Pavlunovsky, who had been arrested one day after Khalatov and Gaister, and the family of Gaister's former boss, Mikhail Chernov, who had been arrested on November 7. The Khalatovs and the Pavlunovskys had been neighbors in Entryway 12. Before being assigned to the People's Commissariat of Heavy Industry,

Pavlunovsky had served as the OGPU plenipotentiary in Siberia and the Caucasus. In Siberia, he had claimed to uncover a counterrevolutionary military organization consisting of White officers, SRs, and kulaks. Pavlunovsky's success had served as a model for Sergei Mironov's discovery of the White-SR-kulak alliance within the "Russian All-Military Union." Mironov's success had served as a model for Ezhov's USSR-wide campaign unveiled on June 23, four days before Pavlunovsky's arrest.[37]

■ ■ ■

The day Gaister and Khalatov were arrested, Arosev returned to Moscow from Leningrad. He had been feeling increasingly isolated and mistrusted. "The time we live in is extraordinarily frightening," he wrote in his diary on August 13, 1936. "Nobody trusts anybody, and even the very principle of a need for trust has been shaken. They are trying to replace trust with cunning. Everyone is afraid of everyone, everyone wears a frown. No one talks about what matters." Arosev's response—the same as Bukharin's— was to prove himself to history by appealing to chosen individuals. He wrote to Stalin: "I feel depressed because of the coldness and even mistrust that I sense around me. If I have done something wrong, there are two ways of dealing with me: either teach me, lift me up, give me more responsibility and more exciting, useful work, or cast me aside and let me look for new paths in a distant world" (by "distant world" he meant his life in art and, in particular, his "historical-psychological" chronicle of the Revolution). He wrote to Voroshilov: "From you, and only from you, I have always seen deep understanding and, most important, intelligent human kindness. It is not only my personal impression, but the feeling shared by everyone who has been in contact with you, directly or indirectly. That is why the affection that I, and the whole nation, have for you is suffused with a profound personal emotion." He kept trying to talk to Molotov, whose biography he was writing. He kept calling Ezhov, who, according to an entry in his diary, received him on at least one occasion (May 8, 1935):[38]

> He seemed utterly exhausted: disheveled, pale, a feverish gleam in his eyes, swollen veins in his thin hands. It's obvious that his work is more than he can take. His khaki tunic was unbuttoned. His secretary kept calling him "Kolia." She's a plump, cheerful, aging woman with a teasing manner.
>
> Ezhov looked at me sharply. I told him about VOKS's "orphanhood." He understood right away. Also understood about American Institute and immediately set things in motion. About wife's trip abroad: agreed right away. Promised to help with apartment, too.[39]

Arosev knew that the general mistrust was justified. The last part of his tetralogy (*Winter*) was going to be about "the falling off of the de facto alien

elements more interested in the process of the revolution than in its results. Trotskyites, Zinovievites. etc." On August 22, 1936, he wrote in his
diary:

> The 19th, 20th, 21st, and today: can't stop thinking about the case of
> Kamenev, Zinoviev, and the others. The Russian revolutionary move-
> ment has always contained demons as well as pure idealists. Degaev
> was a demon, Nechaev was a demon, Malinovsky was a demon, Bo-
> grov was a demon. Kamenev, Zinoviev, and Trotsky are demons. They
> are morally sick. They have a hole in place of moral fiber.
>
> Politics is not the same as ethics, but each politician has and
> must have moral principles. "Demons" do not have them; they have
> only politics.
>
> Sent a letter to Kaganovich the other day: about trust and about
> help with my application to go abroad.[40]

In his letter to Kaganovich, he wrote that he and his wife needed to
spend a month-and-a-half abroad for health reasons. "I have written all
this with the utmost sincerity and leave it up to your judgment," he concluded. "If you find it possible and expedient to help, please do. With sincere respect, yours, faithfully." Kaganovich (who had been left in charge
while Stalin was on vacation) was busy determining the degree of Bukharin's insincerity. He had no way of knowing whether Arosev was also a
demon. The permission was not granted.[41]

On November 6, Arosev's courier arrived at the People's Commissariat
of External Affairs to pick up passes to the Revolution Day parade but was
told there were none left. Arosev wrote to Litvinov and Ezhov reminding
them that he had been one of the leaders of the October insurrection in
Moscow and asking them to investigate the reason for the snub. (He
watched the parade from his House of Government balcony.) On December, 19, *Pravda* published a short notice about Arosev's recently printed
memoir, *October, 1917* (written in 1920). Titled "Advertising for the Enemy,"
it asked why Arosev had chosen to end his account with a mention of
Tomsky. "Why such touching 'concern' for a man who fought against the
Party in the ranks of its most vicious enemies?" In a response published
in *Pravda* ten days later (possibly thanks to Molotov, whom he had asked
to intercede in his behalf), he admitted that the mention of Tomsky had
been a mistake but defended the rest of the memoir as sincere and
accurate.[42]

He believed that he was being followed. According to Voronsky's
daughter, Galina Voronskaia, "once, during those months, my father ran
into his old friend, A. Arosev . . . , who pointed to a man standing nearby.
Arosev and my father were both veterans of the Bolshevik underground
and were quite good at spotting spies. My father said that the man was
probably watching him, but Arosev disagreed, saying that he had first

noticed that he was being followed several days earlier." He had recorded it in his diary. December 20: "Went for a walk in the morning. Followed by spies. At least one on every corner." December 21: "In the morning went for a walk. Spies chasing at my heels. It must seem odd to them for a man to be out just for a walk." He wrote to the Politburo about the constant feeling of being "under assault by something unjust or mistaken" and to tell them about his plan to write a novel about enemies of the people "in the form of interrogation transcripts." He wrote to Stalin on the occasion of Ordzhonikidze's death:

> Perhaps the reason I was so shocked by the news and moved to write to you, of all people, is that I talked to Sergo Ordzhonikidze on two occasions, both at moments of crisis, and met with the deep and, above all, warm understanding that only he was capable of—and that you, dear Iosif Vissarionovich, possess to an enormous degree.
>
> The feeling of loss is painful and acute. It is within me, reaching out to you. For me, for all of us, Sergo was an example and an object of awe; for you, a comrade in arms closer than a brother.
>
> Iosif Vissarionovich, please accept these lines as the sound of my heart, a spasm in my throat rather than words. Yours, Aleksandr Arosev.[43]

Perhaps Stalin was the only one left. According to Arosev's diary, Voroshilov, Ezhov, and Kaganovich were too busy and possibly incapable of a deep and warm understanding. Molotov was becoming increasingly aloof. The world of fraternal comradeship had turned into a Hobbesian state of nature. "I can't remember the last time I heard anyone say anything good, or, at least, not entirely bad, about someone else. When people talk about someone else, they look as if they were chewing and gnawing at a bleeding body. During such conversations, even their mouth movements are repulsive, rodent-like." Arosev was accused of haughtiness and asked to engage in "self-criticism."[44] On March 21, he spoke at a district meeting of Party activists and then wrote down his impressions in his diary:

> They shouted angrily, bared their teeth, asked rude questions— let themselves go and seemed happy to be beating up on an Old Bolshevik.
>
> I responded to every comment, not repenting at all (except to take responsibility for the fact that VOKS had employed some Trotskyites). I concluded by saying that I consider it my duty to tell the truth, whether they like it or not.
>
> No one clapped. Stasova and Yagoda's deputy Prokofiev were there. There was a deathly silence as I walked off the stage. I suddenly felt a chill, as if I were among people from a different social class. I thought of Esenin's "I am a foreigner in my own land."[45]

His daughters disliked their stepmother Gertrude ("Gera"), and she disliked him and his daughters. "My wife has locked herself in her apartment and says she wants a separation. Meanwhile, we are facing much greater tragedies than family troubles. Should we let them deprive us of the chance to at least talk to each other and perhaps make it easier to bear the sense of approaching catastrophe?"[46] On April 15, he was getting ready to leave for Leningrad:

> For several days now, Gera has been refusing to talk to me, coming to my apartment for lunch as if to a restaurant. Yesterday morning I broke the silence. She expressed complete indifference, said she was now fine, feeling better, and did not care at all what I thought or did. She spoke in short sentences, and looked at me as if I were an old, discarded piece of furniture. . . .
>
> When I asked: "So, does this mean the end? Does it mean we're free?" she responded: "What else did you think? Of course we're free." . . .
>
> Just as I was about to leave for the station, Gera walked in—cold and malicious, as always, without a word of greeting, her eyes like ice. The room suddenly turned arctic.
>
> She had come to look for the key to her apartment. After finding it, she disappeared without a word. I walked over to her apartment to say goodbye. With a smile like the ones you sometimes see on corpses, she held out her dry hand and shook mine. Then I left.[47]

Aleksandr Arosev, Gertrude Freund,
and their son, Mitia, in spring 1937

They continued to live together. In early summer 1937, Arosev, Gera, their two-year-old son Mitia, and Arosev's fourteen-year-old daughter Lena went to Sestroretsk, on the Gulf of Finland. (Seventeen-year-old Natalia lived with her mother, and eleven-year-old Olga was in a pioneer camp.) They stopped briefly in Leningrad on the way, and Arosev left his diaries with his sister, Augusta, who hid them at the bottom of a basket filled with firewood.[48] Lena's account begins in Sestroretsk on June 26, one day before Gaister's and Khalatov's arrests:

> One evening there was a knock on the door. Two young men in military uniform walked in, one of them a sailor. They said they had come for Gertrude and that they had an arrest order for her. Gera started to cry. My father got angry and said he would not let her go without him. They said it wasn't allowed, so he told them they would have to wait and ordered a car from the VOKS Leningrad office.
>
> To my surprise, they agreed. This was followed by a strange, unnatural pause. It felt as if life had stopped, or rather, as if a fragment had been edited out of a movie. This went on for quite a while. Finally, we heard a car honk. My father and Gera began to say goodbye. They stood huddled against each other. They were not embracing, but just stood there not moving. Maybe they were silently telling each other something, or perhaps promising . . . I don't know. They were saying goodbye. Suddenly Gera started and turned to walk to the bedroom to say goodbye to her son. She stopped and looked back . . . and I saw her face. I will never forget the look on her face as long as I live. It was pure, indescribable agony. She said softly in German: "No, I cannot do it. Lord, why do you send me such trials?" The two came up on either side and led her away, already under arrest. My father went after them, and I was left alone.

The next morning Arosev and Lena left for Moscow. From the railway station they went straight to the House of Government.

> My father spent a long time walking through the rooms, pondering something, and then came up to me and said: "When they come and ring the doorbell, don't open the door for them." I was surprised: "What do you mean? They'll break it down anyway." "Yes, of course, but we'll gain a little time." I have no idea what he intended to do: I couldn't imagine then, and I can't now. . . .
>
> My father kept pacing around the room and even tried to joke: "I've escaped from exile and prison so many times, but there's no escaping this place. Why did I have to choose an apartment on the tenth floor? I can't even jump out a window, it's so high." He kept trying to reach Molotov, but whoever answered would either hang up or breathe into the receiver without speaking. My father kept saying: "Viacha, I know it's you, I can hear you breathing, please

say something, tell me what to do!" Finally, after one of these calls, Molotov wheezed into the phone: "See that the children are taken care of," and hung up. My father said: "So this is the end," and took me, Mitia, and the nanny to our dacha in Nikolina Gora. There, after lunch, he lay down on the little couch on the terrace, took off his jacket, and covered his face and chest with it. I sat down next to him and refused to budge. Perhaps I sensed that I would never see him again. Finally, he stood up and got ready to leave. We said goodbye. Then he kissed me and said: "Lena, dear, don't worry, I'll be back in the morning. For now, you're in charge. Take care of Mitia."[49]

According to Arosev's secretary, he summoned his limousine, went to see Ezhov at the Lubyanka, and never came back. He was sentenced to death twice: the first time, on November 1, by Molotov, Stalin, Voroshilov, Kaganovich, and Zhdanov, as part of a Category 1 list that contained 292 names of former high officials, and, the second, on November 22, by Stalin and Molotov. The sentence was not formalized by Ulrikh's collegium until February 8, 1938. He was shot two days later. Gera had been shot two months before.[50]

■ ■ ■

Arosev's commander during the October uprising in Moscow, Arkady Rozengolts, had since lost his ability to walk through walls. He was arrested on October 7, 1937. His wife was arrested two weeks later. Their two daughters, ages four and six, were adopted by their maternal grandmother.

Another participant in the Moscow uprising, Osip Piatnitsky, was told at the June plenum that he had lost the Party's trust. His closest Comintern colleagues, Vilgelm Knorin (Wilhelms Knorins, from Apt. 61) and Béla Kun, were arrested during the plenum and soon started testifying against him. Piatnitsky remained in his House of Government study, pacing up and down in his socks. His wife, Yulia, kept a diary. "I really wanted to die. I suggested it to him (the two of us together), knowing it was wrong. He categorically refused, saying that he was as pure before the Party as the first snow and that he couldn't leave without first removing the stain against him." He kept calling Ezhov, asking to be allowed to see his accusers. On the night of July 2, he was summoned to Frinovsky's office for a formal confrontation. "I kept thinking about his sufferings and lay down in his study to wait for him. Finally, at 3 a.m., he came back. He was utterly exhausted and unhappy. All he said was 'Things are very bad, Yulia.' He asked for some water, and I left him." On July 6, Osip and Yulia went for a long walk around their dacha in Serebrianyi Bor. According to Yulia, it was a "gray, rainy day." She told him that life for a Bolshevik would be impossible after that, even if he were exonerated. "He asked me not to talk that way. He said, very earnestly and deliberately: 'After such words, Yulia, it

Aron Piatnitsky   Yulia Piatnitskaia

would, indeed, be better for me to shoot myself, but right now it's out of the question.'"[51] They dropped in on their dacha neighbor, the director of the Special Technology Plant of the Commissariat of Defense Industry, Ilya (Ilko) Tsivtsivadze:

> Ilko looked completely green, with bluish lips and tears in his eyes.
>
> In a quiet, trembling voice, he said: "Yesterday I was expelled from the Party." He told us how it happened.
>
> Piatnitsky was truly something to see. He forgot himself and became just a comrade: he urged Ilko not to torment himself so, comforted him, and offered advice. They parted beautifully. Ilko, shaken and unhappy, gave him his hand. Piatnitsky said: "Think of the things we have done and gone through for the sake of the Party. If the Party requires a sacrifice, no matter how hard, I will bear it all joyfully."
>
> Was he saying this to comfort Ilko or to sanctify his own last, difficult journey? I do not know . . . only the tears were choking me, and no one could have been holier or more beautiful to me at that moment than that man.[52]

The next day, on July 7, Yulia went to work. (She worked as an engineer in a design bureau.) As Yulia wrote in her diary, when Piatnitsky's chauffeur brought her back to the dacha, he told her that the car would not be available the following day. "That's when I understood that the arrest would take place very soon. I did not tell Piatnitsky about it, and we ate in oppressive silence. Piatnitsky had become a shadow of his former self and had lost half his weight. I did not act at all sentimental toward him: those last few days there was something special and otherworldly about him. He and I never discussed mundane things (everyday chores and ordinary feelings), in any case." Their sixteen-year-old son Igor was with them at the dacha. Twelve-year-old Vladimir was at the Artek Young Pioneer Camp (with Svetlana Khalatova, among others).[53]

Piatnitsky and his son Vladimir (*next to him, in the first row*)
with dacha neighbors

That night several NKVD agents came to arrest Piatnitsky. "Before I
could rise, a tall, pale, angry man ran into the room and when I tried to get
up from the bed to get my robe that was hanging in the wardrobe, he
grabbed me hard by the shoulder and pushed me back toward the bed and
away from the wardrobe. He handed me the robe and pushed me out into
the living room. I said: 'So, the black ravens have come. Bastards.' I repeated the word 'bastards' several times." One of the agents heard Yulia
and told her that Soviet citizens did not speak to state officials that way.
She kept trembling. "There were moments or perhaps seconds, I'm not
sure, when I was not aware of what was going on around me, but then I
would come to again . . . and think that I would never see him again, and
get this terrible feeling of helplessness and of the saintliness of his life,
his unstinting devotion to the cause of the working class, and here were
these people—young, rude, shoving me around . . ."

Piatnitsky came up to me and said: "Yulia, I had to apologize to them
for your behavior. Please be reasonable." I decided not to upset him
and immediately apologized to the "man." He extended his hand to
me, but I did not look at him. I took Piatnitsky's two hands in mine
but did not speak to him. That was our farewell. I wanted to kiss the
footprints he had left behind.
     I decided to wait . . . to try to be strong. Igor had not come back yet.
     Finally, Igor came. He immediately understood everything. I told
him that his father had been taken away and asked him to sleep
in his father's room, but he went upstairs to his own room. I did not
get any sleep that night. I don't know who did. I wanted desperately
to die.[54]

Car in Courtyard No. 1

The family—Igor, Yulia, her father (the former priest, whom everyone called "Grandpa"), his second wife, and their daughter—were told to leave their dacha and move from Apt. 400 to Radek's old apartment in the House. It was very hot, so they kept the windows open and could hear the loud knocking of the pump in the river below (the Big Stone Bridge was about to be moved a few hundred meters to the north). Yulia kept smelling something odd. "I've discovered that grief has a certain smell. Igor and I have the same smell, both our bodies and our hair, even though I take a bath every day. Yesterday I even scented the room, but then Grandma came in with her cigarette. She wanted to iron Grandpa's old, torn pillowcases, while he was taking his bath. Igor was ironing his sheets."[55]

■ ■ ■

On July 3, the day Arosev was arrested and Piatnitsky returned home from his confrontation, the Politburo had sent out its letter "On Anti-Soviet Elements," which extended the "extraction" campaign from the former oppositionists and state officials to "kulaks," "criminals," and "others." The arrests began to spread from the House of Government leaseholders and their immediate relatives to the families of the nannies, guards, laundresses, floor-polishers, and stairway cleaners. The German and Polish national operations, launched on July 25 and August 11, added a large new contingent to the target lists, both inside and outside the House. One such person was the former representative of the Communist Party of Poland at the Comintern, Vatslav Bogutsky (Waclaw Bogucki, Apt. 342), whose reaction to the news about Kirov's assassination had made such a strong impression on his son, Vladimir. Bogutsky was arrested on September 2. Vladimir was sent to an orphanage.[56]

On August 15, Ezhov issued Order No. 00486, mandating the arrest and imprisonment of the "wives of traitors to the motherland" and "those of their children over fifteen years of age who are socially dangerous and capable of engaging in anti-Soviet activities." The women were to be sentenced to five to eight years in special camps; the socially dangerous children, to various terms in camps, "correctional labor colonies," or "special-regime orphanages" ("depending on age, degree of danger, and likelihood of rehabilitation"). Children under fifteen were to be placed in regular orphanages; children over fifteen, in orphanages, schools, or workplaces. Adult relatives wishing to "provide full support to the orphans left behind" were "not to be prevented from doing so."[57]

Most wives and children of arrested House of Government leaseholders—including Moroz's, Trifonov's, Gaister's, Khalatov's, Voronsky's, Shumiatsky's, Piatnitsky's, and Bogutsky's—were removed from the House of Government in accordance with this law. Anna Larina was exiled to Astrakhan in June 1937 and then arrested and sent to a camp on September 20; her son was sent to an orphanage. Bukharin's first wife, Nadezhda Lukina, was arrested in their House of Government apartment on April 30, 1938 (and shot two years later). In Astrakhan, Larina had met the wives and children of the recently executed Tukhachevsky and Yakir. She had also seen Radek's wife, Roza Mavrikievna, but refused to talk to her because of Radek's testimony against Bukharin. When both were arrested a month later, Larina received a note from Roza, which said: "Believe me, with N.I. it will all be the same—a trial and false confessions." In the camp, Larina became friends with Sofia Mikhailovna Averbakh (Sverdlov's sister, Leopold Averbakh's mother, and Genrikh Yagoda's mother-in-law), who had been given permission to write to her eight-year-old grandson, Genrikh ("Garik") at the orphanage he had been sent to. According to Larina, he responded twice. The first letter said: "Dear Grandma, again I didn't die! You're the only one I've got in the world, and I'm the only one you've got. If I don't die, when I get big, and you're already very, very old, I'll work and take care of you. Your Garik." The second said: "Dear Grandma, I didn't die this time, either. I don't mean the time I already wrote you about. I keep on not dying. Your grandson."[58]

Transferred back to the Lubyanka in late 1938, Larina first found herself in the same cell with the Central Committee stenographer and, most recently, head of the Political Department of the Northern Sea Route, Valentina Ostroumova (from Apt. 436) and then with Natalia Sats, who "looked like a skinny little girl, but with gray hair" and kept saying: "Where is my Veitser? Surely my Veitser cannot really be dead?"[59]

Natalia Sats had spent the summer of 1937 in the Council of People's Commissars' sanatorium in Barvikha, outside of Moscow, going on daily boat rides and listening to Stanislavsky read new chapters from his *An Actor's Work on Himself*. On August 21, she was scheduled to meet with the recently appointed first deputy chairman of the Committee for the Arts, Naum Rabichev. Her husband had sent his limousine for her (she had her own, but Veitser's was much better). According to her memoirs, in Rabichev's waiting room, there was another person ("a modest, dark-haired young man"), but she was invited in first:

> I enter. He meets me at the door and nods toward the chair facing his. Comrade Rabichev is short. He is almost drowning in the large, oversized armchair. The conversation starts very formally: the chairman asks me to report on my theater's repertoire for the season. I answer eagerly: our plans are well thought through and, I believe, interesting.
>
> There is a notebook in front of him. His right hand is holding a pencil. But he is not writing anything down. He is looking somewhere beyond me. In an indifferent tone of voice, he forces out another question or two.
>
> Suddenly, I notice his left hand. It is resting on the desk opposite his right one. It is small and has—six fingers. I am gripped by fear. No, it cannot be. But yes! One, two, three, four, five, six! Six! Can it be? My nerves must be playing tricks on me.
>
> The chairman has no more questions to ask. He says goodbye.
>
> "Enjoy the rest of your vacation."

In the lobby, she was approached by the dark-haired man, who had been waiting outside. He said he would like to help her clear up some misunderstanding and drove her to the Lubyanka Prison. She was sentenced to five years in a camp for family members of traitors to the motherland. Veitser was arrested two months later. [60]

It had been five months since Rabichev published his article about the counterrevolutionary dregs; three weeks since his closest friend, the former head of the Military Political Academy Boris Ippo, was arrested; and a few days since his son Vladimir left for the School of Aviation in Irkutsk (instead of the History Department at Moscow University, because his father felt that he was spoiled and needed some discipline). Rabichev's main job at the time, as both first deputy chairman of the Committee for the Arts and director of the Lenin Museum, was to prepare the celebrations of the twentieth anniversary of the October Revolution and supervise the depiction of Lenin in film and on stage. Things did not go perfectly smoothly, and on January 15, 1938, the committee's head, Platon Kerzhentsev, was fired and presumed arrested (in part because of an unauthorized appearance of Stalin as an episodic character in N. F. Pogodin's *The Man with the Gun* at the Vakhtangov Theater). On January 21, Rabichev made a speech on the occasion of the thirteenth anniversary of Lenin's death. On

January 24, he shot himself in his study in the House of Government. His wife and mother-in-law were at home at the time.[61]

Rykov's daughter Natalia was, like Anna Larina, first exiled (in her case, to Tomsk) and then arrested. She left the House of Government on September 27, four days after the arrest of Ivan Kuchmin—the prototype for Leonid Leonov's Aleksei Kurilov in *The Road to Ocean*. Kuchmin's family (wife, sister-in-law, and two children) were exiled to Yaroslavl, where they slept in doorways until Kuchmin's wife, Stefania Arkhi-povna, got a job in the provincial education de-

Naum Rabichev

partment. Kuchmin's boss, the director of the Central Administration of Railroad Construction and former director of Berezniki Chemical Works, Mikhail Granovsky, was arrested several days later (soon after the family came back from a trip to Sochi). According to his son, Anatoly, who was fifteen at the time,

On November 5, 1937, my father returned from his office at about 11 o'clock at night, earlier than he usually did. He had with him our pass cards for attendance at the parades on the seventh as well as an invitation to the celebrations at the Bolshoi Theater commemorating the twentieth anniversary of the Revolution. This was to be on the morrow, which would coincide with my father's birthday.

Tired after a hard day's work, he took a glass of vodka and together with mother, brother Valentin and myself, drank the traditional toast to his birthday which would begin in a few minutes' time. We saw his birthday in and all went to bed.

At four o'clock in the morning we were all awakened by a loud knocking on the door of our apartment.[62]

After the search was finished and Granovsky was taken away, the family was told to move one floor down to Apt. 416, which contained several other families of recently arrested officials. They moved the next day, amidst Revolution Day festivities. According to Anatoly, his mother, "who had always been beautiful and had always appeared young, now grew suddenly old and pathetic. She sat all day quite still on a hard chair with her hands in her lap and said nothing. There was something terrifying about her. In her silence and immobility, as though hypnotized, she yet gave the impression of something slowly happening, like the cocoon when a caterpillar becomes a butterfly. Only, she had been the butterfly first."[63]

Kuchmin's and Granovsky's colleague, the head of the Cargo Department of the People's Commissariat of Transportation and Lazar Kaganovich's deputy, Semen ("Siunia") Gaister, from Apt. 98, had been arrested two months earlier. According to his niece, Inna Gaister, "After my father's arrest, Siunia was fired from his job and expelled from the Party. He sat at home waiting to be arrested. Later, the kids from his courtyard told me that the whole entryway had heard him screaming wildly as he was being dragged down the stairs: 'Lazar Moiseevich! Lazar Moiseevich, don't you know what's happening? Lazar Moiseevich, please help me!'"[64]

■ ■ ■

Osinsky's wife and children spent the summer of 1937 on Lake Valdai, fishing, hiking, kayaking, and sleeping in the hayloft of a farmhouse that Osinsky's sister, Galina, had rented. Valia was fifteen, Rem fourteen, and Svetlana twelve. Twenty-five-year-old Dima was there with his pregnant wife, Dina. Suddenly, to everyone's surprise, Osinsky showed up, too. "It was a huge event," wrote Svetlana:

> He brought his work with him, his higher mathematics. Everyone was worried: where was he going to work? Where was he going to sleep? He slept in the hayloft with us and, during the day, surprised everyone by working very little and going for walks with us instead.
>
> I have a small, amateur photograph of my father and me during our trip to the island, which still had a working monastery at that time. We are sitting with our knees pulled up. I'm barefoot, with my arms around my knees, squinting from the bright sun and looking at

Valerian Osinsky and Svetlana at Lake Valdai
(Courtesy of Elena Simakova)

the photographer. I'm wearing a hat with a broad brim, bought at the Valdai market. My father, as always in the summer, is dressed all in white, including his shoes. He had very sensitive skin and suffered from eczema. He is also squinting through his pince-nez, his ears protruding slightly. He has a small moustache, and his hands are clasped behind his knees. He doesn't have his arm around me, and I'm not leaning against him: we are in our own separate worlds. I remember that moment so well! I was happy to be photographed with him, this distant and rather aloof father of mine, who had deigned to go with us to that island and had even chosen to have his picture taken not with Valia, but with me! I felt very grown up and close to him.[65]

Soon after they returned to the House of Government, Dima's wife, Dina, gave birth to a baby boy. They named him Ilya. Svetlana and the two younger boys went back to school. "My father was arrested in the middle of the night on October 14, 1937 (and Dima was taken away with him the same night). The last time I saw him was the evening before his arrest, when he and my mother came to our room to say good night. I remember asking them to buy me some kind of special knee-high socks like the ones a girl in my school had. My father was sitting by the desk and listening absent-mindedly, with an ironic smile that did not seem to fit the occasion."[66]

The agents entered the apartment using their own key. Svetlana was asleep, but "according to Dina, in the middle of the night my mother, who was sleeping in her own room at the opposite end of the corridor from my father's study, was awakened by a bright light flooding the hallway. She ran out, half-dressed, to see what was happening. My father was being escorted to the door. 'Farewell!' he cried out. 'Sell the books, sell everything!'" Svetlana woke up after Osinsky and Dima had been taken away.

The light was on in our room and seemed unusually bright and bare. My brothers were sitting up in their beds, mechanically watching the movements of two or three men, rummaging through our books. "Hush," my mother said—"lie still. Your father and Dima have been arrested."—I froze, frightened by the half-understood words, then sat up and started watching the search, too. The agents were very thorough and deliberate, flipping through and shaking out each book and then, with a look of satisfaction, smoothing out any pieces of paper they came across—notes, probably—and stacking them on the desk. These discoveries made them happy. After that they started pulling out our desk drawers and going through everything in them, and then concluded the search by lifting up each of our mattresses from both ends—the head and the foot, without asking us to get up first, in order to see if there was anything hidden underneath. My mother sat impassively, with a look of contempt on her face, and when they left, stood up, turned off the light, and walked out of the room. We lay there silent and still. Then I fell asleep.[67]

Three days later, the agents came back for Svetlana's mother. Several months later, they came back again:

> They needed to get a suit for my father and some books for him. The list of books, both Russian and foreign, was in his handwriting. They looked for what they needed, but couldn't find everything. They used the phone in our corridor to make a call, and I could hear my father speaking on the other end! He told them where to look for the books. But they still had to ask us for help. Valia and I went into the room where, four months earlier, we had sat on the huge couch next to our father listening to him read Turgenev's *On the Eve*, and where one evening I had been timidly examining Doré's illustrations to the *Divine Comedy* and been caught at it by my father, but he hadn't gotten angry (even though we were forbidden to touch his books without permission) and had said that we would read Dante at some point.[68]

Valia, Rem, and Svetlana were taken to an orphanage. Dina was exiled to Kharkov. Her son, Ilya, was raised by her mother.

■ ■ ■

Svetlana Osinskaia (*right*) with Dina
and Ilya soon after her parents' arrest
(Courtesy of Elena Simakova)

Osinsky had been a recluse—or thought he had, for certain purposes—since the February–March plenum of 1937, when Postyshev, among others, had forced him to account for his silence. Postyshev had also come under attack at the plenum—for nepotism, high-handedness, and suppression of criticism, but had been given a second chance and a new job as first secretary of the Kuibyshev Provincial Party Committee. (His wife, T. S. Postolovskaia, who had been Ukraine's chief ideologist during his tenure there, had been expelled from the Party for her part in the suppression of criticism.) In Kuibyshev, he started slowly and was soon visited by the Politburo member A. A. Andreev, who told him to step up the fight against the enemy underground. Postyshev responded by expelling 3,300 people from the Party and disbandeding thirty-five of the sixty-five district Party committees. According to his deputy, "Comrade Postyshev changed his way of doing things. He started going around yelling that there were no decent people left, and that there were lots of enemies. . . . For two weeks, all the district secretaries and their staffs ran around with magnifying glasses. Comrade Postyshev set the example: he summoned all the district committee representatives to his office, picked up a magnifying glass, and started examining a batch of school notebooks. Later they tore off all the covers of those notebooks because they supposedly found a fascist swastika or some such thing on them. It got to the point where they were finding fascist symbols on cookies, candy, and other items."[69]

In January 1938, Stalin decided to slow down the purge of local Party officials (while intensifying the "mass operations," over which the newly appointed Party officials were to preside). Postyshev was accused of staging a witch hunt against honest Communists, fired from his job in Kuibyshev, and, according to the official statement, "placed at the disposal of the Central Committee." According to Postyshev's son Leonid, who had recently been admitted to the military aviation school in Liubertsy, outside of Moscow (thanks to Voroshilov's intercession), Postyshev was relieved not to receive a harsher punishment, confident of an appointment to the Party Control Commission, and happy to be back in his House of Government apartment. At the hastily convened Central Committee plenum in mid-January 1938, he apologized for his mistakes but continued to assert, in line with the policy he had been sent to Kuibyshev to enforce, that most local officials were enemies. Taunted and interrupted repeatedly ("Weren't there any honest people there?"), he pleaded sincerity, but was told that not all sincerity was worthy of trust. When he was given the floor at the end of the discussion, he said:

I can only say one thing, comrades, and that is that I admit that the speech I made here was fully and totally incorrect and incompatible with the Party spirit. I can't even understand myself how I could have made that speech. I ask the Central Committee plenum to forgive me. Not only have I never associated with enemies, but I have

always fought against enemies. I have always fought against the enemies of the people alongside the Party with all my Bolshevik soul,
and I will always fight against the enemies of the people with all my
Bolshevik soul. I have made many mistakes. I did not understand
them. I may not have understood them completely even now. All I
can say is that I have made an incorrect speech incompatible with
the Party spirit, and that I ask the Central Committee plenum to
forgive me for making it.[70]

He was removed from his position as candidate member of the Politburo and replaced by Khrushchev. A month later, the Control Commission
found that whereas many of the Party members he had expelled as enemies of the people were actually honest Communists, many of those he
had retained as honest Communists were actually enemies of the people.
He was removed from the Central Committee and expelled from the Party.
A day or two later, when Leonid came home for a visit, his father told him
that he and his mother would soon be arrested and that he, Leonid, would
also be arrested—and that it was probably a good thing because he would
become stronger and wiser as a consequence. The next day, on the night
of February 21, a group of NKVD agents came to arrest Postyshev. Several
hours later, a different group of NKVD agents came to arrest his wife, T. S.
Postolovskaia. Leonid's two brothers were arrested soon afterward. Leonid went to see a public prosecutor, who told him that he could not help
because he, too, would soon be arrested. He was, according to Leonid,
shortly thereafter. Leonid himself was not arrested until 1942.[71]

Pavel Postyshev and
Tatiana Semenovna Postolovskaia

. . .

Sergei Mironov returned from Mongolia and moved into the House of Government about two weeks after Postyshev's arrest. One of their new neighbors was their Novosibirsk host, Robert Eikhe, who had since been appointed people's commissar of agriculture and moved into Apt. 234. There is no evidence that they saw each other socially in the House of Government. On April 29, 1938, about three weeks after Mironov's arrival, Eikhe and his wife, Evgenia Evseevna Rubtsova, were arrested.

Another West Siberian top official and Eikhe's and Mironov's close collaborator, the director of the Kuznetsk Steel Plant, Konstantin Butenko, moved in at about the same time as Mironov. In early January 1938, he and his wife Sofia, the women's volunteer movement activist, had traveled by train from Stalinsk (Novokuznetsk) to Moscow to attend the session of the Supreme Soviet. (He was thirty-six; she was thirty-three; and both were beneficiaries of worker-and-peasant promotion programs.) Sofia could still remember a certain day of that journey sixty years later:

> We were in the international car. . . . We had this Novokuznetsk-Moscow express train, and one car was always international. . . . You know, because that's where all the officials would be. Right. So there we were in that train, traveling on and on, and then one night somewhere outside of Omsk, or maybe even before Omsk (I'm not sure, but, in any case, it used to take four and a half days because there weren't any planes back then, or at least not the passenger kind) . . . so anyway, suddenly, in the middle of the night, there was a knock on the door. My husband was sleeping on the upper bunk, so that means I was below. It was a double. . . . I opened the door and it was the conductor. "I'm very sorry, but I have an urgent confidential telegram for your husband." But the train was still going at full speed! I took the piece of paper, unfolded it—and then I quickly turned on the light and woke up my Kostia. . . . He sat with his feet hanging down and read out loud: "Omsk-Tomsk Railway. International Car" . . . But above that it says "Top secret." "To Butenko, director of the Kuznetsk Steel Plant. Butenko, Konstantin Ivanovich. You have been appointed deputy commissar of heavy industry. Cable candidate replacement immediately. Kaganovich."[72]

They were put up in a three-room luxury suite in the recently completed Moscow Hotel in front of the Kremlin while their House of Government apartment (Apt. 141, formerly occupied by the arrested deputy commissar of health of the Russian Federation, Valentin Kangelari) was being cleaned and renovated. In early April, they moved in: Konstantin, Sofia, and Sofia's niece, Tamara, who had been living with them since the famine of 1932. (Sofia's family came from the Greek settlement of Styla, near

Konstantin Butenko

Stalino. Her brother Ivan, a miner, had been arrested in late December, about a week after Ezhov launched the "Greek operation"; her other brother, Nikolai, a collective farmer and Tamara's father, had been arrested in early January, around the time Konstantin received his new appointment.) The apartment had four rooms. The biggest was made into a study for Konstantin and was furnished with a large desk, a desk chair, a rocking chair, and a couple of wardrobes they had brought with them from Stalinsk. The others became Tamara's room, a bedroom for Sofia and Konstantin, and a dining room. They had lived there for about a month and a half when Konstantin was arrested. The agents entered quietly in the middle of the night and surrounded the bed before waking him up. During the search, they took Konstantin's Order of Lenin, but let Sofia keep her Badge of Honor. Several days later, Sofia got a job at a hat factory on Bolshaia Ordynka. She was not used to getting up early and did not have an alarm clock, so the entryway guards, who seemed to have recognized a fellow former peasant, agreed to wake her up every morning by ringing the doorbell. About a month later, Sofia and Tamara were asked to move to a communal apartment on the tenth floor, and were then evicted altogether. Tamara went back to Styla; Sofia found a room in Gorokhovsky Alley and got a job in a medical lab. The Butenkos' House of Government apartment was taken over by the former head of the Gulag, Matvei Berman, who had recently been appointed people's commissar of communications.[73]

■ ■ ■

The Central Committee of the Young Communist League (Komsomol) was purged twice. In August 1937, thirty-five members and candidate members were arrested for trying "to corrupt young people politically and morally, especially through alcohol," and for having become "young 'old men'" married to "grandes dames." One of those elected to replace them was the twenty-seven-year-old Serafim Bogachev, who moved into the House of Government with his wife, Lydia, and their newborn daughter, Natasha. Over the course of the next year, Serafim and Lydia got used to the barrenness of their new apartment, bought two new carpets, found a good nanny, and brought both their peasant mothers to help around the house. They still felt out of place, however, and rarely spent any time at home: he worked long hours in the Central Committee; she prepared for college entrance exams and went to volleyball practice. On November 19–22, 1938, Stalin, Molotov, Kaganovich, and several other Party leaders convened an extraordinary (seventh) plenum of the Komsomol Central Committee and announced that the work of self-cleansing mandated by the Party had not been done; honest young Communists had not been heard; and counter-revolutionary terrorists had not been unmasked. The general secretary of the Komsomol Central Committee, Aleksandr Kosarev (Apt. 209) confessed his errors but claimed that he had "never betrayed the Party and the Soviet people" and that his conscience was clear. His speech was officially characterized as "thoroughly duplicitous and anti-Party." "Are you really such a political newborn," asked Zhdanov, "that you didn't know you were supposed to report to the plenum on everything having to do with the behavior of the Central Committee bureau?" "Perhaps it's a pattern, and not just mistakes?" asked Stalin. Kosarev could not answer these questions, and neither could Bogachev. An incomplete confession was duplicitous and anti-Party; a complete confession meant unmasking oneself as a wrecker. For Bogachev, not denouncing his patron was duplicitous and anti-Party; denouncing him raised the fatal question of why he had not done it before. As the Central Committee member A. A. Andreev put it, "[Bogachev] is following the rotten non-Bolshevik former leadership of the Komsomol Central Committee in everything. In everything! He has not shown any independence. On the contrary, he has adopted all the negative aspects of Kosarev's leadership style."[74]

Bogachev was expelled from the Komsomol Central Committee along with Kosarev. He wrote a letter to Stalin. The Central Committee of the Party told him to expect another assignment. He seemed relieved. On November 27, one week after the plenum, he and Lydia walked over to the Shock Worker to see Aleksandr Macheret's newly released *Swamp Soldiers* (based on Yuri Olesha's screenplay about the arrest, imprisonment, and eventual escape of a group of German antifascists). According to Lydia, at some point she realized that Serafim was not watching. She suggested that they go home, but he said it would not be right to walk out before the end. When they got back to their apartment, he asked her to read aloud to him. She read Jack London's *White Fang* for a while, and then they went to bed.

We were asleep. My husband was by the wall, closer to the window, and I was on the outside. I woke up because there were people staring at me. Just standing there staring in total silence. Our little girl was sick at the time, so I had had to get up during the night. But right then I was asleep. I was terrified. I couldn't speak. I kept rubbing my eyes: "Is this a dream or am I just imagining it?" Then they said: "Who's that sleeping with you?" And I said: "My husband." I told them who we were. "Don't wake him." They told me to leave the bedroom. But first they asked: "Where are your weapons? Put all your weapons on the table!" They asked him, too, when he woke up. But he was confused and couldn't figure out what was going on. So he said: "Ask her where the weapons are, I don't know." He had some kind of engraved gun, it was a gift. And there was a rifle, but it was back in Kolomna. A hunting one. He liked to hunt. The engraved one was in the trunk. I pulled it out. The trunk was right there. I gave them the gun. But I wasn't thinking clearly. I couldn't even talk, let alone scream. I was completely dazed. It was frightening. I was still very young. And he was twenty-seven when we got married, so he must have been twenty-eight at the time.[75]

One NKVD agent who stayed behind after the search seemed friendly. "The first thing he said was: 'Get dressed.' I was still walking around in my nightshirt. I couldn't take anything in. I'd catch the first two letters— but not the rest. My mother kept following me around with my robe for me to cover myself with." A few days later, Lydia, her daughter, and her mother went back to Kolomna, where Lydia got a job as a draftswoman at a factory.[76]

On November 17, 1938, two days before the Komsomol plenum, the Politburo had abolished extrajudicial "troikas" and discontinued the mass operations. A week later (two days before Bogachev's arrest), Ezhov had been fired and replaced by Beria.[77]

When Anatoly Granovsky, now sixteen, heard about Ezhov's dismissal, he went to the NKVD headquarters to ask whether his father's case might not be reviewed, but was turned away at the door. The next day, he went to Red Square and started pacing up and down in front of the Lenin Mausoleum. When a plainclothes NKVD agent asked him what he was doing, he said that he wanted to be arrested in order to talk to Comrade Beria. He was taken to Lubyanka Prison, beaten, and accused of planning an assassination attempt against the members of the Politburo.[78]

27

THE GOOD PEOPLE

The House of Government was in turmoil. Residents had been taken away and replaced by new ones, who had been taken away and replaced by even newer ones. Families of arrested residents were concentrated in vacated apartments before being evicted and replaced by other families of other arrested residents. Rooms had been sealed, settled, resealed and resettled. On May 10, 1938, sixty-eight apartments (162 rooms totaling 3,051 square meters) were occupied by families of arrested residents, and 142 rooms (3,077 square meters) had been sealed by the NKVD. The House commandant, V. A. Irbe, had been arrested as an enemy of the people, and so had the head of the Central Executive Committee's Housekeeping Department, N. I. Pakhomov. An inspection following Pakhomov's arrest (on May 3, 1938) revealed that the department's accounts had been systematically falsified, acts of sabotage deliberately ignored, dachas and sanatoria badly mismanaged, Pakhomov's coconspirators rewarded with watches and automobiles, half the dairy cows in Lenin's Gorki infected with brucellosis, workers' barracks transformed into overcrowded hovels, and House of Government apartments filled with people no longer eligible to live there. Top housekeeping officials and rest home directors were dismissed and arrested. About half the House of Government accountants and warehouse workers were replaced. Emelian Ivchenko, the guard who talked the Leningrad port employee, Anna, into marrying him in order to get registered in Moscow, was appointed political supervisor of all House of Government guards. (At about the same time, the Ivchenkos were told that their little boy Vladimir, who had died in 1936 of pneumonia, had actually been murdered by Kremlin hospital doctors.) In the summer of 1938, not long after Pakhomov's arrest, Ivchenko was put in charge of a large transport of prisoners headed for the labor camps in Kolyma (first by train to Vladivostok and then by boat to Magadan). He stayed on and served as commander of the armed guards in various camps, including Yagodnoe. Ivchenko and his wife had three more sons, one of whom died of meningitis. The surviving children (including the daughter, Elsa) were raised by prisoners who served as nannies and housekeepers.[1]

The entire Swamp was in turmoil. According to the Party secretary of the neighboring Red October candy factory, Comrade Konstantinova, "today, when the whole country is seething with indignation, there is still some vermin left that supports the enemy." The challenge was to annihi-

Emelian Ivchenko

late them once and for all. "Our current director, Comrade Shaposhnikova, is full of energy, and she said that she would get rid of all of them, and I gave her my approval that we need to cleanse ourselves. I agreed that all this scum, which has crept into our socialist factory, must be driven out, and that our party organization must rally even more around our Party and our leader, Comrade Stalin." Several months later, Comrade Shaposhnikova was unmasked as an enemy of the people, and Comrade Konstantinova was no longer Party secretary (Shaposhnikova was eventually executed; Konstantinova's fate is unknown). The Party Committee of the Lenin Municipal District, which governed the Swamp and much of Trans-Moskva, kept up with arrests by means of mass expulsions (including of its own entire leadership) and urgent reappointments. According to the July 31, 1937, report to the district plenum, some of the most dangerous hidden enemies were "people entrusted with conducting political propaganda." The man sent to explain to the Moscow Metro builders the need for vigilance against enemies turned out to be one himself, and at the nearby fur factory, the speaker reporting "On the Goals and Methods of the Work of Foreign Intelligence Services" was arrested while leaving the podium. The new Party secretary of Red October received no instructions concerning Shaposhnikova's disappearance and had no idea how to answer the workers' questions.[2]

In some of the area's schools, teachers and administrators had to devise special policies with regard to the large numbers of students whose parents had been arrested. One proposed solution was to get the children of the enemies of the people involved in volunteer work and to check periodically on their home situation. Most textbooks and teaching guides had to be checked for signs of fascist propaganda smuggled in (often by means of a secret code) by foreign agents posing as school administrators and education theorists. People's Commissar of Enlightenment Andrei Bubnov, who had once said that the enemies should be "squashed like vile vermin," was himself arrested on October 17, 1937, and executed nine months later. Over the course of 1937, 526 Moscow school teachers and 23 principals were "released for political reasons." As the head of the Moscow Department of People's Education, L. V. Dubrovina, put it in April 1937, "on what grounds, I would like to know, should we allow Rykov's daughter, who lived with him up to the moment of his arrest, to work as a teacher? We have every reason to believe that she has not distanced herself from him. We cannot employ her just because she has graduated from the A. S. Bubnov Pedagogical Institute." (After Bubnov's arrest, the institute was named after Lenin.)[3]

News of the public trials of spies and terrorists was reported on the radio, in the newspapers, and at rallies staged in workplaces. During the Radek trial, the first secretary of the Lenin District Party Committee, D. Z. Protopopov, mentioned the case of a sixty-year-old woman who "had a typical woman's reaction and said with pity that maybe it was not necessary to execute them. But when they asked her if she had read the newspapers yesterday and the day before, and explained the situation to her, she said: 'If that's the way it is, I will execute them myself.'" According to a report by the Red October Party secretary, "the rallies in all the shops were conducted with great enthusiasm; everyone was shouting that all these reptiles should be shot. When the workers listened to the radio transmission, there were spontaneous shouts denouncing the scoundrels and demanding their execution." One woman, who had worked at the factory for twenty years, said: "Why waste bullets on this scum? It would be better to pour acid over them and set them on fire." (She was told that such punishments were not being used in the Soviet Union.) At a rally of the House of Government employees held at about the same time, one military training instructor said: "I would agree to take a leave of absence, go to the capitalist countries, track Trotsky down, and kill him." (He was told that this "does not correspond to our Party's program and that we do not accept individual terror.")[4]

In Koltsov's absence, the coverage of the Radek trial had been a collective enterprise. By March 1938, Koltsov was back from Spain, ready to set the tone for *Pravda*'s reporting of the trial of Bukharin's "Anti-Soviet Rightist-Trotskyite Bloc":

> When the scoundrels, whom the court language describes as "defendants," stand up and begin talking about their monstrous crimes— some with the cowering demeanor of penitent sinners, some with the cynical insolence of experienced rogues—one wishes to jump up, scream, bang one's fist on the desk, and grab those dirty, blood-stained bastards by the throat and finish them off on the spot. But no, one has to sit and listen. Listen and understand. Listen and watch. Listen, watch, and remember this last, frightening ghost of fascism—vanquished, sent back into the darkness of the past, destroyed as it attempted in vain to defeat the Soviet people and to darken the bright sun of the Soviet land.[5]

The emphasis, as usual, was on the enemies' beastliness ("cornered rats," "brazen predators," "a pack of bloodhounds," "monsters in human form") and the demonic combination common to all scapegoats: omnipotence (the "endless chain of nightmarish bloody crimes unknown to history") and weakness (of the "perfidious, duplicitous, whiny, and spiteful nonentity"). The wreckers lived underground and, in the tradition shaped by Bukharin and Voronsky, were best described as Dostoevsky's shadows. Chief among them was Bukharin himself: "a tiny Jesus among sinners" and the "Valdai Virgin in a Rightist-Trotskyite brothel."[6]

In open trials, the blinking, shivering creatures of the night were brought to the surface, exposed to the light, and either extinguished forever or sent back to the netherworld, this time to its well-drained, securely sealed-off part. "Only when you leave the courthouse, dust off the nightmarish web of hideous confessions, and inhale the fresh air of loudly resonant evening Moscow," wrote Koltsov in *Pravda*, "can you breathe easily and regain your sense of reality."[7]

Most news of the campaign against anti-Soviet elements was about its carefully scripted public reenactments. The campaign itself was conducted underground and was meant to remain there. Most arrests, searches, and executions took place at night. Family members were not told where their relatives had been taken and had to travel from one prison to another until their parcels were accepted. When the parcels were no longer accepted, they were to conclude that their relative had been transferred or executed. Executions were usually disguised as sentences of "ten years without the right of correspondence." Places of execution were hidden (and, within Sergei Mironov's jurisdiction, camouflaged with previously cut turf). The accused were not informed of the "mass operations" or the individual decisions that had led to their arrests. The interrogators were to banish the numbers of the accused from their minds, "while those who cannot must force themselves to do it anyway" (as Sergei Mironov put it). Large-scale deportations, including those of entire ethnic groups, were carried out in secret and remained largely unknown in the loudly resonant Moscow.

As far as Moscow was concerned, the struggle against spies and terrorists was everywhere at once and nowhere in particular. Everyone was to be incessantly vigilant, but only the officially acknowledged parts of the campaign—purge meetings, exemplary expulsions, show trials—were to be noticed and perhaps commented on. Films and fiction were full of enemies; neighbors' apartments were full of sealed rooms. As Abulkasim Lakhuti, from Apt. 176, had written in a poem, "The Gardener" (dedicated "To the Leader, Comrade, Stalin"), if young vines are to grow, old trunks must be cut down. Or, as he had written in another poem ("We Will Win"), "why can't we all be Chekists, when every possible enemy is sowing treason everywhere?" What Lakhuti could not write or talk about was whose four-room apartment in Entryway 9 he and his family had moved into and which of his other neighbors had also been—or still had to be—cut down. As far as Moscow was concerned, enemies were being caught and punished; one's neighbors vanished tracelessly into the netherworld. Generic spies and terrorists were everywhere; particular names, faces, bodies, stories, nations, people's commissars, and Civil War heroes had never existed.[8]

■ ■ ■

The most common reaction to the multiplying disappearances was silence. Even the show trials were rarely commented on. The people in the government part of the House of Government did not seem to doubt the guilt of the accused or the authenticity of their confessions: they seemed to refrain from mentioning them as a matter of ritual avoidance of the unclean. Only children and very old Old Bolsheviks might ask a question, which no one would consider answering. Even in prison reception rooms, the relatives of the arrested tried, according to Irina Muklevich, "not to talk and not to recognize each other. Hundreds of people would stand in a relatively small room, but it would be quiet and tense. They were all thinking of their own grief, like at a funeral."[9]

On the last day of the Kamenev-Zinoviev trial, Arosev was still in the Sosny rest home on the Moskva, writing in his diary:

In today's papers we read that Kamenev, Zinoviev, Panaev, Mrachkovsky, Evdokimov, Ter-Vaganian, I. N. Smirnov Reingold, Goltsman, M. Lurye, N. Lurye, Dreitser, Olberg, and Perman-Yurgin have all been sentenced—to be shot.

M. P. Tomsky shot himself the other day.

Today Aralov told me that Comrade Piatakov had tried to poison himself, but apparently failed and was taken to the hospital.

No one is saying anything. Everyone talks as if nothing has happened.

"Did you go for a swim today?"

"No, I took a shower."

At the other end of the table:

"Do you play tennis?"

"Of course."

Someone else:

"Have some half-sour pickles. They're delicious."[10]

All Arosev himself had to say was that Kamenev and Zinoviev were "demons." Five months later, on the last day of the Radek trial, he listed the sentences, copied a long excerpt from Feuchtwanger's *Pravda* article, and agreed with the author that "only the pen of a great Soviet writer could explain to the people of western Europe the crime and punishment of the accused." Arosev's own plan was to write a novel in the form of interrogation transcripts. Only "by means of aesthetic impressions," he wrote, could one make sense of "the zigzags that have brought people from the revolution to its opposite." This was true because Arosev was a fiction writer who hoped to represent the age with "the greatest possible generalizability." It was also true because there was no other way to make sense of the zigzags. One of the accused at the trial was Nikolai Muralov, whom Arosev, at Rozengolts's request, had appointed commissar of the Moscow Military District on November 2, 1917.[11]

Another common reaction was to cleanse one's life of all connections to the excommunicated. Some House residents—mostly women—burned books and letters, cut faces out of photographs, changed their children's last names, and avoided contaminated neighbors and relatives. As in most struggles with the onslaught of the unclean, this was both a practical precaution and the extension of ritual silence to new sources of contagion. Some people reduced their possessions to a few things they might need in prison and waited silently for the knock on the door. The former head of the central censorship office, Boris Volin, had a suitcase with warm things stored behind his couch. His wife burned the entire family archive. In the fall of 1937, he had a heart attack and was sent to the Kremlin hospital and then to a sanatorium in Barvikha. When he came back three months later, most of his neighbors and colleagues (he was first deputy of the people's commissar of enlightenment) had disappeared. The former head of the Bookselling Directorate, David Shvarts, would stay up at night, looking out the window. According to his son, "the window looked out onto the courtyard. Whenever a 'black raven' [NKVD car] would enter the courtyard, my father would start getting dressed."[12]

Attempts at self-cleansing and readiness for self-sacrifice were accompanied by vigilance toward others. Two and a half months after Kirov's murder, when he was still chief censor, Boris Volin issued an order informing local censorship offices that the "expertly camouflaged work of the class enemy" had been detected "on the fine arts front":

> By means of different combinations of colors, light and shadow, strokes, and contours disguised according to the method of "mysterious drawings," the enemies are smuggling in counterrevolutionary content.
>
> The symbolic painting by the artist N. Mikhailov, *By Kirov's Coffin*, in which a certain combination of light, shadow, and color represent the outline of a skeleton, has been qualified as a disguised counterrevolutionary act.
>
> The same has been detected on the tin can labels printed by Supply Technology Publishers (a human head instead of a piece of meat surrounded by beans). . . .
>
> In light of the above, I order that:
>
> All censors working with posters, paintings, labels, photo montages, etc. undertake the most thorough scrutiny possible of such material, not limiting themselves to superficial political meaning and overall artistic value, but considering carefully the entire artwork from all angles (contours, ornament, shadows, etc.), frequently resorting to a magnifying glass.[13]

At the height of the campaign against hidden enemies, a magnifying glass was to be directed at everyone, by everyone. On July 27, 1937 (the day Piatnitsky was arrested), Aleksandr Serafimovich received a letter from his old friend, Mirra Gotfrid, asking for the telephone number of the head of the Writers' Union, V. P. Stavsky. She needed to talk to him about the novella she was translating by the Yiddish writer David Bergelson:

In the process of work on the translation I uncovered the petit bourgeois nature of the novella and three subsequent meetings were enough to uncover something quite serious about the author it worries me very much I must see Comrade Stavsky believe me I wouldn't be bothering you for no reason. My observations are serious and this writer must be checked out very carefully. Write to Stavsky and ask him to receive me. You know I wouldn't be making a fuss over nothing. All the best to you. Thank you for all the good things. Warmest regards to Fekola. Why don't you do it this way send me Comrade Stavsky's phone number and drop him a line asking him listen to what I have to say and telling him that I am observant and don't accuse people without evidence and that I would consider it a criminal act to keep silent and not report to the Writers' Union president (who is also a member of the Control Commission now). Help me out. Mirra, 27 July, 1937.[14]

Platon Kerzhentsev also felt the need to be vigilant. In early March 1938, he was at home awaiting arrest after his dismissal from the Committee for the Arts and the suicide of his deputy, Naum Rabichev. On the second day of the Anti-Soviet Rightist-Trotskyite trial, which involved three Kremlin doctors accused of murdering Soviet officials, he sent a handwritten note to Molotov, with a copy to Vyshinsky:

In connection with the charges against D. Pletnev, I consider it necessary to remind you of the circumstances of the death of Comrade Dzerzhinsky.

After his heart attack he was put in the room next to the meeting room. Several hours later the doctors allowed him to go back to his own apartment. When he got home and bent over his bed, he fell down dead.

As is well known, after a heart attack the patient is absolutely forbidden to move in any way (especially walking, bending).

Among the doctors attending to Dzerzhinsky was Pletnev.

By allowing Dzerzhinsky to go, he killed him. . . .

As for Kazakov, I can share my personal experience: my second heart attack happened exactly four hours after the very first injection administered by Kazakov.

Yours, Kerzhentsev, 8 March, 1938[15]

Platon Kerzhentsev

Three days later, after the accused had been given a chance to tell their stories, Feliks Kon wrote to his lover, Maria Komarova, that their next meeting would have to be postponed because of bad weather, but that he would do his best to make up for it when the time was right. "Will I be able to? Will I? But I'll try. Okay?" His late love made him "feel alive, feel young again."[16] And so did the spectacle of the Anti-Soviet Rightist-Trotskyite Trial:

I miss you in earnest. Each time after I read the newspapers, I come close to losing my mind. Have entire generations struggled and have people died at the gallows, in dungeons, at the barricades, and in the Civil War just so these vermin could betray it all? Bukharin trying to kill Lenin and Stalin, Rozengolts with a prayer-amulet in his pocket ready to personally murder Stalin . . . Yagoda, Levin. . . . It's like a villainy contest among scoundrels. And what about the attempt to poison Ezhov? You read something like this and then spend the rest of the day as if someone had spat into your soul. But still, despite all their scheming and their fascist conspiracies, we continue to advance, and now that Ezhov is in charge, things will get even better. If not for my 74 years, I would have approached Ezhov and volunteered to become his assistant. I would not have wavered. I would have killed those monsters with my own hand. I have lived through many assaults, but I never suspected that such creatures existed. Brrrr![17]

For Efim Shchadenko, the struggle against wreckers was a time of revenge for years of humiliation at the hands of "neurotic degenerates" and other clouds in pants from "the intelligentsia in general and the Jewish intelligentsia in particular." Most recently, he had lost a protracted feud with his superiors, the commander of the Frunze Military Academy, August Kork (Apt. 389), and Deputy Commissar of Defense Marshal Tukhachevsky (Apt. 221), both former tsarist officers. On August 17, 1936, Kork wrote to Tukhachevsky: "The state of health of my deputy, Comrade Shchadenko, is extremely precarious. It is my impression that, at any moment, Comrade Shchadenko may succumb to a fit of raving madness. I request that Comrade Shchadenko be relieved of his duties at the academy and transferred to the care of doctors without delay." Tukhachevsky endorsed the request and Shchadenko was dismissed (and spent three and a half months in a hospital). In May 1937, Kork and Tukhachevsky were arrested and, within three weeks, executed. Their close colleague, Deputy People's Commissar of Defense Yan Gamarnik (Yakov Pudikovich), com-

mitted suicide. Shchadenko was sent to Kiev to "liquidate the consequences of wrecking."[18] On July 10, he wrote to an old Civil War comrade:

> We must destroy this treacherous scum without mercy, the way we
> did during the Civil War, no matter what colors they use to camou-
> flage themselves and no matter how leftist their reptile hissing may
> sound.
>
> Death without mercy to the fascist lackeys, spies of the German-
> Japanese imperialism—such is our response to the scheming and
> sabotage on the part of the enemies of the people.
>
> I am, as usual, merciless toward the enemy, hacking at them right
> and left, annihilating them along with their villainous acts.[19]

On November 20, he wrote to another former comrade, reminding him
of his (Shchadenko's) "implacable struggle against the German spy Kork,
the vile governor scum Tukhachevsky, Gamarnik and the whole sellout
gang of the Trotskyite-Bukharinist bloc." But his main correspondent,
confidante, and fellow socialist realist was his wife, Maria. On June 18, he
wrote from Kiev:

> My darling little sun, I miss you so much and worry so much when,
> exhausted, I finally tear myself away from my work and drag myself
> to my—quite literally—soldier's bunk. There is so much work that I
> cannot leave Headquarters until 2 or 3 in the morning. The wrecker
> scum spent years fouling things up, and we only have weeks, or a
> month or two at the most, to not only liquidate all the consequences
> of sabotage, but to start moving forward. The cowardly scoundrels,
> undetected by the cheerful carelessness of our "defenders," sneaked
> into high positions, corrupted the guards, filled the apparently
> watchful sentries with the poison of doubt, and hatched an unimag-
> inably villainous plot.
>
> It is our great fortune that, early on, Stalin himself noticed and
> felt the danger of the fascist terrorist murderers getting close to
> him and began to take measures, not giving in to pleas for mercy for
> Enukidze (that most vile and well-disguised of reptiles), cast him,
> along with the rest of his gang, out of the Kremlin, recruited new,
> reliable guards, and, having appointed Comrade Ezhov, that modest
> and diligent worker, began to untangle the knots and threads of
> fascist designs for the bloody restoration of capitalism. . . .
>
> I have a great deal of work, but working is easy because now I feel
> that I have vast creative freedom to fight with and for the masses,
> and, most important, that the truly great Stalin can, once again, see
> the same ability and selflessness that I demonstrated when he saw
> what I did during the Civil War.

I embrace and kiss you very tenderly, my darling little sun. Soon, no later than early July, I'll be in Moscow and then I'll try to bring my dear family back here with me.[20]

In November, he returned to Moscow as deputy people's commissar of defense in charge of commanding personnel. Meanwhile, Maria herself seems to have succumbed to fits of raving madness. According to Maya Agroskina (Dementieva), who lived in Apt. 17, she once broke into someone's apartment wearing a nightshirt and wielding a gun. According to Ruslan Gelman, who lived in Apt. 13,

She lived in a huge apartment that had been converted from two smaller ones, with a few servants. Occasionally, she'd appear on the landing. She made a strong impression. She was a tall, stout woman with a piercing, menacing glare. Think of Surikov's [sic] painting, *Tsarevna Sofia*: that's her portrait, as if she had posed for it herself. Add to that a long black dress girded by a soldier's leather belt, a kitchen knife stuck into it, and her hand resting on the handle. . . . It was truly a sight to behold! To amuse herself, she used to leave a chair out on the staircase with a vase full of fruit and a tightly packed lady's purse with high-denomination bills sticking out. Sometimes that chair would remain there for several days.

Once she came over to our place. The only ones home at the time were me and our maid, a very young girl, who was deathly afraid of

Ilya Repin, *Tsarevna Sofia*

her. When I opened the door after the bell rang, the maid ran into the bathroom and locked herself in. The fearsome Tsarina swept past me, this time without her knife, but with a retinue: a young man in semi-military uniform. His job must have been to look after her, but he did not dare contradict or restrain her. She spent a long time looking around our apartment and even measuring some things, talking complete gibberish all the while, and finally left, with a parting threat.[21]

∎ ∎ ∎

Maria Denisova was trying to do at home what her husband was doing at work. Both had their sanity questioned by the people they tried to expose, and both were being vindicated by the daily exposure of "monsters in human form."

After the arrest of her seventeen-year-old son, Igor, Yulia Piatnitskaia began to question her own sanity. "I cannot even admit to myself the kinds of thoughts I am having about him," she wrote in her diary on February 25, 1938. "For as long as I have a bit of reason and a lot of love, I'll continue to wait. But I foresee torments terrible for my heart in the coming days." Her heart's most terrible torment concerned the soul of her husband, who had been in prison for seven months. "Who is he?" she asked in her diary. "If he is a professional revolutionary—the kind he described in his book, the kind I saw in him for seventeen years, then he was struck by a terrible misfortune." But what if he was not? What if he actually was a monster in human form?

It is clear that Piatnitsky has never been a professional revolutionary: he has been a professional scoundrel, a spy or secret agent like Malinovsky. That is why he has always been so grim and withdrawn. In the darkness of his soul, there was nothing to do but wait until he was discovered or managed to escape punishment.

We, his wife and children, have never been of much importance to him. Now, the question is: who did he serve? And why? He must have started because tailoring was hard and uninteresting, so he got involved in revolutionary work and, somehow, because of his cowardly nature, became a secret agent. Somebody must have discovered something: how he became a traitor or when he became a traitor, then the revolution happened and he realized how good the real struggle for socialism was, but the spies obviously would not let him work and he spent all those years working for the counterrevolution and surrounding himself with people like him. Piatnitsky's life could have gone like this. But who is he: this one or that one? I don't know, and it hurts. When I think of this first one, I feel so sorry for him and want to die or to fight for him. When I think of that second one, I feel tainted and disgusted, and I want to live in order to see them all caught and have no pity for them. I could spit in his face and call him a "spy." Vova must feel the same way.[22]

Their twelve-year-old son, Vova (Vladimir), wanted to be a sniper and a border guard. "What a bastard Dad is," he said once, "to go and ruin all my dreams like that." On February 25, 1938, he spent all day reading a book about the Red Army. When he finished, he said: "It's too bad Dad hasn't been shot, since he's an enemy of the people." Yulia was not sure it was true. "In the depths of my soul, in my inmost self, I clearly have no feeling of distrust for that man. He cannot possibly be an enemy of the Party he valued above all else in life. He cannot possibly be an enemy of the prole-tariat, whose interests he served all his life, to the best of his ability. It is still too early to talk about this without emotion. But the time will come, and you will still be certain of this, and your heart will sing because you will know that his thoughts and his heart were pure before the Party."[23]

But then, why had he been arrested? The Party did not make mistakes, and Piatnitsky's arrest had been authorized by the Party. "I trust Piat-nitsky, but I trust Ezhov's holy work even more. 'Even the sun can have an eclipse,' but nothing can eclipse the Sun. The Party is the sun of our lives, and nothing can be dearer than its health, and if sacrifices are required (and if your life has been cut down by accident), find the strength to re-main a human being, in spite of everything. My darling little Igor, my sa-cred little boy, I know you will understand everything if you do not die. You are too young to go through something like this."[24]

The only way to reconcile both sides of her heart was to think of Piat-nitsky's arrest as a necessary sacrifice. This meant that Igor's arrest must also be a necessary sacrifice. But it was not. It was a redemptive trial: "As for my Igor, I think along with F. [Engels]: 'Whatever is healthy can with-stand a trial by fire. The unhealthy elements we will happily discard. . . . The day of the great decision, the day of the battle of nations is near, and the victory will be ours.'" She knew that Igor belonged among the chosen and was needed at Armageddon. It was Piatnitsky she was not sure about.[25]

Some relief was provided by the trial of Bukharin, Rykov, and other enemies. They were the ones "who had sowed mistrust, hostility, slander, and cruelty." Their unmasking and destruction would make it "easier to breathe." On March 3, the day Koltsov's article about the pack of blood-hounds came out, Yulia stayed home all day:

I have used up all my physical strength. During the day, while I was alone in the apartment (Grandma had brought me the newspaper), I suddenly woke up with a stomach cramp. Without quite realizing it, I had broken into a "dance of joy" at the decisive routing of those "beasts." To think that I used to respect some of them, although

Piatnitsky had warned me about B. and what a scumbag he was. He told me about how he had sat on the floor in their midst, unshaven and clad in some old suit, and that no one had said hello to him. They already viewed him as a stinking corpse. And now he has turned out to be even more frightening, more treacherous than anybody could have imagined. "Death" is too easy a punishment for them, but the working people should not have to breathe the same air as them. Oh Piatnitsky, you cannot be with them, my heart refuses to accept it.

If it must be, if they haven't withdrawn their accusations against you, then I will adopt the official view in all of my dealings with you and will never be near you, but I cannot think of you as a liar before the Party or a counterrevolutionary. But if it turns out to be true, can I remain among free Soviet citizens? And die? At a time when the dark forces are rising against us, when the last and perhaps decisive battle is coming, and soviets are being formed in other countries? And leave my children behind? I feel like I can't sleep, don't want to see anyone, don't want to move. It frightens me to be wearing Piatnitsky's slippers (flat ones with no heels), and I feel really sick to my stomach after my dance. This was the first time my body has been inspired by anything since Piatnitsky's arrest.[26]

Yulia and Vova followed the trial in the newspapers. Vova read the transcripts every day after school. He asked his mother how the murderers had prepared poison and told her that he thought Koltsov's description of Krestinsky's attempt to retract his testimony was very funny. ("In a brilliant display of cross-questioning, the public prosecutor Comrade Vyshinsky corners the mangy Trotskyite rat. Its squeaking is growing more confused.") They spent their evenings reading Jules Verne's *The Mysterious Island* aloud.[27] On March 13, the sentences were announced.

Today at 4 p.m. they will be liquidated—these terrible villains of our land. They managed to weave such a vast and intricate web that even those who hate them as much as Comrade Ezhov hates them and as much as every honest and conscientious citizen of our country hates them have been caught up in it. In addition to the colossal material damage, they have inflicted moral wounds on us. So much remains to be untangled, pondered, destroyed, cured, and neutralized in time, and among them there is, of course, some of the "living flesh" of Lenin's and Stalin's Party, whose suffering has been immeasurable, even though I have only a dim understanding of it. Who will pay for it? Who will give back the lost months of my life, the possibility of working shoulder to shoulder with my comrades at such a time? Who will make up for this unmarried loneliness? Their disgraceful, vile blood is too small a price for all the grief felt by the

Party and by all those who have some feeling left, for the suffering of those innocent people who have been removed from society, people who have given everything for the revolution, every drop of their strength, not realizing that there existed such two-legged monsters, such cretins who were so good at dissembling. I do not know of a more terrible creature than Bukharin, it is hard for me to express what I feel. Now they will be destroyed, but my hatred will not be diminished. I would like a terrible punishment for them—we could put them in cages built especially for them in a museum, labeled 'counterrevolutionaries,' and take care of them as if they were rare specimens. That would be terrible for them: citizens would come and look at them the way you look at animals. Hatred for them would never die, and they would be forced to see how we fight for a happy life, how united we are in our struggle, how much we love those of our leaders who remain true, how we triumph over fascism while they sit around idle, being fed like animals and not being considered human. . . . I curse you all, curse you for eternity.[28]

On March 9, she went to see the chief military prosecutor, Naum Rozovsky. She was nervous and, according to her diary, "spoke unintelligently and said all the wrong things." So did the prosecutor:

Comrade Rozovsky is also exhausted, he screamed at me angrily, with great emotion. I even felt sorry for him, for I only subsist while he works, and such a hard job it is, too. Oh how dear they are to me, how I wish they could trust me! I would happily give my life for something useful, but coming from me it must sound untrue. . . . I know that the best thing for me is death. But then again, it's probably wrong for me to kill myself. What did I feel in Rozovsky's office? One should always rise above one's private interests—always, but especially in my state, when I have and will have nothing, so I must find work I can live for.[29]

Such work could be found. She needed the NKVD in order to find out what had happened to her husband and son; she admired the NKVD for the difficult work they were doing; and she needed the NKVD's trust in order to resolve her doubts. Working for the NKVD might be the best, and perhaps the only, way to become whole again. On April, 14, she went to see Rozovsky again:

I spoke of my intention of putting myself at the disposal of the NKVD and military organs. He told me that I should express this wish in writing and not be shy about being long-winded, so that I could make myself completely clear. He did not promise anything concrete, but he did promise to try to help me. The letter must be handed to Medvedev. He must have been as humane with me as his position allowed. I could tell that he was exhausted and that he truly cared. I shook his hand firmly, although perhaps that was excessive sentimentality, which I keep trying to overcome, but when I saw in him a person who was doing a job that was difficult yet so necessary at this time, I wanted to express my admiration for those comrades, my heartfelt kinship with those who are uprooting all kinds of scum from our Party.[30]

It did not work. Next time she saw Rozovsky, he was cold and indifferent. She began to doubt the one thing that had seemed solid:

The most frightening thing within me is the growing distrust for the quality of people who conduct investigations and have the right to arrest. Of course, I realize that Ezhov and some others, both top-level and low-level officials, are wonderful, genuine people who are doing extraordinarily difficult work, but the majority—they are also doing difficult work, but as stupid and petty people capable of meanness. It's a shame I feel this way, but the facts (the things I have experienced myself, things I have seen, as single strokes here and there, things I happen to have heard from other people standing in prison lines) make it impossible to feel differently.[31]

She tried to talk to different people, but they would not listen. Some laughed at her. She used to have Piatnitsky to talk to, but he was not there anymore and might or might not be the reason for the silence that surrounded her. The last entry in her diary, under May 28, 1938, is: "I used to talk his ear off, but I never needed anyone else to talk to, and I still won't, except perhaps to someone from the NKVD. In spite of everything, I feel closer to them."[32]

Several weeks later she got a job as an engineer at a hydroelectric power plant in Kandalaksha, on the White Sea. She took Vova with her. On October 27, 1938, she was arrested for telling an NKVD informer that her husband was innocent. Her diary was used as evidence against her. She was sentenced to five years in a labor camp and sent to the Dolinsky Camp in Kazakhstan, where she saw Igor. Vova ran away to Moscow and was taken in by the family of his friend, Zhenia Loginov, from Apt. 89. After three months of living with the Loginovs, Vova overheard one of them say that his stay was causing Zhenia's father problems at work, so he went to the Executive Committee of the Moscow City Council and was sent to an orphanage.[33]

■   ■   ■

According to the grown-up Vladimir Piatnitsky, Zhenia Loginov's father worked in Stalin's secretariat. The Loginovs' act—taking in the enemy's progeny—was uncommon but not unheard of. But most "family members of traitors to the motherland" (as they were described in Order No. 00486) were helped by other family members. And most families' central figure—not targeted by the mass operations and not questioning the duty to help—was the grandmother. Svetlana Osinskaia's maternal grandmother, Ekaterina Nartsissovna Smirnova, was not unusual:

> She was quiet, but firm and unflappable. Short, with soft gray hair cozily pinned back with horn hairpins, she wore long, dark skirts and buttoned-up blouses with a tie or bow at the collar and a small brooch with tiny pearls. Several letters from my grandmother to my mother that I have kept suggest that she was a person of great integrity. Her letters are plain: she talks unaffectedly about her health and simple chores, but her dignity comes through clearly. Those traits of hers bordered on coldness. She was never openly affectionate with us or particularly curious, and never singled anyone out. With the calm of a self-confident and deliberate person, she made jams at the dacha, provoking my great admiration for her ability to remove cherry pits by means of a hairpin, mended clothes, and made wonderful toys for New Year's: a tiny little chest with blue silk lining, a small leather bag stuffed with candy, and little dolls in bright dresses. Spared miraculously by life's upheavals, they stayed with me for a very long time. When my parents were arrested, she did not become frightened, but came over the morning after my father's arrest and stayed with my mother until she was arrested. After that, she came over almost every day and did her best, along with several other people, so that we could go on with our normal lives.[34]

Ekaterina Nartsissovna
Smirnova
(Courtesy of Elena Simakova)

She did eventually take Svetlana (who was twelve), Rem (fourteen), and Valia (fifteen) to an orphanage—she lived with her niece in a twelve-meter room in a communal apartment—but she remained the center of the truncated family and regularly sent news, food, and money to her daughter and grandchildren. The same was true of Arkady Rozengolts's mother-in-law, who took care of her grandchildren until the war made it impossible. Many children, including Inna, Natalia, and Valentina Gaister, Yuri and Tania Trifonov, and Rada Poloz (Tania Miagkova's daughter), were raised by their grandmothers—all of whom were described as dry, unsentimental, and unquestioningly devoted. The fact that two of the three—Tatiana Aleksandrovna Slovatinskaia and Feoktista Yakov-levna Miagkova—were orthodox Bolshevik sectarians does not seem to have diminished their family loyalty. The fact that their families were punished for unexplained reasons does not seem to have diminished their Bolshevik orthodoxy. The two sets of loyalties—shared by their children, instilled in their grandchildren, and maintained painstakingly to the end of their lives—were connected to each other by silence.

Uncles and aunts—the brothers and sisters of arrested enemies—had a more difficult choice to make. They were vulnerable to arrest and had reason to believe that associating with a contaminated relative might increase the risk. Some had children of their own, to whom they owed primary loyalty. Some were members of the Party, to which they owed primary loyalty (and from which they expected extra scrutiny and harsher punishments). Some were both parents and Party members.

The children of the people's commissar of the food industry, Abram Gilinsky, twelve-year-old Nelly and two-year-old Tania, were sent to an orphanage, but Nelly refused to cooperate ("breaking windows, rolling on the floor"), until the principal informed her aunt (her mother's sister, Lydia Mefodievna Stechkina). When the aunt arrived, she asked the principal what would happen to her and her husband, both Party members, if they adopted the two girls. The principal said (accurately, according to Order No. 00486) that there would be no negative consequences, and the aunt took them back with her. The six of them—Nelly and Tania, their aunt and uncle, and their aunt's grown-up adopted daughter and her husband—shared two rooms in a communal apartment. Nelly and Tania were to call their aunt and uncle "mom" and "dad." A month later, the uncle, Vasily Stepanovich Kraiushkin, was arrested. The aunt went on to become the girls' adoptive mother. (Their mother died in exile in 1949.) Their half-brother, the nineteen-year-old David (Gilinsky's son from a previous marriage) became "like a father" to them. Gilinsky's three brothers, who lived in Leningrad, helped out the best they could.[35]

When the deputy commissar of the defense industry, Romuald Mukle-vich, returned home to Apt. 334 after the arrest of his wife, Anna (head of supplies at the State Planning Committee), he was visited by his brother-in-law and old Civil War comrade, the director of the Aviation House, Matvei Yakovlevich Sheiniuk. Muklevich's daughter, Irina, heard her uncle say that, if Muklevich was arrested, he would take Irina to live with him and take care of her as long as he lived. After Muklevich's arrest, he did take her to live with him. Several months later, he, too, was arrested, and Irina was raised by her aunt and grandmother.[36]

Was Sheiniuk arrested because of his loyalty to the Muklevichs? No one knew for sure, but it made sense to assume a connection. When the people's commissar of state farms, N. N. Demchenko, and his wife, Mirra Abramovna, were arrested, their eldest son, nineteen-year-old Kolia, talked his uncle into sheltering his eleven-year-old brother Feliks (named after the founder of the Cheka). When he next came to visit, his uncle opened the door without undoing the chain and told him through the crack that, in order to sever all links with the enemies of the people, he had taken Feliks to an orphanage. At the orphanage, Kolia was told that he was not in a position to adopt his brother. In order to qualify, Kolia married his girlfriend, Tatiana, thereby provoking the "desperate envy" of his roommate, Samuil Moroz. A week later, both Kolia and Samuil were arrested.[37]

Inna Gaister's Uncle Veniamin (a researcher at the Institute of World Economy and International Politics), attempted to cut off all contact with his arrested relatives, but was seemingly left with no choice but to take in his mother, who was visiting from Poland, after three of his sisters (Lipa, Adassa, and Inna's mother, Rakhil) were arrested. Their twenty-year-old brother Lyova was a student at the Bauman Institute at the time. As Inna wrote in her memoirs,

> After my mother and Lipa were arrested, Grandma Gita went to live with Adassa. After Adassa was taken to prison, her son Veniamin took her in. Sometime in early December, Elochka, Aunt Lipa's daughter, came home from school one day to find Grandma Gita sitting on the stairs in front of their apartment. Veniamin, without warning Niuma (Lipa's husband) or Lyova, had brought her there and left her by the locked door. Grandma moved in with them. I would often see her there. She was no longer the same proud and happy Grandma I had seen arrive from Poland. I can still picture her with her red wig all twisted round and her bun hanging over her ear. She could not understand why her children had been imprisoned. She kept pacing up and down the apartment, intoning: "It's all my fault. I have brought grief to my children. I must return home immediately. As soon as I leave, things will get better again." She was saying all this in Yiddish. Of course, Elochka and I did not understand a word of Yiddish, so Lyova had to translate for us.[38]

Inna's mother, Rakhil Kaplan, had been sent to the Akmolinsk Camp for Family Members of Traitors to the Motherland in Kazakhstan. One of her letters contained a note to Veniamin, in which she asked him to take care of her children. "After what had happened with Grandma Gita, I did not want to go to Veniamin. But Niuma and Lyova talked me into taking the note to him, and so Lyova and I went over to his place. He and Sarra were home. They took my mother's note and went into his study. Then Sarra came out and said: 'Go away and never come back.' Veniamin did not come out. Lyova and I left without saying a word. That did not save Veniamin from prison, however."[39]

Dima Osinsky's wife, Dina, was being exiled to Kharkov, which meant that his younger siblings Svetlana and Valia and their adopted brother

Rem Smirnov would have no place to live and be taken to an orphanage. According to Svetlana,

> The matter resolved itself, somehow. We would go to the orphanage, but not for long because, of course, everything would soon be cleared up. But, just in case, Dina sent us over to my father's sister, Galina, who was also my mother's closest friend, to ask for advice. She lived with her husband, the chemist, S. S. Medvedev, the future famous scholar and full member of the Academy of Sciences, and their son, who was a little younger than me. I had been to their place—three small rooms in a communal apartment in a tall building with a dark stairway on the corner of Krivokolenny and Armiansky Alleys—many times before with my mother. The walls of Galina's room were covered with pictures, including a large portrait of her: a handsome, thin, perfectly proportionate face, dark wavy hair, and a blue blouse with a wide-open white collar. Next to it were some of her own drawings. Aunt Galia was an artist and worked at the Vakhtangov Theater.
>
> That spring day in 1938, Valia and I went to Aunt Galia to ask for advice about our future, which had, in fact, already been decided. We climbed up the tall staircase and rang the doorbell. Aunt Galia opened the door. My God how scared she was! She didn't know what to do. We stood in our coats in the large dark entryway, while she disappeared somewhere into the bowels of her rooms. Soon she came back and started stuffing our pockets with candy. "You can't stay here," she said quickly and softly, "Sergey Sergeevich is working. He mustn't be disturbed." She kept pushing us gently toward the door. When we had all walked out onto the stairway, she seemed relieved. "Don't ever come back again, okay? Now go." So we left and walked home in silence. When he got home, Valia, who had never cried once during those six months, buried his face in his pillow and sobbed.[40]

Close friends were in a similar position—and were frequently referred to as "uncles" and "aunts." One of Irina Muklevich's real aunts, her mother's sister Maria, had a friend named Anton Ionych Shpektorov, an official at the People's Commissariat of External Trade (headed, after Rozengolts's arrest, by A. I. Mikoyan). He had "a personal car with a chauffeur, two secretaries, and the use of the government cafeteria, exclusive sanatoria, etc., etc.," but he "was not afraid of anything and came to see us almost every day." (He may have been in love with Irina's aunt, but the risk remained the same, whatever the reason for such open loyalty.)[41] Other friends, according to Irina, acted differently:

> Three days after my father's arrest, my aunts Nina and Meli (my father's sisters) walked into the entryway and saw my parents' close

friend, the Old Bolshevik, Mikhalina Novitskaia [Michalina No-wicka], who had worked for many years at TASS, as Doletsky's per-sonal secretary. They were all waiting for the elevator. When she saw my aunts, Mikhalina did not say hello and did not enter the elevator. She simply stepped aside and turned away. My aunts were shocked. It was as if she had spat in their faces.

Of course, Mikhalina did not know then that a month later her own husband, an Old Bolshevik and top official of the Comintern Executive Committee [Waclaw Bogucki], would be arrested; she would be sent to a camp for eight years; and her son [Vladimir] would be taken to an orphanage. And that after her return she would spend many years looking for her son and that she would never find him because he had been sent to prison for ten years for stealing a watermelon and a cantaloupe from the field when he was hungry. And that she would come to me when she had no place to go in Moscow, and I would take her in. All that happened. She would end her days in a retirement home, lonely and sick.[42]

Vatslav Bogutsky's (Waclaw Bogucki) arrest photographs

Mikhalina Novitskaia's (Michalina Nowicka) arrest photograph

Vladimir Bogutsky (soon after his parents' arrest)

In memoirs and reminiscences, such actions are featured prominently and represented as acts of betrayal, often followed by providential retribution. Most House of Government residents—including those like Piatnitskaia, who thought of themselves as Bolsheviks and were not convinced of their relatives' (or even their own) innocence before the Party—seem to have expected loyalty from their friends, lovers, and relatives, irrespective of whether they were Party members or not. Some self-sacrificial actions and individuals might be singled out for admiration, but most such actions and individuals were mentioned without comment, as part of the normal course of things. Friends, lovers, and relatives were, then and later, depicted as having been subjected to a test of humanity. Some passed, proving themselves to be "true" (in the sense of both "loyal" and "genuine"), and some did not. And since friends, lovers, and relatives were expected to be true, by definition, those who did the right thing might or might not, depending on the other factors involved, be seen as heroic. Those who did not were consistently singled out—and often deliberately exposed—as traitors and "bad people." There were countless shades of gray, forgiven trespasses, and attenuating circumstances in between, but the endpoints on the scale of goodness were clear enough. "Good people" were those who were prepared to risk their own safety and that of their immediate family for the sake of friends, lovers, and other relatives. "Bad people" were those who wished to protect themselves and their immediate family to the exclusion of all other loyalties and commitments. The orthodox Bolsheviks who turned away their nephews and nieces because the only true family was the Party were acting like bad people. In accounts written in the post-sectarian world, these orthodox Bolsheviks and bad people became indistinguishable. Feliks Demchenko's and Inna Gaister's uncles were bad people—both at the time and in the retelling—irrespective of whether their reasons were self-servingly egotistical or self-denyingly sectarian.

Family morality within the House of Government, like the sectarian morality of Party purges, was centered on trust and betrayal. But whereas the purge morality was concerned with secret thoughts as opposed to actions (or rather, with hypothetical actions as emanations of deviant thoughts), family morality was focused on actions as proof of moral choices. Lydia Mefodievna Stechkina, Matvei Yakovlevich Sheiniuk, and Anton Ionych Shpektorov were good people irrespective of whatever private fears they may have had to overcome. Indeed, they were all the more remarkably good people for having overcome their private fears and silently reconciled their sectarian commitments with those toward kith and kin (all three were Party members). The Party itself could not quite make up its mind: it exiled entire clans and punished "family members of traitors to the motherland," while proclaiming, from Stalin's mouth, that "sons do not answer for their fathers" and encouraging, inconsistently but forcefully, the reintegration of those sons into the Soviet family. In a note to her from prison, Irina Muklevich's mother wrote: "Whatever happens to us, always remain a true Soviet." And that is how Irina's aunt, a good person and a true Soviet, brought her up. The key to being a good Soviet while having a mother in prison was silence.[43]

The more intimate the relationship and the thicker the web of mutual obligations, the greater the expectation of loyalty and the more painful the betrayal (very rare in the case of parents and children). The more distant the relationship and less anticipated the favor, the greater the virtue. The Loginovs took in an enemy's son because he was their own son's friend. Irina Muklevich had a school friend, Shura Elchugina, who lived in the dormitory for Military Academy cadets across the river. (Her father was a maintenance worker at the Academy.) After the arrest of Irina's parents, the Elchugins invited her to stay at their place, and Shura's mother made her a dress. Vasily Shuniakov, a former Petrograd worker and Central Control Commission official specializing in purges, and his wife, Iudif Charnaia, a former seamstress and education official specializing in pedology (until it was banned by Volin and Rabichev), let their daughter's friend, Katia Dushechkina (from Apt. 422), stay with them for a while after her parents were arrested. According to their daughter, Tamara, they were visibly frightened by what was happening and burned many of their books; Vasily started drinking.[44]

Boris Ivanov, "the Baker"; his wife, Elena Yakovlevna Zlatkina; and their three children (Volodia, Anatoly, and Galina) occupied two rooms of their three-room apartment and rented out the third. Their first tenant, Professor Lebedev, was arrested very early, perhaps as early as 1935. Their next tenants were a Marxism-Leninism instructor named Krastins (Krastiņš, in Latvian) and his wife and daughter. Once, in the middle of the night, the doorbell rang. Anatoly, who was seventeen at the time, opened the door, saw several NKVD agents, walked over to where his father was sitting at his desk (he used to work late), and said: "Get up, Dad, it turns out you're a bastard. They've come for you." The agents came in, asked everyone for their names, and moved on to the room where the Krastins lived. A few days later, that room was occupied by the wife and two daughters of the recently arrested head of the Cattle-Purchasing Trust, N. A. Bazovsky, from Apt. 377 three floors above. Shortly afterward, Bazovsky's wife was also arrested. Her daughters were not home at the time, and Elena Yakovlevna told Anatoly and Galina (who was fifteen) to save as many of the Bazovskys' belongings as they could. She also told Galina to stand watch downstairs and warn the Bazovskys' older daughter, Nina, not to come up. (The younger one, Olga, was out of town, visiting her aunt.) The guard on duty, named Niura, told Galina to go back to her apartment and promised to call her when Nina showed up. (According to Galina, the guards liked her family and treated them well.) She did; Galina warned Nina; and Nina went to live with her relatives. Meanwhile, the husband of Elena Yakovlevna's sister, an aviation engineer, had been arrested, and the sister had moved in with the Ivanovs. One day, on the Big Stone Bridge, she ran into the fifteen-year-old Olga Bazovskaia, who told her that her aunt had thrown her out and that she had no place to stay. Elena's sister invited her over, and she ended up moving in with them. Boris Ivanov (who had known the Bazovskys as apartment neighbors for about three months) registered her in one of his two rooms. (The third room was now occupied by the Commissariat of Finance official, V. M. Buzarev, and his family.) Galina and Olga became close friends and treated each other like sisters. According to Galina, her parents remained orthodox Bolsheviks. Her father had recently become secretary of the Party organization and head of the personnel department at the People's Commissariat of Food Industry; her mother was a member of the Moscow City Soviet. They never talked about their arrested relatives and neighbors, including Olga's parents. When Krastins returned from prison a year or so later, he stayed with them for several days. According to Galina, he had no teeth and was dressed in rags; he went straight to the bathroom, saw the soap, and started crying. Olga lived with the Ivanovs for about ten years; they raised her as a daughter. When Olga's mother came back from the camps, she also stayed with them for a while. According to Galina, she once said: "If I had been in Elena Yakovlevna's place, would I have done what she did? Would I have taken Galka in? No." The world was divided into good people and bad people. Everyone—Party and non-Party—seemed to agree that Boris Ivanov and his wife, Elena Yakovlevna Zlatkina, were very good people.[45]

■ ■ ■

The Elchugins', Shuniakovs', and Ivanovs' actions may have had something to do with the fact that they were former workers and peasants, not "students," and that they assumed that being a good Soviet was compatible with fulfilling traditional neighborly and kinship obligations (just as it was compatible with not celebrating New Year's Eve and adults' birthdays). Perhaps they found it easier to use silence as a bridge between faith and social practice.

The House of Government's most articulate intellectuals and prominent experts on Bolshevik morality—the author of Soviet family law, Yakov Brandenburgsky, and his coauthor and chess partner, Aron Solts—were not up to this task. In late 1936, Brandenburgsky, who was then chairman of the Collegium for Civil Cases of the Soviet Supreme Court, began to act strangely, telling his family that he was afraid to go to work. In December, his wife and twenty-three-year-old daughter, Elsa, received a call from the mental hospital ("Kanatchikov's Dacha") that he had been picked up on the street

Yakov Brandenburgsky

in a state of complete disorientation. After some time, they were allowed to bring him home, but he refused to eat and was taken to the Pirogov Hospital. "When we came to visit," said his daughter in an interview sixty years later, "we found a complete stranger, suffering from fatigue. A sybarite by nature, he seemed totally unaffected by the company of madmen, screaming, squealing, and crawling on the floor beside him. The room was filled with very sick people, but my father seemed perfectly comfortable there. He had even found a friend—a dwarf with a contorted face—whose company he seemed to enjoy. . . . He would sometimes say things that made no sense to us. Once he became agitated: 'Why did you write my name on the box of chocolates? They might find me that way!'" In late 1938, after the mass operations were over, Brandenburgsky suddenly recovered and returned home. He retired from the Supreme Court and became a volunteer lecturer at the Moscow Party Committee. He died in 1951 at the age of seventy, while playing chess. He never talked about his illness.[46]

Solts was serving as first deputy prosecutor-general for criminal cases and living with his adopted son, Evgeny, and his niece, Anna Grigorievna Zelenskaia. His sister, Esfir, had died in 1935. After the arrest of Anna's former husband, Isaak Zelensky, their two children, eighteen-year-old Elena and sixteen-year-old Andrei, joined their mother in Solts's apartment, and he adopted them, too. On February 14, 1938, he had a violent argument with his boss, Prosecutor-General A. Ya. Vyshinsky, about the case of his friend and disciple, Valentin Trifonov, who had been arrested on June 21, 1937. According to Elena, he came home very upset and said that Vyshinsky had threatened him, too. He decided to stop eating in the hope that Stalin would agree to talk to him. Several days later, he was taken to the ward for the violently insane at the Sokolniki Psycho-Neurological Hospital. According to his doctor, who knew him from her previous work as consultant for the Amnesty Board, which Solts chaired, he blamed the demise of the Old Bolsheviks on the rise of opportunists. "'Who is Ezhov? Why should I believe Ezhov? The Party does not know Ezhov!' Solts would say. 'Vyshinsky, a former Menshevik, is going to interrogate me? A Menshevik is going to sit in judgment over Bolsheviks?!'" He abandoned his hunger strike and, a month and a half later, was allowed to return home in exchange for a guarantee from his niece Anna that he would not pose any danger to himself or others. Two and a half months later, Anna was arrested. Solts wrote a letter to his former colleague, the chairman of the Military Collegium of the Supreme Court, Vasily Ulrikh, but received no response. He was removed from his position and then worked as a literary consultant for the Young Guard Publishers and director of the archive of

Aron Solts

the Museum of the Peoples of the USSR, before retiring in 1940 at the age of sixty-eight. "He suffered terribly from the enforced idleness," wrote Elena. "He spent hours lying in bed reading or pacing around the apartment writing long columns of numbers on pieces of paper or in newspaper margins."[47]

■ ■ ■

Fedor Kaverin's 1933 production of Yuri Smolich's *The Other Side of the Heart* dealt with the problem of Bolshevik trust and damnation. The blue-eyed idealist, Klim, with whom the audience was expected to sympathize, was unmasked as an unreconstructed enemy. His double, the demonic Sixfingers, turned out to be not only his shadow (the other side of his heart), but his true self, the irredeemable evil of his origins. At the discussion in the Commissariat of Enlightenment, Kaverin's main defender against the champions of the still reigning construction/conversion plot had been the State New Theater's administrative director, Sergei Ivanovich Amaglobeli, who claimed that no one had a "fully transparent soul," that naive self-deception was as dangerous as deliberate deception, and that the cat-and-mouse game that the theater was playing with its audiences was, understandably enough, "painful for those who find themselves in the role of the mouse." Kaverin's main critic and the most senior participant in the discussion had been the deputy head of the Theater Department of the Commissariat of Enlightenment, Pavel Ivanovich Novitsky, who argued that the possibility of redemption was at the heart of socialist construction and that the job of every Soviet citizen was to "engage in the inner struggle aimed at reeducating human beings." The right balance, according to Novitsky, had been struck by Kaverin's next production, *Uriel Acosta*, in which the vacilating young idealist who resembled the blue-eyed Klim (and was played by the same actor) overcame his fears, retracted his false confession, and stood up for the tradition of heroic authenticity represented by Galileo, Bruno, and Spinoza, "all the way to Marx, Lenin, and Stalin."[48]

In March 1936, two years after the discussion of *Uriel Acosta*, Novitsky traveled to Sverdlovsk to give a series of lectures on socialist realism. Since there were no rooms available in the local hotels, he stayed at the apartment of his official host, the director of the Sverdlovsk Theater and Entertainment Department, Ya. A. Grinberg. At the end of his visit, he held a confidential meeting with the directors of the local theaters about the recently launched campaign "against all forms of formalism, naturalism, vulgarization, and spineless liberalism." In his talk, he discussed the reasons for the closing down of Moscow's Art Theater II and mentioned a conversation about the Party's theater policy that Stalin had had with Platon Kerzhentsev, the head of the Committee for the Arts, and A. S. Shcherbakov, the Central Committee's supervisor of cultural matters.

Comrade Vinitsky, the head of the Sverdlovsk Committee for the Arts, who was present at the talk, accused Novitsky of slandering Comrade Stalin and reported him to the Provincial Party Committee. Novitsky was briefly detained and interrogated by the NKVD before being allowed to return to Moscow.

Upon his return, he wrote a letter to his boss, Kerzhentsev's deputy for theater affairs, Yakov Iosifovich Boiarsky (Shimshelevich), in which he apologized for exaggerating the virtues of Art Theater II and for revealing the content of Stalin's conversation with Kerzhentsev and Shcherbakov that Boiarsky had related to him "in confidence." His explanation for his "enormous political blunder" was that he had been suffering from severe headaches and that his audience consisted entirely of Party members. He knew that his behavior could not be justified, but he hoped he deserved another chance:

> I am not deluding myself. I know that there are three options: (1) a severe Party reprimand and my retention in the world of Soviet theater; (2) my expulsion from the Party without disgrace and defamation and my retention in the theater world; (3) my expulsion from the Party with disgrace and defamation and my ruin.
>
> Dear Yakov Osipovich, I do not think that you will find it possible to defend me under these circumstances.
>
> But, while making a decision, it is necessary to take into account a person's qualities as a Party member and an employee and his creative potential. I can still do a great deal in this life. I have many ideas and even more willingness to work and create at a time like this, in a country such as ours. Over the last three years, I have been living with a feeling of enormous happiness at the fullness of life and pride in my country and the Party. This feeling has been growing with each day. This feeling is an organic expression of my personality, my sincerity, my honesty toward our epoch. These are not the right words, but it is not the words that matter, it is a person's worth and the way he lives his life. . . . It is easy to destroy a person and turn him into a useless rag. I am asking for the tiniest bit of your understanding and attention.

Novitsky's view of his own predicament was consistent with his position on *The Other Side of the Heart*. His letter's last paragraph dealt with innocence, not redemption:

> Grinberg is not connected to me in any way. He is not guilty of anything. By organizing a meeting between theater directors who are all Party members and a celebrated Party lecturer from Moscow, he did not do anything wrong. Even the fact that he put me up in his apartment is being held against him. I left him in a state of utter dejec-

tion. He and his wife were looking at me with silent reproach. It is impossible to take, it is worse than a formal accusation. I would have left right away, if I had been able to. I vouch for the fact that Grinberg is an honest Party man and a good comrade and that he has nothing to do with the content of my failed improvised talk. I ask you to make sure that Comrade Grinberg does not suffer any consequences, and that this episode does not prevent him from transferring to Moscow (something he dreams of passionately and impatiently).[49]

Boiarsky sent Novitsky's letter to Molotov, assuring him that he had never told Novitsky anything "in confidence" and expressing the hope that the letter as a whole was "sufficient evidence" of Novitsky's guilt. Molotov forwarded both letters to Stalin. Boiarsky was later executed as an enemy of the people (partly for being Ezhov's homosexual partner). So was S. I. Amaglobeli, who believed that no one had a fully transparent soul. The fate of Comrades Vinitsky and Grinberg is unknown. Novitsky survived the purges and died in 1971, at the age of eighty-three.[50]

28

THE SUPREME
PENALTY

The silence ended in prison. New cellmates would begin by asking each other questions about the reason for their arrest and would keep on talking, day after day, as if to make up for lost time ("first cell, first love," Solzhenitsyn called it). They talked about themselves, others, prisons, and freedom, among many other things, but mostly they talked about what was going on. According to two former cellmates, Konstantin F. Shteppa and Fritz Houtermans, "there was no question that excited the prisoners so much as . . . 'Why? What for?' The question was endlessly argued in the wooden waiting-cells, the 'dog kennels' in which prisoners were put before and after interrogation. The words 'Why? What for?' were to be found scratched with smuggled bits of broken glass on the inside walls of the 'black raven' and the coaches of the prison trains. 'Why? What for?'"[1]

One answer was provided by their interrogators. They had been arrested because they were guilty, and they had no choice but to sign their confessions. The principal means of persuasion were torture (usually sleep deprivation, round-the-clock interrogations, and severe beatings) and, in the case of orthodox Bolsheviks, appeals to sectarian logic and Party discipline. Some orthodox Bolsheviks withstood both torture and persuasion and did not plead guilty at their trial: Anna Muklevich, after six months in prison; Ivan Gronsky, after eleven; Filipp Goloshchekin, after twenty-two. Goloshchekin was arrested on October 15, 1939, as part of the roundup of Ezhov's close associates. (Ezhov testified that Goloshchekin "disagreed with the Party line" and that, in 1925 in Kazakhstan, they had lived together as homosexual lovers.) During the interrogation, Goloshchekin insisted that the idea of collectivization had been discredited among the Kazakh population because of "hostile agitation by the enemies of the Soviet state," not deliberate sabotage on his part. On August 12, 1941, he wrote to the "Great Leader and Teacher" that he had been through "140–150 physically and morally excruciating interrogations," but that he was innocent of all charges, committed to "living and struggling for the victory of the cause of Lenin-Stalin around the world and in our country," and "fully convinced that Bolshevik truth would prevail."[2]

The former Party secretary of West Siberia and Sergei Mironov's troika colleague, Robert Eikhe, wrote his letter to Stalin ten days after Goloshchekin: "If I were guilty of even a hundredth of one single crime I am accused of, I would never have dared approach you with this deathbed appeal. But I have not committed any of these crimes and have never harbored any evil thoughts in my heart. I have never uttered even a half-word of untruth to you, and I am telling you the truth now, with both feet in the grave. My case is an example of entrapment, slander, and the violation of the elementary foundations of revolutionary legality."[3] His only crime against the Party and personally against Comrade Stalin, he wrote to Comrade Stalin, was his false confession of counterrevolutionary activity:

> What happened is this. Unable to withstand the torture that Ushakov and Nikolaev inflicted on me, especially the former who skillfully used the fact that my vertebrae, which had not yet healed after the fracture, caused me unbearable pain, I slandered myself and other people. . . .
> I ask and beg you to have my case reconsidered—not because I wish to be spared, but in order to uncover the evil conspiracy that has, like a snake, ensnared many people, partly because of my own cowardice and criminal slander. I have never betrayed you or the Party. I know I am perishing because of the vile, treacherous work of the enemies of the Party and people, who have staged a provocation against me.[4]

At his pro forma trial, on February 2, 1940, Eikhe formally retracted his confession: "In all my supposed testimony there is not a single word of my own, except for my name under the transcripts, which I was forced to sign. The people from 1918 were named under duress, as a result of the pressure by the investigator, who started beating me from the moment of my arrest. After that I started writing all that rubbish. . . . I am awaiting my sentence and the most important thing to me is to tell the court, the Party, and Stalin that I am innocent. I have never participated in any conspiracy. I will die as firm in my faith in the correctness of Party policy as I was over the course of all my work."[5]

He was sentenced to death. When the heads of the NKVD's Commandants' (executions) and Records departments, V. M. Blokhin and L. F. Bashtakov, arrived at the Sukhanovo Prison the next day to pick up the inmates slated for execution, they found Eikhe and two interrogators, A. A. Esaulov and B. V. Rodos, in Beria's office. According to Bashtakov,

> In my presence, Rodos and Esaulov, on Beria's instructions, brutally beat Eikhe with rubber clubs. When Eikhe collapsed from the beatings, they would continue to beat him while he was on the floor. Then they would lift him up and Beria would ask him the same question: "Do you confess to being a spy?" Eikhe would answer: "No, I do not," and Rodos and Esaulov would continue the beating. Just while

I was there, this monstrous treatment of a man already sentenced to death was repeated at least five times. At one point one of Eikhe's eyes was gouged out. Finally, when Beria realized that no confession was forthcoming, he ordered him taken away for execution.[6]

In early February 1937, when Voronsky was arrested, beatings were not commonly used, and his prison interrogations continued the logic of his purge and expulsion ordeals. Because he had maintained "domestic and literary" relations with the Trotskyites, and because domestic and literary relations were, at bottom, political, he was politically allied with the Trotskyites. And since the Trotskyites were, as it turned out, terrorists, so was he. For more than four months, Voronsky insisted on a distinction between the domestic and the literary on the one hand and the political, on the other. In June, he admitted that "Voronskyism" was the expression of Trotskyism in literature. A short time later, after being presented with several eyewitness accounts of his involvement in terrorism, he confessed his guilt. He was subjected to all-night "assembly-line" interrogations and to confrontations with his literary protégés, Boris Guber, Nikolai Zarudin, and Ivan Kataev, who had all accused him of planning to assassinate Ezhov. Faced with his accusers, he retracted his confession. At his trial, on August 13, he said that he was not guilty of terrorism, but that he could not prove that his accusers were lying. The trial lasted twenty minutes. He was shot several hours later. Guber, Zarudin, and Kataev were shot on the same night.[7]

Voronsky's nemesis, Leopold Averbakh, accepted his interrogators' logic as soon as he was arrested. Or rather, he had always shared it, but now he applied it to himself, his family, and friends. "I am in prison, not at home," he wrote in one of his confessions, "and I need paper—not in order to indulge my old habit of talking to myself by writing at night, but to understand the reason for my arrest." The reason, he concluded, was the "atmosphere of all-permissiveness and omnipotence" in which he had been living as Yagoda's brother-in-law. "I am implicated in the Yagoda case because, over the course of several years, I, though not an NKVD employee, lived at NKVD dachas, received NKVD rations, and was often driven around in NKVD cars. The NKVD repaired my apartment and exchanged my old apartment for a new one. The furniture from my apartment was repaired at the NKVD furniture factory." The swamp—"gentry-estate self-satisfaction"—had somehow swallowed him up even as he was fighting it. In the end, he accepted Voronsky's characterization of him and his collaborators ("clever, successful, irrepressible, everywhere-at-once young men, self-confident and self-satisfied to the point of self-abandonment"). "I realized that narcissism, arrogance, intolerance of self-criticism, neurotic instability, flippancy, hollow wit, and other traits of mine are features of a certain nonproletarian social type. During my eighteen years in the Party, I could have developed into a true Bolshevik, but, not having first experienced proletarian education and having always occupied positions of power, I had too high an opinion of myself and got used to living, both politically and personally, in an atmosphere of all-permissiveness."[8]

He was sentenced to death by Stalin and Molotov as part of a "special procedure" reserved for NKVD officials, without the formality of a trial. He was shot a few hours later, one day after Voronsky.[9]

■ ■ ■

Most orthodox Bolsheviks felt guilty by virtue of being Bolsheviks. In the words of Shteppa and Houtermans, "everyone at some time or other had had doubts about the Communist point of view and expressed them. Everyone had made slips and mistakes that could be regarded as crimes from the point of view of the system." The orthodox Bolsheviks were different from everyone else because their point of view was the point of view of the system. Goloshchekin's explanation for what had befallen him ("Why?" "How could all of this have happened, beginning with the fact of my arrest and so on?") was the same as Eikhe's: the enemies had penetrated the Party's inner sanctum and staged a vile provocation that, like a snake, had ensnared many people. But Goloshchekin and Eikhe seemed to believe—or argue, against impossible odds—that their innocence was compatible with the Party's (Stalin's) infallibility. Most Bolsheviks knew better. They understood that, at some point or other, they had suffered from doubt and made slips and mistakes. They were all guilty of "gentry-estate self-satisfaction," of allowing the swamp back into the House of Government, of being surrounded by beds, maids, carpets, nephews, and mothers-in-law. "In these matters it takes but one slip," wrote Averbakh in his confession, "and you find yourself at the mercy of a kind of vicious logic whose vice-like grip it is very difficult to escape. In the way people related to me, I could see a blurring of the line between one's own pocket and the state and a return of the bourgeois attitude to one's material well-being."[10]

But most of all, they were guilty of inner doubt and impure thoughts. Three days after his arrest, before the interrogations got under way, Aron Gaister wrote a letter to Ezhov:

I admit that I am guilty before the Party of having concealed my Trotskyite vacillations in 1923 and of not having reported (or revealed until now) the fact that when I worked in the State Planning Agency, several leading officials (Rozental, Ronin, Gen. Smirnov, Kapitonov, Kaplinsky, Kraval) formed a caucus, which they talked me into joining for a short period of time, and that Rozental, who presided over that caucus, conducted a de facto Rightist-wrecking policy. In addition to this direct provocation, he treacherously submitted to Kuibyshev a proposal concerning the production of sixty million tons of cast iron during the second Five-Year Plan. This caucus, which often convened in the guise of informal dinners, discussed and criticized the Party line concerning industrialization and the policy in the countryside. I admit that, although I attended these gatherings infrequently and soon stopped altogether, I should have reported that fact to the Central Committee and the NKVD promptly or, in any case, after the unmasking of so many double-dealers and scoundrels. I am profoundly guilty of having done so only after my arrest, and not when I should have. I am ready to inform the investigation about all the relevant facts, including my own guilt.[11]

The same, he wrote, was true of his work as deputy commissar of agriculture. He had done well in firing several bad employees, but he had been guilty of mistaking "facts of wrecking" for sloppy work and for not reporting those facts to the Central Committee and the NKVD. Secret doubts had led to criminal inaction, which had led to facts of wrecking. Only a full confession could achieve reconciliation. "I urgently ask you, Nikolai Ivanovich, to interrogate me personally, so I can tell you, without embellishment, everything I know about all the individuals involved and about myself."[12]

A week later, he wrote another letter to Ezhov, in which he acknowledged that criminal inaction was indistinguishable from criminal action:

I readily admit that I am guilty of the fact that, not having overcome my Trotskyite vacillations of 1923, I continued, in subsequent years, to maintain contacts with the Trotskyites known to me from our days as fellow students at the Institute of Red Professors, and that, having transferred to the People's Commissariat of Agriculture, I, de facto, aided, and participated in, counterrevolutionary wrecking activities of the Rightist center in the commissariat.

I stand ready to provide the investigation with a full confession of all the facts of counterrevolutionary wrecking activity by all the individuals known to me, as well as my own actions.[13]

All he had to realize, in the course of his interrogations, was that de facto abetting counterrevolutionary activity was indistinguishable from actually engaging in counterrevolutionary activity. The Bolshevik conception of sin was identical to St. Augustine's ("a thought, words and deed against the Eternal Law"). When it came to crimes against the Party, which stood for the Eternal Law, thoughts were not radically different from words, and words were not radically different from deeds. And when it came to the Party's Inquisition, sins were not radically different from crimes. After four months of interrogations, he fully admitted his guilt, actual as well as de facto. He was sentenced to death on October 21, 1937, by Stalin, Molotov, Kaganovich, and Voroshilov, as part of a list of sixty-eight individuals, including twenty-four of his House of Government neighbors. The sentence was formally announced on October 29, at a trial

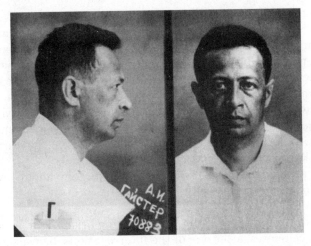

Aron Gaister's arrest photographs (Courtesy of Inna Gaister)

presided over by Vasily Ulrikh. In his last word, Gaister said that his crimes were great and asked the court to allow him to expiate his guilt through honest work. He was shot the next day, on October 30, 1937.[14]

Osinsky, like Gaister and his former friend, Bukharin, wanted his confession of guilt to be part of the sacrament of penance, with the inquisitor as confessor. The record of his interrogation may or may not have been revised and abridged, but his voice is recognizable, and all of the themes are familiar:

QUESTION: You, Osinsky, have been unmasked as an enemy of the people. Do you admit your guilt?

ANSWER: I am surprised to even hear such accusations. Where do such monstrous accusations against me come from? It is simply a misunderstanding. I am an honest person, I fought for Soviet power for many years.

QUESTION: Our advice to you, Osinsky, is to stop juggling terms like "honest person," which are inapplicable to you. Tell us without equivocation: do you intend to supply frank testimony about your crimes?

ANSWER: I would like to talk to you. After all, I am Osinsky. I am known inside and outside the country.

QUESTION: It is good that you are beginning to understand that.

ANSWER: I have made many mistakes, but a betrayal of the Party in the literal sense is out of the question. I am an unusual person, and that means a lot. I am an intelligentsia member of the old formation, with all the individualism characteristic of people of that category. I may disagree with much that is being done in our country, but I have nurtured this disagreement within myself.

Can my personal views be considered treason? I have never been
a Bolshevik in the full sense of the term. I have always wandered
from one opposition to another. <u>In recent years, I have had some</u>
<u>innermost thoughts that were anti-Party in nature</u>, but that is not
quite struggle. I was doing scholarly work, withdrew into myself.
I wanted to leave political work.

QUESTION: Come on, Osinsky, stop posturing! <u>We assure you that</u>
<u>Soviet counterintelligence will be able to make you</u>, an enemy of
the people, tell us everything about the crimes you have committed. We suggest that you stop this equivocation.

ANSWER: Good. I will provide truthful testimony about my work
against the Party.[15]

The rest was a matter of time and blinding bright light. According to
one of his cellmates, after one of the interrogations, he walked into the
cell, "lay down on his bunk, covered his eyes with a wet handkerchief, lay
silently for a while, and suddenly cried out: 'What are they doing to my
eyes? What do they want from my eyes?'"[16]

QUESTION: Osinsky, are you a traitor to the Motherland?

ANSWER: Yes, it is true. I admit my guilt.

QUESTION: Did you use the trust of the Party and the Soviet government for the purpose of betrayal?

ANSWER: That is also true. I acted as a member of a political organization that had the goal of taking power in the Soviet Union.

QUESTION: You acted not as member of a political organization, but
as a traitor and agent provocateur.

ANSWER: Well, that is overdoing it. You must understand that I am a
person of certain political views. I carried out the instructions of
like-minded people as an envoy of the Rightist Center.

QUESTION: You, Osinsky, are the envoy of a gang of murderers. Are
you not the one who tried to drown the working people of our
country in blood? Are you not the one who sold our republics' and
our country's wealth, lock, stock, and barrel?[17]

He was first sentenced to death (by Molotov, Stalin, Voroshilov, Kaganovich, and Zhdanov) on November 1, 1937, along with 291 other high officials, but was left alive as a possible participant in the Bukharin trial. As
in the case of the February–March plenum, he appeared as a witness, not
a defendant. On April 19, 1938, several days after the end of that trial, he
was included in another Category 1 list, but someone (Stalin, Molotov, Kaganovich, or Zhdanov) crossed his name out. Four months later, on August
20, 1938, Stalin and Molotov signed his death sentence (along with those
of 311 other people, including Boris Ivanov's neighbor, N. A. Bazovsky; the
former director of the Berezniki Chemical works, M. A. Granovsky; the

former head of the Party's Jewish Section, S. M. Dimanshtein; the former leader of the Hungarian Soviet Republic, Béla Kun; and a trade representative by the name of Iosif-Samuil Genrikhovich Winzer-Weinzer-Marzelli). Osinsky was executed ten days later, on September 1, 1938. One of his cellmates told his daughter, Svetlana, that he was so weak toward the end that he was allowed to bring a stool to the Lubyanka prison yard. "I picture them beating him—tall, slim, in his gold-rimmed pince-nez, always well groomed, clean shaven, fond of light suits. . . . Of course, it's terrible when anyone is beaten, but this was my father."[18]

∎ ∎ ∎

Bukharin had done most of the inner work needed for a full confession in his letters to Stalin in late 1936, but he had not been able to "disarm" completely. "Interrogate me, turn my skin inside out," he had written to dear Koba on September 24, "but dot the 'i' in such a way that no one will ever dare kick me." The attached condition—"but dot the 'i'"—had demonstrated clearly that he, as Stalin put it at the December plenum, "had no idea what was happening." Bukharin's job—like that of Osinsky, Gaister, Voronsky, and every other Bolshevik, arrested or not—was the same as Job's. It was not to demonstrate guilt or innocence or confess to particular transgressions—it was to submit unconditionally to the eternal truth. It took about three months in prison for him to complete his confession. No bright lights or "assembly-line interrogations" seem to have been required. The "real reason," he said in his last plea at the trial, was the final overcoming of the "split consciousness" in "his own soul." (The transcript of his speech was censored before publication; the deleted words are underlined.)

The <u>real</u> reason is that in prison, <u>where you have to spend a long time permanently suspended between life and death, certain questions appear in a different dimension, and are resolved in a different dimension, compared to the way things are in ordinary, practical life</u>. For, when you ask yourself: if you must die, what are you dying for, <u>particularly at the current stage of the development of the USSR, when it is marching in close formation into the international arena of proletarian struggle</u>? And suddenly, <u>if your consciousness is split,</u> you see with startling vividness the totally black void that opens up before you. There is nothing to die for, if you want to die unrepentant. And, on the other hand, everything positive that shines in the Soviet Union acquires new dimensions in your mind. In the end, this disarms you completely, leads you <u>and forces you</u> to bend your knees before the Party and the country. And when you ask yourself: all right, if you don't die, if, by some miracle, you are allowed to live, then, once again, for the sake of what? As an ostracized enemy of the people, in an inhuman situation, completely separated from everything that makes up the meaning of life? And the answer is the same. At such moments, Citizen Judges, everything personal, everything superfluous and mundane, all the remaining bitterness, pride, and a number of other things, fall away and disappear.[19]

In prison, Bukharin wrote two theoretical works: *Philosophical Arabesques* and *Socialism and Its Culture*. The former was about escaping the black void of individualism; the latter, about everything positive that shines. In the *Arabesques*, the narrator chases away Mephistopheles, "the devil of solipsism," and tells him to hold his "dissolute tongue." The story of *Faust*—the highest of the Pamirs and the model for socialist realism—is interpreted as the defeat of the "insane abstraction" of the lone individual and the rise of the reality of the "socialized man." In late 1937, when Bukharin was in his cell writing the *Arabesques*, that reality consisted of the final unfolding of the last days. The apocalypse, he conceded, had been prophesied before: "Various 'sects' and movements (the Taborites, Moravian Brothers, Herrnhuters, Bogomils, Cathars, et al.) were, in effect, different political factions of the working people, and their leaders, including the executed Thomas Müntzer, John of Leiden, and others deserve the grateful memory of self-emancipating humanity." The peasant warriors had been followed by "the great martyr Campanella," Thomas More, and, in particular, Saint-Simon and Fourier, who had "identified socialism as the goal." Now, in late 1937, that goal had been reached. "All the principal vital functions have been synthesized in the victorious completion of Stalin's five-year plans, with theory and practice becoming one on the scale of the entire society and in every single cell of the social organism." The time had been fulfilled. The *real* real day—"the birth of the new world for mankind"— had arrived.[20]

That new world, according to *Socialism and Its Culture*, was not an abstract socialism theorized by uninformed well-wishers, but the Soviet state as currently constituted. "For that reason, the world-historical task at the moment is not the preaching of universal love, but the preaching of ardent patriotism toward the USSR, which represents the most powerful force of the international socialist movement." This was all the more urgent because of the rise of fascism and the attendant division of the world into two irreconcilable camps (a prerequisite for every apocalypse, including the one chronicled by Bukharin in the summer and early fall of 1917). Fascists deceived the nations by uttering proud words "about totality (i.e., wholeness)," but rather than healing "the rupture of human social existence and the coming apart of man," they "reinforced and institutionalized" them. Fascist totalitarianism was a myth. "*Socialism in the USSR*, on the other hand, is *true* totalitarianism, i.e. wholeness and unity, whose dynamic is the *self-generating growth of that same unity*." The USSR was a "monoideocracy" in the sense that it had created an "ideological unity of the masses" that had no use for the nonsocialized man. The task of socialism was "to overcome the split between will and intelligence" and lead Faust into a world in which "everyone will understand the basic principles of managing things and perform any number of functions." "The directives of the central governing organs, staffed by people who will transfer there for reasons of aptitude and inclination, will be obeyed not as orders issued by superiors, but the way one follows doctors' recommendations or orchestra conductors' instructions. The sins and vices of the old individualistic and authoritarian-hierarchical world will gradually disappear: envy, perfidy, backstabbing will no longer be conceivable as innermost desires or motivations for human behavior; lust for power, vanity, pride, and the desire to subordinate people and rule over them will all disappear."[21]

The "whole society" would be made up of "whole human beings." Whole human beings were inconceivable without a whole society:

> This thesis is in no way contradicted by the fact of the existence of the "harmonious individuals" of the Renaissance or ancient Greece or such phenomena as *Goethe* or our *Pushkin*, the universal geniuses of their time, because we are talking about the average type, not a small sample taken from the "elite." Renaissance humanists were a negligibly small top layer of society; the "ideal human beings" in ancient Greece (idealized to an extraordinary degree in later times) relied on slave labor (as clearly demonstrated in Plato's *Republic*); Goethe was an exception in the whole of Germany (and not only Germany).[22]

Socialist society would be the definitive answer to the call issued by the first Congress of Soviet Writers—a fraternal family of giants "who think and act at the same time," an international constellation of redeemed Faust's remaking the world:

> One of the greatest geniuses of humanity, *Goethe*, said that he was a "collective being" because in his work he expressed the experience of a huge number of his fellow humans [*Mitmenschen*]. In socialist society the lives of fellow humans will be immeasurably richer and more varied, and its *geniuses* will stand on shoulders immeasurably more powerful. Whereas *Goethe*, unlike the modern philistines of capitalism, had a sense of social connection, the geniuses of the socialist period of human history will find the idea of *opposing* themselves to their comrades and contemporaries totally inconceivable. Human *relations* will be entirely different because all traces of *individualism* will disappear.[23]

This future was near, but it had not yet arrived. Socialism was still being shaped, and Bukharin was still in prison, trying to outwit Mephistopheles. The last and decisive battle was still to be fought, and violent coercion—against both Bukharin and Mephistopheles—was still needed.

The more acute the struggle against the still powerful capitalist enemy, the more necessary this element of "authoritarianism," strict discipline, promptness, cohesion, urgency, etc. From an ahistorical point of view, from the point of view of ideal absolutes and empty phraseology one can attack Soviet "authoritarianism" and "hierarchy" as much as one wishes. But such a point of view is itself empty, abstract, and meaningless. The only possible approach in this regard is the historic one, which bases the criteria of rationality on the specific historic circumstances and the common goal as defined by the "giant steps" of the historical process.[24]

After nine and a half months in prison, he had completed his confession and was ready to sacrifice himself to the giant steps of the historical process. On December 19, 1937, he wrote a letter to Stalin:

I've come to the last page of my drama and perhaps of my very life. I agonized over whether I should pick up pen and paper—as I write this, I am shuddering all over from disquiet and from a thousand emotions stirring within me, and I can hardly control myself. But precisely because I have so little time left, I want to *take my leave* of you in advance, before it's too late, before my hand ceases to write, before my eyes close, while my brain somehow still functions.

In order to avoid any misunderstandings, I will say to you from the outset that, as far as the *world at large* (society) is concerned: (a) I have no intention of recanting anything I've written down [confessed]; (b) In *this* sense (or in connection with this), I have no intention of asking you or of pleading with you for anything that might derail my case from the direction in which it is heading. But I am writing to you for your *personal* information. I cannot leave this life without writing to you these last lines because I am in the grip of torments which you should know about.[25]

He still did not understand, still distinguished between his private and public selves, still believed that there was a Koba separate from Comrade Stalin. He was willing to play his role in the upcoming scapegoating ritual, but he was giving his "graveside word of honor" that he was innocent of the crimes he was confessing and that the reason he had admitted his guilt was to avoid the impression that he had not fully disarmed. He had, in fact, not fully disarmed: he continued to insist, like Job before the Lord spoke, that guilt and innocence with regard to specific actions must be relevant to the giant steps of the historical process.

There is something *great and bold about the political idea* of a general purge. It is (a) connected with the prewar situation and (b) connected with the transition to democracy. This purge encompasses (1) the guilty; (2) persons under suspicion; and (3) persons potentially under suspicion. This business could not have been managed without me. Some are neutralized one way, others in another way, and a third group in yet another way. What serves as a guarantee for all this is the fact that people inescapably talk about each other and in doing so arouse an *everlasting* distrust in each other. (I'm judging from my own experience. How I raged against Radek, who had smeared me, and then I myself followed in his wake. . . .) In this way, the leadership is bringing about a *full guarantee* for itself.

For God's sake, don't think that I am engaging here in reproaches, even in my inner thoughts. I wasn't born yesterday. I know all too well that *great* plans, *great* ideas, and *great* interests take precedence over everything, and I know that it would be petty for me to place the question of my own person *on a par* with the *universal-historical* tasks resting, first and foremost, on your shoulders. But it is here that I feel my *deepest* agony and find myself facing my chief, agonizing paradox.

What he needed was some sign of recognition that what he was offering was not utter self-abasement but an act of conscious self-sacrifice for the sake of *great* plans, *great* ideas, and *great* interests. What he needed was a nod from the historical process, a blessing from Koba on behalf of Comrade Stalin:

> *If I* were absolutely sure that your thoughts ran precisely along this path, then I would feel so much more at peace with myself. Well, so what! If it must be so, then so be it! But *believe* me, my heart boils over when I think that you might believe that I am guilty of these crimes and that in your heart of hearts you *yourself* think that I am really guilty of all of these horrors. *In that case*, what would it mean? Would it turn out that I have been helping to deprive [the Party] of many people (beginning with myself!)—that is, that I am wittingly committing an *evil*?! In that case, such action could never be justified. My head is giddy with confusion, and I feel like yelling at the top of my voice. I feel like pounding my head against the wall: for, *in that case*, I have become a cause for the death of others. What am I to do? What am I to do?[26]

In the rest of the letter, he described how difficult it would be for him to go through with the trial; asked for poison, so he would be able to spend his last moments alone; begged to be allowed to see Anna and their son; and suggested various ways in which he might be useful if left alive. He ended his letter with a farewell to Koba.

But I am preparing myself mentally to depart from this vale of tears, and there is nothing in me toward all of you, toward the Party and the cause, but a great and boundless love. I am doing everything that is humanly possible and impossible. I have written to you about all this. I have crossed all the t's and dotted all the i's. I have done all this in *advance,* since I have no idea at all what condition I shall be in tomorrow and the day after tomorrow, etc. *Being* a neurasthenic, I shall perhaps feel such universal apathy that I won't be able even so much as to move my finger.

But now, in spite of a headache and with tears in my eyes, I am writing. My conscience is clear before you now, Koba. I ask you one final time for your forgiveness (only in your heart, not otherwise). For that reason I embrace you in my mind. Farewell forever and remember kindly your wretched

N. Bukharin

10 December 1937[27]

Koba never responded. Stalin's response was the public Trial of the Anti-Soviet Rightist-Trotskyite Bloc, which took place on March 2–13, 1938. Bukharin confessed to "betraying the socialist Motherland, the gravest crime there is, organizing kulak uprisings, preparing terrorist acts, and belonging to an anti-Soviet underground organization," but rejected most of the specific accusations, including the murder of Kirov and Gorky. He was bending his knees before the giant steps of the historical process, but the remaining bitterness and pride did not fall away completely. Or, as he would have it, the remaining bitterness and pride did not fall away completely, but he was bending his knees before the giant steps of the historical process. At the end of his last plea, he said:

I am kneeling before the country, before the Party, before the whole people. The monstrousness of my crimes is immeasurable especially in the new stage of the struggle of the USSR. May this trial be the last severe lesson, and may the great might of the USSR become clear to all. Let it be clear to all that the counterrevolutionary thesis of the national limitedness of the USSR has remained suspended in the air like a wretched rag. Everybody perceives the wise leadership of the country that is ensured by Stalin.

It is in the consciousness of this that I await the verdict. What matters is not the personal feelings of a repentant enemy, but the flourishing progress of the USSR and its international importance.[28]

He was sentenced to death the next day, along with seventeen other defendants, including Rykov, Yagoda, Zelensky, and Rozengolts. The sentence was carried out two days later, on March 15, 1938. "Their disgraceful,

Aleksei Rykov and Nikolai Bukharin at the trial

vile blood" wrote Yulia Piatnitskaia in her diary, "is too small a price for all the grief felt by the Party." And as Koltsov wrote in his *Pravda* article (which may have influenced Piatnitskaia), "The pitiful attempt by the duplicitous, villainous murderer, Bukharin, to paint himself as an 'ideologist,' a creature lost in theoretical mistakes, is hopeless. He will not succeed in separating himself from his gang of accomplices. He will not be able to deflect full responsibility for a series of monstrous crimes. He won't be able to wash his little academic hands. Those little hands are covered in blood. They are the hands of a murderer."[29]

∎ ∎ ∎

Over the course of several months following the Bukharin trial, Koltsov was elected to the Supreme Soviet and to the Academy of Sciences (as a corresponding member), awarded the Order of Red Banner, and praised (by Stalin and everyone else) for *The Spanish Diary*, which was published as a book. On December 12, he delivered a lecture "On the Short Course of the History of the Communist Party" at the Writers' Club. The event was described by the *Pravda* correspondent, Aleksandr Avdeenko:

The oak hall was full of people. Instead of making a speech, Koltsov spoke informally about how our country would gradually move from socialism to communism. First, public transportation would become free, then bread. All other food items would begin to be distributed according to need, in exchange for conscientious labor, as opposed to money, which would lose its current role and turn to dust.

Mikhail Koltsov welcomed at the Belorussky
railway station on his arrival from Spain,
1937. Next to him is his nephew, Mikhail.
(Courtesy of M. B. Efimov)

After his presentation Koltsov hosted a modest dinner for his friends in an adjacent room. I saw him there. He was in a good mood, joked and laughed a lot, made ironic comments, and told stories about Spain that had not made it into the newspapers. The dinner ended at midnight, if not later. A whole crowd of us walked out to say goodbye to Koltsov as he was getting into his car.[30]

The next morning Koltsov's secretary, Nina Gordon, went over to his apartment to take dictation:

When I arrived at the House of Government around 10 a.m. and went into the entryway, I noted subconsciously that the guard, who had always been very friendly and courteous and had even caused me, a young girl, some embarrassment by holding the elevator door for me, did not move and remained seated at his desk with the phone. I said hello to him, as usual. When he did not respond, I was a little surprised, but decided he was in a bad mood and calmly went up to the eighth floor and rang the bell.

The door was opened by Elizaveta Nikolaevna's niece, Lyulia. Elizaveta Nikolaevna [Koltsov's wife] was in Paris at the time.

I entered and noticed that the entrance to Koltsov's study was barred by a white wicker couch, and that the rest of the hallway furniture had been moved, too.

"Are the floor polishers here?" I asked with surprise.

"What," asked Lyulia, amazed, "you haven't heard? Misha was arrested last night. The search has just ended—see, the doors are sealed."[31]

He spent two and a half weeks in a cell before his interrogations began. At first he denied his guilt, but, twenty interrogations later, on February 21, he mentioned several anti-Bolshevik articles he had published in the Kiev newspapers in 1918. A month later, he wrote a long confession about the many "perversions" that had resulted from his secret doubts about Party policy. Most of the perversions concerned his work at *Pravda* and *Ogonyok*, but the problem went deeper: "I also had anti-Party doubts in 1923–27, concerning the struggle against the oppositionists, whom I, for the longest time, considered to be merely ideological opponents, not recognizing their transformation into an anti-Soviet gang, an advance detachment of the counterrevolutionary bourgeoisie. I experienced similar doubts and unhappiness at the end of 1937, when, having returned from Spain, I was shocked by the scale of the repressions against the enemies of the people. I thought it was exaggerated and unneeded."[32]

Similar doubts and unhappiness were shared by many of his friends and colleagues, whose views and traits he went on to describe in his testimony. (Natalia Sats, for example, was "a crafty careerist, who knew how to promote her interests by using her connections to high officials.") Maria Osten was not among those he exposed. He claimed to have maintained an "intimate, familylike relationship" with her until the summer of 1937, when he discovered her affair with the singer of revolutionary songs, Ernst Busch. They had remained close friends, however, and he "continued to help her and support her."[33]

While in Moscow throughout 1938, up to the moment of my arrest, I remained in contact with Maria Osten. She wrote to me several times about her wish to return to Moscow and settle here again. I was in favor of a temporary stay, but was against her moving here permanently because I did not think she could get a job, there were people living in her apartment, and our personal relationship had come to an end earlier.

At an interrogation after my arrest, I was informed that M. Osten had links with spies and was herself under investigation for espionage. Personally, I trusted her and considered her an honest person, but I am not trying to excuse myself and admit my guilt in maintaining this relationship.[34]

After several more months, he had admitted that he, Maria, and most of his friends and colleagues had spent most of their lives working for foreign intelligence services. On December 13, 1939, one year after his arrest, the investigation was completed. "The accused, M. E. Koltsov, has familiarized himself with the materials of the investigation, in two volumes, and stated that he has nothing to add." On January 17, 1940, Stalin signed his death sentence, along with those of 345 other people. At the closed trial two weeks later, Koltsov pleaded not guilty and claimed—as quoted in the official record—that he had never engaged in anti-Soviet work and that "his testimony had been coerced while he was being beaten in the face, in the teeth, and all over his body. The investigator, Kuzminov, had reduced him to such a state that he was ready to provide testimony about working for any number of intelligence services." After withdrawing for deliberation, the court, chaired by Vasily Ulrikh, pronounced the defendant guilty and sentenced him to death. He was shot the following day (probably sometime after midnight, a few hours after the trial).[35]

Having heard about Koltsov's arrest, Maria picked up her four-year-old son, whom she had adopted in Spain in the fall of 1936, and rushed to Moscow. According to Boris Efimov, she went straight to her apartment, but her other adopted son, Hubert, who had turned sixteen and was living there with his girlfriend, did not let her in. "Hubert in Wonderland, indeed," she is supposed to have said. She checked into the Metropole Hotel and applied for Soviet citizenship. Her attempts to contact Koltsov remained unsuccessful. Her friends from the German Communist community in Moscow shunned her. In July 1939, a special committee chaired by Walter Ulbricht expelled her from the Party for an unauthorized relationship with Koltsov and insufficient engagement with "the policy of the Party and the theory of Marxism-Leninism." On June 24, 1941, two days after the German invasion, she was arrested. A month later she was transferred to Saratov. On September 16, 1942, two days after the German troops reached the center of Stalingrad, she was shot. Soon after Maria's arrest, Hubert was exiled to Kazakhstan as part of the deportation of ethnic Germans from European Russia.[36]

Mikhail Koltsov's arrest photograph
(Courtesy of M. B. Efimov)

Maria Osten's arrest photograph
(Courtesy of M. B. Efimov)

■ ■ ■

Tania Miagkova was thirty-nine when she was sent to the labor camp. "I seem to have 'settled,'" she wrote to her mother on August 9, 1936, about a month after her arrival in Magadan. "And although sometimes when I think about everything that has happened to me, I do rebel inside, those are but echoes of the way I felt before. Life around me and its demands are beginning to absorb me. . . . When people tell me 'you'll forget you are a prisoner,' I still smile warily, but the thought that things may actually work out that way does not seem completely crazy anymore. And of course Kolyma is, in its own right, an extremely interesting place that is making seven-league strides in its development (oh what an antediluvian image—please, dear, industrialize it yourself)." The main source of both redemption and despair was her family. To safeguard the happy childhood of her daughter, to keep her bond with her Party-minded mother, to maintain the hope of being reunited with her husband, and possibly to heal what she, like Bukharin, called her "split consciousness," she had to love Kolyma and forget she was a prisoner. And the only way she could love Kolyma and forget she was a prisoner was to stay close to her family and be certain of her daughter's happy childhood. "If I continue to hear that everything is okay with you, then I will not be afraid of anything: I'll keep on building Kolyma—even with pleasure, and even enjoy it, by god, in spite of everything. Well, my dear mommy, I'll just have to muster more patience—for how many years? So I don't make any more mistakes until the end of my life. In the meantime, I'll be waiting patiently for a line from you and from Mikhas."[37]

Tania's mother, Feoktista Yakovlevna, and daughter, Rada, wrote regularly, but there was nothing from her husband, Mikhail ("Mikhas"). Soon after mailing the August 9 letter, Tania went on a partial hunger strike. Her demands were "contact with my husband, the right to leave camp territory, and improved living conditions." Her letters never mentioned the hunger strike, while continuing to describe a split consciousness striving for wholeness. "What can I do? A turn for the better just keeps not happening for me. Still, I continue to believe that the question of who will win (me or my fate) will finally be resolved in my favor." The news of the Kamenev-Zinoviev trial seemed to explain the reason for the latest blow:

You can imagine how that trial has affected me. I would never have believed it was possible, but how can I not believe what they themselves are saying? I was in utter shock. But now the shock is gone, and I'm left with political lessons and conclusions. The fact of their physical execution made little impression on me: after all, what was executed were their political corpses. In general, however, this is a very difficult and painful phase for me. Life has not been easy for me in recent years, my dear, but don't worry about me, my darling: you know that I, like you, can live not only for myself and through my own emotions, and that, whatever my personal circumstances, I remain interested in my environment, which, in the case of Kolyma, is changing as rapidly and excitingly as everywhere else in the USSR.[38]

The environment kept changing. Magadan looked lovely at night when seen from above ("then the lights on the shore remind me of Yalta"), and the colleagues in the planning department and the atmosphere at work were "very good," but hope and comfort came less from Kolyma and the entire USSR than from the simple things of life. "I am beginning to live again," she wrote on October 10, 1936:

I will probably never rid myself of this particular bad habit. Of course, I cannot claim that I am "in seventh heaven," but I have been living on earth for a long time now, and I still endorse life as it is. Or rather, I don't quite feel like endorsing the way I live right now, but, to be honest with you, I am beginning to derive pleasure from certain processes and phenomena, sometimes on the most unlikely occasions—like when I am chopping wood or even doing my wash. It is a joy to swing the axe and watch the log crack, or see the earth covered with frost, or feel that I am alive, doing something. You understand that everything is okay, don't you, and that this feeling is a sure sign of returning spiritual health?[39]

The link to the entire USSR was still a prerequisite for spiritual health, at least in the letters meant for Rada, Feoktista Yakovlevna, and the NKVD censors (on November 7, 1936, Tania sent Rada a telegram congratulating her on "the day of the great holiday"), but the link to the family—the part of it that was still within reach—kept growing in importance. On November 26, she sent one of her shortest letters since the day of her arrest: "My dear little girl: I only have a few minutes, and I want to give you a big, big kiss. My life is still the same. I am in good health, think a lot about you, and love you very much. Kiss everyone for me. Mommy." Her next letter, addressed to her mother and not much longer than the previous one, ended with the words: "My dear, please forgive me for this hasty and slight little note. Oh how I wish you could all feel my huge, ardent love and immeasurable gratitude, especially you, my darling mother! I hug you all very, very tight. To rest a bit, I'll lay my head on your shoulder, the way I did that time on the train to Chelkar, remember? It is so good to rest close to you, my darling. Your Tania."[40]

In late February or early March 1937, Tania stopped her partial hunger strike (her personnel file does not specify what it consisted of). In August, she was transported from Magadan to a remote camp in the settlement of Yagodnoe ("Berrytown"). On September 2, 1937, she wrote to Rada that she was feeling a little sad. "I haven't gotten used to the new place or fallen into a particular routine yet. My job is less interesting, the library is much smaller, and I have no friends. On the other hand, the nature here is much more beautiful, and the weather has been warm, so I have been going for walks. But I am still a little out of sorts. I know I'll be fine soon, but still, I am pining a bit. I don't show it, of course, except that I laugh a lot less often and tend to walk around looking serious. It's a perfect time to remember: 'Smile, Captain, smile.' Okay, I'll start tomorrow."[41]

The injunction to smile came from the film *The Children of Captain Grant*, which also featured "The Jolly Wind" ("those who seek will always find"). The refrain was "Smile, Captain, smile, for a smile is the flag of a ship; be strong, captain, be strong, for only the strong can conquer the seas." Tania's camp was surrounded by water.

> My roommate and I go for walks together. Around here, if you get off the path, you end up in a swamp. It's not scary—it won't suck you in—but it is very, very wet! You hop from one clump of grass to the next, and, before you know it, you slip and there's water in your shoe. There are creeks and ditches everywhere, and you have to cross them on narrow logs. All around are dense bushes and trees. Some trees are large and beautiful, but it is very difficult for them to grow here, probably because of the permafrost and the cold, wet earth. Their roots stretch along the surface and are often rotten inside. As a result, the forests here are filled with bare, dried-out trees, and it makes you sad to look at them.[42]

Her next letter to Rada, sent on September 18, began with a description of the nearby Debin River:

> This river, with its banks covered with bushes, trees, and pebbles and the perpetual sound of running water, is very good for my mood. Sometimes I sit or lie down on a fallen tree trunk and think to myself: "If my little Rada were here, we would be crossing this river and launching little boats together."
> Beyond the river is a swamp. You can't see the water except for a few spots here and there. It is completely covered with an extremely thick layer of very beautiful, colorful moss. Your feet sink into it. It's like walking on springs. There are berries in the swamp. When we first saw them, we couldn't tell what they were: tiny red berries hanging on very thin threads. Actually, both the berry and the thread were lying on top of the moss. There were almost no leaves. We ate them and wondered if they were poisonous or not. They didn't taste good: they were sour, and obviously green. Finally, one of us realized: "These are cranberries!" "If so, I'll have some more. They taste better already." But if you go up into the hills a little, you can find some lingonberries. There aren't many of them, but today they were

so beautiful and delicious: really ripe and a tiny bit frozen. I got a
wonderful little posy. I wanted to take it home and draw it for you,
but you can't paint on this paper: first, because it gets smeared and,
second, because, on the way home, I ate them without thinking.[43]

The letter ended with an urgent request to write more often and send new
photographs. "My life is not very easy these days, my little one, because I
am so far away from you and all alone."[44]

Several days later she was moved back to Magadan. According to her
old Chelkar roommate, Sonia Smirnova, "it was a time of new accusations
and new sentences for political prisoners in Kolyma. They were being
brought from faraway camps, to be informed of their new guilt and new
sentences in labor camps without the right of correspondence. Those with
new sentences were put in large barracks with two rows of bunks. Tania
and I found ourselves in one of them."[45]

Tania was interrogated on September 26, 1937. According to a guard
named Artemy Mikhailovich Kadochnikov, on September 14, when a group
of prisoners being escorted to another camp had stopped by the Yagodnoe
"isolator," she had engaged in conversation with one of them, Mikhail
Alekseevich (Moiseevich) Poliakov. "She did not obey my order to move
away. She wanted to hand something to him. When I threatened to open
fire, she started screaming at the top of her voice: 'Fascists! Fascist lackeys! They spare neither women nor children! Soon it will be the end of you
and your lawlessness!' To which Poliakov shouted: 'That's right, Tania!'
Finally, she left. I knew her from before. On numerous occasions during
my shift, Miagkova attempted to leave the zone at unauthorized times.
When I did not let her, she would shout: 'Fascists! Next you'll forbid fresh
air! All they know is the zone. That's all they understand.'"[46]

Assuming Kadochnikov's story is true, it is impossible to know
whether Tania's protest was Job's rebellion against God or a version of
Eikhe's and Goloshchekin's true-believer theory that the NKVD had been
penetrated by fascist saboteurs (itself a version of Job's tale, since the
idea of testing the righteous was suggested to God by Satan). At the interrogation, Tania denied the truth of Kadochnikov's acount. "I learned of
the passing party of Trotskyites two minutes before its arrival. I did not
hear any orders from the guards. Among the new arrivals was my friend,
Veniamin Alekseevich Poliakov. I talked to him for exactly two minutes. I
have nothing to add." The second of two witnesses was Tania's "roommate" from Yagodnoe, perhaps the one she went berry-picking with, who
testified that T. I. Miagkova was an "unreformed Trotskyite . . . bitterly
hostile to the regime."[47]

On November 3, the NKVD troika of the Far Eastern Territory sentenced
her to death for "maintaining regular contact with convicted Trotskyites,
holding a six-month-long hunger strike, and expressing counterrevolutionary, defeatist ideas." According to Sonia Smirnova's account, recorded

by Tania's daughter, Rada Poloz, "A group of guards would often walk in at night. Their commander would read out yet another list of the convicted, with the order to get ready 'with your possessions.' As we thought then, they were being taken to faraway camps. On one of those nights, they called out your mother's name. I jumped up and helped her pack. We kissed. 'I'll be joining you soon,' I said as she was leaving. But I never saw her again."[48]

The sentence was carried out on November 17, 1937. Tania's husband, Mikhail Poloz, had been executed two weeks earlier. In late October, he had been taken from Solovki to Medvezhyegorsk as part of a group of 1,111 prisoners slated for execution by the NKVD troika of Leningrad Province. One of the accusations against him was "maintaining correspondence with his wife, a Trotskyite." On November 3, he and 264 other prisoners, three of them women, were stripped to their underwear, driven to a place in the woods about nineteen kilometers from town, and told to dig trenches and lie face down inside them. They were shot, one at a time at close range, by the deputy head of the Housekeeping Department of the NKVD Directorate of Leningrad Province, Captain Mikhail Rodionovich Matveev, and his assistant, Deputy Commandant Georgy Leongardovich Alafer. According to Matveev's later deposition, some of the prisoners were beaten before being shot.[49]

Also among the 1,111 was Ivar Smilga's wife, Nadezhda Smilga-Poluian, and her closest friend, Nina Delibash, who had lived with the Smilgas in the House of Government. Delibash was shot one day earlier than Poloz; Smilga-Poluian, one day later.[50]

▪ ▪ ▪

Ivar Smilga and most other arrested leaseholders from the House of Government were shot in or around Moscow, after a formal sentencing by Vasily Ulrikh's Military Collegium of the Supreme Court. One such trial was described by the former overseer of "the Soviet and foreign intelligentsia" and editor of *Izvestia* and *Novyi mir*, Ivan Gronsky:

> There are three men sitting behind a desk. You are brought in.
>
> "Last name, first name, patronymic? You have received the indictment. There is a letter in the file? Okay, the court will consider it."
>
> They take you out. Three or five minutes later, they bring you back in. They read out the sentence. That's it!
>
> At my trial, they let me talk (most unusual). I spoke for one hour and twenty minutes. I ridiculed the testimony used against me, made fun of the investigation, argued that I was completely innocent before my country and my Party. Nobody mentioned any accusations against me. The judges were silent throughout. Only once one of the judges said:

"Didn't you print Bukharin's 'Notes by an Economist'"?

But the presiding judge, Ulrikh, interrupted him:

"Not only did he not print them, he criticized them in print the very next day."

When I finished, I was escorted out. "Now," I thought, "the whole thing will collapse, and I will be set free. After all, no one accused me of anything, and the presiding judge even supported me."

I was brought before the judges again. The same Ulrikh read out the sentence: fifteen years in a camp and five years deprivation of rights.

Although I was very weak then, I flew into a rage:

"Please tell me where I am! What is this, a court or a comedy theater?"

At that moment the soldiers put my arms behind my back and took me down the stairs to the ground floor.

"Death sentence?" somebody asked.

"No, fifteen years."

"To the left."[51]

Most House of Government leaseholders were taken to the right. Most of the approximately twenty-nine thousand people sentenced to death in Moscow in 1937–38 were executed at one of two wooded "special sites" disguised as military shooting ranges: Butovo, used by the Moscow Region NKVD Directory (presided over by Stanislav Redens, who headed the sentencing troika and signed off on all the execution orders), and Kommunarka (Yagoda's former dacha), used by the NKVD's central organs to execute top state and Party officials sentenced by the Supreme Court's Military Collegium. In the case of Butovo, the procedure has been reconstructed on the basis of archival documents and interviews with retired executioners, and described by the historian Lydia Golovkova:[52]

The people sentenced to death were taken to Butovo without being told where they were going or why. . . .

Trucks with twenty to thirty, and sometimes up to fifty people inside approached the area from the direction of the forest at around 1 or 2 a.m. Today's wooden fence did not exist then. The zone was surrounded by barbed wire. The trucks pulled up to an improvised observation tower, in a tree. Nearby were two buildings: a small stone house and a very long barrack, about eighty meters long. The people were taken inside the barrack, supposedly for "sanitary treatment." Immediately before the execution the decision was announced and personal data verified. This was done very thoroughly. Along with reports on executions, archival documents contain letters requesting confirmation of the place of birth, and often the name and patronymic of one of the condemned. . . .

In Butovo, the executions were carried out by one of several so-called execution crews, which, according to a former acting commandant, usually included three or four men. On days with large numbers of executions the crews might be bigger. According to one local resident who worked in the NKVD garage . . . , the entire "special unit" consisted of twelve men, who worked in both Butovo and Kommunarka, as well as in Moscow, in Varsonofiev Alley and Lefortovo Prison.

At first the condemned were buried in small single graves. They were scattered throughout the grounds. But starting in August 1937, executions in Butovo reached such a volume that the "procedure" had to be modified. A bulldozer-excavator dug out several large pits, about 500 meters long, 3 meters wide, and 3 meters deep. . . .

The roll-call, ID verification, and the filtering out of those whose files raised questions appears to have continued until dawn. According to the former acting commandant, the executioners had nothing to do with the verification process and waited, in isolation, in the nearby stone building. . . .

The condemned were led out of the barrack one at a time. At this point, the executioners would appear. The condemned would be handed over to them and they would lead them, each his own victim, to the back of the grounds, toward the pit. The condemned were shot at the edge of the pit, in the back of the head, at point-blank range. The bodies were thrown to the bottom of the pit, until they covered it more or less evenly. Nights with fewer than 100 executions were rare. There were cases of 300, 400, or even over 500 executions in one night. On February 28, 1937, 562 individuals were executed. According to the acting commandant, the executioners used their own Civil War weapons, usually Nagan revolvers, which they considered accurate, convenient, and reliable. Executions were supposed to be witnessed by a doctor and a public prosecutor, but that was not always the case. There was plenty of vodka, however, which was brought to Butovo especially for the executioners. After the shootings forms were filled out and signed, and the executioners, usually completely drunk, were taken to Moscow. In the evening, a local resident whose house stood on the grounds until the 1950s showed up, turned on the bulldozer, and covered the bodies with a thin layer of earth.[53]

It is not known whether the House of Government neighbors executed on the same nights—Kraval, Mikhailov, and Khalatov on September 26, 1937, Gaister and Demchenko on October 30, 1937, Muklevich, Kaminsky, and Serebrovsky, on February 10, 1938, Piatnitsky and Shumiatsky on July 29, 1938, or the accused at the Bukharin trial, who had their sentences publicly announced to them—had a chance or the wish to talk to each other before being shot. As the Cossack corps commander Filipp Mironov had written after his own conviction by Smilga and Poluian, "in battle, death is not frightening: one moment and it's over. What is terrible for the human soul is the awareness of an imminent, inescapable death, when there is no hope for another chance and when you know that nothing in the world can stop the approaching end, when there is less and less time before the terrible moment, and when finally they tell you: 'your grave is ready.'" For most condemned residents of the House of Government, the time of full awareness varied from a few minutes to at least two nights and a day in the case of Bukharin and his codefendants.[54]

∎ ∎ ∎

Witch hunts begin abruptly, as violent reactions to particular events, and die down gradually, for no apparent reason. Participants have difficulty remembering and explaining what has happened and try to avoid talking or thinking about it.

In the second half of November 1938, without a formal announcement or explanation, the mass operations were discontinued, the troikas disbanded, and Ezhov fired. Arrests and killings became sporadic and more carefully targeted. The shootings of some of those arrested earlier, including Postyshev, Eikhe, and Bogachev, can mostly be attributed to the force of inertia. Radek and Sokolnikov, who had been spared after the trial of the "Anti-Soviet Trotskyite Center," were murdered in prison on Stalin's orders, as part of a mopping-up operation. The first assassin planted in Radek's cell in the Verkhneuralsk political isolator provoked a fight but failed to kill Radek. The second one was more successful. According to the report issued by the prison administration on May 19, 1939, "The examination of the body of inmate K. B. Radek revealed bruises around the neck and bleeding from one ear and the throat, which resulted from the forceful impact of the head against the floor. Death resulted from the beatings and strangling inflicted by inmate Varezhnikov, a Trotskyite." The killer's real name was I. I. Stepanov; he was the former commandant (officer in charge of executions) of the Checheno-Ingush NKVD office, who had been arrested three months earlier for official misconduct. Six months later, he was released for performing "a special assignment of particular importance to the state."[55]

The last act of the mass operations was the liquidation of their organizers. Having woken up after the orgy, Stalin and the surviving members of the inner circle needed to get rid of those who had administered it.

The head of the NKVD's First Special (Bookkeeping) Section, Isaak Shapiro, from Apt. 453, who signed the "lists of individuals to be tried by the Military Collegium of the Supreme Court" before they were sent up to the Politburo, was arrested on November 13, 1938. The former head of the Moscow Province NKVD Directorate and the undisputed champion among regional exterminators of the enemies of the people, Stanislav Redens, from Apt. 200, was arrested on November 21, 1938 (one day after being urgently summoned to Moscow from Kazakhstan, where he had been serving as the people's commissar of internal affairs since late January). The former head of the Gulag and, most recently, people's commissar of communications, Matvei Berman, from Apt. 141, was arrested on December 24, 1938 (ten days after his upstairs neighbor from Apt. 143, Mikhail Koltsov, and three months after his brother, Boris Berman, who had been Radek's and Bukharin's interrogator and later head of Belorussian NKVD). The two men who had directed the conduct of the operations were among the last ones to be arrested: Frinovsky, on April 6, 1939, and Ezhov, on April 10. At his trial before Vasily Ulrikh's Collegium, Ezhov said: "During the preliminary investigation, I said that I was not a spy and not a terrorist, but they did not believe me and subjected me to the most violent beatings. During my twenty-five years of Party work I honestly fought and exterminated our enemies. I have committed crimes for which I may deserve to be executed, and I will talk about them shortly, but I have not committed the crimes listed in my indictment and am not guilty of them."

Bukharin had claimed that he was innocent of the crimes listed in his indictment, but guilty of endowing them with moral and intellectual legitimacy. Ezhov argued that he was innocent of the crimes listed in his indictment but guilty of not neutralizing their perpetrators:

> I purged 14,000 Chekists. But my true guilt consists of the fact that I did not purge enough of them. My practice was as follows: directing this or that department head to interrogate an arrested person, I would think to myself: "Today you are doing the interrogating, and tomorrow I'll have you arrested." I was surrounded by enemies of the people, my enemies. I purged Chekists everywhere. It was only in Moscow, Leningrad, and the North Caucasus that I did not purge them. I thought they were honest, but it turned out that I had been harboring saboteurs, wreckers, spies, and enemies of the people of other stripes.

Ezhov, like Bukharin, attempted to justify himself by appealing to Stalin. Bukharin, as the ideologue of what he called "the political idea of a general purge," had hoped for an acknowledgment that he was not a monster in human form but a scapegoat randomly selected for redemptive sacrifice. Ezhov, as the purge's executioner in chief, was hoping for an acknowledgment that the people who were about to execute him were the same enemies he should have had executed as part of the general purge. "I request that Stalin be informed that I have never in my life deceived the Party politically, a fact known to thousands of people who know my honesty and modesty. I request that Stalin be informed that I am a victim of circumstances and that it is possible that some enemies I have missed may have had something to do with this. Tell Stalin that I will die with his name on my lips."[56]

Sergei Mironov, who had spearheaded the implementation of mass operations and proposed the creation of the first "execution troika," was happy in his new apartment and in his new job in the People's Commissariat of Foreign Affairs. According to Agnessa, "The arrests continued. We knew about them, of course. In our House of Government, not a night passed without someone being taken away. At night the 'Black Ravens' still prowled around. But the fear that had closed in on us in Novosibirsk seemed to recede and give us a little breathing room. Not that it disappeared completely—it just subsided, retreated."

For the first time in their life together, Mironov and Agnessa were living as a family surrounded by other families. As Agnessa put it, "We had landed on a safe, lucky island":

> We were so happy! Mirosha loved his new job. He would sometimes even tell me funny stories about his work: about the "Japs," "Chinks," or others he happened to be dealing with. He was often in a good mood and spent a lot of time with the family. Our apartment was always full of children, and he would dream up all kinds of amusements for them, clowning around and joking, and spoiling them terribly.
>
> Once he announced:
>
> "Today is International Women's Day. I am going to do everything myself so the women can relax."
>
> And then he began to set the table, deliberately doing everything wrong. Little Agulia danced around him in delight, choking with laughter. "No, Daddy, not like that. Not like that, Daddy."[57]

Agnessa found a good dressmaker. At the first reception for foreign diplomats to which Mironov was invited, she wore "a strapless brocade evening gown with A-line skirt and train," dress shoes with gold braid trimming, and her hair "piled high." Everyone noticed them, according to Agnessa. "Later I heard that many people at the reception had asked, 'What country are that new ambassador and his wife from?'"[58]

After the transfers of Frinovsky (to the People's Commissariat of the Navy) and Ezhov (to the People's Commissariat of Water Transport) and the intensification of the purge of the Commissariat of Foreign Affairs, the mood changed. Most of Mironov's closest colleagues had been arrested. One night, he got out of bed, told Agnessa that he did not want to be taken by surprise, and barricaded the kitchen elevator door with a chest of drawers. "Suddenly he began to sob hysterically, and cried out in despair, 'They're arresting the wives, too. The wives!'" Agnessa gave him some valerian drops and kept talking to him until he went back to sleep. Before he did, they agreed that if he was arrested, he would try to send her a note.

"I kiss you tenderly" would mean he was fine; "I kiss you" would mean "okay"; and "regards to everyone" would mean things were bad. Several days later, he was the only Commissariat of Foreign Affairs official besides Litvinov to be invited to the New Year's Eve banquet in the Kremlin. Agnessa chose to wear a "severe dress suit" rather than the new black evening gown with the train and a rose at the waist that she had had sewn for another occasion. From their table, they could see Stalin and Molotov's wife, Polina Zhemchuzhina. "After that New Year's invitation, all our fears and worries evaporated, and we spent six calm, blissful days, completely reassured."[59]

January 6, 1939, was a day off. After the maid had straightened the room and made the bed, Agnessa took Mironov's revolver, which he kept under his pillow, and hid it in her closet. Then they took the children to Gorky Park. "Mirosha horsed around with the children, as if he were a kid himself. To Agulia's delight, he would stumble around on his skates and deliberately fall down (though he was a good skater), and slide downhill on a tiny sled and tumble over on his side." Afterward, Mironov, Agnessa, and Agulia went over to the apartment of Mironov's colleague from the Commissariat of Foreign Affairs, Anatoly Kolesnikov. The plan was for both families to take their children to the circus that evening:

We were all having a good time. Suddenly the telephone rang. It was for Mirosha.

He picked up the phone and listened. I could see the puzzled look on his face.

"But everything has already been agreed upon," he said.

The person on the other end seemed to be insisting. Mirosha looked even more puzzled and said,

"All right, I'm on my way."

He slowly put down the receiver, but remained standing by the telephone, staring at it and thinking.

I asked him, "Mirosha, who was that?"

"They asked me to come down to the Commissariat right away—something to do with the fishing concessions with Japan. There's some kind of problem. . . . I don't understand, everything was already settled."

Then he whispered to me, "Maybe it's an arrest?"

I had been dealing with this paranoia of his for quite a while before New Year's, and I was already used to it. So I brushed it aside cheerfully, and said:

"Don't be silly, Mirosha! Just come back quickly, we'll be waiting for you. And try not to be late for the circus."

He put on his coat, still looking anxious. He asked Kolesnikov for the use of his car to take him there and then bring him back afterward. I accompanied him to the stairs.

"Call me as soon as you get to the Commissariat, okay?"

He promised.

It was a very cold day, but Mirosha never wore a scarf, even when it was freezing. I had a nice wool scarf from abroad.

"It's so cold," I said, "and you've been coughing. Take my scarf."

To my surprise, he agreed. Under normal circumstances he would never have agreed, but this time he took it right away. He gazed at the scarf, stroking it gently and tenderly, and then put it around his neck. Now, looking back, I understand: it was something of *mine*—perhaps the only thing he would have left of me.

He was silent for a few seconds. Then he looked into my eyes, hugged me, kissed me very, very hard, gently pushed me away, and, quickly, without looking back, started running down the stairs. I stood watching as he appeared on one landing, then another, lower and lower. He never once looked back. The door to the outside slammed shut. Everything was still.[60]

Twenty minutes later, someone called on the phone and asked for Mironov. Another twenty minutes later, the same person called again. Two hours later, the doorbell rang. A man wearing white felt boots introduced himself as an employee of the Commissariat of Foreign Affairs, apologized for the intrusion, and asked where Mironov was. After he left, Kolesnikov said that he knew everyone who worked at the commissariat and that this man was not one of them. When the telephone rang again, it was the Mironovs' maid asking Agnessa to come back home. When she did, she found several NKVD agents ready to start a search. The man in the white felt boots accused Agnessa of lying about her husband's whereabouts, demanded her address book, and started calling Mironov's relatives. Finally, at 2 a.m., someone called to say that Mironov had been found and taken into custody.

Three weeks later, Agnessa was told to come to the NKVD reception office. From there, she was taken to the main building, where an investigator by the name of Meshik gave her a note from Mironov. The note said: "My darling wife and friend. Only now have I understood the depth of my love for you. I had never realized that it was this strong. Everything will turn out all right, please don't worry. They'll sort things out soon and I'll come back home to you. I kiss you tenderly. Mirosha."[61]

The question that preoccupied Agnessa for the rest of her life was what Mironov had been doing in snowbound Moscow, on a dark and very cold January night, between 5:00 p.m., when he left the Kolesnikovs' apartment, and 2:00 a.m., when he arrived in his office at the commissariat:

I learned from the Kolesnikovs' driver that from their place Mirosha had gone home, and not to the Commissariat. Before reaching the gate, he asked the chauffeur to stop. He got out, thanked the chauffeur, and disappeared from sight.

I thought a lot about what must have happened. The letter that Meshik gave me to read provided some possible clues.

He must have gone home first to get the revolver that he kept under his pillow. He knew, despite all my assurances, that this strange call could mean only one thing—arrest. He had resolved a long time ago not to give himself up. But as soon as he entered the courtyard, his experienced eyes must have spotted the secret agents in the entryway, so he walked out into the still bustling streets of a Moscow winter's evening. He didn't go to see anyone. If he had, I would have been told. What was he hoping to do? Travel to some unknown destination? Run away? Escape? But could he really escape? Wouldn't they find him sooner or later? And what about me? And Agulia?

Should he kill himself some other way, without his Mauser? Throw himself down the stairwell of a tall building or under a bus, or a trolleybus, or a street car?

There were many ways to end one's life. And for him, that would have been easier than what lay ahead. He didn't believe that they would let him go. The list of executed friends and acquaintances that passed before his eyes was too long, all the executed bosses, underlings . . . Balitskii, who, they said, screamed terribly when he was being led out to be shot; Bliukher, who was shot by Ezhov; Uborevich, who was executed immediately after he was sentenced . . .

Should he kill himself? If he did, they would say: aha, you shot yourself, or threw yourself down a stairwell, or under a bus—that means you are guilty, you are an enemy, you know you did something wrong. When Gamarnik killed himself, they denounced him as an "enemy of the people" and arrested his family. The same would happen to Agulia and me if he killed himself.

And so, trying to save his family, he was prepared to submit to physical and moral torture, and that's what he'd meant by that sentence, "Only now have I understood the depth of my love for you."

What must he have suffered that night before he gave himself up?

I have thought and thought about that sentence he wrote about his love for me. Did he sacrifice himself for my sake? I don't mean to say that he didn't love me. He loved me as much as it was possible for him to love another human being—passionately, fiercely. Of course he loved me! But was that the real reason he did not commit suicide? I don't think it was the only one. He must have convinced himself that it was the reason, the only reason. But, in fact, he simply loved life too much and couldn't bring himself to just end it, to do away with himself—so healthy, so full of life and strength—to do away with himself, to take his own life. . . .

And maybe it also helped that, when I was trying to talk him out of killing himself, I said that even if he was arrested, he could still hope to prove his innocence and have justice prevail. He'd been so lucky all his life, after all. Was he hoping to win this last game, too? The chances were slim, but still, there was a chance.[62]

It is not known what Mironov did or thought during those nine hours in snowbound Moscow, or how he understood innocence and justice. He spent a year in prison before being sentenced to death. His sentence was signed by Stalin as part of a list of 346 "active members of a counterrevolutionary, Rightist-Trotskyite, conspiratorial, and espionage organization," submitted by Beria on the previous day. Also on the list were Redens and Shapiro; Ezhov and his brother, Ivan; Frinovsky, his wife, and his older son; Mironov's West Siberian troika colleague, Robert Eikhe; Mironov's deputy in Novosibirsk and later in Mongolia, Mikhail Golubchik; Boris Berman's brother-in-law and the onetime people's commissar of internal affairs of Bashkiria, Solomon Bak; and the NKVD official who directed the executions of about three thousand Trotskyites at the "old brick factory" in Vorkuta in the spring of 1934, Efim Kashketin-Skomorovsky. Included on the same list as the administrators of the great purge were Kerzhentsev's deputy at the Committee for the Arts and director of the Moscow Art Theater, Yakov Boiarsky-Shimshelevich; Bukharin's first wife (an immobile invalid), Nadezhda Lukina-Bukharina; the former Central Committee stenographer and Anna Larina-Bukharina's cellmate, Valentina Ostroumova; the theater director Vsevolod Meyerhold; the writer Isaak Babel; and the chief chronicler of the February Revolution, October Revolution, and socialist construction, Mikhail Koltsov.[63]

Car at the gate of Courtyard No. 1

PART VI
THE AFTERLIFE

29

THE END OF CHILDHOOD

When Maksim Vasilievich Zaitsev, chairman of the Information Section of
the All-Russian Central Executive Committee, and his wife, Vera Vladimirovna Vedeniapina, member of the Presidium of the Supreme Court of
the Russian Federation, from Apt. 468, were arrested in the spring of 1938,
their twelve-year-old son, Igor Zaitsev, wrote a poem titled "Alone":

Nothing made sense to me.
I wandered, and brooded, and cried,
I thought of a Yalta pony
That took me around for a ride.
I called out for Mom and Dad
I broke into a sweat
I bit my lip till it bled,
I lit up a cigarette.
I have to go looking for food,
No one will help me now.
Will I grow up to be good?
Can I be good somehow?[1]

Vladimir (Vova) Osepian, from Apt. 60, was also twelve when his parents (deputy head of the Red Army's Political Department, Gaik Aleksandrovich Osepian, and personnel officer in the Political Department at the
Commissariat of Transportation, Elizaveta Fadeevna Gevorkian) were arrested. Three years later, in June 1940, he wrote a letter to the commander
of the camp where his mother was serving her eight-year sentence as a
family member of a traitor to the motherland. His father had been executed ("sentenced to ten years with no right to correspondence") on September 10, 1937. He had moved in with his mother's father and changed his
last name:

Petition

It has been three years since I last saw my mother. I have been
living with almost complete strangers. It is very hard for me to live

Igor Zaitsev   Vova Gevorkian (Osepian) with his parents

without my dear Mommy. I miss her very much. I ask you, I beg you
to allow me a visit with my Mommy. She is very sick and I am afraid
I may never see her again. I count on your kindness and hope that
you will not refuse. My mother, Elizaveta Fadeevna Gevorkian,
receives our letters at the following address: Novo-Sibirsk
Province, Tomsk Railroad, Station Yaya, P.O. Box No. 247/13.

> Anxiously awaiting your reply at the
> address Marx Street 20, Apartment 12,
> Vova Gevorkian
> Greetings, Vova Gevorkian

The resolution across the page read: "Hand to Prisoner Gevorkian. Write
a petition requesting a visit."[2]

■ ■ ■

Volodia Moroz, the fifteen-year-old son of the former head of the Cheka
Investigations Department, Grigory Moroz, gave up trying to be good.
After his parents' arrest, he and his eight-year-old brother, Aleksandr,
were sent to Orphanage No. 4 in the village of Annenkovo in Kuznetsk
District, Kuibyshev Province. On December 7, 1937, he wrote in his diary:

> Again I feel so miserable and alone. But what can I do? Absolutely
> nothing. The same thought keeps going through my head, over and
> over again: "What am I guilty of?"
> Why did they send me here, into this undeserved exile? . . .
> I thought of writing a letter to Stalin, but then changed my mind:
> he won't believe me anyway and won't understand, even though
> he's considered a genius.
> I'll keep it as a last resort. My only consolations are nature, ciga-
> rettes, and books.

The nature here is really extraordinary. A person from the capital would be amazed by it, while rejecting it as a "pastoral delight."

The vast meadows, covered with crystal snow, the small peasant huts, clean and cozy on the inside and unprepossessing on the outside, the river, the forest, and finally, looming over them all, the white stone building of Orphanage No. 4, in which I have the honor to reside—all this is beautiful but at the same time unpleasant as a reminder of my undeserved exile.

Most of the teachers in the local school were "uncultured and ignorant." Life at school and in the country at large was being poisoned by "sycophancy, lies, slander, infighting, and other squabbles."

But why? Is it because the people are base? No, it's because a few scoundrels holding all the power in their hands are base.

If a person who had fallen into a deep sleep twelve years ago were to wake up now, he would be amazed by the changes that had taken place.

He wouldn't find the old leaders. Instead, he would see a government of callow fools, who had done nothing for the victory of the revolution, or aged scoundrels, who had sold out their comrades for the sake of their personal well-being. He wouldn't see the "former" legendary Red Army commanders, the builders and organizers of the revolution, the talented writers, journalists, engineers, artists, theater directors, diplomats, statesmen, etc. Everything is new: the people, the human relations, the contradictions, the country as a whole. Everything has taken on a new appearance. But have things changed for the better? On the surface, yes. In essence, no. Toadies are respected; slanderers are apparently excoriated but in fact feared; and scoundrels are in fashion.

Thousands of people are unhappy. Thousands of people are badly, dreadfully embittered. This bitterness will burst forth and wash away all this filth. Happiness will triumph!

Volodia's style and imagery were influenced by contemporary political rhetoric, but his main inspiration, both stylistic and programmatic, came from the books he had read in the House of Government (and continued to read in the orphanage school). Amid the crystal snow of distant exile, the aesthetic of Soviet happy childhood reasserted itself along familiar golden age lines. When Volodia heard from his brother that three more women from the House had "followed their husbands," he wrote:

Insatiable beasts, have you not had enough sacrifices? Go on destroying, robbing, and killing, but remember that the day of reckoning will come. Remember Lermontov:

The court and justice may condone your crime
But God's tribunal stands beyond all time.
The dread Judge waits, and on his lips, behold
No smile responds to clink of bribing gold.

According to Volodia's diary, the reign of terror had begun the day Kirov was murdered and had now destroyed the state that Lenin had built:

The whole top layer of the Party and government have been arrested. Meanwhile, their old friends from prerevolutionary prisons and exiles are trying to save themselves by screaming: "Death to the enemy of the people," "Death to the spies," etc. And they call this justice!

It is amazing. A handful of well-fed, fat people are brazenly ruling over a population, 90 percent of whom are unhappy people. Molchalinism and Khlestakovism are flourishing. The facade of general progress is concealing the decline in morality in our country. I feel like crying out:

How much longer will the Russians
Be their masters' mute possessions?
Men and women,
Just like cattle,
How much longer will be sold?[3]

Molchalin is the toady from Aleksandr Griboedov's *Woe from Wit* (1825); Khlestakov is the braggart from Nikolai Gogol's *The Inspector General* (1836); the poem is by the Decembrist Kondraty Ryleev, who was hanged for attempted regicide in 1826.

On January 20, 1938, Volodia wrote a letter to his seventeen-year-old brother Samuil (Mulia), who was sharing Apt. 402 in the House of Government with his friend Nikolai Demchenko while working at the nearby Institute of Local History and Museum Studies (inside the "Little Church"):[4]

Dear Mulia: When are you finally going to write?!

I beg you: write and write again! But don't write anything important in your letter. Remember—absolutely nothing. It's obvious that they are not giving me your letters. Mulia, as soon as you get this letter, send me some cigarettes. I have nothing to smoke. I have no money. I am completely miserable. Soon I will write such a letter to the NKVD that they will put me away in a safe place. Let them, I'll be glad of it!!! They want me to become stupid, they want to make sure I won't be able to fight against evil, which is to say, against them, but that trick is not going to work. The gentlemen from the NKVD have miscalculated. I'll be fighting, screaming, and sounding the bell! I'll be talking about their cruelty and direct violence everywhere! I am not afraid of them now! Down with fear!

Long live the struggle!

Mulia, write to me, and then write again and again. I am waiting for your letter and parcel.

Love,
Vova[5]

Samuil never received the letter because he was arrested on the day it was mailed. On February 18, having heard about Samuil's arrest from a House of Government friend, Volodia wrote to Stalin, describing his parents' unexplained arrest and his own undeserved exile:

Imagine my position in the orphanage. I have turned into a kind of misanthrope: I avoid people, see hidden enemies everywhere, have lost all faith in humanity. Why am I lonely? Only because the general intellectual level of the children in the orphanage and at the local school is so much lower than mine. This is not a boast. And the school? The school is so pathetic, and the teachers, with two exceptions, are so mediocre that I do not even feel like attending. I wish to receive as much knowledge as possible, and here I'm not even receiving the bare minimum. How can I be satisfied in such conditions? You may think that I am too effete and sentimental, but that is not at all the case. All I demand is happiness—genuine, lasting happiness. Lenin said: "In the Land of the Soviets, there should be no destitute children; let all young citizens be happy." But am I happy? No, I am not. So who is happy? You must have heard of the "gilded youth" from the tsarist period. Sad as it sounds, such "gilded youth" exist today, too. They are mostly children of important, esteemed people. These children do not respect anything: they drink, lead dissolute lives, and are rude to others. Most of them are terrible students, although they are given every opportunity to study. They are the ones who are happy! It seems strange, but it's true. Comrade Stalin, I am sinking farther and farther, falling with dizzying speed into a dark abyss from which there is no escape. Please save me, help me, and don't let me perish!

I believe that is everything. I hope you will answer soon and help me.

I await your response with great anticipation. Vl. Moroz.[6]

Two months later he was arrested. At first he denied his guilt, but when the interrogator showed him his letters, he admitted that the arrest of his parents and especially the arrest of his brother had provoked in him the feeling of "hatred toward the Soviet state and the leaders of the Commu-

Volodia Moroz shortly
before his parents' arrest

nist Party and Soviet government." He was found guilty of counterrevolutionary activity, but, as a minor, he could not be formally charged according to article 58–10, part 1, of the criminal code. After a special review by the attorney general's office, he was sentenced to three years in a labor camp.[7]

A year later, on September 9, 1939, Volodia's mother, Fanni Lvovna Kreindel, who was being held in the Temnikovsky Camp for Family Members of Traitors to the Motherland, wrote to the new commissar of internal affairs, Lavrenty Beria, that her sons "could not have committed any crimes independently" and that they had probably been arrested as "family members," in clear violation of Comrade Stalin's statement that sons should not answer for the crimes of their fathers. "I have been working honestly from an early age and even in the camp I have been, since January 1938, working in my professional capacity, as a pharmacist. I am enduring my imprisonment as a family member courageously, but the fact that my children are suffering at such an early age is depriving me of all strength, and only the hope of your legal intervention and review of my children's case gives me the strength to endure this suffering, too."[8]

Kreindel's petition was reviewed by an official of the NKVD's Special Commission, Captain of State Security Chugunikhin, who found that Samuil had been convicted independently as a member of an anti-Soviet organization and that Volodia had revealed himself to be "viciously hostile toward the leaders of the Communist Party and Soviet government." On March 25, 1940, Chugunikhin formally rejected Kreindel's appeal. Neither one of them knew that almost a year earlier, on April 28, 1939, Volodia had died in prison of "tuberculosis of the lungs and intestines."[9]

■ ■ ■

Stalin probably never read Volodia's letter, but he would hear more about the "gilded youth." On June 3, 1943, on the Big Stone Bridge, the fourteen-year-old Volodia Shakhurin (the son of the people's commissar of aviation industry, Aleksei Shakhurin) shot the fifteen-year-old Nina Umanskaia (the daughter of the newly appointed Soviet ambassador to Mexico, Konstantin Umansky) and then shot himself. Nina died on the spot (on the stairs leading to the House of Government). Volodia, who lived on Granovsky Street (the former Fifth House of Soviets) died in the hospital the next day. The police investigation revealed that Volodia had been determined not to allow Nina to follow her father to Mexico; that he had borrowed the gun from Mikoyan's fifteen-year-old son, Vano, who always carried one to school (as did his brother, the thirteen-year-old Sergo); and that he had been the leader of a secret society that included Leonid Barabanov (the fourteen-year-old son of the head of Mikoyan's secretariat, Aleksandr Barabanov), Feliks Kirpichnikov (the fourteen-year-old son of the deputy chairman of Gosplan, Petr Kirpichnikov), Artem Khmelnitsky (the fourteen-year-old son of the director of the Exhibition of Military Trophies, Rafail Khmelnitsky), Petr Bakulev (the fifteen-year-old son of Moscow's surgeon general, Aleksandr Bakulev), Armand Hammer (the nephew of the American "red millionaire" by the same name), Leonid Redens (the fifteen-year-old son of the late Stanislav Redens and Stalin's sister-in-law, Anna Allilueva), and Sergo Mikoyan.

Unlike Volodia Moroz, whose Byronism had stayed within the romantic mode by evolving from scorn for surrounding mediocrity to a self-sacrificial rebellion against injustice, Volodia Shakhurin had moved toward Dostoevsky's Stavrogin—and beyond. His dream had been to create a world government that would combine the might and the ruthlessness of the Soviet Union and Hitler's Germany. He had called it the Fourth Reich and himself the Reichsführer. His bedside reading had been Nietzsche and Hitler's *Mein Kampf* (available in Russian translations to high Party and state officials). The other boys claimed to have been indifferent to his intellectual quest, but they did seem to enjoy the trappings of secrecy and the esoteric reenactment of their fathers' power and privilege. (They were all students in School No. 175, also attended by Svetlana Molotova, who was the same age, and Svetlana Stalina, who was three years older.) After a five-month investigation, the boys were sentenced to one year of exile "in various cities of Siberia, the Urals, and Central Asia."[10]

Anatoly Granovsky (b. 1922), the son of the director of the Berezniki Chemical Plant, Mikhail Granovsky, belonged to an earlier generation of "gilded youth" (which also included Stalin's son Vasily and adopted son Artem Sergeev). According to his memoirs, he and his friends "danced, flirted with girls, went to the theater, had parties and enjoyed [themselves] tremendously" until November 6, 1937, when his father was arrested. On

Volodia Shakhurin   Nina Umanskaia

January 27, 1938, he asked to be arrested, too, in the hope of seeing his father. After almost six months in prison, three severe beatings, several eye-opening conversations with cellmates, and lots of Goethe, Hugo, Balzac, and Tolstoy, he wrote a letter to Beria, pledging his loyalty to the NKVD. On July 20, 1939, he was released in exchange for a formal commitment to serve as a secret agent. His job was to reestablish contact with his old friends from the House of Government and provoke the children of the enemies of the people into revealing their hostility toward the Soviet state.

His first assignments were Igor Peters, the son of the prominent Chekist and Party Control official, Yakov (Jēkabs) Peters, formerly of Apt. 181, and Aleksandr Kulkov, the son of the Party Control and Moscow Party Committee official, Mikhail Kulkov, formerly of Apt. 268. In his memoirs, he describes a sleepless night at the Botkin Hospital, where he was being treated for his prison injuries (a hernia and a damaged cheekbone): "I would have to spy on my friends. And my murdered father, or my imprisoned father, or my tortured father would be a bait to entice their indiscretion." But did he have a choice? Did he need a choice? "It was still dark as I lay there on my back in the comfortable bed and I knew I must think this thing out. Even when one sees one is trapped one must think. Of course, it was quite logical. It was the most logical thing in the world. I belonged to two conflicting parties, one of which could hurt me while the other could not. It was quite logical that I should be asked to serve the former by betraying the latter. What reason had I to expect sentiment to sway the stronger party one way or the other? None. If I was dejected it meant I was still a child."[11]

But he was no longer a child. He was seventeen years old, his father was gone, and he had his helpless mother and two little brothers to look after. And did he really have any friends?

> I remembered Butyrki Prison, and the degradation in which we had lived for a year before that. Had anyone helped us then? Bruskin had helped, but Bruskin had gone, liquidated. But what about the others on our side of the fence, had any of them offered help? Roubles and kopeks apart, the help of a hand to lift a heavy cupboard, the help of a visit, of a kind word? No one had helped, only Erik Korkmasov who had posted a letter to my mother. Who were my friends, then? As I lay quietly awake in the dark, I almost smiled to myself with relief. I had no friends. I owed loyalty to none but those who could exact it from me—and to myself.[12]

Aleksandr Bruskin, the former director of the Cheliabinsk Tractor Plant and people's commissar of machine tool industry (from Apt. 49), had been a friend of his father's who had given him a job as a turner's assistant after his father's arrest. Erik (Jelal-Erast) Korkmasov, the son of the recently arrested former chairman of the Council of People's Commissars of Dagestan and deputy secretary of the Chamber of Nationalities, Jelal-Ed-Din

Korkmasov (from Apt. 401), had been his best friend, whom he had asked to post his farewell letter to his mother before leaving for the NKVD headquarters. Otherwise, he had no friends and was, therefore, in no position to betray anyone. He had become what others called a "bad person," that is, one who owed loyalty to none but those who could exact it from him—and to himself (as well as to his immediate family—something implied in the definition of a "bad person").

When Igor Peters told him that he had renounced his parents, he responded, by way of provocation, that a person who was so quick to betray his parents could not be trusted not to betray his friends and lovers. Igor punched him in the face, but he did not punch back, even though he was stronger. He was going to punish Igor for betraying his parents (and for punching him in the face) by betraying Igor to the secret police. He did, but the chain had come full circle when his NKVD supervisor told him to stop reporting on Igor because Igor was now a secret agent, too. For Granovsky, the Soviet *Faust*—including the cult of self-reflexivity and "work on oneself"—was ultimately about the pact with the devil. He was Lyova Fedotov's evil double: he, too, pursued limitless self-awareness and a seamless blend of experience and reminiscence; he, too, aimed to embody the age of "great planners and future geometers." As he wrote about one of his conversations with Aleksandr Kulkov, "my mind had been fully occupied with the task of recording his conversation and taking care to reply in such a way as would not seem unnatural and would not discourage him from continuing. That is the quality of steel, I thought with pleasure. That is self-mastery and perfect self-subordination to a predetermined objective. Power over others begins with power over oneself."[13]

He did well as an agent and, after the beginning of World War II, was sent to the newly created "special sabotage and reconnaissance training school." There, his "work on the self" became an extension of the state's work toward victory: "Memory, memory, memory, and the mastery of the disciplined mind over the emotions and over the weaknesses of the flesh. There are only two things that must occupy the mind of the true *tchekist*: the objective and the means to attain it. No preconceptions, no absolutes, no principles, no values besides efficiency. The *tchekist* is the perfect servant and guardian of the state. Train, train, train to improve, to achieve perfection, to become a one hundred per cent efficient human machine." He claimed to have benefited from the training and to have performed well on several assassination missions behind enemy lines. "I found that the swift, precise, lethal action that preceded the calculated death exhilarated me. I found with satisfaction that my body responded to urgency with a clean and unhesitant directness and my mind was as cool as if I had been playing a game of chess against an inferior opponent."[14]

In between foreign assignments, he continued to work as a secret agent in Moscow, specializing in seducing and incriminating young women. According to his memoirs, "there was provocation after provocation, investigation after investigation and I introduced myself into the private lives

Anatoly Granovsky

of so many people and so intimately that, were it not for the fact that my memory is as trained as it is, I would by now have become utterly confused with the mass of my recollections." In the spring of 1944, he was told to infiltrate another group of children of arrested high officials (mostly graduates of School No. 175 in their early twenties). Among the group's members was his childhood friend, Erik Korkmasov, who had recently returned from the front because of a shoulder wound, and Romuald Muklevich's daughter, Irina (formerly of Apt. 334).[15]

Irina remembered running into Granovsky in the Metro one day. He was a "fine-looking officer," "handsome and supremely self-confident." He was very happy to see her and later that day he and Erik came over to chat. He started picking her up after college in his limo, to her girlfriends' envy and astonishment. When he found out that Irina was living with her aunt because her room had been occupied by someone else while she was in evacuation, he took her to the courthouse, asked her to wait outside, returned with a judge who told her not to worry, drove over to her old apartment, forced the door open, made a list of the new occupant's possessions, moved them all out, and changed the lock. Soon afterward, Erik told her that Anatoly was being sent somewhere on a special mission. Before leaving, he came over and asked her to marry him, but her aunt did not think it was a good idea, and Irina said no. She never saw Anatoly again. A little while later, Erik Korkmasov and twelve other people were arrested for planning an attempt on Stalin's life. Erik spent five years in prison and several more in exile in Kazakhstan. Later Irina heard that Anatoly had been killed on a mission behind enemy lines. Another friend of theirs, Nadia Belenkaia (the daughter of the arrested NKVD official and, formerly, Lenin's chief bodyguard, Abram Belenky, of Apt. 53) said once that of all of them, Anatoly's fate had been the most tragic. According to Irina, they did not discover Anatoly's book, published in the United States, about his work as an agent provocateur until much later, and she could not help noticing that in his chapter about the people he had betrayed, he mentioned Erik and Nadia, but not her.[16]

∎ ∎ ∎

Granovsky's supervisor in this and several other operations was Yakov Sverdlov's son, Andrei, whom he describes as the Mephistopheles to his Faust—a relentlessly ironic man with an "annoying, conceited air," "the braying laugh of one who is not too sure of himself," and an intense eagerness for "power for its own sake." After a brief imprisonment in 1935 (for saying "Koba must be bumped off"), he had worked as a foreman and shop floor supervisor at the Stalin Automobile Factory before being arrested again in January 1938. It is not clear whether he became an agent after the first or the second arrest. (According to one of his superiors, he had been used as an in-cell agent provocateur during the case of the "Rightist-Trotskyite Bloc.") In December 1938, after almost a year in prison, he was formally released and made a full-time investigator. Ten months later, when Anna Larina was sitting in the office of her Lubyanka interrogator, Yakov Matusov, the door opened and Andrei Sverdlov walked in. She had always believed that her conviction for belonging to a "terrorist youth organization" had something to do with Sverdlov's (and Dima Osinsky's) 1935 arrest, so she immediately assumed he was a fellow prisoner brought in for a confrontation:[17]

> But when I took a closer look at Andrei, I realized that he did not look like a prisoner. He was wearing an elegant gray suit with well-ironed slacks, and his smooth, self-satisfied face projected perfect contentment.
>
> Andrei sat down on a chair next to Matusov and studied me carefully, though not without some emotion.
>
> "Please meet your new investigating officer," said Matusov.
>
> "What do you mean, 'investigating officer'? I exclaimed, in utter bewilderment. "It's Andrei Sverdlov!"
>
> "Yes, Andrei Yakovlevich Sverdlov," said Matusov proudly (as if to say, "see what kinds of investigators we have here"), "the son of Yakov Mikhailovich Sverdlov. He'll be handling your case."
>
> Matusov's announcement terrified me, and I felt completely lost. The hostile confrontation that I had originally expected would have been easier to deal with.
>
> "What, you don't like your investigator?" asked Matusov, noticing my shock and confusion.
>
> "I don't know him as an investigator, but there is no need to introduce us: we have known each other for a long time."
>
> "Was he a friend of yours?" asked Matusov, looking at me curiously.
>
> "Let Andrei Yakovlevich answer that question."
>
> I would not have called Andrei my friend, but I had known him since early childhood. We used to run around the Kremlin and play together. One fall, Adka, as we called him then, snatched my hat off my head and ran away. I ran after him but couldn't catch up. I went over to his place (Yakov Sverdlov's family had continued to live in the Kremlin after his death). Andrei grabbed some scissors, cut off the top part of the hat (it was a knit cap), and threw it in my face. He was around thirteen, and I was around ten. Perhaps that was his first cruel act, and he was cruel by nature. Later we used to spend

our summer vacations in Crimea at the same time. Andrei would come over from Foros to see me in Mukhalatka. That was before his marriage and mine. We used to go walking, hiking, and swimming in the sea together.[18]

Now he was twenty-eight, and she was twenty-five. He asked her why she had mentioned his name in her previous interrogations, and she said that she had assumed that his first arrest would be used against both of them. Two or three days later she was brought in for more questioning:

This time Andrei was gentler and looked at me with more warmth. When walking past me, he put an apple in my hand. But he did not forget his job as an interrogator. He sat behind the desk in the small, narrow office. We looked at each other in silence. My eyes filled with tears. It seemed to me that Andrei, too, became agitated, but maybe I saw what I wanted to see.

We had similar biographies: we were both children of professional revolutionaries. Both our fathers had managed to die in time, we were equally loyal to the Soviet state, and we both admired Bukharin. This had been the topic of a conversation I had with Andrei before my marriage. Finally, we had both suffered a catastrophe—to different degrees, but a catastrophe nonetheless.

Andrei Sverdlov's actions could not be regarded as anything but a betrayal. It was Cain's eyes that were looking at me. But the person responsible for the catastrophe, his and mine, was one and the same—Stalin.

Andrei's silence was unbearable, but I also lost the ability to speak for a while. Finally I exploded:

"What are you going to interrogate me about, Andrei Yakovlevich? Bukharin is dead, so there's no point in trying to obtain more false evidence against him, is there? As for my life, you know it as well as I do, so you don't need to interrogate me about it. And yours, up to a certain point, was pretty clear to me, too. That's why I defended you, saying you couldn't have been involved in any counterrevolutionary organization."

Hunched over his desk, Andrei was looking at me with an enigmatic expression on his face, apparently not having heard a thing I said. Suddenly he blurted out something completely unrelated to the investigation, or rather to the conversation we were having.

"What a pretty blouse you have on, Niuska!" ("Niusia" was the affectionate nickname my parents and friends used.) I believe I felt sorry for the traitor at that moment, thinking that he was in the same trap, but had just entered it from the other end.

"So, you like my blouse" (I also kept switching from the formal to the informal 'you' with Andrei, depending on how I was feeling)— "and what is it that you don't like?"[19]

He responded by saying that she had been slandering the show trials and denying Bukharin's guilt. At the end of the conversation, he told her that, "by the way," his wife, Nina Podvoiskaia, had asked him to say hello.

This "by the way, hello" provoked nothing but irritation in me. I doubt that Andrei's wife knew anything about our dramatic encounter.

I did not remain in his debt for long, however, and responded to his one hello with several of my own. I passed on greetings from his aunt, Yakov Sverdlov's sister Sofia Mikhailovna, whom I had seen in the Tomsk camp, and from his cousin, Sofia Mikhailovna's daughter and Yagoda's wife, whom I had not seen, but said hello anyway. According to camp rumor, Yagoda's wife had been in one of the Kolyma camps before the trial, then transferred back to Moscow after the trial and shot. Finally, I said hello from Andrei's nephew, his cousin's son, and told him about Garik's tragic letters from his orphanage to his grandmother's camp: "Dear, dear Grandma, again I haven't died!"[20]

But there was a lot about Andrei Sverdlov she did not know. She probably had not heard about the execution of his other cousin, Leopold Averbakh; his uncle, Veniamin Sverdlov; or his childhood friend, Dima (Vadim) Osinsky. Nor was she likely to know that Andrei had another uncle, Zinovy Peshkov, who was an officer in the French Foreign Legion, or that his

Andrei Sverdlov (*seated in the middle of the front row*) with friends. Next to him (*front row, right*) is Dima Osinsky.

daughter, Andrei's cousin Elizaveta, had returned to Moscow from Italy in 1937 and had recently been arrested. Anna did find out later that Andrei had also interrogated her aunt, the wife of the former deputy chairman of Gosplan, V. P. Miliutin (from Apt. 163), and that he had been "rude to her, threatened to beat her, and waved his whip in front of her face." Dima Osinsky's sister, Svetlana, considered Andrei "a traitor and vile creature" and claimed that when their mutual friend, Khanna Ganetskaia (Hanna Hanecka, the twenty-one-year-old daughter of the founder of the Polish Social Democratic Party, Jakub Hanecki, from Apt. 10), "entered the investigator's office, saw Andrei, and rushed toward him with a cry of joy, assuming that now everything would be cleared up, he pushed her away, screaming 'you bitch!'" According to Elizaveta Drabkina, whom Andrei had known since early childhood and referred to as "Aunt Liza," he had come to her prison cell sometime after her arrest and said: "Aren't you ashamed of yourself? You used to be Yakov Sverdlov's secretary, and now you are an enemy of the people!" According to Ruf Valbe, Ariadna Efron (the daughter of the poet Maria Tsvetaeva), who had also known Andrei before her arrest, was shaken by his "cynical and vile" behavior when he was interrogating her. And according to Roi Medvedev, the Petrovsky family archive contains documents showing Andrei's participation in the repeated beatings of Grigory Petrovsky's son, Petr Petrovsky.[21]

30

THE PERSISTENCE OF HAPPINESS

Volodia Moroz was a lone rebel. (His brother, Samuil, who also ended up in a camp, "argued furiously" with other inmates in defense of the Party.) Volodia Shakhurin was preparing to become a Reichsführer. Anatoly Granovsky owed loyalty to none but those who could exact it from him. Andrei Sverdlov loved either power for its own sake or Soviet power in its struggle against its enemies (most of whom happened to be his former friends).

Most of Andrei Sverdlov's former friends considered him a traitor but did not question the cause he was serving. They did not feel that they had to choose between their loyalty to the Party and their loyalty to their friends, family, and themselves. No matter how great the catastrophe, they continued to live in a luminous, premillennial world—a world that made sense even if their own exclusion from it did not. The Great Terror spelled the end of most Old Bolshevik families and homes; it did not bring about the end of faith.

Ten days after being sentenced to eight years in a labor camp, Anna Larina wrote a poem dedicated to the tenth anniversary of the October Revolution (a poem that, according to her memoirs, offered a fair reflection of her frame of mind at the time):

> This prison may bring me to tears,
> And make me feel lonely and sad,
> But this day I mark with my dear,
> Beloved Soviet land.
> . . .
> Today I am certain it's near—
> The day I'll reenter the ranks
> And proudly march on Red Square
> Along with my Komsomol friends![1]

Natalia Rykova wrote to Stalin on June 10, 1940, a year after being sentenced to eight years in a labor camp:[2]

> I was accused of conducting anti-Soviet agitation, but not only did I not conduct it, I could not possibly have conducted it because both

before and after the arrest I was faithful to the Soviet state and the Party. I am a person for whom life means work for the benefit of the Soviet people. I was brought up in a Soviet school, in the Pioneer and Komsomol organizations, and in a Soviet university. I am only twenty-two years old, but I have never been able to conceive of any other life than study or work for the benefit of my country, in my own field or in any place the Komsomol chooses to send me, to work first in its ranks and then in the ranks of the Party. This is how I have always thought, and this is how I think now. . . .

I know how odious my last name is, and I understand that I cannot be trusted now the way I was trusted before Rykov's unmasking, and yet I would like to ask you to consider my case because I am not guilty of anything and because I am able and willing to give all of myself for our country's great cause. I was and I remain a Komsomol member, for whom life is worth living only if it means working for the Soviet country.[3]

The Soviet country as one big family continued to exist for most former residents of the House of Government. It took four meetings and a speech by the Party secretary to persuade the Komsomol organization of the Moscow Aviation Institute to expel Nikolai Demchenko (the son of the people's commissar of state farms and Samuil Moroz's best friend). In the case of Leonid Postyshev, four times proved not enough. Only the commissar and Komsomol secretary of his regiment at the Air Force Academy voted for expulsion; everyone else, according to Postyshev, voted against the motion. After the fourth meeting, the commissar called him in and demanded that he surrender his membership card. He did, but said that from now on he considered himself a Party member.[4]

When Inna Gaister and Zaria Khatskevich (the daughter of the recently arrested secretary of the Council of Nationalities of the Central Executive Committee, formerly of Apt. 96) applied to join the Komsomol, they

Natalia Rykova a year and a half before her father's arrest

were both asked about their fathers, and both said that the arrests had been a "tragic mistake." Both were admitted unanimously (Gaister in Moscow and Khatskevich in Mogilev, after several months in an orphanage). Isaak Zelensky's children, Elena and Andrei, were expelled from the Komsomol but appealed to the Central Committee and were reinstated.[5]

Gaister, Khatskevich, the Zelenskys, and most of their friends believed that enemies were, in fact, everywhere and that only their own parents, and perhaps those of their closest friends, were innocent. But even those whose parents they believed to be guilty were not guilty themselves—because Comrade Stalin had said that "sons do not answer for their fathers" and because in their world—the world of happy childhood and the "treasures of world literature"—one did not betray one's friends. There were bad people, tragic mistakes, moments of utter loneliness, enemies posing as commissars, and double-dealers posing as friends, but the Soviet world as a whole was just, transparent, and naturally compatible with private love and friendship. Most of the children who were expelled from the House of Government remained children of the Revolution. Yuri Trifonov's inspirational discussions in the literary club of the Moscow House of Pioneers, led by the editor in chief of the journal *Pioneer*, Comrade Ivanter, took place after the arrests of his parents. Inna Gaister's parents were arrested in the summer of 1937. Two weeks after the beginning of the school year, she and her cousin Igor (whose father, Semen Gaister, had also been arrested) went to see their "class mentor," Inna Fedorovna Grekova, in order to report what had happened: "She looked at us strangely and said: 'So what? What difference does it make? Go and do your work.' And that was that. A little surprised, we went back to our classroom, wondering why she had ignored our declaration. As if nothing had happened."[6]

Inna's other teacher, Anna Zinovievna Klintsova, made the point of looking after Vova Piatnitsky, who needed to re-register at the school after his return from Karelia, and his older brother, Igor, who was one of the stars of the school math club, over which she presided. When, in the fall of 1940, school fees were introduced, Anna Zinovievna paid Inna's tuition and arranged some private lessons for her. And when Inna's grandmother received a telegram with the address of the camp where Inna's mother was being held, she called the school principal, Valentin Nikolaevich, who went and found Inna and escorted her to his office. "When I hung up, I must have looked completely dazed. Valentin Nikolaevich only asked, 'Will you return to class or go home?' I went back to class."[7]

During the Bukharin trial, Inna Gaister's father was mentioned as one of the organizers of the murder of Valerian Kuibyshev (after whom he had named her sister, Valia), but no one in her class held it against her. When the time came to elect a leader for the "Pioneer detachment," they elected Inna. When she said that she could not accept because her father was an enemy of the people, one of her classmates counted all such children in the classroom and produced a list with twenty-five names on it (about three-quarters of the total). The rest of the students felt that he had betrayed their trust and questioned their loyalty, and stopped talking to him. Later, when he did "another dishonorable thing," they decided to teach him a lesson. They caught him on the embankment in front of the British Embassy. The boys formed a semicircle in front of the balustrade, and the girls kept hitting him until one of the policemen posted at the embassy chased them away.[8]

Inna loved her friends and teachers, believed that School No. 19 was unique, and felt vindicated in having refused, as a grade-school student, to transfer to the Moscow Exemplary, where "children were being forced to publicly renounce and disown their parents." The students of the Moscow Exemplary, for their part, seem to have felt that it was their school that was uniquely nurturing (as well as academically distinguished). Svetlana Osinskaia, who was the same age as Inna Gaister (twelve in 1937), remembered telling her class mentor, Kapitolina Georgievna, about her parents' arrest. "She fell back against the wall and said: 'Yours, too?'" Svetlana spent only four years at the school, but she remembered enjoying her time there and admiring Kapitolina Georgievna ("we loved her, even though we were afraid of her"); her choir teacher, Viktor Ivanovich Pototsky (who "wore a velvet jacket with a bow and was not simply a music teacher, but a true artist"); and her physical education teacher, a former imperial army officer, Tikhon Nikolaevich Krasovsky, who was pointedly "attentive and affectionate" toward her after her parents' arrest. Svetlana's brothers, Valia and Rem Smirnov, who were two years older and had spent more time at the Moscow Exemplary, "praised their teachers very highly"; Zaria Khatskevich, who was in the same class as Rem (and believed he was in love with her), did not remember any hostility following her parents' arrest; and Elena Kuchmina, who was a year younger than Svetlana, wrote in a 1991 letter that she had preserved "the most wonderful memories" of the Moscow Exemplary. "I am still amazed at our teachers' nobility of spirit: the school was overflowing with the

Moscow Exemplary School, fifth grade. Svetlana Osinskaia is seated in the front row, third from left. (Courtesy of Elena Simakova)

children of 'enemies of the people,' but we were invariably treated with kindness and forbearance."[9]

Tatiana Smilga, who was five years older and also a Moscow Exemplary student, did not remember any hostility from strangers or betrayal by relatives or friends, but her main "comfort and joy" in those days was her first love, Pushkin. Her nanny made her and her younger sister new dresses for the Pushkin jubilee and someone got her a ticket to a series of lectures on Pushkin at Moscow University—"by Bondi, Brodsky, Grossman—all the best Pushkin scholars." Tatiana's schoolmate, Lydia Libedinskaia (who was two years younger), did remember one Komsomol meeting at which a friend of hers, John Kuriatov, was expelled, but pointed out that the meeting had been presided over by an outsider rather than someone from the school, that John (named for John Reed, the author of *Ten Days That Shook the World*) had refused to renounce his father or surrender his Komsomol card, and that John's friends (including Libedinskaia) had stood by him. One of them, Valentin Litovsky, had run after a little boy who called John an "enemy," caught him, grabbed him by the collar, and said, desperately drawing out his words so as not to stutter: "You creep, how da-a-a-re you? Wha-a-t do you understa-a-and? If his father re-e-eally is an enemy of the people, it is a tra-a-a-agedy, a terrible tra-a-agedy, like sickness or death, you u-u-u-understand? And he-e-e-re you are, atta-a-a-acking him. He is no-o-ot guilty of a-a-a-nything!"[10]

Valentin was the son of the prominent censor, theater critic, Mikhail Bulgakov's nemesis, and *Uriel Acosta*'s champion, Osaf ("Uriel") Litovsky. He had recently returned to school from the set of *The Youth of a Poet*, in which he played the young Pushkin. Lydia Libedinskaia fell in love with him because she was already in love with Pushkin. As she wrote in her memoirs (about herself and her generation), "Might we be fated to relive the days of his lycée fraternity? Might there be a new Pushkin among us? We dedicated our poems, essays, and hopes to Pushkin. We dreamed of Pushkin. We dreamed of a pilgrimage to his Mikhailovskoe estate: to Pskov by train and then on foot, only on foot! In the meantime we walked around Moscow, looking for the buildings that were associated with his life there." Soviet happy childhood was a golden age built on all the previous golden ages, and the most golden of them all was Pushkin's "lycée fraternity." When the boys and girls from the House of Government talked about their beloved country, they meant the center of the world revolution, but they also meant Russia, and the Russia they loved had been created by an eternally young poet, the highest of the Pamirs. In 1937, on the one hundredth anniversary of his death, he stood for both. "We spoke of Pushkin as if he were alive. We kept asking each other if Pushkin would like our Metro, our new bridges that spanned the Moskva, the neon lights on Gorky Street."

After toasting the New Year of 1937, Libedinskaia and her friends went to the Pushkin Monument on Tverskoi Boulevard, in the center of Moscow. That night is one of the central episodes in her memoirs:

The light, transparent snowflakes fluttered down and gathered in the folds of his bronze coat and in his curly hair. The ice-covered tree branches shone in the dark.

We read his poems to him—one after another, on and on: *Eugene Onegin*, "The Forest Sheds Its Purple Attire," "Reminiscences in Tsarskoe Selo," "To the Sea," "Tsar Saltan." . . .

Suddenly, in the frosty silence of that New Year's Eve, a boy's voice, trembling with excitement, rang out:

> While freedom kindles us, my friend,
> While honor calls us and we hear it,
> Come, to our country let us tend
> The noble promptings of the spirit.

It sounded like a vow. That is how, in solemn silence, warriors take their oaths. Happy are those who had such moments in their youth. . . .

The snow kept falling, melting on our flushed faces and silvering our hair. Our hearts were overflowing with love for Pushkin, poetry, Moscow, and our country. We yearned for great deeds and vowed silently to accomplish them. My generation! The children of the 1920s, the men and women of a happy and tragic age! You grew up as equal participants in the building of the Soviet Union, you were proud of your fathers, who had carried out an unheard-of revolution, you dreamed of becoming their worthy successors.[11]

On October 7, 1939, the remnants of the Trifonov family had been expelled from the House of Government. Five weeks later, Yuri, who had just turned fourteen, wrote a poem that seemed to transform his new apartment into Pushkin's Mikhailovskoe and his future life into that of a historian:

Yuri Trifonov

> Faithful Lyova, are you there?
> Oleg, still the jesting man?
> Carefree Misha, do you care
> That I won't be back again?
> Time is counting out the hours,
> Days file by but never end,
> Our past life's no longer ours,
> Long forgotten your old friend.
> Long forgotten my apartment
> And my lyre's timid chord.
> Only I, by fate discarded,
> Will remember every word![12]

■　■　■

Volodia Lande from Apt. 153 was nine years old in December 1937, when several NKVD agents came to arrest his mother, an editor from the Party Publishing House, Maria Yusim. (His father, the head of the Planning Department of the Soviet State Bank, Efim Lande, had been arrested six months earlier.)

> My mother woke me up right before it was time to leave the house. While I, still too sleepy to understand what was happening, was getting dressed, she was nervously packing her things and mine into suitcases. Along with clothes, she put in some family photographs and a few books. In honor of the 100th anniversary of Pushkin's death in 1937, a five-volume edition of his works had been published. My mother packed those small volumes into my suitcase. Right before leaving the apartment, probably with the permission of the NKVD men, she put some money in the pocket of my overcoat. On the surface, my mother appeared calm, but when they led us out into the dark street, she started sobbing, threw her arms around me, and held me tight. The NKVD men literally dragged my sobbing mother away from me, started forcing her into a car, then put me in a different car, and drove us away, in opposite directions.[13]

After a short stay at the Danilovsky Children's Reception Center in the former Danilovsky Monastery, Volodia was taken to an orphanage in the town of Nizhny Lomov, in Penza Province. The local schoolteacher, Antonina Aleksandrovna, welcomed him, introduced him to his new classmates, told him about her own arrested relative, and invited him to her house for a dinner of fried potatoes. "I suppose that for me both the school and Antonina Aleksandrovna's house," he wrote in his memoirs, "were tiny parts of that small world I'd left behind."[14]

His orphanage (also a former monastery) turned out to be yet another part of the same world. When he walked into the 1938 New Year's Eve party soon after he arrived, he saw "a tall New Year's tree, shiny new vinyl tablecloths, a whole stockade of lemon soda bottles, a smiling cook, and girls on cafeteria duty handing out steaming rice porridge with raisins and hot chocolate." Soon, what had first appeared as an imitation of home became home. Volodia liked his new friends (who quickly accepted the new arrivals from Moscow), the church cemetery where they told scary stories, the river Lomovka "with an eddy by the opposite, high bank," the campfires, the orphanage director, with his "big mustache and teasing half-smile," and especially his carpentry teacher, the unflappable Fedor Ivanovich, who "patiently and unobtrusively taught the kids his trade. He would begin by teaching us how to use carpentry tools and how to plane a plank. Lean and agile, Fedor Ivanovich would lift each plank to eye-level and, with a quick stroke of a pencil, mark the places that needed more work. Having learned how to plane, we would begin working on a stool. Having finished his first stool, a newcomer would become a full-fledged member of the carpentry shop and could aspire to other, more complicated tasks. I often remember my first, painstakingly manufactured, unprepossessing, wobbly-legged stool."

In the evenings, Fedor Ivanovich taught an optional photography class. "Everything was almost the same as when, not so long ago, my father and I used to lock ourselves in the bathroom to develop and print photographs." Once he got sick and was taken to the town hospital, where his life story provoked a great deal of curiosity. Among those who came to see him were two "self-assured, insolent" young men who subjected him to "something like an interrogation," but his roommates defended him, saying that he was not responsible for his parents. No one at the orphanage had treated him any differently from the other children, so he was "caught completely by surprise." Later, he discovered that "the unpleasant episode in the hospital was not typical of ordinary people's perception of the events of 1937." After three years in the orphanage, he moved to Leningrad to live with his aunt, a Party official. His suitcase contained family photographs, some shirts and underwear, and the five-volume collected works of Pushkin that his mother had given him on the day she was arrested. After graduating from high school, he was admitted to a military college and eventually became a naval officer.[15]

■ ■ ■

Valia, Rem, and Svetlana Osinsky were sent to an orphanage in the town of Shuya, Ivanovo Province. According to Svetlana, Valia did not change at all. "He found everything interesting, lived a fun-filled, joyous life, and was ready to share his joy with everyone. His future looked bright to him, and he was sure life would not let him down." He loved his orphanage, his school, his teachers (especially the chemistry, geography, and history ones), and his new friends (especially Misha Kristson, who knew the whole of *Eugene Onegin* by heart). He kept up with his Moscow friends, Sasha Kogan and Motia Epstein, who sent him parcels with books and "all sorts of yummy things." He enjoyed acting (his stutter disappeared on stage), singing (especially "Wide Is the Sea," a prerevolutionary ballad revived in 1937 by Leonid Utesov), and sleeping under the stars ("wrapped in a coat with grass for a mattress"). He served with distinction as his ninth-grade elected representative; admired Boris Shchukin in the role of Lenin in *Lenin in October* and *Lenin in 1918*; loved "The Song about Stalin," which he, as a member of his school choir, sang on the third anniversary of the Stalin Constitution; enjoyed a play "about how a bunch of spies and wreckers slander an honest Party member"; rejoiced at being found fit for military service (having read Goethe while waiting for his medical exam); and trained hard in order to pass his "Ready for Labor and Defense" test. Getting ready for labor and defense—and working on oneself as preparation for the general future—involved ascetic self-restraint. "Rem and I," he wrote to his mother, "do not smoke and do not intend to. First, it's bad for your health; second, it's a waste of money; and, third, it would make things harder during a time of war or something else. As for drinking—we don't drink, either. Recently I tried some beer in the theater—I was thirsty, and there was nothing else—and thought it tasted terrible. So no need to worry on that score."[16]

Svetlana and Valia Osinsky
in the orphanage
(Courtesy of Elena Simakova)

But mostly, he read. After a year and a half of searching for their parents, Valia, Rem, and Svetlana found their mother in a "family members' camp" in Mordovia. In his first letter from the orphanage, Valia wrote:

> Mom, in Shuya there is a library—actually, not one, but four. I use all of them, and check out books for Svetlana and Rem, as well as for myself. I've read all three novels by Goncharov, a lot of L. Tolstoy, A. K. Tolstoy, "Kozma Prutkov," a lot of Saltykov-Shchedrin, Chernyshevsky's *What Is to Be Done* and tons more. Of the Europeans, I've read a lot of Heine—the poems in German and the prose in Russian, and Goethe. I particularly liked *Faust* and read Part I three times. I've read a little Balzac—*Le père Goriot* and *Gobseck*, Ibsen—a lot of plays, Hoffmann, and many others whom I can't recall at the moment.[17]

Everything on Valia's list came from his parents' own list, with the usual exception of socioeconomic books. Heine was still the sentimental favorite:

> Recently, I checked out the fifth issue of *October* that you wrote to me about. The Heine biography is very good. And I liked it even more because Heine is now my favorite poet. Remember, Dad once gave me a book of his poems as a present? I didn't read them for a long time, but now that I've read most of them, I'm not sure which I like better—the lyrical or the satirical ones. His long poem *Atta Troll*, in which lyricism and satire are intertwined, is a marvelous work. I also like Heine as a human being. Goncharov, for example, wrote brilliantly, but I don't like him because he was so narrow-minded as a person. With Heine it's completely different. I've read at least three biographies, but none of them so far has been entirely good or complete. I wish the *October* biographer had written a more complete one.[18]

Valia Osinsky (*right*) and his friend, Motia Epstein
(Courtesy of Elena Simakova)

The *Geist* of Soviet happy childhood involved a marriage of lyricism and completeness. "Man's best strivings," as well as the best men who excelled at striving, were to be tenderly loved and methodically appropriated. In the Shuya orphanage, Valia's, Svetlana's, and Rem's motto was: "Life goes on, the most important thing is to study!" All three were excellent students, but the most important studying was done at home—or, in their case, in the orphanage. As Valia wrote to his mother, "I've become fairly well-versed in literature—at least from the historical point of view. But there's a lot I don't know yet. For example, I've barely read any of the French classics. *Le père Goriot, Gobseck*, and *Eugénie Grandet* by Balzac, "A Simple Heart" by Flaubert, and nothing at all by Stendhal. There's still plenty of reading left to do. I've just started on ancient literature—the Greeks. I found Homer a bit boring, but loved Aeschylus, Sophocles, and especially Aristophanes."[19]

Several months later, and now in the tenth grade, he was farther along but still working on filling in the gaps:

> There's still plenty of work to do. Recently I read Voltaire's *Candide* and was very impressed. Too bad I can't get my hands on anything else by Voltaire. I also quite like Anatole France and have made my way through his *The Gods Are Athirst, Penguin Island, The Revolt of the Angels, At the Sign of the Reine Pédauque, The Opinions of Jerome Coignard*, and some stories. On my bookshelf I still have Lucian, Shelley, and *A History of Western Literature*. I read very few contemporary writers: there's no time. I am reading a good novel by Kaverin, *The Two Captains*, which all the critics rightly praise for its resemblance to Dickens.

He never seemed to have enough time to read contemporary Soviet writers because they did not measure up to the Pamirs and because one could not measure anything without conquering the Pamirs first: "I am slowly mastering *Don Quixote*, which is not as difficult as I expected. Sancho Panza is wonderful. I am also reading Romain Rolland's *Jean-Cristophe*, one installment at a time, whenever I can get them. It seems to me that Romain Rolland is not inferior to Dickens or any other writer of that calibre. After Leo Tolstoy, he is my favorite novelist. I have also read Sophocles and find that I like him."

"Completeness" presupposed hierarchy. Only a fully ranked world could be complete. Literary rankings were based on a combination of depth and beauty. At sixteen, Valia had no doubt about which summit was the highest:

> I fell in love with *Faust* for a variety of reasons. First, I like the main characters—Faust and Mephistopheles. Their thoughts are very intelligent and profound. Gretchen is a bit silly, but very touching. *Faust* is good because it is written in simple, clear, but elegant language. Shakespeare uses a lot of metaphors, similes, and elaborate phrases, so it is not always easy to get at the meaning. That's why reading him can be exhausting, in my view. But Goethe has none of that. The play has some very beautiful verses, especially the songs. On the whole, the verse in *Faust* is wooden—written, as Heine said, in the meter of a German puppet theater comedy. But, at the beginning (in the first section), the Archangels' Song, the Chorus of Spirits, and Gretchen's songs are very beautiful. In the second part, too, although it's harder to understand. But it has even more of these beautiful passages.[20]

Because of his perfect grades, he could enroll in any university without taking the entrance exams. He took a long time deciding between biology and philology and ended up choosing classics. His mother wanted him to stay in Moscow, but he decided to go to Leningrad University to study with the legendary Olga Mikhailovna Freidenberg. He spent several nights at the railway station before asking his class representative, Elena Monchadskaia, if she would help him get a place in the dormitory. She took him in, and he spent several days living in her apartment. Her father, the zoologist Aleksandr Samoilovich Monchadsky, whose half-brother had been arrested in 1937, talked to the dean of philology and leading Soviet Assyriologist, Aleksandr Pavlovich Riftin, and Valia was allowed to live in the dorm.[21]

According to Monchadskaia, "He was a brilliant student. He got perfect grades. He stood out from us because of his knowledge of languages (we knew he had been born in Berlin). But he also studied harder." Olga Freidenberg tried to help him with money and started a collection, "but he was proud in such things and would not accept any help." As he wrote to his mother during his first semester at the university, "I sometimes go to the movies and afterward feel that, if it weren't for such occasional outings, things might get pretty bad. I tend to work without a break and without

Valia Osinsky
(Courtesy of Elena Simakova)

realizing how tired I am or noticing that I am not being as efficient. But I won't drive myself into exhaustion. I recently saw *Valery Chkalov*, a very good movie, and *Vasilisa the Beautiful*—which was also not bad." As a member of the Student Scholarly Society, he also worked on his own research projects. "I gave my paper on Racine and Euripides to our department chair, Olga Mikhailovna Freidenberg, and she read it and, contrary to my expectations, said that it was very good. And I had just about decided to burn it. Yet I know that I could have written something better, more substantial. But still, it's good news. We are going to have one of our Society seminars, and Freidenberg herself is going to talk about my paper. I am sure she'll have criticisms, but when they're fair, it doesn't bother me." He had several new friends and reported in detail about their interests and virtues. They talked about history and literature and went to the movies and theater together. According to Monchadskaia, "Valia was an active Komsomol member. Our Marxism instructor, I think his name was Safronov, had a lot of respect for him. During our first class, he asked if he was related to that Osinsky, and Valia told him he was. I remember in seminars they used to have long conversations, talking like equals. And Valia used to gesticulate a lot."[22]

■ ■ ■

Valia's sister, Svetlana, who was two years younger, describes herself as less good-natured, less sociable, and less open to the world. Her first several months in the orphanage were very difficult, but the teachers "showed a great deal of tact," and eventually she understood that there was life—indeed, a more authentic life—outside the House of Government. "I understood," she writes in her memoirs, "that different people had different values, that I was not the moral lawgiver, and that from then on I was equal to everyone else whom fate had brought to that orphanage."[23]

Her memories of orphanage life, like those of her original home, were shaped by the sacred calendar, which centered on the celebration of the New Year.

> For New Year's they used to set up a tree in the assembly hall, and we would stage a masked ball and concert, and sing and dance. Once we performed the children's opera, *The Magic Swan Geese*. I sang in the choir, and Valia acted the silent role of the Wood Sprite. The costumes were borrowed from the theater in town. . . . But in our own theater club, which we organized and led without the help of any of

Children from the Shuya orphanage (Courtesy of Elena Simakova)

Children from the orphanage carrying water in 1941
(Courtesy of Elena Simakova)

Children from the orphanage marching.
Svetlana Osinskaia is in front. (Courtesy of Elena Simakova)

the teachers, we put on a play from prerevolutionary life, in which I played an old laundress, and then we even acted out *Timur and His Crew*, in which I played Zhenia. . . . On New Year's Eve, the teachers from the school used to come sometimes and pass out presents.

We also celebrated November 7 and May 1. Dressed in our sports costumes—short bloomers and light blue T-shirts (they were called vests then) with white collars and white bands on the sleeves—we would perform a trick that was very popular in those days called the pyramid. We older girls would also prepare folk dances of different ethnic groups of the Soviet Union. Our choir would sing both revolutionary and new songs—either military ones or children's ones such as "The Heroic Pilots Are Flying Away," "The Red Flag Is Flying Overhead," "Our Horses, Horses of Steel," "Our Big Brothers Are Marching in Columns," and many others. On Lenin Memorial Day we would create a commemorative bonfire by placing some lightbulbs in a circle on the assembly hall floor and then covering them with a red cloth and some red narrow strips of red fabric that seemed to flicker like flames. We would turn off the light and sit on the floor around the bonfire singing and reciting poetry.[24]

She also remembered trips to the Godless Movie Theater inside an old church and dancing to the accordion at the summer camp, among many other things, but her fondest memories were those of her teachers.

We had a wonderful director, Pavel Ivanovich Zimin. I think it was probably thanks to him that we were always treated the same way as all the other children. Many years later he told me that he had had to report on us and on our behavior, but we never felt any special attention and, of course, knew nothing about it. No one ever reproached us about anything to do with our parents. Only once either a new Pioneer leader or a young teacher started asking me whether I realized who my parents were and whether it might not be better for me to forget them. I listened to him in amazement. Someone interrupted our conversation, and I never heard any more speeches like that again.[25]

What the carpentry shop was to Volodia Lande, the sewing shop was to Svetlana:

Pavel Ivanovich Zimin
(Courtesy of Elena Simakova)

The noise inside the shop was easily tamed by our sewing instructor, Natalia Trofimovna, who, though not noisy herself, was firm and decisive in her own quiet way. Short and thin, she had an attractive face with small, sharp features, gray eyes, small hands, and small feet. She always wore the same carefully ironed, light gray satin smock, under which a silk cream-colored blouse peeked out. She always had a measuring tape around her neck and a row of pins and needles stuck in the lapel of her smock. She would cut the thread with a precise movement of her small teeth, although she warned us not to do this, pointing to a chipped spot on her upper tooth. On my first day Natalia Trofimovna gave me an assignment: to gather a sleeve into a cuff—a five-minute job at most. She showed me how it was done. I worked for at least an hour. When it was finished, she looked at it and, in order to encourage me, showed it to the class as an example of good work. The other girls maintained an ironic silence. Alas, it was probably the only exemplary piece I ever made.

I started coming to the sewing shop every day, on schedule, although I did try to play hooky sometimes. Secretly, I became very attached to Natalia Trofimovna and felt that she, too, liked me and felt sorry for me. I watched her agile movements and listened intently to what she had to say (trying not to be too obvious about it). She was forty, an old woman as far as I was concerned back then. She lived with her son and often talked about him.[26]

The person who helped Svetlana the most during her first difficult days in the orphanage was her "class mentor," Tatiana Nikolaevna Guskova (known to the children as "Tian-Nikolavna"). "Pretty, nervous, thin, quick-tempered, blunt and quite strict, she was wholly devoted to the children and to the orphanage." When she saw that Svetlana did not know how to wash the floor, Tatiana Nikolaevna brought the rag, got down on the floor, and did it with her. But the real test—for both of them—came later, after the orphanage had, for most purposes, become home: "Once, one of my aunts decided, for some reason, to take me home to live with her family in Moscow. In the orphanage everyone was trying to talk me out of it. I wrote to my mother. I remember sitting in a small classroom and suddenly hearing quick footsteps. The door flew open, and in ran a beaming Tatiana Nikolaevna, holding a telegram from my mother in her hand (how did Mother manage to send a telegram from the camp?): 'Do not agree no matter what.' How happy Tatiana Nikolaevna was!"[27]

Svetlana's and Valia's mother, the Old Bolshevik and former senior editor at the Children's Literature Publishing House, Ekaterina Mikhailovna Smirnova, wrote often. Once Pavel Ivanovich, who read all the letters received at the orphanage, took Svetlana into an empty

Tatiana Nikolaevna Guskova
(Courtesy of Elena Simakova)

bedroom, sat her down on the bed, sat down beside her, put his arm around her, and started, "unhurriedly and sympathetically," asking questions about her mother. "Her letters—about books and poetry, and full of advice—not the everyday kind but about life in general—had made a strong impression on him." When love of friends and lovers began to replace love of parents and teachers in Svetlana's life (and letters), her mother responded by quoting from a poem by A. K. Tolstoy: "My love, wide as the sea / Cannot be kept within the shores of life":

> Remember, she wrote, that love between a man and a woman is but one part of that love that cannot be kept within the shores of life and is fuller and wider than the love for one person, which is its earthly incarnation. If love between two people does not contain that all-encompassing force, it is not as interesting and certainly not full. She wrote that most of all she felt the presence of that great feeling in her love for her children, but that she had also known true love for one person, one man, and that she had always tried to make it part of that other, exalted love. I may not be remembering that letter precisely, but I am certain of its lofty meaning, which was exactly what my soul—romantic, like those of most young people of that time—thirsted for.[28]

Svetlana's favorite book, Herzen's *My Past and Thoughts*, seemed to be saying the same thing. "It taught me," she writes, "to see love and friendship as life's highest blessings." It also taught her—to quote from her quote from *My Past and Thoughts*—that "love is passionate friendship" and that "friendship between two young people has all the ardor of love and all of its characteristics."[29]

Svetlana's best memories of her time in Shuya are about a passionate friendship. Her friend's name was Galina Volkova. They met in the Shuya music school. Galina was sixteen, and Svetlana was a year younger. Svetlana had arrived in the middle of the school year and, at first, had not been allowed to enroll, but one of the teachers heard her story and let her in. She was not very good at the piano, but she wanted to recreate her Moscow home life and started coming regularly. The orphanage director, Pavel Ivanovich, gave her the key to the grand piano that stood in the assembly hall, so she could practice "at home." Galina and Svetlana started going on long walks every Sunday after class. They ate ice cream and watched couples dancing to brass bands. "The women had short hair curled at the ends like Liubov Orlova's in the film *Circus* and wore silk dresses that draped loosely below the knee. Young girls wore white blouses, colorful knitted vests, and white canvas shoes with light blue trim and button straps. For young men two-tone zippered jackets were the height of fashion." Sometimes they talked about Svetlana's past life, her parents' fate, the waves of arrests, and the coming war. "But all that lay in some other dimension."[30] Mostly they talked about other things.

> What did we not talk about! We talked about what it means to be a true human being and how one must live by one's conscience. But most of all we talked about books. I remember our endless conversations about Romain Rolland's *The Soul Enchanted*. I read it . . . first, then Galina, at my suggestion. How we loved its heroine, the strong and beautiful Annette; how extraordinary her relationship with her son seemed, and what a beautiful name he had—Marc! And Sylvie, who as an aging woman learned to play the piano! Marc and Assia, Marc's death, Annette's tears. . . . I wanted to be just like her. In our conversations there was never a trace of anything materialistic. Dresses, success? Never! How could they compete with the question of what it meant to become a true human being? It must have been either the times or our youthful romanticism.[31]

It was both, of course. Those were the times of youthful romanticism. Most girls in white blouses and boys in zippered jackets had intimate friends, and the closer they were to the urban professional and artistic world connected by books and music to the House of Government, the more likely it was that they were talking about how to become a true human being (Galina's late father had been a well-known doctor, and she was planning to apply to college in Moscow). They played a lot of music together. "My absolute favorite in those days was Mozart's Fantasia, which she played beautifully and with great feeling, pausing occasionally to tell me how much she liked a certain passage. I did, too: our feelings and opinions always coincided. She played a lot of Chopin—waltzes, mazurkas, one after another, each with its own associations, sometimes quite funny. . . . She also played Mendelssohn, Beethoven, Schubert, Schumann, and Tchaikovsky. I played, too, but I was so bad, it was almost funny."[32]

The romantic age called for romantic music and romantic literature. Svetlana and Galina did not start out by modeling their friendship on Herzen's and Ogarev's: they found their friendship reflected, and then reinforced, in what would become their favorite book in college. Galina had enrolled in the History Department of the Moscow Regional Teachers' College, and Svetlana joined her there. "We were inseparable all through college. . . . Together we 'discovered' Herzen's *My Past and Thoughts*, and it was one of the strongest impressions of our youth. . . . We were struck by the similarity between our relationship and Herzen and Ogarev's friendship. Everything felt the same, and even the vow they swore in the Vorobiev Hills (we made a special trip to find the spot) seemed to be our very own. Except that they had also sworn to be faithful to their cause, and we didn't have one." Herzen's and Ogarev's cause—transformed into the huge

Svetlana Osinskaia (*left*) and Galina Volkova twenty years
after they first met (Courtesy of Elena Simakova)

blacksmith's insatiable utopia—had been fulfilled by Svetlana's father.
Svetlana's and Galina's cause was their friendship.[33]

■ ■ ■

Most of Svetlana's peers from the House of Government shared her cause.
Exiled to camps, orphanages, and communal apartments or surrounded
inside the House by sealed doors and the shadows of departed playmates,
they continued to live in a world of love that could not be kept within the
shores of life, in an "atmosphere of one single family" (as Svetlana Osinskaia would put it many years later). It was a family as wide as the Soviet
Union, a state as close-knit as a sect, a prophecy realized in the body of
believers, and a make-believe world that would remain real for as long as
the believers continued to believe (and for as long as Fedor Ivanovich and
Natalia Trofimovna continued to make it possible).

Aleksandr Serafimovich had a literary protégé by the name of Aleksei
Evgrafovich Kosterin, author of several autobiographical Civil War stories
set in the Caucasus (including *Beyond the Mountain Pass*, an exodus tale
that came out at the same time as *The Iron Flood*). In 1936, he went to
Magadan to work as a reporter for the *Soviet Kolyma* newspaper. In 1938,
he was arrested and sentenced to five years in a camp as a "socially dangerous element." His wife, Anna Mikhailovna, continued to write to Serafimovich asking for help and vouching for Kosterin ("although in his private
life K. could, perhaps, be a bit of a bastard sometimes, in his work and in
the Party he is a pure and loyal person") and for herself ("I swear a terrible
vow on the lives of my three children that I know nothing and am not
guilty of anything").

Their eldest daughter, Nina, was fifteen when her father left Moscow. She did not live in the House of Government, but she belonged to the same world of Soviet happy childhood—urban, romantic, white-collar, self-reflexive, and fervently patriotic. (Her apartment was in No. 19, Trubnikovsky Alley, formerly the People's Commissariat of Nationalities.) She loved Pushkin, Mérimée, Goethe, Heine, Romain Rolland, Levitan, and Beethoven; appeared as Masha (from *The Captain's Daughter*) at the Pushkin masked ball ("in a long orange dress with white lace at the neck and sleeves"); disapproved of the Second Bolshoi production of Gounot's *Faust* (which seemed to trivialize Faust's pact with Mephistopheles); made presentations in the school literary and history societies; worked tirelessly on herself (focusing, at the age of eighteen, on "the wicked emotion of vanity"); thought of knowledge as a "left-luggage room" with separate shelves for labeled suitcases; worried that such different poets as Heine, Esenin, Longfellow, and Mayakovsky could coexist within her "like good neighbors in a large apartment"; "drew up a plan to read all of Feuchtwanger and write an essay 'On Feuchtwanger's Antifascist Novels'"; "resolved to go to the stadium every weekend" (to prepare for the running, jumping, cycling, rowing, and grenade-throwing "Ready for Labor and Defense" tests); wondered how the author of *Victoria* could have "sunk into fascism" and vowed "to become acquainted with the literature on Hamsun"; believed that life without friendship was impossible and that love revealed the "intelligent, genuine essence of life"; measured love according to Stendhal's *De l'amour*; loved her father's Civil War stories and yearned for a moment of self-sacrificial transcendence in her own life; admired Nikolai Ostrovsky's *How the Steel Was Tempered* and "went to see him in his casket"; took pride—at the age of fifteen—in being one of only seven Komsomol members in her class ("that is why we have to do so much volunteer work, but the respect and influence are accordingly great"); helped her Young Pioneer charges make a picture album about Khrushchev and a mock-up model of a border-guard checkpoint; helped the elderly and infirm on election day December 12, 1937 ("this day will remain in my memory for a long time"); cherished her close friendship with her "class mentor" and school Komsomol organizer; struggled against the "swamp of bourgeois domesticity"; and divided the girls in her high school senior class into "the swamp dwellers," "the young misses," and "the Komsomol activists." The Komsomol activists were those who were participating in the building of socialism by doing volunteer work, keeping diaries, acquiring knowledge, going to the theater, realizing that "there is nothing more important in life than friendship and love," and learning how to appreciate Pushkin, Mérimée, Goethe, Heine, Romain Rolland, Levitan, and Beethoven.[34]

Meanwhile, "frightening, incomprehensible things" were happening. Her Uncle Misha, "a Party member since the first days of the revolution," and his wife, Aunt Anya, were arrested, and Nina's cousin Irma was sent to an orphanage. Then "a terrible tragedy" happened to her dacha owners, her friend's father, and her other uncle. When her father sent a telegram that he might lose his job and have to come back early, she wrote in her diary: "I will not deny my father!" When he wrote that he had been expelled from the Party and fired from his job, she wrote, quoting from Gogol's *Taras Bulba*: "I am with you, Father!" When her class mentor, Tatiana Aleksandrovna, seemed to get into trouble, she wrote: "No one and nothing will make me turn my back on Tatiana Aleksandrovna!" When she found out that her father had been arrested, she wrote that it had to be "a terrible mistake." And when her mother, grandmother, and aunts told her that she should not have told the truth about her father to the president of the Geology Institute, she wrote, quoting Saltykov-Shchedrin: "They want me to follow their example and act 'in conformity with meanness.' No, my Komsomol honor is worth more to me!"[35]

"Komsomol honor" stood for a combination of Soviet patriotism ("Party-mindedness) and traditional honor as loyalty to kith and kin. Andrei Sverdlov chose the state (and himself); Volodia Moroz chose his family (and himself); Nina and most children of the Revolution did not have to choose: they were all like Ostap Bulba, for whom faith and father were one and the same. Any suggestion that a choice must be made was a "terrible mistake." The "frightening, incomprehensible" days were also a "time of excitement and joy" (as Nina wrote several months later). On September 10, 1938, she wrote in her diary: "My father and Uncle Misha are supposed to be enemies of the people. How can I, their flesh-and-blood daughter, possibly believe that?" Three days later, she spoke at a Komsomol meeting, arguing "passionately" against admitting a politically passive young man and denouncing several of his friends as equally unworthy. "Our fathers may have been arrested," she wrote, addressing one of them, "but I am not your comrade!" "When he becomes a lawyer," she wrote about another one, "he may become a dangerous enemy of our socialist society." On August 23, 1939, she discovered that she had not been admitted to the Geology Institute because she had told the director the truth about her family. She had joined, she wrote in her diary, the ranks of "lepers for their fathers' sake." Three days later, she conducted a "casual survey" of the most recent additions to her "literary stockpile," which included Anatole France's *The Gods Are Athirst*, a story of a young Jacobin who keeps executing enemies of the people until he is executed himself. "A powerful writer," she wrote, "but I cannot agree with his interpretation of the Jacobins and the French Revolution." Six months later she received an official commendation for her company's performance during some Komsomol war games marking Red Army Day. "In sum, I am ready for war. The only problem is that, because of my poor eyesight, I cannot learn how to shoot properly. I could get glasses, but they don't look good on me."[36]

The world around her seemed to merit her trust. Her class mentor, Tatiana Aleksandrovna, gave her money for her cousin who was in an or-

phanage. Her Komsomol organizer, Nina Andreevna, comforted her when her father was
arrested and, after the "catastrophe" of Nina
Andreevna's husband's arrest, sent her a copy of
Lenin's Materialism and Empiriocriticism with a
dedication that urged her to stop "whimpering"
and to remain "sincere, ... active, and battle-
ready." During the October 1938 elections to the
school Komsomol committee, she wanted desperately to be elected but felt obliged to withdraw her candidacy because of her father's
arrest—and was then elected anyway, by twenty-
nine votes out of thirty-four. Standing in line in

Nina Kosterina

the Committee for Higher Education office after not being admitted to the
Geology Institute, she met a girl who had spent the year after her father's
arrest living in her school principal's office ("an amazingly brave principal"). Having been unsuccessful in Moscow, Nina enrolled in a college in
Baku but was denied a stipend. Her mother wrote a "blunt" letter to Stalin
"asking why the principle that sons did not answer for their fathers was
being violated," and Nina was admitted to the Moscow Geology Institute.
Three weeks later, she celebrated the coming of the New Year 1940. Her
wish was "to study, read, grow."[37]

But her main source of comfort—as well as thrill, worry, joy, and occasional disappointment—were her closest friends: Lena Gershman and
Grisha Grinblat. During her last two years in high school, they saw each
other almost every day: doing homework, visiting Tatiana Aleksandrovna,
preparing Komsomol events, walking in Gorky Park, working in the Lenin
Library, reading each other's diaries, and talking endlessly about love,
friendship, books, and their feelings for each other. Grisha was in love
with Lena, then Nina, then Lena, and then Nina again. He was the only
person who got more votes than Nina in the October 1938 Komsomol committee election. He vowed to devote his life to science and wrote poems
dedicated first to Lena and then to Nina. Nina—"having been spoiled by
poets, from Pushkin to our days"—thought them weak but liked them because they were dedicated to her. Lena cried from happiness when she
was admitted into the Komsomol and "came close to tears" when Grisha
stopped being in love with her. When the three of them were not together,
they wrote letters to each other. Life, "in spite of everything," was "incredibly good." On the night of January 20, 1940, Nina could not sleep, got up
at 3:00 a.m., went for a walk around snowbound Moscow, and "felt an
intense renewed connection to Red Square, the Kremlin, and the scarlet
flag over the Kremlin." When she returned home at 6:00 a.m., she picked
up a book of Goethe's poems, got back into bed, and read the lines that
seemed to define the age:

Wouldst thou ever onward roam?
Lo, the good lies very near.
Learn happiness to seize at home,
For happiness is always here.[38]

The following year, her "New Year's gift" was a "bright and cheerful" letter from her father, with "vivid colors about nature and about the people he was living and working with" (on a labor-camp drilling crew in minus 50-degree Celsius weather). "Before pitching a tent, they had to clear away snow that was a meter deep. . . . And between the lines of the letter was an elusive ironic smile."[39]

■ ■ ■

Earlier that same day, December 31, 1940, Lyova Fedotov stepped off the train in Leningrad and set out for the city center, "trudging through the slushy snow in his galoshes." He stayed with his cousin Raya; her husband, Monya (the cellist Emmanuel Fishman); their little daughter, "Trovatore"; and their maid, Polya, in their large room in a communal apartment on the Moika Canal 95. They celebrated New Year's with the family of the "former baron," cellist, and Leningrad Conservatory professor, Boris Aleksandrovich Struve. (Lyova refused to drink any alcohol, even "for the sake of the New Year.")

The next day, his friend Zhenia Gurov also arrived from Moscow, and they began their journey through Wonderland, with Lyova recording each day's events and conversations in his diary (eighty-nine pages altogether, or about seven and a half pages of dense handwriting per day). They saw the "long-awaited and celebrated" Nevsky Prospect, the "enchanting" monument to Catherine the Great, the "graceful Kazan Cathedral" ("Voronikhin's masterpiece"), the Pushkin Drama Theater (which Lyova called by its prerevolutionary name, "Aleksandrinsky"), the Alexander Column "with the cross-wielding angel on top," the "Peter and Paul Cathedral with its pot-bellied dome and thin belfry and spire," the "heavy, chestlike marble tombs of the tsars with enormous gold crosses on the lids," "an empty fountain surrounded by numerous sculptures depicting Glinka, Lermontov, Nekrasov, and other Russian geniuses," and, of course, the Hermitage. "It was divine: the magnificent gold decorations, combined with the blindingly white marble, created a vision of stunning harmony that produced simultaneous cries of delight from Zhenia and me. . . . Each new room presented us with new marvels: magnificent tables, armchairs, paintings, colonnades, double marble columns, gold plating, malachite, and glass. All of this glittered and sparkled before us—a whole city made up of magnificent rooms and passageways."[40]

They also went to the Russian Museum (where "the masterpieces of our own painters, so dear to our hearts, were collected") and to a Tchaikovsky concert at the Leningrad Conservatory. But just as no composer could compare to Verdi and no Verdi opera could compare to *Aida*, nothing in the incomparable city of Leningrad could compare to St. Isaac's.

> It was stunning. In short, I was looking at St. Isaac's! The somber walls, tinged purple in the winter cold, the powerful crimson colonnades under their triangular porticoes, the numerous sculptures of divinities, the four belfries with their bright gilded domes and, finally, the huge, blindingly yellow main dome presented a breathtaking picture. Under its winter veil it was even more extraordinary than it had been that summer in 1937 when I was here. . . . Winter had softened it, shrouding it in snowy garments, coloring it blue and violet, leaving only the belfry domes and the main dome unchanged. It seemed so solid, heavy and yet majestic, that it made me feel proud for this whole city.[41]

They spent a long time exploring the cathedral's interior and then climbed to the balcony at the base of the main dome. "From here you could see all of Leningrad: the sparkling spire of the Admiralty, the red shape of the famous Winter Palace in the distance, and right below us, the snow-covered *Bronze Horseman* scaling the cliff astride his stallion. The view of this treasure-trove from above was truly world-conquering." Finally, they made it to the very top:

> The bright golden arrows of the sun's rays peeked through the tattered, ghostly, gauzelike clouds and lit up the surroundings. From above, the city seemed like some kind of fairy-tale village with its snow-covered roofs sparkling in the sun. Thick clouds of steam rose from the houses in the devilishly bitter cold, and the shimmering, fluorescent layers of vapor and fog flowed through the air, blurring and obscuring distant buildings and the horizon's edge in an interesting way. . . . In the distance you could see the blue shapes of the churches, the Peter-and-Paul spire, and even, to my delight, the dark dome of the Kazan Cathedral. Right below our little balcony were the gold plates of St. Isaac's dome, curving steeply downward, and looking at them, for some reason, made me feel a little dizzy.[42]

They did their best to see as many of those churches as possible, following predetermined routes through the city and making sketches of as many "architectural treasures" as they could. As Lyova explained to his cousin Raya, his scholarly interests were now concentrated on "geology, particularly mineralogy and paleontology, and biology, in the form of zoology." In the Zoology Museum, he and Zhenia "contemplated the gigantic skeleton of a whale, which took up two floors, fish, mammals, birds, and even some incredibly gorgeous butterflies on the top floor." Lyova kept asking himself if he was dreaming. Describing his walk on the Moika Embankment on January 5, he wrote: "I was walking next to the railing looking down at the icy surface of the river and humming the finale of Act 1 from *Aida* to myself. The joyous thought that I was in Leningrad continued to flutter within me! I had not yet calmed down and could hardly believe it was not a chimera or an illusion." The next morning his first words were: "Dear God, can this really be Leningrad?" The answer, assuming God was paying attention, might have been: "No, not really." They did not go to see the cruiser *Aurora*, which had given the signal for the storming of the Winter Palace; the Smolny Institute, which had served as the Bolshevik headquarters during the October Revolution; or the Kirov Museum, which Lyova had vowed to visit on the fifth anniversary of the assassination. As children of the Soviet Augustinian Age, reared among the Pamirs, they took no interest in revolutionary Petrograd and emerged from St. Petersburg back into Leningrad on only a few rare occasions—such as when they saw Hitler standing next to Molotov in a newsreel ("the executioner was smiling and trying to act polite"); when Lyova told Zhenia that if they were in Germany, they would be hanged "for being, first, Slavs and, second, Jewish"; when they asked a "bearded man who was furiously sweeping the sidewalk" whether there was a museum inside the Church of the Savior on Spilled Blood (built on the site of Alexander II's assassination) and were "totally shocked to hear that it contained a warehouse instead"; and—finally and irreversibly—when the time came to return to Moscow:[43]

> For the last time I looked around the room that I had always found remarkable, trying to engrave every detail in my memory (who knew when I'd be there again?) and left my Leningrad abode. Even the stairway was difficult to say goodbye to!
>
> Walking through the square, I kept looking at the powerful shape of the cathedral, purple in the frost, and, when it disappeared behind the hotel, thought out loud:
>
> "So, that's it!!!"
>
> I walked down the Moika Embankment, past the kindergarten where Trovatore already seemed far removed from me, and turned onto Nevsky Prospect. To cheer myself up, I started humming the march from *Aida* and, to this accompaniment, walked down the prospect to the Fontanka Canal, saying goodbye to the Kazan Cathedral, the Catherine Monument, and various other treasures.[44]

Lyova and Zhenia met at the railway station. Their train left at 1:00 p.m. They "honored the memory of Leningrad" by eating the food that each of their hosts had packed for them, commiserated with each other about having to leave, climbed into their bunks, and went to sleep.

At around seven in the morning, the train stopped at the Leningrad Station in Moscow.

Good old Moscow greeted us with its fiercest morning cold. It was still completely dark, and when we walked out onto the square, we saw that it was lit up by the floodlights on the station roofs.

"Don't even dream, Zhenya, of finding a street that would lead to St. Isaac's!" I said tragically.

"That's right!," he said. " In one short night, we've put so much distance between us. . . . And now it's gone!"

We were both clearly depressed, but the insidious cold drove us into the Metro, and we set off along that underground road for the city center.

We said goodbye at the Lenin Library station.

"Don't worry," said Zhenia cheerfully. "Not all is lost!"

"True! We're still alive, after all," I nodded gravely.[45]

31

THE COMING OF WAR

The next entry in Lyova's diary did not appear until June 5, 1941—almost five months after his return from Leningrad and his eighteenth birthday. He had been thinking of Leningrad, dreaming of Leningrad, drawing Leningrad, and writing letters to Leningrad. Nothing in school or at home seemed interesting or significant in comparison. He had been ill with strep throat and had taken advantage of the month-and-a-half-long stay at home to apply himself to "creative work in the fields of drawing, literature, and the sciences." He had almost finished his series on the Little Church and begun a new one on the Palace of Soviets. He had passed his ninth-grade exams, seen *Aida* at the Bolshoi, and marveled, once again, at the "patriotic, highly emotional, and noble scenes" of the arrival of the prisoners and the duet of Aida and Amonasro on the banks of the Nile. This reminded him of his own patriotism and his "political views, prompted by circumstances and acquired gradually over this entire time."

> Although Germany is at present on friendly terms with us, I am absolutely certain (and it is well known to everyone) that it is all for show. I think that in doing so it is trying to lull us into a false sense of security, so as to stab us in the back when the time comes. This theory of mine is confirmed by the fact that the German armed forces have been focused on occupying Bulgaria and Romania, having sent their divisions there. When the Germans landed in Finland in May, I became fully convinced that they were secretly preparing to attack our country, not only from the former Poland, but also from Romania, Bulgaria, and Finland. . . .
>
> Assuming that, after having spread its troops along our border, Germany will not want to waste time, I have become convinced that the coming summer will be a turbulent one for our country. . . . It is clear that, by the summer, the troop concentration will be complete and, obviously unwilling to attack us in the winter in order to avoid our Russian frosts, the fascists will try to force us into a war in the summer. I think that the war will begin either in the second half of this month (i.e., June), or in early July, but not later, for it is obvious that the Germans will try to finish their war before the onset of winter weather.

Personally, I am completely convinced that it will be the last arrogant action on the part of the German despots because they will not defeat us before the winter, which will finish them off the way it did Bonaparte in 1812. I am as sure of their fear of our winter as I am of the fact that victory will be ours! . . .

A victory, of course, would be a good thing, but we could lose a lot of territory in the first half of the war. . . .

If I am going to be completely frank here, I have to say that, in view of the German war machine, which has been fed by all their industries for so many years, I am sure there will be major territorial advances by the Germans in the first half of the war. Later, when they have been weakened, we'll be able to drive them out of the occupied areas, go on the offensive, and take the fight to enemy territory. . . .

Hard as it is to contemplate, we may have to give up such centers as Zhitomir, Vinnitsa, Vitebsk, Pskov, Gomel, and a few others. As for the capitals of our old republics, Minsk will, in all probability, be abandoned. Kiev may also be taken by the Germans, but with much greater difficulty.

I am afraid to speculate about the fate of Leningrad, Novgorod, Kalinin, Smolensk, Briansk, Krivoi Rog, Nikolaev, and Odessa—all cities lying relatively close to the border. The Germans are so strong that even these cities may be lost, except for Leningrad. I am absolutely certain that the Germans will never take Leningrad. Leningraders are like eagles! If the enemy does manage to take it, it will be only when the last Leningrader has fallen. But for as long as the Leningraders are still standing, the city of Lenin will be ours! It is not unthinkable that we could surrender Kiev because we would be defending it as the capital of Ukraine, not as a vital center. But Leningrad is incomparably more precious and important for our state. . . .

The fascists can surround Leningrad because it is, after all, close to the border, but they won't be able to take it. As for Moscow, even if they do have the strength to surround it, they won't be able to do it simply because of the time factor, for they won't be able to complete the encirclement before the winter: the distances are too great. Come winter, the area around Moscow and beyond will be their grave! . . .

I am not trying to be a prophet: I may be mistaken in all my theories and conclusions. These thoughts occurred to me as a result of the international situation; logical reasoning and guesswork helped me tie them together and add some things. In sum, the future will reveal all!!![1]

A week later, on June 12, Lyova and Zhenia Gurov took the train to Peredelkino, walked through "a green grove and some woods sparkling in the bright sun," and set up camp on the edge of a large field. On one side was "a narrow little river almost completely choked with grass, its steep banks overgrown with luxuriant sedge and young aspens that looked like twisted gray ropes curving upward." On the other, a clear spring "ran along its rusty red bed covered with last year's dark leaves, swollen twigs, and other outcasts of living nature." They spent the whole day "in this heavenly place, frolicking by the river, then drawing the view of the wooden foot-bridge over that same river, then making a rough sketch of the small rail-road bridge that could be seen through the aspens growing along the banks, creating a very interesting effect behind the thick cobweb of young aspen trunks."[2]

Nine days later, on June 21, Lyova wrote: "I can feel my heart pounding whenever I think that any minute might bring news of Hitler's latest ad-venture. To be honest, over the past several days, I have been waking up each morning with the question: 'Perhaps, at this very moment, the first volleys have already been fired across the border?'" The following morning he woke up early, "as usual," and was rereading and editing his diary when the telephone rang. His Aunt Buba told him to turn on the radio. "We are at war with Germany!" she said. "I was amazed at how closely my thoughts had corresponded to reality," he wrote. "I would much rather have been wrong!"[3]

■ ■ ■

The lives of the House of Government residents had been interrupted and remade three times by a telephone call or a doorbell ring: the one on December 1, 1934, which heralded the coming of the last judgment; the one in 1937 or 1938, which doomed individual families; and the one on June 22, 1941, which announced the beginning of the "Great Patriotic War" and the end of the House of Government as the home of top government officials.

The Bolsheviks had been waiting for the great war since the triumph of their Revolution. It had almost broken out during the Civil War and had never retreated definitively. It had been the cause and consequence of the Party's refusal to settle into life as a church, at peace with the world. It had made the Party's greatest accomplishments—industrialization, collectivization, and cultural revolution—urgently necessary as well as inevitable. And it had been the reason why the assassination of an undistinguished official had led to the "general purge" that had consumed the House of Government, along with many other homes. The coming of the war fulfilled a prophecy that was much larger and older than Lyova's. It justified all the previous sacrifices, both voluntary and involuntary, and offered the children of the original revolutionaries the opportunity to prove, through one more sacrifice, that their childhood had been happy, that their fathers had been pure, that their country was their family, and that life was, indeed, beautiful, even in death.

Nina Kosterina did not make any entries in her diary in the spring of 1941, either. On January 6, the day Lyova went to a Tchaikovsky concert at the Leningrad Conservatory, she had gone to a Beethoven concert at the Moscow Conservatory. ("*Egmont* overwhelmed me," she wrote. "I don't know how to describe it: I suddenly wanted to get up and go somewhere—I experienced an almost physical sensation of flying—my heart pounded anxiously, and it was difficult to breathe. I kept clapping for a long time, unable to take my eyes off the conductor, Natan Rakhlin.") That entry had been followed by a short one on February 8 about Grieg's *Peer Gynt* ("I am in total rapture"); one on February 20 about Thackeray's *Vanity Fair* ("unfortunately, in our society, the well-fed, well-behaved philistine is crawling out of the woodwork, too"); one on February 24, about receiving (but not yet reading) Lenin's *Materialism and Empiriocriticism*; and one on March 2 about standing "at the threshold of the enormous and marvelous temple of science and the arts" ("every step forward not only brings a great deal of knowledge, but also opens up horizons that take your breath away"). The next entry came three and a half months later, on June 20, after she had turned twenty and was living and working in the "Tambov forests" as part of a geological expedition:

I have resisted the urge to write for a long time—either from fear of subjecting my actions to serious scrutiny or from an unwillingness to clarify things in my own mind. The same is true of reading: the desire is there, but what I read between the lines are my own thoughts, things that touch me more than the most interesting book. All I can see before my eyes is one single image, one dear face.

The pictures and memories of days gone by rush past like tiresome nurses or guards. Light, superficial thoughts flit by, but then everything falls silent, leaving only the present and my "right now" happiness.

There has been an immense change in my life. I no longer belong to myself. I am "someone else's" now. I feel that my independence is gone, that this time I won't be able to just pick up and leave if I have to. A very strong thread ties me to this man.[4]

His name was Sergei. He was like a "solicitous brother" to the members of the expedition and "amazed everyone with his exceptional decency, sensitivity, and attention." He told her once that he was too simple for her, but she responded, through her diary, that he had a "fine, sensitive soul." She knew that she was "physically in love," but was not sure about intellectual kinship. "It doesn't mean that he must be a model of intellectualism, but he must meet my inner needs. I must see in him a man who understands my thoughts and emotions. He does not have to love what I love and share my every opinion, but we must be on the same level. That is my dream." In the meantime, she was simply happy.

I want to call him by all sorts of tender names, to keep telling him over and over again: "My love, my dear one! Press me closer to your heart, let me fall asleep on your chest, my joy. I love you, my big and tender man . . ." And hundreds more tender, loving words for the man who is sleeping so soundly right now. . . .

The wind is blowing. Somewhere far away I can hear the frightened cry of a passing train. . . .

I told him the truth: "I want a child." I am not afraid that I am too young and that a baby will interfere with my studies. I want our love to leave a mark.[5]

The next entry, in which she addresses herself, was written three days later, after news of the war had reached the forest:

June 23

Do you remember, Nina Alekseevna, how you secretly dreamed of living through some big, dramatic events, of storms and dangers? Now you have it—war. A black vulture has attacked our country without warning, from behind black clouds.

Well, I'm ready. . . . I want to be where the action is, I want to go to the front.[6]

The coming storms and dangers reminded her of her old friends—the ones she could be sure of, the ones who understood her thoughts and emotions. She recited Grisha's poems, and remembering him gave her "a good, warm feeling." On June 28, she wrote to Lena:

Dear Lena, I want to tell you that I never stopped loving you, that not a day went by without my thinking of you. I tried to convince myself: "That's okay, there'll be new friendships!" But I was deceiving myself. There were no new friendships and never could be.

. . . Outside my window is thick, impenetrable darkness. It's the beginning of the new moon. A tiny crescent timidly appeared and quickly disappeared. But the dancing circle of bright stars stirs and thrills the soul in silent symphony. It is warm outside, and I feel like going somewhere, listening to the mysterious whisper of the forest and reveling in the boundless joy of living. But I have no one to do it with. I feel sad without my friends. There is no one I can talk to about what I am feeling. . . . The man I love . . . whom I think I love, won't do for various reasons. The first and most important reason is that he worries about me too much. . . .

I need to get away from here. This is not where I belong right now. Our lives have been interrupted and are moving in a new direction. I need to make some decisions, but, most important, I need to be honest with myself and have the courage to face the hostile winds.[7]

In the absence of Lena and Grisha, her only confessor and confidant was the forest. "It's hard to tell which are more beautiful: the tall, slender, austerely thoughtful pines or the birch trees, as joyous and festive as a circle of dancing girls. The gloomy pine forests are closer to me in spirit, though." On September 3, she came to her favorite spot, "where the pine trees part, creating a tiny gap for a narrow trail to pass through" and cried "sweet and bitter tears":

Fall is coming. Two or three more weeks, and I will part with you, my dear forest; I will leave, I must leave for the place where the great battle is being waged. . . . I feel very sad at the thought of leaving my happiness here . . . in order to look for a different happiness some-where else. But I will find it, I know I will!

The proud pines seem to be telling me: "You should live your life so as to earn the right to hold your head high, proudly and indepen-dently, the way we do."

"But fate breaks such people," rustle the birches fearfully. "Storms break the proud ones, tear them out by their roots. . . . Be humble, bow down. . . ."

"True, but those who withstand the storm will be even stronger and prouder," I can hear in the roar of the mighty pines, "We sing our song to the folly of the brave!"[8]

A month later, she made a "sudden and resolute" decision to leave for Moscow. Sergei was away, preparing the expedition's evacuation to the Urals. The passenger trains were no longer running, but a young sergeant from a military transport train agreed to let her join them and held out his hand to help her climb in. It took the convoy three weeks to reach Moscow. She and the soldiers became "good friends on the very first day." They were "nice, lovely boys."[9]

Her mother, grandmother, aunt, and two little sisters had left for the Urals. She found a note from her mother urging her to do the same. "The empty apartment felt oppressive. I thought that my favorite books might help distract me and chase away my melancholy, but the dead silence weighed upon me. . . . I ran my finger across the cupboard: a line was clearly visible in the layer of dust. I wrote: "Nina—Lena—Grisha!"—then suddenly felt a chill and goosebumps—from the silence and those words in the dust. I quickly erased the inscription and went outside."[10]

Two weeks later she received a letter from Sergei. He agreed with her mother and the birches. "I have always told you," he wrote, "that you are still very young and that you need the advice of older and more experienced friends. I am becoming more and more convinced of this. I hate doing it, but I feel it's my duty to remind you of our last conversation in the forest. I told you then, as a friend and brother, just how dangerous life is for you right now. My dear Ninusha, I am earnestly asking you: be prudent!!! In these times, we must keep our eyes open! At this moment, carelessness can be fatal. Keep yourself safe from harm!" He begged her to show some concern for her friends and relatives at last and hop on any train headed for Gorky and then travel on to the Urals.

> This was his response to my farewell note.
> Yes, it had been a wonderful summer, filled with love, tender caresses, forest magic, "eternal oaths," and other memories—"too many for him to remember them all." He was not there when I made my "insane" decision." I left a letter for him—"don't be sad, forgive me, and farewell," put on my backpack and walked down the forest path toward the railway station. I must go where my country needs me, leaving everything behind: the forest smells, the whisper of the pines, the birches' merry round dances, the wildflower wreaths. . . .
> Today I learned that Grisha is already at the front—he went as a volunteer. Oh how I wish I could stand shoulder to shoulder with him. . . .
> Meanwhile, in the sky over Moscow, my dear beloved Moscow, Messerschmitts roar and drop their firebombs on the dreams of my youth, burning everything that, along with my mother's milk, has fed and nurtured me since I was a tiny baby.
> So there you have it, my dear Sergei. Do not expect an answer from me. Different times call for different tunes. . . .
> Lena's not in Moscow either, she's gone off somewhere.[11]

She walked all over Moscow, observing the destruction and paying no attention to the air-raid sirens. "The days are filled with anxious expectation. Hitler is gathering strength, preparing to pounce on Moscow. I have to make my decision, and the sooner I do, the better. I cannot remain an outside observer. Of course, it is tempting to live like the detached Josephus Flavius from *The Jewish War*, but the future would never forgive me! While I am sitting in my cozy room, people are struggling, suffering, dying." On November 6, she listened to the radio broadcast of Stalin's speech. "We all froze in front of our radios, listening to the leader, while the guns thundered outside. It was so strange and surreal. Stalin's voice sounded calm, steady, never pausing for a moment." The next day, she went to see the parade and "liked the tanks best." Within a week, her decision had been made.

November 13.

. . . On November 16 I am leaving to join a partisan detachment. So, my life is entering the same path as my father's before me.

The Lenin District Komsomol Committee sent me to the Central Committee: "There you'll find what you're looking for." In the Central Committee they talked to us for a long time. Several people were rejected, and some left after realizing the seriousness and extreme danger of the mission. By the end, only three of us were left. "It's a scary, frightening thing," the Central Committee official kept telling us. But I was afraid of only one thing: "What if, in the course of testing and training, they discover that I am near-sighted? They'll kick me out." They said: "You'll have to jump with a parachute." But that's the easiest and least important part. We'll have to go alone, or, if we're lucky, in pairs. Now that is really hard. . . . In the woods, in the snow, in the dark of night, behind enemy lines. . . . Well, never mind, it's not like I'm looking for a safe place! So, November 16, at 12 o'clock, in front of the Coliseum Movie Theater!

November 14.

Of course I'm not as hard as a rock, or even made of stone. That's why it's so hard for me now. I'm all alone here. Do you think I'm not haunted by sneaky little thoughts or that I'm not sorry to leave my cozy shelter behind and step into the unknown? Oh no, that is not the case at all. I feel very lonely and, these past few days especially, I have needed my friends. . . .

As I walk through the empty rooms, images from the past appear and vanish all around me. It's here that I spent my childhood and youth, here that my mind was formed. Lovingly and sadly, I go through my books, letters, and notes, reread passages from my diaries, look at random entries on torn scraps of paper.

Goodbye books, diaries, and all the dear trifles that have been part of my life since childhood: the inkwell made of Ural stone, the stool and little table in the old Russian style, Khudoga's paintings, and the pile of photographs—of father, mother, Lelia and me as children, and of the Volga and Moscow.

I am saying goodbye to this diary, too. For how many years has it been my loyal companion and trusted confidant, the witness of my failures and triumphs, never forsaking me even at the most difficult times. I have been truthful and sincere with it. . . . A day may come when, having lived through the storm, I return to these faded, yellowed pages. Or perhaps . . . But no, I want to live! It may seem like a paradox, but it's true: the reason I am going to the front is that I love life so much and want so badly to live, work, and create . . . to live, to keep living!

MY WILL AND TESTAMENT

If I don't come back, give all my personal papers to Lena. I have only one thought: perhaps by doing this, I will save my father?

Lena! To you and to Grisha, my only friends, I leave all my personal possessions: my friends' letters and my diary. Lena, dear, sweet Lena, why did you leave, I wanted so much to see you.

Nina[12]

On November 16, Nina joined Special Unit No. 9903, devoted to sabotage behind enemy lines and commanded by Major Artur Sprogis. From the meeting place in front of the Coliseum (later Sovremennik) Theater, she and the other volunteers were taken by truck to an abandoned kindergarten building in Zhavoronki, west of Moscow, where they were taught to set fire to buildings, mine roads, blow up bridges, and cut communication lines. Many of the students were young women (about 18 percent of the total). According to one of them, they were told that only one in a hundred would survive. (Among the early casualties was Zoia Kosmodemyanskaia, one of the most widely celebrated Soviet martyr-heroes.) The training lasted several days. On December 8, Nina wrote to her mother that she had just returned from one mission and was about to go on another; that she was warmly dressed and surrounded by young people; and that she had gotten strep throat from sleeping in the snow but was now fine.[13]

She was killed less than two weeks later, on December 19. The official notice, sent on January 20, 1942, stated that she had died "in battle for her socialist Motherland, true to her military oath and having demonstrated heroism and courage." The message took more than a year and a half to reach her mother (who continued to write regularly to Aleksandr Serafimovich, who continued to help her and her husband, who was still in a camp). Valentin Litovsky, who had played Pushkin in *The Youth of a Poet*, went missing in action at about the same time. Grisha (Grigory Abramovich Grinblat) was last heard from a month later. Vova Osepian (Gevorkian), who had written to his mother's camp asking for a visit, was killed in 1943 (at the age of seventeen or eighteen, about three years after writing that letter).[14]

Nina Kosterina in uniform

Valia Osinsky joined the people's militia in the summer of 1941, soon after presenting a paper on Euripides at a Classics Department colloquium. In a letter to his sister, Svetlana, he wrote that he had a feeling that he would come back alive. "Our studies—yours, Rem's, and mine—are probably over for now. But remember that after the war you will go back to school, graduate from college, and become a true, good, worthwhile human being. It will be difficult for a while—maybe a year or two, and for some time after the war. But then, after Hitler has been beaten and everything has been rebuilt, life will be so wonderful that 'there'll be no need to die,' as Chapaev used to say." Svetlana received the letter in her orphanage: "I remember standing in that large classroom, leaning against the round, slightly warm, tall black metal stove. The younger kids were at their desks, and I was there instead of their teacher. I read the letter, written in a terrible, tiny hand and folded into a triangle, in the dim light of the bare lightbulb hanging from the ceiling." Valia disappeared soon after mailing it. Svetlana stayed in the orphanage for another year, until the fall of 1942. Her "dowry" was a warm red flannel dress, which she had made with the help of Natalia Trofimovna. "She looked at me with sadness and warmth, as if wishing to say something. But she did not say anything. She kissed me and gently pushed me away: go. I left."[15]

Anatoly Granovsky, who was a year younger than Nina, survived his missions behind enemy lines and was, in the spring of 1944, transferred back to agent provocateur work under Andrei Sverdlov. His younger brother, Valentin, volunteered for the army ("to wash away the stain on our name," as he told Anatoly) and died of multiple wounds on December 1, 1942. Volodia Ivanov spent the war in the Far East and participated in the August 1945 campaign against Japan. On March 13, 1946, he wrote to his parents from the city of Bei'an, in Manchuria. "About ten days ago I received a letter from you, but I could not respond right away because I was on a trip around Manchuria—its cities and villages (carrying out a special government assignment). We covered 2,000 kilometers and accomplished a large and very important task. What kind of task it was, I can't tell you in a letter, for obvious reasons." Shortly afterward, when his division was crossing the border from Mongolia on its way home, he was accidentally killed by a Soviet border guard.[16]

Lyova Fedotov remained in the House of Government for at least a month after the beginning of the war. "Amazing things have started happening in our plants and factories," he wrote on June 26. "People have begun to overfulfill their tasks by several hundred percent and to achieve the kinds of heroic successes that could only be dreamed about before. I was reading about it in the newspaper and could not help marveling at how high the spirit of the Soviet people could soar." He thought of the war as the last battle of the army of light against the beast, with a possible Gog-and-Magog epilogue at the very end.[17]

Volodia Ivanov's last photograph

Consequently, in this war we can expect every possible departure from the laws of war because it will be the most monstrous confrontation the world has ever known, for it is an encounter of two opposites. It is possible that, after our victory over fascism, about which I have no doubt, we will have to clash with our last enemies, the capitalists of America and England, before the final triumph of communism on Earth. . . .

But when the last den of reaction has been destroyed, I can only imagine what life on Earth will be like! God, how I would like to live to that time! Communism is a magnificent word! How beautiful it sounds next to Lenin's name. When you put the hangman Hitler next to the image of Ilich . . . My God! Can one really compare? They are two absolute opposites: Lenin's luminous mind and that pathetic, vicious little reptile who resembles . . .—but can Hitler really resemble anything? The most wretched creature on the face of the earth would look like an angel next to that reject of the human race.

How I wish Lenin could be resurrected! Oh, if only he were alive now! How I would love for those Fascist beasts, in their war against us, to feel on their own skin the luminous genius of our Ilich! Then they would truly find out what the Russian people are capable of![18]

Lyova Fedotov had almost certainly never read the Book of Revelation, but he had devoted his life to the study of the Pamirs (in the Hermitage and the Conservatory, as well as among the treasures of world literature), absorbed the vocabulary and eschatology of Bolshevism, and kept reading the newspapers, "marveling at how high the spirit of the Soviet people could soar." He defined the Soviet people as "the Russians and other nations that make up the Soviet family," but the other nations, including his own large Jewish family, were but further evidence of what the Russian people were capable of. Lyova's world, like the one he read about in the newspapers, was a heavenly St. Petersburg. Its earthly incarnation was Peter's creation; its future reign was Lenin's bequest. Lenin, who had been absent from Lyova's Leningrad, had been resurrected for one final battle. Stalin's job was that of the Archangel Michael: mentioned in passing as "the leader" in the war against Satan, he was secondary to the Russian people and the luminous prophet of their triumph.[19]

Sometime in the late summer or early fall, the theater in which Lyova's mother worked was evacuated to Zelenodolsk, in Tatarstan. While there, Lyova, according to his mother, "did not draw, did not come near the piano, and did not keep his diary." In the winter of 1942–43, he joined the army. His mother tried to tell the recruitment board that his vision and hearing were bad, but it did not help. On June 14, 1943, he sent her a postcard: "Dear Mom: Your son, the frontline soldier, is sending you his warmest greetings. I receive frontline rations. We live outdoors. I don't worry about myself, so please don't worry about me, either. Tell everyone who writes to you that I am in a combat unit, on the frontline, and that I am very happy and proud about it. The most important thing is for you to be calm and take care of yourself. See you soon on victory day. Lyova." He was killed eleven days later, on June 25, 1943, "having demonstrated heroism and courage," and was buried in the village of Ozerskoe, Tula Province. Roza Lazarevna received the official notification on November 20, 1943. Forty-five years later, she told a documentary filmmaker: "I had some very difficult moments. I wanted to throw myself out the window. I even came up to the window, but then I thought: 'I have been a Party member since 1917, a Bolshevik. What right do I have to do this?' And I walked away."[20]

32

THE RETURN

About 500 House of Government residents (approximately one per apartment) went off to war; 113 of them (23 percent) did not come back. Those who did not leave on their own were evacuated in the late summer and fall of 1941. On October 16, when the German troops came within sixty miles of Moscow and most government agencies were evacuated to Kuibyshev, some of the House accounting records were burned. Within a week or two, most House employees had been let go, apartments sealed, remaining residents evicted, and the building as a whole placed under "conservation regime." According to the official 1942 report, "as a result of the detonation of aerial bombs in the immediate vicinity of the building in the last quarter of 1941, 90 percent of all glass in the windows and stairways has been completely destroyed or partially damaged. Because the damage occurred in the winter, almost the entire heating, plumbing, and sewage systems have been rendered inoperable. There has also been substantial damage to the stucco and even some shifting of partition walls."[1]

In November 1941, an NKVD unit consisting of forty to fifty men arrived at the House in order to carry out a "special assignment" involving apartment searches. They were quartered in Entryways 12 and 17; the remaining members of the House administration, newly rehired guards (three to four per entryway), and an unknown number of repair workers moved into first- to third-floor apartments in other entryways. An investigation conducted in the summer of 1942 found that the NKVD unit and seventeen members of the House administration, including the House commandant and several of his deputies and senior guards, had stolen a wide variety of items (with a particular preference for watches, razors, revolvers, hunting rifles, leather coats, gramophone records, and sewing machines) from at least sixty-eight different apartments. At the same time, 453,638.45 rubles' worth of furniture was evacuated from residents' apartments and the basement warehouse (which was converted into a bomb shelter) "without any records being kept." Items taken from the apartments "on a massive scale and for unknown destinations" included, among other things, 32 mirrors, 126 curtains, 10 radios, 43 desks, 22 dinner tables, 64 coffee/telephone/card tables, 483 chairs, 151 stools, 23 couches, 79 wardrobes, 65 bookcases, 29 silk lampshades, 33 china cabinets, 67 coat racks (including 42 oak), 84 draperies (including 41 tapestry), 28 carpet runners, 129 beds (85 nickel-plated, 38 iron, and 6 oak), 43 armchairs (including 20 children's), 381 mattresses (305 hair, 37 cotton, and 39 bast), 3 pianos, 3 concert pianos, 17 teapots, 10 pendulum clocks, 103 enamel spittoons, 1 billiard table, 1 drum, 1 "Street Urchin" figurine, 1 "Mother and Child" sculpture, and 1 polar bear skin.[2]

In early 1942, some of the evacuees started returning, and the House began to fill up again. By fall 1942, the repair work had been largely completed and most apartments made habitable. By 1945, the theater had been reopened as part of the Council of Ministers Housekeeping Department Club. By 1946, the House had 970 official leaseholders (270 more than before the war) and 3,500 residents (almost a thousand more than before the war). The proportion of communal apartments had increased dramatically. Hundreds of residents who had moved in illegally or "lost the right to reside in the House" were evicted, often after a long series of petitions and court decisions; new Housekeeping Department officials were moved in as part of the "apartment consolidation" program; and many returning old residents complained about strangers living in their apartments. People and things migrated continuously—in, out, up, and down; during 1942, 50 percent of all registered House furniture was transferred between apartments. Mikhail Koltsov's widow was evicted; Lyova Fedotov's mother moved in with two other Old Bolsheviks; and Stalin's daughter moved in, and later moved from a three-bedroom to a five-bedroom apartment. Dachas, suits, special passes, and, increasingly, cars and garages were to be awarded, returned, and reassigned. The House of Government was back, but it was busier, noisier, messier, less exclusive, and less directly connected to the government than it had been before the mass arrests and wartime evacuation.

Many top postwar officials (including Khrushchev, Molotov, Malenkov, Shcherbakov and Marshals Konev, Rokossovsky, and Zhukov) preferred the French baroque Fifth House of Soviets on Granovsky Street (formerly Count Sheremetev's rental apartments) and, after the construction boom

Fifth House of Soviets

Kutuzovsky Avenue. No. 26 is the first building on the left.

of the late 1940s and early 1950s, the "Stalin empire style" buildings along the renovated embankments and the newly laid-out Leninsky and Kutuzovsky Avenues (especially No. 26, Kutuzovsky Ave., where Brezhnev, Suslov, Andropov, and Shchelokov lived). At the same time, twenty-four special housing cooperatives were built for elite actors, artists, writers, doctors, dancers, singers, scholars, musicians, and foreign ministry officials. The Soviet elite was regenerating, reproducing, and spreading around Moscow and beyond.[3]

■ ■ ■

Meanwhile, many of the wives of the original House of Government residents began to return from the camps. "I hadn't seen Mother in five years," wrote Inna Gaister (who had since entered Moscow University's Physics Department). "She was in terrible shape. It was painful for me to look at her. She had declined so much physically and looked glassy-eyed and listless."[4]

Rakhil Kaplan
(Courtesy of Inna Gaister)

Maya Peterson had not seen her mother in seven years. "I remembered Mother as plump, well-dressed, and always smiling. Now I was looking at a small, skinny, wrinkled woman with long dark braids." Maya had spent two years in an orphanage before moving in with her half-brother, Igor. In July 1941, Igor had joined the volunteer militia ("He wanted very much to wash off the shameful stain of being a son of an enemy of the people"), become a candidate Party member, and been killed on December 16, 1941, three days before Nina Kosterina. Maya had walked two hundred miles with a refugee column to Kovrov; spent a hungry and homeless year in

evacuation in the Urals; returned to Moscow in the spring of 1943; graduated from high school with a gold medal ("schoolwork and friends were my
whole life; never in my life had I laughed so much"); been accepted into
Moscow University's Classics Department; and started writing poetry.[5]
Maya was one of three sisters:

> When Mother was arrested and disappeared from our lives for a
> while, Ira was seventeen, I was eleven, and Marina was two. We had
> been growing up and maturing as individuals without her. When we
> met again seven years later, we had been through a lot and gotten
> used to being independent. It was not always easy for Mother and us
> to understand each other. . . . We never really managed to get used
> to each other again.
>   Ira, with whom Mother had lived before her second arrest, fought
> with her all the time. When Mother and I lived together in exile, we
> also had terrible fights. She lived out her final years with Marina,
> and also badly. . . . Mother suffered terribly because of this and felt
> lonely and hurt.[6]

Svetlana Osinskaia went to see her mother, Ekaterina Mikhailovna
Smirnova, in her camp outside Solikamsk, just north of Berezniki, in 1944.
She stayed with her mother's friend Esfir, who had recently been released.

> When Mother came to see me for the first time, we embraced and
> stood silently for a minute. Esfir was crying. But even then I could
> already sense something false in myself, and perhaps in Mother, as
> well. We had not seen each other for seven years. I felt so remote
> from her; everything that interested me was in Moscow, where I was
> studying at the university: my friendship that seemed extraordinary,
> my love that was desperate and hopeless but so intense, the exciting
> research I was doing in the seminar on ancient history, my presenta-
> tion on the tyranny of Peisistratos—which I was telling Mother and
> Esfir about, when I saw the puzzled look on their faces, and Mother
> then cautiously asked: "Does anyone else find this interesting?" I
> could tell that all these things that engrossed me so utterly were not
> interesting to them and that my raptures were incomprehensible to
> them and could not really be understood because they were con-
> nected to events and emotions that I did not—I knew right away—did
> not want to share, since they did not seem to care! I had my young,
> distant, selfish world, not all happy, but still full. They, as camp in-
> mates, must have thought of the things I lived for and worshipped as
> completely crazy. The tyranny of Peisistratos . . .[7]

In 1945, Ekaterina Mikhailovna's camp term ended. She was fifty-six
years old. She wanted to stay as a free employee in the camp hospital, but

the settlement was closed down, and she had to leave. Former prisoners were not allowed to live in Moscow, but she had nowhere else to go. "She could only live in Moscow illegally. But where? In the apartment of my father's brother Pavel, where I was living? It was impossible, and nobody wanted her there. With friends? But how long would they tolerate her? And how would she make a living?" Since she was not allowed to register in Moscow, she could not get a job. More important, according to Svetlana, "The eight years she spent there [in prison and camp] had broken her. She came back a completely different person, and only very rarely could one see a pale reflection of her former brilliance. Those who expected her to return to her former life were disappointed: there was no life left in her, only the wish to survive somehow. 'If we are alive, we must go on living,' she used to say, and there was bitterness and hopelessness in those words. . . . Very soon it became obvious that nobody wanted her and that she should leave as soon as possible." She found a job as a bookkeeper at a dairy factory outside Uglich, and in early 1947 Svetlana visited her there. "It was a cold winter. She had a tiny room in a long barrack with blind windows. You could hear everything through the walls. Outside, in the dark hall, people were constantly walking back and forth, cursing, or having drunken fights."[8]

In late 1948 and 1949, as the Soviet Union returned to a state of siege, some of the recently freed "family members of the traitors to the motherland," including Maria Peterson, were rearrested and sent back into exile. Arrested and exiled along with them were some of the traitors' newly grown children. Maya Peterson (twenty-two years old), Inna Gaister (twenty-three), and Tania Miagkova's daughter, Rada Poloz (twenty-four) were arrested on the same day (April, 23, 1949) and found themselves in the same prison cell. Inna Gaister had defended her thesis that day. The State Security agent who came to arrest her had waited for her to finish before escorting her to the Lubyanka. Rada Poloz had spent the war as a

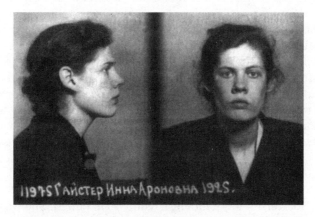

Inna Gaister's arrest photographs (Courtesy of Inna Gaister)

nurse on a hospital train and was, at the time of her arrest, a student at the Bauman Institute of Technology. Maya Peterson remembered feeling "great relief" at not having to prepare for her Latin, Greek, and ancient drama exams or write her thesis on Aristophanes. They were all sentenced to five years in exile as "socially dangerous elements." None was charged with a crime. Maya was sent to Siberia; Inna and Rada, to Kazakhstan.[9]

■   ■   ■

Anatoly Granovsky's specialty of seducing the daughters of the enemies of the people was not as urgently needed anymore. He remembered being summoned once in December 1944 to Andrei Sverdlov's office. "He sat with the rigid immobility of a corpse and only his bright, staring eyes seemed alive as I stood stiffly to attention before him. . . . It would not have been in character for him to have asked me to sit down, and he did not do so while this interview lasted." Granovsky's new assignment was to become a priest and serve as a secret informer within the Russian Orthodox Church. Unhappy at the idea, tired of working as an informer, bored by his current female "subject" (whom he described as a "hungry, despised, and hated mistress"), and desperate to get away from the "sadistic" Sverdlov, he asked for a transfer back to Pavel Sudoplatov's Fourth Section (which directed terror and sabotage activities behind enemy lines), citing his desire to do the "man's work" he had been trained for.[10] The next day he was called in to see Sverdlov again:

> He received me with an exaggerated pantomime of courtesy, bowing to me slightly and waving me to a chair. I remained standing, however.
> "So?" he said. "The great Captain Granovsky does not consider that the Second Section is the place for him? He does not think he is doing a man's work? What is his definition of a man's work, I wonder? . . .
> I remained silent.
> "Please forgive Commissar Sudoplatov, Comrade Granovsky, because he has been unable to grant your request. I am afraid there is no other way for you except to continue obeying orders, my orders." And his manner changed from bantering sarcasm to tight-lipped anger. "You may go now, and if I hear any more of this nonsense, I will see that you are properly punished."[11]

According to his memoirs, Granovsky left that same night for Minsk and then Kiev, seeking the protection of his former Fourth Section commanders. In Kiev, one of his mentors from the sabotage school took him to see the commissar of state security of Ukraine, Sergei Savchenko, who sent him to the recently reoccupied town of Uzhgorod, in West Ukraine, as

Anatoly Granovsky, 1944

part of a team charged with recruiting "sleeper agents" among the departing refugees. The principal method was hostage-taking and blackmail, and the success rate, according to Granovsky, was very high. "In the Trans-Carpathian Ukraine already occupied by Soviet troops there was plenty of material among the Hungarians, Poles, Czechs, Romanians, Slovaks, Jews, Ruthenians, Ukrainians and Austrians who lived there to serve the purpose admirably." Granovsky did well and was retained by the Ukrainian NKVD. His subsequent missions included marrying Uzhgorod's wealthiest woman for the purpose of accompanying her to the West (aborted, in April 1945, owing to the chronic alcoholism of the "subject"); traveling to Berlin in May 1945 in order to recover the secret files taken by the Nazis from the Kiev NKVD offices; and running a spy ring in newly liberated Prague in the winter and early spring of 1946. In late April, he was placed as a secret agent on a Soviet ship that was to travel around Europe.

On September 21, 1946, he offered his services as a defector to the US military attaché in Stockholm. The intelligence officer who flew over from the Allied Command in Berlin to interrogate him found his story unconvincing, and he was handed over to the Swedish authorities. Around mid-October, he was visited in Långholmen Prison by the Soviet ambassador and consul general, who urged him to return home. When he refused, they asked him if he had a message for his mother and twelve-year-old brother, Vladimir. He responded:

> "Tell them that I cannot take part in mass murders and mass enslavement of millions of people in order to secure a few years of existence for my beloved mother and brother in Soviet paradise. If you kill my brother you will kill him, but it is better for him to die as a child than to suffer the torture of life under communism. However, I am sure you will tell them whatever your masters order you to tell them."
>
> "You pretend to be unconcerned, but do you fully realize what it means for them that you should desert the service of your motherland?"
>
> "I realize perfectly."
>
> "And you can so easily send your mother to Siberia?"
>
> "There is nothing I can do to help now."[12]

On October 30, 1946, the Soviet Ministry of External Affairs sent a note to the Swedish Embassy in Moscow demanding Granovsky's extradition. According to the Swedish-Russian report of 2000 on the fate of the "savior of Hungarian Jews," Raoul Wallenberg, arrested in Budapest in January 1945, Soviet officials may have suggested an exchange of Wallenberg for Granovsky. On November 8, the king of Sweden decreed that Granovsky not be released to the Soviet Union, "nor to any country where, presumably, he does not enjoy safety against being returned to his national country." Later that day, he was released from custody. On November 15, the Swedish Ministry of External Affairs informed the Soviet Embassy that Granovsky would be extradited to a country other than the USSR. The Soviet ambassador, I. S. Chernyshev, made several attempts to persuade the Swedish government to reconsider (one of which was described by the prime minister, Tage Erlander, as "so naked and abrupt that one is completely taken aback"), to no avail. Granovsky left Sweden and seems to have spent several years in Brazil before arriving in the United States. Wallenberg was, by most accounts, executed in July 1947. The fate of Granovsky's mother and brother is unknown.[13]

Andrei Sverdlov was arrested in October 1951 as part of the purge of Jewish secret police officials. According to his letter to the chairman of the Council of Ministers, G. Malenkov, he spent nineteen months under investigation, "being groundlessly accused of the most monstrous and preposterous crimes." He was released on May 18, 1953, two and a half months after Stalin's death, but was not readmitted to the secret police. He graduated from the Academy of Social Sciences at the Party's Central Committee, became a Party historian, got a job at the Marx-Engels-Lenin Institute, and collaborated with his mother on her memoir about his father and with his father's employee, Pavel Malkov, on his *Memoirs of a Kremlin Commandant*.

In the 1960s, he and his former fellow interrogator in the Anna Larina-Bukharina case, Yakov Naumovich Matusov, collaborated, under the names of Andrei Yakovlevich Yakovlev and Yakov Naumovich Naumov, on three spy thrillers for adolescents: *A Thin Thread*, *Two-Faced Janus*, and *A Fight with a Werewolf*. In all three, the villain, "embittered against the Soviet system" because of his class or ethnic origins or because of his father's fall from grace, forms an anti-Soviet secret society in the late 1930s, betrays his country to the Nazis during the war, and spies for the Americans in the 1960s. The secret societies, known as "Avenging Our Fathers," are replicas of the ones Anatoly Granovsky, on Sverdlov's orders, used to press his classmates into joining. In *A Thin Thread*, the future spy "socialized with school kids and tried to tempt some of them into joining the 'society' he planned to create. Not with good intentions, you understand. The girls he tried to corrupt, to seduce." The Soviet counterintelligence agents do catch him in the end, but not before one of them is fired for extracting false confessions from innocent people. The reader is given an example of his interrogation technique: "The longer you persist in denial, the worse for you. And what do you expect? If you start talking of your own free will and tell everything, it means that you have laid down your arms

Andrei Sverdlov (*right*) with his uncle, German Mikhailovich
Sverdlov (Yakov Sverdlov's half-brother), from Apt. 169

and stopped fighting against the Soviet state. That will be taken into account. I'll be the first to ask for leniency for you. But if you continue your
denials, there will be no mercy. You will start talking, in any case. Sooner
or later, you will. And the sooner it happens, the better for you."[14]

It is not known whether the authors meant this to be a mockery or a
confession. Andrei Sverdlov died in 1969, the same year the following notice appeared in the underground publication *Chronicle of Current Events*:

> There are at least seven individuals living in Moscow, whom Andrei
> Sverdlov personally interrogated, using torture and abuse. He par-
> ticipated in the investigation of the case of Elizaveta Drabkina, who
> had been Yakov Sverdlov's secretary in 1918–19 and who, at his re-
> quest, had taken his children Andrei and Vera out of his apartment
> several hours before his death. Andrei Sverdlov knew very well that
> Drabkina had not committed the crimes she was accused of com-
> mitting, but still demanded her "confession" and "repentance." . . .
>
>   Andrei Sverdlov's address is: No 2, Serafimovich Street, Apt. 319
> (the very same House of Government, from which so many victims
> were taken away). His telephone numbers are: 231–94–97 (home),
> 181–23–25 (work).[15]

■ ■ ■

On March 5, 1953, Stalin died. The Party had lost what Bukharin called "the
personal embodiment of its mind and will."

Maya Peterson and her mother, Maria, heard the news in the village
of Pikhtovka, in Novosibirsk Province, where they were living in exile.
"In those days, my mother and I did not hold Stalin responsible for the
tragedy whose victims and witnesses we were. My mother saw its causes

in wrecking: a conspiracy against the cream of the Bolshevik Party by the enemies who had made their way to the top, including the Ministry of State Security. When Stalin died, we felt the same grief as everyone around us."[16]

So did Rada Poloz's grandmother (Tania Miagkova's mother), Feoktista Yakovlevna Miagkova, who kept Stalin's portrait on the wall and explained the fate of her daughter and son-in-law by saying that "there were so many enemies that it was impossible not to make a mistake." At the time of Stalin's death, Yuri Trifonov had finished school in Tashkent, worked at an airplane factory in Moscow, graduated from the Literary Institute, gotten married, published his first novel in Tvardovsky's *Novyi mir*, received the Stalin Prize of the Third Category, and turned twenty-seven. "I heard that Tvardovsky cried on stage during the Stalin memorial meeting in the House of Cinema," he wrote many years later. "Those tears were, of course, genuine. I saw the same sincere grief in my own family. My mother, who had passed through the Karaganda and Akmolinsk camps, feared that things would get worse. My grandmother grieved desperately." (Stalin's *On Lenin and Leninism*, with the inscription "To Dear Comrade Slovatinskaia, in memory of joint work underground, from the author," was prominently displayed in her bookcase.)[17]

Fedor Kaverin had been abandoned by most of his actors, ridiculed in the press, chased out of a succession of temporary buildings, and eventually fired as artistic director. He continued to direct in other theaters and dreamed of staging "one final production summing up [his] entire creative life" (rereading *Faust*, among other things, for the purpose). During the war he had produced shows for the cadets of the School of Aviation in Borisoglebsk, wished for a "communion with the Soviet state through blood sacrifice," and hoped to direct a play in which "the Russian soul takes on the salvation of the world and appears before the world and the spectator in all its holy majesty." On the day of Stalin's death he wrote in his diary: "What grief—general for the entire nation and personal for each one."[18]

On the same day, Boris Ivanov wrote: "The radio announcement of the death of our leader and teacher, Comrade Stalin, felt like a stab in the heart. When the announcer's voice died away, I looked out the window at the dark red walls of the Kremlin where, inside the quadrangle formed by those walls, the Great Stalin had lived and worked." Several days later he spoke at a memorial rally at the Kalinin Bread Factory. "I knew what needed to be said, but I could not utter a sound because the sobs rising in my throat were chok-

Boris Ivanov with daughter
Galina and grandson Volodia

ing me and tears were welling in my eyes." Anatoly Ronin, the secretly circumcised son of the planning official, Solomon Ronin, and a friend of Boris Ivanov's younger son, Anatoly, and Stalin's sons, Vasily and Artem, was trampled to death at the funeral.[19]

Stalin's body was embalmed by Boris Zbarsky's deputy, S. R. Mardashev, because Zbarsky (who had recently embalmed Georgi Dimitrov in Bulgaria) had been arrested a year earlier and accused of Jewish nationalism, spying for Germany, ties to Trotsky and Bukharin, former membership in the Socialist Revolutionary Party, and "minimizing Lenin's greatness" by comparing his body to Egyptian mummies.[20]

With his body in the mausoleum, Stalin was no longer the personal embodiment of the mind and will of the Party. The Party, separated from Stalin, needed a new personal embodiment; Stalin, separated from his body and from the Party, became open to critical scrutiny. If his body was comparable to an Egyptian mummy, his rule might be comparable to that of a pharaoh.

Rada Poloz remembered telling her grandmother that it was all Stalin's fault. Yuri Trifonov spent the day of the funeral walking with two friends, one of whom, the future children's writer, Iosif Dik, startled the other two by saying that they would live to see the day when Stalin would be taken out of the mausoleum. Svetlana Osinskaia was taken aback by her mother's reaction: "When Stalin died, our whole school was in shock and I, like everyone around me, was full of worry about how we would live without our dear father. My mother listened to me and said, with a simplicity and certainty that startled me: 'Actually, it's wonderful that he is dead.'"[21]

Three years later, on February 25, 1956, Khrushchev said as much in his "Secret Speech" at the Twentieth Party Congress—on behalf of the Party, history, and the Revolution. The bond that had held the scattered survivors of the House of Government together was broken. Boris Volin, the former chief censor and, more recently, premier ideologue of official Russian nationalism, came home from the congress "completely devastated," according to his daughter, and died within a year, never regaining his for-

Fedor Kaverin

mer self. Yuri Trifonov's grandmother, Tatiana Slovatinskaia, died six months later. The author of *The Road to Ocean*, Leonid Leonov, "went into deep spiritual shock" and lost control of the left side of his face. In the Kremlin Hospital, he ran into the Writers' Union president, Aleksandr Fadeev, who shot himself several weeks later.[22]

Fedor Kaverin compared the news to reading Dostoevsky's *The Possessed*. "How awful," he wrote in his diary. "What terrible things one learns about our Soviet past." He had suffered a stroke but was beginning to recover, spending much of his time at his dacha in Pushkino, work-

Boris Ivanov and Elena Ivanova (Zlatkina)

ing on several new productions, and writing his memoirs. On Sunday, October 20, 1957, he wrote in his diary: "I feel very happy inside. The main thing is that I know I am needed. There's so much to do. And that makes me feel good." Later that evening he, his wife, and their dog Johnny got on the suburban train for Moscow. Johnny was not wearing a muzzle, and the conductor told them they had to pay a fine. In Moscow they were escorted to the Yaroslavl Railway police station. When Kaverin attempted to argue his case, the station chief seized him by the collar and pushed him to the floor. He died on the spot.[23]

Around the same time, Boris Ivanov added a note to his diary entries on Stalin's death: "These entries about the day Stalin died were written on the day of his funeral, they show how when he was alive he was able to deceive us and if my pain at the time was great, equally great today is my hatred for this man who was able to ensnare us so completely in the feeling of love for him, while in fact he was a beast and a sadist with hundreds of thousands of destroyed lives on his conscience among them dozens of my friends and comrades."[24]

■ ■ ■

Meanwhile, the survivors from among the banished House residents kept returning from prisons, camps, and exile. A few were allowed back into the House. The widow of the executed Chekist, Yakov Peters (and the mother of Anatoly Granovsky's "subject," Igor Peters, who had since died in the war), Antonina Zakharovna Peters, moved in with Lyova Fedotov's mother, Roza Lazarevna Markus. Boris Zbarsky's old apartment, one of the largest in the House, had been occupied by the new prosecutor general, former member of the Donetsk execution troika, and lead Soviet prosecutor at the Nuremberg Trial, Roman Rudenko. Zbarsky was given a new apartment (Apt. 197), went back to teaching (but not to the mausoleum), and died in the middle of a lecture he was giving on October 7, 1954, nine months after being let out of prison.[25]

Most of the recently released residents had no chance of returning to the House of Government or recovering their former possessions (hard as some of them tried). They moved in with their children, who had little to say to them; procured rooms in communal apartments; or found refuge in the Home for Party Veterans in Peredelkino, not far from the "heavenly place" where Lyova Fedotov and Zhenia Gurov had spent a day "frolicking by the river" ten days before the start of the war. (When Antonina Zakharovna Peters and Roza Lazarevna Markus could no longer manage by themselves in the House of Government, they moved to the Peredelkino home together. Antonina Zakharovna died soon afterward. Roza Lazarevna lived to the age of ninety-two. Zhenia Gurov was present at her funeral.)

To have the "stain" removed—and to become eligible for better pensions, health care, and living space, the returnees needed to be formally "rehabilitated" (proclaimed legally innocent) and—crucially important for many of them—reinstated in the Party. To save their previous lives from meaninglessness and their families from oblivion, they also needed posthumous rehabilitation and Party readmission for their vanished relatives. What was required for the purpose, among other things, were character references from prominent Old Bolsheviks who had known them before their fall. Finding such people was not easy. Of those who had not been arrested, Platon Kerzhentsev had died in 1940; Feliks Kon, in 1941; Panteleimon Lepeshinsky, in 1944; Sergei Alliluev, Aron Solts, and Vladimir Adoratsky, in 1945; Rozalia Zemliachka, in 1947; Nikolai Podvoisky, in 1948; Aleksandr Serafimovich and Georgi Dimitrov, in 1949 (Dimitrov's body was embalmed by Zbarsky and displayed in a mausoleum in Sofia); Yakov Brandenburgsky, Maksim Litvinov, and Efim Shchadenko, in 1951. Others were not willing to vouch for those who had not been vouched for. Those still in power—with the exception of Anastas Mikoyan—had other things to worry about.[26]

The most prominent exception was the oldest of the Old Bolsheviks, Elena Dmitrievna Stasova. Born in 1873 into a prominent intelligentsia (noble) family, she had met Nadezhda Krupskaia while working for the Political Red Cross in the mid-1890s; joined Lenin's party in 1898; served as a "technical worker" (under the alias "The Absolute") and underground *Iskra* agent; spent time in prison, exile, and emigration; worked as the Central Committee secretary in 1917 (before Sverdlov took over); and held high office in the Comintern, Central Control Commission, and International Red Aid (MOPR) before being removed by Stalin in 1938, for reasons she claimed—in her letter to him—not to understand ("it is especially hard because I have never had, do not have, and will never have a life outside the Party"). From 1938 to 1946 she had worked as editor in chief of the French and English editions of the *International Literature* magazine. In 1948, she had received a "severe reprimand" for saying in a public lecture that "Lenin treated all comrades equally and even called Bukharin

'Bukharchik.'" ("These words slipped off my tongue," she wrote to Khrushchev in 1953, "but of course they constituted a grave political mistake because after the Bukharin trial I had absolutely no right to say what I did.") She was famously humorless, irritable, and difficult to please. (According to Goloshchekin's wife, once, when Goloshchekin made a grave political mistake, Stalin threatened to force him to marry Stasova.) On October 15, 1953, on the occasion of her eightieth birthday, she received her second Order of Lenin. Four years later, on the fortieth anniversary of the October Revolution, she re-

Elena Dmitrievna Stasova

ceived her fourth. She was celebrated as the paradigmatic Old Bolshevik, frequently featured as the keynote speaker at public events, and consulted as a living archive at the Marx-Engels-Lenin Institute. But her main job, after the Twentieth Party Congress, was to affirm the Bolshevik credentials of former enemies of the people. She was a one-woman rehabilitation committee, the last living memorial to the sacred origins, the only bona fide link among the remnants of severed lives. She received hundreds of letters, answered them with the help of a secretary and several volunteer assistants, and signed countless appeals to the Military Procuracy and the Party Central Committee. "In all our meetings, our conversations were always friendly," she wrote in behalf of Valentin Trifonov, "and I have always considered Valentin Andreevich a firm Bolshevik, who always followed the Party line. If you need any further clarifications regarding particular aspects of the Trifonov case, I will be happy to do whatever is necessary."[27]

She wrote such letters for Bukharin, Rykov, Goloshchekin, and Voronsky, among others. She needed help and was impatient with her assistants. On May 17, 1956, she wrote to an old comrade (whom she was helping to return from exile) about her shock over the suicide of the writer Aleksandr Fadeev and her need for a new secretary: "So now my nerves are on edge, and I have to work hard to keep them in check. And here is this young lady, who helps me read in the mornings and afternoons and is so extraordinarily ignorant and stupid that her reading often perplexes me and rattles my nerves. I am looking for a person who could be a real secretary to me—someone with knowledge of another language, typewriting skills, and clear political thinking. I don't include Party membership because if I need help reading strictly confidential materials, one of my Party comrades can always do it for me."[28]

A year later, Voronsky's daughter Galina came from Magadan to Moscow to thank Stasova for her help with her father's rehabilitation and Party reinstatement. Stasova was living in Apt. 291, in Entryway 15. "She opened the door herself. Before me stood a very old, tall, thin, slightly stooped woman with snow-white hair and a long face carved with wrinkles. In the small study, with a balcony overlooking the courtyard and full of old furniture and bookcases, were two portraits of Stalin." A third, very large, portrait of Stalin hung in the bedroom, over her bed. She asked Voronskaia if she had a place to stay and offered her a bed in her apartment. (Voronskaia declined.) Staying with her at the time was Zinoviev's first wife, Sarra Ravich, who had just returned from exile (and died within the next few days, before Stasova had a chance to place her in the Home for Party Veterans).[29]

In the fall of 1960, Voronskaia moved permanently to Moscow and became one of Stasova's assistants.

Elena Dmitrievna had had an operation on her eyes and could barely see. She could not read herself. Each reader had her own day, once a week. My day was first Friday, and then Monday. We always read *Pravda* and *Izvestia*. Elena Dmitrievna preferred *Izvestia*. We used to read the entire newspaper (especially *Izvestia*), but later on she would often say: "This article is boring, let's not read it," or simply announce: "I'm very tired. That's enough for today. Let's play cards instead."

The newspaper was to be read quickly, "without feeling," and God save you if you mispronounced a word: Elena Dmitrievna would correct you and sometimes lose her patience. . . .

Sometimes Elena Dmitrievna would become very irritable, and it would be hard to be around her. "You did not sit down properly," "did not get up properly," "did not respond properly." Sometimes I would leave with a heavy heart: it was not easy to be the object of constant attacks. But sometimes she could be very welcoming, kind, and friendly.[30]

She left no letter unanswered (checking regularly on her assistants' progress), was very generous with money, supported countless relatives, and was rumored to be paying the college tuition of two students. Ainu Kuusinen, the wife of the Finnish Communist Otto Kuusinen (Apt. 19), wrote to her from exile: "You are the best person in the world. You are an angel." Galina Voronskaia had seen too much to fully share that view. At the end of her life, the Old Bolshevik had turned into an old noblewoman.[31]

Kindness, the desire to help, extraordinary selflessness, and complete indifference to money, things, and the material side of life in general coexisted with a contemptuous treatment of those who lived near her. Not wanting her to live alone after the death of a relative, her comrades tried to find a companion for her. But it was simply impossible to live with Elena Dmitrievna. She had no regard for anyone. After they came home from work (and many of them did work), she would make them play cards with her for hours on end, order them around, and humiliate them in the presence of others. No one could stand living in her apartment for long. Different women kept coming and going.[32]

As she approached ninety, she could no longer listen to an entire newspaper or have the radio on all day long. (She used to turn it off only for reading and sleeping.) In 1962, at the age of eighty-nine, she asked for her ashes to be buried in the former Tikhvin Cemetery, currently the Artists' Necropolis in Leningrad, next to her uncle, the famous art and music critic (and whatever other family graves had not been destroyed during the reconstruction after the war). In January 1966, she wrote her will, leaving her archive to the Marx-Engels-Lenin Institute and her savings to her relatives. Several months later, she became ill. In late December, Voronskaia came to visit her. "She was unconscious and mumbling indistinctly, sometimes in French." She died shortly before New Year's, at the age of ninety-three (the same age as Princess Natalia Petrovna Golitsyna, the original Queen of Spades). Her wish to be buried next to her family made no sense for someone who had "never had a life outside the Party." It was, therefore, disregarded. Her ashes were interred in the Kremlin Wall, not far from Otto Kuusinen, Grigory Petrovsky, Rozalia Zemliachka, her friend Nadezhda Krupskaia, and the grave of Joseph Stalin, whose remains had been removed from the mausoleum five years earlier.[33]

■　■　■

Most of Stasova's erstwhile House of Government neighbors who survived "the catastrophe" also died alone. Stanislav Redens's widow and Stalin's sister-in-law, Anna Allilueva, had been arrested in 1948 along with several other members of her family (including Anna's sister-in-law, Evgenia Allilueva; her second husband, N. V. Molochnikov; and daughter Kira). According to Stalin's daughter, Svetlana, whose House of Government apartment shared a balcony with Anna's,

> She came back six years later in the spring of 1954. She had spent part of the time in solitary confinement. But most of it she'd spent in the prison hospital. The curse of heredity—the schizophrenia that plagued my mother's family—had caught up with her. Even Aunt Anna failed to weather all the blows visited on her by fate.
>
> She was in a terrible state. I saw her the first day she was back. She was sitting in her old room unable to recognize her two grown sons, apathetic to everyone. Her eyes were cloudy, and she was staring out the window, indifferent to the news we were trying to tell her about my father's death, about Grandmother's death and the down-

fall of our sworn enemy, Beria. Her only reaction was to shake her head listlessly.[34]

She recovered eventually, "stopped raving and only occasionally talked to herself at night." She was back to the way she had always been (as Svetlana saw it in 1963): "a martyr in the name of goodness, a true saint, a genuine Christian."[35]

> Once again she tries to help everyone else in sight. The day her pension arrives, myriad old ladies appear on her doorstep and she hands out money to them all, knowing perfectly well that none of them will ever be able to pay her back. People she's never seen in her life keep showing up at her apartment to ask for help. One wants a permit to stay in Moscow. Another is looking for a job. An old schoolteacher has trouble at home and nowhere to live. Aunt Anna does what she can for all of them. She goes to the Moscow City Soviet. She spends hours waiting to see someone at the Presidium of the Supreme Soviet. She peppers the Central Committee with appeals, never for herself, of course, but for someone in trouble, some ailing old woman who doesn't have a pension and has nothing to live on.
>   She's a familiar figure everywhere she goes. Everybody respects her and is kind to her, everybody except her two young, good-looking daughters-in-law, who are only out for themselves. Her home life is terrible—no one consults her or pays her any attention. Sometimes they go to the cinema and pay her to baby-sit. When they have friends in for the evening, she is an unwanted guest, a dishevelled, white-haired old woman who is sloppily dressed and keeps butting in at the wrong moment. Instead of a purse, she'll pick up an old muff or sack and go out for a walk. She'll have a long talk with the militiaman on the street, ask the dustman how he's been lately and go for a boat ride on the river. If this were before the Revolution people would treat her like a holy woman and bow down before her on the street.

Neither Anna nor Svetlana knew that Anna's late husband had been officially recognized as the country's number one executioner. Unlike number two, Sergei Mironov, he had since been rehabilitated. "She's convinced Redens is still alive, although she's had official word of his posthumous rehabilitation. She thinks he has a new wife and family somewhere in the far North like Kolyma or Magadan ('After so many years, why not?' she'll ask) and that he just doesn't want to come home. From time to time she'll insist after one of her dreams or hallucinations that she's seen her husband and had a talk with him. She lives in a world of her own, where memories and visions and shadows of bygone years blur into those of the present."[36]

Svetlana Stalina finished her book of memoirs, *Twenty Letters to a Friend*, in August 1963. A year later, she added the footnote: "Anna Redens [Allilueva] died in August 1964, in a section of the Kremlin hospital located outside of Moscow. After prison she had a great fear of locked doors, but despite her protests she was locked up one night in a hospital ward. The next morning she was found dead."[37]

Anna Allilueva

Osinsky's widow, Ekaterina Mikhailovna Smirnova, had died six months earlier. According to her daughter, Svetlana, no one would have recognized in her "the brilliant woman from many years ago or even the intelligent and sad one of more recent years."

Fate was not kind to her in her last years. Her rehabilitation in 1955 provided her with relative comfort, an apartment in Moscow, and a chance to rent a dacha, something she had always dreamed of. But the people she loved were all in their graves, and unknown ones at that. She did have a daughter, but she was unloving, uncaring, and irritable.

When my mother became an invalid, she moved from one rented apartment to another, with her friends' help, until the Academy of Sciences gave her, as an Academician's widow, a room in a communal apartment. She started living with constantly changing maids, who stole from her to the best of their ability or conscience. In 1961 the Academy authorities decided, for some reason, that she was mentally ill and offered her a separate one-bedroom apartment. I moved in, too, with my daughter and against my wishes. She would live for another three years and have two more strokes. Nobody wanted to stay with her permanently, but she could no longer live by herself.

Thus began our three years of torment, which are not worth describing because they are so easy to imagine. I will only say a few words about my mother. Until the very end, she would sit completely straight in a simple, ten-rouble lawn chair made of canvas stretched over aluminum tubes, which I would push around the apartment. With unsteady, indistinct movements of her now completely smooth, "boyish hand" (as my father used to say), she would direct her food toward her mouth, spilling some along the way and greedily devouring the rest. Her main occupation was reading, but only books she had read before. Sometimes, when looking at my mother from behind, I would notice her back begin to quiver and shake. She would suddenly burst into violent sobs while reading something that brought back memories or, more often, when listening to music.

E. M. Smirnova (*left*) (Courtesy of Elena Simakova)

(When the sweet strains of Lakmé's aria "Where will the young Indian girl, a Pariah, go?," poured forth from the radio, Mother, no matter how hard she tried, could not hold back the sobs, which would then turn into almost a howl.)[38]

Sometime during the war, Svetlana had been contacted by Anna Shaternikova, who told her about her twenty-year relationship with her father. They became friends. Anna lived in a communal apartment with her husband, whom she did not love, and son Vsemir, who died soon after the war. She was paid a special Old Bolshevik pension and worked part-time in the district Party committee and as a volunteer in various official campaigns. She was very proud of having joined the Party before the October Revolution. After Khrushchev's Secret Speech, she was contacted by a man who had spent time in the same prison cell with Osinsky. She did not tell Svetlana about it because Svetlana was not a Party member (but did tell Svetlana's nephew, Ilya, who was). Toward the end of her life she spent some time in a psychiatric institution. She once told Svetlana that she had three

Anna Shaternikova
(Courtesy of Elena Simakova)

wishes: not to die alone, to have someone say something at her funeral, and to have her grave taken care of. She died alone in a hospital, sometime in the late 1970s, when she was in her mid-eighties. Svetlana never found out where she was buried. But she did receive the package of her father's letters, which Anna had preserved for forty years, in a variety of hiding places.[39]

Bolshevism, like Christianity, Islam, and most other millenarianisms, started out as a men's movement. Women represented a very small proportion of both the original sect members and House of Government leaseholders. Men could be married to both women and the Revolution. Women had to choose. The great majority of those who moved into the House of Government did so as family members of male Bolsheviks. Many of them were Bolshevik true believers and trained professionals, but they did not qualify for the House of Government in their own right. Those who did tended to be like Stasova: single, childless, politically irrelevant, and recognized for their past service (in auxiliary capacities).

Bolshevism, unlike Christianity, Islam, and a few other millenarianisms, was a one-generation phenomenon. When the leading Bolsheviks were homeless young men, women embodied the "insatiable utopia." When they settled down and formed families, women represented either "the pettiness of existence" or—occasionally and often secretly—the last hope for the luminous faith. When they went to their deaths, women were not present, except possibly as the subject of their last farewell. After their husbands' disappearances, most Bolshevik wives were not accused of any crime but were sent to special camps as "family members." When they came back—old, sick, broken, and unwanted—there was no luminous faith left and no home to return to. They had nothing to say to their children, and their children had nothing to say to them.

Revolutions repeat themselves: first as tragedy and then as family tragedy. They begin as rebellions against the eternal return and end at home, amidst women and children. If they attempt to survive by executing their high priests for betrayal, they end a little later, amidst broken families and old love letters. When it turns out that immortality is impossible, some of the men get punished for it, and acquire a degree of immortality as a consequence (often with the help of their women and children). The women are left to be forgotten and to bear some of the blame—first in general, as carriers of the hen-and-rooster problems, and then at home, for outliving their husbands and their faith.

Valerian Osinsky had once loved his wife, Ekaterina Smirnova; his lover, Anna Shaternikova; his three children, Dima, Valia, and Svetlana (especially the boys), and the insatiable utopia, which promised profound tenderness without shame and charity without embellishment. Dima was executed along with him; Valia went missing in action; and the utopia evaporated a decade or two later, without anyone quite noticing. Ekaterina and Anna died alone. Svetlana deposited her father's letters in the Academy of Sciences archive and published a book of memoirs—as a tribute to her father, brothers, and teachers and a mea culpa to her mother.

Arkady Rozengolts's sister, Eva Levina-Rozengolts, was arrested in August 1949, as part of the campaign against relatives of executed enemies of the people. She was sentenced to ten

Eva Levina-Rozengolts, 1974
(Courtesy of E. B. Levina)

years in exile (as a "socially dangerous element") and spent five years in Siberia as a lumberyard worker, cleaning woman, medical orderly, nurse, and painter on a river barge, and two years in Karaganda, as artist-decorator at the Kazakh Drama Theater. In 1956, she was allowed to return to Moscow.

By the time of her death in 1975, at the age of seventy-seven, she had produced eight graphic cycles: *Trees, Swamps, People, Sky, Portraits, Frescoes, Plastic Compositions,* and *Landscapes.* Her human figures seem to emerge from the netherworld of silent despair into a crowded purgatory of ageless, sexless, anonymous souls. Some are imploring or praying; most seem resigned to whatever judgment awaits them.[40]

Eva Levina-Rozengolts, *People,* Rembrandt series, ink on paper, 1958 (Courtesy of E. B. Levina)

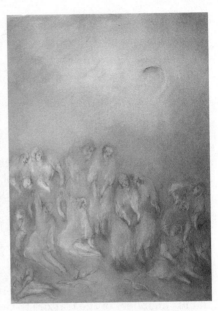

Eva Levina-Rozengolts, *People*, Rembrandt
series, ink on paper, 1960
(Courtesy of E. B. Levina)

Eva Levina-Rozengolts, *People, Plastic
Compositions*, pastel on paper, 1972–74
(Courtesy of E. B. Levina)

Eva Levina-Rozengolts, *Frescoes*, pastel on paper, 1968
(Courtesy of E. B. Levina)

33

THE END

The best of the House of Government children were killed in the war. Or rather, the children who were killed in the war became the best because they had fulfilled their oath to Pushkin and followed him into the temple of eternal youth.

The children who were not killed in the war came back to Moscow and stopped being children, with varying degrees of success. The children of former students fared better than the children of former workers, and both fared better than the children of the workers who had served and guarded them. Most of the children of government officials, including "family members of the traitors to the motherland," graduated from prestigious colleges and (re)joined the postwar Soviet cultural and professional elite (known to both members and nonmembers as the "intelligentsia"). They got married, raised children, bought refrigerators, moved into new apartments (if they did not stay in the House of Government), had more or less successful careers, and never lost their sense of chosenness. They were heartened and briefly rejuvenated by Khrushchev's "thaw" and disillusioned and perhaps amused by Brezhnev's "stagnation." They venerated the memory of their fathers but no longer shared their faith. They thought of Roza Lazarevna Markus and her neighbors in the Home of Party Veterans as shadows of forgotten ancestors. Some of them became dissidents; some emigrated to Israel, the United States, or Germany; most welcomed Gorbachev's *perestroika*. By the time the Soviet state collapsed, no one seemed to take the original prophecy seriously anymore.

The Palace of Soviets was never built. During the war, the metal piles from its foundation were used to make antitank barriers. In 1960, the foundation pit was converted into an outdoor swimming pool. In the 1990s, the pool was drained and the Cathedral of Christ the Savior, rebuilt. The square in front of the House of Government officially reverted to its former name, Swamp Square.

The Russian Revolution ended where it began—in the swamp on the eve of the End. As the Soviet world began to crumble, at first in a few places and then everywhere at once—amidst earthquakes, nuclear explosions, falling stars, and nation rising against nation—people became increasingly talkative, contemplative, and quick-tempered. As Celsus wrote about a similar time two thousand years earlier, "there were many, who, although of no name, with the greatest facility and on the slightest occasion, whether within or without temples, assumed the motions and gestures of inspired persons." They promised a variety of things (mostly disastrous), and "to those promises were added strange and quite unintelligible words," some of them so dark as to have no meaning at all. Some came from afar: Mormons, Christian evangelicals, Sathya Sai Baba, Baba Vanga, and, with particular success, Aum Shinrikyo (which had its own radio and TV shows and filled stadiums for initiation ceremonies). Some were homegrown: Vissarion's Church of the Last Testament, Maria Devi Christ's White Brotherhood, and Blessed John's Mother-of-God Center preached the coming apocalypse; Anatoly Kashpirovsky and Allan Chumak healed and "energized" millions of TV viewers; Pavel Globa and Mikhail Levin transformed astrology into a science and an industry; Sergei Mavrodi built a financial pyramid that offered profits to millions of investors, and Anatoly Fomenko discovered that most recorded history was a hoax.[1]

The last days of the twentieth century were different from the last days of the nineteenth century in that they ended the way most last days do. The fervor subsided, the prophets vanished, the revolution never came, and life in the Swamp resumed its usual course.

One of the most magnificent monuments of that era is Leonid Leonov's novel *The Pyramid*, which reimagines the building of socialism (and Leonov's own previous work) as Satan's deadly joke. Conceived in 1940, after one of his plays was banned and his family "had spent a week sleeping with their clothes on, waiting for a nocturnal knock on the door," it was still unfinished in 1994, when the first edition came out. In the meantime, the author of *The Sot'* and *The Road to Ocean* had been acclaimed and forgotten as the exemplar of socialist realism, elected to the Supreme Soviet and Academy of Sciences, named Hero of Socialist Labor and Distinguished Artist of the Russian Republic, awarded Lenin, Stalin, and state prizes, and presumed dead by most readers. In 1989, he had asked the Bulgarian clairvoyant, Vanga (whom he had consulted on several previous occasions), about his new novel, and she told him to publish it in three years. He published it five years later and died soon afterward, at the age of ninety-five. "Not counting on being able to complete his last book in the time remaining," he wrote in the foreword, "the author has accepted his friends' advice to publish it in its present condition. The urgency of the decision is dictated by the imminence of the most terrible cataclysm—religious, ethnic, and social—we have ever lived through, the last one for all Earthlings. The ever-growing horror of the events of the waning century lead one to interpret it as the preface to humanity's epilogue."[2]

The Pyramid was written as an epitaph to a false apocalypse on the eve of a true one. The action takes place in the fall of 1940 and at various points in the future, to which the narrator, known as "Leonid Leonov," is taken by a succession of guides, not all of them reliable. In 1935, Gorky had written to Leonov about *The Road to Ocean*: "Dostoevsky's gloomy and

Mikhail Gorbachev visiting Leonid Leonov
on the occasion of his ninetieth birthday
(Courtesy of N. A. Makarov)

spiteful shadow hangs over the entire plotline." In 1971, Leonov had written to a friend about his new novel: "Dostoevsky and I stand on opposite sides of the mountain range. I can see with my own eyes the things he was afraid of." In the 1990s, after the experiment has been pronounced a failure, Leonov—and one of the novel's central characters, Father Matvei—agree with Dostoevsky about the meaning of the catastrophe: "Was it not Russia's historic mission to crash to the ground from the height of a thousand-year greatness before the eyes of the world, so as to warn the coming generations against repeated attempts to contrive a heaven on earth?"[3]

In Leonov's creation novel, *The Sot'*, Communism had been a vision of distant buildings glimpsed by the chief of construction. In *The Road to Ocean*, it had been a glorious city that travelers from the present could explore and write books about. In *The Pyramid*, it is—for a while—still hidden behind the gate of a top-secret construction site. Father Matvei's son, Vadim, has been brought there by the mysterious "Comrade Virgil." "While talking to him, Vadim never took his eyes off the unfolding panorama of construction, whose awesome grandeur could only be compared to one of the visions of the apocalyptic cycle. A dwarfed imagination strained in vain for a commensurate episode. It was difficult for the eye to grasp the true dimensions or even the approximate shape of the stone bulk that could only be guessed at by the rising agitation within the soul, while the bewildered mind foresaw the scale of the catastrophe occasioned by the tiniest engineering miscalculation."[4]

At first, all Vadim can see is an enormous rectangular building with tunnel-like round windows. Inside one of them is a tiny puffing locomotive and a stream of overloaded trucks that look "Lilliputian within this monstrous Cyclopean colossus." On top of that rectangular foundation are two pillars "whose frightening scale seemed to rival the ancient wonders of the world. Both cylinders of irregular shape, they served as twin supports for the architecturally indeterminate granite mass towering over them." On closer inspection, the pillars assume "the familiar shape of ordinary shoe heels."

> Then suddenly, some hundred and fifty meters higher up, Vadim perceived the equally impressive accordions of a pair of men's boots, but further identification was complicated by the jagged fringe of the clouds. Thanks to the almost daytime brightness of the illumination over the left block, he could see immeasurably tiny suspension scaffolds with advanced brigades of finishing workers poking around with their polishing machines in the cave-like folds of the boot leg, while the apparent laggards on the right block still swarmed around the welt of the heel. Reason still resisted the conclusions of a perplexed mind, but then, through an accidental tear in the cloud and at a terrible height, there appeared and soon vanished the elongated granite figure eight of a military trench coat half-belt.[5]

The house of socialism, built by the proletarians of all countries, turns out to be a pyramid, and the pyramid turns out to be an enormous statue of Comrade Stalin. Or, as one character in *The Pyramid* suggests, the New Man molded by Comrade Stalin is in fact Comrade Stalin himself. In 1934, at the first Congress of Soviet Writers, Leonov had said that his creative mirror was too small for "the new master, the great planner, the future geometer of our planet." In 1946, he had written, with resignation, that he was "not a sea, not even a tender northern lake that could reflect, to the tiniest degree, the majesty of the celestial body visible today from all corners of the universe." In 1994, in *The Pyramid*, Leonov's doomed alter ego is allowed to see parts of this body from the "dizzying height" of the chief architect's bridge. "Around the entire perimeter of the platform there was not a single railing to lean on in case of a sudden attack, in equal measure, of nausea and vertigo, as the bottomless abyss peered in through the cracks in the wooden planks underfoot."[6]

> The romanticism of this fantastic sight, when viewed through binoculars, shattered into a multiplicity of everyday scenes. Moving upward, isolated sections of the ongoing construction work slid into view. A convoy of heavy trucks gradually climbed the steep slope toward the foot of the statue and disappeared into the enormous

tunnel under the heel, only to reappear a hundred meters higher on a highway built into one of the folds of the boot. Further up, on the left side, a brigade of workers suspended on a block and tackle were using—clearly as a matter of great urgency—dozens of blinding ultraviolet rays to cut through the almost finished outer casing on the statue's chest. "In all the bustle of big history, they seem to have overlooked the trifling matter of the giant's heart," said the guide by way of a poor joke, looking into Vadim's soul and smirking devilishly. Even higher, through the haze of distance, Vadim could see a molding of spiral curls float, suspended on cables, toward the row of powerful cantilevers on the statue's half-shaven upper lip: the mounting of the moustache was nearing completion. Meanwhile, through an open cut in the little finger, Vadim was able to peer, despite the egregious difference in height, into a railwaylike building, where a staff meeting was taking place, and the speaker appeared to be lopping off truths with his hand each time a new one arose.[7]

Most of *The Pyramid*'s world and the whole of socialism are contained within this "universal idol," and the bewildered minds of most of the characters foresee the scale of the catastrophe. The action is propelled by the contest between the angel, Dymkov ("Puff of Smoke"), who comes down to Earth to see what has gone wrong, and the devil, Shatanitsky, who represents "that power which would the evil ever do" (and does). Dymkov is gradually sapped of his miracle-working powers; Shatanitsky works steadily in concert with the Party leaders, who see in him a fellow "activist of forced happiness." Dymkov gets a job as a circus magician; Shatanitsky is "the leading practitioner of the advanced science that resolutely denies its own existence." Dymkov comes out of a door painted on a church pillar and eventually flees in despair; Shatanitsky abandons the pyramid project and lives on in the Swamp, in what used to be the House of Government:[8]

It was an ordinary, overcrowded communal apartment building with rooms off long corridors. A stinging light was coming from a burning lamp somewhere, and the entire host of infernal servitors must have been home, for one could not escape the unbearable, brain-tingling, feverish sound of its vespertine activity: the barking of a dog, a telephone ringing, the unconvincing crying of a dubious infant, a fretsaw cutting glass, furniture being moved around, the hammering in of four-inch nails, and, finally, a coloratura singer calling to her lover, with the help of a gramophone, to come back into her arms. The sound refuse trickling down on all sides dropped resoundingly into the boundless echo of the stairwell.[9]

∎ ∎ ∎

The Soviet government remained an ideocracy (theocracy, hierochracy) until the end. All decisions deemed important were made by the Party, whose legitimacy was based on the original prophecy and whose members were admitted—at least in theory—on the basis of their adherence to that prophecy (as canonized in sacred texts and interpreted by current leaders). The original sect (a fraternal community of the faithful opposed to the surrounding world) had become a priesthood (a hierarchical corporation of professional mediators between the original prophecy and the community of the faithful, redefined as all citizens), but the faith remained the same. The faith remained the same, but the majority of the faithful—including, most vocally, the children of the original "student" sectarians—turned away from it. One could be loyal to the Soviet state and the various rites, myths, practices, and institutions it spawned, but no one seemed to recognize the original prophets as prophetic, the foundational texts as sacred, or the coming of Communism as either inevitable or desirable (no matter how long the delay).

Why was that? Why did Bolshevism die after one generation, like sects that have never become successfully institutionalized (let alone conquered much of the world)? Why did Bolshevism not outlive its own ideocracy? Why could the children of the Bolshevik believers not maintain their fathers' faith while breaking most of its injunctions and ignoring its many false claims and failed prophecies? Why was the fate of Bolshevism so different from that of Christianity, Islam, Mormonism, and countless other millenarian faiths? Most "churches" are vast rhetorical and institutional structures built on broken promises. Why was Bolshevism unable to live with its own failure? The House of Government was meant to stand in the shadow of the Palace of Soviets. Why did the government succeed in building only the shadow?

The assumption that the Communist prophecy was uncommonly factual and therefore easily falsifiable seems insufficient: many millenarians set more or less specific dates for the end of the world, prepare accordingly, miss the deadline, weep from disappointment, postpone the inevitable, and continue to wait, more or less eagerly.

A related, but perhaps more effective, explanation has to do with the place of the supernatural in the Marxist vision of history. The drama of universal degradation and proletarian salvation is preordained and independent of human will (except in the same dialectical sense in which the coming of the Kingdom of God is dependent on Jesus's ministry); Communism is a time beyond time: history without the locomotive. The core of Marxism may, therefore, be seen as supernatural—incapable of empirical verification and ultimately a matter of what Osinsky, following Verhaeren, calls "luminous faith." The doctrine's vocabulary, on the other hand, is primarily sociological and economic, with no overt references to magic, mystery, or transcendence. This strategy—of wrapping faith in logic—offers considerable advantages in the post-Renaissance age, but it suffers from a rigidity that explicitly irrational prophecies do not have. A Christian who misses an end-of-the-world deadline may escape into mysticism or to heaven; a Marxist stuck inside the hollow statue of Comrade Stalin has fewer such resources. The problem is not so much that the original claims were false: it is that they cannot be explained away as riddles or allegories.

Another possible explanation has to do with Marxism's economic determinism—its claim that economics is the "base" that props up the social "superstructure" and the fuel that feeds the locomotive of history. A change in the economic base is the key to a change in human condition. The key to the last and decisive change in the economic base is the abolition of private property. Most millenarian sects are opposed to private property (on account of its obvious incompatibility with sectarian fraternity), but only Marxists believe that control over the economy is the main condition for universal salvation. As committed Marxists, the Bolsheviks built the world's first state devoted above all to the suppression of non-state property. After Stalin's death, that state pledged to fulfill the promise of socialism in providing "to each according to his needs." Its failure to do so in competition with Babylon's money changers was difficult to justify. Capitalism proved better at meeting the needs that it shaped for the purpose.

But Marxism's economic determinism had an even more fatal consequence—one most obviously on display in the House of Government and most pointedly not seen by those who had eyes. Focused on political economy and "base"-derived sociology, Marxism developed a remarkably flat conception of human nature. A revolution in property relations was the only necessary condition for a revolution in human hearts. The dictatorship of unchained proletarians would automatically result in the withering away of whatever got in the way of Communism, from the state to the family. Accordingly, the Bolsheviks never worried very much about the family, never policed the home, and never connected the domestic rites of passage—childbirth, marriage, and death—to their sociology and political economy. Party, Komsomol, and Young Pioneer members were registered and monitored in school and at work, not at home, and the only House of Government residents subject to outside surveillance were those who worked there. Not only did the Bolsheviks never devise a policy analogous to Christian pastoral care or its "child protective" successors in the modern therapeutic state: they had no local parishes (missions) at all. District Party committees supervised work-based primary cells and coordinated plan fulfillment by local enterprises, leaving "hen-and-rooster" problems and whatever their opponents called "spiritual needs" to history and an occasional exhortation campaign.[10]

Most millenarian sects attempt to reform or abolish the family (by decreeing celibacy, promiscuity, or the leader's sexual monopoly), but if they are to survive, they must incorporate it as part of the providential plan.

Jesus said: "If anyone comes to me and does not hate his father, mother, wife, children, brothers, and sisters, as well as his own life, he can't be my disciple." Jesus's disciple, Paul, told his (much more numerous and diverse) disciples: "I say this as a concession, not as a command. I wish that all of you were as I am. But each of you has your own gift from God; one has this gift, another has that. Now to the unmarried and the widows I say: It is good for them to stay unmarried, as I do. But if they cannot control themselves, they should marry, for it is better to marry than to burn with passion." And then, following Augustine's reconciliation with the indefinite postponement of Jesus's return, marriage became a sacrament enforced by the church and, in later Protestant practice, the institution anchoring the community of the faithful. The Bolsheviks' early attempts to reform the family, halfhearted and marginal to begin with, were soon abandoned in favor of an acceptance that remained untheorized and apparently irrelevant to the building of Communism.[11]

Christianity attached itself to the law of Moses and kept devising new ways of monitoring the family. Muhammad codified and reformed Arabian common law. Marx-Engels-Lenin-Stalin had nothing to say about everyday human morality and left their disciples no guidance on how to be good Communists at home.

The Münster Anabaptists banned monogamy and burned all books except the Bible; the Bolsheviks did not realize that by having their children read Tolstoy instead of Marx-Engels-Lenin-Stalin, they were digging the grave of their revolution. That by having children at all, they were digging the grave of their revolution. The house of socialism—as a residential building with family apartments—was a contradiction in terms. The problem with Bolshevism was that it was not totalitarian enough.

The sects that survive the death of the first generation of believers are those that preserve the hope of salvation by maintaining a strict separation from the outside world (physical, ritual, and intellectual—including the unceasing study of sacred texts and a ban on Babylon's art and literature). The Bolsheviks, secure in their economic determinism, assumed that the outside world would join as a matter of course, and they embraced Babylon's art and literature as a prologue and accompaniment to their own. Even at the height of fear and suspicion, when anyone connected to the outside world was subject to sacrificial murder, Soviet readers and writers were expected to learn from Shakespeare, Cervantes, and Goethe. (This changed briefly in the late 1940s, but the fact that the motivation was nationalist, not Marxist, made the paradox all the more obvious.) The children of the Bolshevik millenarians never read Marx-Engels-Lenin-Stalin at home, and, after the educational system was rebuilt around Pushkin, Gogol, and Tolstoy, all Soviet children stopped reading them in school. At home, the children of the Bolshevik millenarians read the "treasures of world literature," with an emphasis on the golden ages (the Renaissance, romanticism, and the realist novel, especially Balzac, Dickens, and Tolstoy) and modern historical novels (especially by Romain Rolland and Lion Feuchtwanger). They almost never read Soviet literature at home: the most common exceptions were Ostrovsky's *How the Steel Was Tempered* and Veniamin Kaverin's *The Two Captains*, but of course *How the Steel Was Tempered* ends in almost the same way as *David Copperfield*, with a marriage and the publication of the hero's autobiography, and *The Two Captains*, according to Valia Osinsky, was praised by the critics, "with good reason, for its resemblance to Dickens."

What most of those books had in common was their antimillenarian humanism. Some particular favorites, including Charles Dickens's *The Tale of Two Cities* and Anatole France's *The Gods Are Athirst*, were expressly antirevolutionary; most did the opposite of what Jesus, Buddha, Muhammad, the Jacobins, and the Bolsheviks preached by embracing the folly and pathos of human existence. The point of the golden ages, as opposed to the silver ones and any number of modernisms, modern or not, is the affirmation of "really existing" humanity. The books proclaimed as models at the first Congress of Soviet Writers and imbibed religiously by the children of the original Bolsheviks were profoundly anti-Bolshevik, none more so than the one routinely described as the best of them all: Tolstoy's *War and Peace*. All rules, plans, grand theories, and historical explanations were vanity, stupidity, or deception. Natasha Rostova "did not deign to be intelligent." The meaning of life was in living it.

Something else all those books had in common was that they represented life at other times and in other places. The children of the original Bolsheviks lived in the House of Government the way Tom Sawyer lived in St. Petersburg, Missouri: there and not there; in the present and in the past; on Serafimovich Street and in the mysterious caves leading to the Kremlin, America, or the center of the earth. Lyova Fedotov's journey from Moscow to St. Petersburg was a heroic quest for a living past, with Verdi's *Aida* as the golden key. Indeed, the books, paintings, and operas Lyova and his friends loved were not just set in other times and places—they were "historical" in the sense of being self-consciously concerned with the passing of time and the past as a foreign country.

The children of the Revolution did not only live in the past—they loved it for being past and, like most readers and writers of historical fiction, tended to focus on lost causes: Scott's Scots, Boussenard's Boers, Cooper's Mohicans, Sienkiewicz's Poles, Mayne Reid's Seminoles, Mérimée's Corsicans, Pushkin's Pugachev, Gogol's Taras Bulba, Stendhal's Napoleon, and everything Dumas's Musketeers pledged to preserve, from Her Majesty's honor to the head of Charles I. Even the great socialist classics, Raffaello Giovagnioli's *Spartacus* and Ethel Voynich's *The Gadfly*, were about romantic self-sacrifice. And of course no one doubted that the greatest of them all was the one that focused on the most hopeless of lost causes: the pursuit of historical causality. Tolstoy did not deign to be intelligent. Georg Lukacs, who worked in the Marx-Engels-Lenin Institute, did. His *The His-*

torical Novel, written in Moscow in 1937, analyzed the books that the House of Government children were reading from the point of view of historical materialism. But the House of Government children who were reading those books never read *The Historical Novel*.

Revolutions do not devour their children; revolutions, like all millenarian experiments, are devoured by the children of the revolutionaries. The Bolsheviks, who did not fear the past and employed God-fearing peasant nannies to bring up their children, were particularly proficient in creating their own gravediggers. As Plato's Socrates says in *The Republic*,

> Shall we just carelessly allow children to hear any casual tales which may be devised by casual persons, and to receive into their minds ideas for the most part the very opposite of those which we should wish them to have when they are grown up?
>
> We cannot.
>
> Then the first thing will be to establish a censorship of the writers of fiction, and let the censors receive any tale of fiction which is good, and reject the bad; and we will desire mothers and nurses to tell their children the authorised ones only. Let them fashion the mind with such tales, even more fondly than they mould the body with their hands; but most of those which are now in use must be discarded.[12]

The Bolsheviks did not agree with Plato, because he was an "idealist." They discarded Plato and most other idealist philosophers, but they did not worry about the writers of fiction and ended up raising their children on ideas that were the very opposite of those they wished them to have (or thought they did, some of the time). The parents lived for the future; their children lived in the past. The parents had their luminous faith; the children had their tastes and knowledge. The parents had comrades (fellow saints who shared their faith); the children had friends (pseudo-kin who shared their tastes and knowledge). The parents started out as sectarians and ended up as priestly rulers or sacred scapegoats; the children started out as romantics and ended up as professionals and intellectuals. The parents considered their sectarianism to be the realization of humanism—until their interrogators forced them to choose, and to die, one way or the other. The children never knew anything but humanism and never understood their parents' last dilemma.

One reason for the fragility of Russian Marxism was Marxism. The other was Russia.

Tsarist Russia was a multinational empire, and the original Bolsheviks were a cosmopolitan sect with a strong overrepresentation of rebellious borderlands (especially Jews, Latvians, Georgians, and Poles). On the central millenarian question of what makes the chosen people chosen, they were much closer to Jesus's proletarian option than to Moses's tribal one.

But as time went on, and in accordance with the logic of common sacrifices and shared living arrangements, the world revolution evolved into "socialism in one country" before becoming a motherland with a Russian pedigree. In early 1931, in the midst of the First Five-Year Plan, Stalin sounded like the Prophet Isaiah, Enoch Mgijima, or any other messianic leader of a scorned nation dreaming of revenge:

> To slacken the tempo would mean falling behind. And those who fall behind get beaten. But we do not want to be beaten. No, we refuse to be beaten! One feature of the history of old Russia was the continual beatings she suffered because of her backwardness. She was beaten by the Mongol khans. She was beaten by the Turkish beys. She was beaten by the Swedish feudal lords. She was beaten by the Polish and Lithuanian gentry. She was beaten by the British and French capitalists. She was beaten by the Japanese barons. All beat her because of her backwardness, military backwardness, cultural backwardness, political backwardness, industrial backwardness, agricultural backwardness. They beat her because to do so was profitable and could be done with impunity. . . .
>
> In the past we had no fatherland, nor could we have one. But now that we have overthrown capitalism and power is in our hands, in the hands of the people, we have a fatherland, and we will defend its independence. Do you want our socialist fatherland to be beaten and to lose its independence? If you do not want this you must put an end to its backwardness in the shortest possible time and develop genuine Bolshevik tempo in building up its socialist system of economy. There is no other way. That is why Lenin said on the eve of the October Revolution: "Either perish, or overtake and outstrip the advanced capitalist countries."[13]

The Soviet Union was a form of retribution for the humiliations of the Russian Empire. It was, ultimately, the same country, but that country was a multinational state without a clear ethnic owner. Stalin may have sounded like a Russian national prophet, but his Russian never sounded native. Soviet Communism never completed its journey away from Jesus's internationalism. It became self-consciously Russo-centric in Stalin's later years, but it never claimed to be the voice of Russian national liberation. And because the House of Government had never become the Russian national home, late Soviet Communism became homeless—and, eventually, a ghost. In most non-Russian nation-states, it was proclaimed to have been a Russian imposition; in the new Russia, it was assumed to have been a flood that, for better or worse, had destroyed much of old Russia.

Marxism as an ideology of rootless proletarians triumphed in the Russian Empire and ended with the Soviet Union. Elsewhere, homegrown Communism—Mao's, Tito's, Hoxha's, Sandino's, Fidel's, Ho-Chi-Minh's,

Kim Il-Sung's, Pol Pot's—was primarily nativist (anticolonial, Israelite). So were Peru's Shining Path and Colombia's FARC. The Chinese and Vietnamese Communist Parties survived the transition to capitalism because they stood, above all, for anticolonial national self-assertion. In the Soviet Union, the decision to embrace private property left the emperor with no clothes at all.

One reason for the fragility of Russian Marxism was that the Party's doctrine was not Russian enough. The other was that the country it took over was too Russian at heart.

The Russian Orthodox, unlike the Russian Jews and Old Believers, had never known Reformation or Counterreformation and had never been taught how to deal with a Big Father who was always watching (and could never be bribed, flattered, or evaded); how to think of salvation as a matter of ceaseless self-improvement (as opposed to happy accident, deathbed repentance, or the sudden descent of collective grace); how to take Jesus's message for the totalitarian demand that it was (the real crimes are thought crimes, and no one is innocent); or how to forestall censorship with self-censorship, police surveillance with mutual denunciation, and state repression with voluntary obedience.[14]

Bolshevism, in other words, was Russia's Reformation: an attempt to transform peasants into Soviets, and Soviets into self-monitoring, morally vigilant modern subjects. The means were familiar—confessions, denunciations, excommunications, and self-criticism sessions accompanied by regular tooth-brushing, ear-washing, and hair-combing—but the results were not comparable. Within the House of Government and in certain well-drained parts of the Swamp, there were plenty of people who felt permanently guilty and worked tirelessly on themselves, but, by the time the children of the Revolution had become parents themselves, there was little doubt that most Russians still drew a rigid line between themselves and authority and still thought of discipline as something imposed from the outside. The Bolshevik Reformation was not a popular movement: it was a massive missionary campaign mounted by a sect that proved strong enough to conquer an empire but not resourceful enough to either convert the barbarians or reproduce itself at home. In the meantime, the founders' children had moved from the romance of those embarking on a new quest to the irony of those who have seen it all before. This is true of all human lifetimes (senile romanticism is almost as unappealing as infantile irony), but not all historical ages (some of which take centuries to complete). The Soviet Age did not last beyond one human lifetime.

EPILOGUE

THE HOUSE ON THE EMBANKMENT

Yuri Trifonov kept the promise he had given his friends when he was fourteen years old. He became a writer and dedicated his "lyre" to not forgetting. "Should one remember?" asks the narrator in his last novel, *Time and Place*. "My God, it's like asking: 'Should one live?' To live and to remember is one and the same thing. You can't destroy one without destroying the other. Together they make up a verb that has no name." Trifonov's life as a writer was a quest for that verb—for himself and on behalf of his generation. To live on and to be remembered was one and the same thing. All houses have histories, but very few have their own historians. The House of Government had Yuri Trifonov.[1]

There were different ways to remember. Leonid Leonov's *The Pyramid* was a reversal of Bolshevik apocalypticism (and of Leonov's novels from the 1930s). The Heavenly Warrior is revealed to have been the Beast, but the story of Armageddon is the same; the memory is the mirror image of the prophecy. Yuri Trifonov abandoned prophetic revelations for irony when he was twelve years old (in a story about four boys writing a story). In his last story, written four months before his death on March 28, 1981, the middle-aged narrator goes to Finland and looks back on his time there in the late 1920s, when he was two years old and his father, "torn away from the world revolution," was head of the Soviet trade mission. All he remembers is the gray sky, some masts, and a chestnut horse. The sky and the masts are the same, and, on his last day in Helsinki, he meets a ninety-four-year-old woman who still remembers his father and the chestnut horse. On the train ride home, he thinks: "The oddest thing is that everything fits into a circle. First there was the horse, and then it appeared again, completely unexpectedly. Everything else is in between."[2]

There were different things to remember. Leonid Leonov remembered the catastrophe that Dostoevsky had warned against. Yuri Trifonov remembered "that irreplaceable something that's called life": the gray sky, the masts, the chestnut horse, his father, the woman who remembered his father, and many other people and things, some more important than others. The memories he turned into stories consisted of two generations and their worlds: the Revolution and its children. "My father," says one of his narrators, "went through life marked by 1917. There are people of the late 1920s and people of the mid-1930s, people of the beginning of the war and people of the end of the war. And like my father, they remain such to the end of their lives." These moments of creation are separated from each other by "gaps, breaks, and lacunae" without which human lives and historical chronicles are unimaginable. "It is like a play: first act, second act, third act, eighteenth act. In each act the characters are slightly changed. But years, decades pass between the acts."[3]

Trifonov's main characters are his contemporaries: the people who went through life marked by their mid-1930s childhood. Act 1 of their story is set in the House of Government, which Trifonov calls "the House on the Embankment" because what matters is the river, not the government. "The air in the courtyards was always damp and the smell of the river penetrated into the rooms." People who grew up there can leave the house, but not the river. "They swim, carried along by the current, paddling with their hands, farther and farther, faster and faster, day after day, year after year: the shores change, the hills recede, the forests thin out and lose their leaves, the sky darkens, the cold sets in, they have to hurry, hurry—and they no longer have the strength to look back at what lies behind, motionless, like a cloud on the edge of the horizon."[4] The current outlives the building; only the embankment is left to connect time to place.

> I once lived in that building. No—*that* building died, disappeared, a long time ago. I lived in another building, but within those same enormous dark-gray fortress-like concrete walls. The apartment house towered over the trivial two-story buildings, private houses, belfries, old factories, and embankments with granite parapets; and the river washed it on both sides. It stood on an island and looked like a ship, unwieldy and ungainly, without masts, rudderless, and without smokestacks, a huge box, an ark, crammed full of people, ready to sail. Where to? No one knew, no one wondered about that. To people who walked down the street past its walls, glimmering with hundreds of small fortress windows, the building seemed indestructible and permanent, like a rock: in thirty years the dark gray color of the walls had not changed.[5]

Seen from the outside, it looked "like an entire city or even an entire country." Seen from the courtyards, it suggested an intricate hierarchy of entryways, stairways, residents, and apartments that the children could only guess at. The apartments "smelled of carpets and old books," as well as the river, and contained a variety of rooms, which contained a variety of mysteries. When uncles, aunts, and cousins came over, the grown-ups would sit around the dining-room table under a "giant orange lampshade," talking "about war, politics, the ancient Hittites, enemies of the people, Schmidt's polar camp, Karl Radek (who had, until recently, lived in the same entryway), the writer Feuchtwanger, the fact that Málaga had fallen and that the attack had been directed by the German Naval Staff from on board the cruiser *Admiral Speer*." In late December, the table would be pushed against the piano to clear a space for the New Year's tree and the

House on the Embankment, childhood drawing by Yuri Trifonov
(Courtesy of Olga Trifonova)

midnight world it promised to reveal. During the rest of the year, the best place for magic was "Father's study," which contained a weapons collection and "very beautiful encyclopedias bound in leather, with gold backs and a great number of pictures inside."[6]

But the real magic of childhood was the other children, and the real hero of their courtyard adventures was Lyova Fedotov. In *The House on the Embankment,* he appears as Anton Ovchinnikov:

> We used to visit Anton in his dark apartment on the first floor, where the sun never penetrated, where his watercolors, in shades of yellow and blue, hung next to the portraits of composers; where a young man with a shaved head and officer's insignia on his collar looked out at us from a photograph in a heavy wooden frame on the piano—Anton's father had died in Central Asia, killed by the Basmachi rebels; where the radio was always on; where in a secret drawer of his desk lay a stack of thick, fifty-five-kopeck school notebooks, every page covered with tiny handwriting; where cockroaches rustled across newspapers in the bathroom (there were cockroaches in all the bathrooms in that section of the building); where in the kitchen we ate cold potatoes sprinkled with salt in between bites of delicious, thickly-sliced black bread; where we laughed, fantasized, reminisced, dreamed, and rejoiced, and always felt happy for some reason, like fools.[7]

The sunniest part of that "sunny, variegated, multifaceted world known as childhood" were the summers at the dacha—"back when people still used to wade across the Moscow River, still used to take the long, red Leyland bus from Theater Square to Serebrianyi Bor, still used to wear India-silk Tolstoy shirts, white linen pants, and canvas shoes, which they rubbed

Pine Grove, childhood drawing by Yuri Trifonov
(Courtesy of Olga Trifonova)

with tooth powder in the evenings so they would look freshly white and release a cloud of white dust with each step the next morning."[8] The river that the dacha stood on was the same river that washed the House on the Embankment on both sides, but it took a little while to reach it from the bus stop:

> The road from the bus stop wound through the pines, past the long-unpainted fences blackened by rain, past the dachas hidden behind lilac bushes, sweetbriar, and elder, their small-paned verandas gleaming through the foliage. You had to walk a long time down the highway until the tarmac ended, and it became a dusty road. On the right, on a little hill, was the pine grove with the large bald spot (in the 1920s a plane had crashed there, and the grove caught fire), and on the left the long line of fences. Behind one of the fences, barely screened by young birches, stood the two-story wooden building that looked less like a dacha than a trading post somewhere in the forests of Canada or a hacienda in the Argentine savannah.[9]

The inside of the house was of little interest. The next stage of the journey was the meadow that separated the house from the river:

> Father liked making kites. On Saturdays he used to come to the dacha, and we would stay up late shaving down sticks, cutting

Riverbank, with the Lykovo Trinity Belfry, childhood drawing
by Yuri Trifonov (Courtesy of Olga Trifonova)

paper, gluing, and drawing scary faces on the paper. Early the next
morning we would walk out the back gate into the meadow, which
stretched all the way to the river, but you could not see the river,
just the high opposite bank, the yellow sandy slope, the pines, the
cottages, and the belfry of the Lykovo Trinity Church, sticking up
from the pines at the highest point of the bank. I would run through
the dewy meadow, letting out string, afraid Father might have done
something wrong and the kite wouldn't fly, and it really wouldn't fly
right away, but would trail through the grass for a while, trying to
fly, failing, and sinking down, fluttering like a frightened hen, before
suddenly, slowly and miraculously, soaring up behind my back, as I
ran on and on as fast as I could.[10]

The final destination was the river, which reappears in story after story,
as both beginning and end. The earliest beginnings, and some special occasions, involve the protagonist's parents. The protagonist could be a
first-person narrator, a third-person character, or both (often as a set of
doubles):

When Mother took her vacation, usually in August, the three of
them would often paddle off in the boat very early in the morning
and go somewhere far away—for the whole day. Mornings on the
river were cool and quiet, with only a few solitary fishermen in
crumpled hats sitting next to their rods and casting disapproving
glances in their direction. The sun would rise, and it would get hot.
Light pale clouds would appear in the sky; the banks would start
filling up with people and the water, with boats. Father would pull up
on a sandbar, and the three of them would spend a long time swimming, sunbathing, looking for pretty shells and "Devil's toenails,"

Trifonovs on the river (Courtesy of Olga Trifonova)

and, if there was no one around, Father would perform funny stunts on the sand, stand on his hands, and might even walk on his hands into the water.[11]

On regular weekday mornings, the boy would run there by himself, through the garden and down the rocky road to the highway. "After running a hundred and fifty steps or so, he turns into the thin pine forest that stretches along the bank. Here he has to tread carefully again because, under the fallen needles, there might be pinecones, pieces of glass, or treacherous pine roots lying in wait to make him stub his toe. At last he is on the river bluff, and sees the others already there, below: Alyosha in his red trunks, fat Rooster, and Chunya, dark as a little devil. He yells happily to them, waving his arms, and then, with a running start, takes a giant leap onto the sand below."[12]

It all ended abruptly, with Father's disappearance. Parts of the pine forest were claimed by new dacha owners. The sandbar and escarpment were washed away after the construction of the Moscow-Volga Canal. "His former life crumbled and collapsed like a sandy bank: quietly and suddenly. The bank collapsed. Gone with it were the pine trees, benches, paths strewn with fine gray sand, the white dust, pinecones, cigarette butts, pine needles, the scraps of old bus tickets, condoms, hairpins, and the kopeck coins that had fallen out of the pockets of those who had once embraced here on warm evenings. Everything was swept downstream in the swirl of water."[13]

The House on the Embankment died, too. "That's what happens to buildings: we leave them, and they die." It died because the boys and girls had left. "Some had been killed in the war, some had died from sickness, some had disappeared without a trace, while others, though still alive, had become different people; and if by some magic means those different people were to meet the ones long gone—in their cotton twill shirts and can-

Yuri Trifonov (*in the middle*) with friends at
the dacha (Courtesy of Olga Trifonova)

vas sneakers—they would not know what to say to them." The tests of will
devised by Lyova Fedotov and his fictional doubles had proved both pre-
scient and premature. "The tests came soon enough: there was no need to
invent them. They poured down upon us like thick, heavy rain—some were
beaten into the ground, some drenched and soaked to the bone, and some
drowned in that torrent."[14]

· · ·

Act 2 in Trifonov's chronicle of his generation is set in the late 1940s and
early 1950s, when those who had survived the torrent were in their twenties and early thirties. It was a time of "packed rooms and accidental
friends," "crowded communal apartments and narrow couches," Stalin's
funeral, and Khrushchev's "thaw." It was springtime—"that unsettling and
opaque season that remained to be deciphered." The lilacs in Lyalia Telep-
neva's garden (in *The Long Goodbye*) "overwhelmed the dusty, nondescript
street" on which her house stood. "Unable to be contained within the confines of the fence, their luxuriant forms spilled over into the street in a
frenzy of lilac flesh." Olga Vasilievna from *Another Life* wore her hair loose
to her shoulders. "It was a dense, luxuriant, dark-auburn thicket, but her
forehead was open, round, and clean, without a single wrinkle. It was
probably the best year of her entire life, the year of her prime."[15]

    The flood that had washed away their childhood continued to carry
them along. They fell in and out of love, got married, had children, met

Yuri Trifonov (*top right, with glasses*) with friends at the
Literary Institute (Courtesy of Olga Trifonova)

Yuri (*left*) and his sister, Tania (*second from right*), with friends
(Courtesy of Olga Trifonova)

in-laws, went to college, got their first jobs, and, in the case of the men, got into fights and wrote their first plays, screenplays, novels, and short stories. The springtime of their lives coincided with the "thaw" in Soviet history. "What had brought about this sudden change in life remained for Lyalia a mystery, nor did she give it much thought. Perhaps the winds in the heavens had shifted direction? Perhaps some place a thousand miles away had been swept by hurricanes? Her late Grandmother used to love the saying: 'Everything comes at its appointed time.' And now Lyalia's time had come—and why not?"[16]

And so they floated on, too keen on what lay ahead to look back at what remained behind. But the faster they floated, the more difficult it became not to look back—at least for those who were paying attention. Fathers were being "rehabilitated" but not restored to history; mothers were coming back as helpless, reproachful strangers; in-laws kept bringing up their

Trifonov (*left*) and friends on the riverbank
(Courtesy of Olga Trifonova)

own, unfamiliar past; and "men of the past"—men "whose time was up"—
were still running construction sites and editorial offices. Khrushchev's
"thaw" was a deliberate but partial recreation of the Stalin revolution.
Trifonov's *The Quenching of Thirst* (1959–62) contains all the key elements
of a First Five-Year-Plan construction novel but is also, typically for the
"thaw," a bildungsroman about a young man whose future remains to be
deciphered. He joins in the building of an irrigation canal in the desert,
but he is too involved in the pettiness of existence to be a full-fledged
participant. He is lost, he fears, "utterly lost," but the harder he tries to find
his way, the more clearly he realizes that he is floating with the current—
the very current he is trying to channel. "It pulls me along like a small chip
of wood, spinning and tossing me around, flinging me onto the shore, then
washing me away again and carrying me further, on and on!" The challenge, he discovers, is not to catch up: the challenge is to be able to stop.
And the only way to stop, or at least slow down a bit, is to swim against the
current. "To know yourself" means going backward.

The spring—that particular spring—was not about what lay ahead: it
was about what remained behind, like a cloud on the edge of the horizon.
What remained to be deciphered was the past.[17]

■ ■ ■

Act 3 is set in the late 1960s and early 1970s, when the main characters are
in their forties and fifties, much farther downstream, ready and not ready
"to take stock." Vadim Glebov, from *The House on the Embankment*, is balding and fat, "with breasts like a woman's, flabby thighs, a big paunch and
sloping shoulders, which obliged him to have his suits tailor-made instead
of buying them off the rack." He is not from the House on the Embankment, but he visited often enough to betray his friends, teacher, and fiancée. He comes from the Swamp and eventually returns to the Swamp, pos-

sibly never having left it. "He wasn't bad and he wasn't good; he wasn't very selfish and he wasn't very generous"—he was lukewarm, "a nothing person." He does not choose to betray anyone; he fails to make choices.[18]

Aleksandr Antipov, the central character of *Time and Place*, is not sure about either time or place. He and his wife Tania keep waiting for an apartment of their own, but he doubts they will ever have a home—or have made any choices:

> The new cooperative building on the outskirts of Moscow was slowly rising, one floor on top of the other; their children were slowly growing older and setting out for unknown territory; the two halves of the cracked raft, with Antipov on one side and Tania, on the other, were slowly moving apart, and there was no horror on their faces: they went on talking, joking, taking pills, getting annoyed, watching movies, while the wooden halves were quietly drifting apart, because nothing could be stopped and everything kept flowing, moving farther away from one thing and closer to another. . . . There is no such thing as still water: the kind that seems stagnant is also moving—by evaporating or festering.[19]

Antipov falls in love with Tania in the spring of 1951. They separate thirty years later, soon after moving into the new cooperative building on the outskirts of Moscow. Most late-Trifonov plots involve moving into new buildings: applying, queuing, buying, and starting over. The goal is "to furnish one's life the way one would furnish an apartment," but all one gets is more furniture. The flood has become a festering swamp, but most people do not know it because they have "unseeing eyes." Antipov is writing a book about "the fear of seeing," and Sonia Ganchuk from *The House on the Embankment* is taken to a special hospital because she is afraid of light. Living in the dark means living without a shadow—not leaving a trace or relying on someone else's memory. Antipov's Tania wears glasses and cannot remember what made their spring possible. Everything remains to be deciphered, everything keeps getting postponed, "and everything that got postponed gradually disappeared somewhere—leaked out the way warm air leaks out of the house."[20]

Trifonov's contemporaries, "the children," are confronted by their parents and grandparents, who care nothing for furniture, take "a broad view of things," and think of themselves as "makers of history," not chips caught in its flow. Their time has passed, but they linger on—as a reproach, reminder, and source of worn-out wisdom. Some of the children are not blind—just near-sighted—and they notice that their parents' asceticism has not prevented them from moving into the House of Government; that "taking a broader view" means interpreting human behavior in accordance with "class theory"; that class theory is applicable in every case except their own; and that "making history" may stand for "typing away in some

Yuri; his sister, Tania; and their grandmother, Tatiana Slovatinskaia
(Courtesy of Olga Trifonova)

army's political department" or serving as purge committee officials. More to the point, taking the broad view seems to stand for an occasional preference for strangers—the stranger the better—over one's own families. In the case of Aleksandra Prokofievna from *Another Life* (based on Trifonov's grandmother, Tatiana Slovatinskaia), the world seems happy to reciprocate. "Her close relatives have no use for her—for good reasons, because her close relatives know exactly what she is like—but strangers respect and even fear her a little." The same is true of Aron Solts's double, David Shvarts, whose adopted son despises and mistreats him. "How could David raise a child when he was always busy educating others at commissions, on committees, and at plenums until late in the evening?"[21]

The parents and grandparents are just as homeless as their children—in the House of Government, in their children's homes, and in the Home for Party Veterans in Peredelkino. They are just as blind, too. One evening, Gorik, in *The Disappearance*, notices that his grandmother's cousin, "Grandmother Vera," cannot see anything "even with a magnifying glass." The only difference is that the children are near-sighted and the parents, far-sighted. Both would have failed the "good person" test: the children, because their primary commitment is to themselves and their homes; the parents, because their primary commitment is to those who threaten their families and homes.[22]

Neither group casts a shadow. Trifonov's Old Bolsheviks talk a great deal about the past, but they do not *remember*. Professor Ganchuk, from *The House on the Embankment*, does not look back any more than his not-quite-son-in-law, Vadim Glebov. "It wasn't because the old man's memory was failing, but because he did not want to remember. He did not find it interesting." The otherwise blameless Grandfather from *The Exchange* said once that he "had no interest in whatever lay behind, in his entire incalculably long life." And Gorik's Grandmother, in *The Disappearance*, "never reminisced about anything. She once said something that stunned Gorik:

'I don't remember what my real first and last names are. And I don't care.'"
Each generation is blind in its own way, and each one despises the other's
blindness. The parents accuse the children of philistinism and bourgeois
acquisitiveness; the children accuse the parents of hypocrisy and arrogance. Both are right—but also, in their blindness, unfair.[23]

. . .

The Revolution ended at home. The surviving revolutionaries and their
children and grandchildren were facing each other across the kitchen
table, unable to see or listen. Everyone seemed to agree that these were
not routine family squabbles or the inevitable fraying of youthful idealism:
something much larger had gone wrong. The residents of the House of
Government, past and present, were living under a curse. Only those who
did not fear the past could discover its origins and perhaps help lift it.

In every one of Trifonov's novels and novellas there is someone whose
job is to remember: a historian, a novelist, a reminiscing narrator (who is
usually a historian or a novelist), or a character who is jolted into regaining his eyesight and forced to look back. In *The House on the Embankment*,
the autobiographical narrator, who is a professional historian, remembers
seeing Anton Ovchinnikov for the last time in a bakery on Polyanka Street,
in late October 1941.

> Winter with its freezing temperatures and snow had come early that
> year, but of course Anton was wearing neither hat nor coat. He said
> that in two days' time he and his mother were being evacuated to the
> Urals, and asked what I thought he should take with him: his diaries,
> the science-fiction novel he was writing, or the albums of his draw-
> ings. His mother had weak arms, so he was the only one who could
> carry heavy things. His question struck me as absurd. How could
> anyone be worrying about albums or novels, when the Germans were
> at the gates of Moscow? Anton drew or wrote something every day. A
> notebook, folded in two, was sticking out of the pocket of his jacket.
> He said, "I'll record our encounter in this bakery, and our entire con-
> versation. Because everything is important for history."[24]

Anton is killed in the war. His mother gives his diaries to the narrator
just as Roza Lazarevna gave Lyova Fedotov's diaries to Yuri Trifonov. History—through diaries, father's studies, and historical novels—is at the
center of their childhood. "Recording everything" is the duty of those who
have stayed behind and dare look back. But what is important for history?
Tania in *Time and Place* cannot remember the most important things. The
historian in *It Was a Summer Afternoon* memorializes a past that has nothing to do with what the only survivor remembers. Gena Klimuk from *Another Life* believes that a historian's job is to identify "historical necessity."

Yuri Trifonov at his old dacha
(Courtesy of Olga Trifonova)

And Olga Vasilievna, who cannot stand Gena Klimuk, imagines history "as an endless line in which epochs, states, great men, kings, generals, and revolutionaries stand tightly pressed together, so that the historian's task is similar to that of the policeman who, on premier nights, stands by the ticket office of the Progress Movie Theater keeping order—to make sure that the epochs and states do not get mixed up or change places, and that the great men do not cut in line, fight, or try to get a ticket to immortality out of turn."[25]

Those for whom the past is a key to the present think of living and remembering as a single verb. When Grisha Rebrov from *The Long Goodbye* is accused of not being "rooted in the soil," he, "for some reason, started talking about his family: how one of his grandmothers had been a Polish political exile; how his great-grandfather had been a serf and his grandfather had been implicated in some student disorders and banished to Siberia; how his other grandmother had taught music in Petersburg; how her father had been born into the soldier class and how Grisha's own father had taken part in both the First World War and the Civil War although he was by nature a peaceful man who had been a statistician before the Revolution and afterward an economist. And all of this taken together, Grisha shouted excitedly, was the soil, was historical experience, was Russia itself."[26]

In *Another Life*, Olga Vasilievna's husband, Sergei Troitsky, is a professional historian "who suffers greatly in his policeman's job" and thinks that historical necessity is "something shapeless and treacherous, like a swamp." He thinks of history as a search for "a thread that connects the past with an even more remote past, as well as with the future." He—like Grisha Rebrov and Yuri Trifonov—had "started with his own father, for whose faint memory he felt a great love. He thought of his father as an extraordinary man, which was probably an exaggeration and, in a certain sense, pride." His father had led him to his grandfather, who had led him to his great-grandfather, who had led him everywhere at once. "He rambled on about his own ancestors, runaway serfs and religious dissenters, who could be traced to a defrocked priest in Penza, who was connected to some settlers who lived in a commune in Saratov, who could be linked to a teacher in the Tura swamps, who produced a future S. Petersburg student who dreamed of change and justice, all of them united by a seething, bubbling urge to *dissent*."[27]

Which threads should one follow? Rebrov and Troitsky are defeated by this question because they are too invested in the present (and too blind as a consequence) to know what they are looking for. But they know where to search. There are times, according to Rebrov, when conscience "flares up" the way diseases do. "At certain times it grows stronger, at other times weaker, depending on—who knows, perhaps on certain explosions of solar matter." And sometimes it becomes overwhelming. Both are writing books about underground revolutionaries connected to them by the threads of personal and spiritual kinship: about a time on the eve of the Revolution when conscience reached crisis proportions and the urge to dissent became irresistible.

Trifonov's 1973 novel, *Impatience*, is the book Rebrov and Troitsky fail to finish. It is a response to Voronsky's biography of Andrei Zheliabov, which was a response to Dostoevsky's *Crime and Punishment*. It goes back to the People's Will terrorism of the 1870s in order to document the birth of a new, eagerly apocalyptic successor to Christianity. As one of the characters, the terrorist Aleksandr Mikhailov, puts it, "I was as influenced by the story of the Gospel as I was by the story of William Tell or the Gracchi brothers. And what about 'the end justifying the means'? Was it invented by the Jesuits? Or by Machiavelli? No, it is contained in Christ's teachings, in its lining, beneath the pretty exterior." His goal is to "blow up the accursed Sodom" and lead the people out of their "swamp sleep." The means include the creation of a fraternal family of true believers and the use of the "everything is permitted" principle in dealing with nonmembers. The result is the explosion of solar matter that will burn the residents of the House on the Embankment and blind their successors.[28]

■ ■ ■

The impatience of the 1870s begat the Bolshevik Revolution. The Bolshevik Revolution begat everything that followed. Trifonov's novel, *The Old Man* (1978), is about the Civil War, "the time everything began."[29]

The chronological present is the same as in *The House on the Embank-ment* and *Impatience*: the hot Moscow summer of 1972. The old man of the title, Pavel Efgrafovich Letunov, lives in an Old Bolshevik dacha settlement. He is surrounded by his children and their spouses, ex-spouses, lovers, children, neighbors, guests, and dogs. He is hard of hearing; they have unseeing eyes. His family is not quite a family; his house is not a home; and his children are involved in a feud over a cottage they may or may not have a right to. "They still live badly," he imagines telling his wife, Galya, who died five years ago, "a cramped, messy, unsettled existence; they live life not as they want to, but as it happens. They're unhappy, Galya." He is unhappy, too—because Galya is not there and his body is failing him, but mostly because he lives in the past, and the past is even more cramped and unsettled than the present. He does not have much time left and thinks that the only reason he has been spared so far is so he can "piece something together, like a vessel from clay shards, and fill it with wine, the sweetest wine, whose name is Truth." He needs the truth to make sense of his own life and to save his children's lives from mean-inglessness. He believes that the truth got lost when it became inextrica-bly fused with faith, and that its final disappearance had something to do with what happened to Corps Commander Migulin. "Corps Commander Migulin" is a double of Filipp Mironov, the Cossack rebel who defied his Bolshevik commissars, went off to fight for his own socialism, was sen-tenced to death as a false prophet, spent a night awaiting "imminent, inescapable death," was pardoned as a matter of political expediency, and then given command of the Second Cavalry Army before being secretly shot in a prison courtyard.[30]

Letunov's quest takes the story back to 1919, the year of de-Cossackization, the "Last Battle," and Migulin's desertion and trial. Letu-nov, an eighteen-year-old Bolshevik volunteer at the time, witnesses the conflagration. "Savage is the year, savage the hour over Russia. Like lava it flows, that savage time flooding and burying with fire everything in its path." The time is fulfilled, "the earth is aflame," history has run out of patience, and a leatherworker with sleepy little eyes and an absurdly long leather coat promises to "pass through Cossack villages like Carthage" (and does). The flare-up of conscience turns into "savage zeal."[31] Everyone and no one is to blame.

My God, were they really so savage: the leatherworker with sleepy little eyes; the Veshenskaia Cossacks, who, that same spring, in a fit of revolutionary enthusiasm, killed off all their officers in one fell swoop and declared themselves supporters of the new regime; the four exhausted Petrograd workers, one Hungarian who barely understood any Russian and three Latvians who had all but for-gotten their home country, and who, for years, had been killing, first Germans, then Ukrainian nationalists, and then, in the name of the great idea, enemies of the Revolution? There are the enemies:

bearded, with animal hatred in their eyes, barefoot, and in their undershirts; one shouts and shakes his fists; another drops to his knees; while their wives wail on the other side of the fence. And here is the man who has returned from exile, where he was beaten and flogged, an old man at thirty, who, his hopeless lungs bursting, manages to wheeze out: "Death to the enemies of the revolution! Fire!"[32]

Were they really so savage? No, claims Letunov, looking back from his dacha settlement. It is the year 1919 that is to blame, not anyone in particular. "And all because of a sort of haste, fear, a mad internal fever: fix, rebuild at once, for all time, for ever and ever!" Some call it "the Vendee"; some, the last and decisive class battle; and one mad seminarian mumbles something about a blazing star falling from the sky ("the name of the star is Wormwood"). Letunov himself—in 1919 and later, as an old man—is unrelenting in his scrutiny of Corps Commander Migulin. "If you could figure out or at least decide for yourself what he was, a lot would become clear."[33]

The matter is to be settled in the fall of 1919, in revolutionary court, with Migulin as defendant, young Letunov as assistant court secretary, and Commissar Janson as chief prosecutor. Janson's speech in *The Old Man* is a partial transcript of Smilga's speech at the Filipp Mironov trial: the eagle of the Revolution has turned out to be a rooster; his vision of socialism is a "semi-Tolstoyan, semi-sentimental melodrama"; there is but one force that "will come out victorious from this terrible, colossal struggle"; and "the litter of petit bourgeois ideology must be swept off the road of the Revolution." Letunov describes Janson as both a Latvian Bolshevik with Ivar Smilga's biography and "historical necessity" in the flesh. "He was twenty-eight at the time. But in that sandy-haired, short-legged little man on the rostrum I did not see—no one saw—his youth or his university past or his Baltic origins. It was the icy words of the Revolution speaking, it was *the course of events*. And one's spirit froze and one's hands became rigid. I remember, I remember . . ."[34]

And the more the old man Letunov remembers, the more obvious it becomes that he is in the same mold as Glebov and his own children and that he, too, had been swimming in the current, the lava, and *the course of events*: when the leatherworker with sleepy little eyes talked him into becoming the chairman of the revolutionary tribunal ("I didn't want it, I tried my best to refuse"); when he agreed to serve as assistant court secretary at the Migulin trial ("a lot of red tape, a lot of papers, names"); and when, "blinded by red foam," he betrayed himself along with the Revolution by accepting Janson's story of Migulin's betrayal of the Revolution. He points to the times, the year, and the lava, and he hopes he has become stronger as a consequence ("Peter, who denied Jesus in the high priest's courtyard, would later earn his name Petros, meaning 'rock,' that is, 'hard'"). And perhaps he is right: sometimes the current slows down to an imperceptible process of festering and evaporating, and sometimes it is so fast one can hardly think. And of course it is true that he is different from Glebov and so many others because he—like Rebrov and Troitsky—keeps looking back, keeps following the threads, keeps trying to see and to remember.[35]

But does he know where to look? Late one evening he walks over to see his wife's old friend, but finds her daughter, Zina, instead. She seems distracted, but he insists on reading a document from his archive. It is Migulin's description of the night he and his comrades spent in a prison cell before their scheduled execution (the text comes directly from Filipp Mironov's papers): "Some people are able to look [death] proudly in the eye; others have to muster whatever is left of their spiritual strength to seem calm; no one wants to appear fainthearted. In an attempt to deceive himself and us, for instance, one of our comrades suddenly leaps up and breaks into a dance, his heels drumming faster and faster on the cement floor. But his face is frozen and his eyes so blank it is terrifying for a live person to look into them." Letunov ("Pavel Evgrafovich") has forgotten that Zina's husband is dying and that Zina's mother, his wife's old friend, is about to move into the Home for Party Veterans.

> "Pavel Evgrafovich . . ." Zina was looking at him in a strange and disturbing way, her eyes red. "There is something I think you should know: in our life today, with no wars or revolutions . . . things still happen . . ."
> "What? What did you say?" asked Pavel Evgrafovich.
> "I, too, sometimes feel like . . . breaking into a dance."[36]

Zina gets up from her chair and leaves the room. Pavel Evgrafovich waits patiently for her to return, "clasping his file to his chest." Perhaps it is not the year, after all. Back in 1919, Letunov's Uncle Shura, based on Trifonov's father, never accepted the "killing arithmetic" and refused to participate in the Migulin trial because trials were needed to establish the facts, not to serve as "a show rehearsed in advance." And now, in 1972, some people have time to look back—and look around—and others do not. And the heat is just as terrible, if not worse. "The cast iron was bearing down; the forests were burning, and Moscow was choking to death, suffocating from the haze—dusky blue, charcoal gray, reddish brown, black—different colors at different times—that filled the streets and houses with a slow rolling, blanketing cloud, like a fog or poisonous gas; the smell of burning penetrated everywhere, there was no escaping it; the lakes turned to sandy shallows, the river revealed its rocks, the water barely trickled from the faucets, the birds did not sing; life on this planet had come to an end, killed by the sun."[37]

Seasons come and go, and the heat—along with conscience—keeps flaring up and cooling off, day after day, year after year. Letunov senses this, but he belongs to the parents' generation and he cannot stop looking for final resolutions: a beginning in 1919, when the lava flowed through the Don Region, and an end in the near future, when the smell of burning will disappear once and for all. "Migulin perished because at a fateful moment two streams of hot and cold, two clouds the size of continents—belief and unbelief—had collided in the heavens and produced a discharge of colossal magnitude, and he had been whisked up and carried away by the hurricane-force wind in which hot and cold, belief and unbelief commingled. Displacement always brings on a thunderstorm, and the downpour drenches the earth. This merciless heat will end in a downpour, too. And I shall rejoice in the coolness if I survive."[38]

At the end of the novel, and at the end of his life, Letunov goes to see Asya, Migulin's wife (Trifonov's version of Filipp Mironov's Nadezhda). She turns out to be a "mummy-like old woman with shining eyes." He asks her where Migulin was headed in August 1919. She understands that her answer is very important to him, but all she can say is: "I have never loved anyone so much in my long and wearisome life.'"[39]

A year later, after Letunov's death, his son gives his documents to a history graduate student from Rostov who is writing his dissertation on Migulin. The graduate student thinks that there are times when truth and faith become so tightly and inextricably intertwined that it is difficult to sort out which is which, but he believes that he can do it. He sets out for home, but he misses his train because of a sudden downpour. It is not the downpour Letunov was waiting for. It signifies the end of faith—his faith—but it is unlikely to be the last one. The novel ends the same way as *The Road to Ocean*, except that there is no Ocean, just the rain, and no guide to accompany the historian. "The rain was coming down in a flood. It smelled of ozone. Two little girls had covered themselves with a sheet of clear plastic and were running barefoot over the asphalt."[40]

■ ■ ■

Sergei Troitsky from *Another Life* has trouble telling truth from faith and defining the subject of his dissertation. One night, when he and his wife, Olga Vasilievna, are in bed, talking, he suddenly says:

> "Do you know why I am having such a hard time?" Barely audibly, he whispered: "Because the threads that stretch out from the past . . . they are fraught. . . . Don't you see? They are really fraught. Don't you understand?"
>
> She did not understand. "Fraught . . . with what?"
>
> "What do you mean, with what?" He laughed. She suddenly felt scared: he seemed to be losing his mind. "Nothing breaks off without leaving a trace of some kind. . . . There is no such thing as a final rupture! Don't you understand? There has to be a continuation, there must be. It's so obvious."[41]

It is only after he dies, defeated by his failure to relate to other lives (in the present as well as in the past), that she finally understands. "Every contact with the past meant pain. Yet life is made up of such contacts, for the threads to the past are a thousandfold and each one must be torn out of living flesh, out of a wound. At first she had thought that peace would come when all those threads, down to the tiniest and thinnest, had been broken. It now appeared, however, that this would never be, because the number of threads was infinite. Every object, every familiar person, every thought, every word—every single thing in the world was linked by some thread to him."[42]

In one of the final scenes of the novel, Olga Vasilievna has a dream. She and Sergei are gathering mushrooms in the forest, but they are too involved in conversation to notice anything, and there aren't any mushrooms, anyway. They go deeper and deeper into the forest. The aspens and birches give way to dense spruce thickets, and it grows dark and damp. They walk faster and faster. "Somewhere ahead there was a glimmer of brighter light, a glimpse or two of a glade or a clearing. That was where another life would begin." They keep going. "The dampness in the air was oppressive, the smell of rotting wood drifted up from the fallen trees and from the bottoms of ravines. Occasionally they had to wade through black swampy water as they walked on and on, talking, enticed by the brightness ahead." Finally, they come to a green fence, walk along it for a while, find a gate, and ask four men sitting on a bench where the bus stop is. The men say that there is no bus stop, but a woman sitting beside them says that the men are patients from an asylum and offers to show them a shortcut through the woods. They walk for a long time. It grows dark. The woman keeps saying that they are almost there. Suddenly she says: "Here we are."

> They were standing in front of a small woodland swamp. "What's this?" Olga Vasilievna asked.
> "This is the road," said the woman. "There's your bus—over there." She stretched out her arm, pointing to a clump of sedge growing on the far side of the swamp.[43]

When the literary historian Ralf Schröder asked Trifonov about the meaning of this scene, Trifonov said that, being German, he must remember Faust's final monologue:

> A swamp still skirts the mountain chain
> And poisons all the land retrieved;
> This marshland I hope yet to drain,
> And thus surpass what we achieved.

Faust's vision of heavenly life on reclaimed land echoes the story of the House of Government, but his conclusion points to "another life," the one that Olga Vasilievna is attempting to come to terms with.

This is the highest wisdom that I own,
The best that mankind ever knew:
Freedom and life are owned by those alone
Who conquer them each day anew.

Blind and about to die, Faust seems to realize something that Moses and Pavel Letunov never do: that life is not about getting to the other side and stopping time; it is about swimming against the current—even if it means staying in one place. Such, at any rate, is the claim made by the angels who wrest Faust's soul from Mephistopheles (who cries foul, not without some justification):

Saved is the spirit kingdom's flower
From evil and the grave:
"Whoever strives with all his power,
We are allowed to save."[44]

And such is Olga Vasilievna's realization at the end of *Another Life*. She conquers each day anew and eventually finds another love. He is middle-aged, married, and often sick. They like to go for walks on a trail that runs through the pine woods along the river. "Moscow had long since surrounded this ancient spot, part village and part dacha settlement, had flowed around it and surged westward, but had somehow not quite swallowed it up: the pine trees were still there, the water-meadow still shimmered in green, and high on a hilltop over the river and above the pines floated the bell tower of the old Spasskoe-Lykovo church, visible from far away on every side." It was the same belfry that the barefooted little boy used to see as he ran through that same meadow chasing his father's kite; the same river that flowed eastward into Moscow and washed the House on the Embankment on both sides; the same man coming back to the spot he never left. As Trifonov's alter ego from *The Old Man* puts it, "life is a system in which everything, in some mysterious way and according to some higher plan, keeps coming back to form a circle."[45]

The story of the Revolution's children does not end in self-immolation or execution. It ends the same way as *The Blue Bird*, which they saw at the Moscow Art Theater when they were little; the same way as *Faust* and *War and Peace*, which their blind parents raised them on; and the same way as Bulgakov's *Master and Margarita*, which they adopted as their *Faust*. What was a swamp to Trifonov's father is Trifonov's life, the only one he has. And what was his father's House of Government is Trifonov's home, the one he keeps coming back to. And Trifonov's home, whatever its particular time and place, will always remain the House on the Embankment—because the river keeps flowing, and the exiles from childhood keep floating downstream or swimming against the current, paddling with their hands, day after day, year after year.

Yuri Trifonov on the riverbank, with the Lykovo Trinity belfry
in the background (Courtesy of Olga Trifonova)

Yuri Trifonov in front of the Lykovo Trinity belfry
(Courtesy of Olga Trifonova)

APPENDIX

PARTIAL LIST OF LEASEHOLDERS

The following is a list of House of Government leaseholders most prominently featured in this book. Entries include selected positions and occupations and names of dependents who lived in the House.

Adoratsky, Vladimir Viktorovich (b. 1878), director of the Marx-Engels-Lenin Institute at the Party Central Committee. Apt. 93.
- His wife, Serafima Mikhailovna (b. 1878).
- Their daughter, Varvara (b. 1904).

Arosev, Aleksandr Yakovlevich (b. 1890), military leader of the Bolshevik uprising in Moscow in October 1917; chairman of the Supreme Revolutionary Tribunal of Ukraine; deputy director of the Lenin Institute; ambassador to Lithuania and Czechoslovakia; chairman of the All-Union Society for Cultural Ties with Foreign Countries (VOKS). Diarist, memoirist, novelist, short-story writer. Apts. 103 and 104.
- His daughters, Natalia (b. 1919), Elena (b. 1923), and Olga (b. 1925).
- His second wife, Gertrude Freund (b. 1909), Czechoslovak citizen, dance teacher.
- Their son, Dmitry (b. 1934).

Berman, Matvei Davydovich (b. 1898), head of the Gulag; people's commissar of communications. Apt. 141.

Bogachev, Serafim Yakovlevich (b. 1909), secretary of the Central Committee of the Komsomol (Young Communist League). Apt. 65.
- His wife, Lydia Aleksandrovna Kozlova (b. 1909).
- Their daughter, Natalia (b. 1937).

Bogutsky, Vatslav Antonovich (Waclaw Bogucki, b. 1884), representative of the Communist Party of Poland at the Comintern Executive Committee; chairman of the Central Committee of the Trade Union of Communications Workers. Apt. 342.
- His wife, Mikhalina Iosifovna Novitskaia (Michalina Nowicka, b. 1896), librarian at the Lenin Institute.
- Their son, Vladimir (b. 1924).

Butenko, Konstantin Ivanovich (b. 1901), director of the Kuznetsk Steel Plant; deputy people's commissar of heavy industry. Apt. 141.
- His wife, Sofia Aleksandrovna (b. 1904), leader of the All-Union Movement of Wives of Managers and Engineers Working in Heavy Industry.
- Their adopted daughter (Sofia's niece), Tamara Nikolaevna Romanova.

Demchenko, Nikolai Nesterovich (b. 1896), first secretary of Kiev and Kharkov Provincial Party Committees; first deputy of the people's commissar of agriculture; people's commissar of grain producing and livestock raising state farms. Apt. 349.
- His wife, Maria (Mirra) Abramovna Shmaenok (b. 1900).
- Their sons, Nikolai (b. 1914) and Feliks (b. 1926).

Eikhe, Robert Indrikovich (Roberts Eihe, b. 1890), first secretary of the West Siberian Party Committee; people's commissar of agriculture. Apt. 234.
- His wife, Evgenia Evseevna Rubtsova (b. 1898).

Fedotov, Fedor Kallistratovich (b. 1897), trade union organizer in the United States; inmate of the Trenton Prison in New Jersey; Central Committee instructor (Central Asian Bureau). Fiction writer. Apt. 262.
- His wife, Roza Lazarevna Markus (b. 1895), costume maker at the Moscow Youth Theater.
- Their son, Lyova (b. 1923), diarist, fiction writer, musician.

Gaister, Aron Izrailevich (b. 1899), deputy chairman of the State Planning Committee (Gosplan); deputy people's commissar of agriculture. Apt. 162.
- His wife, Rakhil Izrailevna Kaplan (b. 1897), economist at the People's Commissariat of Heavy Industry.
- Their children, Inna (b. 1925), Natalia (b. 1930), Valeria (b. 1936).

Goloshchekin, Filipp Isaevich (Shaia Itskov, "Georges," b. 1876), commissar of the Urals Military District (entrusted with the execution of the tsar's family); first secretary of the Party Committee of Kazakhstan; chairman of the State Arbitrage Court. Apt. 228.
- His wife, Elizaveta Arsenievna (b. 1895).
- Her son, Nikolai.
- Her mother, Elizaveta Lukinichna Vinogradova (b. 1868).

Granovsky, Mikhail Aleksandrovich (b. 1893), head of construction and director of the Berezniki Chemical Plant; director of the Central Administration of Railroad Construction. Apt. 418.

- His wife, Zinaida Kolosova.
- Their sons, Anatoly (b. 1922), NKVD agent, English-language memoirist; Valentin (b. 1927); Vladimir (b. 1934).

Gronsky (Fedulov), Ivan Mikhailovich (b. 1894), responsible editor of *Izvestia*; editor in chief of *Novyi mir*; chairman of the Organizing Committee of the first Congress of Soviet Writers. Apts. 144, 18.
- His wife, Lydia Aleksandrovna (b. 1905), theatrical set designer.
- Their children, Vadim (b. 1927), Irina (b. 1934).
- Lydia's son, Igor Levashov (b. 1924).

Iofan, Boris Mikhailovich (b. 1891), chief architect of the House of Government and Palace of Soviets. Apt. 426.
- His wife, Olga Fabritsievna Sasso-Ruffo (b. 1883).
- Her children, Olga Ogareva (b. 1909), Boris Ogarev (b. 1910).
- Olga Ogareva's son, Sergei (b. 1932).

Ivanov, Boris Ivanovich ("the Baker," b. 1887), chairman of the Flour Milling Industry Directorate; deputy chairman of the Main Administration of the Canned Food Industry. Apt. 372.
- His wife, Elena Yakovlevna Zlatkina (b. 1897), seamstress, tannery worker, member of the Moscow City Soviet.
- Their children, Vladimir (b. 1919), diarist, artist, actor, letter-writer; Anatoly (b. 1921); Galina (b. 1923).
- Their adopted daughter, Olga Nikolaevna Bazovskaia (b. 1923).

Ivchenko, Emelian Mikhailovich (b. 1905), House of Government guard; commander of armed labor-camp guards in Kolyma (Gulag). Apt. 107.
- His wife, Anna Vladimirovna (b. 1915), Leningrad port worker; clerk at the House of Government post office.
- Their children, Vladimir (b. 1935), Elsa (b. 1937), Boris (b. 1939), Viacheslav (b. 1941), Aleksandr (b. 1943).
- Anna's mother, Daria Ivanovna Chesheva (b. 1886), bathhouse attendant; cannery worker.

Kerzhentsev (Lebedev), Platon Mikhailovich (b. 1881), ambassador to Sweden and Italy; head of the Russian Telegraphic Agency; chairman of the League of Time; director of the Institute of Literature, Arts, and Language at the Communist Academy; chief administrator of the Council of People's Commissars, chairman of the All-Union Radio Committee; chairman of the Committee for the Arts; director of the Small Soviet Encyclopedia. Apts. 206, 197.
- His wife, Maria Mikhailovna (b. 1901).
- Their daughter, Natalia (b. 1925).

Khalatov, Artemii Bagratovich (Artashes Bagirovich, Bagrationovich, b. 1896), chairman of the Commission for Improving the Living Condition of Scholars; chairman of the Committee on People's Nutrition; head of the Association of State Book and Magazine Publishers (OGIZ). Apt. 229.

- His mother, Ekaterina Gerasimovna (b. 1876), head of collections at the Lenin Library.
- His cousin, Elena Bogdanovna Khalatova, actress at the Moscow Art Theater.
- His wife, Tatiana Pavlovna (b. 1902), graphic artist.
- Their daughter, Svetlana (b. 1926).

Khrushchev, Nikita Sergeevich (b. 1896), first secretary of the Moscow City Party Committee. Apts. 199, 206.

- His wife, Nina Petrovna Kukharchuk (b. 1900).
- Their children, Rada (b. 1929), Sergei (b. 1935), Elena (b. 1937).

Koltsov (Fridliand), Mikhail Efimovich (b. 1898), *Pravda* correspondent and essayist; editor in chief of *Ogonyok, Krokodil,* and *Za rulem;* founder and head of the Newspaper and Magazine Alliance, author of *The Spanish Diary.* Apt. 143.

- His wife, Elizaveta Nikolaevna Ratmanova (b. 1901).
- His common-law wife, Maria Osten (Gresshöner, b. 1908), journalist and fiction writer.
- Their adopted son, Hubert L'Hoste (b. 1923).

Kon, Feliks Yakovlevich (b. 1864), head of the Arts Section of the People's Commissariat of Enlightenment; head of the All-Union Radio Committee. Apt. 198.

- His wife, Khristina Grigorievna (Khasia Girshevna) Grinberg (b. 1857).
- Their grandson, Grigory Grigorievich Usievich (b. 1917).

Kraval, Ivan Adamovich (Jānis Kravalis, b. 1897), deputy people's commissar of labor; deputy chairman of the State Planning Committee (Gosplan); head of the Central Statistical Administration. Apt. 190.

- His daughter, Elena (b. 1921).
- His second wife, Minna Ilinichna.
- Minna's sister, Polina Ilinichna Shtykan.
- Polina's husband, Abram Borisovich Shtykan.

Kritsman, Lev Natanovich (b. 1890), director of the Agrarian Institute of the Communist Academy; deputy chairman of the State Planning Committee (Gosplan). Apt. 186.

- His wife, Sarra Lazarevna Soskina, b. 1891.

Kuchmin, Ivan Fedorovich (b. 1891), secretary of the Stalingrad Party Committee; deputy chairman of the Moscow Province Executive Committee; political commissar and director of the Moscow-Kazan Railway. Prototype of Aleksei Kurilov in Leonid Leonov's novel *The Road to Ocean.* Apt. 226.

- His wife, Stefania Arkhipovna Revenko, biology instructor at the Institute of Chemical Engineering; head of the Women's Council of the Moscow-Kazan Railroad.
- Their children, Oleg (b. 1922), Elena (b. 1926).
- His wife's sister, Anna Arkhipovna Revenko (b. 1903).

Lakhuti (Lohuti), Abulkasim (Abulgasem, Abulqosim, b. 1887), Persian and Tajik poet; *Pravda* and *Izvestia* correspondent; secretary of the Union of Soviet Writers. Apts. 362, 110, 176.

- His wife, Tsetsilia Bentsionovna Banu (Bakaleishchik, b. 1911).
- Their children, Ateia (b. 1931), Delir (b. 1934), Giv (b. 1937), Leila (b. 1947).

Lande, Efim Zosimovich (b. 1898), head of the Economic Planning Department of the State Bank. Apt. 153.

- His wife, Maria Aleksandrovna Yusim (b. 1900), editor at the Party Publishing House.
- Their son, Vladimir (b. 1927).

Lander, Karl Ivanovich (Kārlis Landers, b. 1883), Cheka plenipotentiary for the North Caucasus and the Don Region (1920); head of the Agitprop Department of the Moscow Party Committee; Soviet representative at the foreign Famine Relief missions in 1922–23; member of the Collegium of the People's Commissariat of Foreign Trade. Apt. 307.

Larina-Bukharina, Anna Mikhailovna (b. 1914), wife of Nikolai Bukharin. Apt. 470.

- Her son, Yuri (b. 1936).
- Her husband's father, Ivan Gavrilovich Bukharin (b. 1862).
- Her husband's first wife, Nadezhda Mikhailovna Lukina (b. 1887).

Mikhailov, Vasily Mikhailovich (b. 1894), head of the Moscow Trade Union Council; deputy head of construction of the Dnieper Hydroelectric Dam; head of construction of the Palace of Soviets. Apt. 52.

- His daughters, Yulia (b. 1917), Nasdezhda (b. 1922).
- His second wife, Nadezhda Ivanovna Ushakova (b. 1888).
- Her daughter, Maria Nikolaevna Kulman (Musia, b. 1922).
- Their daughter, Margarita (b. 1929).

Mironov, Sergei Naumovich (Miron Iosifovich Korol, b. 1894), deputy head of the GPU [secret police] Highlands Department; head of the GPU Chechen-Grozny Department; deputy head of the GPU plenipotentiary in Kazakhstan; head of the OGPU Secret-Operational Department in Kazakhstan; head of the NKVD Directorate of Dnepropetrovsk Province; head of the NKVD Directorate of West Siberia; Soviet ambassador to Mongolia; head of the Far Eastern Section of the People's Commissariat of Foreign Affairs. Apt. unknown.
  - His wife, Agnessa Ivanovna Argiropulo (b. 1902), memoirist.
  - Their adopted daughter (Agnessa's niece), Agulia (b. 1930).

Moroz, Grigory Semenovich (b. 1893), head of the Cheka Investigations Department; Cheka plenipotentiary in the Kirgiz Territory; Cheka plenipotentiary in the Urals; secretary of the Urals Party Committee; chairman of the Moscow Control Commission; chairman of the Trade Employees Union. Apt. 39.
  - His wife, Fanni Lvovna Kreindel (b. 1897), pharmacist.
  - Their sons, Samuil (b. 1920), memoirist, poet; Vladimir (b. 1922), diarist; Aleksandr (b. 1928).

Muklevich, Romuald Adamovich (Romuald Muklewicz, b. 1890), commander of Soviet Naval Forces; naval inspector general; deputy people's commissar of defense industries. Apt. 334.
  - His wife, Anna Yakovlevna (b. 1890), head of supplies at the State Planning Committee (Gosplan).
  - Their daughter, Irina (b. 1923).

Murzin, Pavel Gerasimovich (b. 1884), senior inspector, People's Commissariat of Transportation. Apt. 130.
  - His niece, Nina Markelovna Andreeva.
  - His wife, Maria Semenovna (b. 1885).
  - Their children, Mikhail (b. 1913), Nikolai (b. 1915).
  - Mikhail's wife, Zinaida Pavlovna (b. 1909).

Orekhov, Vasily Andreevich (b. 1884), member of the Moscow Revolutionary Tribunal; deputy prosecutor of the Moscow Province; member of the High Court of Crimea; chairman of the Department of Party History of the Party Committee of Crimea. Apt. 384.
  - His wife, Elizaveta Ermolaevna (b. 1888).
  - Their children Vladimir (b. 1912), Tamara (b. 1923).

Osinsky (Obolensky), Valerian Valerianovich (b. 1887), director of the State Bank; chairman of the Supreme Council of the National Economy (VSNKh); deputy people's commissar of agriculture; ambassador to Sweden; director of the Institute of World Economy and Politics; head of the Central Directorate of Statistics; deputy head of the State Planning Committee (Gosplan); director of the Institute of the History of Science and Technology of the Academy of Sciences. Apts. 389, 18.

- His wife, Ekaterina Mikhailovna Smirnova (b. 1889), senior editor at Children's Publishers.
- Their children, Vadim (Dima, b. 1912); Valerian (Valia, b. 1923), classical philologist; Svetlana (b. 1925), memoirist and historian.
- Their adopted son (Ekaterina's nephew), Rem Vladimirovich Smirnov (b. 1923).
- Vadim's wife, Nadezhda (Dina) Dmitrievna Filatova (b. 1912), and their son, Ilya (b. 1937).
- Ekaterina's mother, Ekaterina Nartsissovna Smirnova (Zhurakovskaia).

Ostroumova, Valentina Petrovna (b. 1898), stenographer of the Central Committee of the Party, Council of People's Commissars, Comintern Executive Committee, and Cheka Collegium; head of the Igarka Political Department of the Main Administration of the Northern Sea Route; head of the Secretariat of Main Civil Aviation Directorate. Apt. 436.

Ozersky, Aleksandr Vladimirovich (b. 1891), Soviet trade representative in Great Britain; head of the Central Directorate of Supplies, People's Commissariat of Defense Industry. Apt. 208.

- His wife, Maria Efimovna (Mirra Khaimovna) Kaminskaia (b. 1907).
- Their children, Vladimir (b. 1924), Diana (b. 1935).

Peterson, Rudolf Avgustovich (Rūdolfs Petersons, b. 1897), commander of Trotsky's armored train; commandant of the Kremlin; deputy commander of the Kiev Military District. Apt. unknown.

- His wife, Maria Stepanovna (b. 1894).
- Their children, Irina (b. 1920), Maia (b. 1926), Marina (b. 1935).
- Maria's son, Igor Aleksandrovich Boiarsky (b. 1916).

Petrovsky, Grigory Ivanovich (b. 1878), people's commissar of internal affairs; chairman of the All-Ukrainian Central Executive Committee; co-chairman of the All-Union Central Executive Committee; deputy chairman of the Presidium of the Supreme Soviet. Apt. 321.

- His wife, Domna (Domenika) Fedotovna Sivakova.
- Their children, Leonid (b. 1902), Antonina (b. 1906).
- Leonid's wife, Nadezhda Vasilievna Vikulova (b. 1902).

Piatnitsky (Tarshis), Osip (Iosif) Aronovich (b. 1882), secretary of the Comintern Executive Committee. Apt. 400.

- His wife, Yulia Iosifovna Sokolova (b. 1899), diarist.

- Their sons, Igor (b. 1921), Vladimir (Vova, b. 1925), memoirist, historian.
- Yulia's father, Iosif Sokolov, his second wife, Sofia, and their daughter, Liudmila.

Podvoisky, Nikolai Ilich (b. 1880), head of the Military Organization of the Petrograd Party Committee; chairman of the Military Revolutionary Committee and commander of the storming of the Winter Palace; commander of the Petrograd Military District; people's commissar of military affairs of the Russian Republic; people's commissar of military and naval affairs of Ukraine; chairman of Sports International and Supreme Council of Physical Culture; member of the Party's Central Control Commission. Apt. 280.
- His wife, Nina Avgustovna Didrikil (b. 1882), editor at the Marx-Engels-Lenin Institute.
- Their children, Olga (b. 1908), Lev (b. 1911), Lydia (b. 1913), Nina (b. 1916), Elena (b. 1925).

Poloz (Polozov), Mikhail Nikolaevich (b. 1890), Ukrainian ambassador to the Russian Republic; chairman of the State Planning Committee of Ukraine; people's commissar of finance of Ukraine; deputy chairman of the Budget Committee of the Central Executive Committee of the USSR. Apt. 199.
- His wife, Tatiana Ivanovna Miagkova ("Tania," b. 1897).
- Their daughter, Rada Mikhailovna Poloz (b. 1924).
- Tatiana's mother, Feoktista Yakovlevna Miagkova.

Postyshev, Pavel Petrovich (b. 1887), plenipotentiary of the Government of the Far Eastern Republic; first secretary of the Kiev Provincial Party Committee; first secretary of the Kharkov Provincial Party Committee; second secretary of the Central Committee of the Communist Party of Ukraine; secretary of the Central Committee of the Party; head of the Organizational Bureau and the Agitprop Department of the Central Committee; first secretary of the Kuibyshev Provincial Party Committee. Apt. 274.
- His wife, Tatiana Semenovna Postolovskaia (b. 1899), secretary of the Party Committee of the Ukrainian Association of Marxist-Leninist Academic Institutions.
- Their sons, Valentin (b. 1914), Leonid (b. 1920), Vladimir (b. 1922).
- Tatiana's mother, Maria Ignatievna, and sister, Nina Semenovna.

Rabichev (Zeidenshner, Zaidenshner), Naum Natanovich (b. 1898), director of the Party Press; director of the Central Lenin Museum; deputy director of the Department of Culture and Propaganda of the Central Committee of the Party. Apt. 417.

- His mother, Sofia Markovna (b. 1876), researcher at the Institute of World Economics and Politics.
- His wife, Vera Semenovna Kliachko (b. 1900).
- Their son, Vladimir (b. 1919).

Radek, Karl Berngardovich (Karol Sobelsohn, b. 1885), member of the Executive Committee of Comintern; rector of the Sun Yat-sen Communist University of the Toilers of China; head of the International Information Bureau of the Central Committee of the Communist Party; head of the International Department at *Izvestia.* Apt. 20.
- His wife, Roza Mavrikievna (b. 1885).
- Their daughter, Sofia (b. 1919).

Ronin, Solomon Lazarevich (b. 1895), head of the Financial Department of the State Planning Committee (Gosplan). Apt. 55.
- His brother, Samuil (b. 1910).
- His wife, Tatiana Vladimirovna (b. 1897).
- Their children, Anatoly (b. 1921), Galina (b. 1930).
- Tatiana's mother, Dora Naumovna (b. 1873).

Rozengolts, Arkady Pavlovich (b. 1889), secretary of the Moscow Soviet of Workers' Deputies; head of the Main Directorate of the Air Force; ambassador to Great Britain; people's commissar of foreign trade. Apt. 237.
- His wife, Zoya Aleksandrovna (b. 1898).
- Their daughters, Natalia (b. 1932), Zoya (b. 1934).
- Arkady's sister, Eva Pavlovna Levina-Rozengolts (b. 1898), painter, graphic artist. Her daughter, Elena (b. 1928).
- Zoya Aleksandrovna's brother, Evgeny Riashentsev.

Rykov, Aleksei Ivanovich (b. 1881), people's commissar of internal affairs; chairman of the Supreme Economic Council (VSNKh); chairman of the Council of People's Commissars; people's commissar of communications. Apt. 18.
- His wife, Nina Semenovna Marshak (b. 1884), head of the Children's Health Administration at the People's Commissariat of Health.
- Their daughter, Natalia (b. 1916).

Serafimovich (Popov), Aleksandr Serafimovich (b. 1863), writer; author of *The Iron Flood.* Apt. 82.
- His wife, Fekla (Fekola) Rodionovna Belousova (b. 1892).
- His son, Igor Popov (b. 1903).
- Igor's first wife, Aleksandra Vladimirovna Maniushko (b. 1900).
- Their daughters, Iskra (b. 1933), Svetlana (b. 1937).
- Igor's second wife, Izabella Veniaminovna Arutiuniants (b. 1910).

Shaburova (Karabaeva), Maria Aleksandrovna (b. 1902), head of the Women's Section of the Central Committee Agitation Department; editor in chief of *Rabotnitsa* (Female worker); people's commissar of social welfare of the Russian Republic. Apts. 170, 167.

- Her husband, Nikolai Efimovih Shaburov (b. 1886).
- Their children, Nelli (b. 1925), Lev (b. 1927).

Shapiro, Isaak Ilich (b. 1895), head of the Ninth (secret codes) Section of the Main Directorate of State Security at the People's Commissariat of Internal Affairs (NKVD); head of the NKVD Secretariat; head of the First Special (secret service) Department of the NKVD. Apts. 43, 453.

Shchadenko, Efim Afanasievich (b. 1882), member of the Revolutionary-Military Committees of the First and Second Red Cavalry Armies; deputy president of the Frunze Military Academy; head of the Political Department of the Kiev Military District; deputy people's commissar of defense. Apts. 10, 505.

- His son, Gennady (b. 1929).
- His wife, Maria Aleksandrovna Denisova-Shchadenko (b. 1894), sculptor; prototype of Maria in Vladimir Mayakovsky's poem, *A Cloud in Pants.*
- Maria's daughter, Alisa Vasilievna Stroeva; her husband, Yuri Lvovich Karpov (b. 1912); and their children, Tatiana (b. 1937), Olga (b. 1944).

Shumiatsky, Boris Zakharovich (b. 1886), chairman of the Far Eastern Bureau of the Central Committee of the Party; chairman of the Council of People's Commissars of the Far Eastern Republic; ambassador to Persia; chairman of the All-Union Cinema and Photography Association. Apt. 398.

- His wife, Leah Isaevna Pandre (b. 1889).
- Their daughters, Eleonora (b. 1909), Ekaterina (b. 1922).

Shuniakov, Vasily Petrovich (1889), secretary of the Arkhangelsk Provincial Party Committee; instructor at the Moscow Party Committee. Apt. 429.

- His wife, Iudif Aleksandrovna Charnaia (b. 1902).
- Their daughter, Tamara (b. 1922).
- Iudif's mother, Elena Iosifovna Charnaia (b. 1870).
- Iudif's father, Zasil Iudeleevich Solov (b. 1871).

Smilga, Ivar Tenisovich (Ivars Smilga, b. 1892), chairman of the Executive Committee of the Army, Navy, and Workers of Finland; chairman of the Political Department of the Revolutionary Military Council of the Republic (head commissar of the Red Army); deputy head of the State Planning Committee (Gosplan); member of the Presidium of the Supreme Council of National Economy. Apt. 230.

- His wife, Nadezhda Vasilievna Poluian (b. 1895).
- Their daughters, Tatiana (b. 1919), Natalia (b. 1922).
- Nadezhda's friend, Nina Zakharovna Delibash (b. 1903).

Solts, Aron Aleksandrovich ("The Party's Conscience," b. 1872), member of the Presidium of the Central Control Commission, the International Control Commission of the Comintern, and the Soviet Supreme Court; deputy prosecutor general. Apt. 393.

- His sister, Esfir (b. 1873).
- His adopted son, Evgeny (b. 1927).
- His niece, Anna Grigorievna Zelenskaia, and her children, Elena (b. 1919), Andrei (b. 1921).

Stasova, Elena Dmitrievna (b. 1873), secretary of the Central Committee of the Party; chairwoman of the Central Committee of International Red Aid (MOPR); member of the Central Control Committee and International Control Committee of the Comintern. Apts. 245, 291.

Sverdlova-Novgorodtseva, Klavdia Timofeevna (b. 1876), widow of the chairman of the All-Russian Central Executive Committee, Yakov Sverdlov; employee of the Central Censorship Office (Glavlit). Apt. 319.

- Her son, Andrei (b. 1911), NKVD official.
- Andrei's wife, Nina Nikolaevna Podvoiskaia (b. 1916), and their daughter, Elena (b. 1935).

Terekhov, Roman Yakovlevich (b. 1890), secretary of the Central Committee of the Communist Party of Ukraine; first secretary of the Kharkov Provincial Party Committee; second secretary of the Donetsk Provincial Party Committee; member of the Soviet Control Commission. Apts. 108, 190.

- His wife, Efrosinia Artemovna (b. 1901).
- Their children, Victoria (b. 1924), Gennady (b. 1931).

Trifonov, Valentin Andreevich (b. 1888), commissar of the Special Expeditionary Corps in the Don Area in 1919; chairman of the Military Collegium of the Soviet Supreme Court; deputy military attaché in China; trade representative in Finland; chairman of the Main Committee on Foreign Concessions at the Council of People's Commissars. Apt. 137.

- His wife, Evgenia Abramovna Lurye (b. 1904).
- Their children, Yuri (b. 1925), Tatiana (b. 1927).
- Evgenia's mother, Tatiana Aleksandrovna Slovatinskaia (b. 1879).
- Her adopted son, Andrei Grigorievich Slovatinsky (Undik, b. 1917).

Tuchin, Mikhail Andreevich (b. 1896), foreman and Party secretary, House of Government Construction Organization; senior inspector at Gorky Park. Apt. 4.
- His father, Andrei Gurianovich (b. 1870).
- His mother, Natalia Fedorovna (b. 1867).
- His wife, Tatiana Ivanovna Chizhikova (b. 1901), salesclerk at the House of Government store.
- Their children, Zinaida (b. 1923), Vladimir (b. 1925).

Usievich, Elena Feliksovna (b. 1893), literary critic; widow of Grigory Aleksandrovich Usievich; daughter of Feliks Kon; deputy director of the Institute of Literature and Arts of the Communist Academy. Apts. 194, 193.
- Her second husband, Aleksandr Aleksandrovich Takser
- Their daughter, Iskra-Marina (b. 1926).

Veitser, Izrail Yakovlevich (b. 1889), people's commissar of trade of Ukraine; deputy people's commissar of foreign trade; trade representative in Germany; people's commissar of internal trade. Apt. 159.
- His wife, Natalia Ilinichna Sats (b. 1903), director and artistic director of Moscow Children's Theater (Central Children's Theater).

Volin, Boris Mikhailovich (Iosif Mikhailovich Fradkin, b. 1886), deputy people's commissar of internal affairs of Ukraine; chairman of the Press Department of the People's Commissariat of Foreign Affairs; director of the Main Administration for Literary and Publishing Affairs (Central Censorship Office, Glavlit); head of the Schools Department of the Central Committee of the Party. Apt. 276.
- His wife, Dina Davydovna (b. 1888), gynecologist; editor at Medical Press.
- Their daughter, Victoria (b. 1920).

Voronsky, Aleksandr Konstantinovich ("Valentin," b. 1884), editor in chief of *Red Virgin Soil*; head of the Russian and Foreign Classics Section at State Fiction Publishers; literary theorist, fiction writer, memoirist. Apt. 357.
- His wife, Sima Solomonovna (b. 1889).
- Their daughter, Galina (b. 1916).

Zbarsky, Boris Ilich (Ber Elievich, b. 1885), director of the Lenin Mausoleum Laboratory. Apt. 28.
- His son, Ilya (b. 1913), employee of the Lenin Mausoleum Laboratory.
- His second wife, Evgenia Borisovna (b. 1900).
- Their sons, Feliks-Lev (b. 1931), Viktor (b. 1942).

NOTES

The Library of Congress system of transliterating Russian words, followed in these endnotes, has been modified in the main body of the text in accordance with conventional usage ("Mayakovsky," not "Maiakovskii"; "Lyova," not "Leva"; "Tatiana," not "Tat'iana"). Unless noted otherwise, all translations are my own.

ABBREVIATIONS

AGTsTM	Arkhiv Gosudarstvennogo tsentral'nogo teatral'nogo muzeia (Archive of the State Central Theater Museum)
AMDNN	Arkhiv Muzeiia "Dom na naberezhnoi" (Archive of the "House on the Embankment" Museum)
AOM	Arkhiv Obshchestva "Memorial" (Memorial Society Archive)
APRF	Arkhiv Prezidenta Rossiiskoi federatsii (Archive of the President of the Russian Federation)
ARAN	Arkhiv Rossiiskoi akademii nauk (Archive of the Russian Academy of Sciences)
GARF	Gosudarstvennyi arkhiv Rossiiskoi federatsii (State Archive of the Russian Federation)
RGALI	Rossiiskii gosudarstvennyi arkhiv literatury i iskusstva (Russian State Archive of Literature and the Arts)
RGASPI	Rossiiskii gosudarstvennyi arkhiv sotsial'no-politicheskoi istorii (Russian State Archive of Social and Political History)
RGVA	Rossiiskii gosudarstvennyi voennyi arkhiv (Russian State Military Archive)
TsAFSB	Tsentral'nyi arkhiv Federal'noi sluzhby bezopasnosti (Central Archive of the Federal Security Service)
TsALIM	Tsentral'nyi arkhiv literatury i iskusstva Moskvy (Central Archive of Literature and the Arts, Moscow)
TsANTDM	Tsentral'nyi arkhiv nauchno-tekhnicheckoi dokumentatsii Moskvy (Central Archive of Scientific and Technical Documents, Moscow)
TsAODM	Tsentral'nyi arkhiv obshchestvennykh dvizhenii Moskvy (Central Archive of Social Movements, Moscow)
TsAOPIM	Tsentral'nyi arkhiv obshchestvenno-politicheskoi istorii Moskvy (Central Archive of Social and Political History, Moscow)
TsDNA	Tsentr dokumentatsii "Narodnyi arkhiv" (The "People's Archive" Documentation Center)

TsGAMO   Tsentral'nyi gosudarstvennyi arkhiv Moskovskoi oblasti
(Central State Archive of Moscow Province)
TsIAM   Tsentral'nyi istoricheskii arkhiv Moskvy (Central Historical
Archive, Moscow)
TsMAM   Tsentral'nyi munitsipal'nyi arkhiv Moskvy (Central Municipal
Archive, Moscow)

1. THE SWAMP

1. *Iakimanka* (Moscow: Elita, 1998), 24–38; *Po Moskvie: Progulki po Moskvie i eia khudozhestvennym i prosvetitel'nym uchrezhdeniiam* (Moscow: izd. M i S. Sabashnikovykh, 1917), 301–5; O. Shmidt, *Zamoskvorech'e: Iakimanskaia chast'* (Moscow: Gosudarstvennaia publichnaia istoricheskaia biblioteka Rossii, 1999), 5–22, 36–37.

2. *Iakimanka*, 33–38, 47; Shmidt, *Zamoskvorech'e*, 23–24; E. I. Kirichenko, *Khram Khrista Spasitelia v Moskve: Istoriia proektirovaniia i sozdaniia sobora 1813–1931* (Moscow: Planeta, 1992), 16.

3. O. N. Orobei, ed., *Stroiteli Rossii—XX vek: Moskva nachala veka* (Moscow: O-Master, 2001), 120–21; V. A. Kondrat'eva and V. I. Nevzorova, eds., *Iz istorii fabrik i zavodov Moskvy i moskovskoi gubernii: Konets XVIII–nacchalo XX vv* (Moscow: Tsentral'nyi gosudarstvennyi arkhiv Moskvy, 1968), 97; V. Ruga and A. Kokorev, *Moskva povsednevnaia: Ocherki gorodskoi zhizni nachala XX veka* (Moscow: Olma-Press, 2005), 78–81; "History and Tradition," Red October, http://www.redoct.msk.ru/rus/about/history.shtml; TsIAM, f. 179, op. 62, d. 17680; op. 63, d. 17546; I. Evsenin, *Ot fabrikanta k Krasnomu Oktiabriu* (Moscow: Izdatel'stvo VTsSPS, 1927), 15–20.

4. TsIAM, f. 179, op. 62, dd. 17678, 17679, 17544, 17686; Mikhail Korobko, "Rasstupites', dumnyi d'iak idet! Palaty na Bersenevskoi naberezhnoi," http://testan.narod.ru/article/bersen.htm; Shmidt, *Zamoskvorech'e*, 29–34.

5. Nikolai Bukharin, *Vremena* (Moscow: Progress, 1994), 23.

6. TsIAM, f. 179, op. 62, dd. 17682, 17683, 17684, 17686; op. 63, dd. 17549, 17550; Semen Kanatchikov, *A Radical Worker in Tsarist Russia: The Autobiograpy of Semën Ivanovich Kanatchikov*, ed. and trans. Reginald E. Zelnik (Stanford, CA: Stanford University Press, 1986), 7, 25, 34.

7. TsIAM, f. 179, op. 62, dd. 17693, 17693a; op. 63, dd. 17551, 17559, 17560; Kondrat'eva and Nevzorova, *Iz istorii fabrik i zavodov*, 268; V. V. Pokhlebkin, *Istoriia vodki* (Moscow: Tsentrpoligraf, 2007), attachment 9; Orobei, *Stroiteli Rossii*, 279–80.

8. Joseph Bradley, *Muzhik and Muscovite: Urbanization in Late Imperial Russia* (Berkeley: University of California Press, 1985), 251; Orobei, *Stroiteli Rossii*, 153. The quotations are from Ruga and Kokorev, *Moskva povsednevnaia*, 88–90.

9. TsIAM, f. 179, op. 62, d. 17697, 17694, 17695, 17696; op. 63, d. 17563, 17561; Kanatchikov, *Radical Worker in Tsarist Russia*, 7, 25.

10. TsIAM, f. 179, op. 62, d. 17699; *Iakimanka*, 52; *Vospominaniia o Rakhmaninove* (Moscow: Muzyka, 1988), 1:386–89; S. V. Rakhmaninov, *Pis'ma* (Moscow: Muzykal'noe izdatel'stvo, 1955), 115; V. Briantseva, *S. V. Rakhmaninov* (Moscow: Sovetskii kompozitor, 1976), 206–7; Barrie Martyn, *Rachmaninoff: Composer, Pianist, Conductor* (Aldershot, UK: Scolar Press, 1990), 104–6; Anna Gorkushkina, "Roial' Rakhmaninova," *Vecherniaia Moskva*, October 19, 1992.

11. TsIAM, f. 179, op. 62, d. 17700; Orobei, *Stroiteli Rossii*, 118; Kondrat'eva and Nevzorova, *Iz istorii fabrik i zavodov*, 93, 115.

12. Kanatchikov, *Radical Worker in Tsarist Russia*, 20–21.

13. Ibid., 50–51.

14. Ibid., 10, 12–13, 21, 25, 30, 40, 60, 62.

15. Ibid., 10, 15–17. See also Robert Eugene Johnson, *Peasant and Proletarian: The Working Class of Moscow in the Late Nineteenth Century* (New Brunswick, NJ: Rutgers University Press, 1979); and Victoria E. Bonnell, *Roots of Rebellion: Workers' Politics and Organizations in St. Petersburg and Moscow, 1900–1914* (Berkeley: University of California Press, 1983).

16. Ruga and Kokorev, *Moskva povsednevnaia*, 94–98. See also *Iakimanka*, 40; Orobei, *Stroiteli Rossii*, 153, 181.

17. Bukharin, *Vremena*, 23.

18. Orobei, *Stroiteli Rossii*, 255–56, 261–62, 266–73, 276–80, 285–86, 293–94, 328, 360; Ruga and Kokorev, *Moskva povsednevnaia*, 225, 237–38, 244, 297–318, 339–40 (the foul odor quotation is from 305); Robert W. Thurston, *Liberal City, Conservative State: Moscow and Russia's Urban Crisis, 1906–1914* (New York: Oxford University Press, 1987), 85–89, 154–59; Bradley, *Muzhik and Muscovite*, 299–337; Paul W. Werth, "In the State's Embrace? Civil Acts in an Imperial Order," *Kritika: Explorations in Russian and Eurasian History* 7, no. 3 (2006): 433–58; *Vospominaniia o Rakhmaninove*, 1:125–26; E. Dmitrievskaia and V. Dmitrievskii, *Rakhmaninov v Moskve* (Moscow: Moskovskii rabochii, 1993), 75–76.

19. Bradley, *Muzhik and Muscovite*, 4, 9–40; Orobei, *Stroiteli Rossii*, 29–30; *Vospominaniia o Rakhmaninove*, 1:125–26; Dmitrievskaia and Dmitrievskii, *Rakhmaninov v Moskve*, 75–76.

20. Thurston, *Liberal City, Conservative State*, 87; TsIAM, f. 1272, op. 1, dd. 345–58 (the quotation about commercial establishments is from d. 358); f. 475, op. 19, dd. 167, 168; op. 17, d. 1312, ll. 3–39. See also Jonathan W. Daly, *The Watchful State: Security Police and Opposition in Russia, 1906–1917* (DeKalb: Northern Illinois University Press, 2004).

21. I. V. Spiridonov, *Vserossiiskaia politicheskaia stachka v oktiabre 1905 g.* (Moscow: Gospolitizdat, 1955), 51–52, 57; Laura Engelstein, *Moscow, 1905: Working-Class Organization and Political Conflict* (Stanford, CA: Stanford University Press, 1982), 85–86, 110, 206–8, 214; Kondrat'eva and Nevzorova, *Iz istorii fabrik i zavodov*, 164, 172, 176; Evsenin, *Ot fabrikanta k Krasnomu Oktiabriu*, 26–34, 38–47 (the quotation about St. Bartholomew's night is from 28); Eric Lohr, *Nationalizing the Russian Empire: The Campaign against Enemy Aliens during World War I* (Cambridge, MA: Harvard University Press, 2003), 16, 34. On the flood, see post-1908 entries in TsIAM, f. 179, op. 62 and 63.

22. Christine D. Worobec, "Miraculous Healings," in Mark D. Steinberg and Heather D. Coleman, eds., *Sacred Stories: Religion and Spirituality in Modern Russia* (Bloomington: Indiana University Press, 2007), 22–43; Roy R. Robson, "Transforming Solovki: Pilgrim Narratives, Modernization, and Late Imperial Monastic Life," in Stenberg and Coleman, eds., *Sacred Stories*, 44–60; Mark D. Steinberg, *Proletarian Imagination: Self, Modernity, and the Sacred in Russia, 1910–1925* (Ithaca, NY: Cornell University Press, 2002), 224–46; Nadieszda Kizenko, *A Prodigal Saint: Father John of Kronstadt and the Russian People* (University Park: Pennsylvania State University Press, 2000), 196–200 and passim; Vera Shevzov, *Russian Orthodoxy on the Eve of Revolution* (Oxford: Oxford University Press, 2004); Gregory Freeze, "Subversive Piety: Religion and the Political Crisis in Late Imperial Russia," *Journal of Modern History* 68 (June 1996): 308–50; Heather J. Coleman, *Russian Baptists and Spiritual Revolution, 1905–1929* (Bloomington: Indiana University Press, 2005), 41–60 and passim; A. Etkind, *Khlyst: Sekty, literatura i revoliutsiia* (Moscow: NLO, 1998); Olga Matich, *Erotic Utopia: The Decadent Imagination in Russia's Fin de Siècle* (Madison: University of Wisconsin Press, 2005), 9–10 (the "last of a series" line is from Viacheslav Ivanov, quoted on 3); Irina Paperno, "Introduction" and "The Meaning of Art: Symbolist Theories," in Irina Paperno and Joan Delaney Grossman, eds., *Creating Life: The Aesthetic Utopia of Russian Modernism* (Stanford, CA: Stanford University Press, 1994), 1–23 (the Solov'ev quotation is on 16). See also David M. Bethea, *The Shape of Apocalypse in Modern Russian Fiction* (Princeton, NJ: Princeton University Press, 1989); Irene Masing-Delic, *Abolishing Death: A Salvation Myth of Russian Twentieth-Century Literature* (Stanford, CA: Stanford University Press, 1992); Christopher Read, *Religion, Revolution and the Russian Intelligentsia 1900–1912* (London: Macmillan, 1979); Laura Engelstein, *Castration and the Heavenly Kingdom* (Ithaca,

NY: Cornell University Press, 1999); Mark D. Steinberg, *Petersburg Fin de Siècle* (New Haven, CT: Yale University Press, 2011), 234–67; and Robert C. Williams, "The Russian Revolution and the End of Time: 1900–1940," *Jahrbücher für Geschichte Osteuropas* 43, no. 3 (1995): 364–401.

23. Bukharin, *Vremena*, 179–80; A. Voronskii, *Za zhivoi i mertvoi vodoi* (Moscow: Antikva, 2005), 2:202, 222–34, 267–68, 310. The quotations are from 267–68 and 310; Ezek. 11:19; Ezek. 26:12–13.

24. Nikolai Fedorovich Fedorov, *Sochineniia* (Moscow: Mysl', 1982), 90; Kanatchikov, *Radical Worker in Tsarist Russia*, 34; Polina Dimova, "The Poet of Fire: Aleksandr Skriabin's Synaesthetic Symphony *Prometheus* and the Russian Symbolist Poetics of Light" (unpublished manuscript in author's possession); Martyn, *Rachmaninoff*, 94–104; Briantseva, *Rakhmaninov*, 214–41. The Cui quotation is from Iu. Keldysh, *Rakhmaninov i ego vremia* (Moscow: Muzyka, 1973), 103.

25. Martyn, *Rachmaninoff*, 110; Briantseva, *Rakhmaninov*, 247–49. The "symbol" quotation (Gr. Prokof'ev, "Pevets intimnykh nastroenii," *Russkaia muzykal'naia gazeta* 7 [1910]: col. 195) is from Keldysh, *Rakhmaninov i ego vremia*, 128.

26. Ia. M. Sverdlov, *Izbrannye proizvedeniia* (Moscow: Gospolitizdat, 1957), 1:139.

2. THE PREACHERS

1. A. Etkind, *Khlyst: Sekty, literatura i revoliutsiia* (Moscow: NLO, 1998), esp. 585–674; Christopher Read, *Religion, Revolution and the Russian Intelligentsia 1900–1912* (London: Macmillan, 1979), 57–94; Catherine Evtuhov, *The Cross and the Sickle: Sergei Bulgakov and the Fate of Russian Religious Philosophy, 1890–1920* (Ithaca NY, Cornell University Press, 1997); S. Bulgakov, *Dva grada: Issledovaniia o prirode obshchestvennykh idealov* (St. Petersburg: RGKhI, 1997), esp. 207–47; A. V. Lunacharskii, *Religiia i sotsializm* (St. Petersburg: Shipovnik, 1908–11), vols. 1 and 2; N. A. Berdiaev, "Religioznye osnovy bol'shevizma," in Nikolai Berdiaev, *Sobranie sochinenii* (Paris: YMCA Press, 1990), 4:29–37; N. A. Berdiaev, *Russkaia ideia: Osnovnye napravleniia russkoi mysli XIX veka i nachala XX veka* (Moscow: Svarog, 1997), 168–83; V. D. Bonch-Bruevich, *Izbrannye sochineniia* (Moscow: AN SSSR, 1959), 1:184; Roland Boer, *Lenin, Religion, and Theology* (New York: Palgrave Macmillan, 2013), 59–101; David Graeme Rowley, *Millenarian Bolshevism: Empiriomonism, God-Building, Proletarian Culture* (New York: Garland, 1987); Vatro Murvar, "Messianism in Russia: Religious and Revolutionary," *Journal for the Scientific Study of Religion* 10 (1971): 277–338; A. Voronskii, *Za zhivoi i mertvoi vodoi* (Moscow: Antikva, 2005), 1:137.

2. *Deiateli SSSR i revoliutsionnogo dvizhenia Rossii* (Moscow: Sovetskaia entsiklopediia, 1989), 688, 372, 569; Nikolai Bukharin, *Vremena* (Moscow: Progress, 1994), 27–29; RGASPI, f. 124, op. 1, d. 1848 (A. P. Stankevich), l. 6.

3. Feliks Kon, *Za 50 let* (Moscow: Vsesoiuznoe obshchestvo politkatorzhan i ssyl'no-poselentsev, 1934), 1:7, 17–18.

4. *Deiateli SSSR*, 593, 595. For the non-Russian converts to Bolshevism, see Liliana Riga, *The Bolsheviks and the Russian Empire* (Cambridge: Cambridge University Press, 2012).

5. RGASPI, f. 124, op. 1, d. 603 (Dodonova), l. 4 (the "discomfort and shame" quotation); *Deiateli SSSR*, 701–2. See also *Deiateli SSSR*, 395 (Ganetskii); RGASPI, f. 124, op. 1, d. 1114 (Lepeshinskaia), l. 4 ob.

6. *Deiateli SSSR*, 546, 548.

7. Bukharin, *Vremena*, 309–10.

8. Il'ia Erenburg, *Liudi, gody, zhizn'* (Moscow, Sovetskii pisatel', 1990), 1:73.

9. K. T. Sverdlova, *Iakov Mikhailovich Sverdlov* (Moscow: Molodaia gvardiia, 1985), 59–63; S. M. Sverdlova, S. M. Averbakh-Sverdlova, V. M. Sverdlov, "Brat," in *O Iakove Sverdlove: Vospominaniia, ocherki, stat'i sovremennikov* (Moscow: Izdatel'stvo politicheskoi liteatury, 1985), 25–30. The long quotation is from Ts. Zelikson-Borovskaia, *Professional'nyi revoliu-*

tsioner: Ocherk zhizni i deiatel'nosti Ia. M. Sverdlova (Moscow: Staryi bol'shevik, 1934), 11–12.

10. A. Arosev, *Kazanskie ocherki o revoliutsii 1905 goda* (Kazan: Istpart otdel oblastnogo komiteta RKP(b) Tatarskoi respubliki, 1925), 16.

11. A. Arosev, "Na boevykh putiakh: Vospominaniia," *Novyi mir* 1 (1931): 87–88.

12. Ibid., 82.

13. Voronskii, *Za zhivoi i mertvoi vodoi*, 1:16–18.

14. Arosev, "Na boevykh putiakh: Vospominaniia," 90, 88.

15. Kon, *Za 50 let*, 1:18, 19.

16. Arosev, "Na boevykh putiakh: Vospominaniia," 91; Aleksandr Arosev, *Kak my vstupali v revoliutsionnuiu rabotu* (Moscow: Moskovskii rabochii, 1926), 66–67; *Deiateli SSSR*, 569–70.

17. *Deiateli SSSR*, 570. For the largest collection of Old Bolshevik memoirs, see RGASPI, f. 124, op. 1 (The Society of Old Bolsheviks). All the memoirs from f. 124 quoted in this chapter are by the residents of the House of Government.

18. Arosev, *Kak my vstupali*, 68–71, except the "Those were not letters" and "were met with loud applause" quotations, which are from A. Arosev, "Na boevykh putiakh: Prodolzhenie," *Novyi mir* 2 (1931): 85, 87.

19. The translation of the quotation from Lenin's *What Is to Be Done?* is based on V. I. Lenin, *Collected Works* (Moscow: Foreign Languages Publishing House, 1961), 5:355. For the original, see V. I. Lenin, *Polnoe sobranie sochinenii* (Moscow, Politizdat, 1963), izd. 5, vol. 6, pp. 9–10 (http://uaio.ru/vil/06.htm).

20. Bukharin, *Vremena*, 316–37.

21. *Deiateli SSSR*, 569; A. Voronskii, *Rasskazy i povesti* (Moscow: Sovetskaia literatura, 1933), 30; Kon, *Za 50 let*, 1:18. On the culture and mythology of the revolutionary movement, see Marina Mogil'ner, *Mifologiia 'podpol'nogo cheloveka': Radikal'nyi mikrokosm v Rossii nachala XX veka kak predmet semioticheskogo analiza* (Moscow: NLO, 1999); on student radical culture, see Susan K. Morrissey, *Heralds of Revolution: Russian Students and the Mythologies of Radicalism* (New York: Oxford University Press, 1998); on Jewish radicalism, see Inna Shtakser, *The Making of Jewish Revolutionaries in the Pale of Settlement* (New York: Palgrave Macmillan, 2014).

22. V. V. Kuibyshev, *Epizody iz moei zhizni* (Moscow: Staryi bol'shevik, 1935), 32–55. See also *Valerian Vladimirovich Kuibyshev: Biografiia* (Moscow: Politizdat, 1988), 33–35.

23. Voronskii, *Za zhivoi i mertvoi vodoi*, 2:229–30.

24. Ibid., 2:224–25.

25. Kanatchikov, *Radical Worker in Tsarist Russia*, 290; Voronskii, *Za zhivoi i mertvoi vodoi*, 1:115.

26. Voronskii, *Za zhivoi i mertvoi vodoi*, 1:118.

27. Lenin, *Polnoe sobranie sochinenii*, izd. 5, vol. 6, p. 79 (http://uaio.ru/vil/06.htm); Kanatchikov, *Radical Worker in Tsarist Russia*, 290; Bukharin, *Vremena*, 336.

28. Voronskii, *Za zhivoi i mertvoi vodoi*, 2:229; Kon, *Za 50 let*, 49. See also Kanatchikov, *Radical Worker in Tsarist Russia*, xv–xxx (editor's introduction); and Reginald E. Zelnik, "Russian Bebels: An Introduction to the Memoirs of the Russian Workers Semën Kanatchikov and Matvei Fisher," *Russian Review* 35, no. 3 (July 1976): 288–89.

29. *Deiateli SSSR*, 476–79.

30. *Pavel Postyshev: Vospominaniia, vystupleniia, pis'ma* (Moscow: Politizdat, 1987), 46; Iu. A. Dmitriev et al., *Ulitsy Vladimira* (Iaroslavl': Verkhne-Volzhskoe knizhnoe izdatel'stvo, 1989), 17–19.

31. RGASPI, f. 124, op. 1, d. 1919 (R. Ia. Terekhov), ll. 1–20b.

32. Ibid., d. 1429 (V. A. Orekhov), ll. 3–40b.

33. Kanatchikov, *Radical Worker in Tsarist Russia*, 27–34.

34. Ibid., 100.

35. Ibid., 27; *Deiateli SSSR*, 477; P. M. Bykov, "Moi vstrechi s Ia. M. Sverdlovym," in *O Iakove Sverdlove*, 45; S. M. Sverdlova et al., "Brat," in *O Iakove Sverdlove*, 28.

36. *Pavel Postyshev*, 52.

37. Kanatchikov, *Radical Worker in Tsarist Russia*, 248–49.

38. S. M. Sverdlova et al., "Brat," in *O Iakove Sverdlove*, 25–30 (the quotation is on 29); A. Voronskii, *Izbrannaia proza* (Moscow: Khudozhestvennaia literatura, 1987), 20–21; Voronskii, *Za zhivoi i mertvoi vodoi*, 1:40–41; Kuibyshev, *Epizody*, 30–32.

39. Kanatchikov, *Radical Worker in Tsarist Russia*, 249.

40. Ibid., 102.

41. Ibid., 130. For other vivid workers' autobiographies by future House of Government residents, see RGASPI, f. 124, op. 1, d. 39 (S. Ia. Alliluev); 40 (O. E. Allilueva); 119 (S. M. Balakhnin); 273 (I. L. Bulat); 274 (D. A. Bulatov); 275 (A. S. Bulin); 346 (M. K. Vetoshkin); 411 (A. A. Voronin); 493 (N. K. Goncharov); 518 (L. A. Grebnev); 550 (M. A. Gusev); 596 (K. Ia. Dirik); 745 (B. I. Ivanov); 909 (M. N. Kokovikhin); 953 (V. E. Kosorotov); 1031 (M. M. Kul'kov); 1077 (M. A. Lebedev); 1159 (F. F. Liaksutkin); 1542 (V. I. Polonskii); 1599 (S. F. Redens); 1683 (A. N. Riabov); 1717 (P. F. Sakharova); 1797 (M. I. Smirnov); 1890 (F. F. Syromolotov); 2018 (V. V. Fomin); 2083 (A. A. Chevardin); 2988 (A. A. Cherepanov). On radical workers' culture, including reading circles, see Reginald E. Zelnik, "Russian Bebels: An Introduction to the Memoirs of Semen Kanatchikov and Matvei Fisher," part 1, *Russian Review* 35, no. 3 (July 1976): 249–89, and part 2, *Russian Review* 35, no. 4 (October 1976): 417–47; Reginald E. Zelnik, ed., *Workers and Intelligentsia in Late Imperial Russia: Realities, Representations, Reflections* (Berkeley: University of California Press, 1999); Zelnik, "On the Eve: An Inquiry into the Life Histories and Self-Awareness of Some Worker-Revolutionaries," in Lewis H. Siegelbaum and Ronald Grigor Suny, eds., *Making Workers Soviet: Power, Class, and Identity* (Ithaca, NY: Cornell University Press, 1994), 17–65; Mark D. Steinberg, *Proletarian Imagination: Self, Modernity, and the Sacred in Russia, 1910–1925* (Ithaca, NY: Cornell University Press, 2002); Michael Melancon and Alice K. Pate, eds., *New Labor History: Worker Identity and Experience in Russia* (Bloomington, IN: Slavica, 2002); and Deborah Pearl, *Creating a Culture of Revolution: Workers and the Revolutionary Movement in Late Imperial Russia* (Bloomington, IN: Slavica, 2015), esp. 57–239, on what circle members read. For female revolutionaries, see Anna Hillyar and Jane McDermid, eds., *Revolutionary Women in Russia 1870–1917: A Study in Collective Biography* (Manchester: Manchester University Press, 2000).

42. Arosev, "Na boevykh putiakh: Prodolzhenie," 93–94.

43. Bykov, "Moi vstrechi s Ia. M. Sverdlovym," in *O Iakove Sverdlove*, 50–51.

44. Arosev, "Na boevykh putiakh: Prodolzhenie," 94; RGASPI, f. 124, op. 1, d. 1429 (V. A. Orekhov), ll. 30b., 4; E. Brazhnev (Trifonov), *Stuchit rabochaia krov'* (Moscow: Nedra, 1931), 199; Iurii Trifonov, "Otblesk kostra," in *Sobranie sochinenii* (Moscow: Khudozhestvennaia literatura, 1987), 4:9–10, 14, 32.

45. Arosev, "Na boevykh putiakh: Prodolzhenie," 94.

46. Kon, *Za 50 let*, 2:6; *Deiateli SSSR*, 571, 439, 582 (for Osinksy, Bukharin, Kerzhentsev, and Petrovsky); O. Piatnitskii, *Zapiski bol'shevika* (Moscow: Partizdat, 1936), 43 (for Tarshis).

47. Kanatchikov, *Radical Worker in Tsarist Russia*, 125–26, 250.

48. Voronskii, *Za zhivoi i mertvoi vodoi*, 1:165, 2:5–6.

49. S. M. Sverdlova et al., "Brat," in *O Iakove Sverdlove*, 28; Ia. M. Sverdlov, *Izbrannye proizvedeniia* (Moscow: Gospolitizdat, 1957), 1:172–73, 223, 255, 256, 258–62; K. T. Sverdlova, *Iakov Mikhailovich Sverdlov*, 19, 93–94.

50. Sverdlov, *Izbrannye proizvedeniia*, 1:167, 175, 182; K. T. Sverdlova, *Iakov Mikhailovich Sverdlov*, 119–20.

51. On exile as part of revolutionary mythology, see Mogil'ner, *Mifologiia 'podpol'nogo cheloveka'*, 168–76.

52. Kanatchikov, *Radical Worker in Tsarist Russia*, 367. For the "Bek"/"Mek" question, see Voronskii, *Za zhivoi i mertvoi vodoi*, 2:71; and B. I. Ivanov, *Vospominaniia rabochego bol'shevika* (Moscow: Mysl', 1972), 92.

53. Kanatchikov, *Radical Worker in Tsarist Russia*, 364; Sverdlova, *Iakov Mikhailovich Sverdlov*, 124, 193–94; V. I. Piatnitskii, *Osip Piatnitskii i Komintern na vesakh istorii* (Minsk: Kharvest, 2004), 29; Piatnitskii, *Zapiski*, 244–51; RGASPI, f. 124, op. 1, d. 1308 (O. N. Mitskevich), l. 3; Voronskii, *Za zhivoi i mertvoi vodoi*, 2:74, 180.

54. Trifonov, "Otblesk kostra," 21; Ivanov, *Vospominaniia*, 101; Voronskii, *Za zhivoi i mertvoi vodoi*, 2:85–86.

55. Piatnitskii, *Zapiski*, 249; Ivanov, *Vospominaniia*, 95, 153.

56. Sverdlov, *Izbrannye proizvedeniia*, 1:204, 268; Voronskii, *Za zhivoi i mertvoi vodoi*, 2:177–78; Kanatchikov, *Radical Worker in Tsarist Russia*, 367; *Pavel Postyshev*, 51.

57. Sverdlov, *Izbrannye proizvedeniia*, 1:268, 276–77, 298; Dzhugashvili quoted in Iurii Trifonov, "Iz dnevnikov i rabochikh tetradei," *Druzhba narodov* 6 (1998): 114.

58. Sverdlov, *Izbrannye proizvedeniia*, 1:278, 298, 301; RGASPI, f. 124, op. 1, d. 484 (F. I. Goloshchekin), ll. 14–14 ob.

59. Sverdlov, *Izbrannye proizvedeniia*, 1:281, 214–15.

60. Ivanov, *Vospominaniia*, 151–52, 154.

61. Voronskii, *Za zhivoi i mertvoi vodoi*, 2:181–82.

62. Ivanov, *Vospominaniia*, 95; Sverdlov, *Izbrannye proizvedeniia*, 208.

63. Sverdlov, *Izbrannye proizvedeniia*, 1:215; Voronskii, *Za zhivoi i mertvoi vodoi*, 2:182; Piatnitskii, *Zapiski*, 249–50; Ivanov, *Vospominaniia*, 153.

64. *Pavel Postyshev*, 57.

65. Ibid., 50.

66. Ivanov, *Vospominaniia*, 92.

67. Sverdlova, *Iakov Mikhailovich Sverdlov*, 194–97. See also Ivanov, *Vospominaniia*, 96.

68. Ivanov, *Vospominaniia*, 107–8.

69. Sverdlova, *Iakov Mikhailovich Sverdlov*, 196. On Narym exile, see Ernst Khaziakhmetov, *Bol'sheviki v Narymskoi ssylke* (Novosibirsk: Zapadno-Sibirskoe knizhnoe izdatel'stvo, 1967).

70. Voronskii, *Za zhivoi i mertvoi vodoi*, 2:186, 7, 86.

71. Voronskii, *Za zhivoi i mertvoi vodoi*, 2:268.

72. Ibid., 2:5; E. A. Dinershtein, *A. K. Voronskii v poiskakh zhivoi vody* (Moscow: Rosspen, 2001), 271–72.

73. Voronskii, *Za zhivoi i mertvoi vodoi*, 1:89–90.

74. Voronskii, *Za zhivoi i mertvoi vodoi*, 2:268, 303.

75. Ibid., 2:300–301.

76. Ibid., 2:266–67.

77. Frederick Engels, "The Movements of 1847," in Karl Marx, Frederick Engels, *Collected Works* (London: Lawrence & Wishart, 1975–2004), 6:520. The words "The hangman stands at the door" are from Heinrich Heine's "Ritter Olaf."

78. Voronskii, *Za zhivoi i mertvoi vodoi*, 2:305.

79. Ibid., 2:305, 267, 268, 306, 309.

80. Ibid., 2:304.

81. Max Weber, *Economy and Society* (Berkeley: University of California Press, 1978), 1:284.

82. Ernst Troeltsch, *The Social Teaching of the Christian Churches* (New York: Macmillan, 1931), 1:331–43; for a helpful reconsideration, see Bryan Wilson, *Religious Sects: A Sociological Study* (New York: McGraw Hill, 1970), 26–28. On sects defying states, not churches, see Bryan R. Wilson, *Magic and the Millennium: A Sociological Study of Religious Movements of Protest among Tribal and Third-World Peoples* (New York: Harper and Row, 1973), 14. On the cult/sect distinction, see Rodney Stark and William Sims Bainbridge, *The Future of Religion: Secularization, Revival, and Cult Formation* (Berkeley: University of California Press, 1985), 24–26. On the world-rejection/world-acceptance continuum, see Benton Johnson, "On Church and Sect," *American Sociological Review* 28, no. 4 (August 1963): 539–49; for a strong endorsement (and the source of some of my wording), see Stark and Bainbridge, *The Future of Religion*, 23–24.

83. Job 6: 11; 9:19, 20.

84. Bukharin, *Vremena*, 350–51.

85. Voronskii, *Za zhivoi i mertvoi vodoi*, 1:68–69.

86. Gen. 3:19, 1:28.

87. The "mountain" quotation is from Heb. 3:14.

88. Voronskii, *Za zhivoi i mertvoi vodoi*, 1:151.

89. Cf. Arosev's "Na boevykh putiakh: Vospominaniia," esp. 89 (the theme is proclaimed, but not strongly developed).

90. Voronskii, *Za zhivoi i mertvoi vodoi*, 1:151–52.

91. Voronskii, *Za zhivoi i mertvoi vodoi*, 2:269–71.

92. Sverdlov, *Izbrannye proizvedeniia*, 1:185.

93. Ibid., 1:252.

94. Archpriest Avvakum, *The Life Written by Himself*, trans. Kenneth N. Brostrom (Ann Arbor: University of Michigan, Michigan Slavic Publications, 1979), 68; Voronskii, *Za zhivoi i mertvoi vodoi*, 2:154–55; G. A. Voronskaia, "Esli v serdtse posylaiut puliu," *Istoricheskii arkhiv* 1 (1997): 77; Sverdlov, *Izbrannye proizvedeniia*, 1:185.

95. Sverdlov, *Izbrannye proizvedeniia*, 1:329, 339.

96. Ibid., 1:302.

97. Ibid., 1:247–48, 273.

98. Ibid., 1:349.

99. Sverdlova, *Iakov Mikhailovich Sverdlov*, 217–18.

100. K. A. Egon-Besser, "Volia k zhizni, k bor'be," in *O Iakove Sverdlove*, 104.

101. Sverdlov, *Izbrannye proizvedeniia*, 1:208, 170, 294.

102. Biographical information from Svetlana Valerianovna Obolenskaia, interview with author, September 20, 2009.

103. ARAN, razriad 5, op. 1–0, d. 11, ll. 1–5 ob.

104. Aleksandr Mikhailov, *Zhizn' Maiakovskogo: Ia svoe zemnoe ne dozhil* (Moscow: Tsentrpoligraf, 2001), 121; V. V. Kamenskii, *Zhizn's Maiakovskim* (Moscow, 1940; reprint, Munich: Wilhelm Fink Verlag, 1974), 83–84.

105. Mikhailov, *Zhizn'*, 125; Nina Zainullina, "Kto vdokhnovil Maiakovskogo na 'Oblako v shtanakh'?" *Vechernii Khar'kov*, January 11, 2008, http://www.vecherniy.kharkov.ua/news /18715.

106. Kamenskii, *Zhizn'*, 88–89.

107. Ibid., 97–99.

108. Ibid., 25.

109. Ibid., 20; Vladimir Maiakovskii, "Oblako v shtanakh," Biblioteka Komarova, http://ilibrary .ru/text/1241/p.1/index.html.

3. THE FAITH

1. Steve Bruce, *Religion in the Modern World: From Cathedrals to Cults* (Oxford: Oxford University Press, 1996), 7. See also Rodney Stark and William Sims Bainbridge, *The Future of Religion: Secularization, Revival, and Cult Formation* (Berkeley: University of California Press, 1985), 3–14. For Marxism and Bolshevism as religion or "secular religion," see Arthur Jay Klinghoffer, *Red Apocalypse: The Religious Evolution of Soviet Communism* (New York: University Press of America, 1996); Mikhail Ryklin, *Kommunizm kak religiia: Intellektualy i Oktiabr'skaia revoliutsiia* (Moscow: NLO, 2009); Mikhail Agursky, "L'aspect millénariste de la révolution bolchevique," *Cahiers du monde russe et soviétique* 29 (1988): 487–513; Mary-Barbara Zeldin, "The Religious Nature of Russian Marxism," *Journal for the Scientific Study of Religion* 8 (1969): 100–111; Klaus-Georg Riegel, "Marxism-Leninism as a Political Religion," *Totalitarian Movements and Political Religions* 6 (2005): 97–126.

2. Emile Durkheim, *The Elementary Forms of Religious Life* (Oxford: Oxford University Press, 2001), 26–31.

3. For the history of the concepts of "religion" and "world religions," see Talal Asad, *Genealogies of Religion: Discipline and Reasons of Power in Christianity and Islam* (Baltimore, MD: Johns Hopkins University Press, 1993), 40–42; Leora Batnitzky, *How Judaism Became a Religion: An Introduction to Modern Jewish Thought* (Princeton, NJ: Princeton University Press, 2011); Daniel Dubuisson, *The Western Construction of Religion: Myths, Knowledge, and Ideology* (Baltimore, MD: Johns Hopkins University Press, 2003); Timothy Fitzgerald, *Ideology of Religious Studies* (New York: Oxford University Press, 2003); William Herbrechtsmeier, "Buddhism and the Definition of Religion: One More Time," *Journal for the Scientific Study of Religion* 32, no. 1 (March 1993): 1–18; Jason Ananda Josephson, *The Invention of Religion in Japan* (Chicago: University of Chicago Press, 2012); Tomoko Masuzawa, *The Invention of World Religions, or How European Universalism Was Preserved in the Language of Pluralism* (Chicago: University of Chicago Press, 2005); Brian K. Pennington, *Was Hinduism Invented? Britons, Indians, and the Colonial Construction of Religion* (New York: Oxford University Press, 2003); Wilfried Cantwell Smith, *The Meaning and End of Religion* (New York: Harper and Row, 1963).

4. Durkheim, *The Elementary Forms*, 46, 39, 40; Thomas Luckmann, *The Invisible Religion: The Problem of Religion in Modern Society* (New York: Macmillan, 1967), 48–49; Robert N. Bellah, *Beyond Belief: Essays on Religion in a Post-Traditional World* (New York: Harper and Row, 1970), 21; Clifford Geertz, *The Interpretation of Cultures* (New York: Basic Books, 1973), 90; Mircea Eliade, *The Sacred and the Profane: The Nature of Religion* (New York: Harcourt Brace Jovanovich, 1959), 20–21, 28, 68–69, 30. For general surveys, see Roger O'Toole, *Religion: Classic Sociological Approaches* (Toronto: McGraw-Hill Ryerson, 1984), 10–51; Fitzgerald, *Ideology of Religious Studies*; Andrew M. McKinnon, "Sociological Definitions, Language Games, and the 'Essence' of Religion," *Method and Theory in the Study of Religion* 14, no. 1 (2002): 61–83.

5. Phillip E. Johnson, "Concepts and Compromises in First Amendment Religious Doctrine," *California Law Review*, 72 (1984): 821, 832; Barbara Forrest, "The Wedge at Work: How Intelligent Design Creationism Is Wedging Its Way into the Cultural and Academic Mainstream," in Robert T. Pennock, ed., *Intelligent Design Creationism and Its Critics: Philosophical, Theological, and Scientific Perspectives* (Cambridge, MA: MIT Press, 2001), 6–8.

6. S. N. Eisenstadt, ed., *The Origins and Diversity of Axial Age Civilizations* (Albany: State University of New York Press, 1986), esp. 1–25 (editor's introduction); Karl Jaspers, *The Origin and Goal of History* (New Haven, CT: Yale University Press, 1953); Eric Voegelin, *The New Science of Politics: An Introduction*, in Voegelin, *Modernity without Restraint* (Columbia: University of Missouri Press, 2000), 135–74; Robert N. Bellah, *Religion in Human Evolution: From the Paleolithic to the Axial Age* (Cambridge, MA: Harvard University Press, 2011); Benjamin I. Schwartz, "The Age of Transcendence," *Daedalus* 104, no. 2 (Spring 1975): 1–7, the "standing back and looking beyond" quotation is on 3.

7. Eisenstadt, ed., *Origins and Diversity*; Johann P. Arnason, S. N. Eisenstadt, and Björn Wittrock, eds., *Axial Civilizations and World History* (Leiden: Brill, 2005), esp. Björn Wittrock, "The Meaning of the Axial Age," 51–85; Ernest Gellner, *Plough, Sword and Book: The Structure of Human History* (Chicago: University of Chicago Press, 1988), 70–90; Peter L. Berger, *The Social Reality of Religion* (London: Faber and Faber, 1969), 65–69; Joseph Kitagawa, "Primitive, Classical, and Modern Religions: A Perspective on Understanding the History of Religions," in Joseph Kitagawa, ed., *The History of Religions: Essays on the Problem of Understanding* (Chicago: University of Chicago Press, 1967), 53–54.

8. Eisenstadt, ed., *Origins and Diversity*; Guenter Lewy, *Religion and Revolution* (New York: Oxford University Press, 1974), 11–32, 59–66, 254–57; C. K. Yang, *Religion in Chinese Society: A Study of Contemporary Social Functions of Religion and Some of Their Historical Factors*

(Berkeley: University of California Press, 1967); Richard Shek, "Sectarian Eschatology and Violence," in Jonathan N. Lipman and Stevan Harrell, eds., *Violence in China: Essays in Culture and Counterculture* (Albany: State University of New York Press, 1990), 88–108; Susan Naquin, *Millenarian Rebellion in China: The Eight Trigrams Uprising of 1813* (New Haven, CT: Yale University Press, 1976), 7–66.

9. Norman Cohn, *Cosmos, Chaos, and the World to Come: The Ancient Roots of Apocalyptic Faith* (New Haven, CT: Yale University Press, 1993), 77–115; Robert Gnuse, "Ancient Near Eastern Millennialism," in Catherine Weissinger, ed., *The Oxford Handbook of Millennialism* (New York: Oxford University Press, 2011), 246–49; Philip G. Kreyenbroek, "Millennialism and Eschatology in the Zoroastrian Tradition," in Abbas Amanat and Magnus Bernhardsson, eds., *Imagining the End: Apocalypse from the Ancient Middle East to Modern America* (London: I. B. Tauris, 2002), 33–55.

10. Jan Assmann, "Axial 'Breakthroughs' and Semantic 'Relocations' in Ancient Egypt and Israel," in Arnason et al., *Axial Civilizations and World History*, 133–56; Jan Assmann, *Moses the Egyptian: The Memory of Egypt in Western Monotheism* (Cambridge, MA: Harvard University Press, 1997); Assmann, *The Price of Monotheism* (Stanford, CA: Stanford University Press, 2010); Assmann, *Of God and Gods: Egypt, Israel, and the Rise of Monotheism* (Madison: University of Wisconsin Press, 2008). Cf. Michael Walzer, *Exodus and Revolution* (New York: Basic Books, 1985); Paula Fredriksen, *From Jesus to Christ: The Origins of the New Testament Images of Jesus* (New Haven, CT: Yale University Press, 1988), 72; Deut. 30:11–14.

11. Exod. 34:14.

12. Job 34:22; Deut. 5:9–10.

13. Jer. 5:6; Deut. 7:6; Isa. 49:10.

14. Judg. 11:24; Isa. 45:5, 6. See Cohn, *Cosmos*, 152. Cf. Mic. 4:5.

15. Cohn, *Cosmos*, 143–44.

16. Deut. 7:1–2; Isa. 34:2–3, 8–14.

17. Isa. 49:22–23, 26, 41:11, 45:14; Ezek. 38:18–23.

18. Isa. 65:17, 35:5–10, 11:6.

19. Fredriksen, *From Jesus to Christ*, 81–86; Ezek. 34:28; Dan. 7:27.

20. Cohn, *Cosmos*, 187–93; *Selections from Josephus*, trans. H. St. J. Thackeray (New York: Macmillan, 1919), 73; Lewy, *Religion and Revolution*, 70–91; Cecil Roth, "The Zealots in the War of 66–73," *Journal of Semitic Studies* 4, no. 4 (1959): 351.

21. *Selections from Josephus*, 93, 103–4; Fredriksen, *From Jesus to Christ*, 79–80, 83, 91–92; Howard Clark Kee, *Christian Origins in Sociological Perspective: Methods and Resources* (Philadelphia: Westminster Press, 1980), 57–58.

22. Mark 1:3–6 (cf. *Selections from Josephus*, 80–81; *Origen against Celsus*, bk. 7, chap. 9 (in Christian Classics Etherial Library, http://www.ccel.org/ccel/schaff/anfo4.toc.html).

23. Mark 13:8, 12, 24–25. Kee, *Christian Origins*, 54–72; Geza Vermes, *Jesus the Jew: A Historian's Reading of the Gospels* (New York: Macmillan, 1973), 58–100, 129–31; E. P. Sanders, *Jesus and Judaism* (London: SCM Press, 1985), 222; Dale C. Allison, *Jesus of Nazareth: Millenarian Prophet* (Minneapolis: Fortress Press, 1998), 95–171.

24. Mark 13:19; Luke 13:29; Luke 6:20–21; Christopher Rowland, *Christian Origins: An Account of the Setting and Character of the Most Important Messianic Sect of Judaism* (London: SPCK, 1985), 87–88, 109, 146.

25. Mark 1:15, 13:30; Luke 9:27; Fredriksen, *From Jesus to Christ*, 51–63, 128; Kee, *Christian Origins*, 68; Rowland, *Christian Origins*, 87–88, 109–33.

26. Mark 13:20; Luke 13:24; Matt. 19:28–30; Rowland, *Christian Origins*, 137; Cohn, *Cosmos*, 197.

27. Mark 3:31–35.

28. Luke 14:26 (cf. Mark 10:29–31; Luke 9:59–62; Luke 18:29–30); Luke 10:27 (cf. Matt. 22:36–40); Kee, *Christian Origins*, 77–80.

29. Matt. 19:28. For Jesus addressing his messages only to the Jews, see Matt. 7:6, 15:21–28; Mark 7:24–30.

30. Matt. 18:3 (cf. Mark 10:15; Matt. 10:42).

31. Matt. 5:21–22, 27–28, 33–37.

32. Matt. 15:7–11.

33. Matt. 6:8; Fredriksen, *From Jesus to Christ*, 40; Matt. 10:28, 5:46, 48.

34. Mark 14:25.

35. 1 Cor. 7:29–31; 1 Thess. 4:14–18.

36. 1 Thess. 5:5–8; Rom. 4:16–17; Rom. 9:1–8. Cf. Fredriksen, *From Jesus to Christ*, 60–61; Kee, *Christian Origins*, 92; Cohn, *Cosmos*, 206–11.

37. Rev. 7:1–8, 13:15–17, 3:15–16.

38. Rev. 19:15; Rev. 14:9–11; Rev. 16:1–21; Rev. 20:4–5, 12; Rev. 21:1–4; Rev. 22:10, 20.

39. 2 Pet. 3:3–4; Rowland, *Christian Origins*, 276–96; Voegelin, *New Science of Politics*, 176–77.

40. 2 Pet. 3:8–9.

41. Qur'an 47:19, 3:118, 47:18. See also 54:1, 42:17, 22:7, 45:32, 12:107, 43:66.

42. On Islamic apocalypticism, see David Cook, "Early Islamic and Classical Sunni and Shi'ite Apocalyptic Movements," in Weissinger, *The Oxford Handbook of Millennialism*, 267–83; Cook, "The Beginnings of Islam as an Apocalypic Movement," in Stephen D. O'Leary and Glen S. McGhee, eds., *War in Heaven / Heaven on Earth: Theories of the Apocalypic* (London: Equinox, 2005), 79–93; Cook, *Studies in Muslim Apocalyptic* (Princeton, NJ: Darwin Press, 2002), esp. 15–16, 137–88; Said Amir Arjomand, "Messianism, Millennialism and Revolution in Early Islamic History," in Amanat and Bernhardsson, *Imagining the End*, 106–25; Aziz al-Azmeh, *Islams and Modernities* (London: Verso, 1993), esp. 89–103.

43. al-Azmeh, *Islams and Modernities*, 97–98; Ovamir Anjum, *Politics, Law, and Community in Islamic Thought: The Taymiyyan Moment* (Cambridge: Cambridge University Press, 2012), esp. 1–9, 37–92, and passim; A. Azfar Moin, *The Millennial Sovereign: Sacred Kingship and Sainthood in Islam* (New York: Columbia University Press, 2012), 1–14, 74–80, 161–66, and passim; S. N. Eisenstadt, *Fundamentalism, Sectarianism, and Revolution: The Jacobin Dimension of Modernity* (Cambridge: Cambridge University Press, 1999), 19–23, 33–35, 84–89; Henry Munson, Jr., *Islam and Revolution in the Middle East* (New Haven, CT: Yale University Press, 1988), 7–38; S. N. Eisenstadt, *Jewish Civilization: The Jewish Historical Experience in a Comparative Perspective* (Albany: State University of New York Press, 1992), 35–42; Juan R. I. Cole, "Millennialism in Modern Iranian History," in Amanat and Bernhardsson, *Imagining the End*, 282–311; Stephen Sharot, *Messianism, Mysticism, and Magic: A Sociological Analysis of Jewish Religious Movements* (Chapel Hill: University of North Carolina Press, 1982); Marc Saperstein, ed., *Essential Papers on Messianic Movements and Personalities in Jewish History* (New York: New York University Press, 1992); Yuri Slezkine, *The Jewish Century* (Princeton, NJ: Princeton University Press, 2004), passim.

44. Bruce Lawrence, ed., *Messages to the World: The Statements of Osama bin Laden* (London: Verso, 2005), 121.

45. Norman Cohn, *The Pursuit of the Millennium: Revolutionary Millenarians and Mystical Anarchists in the Middle Ages* (New York: Oxford University Press, 1970), 19–204; Frederic J. Baumgartner, *Longing for the End: A History of Millennialism in Western Civilization* (New York: St. Martin's, 1999), 47–76.

46. Martin Luther, "On Secular Authority," in *Luther and Calvin on Secular Authority*, ed. and trans. Harro Höpfl (Cambridge: Cambridge University Press, 1991), 9–11, 23.

47. Ibid., 28.

48. John Calvin, "On Civil Government" (bk. 4, chap. 20 in *Institutio Christianae reilgionis*), in *Luther and Calvin on Secular Authority*, 48–49; Michael Walzer, *The Revolution of the Saints: A Study in the Origins of Radical Politics* (Cambridge, MA: Harvard University Press, 1965), esp. 2–13, 29–55, 121–25, 185–229, and passim; Harro Höpfl, *The Christian Polity of John Calvin* (Cambridge: Cambridge University Press, 1982), 193–202 (the "diligent watch" quotation is from Geneva's 1560 edict, see 200).

49. Calvin, "On Civil Government," 60; Walzer, *Revolution of the Saints*, 176 (the Cheynell quotation), 223–24; Höpfl, *Christian Polity*, 188–92; Bernard Cottret, *Calvin: A Biography* (Grand Rapids, MI: William B. Eerdmans, 2000), 223 (the Guillaume de Trie quotation).

50. Müntzer quoted in Frank E. Manuel and Fritzie P. Manuel, *Utopian Thought in the Western World* (Cambridge, MA: Belknap Press of Harvard University Press, 1979), 189.

51. Matt. 13:24–30, 37–43.

52. Müntzer quoted in Cohn, *Pursuit of the Millennium*, 239, 242, 237, 238; Cohn, *Pursuit of the Millennium*, 249–50. The Luther quotation is from Manuel and Manuel, *Utopian Thought*, 198.

53. 1 Pet. 2:9; Martin Luther, "On the Babylonish Captivity of the Church," in Henry Wace, ed., *First Principles of the Reformation, or the Ninety-Five Theses and Three Primary Works of Dr. Martin Luther* (London: John Murray, 1883), 235; Martin Malia, *History's Locomotives: Revolutions and the Making of the Modern World* (New Haven, CT: Yale University Press, 2006), 81; Ernst Troeltsch, *The Social Teaching of the Christian Churches* (New York: Macmillan, 1931), 1:331–43.

54. Anthony Arthur, *The Tailor King: The Rise and Fall of the Anabaptist Kingdom of Münster* (New York: St, Martin's 1999), 38–41, 53, 75–78, 93–102, 112, 136–38, 156–78 (the "all that is high" quotation is on 75); Cohn, *Pursuit of the Millennium*, 262–80 (the "amongst us" and "swept" quotations are on 266).

55. *Oliver Cromwell's Letters and Speeches, with Elucidations by Thomas Carlyle* (New York: William H. Colyer, 1846), 203.

56. Ibid.; Rogers quoted in B. S. Capp, *The Fifth Monarchy Men: A Study in Seventeenth-Century English Millenarianism* (London: Faber and Faber, 1972), 67, 162, 138, 132, 140–41; Dan. 2 and 7.

57. On self-immolations, see M. V. Pul'kin, "Samosozhzhenniia staroobriadtsev v kontse XII–XVIII vv.," *Novyi istoricheskii vestnik* 1 (2006): 1–14; and Georg B. Michels, *At War with the Church: Religious Dissent in Seventeenth-Century Russia* (Stanford, CA: Stanford University Press, 1999), 207–9. On Old Believer apocalypticism, see Michael Cherniavsky, "The Old Believers and the New Religion," *Slavic Review* 25, no. 1 (March 1966): 1–39; for general overviews, see S. A. Zenkovskii, *Russkoe staroobriadchestvo* (Minsk: Belorusskii ekzarkhat, 2007); and Robert O. Crummey, *The Old Believers and the World of Antichrist: The Vyg Community and the Russian State, 1694–1855* (Madison: University of Wisconsin Press, 1970).

58. L. Vorontsova and S. Filatov, "Staroobriadchestvo: V poiskakh poteriannogo grada Kitezha," in *Religiia i obshchestvo: Ocherki religioznoi zhizni sovremennoi Rossii* (Moscow: Letnii sad, 2002), 247. On Old Believers and the "Protestant work ethic," see Crummey, *Old Believers and the World of Antichrist*, 135–58.

59. See, esp., Ernest Lee Tuveson, *Redeemer Nation: The Idea of America's Millennial Role* (Chicago: University of Chicago Press, 1968); Ruth H. Bloch, *Visionary Republic: Millennial Themes in American Thought, 1756–1800* (Cambridge: Cambridge University Press, 1985); Robert N. Bellah, *The Broken Covenant: American Civil Religion in Time of Trial* (New York: Searbury Press, 1975); William G. McLoughlin, *Revivals, Awakenings, and Reform* (Chicago: University of Chicago Press, 1978); Conrad Cherry, *God's New Israel: Religious Interpretations of American Destiny* (Englewood Cliffs, NJ: Prentice-Hall, 1971); Jon Butler, *Awash in a Sea of Faith: Christianizing the American People* (Cambridge, MA: Harvard University Press, 1992).

60. James West Davidson, *The Logic of Millennial Thought: Eighteenth-Century New England* (New Haven, CT: Yale University Press, 1977), 13–32, 269, and passim; Tuveson, *Redeemer Nation*, 52–90 and passim. The Jonathan Edwards quotations are from Alan Heimert, *Religion and the American Mind: From the Great Awakening to the Revolution* (Cambridge, MA: Harvard University Press, 1966). See also Baumgartner, *Longing for the End*, 127–30; and Ernest Lee Tuveson, *Millennium and Utopia: A Study in the Background of the Idea of Progress* (Berkeley: University of California Press, 1968), 92–99 and passim; McLoughlin, *Reviv-*

als, 98–140 (the Finney quotation is on 125); Ruth Alden Doan, *The Miller Heresy, Millennialism, and American Culture* (Philadelphia: Temple University Press, 1987), 75 (the last quotation is from Henry Cowles).

61. Quoted in McLoughlin, *Revivals*, 139.

62. William E. Wilson, *The Angel and the Serpent: The Story of New Harmony* (Bloomington: Indiana University Press, 1964); Lawrence Foster, *Women, Family, and Utopia: Communal Experiments of the Shakers, the Oneida Community, and the Mormons* (Syracuse, NY: Syracuse University Press, 1991), 75–120; John W. Friesen and Virginia Lyons Friesen, *The Palgrave Companion to North American Utopias* (New York: Palgrave Macmillan, 2004), 104–16; Robert P. Sutton, *Communal Utopias and the American Experience: Religious Communities, 1732–2000* (Westport, CT: Praeger, 2003), 17–46, 67–86; Spencer Klaw, *Without Sin: The Life and Death of the Oneida Community* (New York: Allen Lane, the Penguin Press, 1993); Bryan Wilson, *Religious Sects: A Sociological Study* (New York: McGraw Hill, 1970), 132–35; Warren Lewis, "What to Do after the Messiah Has Come Again and Gone: Shaker 'Premillennial' Eschatology and Its Spiritual Aftereffects," in M. Darrol Bryant and Donald W. Dayton, eds., *The Coming Kingdom: Essays in American Millennialism and Eschatology* (Barrytown, NY: New Era Books, 1983), 71–109.

63. "The Testimony of the Prophet Joseph Smith," in *The Book of Mormon: Another Testament of Jesus Christ* (N.p.); 1 Nephi 13:37.

64. 3 Nephi 11:15.

65. Edson quoted in Gordon D. Pollock, *In Search of Security: The Mormons and the Kingdom of God on Earth, 1830–1844* (New York: Garland Publishing, 1989); Mark P. Leone, *Roots of Modern Mormonism* (Cambridge, MA: Harvard University Press, 1979); Tuveson, *Redeemer Nation*, 179–84 (the "government" quotation, from Parley Pratt's *The Angel of the Prairies*, is on 183).

66. Edson quoted in Ronald L. Numbers and Jonathan M. Butler, eds., *The Disappointed: Millerism and Millenarianism in the Nineteenth Century* (Bloomington: Indiana University Press, 1987), 215. See also Doan, *Miller Heresy* ("that doctrine" quotation is on 74); and David L. Rowe, *Thunder and Trumpets: Millerites and Dissenting Religion in Upstate New York, 1800–1850* (Chico, CA: Scholars' Press, 1985), esp. 119–39. The "agency of man" was a common formula promulgated by Joseph Smith and rejected by Miller. See, e.g., Doan, *Miller Heresy*, 74.

67. Cecil M. Robeck, Jr., *The Azusa Street Mission and Revival: The Birth of the Global Pentecostal Movement* (Nashville, TN: Thomas Nelson, 2006), 1–186 (the *Los Angeles Herald* quotation is on 1); Douglas J. Nelson, "For Such a Time as This: The Story of Bishop William J. Seymour and the Azusa Street Revival" (PhD diss., University of Birmingham [UK], 1981), 191–245; Frank Bartleman, *Azusa Street: The Roots of Modern-Day Pentecost* (Gainesville, FL: Bridge-Logos, 1980), 49–74; Harvey Cox, *Fire from Heaven: The Rise of Pentecostal Spirituality and the Reshaping of Religion in the Twenty-First Century* (Reading, MA: Addison-Wesley, 1995), esp. 45–66 and 111–22; Grant Wacker, *Heaven Below: Early Pentecostals and American Culture* (Cambridge, MA: Harvard University Press, 2001); Wilson, *Religious Sects*, 98–117; Baumgartner, *Longing for the End*, 175–78.

68. Acts 2:1–21.

69. Michael Adas, *Prophets of Rebellion: Millenarian Protest Movements against the European Colonial Order* (Chapel Hill: University of North Carolina Press, 1979); Anthony F. C. Wallace, *Religion: An Anthropological View* (New York: Random House, 1966), 30–38, 157–66, 209–15.

70. Nathan Wachtel, "Rebeliones y milenarismo," in Juan M. Ossio Acuña, ed., *Ideologia mesiánica del mundo andino* (Lima: Ignacio Prado Pastor, 1973), 118–23; Enrique Florescano, *Memoria mexicana: Ensayo sobre la reconstrucción del pasado; Época prehispanica–1821* (Mexico City: Editorial J. Mortiz, 1987), 222; James Mooney, *The Ghost-Dance Religion and the Sioux Outbreak of 1890* (Lincoln: University of Nebraska Press, 1965); Micheline E.

Pesantubbee, "From Vision to Violence: The Wounded Knee Massacre," in Catherine Wess-inger, ed., *Millennialism, Persecution, and Violence: Historical Cases* (Syracuse, NY: Syracuse University Press, 2000), 62–81; Bryan R. Wilson, *Magic and the Millennium: A Sociological Study of Religious Movements of Protest among Tribal and Third-World Peoples* (New York: Harper and Row, 1973), 221–36, 283–308; Euclides da Cunha, *Os Sertões* (1902), trans. Sam-uel Putnam as *Rebellion in the Backlands* (Chicago: University of Chicago Press, 1944); Robert M. Levine, *Vale of Tears: Revisiting the Canudos Massacre in Northeast Brazil, 1893–1897* (Berkeley: University of California Press, 1992).

71. Christine Steyn, "Millenarian Tragedies in South Africa: The Xhosa Cattle-Killing Move-ment and the Bulhoek Massacre," in Wessinger, *Millennialism*, 189–93; J. B. Peires, *The Dead Will Arise: Nongqawuse and the Great Xhosa Cattle-Killing Movement of 1856–7* (Johannes-burg: Ravan, 1989). See also Wilson, *Magic and the Millennium*, 238–40.

72. Steyn, "Millenarian Tragedies, 193–97. See also Robert Edgar, *Because They Chose the Plan of God: The Story of the Bulhoek Massacre* (Johannesburg: Ravan, 1988); Bengt G. M. Sund-kler, *Bantu Prophets in South Africa* (London: Lutterworth, 1948), 72–73; Wilson, *Magic and the Millennium*, 61–64; Lewy, *Religion and Revolution*, 203–5.

73. Leonard E. Barrett, *The Rastafarians: Sounds of Cultural Dissonance* (Boston: Beacon Press, 1977); Barry Chevannes, *Rastafari: Roots and Ideology* (Syracuse, NY: Syracuse University Press, 1994), 1. The "bright morning" quotation is from Bob Marley's "Rasta Man Chant"; "get up, stand up" is from Bob Marley's song by that name. See also Bob Marley's "Revolution."

74. Rev. 18:3, 12–13.

75. Lewy, *Religion and Revolution*, 227.

76. Peter Worsley, *The Trumpet Shall Sound: A Study of "Cargo" Cults in Melanesia* (New York: Schocken, 1968), esp. 101–8, 207–19; Lamont Lindstrom, "Cargo Cults," in Richard A. Landes, ed., *Encyclopedia of Millennialism and Millennial Movements* (New York: Routledge, 2000), 57–61.

77. Shek, "Sectarian Eschatology and Violence"; Naquin, *Millenarian Rebellion in China*; Yang, *Religion in Chinese Society*; Lewy, *Religion and Revolution*, 11–32, 59–66, 254–57; Jonathan D. Spence, *God's Chinese Son: The Taiping Heavenly Kingdom of Hong Xiuquan* (New York: Norton, 1997). The quotation is from Franz Michael, *The Taiping Rebellion: History and Documents* (Seattle: University of Washington Press, 1971), 2:273.

78. Spence, *God's Chinese Son*, 148, 150, 173, 181; Michael, *Taiping Rebellion*, 2:298 (see also 2:139–41, 312–20).

79. Michael, *Taiping Rebellion*, 2:183; Spence, *God's Chinese Son*, 170, 134.

80. Spence, *God's Chinese Son*, 181 ("the road to Heaven"), 234–332; Michael, *Taiping Rebellion*, 3:1530–32.

81. Some of the classics of the secularization debate (beyond Weber and Durkheim) are Bryan Wilson, *Religion in Secular Society: A Sociological Comment* (London: C. A. Watts, 1966); Bryan Wilson, *Religion in Sociological Perspective* (Oxford: Oxford University Press, 1982), esp. 148–79; David Martin, *A General Theory of Secularization* (Oxford: Basil Blackwell, 1978); David Martin, *On Secularization: Towards a Revised General Theory* (Farnham, UK: Ashgate, 2005); Berger, *The Social Reality of Religion*; Bruce, *Religion in the Modern World*; Steve Bruce, *God Is Dead: Secularization in the West* (Oxford: Blackwell, 2002); Stark and Bain-bridge, *Future of Religion*; Rodney Stark and Roger Finke, *Acts of Faith: Explaining the Human Side of Religion* (Berkeley: University of California Press, 2000); Hugh McLeod and Werner Ustorf, eds., *The Decline of Christendom in Western Europe, 1750–2000* (Cambridge: Cambridge University Press, 2003); José Casanova, *Public Religions in the Modern World* (Chicago: University of Chicago Press, 1994); Charles Taylor, *A Secular Age* (Cambridge, MA: Harvard University Press, 2007).

82. Quoted in Tuveson, *Millennium and Utopia*, 119, 125.

83. Turgot quoted in Manuel and Manuel, *Utopian Thought*, 483.

84. Ibid., 461–518.

85. Ruth Scurr, *Fatal Purity: Robespierre and the French Revolution* (New York: Metropolitan Books, 2006), 230, 232; Maximilien Robespierre, "On the Principles of Political Morality," February 1794, Fordham University Modern History Sourcebook, http://www.fordham .edu/halsall/mod/1794robespierre.html (taken from M. Robespierre, *Report upon the Principles of Political Morality Which Are to Form the Basis of the Administration of the Interior Concerns of the Republic* [Philadelphia, 1794]).

86. Robespierre, "On the Principles of Political Morality"; The Law of 22 Prairial, An II 10 June, 1794, Liberty, Equality, Fraternity: Exploring the French Revolution, https://chnm.gmu .edu/revolution/d/439; Scurr, *Fatal Purity*, 328, 262.

87. Cf. William Wordsworth, *The Prelude*, bk. 11, http://www.bartleby.com/145/ww297.html; Wordsworth, *The Recluse*, bk. 1, "Home at Grasmere," http://www.bartleby.com/145/ww301 .html; M. H. Abrams, *Natural Supernaturalism: Tradition and Revolution in Romantic Literature* (New York: Norton, 1971), 336–38 and passim; and Reinhold Niebuhr, *Faith and History: A Comparison of Christian and Modern Views of History* (New York: Charles Scribner's Sons, 1949), 2–5 and passim.

88. *Oeuvres de Saint-Simon & d'Enfantin* (Aalen, DE: Otto Zeller, 1963), 1:121–22; Manuel and Manuel, *Utopian Thought*, 590–614.

89. See Gianfranco Poggi, *Forms of Power* (Cambridge: Polity, 2001), 58–122.

90. For a different view, see Walzer, *Revolution of the Saints*, 300–319; Walzer, *Exodus and Revolution*, 119–35; J. L. Talmon, *The Origins of Totalitarian Democracy* (London: Secker and Warburg, 1952).

91. Rev. 18:7.

92. Robespierre, "On the Principles of Political Morality."

93. Cf. Martin, *General Theory of Secularization*; Martin, *On Secularization*; Malia, *History's Locomotives*; Slezkine, *Jewish Century*.

94. J. L. Talmon, *Political Messianism: The Romantic Phase* (London: Secker and Warburg, 1960), 265, 266, 269.

95. Karl Marx, "On the Jewish Question," in Karl Marx and Frederick Engels, *Collected Works* (New York: International Publishers, 1975–2005), http://www.marxists.org/archive/marx /works/1844/jewish-question/index.htm.

96. Karl Marx, introduction to *A Contribution to the Critique of Hegel's Philosophy of Right*, in Marx and Engels, *Collected Works*, http://www.marxists.org/archive/marx/works/1843 /critique-hpr/intro.htm (for the quotations beginning with "an anachronism" through this one).

97. Marx, "On the Jewish Question."

98. Rev. 7:3.

99. *Manifesto of the Communist Party*, chaps. 1 and 2, Marxists Internet Archive Library, http:// www.marxists.org/archive/marx/works/1848/communist-manifesto/ch01.htm#007; Rev. 18:12, 3.

100. Rev. 18:8, 21; *Manifesto of the Communist Party*, chaps. 2 and 4.

101. *Manifesto of the Communist Party*, chap. 4.

102. Frederick Engels, *The Origin of the Family, Private Property and the State*, Marxists Internet Archive Library, http://www.marxists.org/archive/marx/works/1884/origin-family/ch03 .htm ("childlike simplicity"); V. I. Lenin, "Tri istochnika i tri sostavnykh chasti marksizma," Kommunisticheskii universitet, http://www.communi.ru/matireals/university/origins /lenin/3sources_3parts_marksizm.htm.

103. Frederick Engels, *Anti-Dühring: Herr Eugen Dühring's Revolution in Science*, Marxists Internet Archive Library, http://www.marxists.org/archive/marx/works/1877/anti-duhring /introduction.htm; *Manifesto of the Communist Party*, chap. 2. Engels, "The Principles of Communism," Marxists Internet Archive Library, http://www.marxists.org/archive/marx /works/1847/11/prin-com.htm.

104. Engels, *Anti-Dühring*, pt. 3, chap. 1, https://www.marxists.org/archive/marx/works/1877 /anti-duhring/ch23.htm.

105. Rev. 19:15, 21:1, 4, 7, 25–27. See also Erik van Ree, *Boundaries of Utopia: Imagining Communism from Plato to Stalin* (London: Routledge, 2015).

106. Karl Marx, "Critique of the Gotha Programme," Marxists Internet Archive Library, http://www.marxists.org/archive/marx/works/1875/gotha/ch01.htm.

107. Karl Marx, "Critique of Modern German Philosophy according to Its Representatives Feuerbach, B. Bauer and Stirner, and of German Socialism according to Its Various Prophets," Marxists Internet Archive Library, http://www.marxists.org/archive/marx/works/1845/german-ideology/ch01a.htm; Engels, *Anti-Dühring*, pt. 1, chap. 11, https://www.marxists.org/archive/marx/works/1877/anti-duhring/ch09.htm.

108. Dante, *Paradiso*, canto 3, trans. Allen Mandelbaum, Electronic Literature Foundation, http://www.divinecomedy.org/divine_comedy.html. For a different interpretation, see Andrzej Walicki, *Marxism and the Leap to the Kingdom of Freedom: The Rise and Fall of the Communist Utopia* (Stanford, CA: Stanford University Press, 1995), 172–79 and passim.

109. George Orwell, *1984*, The Complete Works of George Orwell, http://www.george-orwell.org/1984/22.html.

4. THE REAL DAY

1. Edmund Burke, *Thoughts on French Affairs*, A Theory of Civilisation, http://ourcivilisation.com/smartboard/shop/burkee/frnchaff/index.htm#Principles. This section is based on Irwin Scheiner's unpublished essay, "The Revolution in the Restoration," and many conversations with its author.

2. Crane Brinton, *The Anatomy of Revolution* (New York: Vintage Books, 1965), 16–17, 146; Martin Malia, *History's Locomotives: Revolutions and the Making of the Modern World* (New Haven, CT: Yale University Press, 2006), 299; S. N. Eisenstadt, *The Great Revolutions and the Civilizations of Modernity* (Leiden: Brill, 2006), 4, 13, 15, 17; Charles Dickens, *A Tale of Two Cities*.

3. B. S. Capp, *The Fifth Monarchy Men: A Study in Seventeenth-Century English Millenarianism* (London: Faber and Faber, 1972), 162; Michael Walzer, *The Revolution of the Saints: A Study in the Origins of Radical Politics* (Cambridge, MA: Harvard University Press, 1965), 10–11; Thomas Case, *Two Sermons Lately Preached at Westminster before Sundry of the Honourable House of Commons, Second Sermon* (London, 1641; Ann Arbor, MI: University Microfilms, 1967, *Early English Books, 1641–1700*; 254:E.165, no. 8), 18, 22. Cf. Walzer, *Revolution of the Saints*, 10–11 (Walzer cites different page numbers).

4. Ibid., 22.

5. Ibid., 21.

6. Boris Efimov, *Desiat' desiatiletii* (Moscow: Vagrius, 2000), 6–29; Viktor Fradkin, *Delo Kol'tsova* (Moscow: Vagrius, 2002), 24–30; G. Skorokhodov, *Mikhail Kol'tsov: Kritiko-biograficheskii ocherk* (Moscow: Sovetskii pisatel', 1959), 4–17; A. Rubashkin, *Mikhail Kol'tsov: Kritiko-biograficheskii ocherk* (Leningrad: Khudozhestvennaia literatura, 1971), 5–9.

7. Mikhail Kol'tsov, *Fel'etony i ocherki* (Moscow: Pravda, 1956), 17–20.

8. Barrie Martyn, *Rachmaninoff: Composer, Pianist, Conductor* (Aldershot, UK: Scolar Press, 1990), 257, 269–77; V. Briantseva, *S. V. Rakhmaninov* (Moscow: Sovetskii kompozitor, 1976), 462–63, 481–89; Iu. Keldysh, *Rakhmaninov i ego vremia* (Moscow: Muzyka, 1973), 419, 426–30; A. D. Alekseev, *Rakhmaninov: Zhizn' i tvorcheskaia deiatel'nost'* (Moscow: Muzyka, 1964), 181.

9. K. T. Sverdlova, *Iakov Mikhailovich Sverdlov* (Moscow: Molodaia gvardiia, 1985), 218–20; K. A. Egon-Besser, "Volia k zhizni, k bor'be," in *O Iakove Sverdlove: Vospominaniia, ocherki, stat'i sovremennikov* (Moscow: Izdatel'stvo politicheskoi liteatury, 1985), 104; Vladimir Dmitrevskii, *Piatnitskii* (Moscow: Molodaia gvardiia, 1971), 136; Miklosh Kun, *Bukharin: Ego druz'ia i vragi* (Moscow: Respublika, 1992), 66; Lev Trotskii, *Moia zhizn': Opyt avtobiografii* (Berlin: Granit, 1930), 2:6–7; *Deiateli SSSR i revoliutsionnogo dvizheniia Rossii* (Moscow: Sovetskaia

entsiklopediia, 1989), 96; A. Chernobaev, *V vikhre veka* (Moscow: Moskovskii rabochii, 1987), 45–47; Al. Arosev, *Kak eto proizoshlo (Oktiabrs'skie dni v Moskve)* (Moscow: Krasnaia nov', 1923), 16.

10. Polina Vinogradskaia, *Sobytiia i pamiatnye vstrechi* (Moscow: Politizdat, 1968), 27 ("rallies lasted"); Al. Arosev, *Moskovskii sovet v 1917 g.* (Moscow: Ogonek, 1927), 16, 6.

11. Arosev, *Moskovskii sovet*, 17–18.

12. A. Voronskii, *Glaz uragana* (Voronezh: Tsentral'no-Chernozemnoe knizhnoe izdatel'stvo, 1990), 213–14.

13. Ibid., 167.

14. Arosev quoted in Chernobaev, *V vikhre veka*, 46; Voronskii, *Glaz uragana*, 179–80.

15. Trotskii, *Moia zhizn'*, 2:15–16.

16. Voronskii, *Glaz uragana*, 182.

17. Ibid., 184.

18. Podvoiskii, *God 1917* (Moscow: Gospolitizdat, 1958), 5–15 (the quotations are on 5 and 14–15); E. D. Stasova, *Vospominaniia* (Moscow: Mysl', 1969), 135.

19. Podvoiskii, *God 1917*, 16–18.

20. V. I. Lenin, "Zadachi proletariata v dannoi revoliutsii," Revoliutsiia i Grazhdanskaia voina, http://www.rusrevolution.info/docs/index.shtml?1; Exod. 32:9; Deut. 32:29.

21. Podvoiskii, *God 1917*, 20.

22. Voronskii, *Glaz uragana*, 216–21.

23. Deut. 32:48, 31:16.

24. Stasova, *Vospominaniia*, 137–38.

25. Vinogradskaia, *Sobytiia*, 169–70.

26. Sverdlova, *Iakov Mikhailovich Sverdlov*, 223–46; Egon-Besser, "Volia k zhizni," 104–5.

27. Arosev, *Moskovskii sovet*, 8–9, 14–15, 17–18.

28. N. Bukharin, *Na podstupakh k Oktiabriu: Stat'i i rechi mai–dekabr' 1917* (Moscow: Gosizdat, 1926), 25, 28, 33–34.

29. Ibid., 47, 50–51, 132; *Shestoi s"ezd RSDRP (bol'shevikov): Protokoly* (Moscow: Gospolitizdat, 1958), 104, 107–8, 142; Kun, *Bukharin*, 69–70.

30. N. N. Sukhanov, *Zapiski o revoliutsii* (Moscow: Respublika, 1992), 3:267; *Protokoly tsentral'nogo komiteta RSDRP(b), avgust 1917–fevral' 1918* (Moscow: Gospolitizdat, 1958), 83.

31. Sukhanov, *Zapiski o revoliutsii*, 292–93.

32. Ibid., 289–90.

33. Ibid., 260, 299.

34. A. V. Lunacharskii, *Vospominaniia i vpechatleniia* (Moscow: Sovetskaia Rossiia, 1968), 171.

35. Kol'tsov, *Fel'etony i ocherki*, 74–75.

36. Podvoiskii, *God 1917*, 144–46. On the formation of the canonical memory of October (and the evolution of Podvoisky's memories), see Frederick Corney, *Telling October: Memory and the Making of the Bolshevik Revolution* (Ithaca, NY: Cornell University Press, 2004), esp. 90.

37. Trotskii, *Moia zhizn'*, 2:59.

38. Lunacharskii, *Vospominaniia*, 173; G. A. Bordiugov and E. A. Kotelenets, eds., *Revoliutsionnaia Rossiia: 1917 god v pis'makh A. Lunacharskogo i Iu. Martova* (Moscow: AIRO-XXI, 2007), 288–90.

39. Ibid., 289; Arosev, *Kak eto proizoshlo*, 7, 17–18; *Moskva: Oktiabr'. Revoliutsiia. Dokumenty i vospominaniia* (Moscow: Moskovskii rabochii, 1987), 187.

40. Arosev, *Kak eto proizoshlo*, 7.

41. Arosev, *Moskovskii sovet*, 16–17, 23, 27–28.

42. Vinogradskaia, *Sobytiia*, 49; Arosev, *Moskovskii sovet*, 32.

43. Arosev, *Kak eto proizoshlo*, 12.

44. K. V. Ostrovitianov, ed., *Oktiabr' v Zamoskvorech'e* (Moscow: Goslesbumizdat, 1957), 41, 112–20 (quotation on 117).

45. Arosev, *Kak eto proizoshlo*, 14–15.

46. "Aleksandr Iakovlevich Arosev," *Istoriia SSSR* 4 (1967): 116; Chernobaev, *V vikhre veka*, 108.

47. E. Dmitrievskaia and V. Dmitrievskii, *Rakhmaninov v Moskve* (Moscow: Moskovskii rabochii, 1993), 137–39; Oskar von Riesemann, *Rachmaninoff's Recollections* (New York: Macmillan, 1934), 185–87; Martyn, *Rachmaninoff*, 257, 289n66.

48. L. D. Trotskii, *O Lenine* (Moscow: Gosizdat, 1924), 92; V. I. Lenin, *Polnoe sobranie sochinenii* (hereafter *PSS*) (Moscow: Izdatel'stvo politicheskoi literatury, 1967–70), 35:162–66; L. G. Protasov, *Vserossiiskoe uchreditel'noe sobranie: Istoriia rozhdeniia i gibeli* (Moscow: Rosspen, 1997), 263–307; *Uchreditel'noe sobranie: Rossiia 1918: Stenogramma i drugie dokumenty* (Moscow: Nedra, 1991), 54–64.

49. *Uchreditel'noe sobranie*, 68.

50. Lunacharskii, *Vospominaniia*, 214–16; Elizaveta Drabkina, *Chernye sukhari* (Moscow: Sovetskii pisatel', 1963), 97; Vinogradskaia, *Sobytiia*, 176–77.

51. *Uchreditel'noe sobranie*, 70, 87, 89, 91.

52. Protasov, *Vserossiiskoe*, 318–19.

53. Trotskii, *O Lenine*, 106; Mal. 4:1; Lunacharskii, *Vospominaniia*, 214–15.

54. Sverdlova, *Iakov Mikhailovich Sverdlov*, 305.

55. P. Mal'kov, *Zapiski komendanta moskovskogo Kremlia* (Moscow: Molodaia gvardiia, 1961), 52–67 (the quotations are from 52 and 60); Andrew Ezergailis, *The Latvian Impact on the Bolshevik Revolution* (Boulder, CO: East European Mongraphs, distributed by Columbia University Press, 1983). I am grateful to Dace Dzenovska for help with all things Latvian.

56. Mal'kov, *Zapiski* (1961), 104–39; Sverdlova, *Iakov Mikhailovich Sverdlov*, 321–31; B. Z. Stankina, "O rabote sekretariata TsK RKP(b) (aprel' 1918–mart 1919," in *O Iakove Sverdlove*, 165–70; L. A. Fotieva, "Iz vospominanii o Ia. M. Sverdlove," in *O Iakove Sverdlove*, 180–82; Lunacharskii, *Vospominaniia*, 213; Drabkina, *Chernye sukhari*, 162; Trotskii, *Moia zhizn'*, 2:63, 75–78; B. I. Ivanov, "Ia. M. Sverdlov v turukhanskoi ssylke," in *O Iakove Sverdlove*, 115; Vinogradskaia, *Sobytiia*, 171.

57. Drabkina, *Chernye sukhari*, 249; Heinrich Heine, *Deutschland: A Winter's Tale*, trans. T. J. Reed (London: Angel Books, 1997), 31. The German original, recited by Sverdlov, is

    Ein neues Lied, ein besseres Lied,

    O Freunde, will ich euch dichten!

    Wir wollen hier auf Erden schon

    Das Himmelreich errichten.

58. Sverdlova, *Iakov Mikhailovich Sverdlov*, 331–48; S. V. Obolenskaia, interview with author, October 20, 2009.

59. Sverdlova, *Iakov Mikhailovich Sverdlov*, 334; V. Ia. Sverdlova, "Vsegda s tovarishchami," in *O Iakove Sverdlove*, 211–15; M. Parkhomovskii, *Kniga ob udivitel'noi zhizni Eshua Zolomona Movsheva Sverdlova, stavshego Zinoviem Alekseevichem Peshkovym, i neobyknovennykh liudiakh, s kotorymi on vstrechalsia* (Jerusalem: N.p., 1999); Boris Bazhanov, *Vospominaniia byvshego sekretaria Stalina* (Moscow: III tysiacheletie, 2002), 93–99; Evgeniia Sverdlova, "Slovo ob ottse," *Sovetskaia Rossiia*, June 2, 1985, 4; Roi Medvedev, "Slava i tragediia odnoi sem'i," *Karetnyi riad*, November 5, 1985; Zinovy Pechkoff, *La légion étrangère au Maroc* (Paris: Marcelle Lesage éditeur, 1929).

60. Sverdlova, *Iakov Mikhailovich Sverdlov*, 333–34; V. I. Lenin, *State and Revolution*, chap. 4, Marxists Internet Archive Library, http://www.marxists.org/archive/lenin/works/1917/staterev/ch04.htm#s6.

61. V. I. Vorobchenko, *Publitsist-leninets: Revoliutsionno-publitsisticheskaia deiatel'nost' A. K. Voronskogo (1911–1918)* (Kishinev: Shtiintsa, 1986), 112, 131.

62. Ibid., 132–34.

63. Ibid., 115.

64. V. I. Lenin, *State and Revolution*, chap. 3, http://www.marxists.org/archive/lenin/works/1917/staterev/ch03.htm; I. Evsenin, *Ot fabrikanta k Krasnomu Oktiabriu* (Moscow: Izdatel'stvo VTsSPS, 1927), 54.

65. Ibid., 63.

66. Ibid., 63–73. For the general context, see, esp., Silvana Malle, *The Economic Organization of War Communism* (Cambridge: Cambridge University Press, 1985).

67. V. I. Lenin, "K istorii voprosa o neschastnom mire," *PSS*, 35:243–44; Lenin: Revoliutsioner, myslitel', chelovek, http://leninism.su/works/74-tom-35/1610-k-istorii-voprosa-o-neschastnom-mire.html; V. I. Lenin, "Uspekhi i trudnosti Sovetskoi vlasti," *PSS*, 38:55, http://www.leninism.su/works/tom-38/uspexi-i-trudnosti-sovetskoj-vlasti.html; N. Bukharin, E. Preobrazhenskii, *Azbuka kommunizma* (N.p.: Izd. Ob'edinennoĭ kommunisticheskoĭ partii Ameriki, 1921), 49–50.

68. N. Osinskii, *Gosudarstvennoe regulirovanie krest'ianskogo khoziaistva* (Moscow: Gosizdat, 1920), 9–11, 24; N. Bukharin, *Ekonomika perekhodnogo perioda*, in N. I. Bukharin, *Problemy teorii i praktiki sotsializma* (Moscow: Politizdat, 1989), 122.

69. Karl Marx, "Revelations concerning the Communist Trial in Cologne (1853)," Marxists Internet Archive Library, http://www.marxists.org/archive/marx/works/1853/revelations/ch01.htm; Bukharin, *Ekonomika perekhodnogo perioda*, 95; Lenin, "K istorii voprosa o neschastnom mire," *PSS*, 35:243–44, http://www.leninism.su/works/tom-35/k-istorii-voprosa-o-neschastnom-mire.html; V. I. Lenin, "IV Konferentsiia professional'nykh soiuzov i fabrichno–zavodskikh komitetov Moskvy," *PSS*, 36:439, http://www.leninism.su/works/tom-36/iv-konferencziya-professionalnyx-soyuzov-i-fabrichno-zavodskix-komitetov-moskvy.html; V. I. Lenin, "Prorocheskie slova," *PSS*, 36:472–73, http://www.leninism.su/works/tom-36/prorocheskie-slova-36.html; Frederick Engels, "Zur Erinnerung fur die deutschen Mordspatrioten 1806–1807," English trans. in Lenin, *Collected Works*, 27:494–95, Marxists Internet Archive Library, http://www.marxists.org/archive/lenin/works/1918/jun/29b.htm. For violence in Bolshevik thought, see James Ryan, *Lenin's Terror: The Ideological Origins of Early Soviet State Violence* (London: Routledge, 2012).

70. V. I. Lenin, "Ocherednye zadachi Sovetskoi vlasti," 36:196 http://www.leninism.su/works/tom-36/ocherednye-zadachi-sovetskoj-vlasti.html.

71. V. I. Lenin, "Kak organizovat' sorevnovanie," *PSS*, 35:201: http://www.leninism.su/works/tom-35/kak-organizovat-sorevnovanie.html; Lunacharskii, *Vospominaniia*, 216; L. Trotskii, "Pamiati Sverdlova," in *Iakov Mikhailovich Sverdlov: Sbornik vospominanii i statei* (Moscow: Giz, 1926), http://www.magister.msk.ru/library/trotsky/trotm207.htm.

72. Egon-Besser, "Volia k zhizni," 99–106 (the long quotation is on 106).

73. Lunacharskii, *Vospominaniia*, 226.

74. Vinogradskaia, *Sobytiia*, 153–54.

75. Lunacharskii, *Vospominaniia*, 216–17; Lenin, "Kak organizovat' sorevnovanie," 201, 200, 204. See Victoria E. Bonnell, *Iconography of Power: Soviet Political Posters under Lenin and Stalin* (Berkeley: University of California Press, 1998), 187–204, esp. 202–4.

76. Ia. M. Sverdlov, "Rech' na zasedanii VTsIK chetvertogo sozyva, 20 maia 1918 goda," Biografiia.Ru, http://www.biografia.ru/about/sverdlov27.html.

77. Bukharin, *Ekonomika perekhodnogo perioda*, 163.

78. Rev. 18.

79. Quoted in I. F. Plotnikov, *Pravda istorii: Gibel' tsarskoi sem'i* (Ekaterinburg: Za dukhovnost' i nravstvennost', 2003), 238.

80. Ibid., 227.

81. Ibid., 226; Goloshchekin quoted in V. V. Alekseev, *Gibel' tsarskoi sem'i: Mify i real'nost' (novye dokumnty o tragedii na Urale)* (Ekaterinburg: N.p., 1993), 126–27.

82. For photographs and discussion of the inscription, see N. Sokolov, *Ubiistvo tsarskoi sem'i* (Berlin: Slovo, 1925), 171–72 (figs. 53, 54). See also Plotnikov, *Pravda istorii*, 235. For a useful survey of sources, see L. A. Lykova, *Sledstvie po delu ob ubiistve rossiiskoi imperatorskoi sem'i* (Moscow: Rosspen, 2007).

83. Lev Trotskii, *Dnevniki i pis'ma*, ed. Iu. G. Fel'shtinskii (Tenafly, NJ: Hermitage, 1986), 101.

84. Kol'tsov, *Fel'etony i ocherki*, 24–42.

85. Sokolov, *Ubiistvo tsarskoi sem'i*, 192–218 (on the blade, see 216); Alekseev, *Gibel' tsarskoi sem'I*, 139–59; Plotnikov, *Pravda istorii*, 355–73. See also *Sbornik dokumentov, otnosiashchikh-sia k ubiistvu Imperatora Nikolaia II i ego sem'i*, Rus-Sky, http://rus-sky.com/history /library/docs.htm#1–10; and Viktoriia Luk'ianova, *Poslednie angely na zemle*, RoyalLib .com, http://royallib.com/book/lukyanova_viktoriya/poslednie_angeli_na_zemle.html.

5. THE LAST BATTLE

1. Ia. M. Sverdlov, *Izbrannye proizvedeniia* (Moscow: Gospolitizdat, 1957), 3:5–8. The names for the secret police changed over time: Cheka, 1917–22; GPU, 1922–23; OGPU, 1923–34; NKVD, 1934–41.

2. Semion Lyandres, "The 1918 Attempt on the Life of Lenin: A New Look at the Evidence," *Slavic Review* 48, no. 3 (Autumn 1989): 432–48; K. T. Sverdlova, *Iakov Mikhailovich Sverdlov* (Moscow: Molodaia gvardiia, 1985), 372–73; P. Mal'kov, *Zapiski komendanta moskovskogo Kremlia* (Moscow: Molodaia gvardiia, 1961), 159–62 (the "severe" passage is on 160); P. Mal'kov, "Zapiski komendanta Kremlia," *Moskva* 11 (1958): 136. This is the first edition of Mal'kov's memoirs. The other editions do not have the sentence about Sverdlov's apartment.

3. Mal'kov, *Zapiski* (Moscow: Molodaia gvardiia, 1959), 159–60. This episode is only in the 1959 edition. See also Richard Pipes, *The Russian Revolution* (New York: Vintage Books, 1990), 806–9.

4. Mal'kov, *Zapiski* (1961), 162; N. Bukharin, *Ekonomika perekhodnogo perioda*, in N. I. Bukharin, *Problemy teorii i praktiki sotsializma* (Moscow: Politizdat, 1989), 165–66.

5. Peter Holquist, *Making War, Forging Revolution: Russia's Continuum of Crisis, 1914–1921* (Cambridge, MA: Harvard University Press, 2002), 7–11, 174–75, and passim; I. V. Stalin, "K voennomu polozheniiu na iuge," *Sochineniia*, vol. 4 (Moscow: Gospolitizdat, 1946): Biblioteka Gracheva, http://grachev62.narod.ru/stalin/t4/t4_68.htm. The reference is to Anton Denikin and Alexander Kolchak.

6. R. A. Medvedev and S. P. Starikov, *Zhizn' i gibel' Filippa Kuz'micha Mironova* (Moscow: Patriot, 1989), 61 (the Alekseev quotation).

7. *Filipp Mironov: Tikhii Don v 1917–1921 gg.* (Moscow: Demokratiia, 1997), 35–36.

8. Holquist, *Making War*, 143–65.

9. Medvedev and Starikov, *Zhizn' i gibel'*, 112; V. L. Genis, "Raskazachivanie v Sovetskoi Rossii," *Voprosy istorii* 1 (1994): 43.

10. *Filipp Mironov*, 137–38.

11. Holquist, *Making War*, 180–84; Medvedev and Starikov, *Zhizn' i gibel'*, 154–58; *Filipp Mironov*, 145–46.

12. Ibid.; Medvedev and Starikov, *Zhizn' i gibel'*, 158–59 (the Donburo quotation); Aleksandr Kozlov, "Tragediia Donskogo kazachestva v XX v.," *Istoriia Donskogo kraia* 1 (January 20, 2000): http://www.relga.ru/Environ/WebObjects/tgu-www.woa/wa/Main?textid=1881 &level1=main&level2=articles (Yakir quotation).

13. *Filipp Mironov*, 230; Genis, "Raskazachivanie," 45.

14. *Filipp Mironov*, 224.

15. Ibid., 224, 164.

16. Polina Vinogradskaia, *Sobytiia i pamiatnye vstrechi* (Moscow: Politizdat, 1968), 180–87 (the quotation is on 183); Sverdlova, *Iakov Mikhailovich Sverdlov*, 390–95 (the quotation is on 393).

17. V. I. Lenin, "Rech' pamiati Sverdlova na ekstrennom zasedanii VtsIK," in Lenin, *Polnoe sobranie sochinenii* (Moscow: Izdatel'stvo politicheskoi literatury, 1967–70), 38:74–79, Lenin: Revoliutsioner, myslitel', chelovek, http://leninism.su/works/77-tom-38/1302-rech -pamyati-ya-m-sverdlova-na-ekstrennom-zasedanii-vczik.html. The translation is based

on Lenin, *Collected Works*, 29:89–94, Marxists Internet Archive Library, http://www
.marxists.org/archive/lenin/works/1919/mar/18.htm.

18. Ibid.; *Vos'moi s"ezd RKP(b), mart 1919: Protokoly* (Moscow: Politizdat, 1959), 164 (the Osinsky quotation).

19. K. A. Egon-Besser, "Volia k zhizni, k bor'be," in *O Iakove Sverdlove: Vospominaniia, ocherki, stat'i sovremennikov* (Moscow: Izdatel'stvo politicheskoi liteatury, 1985), 106.

20. *Filipp Mironov*, 163, 164–65 (Trotsky quotation); Kozlov, "Tragediia," http://www.relga.ru /Environ/WebObjects/tgu-www.woa/wa/Main?textid=1881&level1=main&level2=articles.

21. *Filipp Mironov*, 165, 185. The translation is based on Holquist, *Making War*, 192.

22. Quoted in Medvedev and Starikov, *Zhizn' i gibel'*, 173.

23. *Filipp Mironov*, 310–11.

24. Ibid., 204–8.

25. Iurii Trifonov, "Otblesk kostra," in *Sobranie sochinenii* (Moscow: Khudozhestvennaia literatura, 1987), 9–73 (the "whirlpool" quotation is on 46); Trifonov, "Iz dnevnikov i rabochikh tetradei," 114; O. Trifonova-Miroshnichenko, "Zhenshchina iz doma na naberezhnoi," *Komsomol'skaia pravda*, July 3, 1988.

26. *Filipp Mironov*, 152 (the quotation from Filipp Mironov), 737, 741–2.

27. Holquist, *Making War*, 193–4; Medvedev and Starikov, *Zhizn' i gibel'*, 174–5, 194–206; *Filipp Mironov*, 210; Genis, "Raskazachivanie," 50; Trifonov, "Otblesk kostra," 111–17.

28. *Filipp Mironov*, 255–71.

29. Ibid., 272, 277, 280–82.

30. Ibid., 294–95.

31. Ibid., 298–99.

32. Ibid., 661.

33. Ibid., 660–66.

34. Ibid., 666.

35. Ibid., 303–4.

36. Ibid., 313–14, 320.

37. *Deiateli SSSR i revoliutsionnogo dvizhenia Rossii* (Moscow: Sovetskaia entsiklopediia, 1989), 675–76; S. N. Burin, "Sud'by bezvestnye," *Nauka i zhizn'* 12 (1989): 57–64; A. P. Nenarokov, "I. T. Smilga," in Nenarokov, ed., *Revvoensovet respubliki* (Moscow: Politizdat, 1991), 350–59; Tat'iana Ivarovna Smilga, interview with author, January 19, 1998.

38. *Filipp Mironov*, 321–22.

39. Medvedev and Starikov, *Zhizn' i gibel'*, 229–36; *Filipp Mironov*, 323–25, 327, 374–75, 382, 390, 392.

40. *Filipp Mironov*, 434.

41. Ibid., 660, 398, 441, 437.

42. Medvedev and Starikov, *Zhizn' i gibel'*, 246–47.

43. *Filipp Mironov*, 415–23.

44. Ibid., 423–27.

45. Ibid., 427–30; Medvedev and Starikov, *Zhizn' i gibel'*, 260.

46. *Filipp Mironov*, 674, 677.

47. Ibid., 433–44, 449.

48. Medvedev and Starikov, *Zhizn' i gibel'*, 271–80.

49. *Filipp Mironov*, 430, 433; Medvedev and Starikov, *Zhizn' i gibel'*, 266.

50. *Filipp Mironov*, 447–52.

51. Ibid., 452, 460, 628, 651; Medvedev and Starikov, *Zhizn' i gibel'*, 289.

52. Bukharin, *Ekonomika perekhodnogo perioda*, 165–66.

53. *Filipp Mironov*, 498, 504, 588–620, 622 ("what I heard . . ."), 651 ("Mass pilgrimages"); Medvedev and Starikov, *Zhizn' i gibel'*, 300–348; V. G. Iashchenko, *Bol'shevistskoe povstanchestvo v Nizhnem Povolzh'e i na Srednem Donu* (Moscow: Librokom, 2008), 31–46.

54. Medvedev and Starikov, *Zhizn' i gibel'*, 348; *Filipp Mironov*, 640–49.

55. Medvedev and Starikov, *Zhizn' i gibel'*, 360; *Filipp Mironov*, 657–59, 681–84, 734.

6. THE NEW CITY

1. Edward Gibbon, *The History of the Decline and Fall of the Roman Empire* (Philadelphia: Claxton, Remsen and Haffelfinger, 1875), 1:34, http://books.google.com/books?id=V6ELAA AAYAAJ&pg=PA34&lpg=PA34&dq=gibbon+decline+and+fall+were+all+considered+by+the +people+as+equally+true&source=bl&ots=xwI3DNxAX2&sig=gRuocgkDTtV77tk8zliBIv -Da-Y&hl=en&ei=njw_TPrdC4boswOnvuX1CA&sa=X&oi=book_result&ct=result&resnum =11&ved=0CDwQ6AEwCg#v=onepage&q&f=false; Guenter Lewy, *Religion and Revolution* (New York: Oxford University Press, 1974), 23.

2. Cf. Max Weber, *Economy and Society* (Berkeley: University of California Press, 1978), 1:216, 241; Edward Shils, *Center and Periphery* (Chicago: University of Chicago Press, 1975), 256–75; Gianfranco Poggi, *Forms of Power* (Cambridge: Polity, 2001), 89.

3. For "hierocracies," see Weber, *Economy and Society*, 2:1159–63.

4. See, in particular, Gerald M. Easter, *Reconstructing the State: Personal Networks and Elite Identity in Soviet Russia* (Cambridge: Cambridge University Press, 2000).

5. Andrei Platonov, *Gorod Gradov*, EMSU, http://emsu.ru/lm/cc/platonov.htm.

6. RGASPI, f. 124, op. 1, dd. 1429, 1919, 745, 484; Reginald E. Zelnik, "The Fate of a Russian Bebel: Semen Ivanovich Kanatchikov, 1905–1940," *Carl Beck Papers in Russian and East European Studies* 1105 (August 1995). See also *Bol'shaia sovetskaia entsiklopediia* and K. A. Zalesskii, *Imperiia Stalina* (Moscow: Veche, 2000).

7. E. A. Dinershtein, *A. K. Voronskii v poiskakh zhivoi vody* (Moscow: Rosspen 2001), 41–94.

8. A. Voronskii, *Literaturnye portrety* (Moscow: Federatsiia, 1929), 239; *Deiateli SSSR i revo-liutsionnogo dvizhenia Rossii* (Moscow: Sovetskaia entsiklopediia, 1989), 355–56; RGASPI, f. 124. op. 1, dd. 80, 1582, 1526; A. P. Nenarokov, ed., *Revvoensovet respubliki* (Moscow: Politiz-dat, 1991), 318–25, 276–96 (the "iron hand" quotation, taken from from Podvoisky's December 7, 1918, letter to Lenin, is from 285); Dinershtein, *A. K. Voronskii*, 44. See also Zalesskii, *Imperiia Stalina*.

9. Nenarokov, *Revvoensovet respubliki*, 356–59; RGASPI, f. 124, op. 1, d. 1946; op. 2, d. 345; Nicolas Werth, "A State against Its People: Violence, Repression, and Terror in the Soviet Union," in Stéphane Courtois et al., eds., *Black Book of Communism* (Cambridge, MA: Harvard University Press, 1999), 100.

10. *Deiateli SSSR i revoliutsionnogo dvizhenia Rossii* (Moscow: Sovetskaia entsiklopediia, 1989), 573, 439, 374 (quotation); RGASPI, f. 124, op. 1, d. 854, ll. 3–4.

11. P. Mal'kov, *Zapiski komendanta moskovskogo Kremlia* (Moscow: Molodaia gvardiia, 1961), 118–36 (the quotation is on 136); A. Ia. Arosev, *Belaia lestnitsa* (Moscow: Sovremennik, 1989), 414, 416.

12. Mal'kov, *Zapiski* (1961), 121–22 (see also K. T. Sverdlova, *Iakov Mikhailovich Sverdlov* [Moscow: Molodaia gvardiia, 1985], 337–40); Arosev, *Belaia lestnitsa*, 376–79.

13. GARF, f. 551, op. 1, d. 39, ll. 59–108.

14. See, e.g., GARF, f. 551, op. 1, 8, 17, 20, 28, 39, 43, 46, 48, 81–84, 101; and GARF, f. 1235, op. 70, d. 13; op. 133, dd. 10, 174, 175, 215, 375, 420. The quotations are from GARF, f. 551, op. 1, d. 83, l. 2; d. 101, ll. 149–1490b. and l. 139; d. 84, ll. 1–30b.

15. GARF, f. 551, op. 1, d. 1, l. 7; d. 17, l. 42; d. 50, ll. 4, 10–20.

16. GARF, f. 551, op. 1, d. 39, l. 75; d. 48, l. 139; d. 67, ll. 1, 25–26, 256; d. 48, ll. 33, 74, 93–100; f.1235, op. 72, d. 63, ll. 7–8.

17. GARF, f. 551, op. 1, d. 20, l. 6.

18. GARF, f. 551, op. 1, d. 39, ll. 68, 67; d. 20, l. 2; d. 48, l. 139.

19. GARF, f. 551, op. 1, d. 3, d. 39, ll. 76, 95; GARF, f. 1235 op. 133, dd. 7; 10; 185, l. 14; 187; 194, l. 184; 197.

20. GARF, f. 1235, op. 133, d. 181; AOM, f. 2, op. 3. d. 14 (Irina Kalistratovna Gogua), ll. 39–40.
21. GARF, f. 551, op. 1, dd. 22a, 48, 55; f. 1235, op. 133, d. 10, l. 35; f. 9542, op. 1, d. 5, l. 2.
22. GARF, f. 1235, op. 133, d. 10; f. 5446, op. 55, d. 794; f. 336, op. 21, d. 711; f. 9542, op. 7, d. 3, ll. 1050b–106.
23. RGASPI, f. 559, op. 1, d. 132, ll. 10–14.
24. V. Kerzhentsev, *Tvorcheskii teatr: Puti sotsialisticheskogo teatra* (Moscow: Kniga, 1918), 44, 80–82.
25. Ibid., 56.
26. V. V. Maiakovskii, *Misteriia-Buff*, Klassika, http://az.lib.ru/m/majakowskij_w_w/text_0190.shtml.
27. K. Lander, *Nasha teatral'naia politika* (Moscow: Gosizdat, 1921), 9–10; A. Voronskii, *Literaturnye tipy* (Moscow: Krug, n.d.), 17–20, 38.
28. Aleksandr Malyshkin, *Padenie Daira*, Magister, http://www.magister.msk.ru/library/prose/malya001.htm; Rev. 18:3,13; Vsevolod Ivanov, "Bronepoezd No. 14.69," Lib.ru, http://lib.ru/IWANOWWS/bronepoezd.txt.
29. Iurii Libedinskii, *Nedelia. Komissary* (Moscow: Voenizdat, 1968), 8–9.
30. Platonov, *Gorod Gradov*.
31. Isaak Babel', *Sochineniia* (Moscow: Khudozhestvennaia literatura, 1992), 2:43, 101, 70; Boris Pil'niak, *Golyi god*, Biblioteka Aleksandra Belousenko, http://www.belousenko.com/books/Pilnyak/pilnyak_golyj_god.htm; Libedinskii, *Nedelia*, 71.
32. Rev. 18:7.
33. Malyshkin, *Padenie Daira*.
34. Vsevolod Ivanov, *Tsvetnye vetra*, in *Sopki* (Moscow: Gosizdat, 1927), 300–309.
35. Rev. 19:11–13; Boris Lavrenev, *Sorok pervyi*, Lib.ru, http://lib.ru/RUSSLIT/LAWRENEW/41.txt
36. Pil'niak, *Golyi god*.
37. A. Arosev, *Zapiski Terentiia Zabytogo* (Berlin: Russkoe tvorchestvo, 1922), 102–4; A. Voronskii, *Iskusstvo videt' mir* (Moscow: Sovetskii pisatel', 1987), 211–12 (the article "Vsevolod Ivanov" was originally published in 1922).
38. M. M. Bakhtin, *Epos i roman (O metodologii issledovaniia romana)*, Biblioteka Gumer, http://www.gumer.info/bibliotek_Buks/Literat/bahtin/epos_roman.php; Andrei Platonov, *Chevengur*, Infolio, http://www.infoliolib.info/rlit/platonov/chewengur1.html.
39. Based on a still-unfinished translation of *Chevengur* by Robert and Elizabeth Chandler and Olga Meerson. Courtesy of Robert Chandler.
40. Ibid.
41. Isaak Babel', *Sochineniia*, 2:34.
42. Ibid., 2:69.
43. Voronsky, *Literaturnye tipy*, 110–15; *Pervyi vsesoiuznyi s"ezd sovetskikh pisatelei 1934: Stenograficheskii otchet* (Moscow: Khudozhestvennaia literatura, 1934), 279.
44. Dm. Furmanov, *Chapaev*, Lib.ru, http://lib.ru/RUSSLIT/FURMANOW/chapaew.txt.
45. Libedinskii, *Nedelia*, 70.
46. Malyshkin, *Padenie Daira*.
47. Furmanov, *Chapaev*; Malyshkin, *Padenie Daira*; Ivanov, *Tsvetnye vetra*, 326; A. Fadeev, *Razgrom*, translation based on A. Fadeev, *The Rout* (Moscow: Foreign Languages Publishing House, n.d.), 207–8.
48. Platonov, *Chevengur*.
49. Ivanov, "Bronepoezd No. 14.69"; Malyshkin, *Padenie Daira*; Leonid Leonov, *Petushikhinskii prolom*, Leonid Leonov.ru, http://www.leonid-leonov.ru/files/petushihinskiy.txt; Voronsky, *Literaturnye tipy*, 184–85, 189.
50. Ivanov, *Tsvetnye vetra*, 267. For the pioneering interpretation of the master plot of Bolshevik literature, see Katerina Clark, *The Soviet Novel: History as Ritual* (Chicago: University of Chicago Press, 1985).

51. Furmanov, *Chapaev.*

52. Babel', *Sochineniia,* 2:252.

53. Lev Lunts, "V pustyne," Klassika, http://az.lib.ru/l/lunc_l_n/text_0010.shtml.

54. A. S. Serafimovich, *Sobranie sochinenii* (Moscow: Khudozhestvennaia literatura, 1959), 6:191; V. Chalmaev, *Aleksandr Serafimovich* (Volgograd: Nizhne-Volzhskoe knizhnoe izdatel'stvo, 1986), 241–45; A. Volkov, *Tvorcheskii put' A. S. Serafimovicha* (Moscow: Khudozhestvennaia literatura, 1963), passim; N. I. Sats, *Novelly moei zhizni* (Moscow: Iskusstvo, 1984), 1:100– 106; Ol'ga Garbuz, "V shestnadtsat' mal'chisheskikh let," *Sovetskaia Rossiia* 142 (12753), October 27, 2005.

55. The translations below are based on A. Serafimovich, *The Iron Flood,* trans. Ovid Gorchakov (Westport, CT: Hyperion Press, 1973; reprint of the Moscow Progress Publishers edition, 1957), 5, 8.

56. Ibid., 16–18, 54–55.

57. Ibid., 56.

58. Ibid., 153, 40–41, 102, 140, 100, 139.

59. Ibid., 155–56.

60. Ibid., 108, 112, 164.

61. Ibid., 117, 127–28.

62. Ibid., 170.

63. Ibid., 167.

64. Ibid., 206–7, 209.

65. ARAN, f. 528, op. 2, d. 1, ll. 1–2, 16–19; Saul Borovoi, *Vospominaniia* (Moscow: Gesharim, 1993), 46–53. People's Will was a terrorist revolutionary organization responsible for the assassination of Tsar Alexander II.

66. L. Kritsman, *Geroicheskii period Velikoi russkoi revoliutsii (opyt analiza t.n. "voennogo kommunizma")* (Moscow: Gosizdat, 1924), 10–11, 75.

67. Ibid., 77–83, 85–87.

68. Ibid., 59, 61, 64, 127, 43, 227.

69. Ibid., 228, 249–50.

70. Karl Radek, *Portrety i pamflety* (Moscow: Sovetskaia literatura, 1933), 1:36; on Lenin iconography, see Victoria E. Bonnell, *Iconography of Power: Soviet Political Posters under Lenin and Stalin* (Berkeley: University of California Press, 1998), 139–52.

71. Bor. Volin and Mikh. Kol'tsov, eds., *Umer Lenin* (Moscow: Mospoligraf, 1924), 7, 21.

72. Ibid., 7, 21; Mikhail Kol'tsov, *Fel'etony i ocherki* (Moscow: Pravda, 1956), 200–201.

73. Volin and Kol'tsov, *Umer Lenin,* 22; N. Osinskii, "Risunok perom,'" in *Lenin,* comp. V. Krainii and M. Bespalov, ed. D. Lebed' (Kharkov: Molodoi rabochii, 1924), 43; Kol'tsov, *Fel'etony i ocherki,* 199. For a discussion of this synthesis, see Alexei Yurchak, "Bodies of Lenin: The Hidden Science of Communist Sovereignty," *Representations* 129 (Winter 2015): 116–57.

74. Volin and Kol'tsov, *Umer Lenin,* 7–8.

75. Ibid., 8; A. Arosev, *Po sledam Lenina* (Leningrad: Gosizdat, 1924), 39, 42.

76. Kol'tsov, *Fel'etony i ocherki,* 207.

77. Volin and Kol'tsov, *Umer Lenin,* 21.

78. Kol'tsov, *Fel'etony i ocherki,* 201–3.

79. Quoted in M. Ol'minskii, "Lenin ili ne Lenin," *Proletarskaia revoliutsiia* 1 (1931): 149–50; Nina Tumarkin, *Lenin Lives! The Lenin Cult in Soviet Russia* (Cambridge, MA: Harvard University Press, 1983), 136–64, 181; Iu. M. Lopukhin, *Bolezn', smert' i bal'zamirovanie V. I. Lenina: Pravda i mify* (Moscow: Respublika, 1997), 63–68; B. I. Zbarskii, *Mavzolei Lenina* (Leningrad: OGIZ, 1945), 26–32; Timothy Edward O'Connor, *The Engineer of Revolution: L. B. Krasin and the Bolsheviks, 1870–1926* (Boulder, CO: Westview Press, 1992), 58–113; 144–47; 277–81; I. B. Zbarskii, "Ot Rossii do Rossii," in *Pod kryshei Mavzoleiia* (Tver: Polina, 1998), 191–3; Iu. G. Fel'shtinskii, *Vozhd v zakone* (Moscow, Terra, 1999), chap. 1, Lib.ru, http://www.lib.ru/POLI-

TOLOG/felshtinskij.txt. On the idea of immortality, see Nikolai Krementsov, *Revolutionary Experiments: The Quest for Immortality in Bolshevik Science and Fiction* (New York: Oxford University Press, 2013). On Lenin's embalming and its meanings, see Yurchak, "Bodies of Lenin" (for Krasin's plan, see 125).

80. Lopukhin, *Bolezn'*, 67–88; Zbarskii, "Ot Rossii do Rossii," 191–222, 9–27; Il'ia Zbarskii, *Ob"ekt No. 1* (Moscow: Vagrius, 2000), 44–57.

81. Zbarskii, *Mavzolei Lenina*, 43–44.

82. Lopukhin, *Bolezn'*, 92–109; Zbarskii, *Ob"ekt No. 1*, 80–95.

83. A. Chernobaev, *V vikhre veka* (Moscow: Moskovskii rabochii, 1987), 135–47; A. Arosev, *O Vladimire Il'iche* (Moscow: Priboi, 1926), 5–7.

84. A. Arosev, *O Vladimire Il'iche*, 8–13.

85. Ibid., 19–23.

86. Ibid., 24–31. This passage is taken from Lenin, "Zamechaniia na vtoroi proekt programmy Plekhanova," in Lenin, *Polnoe sobranie sochinenii* (Moscow: Izdatel'stvo politicheskoi literatury, 1967–70), vol. 6:231, Lenin: Revoliutsioner, myslitel', chelovek, http://leninism.su /index.php?option=com_content&view=article&id=753:materialy-k-vyrabotke-programmy-rsdrp&catid=44:tom-6&Itemid=53#.Do.97.Do.9o.Do.9C.Do.95.Do.A7.Do.9o.Do.9D .Do.98.Do.AF_.Do.9D.Do.9o_.Do.92.Do.A2.Do.9E.Do.Ao.Do.9E.Do.99_.Do.9F.Do.Ao.Do.9E .Do.95.Do.9A.Do.A2_.Do.9F.Do.Ao.Do.9E.Do.93.Do.Ao.Do.9o.Do.9C.Do.9C.Do.AB_.Do.9F .Do.9B.Do.95.Do.A5.Do.9o.Do.9D.Do.9E.Do.92.Do.9o. The translation is a modified version of "Notes on Plekhanov's Second Draft Version," in Lenin, *Collected Works*, vol. 6, Marxists Internet Archive Library, http://www.marxists.org/archive/lenin/works/1902/draft/04mar07 .htm#fwV06P053F01. The phrase "there is no point in wasting words where the use of power is required" comes from I. A. Krylov's fable "A Cat and a Cook."

87. Rev. 14:14–16.

88. Vladimir Vladimirovih Maiakovskii, *Poemy*, Vladimir Vladimirovich Mayakovsky, http:// www.mayakovsky.velchel.ru/index.php?cnt=7&sub=3&page=14.

89. *Mariia Denisova-Shchadenko, skul'ptor* (Moscow: Gosudarstvennyi muzei V. V. Maiakovskogo, 2000); Natal'ia Dardykina, "Dzhiokonda, kotoruiu ukrali," *Moskovskii komsomolets* 21608 (January 22, 2001).

7. THE GREAT DISAPPOINTMENT

1. RGASPI, f. 124, op. 1, d. 1429, l. 41.

2. Ronald L. Numbers and Jonathan M. Butler, eds., *The Disappointed: Millerism and Millenarianism in the Nineteenth Century* (Bloomington: Indiana University Press, 1987), 215; J. B. Peires, *The Dead Will Arise: Nongqawuse and the Great Xhosa Cattle-Killing Movement of 1856–7* (Johannesburg: Ravan, 1989), 158.

3. The translations are from the *The Portable Platonov: Andrey Platonov, 1899–1999*, comp. and intro. Robert Chandler, trans. Robert and Elisabeth Chandler, with Nadya Bourova, Angela Livingstone, David Macphail and Eric Naiman (Moscow: Glas, 1999), 79–80.

4. G. A. Voronskaia, "Esli v serdtse posylaiut puliu," *Istoricheskii arkhiv* 1 (1997): 80; T. I. Smilga-Poluian, interview with author, January 19, 1998; Natal'ia Aroseva, *Sled na zemle: Dokumental'naia povest' ob ottse* (Moscow: Politizdat, 1987), 147; Olga Nikolaevna Podvoiskaia, interview with author, February 27, 1998; RGASPI, f. 124, op. 1, d. 1429, l. 400b.; V. E. Baranchenko, *Stoikost', neutomimost', otvaga* (Moscow: Moskovskii rabochii, 1988), 47; ARAN, f. 528, op. 2, l. 4; A. M. Larina, *Nezabyvaemoe* (Moscow: APN, 1989), 104.

5. GARF, f. 9542, op. 7, d. 3, ll. 45–46, 104. On the history of Soviet sanatoria and rest homes, see Diane P. Koenker, *Club Red: Vacation Travel and the Soviet Dream* (Ithaca, NY: Cornell University Press, 2013); on the epidemic of nervousness, see Frances L. Bernstein, "Panic, Potency, and the Crisis of Nervousness in the 1920s," in Christina Kiaer and Eric Naiman, eds., *Everyday Life in Early Soviet Russia: Taking the Revolution Inside* (Bloomington: Indi-

ana University Press, 2006), 153–82; and Eric Naiman, *Sex in Public: The Incarnation of Early Soviet Ideology* (Princeton, NJ: Princeton University Press, 1997).

6. GARF, f. 9542, op. 1, d. 11, l. 3.

7. RGASPI, f. 124, op. 1, d. 1308, l. 20.

8. RGASPI, f. 124, op. 1, d. 745, l. 19.

9. RGASPI, f. 124, op. 1, d. 1429, ll. 40–400b.

10. Ibid., ll. 47–61.

11. *Portable Platonov*, 64; A. A. Sol'ts, "O partetike," in *Partiinaia etika: Dokumenty i materialy diskussii 20-kh godov* (Moscow: Politizdat, 1989), 279–80.

12. RGALI, f. 457, d. 225, l. 3 ob.

13. V. I. Lenin, "Kak organizovat' sorevnovanie," 200, and "Detskaia bolezn' levizny v kommunizme," Lenin: Revoliutsioner, myslitel', chelovek, http://leninism.su/index.php ?option=com_content&view=article&id=1189:detskaya-bolezn-levizny-v-kommunizme &catid=80:tom-41&Itemid=53, translation based on Marxists Internet Archive Library, http://www.marxists.org/archive/lenin/works/1920/lwc/cho2.htm.

14. GARF. f. 1235, op. 133, d. 477, l. 257; GARF, f. 551, op. 1, d. 48, l. 82; GARF, f. 155, op. 1, d. 101, l. 62; GARF, f. 9542, op. 1, d. 9, l. 9; GARF, f. 1235, op. 133, d. 477, l. 180; RGASPI, f. 613, op. 4, d. 51, ll. 13–30.

15. GARF, f. 551, op. 1, d. 48, l. 7; GARF, f. 1235 op. 133, d. 477, ll. 180 (the long quotation), 251–52; GARF, f. 551, op. 1, d. 48, l. 82; d. 50. ll. 4, 15, 20, 158; GARF, f. 551, op. 1, d. 82, l. 1 ob., 5; GARF, f. 9542, op. 1, d. 11, l. 7.

16. GARF, f. 551, op. 1, d. 57, ll. 10–100b.; RGASPI, f. 613, op. 4, d. 51, l. 39 (the "retired wives" quotation).

17. N. Bukharin, *Kommunisticheskoe vospitanie molodezhi* (Moscow: Molodaia gvardiia, 1925), 54–57; V. I. Lenin, "Zadachi soiuzov molodezhi," in Lenin, *Polnoe sobranie sochinenii* (hereafter *PSS*) (Moscow: Izdatel'stvo politicheskoi literatury, 1967–70), 41:309–11, Lenin: Revoliutsioner, myslitel', chelovek, http://leninism.su/index.php?option=com_content&view= article&id=1218:zadachi-soyuzov-molodezhi&catid=80:tom-41&Itemid=53; translation in Marxists Internet Archive Library, http://www.marxists.org/archive/lenin/works/1920 /oct/02.htm. For an overview, see David L. Hoffmann, *Stalinist Values: The Cultural Norms of Soviet Modernity, 1917–1941* (Ithaca, NY: Cornell University Press, 2003).

18. A. A. Sol'ts, "O partiinoi etike," in *Partiinaia etika*, 260, 261.

19. "Proekt predlozhenii prezidiuma TsKK II plenumu TsKK RKP(b), 1924," in *Partiinaia etika*, 154; Sol'ts, "O partetike," 277.

20. Sol'ts, "O partiinoi etike," 264–65.

21. Iudit Agracheva, "Chlen partii s 1903 g.," *Vesti* (Israel), June 1, 1995, 10; AMDNN, "Brandenburgsky" file.

22. Ia. N. Brandenburgskii, *Brak i ego pravovye posledstviia* (Moscow: Iuridicheskoe izdatel'stvo, 1926), 7–10; Brandenburgskii, *Brak i sem'ia* (Moscow: Iuridicheskoe izdatel-stvo, 1926), 5.

23. Ia. N. Brandenburgskii, A. Sol'ts, N. Krylenko, S. Prushitskii, *Sem'ia i novyi byt* (Moscow; Gosudarstvennoe izdatel'stvo, 1926), 20; Brandenburgskii, *Brak i sem'ia*, 19. For debates about the 1926 family code, see Wendy Z. Goldman, *Women, the State, and Revolution: Soviet Famly Policy and Social Life, 1917–1936* (Cambridge: Cambridge University Press, 1993), 185–253.

24. Sol'ts, "O partiinoi etike," 263; Sol'ts, "O partetike," 286; Brandenburgskii, *Brak i ego pravovye posledstviia*, 5.

25. Sol'ts, "O partiinoi etike," 263.

26. See, esp., E. M. Iaroslavskii, "O partetike: Doklad na II plenume TsKK RKP(b), October 5, 1924," in *Partiinaia etika*, 170–219.

27. Bukharin, *Kommunisticheskoe vospitanie molodezhi*, 43; L. Trotskii, *Voprosy byta: Epokha "kul'turnichestva" i ee zadachi* (Moscow: Gosizdat, 1926), 47–63. See also Richard Stites, *Revolutionary Dreams: Utopian Vision and Experimental Life in the Russian Revolution* (New

York: Oxford University Press, 1989), 109–23 and passim; and, esp., Victoria Smolkin, *A Sacred Space Is Never Empty: A History of Soviet Atheism* (Princeton, NJ: Princeton University Press, 2018).

28. Trotskii, *Voprosy byta*, 47–63.
29. Mikhail Kol'tsov, *Fel'etony i ocherki* (Moscow: Pravda, 1956), 105–7.
30. Boris Efimov, *Desiat' desiatiletii* (Moscow: Vagrius, 2000), 39, 52; Boris Efimov, interview with author, October 16, 1997; *Mikhail Kol'tsov, kakim on byl: Sbornik vospominanii* (Moscow: Sovetskii pisatel', 1989), 141, 144; Boris Medovoi, *Mikhail i Mariia* (Moscow: Izdatel'stvo politicheskoi literatury, 1991), 57–58; GARF, f. 9542, op. 1, d. 111, ll. 42–48.
31. *Mikhail Kol'tsov*, 136–38, 144–45, and passim; N. I. Sats, *Novelly moei zhizni* (Moscow: Iskusstvo, 1984), 1:170, 181.
32. Mikhail Kol'tsov, *Izbrannye sochineniia v trekh tomakh* (Moscow: Khudozhestvennaia literatura, 1957), 1:193–203; Sats, *Novelly*, 1:108–9, 207–13, 310–14, 362–75 and passim.
33. *Mikhail Kol'tsov*, 205; E. B. Levina, interview with author, September 27, 1998; *Eva Pavlovna Levina-Rozengol'ts, 1898–1975, sbornik materialov* (Moscow: Gosudarstvennaia Tret'iakovskaia galereia, 1996); *Eva Pavlovna Levina-Rozengol'ts, zhivopis' i grafika* (Moscow: Galart, 2006).
34. Efimov, *Desiat' desiatiletii*, 55, 179, 244, 614–25; Roi Medvedev, "Slava i tragediia odnoi sem'i," *Karetnyi riad* 5 (November 1985).
35. Elena Andreevna Sverdlova, interview with author, February 26, 1998; Olga Nikolaevna Podvoiskaia, interview with author, February, 27, 1998; Milena Alekseevna Lozovskaia, interview with author, March 4, 1998 ("Aleksei" was Solomon Lozovsky's Party pseudonym); N. V. Petrov and K. V. Skorkin, eds., *Kto rukovodil NKVD 1934–1941: Spravochnik* (Moscow: Zven'ia, 1999), 93–94; Iurii Doikov, "Mikhail Kedrov i Revekka Plastinina," *Vazhskaia oblast'* 8 (September 8, 1992).
36. N. Efimov, *Tovarishch Nina* (Iaroslavl': Verkhne-Volzhskoe knizhnoe izdatel'stvo, 1969), 62, 115, 110, 111; Olga Nikolaevna Podvoiskaia, interview with author, February 27, 1998.
37. Efimov, *Tovarishch Nina*, 61, 64.
38. Ibid., 112.
39. N. Podvoiskii, *Smychka s solntsem* (Leningrad: Gosizdat, 1925); N. Stepanov, *Podvoiskii* (Moscow: Molodaia gvardiia, 1989), 319–41. For a history of Soviet hygiene, see Tricia Starks, *Body Soviet: Propaganda, Hygiene, and the Revolutionary State* (Madison: University of Wisconsin Press, 2008).
40. Iurii Trifonov, *Sobranie sochinenii* (Moscow: Khudozhestvennaia literatura, 1986), 3:516–18, translation from Yuri Trifonov, *The Old Man* (New York: Simon and Schuster, 1980); RGASPI, f. 124, op. 1, d. 1526, ll. 4–8.
41. Trifonov, *Sobranie sochinenii*, 4:99; Iurii Trifonov, *Ischeznovenie*, RoyalLib.com, http://royallib.ru/read/trifonov_yuriy/ischeznovenie.html#0; A. Shitov, *Iurii Trifonov: Khronika zhizni i tvorchestva* (Ekateringurg: Izdatel'stvo Ural'skogo universiteta, 1997), 72 and passim; O. R. Trifonova-Miroshnichenko, "Zhenshchina iz Doma na naberezhnoi," *Moskovskaia pravda*, June 3, 1988.
42. Trifonov, *Sobranie sochinenii*, 4:21; E. I. Zelenskaia, "A. A. Sol'ts," unpublished manuscript in AMDNN, "Solts" file. See also Trifonov, *Ischeznovenie*, http://royallib.ru/read/trifonov_yuriy/ischeznovenie.html#0.
43. *Mikhail Kol'tsov*, 142; Sol'ts, "O partetike," 286–87.
44. Natal'ia Aroseva, *Sled na zemle*, 78–9, 140–41, 148, 177–79, 184–86, 194–95, 199–200, 225–26; Ol'ga Aroseva, *Bez grima* (Moscow: Tsentrpoligraf, 1999), 7–8, 13–15, 20–21, 93–94; A. Chernobaev, *V vikhre veka* (Moscow: Moskovskii rabochii, 1987), 124–25.
45. V. I. Piatnitskii, comp., *Golgofa* (St. Petersburg: Palitra, 1993), 6–10; V. I. Piatnitskii, *Osip Piatnitskii i Koimintern na vesakh istorii* (Minsk: Kharvest, 2004), 58–63; Mark Grossman, *Da sviatitsia imia tvoe!* (Cheliabinsk: Iuzhno-Ural'skoe knizhnoe izdatel'stvo, 1983), 442–62.

46. Il'ia Zbarskii, *Ob"ekt No. 1* (Moscow: Vagrius, 2000), 10–11, 20, 24–26, 36–38; Anatolii Korolev, "Vsevolodo-Vil'va na perekrestke russkoi kul'tury," *Znamia* 11 (2009): http://magazines .russ.ru/znamia/2009/11/ko29.html; Il'ia Borisovich Zbarskii, interview with author, March 10, 1998; Viktor Borisovich Zbarskii, interview with author, March 22, 1998.

47. Warren Lerner, *Karl Radek: The Last Internationalist* (Stanford, CA: Stanford University Press, 1970), 4.

48. Angelica Balabanoff, *My Life as a Rebel* (New York: Harper and Brothers, 1938), 167, 246–47.

49. Lerner, *Karl Radek*, 17–19, 23–28, 47–48, 60, 69–71, 97, 127–28, 132, and passim (Fischer is quoted in Lerner); Jean-François Fayet, *Karl Radek (1885–1939)* (Bern: Peter Lang, 2004), 11–477, passim; El'mar Giseinov and Vladlen Sirotkin, "Litso i maski Karla Radeka," in *Arkhivy raskryvaiut tainy . . . Mezhdunarodnye voprosy: Sobytiia i liudi* (Moscow: Politizdat, 1991), 343–48; V. A. Artemov, *Karl Radek: Ideiia i sud'ba* (Voronezh: TsChKI, 2000); V. A. Torchinov and A. M. Leontiuk, *Vokrug Stalina: Istoriko-biograficheskii spravochnik* (St. Petersburg: Filologicheskii fakul'tet Sankt-Peterburgskogo gosudarstvennogo universiteta, 2000), 392–94.

50. Mandelstam, Koltsov, Roshal, and Libedinsky quoted in Galina Przhiborovskaia, *Larisa Reisner* (Moscow: Molodaia gvardiia, 2008), 95, 205, 412, 87, 414; Lev Trotskii, *Moia zhizn': Opyt avtobiografii* (Berlin: Granit, 1930), 2:140; Vadim Andreev, *Detstvo* (Moscow: Sovetskii pisatel', 1966), 70–71.

51. Przhiborovskaia, *Larisa Reisner*, 155, 165, 247, 258, 261, 293, and passim; Elizaveta Drabkina, *Chernye sukhari* (Moscow: Sovetskii pisatel', 1963), 213.

52. Andreev, *Detstvo*, 70; Alla Zeride, "Myth as Justification for Life," *Russian Review* 51, no. 2 (April 1992): 172–87.

53. A. Voronskii, *Iskusstvo videt' mir* (Moscow: Sovetskii pisatel', 1987), 332–33.

54. Karl Radek, *Portrety i pamflety* (Moscow: Sovetskaia literatura, 1933), 1:66, 69.

55. Przhiborovskaia, *Larisa Reisner*, 410–77; Feliks Medvedev, "Sof'ia Radek o svoem ottse i o sebe," *Ogonek* 52 (1988): 28–31; Trotskii, *Moia zhizn'*, 2:139.

56. Przhiborovskaia, *Larisa Reisner*, 471–75.

57. Il'ia Erenburg, *Liudi, gody, zhizn'* (Moscow, Sovetskii pisatel', 1990), 1:73; Svetlana Allilueva, *Dvadtsat' pisem k drugu* (Moscow: Zakharov, 2000), 33, translation based on Svetlana Allilueva, *Twenty Letters to a Friend* (New York: Harper and Row, 1967), 31; Larina, *Nezabyvaemoe*, 211.

58. Larina, *Nezabyvaemoe*, 211–12.

59. Miklosh Kun, *Bukharin, ego druz'ia i vragi* (Moscow: Respublika, 1992), 28–29; Larina, *Nezabyvaemoe*, 119–21; Svetlana Gurvich-Bukharina, interview with author, May 1, 1998; Paul R. Gregory, *Politics, Murder, and Love in Stalin's Kremlin: The Story of Nikolai Bukharin and Anna Larina* (Stanford, CA: Hoover Institution Press, 2010), 4, 16–17, 58–60.

60. "No ia to znaiu, chto ia prav," *Istochnik* 3 (2000): 49–50.

61. The English translation is from Knut Hamsun, *Victoria*, trans. Oliver Stallybras (New York: Farrar, Straus and Giroux, 1969), 35–37.

62. Ibid., 152–55; Larina, *Nezabyvaemoe*, 80–86, 106–7.

63. Larina, *Nezabyvaemoe*, 112–27, 221–23.

64. Ibid., 125–27, 119–20.

65. ARAN, razriad 5, op. 1-o, d. 11, l. 28 ob.; cf. Hamsun, *Victoria*, 78.

66. ARAN, razriad 5, op. 1-o, d. 11, l. 23–24ob. (the long quotation is on ll. 24–24ob.); *Deiateli SSSR i revoliutsionnogo dvizhenia Rossii* (Moscow: Sovetskaia entsiklopediia, 1989), 572–73; S. V. Obolenskaia, interview with author, October 20, 2009.

67. S. V. Obolenskaia, interview with author, October 20, 2009.

68. Obolenskaia, *Iz vospominanii*, "Samizdat," http://zhurnal.lib.ru/o/obolenskaja_s_w/o1 .shtml; ARAN, razriad 5, op. 1-o, d. 11, l. 28ob.

69. Obolenskaia, *Iz vospominanii*, http://zhurnal.lib.ru/o/obolenskaja_s_w/o1.shtml; S. V. Obo-

lenskaia, interview with author, October 20, 2009; ARAN, razriad 5, op. 1-o, d. 11, ll. 39–390b. and passim.

70. RGVA, f. 37461, op. 1, d. 128. ll. 32–330b.

71. Ibid., ll. 58–640b.

72. Natal'ia Dardykina, "Dzhiokonda, kotoruiu ukrali," *Moskovskii komsomolets* 21608 (January 22, 2001).

73. Agnessa Mironova-Korol', *Agnessa: From Paradise to Purgatory: A Voice from Stalin's Russia*, trans. Rose Glickman (Bloomington, IN: Slavica, 2012), 41 (translation modified); M. M. Iakovenko, *Agnessa: Ustnye rasskazy Agnessy Ivanovny Mironovoi-Korol'*, Memorial: Istoricheskie programmy, "Nasha zhizn's Miroshei," http://www.memo.ru/history/agnessa.

74. Aleksei Tepliakov, *Oprichniki Stalina* (Moscow: Iauza, 2009), 206–16; Petrov and Skorkin, *Kto rukovodil NKVD*, 301; Iakovenko, *Agnessa*, http://www.memo.ru/history/agnessa; Mironova, *Agnessa: From Paradise to Purgatory*, 35 (translation modified).

75. Mironova, *Agnessa: From Paradise to Purgatory*, 35–36; Iakovenko, *Agnessa*, http://www.memo.ru/history/agnessa.

76. Mironova, *Agnessa: From Paradise to Purgatory*, 41–43 (translation modified); Iakovenko, *Agnessa*, http://www.memo.ru/history/agnessa.

77. ARAN, f. 528, op. 2, d. 65, l. 4 ob.

78. L. Kritsman, *Geroicheskii period Velikoi russkoi revoliutsii (opyt analiza t.n. "voennogo kommunizma")* (Moscow: Gosizdat, 1924), 79; Sheila Fitzpatrick, "Ascribing Class: The Construction of Social Identity in Soviet Russia," *Journal of Modern History* 65, no. 4 (December 1993): 745–70.

79. *Deiateli SSSR i revoliutsionnogo dvizhenia Rossii* (Moscow: Sovetskaia entsiklopediia, 1989), 688; E. I. Zelenskaia, "A. A. Sol'ts"; E. B. Levina, interview with author, September 27, 1998; M. A. Lozovskaia, interview with author, March 4, 1998; Larina, *Nezabyvaemoe*, 194–211; Iakovenko, *Agnessa*, http://www.memo.ru/history/agnessa; ARAN, razriad 5, op. 1-o, d. 11, ll. 74–75; N. I. Bukharin, *Ekonomika perekhodnogo perioda*, in Bukharin, *Problemy teorii i praktiki sotsializma* (Moscow: Politizdat, 1989), 163; Kritsman, *Geroicheskii period Velikoi russkoi revoliutsii*, 79; ARAN, f. 528, op. 2, d. 1, l. 1.

80. ARAN, f. 528, op. 2, d. 80, ll. 1–2; Irena Vladimirski, "Evreiskaia diaspora i ee vklad v ekonomicheskoe razvitie Manchzhurii," *Zametki po evreiskoi istorii* 10 (October 2008): http://berkovich-zametki.com/2008/Zametki/Nomer10/Vladimirski1.php; V. I. Lenin, "Novaia ekonomicheskaia poitika i zadachi politprosvetov," in *PSS*, 44:173, http://leninism.su/index.php?option=com_content&view=article&id=943:novaya-ekonomicheskaya-politika-i-zadachi-politprosvetov&catid=83:tom-44&Itemid=53#.Do.9F.Do.95.Do.Ao.Do.92.Do.AB.Do.99_.Do.92.Do.Ao.Do.90.Do.93_.E2.80.94_.Do.9A.Do.9E.Do.9C.Do.9C.Do.A3.Do.9D.Do.98.Do.A1.Do.A2.Do.98.Do.A7.Do.95.Do.A1.Do.9A.Do.9E.Do.95_.Do.A7.Do.92.Do.90.Do.9D.Do.A1.Do.A2.Do.92.Do.9E.

81. The Kritsman-Shcherbakov family archive (courtesy of Irina Shcherbakova).

82. ARAN, f. 528, op. 2, d. 79; RGASPI, f. 329, op. 2, d. 1, l. 10.

83. A. Arosev, *Belaia lestnitsa* (Moscow: Krug, 1923), 17–30.

84. V. I. Lenin, "Zasedanie petrogradskogo soveta," in *PSS*, 38:15–16, http://leninism.su/index.php?option=com_content&view=article&id=1298:zasedanie-petrogradskogo-soveta&catid=77:tom-38&Itemid=53.

85. This section is greatly indebted to Eric Naiman, *Sex in Public: The Incarnation of Early Soviet Ideology* (Princeton, NJ: Princeton University Press, 1997), esp. 148–207.

86. A. Arosev, *Zapiski Terentiia Zabytogo* (Berlin: Russkoe tvorchestvo, 1922), 14, 96–97, 106–8.

87. A. Ia. Arosev, *Belaia lestnitsa: Roman, povesti, rasskazy* (Moscow: Sovremennik, 1989), 269–307.

88. Fedor Gladkov, *Tsement*, RoyalLib.com, http://royallib.com/book/gladkov_fedor/tsement

.html; V. Kirshon and A. Uspenskii, "Koren'kovshchina," *Molodaia gvardiia* 10 (1926): 36–79; Sergei Malashkin, *Luna s pravoi storony* (Moscow: Molodaia gvardiia, 1928), 120–21.

89. Arosev, *Zapiski*, 27–33, 65–66, 100–101.

90. Aleksandr Arosev, *Nedavnie dni* (Moscow: Gosizdat, 1926), 28–29, 46, 48–52, 97–107, 123–28.

91. Iurii Libedinskii, *Rozhdenie geroia* (Leningrad: GIKhL, 1931), 3, 17–18, 53–56, 78 (the "conciliator" quotation), 82 (the "bitch" quotation), 87–89, 123–24, 153 (the "children's cities" quotation), 185–87.

92. Andrei Platonov, *Chevengur*, Klassika.ru, http://www.klassika.ru/read.html?proza/platonov/chevengur.txt&page=62.

93. A. Voronskii, *Literaturnye portrety* (Moscow: Federatsiia, 1929), 2:229–39. For an extensive discussion, see Eliot Borenstein, *Men without Women: Masculinity and Revolution in Russian Fiction, 1917–1929* (Durham, NC: Duke University Press, 2000). Platonov, *Chevengur*.

94. V. V. Maiakovskii, "Klop," Lib.ru, http://lib.ru/POEZIQ/MAYAKOWSKIJ/klop.txt; V. V. Maiakovskii, "Idilliia," Biblioteka russkoi poezii, http://libverse.ru/mayakovskii/idilliya.html; V. V. Maiakovskii, "Vsem," Vladimir Maiakovskii, http://mayakovsky.narod.ru/; Dardykina, "Dzhiokonda."

8. THE PARTY LINE

1. A. Arosev, *Po sledam Lenina* (Leningrad: Gosizdat, 1924), 42; Boris Schumatsky, *Silvester bei Stalin* (Berlin: Philo, 1999); B. Baabar, *History of Mongolia* (Cambridge: White Horse Press, 1999), 218–26; S. G. Luzianin, *Rossiia—Mongolia—Kitai v pervoi polovine XX veka: Politicheskie vzaimootnosheniia v 1911–1946* (Moscow: Ogni, 2003), 102–47.

2. Mikhail Kol'tsov, *Fel'etony i ocherki* (Moscow: Pravda, 1956), 121–24.

3. Quoted in Michael Walzer, *The Revolution of the Saints: A Study in the Origins of Radical Politics* (Cambridge, MA: Harvard University Press, 1965), 224.

4. Oleg Kharkhordin, *The Collective and the Individual in Russia: A Study of Practices* (Berkeley: University of California Press, 1999), esp. chap. 3.

5. David L. Hoffmann, *Stalinist Values: The Cultural Norms of Soviet Modernity, 1917–1941* (Ithaca, NY: Cornell University Press, 2003).

6. Art. Khalatov, *Rabotnitsa i obshchestvennoe pitanie* (Moscow: Narpit, 1924), 11; Khalatov, *Obshchestvennoe pitanie k desiatiletiiu Oktiabria* (Moscow: Narpit, 1927), 5; Svetlana Artem'evna Khalatova, interview with author, September 6, 1998.

7. N. I. Podvoiskii and A. R. Orlinskii, eds., *Massovoe deistvo: Rukovodstvo k organizatsii i provedeniiu prazdnovaniia desiatiletiia Oktiabria i drugikh revoliutsionnykh prazdnikov* (Moscow: Gosizdat, 1927), 9; N. I. Podvoiskii, ed., *Massovoe deistvo, stsenicheskie igry: Vsemirnyi Oktiabr', postavlennyi na Pervoi vsesoiuznoi spartakiade, i drugie stsenicheskie igry* (Moscow: Teakinopechat', 1929), 10–11.

8. V. Kerzhentsev, *Tvorcheskii teatr: Puti sotsialisticheskogo teatra* (Moscow: Kniga, 1918), 44, 46–47; P. M. Kerzhentsev, *Organizui samogo sebia* (Moscow: Molodaia gvardiia, 1925), 7, 21.

9. P. M. Kerzhentsev, *Bor'ba za vremia* (Moscow: Ktasnaia nov', 1924), 15, 8–9; Kerzhentsev, *Organizui*, 15–16; see also Richard Stites, *Revolutionary Dreams: Utopian Vision and Experimental Life in the Russian Revolution* (New York: Oxford University Press, 1989), 145–64.

10. N. P. Kerzhentseva, interview with author, January 12, 1998; Charles Dickens, *Our Mutual Friend*, chap. 11, eBooks@Adelaide, https://ebooks.adelaide.edu.au/d/dickens/charles/d540u/chapter11.html.

11. Kol'tsov, *Fel'etony i ocherki*, 107–10.

12. G. A. Voronskaia, "Esli v serdtse posylaiut puliu," *Istoricheskii arkhiv* 1 (1997): 76; Vsevolod Ivanov, *Sobranie sochinenii* (Moscow: Gosudarstvennoe izsdatel'stvo khudizhestvennoi literatury, 1958), 1:62 (the Gorky quotation).

13. Voronskaia, "Esli v serdtse posylaiut puliu," 78–79 (the "self-discipline quotation); Ivanov, *Sobranie sochinenii*, 1:63.

14. Ivanov, *Sobranie sochinenii*, 1:63.

15. A. Voronskii, *Za zhivoi i mertvoi vodoi* (Moscow: Antikva, 2005), 2:322; Voronskaia, "Esli v serdtse posylaiut puliu," 77–78, 82–84; Ivanov, *Sobranie sochinenii*, 1:63–64.

16. E. A. Dinershtein, *A. K. Voronskii v poiskakh zhivoi vody* (Moscow: Rosspen 2001), 90 (the censorship quotation); N. A. Trifonov, ed., *Literaturnoe nasledstvo* (Moscow: Nauka, 1983), 93:571; Voronskii, *Za zhivoi i mertvoi vodoi*, 1:165, 2:5–6; Voronskaia, "Esli v serdtse posylaiut puliu," 90.

17. Dinershtein, *A. K. Voronskii*, 81–85, 116–23; Edward J. Brown, *The Proletarian Episode in Russian Literature, 1928–1932* (New York: Columbia University Press, 1953), 13–32; Evgenii Dobrenko, *Formovka sovetskogo pisatelia* (St. Petersburg: Akademicheskii proekt, 1999), 42–62.

18. A. Voronskii, "Mister Britling p'et chashu do dna," *Krasnaia nov'* 5 (1926): 195; Voronskii, "Iskusstvo kak poznanie zhizni i sovremennost'," in Voronskii, *Izbrannye stat'i o literature* (Moscow: Khudozhestvennaia literatura, 1982), 302. For a discussion, see Dobrenko, *Formovka sovetskogo pisatelia*, 88–94.

19. A. Voronskii, "Ob iskusstve pisatelia," in *Kak i nad chem rabotat' pisateliu* (Moscow: Molodaia gvardiia, 1927), 3, 15–16; Voronskii, *Literaturnye tipy* (Moscow: Krug, 1931), 222 (on Pushkin's "The Prophet"); Voronskii, "Iskusstvo videt' mir," in Voronskii, *Izbrannye stat'i o literature*, 419, 415.

20. Voronskii, *Izbrannye stat'i o literature*, 416, 422.

21. Voronskii, "Ob iskusstve pisatelia," 21; A. Voronskii, *Iskusstvo i zhizn'* (Moscow: Krug, 1924), 268–71.

22. A. Voronskii, "O khlestkoi fraze i klassikakh," in Voronskii, *Izbrannye stat'i o literature*, 296–97; Voronskii, "Iskusstvo videt' mir," 416. For more on Voronsky's theory of literature, see Robert E. Maguire, *Red Virgin Soil: Soviet Literature in the 1920s* (Princeton, NJ: Princeton University Press, 1968), 188–259.

23. Dinershtein, *A. K. Voronskii*, 155, 137. Italics in the original. See also "Dneivnik D. A. Furmanova za 1924–1925 gg.," *Istochnik* 1 (1998): 106–41, esp. 116, 121.

24. Aleksandr Isbakh, *Na literaturnykh barrikadakh* (Moscow: Sovetskii pisatel', 1964), 8–10.

25. A. S. Serafimovich, *Sobranie sochinenii* (Moscow: GIKhL, 1960), 7:532; *Vospominaniia sovremennikov ob A.S. Serafimoviche* (Moscow: Sovetskii pisatel', 1977), 103, 121.

26. Isbakh, *Na literaturnykh barrikadakh*, 14.

27. Ibid., 15 ("you're sure to win" quotation); *Vospominaniia sovremennikov ob A. S. Serafimoviche*, 113 ("public discussions" quotation).

28. Andrei Artizov and Oleg Naumov, comps., *Vlast' i khudozhestvennaia intelligentsiia* (Moscow: Demoktaiia, 1999), 53–57.

29. Voronskii, "Mister Britling," 201.

30. Boris Pilniak, *Povest' nepogashennoi luny* (Sofia: N.p., n.d.).

31. *Vlast' i khudozhestvennaia intelligentsiia*, 66–67.

32. T. M. Goriaeva, ed., *Iskliuchit' vsiakie upominaniia . . . Ocherki istorii sovetskoi tsenzury* (Minsk: Staryi svet-print, 1995), 71–72; A. Voronsky, "Pis'mo v redaktsiiu," *Novyi mir* 6 (1926): 184.

33. Voronskii, "Mister Britling," 203.

34. N. I. Bukharin, "Zlye zametki," in N. I. Bukharin, *Revoliutsiia i kul'tura* (Moscow: Fond imeni N. I. Bukharina, 1993), 104–10.

35. A. Voronskii, "Ob industrializatsii i ob iskusstve," in Voronskii, *Iskusstvo videt' mir* (Moscow: Krug, 1928), 167–68.

36. P. Kerzhentsev, "Ob oshibke tt. Trotskogo, Voronskogo i dr.," *Oktiabr'* 1 (1925): 117; Bukharin, "Zlye zametki," 110.

37. Maguire, *Red Virgin Soil*, 177–86; Dinershtein, *A. K. Voronskii*, 175–78.

38. N. I. Bukharin, "Zheleznaia kogorta revoliutsii," in Bukharin, *Izbrannye proizvedeniia* (Moscow: Politizdat, 1988), 35, 38; Nikolai Bukharin, *Vremena* (Moscow: Progress, 1994), 179.

39. A. A. Sol'ts, "O partetike," in *Partiinaia etika: Dokumenty i materialy diskussii 20-kh godov* (Moscow: Politizdat, 1989), 277.

40. Igal Halfin, *Terror in My Soul: Communist Autobiographies on Trial* (Cambridge, MA: Harvard University Press, 2003), 43–95; Charles Lloyd Cohen, *God's Caress: The Psychology of Puritan Religious Experience* (New York: Oxford University Press, 1986), 137–61; Walzer, *Revolution of the Saints*, 222–23.

41. Walzer, *Revolution of the Saints*, 223. See also Philip S. Gorski, *The Disciplinary Revolution: Calvinism and the Rise of the State in Early Modern Europe* (Chicago: University of Chicago Press, 2003), 19–34; Christopher Hill, *Society and Puritanism in Pre-Revolutionary England* (New York: Schoken Books, 1967), 124–32, 225–49.

42. *XIV s"ezd Vsesoiuznoi Kommunisticheskoi partii (b): Stenograficheskii otchet* (Moscow: Gosizdat, 1926), 600–601.

43. "Prostupki protiv partiinoi etiki" and "O partetike: Proekt predlozhenii Prezidiuma TsKK II Plenumu TsKK RKP(b)," in *Partiinaia etika*, 395–463 and 155–70; Kharkhordin, *The Collective and the Individual in Russia*, 35–74.

44. Matt. 24:24.

45. "Zaiavlenie 46-ti v politbiuro TsK RKP(b), October 15, 1923," in *Izvestiia TsK KPSS* 6 (1990): 189–94 (the laity quotation is on 190).

46. N. I. Bukharin, "O Novoi ekonomicheskoi politike i nashikh zadachakh,' in *Izbrannye proizvedeniia*, 135–37; "Proekt platformy bol'shevikov-lenintsev (oppozitsii) k XV s"ezdu VKP(b)," in Iu. Fel'shtinskii, ed., *Kommunisticheskaia oppozitsiia v SSSR, 1923–1927* (Benson, VT: Chalidze Publications, 1988), 4:125.

47. Susan Gross Solomon, *The Soviet Agrarian Debate: A Controversy in Social Science, 1923–1929* (Boulder, CO: Westview Press, 1977); Terry Cox, *Peasants, Class, and Capitalism: The Rural Research of L. N. Kritsman and His School* (Oxford: Clarendon Press, 1986); A. V. Chayanov, *Izbrannye trudy* (Moscow: Kolos, 1993). The Kritsman quotation is from "Desiat' let na agrarnom fronte proletarskoi revoliutsii," in L. Kritsman, *Proletarskaia revoliutsiia i derevnia* (Moscow: Gosizdat, 1929), 8. For the argument that the Agrarian-Marxist findings on class differentiation do not necessarily support the opposition's view at the Fifteenth Party Congress, see A. Gaister, *Rassloenie derevni (dlia propagandistov)* (Moscow: Moskovskii rabochii, 1928). For Lenin's predictions, cf. *The Development of Captalism in Russia* (1899) and "On Cooperation" (1923); see Solomon, *Soviet Agrarian Debate*, 76–86.

48. Fel'shtinskii, *Kommunisticheskaia oppozitsiia*, 2:49–50.

49. *XIV s"ezd Vsesoiuznoi Kommunisticheskoi partii (b)*, 401.

50. *Pravda*, January 13, 1924, 4–5.

51. *XIV s"ezd Vsesoiuznoi Kommunisticheskoi partii (b)*, 165–66, 159. At the Fourth Party Congress in Stockholm, in 1906, the Mensheviks got the majority on the Central Committee.

52. Ibid., 152 (the Bukharin quotation); *XV s"ezd Vsesoiuznoi Kommunisticheskoi partii (b): Stenograficheskii otchet* (Moscow: Partizdat, 1935), 1:171.

53. Bukharin, *Izbrannye proizvedeniia*, 351.

54. *XV s"ezd*, 170 (Goloshchekin); Bukharin, *Izbrannye proizvedeniia*, 363–64.

55. *XV s"ezd*, 248–53, 487.

56. Fel'shtinskii, *Kommunisticheskaia oppozitsiia*, 4:250–52; T. I. Smilga-Poluian, interview with author, January 19, 1998.

57. Fel'shtinskii, *Kommunisticheskaia oppozitsiia*, 4:258–60; T. I. Smilga-Poluian, interview with author, January 19, 1998.

58. Fel'shtinskii, *Kommunisticheskaia oppozitsiia*, 4:253, 258–60.

59. Voronskaia, "Esli v serdtse," 83; RGASPI, f. 329, op. 1, l. 45.

60. I. V. Stalin, "God velikogo pereloma," in Stalin, *Sochineniia*, vol. 12, Marxists Internet Archive Library, https://www.marxists.org/russkij/stalin/t12/t12_06.htm; I. V. Stalin, "Politicheskii

otchet tsentral'nogo komiteta XVImu s"ezdu VKP(b)," in *Sochineniia*, vol. 12. See also *XVI s"ezd Vsesoiuznoi kommunisticheskoi partii (b): Stenograficheskii otchet* (Partizdat TsK VKP(b), 1935), 1:76–77. Cf. V. I. Lenin, *Polnoe sobranie sochinenii* (hereafter *PSS*) (Moscow: Izdatel'stvo politicheskoi literatury, 1967–70), vol. 45:78, Lenin: Revoliutsioner, myslitel', chelovek, http://leninism.su/index.php?option=com_content&view=article&id=452 :xi-sezd-rkpb-45&catid=84:tom-45&Itemid=53#XI_.Do.A1.Do.AA.Do.95.Do.97.Do.94_.Do .Ao.Do.9A.Do.9F.28.Do.B1.2951.

61. Matt. 7:7; Vasilii Lebedev-Kumach, "Veselyi veter" (song from the 1937 film, *Captain Grant's Children*): "kto khochet, tot dob'etsia, kto ishchet, tot vsegda naidet"; I. V. Stalin, "O zadachakh khoziaistvennikov," in *Sochineniia*, vol. 13, Marxists Internet Archive Library, https://www.marxists.org/russkij/stalin/t13/t13_06.htm.

62. P. Kerzhentsev, *Pamiatka bol'shevika* (Moscow: Moskovskii rabochii, 1931), 111; Stalin, "O zadachakh khoziaistvennikov."

63. N. I. Bukharin, "Vystuplenie na ob"edinennom plenume TsK I TsKK VKP(b)," in Bukharin, *Problemy teorii i praktiki sotsializma* (Moscow: Politizdat, 1989), 253–54 (italics in the original).

64. Iu. G. Fel'shtinskii, *Razgovory s Bukharinym* (New York: Teleks, 1993), 37–43; see also Lib .ru, http://lib.ru/HISTORY/FELSHTINSKY/buharin.txt.

65. Ibid., p. 14.

66. Cf., esp., Stalin, "God velikogo pereloma," and N. I. Bukharin, "Politicheskoe zaveshchanie Lenina," in *Ibzrannye proizvedeniia*, 437–48. The recantation was published in *Pravda*; quoted in Miklosh Kun, *Bukharin, ego druz'ia i vragi* (Moscow: Respublika, 1992), 295–96.

67. *XVI s"ezd*, 1:203, 273; A. M. Larina, *Nezabyvaemoe* (Moscow: APN, 1989), 86.

68. *XVI s"ezd*, 1:262, 266, 270.

69. Ibid., 1:286.

70. Lev Trotskii, *Moia zhizn': Opyt avtobiografii* (Berlin: Granit, 1930), 2:300. The Osinsky-Stalin correspondence is reproduced in V. M. Soima, *Zapreshchennyi Stalin* (Moscow: Olma Press, 2005), 10–12 (from APRF, f. 45, op. 1, d. 780, ll. 12–13, 14, 16).

71. *XVI s"ezd*, 1:262, italics in the original.

72. "Protokol doprosa D. S. Azbelia," in *Dokumenty po "Kremlevskomu delu"* (from APRF, f. 3, op. 58, d. 233, ll. 80–87), http://perpetrator2004.narod.ru/Kremlin_Affair.htm; Larina, *Nezabyvaemoe*, 67–69, 234–36.

73. T. I. Smilga, interview with author, January 19, 1998; *Pravda*, 13 July 1929.

74. Voronskaia, "Esli v serdtse," 90–97; Dinershtein, *A. K. Voronsky*, 270–82; Reginald E. Zelnik, "The Fate of a Russian Bebel: Semen Ivanovich Kanatchikov, 1905–1940," *Carl Beck Papers in Russian and East European Studies* 1105 (August 1995): 7–9, 28–30.

75. N. Bukharin, *Kommunisticheskoe vospitanie molodezhi* (Moscow: Molodaia gvardiia, 1925), 54–57; Lenin, "Zadachi soiuzov molodezhi," in *PSS*, 41:309–11.

76. N. I. Bukharin, "Finansovyi kapital v mantii papy," in *Etiudy* (Moscow: Gosudarstvennoe tekhniko–teoreticheskoe izdatel'stvo, 1932), 338, italics in the original.

77. Ibid., 335–38, italics in the original.

78. Voronskaia, "Esli v serdtse," 96–97; Dinershtein, *A. K. Voronsky*, 272; ARAN, razriad 5, op. 1-o, d. 11, ll. 32, 42.

79. ARAN, razriad 5, op. 1-o, d. 11, l. 410b. For Osinsky's role in creating the Soviet automobile industry, see Lewis H. Siegelbaum, *Cars for Comrades: The Life of the Soviet Automobile* (Ithaca, NY: Cornell University Press, 2011), 3–4, 37–39, and passim.

80. ARAN, razriad 5, op. 1-o, d. 11, ll. 31–310b., 39–390b.

81. *Socialist Planned Economy in the Soviet Union* (New York: International Publishers, 1932), 17, 47.

82. Ibid., 80, 81, 98, 100; A. Gaister, *Dostizheniia i trudnosti kolkhoznogo stroitel'stva: Diskussiia v Agrarnom institute Kommunisticheskoi Akademii* (Moscow: Izdatel'stvo Kommunisticheskoi Akademii, 1929), 100 and passim; Inna Shikheeva-Gaister, *Deti vragov naroda: Semein-*

aia khronika vremen kul'ta lichnosti 1925–1953 (Moscow: Vozvrashchenie, 2012), 16–34; "I. A. Kraval'," *Vestnik statistiki* 3 (1975): 60–61; E. I. Gruzinova (Kraval'), interview with author, January 16, 1998; RGASPI, f. 17, op. 8, d. 393, ll. 92–94; G. S. Ronina, interview with author, October 1, 1997.

83. AMDNN, "Poloz" file, "Vospominaniia Mirry Varshavskoi," l. 3; "Astrakhan'"; "Chelkar," l. 1.

84. Ibid., "Vospominaniia Mirry Varshavskoi," l. 1; "Chelkar," ll. 1, 4, 8, and passim.

85. Ibid., "Chelkar," ll. 2, 6, 8, 10.

86. Ibid., "Chelkar," ll. 9, 7.

87. Ibid., "Vospominaniia Mirry Varshavskoi," ll. 3–4.

9. THE ETERNAL HOUSE

1. Andrei Platonov, "Usomnivshiisia Makar," Biblioteka Komarova, http://www.ilibrary.ru/text/1012/p.1/index.html.

2. GARF, f. 3316, op. 21, d. 717, l. 9.

3. I. Iu. Eigel', *Boris Iofan* (Moscow: Stroiizdat, 1978), 19–37; Mikhail Korshunov and Victoria Terekhova, *Tainy i legendy Doma na naberezhnoi* (Moscow: Slovo, 2002), 239–47.

4. TsAFSB, f. 2, op. 6, d. 230, ll. 34–35.

5. GARF, f. 5446, op. 55, d. 1519, ll. 1, 3–5; TsAFSB, f. 2, op. 6, d. 230, l. 40.

6. TsANTDM f. 2, op. 1, d. 448, ll. 120b. and 13 ob.; GARF, f. 5446, op. 82, d. 2, l. 328; TsGAMO, f. 66, op. 14, d. 69, ll. 200–203; TsGAMO, f. 66, op. 14, d. 124, ll. 10, 16; TsAFSB, f. 2, op. 6, d. 230, ll. 91–93; GARF, f. 5446, op. 38, d. 10, ll. 228–30; GARF, f. 1235, op. 72, d. 62, ll. 1–8; GARF, f. 3316, op. 24, d. 517, ll. 2–96 (the quotation is on l. 120b.); T. Shmidt, "Stroitel'stvo Doma TsIK i SNK," *Vestnik arkhivista* 1 (2002): 195–202.

7. TsANTDM, f. 2, op. 1, d. 448, ll. 120b., 130b., 26; Eigel', *Boris Iofan*, 42; Shmidt, "Stroitel'stvo."

8. TsANTDM, f. 2, op. 1, d. 448, ll. 71–800b.; Shmidt, "Stroitel'stvo."

9. B. Iofan, "Postroika doma TsIK I SNK," *Stroitel'stvo Moskvy* 10 (1928): 8–10; TsAFSB, f. 2, op. 6, d. 230, l. 71; TsMAM, f. 589, op. 1, d. 29. l. 337.

10. Platonov, "Usomnivshiisia Makar."

11. TsGAMO, f. 268, op. 1, d. 175, l. 19; d. 31, l. 35; TsAODM, f. 67, op. 1, d. 625, ll. 43–44.

12. GARF, f. 5446, op. 38, d. 10, l. 230; TsMAM, f. 1474, op. 7, d. 50, l. 21; TsAODM, f. 67, op. 1, d. 665, l. 4; TsGAMO, f. 268, op. 1, d. 179, l. 1; TsMAM, f. 1474, op. 7, d. 102, l. 137 (the "powerful tool" quotation); TsGAMO, f. 268, op. 1, d. 175, l. 10 (the activist quotation). Cf. "Our departments are shit, our decrees are shit. . . . Mistrust of decrees, of institutions, of 'reorganizations' and pompous bureaucrats, especially from among Communists; struggle against the swamp of bureaucratism and red tape by means of supervising people and checking the actual work they do; a merciless expulsion of all unneeded officials; a reduction of personnel; and the firing of Communists unwilling to learn the art of governance seriously—such should be the policy of people's commissars and the Council of People's Commissars, its chairman and his deputies." V. I. Lenin, "O perestroike raboty SNK, STO i malogo SNK," *Polnoe sobranie sochinenii* (Moscow: Izdatel'stvo politicheskoi literatury, 1967–70), 44:369–70, Lenin: Revoliutsioner, myslitel', chelovek, http://leninism.su/works/83-tom-44/999-o-perestrojke-raboty-snk-sto-i-malogo-snk.html; Platonov, "Usomnivshiisia Makar."

13. TsAODM, f. 67, op. 1, d. 591, l. 32; d. 815, ll. 65–66; TsMAM, f. 1474, op. 7, d. 104, l. 122; TsGAMO, f. 268, op. 1, d. 175, l. 11.

14. TsGAMO, f. 268, op. 1, d. 31, l. 60; Platonov, "Usomnivshiisia Makar."

15. TsAODM, f. 67, op. 1, d. 735, ll. 9–75 and passim; d. 746, l. 150; d. 755, l. 49; d. 759, l. 96; d. 770, l. 780b.; TsMAM, f. 1474, op. 7, d. 50, l. 29a; d. 102, l. 242; RGASPI, f. 124, op. 1, d. 1298, l. 30b.; Z. M. Tuchina, interview with author, September 8, 1998; TsANTDM, f. 2, op. 1, d. 448, ll. 121–31.

16. Platonov, "Usomnivshiisia Makar."

17. TsAODM, f. 67, op. 1, d. 663, l. 110; d. 733, ll. 93, 185; d. 746, l. 150; *Postroika 40* (April 5, 1928) (copy in TsAFSB, f. 2, op. 6, d. 230, l. 89); *Stroitel'stvo Moskvy* 7 (1928): 13–14 (italics in the original); 8 (1928): 23.

18. GARF, f. 5446, op. 11a, d. 554, ll. 1–64 (quotations on ll. 49 and 64); op. 1, d. 37, l. 45; op. 9, d. 413, ll. 1–15; op. 10, d. 2021, ll. 1–5; op. 13a, d. 981, ll. 1–29; TsAFSB, f. 2, op. 6, d. 230, l. 93.

19. GARF, f. 5446, op. 82, d. 2, ll. 327–28.

20. GARF, f. 5446, op. 11a, d. 554, l. 53; op. 82, d. 2, ll. 26–29, 328ob.; op. 13a, d. 981, ll. 13–18; op. 38, d. 10, ll. 226–34; Shmidt, "Stroitel'stvo."

21. N. K. Krupskaia, *O bytovykh voprosakh* (Moscow: Gosizdat, 1930), 16; V. Voeikov, in "Preniia po dokladu M. Ia. Ginzburga," *Sovremennaia arkhitektura* 1 (1929): 22. See also V. E. Khazanova, *Sovetskaia arkhitektura pervoi piatiletki: Problemy goroda budushchego* (Moscow: Nauka, 1980), 170–71.

22. M. Okhitovich, "K probleme goroda," *Sovremennaia arkhitektura* 4 (1929): 130–34; Karl Radek, *Portrety i pamflety* (Moscow: Khudozhestvennaia literatura, 1934), 2:5.

23. A. Zelenko, "Gorod blizhaishikh let," in *Goroda sotsializma i sotsialisticheskaia rekonstruktsiia byta: Sbornik statei* (Moscow: Rabotnik prosveshcheniia, 1930), 59–60. See also "Ispol'zovat' proekty utopistov," *Pravda*, December 2, 1929, and L. M. Sabsovich, *Sotsialisticheskie goroda* (Moscow: Moskovskii rabochii, 1930).

24. A. Lunacharskii, "Arkhitekturnoe oformlenie sotsialisticheskikh gorodov," in *Goroda sotsializma*, 70.

25. Krupskaia, *O bytovykh voprosakh*, 30–31.

26. Marxists Internet Archive Library, http://www.marxists.org/archive/marx/works/1848/communist-manifesto/ch02.htm.

27. N. A. Miliutin, *Problema stroitel'stva sotsialisticheskikh gorodov* (Moscow: Gosizdat, 1930), 34–35, 39.

28. L. Sabsovich, *Sotsialisticheskie goroda* (Moscow: Moskovskii rabochii, 1930), 75, 48–49.

29. L. Sabsovich, "O proektirovanii zhilykh kombinatov," *Sovremennaia arkhitektura* 3 (1930): 7–8.

30. Ibid.

31. Sabsovich, *Sotsialisticheskie goroda*, 73; L. M. Sabsovich, *Goroda budushchego i organizatsiia sotsialstcheskogo byta* (Moscow: Gosudarstvennoe tekhnicheskoe izdatel'stvo, 1929), 35–41 (quotation is on 35).

32. A. Pasternak, "Spory o budushchem goroda," *Sovremennaia arkhitektura* 1–2 (1930): 58; Aleksandr Pasternak, *Vospominaniia* (Moscow: Progress-Traditsiia, 2002), 5; Alexander Pasternak, *A Vanished Present*, ed. and trans. Ann Pasternak Slater (Ithaca, NY: Cornell University Press, 1984), xviii. See also M. Okhitovich, "Ne gorod, a novyi tip rasseleniia," in *Goroda sotsializma*, 153–55.

33. Sabsovich, *Sotsialisticheskie goroda*, 20; Pasternak, "Spory o budushchem goroda," 60; M. Okhitovich, "K probleme goroda," *Sovremennaia arkhitektura* 4 (1929): 130, 133; M. Okhitovich, "Zametki po teorii rasseleniia," *Sovremennaia arkhitektura* 1–2 (1930): 10, 14.

34. Okhitovich, "Zametki po teorii rasseleniia," 7–9; Pasternak, "Spory o budushchem goroda," 58.

35. Okhitovich, "Zametki po teorii rasseleniia," 12.

36. Ibid., 12–13.

37. Ibid., 15; Pasternak, "Spory o budushchem goroda," 60.

38. Iu. Larin, *Zhilishche i byt* (Moscow: Vlast' sovetov, 1931), 4–5.

39. S. Frederick Starr, *Melnikov: Solo Architect in a Mass Society* (Princeton, NJ: Princeton University Press, 1978), 178–79; N. Kuz'min, "Problema nauchnoi organizatsii byta," *Sovremennaia arkhitektura* 3 (1930): 15.

40. Okhitovich, "Zametki po teorii rasseleniia," 13; A. Lunacharskii, "Kul'tura v sotsialisticheskikh gorodakh," in *Goroda sotsializma*, 82; Kuz'min, "Problema nauchnoi organizatsii byta," 15.

41. M. M. Zarina, *Domovodstvo: Pishcha, zhilishche, odezhda* (Moscow: Gosizdat, 1928), 70. The "velvet-covered albums" quotation is from Iurii Libedinskii, *Nedelia. Komissary* (Moscow: Voenizdat, 1968), pt. 2, chap. 2; see also V. Bazarov's comment during the discussion of A. Zelenko's presentation on November 26, 1929, quoted in Khazanova, *Sovetskaia arkhitektura pervoi piatiletki*, 68 (see also 63–68, 160–61, 203); Victor Buchli, *An Archaeology of Socialism* (Oxford: Berg, 1999), 44–45; "Preniia po dokladu M. Ia. Ginzburga," 16–17; Miliutin, *Problema stroitel'stva*, 39–40.

42. Khazanova, *Sovetskaia arkhitektura pervoi piatiletki*, 194–95, 186–87; Milka Blizniakov, "Soviet Housing during the Experimental Years, 1918 to 1933," in William Craft Brumfield and Blair A. Ruble, eds., *Russian Housing in the Modern Age* (Cambridge: Cambridge University Press, 1993), 120–25; Anatole Kopp, *Town and Revolution: Soviet Architecture and City Planning, 1917–1935* (New York: George Braziller, 1970), 179–84; A. M. Zhuravlev, A. V. Ikonnikov, and A. G. Rochegov, *Arkhitektura sovetskoi Rossii* (Moscow: Stroiizdat, 1987), 87–88; A. V. Ikonnikov, *Arkhitektura Moskvy, XX vek* (Moscow: Moskovskii rabochii, 1984), 71–72; A. V. Ikonnikov, *Arkhitektura XX veka: Utopii i real'nost'* (Moscow: Progress-Traditsiia, 2001), 3, 8–9, 311–12; Ekaterina Sevriukova, "Vozrozhdenie kommuny," *Rossiiskaia gazeta*, April 23, 2007 (no. 4348; incl. the Nikolaev quotation).

43. P. Golubkov, "V novom dome (na postroike opytnogo doma-kommuny na Novinskom bul'vare v Moskve)," in *Goroda sotsializma*, 139–40. See also Buchli, *An Archaeology of Socialism*, 67–76; Khazanova, *Sovetskaia arkhitektura pervoi piatiletki*, 171–73; Ikonnikov, *Arkhitektura Moskvy*, 72.

44. Khazanova, *Sovetskaia arkhitektura pervoi piatiletki*, 107–8, 176–79, 191–92, 191–93, 201 (the "plastic Puritanism" quotation belongs to Novitsky and is cited on 193).

45. Kuz'min, "Problema nauchnoi organizatsii byta," 14–15, 15–16; A. Kurella in "Preniia po dokladu M. Ia. Ginzburga," 12.

46. M. Kol'tsov, "Na poroge svoego doma," *Pravda*, May 1, 1930.

47. "Postanovlenie TsK VKP(b) o rabote po perestroike byta," *Sovremennaia arkhitektura* 1–2 (1930): 3.

48. Arkh. Pasternak, "Problema doma-kommuny," in *Goroda sotsializma*, 135 (italics in the original).

49. G. M. Krzhizhanovskii, "K diskussii o genplane," *Planovoe khoziaistvo* 2 (1930): 7–8, 18–19.

50. Gwendolyn Wright, *Building the Dream: A Social History of Housing in America* (Cambridge, MA: MIT Press, 1983), 139–44; Norbert Schoenauer, *6,000 Years of Housing* (New York: Norton, 2000), 335–37.

51. Eigel', *Boris Iofan*, 37–43, 53–56; Ikonnikov, *Arkhitektura Moskvy*, 74–77.

52. Lunacharskii, "Arkhitekturnoe oformlenie," 67–68.

53. A. V. Ikonnikov, *Arkhitektura i istioriia* (Moscow: Architectura, 1993), 137–38.

54. GARF, f. 5446, op. 1, d. 67; f. 3316, op. 24, d. 517, ll., 32, 95; op. 29, d. 496; Shmidt, "Stroitel'stvo"; M. Kol'tsov, "Moskva-matushka," in Mikhail Kol'tsov, *Vostorg i iarost'* (Moscow: Pravda, 1990), 209–12.

55. B. Strogova, "Moskva—gorod-sprut ili soiuz gorodov?" in *Goroda sotsializma*, 143–44.

56. GARF, f. 3316, op. 24, d. 517, ll. 3–7, 53–55; TsMAM, f. 694, op. 1, d. 3, ll. 65–66; *Dvorets sovetov: Vsesoiznyi konkurs 1932 g.* (Moscow: Vsekokhudozhnik, 1933), 6–8; Sona Stephan Hoisington. "'Ever Higher': The Evolution of the Project for the Palace of Soviets," *Slavic Review* 62, no. 1 (Spring 2003): 41–68; Richard Anderson, "The Future of History: The Cultural Politics of Soviet Architecture, 1928–41," (PhD diss., Columbia University, 2010), 67–71; Karine N. Ter-Akopyan, "The Design and Construction of the Palace of Soviets of the USSR in Moscow," in *Naum Gabo and the Competition for the Palace of Soviets, Moscow 1931–1933* (Berlin: Berlinische Galerie, 1993), 185–96. I am grateful to Katherine Zubovich for her help with this section.

57. *Dvorets sovetov*, 76, 55–56, 101–3, 106–7.

58. Hoisington. "'Ever Higher,'" 57–62; Eigel', *Boris Iofan*, 87–93 (the Lunacharsky quotation

is on 93); *Dvorets sovetov*, 59–60; RGASPI, f. 124, op. 1, d. 1298, l. 3ob.; Anderson, "The Future of History," 71–74; M. V. Mikhailova, interview with author, December 3, 1997.

59. N. Atarov, *Dvorets sovetov* (Moscow: Moskovskii rabochii, 1940), 11, 17–18.

60. Ibid., 19, 109–10.

61. Ibid., 18–19.

62. Ibid., 12.

63. Ibid., 14–15.

64. Ibid., 18; RGASPI, f. 81, op. 3, d. 184, l. 124.

65. For surveys, see Mary A. Nicholas, *Writers at Work: Russian Production Novels and the Construction of Soviet Culture* (Lewisburg, PA: Bucknell University Press, 2010); and Andreas Guski, *Literatur und Arbeit: Produktionsskizze und Produktionsroman im Russland des 1. Fünfjahrplans (1928–1932)* (Wiesbaden: Harrassowitz, 1995).

66. Bruno Iasenskii, *Chelovek meniaet kozhu* (Moscow: GIKhL, 1960), 425.

67. Valentin Kataev, *Vremia, vpered!*, in *Sobranie sochinenii* (Moscow: Khudozhestvennaia literatura, 1983), 2:302, translation based on Valentin Kataev, *Time, Forward!*, trans. Charles Malamuth (Bloomington: Indiana University Press, 1961), 73–74; Il'ia Erenburg, *Den' vtoroi* (Moscow: Sovetskii pisatel', 1935), 9, translation based on Ilya Ehrenburg, *Out of Chaos*, trans. Alexander Bakshy (New York: Henry Holt, 1934), 7; Leonid Leonov, *Sot'* (Moscow: Sovetskii pisatel', 1968), 97–98, translation based on Leonid Leonov, *The River*, trans. Liv Tugde (Moscow: Raduga, 1983), 165–66.

68. Andrey Platonov, *The Foundation Pit*, trans. Robert Chandler, Elizabeth Chandler, and Olga Meerson (New York: New York Review of Books, 2009), 108, 19.

69. Erenburg, *Den' vtoroi*; Andrei Platonov, *The Foundation Pit*, 9; Kataev, *Vremia, vpered!*, 281; Fedor Gladkov, *Energiia* (Moscow: Sovetskii pisatel', 1952), 85, 18.

70. Iasenskii, *Chelovek meniaet kozhu*, 26, 33.

71. A. S. Pushkin, *Mednyi vsadnik*, Biblioteka Komarova, http://ilibrary.ru/text/451/p.1/index .html ("iz t'my lesov, iz topi blat"); Gladkov, *Energiia*, 40, 19; Ehrenburg, *Den' vtoroi*, 99; *Belomorsko-Baltiiskii kanal imeni Stalina* (Moscow: OGIZ, 1934), 93; Leonov, *Sot'*, 48, 7 (86, 20).

72. Kataev, *Vremia, vpered!*, 460, translation based on Kataev, *Time, Forward!*, 257.

73. Platonov, *The Foundation Pit*, 44; Kataev, *Vremia, vpered!*, 359 (140–41).

74. Kataev, *Vremia, vpered!*, 251 (12–13).

75. Yuri Olesha, *Envy*, trans. Marian Schwartz (New York: New York Review of Books), 111, 144–46, 28, 25, 32.

76. Marietta Shaginian, *Gidrotsentral'* (Leningrad: Izdatel'stvo pisatelei, 1933), 39–40.

77. Leonov, *Sot'*, 20, 29, 31 (40, 54, 58).

78. Boris Pilniak, *Volga vpadaet v Kaspiiskoe more* (Pullman, MI: Russian Language Specialties, 1973; reprint of the 1930 Nedra edition), 68, 62, translation based on Boris Pilnyak, *The Volga Flows to the Caspian Sea* (London: Peter Davies, 1932), 90, 84.

79. Ibid., 62 (84); Gladkov, *Energiia*, 126, 184.

80. Gladkov, *Energiia*, 55.

81. Leonov, *Sot'*, 280–81, 178, 262 (456–57, 293, 428).

82. Pilniak, *Volga vpadaet*, 157 (200).

83. Gladkov, *Energiia*, 164; Platonov, *The Foundation Pit*, 15, 58, 56–57.

84. Erenburg, *Den' vtoroi*, 80–98, 246–52; translation based on Erenburg, *Out of Chaos*, 108–30, 357–63.

85. Pilniak, *Volga vpadaet*, 119, 121, 158 (155–57, 201–2).

86. Gladkov, *Energiia*, 165, 167, 172.

87. Pilniak, *Volga vpadaet*, 263–64 (321–22); Leonov, *Sot'*, 80 (137); Shaginian, *Gidrotsentral'*, 41–42.

88. Erenburg, *Den' vtoroi*, 208–9 (299).

89. *Belomorsko-Baltiiskii kanal*, 339–40.

90. Erenburg, *Den' vtoroi*, 45 (50–51).

91. Gladkov, *Energiia*, 68–69; Leonov, *Sot'*, 267 (436); Shaginian, *Gidrotsentral'*, 173.

92. Erenburg, *Den' vtoroi*, 116 (159).

93. Kataev, *Vremia, vpered!*, 404–5 (193).

94. Ilya Ilf and Evgeny Petrov, *The Golden Calf*, trans. Konstantin Gurevich and Helen Anderson (Rochester, NY: Open Letter, 2009), 254.

95. Ibid., 256.

96. Ibid., 327.

97. Olesha, *Envy*, 121–22.

98. Platonov, *The Foundation Pit*, 59; *XVI s"ezd Vsesoiuznoi kommunisticheskoi partii (b): Stenograficheskii otchet* (Moscow: Partizdat, 1935), 500; Leonov, *Sot'*, 175–76 (289, 291).

99. Leonov, *Sot'*, 176, 288 (291, 468–69).

100. Platonov, *The Foundation Pit*, 148, 44, 60.

10. THE NEW TENANTS

1. GARF, f. 5446, op. 82, d. 13, ll. 217–18; GARF, f. 3316, op. 25, d. 987, ll. 3–50b., 8–80b.; GARF, f. 1235, op. 70, d. 13, ll. 5, 14–160b.; T. I. Shmidt, *Dom na naberezhnoi: Liudi i sud'by* (Moscow: Vozvrashchenie, 2009), 14–15, 25–26, 45–47, and passim.

2. E. B. Levina, interview with author, September 27, 1998.

3. RGVA, f. 37461, op. 1, d. 149, l. 93; AMDNN, Museum's questionnaire, responses by R. N. Gel'man and A. N. Leushina; Natal'ia Dardykina, "Dzhiokonda, kotoruiu ukrali," *Moskovskii komsomolets* 21608 (January 22, 2001).

4. Ol'ga Aroseva, *Bez grima* (Moscow: Tsentrpoligraf, 1999), 20–21; Natal'ia Aroseva, *Sled na zemle: Dokumental'naia povest' ob ottse* (Moscow: Politizdat, 1987), 225–27; O. A. Aroseva, interview with author, January 15, 1998; RGASPI, f. 124, op. 1, d. 80, ll. 4–14; A. Arosev, *Korni* (Moscow: OGIZ–GIKhL, 1933), 21.

5. V. I. Piatnitskii, comp., *Golgofa* (St. Petersburg: Palitra, 1993), 18; A. Shitov and Iurii Trifonov, *Khronika zhizni i tvorchestva, 1925–1985* (Ekaterinburg: Izdatel'stvo Ural'skogo universiteta, 1997), 74–79.

6. E. I. Zelenskaia, "A. A. Sol'ts," unpublished manuscript in AMDNN, "Solts" file, 68–70.

7. AMDNN, "Brandenburgsky" file (KP 371/17, KP 3771/18).

8. A. Volkov, *Tvorcheskii put' A. S. Serafimovicha* (Moscow: Khudozhestvennaia literatura, 1963), 301, 342–48; Grigorii Ershov, *Serafimovich: Stranitsy zhizni, bor'by i tvorchestva* (Moscow: Sovremennik, 1982), 304–8; A. S. Serafimovich, *Sbornik neopublikovannykh proizvedenii i materialov* (Moscow: Gosudarstvennoe izdatel'stvo khudozhestvennoi literatury, 1958), 48–78.

9. RGASPI, f. 124, op. 1, d. 854, ll. 2–5; N. P. Kerzhentseva, interview with author, January 12, 1998.

10. RGASPI, f. 124, op. 1, d. 924, ll. 11–12; N. P. Kerzhentseva, interview with author, January 12, 1998.

11. M. A. Usievich, interview with author, January 30, 1998; ARAN, f. 358, op. 3, d. 22; E. Usievich, "Novye formy klassovoi bor'by v sovetskoi literature," in *Sovetskaia literatura na novom etape: Sbornik kriticheskikh statei* (Moscow: GIKhL, 1934), 3–32.

12. Mikhail Kol'tsov, *kakim on byl: Sbornik vospominanii* (Moscow: Sovetskii pisatel', 1989), 384–85; Reinhard Müller, "Exil im 'Wunderland Sowjetunion'—Maria Osten (1908–1942)," *Exil: Forschung, Erkenntnisse, Ergebnisse* 27, no. 1 (2007): 73–95; Ursula El-Akramy, *Transit Moskau: Margarete Steffin und Maria Osten* (Hamburg: Europäische Verlangsanstalt, 1998), 79, 94; Viktor Fradkin, *Delo Kol'tsova* (Moscow: Vagrius, 2002), 95, 99, 176; Boris Medovoi, *Mikhail i Mariia* (Moscow: Gospolitizdat, 1991), 73–86, 150; Boris Efimov, interview with author, October 16, 1997.

13. R. Lavrov, "Vidnyi gosudarstvennyi deiatel'," *Sovetskaia kul'tura*, May 21, 1964; "Papakha

Khalatova," *Sovetskaia torgovlia*, May 1, 1990; *Deiateli SSSR i revoliutsionnogo dvizhenia Rossii* (Moscow: Sovetskaia entsiklopediia, 1989), 742–43; *Gosudarstvennyi teatr detskoi knigi imeni A. B. Khalatova, 1930–1934* (Moscow: Izdanie Teatra detskoi knigi, 1934), 30; Art. Khalatov, *Rabotnitsa i obshchestvennoe pitanie* (Moscow: Narpit, 1924), 11; S. A. Khalatova, interview with author, September 6, 1998.

14. Evgenii Zhirnov, "Vse proiskhodiashchee so mnoi lozhitsia ten'iu na imia ottsa," *Vlast'* 44, no. 647 (November 7, 2005); Roi Medvedev, "Slava i tragediia odnoi sem'i," *Karetnyi riad* 5 (November 1989): 1–6; O. N. Podvoiskaia, interview with author, February 27, 1998; M. A. Lozovskaia, interview with author, March 4, 1998; E. S. Sverdlova, interview with author, February 26, 1998.

15. RGASPI, f. 124, op. 1, d. 745, l. 20.

16. GARF, f. 5449, op. 1, d. 1, l. 1; RGASPI, f. 124, op. 1, d. 745, ll. 25, 27 (the quotation is from l. 27); G. B. Ivanova, interview with author, March 13, 1998; GARF, f. P-7013, op. 1 ("Historical Comment"); RGASPI, f. 124, op. 1, d. 745, ll. 29–42.

17. RGASPI, f. 124, op. 1, d. 1429, ll. 63–77; G. B. Ivanova, interview with author, March 13, 1998.

18. RGASPI, f. 559, op. 1, d. 141, ll. 18–190b., 33; RGASPI, f. 559, op. 1, d. 132, l. 55.

19. RGASPI, f. 124, op. 1, d. 1308, ll. 6–6ob., 25–36; RGASPI, f. 124, op. 2, d. 345, l. 2; V. E. Baranchenko, *Stoikost', neutomimost', otvaga* (Moscow: Moskovskii rabochii, 1988), 48; ARAN, f. 528, op. 2, d. 1, l. 4; op. 4, d. 86, ll. 11, 15.

20. Inna Shikheeva-Gaister, *Deti vragov naroda: Semeinaia khronika vremen kul'ta lichnosti 1925–1953* (Moscow: Vozvrashchenie, 2012), 16–17; I. A. Gaister, interview with author, September 30, 1997; E. I. Gruzinova (Kraval'), interview with author, January 16, 1998; G. S. Ronina, interview with author, October 1, 1997.

21. ARAN, f. 528, op. 4, d. 86, l. 19; AMDNN, "Kisis" file, letter from E. R. Kisis, 10; Warren Lerner, *Karl Radek: The Last Internationalist* (Stanford, CA: Stanford University Press, 1970), 156–57; V. A. Artemov, *Karl Radek: Ideiia i sud'ba* (Voronezh: TsChKI, 2000), 161–63; Karl Radek, *Portrety vreditelei* (Moscow: OGIZ, 1931), 29.

22. T. I. Smilga, interview with author, January 19, 1998.

23. G. A. Voronskaia, "Esli v serdtse posylaiut puliu," *Istoricheskii arkhiv* 1 (1997): 98–101; E. A. Dinershtein, *A. K. Voronskii v poiskakh zhivoi vody* (Moscow: Rosspen 2001), 302–10.

24. R. M. Poloz, interview with author, June 28, 1998; AMDNN, "Poloz" file.

25. RGASPI, f. 613, op. 3, d. 193, ll. 1–5, 9; V. B. Volina, interview with author, September 18, 1997.

26. S. Moroz, "Minuvshee," 2–4, and S. Moroz, "V dome tom . . . ," 5, both in AMDNN, "Moroz" file.

27. AMDNN, "Podvoisky" file; Mikhail Korshunov and Victoria Terekhova, *Tainy i legendy Doma na naberezhnoi* (Moscow: Slovo, 2002), 9–27; O. A. Aroseva, interview with author, January 15, 1998; V. B. Volina, interview with author, September 18, 1997; S. A. Khalatova, interview with author, September 6, 1998; O. N. Podvoiskaia, interview with author, February 27, 1998; N. P. Kerzhentseva, interview with author, January 12, 1998; and G. B. Ivanova, interview with author, March 13, 1998.

28. Korshunov and Terekhova, *Tainy i legendy*, 10; Shikheeva-Gaister, *Deti vragov naroda*, 23; Z. M. Tuchina, interview with author, September 8, 1998; V. N. Rabichev, interview with author, April 14, 1998; G. S. Ronina, interview with author, October 1, 1997; G. B. Ivanova, interview with author, March 13, 1998.

29. GARF, f. 3316, op. 24, d. 517, ll. 2–96.

30. O. Shmidt, *Zamoskvorech'e: Iakimanskaia chast'* (Moscow: Gosudarstvennaia publichnaia istoricheskaia biblioteka Rossii, 1999), 31–44; E. I. Kirichenko, *Khram Khrista Spasitelia v Moskve: Istoriia proektirovaniia i sozdaniia sobora 1813–1931* (Moscow: Planeta, 1992), 216–70; I. Evsenin, *Ot fabrikanta k Krasnomu Oktiabriu* (Moscow: Izdatel'stvo VTsSPS, 1927), 80; Korshunov and Terekhova, *Tainy i legendy*, 289; E. R. Kisis, "Pis'mo v muzei," 5, in AMDNN, "Kisis" file; Z. M. Tuchina, interview with author, September 8, 1998.

31. Korshunov and Terekhova, *Tainy i legendy*, 291; RGASPI, f. 559, op. 1, d. 132, l. 45; Shikheeva-Gaister, *Deti vragov naroda*, 24.

32. GARF, f. 3316, op. 43, d. 593, l. 8; d. 911, ll. 5–7, 200b.–220b.

33. E. E. Ivchenko, interview with author, September 23, 1998. Copies of Emelian and Anna Ivchenko's official autobiographies are in the author's possession.

34. GARF, f. 3316, op. 43, d. 911, l. 190b.; Korshunov and Terekhova, *Tainy i legendy*, 18; Z. M. Tuchina, interview with author, September 8, 1998.

35. GARF, f. 331.6, op. 43, d. 911, l. 200b.–340b.; f. 9542, op. 1, d. 19, l. 61; Korshunov and Terekhova, *Tainy i legendy*, 291.

36. GARF, f. 3316, op. 43, d. 593, ll. 90b., 23–24, 33; d. 801, ll. 6, 33–35; 40–41; f. 9542, op. 1, d. 19, ll. 58–63.

37. GARF, f. 3316, op. 25, d. 686, ll. 12–162; RGASPI, f. 559. op. 1, d. 132, l. 390b.

38. RGALI, f. 2310, op. 1, d. 19, ll. 10, 15. See also AGTsTM, f. 454, d. 90; GARF, f. 3316, op. 25, dd. 690, 1038.

39. F. N. Kaverin, *Vospominaniia i teatral'nye rasskazy* (Moscow: VTO, 1964), 19–20.

40. Ibid., 81 (the "flooding" quotation), 20–21.

41. Aleksandr Kron, *Vechnaia problema* (Moscow: Sovetskii pisatel', 1969), 259–65. The Ruben Simonov quotation is from B. G. Golubovskii, *Bol'shie malen'kie teatry* (Moscow: Izdatel'stvo imeni Sabashnikovykh, 1998), 97.

42. AGTsTM, f. 454, d. 446, ll. 9, 14, 18, 20; Kaverin, *Vospominaniia*, 221.

43. Kaverin, *Vospominaniia*, 38.

44. Ibid., 117.

45. Ibid., 39, 37.

46. Ibid., 266–74. See also Golubovskii, *Bol'shie malen'kie teatry*, 99; N. A. Smirnova, *Vospominaniia* (Moscow: VTO, 1947), 405–9; RGALI, f. 645, op. 1, d. 267, l. 13b; RGALI, f. 649, op. 1, d. 530, l. 7; AGTsTM, f. 454, d. 1283, l. 2.

47. L. D. Snezhnitskii, "Rezhisserskie iskaniia F. N. Kaverina," in Kaverin, *Vospominaniia*, 369–70, 374–77; Smirnova, *Vospominaniia*, 407–12 (the quotation is on 411); RGALI, f. 656, op. 1, d. 3134, l. 68 (the censor's comments).

48. RGALI, f. 645, op. 1, d. 267, ll. 13a; AGTsTM, f. 454, d. 1379, l. 2; d. 1285, ll. 6–8; Snezhnitskii, "Rezhisserskie iskaniia," 380–82.

49. AGTsTM, f. 454, d. 447, l. 4.

50. Ibid., ll. 5, 7, 10–11.

51. Ibid., ll. 4–5, 11; d. 1285, l. 5.

52. A. Artizov and Oleg Naumov, eds., *Vlast' i khudozhestvennaia intelligentsiia* (Moscow: Fond "Demokratiia," 1999), 173; GARF, f. 3316, op. 25, d. 690, ll. 12–14; RGALI, f. 645, op.1. d. 299, l. 6; AGTsTM, f. 454, d. 1285, l. 16; d. 1292, no list numbers (*Sovetskoe iskusstvo* 52 [November 15, 1932]).

53. AGTsTM, f. 454, d. 512, ll. 22–25, 58–62, 66, 113.

54. Smirnova, *Vospominaniia*, 424–25; Golubovskii, *Bol'shie malen'kie teatry*, 104.

55. RGALI, f. 656, op.1, d. 2693, ll. 8, 67, 73–79, and passim; f. 2310, op. 1, d. 19, l. 27.

56. RGALI, f. 656, op.1, d. 2693, l. 79.

57. Ibid., l. 2; RGALI, f. 2310, op.1, d. 19, ll. 12, 30, 44, 39–40.

58. RGALI, f. 2310, op.1, d. 19, ll. 64–65, 25–26.

59. Ibid., ll. 5, 80, 8.

60. RGALI, f. 2310, op.1, d. 19, l. 3a.

61. Ibid., ll. 59–60, 62–63, 50, 55; RGALI, f. 649, op. 2, d. 498, l. 1 (on Boichevskaia).

62. N. I. Bukharin, *Ekonomika perekhodnogo perioda*, in Bukharin, *Problemy teorii i praktiki sotsializma* (Moscow: Politizdat, 1989), 165–66.

63. Ibid., 70.

64. Ibid., 71–72.

11. THE ECONOMIC FOUNDATIONS

1. J. V. Stalin, *Problems of Leninism* (Moscow: Foreign Languages Publishing House, 1953), 528–29. Cf. I. V. Stalin, *Sochineniia* (Moscow: Gospolitizdat, 1951), 13:37–38. For an overview, see David R. Shearer, *Industry, State, and Society in Stalin's Russia, 1926–1934* (Ithaca, NY: Cornell University Press, 1996); for a classic history and interpetation, see Stephen Kotkin, *Magnetic Mountain: Stalinism as Civilization* (Berkeley: University of California Press, 1995).

2. RGASPI, f. 124, op. 1, d. 1298, ll. 3–5; d. 1301, ll. 4–40b.; AMDNN, "Mikhailov" file (letters from M. N. Kul'man); Anne D. Rassweiler, *The Generation of Power: The History of Dneprostroi* (New York: Oxford University Press, 1988), 128; M. V. Mikhailova, "Mariia Nikolaevna Kul'man," Muzei "Dom na naberezhnoi," http://museumdom.narod.ru/bio10/kulman.html; M. V. Mikhailova, interview with author, December 3, 1997.

3. N. S. Khrushchev, *Vremia, liudi, vlast' (vospominaniia)* (Moscow: Moskovskie novosti, 1999), 1:38–91; William Taubman, *Khrushchev: The Man and His Era* (New York: W. W. Norton, 2003), 72–113. On the Moscow Metro, see Josette Bouvard, *Le Métro de Moscou: La contruction d'un mythe soviétique* (Paris: Sextant, 2005); and Dietmar Neutatz, *Die Moskauer Metro: Von den ersten Plänen bis zur Grossbaustelle des Stalinismus* (Cologne: Bohlau, 2001).

4. Il'ia Zbarskii, *Ob"ekt No. 1* (Moscow: Vagrius, 2000), 60, 122, 126, 128–30.

5. K. Paustovskii, *Velikan na Kame: Na stroike Bereznikovskogo kombinata* (Moscow: Gosudarstvennoe khimiko-tekhnicheskoe izdatel'stvo, 1934); O. D. Gaisin, "Opyt proektirovaniia sotsgoroda Berezniki (1930–40 gg.)," Nasledie.perm.ru, http://nasledie.perm.ru/pages002 .htm; I. T. Sidorova, "Stroitel'stvo predpriiatii khimicheskoi promyshlennosti v SSSR na etape industrializatsii 1928–1932 gg. (na primere Bereznikovskogo khimicheskogo kombinata)" (PhD diss., Perm', Permskii gosudarstvennyi tekhnicheskii universitet, 2011), 28–42, 54 (quotation is from 42); "Bereznikovskii khimkombinat," *SSSR na stroike* 5 (1932).

6. Z. Kh. Tsukerman, "Vospominaniia," in *Istoricheskii ocherk o Bereznikovskom azotno-tukovom zavode im. K. E. Voroshilova* (Arkhiv muzeiia trudovoi slavy filiala "Azot" OAO "OkhK" "Uralkhim" in Berezniki, manuscript), 214–15, 238. All the unpublished materials on the Berezniki Chemical Works were sent to me by I. T. Sidorova. I am very grateful for her generosity and expert advice.

7. *Verkhnekam'e: istoriia v litsakh: Konovalovskie chteniia* (Berezniki, 2001), 4:204; Anatoly Granovsky, *I Was an NKVD Agent* (New York: Devin-Adair, 1962), 3–13 (the quotation is on 12–13).

8. Varlam Shalamov, "Vizit mistera Poppa," in Shalamov, *Sobranie sochinenii v chetyrekh tomakh* (Moscow: Khudozhestvennaia literatura, Vagrius, 1998), 2:255, http://shalamov.ru /library/5/27.html; Sidorova, "Stroitel'stvo predpriiatii," 93–106; M. M. Fedorovich, in *Istoricheskii ocherk*, 174.

9. Sidorova, "Stroitel'stvo predpriiatii," 54–82 (the quotations are from 79–80).

10. Ibid., 78, 107–8; A. B. Suslov, *Spetskontingent v Permskoi oblasti: 1929–1953 gg.* (Ekaterinburg and Perm': Ural'skii gosudarstvennyi universitet and Permskii gosudarstvennyi pedagogicheskii universitet, 2003), 126–30.

11. Sidorova, "Stroitel'stvo predpriiatii," 77, 109–13, 208; Suslov, *Spetskontingent*, 64–66; M. B. Smirnov, ed., *Sistema ispravitel'no-trudovykh lagerei v SSSR, 1923–1960* (Moscow: Zven'ia, 1998), 25–27, 184–85; V. Shmyrov, "K probleme stanovleniia GULAGa (Vishlag)," in *Gody terrora: Kniga pamiati zhertv politicheskikh repressii* (Perm': Izdatel'stvo Zdravstvui, 1998), 75–77.

12. Varlam Shalamov, *Vishera*, Shalamov.ru, http://shalamov.ru/library/16/3.html.

13. Ibid., http://shalamov.ru/library/16/5.html.

14. Ibid., http://shalamov.ru/library/16/2.html.

15. Smirnov, *Sistema ispravitel'no-trudovykh lagerei*, 27; A. I. Kokurin and N. V. Petrov, eds., *GULAG (Glavnoe upravlenie lagerei), 1918–1960* (Moscow: Fond "Demokratiia," 2000), 222–26.

16. Shalamov, *Vishera*, http://shalamov.ru/library/16/6.html.

17. Ibid.

18. *Belomorsko-Baltiiskii kanal*, 70–75; N. V. Petrov and K. V. Skorkin, eds., *Kto rukovodil NKVD 1934–1941: Spravochnik* (Moscow: Zven'ia, 1999), 108–9.

19. Shalamov, *Vishera*, http://shalamov.ru/library/16/5.html.

20. Ibid.

21. Sidorova, "Stroitel'stvo predpriiatii," 58–60.

22. S. I. Iur'ev, "Vospominaniia," in *Istoricheskii ocherk*, 1–2 (also listed as Arkhiv muzeia tru- dovoi slavy filiala "Azot" OAO "OkhK" "Uralkhim" in Berezniki, op. 1, d. 102, ll. 1–2); *Nemtsy v Prikam'e. XX v.: Sbornik dokumentov i materialov v 2kh tomakh*, vol. 1, bk. 1: Arkhivnye do- kumenty (Perm': Pushka, 2006), 155; Fedorovich, in *Istoricheskii ocherk*, 169, 174; Tsuker- man, in *Istoricheskii ocherk*, 241; Shalamov, *Vishera*, http://shalamov.ru/library/16/6.html.

23. *Verkhnekam'e: istoriia v litsakh*, 204; Smirnov, *Sistema ispravitel'no-trudovykh lagerei*, 27, 184; Shmyrov, "K probleme stanovleniia GULAGa," 85; Sidorova, "Stroitel'stvo predpriiatii," 120; Granovsky, *I Was an NKVD Agent*, 21–23.

24. G. P. Sidegova, Arkhiv muzeia trudovoi slavy filiala "Azot" OAO "OkhK" "Uralkhim" in Ber- ezniki, audio archive; Granovsky, *I Was an NKVD Agent*, 8.

25. Granovsky, *I Was an NKVD Agent*, 24.

26. Fedorovich, in *Istoricheskii ocherk*, 178.

12. THE VIRGIN LANDS

1. I. V. Stalin, "God velikogo pereloma," in *Sochineniia*, vol. 12, Marxists Internet Archive Li- brary, https://www.marxists.org/russkij/stalin/t12/t12_06.htm.

2. I. V. Stalin, "K voprosam agrarnoi politiki v SSSR. Rech' na Konferentsii agrarnikov- marksistov," in *Sochineniia*, vol. 12, https://www.marxists.org/russkij/stalin/t12/t12_10 .htm; V. Danilov, R. Manning, L. Viola, eds., *Tragediia sovetskoi derevni: Kollektivizatsiia i raskulachivanie* (Moscow: Rosspen, 2000), 2:126–30.

3. Danilov et al., *Tragediia sovetskoi derevni*, 2:126–30, 163–67, 1:727–29; N. A. Ivnitskii, *Repres- sivnaia politika sovetskoi vlasti v derevne, 1928–1933 gg.* (Moscow: Institut istorii RAN), 131; Lynne Viola, *The Unknown Gulag: The Lost World of Stalin's Special Settlements* (New York: Oxford University Press, 2007), 32 and passim; Viktor Kondrashin, *Golod 1932–1933 godov: Tragediia rossiiskoi derevni* (Moscow: Rosspen, 2008), 76.

4. Danilov et al., *Tragediia sovetskoi derevni*, 2:299.

5. On agricultural statistics, see Stephen G. Wheatcroft, "O zernovykh balansakh i otsenkakh urozhainosti v SSSR v 1931–1933," in Danilov et al., *Tragediia sovetskoi derevni*, 3:842–65; Stephen G. Wheatcroft, "O demografisheskikh svidetel'stvakh tragedii sovetskoi derevni v 1931–1933 gg.," in Danilov et al., *Tragediia sovetskoi derevni*, 3:866–67; V. P. Danilov, "Vve- denie," in Danilov et al., *Tragediia sovetskoi derevni*, 1:17; R. W. Davies and Stephen G. Wheat- croft, *The Years of Hunger: Soviet Agriculture, 1931–33* (New York: Palgrave Macmillan, 2004), 123–36, 239–49, and passim. The Bak quotations are from *Tragediia sovetskoi derevni*, 3:394–97; the decree of August 7, 1932, is in *Tragediia sovetskoi derevni*, 3:453–44. For a discussion of the "excess deaths" during the famine, see Davies and Wheatcroft, *Years of Hunger*, 412–20. Wheatcroft's own estimate (on 415) is about 5.7 million deaths.

6. Danilov et al., *Tragediia sovetskoi derevni*, 3:588–97; *Kolektyvizatsyia i golod na Ukraini, 1929–1933* (Kiev: Naukova dumka, 1993), 573–76.

7. I. E. Zelenin, *Stalinskaia "revoliutsiia sverkhu" posle "Velikogo pereloma" 1930–1939: Politika, osushchestvlenie, rezul'taty* (Moscow: Nauka, 2006), 95; *Pravda*, May 26, 1964.

8. N. S. Khrushchev, *Vremia, liudi, vlast' (vospominaniia)* (Moscow: Moskovskie novosti, 1999), 1:32, 71.

9. Davies and Wheatcroft, *Years of Hunger*, 113–14, 118, 145; S. Kul'chitskii, "Obshchii i regional'nyi podkhody k istorii velikoi tragedii narodov Rossii i Ukrainy," in *Sovremennaia*

rossiisko-ukrainskaia istoriografiia goloda 1932–1933 gg. v *SSSR* (Moscow: Rosspen, 2011), 160; Oleg Khlevniuk, *Khoziain: Stalin i utverzhdenie stalinskoi diktatury* (Moscow: Rosspen, 2010), 186–87; Nikolai Zen'kovich, *Elita: Samye sekretnye rodstvenniki* (Moscow: Ol'ma-Press, 2005), 305.

10. Davies and Wheatcroft, *Years of Hunger*, 91, 147, 325. See also Gerald Easter, *Reconstructing the State: Personal Networks and Elite Identity in Soviet Russia* (Cambridge: Cambridge University Press, 2000), 117–32; Kondrashin, *Golod 1932–1933 godov*, 83–84.

11. Danilov et al., *Tragediia sovetskoi derevni*, 1:699, 2:137–38; Iudit Agracheva, "Chlen partii s 1903 goda," *Vesti-2* (Israel), June 1, 1995, 10; G. S. Ronina, interview with author, October 1, 1997; A. M. Larina, *Nezabyvaemoe* (Moscow: APN, 1989), 268; ARAN, razriad 5, op. 1-o, d. 11, l. 54 ob.; Oleg Khlevniuk, *Khoziain: Stalin i utverzhdenie stalinskoi diktatury* (Moscow: Rosspen, 2010), 57–72 (quotations from 60 and 70).

12. Danilov et al., *Tragediia sovetskoi derevni*, 3:12, 575; Kondrashin, *Golod 1932–1933 godov*, 154–62.

13. Danilov et al., *Tragediia sovetskoi derevni*, 3:598–601; Kondrashin, *Golod 1932–1933 godov*, 154–62; Zelenin, *Stalinskaia "revoliutsiia sverkhu,"* 92–94, 100–101; V. Kondrashin, "Golod 1932–1933 v sovremennoi rossiiskoi i zarubezhnoi istoriografii: vzgliad iz Rossii," in Kondrashin, ed., *Sovremennaia rossiisko-ukrainskaia istoriografiia*, 68; L. P. Postyshev, interview with author, October 1, 1998.

14. Isabelle Ohayon, *La sédentarisation des kazakhs dans l'URSS de Staline: Collectivisation et changement social (1928–1945)* (Paris: Maisonneuve et Larose, 2006), 235–40. See also Niccolò Pianciola, "The Collectivization Famine in Kazakhstan, 1931–33," in Halyna Hryn, ed., *Hunger by Design: The Great Ukrainian Famine and Its Soviet Context* (Cambridge, MA: Harvard University Press, 2008), 103, 108; Niccolò Pianciola, "Famine in the Steppe: The Collectivization of Agriculture and the Kazak Herdsmen, 1928–1934," *Cahiers du monde russe* 45, nos. 1–2 (January–June 2004): 137; Zelenin, *Stalinskaia "revoliutsiia sverkhu,"* 107; Danilov et al., *Tragediia sovetskoi derevni*, 3:688.

15. L. S. Akhmetova, V. K. Grigor'ev, *Pervye litsa Kazakhstana v stalinskuiu epokhu* (Almaty: Kazakhskii natsional'nyi universitet im. Al-Farabi, 2010), 26, 44.

16. *XVI s"ezd Vsesoiuznoi kommunisticheskoi partii (b): Stenograficheskii otchet* (Moscow: Partizdat, 1935), 1:232–33.

17. Valerii Mikhailov, *Khronika Velikogo Dzhuta* (Almaty: Zhalyn, 1996), 149–50 (the quotation from Goloshchekin); Akhmetova and Grigor'ev, *Pervye litsa*, 41 (see also 29–31); *XVI s"ezd Vsesoiuznoi kommunisticheskoi partii*, 1:233.

18. Mikhailov, *Khronika Velikogo Dzhuta*, 264–65, 295.

19. Zelenin, *Stalinskaia "revoliutsiia sverkhu,"* 106.

20. N. A. Ivnitskii, *Golod 1932–1933 godov v SSSR* (Moscow: Sobranie, 2009), 120–21; Danilov et al., *Tragediia sovetskoi derevni*, 3:335.

21. Agnessa Mironova-Korol', *Agnessa: From Paradise to Purgatory: A Voice from Stalin's Russia*, trans. Rose Glickman (Bloomington, IN: Slavica, 2012), 48 (translation modified); M. M. Iakovenko, *Agnessa: Ustnye rasskazy Agnessy Ivanovny Mironovoi-Korol'*, Memorial: Istoricheskie programmy, "Nasha zhizn' s Miroshei," http://www.memo.ru/history/agnessa.

22. Mironova, *Agnessa: From Paradise to Purgatory*, 49–51 (translation modified); Iakovenko, *Agnessa*, http://www.memo.ru/history/agnessa.

23. *Nasil'stvennaia kollektivizatsiia i golod v Kazakhstane v 1931–33 gg. Sbornik dokumentov i materialov* (Almaty: Fond "XXI vek," 1998), 88.

24. Mironova, *Agnessa: From Paradise to Purgatory*, 51 (translation modified); Iakovenko, *Agnessa*, http://www.memo.ru/history/agnessa.

25. *Nasil'stvennaia kollektivizatsiia*, 98.

26. Ibid., 99–105, 165.

27. Mikhailov, *Khronika Velikogo Dzhuta*, 9–11.

28. Danilov et al., *Tragediia sovetskoi derevni*, 3:89; *Nasil'stvennaia kollektivizatsiia*, 107–9,

111–14, 117–18; 122–25; Ohayon, *La sédentarisation*, 271–72; Mikhailov, *Khronika Velikogo Dzhuta*, 311–17.

29. *Nasil'stvennaia kollektivizatsiia*, 153–62.

30. Mikhailov, *Khronika Velikogo Dzhuta*, 317–18; *Nasil'stvennaia kollektivizatsiia*, 194–97; Danilov et al., *Tragediia sovetskoi derevni*, 3:548–49, 628; Zelenin, *Stalinskaia "revoliutsiia sverkhu,"* 85.

31. G. A. Voronskaia, "Esli v serdtse posylaiut puliu," *Istoricheskii arkhiv* 1 (1997): 82.

32. Mironova, *Agnessa: From Paradise to Purgatory*, 62 (translation modified); Iakovenko, *Agnessa*, http://www.memo.ru/history/agnessa.

33. Mironova, *Agnessa: From Paradise to Purgatory*, 62, 61 (translation modified); Iakovenko, *Agnessa*, http://www.memo.ru/history/agnessa.

34. Lyova quoted in Mironova, *Agnessa: From Paradise to Purgatory*, 58 (translation modified); Iakovenko, *Agnessa*, http://www.memo.ru/history/agnessa.

35. Aleksei Tepliakov, *Oprichniki Stalina* (Moscow: Iauza, 2009), 215; V. Kondrashin, "Golod 1932–33 gg. v Rossiiskoi Federatsii (RSFSR)," in Kondrashin, ed., *Sovremennaia rossiisko-ukrainskaia istoriografiia*, 278.

36. Mironova, *Agnessa: From Paradise to Purgatory*, 70 (translation modified); Iakovenko, *Agnessa*, http://www.memo.ru/history/agnessa.

37. Mironova, *Agnessa: From Paradise to Purgatory*, 62–63 (translation modified); Iakovenko, *Agnessa*, http://www.memo.ru/history/agnessa.

38. See, esp., Danilov et al., *Tragediia sovetskoi derevni*, 1:111, 236, 685, 715, 744, 746–58; 2:17, 35–37, 39–47, 61–66, 75, 131, 544, 548, 613–32; 3:217; I. S. Sobol', "Narkom zdravookhraneniia bol'shevik Grigorii Kaminskii," *Za meditsinskie kadry* 4 (February 6, 1989); T. M. Belen'kaia-Rybakova, interview with author, October 1, 1997.

39. GARF, f. 9542, op. 1, d. 17, ll. 158–60.

40. TsAODM, f. 75, op. 1, d. 69, l. 325.

41. RGASPI, f. 613, op. 3, d. 156, l. 6; Il'ia Zbarskii, *Ob"ekt No. 1* (Moscow: Vagrius, 2000), 125–26.

42. RGASPI, f. 214, op. 1, d. 853, ll. 30–49.

43. RGASPI, f. 146, op. 1, d. 24, ll. 7–8; d. 211, ll. 3–11, 18–22.

44. RGVA, f. 37461, op. 1, d. 149, ll. 136–136 ob.

45. A. S. Serafimovich, *Sobranie sochinenii* (Moscow: GIKhL, 1960), 7:570.

46. RGALI, f. 457, d. 390, ll. 81, 810b., 110.

47. Ibid., ll. 17–23.

48. Serafimovich, *Sobranie sochinenii*, 7:573.

49. Tat'iana Rybakova, *Schastlivaia ty, Tania* (Moscow: Vagrius, 2005), 12; Elina Robertovna Kisis, letter to the Museum, 6, in AMDNN, "Kisis" file.

50. Kisis, letter to the Museum, 9. The "documentary proof" quotation is from Platonov's *The Foundation Pit*.

51. Ibid., 7; T. I. Smilga, interview with author, January 19, 1998.

52. Serafimovich, *Sobranie sochinenii*, 7:575–76, 574.

53. M. Kol'tsov, "Chernaia zemlia," in *Fel'etony i ocherki* (Moscow: Pravda, 1956), 133–34.

54. A. Platonov, *Vprok*, RoyalLib.com, http://royallib.ru/read/platonov_andrey/vprok.html #133120.

55. N. V. Kornienko and E. D. Shubina, eds., *Andrei Platonov: Vospominaniia sovremennikov; Materialy k biografii* (Moscow: Sovremennyi pisatel', 1994), 268–88 (quotations from 282–83, 278, 274); A. Artizov and Oleg Naumov, eds., *Vlast' i khudozhestvennaia intelligentsiia* (Moscow: Fond "Demokratiia," 1999), 150.

56. Kornienko and Shubina, *Andrei Platonov*, 279; Platonov, *Vprok*, http://royallib.ru/read /platonov_andrey/vprok.html#133120.

57. M. Sholokhov, *Podniataia tselina*, Lib.ru, http://lib.ru/PROZA/SHOLOHOW/celina.txt.

58. Serafimovich, *Sobranie sochinenii*, 7:70–72.

59. Yuri Slezkine, *Arctic Mirrors: Russia and the Small People of the North* (Ithaca, NY: Cornell University Press, 1994), 292–99, 323–35.

60. A. L. Isbakh, *Bol'shaia zhizn'* (Moscow: Khudozhestvennaia literatura, 1936), 282; *Solo truby* (Moscow, 1986), a documentary film, directed by A. Ivankin, screenplay by Lev Roshal'. See also L. Roshal', *Piramida. Solo truby. Kinostsenarii* (Moscow: Iskusstvo, 1989), 63–68.

61. Isbakh, *Bol'shaia zhizn'*, 266–68.

62. Ibid., 284.

63. Cf. F. Fedotov, *Bezrabotnye* (Moscow: Bibliotechka batraka, 1930); Isbakh, *Bol'shaia zhizn'*, 167–261; Mikhail Korshunov and Victoria Terekhova, *Tainy i legendy Doma na naberezhnoi* (Moscow: Slovo, 2002), 168. The quotations are from Isbakh, *Bol'shaia zhizn'*, 167–68, 262.

64. Isbakh, *Bol'shaia zhizn'*, 285–86.

65. F. Fedotov, *Mongolia* (Moscow: OGIZ Molodaia gvardaiia, 1932).

66. F. Fedotov, *Pakhta* (Moscow: OGIZ Molodaia gvardiia, 1933).

67. I. E. Zelenin, "Politotdely MTS—prolozhenie politiki 'chrezvychaishchiny' (1933–1934 gg.)," *Otechestvennaia istoriia* 6 (1992): 42–61; Danilov et al., *Tragediia sovetskoi derevni*, 3:678–97.

68. Isbakh, *Bol'shaia zhizn'*, 299–302.

69. Ibid., 301.

70. Ibid., 305–6.

13. THE IDEOLOGICAL SUBSTANCE

1. A. Platonov, *Vprok*, RoyalLib.com, http://royallib.ru/read/platonov_andrey/vprok.html #133120.

2. Il'ia Zbarskii, *Ob"ekt No. 1* (Moscow: Vagrius, 2000), 98–99.

3. The pioneering work on the subject is Sheila Fitzpatrick, ed., *Cultural Revolution in Russia, 1928–1931* (Bloomington: Indiana University Press, 1978).

4. Susan Gross Solomon, *The Soviet Agrarian Debate: A Controversy in Social Science, 1923–1929* (Boulder, CO: Westview Press, 1977), 148–70; Terry Cox, *Peasants, Class, and Capitalism: The Rural Research of L. N. Kritsman and His School* (Oxford: Clarendon Press, 1986), 201–19; E. A. Tonchu, "Sol' zemli," in *Ekonomicheskoe nasledie Chaianova* (Moscow: Izdatel'skii dom Tonchu, 2006), 658–59; I. V. Stalin, "K voprosam agrarnoi politiki v SSSR. Rech' na Konferentsii agrarnikov-marksistov," in *Sochineniia*, vol. 12, Marxists Internet Archive Library, https://www.marxists.org/russkij/stalin/t12/t12_10.htm; ARAN, f. 528, op. 4, d. 10, l. 3.

5. Tonchu, "Sol' zemli," 659; A. V. Chaianov, *Puteshestvie moego brata*, Klassika, http://az.lib .ru/c/chajanow_a_w/text_0020.shtml; V. Goncharov and V. Nekhotin, comps., *Prosim osvobodit' iz tiuremnogo zakliucheniia: Pis'ma v zashchitu repressirovannykh* (Moscow: Sovremennyi pisatel', 1998), 176–77; *Pis'ma I. V. Stalina V. M. Molotovu, 1925–1936 gg.: Sbornik dokumentov* (Moscow: Rossiia molodaia, 1995), 211, 224.

6. ARAN, f. 528, op. 4, d. 86, ll. 2–5, 14.

7. L. Averbakh, "O tselostnykh masshtabakh i chastnykh Makarakh," in N. V. Kornienko and E. D. Shubina, eds., *Andrei Platonov: Vospominaniia sovremennikov; Materialy k biografii* (Moscow: Sovremennyi pisatel', 1994), 258.

8. Ibid., 265.

9. *Vospominaniia sovremennikov ob A. S. Serafimoviche* (Moscow: Sovetskii pisatel', 1977), 188–89.

10. A. Artizov and Oleg Naumov, eds., *Vlast' i khudozhestvennaia intelligentsiia* (Moscow: Fond "Demokratiia," 1999), 196; G. V. Zhirkov, *Istoriia tsenzury v Rossii XIX–XX vv.* (Moscow: Aspekt Press, 2001), 314–15.

11. Ivan Gronskii, *Iz proshlogo* (Moscow: Izvetiia, 1991), 153.

12. Ibid., 146; Brian Evan Kassof, "The Knowledge Front: Politics, Ideology, and Economics in

the Soviet Book Publishing Industry, 1925–1935" (PhD diss., University of California, Berkeley, 2000), 461–506; L. Gronskaia, *Nabroski po pamiati* (Moscow: Flinta, 2004), 55.

13. TsAOPIM, f. 78, op. 1a, d. 176, ll. 55, 50, 51.
14. Ibid., l. 49.
15. Ibid., ll. 62, 67–68.
16. Ibid., ll. 65, 74–77ob.
17. Ibid., ll. 77–77ob. See also Varlam Shalamov, "Aleksandr Konstantonovich Voronskii," in *Sobranie sochinenii*, 4:577–87, Shalamov.ru, http://shalamov.ru/library/32/4.html.
18. AGTsTM, f. 454, d. 512, l. 12; d. 90, l. 1.
19. Mikhail Romm, *Ia boleiu za "Spartak"* (Alma-Ata: Zhazushi, 1965); RGALI, f. 656, op.1. d. 2505, l. 3.
20. AGTsTM, f. 454, d. 512, ll. 12–38; M. Romm, *Chempion mira: Rezhisserskii kommentarii F. N. Kaverina* (Moscow: GIKhL, 1933), 95–104.
21. AGTsTM, f. 454, d. 158, ll. 1–2; AGTsTM, f. 454, d. 90, l. 1.
22. AGTsTM, f. 454, d. 448, ll. 1–2.
23. Aleksandr Kron, *Vechnaia problema* (Moscow: Sovetskii pisatel', 1969), 266–68. See also B. G. Golubovskii, *Bol'shie malen'kie teatry* (Moscow: Izdatel'stvo imeni Sabashnikovykh, 1998), 106.
24. Oleg Khlevniuk, *Khoziain: Stalin i utverzhdenie stalinskoi diktatury* (Moscow: Rosspen, 2010), 183.
25. *XVII s"ezd Vsesoiuznoi kommunisticheskoi partii (b): Stenografocheskii otchet* (Moscow: Partizdat, 1934), 261.
26. Ibid., 252.
27. Ibid., 67, 351.
28. Ibid., 516.
29. Ibid., 237–38.
30. Ibid., 238.
31. Ibid., 212.
32. Ibid., 125, 496.
33. On the Stalin cult, see Jan Plamper, *The Stalin Cult: A Study in the Alchemy of Power* (New Haven, CT: Yale University Press, 2012). See also Sarah Davies and James Harris, *Stalin's World: Dictating the Soviet Order* (New Haven, CT: Yale University Press, 2014), 133–82.
34. *XVII s"ezd Vsesoiuznoi kommunisticheskoi partii*, 250, 209, 129.
35. Ibid., 238–39.
36. Ibid., 239, 245.
37. Ibid., 627.
38. Ibid., 500, 253.
39. *Izvestiia*, April 24, 1931, 2. See also Grigorii Besedovskii, *Na putiakh k Termidoru* (Moscow: Sovremennik, 1997), 338–44.
40. *XVII s"ezd Vsesoiuznoi kommunisticheskoi partii*, 501, 252–53.
41. Artizov and Naumov, *Vlast' i khudozhestvennaia intelligentsiia*, 175, 184, 190–91, 214; Gronskii, *Iz proshlogo*, 16–154 and passim; Gronskaia, *Nabroski po pamiati*, 14–57 and passim.
42. *Pavel Vasil'ev, materialy i issledovaniia: Sbornik statei* (Omsk: OmGU, 2002), 66–67; Gronsky, *Iz proshlogo*, 149, 234; Gronskaia, *Nabroski po pamiati*, 42–57; K. Zelinskii, "Odna vstrecha u Gor'kogo (Zapis' iz dnevnika)," *Voprosy literatury* (May 1991): 153.
43. Gronsky, *Iz proshlogo*, 153–54; Zelinskii, "Odna vstrecha," 167.
44. *Pervyi vsesoiuznyi s"ezd sovetskikh pisatelei 1934: Stenograficheskii otchet* (Moscow: Sovetskii pisatel', 1990: reprint of the 1934 Khudozhestvennaia literatura edition), 2, 210–11, 279, 151–53.
45. Ibid., 152–53. On Leonov, see Zakhar Prilepin, *Leonid Leonov* (Moscow: Molodaia gvardiia, 2010), 11–271.
46. *Pervyi vsesoiuznyi*, 153.

47. Ibid., 279.
48. Ibid., 280.
49. Ibid., 501–2.
50. Ibid., 502.
51. Ibid., 20, 233, 152, 142. Foma Gordeev is the main character in the eponymous novel by Gorky; Raphael de Valentin is a character from Balzac's *La peau de chagrin*.
52. *Pervyi vsesoiuznyi*, 185.
53. Ibid., 498, 502; Gronskii, *Iz proshlogo*, 141.
54. *Pervyi vsesoiuznyi*, 498, 306; Zelinskii, "Odna vstrecha," 165. On Shakespeare in the 1930s, see Arkady Ostrovsky, "Shakespeare as a Founding Father of Socialist Realism: The Soviet Affair with Shakespeare," in Irena K. Makaryk and Joseph G. Price, eds., *Shakespeare in the Worlds of Communism and Socialism* (Toronto: University of Toronto Press, 2006), 56–83. On the Russian classics, see David Brandenberger, *National Bolshevism: Stalinist Mass Culture and the Formation of Modern Russian National Identity, 1931–1956* (Cambridge, MA: Harvard University Press, 2002), 63–112; and David Brandenberger and Kevin M. F. Platt, eds., *Epic Revisionism: Russian History and Literature as Stalinist Propaganda* (Madison: University of Wisconsin Press, 2006).
55. A. Lunacharskii, "Arkhitekturnoe oformlenie sotsialisticheskikh gorodov," in *Goroda sotsializma i sotsialisticheskaia rekonstruktsiia byta: Sbornik statei* (Moscow: Rabotnik prosveshcheniia, 1930), 67–68; *Dvorets sovetov: Vsesoiuznyi konkurs 1932 g.* (Moscow: Vsekokhudozhnik, 1933), 103. The final quotation is the last line of *Faust*.

14. THE NEW LIFE

1. *XVII s"ezd Vsesoiuznoi kommunisticheskoi partii (b): Stenografocheskii otchet* (Moscow: Partizdat, 1934), 252.
2. RGASPI, f. 124, op. 1, d. 1429, ll. 77–90.
3. GARF, f. 3316, op. 43, d. 1190, l. 112; f. 9542, op. 7, d. 34, l. 111; f. 3316, op. 28, d. 590, l. 17.
4. GARF, f. 9542, op. 7, d. 14, ll. 6–7. See also d. 13, ll. 46, 69; and op. 1, d. 28, ll. 132, 141.
5. AMDNN, "Lakhuti" file; G. G. Lakhuti, interview with author, September 14, 1998; GARF, f. 5446, op. 82, d. 27, l. 164; GARF, f. 9542, op. 1, d. 28, ll. 132, 141; L. V. Maksimenkov, ed., *Bol'shaia tsenzura: Pisateli i zhurnalisty v strane Sovetov 1917–1956* (Moscow: Fond "Demokratiia," izdatel'stvo "Materik," 2005), docs. 271, 272, 302; Abul'gasem Lakhuti, *Dva ordena* (Moscow: Khudozhestvennaia literatura, 1936), 7.
6. According to a 1938 report, 257 apartments out of 420 included in the report belonged, or used to belong, to nomenklatura members. Forty-three apartments (not included in 257) were occupied by personal pensioners. See GARF, f. 9542, op. 7, d. 14, l. 6.
7. RGASPI, f. 124, op. 1, d. 1346, ll. 2–40b., 71, 82, 85, 89, 91–92, 99, 103, 115, 118–200b., 122, 132, 143–52.
8. Ibid., ll. 93–94 ob.
9. RGVA, f. 37461, op. 1, d. 129, ll. 4, 8 ob.; M. V. Mikhailova, interview with author, December 3, 1997; K. Zelinskii, "Odna vstrecha u Gor'kogo (Zapis' iz dnevnika)," *Voprosy literatury* (May 1991): 168; *Pavel Postyshev: Vospominaniia, vystupleniia, pis'ma* (Moscow: Politizdat, 1987), 52.
10. Yuri Slezkine, *The Jewish Century* (Princeton, NJ: Princeton University Press, 2004), 275–86 and passim. The 1935 apartment register lists 506 leaseholders, 116 of them Jews "by nationality." On ethnic contingents within the Soviet elite, see Liliana Riga, *The Bolsheviks and the Russian Empire* (Cambridge: Cambridge University Press, 2012). On Latvians among Soviet military and state security officials, see Ēriks Jēkabsons, "Latyshi v rukovodstve krasnoi armii i Narodnogo komissariata vnutrennikh del SSSR," in A. A. Komarov, ed., *Baltiiskoe sosedstvo: Rossiia, Shvetsiia, strany Baltii na fone epokh i sobytii XIX–XXI vv.* (Moscow: Lenand, 2014), 105–47. I am grateful to the author for a helpful consultation.

11. Ol'ga Aroseva, *Bez grima* (Moscow: Tsentrpoligraf, 1999), 21–22; O. A. Aroseva, interview with author, January 15, 1998; Boris Efimov, interview with author, October 16, 1997; S. V. Obolenskaia (Osinskaia), interview with author, March 26, 1998; V. E. Yusim, interview with author, December 5, 1998; Z. A. Khatskevich, interview with author, September 4, 1998; M. V. Mikhailova, interview with author, December 3, 1997; V. N. Rabichev, interview with author, April 14, 1998; V. D. Shvarts, interview with author, December 10, 1998; V. B. Volina, interview with author, September 18, 1997.

12. O. A. Aroseva, interview with author, January 15, 1998; V. B. Volina, interview with author, September 18, 1997; S. V. Obolenskaia (Osinskaia), interview with author, March 26, 1998; M. V. Mikhailova, interview with author, December 3, 1997; S. A. Khalatova, interview with author, September 6, 1998; V. A. Ozerskii, interview with author, June 26, 1999.

13. K. P. Politkovskaia (Allilueva), interview with author, April 1, 1998; M. V. Mikhailova, interview with author, December 3, 1997; T. I. Smilga, interview with author, January 19, 1998; Vladimir Alliluev, *Khronika odnoi sem'i* (Moscow: Molodaia gvardiia, 2002), 100–101; Aroseva, *Bez grima*, 22; I. K. Gronsky, interview with author, October 9, 1998; Ivan Gronskii, *Iz proshlogo* (Moscow: Izvestiia, 1991), 141; S. A. Khalatova, interview with author, September 6, 1998; I. R. Muklevich, interview with author, November 7, 1997; M. R. Peterson, "O nas," l. 1, in AMDNN, "Peterson" file; Yuri Trifonov, *The Disappearance*, trans. David Lowe (Ann Arbor, MI: Ardis, 1991), 17; cf. Iurii Trifonov, *Ischeznovenie*, RoyalLib.com, http://royallib.ru/read/trifonov_yuriy/ischeznovenie.html#0.

14. E. R. Kisis, "Pis'mo v muzei," 3–4, in AMDNN, "Kisis" file.

15. M. V. Mikhailova, interview with author, December 3, 1997.

16. S. V. Obolenskaia (Osinskaia), interview with author, March 26, 1998; R. M. Poloz, interview with author, June 28, 1998; T. I. Smilga, interview with author, January 19, 1998; G. B. Ivanova, interview with author, March 13, 1998; N. P. Kerzhentseva, interview with author, January 12, 1998; N. A. Iur'eva interview with author, August 21, 1998; M. V. Mikhailova, interview with author, December 3, 1997; G. S. Ronina, interview with author, October 1, 1997; L. N. Shaburov, interview with author, September 25, 1997; S. A. Khalatova, interview with author, September 6, 1998; E. B. Levina, interview with author, September 27, 1998; M. V. Mikhailova, interview with author, December 3, 1997; I. R. Muklevich, interview with author, November 7, 1997; Z. A. Khatskevich, interview with author, September 4, 1998; V. B. Volina, interview with author, September 18, 1997; I. A. Gaister, interview with author, September 30, 1997; V. E. Iusim, interview with author, December 5, 1998; V. D. Shvarts, interview with author, December 10, 1998; M. A. Tsiurupa, interview with author, January 8, 1998.

17. O. N. Podvoiskaia, interview with author, February 27, 1998; Peterson, "O nas," ll. 22; S. V. Obolenskaia (Osinskaia), interview with author, March 26, 1998; R. M. Poloz, interview with author, June 28, 1998; T. I. Smilga, interview with author, January 19, 1998; M. V. Mikhailova, interview with author, December 3, 1997.

18. Z. M. Tuchina, interview with author, September 8, 1998.

19. L. A. Kozlova (Bogacheva), interview with author, September 24, 1997.

20. Peterson, "O nas," ll. 22–23; Z. M. Tuchina, interview with author, September 8, 1998; Z. A. Khatskevich, interview with author, September 4, 1998; T. M. Rybakova (Belen'kaia), interview with author, October 1, 1997; M. V. Mikhailova, interview with author, December 3, 1997; Kira Allilueva, *Plemiannitsa Stalina* (Moscow: Vagrius, 2006), 84; K. P. Politkovskaia (Allilueva), interview with author, April 1, 1998.

21. N. A. Gilinskaia, interview with author, March 2, 1998; E. I. Gruzinova (Kraval'), interview with author, January 16, 1998.

22. RGASPI, f. 559, op. 1, d. 142, ll. 8, 13, 29–30.

23. GARF, f. 9542, op. 1, d. 30, ll. 2–3; I. R. Muklevich, interview with author, November 7, 1997; V. B. Volina, interview with author, September 18, 1997; M. P. Korshunov, interview with

author, November 11, 1997; L. N. Shaburov, interview with author, September 25, 1997; L. P. Postyshev, interview with author, October 1, 1998; T. V. Ignatashvili (Shuniakova), interview with author, April 22, 1998; M. A. Tsiurupa, interview with author, January 8, 1998; M. V. Mikhailova, interview with author, December 3, 1997; K. P. Politkovskaia (Allilueva), interview with author, April 1, 1998; V. N. Rabichev, interview with author, April 14, 1998; Allilueva, *Plemiannitsa Stalina*, 85; M. N. Kul'man, "Pis'mo v muzei," 11, in AMDNN, "Mikhailov" file; GARF, f. 9542, op. 7, d. 90, l. 39.

24. Kul'man, "Pis'mo v muzei," 11.

25. N. S. Khrushchev, *Vremia, liudi, vlast' (vospominaniia)* (Moscow: Moskovskie novosti, 1999), 1:81; Nataliia Sats, *Zhizn'—iavlenie polosatoe* (Moscow: Novosti, 1991), 260, 263, 270–71.

26. Sats, *Zhizn'*, 270–71.

27. Khrushchev, *Vremia, liudi, vlast' (vospominaniia)*, 1:81; Artem Sergeev and Ekaterina Glushik, *Kak zhil, rabotal i vospityval detei I. V. Stalin: Svidetel'stva ochevidtsa* (Moscow: Forum, 2011), 44–45; R. M. Poloz, interview with author, June 28, 1998; T. M. Rybakova (Belen'kaia), interview with author, October 1, 1997; Tat'iana Rybakova, *Schastlivaia ty, Tania* (Moscow: Vagrius, 2005), 14; I. A. Gaister, interview with author, September 30, 1997; S. A. Butenko, interview with author, September 24, 1998; E. I. Gruzinova (Kraval'), interview with author, January 16, 1998; V. A. Ozerskii, interview with author, June 26, 1999; V. N. Rabichev, interview with author, April 14, 1998; Gronskii, *Iz proshlogo*, 135–36.

28. N. Beliaev, in *Mikhail Kol'tsov, kakim on byl: Sbornik vospominanii* (Moscow: Sovetskii pisatel', 1989), 193; S. V. Obolensksia, *Iz vospominanii*, "Samizdat," http://samlib.ru/o /obolenskaja_s_w/01.shtml; M. A. Usievich, interview with author, January 30, 1998.

29. N. Gordon (née Prokof'eva), in *Mikhail Kol'tsov, kakim on byl*, 384–85.

30. Sof'ia Vinogradskaia, in *Mikhail Kol'tsov, kakim on byl*, 136; Sats, *Zhizn'*, 260, 265; E. B. Levina, interview with author, September 27, 1998; Ol'ga Aroseva, *Bez grima*, 22; M. A. Lozovskaia, interview with author, March 4, 1998; Lidiia Shatunovskaia, *Zhizn' v Kremle* (New York: Chalidze, 1982), 21–22.

31. I. A. Gaister, interview with author, September 30, 1997; I. R. Muklevich, interview with author, November 7, 1997; T. I. Smilga, interview with author, January 19, 1998; M. A. Usievich, interview with author, January 30, 1998.

32. L. Gronskaia, *Nabroski po pamiati* (Moscow: Flinta, 2004), 68; M. V. Mikhailova, interview with author, December 3, 1997; Z. A. Khatskevich, interview with author, September 4, 1998; V. A. Ozerskii, interview with author, June 26, 1999; Peterson, "O nas," ll. 14–15.

33. K. P. Politkovskaia (Allilueva), interview with author, April 1, 1998; Allilueva, *Plemiannitsa Stalina*, 84, 137–38.

34. Allilueva, *Plemiannitsa Stalina*, 138.

35. Ibid., 133–35.

36. Kisis, "Pis'mo v muzei," 8; T. I. Smilga, interview with author, January 19, 1998; I. K. Gronsky, interview with author, October 9, 1998; Allilueva, *Plemiannitsa Stalina*, 137.

37. S. A. Butenko, interview with author, September 24, 1998.

38. Nataliia Sats, *Put' k sebe: O mame Natalii Sats, liubvi, iskaniiakh, teatre* (Moscow: Voskresen'e, 1998), 7–9.

39. M. M. Iakovenko, *Agnessa: Ustnye rasskazy Agnessy Ivanovny Mironovoi-Korol'*, Memorial: Istoricheskie programmy, "Nasha zhizn's Miroshei," http://www.memo.ru/history/agnessa. This passage is not included in the English version.

40. Ibid.

41. Agnessa Mironova-Korol', *Agnessa: From Paradise to Purgatory: A Voice from Stalin's Russia*, trans. Rose Glickman (Bloomington, IN: Slavica, 2012), 64–65 (translation modified); Iakovenko, *Agnessa*, http://www.memo.ru/history/agnessa.

42. Mironova, *Agnessa: From Paradise to Purgatory*, 74 (translation modified); Iakovenko, *Agnessa*, http://www.memo.ru/history/agnessa.

15. THE DAYS OFF

1. Eviatar Zerubavel, *The Seven Day Circle: The History and Meaning of the Week* (New York: Free Press, 1985), 35–41; Larin, *Zhilishche i byt*, 4–5.

2. Zerubavel, *Seven Day Circle*, 41–43.

3. Unless otherwise noted, descriptions of life in the House are based on interviews with residents.

4. N. P. Kerzhentseva, interview with author, January 12, 1998.

5. Iudit Agracheva, "Chlen partii s 1903 goda," *Vesti-2* (Israel), June 1, 1995, 10; I. R. Muklevich, "Dorogoi drug," manuscript in AMDNN, "Muklevich" file; N. P. Kerzhentseva, interview with author, January 12, 1998; L. A. Kozlova (Bogacheva), interview with author, September 24, 1997.

6. Maria Osten, *Gubert v strane chudes* (Moscow: Zhurgaz, 1935), 115–16. See also *Teatral'naia Moskva, sezon 1935* (Moscow: Izdanie UTZP Narkomprosa RSFSR, 1935), 264.

7. Osten, *Gubert v strane chudes*, 4; V. B. Volina, interview with author, September 18, 1997; *Teatral'naia Moskva, sezon 1935*, 263–64. See also Katharina Kucher, *Der Gorki-Park: Freizeitkultur im Stalinismus 1928–1941* (Cologne: Böhlau, 2007), esp. 109–13.

8. Olga Aroseva, *Prozhivshaia dvazhdy* (Moscow: AST, 2012), RoyalLib.com, http://royallib.com/book/aroseva_olga/progivshaya_dvagdi.html.

9. Aroseva, *Prozhivshaia dvazhdy*, chap. 4, http://royallib.com/book/aroseva_olga/progivshaya_dvagdi.html; V. D. Shvarts, interview with author, December 10, 1998; S. V. Obolenskaia (Osinskaia), interview with author, March 26, 1998.

10. Aroseva, *Prozhivshaia dvazhdy*, chap. 4, http://royallib.com/book/aroseva_olga/progivshaya_dvagdi.html. VOKS is the All-Union Society for Cultural Ties with Foreign Countries.

11. S. V. Obolenskaia (Osinskaia) interview, 26 March, 1998.

12. S. V. Obolensksia, *Iz vospominanii*, "Samizdat," http://samlib.ru/o/obolenskaja_s_w/01.shtml. In fact, "WOT LARX" are words from Pip's letter to Joe.

13. N. P. Kerzhentseva, interview with author, January 12, 1998; Aroseva, *Prozhivshaia dvazhdy*, May 29, 1935, http://royallib.com/book/aroseva_olga/progivshaya_dvagdi.html; N. A. Yur'eva, interview with author, August 21, 1998.

14. Charles Dickens, *Our Mutual Friend*, Free Library, http://dickens.thefreelibrary.com/Our-Mutual-Friend/1–5.

15. N. A. Gilinskaia, interview with author, March 2, 1998; V. D. Shvarts, interview with author, December 10, 1998; Aleksei Tepliakov, *Oprichniki Stalina* (Moscow: Iauza, 2009), 216.

16. Agnessa Mironova-Korol', *Agnessa: From Paradise to Purgatory: A Voice from Stalin's Russia*, trans. Rose Glickman (Bloomington, IN: Slavica, 2012), 68–70 (translation modified); M. M. Iakovenko, *Agnessa: Ustnye rasskazy Agnessy Ivanovny Mironovoi-Korol'*, Memorial: Istoricheskie programmy, "Nasha zhizn' s Miroshei," http://www.memo.ru/history/agnessa.

17. Mironova, *Agnessa: From Paradise to Purgatory*, 76–77 (translation modified); Iakovenko, *Agnessa*, http://www.memo.ru/history/agnessa.

18. E. R. Kisis, "Pis'mo v muzei," 10, in AMDNN, "Kisis" file; V. D. Shvarts, interview with author, December 10, 1998; I. A. Gaister, interview with author, September 30, 1997; Inna Shikheeva-Gaister, *Deti vragov naroda: Semeinaia khronika vremen kul'ta lichnosti 1925–1953* (Moscow: Vozvrashchenie, 2012), 34–35.

19. Aroseva, *Prozhivshaia dvazhdy*, October 24, 1934, http://royallib.com/book/aroseva_olga/progivshaya_dvagdi.html.

20. Ivo Banac, ed., *The Diary of Georgi Dimitrov, 1933–1949* (New Haven, CT: Yale University Press, 2003), xliii, 9–23 (the quotation is from 23); Sophie Coeuré and Rachem Mazuy, eds., *Cousu de fil rouge: Voyages des intellectuels français en Union Soviétique* (Paris: CNRS Éditions, 2012), 181–82, 250–54, 316–17; Henri Barbusse, *Staline, une monde nouveau vu à travers un homme* (Paris: Flammarion, 1935).

21. Aroseva, *Prozhivshaia dvazhdy*, March 10, 1937, http://royallib.com/book/aroseva_olga/progivshaya_dvagdi.html.

22. *Vospominaniia sovremennikov ob A. S. Serafimoviche* (Moscow: Sovetskii pisatel-, 1977), 116–17; L. Gronskaia, *Nabroski po pamiati* (Moscow: Flinta, 2004), 45.

23. Gronskaia, *Nabroski po pamiati*, 49–50.

24. L. V. Maksimenkov, ed., *Bol'shaia tsenzura: Pisateli i zhurnalisty v Strane Sovetov, 1917–1956* (Moscow: Fond "Demokratiia", 2005), 292–93.

25. Ibid.

26. Gronskaia, *Nabroski po pamiati*, 56–57. See also A. Konovalov, "Vinovnym sebia ne priznal," *Leninskoe znamia*, July 10, 1988.

27. Maksimenkov, ed., *Bol'shaia tsenzura*, 292; S. A. Khalatova, interview with author, September 6, 1998; Richard F. Staar, "The Polish Communist Party, 1918–1948," *Polish Review* 1, nos. 2/3 (1956): 43; I. R. Muklevich, interview with author, November 7, 1997; T. I. Smilga, interview with author, January 19, 1998.

28. Shikheeva-Gaister, *Deti vragov naroda*, 34; Mironova, *Agnessa: From Paradise to Purgatory*, 59–60 (translation modified); Iakovenko, *Agnessa*, http://www.memo.ru/history/agnessa.

29. E. Dushechkina, "Tri veka russkoi elki," *Nauka i zhizn'* 12 (2007) and 1 (2008): http://www.nkj.ru/archive/articles/12362/; http://www.nkj.ru/archive/articles/12680; Elena Dushechkina, "Legenda o cheloveke, podarivshem elku sovetskim detiam," *Otechestvennye zapiski* 1 (2003): http://magazines.russ.ru/oz/2003/1/2003_01_28.html; N. S. Khrushchev, *Vremia, liudi, vlast' (vospominaniia)* (Moscow: Moskovskie novosti, 1999), 1:119–20. At that time, Stanislav Kosior was the first secretary of the Ukrainian Central Committee; Postyshev was the second secretary and head of the Kiev Party Committee; and A. P. Liubchenko, the chairman of the Council of People's Commissars of Ukraine.

30. *Pravda*, December 28, 1935; L. P. Postyshev, "Ob ottse," in *Pavel Postyshev: Vospominaniia, vystupleniia, pis'ma* (Moscow: Politizdat, 1987), 304–5; Dushechkina, "Legenda," http://magazines.russ.ru/oz/2003/1/2003_01_28.html. On Soviet holidays, see Karen Petrone, *Life Has Become More Joyous, Comrades: Celebrations in the Time of Stalin* (Bloomington: Indiana University Press, 2000).

31. M. R. Peterson, "O nas," ll. 25–26, in AMDNN, "Peterson" file.

32. Z. M. Tuchina, interview with author, September 8, 1998; G. B. Ivanova, interview with author, March 13, 1998. See also Petrone, *Life Has Become More Joyous, Comrades*, 85–109.

33. Nataliia Sats, *Zhizn'—iavlenie polosatoe* (Moscow: Novosti, 1991), 266.

34. Ibid., 243–50; Miron Petrovskii, *Knigi nashego detstva* (St. Petersburg: Izdatel'stvo Ivana Limbakha, 2006), 217–324 (the reference to Hubert is on 318); E. D. Tolstaia, "Buratino i podteksty Alekseia Tolstogo," *Izvestiia AN, seriia literatury i iazyka* 56, no. 2 (1997): 28–39; A. N. Gozenpud, *Tsentral'nyi detskii teatr, 1936–1961* (Moscow: Nauka, 1967), 34–44.

35. Sats, *Zhizn'*, 270.

36. RGASPI, f. 559, op. 1, d. 132, ll. 119–119 ob.

37. TsAODM, f. 75, op. 1, d. 72, l. 76; GARF, f. 9542, op. 1, d. 25, ll. 39, 43–44.

38. GARF, f. 9542, op. 1, d. 26, ll. 28–33; E. E. Ivchenko, interview with author, September 23, 1998.

39. Osten, *Gubert v strane chudes*, 118.

40. RGASPI, f. 559, op. 1, d. 132, ll. 118–118 ob.

41. L. Podvoiskii, "Krasnoe solnyshko sem'i—mama," *Sem'ia i shkola* 3 (1965): 10.

42. S. V. Obolenskaia (Osinskaia), interview with author, March 26, 1998; Z. M. Tuchina, interview with author, September 8, 1998.

43. N. A. Perli-Rykova, interview with author, February 12, 1998; G. B. Ivanova, interview with author, March 13, 1998.

44. Kira Allilueva, *Plemiannitsa Stalina* (Moscow: Vagrius, 2006), 145–46.

45. Vladimir Alliluev, *Khronika odnoi sem'i* (Moscow: Molodaia gvardiia, 2002), 84.

46. S. V. Obolenskaia (Osinskaia), interview with author, March 26, 1998; O. A. Aroseva, inter-

view with author, January 15, 1998; E. I. Gruzinova (Kraval'), interview with author, January 16, 1998; N. A. Perli-Rykova, interview with author, February 12, 1998; I. R. Muklevich, interview with author, November 7, 1997; I. R. Muklevich, "Dorogoi drug," l. 58, manuscript in AMDNN, "Muklevich" file; N. P. Kerzhentseva, interview with author, January 12, 1998; G. B. Ivanova, interview with author, March 13, 1998; V. B. Volina, interview with author, September 18, 1997; T. I. Smilga, interview with author, January 19, 1998; Samuil Moroz, "Chlen kollegii VChK," l. 6, manuscript in AMDNN, "Moroz" file; N. Stepanov, *Podvoiskii* (Moscow: Molodaia gvardiia, 1989), 11–23.

47. M. V. Mikhailova, interview with author, December 3, 1997; T. I. Smilga, interview with author, January 19, 1998; I. A. Gaister, interview with author, September 30, 1997; E. B. Levina, interview with author, September 27, 1998; S. V. Obolenskaia (Osinskaia), interview with author, March 26, 1998; Obolenskaia, *Iz vospominanii*, http://zhurnal.lib.ru/o/obolenskaja_s_w/01.shtml; G. B. Ivanova, interview with author, March 13, 1998; Peterson, "O nas," l. 25; Moroz, "Chlen kollegii," l. 6; Aroseva, *Prozhivshaia dvazhdy*, chap. 4, http://royallib.com/book/aroseva_olga/progivshaya_dvagdi.html; O. A. Aroseva, interview with author, January 15, 1998; V. B. Volina, interview with author, September 18, 1997; O. N. Podvoiskaia, interview with author, February 27, 1998; V. D. Shvarts, interview with author, December 10, 1998.

16. THE HOUSES OF REST

1. GARF, f. 9542, op. 7, d. 34, ll. 65–75 (the quotation is from l. 75).

2. GARF, f. 9542, op. 1, d. 16, ll. 30–38; op. 7, d. 34, ll. 65–75; f. 3316, op. 28, d. 1033, ll. 1–2, 17–18; GARF, f. R-5283, op. 1, d. 283, ll. 197–98; Olga Aroseva, *Prozhivshaia dvazhdy* (Moscow: AST, 2012), May 18, 1935, RoyalLib.com, http://royallib.com/book/aroseva_olga/progivshaya_dvagdi.html.

3. RGASPI, f. 559, op. 1, d. 141, l. 66; L. Gronskaia, *Nabroski po pamiati* (Moscow: Flinta, 2004), 53; L. A. Kozlova (Bogacheva), interview with author, September 24, 1997; L. P. Postyshev, interview with author, October 1, 1998; M. P. Korshunov, interview with author, November 11, 1997; E. I. Gruzinova (Kraval'), interview with author, January 16, 1998; V. D. Shvarts, interview with author, December 10, 1998; V. N. Rabichev, interview with author, April 14, 1998; GARF, f. 9542, op. 1, d. 75, l. 2; Mikhail Korshunov and Victoria Terekhova, *Tainy i legendy Doma na naberezhnoi* (Moscow: Slovo, 2002), 107–8.

4. GARF, f. 9542, op. 1, d. 17, ll. 96–96ob.

5. Ibid., ll. 98–98 ob.

6. Anatoly Granovsky, *I Was an NKVD Agent* (New York: Devin-Adair, 1962), 18.

7. GARF, f. 3316, op. 43, d. 1194, ll. 2–4; GARF, f. 9542, op. 1, d. 19, ll. 71–72ob.

8. GARF, f. 9542, op. 1, d. 19, ll. 83–84.

9. Agnessa Mironova-Korol', *Agnessa: From Paradise to Purgatory: A Voice from Stalin's Russia*, trans. Rose Glickman (Bloomington, IN: Slavica, 2012), 64 (translation modified); M. M. Iakovenko, *Agnessa: Ustnye rasskazy Agnessy Ivanovny Mironovoi-Korol'*, Memorial: Istoricheskie programmy, "Nasha zhizn' s Miroshei," http://www.memo.ru/history/agnessa.

10. I. A. Gaister, interview with author, September 30, 1997; I. R. Muklevich, interview with author, November 7, 1997.

11. V. D. Shvarts, interview with author, September 10, 1998; RGASPI, f. 559, op. 1, d. 141, ll. 55 ob., 19, 33; ARAN, razriad 5, op. 1-o, d. 11, ll. 41–42, 51–52ob., 57–58ob., 74–75ob.

12. N. A. Perli-Rykova, interview with author, February 12, 1998.

13. Mironova, *Agnessa: From Paradise to Purgatory*, 65–66 (translation modified); Iakovenko, *Agnessa*, http://www.memo.ru/history/agnessa; N. V. Petrov and K. V. Skorkin, eds., *Kto rukovodil NKVD 1934–1941: Spravochnik* (Moscow: Zven'ia, 1999), 99–100; "Petrovskii, Daniil Ivanovich," Spravochnik po istorii Kommunisticheskoi partii i Sovetskogo soiuza 1898–1991, http://www.knowbysight.info/PPP/04888.asp.

14. O. N. Podvoiskaia, interview with author, February 27, 1998; I. B. Zbarskii, interview with author, April 22, 1998; S. A. Khalatova, interview with author, September 6, 1998; V. B. Volina, interview with author, September 18, 1997; Samuil Moroz, "Chlen kollegii VChK," l. 12, manuscript in AMDNN, "Moroz" file; A. Shitov, *Iurii Trifonov: Khronika zhizni i tvorchestva* (Ekaterinburg: Izdatel'stvo Ural'skogo universiteta, 1997), 104. On Soviet dachas, see Stephen Lovell, *Summerfolk: A History of the Dacha, 1710–2000* (Ithaca, NY: Cornell University Press, 2003), 136–62.

15. Rosa quoted in Lev Roshal', "Vzlety i posadki: Shest' novell iz zhizni rasstreliannogo generala; Stsenarii polnometrazhnogo dokumental'nogo fil'ma" (manuscript in author's possession), 16–17.

16. M. A. Lozovskaia, interview with author, March 4, 1998.

17. S. V. Obolensksia, *Iz vospominanii*, "Samizdat," http://samlib.ru/o/obolenskaja_s_w/01 .shtml.

18. Inna Shikheeva-Gaister, *Deti vragov naroda: Semeinaia khronika vremen kul'ta lichnosti 1925–1953* (Moscow: Vozvrashchenie, 2012), 25–27.

19. N. P. Kerzhentseva, interview with author, January 12, 1998; M. A. Usievich, interview with author, January 30, 1998; E. B. Levina, interview with author, September 27, 1998; Joseph E. Davies, *Mission to Moscow* (New York: Simon and Schuster, 1941), 66; GARF, f. 9542, op. 7, d. 18, ll. 18, 44–70.

20. RGASPI, f. 124, op. 1, d. 80, ll. 34–42; Aroseva, *Prozhivshaia dvazhdy*, http://royallib.com /book/aroseva_olga/progivshaya_dvagdi.html (see entries under 15 June, 1934, 21 September, 1934, 132 and 13 October, 1934, 23–28 May, 1935; 26 May, 1936; 12 July, 1936).

21. Ol'ga Aroseva, *Bez grima* (Moscow: Tsentrpoligraf, 1999), 32–33.

22. Aroseva, *Prozhivshaia dvazhdy*, July 12, 1936, http://royallib.com/book/aroseva_olga /progivshaya_dvagdi.html.

17. THE NEXT OF KIN

1. RGASPI, f. 124, op.1, d. 1105, ll. 3, 18.

2. N. A. Iur'eva, interview with author, August 21, 1998.

3. S. V. Obolenskaia (Osinskaia), interview with author, March 26, 1998. On the place of kinship in Stalinist ideology, see Golfo Alexopoulos, "Stalin and the Politics of Kinship: Practices of Collective Punishment, 1920s–1940s," *Comparative Studies in Society and History* 50, no. 1 (January 2008): 91–117.

4. O. A. Aroseva, interview with author, January 15, 1998; N. V. Petrov and K. V. Skorkin, eds., *Kto rukovodil NKVD 1934–1941: Spravochnik* (Moscow: Zven'ia, 1999), 98–99, 107–8; A. G. Tepliakov, *Mashina terrora: OGPU-NKVD Sibiri v 1929–41 gg.* (Moscow: Novyi khronograf, 2008), 498–500.

5. ARAN, razriad 5, op. 1-o, d. 11; letter to Shaternikova, January 31, 1937 (copy of the original kept in S. V. Obolenskaia's personal archive); S. V. Obolenskaia, interview with author, October 20, 2009.

6. RGASPI, f. 135, op. 2, d. 10, ll. 56, 4, 33, 330b., 22.

7. Ibid., l. 23.

8. Ibid., l. 62.

9. Ibid., l. 58.

10. Ibid., l. 24.

11. A. S. Serafimovich, *Sobranie sochinenii* (Moscow: GIKhL, 1960), 7:569.

12. Ibid., 7:561, 563.

13. Ibid., 7:568.

14. Ibid., 7:564.

15. Ibid., 7:556.

16. Samuil Moroz, "V Dome tom," 4, manuscript in AMDNN, "Moroz" file.

17. Lev Roshal', "Vzlety i posadki: Shest' novell iz zhizni rasstreliannogo generala; Stsenarii polnometrazhnogo dokumental'nogo fil'ma" (manuscript in author's possession), 32–33.

18. Boris Efimov, *Desiat' desiatiletii* (Moscow: Vagrius, 2000), 55, 179, 244, 614–25; E. I. Gruzinova (Kraval'), interview with author, January 16, 1998; V. V. Kuibyshev, interview with author, February 18, 1998; GARF, f. 9542, op. 1, d. 75, ll. 2–3; Nikolai Zen'kovich, *Elita: Samye sekretnye rodstvenniki* (Moscow: Ol'ma-Press, 2005), 205–12; Z. M. Tuchina, interview with author, September 8, 1998.

19. Olga Aroseva, *Prozhivshaia dvazhdy* (Moscow: AST, 2012), RoyalLib.com, http://royallib .com/book/aroseva_olga/progivshaya_dvagdi.html (in "Zaveshchanie moim detiam," in the afterword [Posleslovie]); L. Podvoiskii, "Krasnoe solnyshko sem'i—mama," *Sem'ia i shkola* 3 (1965): 10.

20. Nataliia Sats, *Zhizn'—iavlenie polosatoe* (Moscow: Novosti, 1991), 272.

21. RGALI, f. 457, d. 390, l. 110; d. 391, ll. 203–4; RGVA, f. 37461, op. 1., d. 128, ll. 15, 29; N. S. Khrushchev, *Vremia, liudi, vlast' (vospominaniia)* (Moscow: Moskovskie novosti, 1999), 140.

22. S. A. Butenko, interview with author, September 24, 1998.

23. Agnessa Mironova-Korol', *Agnessa: From Paradise to Purgatory: A Voice from Stalin's Russia*, trans. Rose Glickman (Bloomington, IN: Slavica, 2012), 41 (translation modified); M. M. Iakovenko, *Agnessa: Ustnye rasskazy Agnessy Ivanovny Mironovoi-Korol'*, Memorial: Istoricheskie programmy, "Nasha zhizn' s Miroshei," http://www.memo.ru/history/agnessa.

24. AMDNN, "Poloz" file, "Moskva, 1933, delo No. 1244"; *Reabilitatsiia: Kak eto bylo, ser. 1980kh–1991*, razdel 4, doc. 13, Alexander Yakolev.org, http://www.alexanderyakovlev.org/fond /issues-doc/67974.

25. A. M. Garaseva, *Ia zhila v samoi beschelovechnoi strane* (Moscow: Intergraf-Servis, 1997), 123, http://www.sakharov-center.ru/asfcd/auth/?t=page&num=7753.

26. AMDNN, "Poloz" file, "Verkhneural'skii izoliator," VU-8 (May 18, 1933), VU-10 (May 18, 1933).

27. AMDNN, "Poloz" file, "Verkhneural'skii izoliator," VU-1–VU-2 (May 2, 1933); VU-8 (May 18, 1933); VU-18 (July 12, 1933), VU-29-9 (August 30, 1933), VU-55 (December 31, 1933).

28. Ibid., VU-15 (June 12, 1933), VU-41 (November 12, 1933), VU-49 (December 12, 1933) and passim.

29. Ibid., n.p. (January 12, 1934).

30. Ibid., VU-30 (September 18, 1933); VU-34 (October 17, 1933); n.p. (October 12, 1934; November 18, 1934; November 29, 1934; December 24, 1934; May 30, 1935) and passim; A. Voronskii, *Za zhivoi i mertvoi vodoi* (Moscow: Antikva, 2005), 2:269–71.

31. A. Voronskii, *Zheliabov* (Moscow: Zhurnal'no-gazetnoe ib"edinenie, 1934), 207, 384, 391–92.

32. AMDNN, "Poloz" file, "Verkhneural'skii izoliator," VU-1 (May 2, 1933), VU-6 (May 12, 1933), VU-10 (May 18, 1933), VU-15 (June 12, 1933).

33. Ibid., VU-12 (June 12, 1933), VU-22 (July 30, 1933), VU-33–VU-34 (October 17, 1933), VU-35 (October 23, 1933), VU-43 (November 30, 1933), VU-51 (December 30, 1933), VU-47 (December 12, 1933).

34. Ibid., VU-32 (October 17, 1933); R. M. Poloz, interview with author, June 28, 1998.

35. AMDNN, "Poloz" file, "Verkhneural'skii izoliator," VU-36–VU-37 (October 23, 1933).

36. Ibid., VU-34 (October 17, 1933), VU-39 (October 23, 1933), VU-42 (November 12, 1933), VU-50 (December 30, 1933).

37. Ibid., VU-45 (November 13, 1933), VU-50–VU-51 (December 30, 1933).

38. Ibid., VU-46 (November 30, 1933), VU-51 (December 30, 1933).

39. Ibid., VU-54 (December 31, 1933).

40. Ibid., n.p. (January 12, 1934).

41. Ibid., n.p. (January 24, 1934).

42. AMDNN, "Poloz" file, "Raport Nachal'niku SPO OGPU tov. Molchanovu."

43. R. M. Poloz, interview with author, June 28, 1998.

44. AMDNN, "Poloz" file, "Verkhneural'skii izoliator," n.p. (January 30, 1934).

45. Ibid., n.p. (February 18, 1934; June 4, 1934); R. M. Poloz, interview with author, June 28, 1998.
46. AMDNN, "Poloz" file, "Verkhneural'skii izoliator," n.p. (March 29, 1934; April 17, 1934; May 11, 1934).
47. Ibid., n.p., June 24, 1934.
48. Ibid., n.p., June 28, 1934.
49. Ibid., n.p., March 1, 1934. See Jochen Hellbeck, *Revolution on My Mind: Writing a Diary under Stalin* (Cambridge, MA: Harvard University Press, 2009).
50. AMDNN, "Poloz" file, "Verkhneural'skii izoliator," n.p. (July 27, 1934).
51. Ibid.
52. Ibid.
53. Ibid., n.p., (August 30, 1934; August 6, 1934; August 12, 1934).
54. Ibid., n.p., (August 12, 1934).
55. Ibid., n.p., (August 17, 1934).
56. Ibid., n.p., (August 30, 1934).
57. Ibid., n.p., (September 12, 1934).
58. Ibid., n.p., (November 7, 1934).
59. Ibid., n.p., (November 18, 1934).
60. Ibid., n.p., (November 29, 1934).
61. Ibid., n.p., n.d., last letter of 1934.
62. Ibid., VU-35, l. 1 (May 30, 1935).

18. THE CENTER OF THE WORLD

1. *General'nyi plan rekonstruktsii goroda Moskvy* (Moscow: Moskovskii rabochii, 1935), 1–8 and passim; A. V. Ikonnikov, *Arkhitektura XX veka: Utopii i real'nost'* (Moscow: Progress-Traditsiia, 2001), 83–89; N. Atarov, *Dvorets sovetov* (Moscow: Moskovskii rabochii, 1940), 18 (the "parks" quotation).
2. Rev. 21:9–16; Thomas More, Utopia, International World History Project, http://history-world.org/Utopia_T.pdf; S. Lang, "The Ideal City from Plato to Howard," *Architectural Review* 112, no. 668 (August 1952): 98, 100; Georg Münter, "Die Geschichte der Idealstadt," *Städtebau* 12 (1929): 326–27; Ikonnikov, *Arkhitektura XX veka*, 193.
3. "Plato's Atlantis," Ascending Passage, http://ascendingpassage.com/plato-atlantis-timaeus.htm; Spiro Kostof, *The City Shaped: Urban Patterns and Meanings through History* (Boston: Little, Brown, 1991), 185–86, 163, 194, 202; "Campanella's City of the Sun," The Alchemy, http://www.levity.com/alchemy/citysun.html; Lang, "Ideal City," 98–100.
4. Lang, "Ideal City," 95–97; Kostof, *City Shaped*, 186–87.
5. Mircea Eliade, *The Sacred and the Profane: The Nature of Religion* (New York: Harcourt, Brace, Jovanovich), 32–58; Norbert Schoenauer, *6,000 Years of Housing* (New York: Norton, 2000), 14–93; Joseph Rykwert, *The Idea of a Town: The Anthropology of Urban Form in Rome, Italy and the Ancient World* (Princeton, NJ: Princeton University Press, 1976), 179.
6. Rykwert, *Idea of a Town*, 28–9, 34–35, 68, 98, 163–95, and passim; Kostof, *City Shaped*, 47–52; 164–65.
7. Kostof, *City Shaped*, 209–77.
8. Peter Hall, *Cities of Tomorrow: An Intellectual History of Urban Planning and Design in the Twentieth Century* (Oxford: Blackwell, 2002), 189, 198–206; Wolfgang Sonne, *Representing the State: Capital City Planning in the Twentieth Century* (Munich: Prestel, 2003), 194–99, 201–40 (quotations on 230 and 240).
9. Sonne, *Representing the State*, 199–201, 153–88; 94–100 (quotations on 152 and 95); Peter Proudfoot, *The Secret Plan of Canberra* (Kensington: University of New South Wales, 1994); John Galbraith, *In the New Capital, or, The City of Ottawa in 1999* (Toronto: Toronto News Co., 1897), 139–40.
10. Hall, *Cities of Tomorrow*, 210–15 (quotation from Mussolini on 211); Ikonnikov, *Arkhitektura*

XX veka, 367–96; Albert Speer, *Inside the Third Reich* (New York: Macmillan, 1970), 69, 74–79, 133–35, 139, 147, 155–60.

11. Sonne, *Representing the State*, 140–48, 50 (the "proportional" quotation); Hall, *Cities of Tomorrow*, 189–97; *The Chicago World's Fair of 1893: A Photographic Record*, with text by Stanley Appelbaum (New York: Dover, 1980).

12. Sonne, *Representing the State*, 50–88 (the *National Geographic* quotations are on 60, 59, and 57).

13. Ibid., 65.

14. Brunner quoted in ibid., 69; B. M. Iofan, "Materialy o sovremennoi arkhitekture SShA i Italii," *Akademiia arkhitektury* 4 (1936): 27. I am grateful to Katherine Zubovich for bringing this article to my attention. Cf. Mark Gelernter, *A History of American Architecture: Buildings in Their Cultural and Technological Context* (Hanover, NH: University Press of New England, 1999), 247–48.

15. A. V. Bunin and M. G. Kruglova, *Arkhitekturnaia kompozitsiia gorodov* (Moscow: Akademiia arkhitektury SSSR, Kabinet gradostroitel'stva, 1940), 48–50; *General'nyi plan*, 6; RGASPI, f. 81, op. 3, d. 184, l. 124.

16. For Moscow in time and space, see Karl Schlögel, *Moscow, 1937* (Cambridge: Polity Press, 2012).

17. Olga Aroseva, *Prozhivshaia dvazhdy* (Moscow: AST, 2012), RoyalLib.com, http://royallib .com/book/aroseva_olga/progivshaya_dvagdi.html (under April 13, 1934); R. Amundsen, *Sobranie sochinenii* (Leningrad: Izdatel'stvo Glavsevmorputi).

18. *Pervyi vsesoiuznyi s"ezd sovetskikh pisatelei 1934: Stenograficheskii otchet* (Moscow: Khudozhestvennaia literatura, 1934), 677.

19. M. Gor'kii and M. Kol'tsov, eds., *Den' mira* (Moscow: Zhurgaz, 1937), introductory material (no pagination).

20. *Mikhail Kol'tsov, kakim on byl: Sbornik vospominanii* (Moscow: Sovetskii pisatel', 1989), 283–84, 391–92 (the quotation is from 283).

21. Gor'kii and Kol'tsov, eds., *Den' mira*, 506, 508, 510, 511, 517, 540, 584.

22. André Gide, *Return from the USSR* (New York: Alfred A. Knopf, 1937), 30, 5–7.

23. Lion Feuchtwanger, *Moscow 1937: My Visit Described for My Friends* (London: Victor Gollancz, 1937), 54–55; Michael David-Fox, *Showcasing the Great Experiment: Cultural Diplomacy and Western Visitors to the Soviet Union, 1921–1941* (New York: Oxford University Press, 2012), 207–311; Boris Frezinskii, *Pisateli i sovetskie vozhdi: Izbrannye siuzhety 1919–1960 gg.* (Moscow: Ellis Lak, 2008), 421–34; Schlögel, *Moscow, 1937*, 81–94.

24. A. S. Serafimovich, *Sobranie sochinenii* (Moscow: GIKhL, 1960), 7:586.

25. A. M. Larina, *Nezabyvaemoe* (Moscow: APN, 1989), 248–50.

26. Ibid., 256–57.

27. Iu. G. Fel'shtinskii, *Razgovory s Bukharinym* (New York: Teleks, 1993), 19–35, 61–109; Vadim Rogovin, *1937*, http://trst.narod.ru/rogovin/t4/xiv.htm.

28. I. V. Stalin, "O zadachakh khoziaistvennikov," in *Sochineniia*, vol. 13, Marxists Internet Archive Library, https://www.marxists.org/russkij/stalin/t13/t13_06.htm; Larina, *Nezabyvaemoe*, 244; Kira Allilueva, *Plemiannitsa Stalina* (Moscow: Vagrius, 2006), 137.

29. Aroseva, *Prozhivshaia dvazhdy*, RoyalLib.com, http://royallib.com/book/aroseva_olga /progivshaya_dvagdi.html (under November 7, 1932; October 13, 1934; July 17, 1935); RGASPI, f. 559, op. 1, d. 142, ll. 8, 13, 29–30; Aroseva, *Prozhivshaia dvazhdy* (under November 2, 1932).

30. Ibid. (under June 19, 1935).

31. Ibid. (under November 7, 1932; November 25, 1935; July 17, 1935; December 7, 1935; December 3, 1935; December 4, 1935; December 5, 1935).

32. Ibid. (under November 25, 1935; December 16, 1934; October 4, 1935; July 21, 1936; November 2, 1932; July 17, 1935).

33. ARAN, f. 528, op. 4, d. 1, no pagination, letters dated February 10, 1914, and simply "1914."

34. Ibid., November 2, 1931, and April 30, 1936.

35. Katerina Clark, *Moscow, the Fourth Rome: Stalinism, Cosmopolitanism, and the Evolution of Soviet Culture, 1931–1941* (Cambridge, MA: Harvard University Press, 2011), 156, 179–80; David Pike, *German Writers in Soviet Exile, 1933–1945* (Chapel Hill: University of North Carolina Press, 1982), 51–57; David-Fox, *Showcasing the Soviet Experiment*, 252–59; Eva Oberloskamp, *Fremde neue Welten: Reisen deutscher und französischer Linksintellektueller in die Sowjetunion 1917–1939* (Munich: Oldenbourg, 2011); Jean-François Fayet, *Karl Radek (1885–1939)* (Bern: Peter Lang, 2004), 661–90; Warren Lerner, *Karl Radek: The Last Internationalist* (Stanford, CA: Stanford University Press, 1970), 156–65; Karl Radek, *Podgotovka bor'by za novyi peredel mira* (Moscow: Partiinoe izdatel'stvo, 1934), 39–76; *Pervyi vsesoiuznyi s"ezd*, 313; Gustav Regler, *The Owl of Minerva* (New York: Farrar, Straus and Cudahy, 1959), 211–13.

36. Müller, Reinhard Müller, "Exil im 'Wunderland Sowjetunion'—Maria Osten (1908–1942)," *Exil: Forschung, Erkenntnisse, Ergebnisse* 27, no. 1 (2007): 73–95 (quotation is from 78); Ursula El-Akramy, *Transit Moskau: Margarete Steffin und Maria Osten* (Hamburg: Europäische Verlangsanstalt, 1998), 131, 202–10; Viktor Fradkin, *Delo Kol'tsova* (Moscow: Vagrius, 2002), 91–92, 99.

37. Müller, "Exil im 'Wunderland Sowjetunion,'" 73–79; El-Akramy, *Transit Moskau*, 79–97; Fradkin, *Delo Kol'tsova*, 95, 99, 173, 176–84; Boris Efimov, *Desiat' desiatiletii* (Moscow: Vagrius, 2000), 180–209.

38. Maria Osten, *Gubert v strane chudes* (Moscow: Zhurgaz, 1935), 43.

39. Ibid., 52, 58, 90.

40. Ibid., 75.

41. Ibid., 93–115, 147–61, 176–77; Klaus's diary quoted in Müller, "Exil im 'Wunderland Sowjetunion,'" 80.

42. Schwartzenbach quoted in Müller, "Exil im 'Wunderland Sowjetunion,'" 80.

43. Fradkin, *Delo Kol'tsova*, 95–96; 176, 183; Müller, "Exil im 'Wunderland Sowjetunion,'" 79; El-Akramy, *Transit Moskau*, 136–39.

44. Mikhail Kol'tsov, *Ispanskii dnevnik* (Moscow: Sovetskii pisatel', 1957), 41–42, 189.

45. Ibid., 124–25; Ernest Hemingway, *For Whom the Bell Tolls* (New York: Scribner, 1940), https://books.google.ru/books?id=TdVQAQAAQBAJ&printsec=frontcover&dq=Hemingway+For+Whom+the+Bell+Tolls&hl=en&sa=X&ved=0ahUKEwjSteOMwofRAhWHjSwKHRnNA6cQ6AEIHzAA#v=onepage&q=Hemingway%20For%20Whom%20the%20Bell%20Tolls&f=false.

46. Kol'tsov, *Ispanskii dnevnik*, 193, 234, 323.

47. Ibid., 197, 161, 234. "The Mysteries of the Madrid Court" is a common Russian version of the title of Eugene Scribe's play, *Les contes de la reine de Navarre*.

48. Ibid., 100–101.

49. Ibid., 113–14.

50. Ibid., 406–11.

19. THE PETTINESS OF EXISTENCE

1. AMDNN, "Poloz" file, "Verkhneural'skii izoliator," VU-16 (June 24, 1933); n.p. (February 6, 1934, December 24, 1934); Obolensksia, *Iz vospominanii*, "Samizdat," http://samlib.ru/o/obolenskaja_s_w/01.shtml; S. V. Obolenskaia (Osinskaia), interview with author, March 26, 1998; T. I. Smilga, interview with author, January 19, 1998; G. A. Voronskaia, "Esli v serdtse posylaiut puliu," *Istoricheskii arkhiv* 1 (1997): 90; S. A. Butenko, interview with author, September 24, 1998; I. A. Gaister, interview with author, September 30, 1997; G. B. Ivanova, interview with author, March 13, 1998; N. P. Kerzhentseva, interview with author, January 12, 1998; V. V. Kuibyshev, interview with author, February 18, 1998; Samuil Moroz, "Chlen kollegii VChK," 6, manuscript in AMDNN, "Moroz" file; I. R. Muklevich, interview with author, November 7, 1997; E. B. Levina, interview with author, September 27, 1998; N. A. Perli-Rykova, interview with author, February 12, 1998; RGASPI, f. 559 (Adoratsky), op. 1,

d. 132, ll. 39, 45; K. P. Politkovskaia (Allilueva), interview with author, April 1, 1998; N. A. Iur'eva, interview with author, August 21, 1998; T. M. Rybakova (Belen'kaia), interview with author, October 1, 1997; S. A. Khalatova, interview with author, September 6, 1998; Z. A. Khatskevich, interview with author, September 4, 1998; M. P. Korshunov, interview with author, November 11, 1997; E. I. Gruzinova (Kraval'), interview with author, January 16, 1998; M. A. Lozovskaia, interview with author, March 4, 1998; M. V. Mikhailova, interview with author, December 3, 1997; V. D. Shvarts, interview with author, December 10, 1998; V. B. Volina, interview with author, September 18, 1997.

2. Artem Sergeev and Ekaterina Glushik, *Kak zhil, rabotal i vospityval detei I. V. Stalin: Svidetel'stva ochevidtsa* (Moscow: Forum, 2011), 18.

3. Olga Aroseva, *Prozhivshaia dvazhdy* (Moscow: AST, 2012), RoyalLib.com, http://royallib.com /book/aroseva_olga/progivshaya_dvagdi.html (under April 24, 1937).

4. Aroseva, *Prozhivshaia dvazhdy*, http://royallib.com/book/aroseva_olga/progivshaya _dvagdi.html (under March 10, 1936; February 3, 1934; April 21, 1937).

5. Ibid. (under April 4, 1935).

6. Ibid. (under May 25, 1935; September 21, 1934).

7. Ibid. (under May 19, 1935, "Iz zapisnykh knizhek"; September 6, 1934).

8. Ibid. (under October 20, 1934; September 28, 1934; October 22, 1934; October 3, 1934; November 19, 1933; February 27, 1935; October 16, 1934).

9. *Pravda*, October 27, 1932, http://lib.babr.ru/?book=4652.

10. J. V. Stalin, "Industrialisation and the Grain Problem, Speech Delivered on July 9, 1928," in *Works*, vol. 11 (Moscow: Foreign Languages Publishing House, 1954), Marxists Internet Archive Library, http://www.marxists.org/reference/archive/stalin/works/1928/07/04 .htm#Industrialisation_and_the_Grain_Problem.

11. Aroseva, *Prozhivshaia dvazhdy*, http://royallib.com/book/aroseva_olga/progivshaya _dvagdi.html (under September 28, 1934).

12. GARF, f. 3316, op. 43, d. 911, ll. 19–57; op. 28, d. 621, ll. 8–12, 14–140ob., 19; GARF, f. 9542, op. 1a, d. 15, l. 107; RGALI, f. 645, op. 1, d. 299, ll. 1–2, 40–46; RGALI, f. 2310, op. 1, d. 79. ll. 1–32 (quotations from ll. 31–32); RGALI, f. 2310, op. 1, d. 76 ll. 54–540b. (quotation about Ostrovsky etc.); RGALI, f. 2310, op. 1, d. 41, ll. 130b.–14; AGTsTM, f. 454, d. 7, d. 16.

13. AGTsTM, f. 454, d. 1004, l. 2 (on Levidov); RGALI, f. 656, op. 1, d. 954, l. 1, 3, 24 (censor on UA); RGALI, f. 2310, op. 1, d. 41, ll. 13a ob.; AGTsTM, f. 454, d. 460, ll. 12–19; B. G. Golubovskii, *Bol'shie malen'kie teatry* (Moscow: Izdatel'stvo imeni Sabashnikovykh, 1998), 104–6, 107–8.

14. Golubovskii, *Bol'shie malen'kie teatry*, 108–10; AGTsTM, f. 454, d. 453, l. 21; RGALI, f. 2310, op. 1, d. 121, l. 2; TsALIM, f. 2007, op. 1, d. 1, ll. 31, 60, 69; GARF, f. 3316, op. 28, d. 621, ll. 6–140b., 29–290b. (quotation is on 29); GARF, f. 9542, op. 1, d. 25, ll. 60–71.

15. GARF, f. 9542, op. 1, d. 26, l. 30; f. 3316, op. 28, d. 590, ll. 18–19, 22, 270b.

16. GARF, f. 9542, op. 1, d. 30, ll. 4, 4 ob., 6, 60b., 7, 7 ob., 80b., 9, 90b.

17. Ibid., l. 4 ob.

18. GARF, f. 3316, op. 28, d. 621, ll. 6–140b., 29–290b. (quotation is on 29); GARF, f. 9542, op. 1, d. 25, ll. 60–71; GARF, f. 3316, op. 28, d. 590, l. 18.

19. "Rech' Sof'i Aleksandrovny Butenko," *Sovetskaia Sibir'*, May 16, 1936.

20. GARF, f. 9542, op. 1, d. 30, l. 6; L. A. Kozlova (Bogacheva), interview with author, September 24, 1997; L. N. Shaburov, interview with author, September 25, 1997; E. E. Ivchenko, interview with author, September 23, 1998; Anna Ivchenko's autobiography (including her mother's employee record) is in the author's possession; M. V. Mikhailova, interview with author, December 3, 1997; I. A. Serebrovskaia, interview with author, June 15, 1999; E. B. Levina, interview with author, September 27, 1998; V. A. Ozerskii, interview with author, June 26, 1999; I. Shikheeva-Gaister, interview with author, September 30, 1997; Inna Shikheeva-Gaister, *Deti vragov naroda: Semeinaia khronika vremen kul'ta lichnosti 1925–1953* (Moscow: Vozvrashchenie, 2012), 41–42; L. Gronskaia, *Nabroski po pamiati* (Moscow: Flinta,

2004), 68–69; A. Artizov and Oleg Naumov, eds., *Vlast' i khudozhestvennaia intelligentsiia* (Moscow: Fond "Demokratiia," 1999), 255–56, 763–64; T. I. Smilga, interview with author, January 19, 1998; S. V. Obolenskaia (Osinskaia), interview with author, March 26, 1998; M. M. Iakovenko, *Agnessa: Ustnye rasskazy Agnessy Ivanovny Mironovoi-Korol'*, Memorial: Istoricheskie programmy, "Nasha zhizn' s Miroshei," http://www.memo.ru/history/agnessa; S. A. Butenko, interview with author, September 24, 1998.

20. THE THOUGHT OF DEATH

1. Aleksandr Voronskii, *Gogol'* (Moscow: Molodaia gvardiia, 2009), 414–15.
2. Ibid., 415–16; RGASPI, f. 559, op. 1, d. 152, l. 31.
3. Olga Aroseva, *Prozhivshaia dvazhdy* (Moscow: AST, 2012), RoyalLib.com, http://royallib.com/book/aroseva_olga/progivshaya_dvagdi.html (under August 13, 1936; March 6, 1934; prologue to Tetrad' [notebook] no. 7; January 1937; November 7, 1936). See also Jochen Hellbeck, *Revolution on My Mind: Writing a Diary under Stalin* (Cambridge, MA: Harvard University Press, 2009), 37–114; Igal Halfin, *Terror in My Soul: Communist Autobiographies on Trial* (Cambridge, MA: Harvard University Press, 2003); Halfin, *Stalinist Confessions: Messianism and Terror at the Leningrad Communist University* (Pittsburgh, PA: University of Pittsburgh Press, 2009).
4. GARF, f. 5446, op. 16a, d. 617, ll. 2–20b., 5–6; V. M. Mikhailova, "Pis'mo Marii Nikolaevny Kul'man ot 7 sentiabria 1992 g.," in AMDNN, "Mikhailov" file.
5. Aroseva, *Prozhivshaia dvazhdy*, http://royallib.com/book/aroseva_olga/progivshaya_dvagdi.html (under August 13, 1936; March 17, 1937; February 23, 1935).
6. Translation based on Yuri Trifonov, *The Disappearance*, trans. David Lowe (Ann Arbor, MI: Ardis, 1991), 70–71. Cf. Iurii Trifonov, *Ischeznovenie*, RoyalLib.com, http://royallib.com/book/trifonov_yuriy/ischeznovenie.html.
7. "O khoroshikh rasskazakh i redaktorskoi rutine," *Literaturnyi kritik* 8 (1936): 106–13; Andrei Platonov, "Bessmertie," *Literaturnyi kritik* 8 (1936): 123–24, 127. See also Aleksandr Galushkin, "Andrei Platonov—Stalin—'Literaturnyj kritik,'" in *"Strana filosofov" Andreia Platonova: Problemy tvorchestva* (Moscow: IMLI RAN, "Nasledie," 2000), 4:816–17.
8. Platonov, "Bessmertie," 118.
9. Ibid., 117, 121.
10. Ibid., 127.
11. Ibid., 125.
12. Ibid., 128.
13. A. Gurvich, "Andrei Platonov," *Krasnaia nov'* 10 (1937), reprinted in N. V. Kornienko and E. D. Shubina, eds., *Andrei Platonov: Vospominaniia sovremennikov; Materialy k biografii* (Moscow: Sovremennyi pisatel', 1994), 358–413 (quotations are from 362, 381, 388, 382, and 396); M. A. Usievich, interview with author, January 30, 1998.
14. A. Platonov, "Vozrazhenie bez samozashchity," *Literaturnaia gazeta*, December 20, 1937; A. Gurvich, "Otvet tov. Platonovu" and "Ot redaktsii," *Literaturnaia gazeta*, December 26, 1937 (all reprinted in Kornienko and Shubina, *Andrei Platonov*, 414–18); E. Usievich, "Razgovor o geroe," *Literaturnyi kritik* 9–10 (1938): 171–84.
15. Aleksandr Ovcharenko, *V krugu Leonida Leonova: Iz zapisok 1968–1988 godov* (Moscow: Moskovskii intellektual'no-delovoi klub, 2002), 171, 189; A Voronskii, *Literaturnye tipy* (Moscow: Krug, 1931), 143; L. Leonov, "Prizyv k muzhestvu," *Literaturnaia gazeta*, April 16, 1934.
16. Ovcharenko, *V krugu Leonida Leonova*, 182.
17. Letter from L. M. Leonov to A. Z. Goloborod'ko, August 10, 1955, in AMDNN, "Kuchmin" file; O. I. Kuchmin and E. I. Kuchmina, "Sud'ba soldata revoliutsii," manuscript in AMDNN, "Kuchmin" file; letters to the Museum by E. I. Kuchmina, approx. August–September 1991 and March 17, 2003; E. I. Kuchmina, interviews with author, April 6 and July 25, 2008.

18. Leonid Leonov, *Doroga na Okean* (Moscow: GIKhL, 1936), 6–7, 124, 38 (cf. the translation in Leonid Leonov, *Road to the Ocean*, trans. Norbert Guterman [New York: L. B. Fischer, 1944], 2, 100, 29); on the Prometheus/Hephaestus connection, see Eduard Nadtochii, "Tipologicheskaia problematizatsiia sviazi sub"ekta i affekta v russkoi literature," *Logos* 2 (1999): http://www.ruthenia.ru/logos/number/1999_02/1999_2_04.htm.

19. Leonov, *Doroga na Okean*, 128 (cf. Leonov, *Road*, 104–5).

20. Leonov, *Doroga na Okean*, 550, 442, 547, 35, 33, 43–44, 511, 75 (cf. Leonov, *Road*, 453, 362, 450, 25, 33–34, 420, 60); Zakhar Prilepin, *Leonid Leonov* (Moscow: Molodaia gvardiia, 2010), 273–79; Boris Thomson, *The Art of Compromise: The Life and Work of Leonid Leonov* (Toronto: University of Toronto Press, 2001), 160.

21. Leonov, *Doroga na Okean*, 45–46 (cf. Leonov, *Road*, 35–36).

22. Leonov, *Doroga na Okean*, 460 (cf. Leonov, *Road*, 377); Nadtochii, "Tipologicheskaia problematizatsiia," http://www.ruthenia.ru/logos/number/1999_02/1999_2_04.htm.

23. Leonov, *Doroga na Okean*, 213 (cf. Leonov, *Road*, 174); Thomson, *The Art of Compromise*, 153–55; Leonov, *Doroga na Okean*, 144 (cf. Leonov, *Road*, 116).

24. Leonov, *Doroga na Okean*, 119–23 (cf. Leonov, *Road*, 97–99).

25. Leonov, *Doroga na Okean*, 438 (cf. Leonov, *Road*, 359).

26. Leonov, *Doroga na Okean*, 38, 122 (cf. Leonov, *Road*, 29, 99–100).

27. Leonov, *Doroga na Okean*, 438 (cf. Leonov, *Road*, 358).

28. Leonov, *Doroga na Okean*, 32–33, 513 (cf. Leonov, *Road*, 24–25, 422).

29. Leonov, *Doroga na Okean*, 287–88 (cf. Leonov, *Road*, 234–35).

30. Leonov, *Doroga na Okean*, 289, 237, 300 (cf. Leonov, *Road*, 236, 193, 245).

31. Leonov, *Doroga na Okean*, 297 (cf. Leonov, *Road*, 242).

32. Leonov, *Doroga na Okean*, 29 (cf. Leonov, *Road*, 22); Thomson, *The Art of Compromise*, 152.

33. Leonov, *Doroga na Okean*, 130 (cf. Leonov, *Road*, 106).

34. Leonov, *Doroga na Okean*, 130, 450, 138, 134, 322, 74 (cf. Leonov, *Road*, 106, 369, 112, 108, 262–63, 59). See also S. G. Semenova, "Romany Leonida Leonova 20–30kh godov v filosofskom rakurse," in *Vek Leonida Leonova: Problemy tvorchestva. Vospominaniia* (Moscow: OMLI RAN, 2001), 49–53.

35. Leonov, *Doroga na Okean*, 139–41, 450, 444–45 (cf. Leonov, *Road*, 112–14, 369, 364–65).

36. Leonov, *Doroga na Okean*, 553, 557–61, 46 (cf. Leonov, *Road*, 456, 459–63, 36).

37. Leonov, *Doroga na Okean*, 598–99 (cf. Leonov, *Road*, 494).

38. Leonov, *Doroga na Okean*, 615–16 (cf. Leonov, *Road*, 509–10).

39. "'Doroga na Okean' L. Leonova," *Literaturnaia gazeta*, November 5, 1935; "Obsuzhdenie romana L. Leonova 'Doroga na Okean,'" *Literaturnaia gazeta*, May 10, 1936; I. Vinogradov, "Za sovetskuiu klassiku," *Literaturnyi sovremennik* 5 (1936): 149–50; B. Iasenskii, "Ideinyi rost khudozhnika," *Literaturnaia gazeta*, May 10, 1936; M. Levidov, "Tvorcheskaia vzvolnovannost' i distsiplina," *Literaturnaia gazeta*, May 10, 1936; M. Gor'kii, *Sobranie sochinenii v tridtsati tomakh* (Moscow: GIKhL, 1955), 30:399.

40. "'Doroga na Okean' L. Leonova"; "Obsuzhdenie romana L. Leonova 'Doroga na Okean,'"; Vinogradov, "Za sovetskuiu klassiku," 145, 149–50; Iasenskii, "Ideinyi rost khudozhnika"; Levidov, "Tvorcheskaia vzvolnovannost' i distsiplina"; Gor'kii, *Sobranie sochinenii v tridtsati tomakh*, 30:399–400; E. Usievich, *Pisateli i deistvitel'nost'* (Moscow: Goslitizdat, 1936), 36; A. Selivanovskii, "'Doroga na Okean' Leonida Leonova," *Literaturnyi kritik* 3 (1936): 101; V. Petrsov, *Pisatel' i novaia deistvitel'nost'* (Moscow: Sovetskii pisatel', 1961), 159.

41. I. Grinberg, "Geroi sovetskogo romana," in *Obraz bol'shevika: Sbornik kritiheskikh statei* (Leningrad: Khudozhestvennaia literatura, 1938), 18–19.

42. V. Shklovskii, "Manevry, a ne voiny za budushchee," *Literaturnaia gazeta*, May 10, 1936; Levidov, "Tvorcheskaia vzvolnovannost' i distsiplina."

43. Mikhail Kol'tsov, *Vostorg i iarost'* (Moscow: Pravda, 1990), 159.

44. Ibid., 164.

45. L. A. Anninskii, "Obruchennyi s ideei: Sud'ba romana 'Kak zakalialas' stal' N. A. Ostrov-

skogo,'" in L. A. Anninskii and E. L. Tseitlin, eds., *Vekhi pamiati* (Moscow: Kniga, 1987), 6–33; R. Ostrovskaia, *Nikolai Ostrovskii* (Moscow: Molodaia gvardiia, 1974), 134–229; S. Tregub, *Zhizn' i tvorchestvo Nikolaia Ostrovskogo* (Moscow: Khudozhestvennaia literatura, 1964), 98–117, 167–243; André Gide, *Return from the USSR* (New York: Alfred A. Knopf, 1937), 83–84; Anatolii Osipov, *Korchagintsy piati kontinentov* (Perm': Permskoe knizhnoe izdatel'stvo, 1973); A. Karavaeva, *Kniga, kotoraia oboshla ves' mir* (Moscow: Kniga, 1970); Donghui He, "The Coming of Age in the Brave New World: The Changing Reception of the Soviet Novel, *How the Steel Was Tempered*, in the PRC," in Thomas Bernstein and Hua-Yu Li, eds., *China Learns from the Soviet Union, 1949–present* (Lanham, MD: Rowman and Littlefield, 2010), 393–420.

46. Nikolai Ostrovskii, *Kak zakalialas' stal'* (Leningrad: Lenizdat, 1967), 169, 198, 312, 159, 233, 152; Lilya Kaganovsky, *How the Soviet Man Was Unmade: Cultural Fantasy and Male Subjectivity under Stalin* (Pittsburgh, PA: University of Pittsburgh Press, 2008), 19–41.

47. Anninskii, "Obruchennyi s ideei," 48–49; Leonov, *Doroga na Okean*, 34, 149 (cf. Leonov, *Road*, 26, 121); Ostrovskii, *Kak zakalialas' stal*, 55–56.

48. A. W. Ward, W. P. Trent, et al., *The Cambridge History of English and American Literature* (New York: G. P. Putnam's Sons, 1907–21; New York: Bartleby.com, 2000 [www.bartleby .com/cambridge]), vol. 7, pt. 6, p. 18, http://www.bartleby.com/217/0706.html; James Boswell, *Life of Johnson: Including Boswell's "Journal of a Tour to the Hebrides" and Johnson's "Diary of a Journey into North Wales"* (New York: Bigelow, Brown, and Co; Google eBook), p. 82, http://books.google.co.in/books?id=g4JgCSZ_YPoC&pg=PA82&dq=%22there+ever +yet+anything+written+by+mere+man+that+was+wished+longer+by+its+readers+excepting +Don+Quixote,+Robinson++%22&hl=en&sa=X&ei=J-fNUf6vDYqErQfr_4CoAw&redir _esc=y#v=onepage&q=%22there%20ever%20yet%20anything%20written%20by%20 mere%20man%20that%20was%20wished%20longer%20by%20its%20readers%20 excepting%20Don%20Quixote%2C%20Robinson%20%20%22&f=false.

49. Ostrovskii, *Kak zakalialas' stal*, 364.

50. Ostrovskii, *Kak zakalialas' stal*, 345–47, 337.

51. Ostrovskii, *Kak zakalialas' stal*, 313, 227, 348–51.

21. THE HAPPY CHILDHOOD

1. RGASPI, f. 135, op. 1, d. 10, l. 57.

2. Olga Aroseva, *Prozhivshaia dvazhdy* (Moscow: AST, 2012), RoyalLib.com, http://royallib .com/book/aroseva_olga/progivshaya_dvagdi.html (in "Zaveshchanie moim detiam," in the afterword [Posleslovie], under July 9, 1936; July 21, 1936; January 30, 1937; non-dated first entry under 1937; September 20, 1934).

3. N. Efimov, *Tovarishch Nina* (Iaroslavl': Verkhne-Volzhskoe knizhnoe izdatel'stvo, 1969), 110; L. Podvoiskii, "Krasnoe solnyshko sem'i—mama," *Sem'ia i shkola* 3 (1965): 10; ARAN, razriad 5, op. 1-o, d. 11, l. 75; Aroseva, *Prozhivshaia dvazhdy* (under April 30, 1933, and October 24, 1933.

4. Cf. Gary Saul Morson, *Hidden in Plain View: Narrative and Creative Potentials in War and Peace* (Stanford, CA: Stanford University Press, 1988).

5. M. A. Tsiurupa, interview with author, January 8, 1998; S. V. Obolenskaia (Osinskaia), interview with author, March 26, 1998; I. R. Muklevich, interview with author, November 7, 1997; I. A. Gaister, interview with author, September 30, 1997; N. A. Rykova, interview with author, February 12, 1998; T. M. Rybakova (Belen'kaia), interview with author, October 1, 1997; Tat'iana Rybakova, *Schastlivaia ty, Tania* (Moscow: Vagrius, 2005), 16–17; M. P. Korshunov, interview with author, November 11, 1997; E. I. Kuchmina, interview with author, July 25, 2008; V. N. Rabichev, interview with author, April 14, 1998; T. A. Ter-Egizarian, interview with author, October 8, 1997; M. V. Mikhailova, letter to the Museum, September 1992, 2, in AMDNN, "Mikhailov" file.

6. GARF, f. 9542, op. 7, d. 14, ll. 59 ob.–65ob., 78–80ob.; I. A. Gaister, interview with author, September 30, 1997; N. A. Gilinskaia, interview with author, March 2, 1998; M. A. Tsiurupa, interview with author, January 8, 1998; E. R. Kisis, "Pis'mo v muzei," 5, in AMDNN, "Kisis" file; Inna Shikheeva-Gaister, *Deti vragov naroda: Semeinaia khronika vremen kul'ta lichnosti 1925–1953* (Moscow: Vozvrashchenie, 2012), 17–18.

7. O. A. Aroseva, interview with author, January 15, 1998; I. A. Gaister, interview with author, September 30, 1997; G. B. Ivanova, interview with author, March 13, 1998; N. P. Kerzhentseva, interview with author, January 12, 1998; M. P. Korshunov, interview with author, November 11, 1997; T. V. Shuniakova, interview with author, April 22, 1998; T. I. Smilga, interview with author, January 19, 1998; Kisis, "Pis'mo v muzei," 16–17; Gaister, *Deti vragov naroda*, 21.

8. S. V. Obolenskaia (Osinskaia), interview with author, March 26, 1998; T. I. Smilga, interview with author, January 19, 1998; I. A. Gaister, interview with author, September 30, 1997; N. P. Kerzhentseva, interview with author, January 12, 1998; I. R. Muklevich, interview with author, November 7, 1997; Maria Osten, *Gubert v strane chudes* (Moscow: Zhurgaz, 1935), 105–9, 169–70; T. M. Rybakova (Belen'kaia), interview with author, October 1, 1997; V. N. Rabichev, interview with author, April 14, 1998; G. S. Ronina, interview with author, October 1, 1997; L. N. Shaburov, interview with author, September 25, 1997; Z. M. Tuchina, interview with author, September 8, 1998; M. A. Usievich, interview with author, January 30, 1998; V. B. Volina, interview with author, September 18, 1997; E. I. Gruzinova (Kraval'), interview with author, January 16, 1998.

9. N. P. Kerzhentseva, interview with author, January 12, 1998; I. R. Muklevich, interview with author, November 7, 1997; K. P. Politkovskaia (Allilueva), interview with author, April 1, 1998; L. N. Shaburov, interview with author, September 25, 1997; Shikheeva-Gaister, *Deti vragov naroda*, 24; Kisis, "Pis'mo v muzei," 7.

10. Samuil Moroz, "Chlen kollegii VChK," l. 12, manuscript in AMDNN, "Moroz" file; A. Shitov, *Iurii Trifonov: Khronika zhizni i tvorchestva* (Ekaterinburg: Izdatel'stvo Ural'skogo Universiteta, 1997), 104; Shikheeva-Gaister, *Deti vragov naroda*, 25–27; N. P. Kerzhentseva, interview with author, January 12, 1998; M. A Usievich, interview with author, January 30, 1998. On Soviet childhood, see Catriona Kelly, *Children's World: Growing Up in Russia, 1890–1991* (New Haven, CT: Yale University Press, 2007), esp. 93–102.

11. S. V. Obolensksia, *Iz vospominanii*, "Samizdat," http://samlib.ru/o/obolenskaja_s_w/01 .shtml.

12. Obolensksia, *Iz vospominanii*, http://samlib.ru/o/obolenskaja_s_w/01.shtml; Shikheeva-Gaister, *Deti vragov naroda*, 28–29; Anatoly Granovsky, *I Was an NKVD Agent* (New York: Devin-Adair, 1962), 28–29; I. R. Muklevich, interview with author, November 7, 1997; Kisis, "Pis'mo v muzei," 10, 14; Mikhail Korshunov and Victoria Terekhova, *Tainy i legendy Doma na naberezhnoi* (Moscow: Slovo, 2002), 76; G. S. Ronina, interview with author, October 1, 1997; T. I. Smilga, interview with author, January 19, 1998; Z. M. Tuchina, interview with author, September 8, 1998; M. A. Usievich, interview with author, January 30, 1998.

13. TsDNA, f. 336 (Pavlovy-Shtrom), op. 1, d. 32 (dnevnikovye zapisi Very Pavlovoi-Shtrom), ll. 137–38 (I am grateful to Jochen Hellbeck for making this document available to me); TsAODM, f. 75, op. 1, d. 310, ll. 16, 22.

14. Moroz, "Minuvshee," 8, in AMDNN, "Moroz" file; G. B. Ivanova, interview with author, March 13, 1998; V. N. Rabichev, interview with author, April 14, 1998; E. I. Zelenskaia, "A. A. Sol'ts," unpublished manuscript in AMDNN, "Solts" file, 85. See also Iurii Trifonov, *Ischeznovenie*, RoyalLib.com, http://royallib.ru/read/trifonov_yuriy/ischeznovenie.html#0; cf. Yuri Trifonov, *The Disappearance*, trans. David Lowe (Ann Arbor, MI: Ardis, 1991), 62.

15. Zelenskaia, "A. A. Sol'ts," 85; Moroz, "Minuvshee," 11–13; Moroz, "V Dome tom," 6, in AMDNN, "Moroz" file; G. B. Ivanova, interview with author, March 13, 1998; V. N. Rabichev, interview with author, April 14, 1998; TsDNA, f. 336 (Pavlovy-Shtrom), op. 1, d. 32 (dnevnikovye zapisi Very Pavlovoi-Shtrom), ll. 137–38.

16. TsMAM, f. r-528 (MONO), op. 1, dd. 13, 16; f. 528 (MONO), op. 1, dd. 43, 106, 161, 165, 352 (quotation is on l. 3), 353 (quotations are from l. 6), 379.

17. TsMAM, f. 528, op. 1, dd. 41, 486, 519.

18. G. Lesskis, "Shkola na Sofiiskoi naberezhnoi," *Russkii iazyk* 32, no. 152 (August 1998): 2; Korshunov and Terekhova, *Tainy i legendy*, 109–24, 64; Shikheeva-Gaister, *Deti vragov naroda*, 20.

19. TsMAM, f. 528, op. 1, d. 150; Kisis, "Pis'mo v muzei," 11–12; Lesskis, "Shkola na Sofiiskoi naberezhnoi," 2; Korshunov and Terekhova, *Tainy i legendy*, 109–24, 64; Shikheeva-Gaister, *Deti vragov naroda*, 20; I. A. Gaister, interview with author, September 30, 1997; N. P. Kerzhentseva, interview with author, January 12, 1998; Z. A. Khatskevich, interview with author, September 4, 1998; T. V. Ignatashvili (Shuniakova), interview with author, April 22, 1998; M. A. Usievich, interview with author, January 30, 1998. Also T. I. Smilga, interview with author, January 19, 1998; Aroseva, *Prozhivshaia dvazhdy*, chap. 5; V. N. Rabichev, interview with author, April 14, 1998; V. D. Shvarts, interview with author, December 10, 1998.

20. Moroz, "Minuvshee," 11.

21. E. I. Gruzinova (Kraval'), interview with author, January 16, 1998; T. I. Smilga, interview with author, January 19, 1998; I. A. Shikheeva-Gaister, *Deti vragov naroda*, 20; L. P. Postyshev, interview with author, October 1, 1998; M. Kol'tsov, *Fel'etony i ocherki* (Moscow: Pravda, 1956), 150–63.

22. Osaf Litovskii, "Uriel' Akosta" (Novyi teatr), *Pravda*, May 23, 1934; Aleksandr Leizerovich, "Gore razumu: 'Uriel' Akosta' Karla Gutskova," *Sem' iskusstv* 5, no. 18 (May 2011): http://7iskusstv.com/2011/Nomer5/Lejzerovich1.php.

23. AGTsTM, f. 454, d. 736, ll. 10–24.

24. RGALI, f. 656, op. 1, d. 954, ll. 1–3, 24; f. 2310, op. 1, d. 78, ll. 13–15; Em. Beskin, "Novyi Gutskov," *Literaturnaia gazeta*, August 6, 1934.

25. Litovskii, "Uriel' Akosta"; *MKhAT vtoroi: Opyt vosstanovleniia biografii* (Moscow: Moskovskii khudozhestvennyi teatr, 2010), 190, 300, 611.

22. THE NEW MEN

1. G. B. Ivanova, interview with author, March 13, 1998; Volodia Ivanov's diary, AMDNN, "B. Ivanova" file, April 14, 1937.

2. Volodia Ivanov's letters, AMDNN, "B. Ivanova" file, August 11 and October 20, 1938.

3. Ibid., April 15, 1939; February 7, 1939; and n.d.

4. Ibid., March 10, 1939.

5. Ibid., n.d.; April 15, 1939.

6. Ibid., March 10, 1939.

7. Ibid., n.d.

8. Ibid., September 25, 1939; and n.d.

9. Obolenskaia, *Iz vospominanii*, "Samizdat," http://samlib.ru/o/obolenskaja_s_w/02.shtml; Svetlana Obolenskaia, *Deti Bol'shogo terrora: Vospominaniia* (Moscow: AGRAF, 2013), 88; ARAN, razriad 5, op. 1-o, d. 11, ll. 74–74ob. The English translation is from Heinrich Heine, *Deutshland: A Winter's Tale*, trans. T. J. Reed (London: Angel Books, 1997), 31. The letter cites the original German:

    Ja, Zuckererbsen für jedermann,
    Sobald die Schoten platzen!
    Den Himmel überlassen wir
    Den Engeln und den Spatzen.

10. ARAN, razriad 5, op. 1-o, d. 11, l. 75; Maria Osten, *Gubert v strane chudes* (Moscow: Zhurgaz, 1935), 54.

11. Obolenskia, *Iz vospominanii*, http://samlib.ru/o/obolenskaja_s_w/02.shtml; Obolenskaia, *Deti Bol'shogo terrora*, 87–88.

12. Iurii Trifonov, "Iz dnevnikov i rabochikh tetradei: Publikatsiia i kommentarii Ol'gi Trifonovoi," entry for October 11, 1934, *Druzhba narodov* 5 (1998): http://magazines.russ.ru/druzhba/1998/5/trif.html.

13. Ibid., entry for December 29, 1934.

14. A. Shitov, *Iurii Trifonov: Khronika zhizni i tvorchestva* (Ekaterinburg: Izdatel'stvo Ural'skogo Universiteta, 1997), 102 (the Yaroslav quotation), 78; Trifonov, "Iz dnevnikov," entries for June 2, 1937; January 1, 1938; January 31, 1938, http://magazines.russ.ru/druzhba/1998/5/trif.html.

15. M. Daniel', "Chetyre dnia (Iulis)," in *Teatr narodov SSSR: Al'manakh p'es No. 1* (Moscow: Khudozhestvennaia literatura, 1934), 113–66; S. Rozanov and N. Sats, *Negritenok i obez'iana* (Moscow: Gosizdat, 1930); Shitov, *Iurii Trifonov*, 86.

16. Iurii Trifonov, *Ischeznovenie*, RoyalLib.com, http://royallib.ru/read/trifonov_yuriy/ischeznovenie.html#0; cf. Yuri Trifonov, *The Disappearance*, trans. David Lowe (Ann Arbor, MI: Ardis, 1991), 46.

17. Trifonov, *Ischeznovenie*, http://royallib.ru/read/trifonov_yuriy/ischeznovenie.html#0; cf. Trifonov, *Disappearance*, 49; Shitov, *Iurii Trifonov*, 89.

18. Trifonov, "Iz dnevnikov," *Druzhba narodov*, entry for November 2, 1938.

19. Ibid., February 9, 1938.

20. Iurii Trifonov, "Dobro, chelovechnost', talant" and "Istoriia bolezni," in Trifonov, *Kak slovo nashe otzovetsia* (Moscow: Sovetskaia Rossiia, 1985), 187–88, 200.

21. Mikhail Korshunov and Victoria Terekhova, *Tainy i legendy Doma na naberezhnoi* (Moscow: Slovo, 2002), 48, 47, 51, 45; Trifonov, *Kak slovo nashe*, 200; L. Roshal', *Piramida, Solo truby: Kinostsenarii* (Moscow: Iskusstvo, 1989), 58, 70; Lyova Fedotov's diary, bk. 13 (December 27, 1940), [41]. As of this writing, Lyova's diary has not yet been catalogued at RGALI. I am using Lyova's own notebook numbers (only four have survived: 5, 13, 14, and 15); his pagination, where visible (brackets indicate uncertainty); and his dating (brackets indicate uncertainty). After this manuscript had been completed, Lyova's diary was published as Lev Fedotov, *Dnevnik sovetskogo shkol'nika*, ed. I. V. Volkova (Moscow: AST, 2015). I am adding references to this text in brackets following the original citations.

22. Korshunov and Terekhova, *Tainy i legendy*, 45; Lyova Fedotov's diary, bk. 14 (June [5], 1941), 72 [Fedotov, *Dnevnik*, 284–85]; bk. 13 (August 29, 1940), 5 [Fedotov, *Dnevnik*, 113]; Roshal', *Piramida, Solo truby*, 58, 60–61, 70.

23. Lyova Fedotov's diary, bk. 5 (November 23, 1939), [10] [Fedotov, *Dnevnik*, 60]; bk. 13 (August 29, 1940), 5 [Fedotov, *Dnevnik*, 113]; Roshal', *Piramida, Solo truby*, 53.

24. Roshal', *Piramida, Solo truby*, 53–54.

25. Lyova Fedotov's diary, bk. 13 ([September, 2], 1940), 9 [Fedotov, *Dnevnik*, 118].

26. Ibid., bk. 5 (December 5, 1939), 59 [Fedotov, *Dnevnik*, 87–88].

27. Ibid., bk. 5 (November 23, 1939), 9–11 [Fedotov, *Dnevnik*, 60–61]; Evgenii Gurov, "Chego ne znali Stalin i Gitler, znal Lyova Fedotov," *Prezent* (supplement to *Moskovskie vedomosti*) 37 (December 1993): 1–2. Cf. Irina Paperno, "Tolstoy's Diaries: The Inaccessible Self," in Laura Engelstein and Stephanie Sandler, eds., *Self and Story in Russian History* (Ithaca, NY: Cornell University Press, 2000), 242–65. Lyova's "A Day from My Life" has not survived.

28. Korshunov and Terekhova, *Tainy i legendy*, 129–30; Roshal', *Piramida, Solo truby*, 53–55. My copy of those pages of the diary is illegible, so I am using Korshunov's and Roshal''s transcription [Fedotov, *Dnevnik*, 89].

29. Korshunov and Terekhova, *Tainy i legendy*, 130 [Fedotov, *Dnevnik*, 90].

30. Lyova Fedotov's diary, bk. 5 (December 7, 1939), 66–67 [Fedotov, *Dnevnik*, 91–92].

31. Ibid., (December 8, 1939), 72–73; Korshunov and Terekhova, *Tainy i legendy*, 129–42 [Fedotov, *Dnevnik*, 93–107]; Mark Twain, *The Adventures of Huckleberry Finn*, Google Books, http://books.google.de/books?id=VxcD91Uh4dcC&pg=PT19&lpg=PT19&dq=He+said+if+I+warn't+so+ignorant,+but+had+read+a+book+called+%22Don+Quixote,%22+I+would+know+without+asking&source=bl&ots=IulY-bfDwo&sig=TmCkpDowiuNV-3v-1eUAyuSPBH4

&hl=en&sa=X&ei=LdpkUo3gPMfXtQboiIDIDg&ved=0CEcQ6AEwBA#v=onepage&q=He%20said%20if%20I%20warn't%20so%20ignorant%2C%20but%20had%20read%20a%20book%20called%20%22Don%20Quixote%2C%22%20I%20would%20know%20without%20asking&f=false.

32. Korshunov and Terekhova, *Tainy i legendy*, 169; Roshal', *Piramida, Solo truby*, 69; Lyova Fedotov's diary, bk. 5 (December 8, 1939), page no. illegible [Fedotov, *Dnevnik*, 104].

33. Lyova Fedotov's diary, bk. 14 (January 4, 1941), 6 [Fedotov, *Dnevnik*, 221]; bk. 13 ([December 8], 1940), 33 [Fedotov, *Dnevnik*, 146]; Gurov, "Chego ne znali," 2.

34. Roshal', *Piramida, Solo truby*, 77–79; Lyova Fedotov's diary, bk. 5 (November 23, 1939), 16 [Fedotov, *Dnevnik*, 64].

35. Ibid., 16–17 [Fedotov, *Dnevnik*, 64].

36. Lyova Fedotov's diary, bk. 5 (November 27, 1939), 20 [Fedotov, *Dnevnik*, 66].

37. Ibid., (November 28, 1939), 20 [Fedotov, *Dnevnik*, 66].

38. Roshal', *Piramida, Solo truby*, 59.

39. Lyova Fedotov's diary, bk. 5 (November 28, 1939), 20–22 [Fedotov, *Dnevnik*, 66–68].

40. Ibid., (November 29, 1939), 28 [Fedotov, *Dnevnik*, 71].

41. Ibid., (December 1, 1939), 35–36 [Fedotov, *Dnevnik*, 75].

42. Ibid., (December 1, 1939), 36–37 [Fedotov, *Dnevnik*, 76].

43. Ibid., (November 30, 1939), 39–40 [Fedotov, *Dnevnik*, 77–78].

44. Ibid., bk. 13 (August 27, 1940), 3 [Fedotov, *Dnevnik*, 110–11].

45. Ibid., 4–5 [Fedotov, *Dnevnik*, 112].

46. Ibid., bk. 13 (September 2, 1940), 10 [Fedotov, *Dnevnik*, 119]; (September 10, 1940), 16 [Fedotov, *Dnevnik*, 126].

47. Ibid., (October 10, 1940), 21 [Fedotov, *Dnevnik*, 131].

48. Ibid., (November 9, 1940), 28 [Fedotov, *Dnevnik*, 140]

49. Ibid., (December 25, 1940), 40 [Fedotov, *Dnevnik*, 153].

50. Ibid., (December 29, 1940), 45 [Fedotov, *Dnevnik*, 159].

51. Ibid., (December 27, 1940), 41–42 [Fedotov, *Dnevnik*, 155].

52. Ibid., (December 30, 1940), 47 [Fedotov, *Dnevnik*, 161].

53. Ibid., 48–49 [Fedotov, *Dnevnik*, 163–64].

54. Ibid., 50–51 [Fedotov, *Dnevnik*, 165–66].

55. Ibid., 52 [Lev Fedotov, *Dnevnik*, 167].

56. Ibid. [Fedotov, *Dnevnik*, 168].

57. Ibid., 53–54 [Fedotov, *Dnevnik*, 169–70].

58. Ibid., 55 [Fedotov, *Dnevnik*, 171].

23. THE TELEPHONE CALL

1. N. S. Khrushchev, *Vremia, liudi, vlast'* (*vospominaniia*) (Moscow: Moskovskie novosti, 1999), 1:91.

2. AOM, fond. 2 (memoir collection), V. V. Bogutskii, *Vospominaniia*, p. 2.

3. I. A. Gaister, interview with author, September 30, 1997; Khrushchev, *Vremia, liudi, vlast'* (*vospominaniia*), 1:84.

4. Agnessa Mironova-Korol', *Agnessa: From Paradise to Purgatory: A Voice from Stalin's Russia*, trans. Rose Glickman (Bloomington, IN: Slavica, 2012), 71; M. M. Iakovenko, *Agnessa: Ustnye rasskazy Agnessy Ivanovny Mironovoi-Korol'*, Memorial: Istoricheskie programmy, "Nasha zhizn's Miroshei," http://www.memo.ru/history/agnessa.

5. Simon Sebag Montefiore, *Stalin: The Court of the Red Tsar* (London: Weidenfeld and Nicolson, 2003), 682, n13; Anatoly Granovsky, *I Was an NKVD Agent* (New York: Devin-Adair, 1962), 24. On the Kirov murder and the beginning of the Great Terror, see Matthew E. Lenoe, *The Kirov Murder and Soviet History* (New Haven, CT: Yale University Press, 2010).

6. Lev. 16:6–10.

7. Walter Burkert, *Greek Religion: Archaic and Classical* (Oxford: Blackwell, 1885), 82–84; René Girard, *The Scapegoat* (Baltimore, MD: Johns Hopkins University Press, 1986); Robert G. Hamerton-Kelly, ed., *Violent Origins* (Stanford, CA: Stanford University Press, 1987); Walter Burkert, *Homo Necans: Interpetationen altgriechischer Opferriten und Mythen* (Berlin: Walter de Gruyter, 1972), esp. 60–85.

8. Northrop Frye, *Anatomy of Criticism: Four Essays* (Princeton, NJ: Princeton University Press, 1957), 43–49, 163–86, and passim (the quotation is from 46).

9. Ibid., 35–43, 206–23.

10. Erich Goode and Nachman Ben-Yehuda, *Moral Panics: The Social Construction of Deviance* (Cambridge, MA: Blackwell, 1994), esp. 144–84; Wolfgang Behringer, *Witches and Witch-Hunts: A Global History* (Cambridge: Polity Press, 2004), 4–5, 12–13, 113–31 and passim; David Frankfurter, *Evil Incarnate: Rumors of Demonic Conspiracy and Ritual Abuse in History* (Princeton, NJ: Princeton University Press, 2006).

11. George L. Burr, ed., *The Witch Persecutions in Translations and Reprints from the Original Sources of European History*, 6 vols. (Philadelphia: University of Pennsylvania History Department, 1898–1912), vol. 3, no. 4, pp. 23–24, http://history.hanover.edu/texts/bamberg .html, scanned by Mike Anderson, May 1998. Proofread and pages added by Jonathan Perry, March 2001.

12. Ibid., 26–28.

13. Ibid., 28.

14. James Davidson Hunter, *Culture Wars: The Struggle for America* (New York: Basic Books, 1990); Debbie Nathan and Michael Snedeker, *Satan's Silence: Ritual Abuse and the Making of a Modern American Witch Hunt* (New York: Basic Books, 1995), 2–3, 53–103; Lawrence Wright, *Remembering Satan* (New York: Knopf, 1994), 73–75; Mary de Young, *The Day Care Ritual Abuse Moral Panic* (Jefferson, NC: McFarland, 2004), 152. See also Sex Offender Laws Research, http://www.solresearch.org/~SOLR/rprt/bkgrd/FalsAcCases.htm.

15. Wright, *Remembering Satan*, 3–11, 23–27, 37, 48, 59–62, 75–76, 86, 163–64 and passim (the Ingram quotation is from 7, the Braun quotation is from 83); Jeffrey S. Victor, *Satanic Panic: The Creation of a Contemporary Legend* (Chicago: Open Court, 1993), 104 and passim; Rev. 16:19–20.

16. Wright, *Remembering Satan*, 74; Nathan and Snedeker, *Satan's Silence*, 11–50; Frankfurter, *Evil Incarnate*, 58; Victor, *Satanic Panic*; Philip Jenkins and Daniel Maier-Katkin, "Occult Survivors: The Making of a Myth," in James T. Richardson et al., eds., *The Satanism Scare* (New York: Aldine de Gruyter, 1991), 127–44.

17. Quoted in de Young, *Day Care Ritual Abuse Moral Panic*, 80–81.

18. Frederick Crews, *The Memory Wars: Freud's Legacy in Dispute* (New York: New York Review of Books, 1995), 18–23, 185–87, 219–22; Sherrill Mulhern, "Satanism and Psychotherapy: A Rumor in Search of an Inquisition," in Richardson et al., *Satanism Scare*, 145–72; Victor, *Satanic Panic*, 104; Wright, *Remembering Satan*, 78 (the California poll quotation). The *Malleus Maleficarum* of the campaign was Ellen Bass and Laura Davis, *The Courage to Heal: A Guide for Women Survivors of Child Sexual Abuse* (first published in 1988 by HarperCollins).

19. Wright, *Remembering Satan*, 8, 58, 59.

20. Nathan and Snedeker, *Satan's Silence*, 160–61; Mark Pendergrast, *Victims of Memory: Sex Abuse Accusations and Shattered Lives* (Hinesburg, VT: Upper Access, 1996), 367. For Thomas McEachin's "Pennsylvania Sex Offender Archive Record," see http://www.google .de/imgres?client=safari&sa=X&rls=en&biw=1100&bih=485&tbm=isch&tbnid=41Gt9t5rfy Lu7M:&imgrefurl=http://www.sexoffenderrecord.com/citydirectory/PA/Brookhaven /Thomas_Mceachin_536231&docid=lfgvhmitWoqJWM&itg=1&imgurl=http://www.sex offenderrecord.com/fullsize/14/91/149136605a26abb91748b1aed18oda9e11dd121d.jpg&w =319&h=400&ei=waGcUvrAHonEtQbv6IGICA&zoom=1&iact=rc&dur=650&page=1&tbnh =156&tbnw=118&start=0&ndsp=15&ved=1t:429,r:1,s:0,i:86&tx=59&ty=82.

21. Wright, *Remembering Satan*, 134–92. The quotation is from 188. See also "Listing of information on 159 cases," in Sex Offender Laws Research, http://www.solresearch.org/~SOLR/rprt/bkgrd/FalsAcCases.htm.

22. de Young, *Day Care Ritual Abuse Moral Panic*, 71; Ileana Flores, interview with *Frontline*, July 2001, in "Did Daddy Do It?" PBS *Frontline*, http://www.pbs.org/wgbh/pages/frontline/shows/fuster/interviews/ileana.html; Nathan and Snedeker, *Satan's Silence*, 173–74 (Rappaport quotation).

23. Nathan and Snedeker, *Satan's Silence*, 175.

24. Ibid., 175–77.

25. "Ileana Flores's 1994 Deposition," in "Did Daddy Do It?," http://www.pbs.org/wgbh/pages/frontline/shows/fuster/frank/94recant.html; Ileana Flores, interview with *Frontline*, "Did Daddy Do It?" transcript, http://www.pbs.org/wgbh/pages/frontline/shows/fuster/etc/script.html.

26. Frank Fuster, interview with *Frontline*, in "Did Daddy Do It?" http://www.pbs.org/wgbh/pages/frontline/shows/fuster/interviews/fuster.html.

27. Florida Department of Law Enforcement, Sexual offender/predator flyer, http://offender.fdle.state.fl.us/offender/flyer.do?personId=58857.

28. Behringer, *Witches and Witch-Hunts*, 213–14; Joanna Ball, "The Ritual of the Necklace," publication of the Centre for the Study of Violence and Reconciliation, March 1994, http://www.csvr.org.za/index.php/publications/1632-the-ritual-of-the-necklace.html; Philip S. Gorski, *The Disciplinary Revolution: Calvinism and the Rise of the State in Early Modern Europe* (Chicago: University of Chicago Press, 2003), 121.

29. Ruth Scurr, *Fatal Purity: Robespierre and the French Revolution* (New York: Metropolitan Books, 2006), 182.

30. Exod. 32:26–29.

31. 2 Pet. 2:20–22.

32. Num. 16:3, 19; 12:2, 10; 16: 32; Deut 9:20; Michael Walzer, *Exodus and Revolution* (New York: Basic Books, 1985), 64, 111.

33. 2 Pet. 2:4–9.

34. 2 Pet. 2:12.

35. N. I. Bukharin, *Ekonomika perekhodnogo perioda*, in Bukharin, *Problemy teorii i praktiki sotsializma* (Moscow: Politizdat, 1989), 163.

36. Ibid., 165–66.

37. 2 Pet. 3:8–9, 17.

38. Max Domarus, ed., *Hitler: Speeches and Proclamations, 1932–1945*, vol. 3: *1939–1940* (Würzburg: Domarus Verlag, 1997), 1449. Cf. Max Domarus, *Hitler: Reden und Proklamationen, 1932–1945*, vol. 2: *1939–1945* (Würzburg: Domarus Verlag, 1963), 1057–58. David Regles, *Hitler's Millennial Reich* (New York: New York University Press, 2005), 166 and passim. On the Bolshevik state as a besieged fortress, see Sarah Davies and James Harris, *Stalin's World: Dictating the Soviet Order* (New Haven, CT: Yale University Press, 2014), 59–130; James Harris, *The Great Fear: Stalin's Terror of the 1930s* (Oxford: Oxford University Press, 2016).

24. THE ADMISSION OF GUILT

1. "Postanovlenie TsIK i SNK SSSR ot 1 dekabria 1934 g.," Memorial Society database, http://stalin.memo.ru/images/1934.htm; Matthew E. Lenoe, *The Kirov Murder and Soviet History* (New Haven, CT: Yale University Press, 2010), 251–388 and passim; Oleg Khlevniuk, *Khoziain: Stalin i utverzhdenie stalinskoi diktatury* (Moscow: Rosspen, 2010), 232–34; A. N. Iakovlev, ed., *Reabilitatsiia: Politicheskie protsessy 30–50-kh godov* (Moscow: Izdatel'stvo politicheskoi literatury, 1991), 123–70 (the Ezhov quotation is on 153), 183 (the Liushkov quotation).

2. Iakovlev, *Reabilitatsiia*, 159–64.

3. Iakovlev, *Reabilitatsiia*, 191–95.

4. Vladimir Khaustov and Lennart Samuelson, *Stalin, NKVD i repressii 1936–1938 gg.* (Moscow: Rosspen, 2010), 87, 93; Khlevniuk, *Khoziain*, 235–36, 252–56; Lenoe, *Kirov Murder*, 454–55; J. Arch Getty and Oleg V. Naumov, *The Road to Terror: Stalin and the Self-Destruction of the Bolsheviks, 1932–1939* (New Haven, CT: Yale University Press, 1999), 140–218; *Dokumenty po "Kremlevskomu delu*," Dokumenty Sovetskoi vlasti, http://perpetrator2004.narod.ru /Kremlin_Affair.htm.

5. Khlevniuk, *Khoziain*, 236–39, 302; Khaustov and Samuelson, *Stalin, NKVD i repressii*, 62–69, 80–83; Lenoe, *Kirov Murder*, 455–57; V. N. Khaustov et al., eds., *Lubianka: Stalin i VChK-GPU-OGPU-NKVD, ianvar' 1922—dekabr' 1936* (Moscow: Demokratiia, 2003), 613–16, 654–57, 670–71; A. G. Tepliakov, *Mashina terrora: OGPU-NKVD Sibiri v 1929–41 gg.* (Moscow: Novyi khronograf, 2008), 206–27.

6. Khlevniuk, *Khoziain*, 291–98, 240–41; Khaustov and Samuelson, *Stalin, NKVD i repressii*, 26–56; Maximilien Robespierre, "On the Principles of Political Morality," February 1794, http://www.fordham.edu/halsall/mod/1794robespierre.html (taken from M. Robespierre, *Report upon the Principles of Political Morality Which Are to Form the Basis of the Administration of the Interior Concerns of the Republic* [Philadelphia, 1794]).

7. Iakovlev, *Reabilitatsiia*, 171–84; Aleksandr Orlov, *Tainaia istoriia stalinskikh prestuplenii* (Moscow: Vsemirnoe slovo, 1991), 94–98.

8. Iakovlev, *Reabilitatsiia*, 184.

9. Ibid., 196–210.

10. *Sudebnyi otchet po delu trotskistsko-zinov'evskogo terroristicheskogo tsentra* (Moscow: Narodnyi kommissariat iustitsii SSSR, 1936); Karl Radek, "Trotskistsko-zinov'evskaia fashistskaia banda," *Izvestiia*, August 21, 1936.

11. Khaustov and Samuelson, *Stalin, NKVD i repressii*, 91–99; Getty and Naumov, *Road to Terror*, 255–82; "Stalinskie spiski," Memorial Society database, http://stalin.memo.ru /images/intro.htm.

12. "Pis'ma Bukharina," Dokumenty Sovetskoi vlasti, http://perpetrator2004.narod.ru /Bukharin.htm; A. M. Larina, *Nezabyvaemoe* (Moscow: APN, 1989), 294.

13. "Pis'ma Bukharina."

14. *Pravda*, August 23, 1936.

15. "Pis'ma Bukharina."

16. V. M. Soima, *Zapreshchennyi Stalin* (Moscow: Olma Press, 2005), 186.

17. Khaustov and Samuelson, *Stalin, NKVD i repressii*, 93; Larina, *Nezabyvaemoe*, 305, 310–11; "U menia odna nadezhda na tebia," *Istoricheskii arkhiv* 3 (2001): 69.

18. "U menia odna nadezhda na tebia," 70.

19. Ibid., 71–72.

20. "Fragmenty stenogrammy dekabr'skogo plenuma TsK BKP(b) 1936 goda," *Voprosy istorii* 1 (1995): 2–9.

21. Ibid., 10.

22. Vadim Rogovin, *1937*, http://trst.narod.ru/rogovin/t4/xiv.htm.

23. "Pis'ma Bukharina." See also Getty and Naumov, *Road to Terror*, 300–330. On Bolshevik "subjectivity" and confession rituals, see, esp., J. Arch Getty, "*Samokritika* Rituals in the Stalinist Central Committee, 1933–1938," *Russian Review* (January 1999): 49–70; Igal Halfin, *Terror in My Soul: Communist Autobiographies on Trial* (Cambridge, MA: Harvard University Press, 2003); Jochen Hellbeck, *Revolution on My Mind: Writing a Diary under Stalin* (Cambridge: Harvard University Press, 2006); and Nanci Adler, *Keeping Faith with the Party: Communist Believers Return from the Gulag* (Bloomington: Indiana University Press, 2012).

24. Dmitrii Shelestov, *Vremia Alekseia Rykova* (Moscow: Progress, 1990), 286–87; N. A. Perli-Rykova, interview with author, February 12, 1998; L. Gronskaia, *Nabroski po pamiati* (Moscow: Flinta, 2004), 77.

25. Larina, *Nezabyvaemoe*, 317, 326.

26. *Pravda*, December 15, 1936; "U menia odna nadezhda na tebia," 76–77; "Stenogrammy ochnykh stavok v TsK VKP(b): Dekabr' 1936," *Voprosy istorii* 4 (2002): 7–11.

27. "O partiinosti lits, prokhodivshikh po delu tak nazyvaemogo 'antosovetskogo pravotrotskistskogo bloka," *Izvestiia TsK KPSS* 5 (1989): 72–75.

28. "'Vse, chto govorit Radek—eto absoliutno zlostnaia kleveta . . .': Ochnaia stavka K. Radeka i N. Bukharina v TsK VKP(b) 13 ianvaria 1937," *Istochnik* 1 (2001): 67.

29. "Ia ikh, eti navety, otvergaiu i budu otvergat'," *Istochnik* 3 (2001): 32–37.

30. Ibid., 31–32.

31. *Sudebnyi otchet po delu antisovetskogo trotskistskogo tsentra* (Moscow: Iuridicheskoe izdatel'stvo, 1937), 230.

32. Ibid., 231.

33. Ibid., 225.

34. Ibid., 231.

35. Lion Feuchtwanger, *Moscow 1937* (London: Victor Gollancz, 1937), 147–49.

36. *Sudebnyi otchet po delu antisovetskogo trotskistskogo tsentra*, 58.

37. *Pravda*, January, 25, 1937.

38. *Sudebnyi otchet po delu antisovetskogo trotskistskogo tsentra*, 187; *Pravda*, January 25, 1937.

39. Feuchtwanger, *Moscow 1937*, 135.

40. G. A. Voronskaia, "Esli v serdtse posylaiut puliu," *Istoricheskii arkhiv* 1 (1997): 109.

41. "Materialy fevral'sko-martovskogo plenuma TsK VKP(b) 1937 g.," *Voprosy istorii* 2–3 (1992): 4–43; "U menia odna nadezhda na tebia," 77–78.

42. Larina, *Nezabyvaemoe*, 332, 341–42.

43. Shelestov, *Vremia Alekseia Rykova*, 287.

44. Larina, *Nezabyvaemoe*, 333–34.

45. Ibid., 363–64.

46. "Materialy fevral'sko-martovskogo plenuma TsK VKP(b) 1937 goda," *Voprosy istorii* 10 (1992): 4–5, see also in http://www.memo.ru/history/1937.

47. Ibid., *Voprosy istorii* 2 (1993): 7, http://www.memo.ru/history/1937.

48. Ibid., *Voprosy istorii* 4–5 (1992): 23, http://www.memo.ru/history/1937.

49. Larina, *Nezabyvaemoe*, 349.

50. "Materialy fevral'sko-martovskogo plenuma TsK VKP(b) 1937 goda", *Voprosy istorii* 6–7 (1992): 2.

51. Ibid., *Voprosy istorii* 2 (1993): 3.

52. Ibid., *Voprosy istorii* 10 (1992): 25

53. Ibid., *Voprosy istorii* 8–9 (1992): 10.

54. Ibid., *Voprosy istorii* 8–9 (1992): 24.

55. Ibid., *Voprosy istorii* 10 (1992): 7.

56. Ibid., *Voprosy istorii* 2 (1993): 5–6.

57. Ibid., 17.

58. Ibid., 19.

59. Ibid., *Voprosy istorii* 10 (1992): 20–22.

60. Ibid., 15.

61. Ibid., *Voprosy istorii* 11–12 (1992): 2–3.

62. Ibid., 3.

63. Ibid., 5.

64. Ibid., *Voprosy istorii* 2 (1993): 25.

65. Ibid., 16. For more excerpts and discussion of the plenum, see Getty and Naumov, *Road to Terror*, 364–419.

66. Shelestov, *Vremia Alekseia Rykova*, 289.

67. N. A. Perli-Rykova, interview with author, February 12, 1998.

68. Shelestov, *Vremia Alekseia Rykova*, 290.

69. Larina, *Nezabyvaemoe*, 352–53.

70. Ibid., 354–55.

71. Ibid., 151.

72. N. A. Perli-Rykova, interview with author, February 12, 1998.

73. Ibid.

74. Ibid.; S. V. Obolenskaia, interview with author, March 26, 1998; Obolenskaia, *Iz vospomina-nii*, "Samizdat," http://samlib.ru/o/obolenskaja_s_w/01.shtml; Obolenskaia, *Deti bol'shogo terrora*, 36–7.

75. Obolenskaia, *Iz vospominanii*, http://samlib.ru/o/obolenskaja_s_w/01.shtml; Svetlana Obo-lenskaia, *Deti Bol'shogo terrora: Vospominaniia* (Moscow: AGRAF, 2013), 26–27, 36–37; Vladi-mir Volkov, "Portrety liderov revoliutsii i bor'by protiv stalinizma 20kh i 30kh godov: V. M. Smirnov i gruppa demokraticheskogo tsentralizma," World Socialist Website, http://www.wsws.org/ru/2000/mai2000/smir-m25.shtml; http://lists.memo.ru/index18.htm.

76. Obolenskaia, *Iz vospominanii*; Samlib, http://zhurnal.lib.ru/o/obolenskaja_s_w/01.shtml; "Protokol doprosa D. S. Azbelia," in *Dokumenty po "Kremlevskomu delu"* (from APRF, f. 3, op. 58, d. 233, ll. 80–87), http://perpetrator2004.narod.ru/Kremlin_Affair.htm; Larina, *Nezaby-vaemoe*, 67–69, 234–36.

77. Osinsky's letter to Anna Shaternikova, dated January 31, 1937, and mailed on February 2, 1937, is in Svetlana Obolenskaia's (Osinskaia's) family archive; I have a typed copy in my possession.

78. Ibid., 2.

79. GARF, f. 5446, op. 82, d. 36, l. 126.

80. Osinsky, letter to Anna Shaternikova, January 31, 1937, 3.

81. Ibid., 2.

82. Ibid., 6.

25. THE VALLEY OF THE DEAD

1. Vladimir Khaustov and Lennart Samuelson, *Stalin, NKVD i repressii 1936–1938 gg.* (Moscow: Rosspen, 2010), 73–74; Jeffrey S. Victor, *Satanic Panic: The Creation of a Contemporary Leg-end* (Chicago: Open Court, 1993), 104; N. Rabichev, "Gnilaia i opasnaia teoriia prevrashche-niia klassovykh vragov v ruchnykh," *Bol'shevik* 7 (April 1, 1937): 55; V. Rabichev, interview with author, April 14, 1998.

2. Rabichev, "Gnilaia i opasnaia teoriia," 56; Khaustov and Samuelson, *Stalin, NKVD i repressii*, 77, 130–141; "Materialy fevral'sko-martovskogo plenuma TsK VKP(b) 1937 goda", *Voprosy istorii* 10 (1992): 18.

3. "Stalinskie spiski," Memorial Society database, http://stalin.memo.ru/images/intro.htm, http://stalin.memo.ru/spiski/index.htm, http://stalin.memo.ru/images/gb537.htm; J. Arch Getty and Oleg V. Naumov, *The Road to Terror: Stalin and the Self-Destruction of the Bolsheviks, 1932–1939* (New Haven, CT: Yale University Press, 1999), 1–5; "Rasstreliannye v Moskve," http://mos.memo.ru; "Dimanshtein Semen Markovich," *Spravochnik po istorii Kommunisticheskoi partii i Sovetskogo Soiuza*, http://www.knowbysight.info/DDD/02430.asp; "Repressii uchenykh: Biograficheskie materialy," Institut istorii estestvoznaniia i tekhniki im. S. I. Vavilova RAN, http://www.ihst.ru/projects/sohist/repress/kom/1938/dimanshtein.htm.

4. Agnessa Mironova-Korol', *Agnessa: From Paradise to Purgatory: A Voice from Stalin's Russia*, trans. Rose Glickman (Bloomington, IN: Slavica, 2012), 77–78; M. M. Iakovenko, *Agnessa: Ustnye rasskazy Agnessy Ivanovny Mironovoi-Korol'*, Memorial: Istoricheskie programmy, "Nasha zhizn's Miroshei," http://www.memo.ru/history/agnessa. Eikhe's wife's name was Evgenia Evseevna Rubtsova.

5. S. A. Papkov, *Stalinskii terror v Sibiri 1928–1941* (Novosibirsk: Izdatel'stvo Novosibirskogo otdeleniia RAN, 1997), 184–85.

6. Ibid., 189–91.

7. Aleksei Tepliakov, *Oprichniki Stalina* (Moscow: Iauza, 2009), 228; A. G. Tepliakov, *Mashina terrora: OGPU-NKVD Sibiri v 1929–1941 gg.* (Moscow: Novyi Khronograf, 2008), 477; Mironova, *Agnessa: From Paradise to Purgatory*, 79; Iakovenko, *Agnessa*, http://www.memo.ru/history/agnessa.

8. Tepliakov, *Oprichniki Stalina*, 229–30; Tepliakov, *Mashina terrora*, 478; Papkov, *Stalinskii terror v Sibiri*, 203–5.

9. Tepliakov, *Oprichniki Stalina*, 226–30, 247–48; Tepliakov, *Mashina terrora*, 356–63; Papkov, *Stalinskii terror v Sibiri*, 187–207; Mironova, *Agnessa: From Paradise to Purgatory*, 80; Iakovenko, *Agnessa*, http://www.memo.ru/history/agnessa.

10. Papkov, *Stalinskii terror v Sibiri*, 196.

11. Mironova, *Agnessa: From Paradise to Purgatory*, 85; Iakovenko, *Agnessa*, http://www.memo.ru/history/agnessa.

12. Mironova, *Agnessa: From Paradise to Purgatory*, 200; Iakovenko, *Agnessa*, http://www.memo.ru/history/agnessa; Tepliakov, *Oprichniki Stalina*, 233–43; Khaustov and Samuelson, *Stalin, NKVD i repressii*, 127; N. V. Petrov and K. V. Skorkin, eds., *Kto rukovodil, NKVD 1934–1941: Spravochnik* (Moscow: Zven'ia, 1999), 99–100, 300–301.

13. Khaustov and Samuelson, *Stalin, NKVD i repressii*, 262–63; V. Danilov, R. Manning, L. Viola, eds., *Tragediia sovetskoi derevni: Kollektivizatsiia i raskulachivanie* (Moscow: Rosspen, 2000), vol. 5, bk. 1 (Moscow: Rosspen, 2004), 256–57, 601–2; Khaustov and Samuelson, *Stalin, NKVD i repressii*, 332–35.

14. Khaustov and Samuelson, *Stalin, NKVD i repressii*, 332; *Tragediia sovetskoi derevni*, 5:258.

15. Mark Iunge [Marc Junge], Gennadii Bordiugov, and Rolf Binner, *Vertikal' bol'shogo terrora: Istoriia operatsii po prikazu NKVD No. 00447* (Moscow: Novyi Khronograf, 2008), 57.

16. Iunge, Bordiugov, and Binner, *Vertikal' bol'shogo terrora*, 58; M. Vyltsan and V. Danilov, "Primenenie VMN 'nami garantiruetsia,'" *Nauka i zhizn'* 9 (1997): 70; Tepliakov, *Mashina terrora*, 273–74, 347–48; Khaustov and Samuelson, *Stalin, NKVD i repressii*, 265.

17. *Tragediia sovetskoi derevni*, 5:602; Iunge, Bordiugov, and Binner, *Vertikal' bol'shogo terrora*, 32–33; Khaustov and Samuelson, *Stalin, NKVD i repressii*, 264; Tepliakov, *Oprichniki Stalina*, 253–54.

18. Iunge, Bordiugov, and Binner, *Vertikal' bol'shogo terrora*, 94–96.

19. Ibid., 451.

20. Ibid., 98–114, 176, 597.

21. *Reabilitatsiia: Kak eto bylo* (Moscow, Demokratiia, 2000), 1:319; Iunge, Bordiugov, and Binner, *Vertikal' bol'shogo terrora*, 48, 149, 214, 187.

22. Iunge, Bordiugov, Binner, *Vertikal' bol'shogo terrora*, 100; Khaustov and Samuelson, *Stalin, NKVD i repressii*, 267.

23. Khaustov and Samuelson, *Stalin, NKVD i repressii*, 286–304; Viktor Dönninghaus [Deninghaus], *V teni 'Bol'shogo brata': Zapadnye natsional'nye menshinstva v SSSR, 1917–1938 gg.* (Moscow: Rosspen, 2011), 587–628; Oleg Khlevniuk, *Khoziain: Stalin i utverzhdenie stalinskoi diktatury* (Moscow: Rosspen, 2010), 315–22; Tepliakov, *Mashina terrora*, 365–88; N. V. Petrov and A. B. Roginskii, "Pol'skaia operatsiia NKVD 1937–1938 gg.," in A. E. Gur'ianov, ed., *Repressii protiv poliakov i pol'skikh grazhdan* (Moscow: Zven'ia, 1997), 22–43; Marc Jensen and Nikita Petrov, *Stalin's Loyal Executioner: People's Commissar Nikolai Ezhov, 1895–1940* (Stanford, CA: Hoover Institution Press, 2002), 93–100.

24. Iunge, Bordiugov, and Binner, *Vertikal' bol'shogo terrora*, 598, 622–23; Petrov and Roginskii, "Pol'skaia operatsiia NKVD 1937–1938 gg.," 33; Khlevniuk, *Khoziain*, 320; Jensen and Petrov, *Stalin's Loyal Executioner*, 205–6.

25. Tepliakov, *Mashina terrora*, 484, 518; Tepliakov, *Oprichniki Stalina*, 263–64, 238.

26. Tepliakov, *Mashina terrora*, 496.

27. Mironova, *Agnessa: From Paradise to Purgatory*, 85–86; Iakovenko, *Agnessa*, http://www.memo.ru/history/agnessa.

28. Jensen and Petrov, *Stalin's Loyal Executioner*, 91–92; Tepliakov, *Oprichniki Stalina*, 217–18, 229–31, 242–43, 264–65.

29. Mironova, *Agnessa: From Paradise to Purgatory*, 86; Iakovenko, *Agnessa*, http://www.memo.ru/history/agnessa.

30. A. G. Tepliakov, "Personal i povsednevost' Novosibirskogo NKVD v 1936–1946," in *Minuvshee: Istoricheskii al'manakh* (Moscow: Atheneum-Feniks, 1997), 21:254; Tepliakov, *Oprichniki Stalina*, 263–65.

31. Mironova, *Agnessa: From Paradise to Purgatory*, 87; Iakovenko, *Agnessa*, http://www.memo.ru/history/agnessa.

32. Mironova, *Agnessa: From Paradise to Purgatory*, 89; Iakovenko, *Agnessa*, http://www.memo.ru/history/agnessa.

33. Mironova, *Agnessa: From Paradise to Purgatory*, 90; Iakovenko, *Agnessa*, http://www.memo.ru/history/agnessa.

34. Tepliakov, *Oprichniki Stalina*, 266; Papkov, *Stalinskii terror v Sibiri*, 269; Tepliakov, *Mashina terrora*, 92.

35. Mironova, *Agnessa: From Paradise to Purgatory*, 90; Iakovenko, *Agnessa*, http://www.memo.ru/history/agnessa.

36. Baabar, *From World Power to Soviet Satellite: History of Mongolia* (Winwick, UK: White Horse Press, 1999), 356–63; S. G. Luzianin, *Rossiia-Mongoliia-Kitai v pervoi polovine XX veka* (Moscow: Ogni, 2003), 229–41; Shagdariin Sandag and Harry H. Kendall, *Poisoned Arrows: The Stalin-Choibalsan Mongolian Massacres, 1921–1941* (Boulder, CO: Westview, 2000), 84, 95, 104.

37. Baabar, *From World Power to Soviet Satellite*, 361–65; Sandag and Kendall, *Poisoned Arrows*, 119–32; I. I. Kudriavtsev, ed., *Arkhivy Kremlia i Staroi ploshchadi: Dokumenty po "Delu KPSS"* (Novosibirsk: Sibirskii Khronograf, 1995), 20.

38. Mironova, *Agnessa: From Paradise to Purgatory*, 93; Iakovenko, *Agnessa*, http://www.memo.ru/history/agnessa.

39. Mironova, *Agnessa: From Paradise to Purgatory*, 95; Iakovenko, *Agnessa*, http://www.memo.ru/history/agnessa.

40. Mironova, *Agnessa: From Paradise to Purgatory*, 98–99; Iakovenko, *Agnessa*, http://www.memo.ru/history/agnessa.

26. THE KNOCK ON THE DOOR

1. T. I. Shmidt, *Dom na naberezhnoi: Liudi i sud'by* (Moscow: Vozvrashchenie, 2009), 21–34; T. I. Smilga, interview with author, January 19, 1998; I. Smilga, "Charl'z Dikens (lichnost' i tvorchestvo)," in *Charl'z Dikkens* [Charles Dickens], *Posmertnye zapiski Pikvikskogo kluba*, trans. A. V. Krivtsov and Evgenii Lann, with the participation of G. G. Shpet, introduction by I. T. Smilga (Moscow Academia, 1933), xiii.

2. T. I. Smilga, interview with author, January 19, 1998.

3. Ibid.; "Zhertvy politicheskogo terrora v SSSR," Memorial Society database, http://lists.memo.ru/index1.htm; "Frenkel' Aron Abramovich," Spravochnik po istorii Kommunisticheskoi partii Sovetskogo Soiuza, http://www.knowbysight.info/FFF/06548.asp; "Stalinskie spiski," Memorial Society database, http://stalin.memo.ru/names/index.htm; M. R. Peterson, "O nas," 11a–12, 26–27, in AMDNN, "Peterson" file.

4. A. Shitov, *Iurii Trifonov: Khronika zhizni i tvorchestva* (Ekaterinburg: Izdatel'stvo Ural'skogo Universiteta, 1997), 98–99; Iurii Trifonov, "Otblesk kostra," in *Sobranie sochinenii* (Moscow: Khudozhestvennaia literatura, 1987), 143–44 (also http://lib.misto.kiev.ua/TRIFONOW/campfire.txt); Iurii Trifonov, "Iz dnevnikov i rabochikh tetradei: Publikatsiia i kommentarii Ol'gi Trifonovoi," *Druzhba narodov* 5 (1998): http://magazines.russ.ru/druzhba/1998/5/trif.html.

5. "Pervyi predsedatel' voennoi kollegii Verkhovnogo suda SSSR," *Sotsialisticheskaia zakonnost'* 11 (1988): 59–60; Trifonov, "Iz dnevnikov," June 22, 1937.

6. Trifonov, "Iz dnevnikov"; Shitov, *Iurii Trifonov*, 102–27.
7. E. A. Dinershtein, *A. K. Voronskii v poiskakh zhivoi vody* (Moscow: Rosspen 2001), 310–11; G. A. Voronskaia, "Esli v serdtse posylaiut puliu," *Istoricheskii arkhiv* 1 (1997): 102; TsAOPIM, f. 78, op. 1a, d. 176, ll. 67–68.
8. "Mozhet byt', pozzhe mnogoe stanet bolee ochevidnym i iasnym (Iz dokumentov 'Partiinogo dela' A. K. Voronskogo)," *Voprosy literatury* 3 (1995): 274–75, 288–89.
9. "Fragmenty stenogrammy dekabr'skogo plenuma TsK BKP(b) 1936 goda," *Voprosy istorii* 1 (1995): 2–9.
10. "Mozhet byt,'" 289–90.
11. Voronskaia, "Esli v serdtse," 107; "Protokol doprosa Zorina (Gombarga) Sergeia Semenovicha ot 21 ianvaria 1935 goda," Spravochnik po istorii Kommunisticheskoi partii i Sovetskogo soiuza 1898–1991, http://www.knowbysight.info/5_DOC/08413.asp.
12. A. Voronskii, *Iskusstvo i zhizn'* (Moscow: Krug, 1924), 71.
13. Voronskaia, "Esli v serdtse," 102.
14. Nikolai Gogol, *The Collected Tales of Nikolai Gogol*, trans. Richard Pevear and Larissa Volokhonsky (New York: Vintage Books, 1998), 190–92. I have substituted "memorial service" for the untranslated (and footnoted) word *panikhida*.
15. A. Voronskii, "Mister Britling p'et chashu do dna," *Krasnaia nov'* 5 (1926): 195, 201; Voronskii, *Iskusstvo i zhizn'*, 268–71.
16. Aleksandr Voronskii, *Gogol'* (Moscow: Molodaia gvardiia, 2009), 119–20.
17. A. Voronskii, "Ob iskusstve pisatelia," in *Kak i nad chem rabotat' pisateliu* (Moscow: Molodaia gvardiia, 1927), 15.
18. Voronskii, *Gogol'*, 439.
19. Voronskaia, "Esli v serdtse," 109–10.
20. Voronskaia, "Esli v serdtse," 111; G. Nurmina, *Na dal'nem priiske* (Magadan: Gobi, 1992), 8–9, http://www.sakharov-center.ru/asfcd/auth/?t=page&num=8718.
21. M. V. Zelenov, "Glavlit i istoricheskaia nauka v 20–30-e gody," *Voprosy istorii* 3 (1997): 30; Stalinskie spiski," http://stalin.memo.ru/names/index.htm; I. L. Averbakh, *Ot prestupleniia k trudu* (Moscow: OGIZ, 1936); Roi Medvedev, "Slava i tragediia odnoi sem'i," *Karetnyi riad* 5 (November 1989); Evgenii Zhirnov, "Vse proiskhodiashchee so mnoi lozhitsia ten'iu na imia ottsa," *Kommersant-Vlast'*, November 7, 2005, http://www.kommersant.ru/doc/624225; Boris Efimov, *Desiat' desiatiletii* (Moscow: Vagrius, 2000), 621–23; Mikhail Shreider, "NKVD iznutri: Zapiski chekista," Urnatia-s.com, http://www.urantia-s.com/library/shreider/nkvd/3.
22. AMDNN, "Poloz" file, letters, K-1–K-11 (February 18, 1936; February 27, 1936; February 28, 1936); AMDNN, "Poloz" file, R. M. Poloz's letter to the Museum, October 7, 2000.
23. AMDNN, "Poloz" file, letters, K-10–K-11 (February 28, 1936).
24. Ibid., K-11 (February 29, 1936); K-7 (February 27, 1936); K-3 (n.d., between February 21 and 27, 1936); K-15 (March 25, 1936); K-16 (March 30, 1936).
25. Ibid., K-17–K-19 (April 1, 1936; April 5, 1936).
26. AMDNN, "Poloz" file, letters, K-25 (April 10, 1936); Matthew 6:31–34.
27. AMDNN, "Poloz" file, letters, K-29 (April 30, 1936); K-32, K-30 (May 20, 1936); R. M. Poloz, interview with author, June 28, 1998; AMDNN, "Poloz" file, letters, K-31 (April 9, 1936 [there is a mistake in the typescript; should be May 9, 1936]).
28. AMDNN, "Poloz" file, letters, K-32–K-33 (May 20, 1936); K-34–K-35 (May 31, 1936).
29. AMDNN, "Poloz" file, R. M. Poloz's letter to the Museum, October 7, 2000; R. M. Poloz, interview with author, June 28, 1998.
30. AMDNN, "Poloz" file, letters, M-1, July 1936.
31. Ibid., M-1–M-2 (July 18, 1936).
32. Ibid., M-3 (July 29, 1936).
33. AMDNN, "Poloz" file, "Vospominaniia Mirry Varshavskoi," ll. 3–4.
34. "Zhertvy politicheskogo terrora v SSSR," Memorial Society database, http://lists.memo.;

ru/index1.htm; Moroz, "Minuvshee," 16–20, in AMDNN, "Moroz" file; N. N. Demchenko, "Kanikuly dlinoi v 18 let," *Mendeleevets* 36, no. 1799 (November 30, 1988): 3.

35. "Zhertvy politicheskogo terrora v SSSR," http://lists.memo.; ru/index1.htm; Schumatsky, *Silvester bei Stalin*, 21–2; N. V. Petrov and K. V. Skorkin, eds., *Kto rukovodil, NKVD 1934–1941: Spravochnik* (Moscow: Zven'ia, 1999), 82–83.

36. Inna Shikheeva-Gaister, *Deti vragov naroda: Semeinaia khronika vremen kul'ta lichnosti 1925–1953* (Moscow: Vozvrashchenie, 2012), 43–49 (the quotation is from 47–48); "Zhertvy politicheskogo terrora v SSSR," http://lists.memo.; ru/index1.htm.

37. S. A. Khalatova, interview with author, September 6, 1998; "Zhertvy politicheskogo terrora v SSSR," http://lists.memo.; ru/index1.htm; A. G. Tepliakov, *"Nepronitsaemye nedra": VChK-OGPU v Sibiri, 1918–29 gg.* (Moscow: AIRO-XXI, 2007), 137–47; Tepliakov, *Mashina terrora*, 356.

38. Olga Aroseva, *Prozhivshaia dvazhdy* (Moscow: AST, 2012), RoyalLib.com, http://royallib .com/book/aroseva_olga/progivshaya_dvagdi.html (under August 24, 1936; July 21, 1936; July 31, 1936).

39. Ibid. (under May 8, 1935).

40. Ibid. (under July 21, 1936; August 22, 1936).

41. Ibid. (under August 22, 1936).

42. Ibid. (under October 25, 1936; November 7, 1936); *Pravda*, December 19 and 29, 1936; GARF, f. 5446, op. 82, d. 49, ll. 60–62.

43. Voronskaia, "Esli v serdtse," 106; Aroseva, *Prozhivshaia dvazhdy*, http://royallib.com /book/aroseva_olga/progivshaya_dvagdi.html (under December 20, 1936, December 21, 1936; January 6, 1937; January 30, 1937; February 19, 1937).

44. Aroseva, *Prozhivshaia dvazhdy*, http://royallib.com/book/aroseva_olga/progivshaya _dvagdi.html (under February 9, 1937).

45. Ibid. (under March 21, 1937).

46. Ibid. (under February 19, 1937).

47. Ibid. (under April 16, 1937).

48. Ibid., chaps. 6 and 7; "Zhertvy politicheskogo terrora v SSSR," http://lists.memo.; ru /index1.htm.

49. Aroseva, *Prozhivshaia dvazhdy*, chap. 7, http://royallib.com/book/aroseva_olga/progiv shaya_dvagdi.html.

50. Ibid.; "Stalinskie spiski," http://stalin.memo.ru/names/index.htm; "Zhertvy politicheskogo terrora v SSSR," http://lists.memo.; ru/index1.htm.

51. V. I. Piatnitskii, comp., *Golgofa* (St. Petersburg: Palitra, 1993), 18–24; V. I. Piatnitskii, *Osip Piatnitskii i Komintern na vesakh istorii* (Minsk: Kharvest, 2004), 452–72.

52. Piatnitskii, *Golgofa*, 25.

53. Ibid., 25.

54. Ibid., 25–27.

55. Ibid., 32.

56. Vladimir Khaustov and Lennart Samuelson, *Stalin, NKVD i repressii 1936–1938 gg.* (Moscow: Rosspen, 2010), 265; Petrov and Skorkin, *Kto rukovodil NKVD*, 97–98; AOM, fond. 2 (memoir collection), V. V. Bogutskii, *Vospominaniia*, pp. 7–9.

57. "Operativnyi prikaz Narodnogo kommissara vnutrennikh del Soiuza SSR No. 00486," Memorial Society database, http://www.memo.ru/history/document/00486.htm.

58. "Zhertvy politicheskogo terrora v SSSR," http://lists.memo.; ru/index1.htm; A. M. Larina, *Nezabyvaemoe* (Moscow: APN, 1989), 28–32, 70–71, 151, 167.

59. Larina, *Nezabyvaemoe*, 224–27.

60. Nataliia Sats, *Zhizn'—iavlenie polosatoe* (Moscow: Novosti, 1991), 273–86.

61. V. N. Rabichev, interview with author, April 14, 1998; L. V. Maksimenkov, *Sumbur vmesto muzyki: Stalinskaia kul'turnaia revoliutsiia 1936–1938* (Moscow: Iuridicheskaia kniga, 1997), 283–98.

62. N. A. Perli (Rykova), interview with author, February 12, 1998; in AMDNN, "Kuchmin" file, O. I. Kuchmin and E. I. Kuchmina, "Sud'ba soldata revoliutsii," manuscript; letters to the Museum by E. I. Kuchmina, approx. August–September, 1991, and March 17, 2003; E. I. Kuchmina, interviews with author, April 6 and July 25, 2008; Anatoly Granovsky, *I Was an NKVD Agent* (New Yrk: Devin-Adair, 1962), 36–37.

63. Granovsky, *I Was an NKVD Agent*, 40–41.

64. Gaister, *Deti vragov naroda*, 52.

65. Obolenskaia, *Iz vospominanii*, "Samizdat," http://samlib.ru/o/obolenskaja_s_w/01.shtml; Svetlana Obolenskaia, *Deti Bol'shogo terrora: Vospominaniia* (Moscow: AGRAF, 2013), 31–33.

66. Obolenskaia, *Iz vospominanii*, http://samlib.ru/o/obolenskaja_s_w/01.shtml; Obolenskaia, *Deti Bol'shogo terrora*, 33.

67. Obolenskaia, *Iz vospominanii*, http://samlib.ru/o/obolenskaja_s_w/01.shtml; Obolenskaia, *Deti Bol'shogo terrora*, 38–39.

68. Obolenskaia, *Iz vospominanii*, http://samlib.ru/o/obolenskaja_s_w/01.shtml; Obolenskaia, *Deti Bol'shogo terrora*, 33.

69. O. V. Khlevniuk, *1937oi: Stalin, NKVD i sovetskoe obshchestvo* (Moscow: Respublika, 1992), 100–111 (the quotation is from 110); Khaustov and Samuelson, *Stalin, NKVD i repressii*, 170–1.

70. Khlevniuk, *1937*, 110–4 (the quotation is on p. 113); Getty, *The Road to Terror*, 493–512 (the quotation is on p. 510).

71. Getty, *The Road to Terror*, 514–6; L. P. Postyshev, interview with author, October 1, 1998.

72. S. A. Butenko, interview with author, September 24, 1998.

73. Zhertvy politicheskogo terrora v SSSR," http://lists.memo.; ru/index1.htm; http://ru.rodovid.org/wk/Запись:798224; Ivan Dzhukha, *Grecheskaia operatsiia. Istoriia repressii protiv grekov v SSSR* (St. Petersburg: Aleteia, 2006); S. A. Butenko, interview with author, September 24, 1998.

74. RGASPI (molodezhnye organizatsii), f. M-1, op. 2, d. 133, ll. 13, 53, 61–66; d. 157, l. 147; d. 161, l. 110; d. 156, l. 67; d. 161, l. 101, 63.

75. L. A. Kozlova (Bogacheva), interview with author, September 24, 1997.

76. Ibid.

77. Khlevniuk, *Khoziain*, 345–59; Khaustov and Samuelson, *Stalin, NKVD i repressii*, 304–24.

78. Granovsky, *I Was an NKVD Agent*, 51–77.

27. THE GOOD PEOPLE

1. GARF, f. 9542, op. 7, d. 13, ll. 43–47; d. 14, ll. 1, 1 ob., 6–7, 96–96ob., 150b–150v; d. 34, ll. 27–54; E. E. Ivchenko, interview with author, September 23, 1998; E. I. Ivchenko's autobiography (in the author's possession).

2. TsAODM, f. 75, op. 1, dd. 176, 177 (quotations from ll. 6, 14, 41), 196 (quotation from l. 12), 200, 225, ll. 3–4; "Zhertvy politicheskogo terrora v SSSR," Memorial Society database, http://lists.memo.ru/index1.htm; RGASPI, f. 124, op. 1, d. 264, ll. 7, 8; Nikolai Zen'kovich, *Elita: Samye sekretnye rodstvenniki* (Moscow: Ol'ma-Press, 2005), 53–54.

3. TsMAM, f. 528, op. 1, dd. 493, 499 (quotation on l. 4), 504 (Dubrovina quotation on l. 15), 528, 575 (info on numbers on ll. 26 and 59).

4. TsAODM, f. 75, op. 1, d. 196, ll. 9–10, 30–32, 35.

5. Mikhail Kol'tsov, "Svora krovavykh sobak," *Pravda*, March 3, 1938.

6. Ibid.; Mikhail Kol'tsov, "Ubiitsa s pretenziiami," *Pravda*, March 7, 1938.

7. Kol'tsov, "Svora krovavykh sobak."

8. A. Lakhuti, *Izbrannye poemy* (Moscow: Khudozhestvennaia literatura, 1936), 29, 63–67.

9. I. R. Muklevich, "Dorogoi drug," manuscript in AMDNN, "Muklevich" file, 28.

10. Olga Aroseva, *Prozhivshaia dvazhdy* (Moscow: AST, 2012), RoyalLib.com, http://royallib.com

/book/aroseva_olga/progivshaya_dvagdi.html, V. M. Soima, *Zapreshchennyi Stalin* (Moscow: Olma Press, 2005) http://lib.rus.ec/b/387149/read (under August 24, 1936).

11. Ibid. (under January 30, 1937).

12. V. B. Volina, interview with author, September 18, 1997; V. D. Shvarts, interview with author, September 10, 1998. "Black raven" was a colloquial term for "prison van."

13. V. M. Soima, *Zapreshchennyi Stalin* (Moscow: Olma Press, 2005), 97–98.

14. RGALI, f. 457, d. 391, ll. 199–1990b.

15. GARF, f. 5446, op. 82, d. 65, ll. 182–84.

16. RGASPI, f. 135, op. 2, d. 19, l. 57.

17. Ibid., ll. 56–560b.

18. RGASPI, f. 74, op. 2, d. 105, ll. 41–42, 47, 51, 55, 59–60 (cited in Boris Sokolov, "Dva marshala: Tragicheskii roman v pis'makh," *Grani.ru*, February 21, 2003, http://grani.ru/Society /History/m.23664.html); RGVA, f. 37461, op. 1, d. 134, l. 25.

19. RGVA, f. 37461, op. 1, d. 134, ll. 15–150b.

20. Ibid., l. 25; d. 128, ll. 7–9.

21. AMDNN, "Ankety" file, "Otvety M. I. Dement'evoi (Agroskinoi)"; AMDNN, "Ankety" file, Ruslan Nikolaevich Gel'man's, letter to the Museum.

22. V. I. Piatnitskii, comp., *Golgofa* (St. Petersburg: Palitra, 1993), 46, 41–42.

23. Ibid., 56, 46.

24. Ibid., 63–64.

25. Ibid., 61.

26. Ibid., 51–53.

27. Ibid., 57; Kol'tsov, "Svora krovavykh sobak."

28. Piatnitskii, *Golgofa*, 57, 60–61.

29. Ibid., 79.

30. Ibid., 82–83.

31. Ibid., 103.

32. Ibid.

33. Ibid., 13–16, 104–20; Inna Shikheeva-Gaister, *Deti vragov naroda: Semeinaia khronika vremen kul'ta lichnosti 1925–1953* (Moscow: Vozvrashchenie, 2012), 55–57.

34. Obolenskaia, *Iz vospominanii*, "Samizdat," http://samlib.ru/o/obolenskaja_s_w/01.shtml.

35. N. A. Gilinskaia, interview with author, March 2, 1998.

36. Muklevich, "Dorogoi drug," 12; I. R. Muklevich, interview with author, November 7, 1997.

37. N. N. Demchenko, "Kanikuly dlinoi v 18 let," *Mendeleevets* 36, no. 1799 (November 30, 1988): 3.

38. Gaister, *Deti vragov*, 57–58.

39. Ibid., 66.

40. Obolenskaia, *Iz vospominanii*, http://samlib.ru/o/obolenskaja_s_w/01.shtml; Svetlana Obolenskaia, *Deti Bol'shogo terrora: Vospominaniia* (Moscow: AGRAF, 2013), 55–56.

41. Muklevich, "Dorogoi drug," 62–63.

42. Ibid., 24–25. Cf. AOM, fond. 2 (memoir collection), V. V. Bogutskii, *Vospominaniia*, pp. 7–8.

43. See Golfo Alexopoulos, "Stalin and the Politics of Kinship: Practices of Collective Punishment, 1920s–1940s," *Comparative Studies in Society and History* 1 (2008): 91–117; Cynthia Hooper, "Terror of Intimacy: Family Politics in the 1930s Soviet Union," in Christina Kiaer and Eric Naiman, eds., *Everyday Life in Early Soviet Russia: Taking the Revolution Inside* (Bloomington: Indiana University Press, 2006); Amir Weiner, "Nature, Nurture, and Memory in a Socialist Utopia: Delineating the Socio-Ethnic Body in the Age of Socialism," *American Historical Review* 104, no. 4 (October 1999): 1114–55.

44. Muklevich, "Dorogoi drug," 30–31; I. R. Muklevich, interview with author, November 7, 1997; T. V. Shuniakova (Ignatashvili), interview with author, April 22, 1998.

45. G. B. Ivanova, interview with author, March 13, 1998.

46. Iudit Agracheva, "Chlen partii s 1903 goda," *Vesti-2*, June 1, 1995; "Biografiia" and "Avtobiografiia," in AMDNN, "Brandenburgsky" file (KP-371/17, KP-3771/18).

47. E. I. Zelenskaia, "A. A. Sol'ts," unpublished manuscript in AMDNN, "Solts" file, 68–92. Cf.

Yury Trifonov, *The Disappearance*, trans. David Lowe (Ann Arbor, MI: Ardis, 1991), 99–100. Cf. Iurii Trifonov, *Ischeznovenie*, RoyalLib.com, http://royallib.ru/read/trifonov_yuriy /ischeznovenie.html#0.

48. RGALI, f. 2310, op.1. d. 19, ll. 55, 70–72; d. 78, ll. 13–15. On the similarity between Uriel Acosta and "blue-eyed Kim," see Iakov Grinval'd, "Peresmotrennyi Gutskov: 'Uriel' Akost' v Novom teatra," *Vecherniaia Moskva*, May 7, 1934.

49. GARF, f. 5446, op. 82, d. 51, ll. 121–25.

50. GARF, f. 5446, op. 82, d. 51, ll. 126; Nikita Petrov and Mark Iansen [Jansen], *"Stalinskii pito-mets"—Nikolai Ezhov* (Moscow: Rossiiskaia politicgeskaia entsiklopediia, 2008), 29, 204, 366; "Zhertvy politicheskogo terrora v SSSR," Memorial Society database, http://lists .memo.; ru/index1.htm; http://www.kino-teatr.ru/teatr/activist/m/283730/bio/; http:// www.alexanderyakovlev.org/almanah/almanah-dict-bio/1021729/0; *Stalin's Lists on Geor-gia*, forthcoming, see Heinrich Böll Stiftung, https://ge.boell.org/en/2014/01/20/stalins -lists-georgia-2011-2013 and https://idfi.ge/en/stalins-lists-on-georgia.

28. THE SUPREME PENALTY

1. F. Beck and W. Godin [Konstantin Shteppa and Fritz Houtermans], *Russian Purge and the Extraction of Confession* (New York: Viking Press, 1951), 215.

2. "Zhertvy politicheskogo terrora v SSSR," Memorial Society database, http://lists.memo.; ru/index1.htm; Teatral'nye deiateli, http://www.kino-teatr.ru/teatr/activist/m/283730 /bio; Al'manakh "Rossiia: XX vek," Alexander Yakolev.org, http://www.alexanderyakovlev .org/almanah/almanah-dict-bio/1021729/0; Ivan Gronskii, *Iz proshlogo* (Moscow: Izvestiia, 1991), 162–69; Igor' Nepein, "Tsareubiitsa v rukakh NKVD," *Cheliabinskii rabochii*, July 17, 2004 (http://www.chelpress.ru/newspapers/chelrab/archive/17-07-2004/2/A121270.DOC .shtml.ru) and July 21, 2004 (http://mediazavod.ru/articles/15797).

3. Eikhe quoted in N. S Khrushchev, "O kul'te lichnosti i ego posledstviiakh," Wikisource, http://ru.wikisource.org/wiki/О_культе_личности_и_его_последствиях._Доклад_XX _съезду_КПСС_(Н.С._Хрущев).

4. Ibid.; see also *Reabilitatsiia: Kak eto bylo; Dokumenty prezidiuma TsK KPSS i drugie mate-rialy* (Moscow: MFD, 2003), 2:646–47.

5. *Reabilitatsiia: Kak eto bylo*, 2:647.

6. Ibid., 647–48.

7. Vitalii Shentalinskii, "Rasstrel'nye nochi," *Zvezda* 5 (2007): 67–78.

8. Ibid., 83–84.

9. "Stalinskie spiski," Memorial Society database, http://stalin.memo.ru/names/index.htm.

10. Beck and Godin, *Russian Purge and the Extraction of Confession*, 215; Shentalinskii, "Rasstrel'nye nochi," 82.

11. Inna Shikheeva-Gaister, *Deti vragov naroda: Semeinaia khronika vremen kul'ta lichnosti 1925-1953* (Moscow: Vozvrashchenie, 2012), 234–35.

12. Ibid., 235.

13. Ibid., 236.

14. Ibid., 236–44; "Stalinskie spiski," http://stalin.memo.ru/names/index.htm.

15. Obolenskaia, *Iz vospominanii*, "Samizdat," http://samlib.ru/o/obolenskaja_s_w/01.shtml; Svetlana Obolenskaia, *Deti Bol'shogo terrora: Vospominaniia* (Moscow: AGRAF, 2013), 15–66.

16. Obolenskaia, *Iz vospominanii*, http://samlib.ru/o/obolenskaja_s_w/01.shtml; Obolenskaia, *Deti Bol'shogo terrora*, 20.

17. Obolenskaia, *Iz vospominanii*, http://samlib.ru/o/obolenskaja_s_w/01.shtml; Obolenskaia, *Deti Bol'shogo terrora*, 16–17.

18. Obolenskaia, *Iz vospominanii*, http://samlib.ru/o/obolenskaja_s_w/01.shtml; Obolenskaia, *Deti Bol'shogo terrora*, 20; "Stalinskie spiski," http://stalin.memo.ru/names/index.htm.

19. "Moe poslednee slovo na sude, veroiatno, budet moim poslednim slovom voobshche," *Is-*

tochnik 4 (1996): 89–90 (underlined lines were crossed out by the censor); Jochen Hellbeck, "With Hegel to Salvation: Bukharin's Other Trial," *Representations* 107 (Summer 2009): 67–68.

20. Gennadii Bordiugov, ed., *Tiuremnye rukopisi N. I. Bukharina* (Moscow: AIRO-XX, 1996), 2:34, 37, 39, 321, 324, 333, 30. I am indebted to Jochen Hellbeck, "With Hegel to Salvation," 56–90.

21. Bordiugov, *Tiuremnye rukopisi N. I. Bukharina*, 2:63, 80, 216, 175, 82, 159.

22. Ibid., 2:92.

23. Ibid., 2:131.

24. Ibid., 2:157–58.

25. "'Prosti menia, Koba': Neizvestnoe pis'mo N. I. Bukharina," *Istochnik* o [sic] (1993): 23–25. English translation (by Benjamin Sher) from J. Arch Getty and Oleg V. Naumov, eds., *The Road to Terror: Stalin and the Self-Destruction of the Bolsheviks* (New Haven, CT: Yale University Press, 1999), 556–59 (doc. 198).

26. Ibid.

27. Ibid.

28. "Moe poslednee slovo na sude," 90–91. English translation from Robert C. Tucker and Stephen F. Cohen, eds., *The Great Purge Trial* (New York: Grosset and Dunlap, 1965), 668.

29. V. I. Piatnitskii, comp., *Golgofa* (St. Petersburg: Palitra, 1993), 60–61; Mikhail Kol'tsov, "Ubiitsa s pretenziiami," *Pravda*, March 7, 1938.

30. Aleksandr Avdeenko, "Otluchenie," *Znamia* 4 (April 1989): 91–92.

31. Gordon, in *Mikhail Kol'tsov, kakim on byl: Sbornik vospominanii* (Moscow: Sovetskii pisatel', 1989), 400–401.

32. Viktor Fradkin, *Delo Kol'tsova* (Moscow: Vagrius, 2002), 19–31, 74–94 (quotation from 86).

33. Ibid., 247, 95; Boris Sopel'niak, *Smert' v rassrochku* (Moscow: Olma-Press, 2004), 141.

34. Fradkin, *Delo Kol'tsova*, 95–96.

35. Ibid., 95–119, 321–29; Sopel'niak, *Smert' v rassrochku*, 129–59.

36. Ursula El-Akramy, *Transit Moskau: Margarete Steffin und Maria Osten* (Hamburg: Europäische Verlagsanstalt, 1998), 13, 229–33, 262–72; Boris Efimov, *Desiat' desiatiletii* (Moscow: Vagrius, 2000), 320–22; V. F. Koliazin, ed., *Vernite mne svobodu! Deiateli literatury i iskusstva Rossii i Germanii–zhertvy stalinskogio terrora* (Moscow: Medium, 1997), 284–302; Fradkin, *Delo Kol'tsova*, 171–94.

37. AMDNN, "Poloz" file, letters, M-4–M-5 (August 9, 1936); M-9 (October 9, 1936).

38. Ibid., M-8 (September 25, 1936); AMDNN, "Poloz" file, "Lichnoe delo No. 90365."

39. AMDNN, "Poloz" file, letters, M-7 (August 31, 1936); M-12 (November 17, 1936); M-9 (October 10, 1936).

40. Ibid., M-13 (November 26, 1936); M-13 (December 1936).

41. Ibid., M-14 (September 2, 1937).

42. Ibid.

43. Ibid., M-15–M-16 (September 18, 1937).

44. Ibid.

45. T. I. Miagkova, "Poslednee pis'mo k docheri," introduction by R. M. Poloz, in S. S. Vilenskii, ed., *Dodnes' tiagoteet* (Moscow: Vozvrashchenie, 2004), 2:139–42.

46. AMDNN, "Poloz" file, "Lichnoe delo No. 90365."

47. Ibid.

48. Ibid.; Miagkova, "Poslednee pis'mo," 142–45.

49. *Solovki-entsiklopediia*, bk. 10, chap. 4, "Rasstrel solovetskogo etapa v urochishche Sandarmokh (Sandormokh)," http://www.solovki.ca/camp_20/sandarmoh.php; AMDNN, "Poloz" file, R. M. Poloz, letter to the Museum," October 7, 2000, l. 9; *Memorial'noe kladbishche Sandormokh, 1937, 27 oktiabria–4 noiabria (Solovetskii etap)* (St. Petersburg: Memorial, 1997), 87–124, 160–71.

50. *Memorial'noe kladbishche Sandormokh*, 69, 150.

51. Gronskii, *Iz proshlogo*, 168–69.
52. "Zakhoronenie v Kommunarke, spisok po godam: Posleslovie," Memorial Society database, http://www.memo.ru/memory/communarka/index.htm.
53. L. Golovkova, "Spetsob"ekt 'Butovskii poligon' (istoriia, dokumenty, vospominaniia)," in *Butovskii poligon, 1937–38: Kniga pamiati zhertv politicheskikh repressii* (Moscow: Institut eksperimental'noi sotsiologii, 1997), 24–26.
54. "Zhertvy politicheskogo terrora v SSSR," http://lists.memo.ru/index1.htm.
55. N. V. Petrov, "Stalinskii zakaz: Kak ubivali Sokol'nikova i Radeka," *Novaia gazeta*, June 5, 2008.
56. L. S. Redens (Alliluev), interview with author, June 24, 1999; Vladimir Alliluev, *Khronika odnoi sem'i* (Moscow: Molodaia gvardiia, 2002), 97; "Poslednee slovo N. I. Ezhova," Dokumenty o deiatel'nosti N. I. Ezhova, http://perpetrator2004.narod.ru/documents/Yezhov /Yezhov.htm; cf. English translation in Getty and Naumov, *Road to Terror*, 561–62.
57. Agnessa Mironova-Korol', *Agnessa: From Paradise to Purgatory: A Voice from Stalin's Russia*, trans. Rose Glickman (Bloomington, IN: Slavica, 2012), 101–2, 103; M. M. Iakovenko, *Agnessa: Ustnye rasskazy Agnessy Ivanovny Mironovoi-Korol'*, Memorial: Istoricheskie programmy, "Nasha zhizn's Miroshei," http://www.memo.ru/history/agnessa.
58. Mironova, *Agnessa: From Paradise to Purgatory*, 100–101; Iakovenko, *Agnessa*, http://www .memo.ru/history/agnessa.
59. Mironova, *Agnessa: From Paradise to Purgatory*, 114–17; Iakovenko, *Agnessa*, http://www .memo.ru/history/agnessa.
60. Mironova, *Agnessa: From Paradise to Purgatory*, 117–18; Iakovenko, *Agnessa*, http://www .memo.ru/history/agnessa.
61. Mironova, *Agnessa: From Paradise to Purgatory*, 122; Iakovenko, *Agnessa*, http://www .memo.ru/history/agnessa.
62. Mironova, *Agnessa: From Paradise to Purgatory*, 123–25; Iakovenko, *Agnessa*, http://www .memo.ru/history/agnessa.
63. "Stalinskie spiski," http://stalin.memo.ru/names/index.htm. On "Kashketin executions," see Vadim Rogovin, *Partiia rasstreliannykh* (Moscow: N.p., 1997), 299–305, http://trst .narod.ru/rogovin/t5/xxxiv.htm; Ia. I. Kaminskii, *"Minuvshee prokhodit predo mnoiu . . .": Izbrannoe iz lichnogo arkhiva* (Odessa: Aspekt, 1995), 95–98; A. V. Antonov-Ovseenko, *Vragi naroda* (Moscow: Intellekt, 1996), 98–102. When Agnessa Argiropulo was told that Mironov had been sentenced to ten years "without the right to correspondence," she married his cousin, Mikhail Davydovich Korol (who had recently returned to the Soviet Union after serving as an undercover agent in the United States). In 1942, she was arrested for "anti-Soviet conversations" and sentenced to five years in a labor camp. After her release in 1947, she started working as a nurse. She died in Moscow in 1981, at the age of seventy-eight.

29. THE END OF CHILDHOOD

1. AMDNN, "Zaitsev" file; T. I. Shmidt, *Dom na naberezhnoi: Liudi i sud'by* (Moscow: Vozvrashchenie, 2009), 24–27; Memorial Society database, http://lists.memo.ru/index3.htm. See also Cathy A. Frierson and Semyon S. Vilensky, *Children of the Gulag* (New Haven, CT: Yale University Press, 2010), esp. 136–232.
2. AMDNN, "Osepian" file; Shmidt, *Dom na naberezhnoi*, 62–63; Memorial Society database, http://lists.memo.ru/index3.htm; Gamlet Mirzoian, "Ovsepian, A. A.," *Noev kovcheg* 11, no.134 (November 2008): http://www.noev-kovcheg.ru/mag/2008-11/1432.html.
3. AMDNN, "Moroz" file; S. S. Vilenskii et al., eds., *Deti Gulaga, 1918–1956* (Mosow: Demokratiia, 2002), 291–93, http://www.alexanderyakovlev.org/almanah/inside/almanah-doc/129; Mikhail Korshunov and Victoria Terekhova, *Tainy i legendy Doma na naberezhnoi* (Moscow: Slovo, 2002), 355–58. Lermontov's "The Death of a Poet," trans. Robert Hillyer, in Samuel

H. Gross and Ernest J. Simmons, eds., *Centennial Essays for Pushkin* (New York: Russell and Russell, 1967), 225–26.

4. Moroz, "Minuvshee," 16–20, in AMDNN, "Moroz" file.

5. Vilenskii et al., *Deti Gulaga*, 291; Korshunov and Terekhova, *Tainy i legendy*, 359.

6. AMDNN, "Moroz" file; Vilenskii et al., *Deti Gulaga*, 290.

7. AMDNN, "Moroz" file; Vilenskii et al., *Deti Gulaga*, 285–86.

8. AMDNN, "Moroz" file; Vilenskii et al., *Deti Gulaga*, 287–88.

9. AMDNN, "Moroz" file.

10. AMDNN, "Letter from deputy director of the Central State Security Archive, V. P. Gusachenko, to the House on the Embankment People's Museum, August 31, 1993," copy; "Spravka Tsentral'nogo arkhiva FSB Rossii," n.d., no number (in author's possession); Leonid Redens, interview with author, June 24, 1999. Aleksei Kirpichnikov's *Stalin''iugend* (Moscow: Veche, 2010), http://lib.rin.ru/doc/i/221529p19.html, is a fictionalized account based on interviews and documentary evidence, including the fully reprinted text of the indictment.

11. Anatoly Granovsky, *I Was an NKVD Agent* (New York: Devin-Adair, 1962), 31, 51–96, 107–11, 116–34 (the quotations are from 111).

12. Ibid., 111.

13. Ibid., 46–47, 51, 130.

14. Ibid., 161, 190. See also O. B. Mozokhin, "Organy gosudarstvennoi bezopasnosti SSSR v gody Velikoi Otehestvennoi voiny," vol. 2, bk. 2 (September 1–December 31, 1941), doc. no. 564, http://mozohin.ru/article/a-114.html. Granovsky's presence in the school is confirmed by Pavel Sudoplatov in P. A. Sudoplatov, *Raznye dni tainoi voiny i diplomatii: 1941 god* (Moscow: Olma Press, 2001), 270, also http://www.pseudology.org/Abel/Sudoplatov1941/12.htm.

15. Granovsky, *I Was an NKVD Agent*, 194–206.

16. Ibid., Irina Muklevich, interview with author, December 4, 1997; Valerii Frid, *58 ½: Zapiski lagernogo pridurka* (Moscow: Izdatel'skii dom Rusanova, 1996), 7–40; Viktor Levenshtein, "Za Butyrskoi kamennoi stenoi," *Kontinent* 132 (2007): http://magazines.russ.ru/conti nent/2007/132/le14.html; Anatolii Korkmasov, "Korkmasov Dzhelal-Erast (Erik) Dzhelal -Ed-Dinovich," Gazavat.ru, http://www.gazavat.ru/history3.php?rub=31&art=411. Frid's and Levenshtein's accounts of the affair differ considerably from Granovsky's.

17. Granovsky, *I Was an NKVD Agent*, 145, 214, 223; Evgenii Zhirov, "Vse proiskhodiashchee so mnoi lozhitsia ten'iu na moego ottsa," *Kommersant-Vlast'*, November 7, 2005, http://www .kommersant.ru/doc/624225; Roi Medvedev, "Slava i tragediia odnoi sem'i," *Karetnyi riad* 5 (November 1989); R. I. Medvedev, *Oni okruzhali Stalina* (Moscow: Vremia, 2012), 407–10, Google Books, https://books.google.com/books?id=u1P4TUgiqncCⲷpg=PA408⳹lpg=PA40 8⳹dq=елизавета+драбкина+андрей+свердлов⳹source=bl⳹ots=xK3_KjSVqa⳹sig =PpSLDdaaysZ5zmvUm0-DWxKQQog⳹hl=en⳹sa=X⳹ei=VxSXVN-pOJawogTr8IDACQ⳹ved =oCCAQ6AEwAA#v=onepage⳹q=елизавета%20драбкина%20андрей%20свердлов⳹f =false.

18. A. M. Larina, *Nezabyvaemoe* (Moscow: APN, 1989), 234–36.

19. Ibid., 237–38.

20. Ibid., 239–40.

21. "Zhertvy politicheskogo terrora v SSSR," http://lists.memo.ru/index18.htm; M. Parkhomovskii, *Kniga ob udivitel'noi zhizni Eshua Zolomona Movsheva Sverdlova, stavshego Zinoviem Alekseevichem Peshkovym, i neobyknovennykh liudiakh, s kotorymi on vstrechalsia* (Jerusalem: N.p., 1999), 198–209, 222; Larina, *Nezabyvaemoe*, 240n; Obolenskaia, *Iz vospo-minanii*, "Samizdat," http://samlib.ru/o/obolenskaja_s_w/01.shtml; Irina Chaikovskaia, "Vgliadet'sia v postup' roka: Interv'iu s Ruf'iu Val'be," *Chaika* 17, no. 148 (September 1, 2009): http://www.chayka.org/node/2464; Nadezhda Kataeva-Lytkina, "145 dnei posle Parizha," *Vestnik* 1, no. 312 (January 8, 2003): http://www.vestnik.com/issues/2003/0108/win /lytkina.htm; Irma Kudrova, *Gibel' Mariny Tsvetaevoi* (Moscow: Nezavisimaia gazeta, 1995),

http://tsvetaeva.synnegoria.com/WIN/about/kudrovG3.html; Medvedev, "Slava i tragediia," 6; Medvedev, *Oni okruzhali Stalina*, 408–9.

30. THE PERSISTENCE OF HAPPINESS

1. A. M. Larina, *Nezabyvaemoe* (Moscow: APN, 1989), 140–41.
2. Moroz, "Minuvshee," 43, in AMDNN, "Moroz" file.
3. B. H. Uimanov, *Repressii: Kak eto bylo (Zapadnaia Sibir'v kontse 20kh–nachale 50-kh godov)* (Tomsk: Izdatel'stva Tomskogo universiteta, 1995), 288–91.
4. N. N. Demchenko, "Kanikuly dlinoi v 18 let," *Mendeleevets* 36, no. 1799 (November 30, 1988): 3; L. P. Postyshev, interview with author, October 1, 1998.
5. Inna Shikheeva-Gaister, *Deti vragov naroda: Semeinaia khronika vremen kul'ta lichnosti 1925–1953* (Moscow: Vozvrashchenie, 2012), 73–74; Z. A. Khatskevich (Volkova), interview with author, September 4, 1998.
6. Gaister, *Deti vragov naroda*, 54.
7. Ibid., 55, 62–63, 72–73.
8. Ibid., 56, 59.
9. Ibid., 54; Obolenskaia, *Iz vospominanii*, "Samizdat," http://samlib.ru/o/obolenskaja_s_w/01.shtml; Z. A. Khatskevich (Volkova), interview with author, September 4, 1998; E. I. Kuchmina, letter to the Museum, August–September 1991, in AMDNN, "Kuchmin" file. For a history of the Moscow Exemplary, see Larry E. Holmes, *Stalin's School: Moscow's Model Schoool No. 25, 1931–1937* (Pittsburgh, PA: University of Pittsburgh Press, 1999).
10. Lidiia Libedinskaia, *Zelenaia lampa*, LitRes, http://www.litres.ru/lidiya-libedinskaya/zelenaya-lampa-2/chitat-onlayn/page-7.
11. Ibid. The Pushkin translation ("To Chaadaev") is from Avrahm Yarmolinsky, ed., *The Poems, Prose, and Plays of Alexander Pushkin* (New York: Modern Library, 1936), 51. On the Pushkin jubilee, see Karen Petrone, *Life Has Become More Joyous, Comrades: Celebrations in the Time of Stalin* (Bloomington: Indiana University Press, 2000), 113–48.
12. A. Shitov, *Iurii Trifonov: Khronika zhizni i tvorchestva* (Ekaterinburg: Izdatel'stvo Ural'skogo Universiteta, 1997), 144–45.
13. V. E. Iusim, "Detskie gody," 12–13, in AMDNN, "Efim Lande" file.
14. Ibid., 24.
15. Ibid., 20–38 (the long quotation is from 28); V. E. Iusim, interview with author, December 5, 1998.
16. Obolenskaia, *Iz vospominanii*, http://samlib.ru/o/obolenskaja_s_w/02.shtml; Svetlana Obolenskaia, *Deti Bol'shogo terrora: Vospominaniia* (Moscow: AGRAF, 2013), 89–90.
17. Obolenskaia, *Iz vospominanii*, http://samlib.ru/o/obolenskaja_s_w/02.shtml; Obolenskaia, *Deti Bol'shogo terrora*, 90.
18. Obolenskaia, *Iz vospominanii*, http://samlib.ru/o/obolenskaja_s_w/02.shtml.
19. Obolenskaia, *Deti Bol'shogo terrora*, 90; Obolenskaia, *Iz vospominanii*, http://samlib.ru/o/obolenskaja_s_w/02.shtml.
20. Obolenskaia, *Iz vospominanii*, http://samlib.ru/o/obolenskaja_s_w/02.shtml.
21. Obolenskaia, *Iz vospominanii*, http://samlib.ru/o/obolenskaja_s_w/02.shtml; Obolenskaia, *Deti Bol'shogo terrora*, 91.
22. Obolenskaia, *Iz vospominanii*, http://samlib.ru/o/obolenskaja_s_w/02.shtml; Obolenskaia, *Deti Bol'shogo terrora*, 91–93.
23. Obolenskaia, *Iz vospominanii*, http://samlib.ru/o/obolenskaja_s_w/02.shtml; Obolenskaia, *Deti Bol'shogo terrora*, 64, 72.
24. Obolenskaia, *Iz vospominanii*, http://samlib.ru/o/obolenskaja_s_w/02.shtml; Obolenskaia, *Deti Bol'shogo terrora*, 73.
25. Obolenskaia, *Iz vospominanii*, http://samlib.ru/o/obolenskaja_s_w/02.shtml; Obolenskaia, *Deti Bol'shogo terrora*, 72.

26. Obolenskaia, *Iz vospominanii*, http://samlib.ru/o/obolenskaja_s_w/o2.shtml; Obolenskaia, *Deti Bol'shogo terrora*, 75.

27. Obolenskaia, *Iz vospominanii*, http://samlib.ru/o/obolenskaja_s_w/o2.shtml; Obolenskaia, *Deti Bol'shogo terrora*, 69–70.

28. Obolenskaia, *Iz vospominanii*, http://samlib.ru/o/obolenskaja_s_w/o2.shtml; Obolenskaia, *Deti Bol'shogo terrora*, 78–79.

29. Obolenskaia, "Vspominaiu o druzhbe," Lib.ru, http://samlib.ru/o/obolenskaja_s_w/o3b .shtml.

30. Obolenskaia, "Vspominaiu o druzhbe," http://samlib.ru/o/obolenskaja_s_w/o3b.shtml; Obolenskaia, *Deti Bol'shogo terrora*, 81–82.

31. Obolenskaia, "Vspominaiu o druzhbe," http://samlib.ru/o/obolenskaja_s_w/o3b.shtml; Obolenskaia, *Deti Bol'shogo terrora*, 83.

32. Obolenskaia, "Vspominaiu o druzhbe," http://samlib.ru/o/obolenskaja_s_w/o3b.shtml; Obolenskaia, *Deti Bol'shogo terrora*, 82–83.

33. Obolenskaia, "Vspominaiu o druzhbe," http://samlib.ru/o/obolenskaja_s_w/o3b.shtml; Obolenskaia, *Deti Bol'shogo terrora*, 83–84.

34. A. Kosterin, "Za pereval," in *V potoke dnei* (Moscow: Sovetskii pisatel', 1958), 223–49; RGALI, f. 457, d. 392, ll. 54, 57; *Dnevnik Niny Kosterinoi* (Moscow: Detskaia literatura, 1964), 21–22, 67–68, 83, 77–78, 71, 58, 91, 89, 105, 12, 20, 19, 32–34, 33, 60, 68, 63, 88–89 and passim. For the uncensored version, see *Dnevnik Niny Kosterinoi*, http://gendirector1.blogspot.com/p /blog-page_4833.html. See also Il'ia Okunev, "Dom, v kororom proshli moe detstvo i iunost,'" http://www.liveinternet.ru/showjournal.php?journalid=4298821&jday=14&jyear =2012&jmonth=8.

35. *Dnevnik Niny Kosterinoi*, 23, 49, 28, 30, 34, 53, 77, 81. Cf. http://gendirector1.blogspot .com/p/blog-page_4833.html.

36. Ibid., 31, 56–57, 59, 81–83, 94. Cf. http://gendirector1.blogspot.com/p/blog-page_4833.html.

37. Ibid., 36, 54, 102, 104, 62–63, 83, 86–87, 93. Cf. http://gendirector1.blogspot.com/p/blog -page_4833.html.

38. Ibid., 37, 41–47, 72–73, 76, 84, 88–89, 94, and passim. Cf. http://gendirector1.blogspot .com/p/blog-page_4833.html. The German original is "Erinnerung": "Willst du immer weiter schweifen? / Sieh, das Gute liegt so nah. / Lerne nur das Glück ergreifen, / Denn das Glück ist immer da." The English translation is from Paul Carus, *Goethe, with Special Consideration of His Philosophy. Containing One Hundred and Eighty-Five Portraits and Other Historical Illustrations* (Chicago: Open Court, 1915), 335.

39. Ibid., 103; Cf. http://gendirector1.blogspot.com/p/blog-page_4833.html.

40. Lyova Fedotov's diary, bk. 13 (January 2 and 3, 1941), 56–58, 89–90, 92; bk. 14 (January 5 and 6, 1941), 7, 13–14 [Fedotov, *Dnevnik*, 171–92, 211–15]. See chapter 22, note 22, for how this work is cited.

41. Lyova Fedotov's diary, bk. 14 (January 6, 1941), 16; bk. 14 (January 8, 1941) 27; bk. 13 (December 31, 1940), 59 [Fedotov, *Dnevnik*, 231–32, 176].

42. Lyova Fedotov's diary, bk. 14 (January 2, 1941), 86–87 [Fedotov, *Dnevnik*, 207].

43. Lyova Fedotov's diary, bk. 14 (January 5–9, 1941), 8, 11–12, 39, 25–26, 14 [Fedotov, *Dnevnik*, 223, 226–27, 240, 253, 230].

44. Lyova Fedotov's diary, bk. 14 (January 12, 1941), 50 [Fedotov, *Dnevnik*, 264].

45. Ibid., 52 [Fedotov, *Dnevnik*, 266].

31. THE COMING OF WAR

1. Lyova Fedotov's diary, bk. 14 (June 5, 1941), 77–83 [Fedotov, *Dnevnik*, 289–95]. See chapter 22, note 22, for how this work is cited.

2. Lyova Fedotov's diary, bk. 14 (June 12, 1941), 96 [Fedotov, *Dnevnik*, 306–7]; Evgenii Gurov,

"Chego ne znali Stalin i Gitler, znal Leva Fedotov," *Prezent* (supplement to *Moskovskie vedomosti*) 37 (December 1993): 6, 8.

3. Lyova Fedotov's diary, bk. 15 (June 22, 1941), 4–5 [Fedotov, *Dnevnik*, 311–13].
4. *Dnevnik Niny Kosterinoi* (Moscow: Detskaia literatura, 1964), 103–5. Cf. Dnevnik Niny Kosterinoi, http://gendirector1.blogspot.com/p/blog-page_4833.html.
5. Ibid., 105–7. Cf. http://gendirector1.blogspot.com/p/blog-page_4833.html (unabridged).
6. Ibid. Cf. http://gendirector1.blogspot.com/p/blog-page_4833.html.
7. Ibid., 107–8. Cf. http://gendirector1.blogspot.com/p/blog-page_4833.html.
8. Ibid., 109–10. Cf. http://gendirector1.blogspot.com/p/blog-page_4833.html. The last sentence comes from Gorky's "The Song of the Stormy Petrel."
9. Ibid., 112. Cf. http://gendirector1.blogspot.com/p/blog-page_4833.html.
10. Ibid., 113. Cf. http://gendirector1.blogspot.com/p/blog-page_4833.html.
11. Ibid., 114–15. Cf. http://gendirector1.blogspot.com/p/blog-page_4833.html. The lines "too many for him to remember them all" are from *The Demon*, by Mikhail Lermontov.
12. Ibid., 115, 118–19. Cf. http://gendirector1.blogspot.com/p/blog-page_4833.html. *The Jewish War* is a novel by Lion Feuchtwanger.
13. Ibid., 119–20. Cf. http://gendirector1.blogspot.com/p/blog-page_4833.html; Viacheskav Boiarskii, *Diversanty zapadnogo fronta: Artur Sprogis i drugie* (Moscow: Krasnaia zvezda, 2007), 77, 96–97, 107–61, 232–34, 297–355, and passim; A. K. Megera, "V tylu vraga (o boevoi deiatel'nosti razvedyvatel'no-podryvnykh grupp na vremenno okkupirovannoi territorii Podmoskov'ia)," in *Kliatvu vernosti sderzhali: Partizanskoe Podmoskov'ie v dokumentakh i materialakh* (Moscow: Moskovskii rabochii, 1982), 297–306; F. S. Fazliakhmetov, "Reidy komsomol'tsev-razvedchikov po tylam vraga," in *Kliatvu vernosti*, 307–16; Nadezhda Arabkina, "Krestnyi put' Zoi," *Moskovskii komsomolets*, December 8, 2001, http://www.mk.ru/editions/daily/article/2001/12/08/100549-krestnyiy-put-zoi.html; "Legendy Velikoi Otechestvennoi: Zoia Kosmodem'ianskaia," Rossiia v kraskakh, http://ricolor.org/history/rsv/ist/7/3, and Russkaia narodnaia liniia, http://ruskline.ru/monitoring_smi/2005/04/13/legendy_velikoj_otechestvennoj_zoya_kosmodem_yanskaya.
14. *Dnevnik Niny Kosterinoi*, 120. Cf. http://gendirector1.blogspot.com/p/blog-page_4833.html; Viacheslav Otshel'nik, "Tvoi lichnyi dnevnik: Interv'iu Eleny Alekseevny Kosterinoi," Tvoi lichnyi dnevnik: Proekt Viacheslava Otshel'nika, http://subscribe.ru/archive/lit.graph.dnevnikovedenie/200902/05065454.html; RGALI, f. 457, d. 392, ll. 65–66; *Memorial: Obobshchennyi bank dannykh o zashchitnikakh otechestva, pogibshikh ili propavshikh bez vesti v period Velikoi otechestvennoi voiny i poslevoennyi period,* http://www.obd-memorial.ru/html/default.htm; Gamlet Mirzoian, "Ovsepian, A. A.," *Noev kovcheg* 11, no. 134 (November 2008): http://www.noev-kovcheg.ru/mag/2008-11/1432.html.
15. Obolenskaia, *Iz vospominanii*, "Samizdat," http://samlib.ru/o/obolenskaja_s_w/02.shtml; Svetlana Obolenskaia, *Deti Bol'shogo terrora: Vospominaniia* (Moscow: AGRAF, 2013), 93–95, 77.
16. P. A. Sudoplatov, *Raznye dni tainoi voiny i diplomatii. 1941 god* (Moscow: Olma Press, 2001), chap. 12, http://www.pseudology.org/Abel/Sudoplatov1941/12.htm; Anatoly Granovsky, *I Was an NKVD Agent* (New York: Devin-Adair, 1962), 142, 165–68; *Memorial: Obobshchennyi bank dannykh o zashchitnikakh otechestva,* http://www.obd-memorial.ru/html/info.htm?id=53081753; Volodia Ivanov's letters, AMDNN, "B. Ivanov" file, letter of March 13, 1946; G. B. Ivanova, interview with author, March 13, 1998.
17. Lyova Fedotov's diary, bk. 15 (June 26, 1941), 8 [Fedotov, *Dnevnik*, 320].
18. Ibid., 10 [Fedotov, *Dnevnik*, 321–22].
19. Ibid. 8, and (July 11, 1941), 19 [Fedotov, *Dnevnik*, 320, 334].
20. L. Roshal', *Piramida, Solo truby: Kinostsenarii* (Moscow: Iskusstvo, 1989), 87–89; Gurov, "Chego ne znali Stalin i Gitler," 8; Mikhail Korshunov and Victoria Terekhova, *Tainy i legendy: Doma na naberezhnoi* (Moscow: Slovo, 2002), 184–90; *Memorial: Obobshchennyi*

bank dannykh o zashchitnikakh otechestva, http://www.obd-memorial.ru/html/info.htm
?id=87025470.

32. THE RETURN

1. GARF, f. 9542, op. 7, d. 216, ll. 2–9; d. 265, l. 1.

2. GARF, f. 9542, op. 7, d. 565, l. 3; d. 263, ll. 5–119; op. 1, d. 82, ll. 2–28.

3. GARF, f. 9542, op. 7, d. 263, l. 5; d. 265, ll. 1–2; d. 565, l. 3; d. 374, l. 4; d. 427, l. 1; d. 243, ll. 5–6; d. 462, l. 30b.; d. 485, ll. 4, 81–93; op. 1a, d. 28, l. 186; d. 32, ll. 153–63; op. 1, d. 53, ll. 11–63; d. 18, ll. 105–8; d. 92, ll. 1–50b.; d. 83, ll. 11–29; d. 96, ll. 16–17, 31; d. 102, ll. 1–2; d. 103; d. 107, l. 1; d. 108, ll. 1–7; d. 111, ll. 40–41; d. 112; d. 113, ll. 1–2; d. 135, ll. 1–4; d. 139, ll. 1–2; d. 145, ll. 1–4; Viktoriia Il'inichna Vakhrusheva, interview with author, January 9, 1998; Timothy J. Colton, *Moscow: Governing the Socialist Metropolis* (Cambridge, MA: Harvard University Press, 1995), 502–10; Steven E. Harris, *Communism on Tomorrow Street: Mass Housing and Everyday Life after Stalin* (Washington. DC: Woodrow Wilson Center Press; Baltimore, MD: Johns Hopkins University Press, 2013), 178–80, 336.

4. Inna Shikheeva-Gaister, *Deti vragov naroda: Semeinaia khronika vremen kul'ta lichnosti 1925–1953* (Moscow: Vozvrashchenie, 2012), 102. On post-Gulag reunions, see Cathy A. Frierson and Semyon S. Vilensky, *Children of the Gulag* (New Haven, CT: Yale University Press, 2010), 301–51.

5. M. R. Peterson, "O nas," ll. 17, 19–20, 27–34, in AMDNN, "Peterson" file.

6. Peterson, "O nas," l. 17.

7. Obolenskaia, *Iz vozpominanii*, "Samizdat," http://samlib.ru/o/obolenskaja_s_w/01.shtml; Svetlana Obolenskaia, *Deti Bol'shogo terrora: Vospominaniia* (Moscow: AGRAF, 2013), 47.

8. Obolenskaia, *Iz vozpominanii*, http://samlib.ru/o/obolenskaja_s_w/01.shtml; Obolenskaia, *Deti Bol'shogo terrora*, 48, 49.

9. T. I. Shmidt, *Dom na naberezhnoi: Liudi i sud'by* (Moscow: Vozvrashchenie, 2009), 80–81; Shikheeva-Gaister, *Deti vragov naroda*, 113–64; Peterson, "O nas," ll. 33–35, 53.

10. Anatoly Granovsky, *I Was an NKVD Agent* (New York: Devin-Adair, 1962), 214, 222–24.

11. Ibid., 223–24.

12. Ibid., 178, 225–341.

13. *Raoul Wallenberg: Report of the Swedish-Russian Working Group* (Stockholm: Ministry for Foreign Affairs, Department for Central and Eastern Europe, 2000), 68–69, 92, 129–49, 177, 188, http://www.raoulwallenberg.net/wp-content/files_mf/2836.pdf; Granovsky, *I Was an NKVD Agent*, insert between 179 and 180.

14. Evgenii Zhirnov, "Vse proiskhodiashchee so mnoi lozhitsia ten'iu na imia ottsa," *Kommersant-Vlast'*, November 7, 2005, http://www.kommersant.ru/doc/624225; Roi Medvedev, "Slava i tragediia odnoi sem'i," *Karetnyi riad* 5 (November 1989): 6; Ia. N. Naumov and A. Ia. Iakovlev, *Tonkaia nit'* (Moscow: Detskaia literatura, 1965), 71–72, 342, 77–93 (the interrogation technique quotation is on 82). See also Ia. N. Naumov and A. Ia. Iakovlev, *Dvulikii Ianus* (Moscow: Detskaia literatura, 1967); and Ia. Naumov and A. Iakovlev, *Skhvatka s oborotnem* (Moscow: Veche, 2008; originally published in 1969).

15. *Khronika tekushchikh sobytii*, No. 7, http://www.memo.ru/history/diss/chr/chr7.htm.

16. Peterson, "O nas," l. 20.

17. R. M. Poloz, interview with author, June 28, 1998; Iurii Trifonov, "Zapiski soseda," in *Iurii i Ol'ga Trifonovy vspominaiut* (Moscow: Soverwenno sekretno, 2003), 180.

18. B. G. Golubovskii, *Bol'shie malen'kie teatry* (Moscow: Izdatel'stvo imeni Sabashnikovykh, 1998), 108–23; AGTsTM, f. 454, d. 1294, l. 3; d. 4, l. 1; d. 455, ll. 106–7; d. 1377, n.p.

19. GARF, f. R-5449, op. 1, d. 63, ll. 33, 52; G. S. Ronina, interview with author, October 1, 1997.

20. Il'ia Zbarskii, *Ob"ekt No. 1* (Moscow: Vagrius, 2000), 233–36; V. I. Zbarskii, interview with author, March 10, 1998.

21. R. M. Poloz, interview with author, June 28, 1998; A. Shitov, *Iurii Trifonov: Khronika zhizni*

i tvorchestva (Ekateringurg: Izdatel'stvo Ural'skogo Universiteta, 1997), 249–50; Obolenskaia, *Iz vozpominanii*, http://samlib.ru/o/obolenskaja_s_w/01.shtml.

22. V. B. Volina, interview with author, September 18, 1997; Shitov, *Iurii Trifonov*, 271; Zakhar Prilepin, *Leonid Leonov* (Moscow: Molodaia gvardiia, 2010), 409.

23. Golubovskii, *Bol'shie malen'kie teatry*, 119–20; AGTsTM, f. 454, d. 1377, l. 128.

24. GARF, f. R-5449, op. 1, d. 63, ll. 31–32.

25. Evgenii Gurov, "Chego ne znali Stalin i Gitler, znal Leva Fedotov," *Prezent* (supplement to *Moskovskie vedomosti*) 37 (December 1993): 8; Shmidt, *Dom na naberezhnoi*, 90–93; Zbarskii, *Ob"ekt No. 1*, 233–36; V. B. Zbarskii, interview with author, March 10, 1998.

26. Gurov, "Chego ne znali Stalin i Gitler," 8; Shmidt, *Dom na naberezhnoi*, 91–92. On rehabilitations, see N. F. Bugai, *Reabilitatsiia repressirovannykh grazhdan Rossii (XX-nachalo XXI veka)* (Moscow: MSNK-Press, 2005); A. G. Petrov, *Reabilitatsiia zhertv politicheskikh repressii: Opyt istoriko-pravovogo analiza* (Moscow: INION RAN, 2005); A. Artizov et al., eds., *Reabiitatsiia: Kak eto bylo*, vols. 1–3 (Moscow: Demokratiia, 2000); and, esp., Nanci Adler, *Keeping Faith with the Party: Communist Believers Return from the Gulag* (Bloomington: Indiana University Press, 2012).

27. E. D. Stasova, *Stranitsy zhizni i bor'by* (Moscow: Gospolitizdat, 1960); RGASPI, f. 356, op. 2, d. 32, l. 1; d. 24, ll. 159–60 and passim; G. A. Voronskaia, *Vospominaniia* (Moscow: Protei, 2002), 70; RGASPI, f. 356, op. 2, d. 24, l. 160.

28. RGASPI, f. 356, op. 2, d. 34, l. 480b.

29. Voronskaia, *Vospominaniia*, 64, 68.

30. Ibid., 66–67.

31. Ibid., 64–65, 69; RGASPI, f. 356, op. 2, d. 6, l. 113.

32. Voronskaia, *Vospominaniia*, 69.

33. Ibid., 71–72; RGASPI, f. 356, op. 1, d. 19, ll. 1–3.

34. Svetlana Allilueva, *Dvadtsat' pisem k drugu* (Moscow: Zakharov, 2000), 59–60; translation from Svetlana Allilueva, *Twenty Letters to a Friend* (New York: Harper and Row, 1967), 61–62.

35. Allilueva, *Dvadtsat' pisem*, 60–61.

36. Allilueva, *Dvadtsat' pisem*, 59–62; translation from Allilueva, *Twenty Letters to a Friend*, 62–64. See also Vladimir Alliluev, *Khronika odnoi sem'i* (Moscow: Molodaia gvardiia, 2002), 225–61, 274, 281; Kira Allilueva, *Plemiannitsa Stalina* (Moscow: Vagrius, 2006), 210–52.

37. Allilueva, *Dvadtsat' pisem*, 62, translation from Allilueva, *Twenty Letters to a Friend*, 64. See also Alliluev, *Khronika odnoi sem'i*, 281.

38. Obolenskaia, *Iz vospominanii*, http://samlib.ru/o/obolenskaja_s_w/01.shtml; Obolenskaia, *Deti Bol'shogo terrora*, 52–53.

39. S. V. Obolenskaia, interview with author, October 20, 2009.

40. For the catalog, see *Eva Pavlovna Levina-Rozengolts, 1898–1975: Sbornik materialov; Katalog vystavki proizvedenii* (Moscow: Gosudarstvennaia Tret'iakovskaia galereia, Gosudarstvennyi muzei izobrazitel'nykh iskusstv im. A. S. Pushkina, 1996). See also E. B. Levina, comp., *Eva Pavlovna Levina-Rozengol'ts: Zhivopis' i grafika* (Moscow: Galart, 2006); *Eva Levina-Rozengolts: Her Life and Work* (Washington, DC: National Museum of Women in the Arts, 1999).

33. THE END

1. Joseph Kellner, "The End of History: Radical Responses to the Soviet Collapse" (PhD diss., University of California, Berkeley, forthcoming, 2018).

2. Aleksandr Ovcharenko, *V krugu Leonida Leonova: Iz zapisok 1968–1988 gg.* (Moscow: Moskoskii intellektual'no-delovoi klub, 2002), 158; M. A. Kanazirska, "Zagadka Leonova (Iz besed s pisatelem)," in *Vek Leonida Leonova: Problemy tvorchestva; Vospominaniia* (Moscow: IMLI RAN, 2001), 347–48; Zakhar Prilepin, *Leonid Leonov* (Moscow: Molodaia gvardiia, 2010), 328–37, 485–500, 507–8; Leonid Leonov, *Piramida* (Moscow: Nash sovremennik, 1994), 1:6.

3. Leonov, *Piramida*, 3:72; M. Gor'kii, *Sobranie sochinenii* (Moscow: GiKhL, 1955), 30:400; *Leonid Leonov v vospominaniiakh, dnevnikakh, interv'iu* (Moscow: Golos, 1999), 223; Leonov, *Piramida*, 1:32.

4. Ibid., 2:252.

5. Ibid.

6. Leonid Leonov, "Slovo o pervom deputate," Leonid Leonov, http://www.leonid-leonov.ru /slovo-o-pervom-deputate.htm; Leonov, *Piramida*, 3:6.

7. Leonov, *Piramida*, 3:8–9.

8. Ibid., 2:254; 1:14, 19.

9. Ibid., 1:67–68.

10. Victoria Smolkin, *A Sacred Space Is Never Empty: A History of Soviet Atheism* (Princeton, NJ: Princeton University Press, 2018).

11. Luke 14:26; 1 Cor.: 8–9.

12. Plato, *The Republic*, Internet Classics Archive, http://classics.mit.edu/Plato/republic.3.ii .html.

13. J. V. Stalin, *Problems of Leninism* (Moscow: Foreign Languages Publishing House, 1953) 528–29. Cf. I. V. Stalin, *Sochineniia* (Moscow: Gospolitizdat, 1951), 13:37–38.

14. Philip S. Gorski, *The Disciplinary Revolution: Calvinism and the Rise of the State in Early Modern Europe* (Chicago: University of Chicago Press, 2003); Viktor Zhivov, "Osobyi put' i puti spaseniia v Rossii," manuscript in author's possession.

EPILOGUE

1. Iurii Trifonov, *Vremia i mesto*, in *Sobranie sochinenii* (Moscow: Khudozhestvennaia literatura, 1985), 4:260.

2. Iurii Trifonov, "Seroe nebo, machty i ryzhaia loshad'," in *Sobranie sochinenii*, 4:260.

3. Trifonov, *Utolenie zhazhdy*, in *Sobranie sochinenii* (Moscow: Khudozhestvennaia literatura, 1985), 1:715–16, Trifonov, "Pravda i krasota," in Iurii Trifonov, *Stat'i*, Litmir, http://www.lit-mir.co/br/?b=71204&p=1; Yuri Trifonov, *The House on the Embankment*, in *"Another Life" and "The House on the Embankment,"* trans. Michael Glenny (Evanston, IL: Northwestern University Press, 1999), 197–98 (translation modified). Cf. Iurii Trifonov, *Dom na naberezhnoi*, in *Sobranie sochinenii*, 2:370.

4. Trifonov, "The House on the Embankment," 222, 189 (translation modified).

5. Yury Trifonov, *The Disappearance*, trans. David Lowe (Ann Arbor, MI: Ardis, 1991), 7.

6. Trifonov, "The House on the Embankment," 201 (translation modified); Trifonov, *The Disappearance*, 78 (translation modified), 15–17.

7. Trifonov, "The House on the Embankment," 226 (translation modified).

8. Yury Trifonov, "Games at Dusk," in *The Exchange and Other Stories*, trans. Jim Somers (Evanston, IL: Northwestern University Press, 1991), 175 (translation modified). Cf. Trifonov, "Igry v sumerkakh," TheLib.ru, http://thelib.ru/books/trifonov_yuriy/igry_v _sumerkah.html.

9. Yury Trifonov, "The Exchange," trans. Ellendea Proffer, in *The Exchange and Other Stories*, 40–41 (translation modified). Cf. Trifonov, "Obmen," Solnechnyi veter, http://www.vilavi .ru/raz/trif/1.shtml.

10. Iurii Trifonov, "Otblesk kostra," in *Sobranie sochinenii* (Moscow: Khudozhestvennaia literatura, 1987), 4:7.

11. Trifonov, *Studenty*, in *Sobranie sochinenii*, 1:238.

12. Trifonov, *Vremia i mesto*, in *Sobranie sochinenii*, 4:254–55.

13. Yuri Trifonov, *The Old Man*, trans. Jacqueline Edwards and Mitchell Schneider (New York: Simon and Schuster, 1984), 153 (translation modified).

14. Trifonov, *The Disappearance*, 7; Trifonov, "The House on the Embankment," 189, 280 (translation modified).

15. *Drugaia zhizn, Dom na naberezhnoi, Predvaritel'nye itogi, Vremia i mesto.* The last quotation is from *The Long Goodbye,* in Yury Trifonov, *The Long Goodbye: Three Novellas* (New York: Harper and Row, 1978), 203.

16. Trifonov, *The Long Goodbye,* 232 (translations modified).

17. Trifonov, *Utolenie zhazhdy.*

18. Trifonov, "The House on the Embankment," 272–73, 274 (translation modified).

19. Trifonov, *Vremia i mesto.*

20. *Vremia i mesto, Dom na Naberezhnoi, Predvaritel'nye itogi, Starik.* On blindness, see Natal'ia Ivanova, *Proza Iuriia Trifonova* (Moscow: Sovetskii pisatel', 1984), 258.

21. The David Shvarts quotation is from *The Disappearance,* 58.

22. Trifonov, *The Disappearance,* 116.

23. The grandmother quotation is from *The Disappearance,* 114. See Ivanova, *Proza,* 227.

24. Trifonov, "The House on the Embankment," 333–34 (translation modified).

25. Trifonov, *Another Life,* in *"Another Life" and "The House on the Embankment,"* 107 (translation modified).

26. Trifonov, *The Long Goodbye,* 276 (translations modified).

27. Trifonov, *Another Life,* 112, 128 (translation modified).

28. Trifonov, *The Old Man,* 261; Trifonov, *The Long Goodbye,* 276 (translations modified). Iu. Trifonov, *Neterpenie, Otkrytyi tekst,* http://opentextnn.ru/man/?id=2806.

29. "The time we began" quotation is from Iurii Trifonov, "Otblesk kostra."

30. Trifonov, *The Old Man,* 114, 247, 251, 185 (translations modified).

31. Ibid., 91–92, 76, 87–90 (translations modified). For the original report, including the "Carthage" quotation, see *The Last Battle,* based on *Filipp Mironov: Tikhii Don v 1917–1921 gg.* (Moscow: Demokratiia, 1997), 224, reprinted from GARF, f. 1235, op. 83., d. 8, ll. 43–52.

32. Trifonov, *The Old Man,* 90 (translation modified).

33. Ibid., 99–100, 171–72, 71–72 (translations modified), cf. Rev. 8:10–11.

34. Ibid., 225–29 (translations modified). The original is in *Filipp Mironov,* 415–23 (see *The Last Battle*).

35. Ibid., 178, 41 (translations modified).

36. Ibid., 243–44 (translation modified).

37. Ibid., 165 (translation modified).

38. Ibid., 185–86 (translation modified).

39. Ibid., 255–60 (translation modified).

40. Ibid., 261 (translation modified).

41. Trifonov, *Another Life,* 127–28 (translation modified)

42. Ibid., 77–78 (translation modified)

43. Ibid., 183–84.

44. English translation by Walter Kaufmann, in *Goethe's Faust* (New York: Doubleday, 1961), 467–69, 493.

45. Trifonov, *Another Life,* 185–86 (translation modified); Trifonov, *The Old Man,* 152–53 (translation modified).

INDEX

Page numbers in italics refer to maps or photographs.

"An incomparable masterpiece, Slezkine's account of the lives of elite Bolshevik families is as fascinating as a nineteenth-century Russian novel. He builds real drama and pathos into the stories of these people, and we find ourselves hoping against hope that they will survive. Yet this is history of the highest rigor. It would take several lifetimes for mere mortals to locate, read, and figure out what to do with the diaries, letters, notebooks, and drawings Slezkine found in the archives. This family saga heightens the tragedy of the Russian Revolution and gives the reader a quality of understanding rarely achieved by any work of history."

LEWIS H. SIEGELBAUM, coeditor of *Stalinism as a Way of Life* and author of *Cars for Comrades*

"Using the House of Government as a microcosm of the rise and fall of the first generation of Soviet leaders and their utopian ideas, Yuri Slezkine's remarkable book illuminates the entire experience of Stalinism. Drawing on memoirs, letters, and literature, he lays bare the emotions of the Russian Revolution and its Bolshevik beneficiaries, from love and friendship to a commitment to the end that justified the most vicious means. Perpetrators became victims as hundreds of once-powerful residents of the House were imprisoned, exiled, tortured, and shot. *The House of Government* is extraordinarily ambitious, exciting, and disturbing."

RONALD GRIGOR SUNY, author of *The Soviet Experiment*

"In this monumental study, Yuri Slezkine tells the story of the first Soviet ruling generation by looking through the windows of the remarkable building where many of them lived. Fittingly built in an area called the Swamp, the House of Government saw more than a third of its elite tenants evicted and arrested in the terror of the 1930s. Drawing on an amazing array of archives, memoirs, and interviews, Slezkine's unique narrative becomes a history of the Soviet Union itself. Nobody interested in Soviet history can afford to miss it."

J. ARCH GETTY, University of California, Los Angeles

"Boldly conceived and brilliantly executed, *The House of Government* is a major scholarly and literary achievement."

DOUGLAS SMITH, author of *Former People: The Final Days of the Russian Aristocracy*